National Income and Related Statistics for Selected Years, 1929-1993

Basic National Income Accounts **	1929	1933	1939	1941	1945	1950	1951	1952	1953	1954
Personal Consumption Expenditures*	77.3	45.8	67.0	80.8	119.6	192.1	208.1	219.1	232.6	239.8
Gross Private Domestic Investment*	16.7	1.6	9.5	18.3	11.3	55.1	60.5	53.5	54.9	54.1
Government Purchases*	8.9	8.3	13.6	25.0	83.0	38.8	60.4	75.8	82.8	76.0
Net Exports*	1.1	0.4	1.2	1.5	-0.5	2.2	4.5	3.2	1.3	2.6
SUM TO: Gross Domestic Product***	103.9	56.0	91.3	125.5	213.4	288.3	333.4	351.6	371.6	372.5
MINUS: Depreciation Allowance*	9.9	7.6	9.0	10.3	12.4	23.6	27.2	29.2	30.9	32.5
EQUALS: Net Domestic Product	94.0	48.4	82.3	115.2	201.0	264.7	306.2	322.4	340.7	340.0
MINUS: Indirect Business Taxes*	9.3	9.0	11.1	12.5	18.4	24.6	28.9	30.9	34.1	33.7
EQUALS: National Income	84.7	39.4	71.2	102.7	182.6	240.1	277.3	291.5	306.6	306.3
MINUS: Social Security Contributions	0.3	0.3	2.2	2.8	6.3	7.4	8.8	9.3	9.6	10.6
MINUS: Corporate Income Taxes*	1.4	0.5	1.4	7.6	10.7	17.9	22.6	19.4	20.3	17.6
MINUS: Undistributed Corp. Profits*	2.4	-4.1	0.3	2.3	4.4	8.2	8.8	9.6	8.6	9.8
PLUS: Transfer Payments*	3.7	3.7	4.8	4.1	9.8	21.8	19.4	20.5	22.4	24.8
EQUALS: Personal Income	84.3	46.4	72.1	94.1	171.0	228.4	256.5	273.7	290.5	293.1
MINUS: Personal Taxes*	2.6	1.4	2.4	3.3	20.8	20.6	28.9	34.0	35.5	32.5
EQUALS: Disposable Income	81.7	45.0	69.7	90.8	150.2	207.8	227.6	239.7	255.0	260.6
REAL GDP (in $1987 Billions)	709.6	498.5	716.6	909.4	1354.8	1203.7	1328.2	1328.2	1435.3	1416.2
Real Per Capita Disposable Income ($1982)	$3,923	$2,771	$3,834	$4,686	$5,991	$5,653	$5,651	$5,742	$5,964	$5,941
Annual Percent Change in Per Capita DI	0.0	-2.1	7.9	7.7	0.2	6.8	0.0	1.6	3.9	-0.4
Money and the Price Level										
Consumer Price Index (1982-4 = 100)	17.1	12.9	13.9	14.7	17.8	24.1	26.0	26.5	26.7	26.9
Percentage Inflation Rate	0.0	-5.1	-1.4	5.0	2.3	1.3	7.9	1.9	0.8	0.7
Supply of Money, M1*	26.3	19.2	33.3	45.0	98.7	115.6	122.2	126.8	128.2	131.6
Population / Labor Force										
Population (Millions)	121.8	125.6	130.8	133.4	139.9	152.3	154.9	157.6	160.2	163.0
Civilian Labor Force (Millions)	49.2	51.6	55.2	55.9	53.8	62.2	62.0	62.1	63.0	63.6
Unemployment (Millions)	1.6	12.8	9.5	5.6	1.0	3.3	2.1	1.9	1.8	3.5
Percent Unemployment / Total Labor	3.2	24.9	17.2	9.9	1.9	5.3	3.3	3.0	2.9	5.5
International Trade										
Exports*	7.1	2.4	4.6	6.1	7.4	14.5	19.8	19.2	18.1	18.8
Imports*	5.9	2.1	3.4	4.7	7.9	12.3	15.3	16.0	16.8	16.3
The Federal Budget										
Federal Government Receipts*	3.9	2.0	6.3	8.7	45.2	39.4	51.6	66.2	69.6	69.7
Federal Outlays*	3.1	4.6	9.1	13.7	92.7	42.6	45.5	67.7	76.1	70.9
Federal Surplus (+) or Deficit (-)*	0.7	-2.6	-2.8	-4.9	-47.6	-3.1	6.1	-1.5	-6.5	-1.2

*Billions of Dollars

**GNP data are presented for years prior of 1959

Economics

Sixth Edition

Ralph T. Byrns

University of Colorado, Boulder

Gerald W. Stone

Metropolitan State College of Denver

HarperCollins*CollegePublishers*

Acquisitions Editor: Bruce Kaplan
Developmental Editor: Mimi Melek
Project Coordination and Text Design: Innodata Corporation
Cover Designer: Sheila Stoneham
Cover Illustration: Steve Karchin
Art Studio: ElectraGraphics, Inc.
Manufacturing Manager: Willie Lane
Printer and Binder: R.R. Donnelley & Sons Company
Cover Printer: The Lehigh Press, Inc.

Economics, Sixth Edition

Library of Congress Cataloging-in-Publication Data

Byrns, Ralph T.
    Economics/Ralph T. Byrns, Gerald W. Stone, Jr.
  6th ed.
      p.   cm.
    Includes index.
    ISBN 0-673-99316-7. (student edition)
    ISBN 0-673-99869-X (instructor's edition).
    1. Economics.   I. Stone, Gerald W.   II. Title.
  HB171.5.B99   1995
    330–dc20   94-48159
                                                    CIP

95   96   97   98   9   8   7   6   5   4   3   2   1

Brief Contents

The following is a cross-reference to the chapters in *Economics* (hard-cover edition) and *Macroeconomics* and *Microeconomics* (the two paper-back editions).

Detailed Contents

*Chapter Review: Key Points and Questions for Thought and Discussion appear in every chapter.

Chapter 3   Demand and Supply   58

Macroeconomics

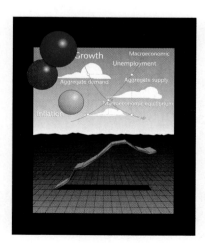

Chapter 6   Employment and Unemployment   133

Chapter 7   Inflation   153

Chapter 8   Measuring Economic Performance and Growth   170

Part 3

Foundations of Macroeconomic Theory   191

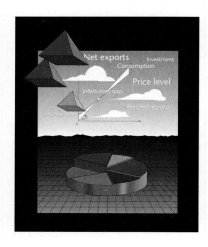

Chapter 10   Macroeconomic Equilibrium   215

Chapter 11   Fiscal Policy   235

Part 4   The Financial System   259

Chapter 12   Money and Banking   260

Chapter 13   Central Banking: The Federal Reserve System   280

Chapter 14   Monetary Theory and Policy   297

Chapter 15   Budget Deficits and Public Debt   326

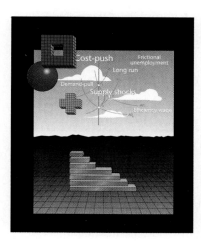

Chapter 18   Limitations of Stabilization Policy   404

Chapter 19   Economic Growth and Development   423

Microeconomics

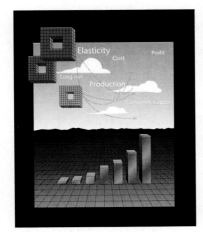

Part 6

Core Concepts in Microeconomics

447

Chapter 20   Elasticity

448

Chapter 23   Production and Costs   509

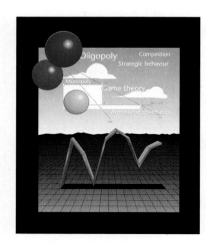

Chapter 26   Imperfect Competition and Strategic Behavior   581

Chapter 27   Antitrust and Regulation   606

Part 8   **Resource Markets**   **635**

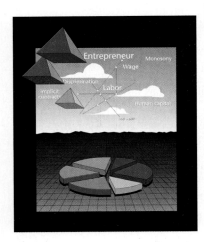

Chapter 28   Competitive Labor Markets   636

Chapter 31   Income Distribution and Poverty   704

Global Economics

Chapter 37   International Finance   847

To the Instructor

The major objective in this edition of *Economics* is to ensure that students learn basic principles that provide insights into how things work in an increasingly internationalized world. Powerful examples and engaging writing can overcome student apathy and a frequent failure to connect "textbook" economics with real-world events. The *Economics* package constantly applies theory to a variety of everyday experiences, historical events, and recent headlines. Integrated sets of extensively reviewed and class-tested materials are at the heart of this revision. Smooth and logical flow derive from contemplation of learning processes, revision, external reviews—and then more reflection and revision.

Each edition of *Economics* seems livelier and more polished than its predecessor. We are gratified that so many previous adopters continue to use our package for teaching—and learning—economics. Even if you have not used *Economics* previously, our conventional organization should make it unnecessary to radically alter your syllabus. Our approach to principles of economics is intended to be a tool that makes your teaching experience—and the learning experience of your students—especially rewarding.

KEY CHANGES IN THIS EDITION

Major and minor updates and improvements pervade these pages. Four increasingly powerful threads of economic theory—and the realities of everyday life—are more completely interwoven through the body of this edition of *Economics* than ever before:

- the globalization of economic activity
- the dynamics of labor markets
- the pervasiveness of imperfect information and strategic behavior
- an emerging consensus among economists about foundations for theory

In addition, this edition of *Economics* has a new chapter about an increasingly critical topic, "The Economics of Health Care." Some of these changes may affect the structure of your course if you taught from a previous edition.

The Global Economy

International economics was once relegated to a few chapters near the end of most texts. But today's students require exposure to developments east of Maine and west of Maui.

International competition spreads technology and speeds economic growth, as evidenced by developments along the Pacific Rim and elsewhere. But progress can disturb those who prospered in a more insular age. Traditions and institutions that fail to keep pace are being swept away. Symptoms of invigorated global competition include the toppling of long established governments (e.g., the Soviet Union); the emergence of dozens of newly independent nations, such as Russia, the Ukraine, and Mongolia; and the awakening of such potential industrial powerhouses as China and India.

Important changes can set off chain reactions that reverberate around the world. For example, the dissolution of the Soviet empire dissipated the prospects for conflict between major powers, diminishing needs for large armies and defense industries. But major structural changes following declines of U.S. military spending have combined with increasing international competition to disrupt both product and resource markets, reigniting waves of corporate downsizing and unemployment among workers who once considered themselves career employees.

Economic integration is paralleled by a revolution in telecommunications. Couch potatoes are now presented a menu of prime-time viewing that includes Australian rugby, Mexican soap operas, stock market reports from Japan and Hong Kong, the BBC's *Masterpiece Theater*, and on-location coverage of current events around the world. New information and transportation technologies are critical if entrepreneurs are to stimulate economic development. The spread of technology is also emphasized in this edition of *Economics*, which reflects our continuing determination to integrate international issues and examples through both macroeconomics and microeconomics courses.

Recent Developments in Labor Markets

Recent theories of employment and unemployment merit the expanded treatment given them in this edition. Typical patterns of work and joblessness seem decreasingly stable. Consequently, unemployment and inflation are now covered in separate chapters. Chapter 6, "Employment and Unemployment," describes how aggregate labor markets—and the careers of your students—are affected by vigorous global competition, evolving technologies, corporate restructuring, and the growing wedge between wage rates and hiring costs caused by new taxes and regulations. *Sticky wages* are another possible impediment to smooth adjustments in labor markets. The growth of the *contingency labor force*, composed of temporaries, part-timers, and consultants, is another facet of how labor markets manifest global change.

Burgeoning labor force participation among women is another development. Careers are becoming less secure, so the role of breadwinner is increasingly shared. More than ever before, unemployed workers rely on a spouse to cushion the shock of lost income, but job security is increasingly tenuous, especially for growing numbers of single-parent households that, too often, survive only at the fringe.

The changing nature of work and modern theories of labor markets are continuing themes in the sixth edition. Employment and unemployment are issues for both macroeconomics and microeconomics. Chapter 6 and Parts 5 and 8 of this book emphasize labor market dynamics—such topics for theory as *efficiency wages, implicit contracting*, and *imperfect information*—to help provide microeconomic foundations for macropolicy.

Imperfect Information and Strategic Behavior

Our experience is that students have little difficulty understanding recent theories that recognize that information is costly and that people behave strategically—topics largely consolidated in a single chapter in our previous edition. Thus, this edition of *Economics* integrates discussions about how imperfect and asymmetric information affect outcomes. For example, *asymmetric information* and the *principal-agent problem* are discussed in our chapters on consumer behavior, the theory of the firm, market structures, resource markets, and health care. Similarly, *screening* and *signaling* in labor markets are described in both macroeconomic and microeconomic contexts.

An Emerging Consensus About Theory

Although theory is constantly being refined, substantial consensus has long existed about much of microeconomics. Macroeconomics, however, has a long history of theories that, too often, seemed diametrically opposed. For example, the quantity-adjusting flavor of Keynesian theory seems at odds with the price adjustments relied on by classical theorists to quickly clear all markets. It appeared that little middle ground existed between competing schools of thought. This dichotomy in theory is slowly fading.

We continue to contrast classical and Keynesian theories, but primarily as a teaching device. Practicing economists draw from an increasingly eclectic mix of theories. A consensus has existed for more than two decades that macroeconomics and microeconomics should have reasonably consistent foundations. Partisans of particular refinements of theory continue to argue emphatically, but a consensus is growing about microfoundations for macroeconomic theory. This confluence of theory has made it necessary to more frequently consider microeconomic phenomena in parts of *Economics* that deal with macroeconomics, and vice versa.

Debates traditionally centered on which sets of mutually exclusive assumptions applied, but disagreement seems increasingly to turn on assumptions about the relative power of nonexclusive effects. Thus, for example, most new Keynesians and new classical economists now agree that incentives have powerful macroeconomic consequences, and most now recognize that, contrary to a central conclusion of classical theory, high rates of unemployment can persist because of a host of behavioral and institutional factors. In this edition, we highlight emerging areas of agreement about macroeconomic theory.

Health-Care Economics

No text would be complete today without an overview of the economics of the health-care industry. Our new chapter 35, "The Economics of Health Care," focuses on why health-care reform has hit center stage, and it applies many of the microeconomic tools students learn in earlier chapters. Equity issues such as universal access are balanced against efficiency issues and cost containment. The dominant role of third party payers is addressed, along with problems of *adverse selection* and *moral hazard*. We examine the nature and growth of health-care spending, how health care traditionally has been provided and paid for, and then compare this to how health care is delivered and financed in other industrialized countries. This chapter thus provides a framework for analyzing current health-care reform proposals before Congress.

SPECIAL FEATURES

This *Economics* package is intended to accommodate both the varied learning styles of students and the different teaching styles of instructors. Our supplements for *Economics* emphasize "learning in different ways." Our *Economics, Sixth Edition, Student Guide for Learning Economics, Homework Sets,* and computer software are integrated into a comprehensive learning package to help students understand economic analysis—and enjoy the process. Each component addresses the needs of student learning in a different but interrelated way.

For the Student

• **Text**   Each part of *Economics* opens with a broad introduction to identify how sequential chapters fit together, and each chapter begins with an overview of the topics it covers. Numerous other instructional aids run through the text:

1. Major points are *italicized*, and **key terms** and **economic laws** are **boldfaced** when introduced, with

    Definitions *that are set off from the rest of the text.*

2. Analytical graphs are rendered simply, with important points clearly labeled to efficiently convey economic concepts, and attractively, to pique student interest. Standardized notation in graphs and equations aids student comprehension. Descriptive and historical data are illustrated through modern techniques paralleling presentations in TV news broadcasts, in such newspapers as the *Wall Street Journal* or *USA Today*, and in such magazines as *Newsweek* or *Fortune*.

3. Boxed focuses (e.g., Is Life Priceless?; Innovation, Entrepreneurship, and Economic Growth; and Should We Export Pollution?) and biographical sketches of famous economists provide a well-rounded introduction to economics.

4. Chapters conclude with (*a*) a comprehensive Chapter Review to cover key points and (*b*) Questions for Thought and Discussion. (Solutions are provided only in our *Instructor's Manual.*)

5. Optional Materials covering selected analytical concepts (e.g., Graphing, Mathematics of Multipliers, Indifference Curves, and Isoquants) are appended to some

chapters for instructors who seek intensive coverage of more advanced topics.

6. Thorough Indexes and a Glossary at the end of the book provide handy references for students.

• **Study Guide**   Each chapter of our *Student Guide for Learning Economics* includes a chapter review, matching problems, true-false questions, fill-in reviews, multiple-choice questions, and problem sets, and some have specialized exercises as well. Each chapter concludes with complete answers and step-by-step solutions to especially challenging problems.

• **Homework Sets**   *Homework Sets* are new to the *Economics* learning package. They include two sets of 10 homework assignments each for *Macroeconomics* and *Microeconomics* (for a total of 40 homework assignments). Major concepts are first addressed with straightforward applications and, step-by-step, students are guided to solutions for more challenging problems.

Our colleagues have class-tested the *Homework Sets* to reinforce student learning in several ways:

1. These sets may be assigned as straightforward homework. Students hand in scanner-readable answer sheets; the graded materials are part of their final grades.
2. *Homework Sets* can be optional assignments. Some instructors then post solution sets on their office doors.
3. Lectures can be based on working through home work problems. (Transparencies of all figures and answers are provided as part of the Instructor's Package.)
4. Finally, these problems are useful for team projects during class. Students, by working in teams, often discover that helping other students is an extraordinarily powerful way to learn. Monitoring the progress of student teams is also a useful way to identify concepts that require greater emphasis in class lectures.

Homework Sets are constructed for efficient processing with automatic grading systems such as Scantron. Detailed solution sets provided in the *Instructor's Manual* can be copied and posted on your office door or distributed to your students. These homework problems are a stand-alone supplement. Use them if they suit your style; ignore them if they do not.

• **Software Supplements for Students**   Educational research has reached an unambiguous conclusion: students learn more—and have more interest in material—if lectures and reading are augmented by interactive software that reinforces and tests their knowledge. Each chapter of *Economics* is paralleled by a rich array of *MacroStudy* or *MicroStudy* exercises (in Macintosh, Windows, and MS-DOS formats) that allow individual printouts of student performance. Schedules detailing exercises appropriate for each week of a typical course are included in the "Sample Syllabi" provided in the *Instructor's Manual* and on diskette.

• *MacroTutor* integrates computer graphics into a rich tutorial allowing students of macroeconomics to review concepts that include graphical techniques, production possibilities, demand and supply, GDP accounting, unemployment and inflation, classical versus Keynesian theories, Aggregate Demand and Aggregate Supply, money and banking, active versus passive macroeconomic policy-making, new classical macroeconomics, and international trade and finance.

• *MacroSim*, a computer-based simulation in its sixth revision, allows macroeconomics students in the last five to seven weeks of a course to manipulate such policy instruments as government spending, tax rates, and the money supply in attempts to stabilize economic activity and stimulate growth.

• *MicroTutor* provides an interactive tutorial designed to enhance student mastery of graphical analysis, production possibilities, simple demand and supply analysis, elasticity, consumer analysis, the theory of the firm, market structures for outputs and resources, applied topics, and international trade.

- *Entrepreneur* is a microeconomic simulation and tutorial that leads a student along a career path that starts with work in a mailroom and ends after the student attains power as one of the world's movers and shakers. Along the way, the student must solve problems ranging from simple demand and supply analysis to complex markets in which decisions are interdependent.
- *Quizzer* provides students opportunities to test their understanding of economic concepts with sets of randomly generated multiple-choice, true-false, and matching questions drawn from a bank containing roughly 4,000 items. Answers are provided after the student takes a practice quiz so that students can assess their own progress.

For the Instructor

The *Instructor's Package for Economics* provides a variety of quality teaching supplements:

- The *Instructor's Manual for Teaching Economics* contains chapter outlines, lecture suggestions, answers to end-of-chapter questions, and detailed solution sheets for *Homework Sets* that can posted or reproduced as class handouts.
- Two *Test Banks for Economics* hold 5,000 multiple choice items (*not* duplicated in the student *Quizzer* program) to allow you to alternate between semesters. Over 10,000 questions were highgraded; we discarded items unlikely to suit your needs. Electronic versions of these class-tested *Test Banks* are available.
- *Great Ideas for Teaching Economics* now includes more than 600 analogies, anecdotes, exercises, and general teaching tips contributed by more than 350 instructors from across the country.
- *Transparencies* are available in a full-color format for all important figures and tables from the text. Transparencies also cover complex elements from the *Homework Sets*.

To the Student

Although economic problems are universal, roughly 90% of the world's population was relatively sheltered from distant events for over 95% of human history. Such isolation, however, is no longer possible—nor would it be desirable. A relatively quiet revolution has been sweeping the world—the globalization of economic activity. The prices of the food we eat, the types of transportation we use, and the occupations we pursue are among the myriad activities that may be powerfully affected by events half a world away.

The basic economic problem confronting you, if you are typical, is that you would like far more than you can afford. Tuition and books probably absorb much of the income you would like to devote to clothes, cars, and entertainment. You would probably also like more time to study, a more gratifying social life, or more sleep. Your limited budget and time require decisions about how you will spend your hours and money. In a similar way, all societies must choose among alternatives. How individuals and societies choose, and the effects of their choices, are the focal points of economics.

Economics can be as fascinating as anything you will ever study and, if you are diligent, it will seem natural and logical. Understanding microeconomics enables you to systematically address issues ranging from national policies to your professional and personal life. Insights gained from an economic perspective can provide you with advantages that most people lack.

HOW TO STUDY ECONOMICS

Superficial cramming is unlikely to succeed in economics. Keeping up is crucial. Most people learn most effectively if exposed to concepts in several ways over a period of time. You will learn more economics and retain it longer if you read, see, hear, communicate, and then apply economic reasoning. This material is much more than a few facts and glib generalizations; understanding economics requires reflection. Here is one strategy that students have found helpful for studying economics; many students have also adapted these techniques for other classes.

Visual Information

Don't let the extensive graphs in economics frighten you. There is a brief review of graphical analysis at the end of Chapter 1. In addition, our *Student Guide* opens with a set of helpful exercises, and there is another review of how to use and interpret graphical analysis at the beginning of *Homework Sets*. Avoid the agony of trying to memorize each graph by taking the time now to learn how graphs work. Proceed to Chapter 2 only after you quell your anxiety a bit. As you become familiar with graphs, you may be surprised to find yourself mentally graphing many noneconomic relationships and even more amazed to find this process enjoyable.

Be sure that you also understand simple algebra. The elementary algebra used in this book should pose no problem if you remember the material from a basic course. A short review of algebraic concepts is included in the graphical review at the front of *Homework Sets*.

Reading

Schedule ample time to read your assignments, and try to use the same quiet and cool (but not cold) room every day. Avoid drowsiness by sitting in a hard chair in front of a desk or table. Think about the material as you read. Many students spend hours highlighting important points for later study, for which they somehow never find time. Too frequently, busywork substitutes for thinking about economics. Try to skim a chapter; then go back and really focus on five or six pages. Don't touch a pen or pencil except to make margin notes cross-referencing related materials you already know.

Writing

After a healthy dose of serious reading, close your text and outline the important points with a half-page of notes. If you cannot briefly summarize what you just read, put your pen down and reread the material. You have not yet digested the central ideas. Don't be surprised if some concepts require several readings. Be alert for graphs and tables that recapitulate important areas. When you finish each chapter, read its Chapter Review, and work through all Questions for Thought and Discussion.

Listening

Most lectures blend your instructor's own insights and examples with materials from the text, but few students conscientiously work through assignments before lectures. You will have a major advantage over most of your classmates if you do, and you will be able to take notes selectively. Focus on topics that your instructor stresses but which are not covered in depth in the text. Notes from lectures should supplement, not duplicate, your text.

Teaching

Your instructors know that they learn their subject in greater depth every time they teach it. Teaching exposes you to previously unfamiliar aspects of a topic because you must conceptualize and verbalize ideas so that other people can understand them. Take turns with a classmate in reading the Key Points (in the Chapter Review) to each other. After one person reads a key point aloud, the other should explain it in his or her own words. Study groups work well in this way, but you may learn economics even more thoroughly if you simply explain economic concepts to a friend who has never studied it.

Applications

Working through the parallel materials from our *Student Guide for Learning Economics* and our economic software for each chapter of the text you study will make it easier to comprehend economic events regularly featured in the news. When this happens, you will be among the minority who truly understand economic and financial news. Use economic reasoning to interpret your day-to-day behavior and that of your friends and relatives. This will provide unique insights into how people function and how the world works.

Examinations

Following the preceding suggestions should prepare you for minor tests and quizzes. To prepare for major exams and finals

1. Read the Chapter Reviews for all material to be covered on the examination. Keep a record of any key points you could not explain to a friend who had never taken economics.
2. Return to each key point that you do not grasp adequately. Read the text material that covers it and rework the parallel parts of the accompanying chapter from your *Student Guide*.
3. Discuss any key point that is not clear to you with a friend.
4. Skim the glossary for a last-minute refresher before your final exam.

We know that this is a tall order, but if you conscientiously follow these study tips, we guarantee you an enjoyable and enlightening course.

CAREERS IN ECONOMICS

Many students find studying economics a pleasant surprise, but wonder if this interesting field is practical. Professors are often asked, "Can I get a good job with a bachelor's degree in economics?" We won't promise anything, but new economics graduates have job opportunities in such areas as public administration, operations analysis, management trainee and internships, sales, real estate appraisal, production management, insurance, or investment and financial analysis. What you might do as an economist depends on your specific areas of study, your minor, and how far you continue your training.

Economists are employed in most large business firms, government agencies, and nonprofit organizations. Many economists teach because effective personal, business, and political decision-making increasingly requires economic literacy. Others find that there are substantial and remunerative demands for their services as consultants or researchers.

Business

Executives are increasingly aware that workable business strategies and policies require applied economic reasoning. Roughly one-third of economists are employed by private firms and trade associations. Most medium-to-large firms in manufacturing, transportation, energy, investment, communications, banking, insurance, retailing, utilities, finance, and mining employ one or more economists. Many have staffs of economists. The median annual income of business economists is above $60,000, with entry salaries exceeding $26,000. Most business economists have advanced degrees, but there are opportunities for bright, hard-working people with bachelor's degrees. Business economists with only bachelor's degrees average over $40,000 annually.

Government and Nonprofit Organizations

One economist in five works for government or a nonprofit corporation. For example, more than 20 different economists have filled seven different cabinet-level posts during the Carter, Reagan, Bush, and Clinton administrations. Local, state, and federal agencies offer job opportunities for people with training in economics ranging from a bachelor's degree through postdoctoral training.

Teaching

Roughly half of all economists with advanced degrees are teacher-researchers employed by colleges and universities. At the university level, there are ample opportunities and rewards for economic research and consulting. Academic economists average annual incomes of roughly $50,000. Many states have recently made economics a requirement for a high-school diploma. People who are motivated to teach economics, but not to endure extended graduate training, are finding a growing demand for their services as teachers in secondary schools.

Acknowledgments

Numerous economists and students have made suggestions that have improved the sixth edition of *Economics*.

A few ideas from reviewers of this edition were not implemented because of onrushing deadlines and so must await the next revision. Most, however, are reflected in these pages or in our supplements. We deeply appreciate the many useful suggestions provided for this (and, in several cases, previous) editions by

Sophie Aguirre   *Catholic University of America*

James Alm   *University of Colorado, Boulder*

D. Andrew Austin   *University of Houston*

Raul Barreto   *University of Colorado, Boulder*

Frances F. Bedell   *Westark Community College*

Lynn Bennett   *Yale University*

Scott Bloom   *North Dakota State University*

W. David Bradford   *University of New Hampshire*

Andrew Buck   *Temple University*

Patricia J. Byrns   *University of Colorado Health Sciences Center*

Michael C. Carroll   *Colorado State University*

David L. Cleeton   *Oberlin College*

John P. Cochran   *Metropolitan State College of Denver*

Bobby Corcoran   *Middle Tennessee State University*

Lucinda Coulter-Burbach   *Seminole Community College*

Mark Cronshaw   *University of Colorado, Boulder*

John David   *West Virginia Institute of Technology*

Gregg E. Davis   *Marshall University*

Michael Ellis   *Kent State University*

Fred Engle   *Eastern Kentucky University*

Fred Englander   *Fairleigh Dickinson University*

Valerie Englander   *St. John's University*

Scott W. Fausti   *South Dakota State University*

JoAnn Feeney   *University of Colorado, Boulder*

Trey Fleisher   *Metropolitan State College of Denver*

David E. R. Gay   *University of Arkansas*

Lori F. Gerring   *Xavier University*

George Gillen   *Oral Roberts University*

Judith Glazner   *University of Colorado Health Sciences Center*

Stuart M. Glosser   *University of Wisconsin, Whitewater*

Harold M. Goldstein   *Northeastern University*

Glenn Graham   *State University of New York College at Oswego*

Phillip Graves   *University of Colorado, Boulder*

Louis C. Green   *San Diego State University*

Ralph Gunderson   *University of Wisconsin, Oshkosh*

Clifford B. Hawley   *West Virginia University*

Jeanne C. Hey   *Lebanon Valley College*

Tony Hirad   *Tulsa Junior College*

William Hogan   *University of Massachusetts, Dartmouth*

Chuck Howe   *University of Colorado, Boulder*

Calvin M. Hoy   *County College of Morris*

Joan Huckaby   *University of Washington*

Beth Ingram   *University of Iowa*

Anisul M. Islam   *University of Houston, Downtown*

Hyman Joseph   *University of Iowa*

William Kaempfer   *University of Colorado, Boulder*

Arthur E. Kartman   *San Diego State University*

Amin Kianian   *Metropolitan State College of Denver*

Seth King, Jr.   *University of Colorado, Boulder*

Kishore Kulkarni   *Metropolitan State College of Denver*

Jamie Brown Kruse   *University of Colorado, Boulder*

Michael Magura   *University of Toledo*

Akbar Marvasti   *University of Houston, Downtown*

Keith Maskus   *University of Colorado, Boulder*

Vijay K. Mathur   *Cleveland State University*

Jessica J. McCraw   *University of Texas at Arlington*

Edward B. Mills   *Clackamas Community College*

Laurence Miners   *Fairfield University*

Sam Mirmirani   *Bryant College*

Thom Mitchell   *Southern Illinois University at Carbondale*

Majed R. Muhtaseb   *California State Polytechnic University, Pomona*

Dana Mukamel   *University of Rochester*

Catherine P. Mulder   *Temple University*

Frank W. Musgrave   *Ithaca College*

Phil O'Reilly   *University of Colorado, Boulder*

Eliot S. Orton   *New Mexico State University*

Jack W. Osman   *San Francisco State University*

W. Alton Parish   *Tarrant County Junior College*

John Rapczak   *Community College of Rhode Island*

Margaret A. Ray   *Texas Christian University*

Janet M. Rives   *University of Northern Iowa*

Barbara Robles   *University of Colorado, Boulder*

Robert Rosenman   *Washington State University*

Jeffrey Rubin   *Rutgers-The State University of New Jersey*

Mark Rush   *University of Florida*

Reza Saidi   *Catholic University of America*

Dorothy Sanford   *College of Notre Dame*

Jolyne Sanjak   *State University of New York at Albany*

William C. Schaniel   *West Georgia College*

Dean Schau   *Columbia Basin College*

Martin Bryan Schmidt   *Colorado State University*

Ramon C. Schreffler   *Houston Community College*

Edwin A. Sexton   *Virginia Military Institute*

Dennis Shannon   *Belleville Area College*

Ruth Shen   *San Francisco State University*

Alan Sorkin   *University of Maryland, Baltimore County*

Stephen P. Stageberg   *Mary Washington College*

Steven G. Thorpe   *University of Colorado, Boulder*

Bob Tokle   *Idaho State University*

Abdul M. Touray   *Radford University*

Ronald J. Vogel   *University of Arizona*

James D. Wadley   *Tulsa Junior College*

Andrew Weintraub   *Temple University*

Jeanne Wendel   *University of Nevada, Reno*

Everett White   *California State University, Stanislaus*

David F. Wihry   *University of Maine*

Virginia B. Wright   *Eastern Kentucky University*

S. Lawrence Yun   *Radford University*

Hassan Zavareei   *West Virginia Institute of Technology*

We are especially indebted to the following economists for their diligence in checking—and double checking—our manuscript to ensure accuracy, and for their helpful reviews as well. Of course, we retain responsibility for any errors that may remain.

Barbara Connelly   *Westchester Community College*

Louis C. Green   *San Diego State University*

Ann Hanson   *Westminster College*

Mike Hayes   *Radford University*

Anisul M. Islam   *University of Houston, Downtown*

Roger Mack   *DeAnza College*

Jessica J. McCraw   *University of Texas at Arlington*

Edward B. Mills   *Clackamas Community College*

Jan Palmer   *Ohio University*

Steve Pitts   *Houston Community College*

Doug Pressel   *Cochise College*

Donald Pursell   *University of Nebraska, Lincoln*

Some reviewers of earlier editions offered comments not implemented until now. We remain deeply indebted to those who reviewed previous editions of our *Economics* teaching package and to those who helped develop supplements for earlier editions.

Jack Adams, John Appleyard, Robert Arnold, Jim Aylsworth, Gerry Babb, John Baden, Dale Bails, Greg Ballentine, Bill Barber, Andy Barnett, Donna Bialik, Brian Binger, Carl Biven, David Black, Dudley Blair, John Bockino, Bruce Bolnick, John Booth, Kenneth Boulding, Michael Brand, Josef Broder, William Brown, Maureen Burton, Jeffrey Buser, Amelia Sue Cain, Lou Cain, Steven Call, Colleen Cameron, Ray Canterbery, Michael Carter, Ann Carlos, Richard Chalecki, Ted Chiles, Mikel Cohick, David Colander, Chip Condon, Eleanor Craig, Jane Crouch, Frank Curtis, Larry Daellenbach, Clinton Daniels, Edward Day, Larry DeBoer, Norbert Dorow, Pat Dumoulin, Randall Eberts, Keith Edwards, John Elliott, Harry

Ellis, Don Evans, Gordon Erlandson, James Esmay, Patricia Euzent, Rudy Fichtenbaum, Ronald C. Fisher, Ronald L. Friesen, Gary Galles, Patricia Garland, Mark Gertler, Frank Giesber, Gary Gigliotti, Fred Glahe, Rob Graham, Steven Greenlaw, Joseph Grens, James Grunloh, Joseph Guerin, Harish Gupta, Robert Gustavson, Dan Hagen, Reza Hamzaee, Robert Harris, Will Harris, Michael Haynes, Robert Hebert, John Henderson, Stan Herren, Gus Herring, Thor Hertsgaard, Jack High, Elizabeth Hoffman, Janos Horvath, Hong Hwang, Bruce Hutchinson, Thomas Ireland, Dilmus James, Ray Johns, Janet Johnson, Robert Johnson, Walter Johnson, Jonathan Jones, Pat Joyce, Monte Juillerat, John Kaatz, Veronica Kalich, Jay Kaplan, Nicholas Karatjas, Sol Kauffler, Ziad Keilany, Larry Kendra, Kevin Klein, Jerry Knarr, William Kordsmeir, Tom Koplin, Maureen Lage, Jerry Langin-Hooper, Daniel Lee, Stephen Lile, Jane Lillydahl, Kenneth Long, Richard Long, Tony Loviscek, Marjorie Mabrey, Rodney Mabry, Hugh Macaulay, Larry Mack, Michael Maloney, Don Mar, Denise Markovich, Drew Mattson, Pete Mavrokordatos, Bruce McCrea, John McCurin, John McDowell, Michael McElroy, Mike McKee, Charles McLure, Patrick McMurray, Robert McNown, Mark McNulty, Tommy Meadows, Steven Medema, Stephen Mehay, Mostafa Mehdizadeh, Peter Meyer, Peter Mezer, Ed Morey, Michael Morgan, Ronald Moses, Richard Moss, Steve Myers, Panos Mourdoukoutas, William Nelson, Michael Nieswiadomy, Tom Oberhofer, Allan Olsen, Dennis Olson, James O'Neill, Vincent Panzone, G. W. Parker, Dilip Pendse, Diana Petersdorf, Steve Peterson, Tim Petry, Maurice Pfannestiel, Michael Pippenger, Hassan Pirasteh, Wayne Plumly, Joseph Pluta, Tom Porebski, Barry W. Poulson, Mark Prell, Ronald G. Reddall, W. Robert Reed, Delores Roman, Dwayne Rosa, Clark Ross, Mason Russell, Edward Sattler, Elizabeth Savoca, Mark E. Schaefer, Dean Schiffman, Richard Schimming, Walter Scott, Donald Shadoan, Michael Shelby, David Shorow, John Simonson, Timothy Smeeding, Gordon Smith, Lynn A. Smith, Abdul Soofi, George A. Spiva, Richard Spivak, Bruce Stecker, James Stephenson, Dudley Stewart, Eugene Swann, James Swofford, Victor Tabbush, Claude Talley, Danny Taylor, Tom Teitenberg, Lydia Thackray, Stephen Trimby, Holley Ulbrich, Edwin Ulveling, Tony Uremovic, Percy Vera, Jim Vincent, Frank Vorhies, C. Richard Waits, Dale Warnice, Michael Watts, Robert Welch, Allison Wellington, Arthur Welsh, Steve Weiss, Don Wells, Leonard White, Jonathan Wight, Allan Wilkens, Richard Winkelman, Peter Zaleski, Joseph Ziegler, William Zeis, and George Zodrow.

Mark Arnold, John Cochran, Karim Esmail, Verna Organ, Candy Payne, Robert Payne, and Steven Thorpe helped ensure the quality and timeliness of our extensive print and software supplements. Parts of the analysis in several software modules reflect work by Raul Barreto and Phil O'Reilly, both of the University of Colorado, Boulder. Software programmers for this edition include Rick Kelsven (*Examiner*), Tim Senecal (implementations of Student Software drivers for MS-DOS, Macintosh, and Windows), and Jenny Vance (*TestPerfect*).

Support from Susan Katz, Publisher at HarperCollins, is also much appreciated. The creative insights of our Senior Acquisitions Editor, Bruce Kaplan, have now been reflected in improvements across four editions. This edition also owes much of its polish and cohesiveness to Mimi Melek, our Developmental Editor. The professionalism of our Project Editors, Paula Soloway of HarperCollins and Betsy Winship of Innodata, has made working with them a delight. Our distinctive design reflects the aesthetic sensibilities of Sheila Stoneham and Bobby Starnes, and our fine artwork was rendered by ElectraGraphics. Last, but not least, we thank James B. Strandberg for his meticulous accuracy checking.

This book remains dedicated to Jennifer, Melissa, Rachel, Matthew, Sheila, and Trish for their support during this revision; we hope that seeing their names in print is still a thrill.

Any principles text is always in process. Suggestions that aid us in making the next edition of *Economics* or its supplements clearer, more accurate, or more complete will be deeply appreciated and gratefully acknowledged. Please send us your comments, c/o HarperCollins Publishers, 10 East 53rd Street, New York, NY, 10022-5299.

Ralph T. Byrns
Gerald W. Stone

A Visual Guide To:

Economics

Sixth Edition
ISBN 0-673-99316-7

Macroeconomics
ISBN 0-673-99329-9

Microeconomics
ISBN 0-673-99328-0

Ralph T. Byrns
University of Colorado, Boulder

Gerald W. Stone
Metropolitan State College of Denver

A market leader and innovator in the principles of economics course, Byrns and Stone's *Economics* is known for its clear models, modern topic coverage, engaging writing style, real-life examples, and attractive visuals that enhance students' understanding of economic concepts. Its comprehensive learning package has long been known for its interactive and exciting text-related software that can be used by students and instructors. This new sixth edition continues to set the standard for the principles market in terms of content and supplements.

The sixth edition includes a new chapter on health-care economics which is unique to the principles market. This chapter applies standard microeconomic tools to the health care issue and provides a framework for understanding the various policy proposals now before Congress. Coverage of labor market issues is enhanced throughout the macroeconomics part of the text, starting with a new chapter on employment and unemployment that analyzes trends in the '90s, and also appears prominently in a discussion of the microfoundations of macroeconomics. The learning package has been further improved not only with new separate homework sets for all major parts of the text that instructors can additionally assign to students, but also by an upgraded and enhanced software package. This sixth edition offers professors and students an unprecedented, complete learning package to enhance the principles of economics course.

The emergence of AIDS and other new diseases is among the reasons health care is now viewed as a critical issue, as is a resurgence of some ancient diseases because certain strains of bacteria and viruses have become drug resistant (e.g., tuberculosis and malaria). Another source of concern is that modern medicine now enables most of us to live longer. Many people fear bankruptcy if costly treatments that would prolong life are not covered by insurance. These sorts of concerns date back to antiquity, but certain interrelated factors come to the fore when experts itemize pressing issues for health-care reform: (*a*) soaring costs, (*b*) uneven quality, and (*c*) lack of universal access, or inadequate health insurance coverage for many Americans.

How we prioritize health-care problems depends on our positions. For most firms and many employees, rising health insurance costs, despite decreasing coverage, are a major concern. For many of the poor and for the uninsured, access is a central issue. Access to care is generally available, but too often, too little health care is accessible too late. For taxpayers, rising shares of tax dollars are absorbed by outlays for Medicare and Medicaid. For health-care providers (e.g., doctors and hospitals), major issues include (*a*) the growth of bureaucracy to oversee payments, leading to micromanagement of medical decisions; (*b*) the prospect of price controls in the guise of *cost containment*; and (*c*) malpractice suits that, regardless of fault, often arise from poor outcomes. (Some of us acknowledge the inevitable only reluctantly, but everyone ultimately recognizes that we all eventually die—a basic health problem beyond medical remedies.)

As is true of so many other economic issues, concerns about health care can be boiled down to trade-offs between *efficiency* (cost containment) and *equity* (improved access). Thus, health-care reform predictably has broad support in the abstract, but little consensus exists about concrete directions for specific reforms.

HEALTH CARE TODAY: SOME VITAL SIGNS

Annual spending on health care in the United States exceeds $1 trillion. It is not surprising that Americans have strong opinions about an industry that now absorbs more than 15 cents out of every dollar of our gross domestic product

FIGURE 1   Health Care Spending as a Percent of GNP

Chapter 35   The Economics of Health Care

COMPREHENSIVE COVERAGE OF CURRENT POLICY CONCERNS

Economics 6/e is the first introductory text to devote a full chapter (35) to the economics of health care. This chapter applies standard microeconomic concepts to this controversial topic, providing a framework that enables students to better understand the issues involved in health care and analyze the current policy debate in Congress.

FIGURE 1 Immigration as a Growing Share of Population Increases 1960-1990

1960–70	11%
1970–80	33%
1980–90	39%

millions 0   2   4   6   8   10

Immigrants as % Share of Total U.S. Population Growth

Source: *Business Week, July 13, 1992*

Two other demographic trends have profoundly affected labor supplies: the growth in the number of two-income households and in the number of households headed by women. Nearly 13 percent of all working women today are primary breadwinners for their families. These trends have led to growing numbers of households that are relatively better-off (two earners) and growing numbers that are relatively poor (women who support families), leaving middle-income families in America declining as a percentage of all households.

Changes in the Demand for Labor

Broad changes to the supply side of our national labor market have been matched by dramatic changes in demands for labor. The demand for labor ultimately derives from consumer demands for goods and depends on workers' productivity. Certain ongoing changes in product

TABLE 1 Population, Labor Force, and Other Labor Market Measures (1960–1993)

Selected Indicator	1960	1970	1980	1993	Percentage change 1960–1993
Population (Pop = age ≥ 16)	117,245	137,085	167,745	193,971	65.4
Labor Force (LF)	69,628	82,771	106,940	127,975	83.8
Employed (E)	65,778	78,678	99,303	119,457	81.6
Unemployed (U)	3,852	4,093	7,637	8,517	—
Employment to Population Ratio (E/Pop)	56.1	57.4	59.2	61.6	9.8
Unemployment Rate (U/LF)	5.5	4.9	7.1	6.7	121.1
Labor Force Participation Rates (LF/Pop)	59.4	60.4	63.8	66.0	11.1
Males	83.3	79.7	77.4	76.7	–7.9
16–19	56.1	56.1	60.5	49.4	–11.1
20–54					
55–64	86.8	83	72.1	67.0	–22.8
Over 65	33.1	26.8	19.0	16.1	–51.4
Females	37.7	43.3	51.5	58.3	54.6
16–19	39.3	44	52.9	48.4	23.1
35–44	43.3	51.1	65.5	85.2	96.8
Over 65	10.8	9.7	8.1	8.6	–20.4
White	58.8	60.2	64.1	66.6	13.3
Other	64.5	61.8	61.7	62.2	–3.6

Source: *Economic Report of the President*, 1994 and U.S. Department of Labor, Bureau of Labor Statistics, *Employment Hours and Earnings* and *Monthly Labor Review*, various dates.

...vironment

Economic Systems as Information Processors

Central planning centralizes data that would be disseminated widely in a market economy. One way to retain power is to monopolize information, so secrecy is common under all forms of totalitarianism. But sustained growth requires information flows across all levels of society and between centers for production. Shared information is vital for advancing technological frontiers. (Otherwise, all scientists would be forced to start by reinventing the wheel.) Thus, closed societies tend to stagnate and seldom compete successfully when pitted against open societies.

The isolation of closed societies usually drives them into ruts, using the same policy recipes over and over. For example, public buildings are uniformly drab when built according to architectural standards established by unmotivated central planners decades ago. The result? An American tourist observed that, in 1994 "buildings all over the ex-communist world look like Cabrini-Green" (a Chicago public housing project notorious for ugly, dysfunctional architecture).

Political freedom and decentralized markets expedite flows of information and technological advances. Anyone who has explored some of the data bases available on computer bulletin boards in the United States quickly realizes that far more information is available on most topics than anyone could completely digest. One result of modern communications networks and the globalization of markets is that, although significant regional variation remains, open societies have become more internally diverse, with ever broadening ranges of choices available to people regardless of where they live. For example, American fast food outlets are more available around the world than ever before, but so are restaurants featuring Chinese, Mexican, Vietnamese, Italian, Thai, or Ethiopian cuisine. Another result is that open societies are increasingly prosperous, and closed societies are being pressured to match their success.

Are Economic Systems Converging?

Exposure (communication and trade) facilitates political and economic imitation of successful patterns. Dramatic advances in standards of living in Western Europe, North America, and some Pacific Rim countries (e.g., Japan, Korea, Taiwan, Hong Kong, and Singapore) have publicized the gains available from allowing market forces to channel specialized production and exchange.

Reforms to decentralize decisions in the USSR accelerated in 1986, when then President Gorbachev launched policies of *perestroika* (economic reform) and *glasnost* (openness) with more internal freedom and greater accommodation with the United States and its allies. He learned, however, that the taste of political and economic freedom is addictive. The results of Gorbachev's experiments? He lost power while communist regimes toppled like rows of dominoes from 1989 to 1992 in Afghanistan, Albania, Bulgaria, Czechoslovakia (now split into the Czech and Slovakia Republics), Hungary, Mongolia, Nicaragua, Poland, Romania, Russia (the USSR dissolved into 15 independent nations), and Yugoslavia (rocked by civil war and shattered into three countries).

Another old-line communist regime is under fire in Cuba, and it seems unlikely that communism will long outlive aged party leaders in China or North Korea. China gradually began to decentralize economic decisions in 1978, shortly after diplomatic relations were reestablished with the United States. China has more successfully decollectivized (privatized) agriculture than the former USSR. In the early 1980s, China stopped being a net importer of rice and grain and became a net exporter. Russia remains a net importer of food.

China and most of the 15 countries carved out of the USSR increasingly rely on market forces in hopes of matching growth recorded in Europe, North America, and much of the Pacific Rim. Political freedom remains problematic in China, but its introduction of a market system has transformed it into the world's second

This sixth edition fully integrates current economic theories. Strategic behavior is woven into the traditional micro theory chapters to enhance students' understanding of modern micro topics, such as game theory, moral hazard, and adverse selections. Labor markets issues, such as wage stickiness and efficiency wages, are included in the traditional macro theory chapters.

UNEMPLOYMENT

Excessive unemployment reduces output and income, erodes human capital, and imposes widespread suffering. Classical analysis suggests that in the longer-term, the economy will equilibrate at full employment. In contrast, traditional Keynesian analysis indicates that adjustments to Aggregate Demand can restore full employment even in the shorter term. But as Figure 6 illustrates, in recent years unemployment has been not only persistent, but growing. And increasing numbers of workers are left jobless for increasingly long periods.

The traditional Keynesian model, as we have seen, explains unemployment as a consequence of inadequate Aggregate Demand and **sticky wages**. Labor markets, according to Keynes, may not clear. For example, workers are often not willing to accept a reduction in their money wages, setting a floor on wages and preventing the market from clearing. Thus the price of labor may not adjust so that the quantity demanded equals the quantity supplied. Modern Keynesians (or **new Keynesians**, as they are called) have developed richer theoretical microfoundations to explain why labor markets sometimes fail to clear, which can lead to persistent involuntary unemployment. Within this ongoing area of research, explanations for failures of labor markets to clear can be grouped under *labor contract* considerations, *efficiency wage* theories, and *dual labor markets* (insiders and outsiders). Before we look at the U.S. record on unemployment, we will examine each of these microeconomic foundations for new Keynesian analysis.

Labor Contracts

Unlike wheat, corn, or soybeans, labor is not traded on spot markets. (Almost no workers are employed one hour at a time, with constant recontracting.) Transaction costs are significant in most labor negotiations. Individuals negotiate either directly or through unions with firms about wage rates and the conditions of their employment. The high costs of information and

mobility (moving between jobs or hiring new employees) are the major reason that most employment relationships take on a long-term nature. Even though most workers today can expect to have five to seven jobs over the course of their careers, this still means that the average job is held six or seven years.

Such long-term relationships imply that wages and working conditions are usually negotiated only periodically; once a year is typical. Union contracts usually extend from two to three years, with wage rates being negotiated in nominal terms and often with escalator clauses to adjust wages for inflation. Even where union agreements are not in effect, federal and/or state laws, or both, often require that overtime pay rises as the hours of work increase beyond some point.

These **labor contracts**, whether written (*explicit*) or unwritten (*implicit*), mean that wages and benefits are set for lengthy periods and adjust in a lagged fashion to changes in economic conditions. Thus, when the economy turns downward, wages fall only slowly to create job openings for the unemployed. Another reason many firms reduce their wage offers only slowly during recessions is found in the notion of efficiency wages.

Efficiency Wages

The existence of substantial and sustained unemployment clashes with standard theories of competitive markets. According to classical theories of competitive labor markets, wage cuts would quickly and automatically eliminate unemployment (surpluses of labor). But the new Keynesians are skeptical that this is how the real world actually works.

The supply and demand for labor shown in Figure 7 yield an equilibrium of q_L and employment at wage w_L under standard assumptions. A worker who failed to perform conscientiously (a problem known as *shirking*) could be fired. However, if this labor market were competitive, this worker would almost immediately find another job at wage w_L. Thus, the threat of being fired would be ineffective as a

onomic Policy Making

Solid Waste Recycling

The problem with waste is that everyone wants you to pick it up and no one wants you to put it down.
William Ruckelshaus
(former EPA Director)

Recycling and waste management are growth industries. Americans will discard over 150 million tons of solid waste this year—enough to fill 80 lanes of garbage trucks extending from coast to coast. Nearly half of all states will fill their existing landfills by the year 2000. Stiff environmental regulations make average costs for new landfills nearly $60 million, but a NIMBY (not in my backyard) syndrome largely prevents their development. Figure 1 indicates the composition of this 150 million tons of garbage.

Moral suasion has swayed the American psyche favorably toward recycling as a remedy for environmental waste. Paper, plastics, metals, and glass are popular candidates for recycling. Aluminum cans represent a huge success cited by proponents of recycling. Virgin aluminum from bauxite is ten times more expensive than ingots from recycled cans. The relatively high prices paid for scrap aluminum have resulted in more than half of all aluminum beverage cans being recycled.

Too many recycling efforts, unfortunately, merely alter the form and place of environmental decay. Filtering airborne and waterborne pollutants, for example, results in dirty filters and mounds of solid waste. Burning solid waste, in turn, increases air pollution. Most cities have abandoned experiments with incinerators, which reflected attempts to increase the longevity of existing landfill space and produce energy as a by-product. Los Angeles, for example, dropped its incinerator project after one study indicated that burning trash might cause one additional Californian to develop cancer each year.

Consider paper and cardboard, which represent nearly 40% of all solid waste. Too few recycling paper mills are available to accomplish the recycling many municipalities now mandate; only eight mills are operating, and most are too remote from urban centers for cost-effective collection and transport. Buyer reluctance to use recycled newsprint—because it tears easily, disrupting tight deadlines by jamming high-speed presses—is another problem.

Paper bundles presented for recycling vary in quality. Recycling is impeded by dirty bundles: mixtures of newsprint, shopping bags,

junk mail, cardboard, catalogs, phone books, magazines, and so on. Equipment cannot satisfactorily sort dirty bundles, necessitating human labor. Clean bundles fetch $12 per ton, but municipalities are charged $20 per ton for the processing of dirty bundles. Teaching consumers who conscientiously try to recycle about the importance of keeping bundles clean is a key to making it economically viable. More than a million tons of dirty bundles of newsprint awaited recycling in 1994.

Switching packaging materials can be a complex and costly decision for firms. For example, over a decade ago, McDonald's switched from paper to plastic packaging in response to concerns about disappearing forests and pollution from paper mills. Then, just recently, McDonald's received a black eye over its use of plastic foam containers. It has returned to paper, but can buy only new paper packaging; satisfactory decontamination of recycled paper is not feasible. And policy flip-flops continue to be a problem. The latest word from the EPA is that paper containers are now considered more damaging than styrofoam.

Restructuring local government trash collection policies might enhance the success of recycling efforts. Most cities charge flat fees or pay for garbage collection through property taxes. To homeowners or tenants, adding additional cans for trash pickups entails only the cost of a new can and the effort required to move it to the curb. Some cities now use a per-can charge to encourage citizens to recycle and to selective in the products they purchase. Residents who pay by their volume of trash tend to avoid relatively small products enclosed in large bulky packages. Trash collection has declined by an average of 25% in cities

Recyclable

Paper & Cardboard 38%
Metals 14%
Plastics 18%

Nonrecyclable

Food Waste 4%
Yard Waste 11%
Other Nonrecyclable 13%
Glass 2%

Focusing on real-world issues from today's news and events, these boxed features reinforce and emphasize the text's themes which will allow students to apply economics to real life and expand their focus of learning.

ANALYTICAL GRAPHS

These clearly-labeled and designed graphs lay out major economics concepts for students with detailed captions that explain each graph and parallel the text discussion. This presentation allows students to clearly visualize and analyze issues while increasing their understanding of difficult topics.

FIGURE 11   Equilibrium in the Paperback Book Market

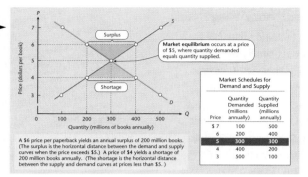

A $6 price per paperback yields an annual surplus of 200 million books. (The surplus is the horizontal distance between the demand and supply curves when the price exceeds $5.) A price of $4 yields a shortage of 200 million books annually. (The shortage is the horizontal distance between the supply and demand curves at prices less than $5.)

Market Schedules for Demand and Supply

Price	Quantity Demanded (millions annually)	Quantity Supplied (millions annually)
$7	100	500
6	200	400
5	300	300
4	400	200
3	500	100

The amounts buyers will purchase at the *equilibrium price* exactly equal the amounts producers are willing to sell. Let's examine the sense in which this is an equilibrium.

Figure 11 summarizes the market supplies and demands for paperbacks. (Note that there are more buyers and sellers than in our earlier examples.) After studying the supply and demand schedules, our auctioneer ascertains that at $5 per book the quantities demanded and supplied both equal 300 million books annually. Sellers will provide exactly as many novels as readers will buy at this price, so the market clears.

But what if the auctioneer set a price of $6 per book, or $4 per book? First, let us deal with the problem of a price set above equilibrium.

*A **surplus** is the excess of the quantity supplied over quantity demanded when the price is above equilibrium.*

At $6 per book, publishers would print 400 million books annually, but readers would only buy 200 million books. The surplus of 200 million books shown in Figure 11 would wind up as excess inventories in the hands of publishers.

Most firms would cut production as their inventories grew, and some might cut prices, hoping to unload surplus paperbacks on bargain hunters. (Publishers call this remaindering.) Other firms with swollen inventories would join in the price war. Prices would fall until all surplus inventories were depleted. Some firms might stop production as prices fell; others might permanently abandon the publishing industry.

How much the quantity supplied would decline is shown in the table accompanying Figure 11. When the price falls to $5 per book, consumers will buy 300 million books annually, while publishers will supply 300 million books; the quantity demanded equals the quantity sup-

...mics

FIGURE 5   Summary of Price and Quantity Responses to Changing Demands and Supplies

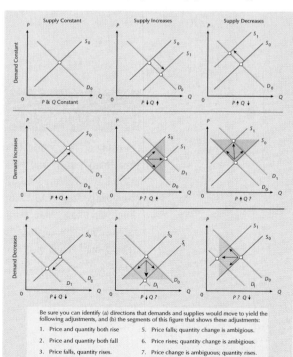

Be sure you can identify (a) directions that demands and supplies would move to yield the following adjustments, and (b) the segments of this figure that shows these adjustments:

1. Price and quantity both rise
2. Price and quantity both fall
3. Price falls, quantity rises.
4. Price rises, quantity falls.
5. Price falls; quantity change is ambiguous.
6. Price rises; quantity change is ambiguous.
7. Price change is ambiguous; quantity rises.
8. Price change is ambiguous; quantity falls.

Chapter 4   Markets and Equilibrium

SUMMARY FIGURES

These figures, which graphically summarize economic concepts, serve as excellent tools with which students can review more difficult economic theories.

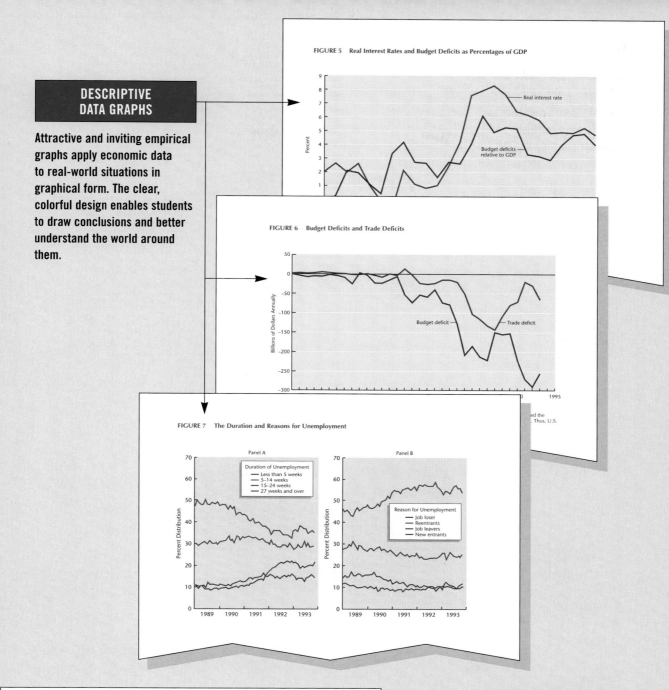

DESCRIPTIVE DATA GRAPHS

Attractive and inviting empirical graphs apply economic data to real-world situations in graphical form. The clear, colorful design enables students to draw conclusions and better understand the world around them.

FIGURE 5   Real Interest Rates and Budget Deficits as Percentages of GDP

Real interest rate

Budget deficits relative to GDP

FIGURE 6   Budget Deficits and Trade Deficits

Budget deficit

Trade deficit

1995

FIGURE 7   The Duration and Reasons for Unemployment

Panel A

Duration of Unemployment
— Less than 5 weeks
— 5–14 weeks
— 15–24 weeks
— 27 weeks and over

1989   1990   1991   1992   1993

Panel B

Reason for Unemployment
— Job loser
— Reentrants
— Job leavers
— New entrants

1989   1990   1991   1992   1993

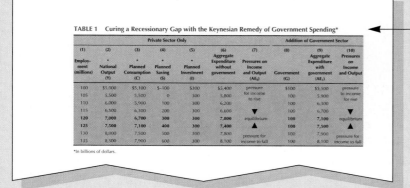

TABLE 1   Curing a Recessionary Gap with the Keynesian Remedy of Government Spending*

TABLES

Economic information is also presented in both analytical tables and empirical tables. These features are linked to corresponding graphs which promote a more complete understanding of economic concepts.

Third, new diagnostic technologies like magnetic resonance imaging (MRI) permit doctors to acquire diagnostic information that previously entailed rare and dangerous surgery. For example, computerized axial tomography (CAT scans) and MRI scanning equipment involve extremely high fixed costs and low variable costs. Consequently, there are tremendous incentives to use the equipment to spread overhead across increased volume. In addition, these expensive scanning techniques are essentially without risk. The result is that savings in surgical costs may be more than offset by the costs of newer high-volume diagnostic scanning.

• **Insurance, Medical Technology and Rising Medical Costs** Typical cities now have fewer five-star restaurants than five-star hospitals equipped to provide organ transplants, CAT scans, and other high-tech treatments. Why so few outstanding restaurants? The answer can be found by imagining what would happen if employers issued every worker in America a meal ticket permitting employees and their families to eat in *any* restaurant at any time, as often as they wished. All employees would do is leave the tip. Five-star restaurants would pop up like convenience stores. Five-star home food delivery services would supplant Domino's Pizza (unless Domino's upgraded its menus). Home cooked meals would become endangered species. Why cook? For the cost of a tip, you can enjoy a piping hot gourmet meal delivered to your door.

future. When a new high-tech treatment is developed, pressure grows for insurance policies to cover the treatment. Competition compels insurance companies to cover such treatments to maintain their market shares. Pharmaceutical and medical equipment companies know this and finance immense R&D projects with confidence that, once a successful treatment is developed, insurance payments will be made available *no matter what the cost.* Thus, firms expect solid rates of return on their R&D dollars.

The insurance and R&D relationship has an unfortunate bias in favor of high-tech, high-cost treatments. There is some evidence that by merely eliminating care that provides little or no benefit, health-care expenditures could be reduced by nearly 30%.[17] For example, while tests for prostate specific antigens (PSA) can help monitor recurrence in cancer patients, they are not cost-effective in screening patients without histories of prostate cancer. When trials were still underway (the R&D component), insurance companies were prematurely pressured to pay for PSA testing on healthy males. Most of this pressure came from the insured population who, individually, did not pick up the tab. Many other countries understandably have tried to contain rising health-care costs by limiting the use of high-tech treatments.

• **Summary** What can we conclude from our review of this market? First, our demand for health care derives from desires for health and ... efits. Second, ... h care, its ... rom fed-

---

Rules vs. Discretionary Policies

Most economists who draw ideas heavily from the classical school believe that designing discretionary monetary and fiscal policies to buffer business cycles is an impossible task. They favor doing away with all discretion in policymaking and adopting stable and permanent monetary and fiscal rules. These critics believe that the market system is inherently stable and that severe swings in business activity inevitably follow ill-advised discretionary policies. One mechanism to eliminate discretion in monetary policymaking is a monetary growth rule.

A monetary growth rule would dictate that the money supply be increased at a rate compatible with historical growth of GDP, say 3% annually.

Suppose you are driving a high-powered car on a fairly straight highway that is banked slightly along the edges to keep you on the road. Unfortunately, someone has blackened the front and side windows—you cannot see where you are or what lies ahead. To make matters worse, your gas pedal sticks at times, the steering wheel is loose, and your brakes alternate between pure mush and grabbing so sharply that you skid. You can vaguely see where you have been through a fogged-over rearview mirror. What is your best strategy?

If you press the gas pedal too hard, you may go so fast that the curbs at the edge of the road will fail to keep you on course. If you try to steer, you may guide yourself over the side. Your best strategy will be to carefully adjust the accelerator to maintain a slow but steady speed and let

viewed as the fumblings of people who barely deserve learners' permits playing with the controls of an Indianapolis 500 racer. They tend to oversteer and to jump back and forth from the accelerator to the brake. The resulting stop-and-go economic pattern might resemble your path when you were learning to drive—and, unlike policymakers, you knew what you were passing and could see what lay ahead. We also hope that the steering, braking, and acceleration of the car you drove responded more precisely than the cumbersome tools available to monetary and fiscal policymakers.

In addition to a monetary growth rule, most economists opposed to discretion in policymaking advocate certain fiscal rules:

1. Government spending should be set at the amounts of government goods and services that the public would demand if the economy were at full employment; no make-work projects should be permitted.
2. Tax rates should then be structured so that the federal budget would be roughly in balance if the economy were at full employment.

Although monetarists perceive some problems emerging from improper spending and tax policies (e.g., Hoover's tax hike in 1930–1932, Johnson's simultaneous wars on poverty and in Vietnam, and the enormous budget deficits of the Reagan years), they cast central bankers (the Fed) as the major villains in their explanations of cyclical chaos in market economies.

The Culpability of the FED

... rists view the market system as largely ... ing and predictable; the ... er- ... nment ...

BIOGRAPHY
Joan Robinson and E. H. Chamberlin: Bringing Realism to Theories of Market Structure

Until Edward Hastings Chamberlin (1899–1967) attempted to fuse the theories of monopoly and competition, the case of many sellers offering differentiated products had been overlooked. Earlier mainstream economists concentrated on the theory of pure competition, which assumes many sellers of homogeneous products. Chamberlin instead saw close competitors in nearly every market trying to gain market power by differentiating their products. For example, firms often allege the superiority of their products over others.

Chamberlin revised his Harvard Ph.D. dissertation and published *The Theory of Monopolistic Competition* in 1933. His was among the few dissertations to ever profoundly alter economic theory. The central feature of his analysis is that it portrays the demand curves facing firms with differentiated products as being negatively sloped.

In other words, firms that compete on the basis of product differences could raise prices without losing all their customers, but they would sell less output. This fact mirrors elements of monopoly. However, competition tends to lower this negatively sloped de-

mand curve to a point of tangency with the firm's average total cost curve, so that no monopoly profits are realized in the long run. Chamberlin's theory was combined with Joan Robinson's ideas to spark numerous studies of industrial markets in the 1940s and 1950s. These analytical feats have provided useful insights into numerous market situations. In Robinson's phrase, she and Chamberlin introduced a "box of tools" sharper and more generally applicable than those that preceded their works.

> *I don't know much math, so I have to think.*
>
> Joan Robinson

The iconoclastic British economist Joan Robinson (1903–1983) was a combatant in virtually every major controversy in economic theory and policy between 1930 and 1983. However, her foes joined her friends in admiring the innovative quality of her ideas and research. She married E. A. G. Robinson (another distinguished British economist) after completing her formal studies in economics and was among the small group of Cambridge University economists who aided John Maynard Keynes

in launching the Keynesian Revolution.

An avowed radical and Marxist, she blended the insights of Keynes, Marx, and neoclassical reasoning in a manner uniquely her own. Robinson's work bridged capital theory, the theories of value and distribution, macroeconomics, and the economics of policymaking, but her most noteworthy contributions were in the area of imperfect competition. At almost exactly the same time that Chamberlin issued his theory of monopolistic competition from Cambridge, Massachusetts, Joan Robinson launched a parallel theory from Cambridge, England, in *The Economics of Imperfect Competition.*

Robinson's imperfect competition, however, stresses oligopolistic interdependence and views competition and monopoly as mutually exclusive, while Chamberlin identified modern business as a blending of the two. Robinson refined the theory of price discrimination, introduced the concept of *monopsony power* (that is, the ability of powerful buyers to control prices), and separated average revenue (demand) and marginal revenue curves.

SUMMARY

1. According to standard theory, the major economic problem posed by the exercise of market power is economic inefficiency. Studies that have attempted to measure the "welfare loss" caused by monopoly have, however, yielded tiny estimates of loss. No serious empirical study suggest that more than 1% to 2% of GDP is lost because of market power, with most estimates being much less than 1%.8 Is antitrust action a waste of taxpayers' resources if these estimates are correct? Are there other socially important reasons to limit industrial concentration? If so, what are they?

2. When the Oakland Raiders moved to Los Angeles in 1982, they touched a vital nerve in the National Football League. This move, which was subsequently upheld by the courts, weakened the NFL's influence over the movement of franchises and threatened to undercut the pooling of network television revenues (60% of NFL income). The NFL is now lobbying Congress for a blanket antitrust exemption. Do you think professional sports should be exempt from antitrust laws? Should owners of professional teams be permitted to move their teams at their discretion? NFL critics argue that the league is more interested in limiting the number of tams and ensuring profits for the existing 28 owners. Do you agree?

3. Are the interests of the general public, the regulated industry, competing industries, of government regulators most obviously served by the following types of regulations? Which industries gain and which lose in each case?

    a. An AIDS vaccine is kept off the market for two years while the Food and Drug Administration tests it on animals to ascertain whether it is safe for humans.

    b. Gasoline must contain 15% fuel alcohol additives each winter in an attempt to reduce Denver's brown cloud of air pollution.

    c. Penalties on clerks in stores are raised if they sell beer to minors.

    d. Restaurants must be inspected every 180 days by the Department of Health.

    e. Installation of new, safer toilet seats is mandated for every facility serving the public or employing more than six workers.

    f. Should the heirs of smokers who ultimately died because of their addiction be able to collect for damages from tobacco companies?

4. The Occupational Safety and Health Act (OSHA) requires that workplaces be made as safe as possible (or more so, according to some critics), with little or no regard for costs. How would you expect OSHA regulations to affect prices for goods previously produced under hazardous conditions relative to the prices of those that have always been produced in safe work environments? What would you expect to happen to wages in previously hazardous industries? In previously safe industries? What will happen to real wages economy-wide? To health insurance rates? Should it matter for the purposes of OSHA regulation whether the risks of particular occupations are well known or not? If so, why?

5. Suppose you were a Food and Drug Administration (FDA) official charged with licensing new drugs. There are two types of errors to which you might fall prey: (a) you might license a harmful drug or (b) you might keep a very beneficial drug off the market. What do you think is the nature of the trade-off between these types of errors? Which of these two types of errors would you wish

Economics

Cornerstones of Economics

People often refer to the financial aspects of business or their personal lives as economics, but the subject of economics encompasses a much broader spectrum of human behavior than money and business alone. Just as connecting the straight-edged pieces is a good start in solving a jigsaw puzzle, this first part of this book introduces building blocks for an understanding of economics. These basic concepts are then applied to a variety of problems in the rest of this text to provide a relatively complete picture of the scope of economics.

Core economics concepts are the themes of Chapter 1. Our first topic, *scarcity*, arises because the sum of human wants exceeds the world's capacity to produce goods —economics would be unnecessary if scarcity evaporated. We then survey various *resources* and examine how scarcity makes *choices* necessary and *opportunity costs* unavoidable. Economists assume that people make rational decisions that they (at times, incorrectly) expect to serve their own self-interest. Attempts to maximize self-interest tend to yield *economic efficiency* because net benefits are maximized.

Our second set of building blocks centers on methods economists use to study the way the world works and the division of economics into *positive* (scientific) versus *normative* (prescriptive) components. We also distinguish *microeconomics*, which examines choices by individual decision-makers and patterns of exchange (trade) between individuals and between nations, from *macroeconomics*, which focuses on such national economic issues as *unemployment*, *inflation*, and *economic growth*, and many international financial issues as well (e.g., exchange rates among currencies). The increasing influence of international trade and finance in countries everywhere raises a variety of both microeconomic and macroeconomic issues.

Chapter 2 opens with an overview of the broad roles played by such institutions as *households*, *business firms*, and *governments* in the market economy. Basic interactions among these social organizations are shown in a simple *circular flow model*. Then we explore how *comparative advantage* governs efficient patterns of production and trade within and between countries. This provides a background for the *production possibilities frontier*, a depiction of scarcity and the inevitability of trade-offs. We also survey several allocative mechanisms (e.g., government or the market system) that people use to deal with scarcity in a changing world.

This overview of capitalism and its alternatives leads to Chapter 3, where *supply and demand* are introduced. Supply and demand analysis provides insights into how a market system determines prices and outputs and allows us to interpret a wide range of human behavior, including ways people fine-tune their choices based on how they expect *marginal* (small) changes to affect them. In Chapter 4, we apply supply and demand to a variety of public policy topics, ranging from agriculture to wage and price controls to the waves of change inundating the international economy.

Can we achieve the standard of living our parents have enjoyed? Will increasingly aggressive foreign competition destroy American jobs and businesses? Are deficits sapping U.S. power and prestige? And why are most formerly socialist countries experiencing such bumpy paths in converting to the market system? These and similar questions are parts of the puzzle as we strive toward the ultimate economic goal—high standards of living for people everywhere.

History books are filled with tales about politicians who lost power because of economic crises. Recent reform movements in Asia, Eastern Europe, and South Africa sprouted from mixtures of despair about economic stagnation and hunger for political freedom. Policies to foster prosperity have been key issues in every U.S. election from 1792 through 1992. (Bill Clinton had "It's the economy, stupid!" taped to a bathroom mirror at his campaign headquarters as a daily reminder during his 1992 march to the White House.)

Before you dismiss economics as relevant only for politics or business, we should mention that *economics focuses on* all *the choices people make as well as the personal and social consequences of these choices.* Some choices involve money, but all de-

cisions fall within the realm of economics. Most decisions involve balancing costs versus benefits, which are not easily always measurable with money; many costs and benefits are ultimately psychological.

Will you finish college? (Potential benefits include higher lifetime income, meeting people with shared interests, and the joy of learning; costs include outlays for tuition and books, the drudgery of dull classes, and the income you could be making right now.) What will you choose for a major? (Will your basic interests be as important as whether subjects are potentially lucrative?) Where will you live and work? Should you marry? (Marriage involves both financial and psychological costs and benefits.) Should you have children? If so, how many? How will your limited income be spent? Decisions about these and other economic choices shape the course of your life.

Right now, economics may seem a mystery, but you have heard such terms as *costs, profit, prices,* and *supply and demand* all your life. Other concepts may seem overly abstract at first, but most are merely precise descriptions of everyday events. You may be skeptical about the theories and graphs economists use to interpret how the world works, but when you finish this book, we think you will join us in the view that the economic way of thinking offers valuable insights into people's everyday behavior.

Your study of economics is launched in this chapter by looking at core concepts that will help you discern why people make certain choices and avoid others. We first survey how scarcity emerges when relatively unlimited wants clash with limited resources. Scarcity implies that every decision involves *opportunity costs*, another key concept. You will also learn how people try to adjust to scarcity efficiently. Our final task in this chapter is an overview of methods economists use to study human behavior.

SCARCITY

I did the best I could with what I had.
Supreme Court Justice Thurgood Marshall,
1908–1993

Human wants can never be completely fulfilled. Whether your goal is as mundane as consuming more goods or as lofty as world peace, you face the constraint Justice Marshall described. Production is a prerequisite for all income and spending. But productive resources and time are limited, while human wants are virtually unlimited. Pitting our insatiable wants against our limited time and resources, as shown in Figure 1, yields the basic economic problem—scarcity.

> **Scarcity** *occurs because human wants exceed the production possible with our limited time and resources.*

Scarcity necessitates *trade-offs*; you can select only a few of all available alternatives. For example, in only two hours, you cannot go hiking, study for a test, and see a film. Thus, scarcity forces us to choose, a fact reflected in a broad definition of economics:

> **Economics** *is the study of how people, individually and collectively, allocate their limited resources to try to satisfy their unlimited wants.*

Scarcity occurs because our limited resources and time can only yield limited production and income, but people's wants are virtually unlimited. Output is produced by using knowledge (technology) to apply energy to a blend of resources. Production, in turn, generates the income people spend on the limited goods and services available.

FIGURE 1 The Origins of Scarcity

Apples, public parks, apartments, or cars are examples of economic goods that help satisfy these wants.

*A **good** is any item or service that adds to human happiness.*

Goods are scarce if the amounts people want exceed the amounts freely available. *Commodities* are tangible goods that can be bought and sold, such as cars or VCRs. Such *services* as haircuts or police protection are also goods because they add to our happiness. Garbage, an economic *bad* (anything that reduces happiness) is, unfortunately, not scarce, so trash collection is a scarce good.

Desirable things that are not scarce are *free goods*. Heat from the sun that warms our earth so we don't all freeze is a free good. But identifying other truly free goods is difficult because our enjoyment is constrained by time and access. For example, you can have all the sea water you want at nearly zero cost (but only if you are already on the beach), or look at a sunset all you like—but even these activities are free only if you truly have nothing else to do with your time. You can freely breathe all the air your lungs will hold (accepting current pollution levels). But even impure air may be scarce for scuba divers, astronauts, or victims of flat tires.

That virtually nothing people enjoy is truly free is reflected in the saying, "There is no such thing as a free lunch" (TINSTAAFL).[1] Limited time and resources constrain production so that our insatiable desires for goods are never fully satisfied. Even billionaires face scarcity—of their time or health, for example, or in their desires for fame, inner peace, or a cleaner environment.

For a specific individual, the possession of a specific unit of a given good has (*a*) value in use, or (*b*) value in exchange. Suppose your idea of heaven is snowboarding down a steep snowy mountain slope. Your snowboard's *value in use* is ultimately subjective. Now suppose you owned a snowboard factory, but you hate the

cold, the snow, and almost everything associated with actually using a snowboard. A snowboard would still be valuable to you because of its *value in exchange*—the value of other things you could buy if you sold it. Value in exchange is the motivating factor behind the production of goods by firms and is the foundation for most economic transactions.

Production and Resources

Hamburgers, mouse traps, and houses are, obviously, produced goods, but services also require production.

***Production** entails using technology to apply energy to materials in ways that make the materials more valuable, or that otherwise help satisfy human wants.*

For example, pouring a cup of coffee is productive—the coffee is more valuable in your cup than in the coffee pot. Studying is also productive: economic concepts on printed paper increase in value when integrated into your thinking processes.

Productive resources (frequently called *factors of production* or *inputs*) come in all types, shapes, and sizes, and all are limited. Economists conventionally refer to four broad categories of resources: *labor, land, capital,* and *entrepreneurship*. These resources provide the energy and materials that, combined through technology, make production possible. Knowledge is integral to technology.

***Technology** consists of the "recipes" available for use in combining and reshaping resources in production processes.*

The technology to grow roses is a simple example. If you know that roses need sunlight and moisture, you (being entrepreneurial and willing to bear the risk of failure) find a sunny spot and apply energy (labor) to a shovel (capital) to dig a hole in the earth (land). Insert a rosebush, add fertilizer, dirt, and water (materials), and, with luck, roses will soon bloom—but never unlimited amounts of roses.

---

[1]This phrase originated as TANSTAAFL ("there ain't no such thing as a free lunch") in a novel by Robert Heinlein, but we'll try to be more grammatical.

How resources can be combined productively clearly depends on technology. Indeed, technology determines whether some materials are even seen as resources. For example, prior to the time when our nomadic ancestors began settling down and planting crops, land was not recognized as a scarce resource. Before our understanding of potential uses for silicon in electronics advanced (e.g., computer chips), clean sand was used primarily to make glass and bricks. Rust was merely an irritant to blacksmiths until someone thought to use it as a pigment in paints. Today, iron oxides underpin another visual revolution—video tapes. And imbedding other types of "rust" in tape and plastic yields computer tapes and diskettes.

Knowledge and technology are closely intertwined. Society increasingly recognizes how industrial technologies may foul clean air and water. Consequently, environmental quality is now recognized as a scarce resource and as an international issue for policy makers. How resources, technology, and production are related is summarized in Table 1.

● **Labor** Labor resources are the physical and mental talents that people can make available for production; labor is typically measured by time available for work during a period. Farm hands, CPAs, and NFL quarterbacks all provide labor services. All payments per period for labor services (including salaries, commissions, fringe benefits, etc.) are called *wages*.

● **Land** Economists define "land" to include all natural resources, such as raw land, miner-

TABLE 1 Resources and Production

Resources	Characteristics	Contributions	Productive Types of Production
Human resources Labor (*wages*)	Productive talents (mental and physical) and energy	Technology (especially skills and knowledge) and energy (effort)	Tangible consumer goods (commodities and services)
Entrepreneurs (*profits*)	Organization of production, innovation of new goods and technologies, and the bearing of risk and uncertainty		Gross investment (new capital)
Natural resources Land (rents)	Acreage, minerals, and the natural environment	Materials and energy	*minus* depreciation
Produced resources Capital* (*interest*)	Buildings, equipment, and other refined materials or incomplete outputs	Technology, energy, and materials	*equals* net new capital

*Note that financial capital (e.g., stocks, bonds, and currency) is not economic capital, nor is it a resource.

Resources (in column 1) have characteristics and provide services (columns 2 and 3) that allow them to be combined productively, through the organizational talents of entrepreneurs. Production (column 4) breaks down into: (a) Consumption goods, or (b) Investment goods. In turn, consumption goods comprise either services (e.g., having your lawn mowed) or commodities (e.g., food and clothing). Subtracting depreciation from the output of gross investment goods (e.g., machine tools) yields net investment.

als, water, climate, and forests. Payments per period for the use of land are called *rent*.

• **Capital** Improvements that make natural resources more productive are *capital*, which includes all produced resources—such things as buildings, machinery, and roads. The production of new capital is *investment*. Some capital wears out each year; this decline in value is *depreciation*. A bulldozer, for example, loses value as it ages and suffers wear and tear. Total investment each year is gross investment. Subtracting depreciation leaves net investment—the change in the nation's capital stock.[2] If $1 trillion is paid for new capital in 1996 while existing capital depreciates by $700 billion, net investment for the year is only $300 billion.

Much of capital investment in the United States is undertaken by business firms, but the government also invests in capital; schools, roads, and dams are examples of investment spending on capital *infrastructure*. Many economists identify development of a rich economic infrastructure—transportation and communications networks are other examples—as keys for growth and development. And, increasingly, economists refer to such activities as on-the-job training or acquisition of a college degree as investments in *human capital*.

However, from the economic perspective, the terms "investment" and "capital" are often misused. Paper assets like currency or stocks and bonds are *financial capital*, which ultimately permits the purchase and use of finished goods or resources, including economic capital. People often fail to distinguish economic (physical) capital from financial capital, which is normally represented by a document of some sort. A deed to a house is financial capital; the house itself is economic capital. Throughout this book, the term "capital" normally refers to economic capital. Payments for both physical capital and financial capital are called *interest*. Note that capital providers receive *interest*, not profit; all profit goes to entrepreneurs.

• **Entrepreneurship** *Entrepreneurs* provide a specialized human resource; they combine labor, land, and capital to produce goods while incurring risk in their quest for profits. After paying wages, rent, and interest for the use of other resources, entrepreneurs keep any funds left over from their sales revenue. An entrepreneur's *profit* is a reward for organizing production, bearing risks, or introducing innovations that improve the quality of life.

The most successful entrepreneurs tend to be innovators of new technologies—better production methods or new products. Advances in communications (e.g., the information highway) and biogenetics are hot areas right now. But risk of *loss* (negative profit) to an entrepreneur is often enormous. Over half of all ventures fail within their first two years. Thousands of oil companies went bankrupt when oil prices plummeted in the 1980s, and hundreds of firms have lost fortunes trying to develop personal computers and software. In 1993, Sears closed its catalogue division because of aggressive competition from Walmart and other discounters. On the other hand, Bill Gates established Microsoft (a major software developer) after dropping out of Harvard, and quickly became the world's youngest self-made billionaire. By 1993, the total value of Microsoft stock exceeded that for IBM. Only prospects of profit can overcome fears of loss.

Unlimited Human Wants

> (*Economists have*) . . . *an irrational passion for dispassionate rationality.*
>
> John Maurice Clark

---

[2]"Stock" in this context does not refer to the corporate stock traded on Wall Street. Instead, it refers to the amount of capital available to society at a point in time. Economists refer to *flow* variables and *stock* variables. A flow variable makes no sense without a time reference. For example, if your salary is $100, it matters greatly whether it is $100 per hour or $100 per week. Thus, income is a flow variable. Stock variables, on the other hand, require no time referent. A sack of groceries is a stock; so is your bike. Refering to such stocks as your bicycle "per hour" would be nonsense, but you can compute such flow variables as hourly income or hourly production. One subtle distinction is between "saving" (a flow—the amount you save per period) and "savings" (a stock—the accumulation of your past efforts to save).

Is Self-Interest Immoral or Unavoidable?

If you sliced off a fingertip while buttering your toast just minutes after hearing on the "Today" show that an earthquake had swallowed China and its 1.3 billion people, which event would dismay you more? In his *Theory of Moral Sentiments* (1759), Adam Smith argued that loss of a little finger would keep the average European from sleeping that night, "but, provided he never saw them, he will snore with the most profound security over the loss of millions of his brethren, and the destruction of that immense multitude seems plainly an object less interesting to him than this paltry misfortune of his own."

Smith illustrated the power of self-interest with this example, arguing that disasters to others arouse sympathy only to the extent that you can imagine yourself in similar straits. Suppose poking your pinkie into a crack in the space-time continuum would prevent the catastrophe in China, but you would lose your finger in the process. Would you do it? Smith thought most of us would, not out of love for humanity, but rather because of ". . . love of what is honourable and noble, of the grandeur, and dignity, and superiority of our own characters." That is, you probably could not live with yourself if you failed to sacrifice your finger.

Self-interest tends to limit and put a different spin on, but not eliminate, charitable acts. Our personal senses of morality yield a spectrum of willingness to sacrifice for others. If you would surrender your finger for the lives of 1.3 billion anonymous Chinese, would you give up an arm? (Would whether others knew about your sacrifice matter?) Would you sacrifice your life? Only a saint could automatically answer this last question.

Constraints on resources and time are only one of two important dimensions of scarcity. The other dimension of scarcity stems from our unlimited wants. Try to imagine consuming all the cars, clothes, or gourmet meals you would want if they were costless. Even if all your desires for some goods were met, it is hard to imagine being so satisfied that you could think of nothing else that would add to your happiness—for example, more interesting conversations, intriguing films, or closer friends. You will always want more goods and pleasures for as long as you live. If all wants could be met, economics would be irrelevant because decisions would never be required. But most people thrive on a bit of adversity and would find this imaginary world boring.

• **Rational Self-Interest** Most economists follow the lead of Adam Smith, the eighteenth-century philosopher who laid the foundations for modern economics, by assuming that people act purposefully to maximize their satisfactions, given their limited time, information, resources, and budgets. The economist's characterization of *Homo sapiens* as *Homo economicus* views all human behavior as rationally self-interested. Why Smith adopted this approach is addressed in Focus 1.

You may object that a lot of people seem irrational, but the economist's notion that people act rationally merely implies that people try to act in ways consistent with their own objectives, even if their goals seem absurd to most outsiders. For example, if misanthropes used grotesque, full-facial tattoos to signal their contempt for society, economists would view this disfigurement as rational—the tattoos are consistent with their objectives. But we would not try to explain why the group was so intensely anti-establishment. (Economists are not psychiatrists!)

The assumption of self-interest need not imply total selfishness or that people never worry about other people's well-being. Personal values powerfully influence our perceptions of costs and benefits. No society could function, for example, if everyone was willing to use a $1 bullet to gain a $99 profit by shooting any stranger flashing a $100 bill in a dark alley. But we all recognize that some sociopaths will maximize these sorts of "profits" in a flash.

Fortunately, most of us consider others to some extent; we want our actions to benefit others and try to do more good than harm. Thus, humanitarianism is not an exception to self-interested behavior. People's self-esteem and their reputations are boosted by picking up litter or contributing to charity. Audience members often share in a "warm glow" when benefit concerts generate funds to support human rights, aid the homeless, or improve environmental quality.

You may agree with philosophers who deny that behavior universally reflects attempts to maximize pleasure and minimize pain—a notion that seems to reduce motivation to its lowest common denominator. Nevertheless, theories based on individual happiness maximization or wealth maximization are usually more realistic and predictive than models based on purely humanitarian motives. Moreover, even people who view behavior as driven by loftier motives concede that personal interest is important at the margin.

Self-interest need not condemn humanity to constant conflict. You will learn in Chapters 3 and 4 why most economists view self-interest as a powerful force that helps coordinate people's plans, indirectly leading to broad forms of social cooperation. In fact, so-called selfish people and so-called altruists react similarly to many events. For example, if the price of fruit falls relative to the prices of other foods, both a selfish person and an altruist may buy more—the selfish person to personally devour the fruit and the altruist to distribute it to needy children. And economics is more focused on the fact that both groups buy more fruit than on who eats it.

Some Basic Choices

Limits on time and resources make it impossible to produce all that we want. We can have some things we want, but not everything. Thus, scarcity forces every society to make choices in trying to resolve three *basic economic questions*:

1. *What* economic goods will be produced?
2. *How* will resources be used in production?
3. *Who* will get to consume economic goods?

How society answers these basic questions ultimately determines our economic structure and level of prosperity.

• **What?**   Current resources and technology limit a society to choosing one combination from the innumerable mixes of goods that could feasibly be produced in a given period. More of any one good means less of another. How much of each good would we like? Shall we have bigger government and a smaller private sector? More health care and less housing? More leisure and less work? Should we protect such endangered species as spotted owls if this drives up the costs of lumber and new housing and reduces job opportunities in the Pacific Northwest?

• **How?**   Most goods can be produced with many different mixes of resources. Farm crops can be harvested by hand or by machine. A swimming pool can be excavated in 1 day by 1 operator and a bulldozer, by 30 shovel-wielders in 1 week, or by 300 people with teaspoons in 1 month. Each day, thousands of Chinese push brooms along the streets of Beijing, while major U.S. cities use giant street sweepers to rid our roads of debris.

• **Who?**   Even if we know what goods we want and how they will be produced, we still must address the question of *who* will get (*a*) income and wealth and (*b*) specific goods. Every society faces hard questions about *equity* (fairness). Our personal views of equity often turn on the distribution of income or wealth, broad claims that permit people to use goods and resources. But this is only one aspect of the "Who?" question. Some of your friends, for example, may work two jobs and sacrifice almost everything else so they can drive sporty modern cars, while some rich eccentrics happily drive rusty old pickups. Answers to the "Who?" question ideally accommodate differences in people's tastes and preferences.

These three basic questions—*what, how,* and *for whom*—seem simple, but each must be addressed almost countless times.[3] For example, "What?" covers not only the types of goods to be produced from *a* to *z*, but also how much of each good. And each basic question is faced at different levels by individuals, families, business firms, government, or other social groups.

For example, college administrators must decide *what* courses to offer, *how* they will be taught (huge lectures, computer labs, or small seminars), and *who* will receive admission and loans or scholarships. Students must choose *what* courses to take, *whom* to take them with, and *how* to study. (Will you attend class and do all homework, or party hearty and cram for your finals?) Families must choose. Shall family funds be used for extravagant vacations? Or your education? Or ballet lessons for Baby? Government officials also choose. Should more or fewer resources be devoted to education? Health care? Reducing the federal deficit?

The economic fabric of a society is woven from the composite of all the answers to these three basic questions by all of its decision-making units. And our combined choices about what, how, and for whom automatically answer a related issue: *When* will goods or resources be used? Perishables such as ice cream cones or newspapers lose value relatively soon after their production, but durable goods such as stained glass windows or canned coffee can be stored for years. Similarly, some productive resources are perishable, while others last for centuries. For example, eight hours of labor are lost forever each day that a worker is unemployed, but a vein of silver or a barrel of oil can be stored indefinitely. Each generation decides how much capital to accumulate and how many natural resources (rain forests, energy reserves) to leave for use by future generations.

---

[3]Another major issue, who decides, is addressed in Chapter 2.

Different aspects of these basic questions recur throughout economics. Relative scarcities of various goods are indicated by their prices—vital information (another scarce good) when choosing among limited alternatives. But what does "price" or "cost" mean? The answer is less obvious than you may think.

Opportunity Costs

Choosing any scarce thing forecloses other options; such lost options are economic costs. Suppose you drive a gas guzzler. Buying an extra gallon of gasoline per week may preclude an extra slice of pizza weekly, but buying the pizza instead of the gas may force you to drive less and walk more. Economists view economic (or *opportunity*) cost as the value of the next best option forgone because of a decision.

> *Opportunity cost* is the value of the best alternative surrendered when a choice is made.

Most people think costs are measured solely by the money paid to produce or acquire goods, but opportunity costs are ultimately personal and involve far more than money alone. Have you ever estimated the cost of your education? Fill in the blanks in Table 2, which verifies that these costs extend far beyond payments for tuition and books. Consider the value of your time. Instead of studying and attending class, you could be holding a full-time job (or maybe two jobs). You may be sacrificing better food and clothes, a nice car, and a comfortable apartment. The values of all forgone alternatives are the true costs of education. But suppose you quit school. The costs of your nice car, apartment, food, and clothing would include the sacrificed enjoyment of learning and campus life and the higher future income and consumption your degree might have made possible.

To show how broad the concept of opportunity cost is, suppose that Bob and Dan both love Liz. Liz reciprocates both Bob's and Dan's love. Unfortunately, Bob threatens to find someone new if Liz does not quit seeing Dan. Soap opera fans might commiserate with Liz's

TABLE 2 The Costs of a College Education, 1995

National Average (annual)		Your Costs
Tuition	$2,100 (public)	_____
	$10,200 (private)	_____
Books and miscellaneous supplies	$ 1,100	_____
Forgone income (conservatively)	$10,000 (minimum wage)	_____
Annual total	$13,200 to $21,300	_____
Typical total for a four-year degree	$52,800 to $85,200	_____

Sources: American Council of Education, Department of Education Estimates for 1993, and author estimates and updates.

dilemma, but economists view the real cost to Liz of a continued relationship with Bob as giving up Dan, and vice versa.

What people do often differs from what they say, so economists concentrate on behavior instead of words alone. For example, Focus 2 suggests that people usually exaggerate when describing something as priceless, implying that its value is so high that trying to estimate cost is futile. Fortunately, most people are very ingenious in finding and selecting good alternatives.

Monetary (Absolute) Prices

Opportunity costs may be only loosely related to monetary (absolute) prices.

> **Absolute prices** *are prices in terms of some* **monetary** *unit.*

Prices in the United States are commonly stated in dollars and cents, but these absolute prices could also be stated in francs, pesos, or yen. For example, if dollars and yen were equally acceptable for purchases and $1 could be exchanged for 100 yen, you would divide any price stated in yen by 100 to figure the dollar price. Tourists and international traders quickly master such mental gymnastics and become indifferent about which currency is used to state absolute prices.

• **Relative Prices**   Opportunity costs as measured by *relative prices* shape most decisions: how many hot fudge sundaes must be sacrificed for

a new compact disk? For a ski vacation? Answers to such questions entail comparisons of monetary prices.

> **Relative prices** *are the prices of goods or resources in terms of each other, and are computed by dividing their absolute prices by one another.*

Rational decision-making focuses on relative prices, which embody tremendous amounts of information about sacrificed alternatives. If hot fudge sundaes are $2 while CDs are $14 and ski vacations are $560, then a CD costs 7 sundaes and a ski vacation costs 280 sundaes or 40 CDs ($14/2 = 7; 560/2 = 280; 560/14 = 40$).

Monetary (absolute) prices bear little on rational decisions until, perhaps unconsciously, we convert them to relative prices. Relative prices are unaffected if all absolute prices change on a one-time, proportional basis. Try this mental experiment: How would you react if your income, assets, liabilities, and all prices for goods and resources doubled, once and for all time? *Answer*: You would handle twice as many dollars, but otherwise your behavior would not change. *Conclusion*: Relative prices guide decisions; changes in absolute prices ultimately affect most decisions only to the extent that relative prices are distorted. Changes in absolute prices can, however, pose problems during inflation, which is harmful primarily because it increases uncertainty and distorts relative prices; some absolute prices zoom up in an inflationary period, while others are somewhat sticky. Thus, inflation garbles the quality of information about relative scarcity, a problem dealt with later in this book.

Is Life Priceless?

The cliché, "human life is priceless," is often heard in debates about public policy, but, in reality, people constantly assign prices to their own lives and those of others. Here are a few examples:

1. Choosing more dangerous over less dangerous activities. If you fail to buckle up, you (subconsciously) weigh the inconvenience of a seat belt against a higher probability of death or injury. In so doing, you implicitly assign prices to your life and body parts. And parents assign prices for their children when they fail to immunize them. Hitchhiking, skydiving, or even taking a walk all involve risks that implicitly assign prices to life.

2. High medical costs cause some people to forgo treatment that would prolong their lives or the lives of seriously ill relatives.

3. A few dollars per child could save children from starvation in famine-plagued countries.

4. Major wars of any duration are usually fought with draftees, whose lives are implicitly priced by politicians and military strategists.

5. We could cut murder rates by surer and swifter law enforcement, but reforming or expanding our police forces, the judicial system, and prisons seems too costly.

6. Paid killers' fees range from $200 to $500,000.

7. After adjusting for training and the pleasantness of working conditions, higher wages are paid for riskier jobs. Numerous studies conclude that, in the United States, an annual wage premium of about $2,000 is paid for each additional 0.1% probability of dying on the job. This translates into roughly $2 million as the average value for the life of a worker.

Estimating the value of a human life partially depends on whose life it is. Most of us would assign high values to the lives of our loved ones, but what about the life of a single person randomly selected from the entire population—in all probability, a stranger? The setting of safety standards for highways is an example of this universal problem. Typical results for several countries are reported in Table 3.

Table 3 Cost per Traffic Fatality	
United States*	$2,600,000
Sweden*	1,236,000
New Zealand*	1,150,000
Britain*	1,100,000
Germany**	928,000
Belgium**	400,000
France**	350,000
Holland**	130,000
Portugal**	20,000

* Willingness-to-pay basis
** Human-capital basis
Source: "The Price of Life," *The Economist*, Dec. 4, 1993, p. 74.

The "willingness-to-pay" estimates in Table 3 report the amounts citizens are willing to pay for greater safety that, in a statistical sense, will stop one traffic fatality. "Human-capital" estimates, on the other hand, are based on the lost earnings of a typical fatality victim. Notice that the human capital approach distills the value of a life down to production, but most of us view people as far more than the sums of their lifetime earnings, so reliance on human capital-based estimates yield far less spending on safety than a country's taxpayers would be willing to pay for greater safety.

Frequently, the price of safety is not monetary. Thomas Hobbes, a sixteenth-century English philosopher, pointed out that greater security entails losses of freedom. Ongoing political debates about handgun control laws are one part of price-setting for human life: how much is society willing to limit the rights of gun fanciers to save each life that might otherwise be ended by a bullet from a Saturday night special?

The next time you see someone run a red light or light a cigarette, or if you ever again eat too many potato chips, we hope it will bring to mind the issue of the value of life.

● **Prices as Information**   Relative prices compress immense amounts of information about buyers' desires and sellers' costs. For example, farmers aware that grapes consistently sell for $2 per pound while limes sell for $1 per pound also know (perhaps unconsciously) that consumers value more grapes roughly twice as much as they do more limes. And consumers know that extra grapes cost roughly twice as much as additional limes to produce.

Information embedded in relative prices spurs action. A tour of a shopping mall can provide thousands of prices to guide your purchases. Low-paying job openings are passed over when a skilled job seeker scans the want ads, while more attractive wage offers are circled for follow-up. And entrepreneurs are steered by expected prices and costs into forms of production where they perceive the greatest profit opportunities.

• **Prices as Incentives** Relative prices signal opportunities for pleasure and prospects of pain. Most people seek pleasure and avoid pain, but life is a series of trade-offs. Renting one video tape, for example, absorbs funds you could use to rent another film that received two "thumbs up" from the critics. A child's dawdling on family chores may be overcome by either a reward (an allowance) or a punishment (no TV tonight). Grades can be thought of as prices. Prospects of an A may induce you to forgo an intriguing film for two hours of study, while only fear of failing drives your roommate to study.

Sellers view relatively *high* prices for goods (relative to their production costs) as *incentives* that stimulate production, while *low* prices are *disincentives* that push resources into alternative types of production. High wage rates, for example, reward work, but an offer of only a low wage may cause a worker to opt for little work and much leisure.

• **Prices as Rationing Devices** Especially scarce goods will ideally be reserved for their more important possible uses, and, where feasible, people will tend to conserve relatively less on more abundant goods and resources. For example, daubing polish on shoes with designer silk scarves would be wasteful; using cotton rags instead seems to make sense. Relatively higher prices for goods or resources signal greater relative scarcity and discourage lower-valued uses of goods. Thus, prices act as *rationing devices*. Buyers are encouraged to use lower-priced goods more and higher-priced goods less.

The information conveyed by relative prices and their incentive and rationing effects are central to our discussions of supply and demand in Chapters 3 and 4, and it explains why many economists refer to private transactions as

the price system. Societies everywhere increasingly rely on the price system, which governs flows of international trade that increasingly dominate the economic landscape. A major virtue of the price system is that it helps allocate goods and resources into economically efficient patterns.

Economic Efficiency

Physicists call a system efficient if it minimizes the energy expended in accomplishing some task, while environmentalists talk about efficiency as the absence of waste in an ecological system. Economists take a different approach to efficiency.

> **Economic efficiency** is achieved when we produce the combination of outputs with the highest attainable total value, given our limited resources.

Efficiency may seem an abstract concept, but it becomes more concrete when decomposed to parallel the three basic economic questions: (*a*) *allocative efficiency* addresses *what* things will be produced; (*b*) *productive efficiency* addresses *how* to produce them; and (*c*) *distributive efficiency* addresses *who* will use specific outputs.

• **Allocative Efficiency—What?** Using all of society's resources to produce mustard and sawdust instead of a mix of more useful goods would obviously waste resources.

> **Allocative efficiency** requires the pattern of national output to mirror what people want and are willing and able to buy.

The social value of output from given resources is maximized in an allocatively efficient economy.

It is usually easier to identify inefficiency than to describe an efficient situation. Mountains of mustard and sawdust would be allocatively *in*efficient nuisances. Another example: England's nationalized auto industry built taxis according to the same design from World War II into the 1970s, long after the rest of the world had abandoned unreliable 1940s technologies and archaic 1940s styles.

• **Productive Efficiency—How?**   Expending more resources than the minimum required to produce a given level of a specific product is also wasteful.

> *Productive (technical) efficiency requires minimizing opportunity cost for a given value of output.*

This requirement also ensures maximum output for a given cost, or using given resources. Production is *technically inefficient* whenever production costs are unnecessarily high or if more output could be produced without raising costs or using more resources.

For example, the saying that "too many cooks spoil the broth" implies that excess company in the kitchen is economically inefficient. More good-quality food presumably could be produced at lower cost using fewer resources if some of the cook's helpers left. Society as a whole is also productively inefficient if excessive unemployment holds output below the maximum possible from the resources available.

• **Distributive Efficiency—Who?**   The question of "Who?" is divisible into issues of (*a*) the distribution of income and wealth, and (*b*) the distribution of goods. Suppose the distribution of income and wealth (discussed later in the book) is a settled issue and that our economy produces precisely what people want. Ensuring that the goods get to the right people may still be a problem.

> *Distributive efficiency requires that specific goods be used by the people who value them **relatively** the most.*

By *relatively*, we mean one person's preferences for certain goods relative to other goods, when compared to other people's preferences among goods. Relative likes and dislikes are important in determining who will gain the most from which goods.

Suppose, for example, that you have gallons of orange soda (which nauseates you) but lack broccoli, your favorite food, while I have bushels of broccoli (which I despise), and I love orange soda. An exchange of your orange soda for my broccoli is obviously in order. Such exchanges are automatic when people buy and sell things.

Distributive efficiency to accommodate people's preferences requires that consumers *maximize* the satisfaction available from their individual budgets. (Relative budget sizes are a separate issue of distribution.) When this occurs, all individuals also *minimize* their outlays to obtain goods yielding a given total amount of satisfaction to them. You currently consume inefficiently if you could gain by changing the mix of goods you now buy for a given cash outlay. Alternatively, you could cut your total spending and maintain the satisfaction now yielded by your inefficient purchasing pattern.

People try to act efficiently, expanding particular activities wherever the extra benefits are expected to exceed the extra costs and reducing activities for which cost saving is expected to exceed any benefits forgone. You could always turn off all lights and adjust your thermostat when you leave home to prevent wasting electricity or gas, but many of us absentmindedly leave on lights and heat or cool empty buildings. Conscientiously saving energy may absorb time more valuably used in other ways, but recognition that a current buying pattern is inefficient prompts changes in behavior. A $700 utility bill might shock you into trying harder to conserve energy, another example of a relative price acting as an incentive.

• **Economy-wide Efficiency**   All opportunity costs must be minimized to attain an economy-wide state of efficiency that combines allocative, productive, and distributive efficiency. Consumption patterns and the production of goods are both efficient whenever any change from the current situation must harm at least one person. This implies that resources are allocated so that they produce the most valuable combination of goods possible—every drop of potential net benefit must be squeezed from the resources available.

Economic efficiency, broadly considered, means that it is impossible for anyone to gain unless someone else loses.

Alternatively, economic inefficiency exists if altering production or exchanging goods could allow at least one person to gain, with no one else losing. Thus, whenever there are potential but unrealized gains to someone entailing losses to none, the current situation is inefficient. Inefficiency means that appropriate corrections would enable society to cope better with scarcity.

The bargains people make usually represent moves toward greater efficiency. All direct parties to a voluntary transaction expect to gain or they would not bother. For example, you will not trade an apple for my orange unless you value the orange more than the apple, and vice versa. Trading your apple for my orange raises your satisfaction from a given outlay because you now have a subjectively (to you) more valuable orange. I gain in a similar fashion. Thus, efficiency is usually enhanced through trade, and a failure to trade when such gains are possible is inefficient. In fact, if only one of us would gain by a trade but no other party would be harmed, failure to trade is inefficient, even if the trade is deemed by some people to harm equity.

We have probed why scarcity makes opportunity costs and decisions unavoidable, and have suggested that people try, not always successfully, to cope with scarcity in efficient ways. Now that you know a bit about the economic problem, the rest of this chapter surveys methods economists have developed to try to understand economic behavior.

ECONOMIC ANALYSIS

Good economic analysis blends both art and science and borrows ideas heavily from philosophers, behavioral scientists, legal scholars, and historians, all of whom offer alternatives to the economic way of thinking. Economics is an art because it requires qualitative judgments about seemingly contradictory evidence; it is also a science that requires organizing a maze of ideas and phenomena into a coherent whole. Understanding economics thoroughly can help you adjust to an ever-changing world.

Areas traditionally within the domain of economics include consumer and business behavior, taxes, international trade, inflation, and unemployment. More recently, economic analysis has been applied to areas ranging from marriage to criminal behavior and war, and from how our political and legal systems operate to questions about education and environmental quality. No short description can cover all the varied concerns of economists.[4] One famous economist, John Maynard Keynes, summarized economics as "a method rather than a doctrine, an apparatus of the mind, a technique of thinking which helps its possessor to draw correct conclusions." Sound theory is a key to the scientific side of economics.

Common Sense and Theory

Everything should be made as simple as possible, but not more so.

Albert Einstein

Some people ridicule *theory*, believing that theorists cannot cope in the real world and find it hard to walk and chew gum simultaneously. These critics favor *common sense* as a practical guide for life. How can we judge theory or common sense? Good theories or common sense must correctly describe how the world works. In other words, we judge both theory and common sense by their accuracy!

In fact, most common sense is merely a blend of time-tested theories. Progress occurs when new knowledge disproves old theories, causing better theories to be absorbed, albeit slowly, into our common sense. Thus, common sense can become outdated—and clearly wrong, given our evolving knowledge. But how may today's new theories become tomorrow's common sense?

---

[4]Evidence of the diversity of economics is that about half of all academic Economics Departments are in Schools of Business, with most of the rest being housed with Social Sciences or Liberal Arts.

The process of theorizing consists, first, of identifying a problem area. Then we collect facts that seem germane. Of course, we cannot gather all the facts, because some things cannot be sensed directly. For example, sophisticated equipment can discern microwaves, but sub-atomic particles cannot be viewed directly, even using our most advanced technology; their existence is inferred. Moreover, we cannot concentrate on everything that can be sensed. Our senses are selective. (If you live near the tracks, after awhile you become habituated and barely hear the trains.) Finally, gathering all potentially helpful data is too costly, so we deal with incomplete information.

After we collect some data that seem relevant, we try to figure out how they are related. That is, we develop a theory that can be tested to see how well it explains how things work. New theory that passes this test gradually replaces older theory and becomes part of our common sense, a pattern summarized in Figure 2.

Exceptions usually compel revision of scientific rules. For example, prior to Columbus's voyages, conventional European wisdom viewed the earth as flat—it looks irregular but relatively flat from your window. The flat earth theory was gradually replaced by a better theory after ships sailed around the world, but some eccentrics still deny that earth is spherical. (The British Flat Earth Society still meets regularly.)

Models are representations of theories; these two terms are synonyms for many purposes. Some models are physical, such as a watch, which models the passage of time. Others exist as mental images or mathematical equations. Still others are graphical, such as an architect's blueprints or the maps you consult on your vacation. Many people are unaware that their heads are filled with models. For example, most single people who ultimately plan to marry have imagined general models of their prospective spouses (appearance, intelligence, sense of humor, etc.).

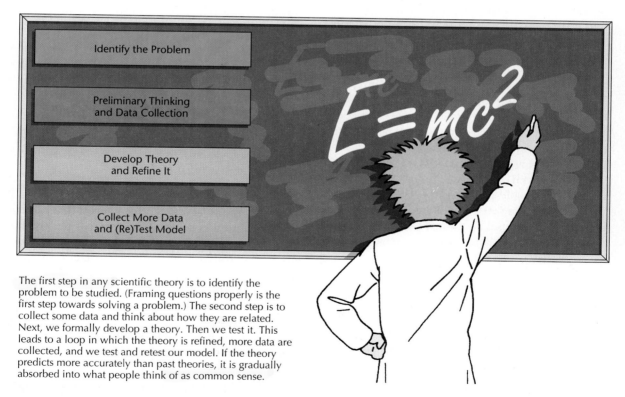

The first step in any scientific theory is to identify the problem to be studied. (Framing questions properly is the first step towards solving a problem.) The second step is to collect some data and think about how they are related. Next, we formally develop a theory. Then we test it. This leads to a loop in which the theory is refined, more data are collected, and we test and retest our model. If the theory predicts more accurately than past theories, it is gradually absorbed into what people think of as common sense.

FIGURE 2   How a Theory Is Developed and Refined

A wag once remarked that "economics is common sense made hard." But theory necessitates *abstraction* (generalization), which is intended to simplify analysis. We try to focus on important relationships and to ignore insignificant tangents. In fact, most scientists prefer simple but accurate theories to complex ones.

Occam's razor is the idea that the simplest workable theories are also the most useful and the best.

For example, earth once was thought to be a fixed point about which all the universe spun. Incredibly complex equations were developed to trace movements of the then-observable planets and stars. Modern astronomy applies Occam's razor to explain cosmic acts in a simpler fashion; all the universe is in motion, and earth orbits the sun, not vice versa.

A good model may be so simple that it is unrealistic except for its intended use. Would finding a particular intersection be aided by an exact replica of a city? Hardly! Any out-of-towner would find a simple paper street map far more useful. Simple models are usually less costly than complex ones. For example, intricate plastic models can show how an airplane looks, but tossing a cheap balsa glider into the air will give you a better understanding of aerodynamics. Watches come in solar, quartz crystal, and other varieties. Which is best? If you care only about knowing the time, the best one most simply, accurately, reliably (and cheaply) reflects the passage of time.

To summarize, a good theory or model as simply as possible predicts how the real world works. Common sense evolves as exceptions to old theories compel acceptance of better theories, if they seem reliable after extensive testing.

Positive vs. Normative Economics

If you took all of the economists in the country and laid them end to end, they'd never reach a conclusion.

George Bernard Shaw

Shaw's line echoes a popular view that economists seldom agree, but 90 percent of economists would probably accept 90 percent of the theory in this book, with only nit-picking differences about which 90 percent to accept. How can this reputation for discord be reconciled with the fact of widespread agreement? Part of the answer is that economists may differ sharply about how even widely accepted theory applies in a specific case. Economists' disputes about how to translate theory into policy get a lot of press, while broad areas of agreement tend to be ignored.

Even if economists reach consensus, politicians often reject their advice. For example, over 90 percent of economists—irrespective of their personal leanings about politics—favor freer international trade, but tariff barriers are standard responses when imports threaten significant groups of voters' jobs. A similar consensus exists about most price controls, which include such things as minimum wage laws and the rent controls some cities enforce—economists almost uniformly view price controls as inefficient. Apparent discord also arises when economists in government agree publicly (but disagree privately) with politicians who appoint them, even if economic logic supports policies the politicos won't enact.

Economists tend to agree most about positive economics, which, ideally, generates ideas that are free of value judgments and which can be tested for accuracy.

Positive economics addresses "what is" and predicts observable and testable tendencies in economic relationships.

The statement "A poor coffee harvest that raises its price induces substitution towards tea" is an example of a positive economic statement. But be wary. Positive statements may be either true or false. The assertion "Grass is pink" is a positive statement. But is it fact? Clearly not. Most grass ranges from green to brown, depending on the season.

Disagreement is most common when value judgments are central to a problem.

Normative economics depends on value judgments and addresses what "should be."

Most statements containing the prescriptive words "should" or "ought" are normative. For example, you might agree with the army of economists who think that federal budgeting and regulation "should" be reformed whenever a particular policy is unarguably inefficient, but even this view is intrinsically normative.

Positive and normative elements are often intertwined. For example, economists may differ sharply about the normative issue of whether government should ever execute murderers. The prediction that quicker, stiffer, and surer penalties deter crime is, however, a positive theory with which most economists would concur.

Normative issues frequently turn on questions of equity and provoke debate among economists and the public alike. Policy is inherently more normative than theory. For example, the statement "We should redistribute wealth from the rich to the poor" implies a value judgment that benefits to the poor would outweigh the harm done to the rich. There is little reason to suppose that an economist's value judgments are superior to those of other people, but economic reasoning can offer unique insights into the effectiveness of alternative policies in achieving specific normative goals.

Few normative issues are settled by looking at evidence because value judgments involve faith and argument, not scientific proof. Disputes about positive economics can ultimately be settled by evidence, but even economists with shared values may disagree because some areas of positive economics remain unsettled for generations. For example, virtually everyone favors price-level stability and high employment, but economists may disagree about how to cure economic instability because of difficulty in finding the right evidence and then digesting and accurately interpreting it in changing circumstances.

Understanding economic reality is useful primarily because it helps us develop strategies to deal with the problem of scarcity. All policies hinge on normative issues, but if economists design policies intended to achieve goals set by policy makers, then their quest is positive in nature. For example, if minimizing unemployment is a goal, then developing policies to accomplish this goal involves positive economics. We can evaluate policies by how well they accomplish our goals, but positive economics cannot determine whether any goal is good or bad. The complex interactions of positive theory, empirical (observable) facts, normative goals, and economic policies are summarized in Figure 3.

Macroeconomics and Microeconomics

Economics is also divided into macroeconomics and microeconomics. (*Macro* and *micro* derive from Greek words for "large" and "small," respectively.) Macroeconomics (the big picture) involves study of the entire society—sums of sets of micro variables (e.g., numbers of workers employed by various firms) yield *aggregate* (macro) variables (e.g., national employment). Microeconomics focuses on the detailed behavior of specific households, firms, or industries. By analogy, macroeconomic tools are telescopes, while microeconomic tools are microscopes.

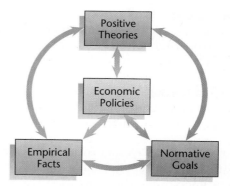

Positive economic theories are derived by applying logic to observed reality (*empirical data*), but even positive theory is influenced by (a) the desires of the policy makers who provide research funding, and (b) normative goals that help us decide which questions to examine. Some empirical observations are filtered through our sense of equity to shape normative goals, but most people want their goals to be attainable, which requires consistency with their positive theories. Normative goals, positive theories, and economic policies all cause us to focus on certain empirical data, and to ignore other real-world data. Directions for policies, in turn, are distilled from a mix of (a) observations about empirical reality, (b) normative goals, and (c) positive theories of economics.

FIGURE 3   Positive Theories, Empirical Facts, Normative Goals, and Economic Policies

- **Macroeconomics**   Macro and micro differ more by degree than kind. In a sense, macro involves the study of the forest whereas micro focuses on individual trees. Thus, macroeconomics considers how national income, unemployment, inflation, and economic growth are determined.

> **Macroeconomics** *focuses on aggregate variables relevant for an entire national economy, or even the world economy.*

The growing influence of international trade and finance on economies everywhere is increasingly incorporated into modern macroeconomic models. Macroeconomic policy addresses the total effects of changing taxes and government spending, or growth in the money supply.

Commonly agreed-upon normative goals of macro policy include:

1. *High employment.* People suffer when many workers cannot find jobs and many manufacturing plants and much machinery sit idle.
2. *Price-level stability.* If average prices are volatile, people may be uncertain about how much their wages will buy or whether to consume now or invest in hopes of future returns.
3. *Economic growth.* People want higher incomes each year and most hope their children will be even more prosperous than they are.

Economic security is closely related to achieving these three goals. People want to retain their jobs and the good things they have. Security may be threatened by such possibilities as nuclear war or by changes in what society wants. The birth of the auto put buggy-whip braiders out of work, and today powerful personal computers are shrinking the market for mainframe computing (e.g., IBM, with its dependence on mainframes, has been in trouble recently).

We mentioned earlier that absolute (monetary) prices influence economic behavior only when translated into relative prices. Thus, for example, inflation (a hike in average monetary prices) is important only if it alters relative prices or the income distribution. But inflation always disrupts both, destabilizing economic activity and distorting patterns of growth, so it is a major concern for macro policymakers.

- **Microeconomics**   Modern macroeconomics increasingly relies on sound foundations from microeconomics. Thus, microeconomics addresses interactions among households, firms, and government agencies in much finer detail than macroeconomics.

> **Microeconomics** *is the study of individual decision-making, resource allocation, and how relative prices, outputs, and the distribution of income are determined.*

Three major goals dominate micro policy:

1. *Efficiency.* An inefficient economy wastes resources and fails to provide the highest possible standard of living for consumers.
2. *Equity.* Huge gaps between the "haves" and "have-nots" may leave most people impoverished while a privileged few live luxuriously.
3. *Freedom.* Maximum freedom requires people to have the widest possible range of choices available. As with equity, however, more freedom for some may leave less for others. Freedom for stick-up artists to practice their professions, for example, imposes high costs and reduces freedom for the rest of us. Thus, society limits the freedom of robbers by putting them in jail at times.

Efficiency is a generally accepted normative goal, but equity and freedom hinge on more controversial value judgments.

All goals involve trade-offs. For example, efficient policies may be seen as inequitable. Granting patents for an AIDS vaccine might be efficient if potential profits stimulated successful research, but it might seem unfair not to immunize all those unable to afford the vaccine after its discovery. Alternatively, freedom and efficiency conflict if, for example, one person exercises freedom to declare bankruptcy, hindering another's production—the ability to make loans.

Such trade-offs are among reasons why legal systems are implemented to govern people's relationships. Acceptably balancing freedom, efficiency, and equity is among society's major challenges.[5] Unfortunately, equity is almost always a bit nebulous and subject to widely different normative interpretations. Efficiency is the micro goal most susceptible to economic reasoning.

Our ability to achieve macro goals depends on micro policy, and vice versa. For example, excessive unemployment is a macro symptom of micro inefficiency: output is lost when resources are idle. Similarly, inefficient regulations may both squelch production in key industries at the micro level and inhibit growth at the macro level. Efficiency facilitates achieving all other goals. Inefficiency wastes resources that could be used to enhance stability, growth, freedom, and equity.

Most early economists stressed microeconomics, believing that macroeconomics merely entailed summing micro variables and tacking on changes in the money supply to account for inflation. Inadequate analysis of macro phenomena may have contributed to boom-bust cycles that culminated in the worldwide Great Depression of the 1930s. That slump forced us to realize that one decision-maker's acts may yield far different results than if all decision-makers take the same action at once. For example, one person in the bleachers may see a ball game better by standing up, but when others also stand (as they will) this advantage is lost. It is now clear that reaching our micro goals depends on achieving our macro goals, and vice versa. Understanding both is essential for an accurate perception of how any economy operates.

You will repeatedly encounter the building blocks from this chapter when we investigate more advanced topics later in this book. If graphs make you at all queasy, you should study the optional material at the end of this chapter before you move on to Chapter 2. In Chapter 2, we explore *comparative advantage*, a concept that uses opportunity costs to help explain why different people and countries specialize in some types of production and exchange their outputs for goods produced by others. We also discuss graphical devices called *production possibilities frontiers* to illustrate how scarcity limits our available choices, and we examine some mechanisms that people use in trying to cope with scarcity.

---

[5]Conflicts between efficiency and equity are common. Efficiency is more easily analyzed with economic reasoning; issues of equity are unavoidable, inescapably normative, and a bit nebulous. Such conflicts are detailed in Arthur Okun's *Efficiency vs. Equity: The Big Tradeoff* (Washington, D.C.: Brookings, 1973).

CHAPTER REVIEW: KEY POINTS

1. **Economics** focuses on choices and their consequences, and addresses how individuals and societies allocate limited resources to try to satisfy relatively unlimited wants.
2. **Goods** include anything that adds to human happiness, while **bads** are things that detract from it. *Economic goods* are costly; *free goods* are not—if any truly free goods actually exist.
3. **Scarcity** occurs because our relatively unlimited wants cannot be completely met, given the limited resources available. A good is scarce if people cannot freely get all they want, so that the good commands a positive price. Scarcity forces all levels of decision-makers, from individuals to society at large, to resolve three basic economic questions:
   a. *What* will be produced?
   b. *How* will production occur?
   c. *Who* will use the goods produced?
4. **Production** occurs when knowledge or *technology* is used to apply energy to materials to make them more valuable.

5. **Productive Resources** (factors of production) include:

   a. **Labor.** Productive efforts made available by human beings. Payments for labor services are called **wages**.

   b. **Entrepreneurship.** The organizing, innovating, and risk-taking function that combines other factors to enable production. Entrepreneurs are rewarded with **profits**.

   c. **Land.** All natural resources. Payments for land are called **rents**.

   d. **Capital.** Improvements that increase the productive potential of other resources. Payments for the use of capital are called **interest**. When economists refer to capital, they mean physical capital rather than financial capital, which consists of paper claims to goods or resources.

6. The **opportunity costs** of choices are measured by the subjective values of the best alternative you sacrifice. **Absolute prices** are monetary and are useful primarily as indicators of **relative prices**, which are the prices of goods or resources in terms of each other and which provide information and incentives to guide our decisions.

7. **Economic efficiency** occurs when a given amount of resources produces the most valuable combination of outputs possible. In an efficient economy, no transactions are possible from which anyone can gain without someone else losing.

   a. **Allocative efficiency** requires production of the things people want.

   b. **Productive (technical) efficiency** requires producing given outputs at the lowest possible cost.

   c. **Distributive efficiency** requires people to adjust their purchasing patterns to maximize their satisfactions from given budgets.

8. *Common sense* is theory tested over a long period and found useful, although it may be wrong or outdated. In general, good theory accurately predicts how the real world operates. **Occam's razor** suggests that the simplest workable theories are the most useful or "best."

9. **Positive economics** is scientifically testable and involves value-free descriptions of economic relationships, dealing with "what is." **Normative economics** involves value judgments about economic relationships and addresses "what should be." Normative theory can be neither scientifically verified nor proven false.

10. **Macroeconomics** is concerned with aggregate (the total levels of) economic phenomena, including such items as gross domestic product, unemployment, and inflation. **Microeconomics** concentrates on individual decision-making, resource allocation, and how prices and output are determined.

QUESTIONS FOR THOUGHT AND DISCUSSION

1. Why do people often let water run onto sidewalks and into the street when they water their lawns? Is this wasted water a sign of inefficiency?

2. Do you agree with the adage "You can't get rich working for someone else"? Must successful entrepreneurs serve others to enrich themselves? Can wage earners achieve great wealth without investing? How might you test the correctness of your answers to these questions?

3. Whose lives are potentially assigned lower prices when a drunk decides to drive home without waiting to sober up? (Pedestrians? People in other cars? The drunk? The drunk's family?)

4. Why is class attendance almost always higher on exam days? And why is it probably accurate to believe that you can think of nothing better to do with your time right now than to study this book?

5. Does everything have a price? Are there some things you would not do regardless of price? (*Remember*: prices and money are not synonyms; prices may be nonmonetary.)

OPTIONAL MATERIAL: GRAPHICAL TECHNIQUES IN ECONOMICS

Are you as likely to suffer nightmares after exposure to equations or graphs as you are after watching Freddy Kruger terrorize people in a horror film? We have a possible cure if you are afflicted with "math-graph-phobia." Try to subdue your anxiety and spend an hour or two studying this material and working the applications. The *Graph-Tutor* software program and the parallel exercises in our *Student Guide for Learning Economics* (both are included in your *Economics* package) can also help clarify analytical material in economics and may facilitate your work in other courses. In this section, we will see how to read, interpret, and use graphs.

GRAPHICAL ANALYSIS

[T]here is just no substitute for the [economic] intuition one acquires with lots of curve bending.

James P. Quirk (1976)

Words, graphs, tables, and equations are all useful in describing economic relationships. Familiarity with all four techniques is a key to understanding economics. Learning how graphs work is a lot easier than trying to memorize all the graphs in this book. Graphs are snapshots of information that can be used descriptively, as in maps and charts, or analytically, to gain insights into economic theory.

*A **graph** is a picture of a relationship between two or more **variables**, which are items that can be described by numbers and include such things as time, distance, income, prices, and outputs.*

You should gain confidence in dealing with graphs if you focus on understanding all figures in the first few chapters of this text.

Maps are descriptive graphs that use grid systems called *Cartesian coordinates* to specify locations. A first step in locating Miami on the map in Figure 4, for example, is to find it in the alphabetical index of the map of Florida in Figure 4. Miami's coordinates, I-10, help pinpoint where to look for Miami. Coordinate I at the side of the map tells you how far north or south Miami is. Coordinate 10 at the bottom indicates Miami's east-west orientation. Aha! Miami!

Cartesian Coordinates

Just as maps plot geographic relationships, most graphs use Cartesian coordinates to show how variables are related. Cartesian coordinate systems entail two perpendicular lines, or *axes*, labeled *x* and *y*, that usually intersect at their respective zeros, the origin. The black lines in Figure 5 are axes for standard Cartesian coor-

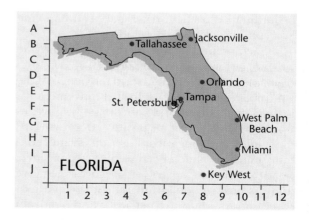

FIGURE 4   A Map of Florida

FIGURE 5 Cartesian Coordinates

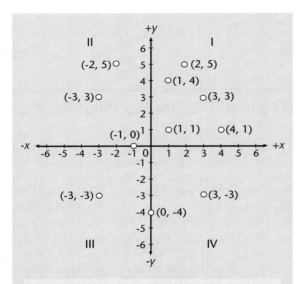

Coordinate areas are divided into four *quadrants*; moving counterclockwise from the northeast, they are I, II, III, and IV. A point is located numerically by an ordered pair denoted (*x,y*). Various ordered pairs are located on this graph. The *x* value reflects rightward movement from the vertical axis if *x* is positive, and vice versa. The *y* value measures vertical distance---upward from the horizontal axis for positive numbers; downward if *y* is negative.

dinates and divide a space into four areas called *quadrants*, which are numbered I through IV, beginning from the northeast area and moving in a counterclockwise direction.

Each point in this space is identified by an *ordered pair* of numbers denoted (*x, y*). The first coordinate, *x*, directs rightward movement if the *x* number is positive, or leftward movement if *x* is negative. The second coordinate, *y*, governs upward movement if *y* is positive, or downward movement if *y* is negative. Thus, quadrant I contains pairs for which both *x* and *y* are positive; quadrant II shows pairs for which *x* is negative and *y* is positive; quadrant III shows situations where both *x* and *y* are negative; and quadrant IV depicts positive values of *x* paired with negative values of *y*. Coordinates for the following

points are depicted in Figure 5: (1, 1), (1, 4), (3, 3), (4, 1), (2, 5), (–2, 5), (–3, 3), (–1, 0), (–3, –3), (0, –4), and (3, –3). Be sure you can locate these coordinates before proceeding.

Remember, each pair gives two pieces of information: left-right for the value of *x*, then up-down for the value of *y*. Even though economists consider multidimensional problems, this technique allows us to deal with very complex issues by considering only two dimensions of a problem at a time. Most economic analyses use only the first, or positive, quadrant (quadrant I). Negative values for many economic variables would be meaningless, (e.g., negative unemployment rates or negative consumption of a good are nonsensical concepts).

Descriptive Graphs

Computerized graphics allow economic data reported in news broadcasts and articles in magazines or newspapers to be imaginatively presented. The ad for Macron in Panel A of Figure 6, for example, dramatizes its sales growth from 1991 to 1995 with vertical bars; Panels B, C, and D superimpose grids on these data to help identify their Cartesian coordinates. Revenues (on the vertical axis) are plotted against years (on the horizontal axis). Panels A and B are called *bar graphs* because they use bars to represent revenue in each year. *Line graphs* depicting annualized sales data over time are shown in Panels C and D. All four panels illustrate the same information.

Analytical Graphs

Economic analysis often hinges on how much one variable responds to a change in another. Graphs can be used to present complex relationships among variables, but reading them is easy if you concentrate on what a figure shows. Variables may be unrelated or related to each other either positively or negatively. That is, higher values of *x* will be associated either with higher values of *y* (a *positive relationship*) or with lower values of *y* (a *negative relationship*).

FIGURE 6 Different Ways to Display the Same Economic Data

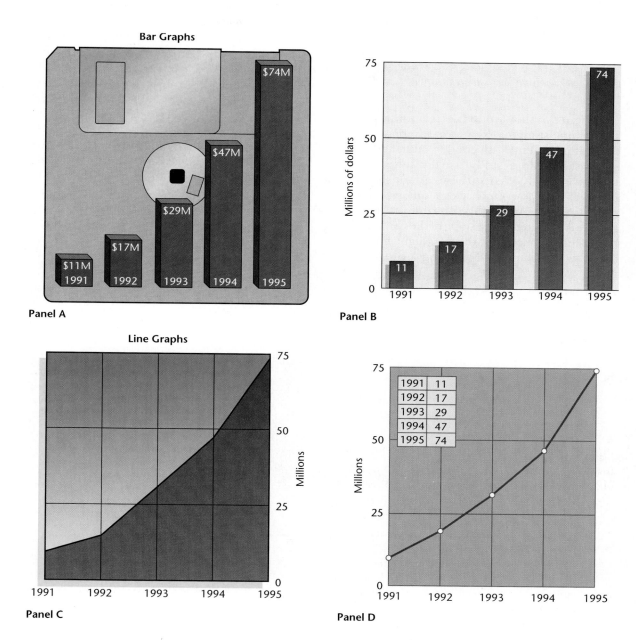

Bar Graphs

Panel A

Panel B

Line Graphs

Panel C

Panel D

The sales data shown in the Macron advertisement are converted directly into the bar graphs, and then into the line graphs, using the Cartesian coordinate system.

- **Slope of a Line**   Graphically, such relationships are equivalent to the slope of the line depicting how the two variables are related. Slope is often described as "rise over run," or rise/run.

*The **slope** of a line is the ratio of its vertical change (**rise**) to its horizontal change (**run**) as we move along it from left to right.*

Figure 7 shows possible relationships between time studying (*x*) and grade point average (*y*) for students with good, typical, and poor study skills. More study usually raises grade point averages (GPAs), so these relationships are positive. But how much extra time must you study to raise your average one full grade? The answer is reflected in the slope of the GPA/study-hours line. Notice that these straight lines are described as "curves." Following a convention among most mathematicians and economists, functional relationships that are straight (linear) are, nevertheless, described as "curves." Don't let this convention throw you for a loop as you proceed through this book.

In this case, the grade (on the vertical axis) is the rise; study hours (along the horizontal axis) is the run. Suppose you have average study skills and study each subject 30 hours a semester, so your GPA is 2.0 (point *c*). Boosting your study time to 45 hours per subject (run = 45 − 30 = 15 hours) will raise your average (point *b*) to 3.0 (rise = 3.0 − 2.0 = 1.0). Fifteen extra hours of study per subject will raise your GPA by one full point (*rise/run* = 1.0/15) if the middle line in Figure 7 corresponds to the relationship between your GPA and the hours you study. Note that steeper lines yield higher values for slope and that the slope of each line reflects the efficiency of study. Students with good study skills

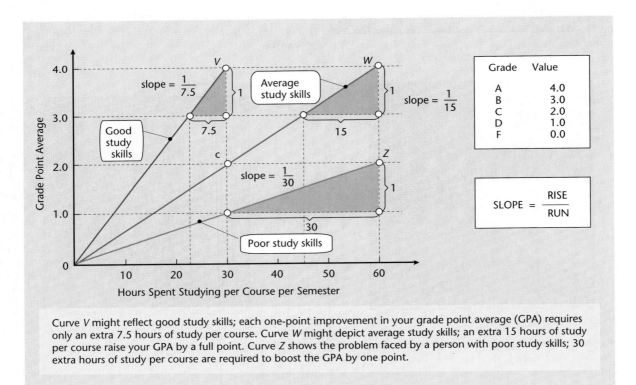

Curve *V* might reflect good study skills; each one-point improvement in your grade point average (GPA) requires only an extra 7.5 hours of study per course. Curve *W* might depict average study skills; an extra 15 hours of study per course raise your GPA by a full point. Curve *Z* shows the problem faced by a person with poor study skills; 30 extra hours of study per course are required to boost the GPA by one point.

FIGURE 7   How Studying and Grade Point Averages Might Be Related

raise their GPAs a full point with only 7.5 extra hours of study, but 30 extra hours are required for people with poor skills; the slopes of these relationships are 1/7.5 and 1/30, respectively.

The slope of a line can also be negative. Excessive partying usually lowers grades, a negative relationship reflected in Figure 8. As the graph suggests, you can party for up to 25 hours per semester without harm to your grade point average (point *b*); there is no relationship between your recreation and your grades within this range. Beyond point *b*, however, each 25 extra hours of partying reduces your grade average by one grade point until point *c* is reached (1.0 GPA and 100 hours of partying).

Your grades drop to 0.0, or failing, when you party beyond 100 hours. Thus, between points *a* and *b*, slope is zero (i.e., change in partying has no effect on grades or, alternatively, the two variables are unrelated). The slope of the line is −1/25 between 25 hours and 100 hours of party time (between points *b* and *c*); each 25 hours partied drops your grade average by one full point. The slope is infinite if you party 100

hours (between points *c* and *d*), so as little as one second may increase or decrease your average by a full grade point.

• **Intercepts**   For simplicity, we often assume that economic relationships are linear, which means that a graph of the relationship has a constant slope. The only information we need beyond slope to fully specify a linear relationship is its intercept, which is the value of the *y* variable when the *x* variable has a value of zero.

For example, Figure 9 shows a hypothetical relationship between lumber yields and annual maintenance per acre of forest to control tree diseases and clear debris (reducing fire hazards). Even with zero maintenance ($x = 0$) we may harvest some lumber ($y = 10,000$), and the harvest rate rises as maintenance increases. Each extra hour of maintenance per acre raises annual lumber yields by 1,000 board feet. This continues (given the linear relationship) until the ability to harvest lumber peaks when 40 hours of annual maintenance are devoted to each acre of forest.

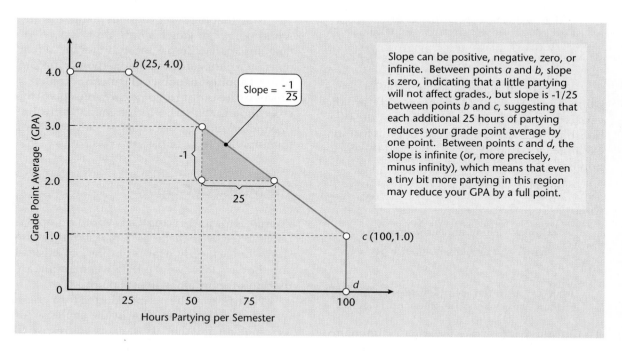

FIGURE 8   How Partying and Grade Point Averages Might Be Related

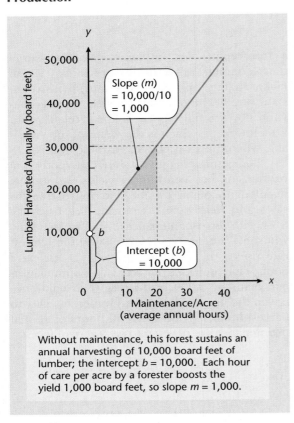

FIGURE 9 Forest Maintenance and Lumber Production

Without maintenance, this forest sustains an annual harvesting of 10,000 board feet of lumber; the intercept $b = 10,000$. Each hour of care per acre by a forester boosts the yield 1,000 board feet, so slope $m = 1,000$.

The general algebraic formula for linear relationships is $y = mx + b$, where y and x are the variables considered, m is the slope of the relationship, and b is the y intercept. For this forestry example, $b = 10,000$, $m = 1,000$, and the equation is:

$$y = 1,000x + 10,000$$

where

y = annual yield of lumber in board feet,

x = hours of annual maintenance per acre,

and

10,000 = the intercept [the value of y (board feet annually) when x (maintenance) is zero].

To find the harvest rate for each maintenance level, just multiply each possible value of x by 1,000 and add 10,000.

To ensure that you understand how the intercept and slope of a line are influenced by how variables interact, you should construct graphs of $y = mx + b$, where you select values of m and b as if you were blindly drawing them out of a hat.

• **Nonlinear Curves** Some economic relationships tend to swing from positive to negative, or vice versa, just as temperature in Alaska varies from summer to winter to spring. Assuming a constant slope for such *nonlinear* relationships is nonsensical. Solid understanding of some relationships later in this book requires you to know a bit of terminology.

Slope may change persistently along nonlinear curves, which may be *decreasingly positive* (curve segment *abc* in Panel A of Figure 10), *increasingly negative* (segment *cd* in Panel A), *decreasingly negative* (segment *ab* in Panel B), or *increasingly positive* (segment *bc* in Panel B). The rise/run formula for the slope of its *tangent* (a straight line that touches the curve at that point) measures slope on nonlinear functions. The slope at point *b* in panel A, for example, is 0.5.

Note that the curves at both point *c* in Panel A and point *b* in Panel B have zero slope; these tangents are flat. Zero slope indicates that a relationship is either at its maximum (point *c* in Panel A) or its minimum (point *b* in Panel B). Nonlinear functions are central to some core concepts of microeconomic analysis, which frequently involves maximization (e.g., of profits or satisfaction) or minimization (e.g., of risks or costs).

The Misuse of Graphs

Darrell Huff and Irving Geis wrote a popular book called *How to Lie with Statistics* that also shows how cleverly drawn graphs can mislead you. Be alert for several pitfalls when graphs are used to support an analytical point.

First, be sure the period selected for a graph is typical for the point made by the analysis. For example, during the 1980s, many aggressive financial investors bought California real estate based on its earlier performance. It seemed that

FIGURE 10   Nonlinear Relationships: Slopes, Maxima, and Minima

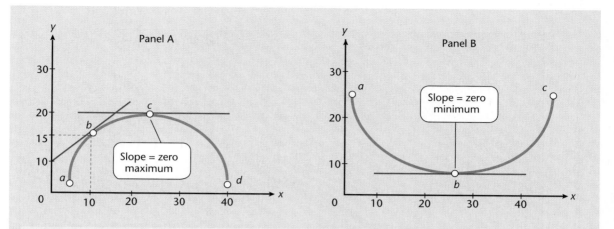

Along nonlinear curves, the slope may be *decreasingly positive* (segment *abc* in Panel A), *increasingly negative* (segment *cd* in Panel A), *decreasingly negative* (segment *ab* in Panel B), or *increasingly positive* (segment *bc* in Panel B). Slope is measured with the familiar "rise/run" formula for the tangent (a straight line barely touching the curve). The slope at point *b* in Panel A, for example, is 0.5 (rise = 15 - 10 = 5; run = 10 - 0 = 10). Point *c* in Panel A and point *b* in Panel B have zero slope because these tangents are flat. Zero slope indicates a *maximum* (point *c* in Panel A) or a *minimum* (point *b* in Panel B).

property and land prices could only rise. But commercial real estate in California crashed by roughly 40% between 1989 and 1993, leaving widespread bankruptcy in its wake. This was not the first boom-bust cycle in real estate. Real estate buyers would have been way ahead if they had seen graphs depicting historical booms and busts, instead of the 1970–1985 boom in isolation.

Second, carefully scrutinize the choice of measurement units. One distortion caused by using different units on the axes is shown in Figure 11. The curve in Panel A appears to have a greater slope than that in Panel B, but both curves accurately portray the same data, so this is impossible. The vertical axes are measured on different scales, accounting for the illusion that the two curves have different slopes.

Finally, the data used should be tightly linked to the analysis. Thus, comparing standards of living between countries cannot be done by simply looking at countries' total production or income; India is much bigger but far less prosperous than the United Arab Emirates.

Income per capita is a more informative measure.

You will confront both analytical and descriptive graphs repeatedly as you read this book. We hope this section has helped ease your mind and that you will find graphs helpful in learning economics. You should return to these materials on graphs if you find yourself perplexed by some of our more advanced topics. The adage that one picture is worth a thousand words is especially true in economics.

Applications

Graph paper will make many economics exercises easier, including these, but you can use a ruler to do problems 1 through 7 on plain paper. For questions 5 through 7, you may need to approximate (guess) what some data might be like. For each question, do the following:

A.   Draw sets of axes for each problem (a horizontal *x* axis and a vertical *y* axis that intersect at the origin where *x* = 0 and *y* = 0).

FIGURE 11   Consumer Prices

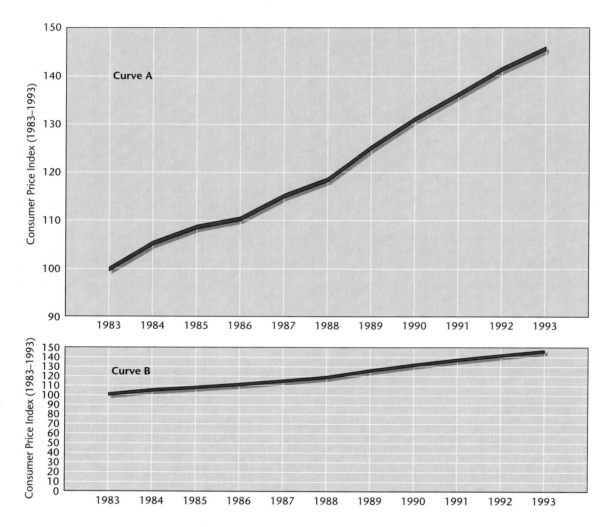

Units of measurement on the axes can make a line appear steeper (have a greater slope), even though its slope remains constant. Both of these curves have the same slope; the units of measurement on the vertical axes are expanded in Curve A.

Place measurement "ticks" at intervals along each pair of axes after you have read each problem.

B. Plot the relationship specified (questions 1–4) or the one you might expect (questions 5–7) between pairs of variables.

C. Identify each relationship as positive, negative, or nonexistent. (Slope = zero for unrelated variables.)

D. In questions 1 through 4, information allows specification of m and b. Calculate m and b and then write an appropriate equation using the formula, $y = mx + b$, where b = the y intercept and m = the slope. Thus, with an intercept of 100 and slope of –0.5, write $y = -0.5x + 100$.

E. Identify each relationship as linear or nonlinear. For nonlinear cases, specify the relationship as increasingly positive, decreasingly positive, increasingly negative, or decreasingly negative, and identify the minimum or maximum if one exists.

1. Plot the ordered pairs (–5, 0), (–2, 7), (0, 5), (3, 2), (5, 0), (8, –3), (10, –5). Connect these plotted ordered pairs with a line. Randomly select a point [e.g., (5, 0)] and call it (x_1, y_1), and then a second point, say (–2, 7), and label it (x_2, y_2). Calculate the slope of the line by plugging these values into the formula $(y_1 - y_2)/(x_1 - x_2)$.

2. Repeat question 1, using the following ordered pairs: (–5, –10), (–2, –7), (0, 5), (3, –2), (5, 0), (7, 2), (10, 5).

3. Suppose income tax rates were zero for the first $5,000 in annual income and 25% for each dollar of income over $5,000. Plot the relationship between people's income (up to a maximum of $100,000) on the horizontal (x) axis and their income taxes on the vertical (y) axis. How much income tax does an entrepreneur who gains $100,000 pay? How much income tax does a bus driver who makes $20,000 annually pay?

4. Each week has 168 hours. Any hours not worked are considered leisure. Put *hours of leisure* (nonwork) on the horizontal axis and *total income* at $10 per hour worked on the vertical axis. Draw a graph showing alternative weekly income levels for hours of leisure ranging from 0 to 168.

5. Put adult women's *height* on the x axis and their average *weight* for each possible height from 3′6″ to 6′6″ on the y axis. (Hint: Would an average woman 6′ tall weigh only 20% more than an average woman who was 5′ tall?)

6. For all possible automobiles with model years from 1930 through 1995, put the *average ages* of cars being traded in on a new car on the horizontal axis, and what you expect would be the *average trade-in allowance* in hundreds of dollars on the vertical axis. (Hint: Your curve should be Ù-shaped. Why?)

7. Many supermarkets in big cities now operate 24 hours a day all year round. Suppose you operate the only store in a very isolated small town and that you would sell $1,000 worth of groceries daily if you operated 1 hour each day. Put all possible numbers of *hours per day* you could be open on the x axis and the resulting *expected weekly sales revenue* on the y axis. (Hint: People would try to ensure purchases of things they consider necessities but might skip frivolous and inconvenient purchases, or they might drive long distances to shop elsewhere if your service were too limited.)

Chapter 2

Scarcity in a World in Transition

Modern communication and transportation networks increasingly link markets everywhere–you can now have a Big Mac in Boston, Budapest, or Beijing. Old political boundaries and alliances are crumbling because time and distance are compressed, while people all over the world have better information about how other people live–international news broadcasts are partially responsible for reform movements in Eastern Europe and parts of Asia. Yet we Americans seem largely oblivious to global events that profoundly affect our lives; typical surveys reveal that fewer than half of all high school seniors can locate Japan on a map, and only a tiny minority of adults can identify Canada as the United States' most important trading partner.

A framework for understanding our dynamic international economy is introduced in this chapter, which opens by discussing a *circular flow model*–how income and resources flow between households and business firms. Then we consider why efficiently maximizing the world's output requires (*a*) cooperative production based on a *division of labor*, and (*b*) special-

ized production and exchange according to *comparative advantage*. This leads us to *production possibilities frontiers*: graphic portrayals of a nation's productive capacity that, among other things, can be used to describe why countries import some things and export others. We also examine some allocative mechanisms used to cope with scarcity: shall economic questions be resolved by government, the market system, or some other device? Finally, we explore the different ways capitalism and socialism resolve economic issues and discuss dramatic trends in the international economy.

CIRCULAR FLOWS OF INCOME

People sometimes act collectively, but organizations cannot make decisions apart from those of the people who operate through them. Thus, although which individuals' choices count most depends on organizational structures, business organizations and government exist primarily to channel interactions among people in households. Markets pivot on the decisions of house-

FIGURE 1 Circular Flows of Income, Resources, and Goods

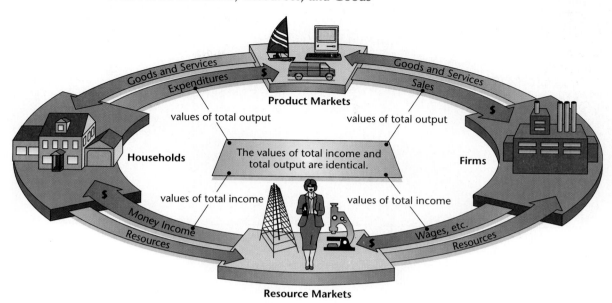

This circular flow model of the private sector depicts flows of income, resources, and outputs between households and business firms. Households provide resources to business firms in exchange for money income, which is used to purchase goods from businesses. Firms provide goods to households and, in return, receive payments, which are conveyed to households as income. All output ultimately generates comparable amounts of income, and all income is ultimately spent on output.

holds and businesses, which together are called the *private sector*. In our mixed economy, government, the *public sector*, takes a back seat only to the marketplace as a dominant allocative mechanism. The **circular flow** shown in Figure 1 models interactions between private households and firms. (We will integrate government into a circular flow model a bit later.)

Households

More than 260 million Americans now inhabit over 92 million *households*, a catchall term covering groups ranging from individuals who live alone to extended families in which several adults and a flock of children share a home.

> **Households** *are centers for consumption and ultimately own all wealth, including resources that they make available to businesses or government in exchange for income.*

Labor is the principal asset of most households, as indicated by the *functional distribution of income* in Table 1, which also broadly breaks down the uses of household income. Wages (including all salaries and such fringe benefits as health insurance) account for roughly three-fourths of income, with the rest being derived from rent, interest, and profit. Part of household income flows to government as taxes, with the rest being either spent on consumer goods or saved. Household saving is the primary source of investment funds for business firms. (Before continuing, see if you can use data from Table 1 to interpret certain long term trends you know about from American history; for example, how do these data reflect continuing population shifts from rural agriculture to employment in urban areas?)

Firms

Some of U.S. national output is produced by households (e.g., cooking, home maintenance, and do-it-yourself projects), nonprofit organi-

TABLE 1 Sources and Uses of Income, 1929–1993

Year	Total Income ($billions)	Functional Distribution of Income*					Uses of Income*		
		Employee's Compensation	Proprietor Income	Net Rents	Corporate Profits	Interest	Consumption	Saving	Taxes
1929	**$84.7**	**60.3**	**17.6**	**5.8**	**10.8**	**5.5**	**91.2**	**3.1**	**4.5**
1933	39.4	73.9	14.5	5.5	4.3	10.3	116.2	0.9	10.2
1940	79.6	65.4	16.2	3.4	10.9	4.1	89.2	3.8	12.6
1950	239.8	65.5	16.3	3.0	14.3	1.0	80.0	5.0	17.5
1960	425.7	71.6	11.4	3.3	11.3	2.4	77.8	4.9	22.1
1970	833.5	76.3	8.2	2.3	8.5	4.7	76.9	4.9	25.0
1980	2198.2	75.5	5.7	3.1	8.6	8.9	78.6	6.9	27.9
1990	4491.0	173.4	9.1	0.2	6.7	10.6	83.8	3.8	38.0
1993	5143.2	73.8	8.2	0.2	9.1	8.6	85.9	3.5	38.5

Source: Economic Report of the President, miscellaneous issues, 1980–1994.

*Percentages of totals for selected years.

Note: Total percentages for Uses of Income frequently exceed 100% because certain taxes appear in GDP accounting but, as you will see, are subtracted before National Income is computed.

Across time, these percentage breakdowns of national income seem to change only at a snail's pace. However, scrutiny of these data discloses such broad trends in American history as (a) long term growth of government, (b) an expansion in labor's share of total income, and (c) a rebirth of entrepreneurship since 1980, after a long decline in the significance of small business (e.g., family farms). Are you aware of forces that might explain persistent declines in rental income? The growth of income from interest? (You should be better able to address these and similar issues after you've progressed further through this book.)

zations (e.g., many hospitals), or government controlled industries (e.g., public schools), but the bulk is produced within privately owned *firms*. Figure 1 indicates that firms use their sales revenues to pay for the resources households provide.

> *A **business firm** is a privately owned and operated center for production.*

Entrepreneurs and managers of firms interpret prices and profits as signals about individual wants or collective wants (expressed through government). Firms prompt households to provide specific resources with incentives in the forms of wage rates paid for specific labor skills, rental rates for land, or rates of return on capital.

• **Government**   *Government* directly provides some goods and services, and indirectly channels resources and the production and consumption of other goods via taxes and regulations. Taxes are the primary sources of government revenue.

Political processes transform this command over resources into governmental provision for collective wants (e.g., police protection, public schools, highways, and national defense) and into income redistributions that politicians view as reflecting voters' desires for equity.[1]

A critical point in the circular flow model is that firms are not the final owners of resources or products, because all firms are ultimately owned by people in households. Nor does government ultimately own anything in a democratic society in which, ideally, it is responsive to the people, who bear the consequences of policies formulated within firms or government. Firms, for example, cannot bear tax burdens; only their resource suppliers, owners, or customers truly pay taxes. It is common to speak of government changing its economic policies, or of firms profiting, changing prices, or introducing new products, but such institutions only shape the flow of

-----

[1]Possible economic roles for government in a market economy are surveyed in Chapter 4 and are considered in more detail throughout this book.

individual decisions. Activities that matter affect people, not organizations per se.

More detailed circular flow models show how goods, resources, and incomes move among households through firms and government, and across international borders. But are resources used in allocatively and productively efficient ways? And do goods and resources flow in distributively efficient ways to those who desire them relatively most?

SPECIALIZATION AND TRADE

Imagine how miserable life would be if you had to be totally self-sufficient—no cars or convenience foods, no ready-made clothing, and no electricity. If you consumed only what you produced, life would be "nasty, brutish, and short."[2] Both living above bare subsistence and economic efficiency require (a) production entailing a division of labor and (b) specialization and exchange according to comparative advantage.

Division of Labor

Romance may motivate most modern marriages, but mundane considerations also play a role. People wed, in part, to share gains from a division of labor. Household chores, for example, involve less drudgery if one spouse cooks and mows the lawn while the other pays the bills and buys the groceries. And cleaning a kitchen takes *less* than half the time when one person rinses crockery while the other loads the dishwasher.

> The **division of labor** entails dividing the work required to produce a given good or accomplish a particular task.

Gains from the division of labor arise because (a) teamwork fosters productivity (no one could do heart transplant surgery alone) and (b) people develop expertise in particular jobs (practice improves quality and reduces error). What is a

---

[2]This phrase was originated, but in a different context, by the sixteenth-century philosopher Thomas Hobbes in his treatise, *Leviathan*.

"key grip?" A "best boy?" Long lists of credits that scroll on-screen at the ends of films barely hint at the divisions of labor behind such complex forms of production as blockbuster movies, skyscrapers, or jumbo jets.

Comparative Advantage

The division of labor facilitates production of a given good, but in what specific goods or services should particular individuals or groups specialize? All potential gains are realized if you concentrate on doing that which you can do at the lowest cost relative to other people's costs. In 1817, David Ricardo, an influential early economist, was focusing on international trade when he generalized this idea into an economic law.

> The **law of comparative advantage**: Mutually beneficial exchange is possible whenever **relative** production costs differ prior to trade.

This law applies to all exchanges, whether between individuals or nations.

Opportunity cost is the key to comparative advantage: *Individuals and nations gain by producing goods at relatively low costs and exchanging their outputs for different goods produced by others at relatively low cost.* All potential trading partners can gain enormously through appropriate specialization and exchange.

Oranges are grown at lower cost in Florida than in Iowa, for example, while Iowa excels in corn production. Floridians and Iowans share gains from exchange according to comparative advantage by trading Florida oranges for Iowa corn. Similar gains are realized when Americans trade with foreigners; efficiency requires using all the world's resources in the relatively most productive ways.

Suppose Brazilians can grow coffee more easily than they can catch salmon, while Alaskans find it relatively easier to catch salmon than to grow coffee. Alaskans have a comparative advantage in salmon fishing, the Brazilians in coffee production. Trading Alaskan salmon for Brazilian coffee clearly yields gains to both parties. Table 2 shows how both parties to a trade

TABLE 2   Opportunity Costs and Efficiency

Before Specialization	Hours Worked	Production and Consumption	
Alaskan	4	5 pounds of salmon	
	4	*1 pound of coffee*	
Brazilian	4	*1 pound of salmon*	
	4	5 pounds of coffee	

After Specialization	Hours Worked	Production	Consumption
Alaskan	8	10 pounds of salmon	5 pounds of salmon
			5 pounds of coffee
Brazilian	8	10 pounds of coffee	5 pounds of coffee
			5 pounds of salmon

Trade enables Alaskans to consume an additional 4 pounds of coffee per day and Brazilians to consume an extra 4 pounds of fish per day. Each group specializes in the form of production in which it enjoys a comparative advantage, and virtually everyone ultimately gains through this process of trade.

can gain as long as their opportunity costs are not identical. If Alaskans and Brazilians each specialize in their areas of comparative advantage, and if 1 pound of salmon trades for, say, 1 pound of coffee, then Alaskans can consume an extra 4 pounds of coffee daily while Brazilians can consume an additional 4 pounds of salmon. Note that the Alaskan opportunity cost of producing 1 pound of coffee is 5 pounds of salmon before trade, while the Brazilian cost of 1 pound of coffee is only 1/5 of a pound of salmon.

But what if Alaskans had *absolute advantages* in everything–they could do every task faster and easier than Brazilians? You might think that Alaskans must lose if Brazilians gain from trade but, surprisingly, both sides can gain.[3] Suppose, for example, that a lawyer whose fees run $100 an hour types twice as fast as her secretary, whose wage is $10 hourly. She still gains by hiring the secretary despite her absolute advantage as a typist–her time is worth more in court. Similarly, many professional athletes probably have absolute advantages in lifting and carrying compared to furniture movers. Nevertheless,

few pro athletes move their furniture when traded between teams. Athletes and movers both gain by concentrating in their own areas of comparative advantage.

It is important to notice that, in these last two examples, absolute advantages do not translate into comparative advantages. Indeed, the lawyer's absolute advantage in typing still yields a comparative *dis*advantage in secretarial work, and, although furniture movers have absolute *dis*advantages at both athletics and furniture moving, their absolute disadvantage is relatively the least in moving furniture, so this is their area of comparative advantage.

• **Roots of Comparative Advantage** Relative resource abundance is often cited as the primary determinant of comparative advantage. It seems natural for a nation with fertile soil to have comparative advantages in agriculture, that huge oil reserves give the Middle East an edge in oil, and that plentiful low-wage workers yield advantages to China in labor-intensive goods. But why is Argentina, which is rich in resources, relatively poor, while Switzerland, with few natural resources, enjoys one of the world's highest standards of living? And why is India's economy stagnant while Singapore thrives despite even

---

[3]Tables and graphs of numerical examples where absolute advantages in all activities still yield comparative advantages to all parties are provided in our chapter on international trade.

greater population density and fewer natural resources?

One answer to such riddles is that comparative advantage is also molded by (a) climate and location, (b) institutional and cultural factors, (c) government policies, (d) the skills and education of the populace, (e) the vigor of internal competition and size of domestic markets, and (f) the commitment of domestic entrepreneurs to innovate new technologies and cultivate global markets. How resources are combined is as important as the mix of resources available.

A detailed multinational study by Michael Porter, a professor at the Harvard Business School, concludes that government policies intended to promote targeted domestic industries (e.g., export subsidies or tariffs against imports) fail as often as they succeed.[4] In this view, government is not very successful in picking industries that are winners. Porter argues that government policy should be broadly limited to (a) encouraging domestic rivalry (which rewards success in lowering costs and improving quality), (b) investing in human resource skills that enhance productivity, and (c) emphasizing quality as a national priority.

U.S. exports have recently been swamped by imports, and many industries once dominated by U.S. firms have been invaded by aggressive foreign exporters. Does this mean that we are losing all comparative advantages? No! Being comparatively disadvantaged in all areas is impossible because relative magnitudes determine comparative advantage. Focus 1 identifies a few of the many areas in which U.S. producers continue to enjoy a substantial competitive edge. The shapes of *production possibilities frontiers* (graphs of the limits to productive capacity) help show how comparative advantages differ internationally.

PRODUCTION POSSIBILITIES

Can you afford a flight in a hot air balloon if you already spend all your income each week? Of course, but only by buying less of something else.

You can eat peanut butter and jelly instead of having pizza delivered, walk instead of filling your gas tank, or drive on bald tires till they go flat. But something has to give! Just as your budget constrains your purchases, scarcity forces society as a whole to make choices about the goods we produce and consume.

Production Possibilities Frontiers

A *production possibilities frontier (PPF)* is among the simplest models of an economy.

> A **production possibilities frontier** depicts the maximum combinations of goods a society can produce in a given period.

This model relies on three critical assumptions.[5]

1. The amounts of labor, capital, land, and entrepreneurship are fixed, but can be allocated among different types of production.
2. Technology, which includes such things as the state of knowledge about production and the qualities of resources, is assumed constant.
3. All scarce resources are fully and efficiently employed.

Suppose you live in Tyrania, a mythical empire ruled by the dictator Atilla. Tyrania contains 1,000 units each of capital, land, and labor. Atilla believes that "balanced" production requires all industries to use the same proportional mix of resources. (In a moment, you will see how dopey this constraint on technology is.)

Some production possibilities for Tyrania using Atilla's technology are detailed in the table in Figure 2. Points a, b, c, d, and e denote five possible combinations of armaments and bread that can be produced per day. (For simplicity, we assume that only two goods are produced.) As resources are shifted from armaments to

---

[4]Michael E. Porter, *The Competitive Advantage of Nations* (New York: The Free Press, 1990).

[5]If lack of realism in these assumptions disturbs you, remember (from Chapter 1) that a model needs to be no more realistic than is necessary for the purpose at hand.

Is the United States at a Comparative Disadvantage?

The U.S. economy was the world's undisputed heavyweight champion from World War II into the 1960s. We found ready export markets for almost everything we produced, e.g., steel, cars, planes, and construction equipment. Today, one new car in four bought by Americans is foreign. U.S. imports have exceeded exports each year from 1982 to the present. We now import shiploads of oil and steel, many of our clothes, and most of our shoes. Such facts dismay people who believe we are losing our ability to compete in world markets.

First, ongoing internationalization in most economies is one major explanation for concern that the United States has lost its ability to compete. Countries everywhere are both exporting and importing record shares of their output and income, so most societies have an increasingly international flavor—an alarming fact to traditionalists all over the globe who fear foreign influence, e.g., adherents to some of the doctrines of Ross Perot and Pat Buchanan.

Second, some countries' exports have grown faster than U.S. exports. This is, in part, a consequence of technological changes and shifts in resource usage that accompany changes in areas of comparative advantage. Signs are emerging, however, that rates of gain are shrinking for countries

that played catch up in recent decades. For example, our average labor productivity growth lagged behind that of Japan and parts of Western Europe during much of the period from 1950 to 1980.* This pattern reversed after 1985, while wages in those countries grew faster than U.S. wages. Consequently, average U.S. labor costs per unit of output, which formerly exceeded those in other major industrial powers, had fallen to roughly average by 1994.

Third, the international value of the dollar was at record highs in the mid-1980s. Foreign suppliers sought high prices and profits by exporting goods to the U.S., while foreign buyers were discouraged from buying high-priced U.S. exports, partially accounting for huge imbalances of trade during 1983–1990. From 1990 to 1993, however, the dollar fell relative to other major currencies. Coupled with the relative decline in U.S. labor costs, this drop in the value of the dollar helped bolster U.S. exports and restrain imports in the 1990s. Thus, our trade imbalance was narrowing by 1993.

Germany briefly displaced the United States as the world's greatest exporter from 1989 to 1991, but by 1992 we had regained that title. If we are the world's biggest exporter, why do we continue to run deficits in our balance of

trade? Answer: we also hold the title of the world's biggest importer. Voracious national consumption sometimes means that we import even some goods at which we excel as producers. For example, the United States is the world's #2 steel producer, but we still import steel.

Robust international competition has made it easy to forget that the U.S. continues to be the world's largest producer across a vast range of major industries, including aircraft, aluminum, computers, education (we "export" degrees earned by foreign students), entertainment, financial services (e.g., credit cards), paper, petrochemicals, plastics, scientific instruments, semiconductors, and software. We remain the world's largest high tech exporter and dominate exports of films, music, and agricultural products. (The topsoil in our farm belt and our agricultural technology are the envy of the rest of the world.) And even our auto industry is the #3 exporter in world markets. If you are in another country and see a new foreign car, chances are one in nine that it was "Made in the U.S.A."

* Average U.S. labor productivity continues to be the highest of any nation, but labor in some countries has gained in productivity relative to that of typical U.S. workers.

---

bread, weaponry output falls and bread output rises. When all resources are used to produce guns, no bread is produced, and vice versa.

Alternatives *a* through *e* are only five of many feasible combinations. Atilla can choose any point on the production possibilities fron-

tier (PPF) graphed by connecting combinations *a* through *e* with a smooth line. The point chosen (answering the question of *what* will be produced) depends on whether he wants people better fed and less well defended, or vice versa. Atilla would never knowingly choose a point

FIGURE 2   A Primitive Production Possibilities Frontier

Production Alternatives	Production Possibilities Schedule		
	Arms (machine guns per day)	Bread (boxcars per day)	Machine guns sacrificed per extra boxcar of bread
a	1,000	- 0 -	1
b	750	250	1
c	500	500	1
d	250	750	1
e	- 0 -	1,000	1

This straight-line PPF reflects resource availability (1,000 units each of land, labor, and capital) and the crude technology used (Atilla's "balanced" production formula). If outputs of both arms and bread are exactly proportional to the amounts of resources used and a maximum of either 1,000 guns or 1,000 boxcars of bread can be produced daily, then output with full resource employment totals to 1,000 total units of bread + weapons. Each gun produced costs 1 boxcar of bread, and vice versa.

such as *x* because some resources would either be wastefully used or idle. Productive efficiency (addressing *how* production will occur) requires being somewhere on the PPF. Any inefficiency (e.g., underemployment) could be eliminated by moving from *x* to a point between *c* and *d* so that more of both goods was produced.

Producing 1,250 units of each commodity at point *z* is clearly preferable to all points on the existing frontier. Resources cannot be stretched to attain point *z*, however, in part because Atilla's neurotic fixation on balanced production yields a limited technology. Remember that an economy produces efficiently, given its technology, when it operates on its production possibilities frontier.

What does bread cost in our example? If Tyranians move from point *c* in Figure 2 to production possibility *d*, they gain 250 boxcars of bread but lose 250 machine guns; the cost of each extra boxcar of bread is 1 machine gun. The guns forgone for extra bread are the opportunity costs (in guns) of producing and consuming more bread, and vice versa. Thus, slope at any given point on a PPF reflects the oppor-

tunity costs of shifting toward greater production of a good from that point. A straight-line PPF such as this one yields constant costs because producing an extra boxcar of bread costs 1 machine gun at every point along the curve. But constant cost is actually an unlikely case—in fact, because of *diminishing returns* in production, increasing costs are the norm.

Diminishing Returns

Here is a very general statement of the law of diminishing returns:

> The **law of diminishing returns**: As any activity is extended, it eventually becomes increasingly difficult to pursue the activity further.[6]

---

[6] The law of diminishing *marginal* returns that economists apply to production is a narrow application of the much broader tendency described here, which, for math purists, is equivalent to the idea that all economic functions are bounded by a strictly convex hull.

For example, the faster you drive, the more gas your engine burns per mile, and it becomes ever harder for your car to accelerate another 10 miles per hour.

Diminishing returns are encountered in many areas, including physics and biology, and the law of diminishing returns has wide and varied applications within economics: expanding any type of production eventually becomes ever more difficult and costly. Increasing your total satisfaction from any good ultimately becomes harder the more of the good you have already consumed. Would four candy bars daily quadruple the enjoyment you got from eating the first?

● **Increasing Opportunity Costs** The inevitable occurrence of diminishing returns in all forms of production generates increasing opportunity costs.

> The **principle of increasing costs**: Repeatedly increasing output by some set proportion ultimately requires more than proportional increases in resources and, thus, higher costs.

For example, grades tend to improve the more you study–a C requires more effort than a D. But boosting a B to an A usually requires far more extra work than moving from a D to a C. Thus, raising your grade point average entails increasing costs. Let's see how this concept applies to the production possibilities frontier.

Atilla's "balanced" technology naively mandated identical resource mixes for all outputs. Suppose he appointed you production minister. You might reason that, relative to arms, efficient bread output requires more land and less capital, while arms should use relatively more capital. This is a technological breakthrough! Your insight allows both outputs to grow! After tinkering to find the best resource mixes, you will find that increasing costs are encountered as either output expands, causing the production possibilities curve to be concave (bowed away) from the origin. Here's why.

Tyrania's production possibilities frontier with this new technology is shown in Figure 3. When bread production is raised from 0 to 200 boxcars daily, machine gun output falls only from 1,000 units to 980 daily (from point *a* to

If the resources available (1,000 each of land, labor, and capital) are combined in the ways that best fit various forms of production, the PPF will be concave from the origin. In this example, arms are capital intensive and bread is land intensive. Differences in the appropriate ratios of capital-to-labor-to-land yield diminishing returns (increasing costs) as more and more bread (or arms) are produced.

Production Possibilities and Increasing Costs

(1)	(2)	(3)	(4)
	Average Daily Production		Average Opportunity Costs (average machine guns sacrificed per extra boxcar of bread)
Point	Arms	Bread	
a	1,000	- 0 -	--
b	980	200	0.100
c	917	400	0.315
d	800	600	0.915
e	600	800	1.000
f	- 0 -	1,000	3.000

FIGURE 3   A More Realistic PPF that Reflects Increasing Costs

point *b*). Why do the first 200 boxcars of bread cost only 20 machine guns? Because the first resources shifted into food production will be those relatively best suited for bread and least suited for weapons. Far more land than capital will be transferred to bread production. But as bread output is continually increased, the resources shifted are less and less suited for bread production relative to production of armaments, and the cost of extra bread rises. Thus, moving from point *b* to point *c* yields an extra 200 boxcars of bread daily, but costs 63 machine guns, while moving from point *c* to point *d* also yields 200 extra boxcars of bread, but the cost is higher: 117 machine guns.

When bread output finally grows from 800 to 1,000 boxcars daily (point *e* to point *f*), the last few resources shifted from armaments are well suited for producing guns but not for producing food. Thus, 600 machine guns are sacrificed for the last 200 boxcars of bread. Less and less land is available for shifting, so more and more capital moves into farming. Note that the slope of the production possibilities frontier reflects relative production costs: as more and more bread is produced, the production possibilities curve becomes ever steeper, so bread becomes increasingly costly relative to machine guns.

The ever-rising cost of extra bread in terms of forgone machine guns, as shown in the table in Figure 3, is graphed in Figure 4. You will learn in the next chapter that this shows the typical shape of a society's long-run supply curve for bread.

To summarize, the production possibilities model illustrates scarcity, choice, opportunity costs, and diminishing returns. Desires for "more" are boundless but resources are scarce, so only limited production is possible. Scarcity forces every society to choose among competing goods, so we face opportunity costs. Finally, opportunity costs eventually rise if we repeatedly expand the production of any good.

ECONOMIC GROWTH

All else being equal, allocating resources more efficiently allows movement from inside a production possibilities frontier to its border— productive capacity is not affected, but total output

FIGURE 4   Rising Opportunity Cost of Bread

Diminishing returns raise the cost of bread as production expands. Thus, more and more guns must be sacrificed for extra bread as bread output rises. (This figure roughly reflects the costs from column 4 of the table in Figure 3.)

does rise. In contrast, economic growth occurs when (*a*) production possibilities frontiers shift outwards, so that more of all goods can be produced, or when (*b*) the value in exchange of a national output increases for purposes of international trade.

> **Economic growth** entails increases in the value of a nation's productive capacity.

Growth is driven by (*a*) technological advances, (*b*) increases in the availability of resources or improvements in their quality, or (*c*) increased values for the goods in which a country specializes. (In a few pages, you will learn how expanded international trade is one major way national output can gain in value.)

Technological Advances

Growth occurs when entrepreneurs implement technologies allowing given amounts of resources to produce more output. It may seem

Innovation, Entrepreneurship, and Economic Growth

Economic growth is meaningless unless it improves the quality of our lives. A prominent scientist once recommended closing the U.S. Patent Office because everything conceivable had already been invented. His proposal to reduce taxes was written to President Grover Cleveland in 1887. The scientist assumed that because he could envision nothing worthwhile not already available, no one could. Fortunately, Cleveland ignored his advice. By most measures (e.g., average lifespans, variety in diet, education, access to transportation or health care, or square feet of housing) average Americans are now materially better off than in any previous generation.

If your background is middle-class, you probably cannot remember when your family lacked a car, remote-controlled color TVs, stereos, microwave ovens, dishwashers, automatic garage door openers—the list goes on and on. Nor did your parents grow up as their parents had. As children, your parents probably watched flickering monochrome TVs, traveled by car or train until airline flights began reducing the time absorbed for cross-country jaunts, and washed dishes by hand as a family chore. Your grandparents, however, probably recall their youth as an era when cars were hand-cranked, films were silent, and listening to the radio was a treat. You will probably tell your own children how tough life was before, for example, most families had computers and instant access to 500 channels on cable TV. (Every generation of parents exaggerates only a little when describing how much tougher things were when they were kids.)

Economic progress is proceeding much faster today than ever before, but probably not as fast as it soon will be. From the dawn of history until the Industrial Revolution (roughly 200 years ago), lifestyles changed only at a snail's pace. For centuries, people lived much as their immediate ancestors had. What accounts for the astonishing pace of technological advances?

Science, which is sometimes characterized as research and development (R&D), is usually accorded much of the credit (or blame). However, the scientific part of R&D usually focuses on research, with development (implementations of new technology) being left to entrepreneurs. Thus, science might be relatively stagnant without support from entrepreneurs, who transform new knowledge from research into practical uses, a process called "innovation."

In their search for profits, entrepreneurs constantly seek better ways to fulfill people's unmet needs. People may be unaware of these needs until someone markets a new product. You probably identify Thomas Edison as the inventor of the electric light bulb, but did you also know that, while still engaged in research, he became a business tycoon after founding General Electric? During his lifetime, hundreds of major patents were granted for all sorts of electric gizmos developed in GE laboratories. Other inventors who made the transition to successful entrepreneurship include Eli Whitney, who invented the cotton gin and the concept of standardized parts (which he put to use making rifles shortly before the Civil War), and George Eastman,

who founded Kodak after patenting a camera.

Few entrepreneurs, however, are full-time inventors. Instead they focus on improving the inventions of others to move new processes and products to market. For example, Henry Ford did not invent the automobile, but he did develop assembly-line production to make standardized cars affordable for average people. Nor did Thomas Watson invent computers—they originated with designs by Charles Babbage for mechanical calculating machines almost 120 years ago. However, Watson, who inherited a small office machines company, did have a vision.

Every major firm processes tremendous amounts of information about billings, expenses, inventories, and taxes. Until the 1950s, armies of bookkeepers recorded these data. Watson thought that business information could be processed more cheaply and reliably with electronic computers, which had been refined in government-subsidized laboratories during the 1940s. The result? Watson's International Business Machines (IBM) came close to monopolizing business computers for almost three decades—a period of enormous growth in the U.S. economy. A major benefit of new technology is the time it saves. IBM's computers, by freeing millions of workers from bean-counting drudgery, substantially contributed to this growth.

Successful entrepreneurs often establish companies that prosper for long periods, but this success is at risk because other entrepreneurs look for ways to do things better and cheaper. One technique is to import new technology into a moribund industry. Sears,

Montgomery Ward, JC Penney, and Woolworth's pioneered mass-market retailing, but Sam Walton, among others, laid waste to these giants by coupling computerized inventory systems with discount prices.

The most imitated computer to date was launched in 1982: the IBM PC. For almost a decade, however, IBM executives remained convinced that only a few hobbyists would ever buy personal computers—only giant mainframes would ever have a large market. IBM's myopia set the stage for a wave of techie entrepreneurs, among others, Bill Gates of Microsoft and Steve Jobs and Steve Wosniak of Apple.

Today, highly publicized alarmists are convinced that the future looks bleak. According to them, the world will soon run out of most natural resources: petroleum, iron ore, forests, and even breathable air. Similar alarms were raised shortly after the Civil War because of worldwide oil shortages: Americans would soon be without adequate lighting from oil lamps. In that case, "oil" was whale oil. Why did their gloom-and-doom forecasts prove so inaccurate? In large measure, they failed to recognize human ingenuity, especially that of entrepreneurs. Petroleum, which until then had been considered a nuisance when it bubbled up out of the ground, filled the hole left by the declining availability of whale oil. And then, shortly thereafter, Edison, developed the light bulb. New technology has a way of curing all sorts of problems. And entrepreneurs are the chefs who make raw technological advances suitable for human consumption.

Others alarmists view technological advances with dismay. (Perhaps they were terrified by *Jurassic Park* or other films about science run amok.) Genetic engineering is a favorite target. Recognize, however, that any type of knowledge can be used improperly. For example, the types of medical research that cured smallpox, polio, and plague also generated the knowledge used for germ warfare. This does not mean that less knowledge is better than more: ignorance can kill you. However, it can mean that, in some cases, due care should be exercised.

Today, adventurous entrepreneurs plot changes to the world as we know it, much as Columbus did in 1492. Columbus sought only a shorter route to India, but he discovered a whole new world (new, at least, to Medieval Europe). These entrepreneurs foresee smart TVs and multimedia systems, rich information highways, and amazing advances in bioengineering. Who knows what new worlds they will discover? Skepticism abounds that their visions will soon be realized, but such critics' batting averages are lousy. Columbus's critics were sure that the world was flat. The scientist who wrote President Cleveland felt certain that everything worth learning was known by 1887. And IBM executives did not realize until the early 1990s that personal computers were not a dead end.

surprising, but technological advances in any active industry expand production possibilities for all other industries.[7] The reason is that, say, installing advanced robots on an auto assembly line would permit fewer resources to produce more cars. Resources would be freed from automaking to produce more food, textiles, housing, and other goods. The innovation of new technologies is a key for economic growth—and for successful entrepreneurship. These relationships are explored in Focus 2.

Expanding the Resource Base

New technology is one path toward growth. Enhancements to the resource base are another.

---

[7]Major exceptions to this statement are cases of technological advances in industries not previously operational.

● **Natural Resources: Land**   Opening up new land could be a source of growth, but there is little unexplored land on earth and settling other planets remains in the realm of science fiction. However, finding better uses for existing natural resources effectively increases the quality of the land available. For example, intricate networks of dams and dikes have allowed the Netherlands to increase its territory—much of its land, once part of the ocean, remains below sea level. Similarly, extensive water desalinization and irrigation projects in Israel have turned what was once arid desert into productive farms. Increases in quality may be thought of as technological advances, or as comparable to increases in the resources available. Either perspective recognizes that better resource quality will expand the production possibilities frontier.

Wiser land-use policies (another form of technological advance) are also possible ways to boost the productivity of existing land, effectively increasing land resources and fostering growth. This could entail reform of overly restrictive zoning laws, or updating inadequate fee structures for use of federal land by ranchers and farmers, as well as logging and mining companies. Or should much of federal land (half or more of all acreage in some states, e.g., Alaska) simply be sold to private developers? Alternatively, should we preserve even more land in public parks? Any resolution of such questions about land use involves trade-offs between economic growth and environmental quality.

• **Labor** Growth of the labor force and, thus, economic growth, can be fostered through (*a*) increases in the number of workers or (*b*) improvements in their productivity. Both the quantity and quality of the work force affect national output and how it grows. One way government could expand the work force would be to allow freer immigration into the United States, especially of skilled workers. Other options include such strategies as (*a*) more support for education or on-the-job training programs to facilitate investment in human capital, or (*b*) provision of daycare for the children of people who want to work, but who, instead, spend the bulk of their time tending their kids because affordable and reasonably convenient daycare is not available. More efficient policies in areas such as health care and safety in the workplace also might foster growth of the work force and the economy, both quantitatively and qualitatively.

• **Capital: Saving and Investment** New capital is a major avenue for growth. National income that is not consumed, freeing resources for new investment, is called saving.

> *Consuming less than we produce is **saving**, which allows resources to be channeled into productive **investment**.*

Scarcity forces us to choose between work and leisure, among various commodities, and between current and future consumption. Investment requires saving—forgoing some of our potential current consumption. Positive interest rates make it possible to consume more if we save, thus waiting a bit before we or our heirs consume. But if perishable consumer goods dominate output, society invests little in new machinery and manufacturing plants. This shrinks the amount of goods available in the future.

Rapid investment boosts production possibilities in two ways. First, more capital is available. Second, new capital embodies more advanced technology than that embodied in older buildings and machinery. Higher labor productivity and the availability of new products are common side benefits. But productive capacity is eroded if depreciation exceeds investment; failure to replace worn-out capital yields stagnation. In such cases, the production possibilities frontier shrinks toward the origin. Thus, choices between current consumption and saving (to allow investment) determine future prosperity, as shown in Figure 5.

Panel A depicts possible choices between consuming and investing in the year 2000, with point *a* reflecting greater consumption (and less investment) than point *b*, point *b* more consumption than point *c*, and so on. Curves PPF_a through PPF_e in Panel B show the production possibilities for year 2020 that result from choices in 2000 of *a*, *b*, *c*, *d*, and *e*, respectively. In sum, growth in an efficient economy is stimulated by rapid investment, which requires more saving (less consumption).

Relatively low U.S. saving rates partially explain why, on average, our economic growth since 1970 has been anemic compared to some other countries. Modern Americans tend to save only 4% to 6% of their income, while the Japanese, for example, save and invest 17% or so of their national income. Consequently, many U.S. industries now try to compete with foreign firms that use better technology and more machinery. Our auto industry, for example, is reeling under competition from Japanese carmakers, who rely more heavily on industrial robots on their assembly lines.

How people's saving is used is as important as different saving rates in explaining international differences in growth rates. Economic

FIGURE 5 The Dilemma of Economic Growth

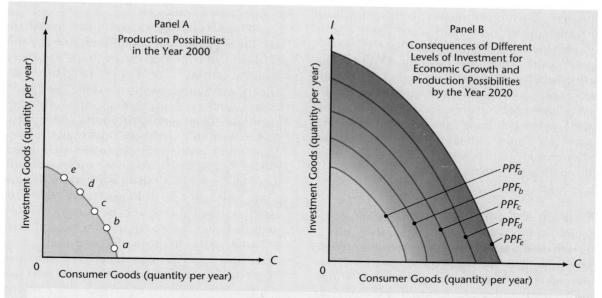

Panel B illustrates economic growth as a movement from PPF_a to PPF_b (or even PPF_e)---more of both goods can be produced, and any two goods could be on these axes. Society faces a trade-off between current and future consumption. If in year 2000 this society chooses a mix of goods that emphasizes consumption (e.g., point *a* in Panel A) instead of investment (capital) goods (as at point *e* in Panel A), the PPF in 2020 will be relatively smaller ---PPF_a in Panel B instead of PPF_b. Choice *a* in Panel A yields only enough new investment to replace capital that depreciates; so PPF_a is identical in both panels. Moving from *a* to *b* in Panel A yields more investment, so in Panel B, more of both consumption and investment are available on PPF_b than on PPF_a. Moving to point *c* in Panel A yields even greater growth, to PPF_c in Panel B. And so on.

growth is stimulated if saving is channeled into productive investments. Interest rates are signals that help channel investment flows. But if, say, government uses most private saving to fund a war, capital accumulation and economic growth will both be hampered. Religious prohibitions on payments of interest may be one reason the middle ages were economically stagnant in Europe. Similar bans against interest may partially account for slow growth in other parts of our world today.

Growth is squelched when saving is funneled into obsolete and inefficient industries. England's experience between 1945 and 1980 provides an example: most private saving was invested in nationalized industries in which England had lost its comparative advantage.

The result was stagnation relative to the U.S. economy, despite relatively higher saving rates by the English than by Americans. Similar stagnation prompted drastic reforms in Eastern Europe where, historically, growth was weak despite suppression of consumption to create high rates of saving and investment.

Another reason for sluggish U.S. economic growth in recent years is that much of private saving has been absorbed by gargantuan federal budget deficits; newly issued U.S. Treasury bonds absorb financial investment that otherwise would flow into private investment in new economic capital. In the 1990s, the eternal trade-off between guns and butter has transformed into a broader controversy: government spending versus private spending. Will the higher taxes or budget deficits needed to finance ambitious new federal programs (e.g., universal health care, improved environment quality) constrain private investment and consumption too tightly? Most public opinion polls find a majority of voters opposed to tax hikes and favoring broad budget cuts, but every proposal for some cut in spending elicits squeals from special interests. (And we are all members of some such groups). A standard result? Political gridlock. However, the expansion of international trade may provide an alternative path to accelerated growth, but even this path is politically daunting.

Growth and International Trade

International trade is another major source of economic growth; sales to foreigners increase the value in exchange of a country's output, while buying low-cost imports increases the availability of goods to consumers and lowers their price. Thus, specialization and exchange according to comparative advantage allows any society's consumption to exceed its PPF in isolation. Figure 6 portrays production possibilities for Alaska and Brazil drawn from a previous

example. Note the relative shapes of the two PPFs, which reflect these two regions' respective comparative advantages.

If trade results in one pound of salmon costing the same as one pound of coffee, both Alaskans and Brazilians can consume anywhere on the negatively sloped line just tangent to both PPFs. Options for consumers expand; people in both countries gain through trade-induced growth of their *consumption possibilities frontiers*. As a general rule, the more relative production costs differ among trading countries, the greater will be the gains from trade: consumers can buy more imported goods that were previously very costly when produced domestically, while producers can sell at relatively higher prices those outputs that, prior to trade, commanded relatively low prices in the domestic market.

Attaining a PPF requires technical efficiency in production. Inefficient methods for selecting what and how to produce preclude ever reaching capacity (recall Atilla's "balanced" production formula). But even if production is efficient, some mechanisms for choosing may inhibit allocative or distributive efficiency. (Would you dine at a sushi restaurant that forced you to select food by tossing darts at its menu?) Significant insights into

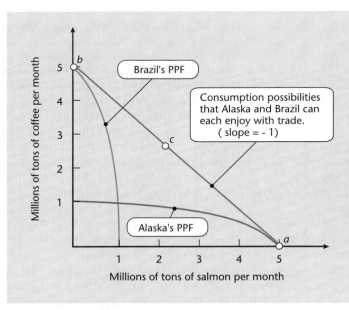

Without trade, consumption in Alaska and Brazil beyond their respective PPFs could not be sustained. Trade according to comparative advantage permits both countries to expand consumption to a consumption possibilities frontier like the green line *acb*, so that either could choose to consume at a point such as *c*.

Note:

These PPFs are based on simplifying assumptions that, if all resources were used in a single industry, Brazil could produce 5 times as much coffee as Alaska, which could produce 5 times as much salmon as Brazil, that maximum Brazilian coffee output exactly equals maximum Alaskan salmon output, and that coffee and fish are normal goods.

FIGURE 6   Production Possibilities and Comparative Advantage

scarcity and choice are gained by examining various mechanisms used to resolve competition among people for scarce goods.

ALLOCATIVE MECHANISMS

Human society is based on a blend of cooperation and competition. The form competition takes is shaped by such **allocative mechanisms** as markets or government. Some mechanisms alter overt behavior, but self-interest appears to be a universal motive that can be channeled, but not eliminated. For example, punishing children for not sharing toys may yield more sharing, but only because they learn to see their self-interests in a different light. Policies intended to stamp out self-interested behavior have uniformly failed in tragic ways (e.g., China from 1948 until the death of Mao, especially during the Great Leap Forward (1958–1961), during which an estimated 20 million to 30 million Chinese died of starvation; and Kampuchea (Cambodia) in the 1970s).

Every allocative mechanism we will discuss is used in some situations and in all countries. Thus, societies everywhere have *mixed* economic systems. But people try to beat the system no matter which mechanism is used. Each mechanism may work well in certain circumstances, but improper use of some mechanisms can be disastrous.

The Market System

The market system is the dominant device used in the United States and much of the industrialized world to address economic problems. Every market is somewhat unique, but all share certain characteristics: (*a*) buyers who demand goods or the resources that produce them if prices are acceptable, and (*b*) suppliers who make products or resources available if the price is right. Private buyers and sellers trade money for resources or goods in a market economy.

Markets enable buyers and sellers to transact business so that people can share in the gains possible through specialization and exchange according to comparative advantage. Markets range from commodity exchanges, where millions of bushels of grain change hands in thousands of daily trades, to markets where one huge transaction requires years to complete (huge construction contracts). Markets also range from geographically limited (local laundries) to global (international markets for petroleum engineers). Some deal in a single type of good (brickyards), while others offer thousands of products (shopping centers).

Much of this book describes how markets allocate resources and distribute income and production. But before we investigate supply and demand in the next two chapters to see how markets resolve economic issues, we will look at some nonmarket methods of choosing.

Brute Force

Brute force is a way to decide who gets what. You could lose your life, limbs, or loved ones if you refused to hand over your goods to a bully. Thugs might view brute force as a fine system, but parts I, II, III, and IV of *The Godfather* films illustrate how violence often inspires cycles of violence (and how successful films inspire sequels).

Brute force also wastes resources. The arms race between the United States and the USSR from 1945 to 1990 absorbed mountains of resources that could have been used to improve standards of living in both countries and elsewhere. And why should people bother to produce if their output will just be seized?

Queuing

Queuing (lining up) is another way to decide who gets what. First-come, first-served systems operate for mining claims or purchases at bookstores. Queuing can sometimes be efficient. For example, there is a trade-off between time you spend in a grocery checkout line and time cashiers would wait for customers if enough checkout lines were always open to provide instant service to everyone. (Your time is costly, but so is theirs.) But if queuing were the dominant allocation mechanism, so much time would be spent in lines that little production would occur, and you would be forced to be very selective about which long waiting line you chose. Should production then be oriented toward goods that have the longest queues? It's hard to say, because people's priorities change. Winter coats attract few buyers in July.

Random Selection

What if all economic questions were decided by *random selection*? Once again little production is likely. For example, if your job were assigned by throwing dice or other games based on pure luck, you probably would lack ambition, and the bulk of the potential gains from specialization would be wasted. Many of us would be round pegs in square holes. Young men are now required to register with the Selective Service System. Would using a lottery to determine who will serve in the Army be fair? Is a draft efficient? Would you want college degrees, new cars, or medical care to be allocated by lottery?

Tradition

Tradition may also be used to resolve economic questions. Feudal European monarchies operated largely on this basis, and the caste system in India still does. In our society, women and members of minority groups have often been pushed into low-paying jobs because tradition restricted access to better positions. Most of us reject the notion that only senators' children should become senators, or that garbage collectors' kids should necessarily haul tomorrow's trash. Resources and human talent are wasted when tradition alone rules.

There are cases, however, where tradition merely codifies efficient modes of resource allocation. For example, the carnage on U.S. highways would be far worse if people failed to follow the convention of driving on the right side of the street. This tradition enhances efficiency.

Such efficient traditions are often reinforced by laws and government regulations.

Government

Government decision-makers play dominant roles in resolving some issues, but how should they decide? Even if everyone agreed that a democratic government should make all economic decisions, we would still confront the questions of who should be given what and how to produce the things to be distributed. Among the criteria government leaders might use to distribute production are equal shares and need.

• **Equal Shares** An egalitarian approach entitling everyone to equal shares might seem a fair way to distribute goods, but equal amounts of food may be more than can be eaten by a 100-pound jockey, yet a starvation diet for a 250-pound all-pro linebacker. Should we all be issued equal paychecks and identical housing and clothing? Egalitarianism, moreover, offers few incentives for production. Why should an American farm family work hard to produce wheat if its share is only 1/92 millionth of farm production?

Another problem arises because policymakers are as self-interested as any of us. If you could decide what is equal or fair, you would probably give yourself and your friends the benefit of every doubt. Egalitarianism may regress to the state of George Orwell's *Animal Farm*: "All animals are equal, but some animals are more equal than others."

• **Need** An alternative is for government to distribute goods according to need. Unfortunately, it is difficult for anyone to judge someone else's needs. Distribution according to need is inherently costly and imprecise and causes people to exaggerate their needs. For example, beggars in underdeveloped countries sometimes cripple their children so the children appear more pathetic to compassionate strangers.

The 1950s TV game show "Queen for a Day" was less brutal. Contestants told tales about emergency operations, unemployed husbands, and foreclosed mortgages. The woman drawing the loudest audience applause was crowned queen and awarded a washer and dryer or trip to Las Vegas. Might you have stretched the truth if you had been a contestant? Do you think even well-intentioned decision-makers might become calloused to the plights of the truly unfortunate and especially sensitive to their own material needs if all allocations were based on need?

Still another difficulty is that distribution by need causes special-interest groups to devote resources to lobbying to make decision-makers aware of their special needs. And what better way to make your needs known than through hefty campaign contributions? The potential for graft and corruption is enormous—few politicians can be expected to be Good Samaritans. Finally, only minimal production is likely. How many people would exert themselves to produce things if all of it were going to be redistributed to the needy?

Despite the drawbacks of needs-based redistributions, no compassionate society ignores the problems of the truly destitute. Much of our welfare system is based on criteria thought to be related to needs. Examples include Medicaid, unemployment compensation, Social Security, food-stamp programs, Aid to Families with Dependent Children, and housing subsidies. Few people are so hard-hearted that they willingly tolerate poor people starving or remaining homeless for long periods. But many Americans now seem convinced that our current welfare system creates poverty because some able-bodied people choose to be "on the dole" when they could work. The continuing growth of this perception partially motivated ambitious welfare reform proposals unveiled by the Clinton administration in 1994. Similar proposals are being advanced in much of Europe—especially Great Britain, Sweden, and Germany.

• **Misallocation**   If government dictated production and consumption in detail, we could count on policymakers' preferences being reflected but should not be surprised if there were only two sizes of everything—too big and too little. Government decision-makers face tough dilemmas even if they scrupulously try to mirror the desires of millions of consumers. People's subjective preferences are often idiosyncratic. A national vote to mandate what everyone will eat during Thanksgiving, for example, would ignore those who prefer roast beef or ham to turkey. Such decisions are more efficiently left up to individuals and their families so that each family can have its first choice.

Another problem is that most people work better when their expertise is valued and they are rewarded for good performance. Workers who feel powerless tend to perform lethargically and may indulge in sabotage. (As a youngster, were you ever tempted to break dishes in hopes that your parents would take over your chores?) The quality and amount of output suffers when rigid decisions emerge from distant managers unaware of local conditions, a common failure in all bureaucracies (large organizations), including government. Bureaucratic decisions often fail to allow workers latitude to make intricate decisions that yield high-quality output.

Landscaping a building located on uneven ground, for example, requires adjusting for soil quality and knowing how much moisture, sunlight, and fertilizer suit different plants and trees. These factors will not be reflected in blueprints intended for thousands of buildings and mandated by a Landscape Architecture Commission that never visits the specific site. The point here is that government decision-making is often crude relative to the fine-tuning made possible through individual choice (*a*) in consumption, when people have differing preferences, and (*b*) in production, when policies specified centrally are not attuned to local conditions.

You can probably identify situations in which each of the preceding allocative mechanisms seems to work. Most economic decisions in the United States rely on markets in which prices and productivity largely determine what is produced and who gets it. One important exception is the family, whose decisions are based on varying degrees of command, tradition, and communal sharing, whether equally, by need, or based on some other criterion. Government is the second most important mechanism for decision-making in our mixed economy; taxes, regulations, public spending, and transfer payments have all grown rapidly in recent decades.

The past decade or so has seen government's size and scope shrink in countries where it dominated economic decisions for decades, or even centuries. Paradoxically, government has grown most rapidly in countries that historically relied more on markets. We need to explore how the balance between governmental decision-making and decision-making through the market system differs between different economic systems.

ECONOMIC SYSTEMS IN TRANSITION

> [W]hen authoritarian regimes promote economic progress, they are likely to lose their authority, because students, intellectuals, and executives will demand greater civil and political freedom.
>
> Nobel Laureate Gary Becker[8]

Every society attempts to cope with scarcity in certain basic ways: (a) use of money to convey information about relative prices, (b) specialization according to comparative advantage, and (c) division of labor. How and when different allocative mechanisms are used determines how efficiently a society produces and delivers goods to its members. Economic systems are conventionally classified by *who makes decisions* and *who owns which resources*, crucial issues in determining the importance of government relative to the market system. Figure 7 summarizes four basic economic systems and lists some countries where each system has dominated, and it shows that whether resources are privately or publicly owned is not rigidly linked to whether decisions are primarily centralized or decentralized.

---

[8]"Democracy Is the Soil Where Capitalism Flourishes Best," *Business Week*, 28 Jan 1991, p. 18.

Foundations of Capitalism

> *Capitalism is not like it used to be, and never was.*
>
> Unknown

Figure 7 also indicates that societies previously based on centralized ownership and control are increasingly relying on market forces. But why? The foundations of capitalism are a starting point in answering this question. Capitalism is only a few centuries old, but its ideological roots first emerged when our early ancestors started staking claims to territory. Hallmarks of pure capitalism are private property and decentralized, laissez-faire policies by government.

• **Private Property Rights**   Things are often described as owned by someone. You probably own books, sports equipment, and perhaps a car, but what does ownership mean? Generally it means that you have certain rights to use these things in certain ways. *Fee-simple property rights*, the broadest of private property rights, include rights to (a) use a good as you choose as long as no one else's rights are violated, (b) trade or give these rights to other people, and (c) deny use of the good to others.

Many property rights, however, are much more limited. For example, you cannot shoot people who trespass on your land, nor may you burn leaded gas in most new cars. You cannot raise hogs in New York City or Des Moines, Iowa. You cannot abuse your children, burn your house for the insurance money–the list goes on and on. The critical point is that most property rights are circumscribed.

How does anyone acquire property? John Locke, a seventeenth-century English philosopher, offered the labor theory of value to justify natural property rights. The *labor theory of value* asserts that human labor is the source of all value. According to Locke, mixing your labor with "gifts of nature" makes land and the crops it produces valuable. Thus, he viewed improvements to natural resources as ethical cornerstones for original property rights, which could then be legally transferred to others.

FIGURE 7   The Changing Structure of Economic Decision-Making

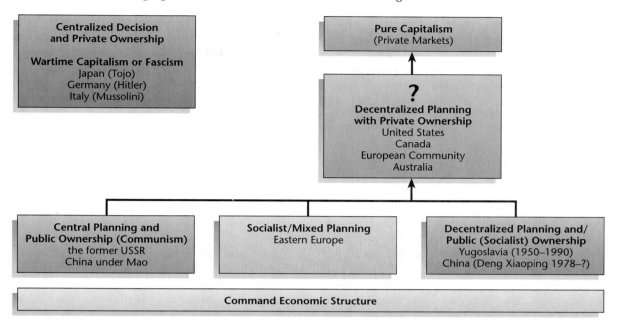

At the upper left, the mixture of private ownership and centralized decision-making occurs in economies that are primarily capitalistic but engaged in war. This configuration also characterizes fascist states. In the command economy (lower left), central decision-making (planning) was the rule, along with social (public) ownership of most resources. Until 1980, "worker management" accompanied by social ownership of resources characterized the decentralized Yugoslavian economy (lower right). The system of maximally decentralized decision-making and private ownership that would characterize pure capitalism (upper right) has never been tried, but has been most closely approached in parts of Western Europe, modern Japan, and North America. The list of countries that have abandoned a central-planning model of socialism to experiment with ever greater reliance on private ownership and decentralized markets is quite long: Albania, Armenia, Bulgaria, Chile, Estonia, Hungary, Kazakistan, Latvia, Lithuania, Nicaragua, Poland, Russia, Ukraine, ... China has grown at roughly a 10% annual clip since it loosened controls that severely limited private markets. Cuba is tottering, the last vestige of centralized socialism in the western hemisphere. The road toward a market system has been rocky in many of these formerly communist countries, with some (e.g., the former Yugoslavia) being dismembered by bloody civil wars. Privatization has been a trend that may cause previously market-oriented economies to become even moreso.

The idea that mixing labor with natural resources creates property rights raises both moral and practical problems. Should those who encounter gifts of nature have property rights on a first-come, first-served basis? If you were the first to pour your blood into the sea, should the oceans and all their riches be yours? And what about rules for transferring property? Who should have property rights to things produced by employees? By slaves? Should you own a piece of land, not by dint of personal effort, but because you inherited it from your parents who inherited it from their parents who bought it from the family who cleared the land? What if the family who cleared it murdered the previous owners? Should property rights become stronger over time, regardless of whether a property transfer long ago was legal or illicit? Difficulties posed by these types of questions for Locke's *natural rights* theory suggest a need for more practical foundations for property rights.

Basing property rights on brute force would be both violent and inefficient. If your claims held only to the extent that you have the muscle to enforce them, too many resources would be absorbed protecting your rights and aggressively trying to take from others. To avoid such problems, we grant government a near-monopoly on the use of legitimate force. Most legal scholars would argue that your property rights are determined by law: what the law says is yours is yours, neither more nor less. Society can be viewed as specifying sets of rights by law and then redefining rights through changes in statutes or legal opinions.

Property rights and legal rights are almost synonymous to economists. For example, zoning confers property rights that regulate how we may use land and buildings, traffic laws specify how we may drive our cars, and criminal laws limit how we may treat our neighbors. You cannot legally slander your neighbor, litter, or shout "Fire!" in a crowded theater. Property rights are also implicit in laws establishing such things as welfare programs or tariffs on imports.

Thus, laws govern the ways we use both our own and our neighbors' property. Government in a capitalist society establishes who owns what and how ownership rights can be transferred. Naturally, changes in rights accompany changes in laws; just as laws create property rights, they can take them away. But too frequent legal changes may create uncertainty and discourage production and investment.

Socialism is capitalism's most significant challenger.

> **Socialism** holds that most nonhuman resources should be owned by the state, acting as a trustee for all the people in society, and not by private individuals.

Differences between capitalism and socialism also tend to be pronounced in specifying appropriate roles for government.

> *That government is best which governs least.*
>
> Thomas Jefferson

• **Laissez-Faire Policies** Feudal monarchs ruled by divine right, claiming they were chosen by God to lead their countries. Even so, their policies often failed. Vexed by stagnation in seventeenth-century France, Louis XIV's finance minister sought advice from a leading industrialist. The manufacturer immediately responded, "Laissez-nous faire," meaning roughly, "Leave us alone." Laissez faire has ever since been a rally-ing cry for those who believe the market system works best with minimal government.

But what specific roles should government play? Nearly everyone recognizes needs for national defense and police protection.[9] In the economic sphere, a laissez-faire government only specifies property rights and enforces contracts. Under pure capitalism, private individuals own virtually all resources and control their uses. Thus, decision-making is private and *decentralized*. Market prices determine the range of choices available to us, given our budgets, which are in turn determined by the resources we individually own.

Private property and laissez-faire policies distinguish capitalism from alternative systems. Capitalism's defenders cite many virtues of the price system, but the two most important are freedom and efficiency. Capitalism, it is argued, allows people maximum freedom because it requires only minimal government. A tradition predating the American Revolution abhors "Big Brother" government as an enemy of freedom.

Central Planning in a Command Economy

Capitalist firms compete for profits by trying to produce better products at lower costs and prices. How a society governs economic activity pivots on a different type of rivalry. From the 1917 October Revolution that swept Marxists into power in the Soviet Union through the 1980s, international relations were dominated by competition (at times, in the form of war) between communist countries and nations based on mixed capitalism. Communism replaces the decentralized decisions of a market system with central planning.

> Under Marxist communism, **central planning** (centralized decision-making) accompanies socialist resource ownership in a command economy.

---

[9] Possible roles for government in a market economy are surveyed at the end of Chapter 4.

The Soviet Union relied on rigid central planning from 1929, with Premier Joseph Stalin's first Five-Year Plan, until Premier Nikita Khrushchev tried modest reforms in the 1960s. China has been ruled by communists since they won a civil war in 1949, after which central planning was quickly instituted. But dismay about stagnation under central planning mounted for decades. Rampant shortages and long queues to acquire food or shoes, for example, became routine. Most Soviet citizens spent as much time waiting in lines as average Americans spend watching TV.

Experiments with market forces (*privatization*) have recently swept through most former Iron Curtain countries. Why is communism being abandoned? One reason is that relative prosperity under different systems becomes clear when magazines and radio or TV signals cross national borders. International broadcasts made it obvious to Soviet citizens that their living standards were falling ever further behind those in more market-oriented economies.[10]

Economic Systems as Information Processors

Central planning centralizes data that would be disseminated widely in a market economy. One way to retain power is to monopolize information, so secrecy is common under all forms of totalitarianism. But sustained growth requires information flows across all levels of society and between centers for production. Shared information is vital for advancing technological frontiers. (Otherwise, all scientists would be forced to start by reinventing the wheel.) Thus, closed societies tend to stagnate and seldom compete successfully when pitted against open societies.

The isolation of closed societies usually drives them into ruts, using the same policy recipes over and over. For example, public buildings are uniformly drab when built according to architectural standards established by unmotivated central planners decades ago. The result? An American tourist observed that, in 1994, "buildings all over the ex-communist world look like Cabrini-Green" (a Chicago public housing project notorious for ugly, dysfunctional architecture).

Political freedom and decentralized markets expedite flows of information and technological advances. Anyone who has explored some of the databases available on computer bulletin boards in the United States quickly realizes that far more information is available on most topics than anyone could completely digest. One result of modern communications networks and the globalization of markets is that, although significant regional variation remains, open societies have become more internally diverse, with ever broadening ranges of choices available to people regardless of where they live. For example, American fast-food outlets are more available around the world than ever before, but so are restaurants featuring Chinese, Mexican, Vietnamese, Italian, Thai, or Ethiopian cuisine. Another result is that open societies are increasingly prosperous, and closed societies are being pressured to match their success.

Are Economic Systems Converging?

Exposure (communication and trade) facilitates political and economic imitation of successful patterns. Dramatic advances in standards of living in Western Europe, North America, and some Pacific Rim countries (e.g., Japan, Korea, Taiwan, Hong Kong, and Singapore) have publicized the gains available from allowing market forces to channel specialized production and exchange.

Reforms to decentralize decisions in the USSR accelerated in 1986, when President Gorbachev launched policies of *perestroika* (economic reform) and *glasnost* (openness) with more internal freedom and greater accommodation with the United States and its allies. He

---

[10]Testimony in 1990 by Abram Bergson (an expert on the Soviet economy) before a U.S. Senate committee indicated that, contrary to misleading official statistics, per capita consumption in the former USSR was exceeded in such emerging nations as, for example, Mexico—less than 25% of the level enjoyed by typical Americans.

learned, however, that the taste of political and economic freedom is addictive. The results of Gorbachev's experiments? He lost power while communist regimes toppled like rows of dominoes from 1989 to 1992 in Afghanistan, Albania, Bulgaria, Czechoslovakia (now split into the Czech and Slovakia Republics), Hungary, Mongolia, Nicaragua, Poland, Romania, Russia (the USSR dissolved into 15 independent nations), and Yugoslavia (rocked by civil war and shattered into three countries).

Another old-line communist regime is under fire in Cuba, and it seems unlikely that communism will long outlive aged party leaders in China or North Korea. China gradually began to decentralize economic decisions in 1978, shortly after diplomatic relations were reestablished with the United States. China has more successfully decollectivized (privatized) agriculture than the former USSR. In the early 1980s, China stopped being a net importer of rice and grain and became a net exporter. Russia remains a net importer of food.

China and most of the 15 countries carved out of the USSR increasingly rely on market forces in hopes of matching growth recorded in Europe, North America, and much of the Pacific Rim. Political freedom remains problematic in China, but its introduction of a market system has transformed it into the world's second largest economy. If its recent 10+% annual growth can be sustained, the Chinese economy may surpass that of the United States by the year 2010.

Pressures for modernization have not been limited to economies once ruled by central planners. Throughout the Americas, Europe, Australia, and New Zealand, there is a broad trend toward privatization—trash collection, highway construction, maintenance of public roads and buildings, the operation of prisons and public hospitals, and some educational activities are among functions traditionally performed by government but increasingly contracted to private firms. The drive for political and economic freedom has also prompted more democratic policies in several South American nations and South Africa. And a united Germany now figures prominently in economic and political developments in Western Europe.

The expanding scope of international trade and modern telecommunications is reducing differences among people and countries. Superior new technologies spread rapidly and are adapted to local conditions in almost all societies. International trade increasingly makes goods that are available anywhere available everywhere. But progress is not always smooth.

• **Impediments to Economic Progress** Market systems require structures of property rights roundly condemned by traditional socialists as leading to an unfair and exploitative class system.[11] Rapid transition from a familiar to a radically different economic system can be chaotic, eliciting outcries from some (especially those who were on top under the old system) for a return to the good old days. Thus, policies in former communist countries vacillate while moving toward greater reliance on markets, reflecting changes in the balances of political power between supporters and opponents of reforms. Figure 8 indicates how some countries are faring under mounting pressures for greater efficiency, political freedom, and international competitiveness.

All societies blend elements of both capitalism and socialism, so people everywhere live in mixed economies. For example, in the United States, socialism appears in the form of government-provided education and highways. And subsidized medical insurance for the aged, disabled, and poor is likely to be broadened to cover all Americans, according to a Clinton administration proposal for health-care reform.

When trends away from rigid central planning are coupled with the growth of economic regulation in societies that have long relied on markets, it appears that "we" may be becom-

---

[11]Command economies did not avoid this problem, instead concealing special privileges for elite groups. For example, stores limited to communist elites typically had a wide variety of quality goods at low prices, while the stores open to the masses had frequent shortages, lower quality, fewer goods, and higher prices.

FIGURE 8 Dynamic Changes in Our Global Economy

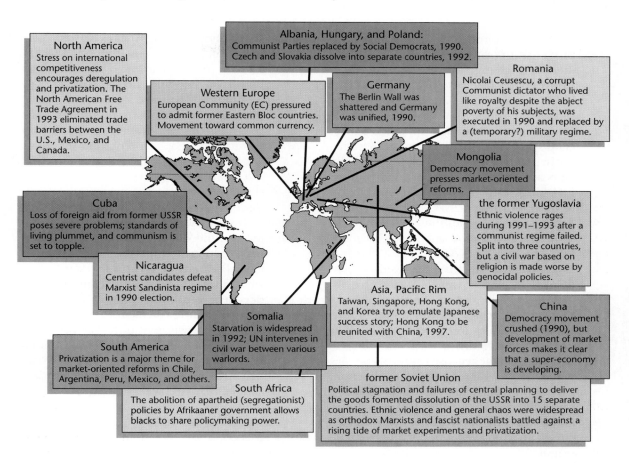

North America
Stress on international competitiveness encourages deregulation and privatization. The North American Free Trade Agreement in 1993 eliminated trade barriers between the U.S., Mexico, and Canada.

Albania, Hungary, and Poland:
Communist Parties replaced by Social Democrats, 1990. Czech and Slovakia dissolve into separate countries, 1992.

Romania
Nicolai Ceusescu, a corrupt Communist dictator who lived like royalty despite the abject poverty of his subjects, was executed in 1990 and replaced by a (temporary?) military regime.

Western Europe
European Community (EC) pressured to admit former Eastern Bloc countries. Movement toward common currency.

Germany
The Berlin Wall was shattered and Germany was unified, 1990.

Mongolia
Democracy movement presses market-oriented reforms.

Cuba
Loss of foreign aid from former USSR poses severe problems; standards of living plummet, and communism is set to topple.

the former Yugoslavia
Ethnic violence rages during 1991–1993 after a communist regime failed. Split into three countries, but a civil war based on religion is made worse by genocidal policies.

Nicaragua
Centrist candidates defeat Marxist Sandinista regime in 1990 election.

Asia, Pacific Rim
Taiwan, Singapore, Hong Kong, and Korea try to emulate Japanese success story; Hong Kong to be reunited with China, 1997.

China
Democracy movement crushed (1990), but development of market forces makes it clear that a super-economy is developing.

Somalia
Starvation is widespread in 1992; UN intervenes in civil war between various warlords.

South America
Privatization is a major theme for market-oriented reforms in Chile, Argentina, Peru, Mexico, and others.

South Africa
The abolition of apartheid (segregationist) policies by Afrikaaner government allows blacks to share policymaking power.

former Soviet Union
Political stagnation and failures of central planning to deliver the goods fomented dissolution of the USSR into 15 separate countries. Ethnic violence and general chaos were widespread as orthodox Marxists and fascist nationalists battled against a rising tide of market experiments and privatization.

More governments have totally changed direction in the past decade (or had it changed for them) than during any comparable period of (relative) peace since the Industrial Revolution. Progress toward political freedom and increased reliance on allocations by markets has proceeded erratically in many of these countries, in part because ethnic violence has often accompanied dramatic changes in national boundaries and forms of government.

ing slightly more like "them" while "they" are becoming a lot more like "us." However, privatization is a strong trend in nations with traditions of mixed capitalism, and, in recent years, deregulation in many industries has been another trend in relationships between government and business. Thus, economies everywhere seem to be moving towards greater reliance on decentralized capitalism, but not necessarily along a smooth path.

In countries characterized by mixed capitalism, government policies often reflect attempts to achieve what some people perceive as greater equity. But where efficiency is our primary goal, we tend to rely on the marketplace to provide most goods. The efficiency of capitalism depends on how well it meets consumer wants, given the resources available. Market allocations of goods and resources are a key element of capitalism. In the next two chapters, we examine the forces of supply and demand, which are the devices determining *What? How?* and *For whom?* in a market system.

CHAPTER REVIEW: KEY POINTS

1. **Households** ultimately own all wealth and provide all resources to firms or government in exchange for income with which to buy goods. Interactions between households, business firms, and government are shown in **circular flow** models.

2. **Comparative advantage** is a guide to efficient specialization; you gain by specializing in production where your opportunity costs are lowest and trading your output for things other people can produce at lower opportunity cost.

3. A **production possibilities frontier (PPF)** shows the maximum combinations of goods that a society can produce. The PPF curve assumes that (*a*) resources are fixed, (*b*) technology is constant, and (*c*) all scarce resources are fully and efficiently employed.

4. **Opportunity costs** are the values of outputs if resources were deployed in their next best alternatives. Opportunity costs are not constant because resources are not equally suited for all types of production. Increasing a particular form of production invariably leads to **diminishing returns** and **increasing opportunity costs**, so PPF curves are concave (bowed away) from the origin.

5. The idea that "a point of diminishing returns" has been reached is sometimes cited as a reason for ceasing an activity. This is usually a misuse of this phrase: people intend to say that a point of **negative** returns has been reached. An activity is often worth doing even though diminishing returns are encountered.

6. **Economic growth** occurs when the value of potential output increases because technology advances or the amounts of resources available for production increase, or freer trade increases the value of national output in exchange. Economic growth is reflected in outward shifts of the production possibilities frontier or the consumption possibilities curve; more of all goods can be produced or enjoyed.

7. The choices a society makes between consumption and investment goods affect its future production possibilities curve. Lower **saving** and **investment** restricts economic growth and PPF expansion.

8. The shapes of PPFs illustrate different countries' comparative advantages. Trade allows a country's people to consume far more goods than they could produce in isolation.

9. Alternative **allocative mechanisms** include (*a*) the **market system**, (*b*) **brute force**, (*c*) **queuing**, (*d*) **random selection**, (*e*) **tradition**, and (*f*) **government**.

10. Many different economic systems have been used in attempts to resolve the problem of scarcity. They can be classified by who makes the decisions (**centralized** or **decentralized**) and who owns the resources (**public** versus **private**).

11. Property is privately owned under pure **capitalism** and government follows **laissez-faire** (hands-off) policies. Thus, decisions that answer the basic questions of *what, how,* and *for whom* are decentralized and rely on individual choices in a market system. Under **socialism**, government acts as a trustee over the nonhuman resources jointly owned by all citizens. Many socialist economies traditionally relied on centralized production and distribution decisions.

12. Although the market system has many critics, communications networks and the obvious prosperity of most mixed capitalist economies began to alter policies in nations everywhere toward greater reliance on market allocations of resources and incomes during the 1980s. This trend is accelerating in the 1990s.

13. Reforms in former communist nations have aimed at replacing the cronyism, corruption, and inefficiency of central planning with the efficiency of a market system.

14. National borders, which once were transformed primarily through military conquest, are increasingly open to facilitate international trade.

QUESTIONS FOR THOUGHT AND DISCUSSION

1. How does the opportunity cost of time help explain why our welfare system involves long queues for people seeking food stamps, housing subsidies, or aid for dependent children?

2. In what kinds of goods do Americans enjoy comparative advantages over production by foreigners? Is this related primarily to the relative abundance of certain resources here in the United States compared with that abroad, or are such influences as technological leads, government policies, highly skilled labor, market competition, aggressive entrepreneurs, or sophisticated consumers also powerful in shaping comparative advantage?

3. What mix of allocative mechanisms is used within most American families to decide which family members get what, given limited family income? How are different mechanisms used for different kinds of decisions?

4. Explain why a family with a fixed budget has a "purchasing possibilities" frontier that is a straight line. A family's budget, however, is seldom fixed. Instead, it depends on the activities of family members. Suppose that different family members can work for different hourly incomes, and that they differ in their ability to do tasks for the family (e.g., cooking, cleaning, gardening, painting, and household repairs). Discuss whether production and the generation of income within the family is characterized by a family production possibilities frontier that is straight or concave from below.

5. What would happen to our PPF if outlays (spending) on human capital were increased? (Human capital refers to the education and skills embodied in an individual.) What does this suggest about countries or cultures that place a high priority on education?

Why are people ranging from Shaquille O'Neal to Garth Brooks paid more than the President? Why are airline ticket prices so volatile? And why are frivolities such as jewelry so costly, while such necessities as water or salt are relatively cheap? These and similar questions about why prices are what they are, and why outputs rise and fall, are all answered by the phrase "*demand and supply.*"

The tools of demand and supply are as integral to economic analysis as saws and hammers are to carpentry. For simplicity, the analysis developed in this chapter assumes vigorous competition—every market is assumed to contain many potential buyers and sellers. But even if competition is weak, or when other mechanisms (e.g., brute force, tradition, or government) are used, market forces powerfully influence resource allocations. Your basic goal for this chapter is a tall order that requires only a short sentence: learn how demand and supply interact in markets to determine prices and outputs.

We launch this chapter with a discussion of *marginalism*, the idea that most decisions entail weighing the relative costs and benefits of *small* changes in behavior (e.g., purchases or sales). Then we survey influences on the amounts of goods people buy or sell and show how demand and supply are linked in markets. After you have worked through this chapter and the next, you should be able to use supply and demand to interpret price and quantity changes in markets for goods and resources as varied as oil, grand pianos, student loans, tour ship cruises, film stars, real estate, or foreign currency.

THINKING AT THE MARGIN

All decisions are at the margin.

Unknown

Adjusting rational decisions to changes in relative costs and benefits tends to be a *marginal*, or *incremental, process.* Just as a sheet of paper is bordered by margins, the last few bits of a thing are its margins. Bankruptcy looms for marginal firms; marginally passing an exam puts you in danger of failing.

Even large changes can be treated as a series of small changes. For example, people seldom decide in advance to have three brownies. Suppose you just ate a brownie. You then weigh the cost of a second (market price, calories, etc.) against its expected ability to satisfy your appetite. When the marginal benefits of extending any activity exceed its marginal costs, you proceed; but if marginal costs exceed marginal benefits, you stop (or even reduce the activity's level slightly). If you eat the second, comparable analysis determines whether you will eat a third. Similarly, firm managers usually adjust operations a bit (marginally) rather than deciding whether to shut down or hire 10,000 workers.

Economists often refer to a marginal unit of something as its *extra* or *last* unit, which is often misinterpreted as a specific unit. For example, if there are 30 students in your class, who is the thirtieth? If anyone drops the course, only 29 students would be enrolled. Thus, each of you is the thirtieth (marginal) student. Similarly, there is no way to identify the last (marginal) slice from a cherry pie until the rest are eaten, nor is there a way to detect the marginal (last?) worker hired—or fired—by IBM. Each unit of any group may, in a sense, be the marginal unit. [Marginal changes are commonly written by preceding the symbol for the changing variable with a Greek capital delta (Δ), e.g., a price (P) change is written ΔP.][1]

Decisions about buying (demanding) or selling (supplying) are based on opportunity costs, which ultimately depend on the relative marginal benefits and costs of goods. For example, you probably eat less from a menu where prices are à la carte than if a restaurant charges a fixed price for a buffet; all-you-can-eat pricing causes you to view the cost of extra food as zero.

---

[1]Economic *marginals* often refer to the ratios of changes in one thing in response to small changes in another. For example, the *marginal physical product of labor* is output generated by adding a worker to a production process (Δoutput/Δlabor), and the *marginal propensity to consume* is the proportion spent on consumer goods out of any extra income (Δspending/Δincome).

DEMAND

Buying goods is like voting with money. Firms view dollar votes as signals about how to most profitably satisfy consumer wants. Items with the highest prices relative to their production costs earn the greatest profits. Firms compete to provide these items so that the wants consumers perceive as most pressing tend to receive top priority.

You may wonder if available resources can accommodate everyone's needs, but needs are ambiguous. Most Americans find a car a necessity, and many of us suffer withdrawal symptoms when deprived of television for a day or two. And in a wealthy society like ours, even meals are often recreational and unnecessary.

What is absolutely required for survival? Life could be sustained for $1,000 a year if, for example, you lived in a cardboard shack, ate soybean curd and vitamins, and wore secondhand clothes to prevent sunstroke or frostbite. Most of us, however, view people living so meagerly as still needy. Economists stress consumer demands because needs are both vague and normative.

> **Demand** *is the quantity of a specific good that people are willing and able to buy during a specific period, given the choices available.*

Consider a typical consumption choice. You probably attend concerts, buy CDs, and watch television. The market price of watching an extra hour of TV is roughly $0, CDs are about $15, and concert tickets range from $16 to $100 apiece. If you are typical, you spend a lot more time watching TV than attending concerts, with listening to CDs or tapes falling somewhere in between. This example suggests that the market prices of goods and the amounts consumers purchase are negatively related. Purchasing patterns depend on two sets of relative prices:

> **Market prices** *are the prices charged for goods whether we buy them or not;* **demand prices** *reflect the relative values an individual subjectively places on having a bit more or less of a good.*

You buy gum or a Frisbee only if they are subjectively worth their market prices to you. Whether market prices and our demand prices are aligned is partially determined by our budgets. BMWs are worth the money to their owners, but the rest of us have demand prices for BMWs far below their market price. Given our budgets, a BMW subjectively is not worth the price to us, and we drive cheaper cars, if we drive at all.

The Law of Demand

Most goods have many possible uses. How extensively a good is used depends on its price. When a good's relative price falls, it becomes more advantageous to substitute it for other goods, and substitutes are used to displace goods that become more expensive. This *substitution effect* of a change in relative prices is the foundation for the law of demand, a basic concept in the economics of consumer behavior.

> The *law of demand*: *All else being equal, consumers buy more of a good during a given period the lower its relative price, and vice versa.*

Substitution is pervasive. For example, caviar is now a high-priced delicacy, but it might replace baloney on children's sandwiches if its price fell to $0.50 per pound. Were it free, we might use it for dog food, hog slop, and fertilizer. We would use diamonds as a base for highways if they cost less than gravel. On the other hand, if gasoline was $10 a gallon, cities would be more compact and we would rely far more on bicycles, walking, or public transit; few people would waste fuel on meandering pleasure trips or hit-and-run shopping. If peanut butter were $50 per pound, gourmets might consider it a delicacy to be savored on fancy crackers at posh parties.

The critical point is that people find substitutes for goods that become relatively more costly and wider uses for goods that become cheaper. Focus 1 indicates how even people's use of water changes as its price varies.

A facet of the law of diminishing returns partially explains why substitution occurs:

> The *principle of diminishing marginal utility (satisfaction)*: *The more you have of any good relative to other goods, the less you desire and are willing to pay for additional units of that good.*

For example, you would probably not find a ninth chocolate chip ice cream cone as satisfying as the first you ate on a given day. This principle applies to demands for windsurfing, hair transplants, affection and kisses from your current heartthrob, or any other good.

Another reason purchases of a good rise when its price falls is that the purchasing power of a given money income increases, so you can buy more of the good while maintaining or even increasing your other purchases. This is the **income effect** of a price change. Income effects usually reinforce the negative slopes of demand curves, but they tend to be less direct and far less important than substitution effects. Only if the good for which price fell absorbed big chunks of your budget (e.g., rent) would the income effect of a price change be very large.[2]

• **The All-Else-Being-Equal (*Ceteris Paribus*) Assumption** Note that all influences on consumption of a good other than its own price are assumed constant in deriving the law of demand. The Latin term *ceteris paribus* refers to the idea that "all other influences" on some *dependent* variable are assumed to be constant while examining the effect of changing a single *independent* variable. Thus, the law of demand deals with the independent influence of price on the quantity demanded (the dependent variable), *ceteris paribus*. Much of economic analysis follows the lead of Alfred Marshall, a great nineteenth-century scholar, in using this all-else-being-equal methodology so that we can examine, one at a time, the variables that affect human behavior. Indeed, this is exactly the controlled experiment approach used throughout science to gain insights into how the world works.

---

[2]Income effects are dealt with much more extensively in the micro portions of economics.

Substitution and the Uses of Water as Its Price Changes

How much purchases are affected by prices depends on the options available. If a good has close substitutes (cotton and wool are examples), we may readily switch from one good to another as their relative prices change. In other situations, substitution entails major losses of efficiency or quality (replacing light bulbs with candles, for instance). In extreme cases, adjusting to higher prices may require that we simply do without.

Figure 1 shows how water usage might be influenced by different prices. If water were incredibly scarce and costly because you were stranded in the desert, you might sip only a little to avoid feeling parched and trust your camel to make it to the next oasis without a drink. Once there, the subjective value of extra water decreases and you would find ever broader uses for water (e.g., brushing your teeth, washing, and so on). Water flows down city streets when people water their lawns only if its price is incredibly low. Of course, water must be clean enough for its intended use; unrelenting rain storms during the spring of 1993 flooded sewage systems along the Mississippi River, leaving many communities without potable water for weeks.

People use water sparingly when it is especially scarce and costly, As the price declines, more and more uses are considered economical, and more water will tend to be devoted to each use.

FIGURE 1 How Water Usage Expands as Its Price Falls

Individuals' Demand Curves

The law of demand's negative relationship between the price of any good and the quantity consumed yields a negatively sloped demand curve.

*A **demand curve** depicts the maximum quantities of a good that given individuals are willing and able to purchase at various prices during a given period, all else assumed equal.*

An equivalent perspective that, in some cases, is also useful, views demand curves as reflecting the maximum price people are willing to pay for an additional unit of a good, given their current consumption. Thus, demand curves re-

BIOGRAPHY

Alfred Marshall: Tools That Simplify Analysis

Few economists extend knowledge in any but their narrow areas of specialization. A handful of master economists, however, have broadly expanded the frontiers of economic science. Their names and ideas are scattered across these pages. Adam Smith, David Ricardo, John Maynard Keynes, and, in our own time, Paul Samuelson and Milton Friedman, have covered the gamut of economic theory. Alfred Marshall (1842–1924) belongs in this elite group.

Born in a middle-class London suburb, Marshall was destined for the ministry, according to his stern, evangelical father. An independent sort, he declined a classics scholarship at Oxford and instead studied math at Cambridge. Marshall's exposure to philosophy led to a lifelong concern with poverty and other social problems that plagued industrial England and, in turn, to the study of economics, in which he excelled. His most famous student, John Maynard Keynes, described Marshall as the greatest economist of the nineteenth century.

Many ideas expressed in Marshall's *Principles of Economics* (1890) had been developed much earlier, but his patience and diligence paid lasting dividends. Despite advances in theory since his death, large parts of economics remain distinctly Marshallian. His major contributions include the concepts of competitive equilibria,

price elasticity of demand, internal and external economies of scale, increasing and decreasing cost industries, quasi-rent, and consumer surplus.

Before Marshall, a hodgepodge of theories competed in explaining pricing and value. An English tradition had refined John Locke's labor theory of value into the idea that value depends only on supply—the costs of the labor, capital, and land absorbed to produce a good. However, the Austrian economists Carl Menger (1840–1921) and Eugen von Bohm-Bawerk (1851–1914) had developed a subjective, demand-oriented view of prices as determined solely by buyers' willingness to pay. Debates raged between supply-side and demand-side theories until, with support from his compatriots F. Y. Edgeworth(1845–1926) and W. S. Jevons (1835–1882),* Marshall ridiculed the debate as empty, comparable to an argument about whether the top blade or the bottom blade of a pair of scissors cuts cloth. To Marshall, prices were about equally dependent on supply and demand—a solution that still satisfies most mainstream economists.

Perhaps Marshall's greatest contribution to economic methodology was the way he wove time into his analysis, bequeathing to subsequent generations of economists not only a powerful tool, but also rules for its effective use.

Marshall handled continuous change by invoking conditional clauses that he grouped under the term *ceteris paribus*. *Ceteris paribus* allows analysts to study the issue at hand narrowly and precisely by temporarily ignoring other disturbances. This step-by-step approach facilitates treatment of broader issues that contain the narrow one; each bit of new knowledge allows more and more restrictions to be relaxed.

This method, known as *partial equilibrium analysis*, is illustrated in Marshall's treatment of demand, in which the number of consumers, their tastes, expectations, and money incomes, and the prices of other goods are all assumed constant when studying how equilibrium price and quantity are determined. As things change over time, however, each restrictive assumption may be relaxed in turn so that the analysis proceeds to a new equilibrium. He also applied this approach with fruitful results to the theories of value and production. In so doing, Alfred Marshall developed an analytical technique used to this day.

---

*Marshall has been credited with welding supply and demand together in market analysis, but most specialists in the history of economic thought identify Jevons as "the minister who joined supply and demand in marriage, nevermore to be considered entirely independently."

flect subjectively determined marginal benefits of goods.

Figure 2 shows how lower market prices for paperbacks could induce Arlene to buy more.[3] She buys 30 novels annually when each is $1, only 10 at $5, and none if prices rise to $7 (she might watch more TV or renew her library card instead). Suppose she currently buys 14 books at an average of $4.20 apiece. Her demand price (the maximum she would pay) for a 15th book is $4 (point *a*).

Notice that Arlene's demand curve for books does not move when prices change. Instead, a price change causes a move along her demand curve for books, not a shift of the entire curve. Figure 2 also includes Arlene's *demand schedule*—

a table that summarizes important points (price-quantity combinations) on a demand curve.

Market Demand Curves

Business firms and government policymakers are far more interested in market demands than in individual demands. Firms, for example, are much more concerned about how much they will sell at various prices than about which individuals buy which good.

> *A **market demand curve** is the horizontal summation of the individual demand curves of all potential buyers of a good.*

Figure 3 depicts the demand curves of Arlene and Bert, the market demand curve if they are the only paperback buyers, and the corresponding demand schedules. *Horizontal summation* involves summing the quantities per period that individuals buy at each price. At $5 each, Arlene buys 10 paperbacks annually while

---

[3]For math purists: You may be disturbed because, by convention, economists place price (presumably the independent variable) on the vertical axis, with quantity (presumably, the dependent variable) on the horizontal axis. However, demand functions can be expressed as $Qd = f(P)$ and supply functions can be expressed as $Qs = g(P)$, where, respectively, f and g are implicit functions for purposes of calculus—prices and quantities are interdependent, so neither is purely a dependent variable, nor is either a purely independent variable.

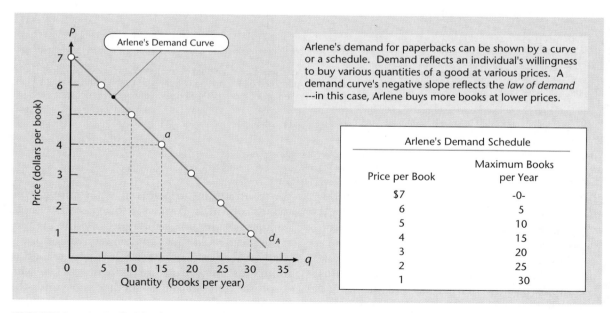

Arlene's demand for paperbacks can be shown by a curve or a schedule. Demand reflects an individual's willingness to buy various quantities of a good at various prices. A demand curve's negative slope reflects the *law of demand* ---in this case, Arlene buys more books at lower prices.

Arlene's Demand Schedule

Price per Book	Maximum Books per Year
$7	-0-
6	5
5	10
4	15
3	20
2	25
1	30

FIGURE 2   An Individual's Demand Curve for Paperback Books

FIGURE 3   Individual and Market Demands for Paperbacks

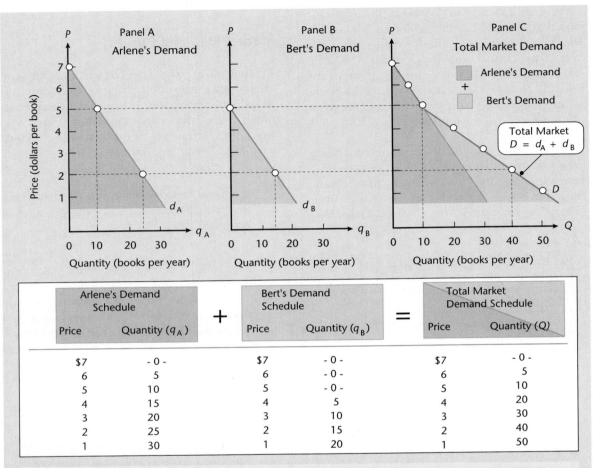

Arlene's Demand Schedule			Bert's Demand Schedule			Total Market Demand Schedule	
Price	Quantity (q_A)	+	Price	Quantity (q_B)	=	Price	Quantity (Q)
$7	- 0 -		$7	- 0 -		$7	- 0 -
6	5		6	- 0 -		6	5
5	10		5	- 0 -		5	10
4	15		4	5		4	20
3	20		3	10		3	30
2	25		2	15		2	40
1	30		1	20		1	50

A market demand curve is derived by horizontally summing a series of individual demand curves: For each price, we add the quantities that each individual will purchase. At a price of $2, Arlene is willing to buy 25 books, while Bert demands 15 books. Thus, the market quantity demanded at a $2 price is 40 books. Follow this process at each price to obtain market demand.

Bert buys none. Thus, at $5, the quantity demanded in this market is 10 books (10 + 0). At $2, Arlene buys 25 books and Bert buys 15, so the quantity demanded is 40 (25 + 15), and so on.

Market behavior is a somewhat erratic process of discovery. Measuring actual demands is complex because markets are volatile and all else is seldom equal. (Whether a shopper has eaten recently, or whether a child is along may be as important as prices in determining what winds up in a family's grocery cart.) Rapid changes in the many influences on buying and selling can yield foggy information about prices and quantities. Economists who estimate market demands must unravel fragmentary data with sophisticated statistical methods beyond the scope of this book. Nevertheless, most influences on buying patterns are conceptually simple.

Other Influences on Demand

A good's relative price is joined by six other broad determinants of the amounts consumers purchase: (a) tastes and preferences; (b) income and its distribution; (c) prices of related goods; (d) numbers and ages of buyers; (e) expectations about future prices, incomes, and availability; and (f) government taxes, subsidies, and regulations.

- **Tastes and Preferences**   Preferences mirror our perceptions of the desirability of goods (e.g., quality, types, and styles) and our individual idiosyncrasies (experiential, biological, or neural differences, reactions to peer pressure or government regulations, etc.). Most advertising is intended to alter preferences among goods subject to people's whims, including cars, clothes, and music. When male beer drinkers worried about calories but viewed light beers as tasteless and unmacho, one brewer's ads featured retired jocks debating whether the beer is "less filling" or "tastes great." Demand increased, and the suds flowed and flowed.

    Tastes and preferences cannot be measured precisely, but you should be able to evaluate how certain trends affect specific demands. For example, how have animal-rights campaigns affected demands for fur coats? And what would happen to the total demand for nose rings if they became signals of status because corporate executives began wearing them?

- **Income and Its Distribution**   Demands for higher quality goods tend to rise if income grows. Goods for which demand is positively related to income are *normal goods*. Most products and services are normal goods, which include luxuries that are especially responsive to changes in income—examples include resort vacations, jewelry, yachts, and live entertainment. On the other hand, when a poor family's income rises, its demands fall for such *inferior goods* as lye soap and pinto beans. When students graduate and get real jobs, their higher incomes typically cause them to buy fewer inferior goods,

such as used tires, macaroni and cheese, or instant noodle soup.

With all else being equal, it follows that income redistribution alters the structure of demands: transferring income from the rich to the poor causes declines in demands for both inferior goods and luxuries, while rising inequality stimulates demands for both. Be aware, however, that one family's inferior good can be another's luxury good. For example, consider a middle-class family trading in a beat-up old car they view as an inferior heap. A poor family that scrimped to save a down payment might view that same car as an incredible luxury.

- **Prices of Related Goods**   A good's own price is important, but prices of related products also influence demand. Most goods are at least weak *substitutes* for one another.

    > *Substitutes* are the goods increasingly purchased in place of the item in question when its price rises, or vice versa.

    For example, if a new tax boosted golf ball prices to $5 each, you would golf less frequently, but your consumption of such substitute goods as tennis balls and racquets might rise. This is especially true for duffers who drop at least one golf ball in every water hazard. When coffee prices soar, tea sales climb. Like golf and tennis, coffee and tea are close substitutes. Other examples include hot dogs, hamburgers, or lasagna; phone calls, letters, faxes, and overnight mail services; or hot tubs, Jacuzzis, and saunas.

    Coffee, cream, and sugar are examples of goods typically consumed together.

    > *Complementary goods* generate more consumer satisfaction if consumed together. Increases in the price of a good tend to reduce demands for its complements, and vice versa.

Other sets of *complements* are tuition and textbooks; videotapes and VCRs; gas, tires, and cars; or microwaves and TV dinners.

• **Numbers and Ages of Buyers** Population growth or the opening of foreign markets expands the numbers of potential buyers and, therefore, the market demands for most goods. The public's age structure is also a factor. Demands for baby products slumped when U.S. birth rates fell in the 1960s, but incomes for producers of diapers and formula—and then orthodontists—recovered somewhat when baby boomers began their families. Lengthened average life spans have swollen demands for golf courses, Ben-Gay, retirement communities, and medical services.

• **Expectations About Prices, Incomes, or Availability** Consumers who expect shortages or price hikes in the near future may rush to buy storable products now, thus boosting current demands. The onset of the Korean War in 1950 triggered memories of the shortages, spiraling prices, and tight rationing rampant during World War II; many Americans raced to stockpile sugar, flour, appliances, tires, and cars. Similarly, most citizens of formerly communist countries have been programmed to react with queues and hoarding whenever potential shortages are rumored. (Shortages were the rule rather than the exception until quite recently.) This pattern should diminish as these nations progress down the path towards a market system.

Expectations of higher income often tempt people to splurge. You might buy a car on credit before receiving your first paycheck from a new job; many people fall deeply in debt by spending income faster than they make it. On the other hand, people tend to postpone purchases when they expect prices to fall or if they fear losing their jobs. Expectations of recessions typically reduce consumption, causing overall demand to decline throughout an economy.

Expectations about government actions also affect buying patterns. Before Nutra-Sweet finally made the issue moot, the Food and Drug Administration repeatedly proposed bans on saccharin as a possible carcinogen. Each time the proposal resurfaced, shoppers stripped grocers' shelves. These consumers worried more about fat attacks than about greater risks from cancer.

• **Taxes, Subsidies, and Regulations** We have focused on how private behavior shifts demands, but regulations and taxes or subsidies also influence demands. From a buyer's perspective, demand is a relationship between the quantity bought and the price paid. Sellers, however, view demand as the relationship between the quantity sold and the price received. These approaches normally yield the same results, but taxes or subsidies can drive a wedge between the demand price that buyers are willing to pay and the price the seller receives. Figure 4 illustrates this.

Consider a new tax of $1 per paperback. Buyers perceive no change in their willingness to purchase, so they view their demand for paperback books as being stable at D_0. They are still willing to buy 400 million books annually at a demand price of $5. However, publishers view demand as having declined to D_1 because the after-tax prices they receive drop $1 for each novel sold. They would receive only $4 per book if they priced books so that 400 million were bought.

Now suppose the government offered publishers a $1 subsidy per book sold to encourage national literacy. Buyers would view their demand curves as stable at D_0, but from the vantage points of publishers, demand would rise to D_2. They would receive $1 more per paperback at every output level. Regulation may either stifle demand, as it does for such illicit goods as narcotics, or bolster it, as the effect of compulsory education on demands for chalk and erasers demonstrates. (In Chapter 4, we delve into more ways that government actions affect buying patterns.)

To summarize, demand grows when (a) preferences change so that people are more inclined to buy a good; (b) consumer incomes rise in the case of a normal good; (c) the price of a substitute good rises or the price of a complement falls; (d) the population of consumers expands; (e) consumers expect higher prices or incomes or anticipate shortages of the good; or when (f) favorable regulation is adopted, taxes are cut, or government subsidizes the good. Demands would decline if these changes were reversed.

FIGURE 4 How Taxes and Subsidies Affect Market Demands

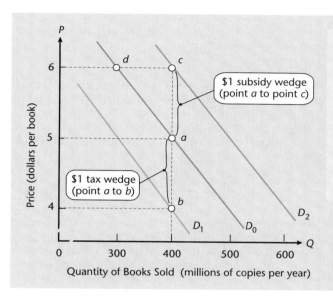

$1 subsidy wedge
(point a to point c)

$1 tax wedge
(point a to b)

From sellers' points of view, a $1 tax would shrink demand from original D_0 to D_1, while a $1 subsidy would boost demand to D_2. If sellers were originally selling 400 million books at a $5 price (point a) and, after a $1 tax was imposed, continued to price books at a $5 retail price, they would continue to sell 400 million books, but the $1 tax wedge would reduce the after-tax price sellers received to only $4 (point b). A subsidy of $1, however, would generate a $6 net price to sellers if they continued to sell only 400 million books annually (point c). From buyers' perspectives, neither taxes nor subsidies would affect their demand, which would remain at D_0.

Changes in Demand

A demand curve shows the negative relationship between the price and the quantity of a good demanded during a given interval, holding all other influences constant. But what happens if influences on the demand for a good other than its own price change?

> *If a determinant of demand other than a good's own price changes, there is a* **change in demand** *and a shift in the demand curve.*

Most marketing strategies are aimed at tastes and preferences. Knockoffs of the latest fashions and the numerous clones of hit TV shows are evidence that firms can react quickly to fads. Kids' lunch boxes, underwear, and toys regularly mirror the latest crazes, from "Barney" to *Jurassic Park* dinosaurs. Media firms often mail novels to reviewers gratis, hoping to promote a bestseller or to swell both book receipts and the box office by linking the advertising of their books and films. For example, in Panel B of Figure 5, successful promotion could

shift the demand curve to the right from D_0 to D_1 so that more books were demanded at every price.

If paperbacks are normal goods, demand will grow if income rises, and vice versa. A drop in income normally shrinks demand; the demand curve in Panel A of Figure 5 shifts toward the origin from D_0 to D_2. In Panel B, pay raises cause consumers (beginning on D_0) to buy more books at every price, moving demand to D_1. Naturally, such effects would be reversed if paperbacks were inferior goods.

Now consider changes in the availability or prices of related goods. Improved cable service, for example, might transform more readers into couch potatoes, shrinking the demand for books (again in Panel A, from D_0 to D_2). Or if ticket prices for movies fell, substitution could squelch demands for novels. Take a moment to consider how demand would shift if illiteracy were eliminated or if consumers' expectations changed.

Thus, a change in demand means a shift in the demand curve. Shifts to the left show falling demand, while rightward shifts show growth of demand. These shifts result from changes in tastes, incomes, related prices, numbers of con-

FIGURE 5 Changes in Demand vs. Changes in Quantity Demanded

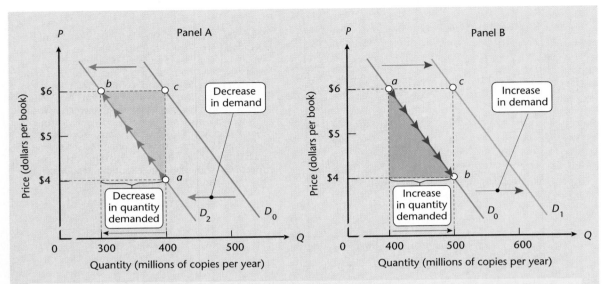

Quantity demanded responds to a price change, but the demand curve itself does not shift. Thus, a price hike from $4 to $6 per book in Panel A does not change demand---instead, it moves consumers from point a to point b, reducing the *quantity demanded* by 100 million books, while a symmetric price cut in Panel B increases the *quantity demanded* by 100 million books. By way of contrast, the shift of the demand curve from D_0 to D_2 in Panel A (point c to point b) reflects a *decrease in demand*, and a shift from D_0 to D_1 in Panel B (point a to point c) reflects an *increase in demand*. These shifts result from changes in influences other than the product price itself. For example, demand expands for most goods when income grows; demand declines if consumers begin viewing a good with distaste.

sumers, expectations, or government policies. Demand rises when consumers become willing to purchase more of a good at every price or to pay a higher demand price for a given quantity of the good, and vice versa.

Changes in Quantity Demanded vs. Changes in Demand

You will spare yourself a lot of grief by learning to carefully differentiate *changes in demand* from *changes in quantity demanded*. Changes in the quantity of a good demanded are movements along a demand curve and are caused by only one thing: a change in its price. Changes in demand, on the other hand, involve shifts of de-

mand curves and occur whenever other determinants of demand change.

A rightward shift from D_0 to D_1 in Panel B of Figure 5 reflects an increase *in demand*. In contrast, *quantity demanded* increases from the original 400 million to 500 million copies sold annually along demand curve D_0 when book prices drop from $6 to $4. (If you were a publisher, would you prefer your novels to face growth in demand—say, point a to point c in Panel B—or similar growth in the amount of output sold, but resulting from an increase in quantity demanded—point a to point b? Why?) Why might paperback sales fall? One possibility is a decline in demand, illustrated by the leftward shift from D_0 to D_2 in Panel A. Another potential reason for falling sales is a price hike from $4 to $6 along demand curve D_0, which yields a decrease in quantity demanded—annual sales fall from the original 400 million to 300 million in either of these cases.

In summary, *changes in demand* reflect changes in influences on purchases other than a good's own price; *changes in the quantity demanded* follow changes in the price of the good. Thus, a price change for computer diskettes yields a change in the quantity demanded, but changes in the prices of computer software or in consumers' incomes will change the demand for diskettes. (How various influences shift demand curves is summarized in Figure 6.) The importance of this distinction will become clear after we show how demand and supply are linked in markets.

SUPPLY

Transactions require both buyers and sellers. Thus, demand is only one aspect of decisions about prices and the amounts of goods traded; supply is the other.

> **Supply** *refers to the quantity of a specific good that sellers will provide under alternative conditions during a given period.*

One critical condition is that producers must expect to gain (added profit) by selling their outputs, or they will refuse to incur production costs. This section outlines some influences on firms' decisions to produce and sell.

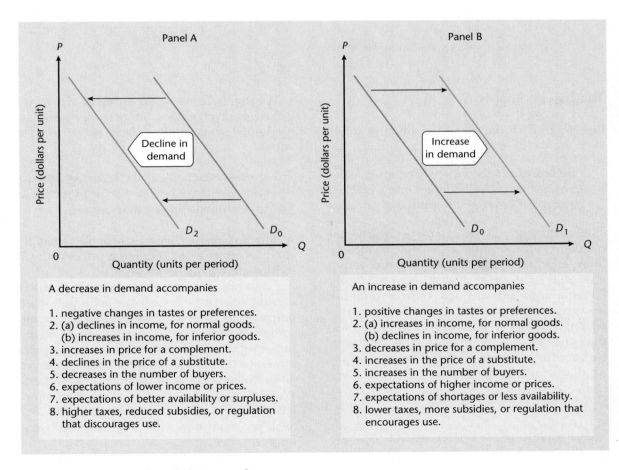

A decrease in demand accompanies

1. negative changes in tastes or preferences.
2. (a) declines in income, for normal goods.
   (b) increases in income, for inferior goods.
3. increases in price for a complement.
4. declines in the price of a substitute.
5. decreases in the number of buyers.
6. expectations of lower income or prices.
7. expectations of better availability or surpluses.
8. higher taxes, reduced subsidies, or regulation that discourages use.

An increase in demand accompanies

1. positive changes in tastes or preferences.
2. (a) increases in income, for normal goods.
   (b) declines in income, for inferior goods.
3. decreases in price for a complement.
4. increases in the price of a substitute.
5. increases in the number of buyers.
6. expectations of higher income or prices.
7. expectations of shortages or less availability.
8. lower taxes, more subsidies, or regulation that encourages use.

FIGURE 6   Factors that Shift Demand

FIGURE 7   Supply Curve of Paperback Books for Dell Publishing Co.

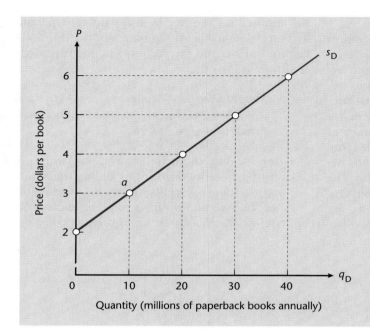

The supply curve and schedule reflect the maximum amounts of a good firms are willing to produce and sell during a given period at various prices. This supply curve reflects the *law of supply*--- at higher prices, more of a good will be offered to the market.

Supply Schedule
Dell Publishing Co.

Price	Quantity (millions)
$ 6	40
5	30
4	20
3	10
2	- 0 -

The Law of Supply

Producers' decisions about the amounts to sell yield the law of supply.

>The **law of supply**: *All else being equal, higher prices induce greater production and offers to sell more output during a given period, and vice versa.*

The law of supply occurs, in part, because higher prices provide incentives to expand production. More importantly, attempts to expand output ultimately succumb to diminishing returns; increasing costs occur when returns diminish because, as larger numbers of costly doses of resources are applied, output may grow, but less than proportionally.[4] When this happens, higher prices are needed to induce suppliers to produce and sell their goods.

_____

[4]The law of supply applies to all produced goods. Substitution effects create similar powerful tendencies in most resource markets, but powerful income effects may cause, for example, supply curves for some types of labor to bend backwards.

• **The Supply Curve**   Just as the law of demand yields negatively sloped demand curves, the law of supply generates positively sloped supply curves.

>A **supply curve** *shows the maximum amounts of a good that firms are willing to furnish at various prices during a given period.*

A different perspective views the same supply curve as showing the minimum prices that will induce specific quantities supplied.

The positive slopes of supply curves reflect eventual increases in costs per extra unit when output grows, because firms (*a*) ultimately encounter diminishing returns, (*b*) may be forced to pay current workers overtime wages for extra hours, or (*c*) successfully attract more labor or other resources only by paying more for them. Working closer to capacity also causes more scheduling errors and equipment breakdowns. Such problems raise costs when firms increase output.

A typical supply curve and schedule are shown in Figure 7. Dell will produce and sell 40 million paperbacks annually at $6, but only 10 million books if the price falls to $3.

> *A **supply price** is the minimum price that will induce a seller to increase production beyond its current level.*

For example, if Dell were selling 9 million books annually at a price of $2.95, the market price would have to grow to Dell's supply price of $3 (point *a*) before annual production would be expanded to 10 million books.

Market demand curves horizontally sum individual demands. Similarly, *market supply curves* entail horizontally summing all firms' supply

curves. Figure 8 assumes only two firms in the book market, Dell and Bantam. At $3, Dell will produce and sell 10 million books, and Bantam, 15 million, making the annual quantity supplied 25 million books, and so on. The law of supply asserts that quantities supplied per period are positively related to prices; as a good's price rises, the quantity supplied grows.

Other Influences on Supply

Just as several types of determinants influence demands, the market supply of a good depends on several broad influences other than its own

Dell's Supply Schedule		Bantam's Supply Schedule		Market Supply Schedule (Dell + Bantam)	
Price	Quantity (q_D) (millions)	Price	Quantity (q_B) (millions)	Price	Quantity (Q) (millions)
$ 6	40	$ 6	60	$ 6	100
5	30	5	45	5	75
4	20	4	30	4	50
3	10	3	15	3	25
2	- 0 -	2	- 0 -	2	-0-

The supplies of all producing firms are summed *horizontally* to obtain market supply. For example, at $6 per paperback, Dell will furnish 40 million and Bantam, 60 million books. Thus, the quantity supplied at $6 per paperback is 100 million books. Repeating the same procedure for all possible prices yields the market supply curve: $s_D + s_B = S$.

FIGURE 8   Individual Firm and Market Supply Curves for Paperbacks

price. A supply curve reflects the positive relationship between price and quantity supplied per period, holding constant (a) technology; (b) resource costs; (c) prices of other producible goods; (d) expectations; (e) the number of sellers in the market; and (f) taxes, subsidies, and government regulations. The supply curve shifts when there are changes in any of these influences, which operate primarily by altering the opportunity costs of producing and selling.

Changes in Supply

Figure 9 illustrates increases in supply by shifts of the supply curve outward and to the right, while movements upward and to the left reflect declines in supply. Along supply curve S_0, 500 million books are supplied at \$5 per novel. If supply grows to S_1, 700 million are supplied at \$5. If supply falls to S_2, only 300 million books will be offered at \$5 each. Thus, an increase in the supply of a good means that more is available at each price; the supply price required for each output level falls. On the other hand, decreases in supply raise supply prices (the minimum required per unit to induce extra production).

Caution: Supply curve movements may seem confusing; the shift from S_0 to S_1 is vertically downward even though supply is rising. Always think of rightward horizontal movements away from the price axis as increases (more is available at each price), and leftward shifts toward the price axis as decreases (less is available at each price). This rule also works for shifts of demand curves because quantity is measured along the horizontal axis.

Parallels between our development of supply and earlier discussions of demand may correctly have led you to expect that shifts in supply result from changes in one or more influences on supply. Supply shifts when these influences affect production costs.

• **Production Technology** Technology encompasses the environment within which resources are transformed into outputs. It includes such influences on production costs as the state of knowledge, the qualities of resources, the legal environment, and such natural phenomena as physical laws (e.g., gravity) and weather. Costs fall and supply grows when technology advances.

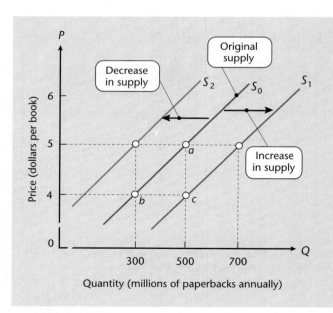

Movements along supply curves reflect how sellers respond to a change in price by adjusting the quantities they supply. For example, along supply curve S_0, a price cut from \$5 to \$4 moves suppliers from point *a* to point *b*, shrinking the quantity supplied from 500 million to 300 million. You need to distinguish such seller responses to a price change (i.e., changes in quantity supplied = moves along a single supply curve) from shifts in supply that follow changes in determinants of supply other than the price of the good itself. Except for more or fewer sellers, these determinants operate by changing opportunity costs. For example, a drop in price for paper could boost supply from S_0 to S_1. Or if publishing rights for translations of foreign novels rose in cost, supply might fall from S_0 to S_2.

FIGURE 9   Changes in the Supply of Paperback Books

Consider innovations in markets for calculators and computers. Massive desktop calculators cost $400 to $2,000 in the 1960s. New technology enabled cheap microchip processors to displace mechanical calculators from the market. Supplies soared and prices fell, so that $4 hand-held calculators are now common, and computer capacity that once would have filled a domed stadium now fits in a briefcase. If transportation technology had advanced as rapidly, you could now travel to Mars and back on a teacup of gasoline.

There are occasions, however, when technology regresses and drives up costs. For example, a plague of locusts might shrivel food output, or a nuclear war could blast us back to the Stone Age. Although technology is hard to quantify, you should be prepared to predict whether a given technological change will boost or inhibit supply.

• **Resource Costs** Supply declines when resource costs rise. Higher wages, rents, interest rates, or prices for raw materials raise costs, squeeze profits, and shrink supplies. For example, higher coal prices raise the cost of steel and reduce incentives to produce. Conversely, falling resource prices stimulate supply. Thus, lower fertilizer prices expand farm outputs.

• **Prices of Related Producible Goods** Most firms can produce a variety of goods, so changes in the prices of other potential outputs can shift the supply of the current good. Price hikes increase the quantity of a good supplied by using resources that would have been devoted to other types of production. Shirtmakers, for example, might switch to sewing parachutes if skydiving became more popular and profits from sewing parachutes grew. The supply of shirts would fall because their opportunity costs of production (the value of the parachutes sacrificed by producing shirts) would rise. Similarly, if corn prices rose, farmers might plant more corn, reducing the soybean supply. These sets of goods are examples of *substitutes in production*.

On the other hand, when goods are byproducts (beef and leather, for example), an increase in the price of one *joint product* yields an increase in the supply of the other; production is complementary among such goods. For example, hikes in the price of honey will induce a greater quantity of honey supplied, and the supply of beeswax will grow automatically even if its price falls.

• **Producers' Expectations** Firms that expect higher output prices in the near future usually increase production quickly. They may also expand their productive capacity by, for example, acquiring new buildings or investing in new equipment and machinery.

Some goods are easily stored, including such durable goods as art and most capital goods. (*Durable goods* provide benefits across time—a house can provide shelter across decades of use, a stereo can be played for years. In contrast, nondurables (*perishable goods*) such as strawberries or newspapers can become worthless unless consumed soon after production.) Producers of storable products who expect prices to rise will try to temporarily stockpile their output, intending to sell their expanded inventories after prices rise. Short-term withholding of products from the market triggers higher prices that, in the longer term, generate larger supplies. Focus 2 illustrates, however, how such short-term reductions of supply often dismay consumers.

The longer term effect of expectations of rising prices is that supplies of durable goods grow when (*a*) swollen inventories are sold and (*b*) new investments become productive. Such adjustments tend to reduce supply when prices are expected to rise, but if producers' expectations are correct, supply will be larger in the future to partially buffer upward pressures on prices. Conversely, firms may try to liquidate inventories if they expect prices to fall; the short-run supply grows and consumers enjoy lower prices temporarily, but smaller long-run supplies eventually drive up prices.

Adjustments of this type occur regularly when agricultural firms try to time their sales to obtain the highest prices. For example, in 1992, many wheat farmers, anticipating a presidential

Expectations and Opportunity Costs

Many people think that only "objective" costs such as the quantity of physical resources used in production truly affect production costs, but expectations and other subjective or psychological factors also frequently alter costs. For example, fear of an "energy crisis" grows whenever major oil-producing regions become embroiled in conflicts. Iraq's invasion of Kuwait quickly pushed up oil prices; gasoline prices rose an average of 30 cents per gallon within days.

Many American drivers viewed this as evidence of unethical profiteering by U.S. oil companies. After all, how can the cost of gaso-line already stocked in a service station's storage tank be affected by events thousands of miles away? But firms dealing with storable goods have alternatives to sell now or later. Gasoline sold today is not available for sale at a later date at a potentially higher price. Thus, expected price hikes immediately raise the opportunity costs of goods sold today.

The Iraqi invasion of Kuwait created expectations of price hikes that immediately raised the opportunity cost of oil, and thus reduced the supply of gasoline. Many U.S. oil companies did gain from this conflict—their inventories increased in value immediately, just as homeowners gain when housing prices climb. But did consumers necessarily lose because of "profiteering"?

When dealers raised prices, the amount of gasoline drivers demanded fell. This conserved fuel and consequently increased the supply of gasoline available in those later periods when higher gasoline prices were expected. (Incorrectly, as it turned out.) This enforced form of conservation, though unpleasant from the short-run vantage point of drivers, undoubtedly contributed to cuts in gas prices in early 1991.

---

change that would be more supportive of agriculture, planted more but reduced shipments to the market temporarily. This raised prices for bread and pasta slightly, but prices fell in 1993 when this extra wheat was finally marketed.

Many goods, however, are not easily inventoried. Adjustments to expected price hikes are very different if storage is impossible. For example, a newspaper publisher who expected a booming market to soon justify higher prices could not store news, but would probably increase the supply of newspapers quickly, partially to justify expanding capacity and partially to hook more customers into reading the firm's paper each day.

Other types of expectations also sway production and sales. For example, a steel company may cut current supplies and try to expand output and inventories if it expects a strike. This allows the firm to serve some customers during the strike. Generalizing about how changing expectations affect supply is difficult, however, because these effects vary with the types of expectations, products, and technologies. Us-ually, though, extraordinary profits in any market will quickly attract a swarm of new sellers, boosting supply.

• **Number of Sellers**   More producers generate more output. Thus, as the number of sellers in a particular market increases, the supply also increases (shifts to the right), and vice versa.

• **Taxes, Subsidies, and Government Regulation** Government policies affect supply as powerfully as they influence demand. From the sellers' vantage point, supply is the relationship between the price received and the units produced and sold. Buyers perceive supply as the relationship between the quantities available and the prices paid. Again, taxes or subsidies cause these prices to differ. In Figure 9, a subsidy to buyers of $1 per book yields no change in the original supply curve (S_0) from the perspective of sellers. But buyers would perceive an increase in supply from S_0 to S_1, which is the same as a price cut of

$1 for every quantity purchased. For example, 500 million paperbacks could now be purchased for a $4 retail price (point *c*).

Taxes and subsidies provide simple examples of how government policies create differences between sellers' supply curves and those that buyers confront. Regulations may either raise or lower supplies, depending on how they affect production costs. For example, policies to protect the environment drive up costs and reduce supply when production processes generate pollution (e.g., tanning leather, which fouls water) while reducing the costs and increasing the supplies of certain other goods (e.g., fresh fish).

In sum, supply decisions are molded by several influences other than a product's price. Specifically, the supply of a good grows (the curve shifts rightward) if (*a*) costs decline because resource prices fall or technology improves, (*b*) substitute goods that firms can produce decline in price, (*c*) the price of a joint product rises, or (*d*) the number of suppliers increases. Expectations of higher prices normally reduce supplies in the short term and enlarge supplies in a longer term if goods can be inventoried, but results are uncertain for less durable goods. Subsidies tend to expand supply from buyers' perspectives, but taxes tend to shrink supply. Regulation can either decrease or increase supply, depending on whether the specific regulation raises or lowers production costs. The only determinant of supply that does not operate primarily by changing the opportunity costs of production is the number of sellers.

Changes in Quantity Supplied vs. Changes in Supply

A *change in supply* occurs only when the supply curve shifts. A *change in the quantity supplied* (movement along the curve) is caused only by a change in the price of the good in question. Consider an adjustment in quantity supplied caused by a change in the market price. The supply curve stays constant because it is defined by the entire relationship between price and quantity. A change in supply (caused by a change in a determinant other than a good's own price) shifts the supply curve

because this price–quantity relationship is altered. (You will appreciate why this distinction is not trivial after we combine supply and demand curves in a market.) Figure 10 summarizes categories of influences that shift supply curves.

MARKET EQUILIBRIUM

It's easy to train economists. Just teach a parrot to say "Supply and Demand."

Thomas Carlyle

Buyers and sellers use prices to signal their respective wants and then exchange money for goods or resources, or vice versa. You accept or reject thousands of offers during every trip to a shopping center or perusal of a newspaper. Prices efficiently transmit incredible amounts of information that is relevant for decisions to buy or sell and make a lot of other information (or misinformation) irrelevant. For example, during the nineteenth century, Ghanians exported cocoa to England, believing that the British used it for fuel. Their mistake was not a problem, however, because their decision to produce depended on the price of cocoa, not its final use.

Supply and demand jointly determine prices and quantities so that markets achieve *equilibrium*.

> In an **equilibrium**, any pressures for change must be offset by opposing forces.

All sciences, including economics, use this powerful concept extensively. Astronomers, for example, describe the moon as following a fairly stable equilibrium path as it circles our earth. But what creates an equilibrium in a market?

Suppose every potential buyer and seller of a good submitted demand and supply schedules to an auctioneer, who then calculated the price at which the quantities demanded and supplied were equal. All buyers' demand prices (the maximum they are willing to pay) and all sellers' supply prices (the minimum they will accept per unit for a given amount) are equal. There is market equilibrium, so the market clears.

FIGURE 10 Factors that Shift Supplies

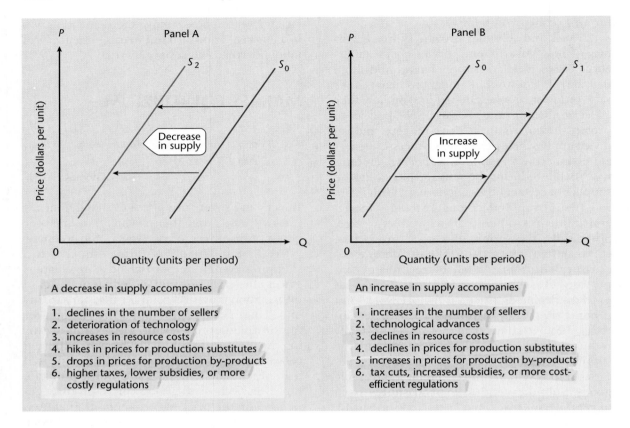

Panel A

A decrease in supply accompanies

1. declines in the number of sellers
2. deterioration of technology
3. increases in resource costs
4. hikes in prices for production substitutes
5. drops in prices for production by-products
6. higher taxes, lower subsidies, or more costly regulations

Panel B

An increase in supply accompanies

1. increases in the number of sellers
2. technological advances
3. declines in resource costs
4. declines in prices for production substitutes
5. increases in prices for production by-products
6. tax cuts, increased subsidies, or more cost-efficient regulations

---

Market equilibrium *occurs at the price–quantity combination where the quantities demanded and supplied are equal.*

The amounts buyers will purchase at the *equilibrium price* exactly equal the amounts producers are willing to sell. Let's examine the sense in which this is an equilibrium.

Figure 11 summarizes the market supplies and demands for paperbacks. (Note that there are more buyers and sellers than in our earlier examples.) After studying the supply and demand schedules, our auctioneer ascertains that at $5 per book the quantities demanded and supplied both equal 300 million books annually. Sellers will provide exactly as many novels as readers will buy at this price, so the market clears.

But what if the auctioneer set a price of $6 per book, or $4 per book? First, let us deal with the problem of a price set above equilibrium.

*A **surplus** is the excess of the quantity supplied over quantity demanded when the price is above equilibrium.*

At $6 per book, publishers would print 400 million books annually, but readers would only buy 200 million books. The surplus of 200 million books shown in Figure 11 would wind up as excess inventories in the hands of publishers.

Most firms would cut production as their inventories grew, and some might cut prices, hoping to unload surplus paperbacks on bargain hunters. (Publishers call this remainder-

FIGURE 11   Equilibrium in the Paperback Book Market

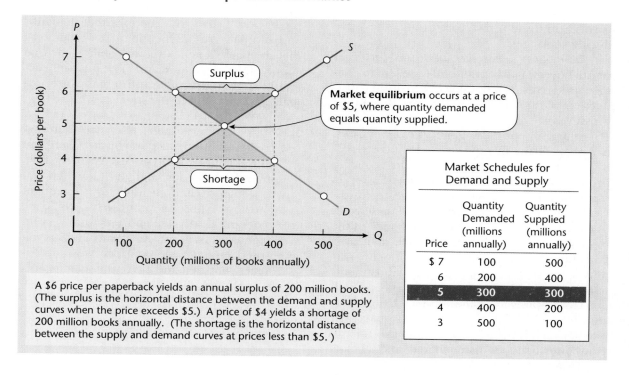

Market equilibrium occurs at a price of $5, where quantity demanded equals quantity supplied.

A $6 price per paperback yields an annual surplus of 200 million books. (The surplus is the horizontal distance between the demand and supply curves when the price exceeds $5.) A price of $4 yields a shortage of 200 million books annually. (The shortage is the horizontal distance between the supply and demand curves at prices less than $5.)

Market Schedules for Demand and Supply		
Price	Quantity Demanded (millions annually)	Quantity Supplied (millions annually)
$ 7	100	500
6	200	400
5	300	300
4	400	200
3	500	100

ing.) Other firms with swollen inventories would join in the price war. Prices would fall until all surplus inventories were depleted. Some firms might stop production as prices fell; others might permanently abandon the publishing industry.

How much the quantity supplied would decline is shown in the table accompanying Figure 11. When the price falls to $5 per book, consumers will buy 300 million books annually, while publishers will supply 300 million books; the quantity demanded equals the quantity supplied. The market-clearing price is $5 per book. At this market equilibrium, any pressures for price or quantity changes are exactly counterbalanced by opposite pressures.

A shortage is created when the price is below equilibrium.

*A **shortage** is the excess of quantity demanded over quantity supplied when the price is below equilibrium.*

At $4 per book, readers demand 400 million books, but firms only print 200 million; a shortage of 200 million books annually is depicted in Figure 11. Publishers will try to satisfy unhappy, bookless customers who clamor for the limited quantities available by raising the price until the market clears; then books will be readily available for the people most desperate to buy them. (Clearing occurs because quantity supplied rises as price rises while quantity demanded falls; they become equal at the equilibrium price.)

Equilibration is not instantaneous. Firms experiment with output prices in a process resembling an auction. Inventories vanishing from store shelves are signals that prices may be too low. Retailers will order more goods and, because the market will bear it, may also raise prices. If retail orders grow rapidly, prices also tend to rise at the wholesale level, quickly eliminating most shortages. People refer to tight markets, or sellers' markets, when shortages are widespread. Suppliers easily sell all they produce, so quality may decline somewhat while sellers raise prices. Many sellers also exercise favoritism in deciding which customers to serve during shortages.

When prices exceed equilibrium, surpluses create buyers' markets and force sellers to consider price cuts. This is especially painful if production costs are resistant to downward pressures even though sales drop. (Most workers stubbornly oppose wage cuts.) In many cases, firms can shrink inventories and cut costs only by laying workers off and drastically reducing production. The price system ultimately forces prices down if there are continuing surpluses.

In 1776, Adam Smith described these types of self-corrections as the "invisible hand" of the marketplace. Price hikes eliminate shortages fairly rapidly, and price cuts eventually cure surpluses, but such automatic market adjustments may seem like slow torture to buyers and sellers. How rapidly markets adjust to changed circumstances depends on (a) the quality of information and how widely and quickly the relevant information is disseminated, and (b) market structure—the vigor or lack of competition.

Evidence that adjustment processes may be long and traumatic includes huge losses by major firms and sluggish economies in many industrial states during the recession of 1990–1991. Contrary evidence includes rapid changes in the prices of stocks in response to changes in profits reported by major corporations. Different views about the speed of typical market mechanisms in the economy as a whole are central to debates between modern advocates of various schools of macroeconomic thought. Most economists agree, however, that long-term shortages or surpluses are, almost without exception, consequences of governmental price controls. We discuss price controls and other applications of supply and demand in Chapter 4.

Supplies and Demands Are Independent

Although specific demands and supplies jointly determine prices and quantities, it is important to realize that they are normally independent of each other, at least in the short run. Many people have difficulty with the idea that demands and supplies are independent. It would seem that demand depends on availability—or that supply depends on demand. The following examples show that supplies and demands are normally independent in the short run.

1. Suppose nonreusable "teleporter buttons" could instantly transport you anywhere you chose. Your demand price to go on the first, most valuable tour might be quite high, but it would decline steadily for subsequent journeys. Short shopping trips would be economical only if teleporters were very inexpensive. By asking how many buttons you would buy at various prices, we can construct your demand curve for such devices even though there is no supply.

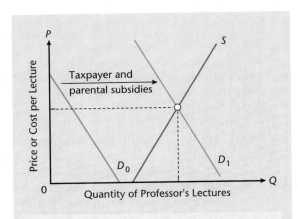

Without subsidies from taxpayers and parents, no positive price would be paid for this loquacious professor's lectures because unsubsidized student demand is only D_0. Tuition subsidies and alumni contributions boost demand to D_1, so the prof is not forced to lecture for free---and, at times, to an empty room (S and D_0 do not intersect at any positive price and quantity).

FIGURE 12   The Demand and Supply of a Professor's Lectures

2. Would you have made more mud pies when you were a kid if your parents had paid you a penny for each one? At two cents each, might you have hired playmates to help you? If mud pies sold for $1 each today, might you be a mud pie entrepreneur? Our point is that supply curves can be constructed for mud pies even if there is no demand for them.

3. You might be willing to pay a little to hear some professors' lectures even if you did not receive college credit for gathering the pearls of wisdom they offer. Some professors, however, like to talk even more than you like to listen. A set of such demand and supply curves is illustrated in Figure 12. It is fortunate for both you and your professors that your demands for their lectures are supplemented by contributions from taxpayers, alumni, and possibly your parents—because only later and upon mature reflection will you realize how valuable those lectures really were.

We hope these examples convince you that specific supplies and demands are largely independent of each other and that they are relevant for markets only when they intersect at positive prices. Markets establish whether the interests of buyers from the demand side are compatible with the interests of sellers from the supply side and then coordinate decisions where mutually beneficial exchange is possible. Keep this in mind as you study the applications of supply and demand in the next chapter.

CHAPTER REVIEW: KEY POINTS

1. Rational decision-making is governed by evaluations of the relative benefits and costs of *incremental* or *marginal changes*.

2. The *law of demand*. People buy less of a good per period at high prices than at low prices, and vice versa. **Demand curves** slope downward and to the right and show the quantities demanded at various prices for a good.

3. Consumers buy more of a good per period only at lower prices because of
   a. The **substitution effect**–the cheaper good will now be used more ways as it is substituted for higher-priced goods. This effect is related to **diminishing marginal utility**–consuming additional units ultimately does not yield as much satisfaction as consuming previous units, so demand prices fall as consumption rises.
   b. The **income effect**–a lower price for any good means that the purchasing power of a given monetary income rises.

4. Changes in relative market prices cause changes in *quantity demanded*. There is a **change in demand** (the demand curve shifts) when there are changes in influences other than a good's own price. These determinants include
   a. Tastes and preferences
   b. Income and its distribution
   c. Prices of related goods
   d. Numbers and ages of buyers
   e. Expectations about prices, income, and availability
   f. Taxes, subsidies, and regulations
   Taxes and subsidies shift demand curves from the perspectives of sellers, who are concerned with the price received when a good is sold, while buyers focus on the price paid. Taxes or subsidies make these two prices differ.

5. The **law of supply**. Higher prices cause sellers to make more of a good available per period. The **supply curve** shows the posi-

tive relationship between the price of a good and the quantity supplied. Supply curves generally slope upward and to the right because

   a. *Diminishing returns* cause opportunity costs to increase.

   b. To expand output, firms must bid resources away from competing producers or use other methods (such as overtime) that increase cost.

   c. Profit incentives are greater at higher prices.

6. In addition to the price paid to producers of a good, supply depends on

   a. the number of sellers

   b. technology

   c. resource costs

   d. prices of other producible goods

   e. producer's expectations

   f. specific taxes, subsidies, and government regulations

Changes in prices cause *changes in quantities supplied*, while changes in other influences on production or sales of goods cause shifts in supply curves that are termed *changes in supply*.

7. When markets operate without government intervention, prices tend to move toward **market equilibrium**, so quantity supplied equals quantity demanded. At this point, the demand price equals the supply price.

8. When the market price of a good is below the intersection of the supply and demand curves, there will be **shortages** and pressures for increases in price. If the market price is above the intersection of the supply and demand curves, there will be **surpluses** and pressures for reduction in price.

9. Supply and demand for a specific good are largely independent in the short run.

QUESTIONS FOR THOUGHT AND DISCUSSION

Use scratch paper to draw graphs illustrating the changes in supply or demand described in problems 1 through 5. If only one curve shifts, assume that the other is stationary.

1. What happens in the market for bananas if the Food and Drug Administration announces research results that eating 5 pounds of bananas monthly raises IQ scores by an average of 10 points? What would happen in the markets for apples or other fruit?

2. What happens to the demand for college professors in the short run if government raises its funding of graduate school education? What happens to the supply of college professors over a longer time span? What will happen to their wages during the adjustment periods?

3. What happens if new miracle seeds allow grain to be grown in shorter periods and colder climates? If the world population mushrooms because starvation ceases to be so widespread?

4. What happens in the U.S. clothing market if freer trade with the People's Republic of China expands our imports of textiles? If, after two years, import tariffs and quotas are imposed? (Tariffs are special taxes on goods that cross international borders, while quotas are quantitative limits.)

5. Around the middle of every January, the annual crop of mink furs is put on the auction block. How will the following affect the supplies and demands for mink pelts?

   a. Wearing fur in public increasingly elicits jeers and harassment from strangers.

   b. More fur-bearing animals are classified as endangered species.

   c. The price of mink food rises.

   d. A sharp, worldwide (1929-type) depression occurs.

   e. Higher income tax rates and a new wealth tax are imposed, and the added revenues are used to raise welfare payments.

*Every individual endeavors to employ his capital so that its produce may be of greatest value. He generally neither intends to promote the public interest, nor knows how much he is promoting it. He intends only his own security, only his own gain. And he is in this led [as if] by an **invisible hand** to promote an end which was not part of his intention. By pursuing his own interest he frequently promotes that of society more effectually than when he really intends to promote it.*

Adam Smith, *Wealth of Nations* (1776)

How do the prices and quantities set by market forces measure up against the standard of efficiency? Are supply and demand unfailingly preferable to alternative mechanisms? Answers to such questions depend on such specifics as the vigor of competition, the characteristics of the goods or resources being exchanged, the quality of information, and the extent of government regulation. We can be sure, however, that market forces shape allocative decisions even when nonmarket mechanisms appear dominant. For example, at times and in some places, laws forbid certain activities (e.g., smuggling, pornography, or gambling), but supplies and demands still underpin prices and quantities for them.

Our first task in this chapter is exploration of how prices and outputs move when supply or demand curves shift. Then we examine how transaction costs prevent equilibration from being instantaneous, and why these costs may cause apparently identical goods to have multiple prices. We also explore how firms, in their roles as intermediaries, help reduce transaction costs and stabilize markets. Our analysis then turns to how market forces may cause such policies as price controls, minimum wage laws, or the war on drugs to yield undesirable side effects incompatible with policymakers' stated goals.

Staunch defenders of laissez-faire capitalism sometimes assert that market outcomes are the best we can ever expect in this imperfect world. Nevertheless, even most die-hards accept the idea that some government is necessary. Our final task is to explore roles for government that are consistent with the operations of a market economy.

THE SEARCH FOR EQUILIBRIUM

Markets can be relatively erratic if consumers are fickle, forever changing their minds. Changes in income, the prices of related goods, expectations, or taxes also shift demand curves. Fluctuations in the business climate disrupt the supply side; resource prices vary, and technology advances, altering costs and, thus, supplies. Changes in the prices of related products, producer expectations, or taxes and regulations also shift supply curves.

Let's examine how changes in supplies and demands typically affect prices and quantities. (You should use a pencil and paper to duplicate the graphing in this section.) We will use the wheat market to explore how Adam Smith's "invisible hand" accommodates changes in the forces that affect markets.

Changes in Supply

Suppose the initial supply and demand for American wheat are S_0 and D_0 in Figure 1; Q_0 bushels of wheat sell at price P_0 at equilibrium point a. If fantastic weather yields a bumper crop, expanding supply from S_0 to S_1 in Panel A, the market now clears at point b. Price drops from P_0 to P_1, and the equilibrium quantity rises from Q_0 to Q_1. Conclusion? Expanding supplies push down prices and increase the quantities sold.

Now consider what happens if higher seed or fuel prices raise farmers' costs. Starting at the original equilibrium point a, now shown in Panel B, supply declines from S_0 to S_2. The equilibrium price rises from P_0 to P_2 at point c, while equilibrium quantity falls from Q_0 to Q_2. Thus, decreases in supply exert upward pressures on prices and decrease the quantities traded in the market.

We have held demand constant while shifting supply. Let's hold supply constant to see how shifts of demand curves affect equilibrium prices and quantities.

Panel A illustrates that increases in supply put downward pressures on prices. When supply increases from S_0 to S_1, prices fall to P_1 and quanities sold rise from Q_0 to Q_1 (equilibrium point a to point b). The opposite is true when supply falls, as depicted in Panel B. Supply declines from S_0 to S_2, causing prices to rise and quantity sold to fall (from point a to point c).

FIGURE 1 **Price and Quantity Effects of Changes in Supply**

BIOGRAPHY

Adam Smith: Father of Economics

Modern economics is by no means the product of a single mind, but no one has a better claim to the title of "Father of Economics" than Adam Smith (1723–1790), a Scottish philosopher who was renowned even before he published *An Inquiry into the Nature and Causes of the Wealth of Nations* in 1776. The international attention given to this work helped establish economics as a field of study apart from moral philosophy.

The eccentric Smith was a lifelong bachelor who described himself as "a beau in nothing but my books." He burned sixteen lengthy manuscripts shortly before he died, but his published remains are literary classics. Smith's *Wealth of Nations* spanned the spectrum of the then current knowledge of economics and was a starting point for virtually every major economic treatise until 1850.

This work provided (a) an impressive array of economic data gleaned from his wide reading of history and keen insights into human affairs, (b) an ambitious attempt to detail economic processes in an individualistic society, and (c) a radical critique of existing government policies. Smith advocated replacing government activities with laissez-faire policies in most economic matters.

Laissez-faire theory greatly differed from *mercantilism*, the conventional wisdom of Smith's era. Among other policies, mercantilism supported (a) imperialism in an era when European monarchs competed to colonize the rest of the world, (b) grants of monopoly by government to private firms, and (c) import restrictions, because it was erroneously thought that countries gained power by exporting goods in exchange for gold. Smith exposed the fallacy of protectionist trade policies by pointing out that the real wealth of a nation consists of productive capacity and the goods available for its people, not shiny metal.

Smith strongly dissented from the interventionist policies prevalent in the eighteenth century and called for a minimal economic role for government. A major point of his argument is that economic freedom is an efficient way to organize an economy—people never trade with each other unless both sides expect to gain. The model of society, and (c) a radical critique of existing government policies. Smith advocated replacing government activities with laissez-faire policies in most economic matters.

the marketplace was the centerpiece of Smith's inquiry. The decisions of buyers and sellers are coordinated in the marketplace by what he called the *invisible hand* of self-interest, which harmonizes the forces of competition with the public interest to generate real national wealth.

The freshest idea in Smith's argument is that the public interest is not served best by those who intend (or pretend) to promote it through government, but rather by those who actively seek their own gain in disregard of the public interest. The quest for higher incomes and profits redirects resources into more efficient configurations, facilitates technological advances, and accommodates changing patterns of demand. Self-interested merchants engaged in competition can gain advantages over rivals and increase their sales only by better serving consumers. Monopoly, on the other hand, harms the public interest by restricting outputs to force prices up. Smith thought that virtually all monopoly power would succumb to competitive forces if not for governmental protection of monopolies.

Changes in Demand

The original demand (D_0) and supply (S_0) from Figure 1 are replicated in Figure 2. If rising oil prices stimulated gasohol production from grain, the demand for wheat would grow to, say, D_1 in panel A. Equilibrium price would rise to P_1, and quantity to Q_1 (point b). Thus, expanding demand exerts upward pressure on both prices and quantities.

Now suppose that a horde of dietary faddists replace wheat bread with oat bran loaf, reducing demand for U.S. wheat from D_0 to D_2 in Panel B of Figure 2. Equilibrium price and quantity both fall (point c). Thus, declines in demand exert downward pressures on both prices and quantities.

FIGURE 2 Price and Quantity Effects of Changes in Demand

Increases in demand put upward pressure on price. In Panel A, when demand increases from D_0 to D_1, equilibrium price rises to P_1 and equilibrium quantity sold rises as well, to Q_1. As Panel B illustrates, declines in demand (from D_0 to D_2) cause prices to fall (from P_0 to P_2) and equilibrium quantity to decline (from Q_0 to Q_2).

In Chapter 3, we distinguished a change in demand from a change in the quantity demanded and changes in supply from changes in the quantity supplied: changes in demand (or supply) refer to shifts of the curve, while changes in the quantity demanded (or supplied) refer to movements along a curve. Compare the two equilibrium positions in Figure 1. Notice that changes in the quantities demanded result from changes in supply. It would be wrong to say that demand changed; it was supply that shifted. Similarly, Figure 2 shows that changes in quantities supplied are caused by changes in demand. Demand shifted; supply did not change. This illustrates how failing to keep your terminology straight in this area can lead to confusion and error.

Please review any of this analysis that seems a bit murky before reading on because now we are going to shift supply and demand curves simultaneously.

Shifts in Supply and Demand

Multiple and conflicting forces sometimes bombard markets. For example, technology may advance when consumer tastes are also changing. We need to fit each change into our supply and demand framework to assess net changes in equilibrium prices and quantities, which depend on the relative magnitudes of shifts in supplies and demands.

The wheat market is now shown in Figure 3, allowing us to examine what happens when supply and demand curves shift in the same direction. Demand and supply are originally at D_0 and S_0, respectively, with equilibrium price at P_0 and equilibrium output at Q_0 (point a).

Assume that Russia began buying more U.S. wheat in a year we experienced a bumper crop. These events would increase *both* demand and supply in Figure 3. This information by it-

FIGURE 3   Price and Quantity Effects of Increases in Both Supply and Demand

When both supply and demand increase (decrease), equilibrium quantity traded must rise (fall), but the change in price depends upon the relative magnitudes of the two shifts.

creases, or remains constant. In this case, quantity changes depend on the relative magnitudes of shifts and relative slopes of the demand curves and supply curves. Thus, if demand rises while supply falls, the price rises, but we cannot predict quantity changes without more information.

Similar results occur if demand falls and supply rises. Thus, declines in demand and increases in supply cause prices to fall, but predicting quantity changes requires more data. Figure 5 summarizes how changes in supplies and demands affect prices and quantities in the short run. A good review of this section is to match the relevant segments of Figure 5 with the possible adjustments listed in its caption.

Market economies are sometimes plagued by volatile prices and production. High prices and abundant profit opportunities cause existing firms to expand and new firms to enter the market, boosting supply and driving the high

self leaves us unsure whether the price at the new equilibrium (point b) is higher or lower than P_0, but equilibrium quantity (now Q_1) is definitely higher than its old value of Q_0. The lesson here is that when both demand and supply grow, quantity increases but price changes are unknowable without more information.

You may have perceived that whether the new price of wheat will be above or below P_0 depends on the relative magnitudes of the two shifts. For example, if Russia's new demand were relatively large and drove market demand to D_2, equilibrium price would rise (point c). Symmetric results occur if both demand and supply decrease, say, from D_1 and S_1 to D_0 and S_0: quantity falls, but price changes cannot be predicted without more information.

What happens if supplies and demands move in opposite directions? The wheat market is again initially in equilibrium at point a in Figure 4. Equilibrium moves to point b if population growth boosts demand to D_1 while drought cuts supply to S_1. Price increases to P_1, but we need more information to be sure whether quantity increases, de-

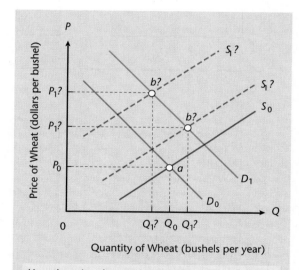

How the price changes is predictable when demand and supply curves move in opposite directions, but the quantity adjustment is not. When demand grows and supply falls, price will rise, but the change in equilibrium quantity depends on the nature of the two shifts. When demand declines and supply increases, prices will fall, but again the change in quantity is uncertain without more information.

FIGURE 4   The Effects of an Increase in Demand and a Decrease in Supply

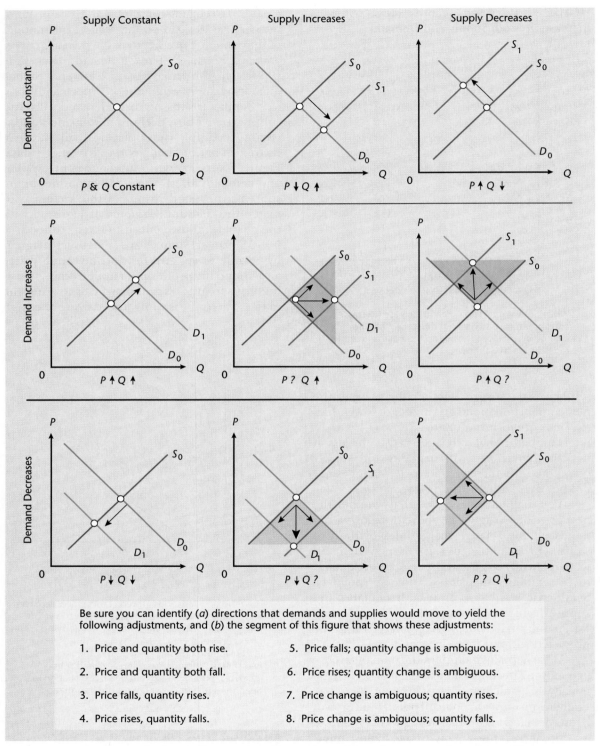

FIGURE 5 Summary of Price and Quantity Responses to Changing Demands and Supplies

price down. Low prices and inadequate profits, on the other hand, cause some firms to exit an industry, while the survivors cut back on output and reduce their hiring. This pushes low prices up. There may be long lags between planning for production and selling output, so prices and outputs can swing wildly before finally settling at equilibrium.

Suppose, for example, that wheat prices soared after a drought devastated a crop. The high price relative to cost could cause wheat farmers to overproduce in the next year, driving the price down. This low price could cause discouraged farmers to cut production back too much in the third year, causing the price to again rise far above production costs. And so on. Similarly cyclical price swings have been observed for engineering wages (it takes four years to get an engineering degree) and in other markets in which training or production, or both, take a long time.

TRANSACTION COSTS

Economists often refer to "the price" as if each good had only one price at a given time. But gas prices differ between service stations, and grocers commonly charge different prices for what seem to be the same foods. How can this be reconciled with economic models that arrive at a single price? The answer is that *transaction costs* create opportunity cost wedges between the various market prices for a good.

> **Transaction costs** *are the costs associated with (a) gathering information about prices and availability and (b) mobility, or transporting goods, resources, or potential buyers between markets.*

The value of the time you take reading ads and driving to a store to take advantage of a bargain is one form of transaction costs. Gasoline used and wear and tear on your car in gathering information and locating goods are also transaction costs. Would you knowingly drive 50 miles from store to store to save $5, or would you prefer to buy at a nearby shopping mall?

Sellers would always sell at the highest possible price if transaction costs were zero, while buyers would only pay the lowest possible price.

If so, the highest and lowest possible prices must be identical—only one price could exist for identical goods. Thus, transaction costs, in which the value of time plays an important role, account for ranges in the monetary prices of any single good. Paying a higher monetary price is often efficient if acquiring the good at a lower monetary price entails high transaction costs.

Transaction costs also help explain why prices sometimes move erratically towards equilibrium. If information were perfect and mobility instantaneous and costless, prices would be driven to equilibrium like arrows shot at a bull's-eye by an expert archer. Instead, prices may resemble basketballs, bouncing up, down, and sideways before finally "reaching equilibrium" by going through the hoop. The speed of equilibration is negatively related to the costs of mobility and information.

People search for bargains only to the extent that they expect the benefits from shopping (lower prices) to exceed the transaction costs they expect to incur. We constantly make decisions based on incomplete or inaccurate information in our uncertain world. Acquiring better market information is a costly process, as is moving goods or resources between markets. *Intermediaries* help minimize these transaction costs.

Intermediaries

Retail stores and wholesalers are examples of operations that cut transaction costs.

> **Intermediaries** *specialize in reducing uncertainty and cutting the transaction costs of conveying goods from original producers to the final users, often transforming the good to make it more compatible with ultimate users' demands.*

Many people are surprised to learn that price swings are moderated by successful *speculators*, who are special types of intermediaries.

Intermediaries are sometimes condemned as profiteers—villains who cause inflation, shortages, or other economic maladies. For example, people who trundled flashlights and bottled water to Los Angeles after earthquakes in 1994 were castigated by the media for charging prices that seemed exorbitant. But the real problems were power outages and the tiny supply of drinkable water. If more people had followed their example and tried to profiteer, prices would have been lower. Like all intermediaries, profiteers absorb risks and help move prices toward equilibrium. This reduces transaction costs and conveys goods to those who desire them most while boosting the incomes of original suppliers. In fact, intermediaries reduce opportunity costs to consumers, and speculators tend to reduce both the volatility of prices and net costs of products.

Have you ever paid more than you had to for anything? Your answer must be no if you behave rationally. You might object that, say, buying apples from a grocer costs more than buying them from an apple grower. But if you bought from a store, it must have charged less than if you had bought apples directly from an orchard, after considering information costs, travel, potential spoilage, and the time entailed in going to the orchard. Otherwise, you would have bought directly from the apple grower.

Similarly, monetary prices at convenience stores exceed those at supermarkets. However, after we adjust for greater accessibility because of the longer hours typical of convenience stores and the frequent extended waits at supermarket checkouts, customers of convenience stores must be paying less (after considering all transaction costs) or they would buy elsewhere.

One important way in which intermediaries reduce transaction costs is by absorbing risk. Quality is often variable. Apples, for example, range from rotten to those that win prizes at county fairs. Consumers would be distraught if they bought a few apples to eat fresh, but wound up with mush unsuitable even for applesauce. Orchard owners specialize in growing apples but may not be geared to assure top quality to every consumer of every apple. Another problem is that an individual customer may buy apples only at irregular intervals, while individual orchards have tons of apples available at some times, and none at others. Timing between individual purchases and harvesting at a given orchard may not be synchronous.

Apple wholesalers and grocers, however, purchase such large quantities that they are accustomed to dealing with a mix of good and bad apples. They also sell to so many customers that no sale to any single final buyer is crucial. This assures apple eaters high quality and allows orchard owners to concentrate on production. Thus, those ultimate producers and consumers who want to reduce risk can shift it to intermediaries who are more willing to bear risk (perhaps because, by pooling numerous transactions, intermediaries may be able to reduce the cost of risk).

Transportation and information costs, time, and risk all contribute to transaction costs. No matter how hard you try, we doubt that you can come up with a single example where, after considering all transaction costs, at the time you bought something, you paid more than the lowest price possible for it.

- **Arbitrage** Positive returns are ensured if you can buy low and sell high.

> *Arbitrage* is the process of buying at a lower price in one market and selling at a higher price in another, where the arbitrageur knows both prices and the price differential exceeds transaction costs.

For example, if gold is $328 per ounce in London while the New York price is $337 per ounce, an arbitrageur can make $9 per ounce (minus transaction costs) by buying in London and selling in New York.

Traders relentlessly seek riskless profits through arbitrage. When intermediaries buy in a market with a lower price, demand grows, driving up the price. When they sell in the market with the higher price, the greater supply pushes the price down. Thus, arbitrage reduces transaction costs and pushes relative prices toward equality in all markets. For example, arbitrageurs finesse any need for you to travel to London to take advantage of better deals on gold available there. Intermediation promotes economic efficiency by linking markets that are spread geographically, so goods are moved from areas where they have a relatively low value to markets where the goods are more highly valued.

- **Speculators** Speculation is unlike arbitrage because positive returns are not guaranteed.

Speculators derive income by buying something at a low price and storing it in the hope of selling it later at a higher price.

Nobody can predict the future with certainty, so this time delay makes speculation risky. Speculators who predict correctly can make fortunes, but they go broke and cease being speculators if they are frequently wrong.

If speculators believe that prices will soon rise, then they expect demands to grow faster than supplies. They respond by buying now, increasing the current demand and price. For example, expectations that bacon prices will soon rise cause speculators to buy and store pork bellies (the source of bacon) right now, driving up the current price. Does this raise prices later? No. If speculators are more often right than wrong, they sell when prices are high and add to the supply at that time. When bacon speculators sell the stored pork bellies, the price of bacon is reduced relative to what it otherwise would have been. Thus, successful speculation shifts the consumption of a good from a period in which it would have a relatively low value into a period when its value to consumers is higher.

Correct speculation reduces price peaks and boosts depressed prices. Thus, successful speculators dampen price swings and, by absorbing some risks to others of doing business, raise net incomes for ultimate suppliers. Overall, costs fall because speculators absorb risks and the prices consumers pay are lower and more predictable. All types of intermediation tend to be very competitive, so on average after adjusting for risk, incomes from these activities tend to be about the same as the incomes intermediaries could have earned in their best alternative employment.

MARKETS AND PUBLIC POLICY

The level of the sea is not more surely kept than is the equilibrium of value in society by supply and demand; and artifice or legislation punishes itself by reactions, gluts, and bankruptcies.

Ralph Waldo Emerson

No mechanism distributes income and allocates resources to everyone's satisfaction. Our mixed economy relies most on the market system, with government coming in a close second—the list of laws and governmentally provided goods and services ranges from police and fire protection to dog leash laws and financial regulations, from national defense to education and interstate highways, and on and on.

In this section, we look at the effects of some government policies. Some regulations are inefficient. An inefficient wedge between buyers and sellers is created if a regulation's costs exceed its benefits. Let's see how specific laws may cause inefficiency in the forms of excessive costs or persistent shortages or surpluses.

Price Controls

You can't repeal the Laws of Supply and Demand.

Anonymous

Supplies and demands change continuously, so we might expect relative prices to bounce around like ping-pong balls. We all want low prices for things we buy and high prices for things we sell. When prices rise or fall, some people gain while others lose, but any lone individual has little influence on market forces. Special-interest groups, however, often persuade government to establish price controls.

• **Price Ceilings**   Price ceilings ostensibly reflect attempts to curb inflation, control monopoly power, or to help the poor by holding down prices for "essentials." Unfortunately, ceilings are seldom appropriate tools for any of these tasks.

*A **price ceiling** is a **maximum** legal price.*

A price ceiling set above the equilibrium market-clearing price is usually as irrelevant as a law limiting joggers to 65 miles per hour. But price ceilings below equilibrium create shortages and drive up opportunity costs; only the legal monetary price is kept from rising. Shortages waste resources because less efficient mechanisms prevail when prices cannot adjust. Ceilings induced erratic shortages of thousands of items (e.g., gasoline, auto parts, and some types of food and clothing) during World Wars I and II. Widespread shortages also followed President Nixon's 1971 wage-price freeze, which was phased out and then largely abandoned by 1976.

Suppose a price ceiling of $1 per gallon were imposed in the gasoline market shown in Figure 6. The quantity of fuel demanded daily will be 75 million gallons, with quantity supplied being only 30 million gallons. An excess demand (or shortage) of 45 million gallons exists. Who will get gasoline? People who bribe service station attendants, those who persuade government to give them priority access, or those who wait through long lines. Even people who waited 2 to 4 hours in gasoline queues in 1974 and 1975 often went without because the pumps ran dry. Note that, unlike a higher price, these long lines generated no corresponding benefits for suppliers, so time spent queuing is a *dead-weight* loss; if prices had been allowed to rise, suppliers would have had more incentives to produce.

But ceilings keep average prices down, don't they? Sorry, but no. The people who most value the 30 million gallons of gas available daily tend to get it. They are willing to pay at least $2 per gallon for gasoline; that is, an extra dollar per gallon in waiting time, lobbying, or as a black market premium.

> A **black market** is an illegal market where price controls are ignored.

Had the price ceiling not been imposed, the price of a gallon of gasoline would have been roughly $1.25. Although the legal monetary price of gas is held at $1 per gallon by this ceiling, its opportunity cost rises to $2 to typical customers.

The costs of queuing, however, tend to be lower for the impoverished or jobless. Poor people may gain from ceilings because waiting in line secures gas that they might lack funds to buy if its monetary price rose. Some people view such redistributions as worth the inefficiency price controls create. Nevertheless, price ceilings create shortages so that opportunity costs—including money, time wasted in lines, and illegal side payments—unnecessarily exceed free-market prices. Only pump prices are controlled; real costs to average consumers are not.

• **Price Floors** Price controls of a different type are aimed primarily at redistributing incomes.

> A **price floor** is a **minimum** legal price.

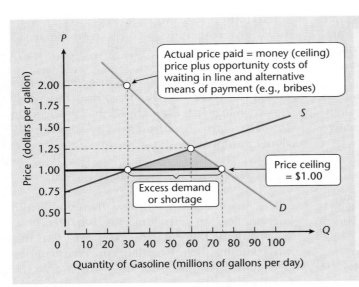

This figure shows the effect of a $1-per-gallon ceiling on the price of gasoline. At $1 per gallon, 75 million gallons will be demanded but only 30 million will be supplied. This creates shortages and stimulates non-price allocation methods: Queueing, black market deals, and so on.

Price controls maintained for long periods are especially inefficient. They (*a*) require a growing enforcement bureaucracy, (*b*) stimulate costly lobbying for "exceptions" to allow certain prices to rise, (*c*) create immense pressures for corruption of the officials in charge of enforcement, and (*d*) thwart the expansion of output that would normally follow higher prices.

Actual price paid = money (ceiling) price plus opportunity costs of waiting in line and alternative means of payment (e.g., bribes)

Price ceiling = $1.00

Excess demand or shortage

FIGURE 6 **Governmentally Induced Shortages in the Gasoline Market**

Price floors set below equilibrium tend to be as irrelevant as laws requiring pilots to fly above sea level, but floors exceeding equilibrium create artificial surpluses and raise costs. Price floors are most common in labor markets (minimum wage laws) and agriculture, where government attempts to boost farm incomes by maintaining farm commodity prices above equilibrium. Figure 7 depicts the consequence of price floors in the cotton market.

Equilibrium occurs at 4 million bales annually at $0.60 per pound of cotton (point *e*). A floor at $0.75 per pound yields a quantity supplied of 5 million bales, but only 3 million bales are demanded; excess supply (surplus) is 2 million bales annually. Government can ensure the $0.75 price by buying and storing excess supplies. (Federal warehouses often hold mountains of surplus wheat, cotton, corn, beet sugar, peanuts, and soybeans.) Alternatively, the government can pay cotton farmers not to produce or limit the amount of planting. (It has done both.)

Inefficiency is a major problem. In our example, consumers view the 5-millionth bale as worth only $0.45 per pound, even though this last bale cost $0.75 per pound to grow and harvest. Worse than that, people do not get to use the surplus 2 million bales society (via government) buys from farmers. Hardly a bargain.

In summary, price ceilings cause shortages and do not hold down the real prices paid by most consumers. Shortages drive up transaction costs, so price ceilings actually raise the opportunity costs incurred in acquiring goods. Some desperate buyers must go without even after enduring long queues or extended shopping trips intended to acquire information and locate goods. On the other hand, price floors cause surpluses. Production costs of the surplus goods exceed their values to consumers.

If price controls tend to be counterproductive, why are they so common? In some cases, price ceilings are enacted because voters favor them, mistakenly perceiving controls as a solution for inflation. Most of the time, however, controls are political responses to pressures from special-interest groups. Some beneficiaries of controls are obvious: price floors in agriculture survive because of bloc voting by generations of farmers. Other gainers are less obvious: farm machinery manufacturers, for example.

Even price supports have not prevented recurrent crises in agriculture, however, as evidenced by rampant farm foreclosures from 1981 to 1987. Technological advances allow ever decreasing numbers of farmers to feed our growing population. Price supports have merely

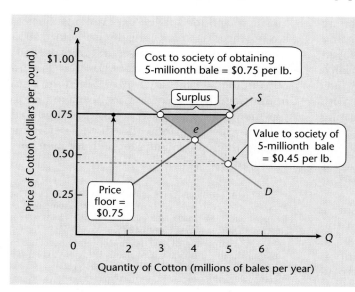

Price floors generate surpluses, as this figure illustrates. If government maintains the price of cotton at $0.75 per pound, quantity supplied exceeds that demanded by 2 million bales. The surplus ends up in the hands of government, which must buy the surplus to maintain the price at $0.75. Thus taxpayers pay $0.75 per pound for cotton for which they then pay storage costs. Furthermore, the opportunity cost to society of producing the 5-millionth bale far exceeds its value. Thus, such policies tend to waste scarce resources.

FIGURE 7   Surpluses in the Cotton Market

slowed the painful flow of people from agriculture into other work.

Rent controls have been enforced for long periods in some cities, including New York City and Santa Monica, California. Long-term tenants are only one group that gains from rent controls. Current homeowners and home builders, for example, gain if apartment shortages cause potential renters to switch into buying rather than renting. Rent controls drive up prices for both new and existing housing. Losers from rent controls include landlords and potential renters who seek vacant apartments.

Most direct gainers from controls are very conscious of their gains, but long-run losers from controls may not recognize their losses. For example, you might favor rent controls limiting the rent your current landlord sets. But will you blame controls if you decide to relocate and cannot find an apartment? Rent control tends to squelch apartment construction and turn older rental units into slums. Shortages of rentals and inadequate maintenance by landlords are predictable consequences of rent controls.

Special interest groups that lobby for controls tend to be among the winners, but even their gains are eroded by lobbying costs and related inefficiencies. One lesson from price controls is that market forces often thwart policies that, on the surface, seem compatible with good intentions and intuition. Economic reasoning may be a better guide in designing efficient and humane policies for areas ranging from farming to rentals to minimum wage laws to illicit drugs. Minimum-wage laws, for example, may hurt far more workers than they help, with young workers and members of minorities being especially hard hit.

Minimum Wages and Unemployment

Minimum wage laws are intended to ensure a living wage. This goal is achieved only if unskilled or inexperienced workers can find and keep jobs. Figure 8 shows the effect of imposing a $6 minimum hourly wage in a competitive labor market for unskilled workers, where the equilibrium wage is $5 and equilibrium employment is 7 million workers. As Panel A illustrates, 2 million unskilled workers are laid off when a $6 legal floor is imposed on hourly wages. Another million enter the job market at this higher wage, so 3 million out of 8 million are now unemployed, and the unemployment rate among the unskilled rises from 0% to 37.5%.

Jobless workers adjust in several ways. The million who entered the market will seek work elsewhere, but lower wages elsewhere will cause most to leave the market. The two million disemployed workers will seek work in labor markets not covered by minimum wage laws (mowing lawns, delivering papers, etc.), shown in Panel B. This increases the labor supply in this uncovered market by 2 million workers, and wages fall to $4.50 per hour. A million workers find work, but a million do not. Thus, wage floors create surpluses of workers and unemployment just as surely as price floors for goods cause surpluses of goods. Minimum wage laws deprive some unemployed workers of job opportunities and can cause them to give up hope.

Our society has tried numerous cures for teenage unemployment. Asked if he was making any progress toward inventing a light bulb, Thomas Edison replied, "Why certainly. I've learned 1,000 ways you can't make a light bulb."[1] Edison eventually developed a good light bulb, but he abandoned failed experiments. Society has not fared as well. In the 8 years before 1955 when minimum hourly wages first crept over $1, teenage unemployment rates hovered around 10%; in the 20 years after 1974, when the minimum wage first exceeded $2, teenage unemployment averaged over 18%.[2] Misguided policies may contribute heavily to persistent teenage unemployment, especially for members of minority groups.

[1]This anecdote is related by Steven P. Zell in "The Problem of Rising Teenage Unemployment: A Reappraisal," *Economic Review*, March 1978. Federal Reserve of Kansas City, March 1978.

[2]The dampening of this disemployment effect due to inflation during this era was probably offset by expanded coverage of the labor force by minimum-wage laws, which increase disemployment. Restaurant and grocery store employees, for example, are now covered by federal minimum-wage laws, but were not in the early 1950s.

FIGURE 8 Minimum Wages and Unemployment

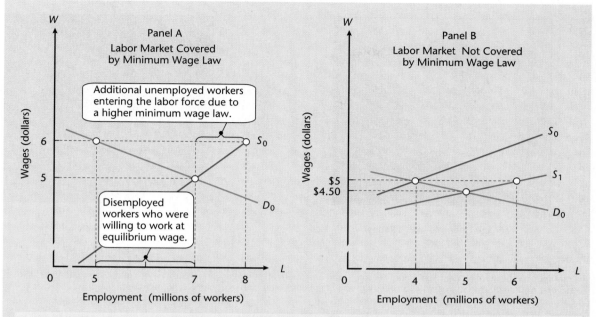

Minimum wage laws can cause involuntary unemployment among workers with few marketable skills. This especially harms young people denied experience that would enhance their future employability. As workers are disemployed in markets covered by minimum wages (Panel A), they move to uncovered markets (Panel B) paying lower wages--- delivering papers, mowing lawns, or odd-job self employment. Or they may take "off-the-book" jobs that violate the minimum wage law. But not all workers are absorbed in uncovered markets. Some become "hard-core" unemployed; others drop out of the work force. Still others may become criminals.

Figure 9 shows that between 1948 and 1951, male African-American teenagers had lower average unemployment than white males. African American teenagers lost steadily thereafter, now suffering twice the unemployment experienced by white teenagers. Panel B suggests that many male African-American teenagers may be so discouraged that declining proportions try to find work, while labor-force participation rates among white teenagers have grown slightly over time.

Minimum wage laws also illustrate how regulations may subtly benefit special-interest groups. These laws create surpluses of unemployed workers who are primarily young and unskilled. Why do labor unions lobby for higher minimum wages even though union workers earn wages much higher than these floors? Misguided humanitarianism may play a role,

but another reason is that wage floors limit the ability of unskilled workers to compete with skilled workers. For example, if two unskilled workers willing to work for $4.50 hourly apiece can, together, do the same job as a $10-per-hour union worker; a $5.50 minimum wage eliminates their ability to compete.

Virtually all studies confirm a positive relationship between teen unemployment and the minimum-wage rate, but the power of this effect remains controversial. Unemployment rates among teenagers—especially minority-member males—have shown a strong upward trend since the 1950s. Is only 20% of this trend attributable to higher minimum wages as some analysts have concluded, or is the number more like 80% as other researchers indicate? Even specialists in this area continue to disagree.

FIGURE 9 Teenagers and the Minimum Wage

Panel A

Teenage Unemployment Ratios
and Minimum Wage

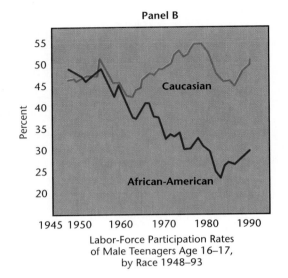

Panel B

Labor-Force Participation Rates
of Male Teenagers Age 16–17,
by Race 1948–93

As minimum legal wages have risen (Panel A), male African-American teenagers apparently have lost jobs to male Caucasian teenagers. As a result, many male African-American teenagers have dropped out of the labor market (Panel B).

The War on Drugs

Substance abuse has been on the political front burner for decades. Standard approaches to this problem emphasize punishing users somewhat, but dealers much more harshly. This retards demands for drugs somewhat, but shrinks their supplies much more. The result is that illicit drug prices are much higher than free-market prices would be, and addiction poses more problems for the rest of society.

Suppose S_0 and D_0 in Figure 10 represent the demand and supply of cocaine if it were legal. The price, P_0, would probably fall somewhere between the prices of aspirin and antibiotics because cocaine production is not complex, nor are currently legal narcotics very expensive. (Some estimates suggest that completely legalized and untaxed marijuana would sell for about $8 a bale, roughly the price of prime hay.)

Penalizing cocaine users reduces demand to D_1, while the stiffer punishment of dealers reduces supply to S_1, boosting the price to P_1. This higher price makes dealing extraordinarily profitable for criminals willing to live dangerously; successful dealers live lives of luxury.

Violence in pursuit of high profits from dealing has become the norm in the drug business. But impoverished users often move into prostitution, burglary, mugging, and other street crimes. Thus, higher crime rates are among the social costs of policies that reduce the supply of cocaine more than the demand for it.[3]

One alternative approach is complete legalization. Advocates of allowing drugs to be governed strictly by demand and supply argue that they would be so cheap that few addicts would feel driven to commit crimes against others. Heroin addicts, for example, would tend to spend a lot of time nodding off, bothering people no more than derelict alcoholics. Most people, however, are unwilling to let others waste away their lives in such a fashion.

What policies might slash drug abuse below Q_0 (the free-market amount, shown in Figure 10) without pushing addicts to commit crimes? Punishing users far more than currently would

---

[3]Analysis to support a focus on demand rather than on supply can be traced to Billy J. Eatherly, "Drug-Law Enforcement: Should We Arrest Pushers or Users?," *Journal of Political Economy*, 82, no. 1 (January–February 1974): 210–214.

FIGURE 10 The Market for Cocaine

Prosecuting dealers reduces supply more than demand, boosting the price from P_0 to P_1. This makes dealing extremely profitable. Harsher prosecution of addicts might reduce demand to D_2, eliminating much of this profit. Alternatively, giving drugs to addicts through government clinics might dry up both the demands and supplies. Supply would shrink because catching and prosecuting dealers would be easier.

reduce demand to, say, D_2 and could cut cocaine prices, dealers' profits, and rates of addiction to Q_2. Most people, however, are reluctant to impose life sentences or the death penalty to punish drug users, especially when minors or experimenters are involved.

Paradoxically, allowing clinics to freely provide drugs to proven addicts while stiffly penalizing dealers might suppress both addiction and the crime it fosters. Suppliers would be left with only experimenters as potential customers, so over time, this policy could reduce the illicit demand for drugs below D_2. Dealers would be more exposed to undercover investigation because they would not know their customers, and illegal supplies of drugs should dry up. A similar approach used in England for almost three decades appears to work reasonably well. However, it does not cure all addicts, which causes some people to criticize the program as a failure.

Do simple solutions exist for such problems as teenage unemployment and drug abuse? Should market forces operate without controls? Answers to such questions depend, in part, on specific market conditions. Any answer is normative; economists cannot definitively say what we should do, but we can point out how various policies operate in hopes that laws consistent with economic theory will eventually be enacted. The Clinton administration announced a shift of emphasis to curbs on demand—educational programs and rehabilitation—in place of the supply-side emphasis long relied on to cope with substance abuse. Most economists would applaud this shift in approach.

Supply and demand exert considerable muscle regardless of which allocative mechanism is used to resolve any problem. We hope that these brief overviews of price controls, minimum-wage laws, and the market for drugs convince you that market forces cannot be ignored when structuring social policies, even in areas closely tied to people's views of morality.

THE MARKET IN OPERATION

Our overview of supply and demand in action has set the stage for addressing how efficiently and equitably market mechanisms answer the basic questions of "*What?*" "*How?*" and "*For Whom?*"

What?

Our exploration of the price system has relied on two critical assumptions:

1. *Individuals are self-interested* and try to maximize their personal satisfaction through the goods they consume. If goods add less to your satisfaction (valued in terms of money) than they cost, you will not buy them. Consumer willingness to pay underpins the demands for goods.
2. *Firms try to maximize profits* when they sell goods to consumers willing to pay for them. The drive for profit underpins the supply side of the market.

Thus, the market system answers the What? question by producing the things people demand.

How?

A firm's ability to exploit consumers is limited. First, competition keeps prices from straying much above costs for long; high profits attract new firms, increasing supply, so prices and profits fall. Second, suppliers try to be efficient; firms that cut costs or innovate a successful technology temporarily reap higher profits. Before long, any firm not using a superior technology is left trying to sell outdated products, or its costs will exceed its competitors' prices and it will fail.

Competition ensures that price is approximately equal to the opportunity cost (sacrifice to society) incurred in production. International competition exerts pressure for specialized output and exchange according to comparative advantage. Thus, competitive markets answer the How? question by shifting resources into goods where production costs are relatively the lowest. This normally means that countries with abundant labor and scarce capital gain most by concentrating on labor-intensive goods (e.g., apparel), while countries with ample capital relative to labor gain by producing capital-intensive goods (e.g., aircraft or scientific instruments).

For Whom?

How markets answer this for Whom? question is relatively simple. Consumers who hold dollar votes and are willing to pay market prices purchase and consume goods. Those who do not own many resources cannot buy very much. It is this distributional side that seems to cause the most problems for critics of the market system.

Many people perceive the price system as impersonal and inequitable. However, the market offers some major compensating advantages. Decisions are decentralized: no government agency dictates what everyone must (or cannot) buy or produce. Moreover, markets tend to be efficient. Consumers usually pay prices for goods that roughly reflect the minimal costs of producing these goods. Finally, although markets may not provide perfect stability, the forces that drive markets toward equilibrium tend to yield more stability than most other mechanisms.

Although markets seem to excel in the production and distribution of a wide array of goods, there are circumstances where the market system may fail. This opens the door for an economic role for government in a market economy.

GOVERNMENT IN A MARKET ECONOMY

Government directly provides some goods, and indirectly channels resources into the production and consumption of other goods via taxes and regulations. As we approach the twenty-first century, our society is more regulated and taxed than when economic policies followed a more laissez-faire philosophy: federal, state, and local governments now directly allocate roughly one-fifth of national production; another 15% is redistributed through transfer payments, with two-thirds of all transfers being made by the federal government. Transfer payments include welfare outlays, loans to farmers and students, and similar expenditures. Figure 11 illustrates some facets of the size and recent growth of total government activity.

Many people see government action as necessary whenever markets apparently fail to respond to our desires for equity, efficiency, full employment, stable prices, and prosperous growth. Widely accepted economic goals for government in a market economy are

1. to provide a stable legal environment for business activity
2. to promote and maintain competitive markets
3. to allocate resources to meet public wants efficiently
4. to facilitate equity through redistributions of income
5. to ensure full employment, a stable price level, economic security, and a growing standard of living

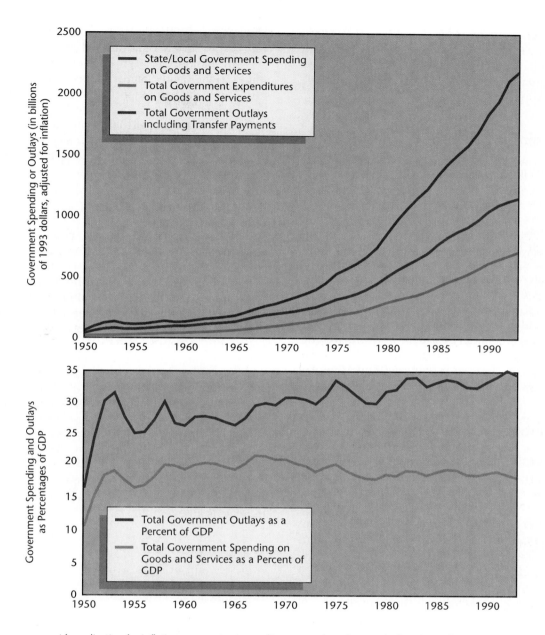

After adjusting for inflation, government spending on goods and resources has risen a bit more rapidly than our national output over recent decades. Total government outlays (which include such transfer payments as, e.g., Social Security and Aid for Dependent Children) have grown even more rapidly. The conclusion that the role of government has expanded in the U.S. economy is inescapable.

FIGURE 11   The Growth of Government Outlays

Although macroeconomic and microeconomic policies are unavoidably intertwined, goals 1 through 4 tend to be microeconomic concerns, while goal 5 is the focus of macroeconomic policymaking.

Providing a Stable Legal Environment

A reasonably certain legal environment helps prevent chaos. Could any system operate efficiently if ownership rights or the rules of business were uncertain? Property rights or contracts, if they existed, would be enforced only through brute force or individual persuasion. Primitive trading could occur, but complex financial transactions—especially those involving time—would be impossible.

In a market economy, government establishes rules about legal relationships between parties, sets standards for money and weights and measures, sometimes insures bank deposits, and engages in other activities intended to promote the public welfare.

Promoting Competition

Competition allows us to enjoy the benefits of efficient markets. Profits signal that consumers want more of certain goods; losses signal that too much is being offered. New technologies that create better and cheaper products force older firms to adapt or perish. Thus, hand-cranked autos don't clog our highways and motor-driven calculators don't clutter our desks.

Monopoly, which occurs when a single firm dominates a market, lies at the opposite end of the spectrum of market structures from competition. *Market power* (also known as monopoly power) exists whenever individual firms significantly influence the supply and price of a good and may be present even if several firms share a market. In contrast, competitive buyers and sellers are each so small relative to the entire market that, alone, none can noticeably affect total output or prices. Firms with market power boost profits by restricting output and setting higher prices. This is inefficient because equilibrium monopoly prices exceed the opportunity cost to society of additional production.

The basic approach to controlling monopoly power in the United States has been through antitrust laws and regulation. Antitrust laws attempt to curb unfair business practices and prevent huge firms from absorbing all their competitors. Where competition is impractical (e.g., electricity and natural gas companies), regulation is used to limit the abuse of monopoly power.

Providing for Public Wants

No private firm could sell you a cleaner environment without simultaneously providing it for your neighbors. Nor could a neighbor privately buy national defense without protecting you. Because no individual willingly bears the costs of adequately accommodating everyone's desires for goods of these types, price signals emitted by consumers are distorted and firms cannot privately market these goods profitably.

Even if firms operate in a stable and competitive environment, certain market failures may still seem to justify government action. Externalities, of which pollution is one form, can warp price signals so that our demands are not accurately reflected. A difficulty called the public goods problem results when shared consumption is possible but people cannot be denied access to the benefits of a good. National defense is an example.

• **Externalities** Externalities occur when some benefits or costs of an activity spill over to parties not directly involved in the activity. For example, when farmers spray their crops, some pesticide may eventually wash into nearby lakes or streams. If the pesticide is absorbed by microorganisms and works its way up the ecological chain, your fishing or health may deteriorate so that you partially bear the cost of the use of chemical sprays. Most human activities generate externalities, some trivial and some of major concern. Cooking creates heat and smoke, cars emit noxious fumes, and loud stereos annoy neighbors. All forms of pollution—chemical, air, noise, and litter, are negative externalities.

Producers who generate negative externalities tend to ignore costs imposed on others, and the prices they charge reflect only their private costs. Pollution-generating goods consequently tend to be overproduced and underpriced. The government uses regulation to limit various pollutants because a total ban on pollution would probably eliminate all production. There are trade-offs between the cleaner environment most of us would like and the higher consumption levels most of us desire.

Inefficiency may also occur when positive externalities spill over from an activity. Immunization against contagious diseases is an example. You are less likely to suffer from the flu if you are inoculated, and we who are your neighbors are less likely to catch it as well. But you tend to ignore our benefits when you decide whether or not to be immunized and so are less likely to get a flu shot than is socially optimal. Thus, private decisions result in underproduction and overpricing of goods that generate positive externalities because the value to society exceeds the demand price individuals willingly pay when they are uncompensated for external benefits.

• **Public Goods**   Keeping violent criminals behind bars makes the world more secure for the rest of us, so the safety a prison system provides to society is an example of a public good. *Public goods* are both *nonrival* because numerous people can consume *the same unit* of such a good simultaneously, and *nonexclusive*, because denying access to such goods is prohibitively expensive. Most goods are private goods. If you eat a corn chip laden with guacamole, no one else can enjoy that particular morsel—such private goods as food, raincoats, or shaving cream are rival and exclusive.

But we need not compete with each other to use public goods once they are produced because their use does not involve rivalry. Most cities would suffer terminal gridlock without traffic lights, which smooth traffic flows and cut accident rates. All drivers benefit simultaneously. Other public goods include research on such things as weather or cancer, democratic government, and national defense. Once the armed forces are maintained and ready, every person in the United States consumes defense services simultaneously, and we all receive this protection whether we pay (through taxes) or not and whether we want it or not.

Public goods cannot be privately and profitably marketed to efficiently service our collective demands for them. A few people might contribute funds for a nonrival good from which exclusion was impossible, but not enough for efficient provision. There is little incentive to reveal your demands for police protection, space exploration, spraying against mosquitoes, landscaping along a public highway, or maintaining courts and prisons if you will be taxed accordingly. Why not be a free rider? Private firms could not adequately market such services, so government provides a variety of public goods and forces us to pay for them through taxes.

Public provision does not, however, require public production. For example, NASA space probes use equipment built by private firms. Alan Shepard, the first American in space, reported that the last thought that flashed through his mind before his rocket was launched was that it was made of millions of parts, ". . . all built by the lowest bidder."

Income Redistribution

Market mechanisms seem impersonal and yield distributions of income and wealth that many people view as inequitable. Goods are channeled to those who own valuable resources, whether they "need" them or not. And how valuable a resource is depends on demand. World class ping-pong players must work at other jobs in the United States, while equally skilled basketball players are millionaires.

Most people are distressed by the suffering of those who live in abject poverty and, if they are modestly prosperous, will donate to charities to help starving children or the unfortunate poor. But private charity may be inadequate to fulfill society's collective desire for equity because curing poverty is a public good—I may not donate if your charitable contribution makes me more comfortable when thinking about the poor. This leads to such government programs as welfare and disaster relief.

Stabilizing Income, Prices, and Employment

Market systems may lack strong natural mechanisms that consistently yield full employment without inflation. In fact, wide swings in economic activity, called *business cycles*, may be a natural tendency in market economies. Employment and the price level fluctuate during business cycles, dislocating workers, firms, and consumers, and generally disrupting our institutions.

Shortly after World War II, Congress stated some general goals in the Employment Act of 1946:

> *The Congress hereby declares that it is the continuing policy and responsibility of the federal government to . . . promote maximum employment, production, and purchasing power.*

The major tools government uses to try to achieve these macroeconomic goals include variations in taxes, government spending, and the supply of money.

International policies also have macroeconomic ramifications. Throughout the world, governments are reducing trade barriers to hasten economic growth and hold down price levels; international trade fosters growth because of incentives to allocate resources more efficiently, and consumers will not buy imports unless they judge the imports to be lower priced or possessing superior quality. However, in the short run, freer trade may worsen unemployment because labor needs to flow towards domestic industries that are internationally competitive and away from industries producing at comparative disadvantages relative to foreign producers—another example of how government faces trade-offs in the pursuit of its goals.

THE SCOPE OF GOVERNMENT

Now that you know some reasons for government action in a market economy, we will briefly survey the extent of the public sector. Total government spending on goods and services now tops $1 trillion annually, over 20% of our national production. When we include transfer payments (Social Security, welfare, and other income payments not tied to production), government outlays exceed one-third of all spending.

Figure 12 breaks down government spending by its major functions. Nearly half of the 1970 federal budget was devoted to national defense; today that figure is about one-fifth. For the next quarter century, outlays on such domestic programs as income security, health, education, natural resources, environmental protection, and energy policy more than absorbed funds freed by reductions in national defense.

Federal expenditures tend to focus on activities with national implications. State and local government spending is directed at services that affect people in more limited geographical areas. In contrast to federal outlays, the composition of state and local spending has changed little since the early 1960s, although there has been a relative reduction in highway spending and a rising proportion of outlays for welfare.

Figure 12 also shows that different levels of government rely on different taxes as revenue sources. State and local governments generate roughly two-thirds of their revenues from three major sources: (*a*) grants from the federal government, (*b*) property taxes, and (*c*) sales taxes. On the other hand, almost 60% of federal revenues come from taxes on individual or corporate incomes. When we include the second largest source of federal revenues, Social Security taxes (which are based solely on wage incomes), the figure is over 90%. Thus, less than 10% of total federal tax revenues rely on sources other than income.

You may have heard our income tax system referred to as progressive, which means the rich pay a greater percentage of their income as taxes than do the poor. Taxes can be related to income in three basic ways:

1. *Progressive.* A tax is progressive if the percentage tax rate rises as income rises; higher incomes are taxed proportionally higher than lower incomes.

FIGURE 12   Revenue Sources and Expenditures for Federal, State, and Local Governments

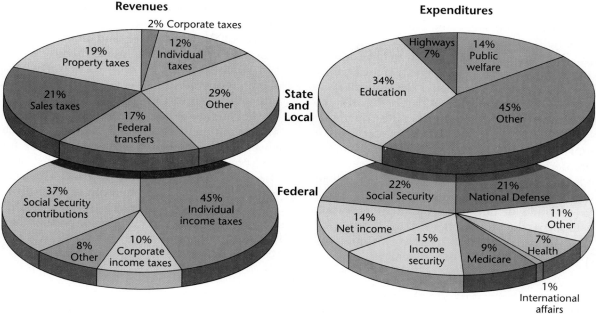

Source: *Statistical Abstract of the United States,* 1994.

The bulk of federal revenues are based on personal, corporate, and wage incomes, and most federal outlays are relatively national in scope. State and local government revenues, on the other hand, tend to derive from property and sales taxes, with outlays being aimed at more local concerns.

2. *Proportional.* Taxes collected are a fixed percentage of income. The flat-rate tax proposal would institute a proportional tax.
3. *Regressive.* A tax is regressive if the percentage of income paid as taxes declines as income rises.

The Budget Bill of 1993 reinstituted much of the progressivity of taxes on income that had been flattened by a 1986 reform of federal taxes. Although more tax loopholes were also opened up, the resulting pattern of collection is moderately progressive: people with higher incomes tend to pay greater percentages of their incomes as taxes.

Social Security taxes totaling roughly 15% of the first $60,000 of an individual's wages are collected, and the tax is roughly proportional in the $0 to $60,000 range of wage income. Because Social Security taxes are not collected beyond $60,000 in wages, this tax is regressive when the entire income range is considered.

Sales taxes also tend to be regressive because low income families commonly spend larger proportions (and save smaller proportions) of their income than high income families.

Taxing and spending are only two of the tools that government uses to mold economic activity. Laws and regulations also have very powerful economic effects. Several studies have concluded that compliance with regulation absorbs 5% to 15% of national income.

In Chapter 2 we surveyed some allocative mechanisms used to resolve economic questions. If the effects of people's choices were perfectly foreseeable and if everyone could, as costlessly as possible, acquire all the information bearing on every decision, the most useful mechanisms would be fairly obvious. Information is costly, and the future, unfortunately, is uncertain. Information for decision-making is sought only as long as the benefits expected from acquiring a bit more information exceed the costs. Beyond that point, we as individuals rationally choose to be ignorant. Thus, private decisions inevitably result in some mistakes because we are all somewhat *rationally ignorant* when we choose, and cannot know what the future holds.

One question is whether, in an environment of rational ignorance and pervasive uncertainty, government can make better decisions than we would make for ourselves. A part of the answer is that government decision-makers also operate in an uncertain environment and base decisions on only limited information. No perfect mechanisms for decision-making exist. If you voted in the last election, how much did you know about individual candidates and important issues? How certain were you about the policies your candidates would support as the future unfolded?

An inequitable distribution of income is one perceived flaw of a market system, and markets tend to be inefficient when firms exercise market power or when property rights are uncertain or unenforceable. At the macroeconomic level, persistent high unemployment, erratic swings of the price level, and unbalanced or sluggish growth may also signal inefficiency.

Much of this book addresses how a market economy operates and how government policies intended to correct for possible failures of the market might operate. Although government is growing in the U.S. economy, regions in which government dominated economic activity for decades (e.g., Eastern Europe, China, and Vietnam) increasingly rely on market mechanisms. The growing momentum of forces from international markets is powerful evidence that no tools of economics are more important than supply and demand.

CHAPTER REVIEW: KEY POINTS

1. Increases in supplies or decreases in demands reduce prices. Decreases in supplies or increases in demands raise prices. Increases in either supplies or demands tend to raise quantities exchanged. Declines in either supplies or demands tend to shrink quantities exchanged. If both demand and supply shift, the effects on price and quantity may be either reinforcing or offsetting.

2. **Transaction costs** arise because information and mobility are costly. This allows the price of a good to vary between markets and to approach its equilibrium erratically.

3. **Intermediaries** prosper only by reducing the transaction costs incurred in getting goods from the ultimate producers to the ultimate consumers. *Speculators* facilitate movements toward equilibrium because they increase demand by trying to buy when prices are below equilibrium, and increase supply by selling when prices are above equilibrium. This dampens price swings and reduces the costs and risks to others of doing business.

4. **Arbitrage** involves buying in a market where the price is low and selling in a market where the price is higher. If this price spread is greater than the transaction costs, arbitrage is risklessly profitable. Competition for opportunities to arbitrage dampens profit opportunities and facilitates efficiency by ensuring that price spreads between markets are minimal.

5. Government can set monetary prices at values other than equilibrium price, but **price ceilings** or **price floors** do not freeze opportunity costs; instead, these **price controls** create economic inefficiency and either shortages or surpluses, respectively.

6. Markets, through the magic of Adam Smith's *invisible hand*, respond to consumers' demands to answer the question of *what* will be produced. Competition tends to compel efficiency in production to answer *how* production occurs. Markets answer the *for whom* question by producing for the owners of resources that generate income.

7. Where the price system is incapable of providing certain goods or fails to supply the

socially optimal levels, government steps in to supplement the private sector in five major ways. It attempts (not always successfully) to

    a.   provide a legal, social, and business environment for stable growth;

    b.   promote and maintain competitive markets;

    c.   redistribute income and wealth equitably;

    d.   alter resource allocations in an efficient manner where public goods or externalities are present; and

    e.   stabilize income, employment, and prices.

8.   **Externalities** occur when some benefits or costs of an activity spill over to parties not directly involved in the activity. If **negative externalities** (costs) exist, the private market will provide too much of the product and the market price will be too low because full production costs are not being charged to consumers. If **positive externalities** (benefits) exist, too little of the product will be produced by the private market and market price will be too high, requiring a government subsidy or government production or provision of the commodity.

9.   Once **public goods** are produced, excluding people from their use is costly (*nonexclusion*), and everybody can consume the goods simultaneously with everyone else (*nonrivalry*). The free market fails to provide public goods efficiently because of the free-rider problem.

10.   Total spending on goods and services by all three levels of government exceeds 20% of U.S. Gross Domestic Product (GDP). State and local governments spend the bulk of their revenues on services that primarily benefit people in their community and rely heavily on the property and sales taxes as a source of revenue. Federal spending is generally aimed at activities that are national in scope. Over 90% of federal revenue comes from individual and corporate income taxes plus Social Security and other employment taxes.

QUESTIONS FOR THOUGHT AND DISCUSSION

1.   Is the assertion that "everyone always buys everything at the lowest possible price" correct? Have you ever paid more than you had to for any good, after allowing for all transaction costs?

2.   Ticket scalpers enable latecomers to avoid standing in line for tickets and allow people to wait until the last moment before deciding to attend concerts or athletic events. Are promoters of an event harmed by scalping? Should ticket scalpers' services be free? See if you can devise graphs to explain this form of speculation.

3.   Financial institutions such as banks act as intermediaries. They lend their depositors' savings to ultimate borrowers, charging higher interest to borrowers than the banks pay to depositors, who are the ultimate providers of loans. How does this reduce the transaction costs incurred in making private savings available to borrowers?

4.   Casual surveys of our students at the beginning of each semester reveal an amused but overwhelming support for a proposal to raise the legal minimum wages of college graduates to $50,000 per year. (They assumed our proposal was facetious.) After covering this chapter, student support for this idea evaporated. How might such a minimum-wage law be harmful to most new college graduates?

5.   Pharmaceutical companies have recently developed and tested drugs that reverse the influence of alcohol on the brain within a half-hour. These pills enable drivers to sober up before driving and to reduce the severity of hangovers. In the past few years, many states have imposed stiff mandatory penalties for drunk driving convictions. How do you think these two separate events will interact to influence alcohol consumption?

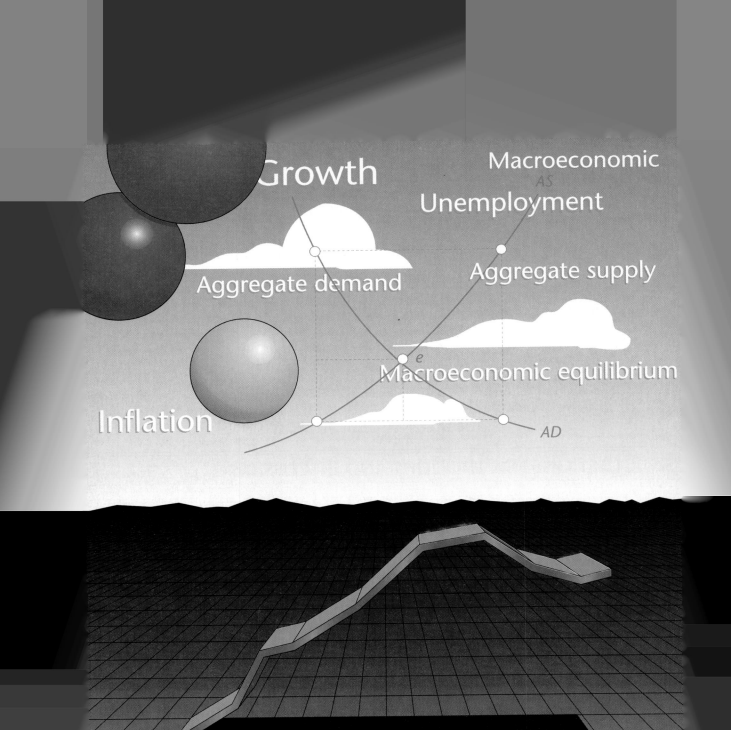

The Macroeconomic Environment

The ultimate macroeconomic goal is ensuring a prosperous stability so that people have opportunities for good jobs and secure standards of living. Thus, the central concern of macroeconomic theory is erratic growth of national income. An overview of business cycles (ups and downs in national income and output) and the tools used to measure economic fluctuations are the central themes of Part 2. Business cycles are sometimes isolated within a country, but more often, prosperity or stagnation is contagious internationally. Cornerstones for macroeconomic models and policies designed to achieve *high employment, price-level stability,* and *economic growth* include consistent measures of such aggregate variables as *Gross Domestic Product* and the *price level* (an index of average prices).

Chapter 5 provides a broad overview of the domain of macroeconomics, opening with a discussion of business cycles followed by a survey of theories developed by early economists to explain macroeconomics instability. Many insights from these early theories have been incorporated into modern views of business cycles. An Aggregate Demand–Aggregate Supply model is then introduced to describe historical swings in unemployment, inflation, and economic growth. The chapter concludes by interpreting the course of twentieth-century American business cycles through the lens of this powerful model.

How unemployment and inflation are measured is addressed in Chapters 6 and 7, respectively, where we also investigate weaknesses of current measurement techniques and lay the groundwork for understanding some root causes of unemployment and inflation and some possible cures.

Achieving prosperity requires policymakers to weigh trade-offs. For example, policies to curb inflation may temporarily push hordes of workers into unemployment lines, whereas attempts to boost employment can stimulate inflationary pressure. Economic growth tends to ease excessive unemployment or inflation. Tracing growth or stagnation in an economy requires measurements of National Income and Gross Domestic Product (*GDP*), which are our focus in Chapter 8.

The concepts presented in Part 2 should prepare you for the macroeconomic theory and policy in more advanced parts of this book. Every modern economy has suffered at times from inadequate growth, volatile price levels, and excessive unemployment. This international experience illustrates the ultimate challenge facing policymakers: maintaining stable rates of healthy economic growth.

Chapter 5

Foundations of Macroeconomics

Macroeconomic fluctuations are a recurring theme throughout history. In primitive societies, periods of famine alternated with periods of plenty. Booms and busts in modern economies periodically wipe out workers' jobs, push business firms into bankruptcy, and oust politicians from power. The survival of firms and the reelection of political incumbents are only a few of many things that depend strongly on the state of the economy. Your job prospects may shrivel if the economy is mired in a recession when you graduate; campus recruiting is one of the first items on most big firms' chopping blocks. And how much your wages will buy will depend on how much inflation the country experiences.

A grasp of macroeconomic theory will enable you to evaluate the benefits and costs of different policies intended to promote the central macroeconomic goals introduced in Chapter 1: (*a*) *high employment* (and thus low unemployment), (*b*) *price level stability* (keeping inflation in check), and (*c*) *economic growth*. The "Big Three" variables that signal macroeconomic performance—unemployment rates, the rate of infla-

tion, and the rate of economic growth—are traced in Figure 1 for both the United States and the European Community (EC) over the past two decades. As this figure illustrates, unemployment, inflation, and growth in both regions tend to move in tandem, evidence that the world economy is increasingly interdependent.

Figure 1 also illustrates that unemployment rates rose in the early 1980s in both economies, but excessive unemployment has lingered far longer in Europe. The U.S. economy has generated about 30 million new jobs since 1980, while Europe created fewer than 13 million. Sluggish economic growth in Europe has been blamed on a mix of problems ranging from militant labor unions to inefficient government bureaucracies, and from excessive monopoly in important industries to overly restrictive anti-inflationary policies.[1] Panel B indicates that inflation spurted internationally in the 1970s but had largely abated by the mid-1980s. Finally,

---

[1]John Cornwall's *The Theory of Economic Breakdown: An Institutional-Analytical Approach* (Cambridge, MA: Basil Blackwell, Ltd., 1990) provides an overview of these issues.

FIGURE 1   Unemployment, Inflation, and Economic Growth in the United States and the European Commuity (EC)—1969–1993

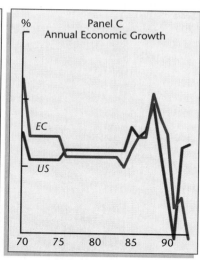

Source: *Economic Report of the President, 1994.*

Loosely parallel paths have been recorded recently in the United States and the European Community for the "Big Three" macroeconomic variables—unemployment, inflation, and economic growth. For example, unemployment rose in both economies during the early 1980s. High unemployment has, however, been more sustained in the EC in recent years.

Panel C shows that both the U.S. and EC economies continue to grow, but at erratic rates.

Modern macroeconomic theories have borrowed heavily from earlier theories intended to explain financial panics and cycles in agricultural and general business activity. This chapter begins with descriptions of business cycles and some of their consequences. Early business cycle theories, ranging from "external shock" theories to the Marxist approach, are surveyed to provide insights into some possible causes of macroeconomic instability. We then introduce an Aggregate Demand–Aggregate Supply model to interpret historic swings in unemployment, inflation, and economic growth.

This Aggregate Demand–Aggregate Supply framework is applied through the rest of our treatment of macroeconomics to interpret similarities and differences between modern classical and Keynesian macroeconomic theories. The foundations of Aggregate Demands and Supplies sketched in this chapter are elaborated more fully after interactions between individual behavior and macroeconomic activity have been explored in greater depth.

BUSINESS CYCLES

Unemployment rises when national output declines, while inflation climbs when productive capacity shrinks or pressure is exerted for output to exceed an economy's capacity.

*Periods of economic expansion and contraction alternate over a **business cycle**.*

Expansions seem to be lengthening, while contractions tend to be shorter than in earlier periods. Consequently, most economists are optimistic that an improved ability to measure and adapt to cyclic pressures may help us avoid the violent fluctuations of earlier times. Less traumatic disruptions, however, will undoubtedly continue to nag all societies.

• A Typical Business Cycle   The comparatively smooth business cycle extracted in Figure 2 shows how cycles are divisible into four subperiods: (*a*) the *peak* or *boom*, (*b*) a *recession* or *contraction* (*c*) a *depression* or *trough*, and (*d*) a *recovery* or *expansion*. The severity of a cycle is somewhat

FIGURE 2 Business Activity, 1880–1994

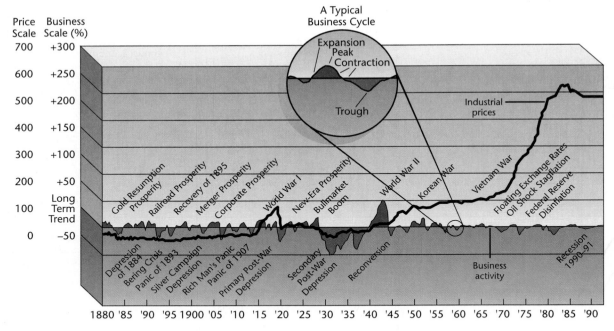

Source: *American Business Activity from 1790 to Today, 65th ed., AmeriTrust Co. (Cleveland), Jan., 1994.*

The business cycle is divided into four phases: the *peak* (boom), *contraction* (recession), *trough* (depression) and *expansion* (recovery). The intensity and timing of business cycles vary considerably, with expansions apparently lengthening in recent years while contractions seem to be growing shorter. (These data series "subtract" long-run trends.)

subjective,[2] but smooth fluctuations are rare. Expansions have lasted from as little as 10 months to as long as 108 months, while contractions have ranged from 7 months to 65 months in length. Notice that long contractions (e.g., 1929–1940) may be followed by short expansions (1940–1944), and vice versa (e.g., 1981–1983 and 1984–1990).

Turning Points in Business Cycles

Methodical analyses of business cycles began in 1920 with the founding of the National Bureau for Economic Research, a privately funded think tank. Tracing economic history is now a relatively systematic process, but forecasting remains an inexact science. Nevertheless, sophisticated models are used to simultaneously forecast every major sector of the economy.

---

[2]An old joke: "It's a recession when your neighbors lose their jobs, but when you lose your job, it's a depression."

Unemployment rates and the Dow Jones stock index are among the more than 5,000 data series now used to analyze and date U.S. business cycles. *Troughs* of the cycle occur when most measures of business activity indicate low points; *peaks* are dated when most data point to cyclic highs. These **turning points** are unofficial until the next peak or trough is passed. For example, the latest trough, tentatively dated November 1990, will not be official until the expansion that began in 1991 is at an end.

Social Aspects of the Business Cycle

Emphasizing the losses of output and income during economic downturns sometimes causes analysts to lose sight of social losses from recessions: waves of crime, illness, and breakdowns of family structures. Marriage and divorce are both positively related to economic swings. Many couples who face hard times delay marriage. Rates of illegitimate birth soar, and unhappy couples postpone divorce. Changes in marital status seem to be luxuries demanded primarily when income is secure. Would you be as prone to marry if your job seemed insecure? Would couples with young children be as apt to divorce during hard times?

Protracted downturns also trigger epidemics of stress-related diseases: heart attacks, alcoholism, mental illness, etc. Suicide rates were 60% to 70% above normal during the depths of the Great Depression, reflecting the gloom caused by forced idleness and sharp losses of income. One study indicates that roughly 260 more males aged 20 to 60 years commit suicide annually with each 1% hike in unemployment rates. Widespread unemployment also tends to fill prisons. Fraud, robberies, and other property crimes soar when legitimate income-earning opportunities shrink. Violence also becomes more widespread during recessions, while prosperity reduces most crime rates.

Policymakers feel pressure from voters to react to the repercussions of severe downturns. Social Security, unemployment compensation, and other relief systems were enacted in the 1930s to aid victims of the Great Depression. Recent recessions have tended to be shorter and milder, but the social maladies of business cycles have not evaporated.

BUSINESS CYCLE THEORIES

Accurately forecasting the next boom or bust provides strategic advantages to business firms and can be an easy path to personal riches. (Perhaps you thought fortunetellers were used only for romantic forecasts.) Even though scant and unreliable statistics limited early economists to impressionistic theorizing about swings in economic activity, their thoughts provide important and lasting insights into the nature of macroeconomic fluctuations.

External Shock Theories

Many early business cycle theories focused on such external shocks as wars or weather.

External shocks are economic disturbances that originate outside an economy.

External shocks remain potent disrupters of an economy. For example, shocks from soaring oil prices severely weakened the economies of most oil-importing nations in the 1970s.

And then there is the shock of war. Some sectors of an economy may flourish (e.g., weapons manufacturing), but conflict wreaks havoc on both victorious and vanquished nations. Wars divert output away from capital investment and destroy equipment (e.g., factories), infrastructure (e.g., bridges and roads), and labor (e.g., soldiers). Today, agriculture dominates few economies, but weather cycles—another external shock—are still studied to help predict the effects of erratic crop yields. For example, in 1993, record floods in parts of the U.S. farm belt and severe drought in other areas drove up food prices internationally. Unless crop failures are global, however, countries are now buffered somewhat by increased ability to import from regions blessed by bumper crops.

The *sunspot theory* is an exotic external shock theory developed in 1875 by W. Stanley Jevons, a pioneering mathematical economist. Jevons reasoned that sunspots (nuclear storms on the sun's surface) affect weather and, hence, agriculture. Although Jevons' theory has been discredited (along with reading tea leaves or the entrails of goats), new sunspot theories may develop if we ever depend heavily on solar energy.

Population Dynamics Theories

Early economists often pondered the long-term effects of such events as wars or the opening of new territory. Thomas Malthus (1766–1834) popularized a *population dynamics* approach, which concludes that bare subsistence is all that people can ultimately expect. A theory from biology illustrates why these early forecasts were pessimistic.

• Subsistence and Population S-Curves
Suppose that at time = *0* in Figure 3, a few rabbits are set loose in a new territory (as in Australia

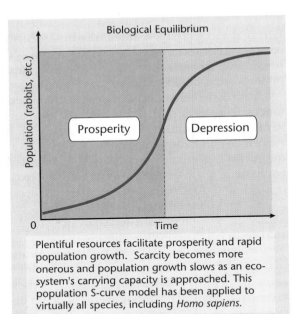

FIGURE 3   An S-Curve for a Rabbit Population

Biological Equilibrium

Population (rabbits, etc.)

Prosperity

Depression

0   Time

Plentiful resources facilitate prosperity and rapid population growth. Scarcity becomes more onerous and population growth slows as an ecosystem's carrying capacity is approached. This population S-curve model has been applied to virtually all species, including *Homo sapiens*.

at the beginning of European colonization). With ample space and food, rabbits prosper and their population growth accelerates. Competition for food and territory mounts, however, when rabbits reproduce excessively (as they will). Malnutrition and a parallel population explosion of predators (packs of wild dingo dogs) eventually depresses the rabbits' population growth. Survival of the fittest means rabbits that fail to secure territory starve. An equilibrium population entails shorter lifespans. This sequence is called a *population S-curve*.

Malthus used a similar model to describe the growth of human populations. He viewed our procreative urges as constant, but argued that birth rates depend primarily on maternal health. Favorable events trigger population explosions because birth rates rise while death rates fall. But population pressures against available resources eventually stifle economic activity, leaving only plagues, famine, or war to impede population growth. Booms and then busts, according to this line of reasoning, should alternate across generations.

Early fans of Malthus's model failed to anticipate technological advances and generally opposed birth control programs. Their speculations now apply more to primitive economies than to modern industrial giants. To this day, however, modernization in less developed countries is often offset by population growth that constrains standards of living to subsistence levels for the majority of the population; starvation is the ultimate population check in Malthus's theory. Small wonder that the historian Thomas Carlyle, a contemporary of Malthus, characterized economics as "the dismal science."

Marxian Capitalistic Crises

Contrary to popular stereotypes, Karl Marx was in awe of economic progress under the market system. In *The Communist Manifesto* (1848), he marveled that capitalism

> *has created more massive and more colossal forces than have all preceding generations together. . . . It has accomplished wonders far surpassing Egyptian pyramids, Roman aqueducts, and Gothic cathedrals; it has conducted expeditions that put in the shade all former migrations of nations and crusades.*

Nevertheless, Marx condemned markets as permitting the rich and powerful to exploit workers.[3] Describing his views as "scientific socialism," he predicted that capitalism would spasmodically expand and then contract, with each peak higher than its predecessor and each successive crash deeper than the last.

Marxists view business cycles as driven by increasing concentrations of wealth in the hands of capitalists. *Underconsumption* is inevitable when, because rapid investment and growth distribute income inequitably, workers lack income to buy all the goods they produce. Glutted markets then plunge capitalism into depressions or imperialistic wars. An upswing emerges when new markets open, new raw materials are discovered, or a successful war yields plunder for capitalists to exploit. This plants the seeds for the next downswing, and so on. Finally, the

[3]An old Soviet joke: "Under capitalism, man exploits man. Under socialism, it's vice versa."

working class overthrows its exploiters, the spark of a revolution igniting during the abyss of a deep depression.

Marx's ideas inspired generations of radical critics of capitalism, and he provided a number of predictions about the course of history. Most have proven wrong. The recent collapse of most communist governments and their replacement by market-oriented systems, for example, is absolutely contrary to Marx's predictions.

Long Waves and Innovations

The resurgence of entrepreneurial instincts in former Eastern bloc nations might also have surprised Joseph Schumpeter, whose writings celebrated the creative vigor of capitalism. In 1911, he proposed a long-wave theory of business cycles in which development is fueled when entrepreneurs initiate such *innovations* as (*a*) discoveries of raw materials, (*b*) new goods or new quality in familiar products, (*c*) technological advances, (*d*) the opening of new markets, or (*e*) major reorganizations of industries.

Major innovations generate *spinoffs*, which are related inventions, mimicries of an original innovation, or the births of new industries. Such advances as microelectronics, Teflon, and laser surgery, for example, were spinoffs of the space program. Economic growth peaks by the time society fully adapts to a major innovation; saturated markets cannot absorb further supply increases or emulation of the new technology. When firms retrench, the economy slumps while awaiting fresh innovations. The next long-wave process is sparked (but only after a delay) by a new wave of innovation. Of course, minor innovations might explain shorter cycles.

Schumpeter identified certain institutional features in a society as essential for innovation and economic vitality. First, entrepreneurs must have broad discretion about how to operate. Second, well-developed financial markets must channel credit to entrepreneurs, allowing investment in new capital and R&D even before they actually contribute anything to national income.

Schumpeter used railroads to illustrate major innovations.[4] Cars, planes, and advances in agriculture have also driven U.S. economic development. More recently, computers have enabled some firms to grow to sizes that were impossible when information processing was primitive, and microprocessors have thrust an array of new consumer goods (e.g., garage door openers, electronic toys, and microwave ovens) into the realm of necessities for many Americans. Perhaps the most underrated innovation of the past century is the supermarket, which reduces transaction costs for an incredible variety of goods. Supermarkets provide outlets for specialized firms that would have been denied shelf space in old-fashioned general stores.

In the past few decades, economically less developed areas such as Japan, Taiwan, Hong Kong, South Korea, Malaysia, Mexico, and, most recently, China and India, have experienced dramatic growth, largely through the implementation of market incentives.[5] Schumpeter would not have been surprised by the progress made possible by competition among ambitious entrepreneurs. One major prediction extended beyond even Schumpeter's own long-wave theory (30 to 60 years). It seems strange, but Schumpeter, a devotee of capitalism, was almost as convinced as Marx that capitalism might ultimately self-destruct. However, he hypothesized a very different mechanism.

Schumpeter thought that prosperity created by capitalism (and not, as Marx thought, a capitalist depression) would ultimately create irresistible pressure for redistribution of income from the haves to the have-nots. This, in turn,

---

[4]"Expenditures on, and the opening of, a new line has some immediate effects on business in general, on competing means of transport, and on the relative position of centers of production. It requires more time to bring into use the opportunities of production newly created by the railroad and to annihilate others. And it takes still longer for population to shift, cities to decay, and, generally, the new face of the country to take a shape that is adapted to the environment as altered by railroadization." J. A. Schumpeter, *Business Cycles: A Theoretical, Historical, and Statistical Analysis of the Capitalist Process* (New York: McGraw-Hill, 1939).

[5]See J. McMillan and B. Naughton, "How to Reform a Planned Economy: Lessons from China," *Oxford Review of Economic Policy* 8, no. 1 (1992): 130–143.

Joseph A. Schumpeter: "Creative Destruction" and Growth

Renowned as a master of economics, mathematics, statistics, history, and philosophy, Joseph Schumpeter (1883–1950) was both a scholar and an active participant in world affairs. At one time or another he was lawyer, banker, and public official, serving a stint as finance minister in his native Austria. Two books, *Economic Development* and *Capitalism, Socialism, and Democracy*, both published before he reached 30, are still highly regarded. In 1932, he accepted a chair in economics at Harvard, where he taught until his death 18 years later.

Schumpeter's writings span the entire economic process: equilibrium, business cycles, and the sur-vival prospects of capitalism. He viewed competition as a process of discovery and as an ordering force. Somewhat paradoxically, he viewed business cycles as vital to economic progress. Cycles occur because equilibrium is destroyed by entrepreneurial innovations, but innovation is an engine for social progress, so this type of destruction is "creative."

Schumpeter distinguished three types of business cycles, naming them for earlier pioneers in business cycle theory. The length of each depends on the disturbance that causes it. The shortest (*Kitchin*) cycle derives from inventory changes and usually lasts about 3 years. An intermediate (*Juglar*) cycle depends on relatively minor innovations, such as radar or electronic calculators, and runs its course in 8 to 11 years. The long (*Kondratieff*) cycle lasts 40 to 60 years and is caused by sweeping innovations such as electrification or jet flight.

Schumpeter's writings failed to attract an active school of disciples. However, the modern Austrian school of thought draws from many of Schumpeter's insights. Modern theories of how a backward economy can shift to a path of dynamic growth also increasingly rely on his insights into capitalism and entrepreneurship.

would diminish entrepreneurial incentives, draining capitalism's creative vigor. Thus, in essence, his most sweeping forecast was that capitalism would fall victim to its own success. Many modern economists who share Schumpeter's enthusiasm for entrepreneurs as innovative heroes also see governmental growth in developed countries as an omen that Schumpeter's worst fears are being realized.

Psychological Theories

Predictions of collapse or expectations of prosperity can be self-fulfilling. **Psychological theories** of cycles focus on how human herd instincts make prolonged optimism or pessimism contagious. These theories help explain the momentum of swings initiated by such external shocks as wars and natural disasters, or by changes in the expected profitability of investment or in the availability of natural resources.

When a real disturbance occurs in the form, say, of some external shock (e.g., a hike in energy costs), decision-makers' reactions set off secondary shock waves, the psychological part of a cycle. Information is costly, so decisions often rely on educated guesses (much as you sometimes answer multiple-choice questions). Most business managers operate from the same forecasts and information bases, which include government and market research data; thus it is not surprising that firms often move in the same directions.

Business cycles unfold when firms adapt their plans to similar expectations. Once set off, waves of pessimism or optimism seem to have lives of their own. For example, pessimistic firms might slash output, lay off workers, and postpone investments. If workers then curb their own spending, firms with shrinking sales lay off even more workers. Thus, expectations of economic collapse may be self-fulfilling. (With psychology involved, is there any wonder at the term "depression"?)

A wave of optimism operates in the opposite direction. Recoveries commence when firms begin expanding output. More labor is hired, bolstering household optimism and spending, creating more employment, and so on. Psychological theories help explain inertia in a recovery or downturn, but cannot predict turning points in business cycles.

The emphasis on shared expectations from psychological theories has become central to modern business cycle theories. But how are expectations formed? One possibility is that investors and other interest groups often closely monitor government policies for signs about future events. For example, some analysts have nightmares that policy errors from the 1930s will be repeated. This group blames the Great Depression on a trade war set off by the Smoot-Hawley Tariff of 1930. In their view, the 1929 stock market crash was precipitated when it became apparent that Smoot-Hawley, the highest set of U.S. tariffs ever, would be enacted.[6] Expectations that international trade would break down in the 1930s triggered a worldwide depression that began in 1929. This group views sentiment for governmental protection against international trade as a threat that could collapse economies everywhere.

Classical Macroeconomic Theory

The preceding theories provide important insights into economic fluctuations, but most modern economists now focus on two general theories that compete in explaining broad cyclic activity: classical theory and Keynesian theory. Classical economics was not the creation of a single mind. Instead, it melds the thoughts of mainstream economists dating back to Adam Smith.

---

[6]"The Trade Bill Fluffs Its Feathers," *The Economist*, 19 March 1988, pp. 21–22.

Classical macroeconomic theory stresses coping with scarcity from the supply side as the key to macroeconomic vitality and supports (a) market solutions to problems and (b) laissez-faire (minimal) government policies.

Classical economics relies heavily on the self-correcting power of automatic market adjustments (Smith's "invisible hand") to cure macroeconomic instability, including excessive unemployment. Recessions create pressures for wages and prices to fall, which in turn, leads to growth of sales and expanding demands for labor. Opposite adjustments help prevent a rapid boom from overheating the economy.

Keynesian Theory

Persistent high unemployment during the Great Depression of the 1930s clashed with classical predictions. Might decades pass before an economy self-corrected? Or was classical reasoning flawed? John Maynard Keynes (1883–1946), the most influential economist of this century, concluded that capitalism might neither automatically nor quickly recover from a depression.

Keynesian theory views inadequate demand as the cause of cyclic downturns and recommends actively adjusting government policies to combat instability.

The demand-oriented model in Keynes's *The General Theory of Employment, Interest, and Money* (1936) dominated macroeconomics from the 1940s through the 1960s, but classical theory bounced back when Keynesian policies failed to cure the economic stagnation of the 1970s.

Some modern economists still stress demand-oriented Keynesian analysis; others view the supply-side orientation of new classical macroeconomics as the major recent advance in economic knowledge. However, most economists of either persuasion now recognize that an appropriate mix of both market forces and government policies is a key to economic stability. Disagreements abound, however, about what constitutes an appropriate mix.

Economists inspired by classical reasoning would rely primarily on market forces, with changes in government policies being used only as a last resort to cure an economy in tumult. On the other hand, economists who follow in the footsteps of Keynes tend to advocate activist government policies, with less reliance on market forces. Virtually all economists agree, however, that Aggregate Supply and Aggregate Demand are both important in explaining the course of economic growth, unemployment, and inflation.

AGGREGATE DEMAND AND AGGREGATE SUPPLY

Demand and supply analysis describes not only movements in the prices and quantities of individual goods, but also trends in such broad macroeconomic aggregates as national income and the price level (using an index that averages changes in nominal prices relative to a specified base year). Aggregate Demand and Aggregate Supply curves are useful in tracing business cycles and describing the broad effects of changes in macroeconomic policies. The Aggregate Demand–Aggregate Supply framework developed next also helps highlight both areas of agreement and some critical differences among major modern macroeconomic theories, which are explored in more depth in the remainder of this book.

AGGREGATE DEMAND CURVES

Aggregate Demand for national output is underpinned by the purchases of four groups of ultimate buyers: (a) consumers, (b) investors, (c) government, and (d) foreigners. Their spending plans are interdependent,[7] and are combined in an Aggregate Demand curve. The amount of national output each group buys depends, in part, on the price level.

*An **Aggregate Demand curve** depicts a negative relationship between the price level and purchases of national output.*

If the price level rises, purchases of our national output fall, and vice versa.

Foundations for the negative slopes of Aggregate Demand curves are variations on the substitution and income effects used to justify negative slopes of individual demands in Chapter 3. The Aggregate Demand curve is negatively sloped because of (a) the *wealth effect*, (b) the *foreign-sector substitution effect*, and (c) the *interest rate effect*. The negatively sloped Aggregate Demand curve in Figure 4 is based on these effects.

• **The Wealth Effect** Will your money buy as much if prices soar? Of course not. A higher price level reduces the purchasing power of financial wealth. Assets such as stocks, bonds,

The Aggregate Demand curve slopes negatively because a rise in the price level generates (a) *wealth effects*, (b) *foreign sector substitution effects*, and (c) *interest rate effects* that result in a lower level of domestic output sold.

FIGURE 4 The Slope of the Aggregate Demand Curve

---

[7]Consumption, for example, depends on national income, which in turn depends on all sources of demand. These sorts of interdependencies (detailed in later chapters) preclude the type of horizontal summation used to calculate, for example, the market demand for a good.

cash, and checking account balances are worth less, which shrinks the amounts you can buy.[8] Thus, higher average prices reduce the amount of domestic production sold along an Aggregate Demand curve.

- **The Foreign-Sector Substitution Effect** Might buyers tend to switch from Buicks to Saabs if prices of American cars rose relative to those for imports? Of course. Higher U.S. prices cause domestic consumers to buy more imports and fewer American goods. Foreign buyers respond similarly, shrinking U.S. exports.

Investment is affected in a similar fashion. Hikes in the price level drive up domestic production costs. If you headed a firm considering a new manufacturing facility, you would be more likely to build it in Mexico if U.S. prices and costs rose. Thus, a higher price level shrinks investment in this country because both foreign and U.S. firms would find it relatively more profitable to invest abroad. In sum, trends toward imports and foreign investments reinforce the wealth effect in making Aggregate Demand curves negatively sloped.[9]

- **The Interest Rate Effect** The amount of borrowing required to finance a major purchase rises if the price level rises. For example, you might need to borrow more to finance your education if tuition costs were to rise. Thus, a higher price level increases the demand for loanable funds and, consequently, increases the interest rate, which is the cost of credit. This increase in interest rates reduces investment and such consumer purchases as new homes, cars, or appliances. Figure 5 summarizes how these effects cause movements along Aggregate Demand curves as the price level changes.

SHIFTS OF AGGREGATE DEMAND CURVES

Now that you have seen why the Aggregate Demand curve slopes downward, we need to explore why these curves shift. National income (output) is a major determinant of market demands for specific goods, but, in conjunction with the price level, it only identifies a specific point on an Aggregate Demand curve.[10] Thus, the horizontal axis measures both national income and output. Changes in national income and the price level reflect movements along the Aggregate Demand curve; they do not cause it to shift. Aggregate Demand curves shift when planned spending changes for consumption (C), investment (I), government (G), or net exports to foreigners ($X - M$, or exports minus imports).

Consumer Spending (C)

Customary living standards and buying habits help shape consumption spending, which represents about two-thirds of Aggregate Demand. Planned **consumption** is also influenced by (*a*) disposable income, (*b*) wealth, (*c*) average size and ages of households, (*d*) stocks of consumer goods on hand and household balance sheets, and (*e*) consumer expectations about future prices, incomes, and availability of goods.

- **Disposable Income** People are often upset by how sharply withholding taxes shrink their take-home pay below their stated salaries. Your disposable income is the amount available to spend after subtracting federal and state taxes and then adding any transfer payments (such incomes received, but not earned, as unemployment compensation or Social Security). On balance, these adjustments shrink aggregate disposable income to less than national income.

---

[8]Note that this wealth effect resembles the income effect discussed in Chapter 3 as a minor reason for the negative slope of a market demand curve.

[9]Foreign sector substitution resembles the substitution effect introduced in Chapter 3.

[10]The accounting differences between national output and income described later in this part of the book can be ignored for simplicity in this simple Aggregate Demand–Aggregate Supply model.

FIGURE 5   The Effects of Price Changes Along Aggregate Demand Curves

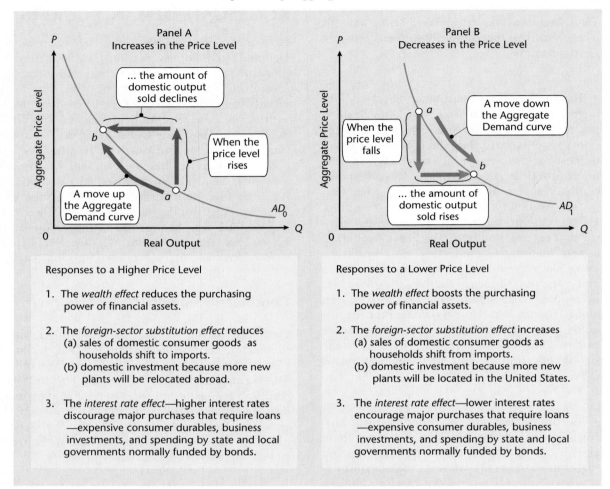

Responses to a Higher Price Level

1. The *wealth effect* reduces the purchasing power of financial assets.

2. The *foreign-sector substitution effect* reduces
   (a) sales of domestic consumer goods as households shift to imports.
   (b) domestic investment because more new plants will be relocated abroad.

3. The *interest rate effect*—higher interest rates discourage major purchases that require loans —expensive consumer durables, business investments, and spending by state and local governments normally funded by bonds.

Responses to a Lower Price Level

1. The *wealth effect* boosts the purchasing power of financial assets.

2. The *foreign-sector substitution effect* increases
   (a) sales of domestic consumer goods as households shift from imports.
   (b) domestic investment because more new plants will be located in the United States.

3. The *interest rate effect*—lower interest rates encourage major purchases that require loans —expensive consumer durables, business investments, and spending by state and local governments normally funded by bonds.

Keynesian theory (detailed in the next part of this book) emphasizes disposable income as the driving force behind consumer spending. Increases in disposable income stimulate saving somewhat, but most of it will be spent. Thus, changing relationships between national income and disposable income (e.g., new taxes or transfer payments) alter consumers' spending plans and shift Aggregate Demand.

• **Wealth or Expected Income**   Is a new car purchase more likely for a senior accounting major at your college, or one majoring in philosophy? Expected higher income after graduation makes the accountant the more probable buyer.

Now consider relative spending by a retired tycoon and a retired postal employee. Even a tycoon suffering huge stock market losses this year is likely to spend significantly more. The point is that wealthy people or those who expect higher incomes typically spend more than poorer people with identical current incomes. Similarly, people who fear losing their jobs tend to decrease their consumption. When expectations change, the Aggregate Demand curve shifts.

• **Household Size and Ages**   Big families spend proportionally more from income than small families. Young families busily acquire durables (e.g., cars and appliances), while established families tend to replace only worn-out durables. Thus, societies full of young or large families consume proportionally more from a given current income than societies composed of older or smaller families. Thus, as an economy's demographics shift, so does Aggregate Demand.

• **Household Balance Sheets** A household's assets include such things as its productive resources, durable goods, and financial wealth; its debts are liabilities. Most families that are deeply in debt try to postpone spending to reduce their indebtedness. Financially secure families typically spend proportionally more from current income. Thus, shrinking debt stimulates consumption. Families may also spend more if more money becomes available.[11]

• **Consumer Expectations** Consumer debt usually climbs when buyers stockpile goods to guard against inflation, but shaky confidence may reduce use of credit. If soaring prices for housing convince many young couples that they will never afford homes if they wait, panic buying pushes up housing prices even faster. When people expect widespread shortages, they hoard almost anything that can be stored. Outputs for consumers were limited during World War II, and shortages were rampant. Most consumers had long wish lists and went on spending binges at the war's end. Opposite trends occur if people have recently been on buying sprees: large household stocks of new durable goods diminish the need to purchase more.

Investment (*I*)

Economic investment enhances future consumption. (Remember that financial investments are merely specialized forms of saving.) Circular flow models identify firms as channels that convert household saving into investment, which falls into three basic categories: (*a*) new buildings and all other construction, (*b*) new equipment, and (*c*) inventory accumulation.

All **investment** is cyclically sensitive, but inventories are especially volatile. Erratic customer purchases allow firms only partial control over their inventories. Firms unintentionally invest in new inventories if sales are unexpectedly low, but inventories dwindle and unintentional disinvestment occurs if sales exceed forecasts. Unexpected inventory changes signal firms to adjust their hiring of resources and their orders to suppliers.

• **Expected Rates of Return** Planned investment spending depends powerfully on expected rates of return. Firms invest only if the new capital's revenue stream is expected to exceed all costs.

*A **rate of return** is the annual percentage earned from an investment after all costs are considered.*[12]

Rates of return, the level of investment, and Aggregate Demand are positively related to the net revenues expected from investment across time. Investors (and most other people) prefer more income to less and lower costs to higher costs. And, because time is valuable, they prefer current income to delayed income and try to postpone costs wherever possible. (Would you prefer an extra $1,000 now or a year from now? Would you rather pay $1,000 to the Internal Revenue Service now or ten years from now?) Another major influence on rates of return and investment is risk, which, all else being equal, investors try to avoid. Therefore, rates of return rise when expected revenues are greater, are expected sooner, or appear more certain, or when expected costs (including taxes) fall, are postponed, or involve less risk.

Investment is stimulated when technological advances are innovated. Innovations yielding high rates of return tend to arrive erratically and in waves. Consequently, investments to implement technological advances tend to be clustered over time.

---

[11]How a central bank regulates a nation's money supply is addressed a few chapters hence.

[12]The math for computing rates of return parallels that used for compounding interest rates.

- **Costs of Investment** Expected returns rise when capital prices fall and shrink when construction or machinery costs rise. Upswings stimulate demands for such capital as lathes or computers, boosting capital prices and inhibiting surges in investment. Conversely, investor pessimism during downturns reduces orders for new capital goods. Capital suppliers then cut prices for new equipment to liquidate their excess inventories, slightly dampening drops in investment.

Interest, however, is the major cost of investment. Investors' opportunity costs rise when interest rates rise; investors with ample funds might make loans instead of buying investment goods, and higher interest rates make investment less attractive for potential investors who must borrow. Taxes on investment income are another consideration. For example, higher corporate taxes shrink after-tax rates of return. Investment tax credits, on the other hand, boost rates of return and, consequently, demands for investment goods. Higher expected rates of return bolster both investment and Aggregate Demand, but investor pessimism shrinks both investment and Aggregate Demand (shifts it leftward).

Government (G)

Expectations about government policies also affect investment. For example, firms that rely on exports or imports might cancel new capital orders if restrictions on foreign trade were expected. Defense contractors invest heavily when war clouds loom and cut back investment with the advent of peace. But government affects Aggregate Demand most directly through its spending and its tax policies.

- **Government Purchases** Government purchases such as highways or education resemble private investment by generating benefits over time. Other purchases immediately exhaust resources and resemble private consumption (e.g., police protection and Medicare). Both consumption and investment types of government purchases directly increase Aggregate Demand. Some government outlays, however, do not entail direct spending. For example, cash transfer payments are only translated into Aggregate Demand when the recipients spend these funds on consumer goods. Thus, these government outlays are not lumped into government purchases.

The percentage of output absorbed by government purchases rose substantially but erratically over this nation's first two centuries, growing most rapidly during wars. The Civil War, World Wars I and II, the Korean conflict, and the Vietnam War were peaks for government demands. Government purchases tend to shrink when a war ends, but rarely to earlier levels. One possible reason for upward trends in government spending is that rising standards of living may make voters willing to devote ever larger shares of income to such publicly provided goods as education or parks.

- **Tax Rates** Consumption depends on disposable income, investment depends on after-tax rates of return, and how much (and what) we import depends on tariffs and import quotas, while how competitively we can produce goods for export depends, in part, on the burdens of taxation. Thus, higher tax rates generally decrease Aggregate Demand.

- **Money** When people have more money, they tend to spend it. A larger money supply, all else being equal, allows a greater supply of loanable funds, so interest rates will be lower. Lower interest rates stimulate borrowing and spending by both consumers and investors. The central bank of the United States is the Federal Reserve System. How this arm of government regulates the supply of money is detailed later in this book.

The Foreign Sector (X-M)

Exports (X) reflect foreign demands for U.S. goods. Thus, they increase Aggregate Demand.

Imports (*M*) are goods produced by foreigners but used by American consumers, investors, or government. In fact, the accounting categories of consumption, investment, and government spending include many goods produced abroad. These imports augment Aggregate Supply but may reduce Aggregate Demand for domestic production because imports sometimes replace purchases of domestic output. This is one reason declining industries vigorously lobby for protection from foreign competition. For example, the auto, clothing, and steel industries have advocated tariffs and quotas for decades; computer makers have recently voiced similar pleas.

It is conventional to look only at net effects of the foreign sector on Aggregate Demand. National income undoubtedly influences U.S. imports. Domestic prosperity inspires imports of Mercedes-Benz cars, French champagne, and Nikon cameras, and our vacations and booming industrial output require more foreign oil. But U.S. exports depend primarily on economic conditions abroad, which may be in the doldrums even if the U.S. economy is prosperous.

Economic interdependence is, however, accurately characterized by the saying "When America sneezes, the rest of the world catches a cold." Although foreign trade is vital for economic vitality, the foreign sector's net effect on Aggregate Demand in the United States is relatively small. Exports and imports each average around 10% of our national income, so **net exports (*X* – *M*)** are usually only a negligible percentage of Aggregate Spending.

Review how all these influences shift the Aggregate Demand curves in Figure 6 before reading our overview of Aggregate Supply.

AGGREGATE SUPPLY

Just as the negative slopes of Aggregate Demand curves resemble those of market demands, the positive slopes of Aggregate Supply curves mirror those of market supplies.

> The **Aggregate Supply curve** reflects a positive relationship between the price level and the real quantity of national output.

The foundations of Aggregate Supply curves have some parallels in the foundations of market supply curves, but there are also some major differences.

Slope of the Aggregate Supply Curve

The general law of diminishing returns partially accounts for the upward slope of supply curves for individual firms and for market supply curves. Additional production eventually becomes ever more costly as output levels grow. Thus, firms may require higher prices to justify expanding their outputs. Moreover, higher prices embody greater incentives for firms to produce more output because profit opportunities are enhanced. A similar logic applies for the economy as a whole.

• **Capacity and Price–Cost Dynamics** The positive slope of the Aggregate Supply curve in Figure 7 reflects the fact that prices adjust more rapidly than production costs; costs are relatively more "sticky." When the price level rises, delayed hikes in costs yield profit incentives to expand production.

Idle resources become less available when higher employment presses against a society's productive capacity. The prices a firm can charge in a growing economy tend to rise faster than its resource costs. Thus, profit per unit of output grows during a business upturn. Firms naturally respond by producing and selling more goods. But prices tend to fall faster than costs when business activity slows down, and profit per unit of output may even become negative. Firms facing declining profit margins may drastically cut back production and lay off workers to cut their costs.

For example, an increase in the demand for food at your local supermarket would cause movement along its supply curve. The manager will order more goods and quickly mark up prices. Grocers will also hire more workers. Employees' wages and other costs will rise, but much less rapidly than prices, so total profits will swell. What happens if this demand collapses?

FIGURE 6   Shifts of Aggregate Demand Curves

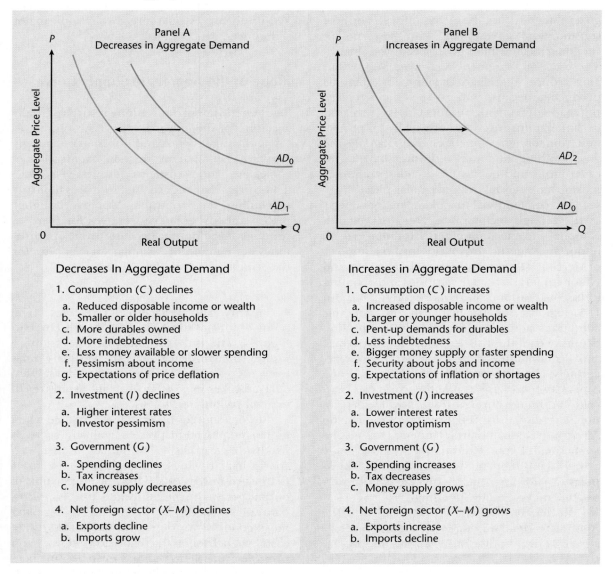

Panel A
Decreases in Aggregate Demand

P — Aggregate Price Level
Q — Real Output

AD_0
AD_1

Panel B
Increases in Aggregate Demand

P — Aggregate Price Level
Q — Real Output

AD_2
AD_0

Decreases In Aggregate Demand

1. Consumption (C) declines

    a. Reduced disposable income or wealth
    b. Smaller or older households
    c. More durables owned
    d. More indebtedness
    e. Less money available or slower spending
    f. Pessimism about income
    g. Expectations of price deflation

2. Investment (I) declines

    a. Higher interest rates
    b. Investor pessimism

3. Government (G)

    a. Spending declines
    b. Tax increases
    c. Money supply decreases

4. Net foreign sector (X–M) declines

    a. Exports decline
    b. Imports grow

Increases in Aggregate Demand

1. Consumption (C) increases

    a. Increased disposable income or wealth
    b. Larger or younger households
    c. Pent-up demands for durables
    d. Less indebtedness
    e. Bigger money supply or faster spending
    f. Security about jobs and income
    g. Expectations of inflation or shortages

2. Investment (I) increases

    a. Lower interest rates
    b. Investor optimism

3. Government (G)

    a. Spending increases
    b. Tax decreases
    c. Money supply grows

4. Net foreign sector (X–M) grows

    a. Exports increase
    b. Imports decline

The prices the grocer charges will fall much faster than wages or other production costs. Profits plummet, so grocery workers will lose their jobs.

Conclusion? Production costs per unit are much slower to adjust to changes in Aggregate Demand than are the prices of output. This is the major reason why a society's Aggregate Supply is positively sloped in the short run, as shown in Figure 7.

• **National Output and the Work Force**
National output expands when more workers become employed, but because of diminishing returns, beyond some point, extra workers decreasingly add to total output. Labor markets are based on supply and demand, much like markets for goods. Higher wages may induce greater effort or attract more people into the labor force, or the unemployed may find acceptable positions after shorter periods of job-

FIGURE 7   The Slope of Aggregate Supply Curves

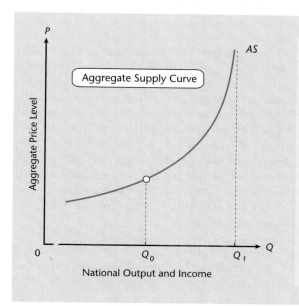

Aggregate Supply Curve

The Aggregate Supply curve is a positive relationship between aggregate real output and the price level in the short run. When the economy has substantial slack and unemployment is high ($Q_0 < Q_f$), output can be increased without substantial increases in prices. As the economy approaches full employment (Q_f), all prices and costs adjust rapidly and completely and the Aggregate Supply curve becomes vertical. This capacity level of output can be exceeded in the short run, but only through force (e.g., slavery) or by fooling workers (e.g., by paying wages that lack the purchasing power workers expected). The prices of outputs tend to adjust faster than production costs when economic conditions change. Thus, profit per unit rises during expansions, or falls during contractions. Aggregate Supply is positively sloped in the short run because firms hire more (or fewer) workers to produce more (or less) output when profit per unit rises (or falls) during an expansion (or contraction).

lessness. Thus, unless the economy is extremely slack, supply curves for labor have a positive slope.

When aggregate output is low and unemployment is high (output below Q_f in Figure 7), economic slack allows most firms to expand output without incurring higher average costs; upward pressure on prices is minimal. As the economy approaches its capacity (Q_f), additional output becomes increasingly costly, pushing prices up sharply. Classical theory relies on market forces to automatically drive an economy to full employment. Output levels ultimately depend on resources and technology, not on the price level per se. Thus, classical economics predicts a vertical long-run Aggregate Supply curve. Keynesian theory, on the other hand, deals best with depressed economies plagued by so many idle resources that the short-run Aggregate Supply curve is horizontal. Consequently, the Aggregate Supply curve is positively sloped when the economy operates between the extremes of classical full employment and a severe Keynesian depression, as shown in Figure 7.

In summary, rising employment and output levels generate pressure for hikes in wages and prices, while falling employment and output create pressure for wage and price cuts. (How the short-run and long-run adjustments differ will be explored more thoroughly after we have surveyed classical and Keynesian macroeconomics in more depth.)

Shifts in Aggregate Supply

Aggregate Supply is determined by how technology is used to combine the available quantities and qualities of labor, land, capital, and entrepreneurship, ultimately determining productive capacity and costs. Our discussion of shifts of Aggregate Supply curves opens with a quick review of the influences on market supply curves detailed in Chapter 3. In addition to price, the major determinants are (*a*) resource costs, (*b*) production technology; (*c*) expectations, (*d*) taxes or subsidies or regulations on producers, (*e*) the prices of other producible goods, and (*f*) the number of producers in the market.

Changes in influences other than its own price cause a good's market supply to shift. An Aggregate Supply curve, however, encompasses all outputs, all producers, and an average of all domestic prices (the price level). Thus, because substitutions between various domestic outputs tend to be offsetting, we will ignore changes in the prices of other producible goods. We are left with (a) the costs and availability of resources, (b) technology, (c) expectations, and (d) government policies as the four major shifters of the Aggregate Supply curve.

• **Resource Costs** Production absorbs resources, so any shock boosting resource costs reduces Aggregate Supply. As resource costs (e.g., wages for labor) climb, Aggregate Supply falls (shifts leftward), and vice versa. Labor supplies depend on how individuals balance income from work against their enjoyment of leisure. Today, people increasingly opt for more leisure through shorter workweeks, part-time employment, or other forms of work sharing. Growing preferences for leisure over work cause leftward shifts of labor supply curves. This shifts Aggregate Supply leftward, as shown in Panel A of Figure 8 by the shift from AS_0 to AS_1. Alternatively, if more people chose to work or began working longer hours, Aggregate Supply might shift from AS_0 to AS_2 in Panel B. Another type of labor market disturbance would occur if the power of unions grew and organized labor negotiated higher wages: Aggregate Supply would shrink.

Other resource costs are also important. Most oil-importing countries endured painful leftward shifts in their Aggregate Supply curves during 1973–1975 after OPEC quadrupled oil prices. Rightward shifts occur when new resources are discovered and push prices down. Discoveries of huge pools of oil in Mexico, Alaska, and the North Sea eventually created a world oil glut that drove prices down in the 1980s, boosting Aggregate Supply to the right.

Some costs may rise artificially if economic power becomes more concentrated. Aggregate Supply shrinks when firms that gain market power cut output to extract higher prices and profits. Alternatively, Aggregate Supply grows if competition intensifies because of (a) external firms' quests for shares of monopolists' profits,

(b) vigorous antitrust actions, or (c) the invasion of a market by imports.

• **Technology** Technological advances shift Aggregate Supply curves rightward. Microchips spun off from the space program, for example, enhanced Aggregate Supplies internationally, in part because robots do boring or repetitive tasks with less physical and mental burnout than most humans suffer. Sophisticated but cheap microcomputers have automated office work, permitting firms to grow to sizes once thought hopelessly inefficient. Such innovations permit a society to produce more from existing resources and talent.

• **Expectations** Changing expectations about inflation or future prosperity acutely affect Aggregate Supply. For example, investors' willingness to buy new machinery or to plan new construction depends on their profit forecasts. New investments enhance productivity and, consequently, Aggregate Supply.

Inflationary expectations can be especially powerful. For example, labor supply curves will shift leftward continuously if workers feel that inflation threatens the purchasing power of their earnings. If you were a union wage negotiator, your wage demands would be closely tied to your view of how rapid inflation might be over the life of a contract. Expectations of inflation shift Aggregate Supply to the left. Naturally, declining inflationary expectations stabilize labor supplies and may shift the Aggregate Supply curve to the right.

• **Government Policies** Work versus leisure choices are influenced by taxes and social welfare policies. Suppose, for example, that income tax rates rise. Some people might try to maintain their disposable incomes by working longer and harder. Even more workers would work less, however, and some might choose not to work at all. These leftward shifts of labor supply curves occur because higher taxes make earning additional income worth less. Workers base

FIGURE 8 Shifts of Aggregate Supply Curves

Panel A
Decreases in Aggregate Supply

Panel B
Increases in Aggregate Supply

Decreases in Aggregate Supply

1. Resource Costs Rise

   a. Workers prefer more leisure
   b. Less education and training
   c. Shrinking work force
   d. Inflationary expectations shrink labor supplies
      Unions become more powerful
   e. Decreased saving and investment
   f. Investor pessimism
   g. Shrinking supplies of raw materials
   h. Competition reduced

2. Technology declines (e.g., nuclear war)

3. Government policies worsen

   a. Inefficient new regulations
   b. Higher taxes on productive effort
   c. Welfare programs discouraging productivity

4. The foreign sector

   a. Increases in exports
   b. New barriers to imports

Increases in Aggregate Supply

1. Resource Costs Fall

   a. Workers desire more income
   b. More education and training
   c. Increased labor supplies
   d. Decreasing inflationary expectations
      Union power declines
   e. Higher saving and investment
   f. Investor optimism
   g. Discoveries of new raw materials
   h. Competition increases

2. Technological advances

3. Government policies improve

   a. More efficient regulatory environment
   b. Reduced taxes on productivity
   c. Efficient welfare reform

4. The foreign sector

   a. Increases in imports
   b. Lower trade barriers

work–leisure decisions on take-home pay, not gross wages. Higher Social Security taxes or increased unemployment compensation or welfare payments may also hinder labor force participation and, thus, shift Aggregate Supply to the left.

Critics argue that massive growth of government regulation causes inefficiency. Some estimates suggest that complying with federal regulations absorbs between 5% and 15% of our national income.[13] If inefficient new regulations (e.g., rigid wage and price controls) smother

[13]See M. Weidenbaum and R. DeFina, *The Rising Cost of Government Regulation* (St. Louis: Center for the Study of American Business, 1981): and U.S. Office of Management and Budget, *Regulatory Program of the United States Government, April 1, 1990–March 31, 1991* (Washington D.C.: U.S. Government Printing Office, 1990).

private business activity, the Aggregate Supply curve shifts to the left (a movement from AS_0 to AS_1 in Figure 8). Abolishing burdensome regulations shifts Aggregate Supply rightward.

For example, airline deregulation resulted in sharp declines in fares and the emergence of new airlines; passenger miles more than doubled after deregulation in 1978.[14] On the other hand, efficient regulations expand Aggregate Supply. For example, supplies of professional services grew after the Federal Trade Commission outlawed fee-setting practices (wrapped in rhetoric about professional ethics) by the American Medical Association and American Bar Association and barred these organizations from limiting advertising by doctors and lawyers.

Policies that dampen incentives to introduce new technologies or to accumulate capital hamper economic growth. If policies impede technological advances and investment, the economy declines (or fails to grow as fast as it could), and the Aggregate Supply curve shifts to the left (or is held back). Government policies encouraging capital accumulation (e.g., reduced taxes on capital gains) or speeding introduction of modern equipment (investment tax credits) shift the Aggregate Supply curve to the right.

Government may also enhance Aggregate Supply through (a) direct funding of research and development (R&D) that advance technology, (b) subsidies or tax incentives that stimulate private R&D, or (c) patent or copyright protection. Incomes to private developers of new technologies or discoverers of basic scientific knowledge are generally less than the values of such advances to the society at large, in part because competitors quickly jump on the bandwagon whenever an innovation appears profitable. Consequently, much of the basic R&D in this country is done in government laboratories (e.g., the National Institutes of Health) or through governmental funding of research projects at colleges and universities.

The major influences that shift Aggregate Supply are listed below Figure 8. Be sure that you understand why Aggregate Supply shifts as it does.

---

[14]U.S. Aviation Safety Commission, April 18, 1988.

MACROECONOMIC EQUILIBRIUM

Aggregate Demand and Aggregate Supply meet to yield a unique short-run equilibrium for aggregate levels of prices and outputs. This is illustrated in Figure 9 with an equilibrium price level of P_e and equilibrium output equal to Q_e (point e). To see why this is an equilibrium point, consider the consequences of the lower price level P_1. This price level is below equilibrium, so consumers will demand output level Q_2—more than the Q_1 currently supplied. Retailers will experience growth in sales and declining inventories, and will order more from wholesalers and manufacturers.

Manufacturers react to growing orders by boosting both production and their own orders for raw materials and intermediate goods. Some may expand output by paying overtime wages to current employees; others will hire additional workers. But this additional output will be increasingly costly, raising the prices firms charge. The economy moves from Q_1 to Q_e as aggregate output and employment expand. Equilibrium is achieved at Q_e and P_e (point e), and economy-wide excess demands for goods evaporate.

Pressures in the opposite direction would occur if this economy were at price level P_2. Sales fall and inventories rise, precipitating layoffs and declining aggregate output. Ultimately, these pressures again result in an economy-wide equilibrium at point e.

Comparing equilibrium points when Aggregate Demand and Aggregate Supply curves shift provides insights into problems macroeconomic policymakers face. All major American depressions before World War II were periods when the price level, output, and employment all declined. Note that in Panel A of Figure 10, if Aggregate Demand falls from AD_0 to AD_1 both the price level (P) and the level of real national income (Q) decline. Thus, one explanation for recessions or depressions is a drop in Aggregate Demand. Conversely, if Aggregate Demand rises from AD_1 to AD_0 (Panel A), the price level and real output both rise. Thus, real growth accompanied by mild inflation conform to expansion of Aggregate Demand relative to Aggregate Supply.

FIGURE 9   Macroeconomic Equilibrium

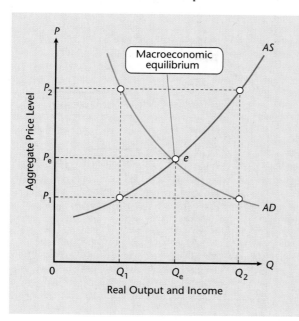

Macroeconomic equilibrium occurs where Aggregate Demand meets Aggregate Supply. If the price level deviates from this equilibrium (P_e), pressures on business and consumers will move the economy back toward point e. For example, if the price level were initially at P_1, excess demands for goods would yield greater sales, shrinking inventories, and more new orders to manufacurers. Manufacturers respond by hiring additional workers, resulting in greater output and employment, but at higher prices (diminishing returns partly explains this). Opposite pressures exist when the price level exceeds P_e.

In a similar vein, changes in Aggregate Supply can lead to growth or stagflation. First, as Panel B of Figure 10 illustrates, growth that exerts downward pressure on prices (called *deflationary growth*) can occur if Aggregate Supply increases faster than Aggregate Demand. This pattern prevailed between 1865 and 1890, when growth was stimulated by new inventions, the settling of the west, and waves of immigration. Alternatively, if Aggregate Supply shrinks, rising prices accompany declines in output and more unemployment, a condition known as *stagflation*, shown in Panel B by a shift in Aggregate Supply from AS_2 to AS_0. Prices rise from P_2 to P_0 while real output falls from Q_2 to Q_0—an incumbent politician's nightmare.

THE AMERICAN BUSINESS CYCLE

The Aggregate Demand–Aggregate Supply framework helps describe macroeconomic problems and enables us to interpret recent economic history. This section provides an overview of U.S. business cycles in the twentieth century. Our discussion begins with the 1920s because the events of that decade and the next profoundly changed American perspectives on capitalism.

The Prosperous 1920s

The 1920s were prosperous by any yardstick. Following a minor dip in business activity after World War I, the United States enjoyed a boom lasting until 1929. Prosperity was sparked by (*a*) rapid growth of technology, labor productivity, and productive capacity; (*b*) the popularity of such new and important goods as telephones, radios, and autos; (*c*) the electrification of homes and industries; and (*d*) a wave of optimism lasting until 1929.

Rising auto production propelled such subsidiary industries as oil and rubber. Nationwide electrification also spurred demands for capital equipment and consumer goods. These were key ingredients for record growth. Rapid technological advances allowed growth without in-

FIGURE 10 Macroequilibrium and Shifts in Aggregate Demand and Supply

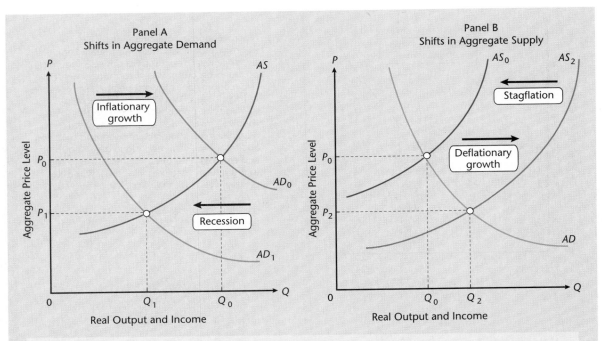

Employment, income, and the price level all fall if Aggregate Demand falls (*AD*₀ to *AD*₁ in Panel A); society then suffers the hardship of recession or depression. Expansion of Aggregate Demand in Panel A from *AD*₁ to *AD*₀, on the other hand, precipitates booming employment and real growth of income accompanied by inflationary pressure. When Aggregate Demand is stable and Aggregate Supply increases (*AS*₀ to *AS*₂ in Panel B), the economy experiences deflationary growth as real output rises but prices fall. When Aggregae Supply declines (*AS*₂ to *AS*₀ in Panel B), the economy is hit simultaneously with the twin evils of reduced employment and real output (or higher unemployment) plus inflation. This has been named *stagflation*.

flation because Aggregate Supply kept pace with growing Aggregate Demand.

The Great Depression of the 1930s

The year 1929 began with optimism that the boom would continue, but by October, a business slump was clearly under way. Then the economy collapsed, not to recover fully until the eve of World War II.[15] Real disposable income fell more than 26% between 1929 and 1933,

while unemployment rates mounted from 3.2% to nearly 25%. The 6% to 8% annual drop in average prices between 1929 and 1933 may sound great, but lower prices were almost meaningless to jobless workers. Family incomes and assets melted away. Despite sharp cuts in consumption spending, years of accumulated savings evaporated, and investment was insignificant.

Public welfare programs were meager, so the burden of relief fell primarily on private charities. But harsh times squelched donations. Average people in some countries suffered even more than most Americans; the Great Depression was worldwide. Many families became homeless when they could not afford rent. Other more fortunate families who were evicted

---

[15]Economists have largely reached a consensus that the infamous stock market crash of 1929 was a symptom rather than, as some people still think, the primary cause of the bad times of the 1930s.

from their homes lived with relatives for as long as possible. It was as if large parts of our population had been swept into the Dark Ages. Entire families spent their days prowling garbage dumps and foraging for scraps of clothing and food with which to stay warm and alive.

Hindsight provides explanations for the Great Depression that could not be derived from the supply-side emphasis of classical theory that dominated economic thinking into the 1930s. In Figure 11, if the Aggregate Demand curve falls from AD_0 to AD_1 (Panel B) the price level and real national income (Q) both decline. Employment is closely tied to national output, so employment also falls and unemployment rates tend to rise. Thus, recessions and depressions are almost uniformly periods when Aggregate Demand has plummeted.

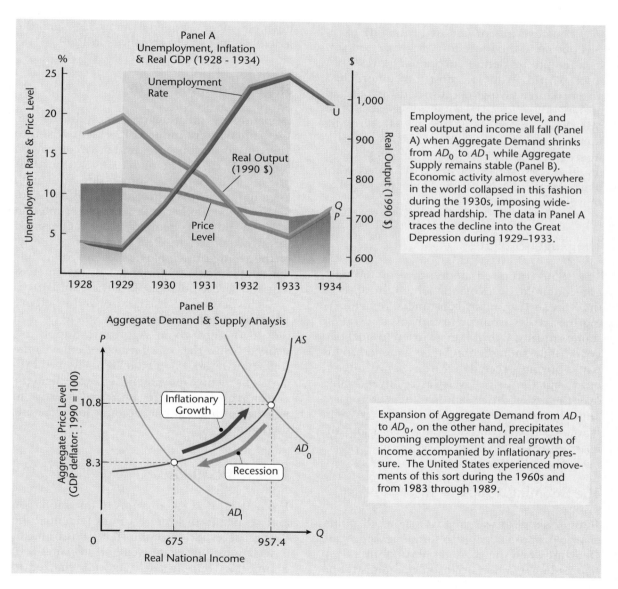

Employment, the price level, and real output and income all fall (Panel A) when Aggregate Demand shrinks from AD_0 to AD_1 while Aggregate Supply remains stable (Panel B). Economic activity almost everywhere in the world collapsed in this fashion during the 1930s, imposing widespread hardship. The data in Panel A traces the decline into the Great Depression during 1929–1933.

Expansion of Aggregate Demand from AD_1 to AD_0, on the other hand, precipitates booming employment and real growth of income accompanied by inflationary pressure. The United States experienced movements of this sort during the 1960s and from 1983 through 1989.

FIGURE 11   Recessions and Inflationary Prosperity

War and Its Aftermath in the 1940s

The economy falteringly began to recover after the trough of 1933, but unemployment still hovered at 15% in 1940. Massive defense spending during World War II snapped the economy out of the depression in the early 1940s, apparently confirming John Maynard Keynes's ideas in his *General Theory* that recessionary trends could be overcome by boosting Aggregate Demand with massive doses of government spending.

The government imposed rationing to divert output to the war effort and price controls in attempts to defuse inflationary pressures. After World War II, most consumers had amassed huge savings because many goods had been tightly rationed or not produced at all. The price level jumped about 10% in 1946, after the war had ended and price controls were lifted. Aggregate Demand grew when families binged on new cars and appliances; manufacturing plants for these products had been restricted to war goods.

The Sluggish 1950s

The 1950s witnessed modest growth and nagging, but mild, doses of inflation. At the onset of the Korean War, many consumers, remembering the hassles from price controls and ration stamps during World War II, tried to stockpile goods they thought might be rationed. This panic buying precipitated a brief inflationary burst, but the price level was relatively stable over the rest of the decade, climbing at average annual rates of only 1% to 2%. A mild recession followed the Korean War (1950–1953), and another ended the decade.

The Booming 1960s

John F. Kennedy was the first major U.S. politician to propose tax cuts to stimulate Aggregate Demand when the economy was not in a deep depression. Lyndon Johnson's administration followed through with sharp cuts in tax rates. The experiment worked, and the nation her-alded an era of prosperity under the guiding hands of Washington economists.

Panel B in Figure 11 helps characterize trends in the 1960s. Growth of Aggregate Demand from AD_1 to AD_0 increases employment, national income, and the price level. Many economists thought that macroeconomic fine-tuning could reduce an apparent trade-off between unemployment and inflation to a minor irritant. Then pressure from the Vietnam War began overheating our economic engine. Nevertheless, unemployment dropped to a low 3.2%, and the federal budget was last balanced in 1969.

Stagflation in the 1970s

Demand-side inflationary forces during the Vietnam War era induced President Nixon to introduce peacetime wage and price controls on August 15, 1971. The mid-1970s saw our first brush with serious supply-side inflation. Lagging productivity growth and rising prices for energy and other raw materials erupted in inflation and high unemployment that persisted through the decade. Real output grew slowly; on the average, unemployment rates rose, while the United States experienced its most persistent and severe inflation since the Civil War.

This stagflation is characterized in Figure 12. Although the economy as a whole grew in the 1970s, growth in Aggregate Supply remained below that of Aggregate Demand; the shift from AS_0 to AS_1 in Panel B of Figure 12 reflects this relative movement. Thus, declines (or slower growth) in Aggregate Supply relative to Aggregate Demand may account for economic stagnation.

The Erratic 1980s

From 1981 to 1983, attempts to quell inflation and reduce record interest rates fomented the deepest recession since the 1930s, illustrated as a decline in Aggregate Demand in panel B of Figure 10. "Supply-side" tax cuts enacted in 1981 eventually stimulated both Aggregate Demand and economic growth. By the mid-

FIGURE 12 The Stagflation of 1973–1975

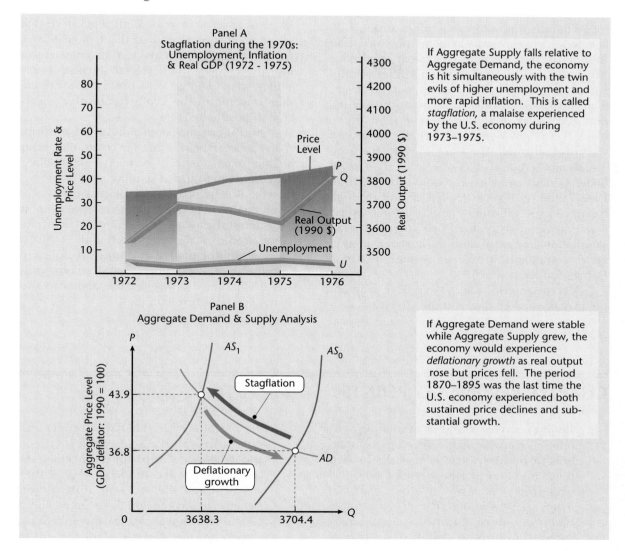

Panel A
Stagflation during the 1970s: Unemployment, Inflation & Real GDP (1972 - 1975)

If Aggregate Supply falls relative to Aggregate Demand, the economy is hit simultaneously with the twin evils of higher unemployment and more rapid inflation. This is called *stagflation*, a malaise experienced by the U.S. economy during 1973–1975.

Panel B
Aggregate Demand & Supply Analysis

If Aggregate Demand were stable while Aggregate Supply grew, the economy would experience *deflationary growth* as real output rose but prices fell. The period 1870–1895 was the last time the U.S. economy experienced both sustained price declines and substantial growth.

1980s, inflation and unemployment were both relatively low, but federal deficits continued to mushroom. The U.S. national debt, which had tripled in the 1970s, tripled again between 1980 and 1990.

The international competitiveness of the U.S. economy became a paramount issue when goods from Pacific Rim countries (Japan, Taiwan, Hong Kong, . . .) and the European Community began flooding world markets, dislodging American products from markets they had once dominated. The dollar's status as the world's premier currency, which had begun to erode in the 1970s, continued to drift during the 1980s, and U.S. balances of payments and trade experienced huge deficits from 1982 into the 1990s. In the late 1980s, communist governments in Eastern Europe tumbled like rows of dominoes, heralding an end to a Cold War that had begun at the end of World War II. The decade closed with the United States in the midst of a prolonged but relatively minor recession.

Muddling Through in the 1990s

Huge deficits in the federal budget and in U.S. balances of trade and payments persisted into the mid-1990s, despite enactment of Deficit Reduction Acts in 1990 and 1993. Interest rates fell to the lowest rates in decades, but a recovery from a shallow worldwide recession proceeded only slowly after an upturn began in 1992. Trade barriers were lowered or largely eliminated worldwide through the General Agreement on Tariffs and Trade (GATT), between the United States, Canada and Mexico in the North American Free Trade Agreement (NAFTA), and through treaties in several other regions. People everywhere increasingly realized that adapting to the internationalization of almost all economies might be as formidable a task as curing the Great Depression seemed in 1933.

Macroeconomic analysts and government policymakers alike increasingly advocate cures for structural inefficiencies as ways to boost Aggregate Supply into the twenty-first century, with emphasis on increased efficiency in certain sectors of the economy. In the United States, movements were launched to reinvent (streamline) government and to reform the health-care system, which had grown from about 5% of national income in the 1950s to absorb roughly 14% of income by 1994.

Our Aggregate Demand–Aggregate Supply framework helps illustrate economic events and the major goals of macroeconomic policy: full employment, price stability, and economic growth. But before we can discuss macroeconomic goals and policy options, we need to know more about the anatomy of unemployment, inflation, and growth. Chapters 6 and 7 address reasons for unemployment and inflation and describe how these important concepts are measured. Chapter 8 addresses the issue of measuring economic growth.

CHAPTER REVIEW: KEY POINTS

1. **Business cycles** consist of alternating periods of economic expansion and contraction. A business cycle is typically broken down into four phases: (a) *peak* (boom), (b) *contraction* (recession or downturn), (c) *trough* (depression), and (d) *expansion* (recovery or upturn). Business cycles are measured from peak to peak by the National Bureau of Economic Research and have averaged roughly 4 years, although some have been as short as 10 months, while others have lasted a decade. Reference dates are established by a detailed examination of data from past cycles.

2. Such social problems as mental and physical illness, marital tensions, divorces, suicides, alcoholism, prostitution, illegitimate births, and crimes against both people and property are closely related to changes in business conditions. Marriages and divorces alike tend to be positively related to the business cycle. Mental disorders and some physical diseases, suicides, crimes, and illegitimate births appear inversely related to business conditions—that is, they all rise when the economy turns down. Declines in income and the negative social effects of business slumps together have prompted policymakers to look for ways to keep the economy on a steady path.

3. Many early business cycle theories were **external shock** theories, focusing on such sources of instability from outside the economic system as bad weather and war.

4. Joseph Schumpeter developed a business cycle theory around major **innovations** that may partially explain major long-term business fluctuations. He cited the development of railroads, automobiles, and similar innovations as generating significant investment leading to tremendous economic growth for extended periods.

5. **Psychological theories** of the business cycle use people's herd instincts to explain the effects of extended periods of optimism or pessimism. These theories may partially account for the cumulative nature of business cycle downturns or recoveries but provide little insight into the reasons for **turning points**.

6. <u>**Classical macroeconomics** focuses on resolving scarcity from the supply side.</u> It relies on market forces to automatically move the economy to full employment and views recessions as self-extinguishing without a role for government.

7. The persistence of the Great Depression seemed to refute classical theory, which was dominated by the demand-oriented theories of John Maynard Keynes from 1936 through the 1960s. <u>**Keynesian macroeconomics** concludes that government can counter business cycles by adjusting Aggregate Demand through government tax and spending policies.</u>

8. **Aggregate Demand** is based on spending by (*a*) consumers, (*b*) investors, (*c*) government, and (*d*) foreigners (i.e., net exports). The Aggregate Demand curve is negatively sloped because a higher price level causes reduced spending on our domestic output due to (*a*) the **wealth effect**, (*b*) the **foreign-sector substitution effect**, and (*c*) the **interest rate effect**.

9. The single most important determinant of *consumer spending* (*c*) is **disposable income**. Other important determinants of *consumption* and *saving* include (*a*) wealth and expectations of future income, (*b*) the average size and age composition of typical households, (*c*) household balance sheets and stocks of consumer goods, and (*d*) consumer expectations regarding prices and availability of products.

10. **Investment** (*I*) in capital refers to purchases of new output that can be used in the future to produce other goods and services. The three categories of investment are (*a*) new business and residential structures, (*b*) machinery and equipment, and (*c*) inventory accumulation.

11. The quantity of investment is determined primarily by expected **rates of return** from investment, which, in turn, depend on (*a*) expectations about the business environment, (*b*) rates of technological change and innovation, (*c*) existing stocks of capital relative to total production, and (*d*) investment costs, which depend most on the interest rate.

12. **Exports** (**X**) add to Aggregate Demand and detract from Aggregate Supply. (Goods sold to foreigners are not available to Americans.) **Imports** (**M**) enhance Aggregate Supply and may reduce Aggregate Demand. (Buyers of imported goods may spend less on American goods.) Exports and imports are reasonably balanced, so **net exports** (**X − M**) have a comparatively small net effect on Aggregate Demand. The foreign sector is vital to our economic strength, however, because it provides (*a*) markets for our production and (*b*) imported goods that would be much more costly if produced only domestically.

13. The **Aggregate Supply curve** is positively sloped, because when business conditions change, a firm can adjust its prices more rapidly than its production costs. Prosperity increases per-unit profit, so firms hire more resources and produce more output.

14. Aggregate Supply curves shift in response to changes in (*a*) cost and availabilities of resources, (*b*) technology, (*c*) expectations, (*d*) government policies that affect costs or (*e*) net imports.

15. Increases in Aggregate Demand tend to raise national income and output, employment, and the price level. Increases in Aggregate Supply exert downward pressures on prices and facilitate growth of employment and national income and output.

QUESTIONS FOR THOUGHT AND DISCUSSION

1. How might your standard of living be affected by the business cycle over the next five years or so? Does your answer apply to most other college students? Why or why not?

2. Why might expectations of economic collapse prove prophetic? Might widespread expectations of prosperity also be self-fulfilling? Why? Can you identify social mechanisms through which people might prevent the enactment of proposed restrictions on international trade if they feared that a trade war could push us into a global recession?

3. Does explosive population growth doom people to declining standards of living? Some economies in which growth has been the most rapid in recent years are also among the most densely populated areas on earth and among the least richly endowed with natural resources (e.g., Japan and Hong Kong). Torrents of entrepreneurial energy and innovation are among the forces cited as driving this growth. Are modern market institutions or natural resources more important as potential sources of growth and development? Can expanded international trade and the spread of market incentive structures improve average standards of living in areas experiencing population explosions (e.g., parts of Asia, Africa, and South America)? What makes you think that Malthus was more correct about the prospects of humankind than Joseph Schumpeter, or vice versa?

4. How would Aggregate Demands and Aggregate Supplies, respectively, be affected by reforms that made government more efficient? Is the answer to this question clear-cut? Why or why not?

5. The price of gold is a barometer of the expectations of some financial investors who some characterize as managing "smart money." How would you expect expectations about inflation, political instability, or a recession to affect the price of gold in international capital markets?

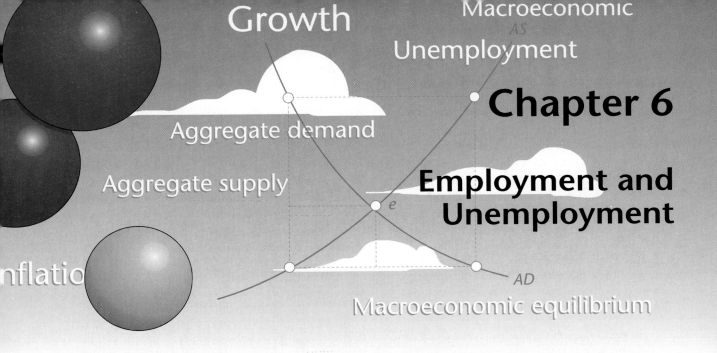

Growth

Macroeconomic
Unemployment

Aggregate demand

Aggregate supply

nflatio

AS

Chapter 6

Employment and Unemployment

e

AD

Macroeconomic equilibrium

Some goods are truly homogeneous—one bushel of #2 winter wheat is almost indistinguishable from another, at least in the eyes of potential buyers. Units of other goods tend to vary more—pieces of original art, for example. In resource markets, the story is similar. One acre of Kansas farmland may be 100% substitutable with another that lies 100 miles distant (i.e., they are identically productive). But no worker is precisely interchangeable with any other worker, from either workers' perspectives or from the perspectives of their employers.

Labor markets require special consideration because the well-being of individuals and families is our ultimate concern when designing economic policies. Every worker brings to the labor market and the job unique mixes of skills, diligence, and personal problems. Some workers are laid off or fired numerous times in their careers. Prolonged joblessness, which can rise to epidemic proportions during downturns in the business cycle, can be even more devastating. Recessions often leave unemployed workers and their families destitute, unable to afford what most people view as life's necessities. Thus, wide-spread joblessness is a major social problem and poses a serious dilemma for macroeconomic policymakers.

In this chapter, we first examine how labor markets are changing. Next, we focus on the nature of employment and the meaning of unemployment, how it is measured, its possible causes, and its costs and benefits. Only after we see how unemployment, inflation, and economic growth are related can we reasonably address the problem of limiting unemployment to tolerable levels. These three concepts comprise the core of this and the next two chapters. First, let's look at how labor markets have changed over recent decades.

LABOR MARKETS IN THE TWENTY-FIRST CENTURY

Since World War II, the economy has been buffeted by powerful forces, both internal and external: the globalization of markets for most products and some resources, widespread corporate downsizing and streamlining, shifts from the production of commodities to jobs focused on services, increased immigration, broad movements of women into labor markets, growing cadres of temporary and part-time workers, major changes in where people work, the birth of several major industries (e.g., microelectronics and bioengineering), and the virtual demise of some minor ones (e.g., typewriter production or blacksmith shops).

Changes in the Supply of Labor

Two-thirds of all Americans over 16 years of age are now in the labor force. The Department of Labor classifies adults as employed, unemployed, and as either in or out of the labor force.

*The **labor force** (LF) consists of all employed (E) or unemployed (U) civilians over age 16 plus members of the Armed Forces stationed in the United States. Thus, LF = E + U.*

*A **labor force participation rate** (LFPR) is the proportion in the labor force from a specific group. For the total labor force, the LFPR = LF/Population of the specific group.*

*The **employment to population ratio** is total employment (E) relative to that population (Pop), or E/Pop.*

*The **unemployment rate** is the number unemployed as a percentage of the labor force, or U/LF.*

Table 1 lists these data for the United States for selected years since 1960. The growth rate of the U.S. labor force over this period exceeded population growth by nearly 30%, which is reflected in a rising employment to population ratio. The labor force almost doubled. This growth

TABLE 1   Population, Labor Force, and Other Labor Market Measures (1960–1993)

Selected Indicator	1960	1970	1980	1993	Percentage change 1960–1993
Population (Pop = age ≥ 16)	117,245	137,085	167,745	193,971	65.4
Labor Force (LF)	69,628	82,771	106,940	127,975	83.8
Employed (E)	65,778	78,678	99,303	119,457	81.6
Unemployed (U)	3,852	4,093	7,637	8,517	—
Employment to Population Ratio (E/Pop)	56.1	57.4	59.2	61.6	9.8
Unemployment Rate (U/LF)	5.5	4.9	7.1	6.7	121.1
Labor Force Participation Rates (LF/Pop)	59.4	60.4	63.8	66.0	11.1
Males	83.3	79.7	77.4	76.7	–7.9
16–19	56.1	56.1	60.5	49.4	–11.1
20–54					
55–64	86.8	83	72.1	67.0	–22.8
Over 65	33.1	26.8	19.0	16.1	–51.4
Females	37.7	43.3	51.5	58.3	54.6
16–19	39.3	44	52.9	48.4	23.1
35–44	43.3	51.1	65.5	85.2	96.8
Over 65	10.8	9.7	8.1	8.6	–20.4
White	58.8	60.2	64.1	66.6	13.3
Other	64.5	61.8	61.7	62.2	–3.6

Source: *Economic Report of the President,* 1994 and U.S. Department of Labor, Bureau of Labor Statistics, *Employment Hours and Earnings* and *Monthly Labor Review,* various dates.

came primarily from increased female labor-force participation (shown in Table 1) and immigration (shown in Figure 1).

Total labor-force participation rates have grown by slightly over 10% since 1960, primarily because women increasingly pursue careers outside their homes; labor-force participation rates for females grew almost 55% between 1960 and 1995. Although a majority of workers are male, labor force participation among males fell almost 8% during this period. In the last two decades, immigration has accounted for over one-third of total U.S. population growth and has been the second largest source of gain in human resources. Nearly a quarter of new immigrants have college degrees (about the same proportion as for the economy as a whole), adding to our stock of skilled workers.

Two other demographic trends have profoundly affected labor supplies: the growth in the number of two-income households and in the number of households headed by women. Nearly 13% of all working women today are primary breadwinners for their families. These trends have led to growing numbers of households that are relatively better-off (two earners) and growing numbers that are relatively poor (women who support families), leaving middle-income families in America declining as a percentage of all households.

Changes in the Demand for Labor

Broad changes to the supply side of our national labor market have been matched by dramatic changes in demands for labor. The demand for labor ultimately derives from consumer demands for goods and depends on workers' productivity. Certain ongoing changes in product markets profoundly affect labor productivity.

First, globalization, especially in markets for manufactured goods, has intensified competition in numerous industries. For example, not too many years ago, carmakers based in Michigan virtually owned the international automobile market. Today, foreign assembly plants provide one-fourth of all new cars sold in the United States, and several foreign-based carmakers (e.g., Toyota, Honda, and Mercedes-Benz) now operate production facilities in the United States.

International competition is changing domestic labor requirements. Today, few young Americans expect to be employed by one firm for the bulk of their careers. The drive for cost-efficiency means that skilled labor commands premium wages. However, less-skilled Americans increasingly must compete with lower-cost foreign labor. International trade tends to equalize the wages of domestic workers with those of comparably skilled foreign workers. Thus, free international trade erodes the incomes of less-skilled Americans while boosting wages for low-skilled foreign workers. At the same time, skilled Americans gain by producing for foreign markets and by buying imported goods at lower prices. Some American firms and industries will prosper in this competitive environment, but others will fail. Competing successfully in the global economy requires flexibility: workers must possess

Source: *Business Week,* July 13, 1992.

Immigration has become a more important source of population growth in recent decades. Immigrant workers are often highly skilled (one-quarter are college graduates) and come primarily from Asia and Latin America.

FIGURE 1   Immigration as a Growing Share of Population Increases 1960–1990

portable skills that allow career moves between firms and, perhaps, industries. These issues are addressed in Focus 1.

Second, for several decades U.S. employment has been shifting from commodity production to the provision of services. High wages in service industries tend to be earned primarily by skilled professionals (e.g., medical doctors, accountants, and engineers), but many workers in service industries tend to be relatively unskilled. As shown in Figure 2, jobs in manufacturing as a percent of total employment have fallen by half since 1950. Productivity gains historically have been most rapid in the manufacturing sector, with rising productivity then boosting wages and standards of living. The decline in the relative importance of U.S. manufacturing has slowed productivity gains. In part because service productivity has grown relatively slowly, our standard of living has improved at only sluggish rates in recent decades.

Third, recent government policies about labor markets have altered employer–employee relationships. Laws governing health, safety, disability, family leave, plant closure, and civil rights have combined with increased Social Security taxes and pension reform legislation to increase the cost of hiring, retaining, firing, and laying off workers. Many of these policies, while desirable, raise both labor costs and the legal exposure for firms. The fastest growing division in many firms is the human resource department, which deals with employee issues raised by expanded legislation. As both the wage and nonwage costs of labor rise relative to other resources, business firms seek lower-cost substitute resources. At the margin, such increases ultimately result in fewer employees being hired, especially full-time career employees.

Firms increasingly rely on part-time and temporary help. Workers who once viewed themselves as career employees are often cast adrift. Growing numbers of workers are lumped together as the contingency work force.

*The **contingency work force** consists of part-time and temporary employees plus business service providers plus the self-employed.*

Figure 3 shows that the ranks of contingent workers are growing as firms adjust their hiring practices to use more part-timers, freelancers, independent subcontractors, consultants, and "temps" from agencies. These temporary employees can be contracted and dismissed with relative ease, permitting firms to cope with unexpected changes in workflow. Current projections suggest that as many as half of all workers may be in the contingency work force by 2010.

Many individuals trickled into the contingency work force as a consequence of corporate downsizing, but for perhaps as many others, becoming a contingent worker has been a conscious choice that was largely unavailable before the revolution in information technology. These workers find constant change a pleasurable challenge, or they enjoy the freedom of working at home, consulting or pounding away on the keyboard of a PC, and communicating via *e*-mail, cellular phones, or fax machines.

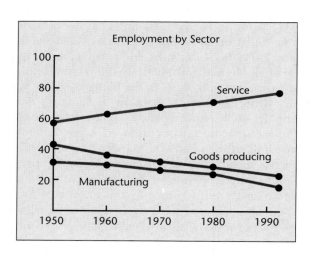

Production in the United States has been shifting from goods-producing to service industries. Today, 4 out of 5 workers are engaged in providing a service. This shift partially explains overall slowing of our productivity gains—productivity tends to grow much slower in service industries than in manufacturing or goods production.

FIGURE 2   Employment in the Goods-Producing, Service, and Manufacturing Sectors, 1950–1993

FIGURE 3 The Contingent Work Force

Contingent Employment Trends

Source: Federal Reserve Bank of Cleveland, *Economic Trends,* November 1993
The contingent work force includes part-time and temporary workers, business service providers, and the self-employed. This group of workers has been growing as a percent of the labor force over recent decades. Contingent workers allow business to quickly adjust to changing market needs. Some economists argue that this trend toward use of contingent workers arises, in part, from labor market regulations that have substantially increased the costs of full-time employees.

All of these changes pose problems for the measurement and interpretation of statistics about employment and unemployment.

THE CONCEPT OF UNEMPLOYMENT

Friday began with the familiar beep-beep-beep of the alarm, a steamy shower, and the aroma of brewing coffee. Commuting was, as usual, a hassle. Morning meetings seemed standard fare, mixed with daydreaming about possible weekend activities. The plant manager dropped the bomb at 2 PM—loss of a major contract. Layoffs would affect not only assembly line workers this time, but executives as well. Two months' severance pay and accrued vacation were in a final check. Firm handshakes accompanied sincere wishes for "Best of luck." Then, out the door, lugging a box full of personal items. Driving home was a nightmare. "My skills are strong; some competitors have expressed interest in my expertise. But are they hiring now? Recession has been in the news. Can we afford health insurance? How will

the mortgage be paid? Do I need to move to find work?" The happily anticipated weekend has dissolved into pure gloom—a reaction typical for workers cut adrift without a job.

Unemployment during the Great Depression cut a wide swath across American society and ultimately led to the Employment Act of 1946, which specified "maintaining maximum employment" as one government goal. Assessing how well this goal has been met usually begins with the overall unemployment rate, a statistic heard regularly in the news. But this single measure is only a crude guide to policy because unemployment occurs for multiple reasons. Before examining various types of unemployment, we must discover who the unemployed are.

Half of the 260 million people in the United States are in the labor force, but this does not mean the rest are unemployed. (Any notion that homemakers are not working is quickly cured by a short stint managing a household and a cou-

How Can You Compete in a Global Economy?

Armies of low-wage foreign workers haunt the dreams of many Americans. Are there ways to protect your financial future? Might pressures from international trade even boost your income? Fortunately, the answer to both questions is yes. Before we outline a possible plan of action, however, you need some background information.

Standards of living everywhere are improved through specialization and exchange. International competition is also a powerful force to equalize prices globally, both for goods and for resources. Some economists describe a *law of one price*; others invoke a *factor price equalization theorem*.

A stereo sold in Budapest must generate the same net revenue to a competitive producer (after transportation costs, taxes, etc.) as one sold in Québec City. International competition in certain labor markets also tends to equalize pay for, say, basketball players in Orlando and Rome (after adjusting for costs of living, regional preferences, etc.). But how does trade exert pressure to equalize wages for all comparable occupations in Barcelona, Melbourne, and San Diego?

One part of the answer is that, under fairly reasonable assumptions, free trade almost perfectly substitutes for resource mobility. A Russian computer programmer need not physically relocate to Moscow, Idaho to compete with Idaho programmers. (*Tetris*, a computer game developed in Russia, is internationally popular.)

Similarly, a French vintner can stay in Bordeaux while competing with California winemakers.

International trade intensifies pressures for firms everywhere to adopt similar technology. Microchip makers in Malaysia use the same basic technologies as firms in Silicon Valley, which ultimately translates into similar productivities for labor, and, consequently, similar wages.

A second form of international competition among workers arises from location decisions by multinational corporations. Consider a janitor in an Indiana plant that manufactures mirrors. If the company operating this plant could produce mirrors in Manila instead, then the Indiana janitor must compete for a job with a Filipino janitor. If the Indiana plant is relatively more costly, manufacturing will shift to the Philippines.

The third part of the answer is that workers compete with other workers within their national borders. If, say, bankers enjoy higher returns on their investments in human capital than lawyers do, then some Americans considering careers in law will switch to banking instead. These adjustments will continue until returns on comparable investments in human capital are roughly equalized.

How does this analysis help answer the title question of this focus? Competitive forces combine to equalize wages, interest rates, and rents for comparable land throughout the world. This means that if the resources you control are relatively scarce inter-

nationally, then your share of the gains from international trade (the increased purchasing power of your income) will exceed the average. But if your resources are even more abundant internationally than within your own country (e.g., unskilled labor), then your gains from trade will be less than average.

A sad reality is that unskilled Americans gain less from international trade than those with more human capital do, both absolutely and relatively, because they must compete with abundant unskilled foreign labor. This may be the major reason why the share of earned income going to Americans at the bottom of the economic spectrum has declined over the past decade or so, while the share going to Americans toward the top of the spectrum has been rising.

One Strategy The world is full of bright, industrious people. The trick is to tailor your resources so that they are relatively scarce in the rest of the world, even if relatively abundant in the United States. This usually entails acquisition of human capital. On average, Americans have better access to education than most people, although many foreigners are catching up quickly. Thus, the answer to our major question is almost a cliché: Get as much education as you can stand, and try to develop expertise that will be increasingly in demand as internationalization continues into the twenty-first century.

ple of kids.) Adults can elect to be, or not to be, members of the labor force. Economists classify people as "employed" or "unemployed" only if they choose to be in the labor force.

*Conceptually, **unemployment** occurs when people are able to work and would willingly accept the prevailing wage paid to someone with their skills, but either cannot find or have not yet secured suitable employment.*

Figure 4 illustrates unemployment as a labor market surplus. At prevailing average hourly wages of $12, Americans want to sell 260 billion hours of labor, but firms will hire only 240 billion hours. Thus, 20 billion hours of labor are unemployed, almost 8% of total hours available.

Standard theories of markets identify cuts in prices (or wages) as a cure for any surplus. Although markets for most goods remedy surpluses rapidly through price cuts, similar remedies do not seem to work as quickly in labor markets when there are gluts of workers. In Figure 4, there would be full employment if wages dropped to an average of $10 per hour. But wages are seldom perfectly flexible; they

tend to be downwardly sticky, which prolongs unemployment. Economists and the public at large differ about whether individual workers control *wage stickiness,* or whether certain institutional factors cause this stickiness.

Voluntary vs. Involuntary Unemployment

Unemployment can be viewed as either voluntary or involuntary.

***Voluntary unemployment** occurs when people could find work quickly, but choose to search for what they view as better jobs in terms of pay or working conditions.*

For example, you would be voluntarily unemployed if you turned down a night job that required a 50-mile commute, looking instead for 9-to-5 work closer to your home.

Some people view all unemployment as voluntary: If you really want a job and are willing to work for "what you're worth," you can find work almost immediately. I am willing to hire

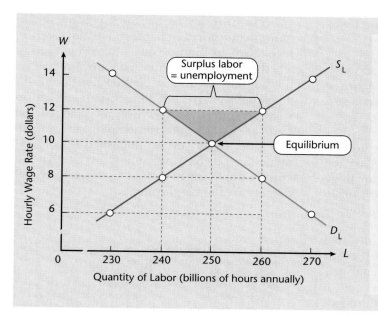

A prevailing average hourly wage of $12 yields an annual *surplus* of 20 billion hours of labor effort. Households would supply 260 billion hours of labor at this wage, but firms would hire only 240 million hours—*unemployment* equals 20 billion hours of labor time, yielding an *unemployment rate* of roughly 7.7% (20/260 = 7.6923).

This unemployment would be eliminated if wage rates fell to a $10 hourly average, but the speed of such adjustments is limited by *wage stickiness,* a problem that may vary markedly across different labor markets.

Note: These numbers roughly reflect the current U.S. work force of 130 million workers and typical full-time work of 2,000 hours (40 hours ×50 weeks).

FIGURE 4   Unemployment as a Surplus in the Labor Market

you to paint my home, mow my lawn, or baby-sit as long as you accept a wage equal to what these activities are worth to me. My neighbor would do the same. Thus, if you are unemployed for more than a few hours, it must be voluntary.

The counterargument is that people should not be forced to accept just any job.

> *Involuntary unemployment* occurs when people lack jobs, but they are willing, able, and even eager to work at wages commensurate with their skills.

According to this point of view, work should neither underemploy people's skills nor insult their human worth, but wretched business conditions and corporate restructuring may yield times and places in which job openings are almost non-existent.

Sticky Wages

Those who argue that all unemployment is voluntary assert that vacancies always exist for anyone who is (a) productive and (b) willing to accept a sufficiently low wage. But how much discretion do individual workers have about whether to accept a lower wage? At times, the answer may be "Not much."

> *Sticky wages and prices* occur whenever wages or prices fail to instantaneously adjust to clear a market at the point where the quantities demanded and supplied are equal.

Even workers who overcome a widespread psychological aversion to accept wage cuts may be unable to agree to a lower wage. Minimum wage laws are one example of restrictions that make some wages downwardly sticky—less than perfectly flexible.

Wages are also sticky because individual workers cannot negotiate their own wages with unionized employers. Union wage contracts typically govern wage structures from two to three years. It would be futile for any individual facing a layoff to try to offer to work for a lower wage in hopes that the firm would lay off someone unwilling to accept a wage cut. Unionized firms lack this discretion, and such a strategy would aggravate other workers. Most union workers are hostile to "scabs"—workers willing to accept pay cuts while union members get bumped.

Seniority rules are another barrier to wage cuts as ways to keep your job at the expense of another employee. Even the personnel manuals of non-unionized firms often specify something on the order of last hired, first fired. Seniority rules are attempts on the part of management to appear fair when allocating pay hikes, promotions, or even work itself. Productivity partly depends on morale. Almost any partial layoff by a firm, whether unionized or not, is governed by rules intended to maintain employee morale, especially that of career employees. Consequently, firms under pressure because of weak demands for their products will be reluctant to hire job applicants merely because the applicants are willing to accept lower wages. However, even if wages are sticky in the short run, they ultimately fall if business is depressed for a sufficient period. In 1993, United Airlines sold roughly 40% of the company to its unions for cash plus wage and benefit concessions to obtain a more competitive wage structure.

The issue of wage stickiness is addressed in more detail in later chapters.[1] In the interim, recognize its importance for determining whether unemployment can be involuntary, or if it is always voluntary. Neither position is unambiguously correct. Willingness to work at prevailing wages is not objectively ascertainable, so estimates of involuntary unemployment tend to be crude. In any event, published unemployment data rely on government surveys that use criteria only loosely related to our conceptual definition of unemployment.

---

[1]We will explore the theories that persistent unemployment for some workers arises because (a) *implicit contracts* between firms and career employees provide some workers with job security when business is slack in exchange for less pressure for raises during prosperous periods, and (b) systems of *efficiency wages* limit jobs for some workers while ensuring premium wages and jobs for workers who are expected to be especially reliable.

MEASURING UNEMPLOYMENT

The major source of U.S. unemployment statistics is a monthly Department of Labor survey of about 60,000 households, a sample sufficiently large that it ensures that the statistics collected are reasonably representative. This survey (broadly outlined in Figure 5) by the Bureau of Labor Statistics (BLS) is intended to determine the labor force status of each adult family member.

Employed persons include (a) anyone who worked for pay any time during the week that includes the 12th day of the month or without pay for 15 hours or more in a family-operated firm, and (b) those temporarily absent from regular jobs because of illness, vacation, strikes, or similar reasons. Armed Forces personnel stationed in the United States are also counted as employed.

Unemployed persons are those who did not work during the survey week but were available for

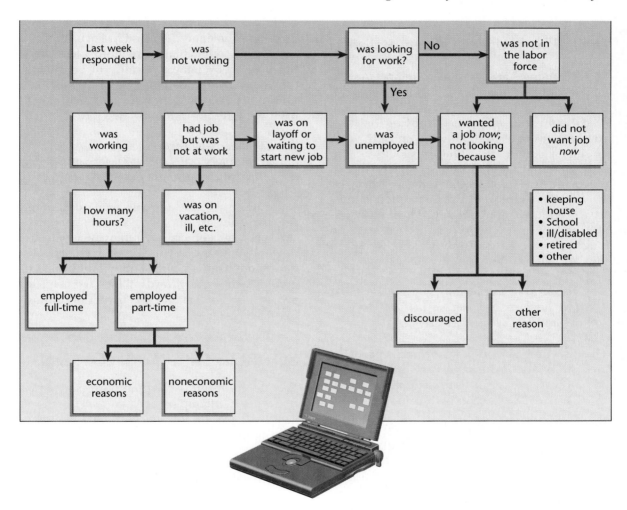

A monthly questionnaire administered to roughly 60,000 families randomly selected by the Bureau of Labor Statistics uses the logical chains in this figure to ascertain the work force status of people aged 16 and over. Computerized responses have reduced ambiguities in this process.

FIGURE 5   Determining Who Is Unemployed

work, except for temporary illness, and who looked for jobs within the preceding four weeks. Persons who did not look for work because they were on layoff or waiting to start new jobs within the next 30 days are also counted as unemployed.

Refined survey questions and computerized technology introduced by the BLS in 1994 reduced the ambiguity of questions and the subjectivity of the interviewing process. Follow-up questions on the survey are now directed by computers, standardizing interview processes.

Limitations of Unemployment Statistics

Most economic statistics reflect attempts to summarize, but keep in mind that a lot of detail can be lost in any summary. (You may have discovered this for yourself if, when studying for a test, you have ever relied too heavily on Cliff Notes or similar summaries.) One possibility is that published statistics may understate true unemployment. One reason is that some workers who are truly unemployed are uncounted if they have given up looking for jobs. Those individuals who have given up looking for work are no longer classified as "actively seeking work," so they are not counted as in the labor force.

Discouraged workers are so pessimistic about their prospects that they do not look for jobs, although they would like to work.

The discouraged worker syndrome is probably most pronounced during recessions, when job openings are perceived as few and far between.

Earlier BLS estimates of discouraged workers were widely criticized as too subjective; whether or not a worker was "discouraged" was inferred from answers to other questions. The refined survey introduced in 1994 asks questions that more carefully identify discouraged workers. Preliminary tests of the new questionnaire revealed that many of those previously classified as discouraged actually "had looked for work in the last year, found a job, lost or left the job, and had not looked for a job since." The new BLS survey explicitly asks individuals for the main reason they are not looking for work and to prioritize their reasons. As a result, the discouraged worker category will probably be cut in half relative to previous estimates.[2]

Another major reason unemployment rates may be understated is that all part-time employees are considered employed: the BLS unemployment rate does not weigh the problem of *part-time unemployment*. For example, if you want a full-time job but only work half-time, ideally, the official unemployment rate should weight you as half of an unemployed worker. But it does not. That part-time unemployment may be a growing problem is discussed in Focus 2.

On the other hand, unemployment statistics may be overstated because of our unemployment compensation system. (Have you known people who drew unemployment checks even though they did not want a job?)

Dishonest nonworkers claim to be available for work so they can draw unemployment benefits, even though they do not intend to work.

Failure to include discouraged workers and the part-time unemployed in unemployment statistics biases official unemployment statistics downward: unemployment is understated. Dishonest nonworkers, on the other hand, bias unemployment data upwards. Which sets of effects are stronger, on balance, is a matter of continuing debate.

SOURCES OF UNEMPLOYMENT

Five different but overlapping forces generate five types of unemployment: *frictional*, *seasonal*, *structural*, *cyclical*, and *induced*. Each poses somewhat unique problems for government policy.

Frictional Unemployment

People enter or reenter the work force, are fired or permanently laid off, or voluntarily quit one

---

[2]U.S. Department of Labor, Bureau of Labor Statistics, *Monthly Labor Review*, September 1993.

Part-Time Unemployment?

From the vantage point of economics, unemployment exists whenever a potential worker has time for sale at the going wage rate, but no buyer (employer) has offered a position that absorbs all the worker's surplus time and effort. Thus, ideally, unemployment rates would measure such surpluses of labor as a proportion of the total labor available at prevailing wage rates. For example, if households would willingly supply 10% more labor time and effort than firms currently hire, the unemployment rate is, conceptually, 10%. If, however, every worker worked exactly 90% as much as he or she liked, the official unemployment rate would be zero: all people who wanted work would have jobs, so no one would be counted as unemployed.

This type of uncounted unemployment may be especially pronounced among part-time workers. Large numbers of people, including a lot of full-time students and homemakers with school-aged children, truly want to work only part-time. In many cases, however, workers who have been laid off take part-time jobs as a holding action to keep food on the table and a roof overhead. Continuing waves of restructuring (downsizing) in corporate America have clobbered large numbers of midlevel professionals and managers, many of whom lost jobs they secured only after several promotions during decades of work with an established firm. An increasingly common pattern is for these individuals to operate as consultants from their home offices or to work part-time (e.g., filling out tax forms for H&R Block at $5 per hour during the tax season) while desperately seeking jobs comparable to those they have lost. Too frequently, however, these people ultimately find full-time employment at salaries of only 40% to 60% of what they earned in their previous positions.

A related problem is that some people with full-time jobs supplement their income with a part-time, after-hours, second job. If they lose their part-time jobs, their idle time is not counted as unemployment. All of these people who would like to work more, but who are currently working either part-time or 40 hours per week, are not counted as "partially unemployed" by the Bureau of Labor Statistics.

The prevalence of part-time employment has grown over the decades, and the number of part-timers who would like full-time jobs appears to be growing even faster. (In 1994, over 13,000,000 workers had two or more part-time jobs that summed to more than 38 hours per week.) Therefore, statistics for total unemployment rates may not be comparable across time. In 1994, the BLS revised its monthly questionnaire to more accurately track the numbers of part-time workers who want full-time jobs. Nevertheless, official unemployment rates remain unadjusted for part-time unemployment.

job to look for another. Both firms and workers expend resources trying to match job applicants with job openings. Information about job openings and applicants is far from perfect, and mobility (e.g., relocating an employee or moving to get a job) is costly.

Frictional unemployment *arises from transaction costs incurred in matching workers with jobs.*

In a narrow sense, almost all unemployment is frictional. Suppose transaction costs were zero. Every potential worker would know about all possible jobs, and every firm would know about all potential workers. Moreover, mobility would be costless and instantaneous. In such a world, people willing and able to work could instantly move into the (relatively) best jobs available to them, and firms could instantly fill every available job with the worker having the greatest comparative advantage in that job. The fit between workers and jobs would be optimal.

However, it actually takes time for workers to move between jobs and for firms to find suitable employees. Thus, many economists refer to frictional unemployment as *search unemployment*. Search processes can be viewed as investments in information. Workers search for satisfying and remunerative employment, sometimes turning down several jobs before finding a position that suits them. They will continue to look for a better job until the expected marginal benefits from further search (e.g., higher wage offers) no longer exceed their expected marginal costs (wages forgone while looking).

Similarly, firms search for workers with skills honed to accomplish the work required until the firms' marginal benefits (better workers or lower wages) no longer exceed their marginal costs (e.g., forgone output and profit). Firms may make many job offers before finding someone acceptable who agrees to fill a job. (Most fast-food restaurants post semi-permanent HELP WANTED signs.) Unemployed workers often offer their labor dozens of times before landing an acceptable job. Thus, frictional unemployment is an unavoidable byproduct of normal economic activity. Unemployment rates naturally rise as the average duration of search increases.

The existence of frictional unemployment implies that a target of zero unemployment would be neither reasonable nor desirable. Zero unemployment would freeze all workers in their current jobs, no matter how unsatisfactory. And firms would be stuck with their current workers, no matter how bad the mismatch. In fact, the employed and unemployed both experience considerable *turnover*, a term used when workers change jobs. For example, employment in 1993 averaged nearly 120 million persons per month, but about 130 million different persons worked at some time during the year. While unemployment averaged around 8.7 million per month, nearly 30 million people were unemployed at some time during those 12 months.

Seasonal Unemployment

Vacations, football, tomato harvests, and holidays are seasonal activities. Seasonal unemployment also varies systematically over the year. For example, most lifeguards are only employed during the summer months, and department store Santas work only a few weeks annually. Economic data published for activities that vary regularly over the year, including unemployment, must be seasonally adjusted to make them comparable.

Seasonal unemployment varies systematically over the year.

Weather, for example, operates from the demand side to drive patterns of employment and joblessness in agriculture and construction. Beach towns and ski resorts also experience seasonal swings in employment. Seasonal influences emerge on the supply side as well. School vacations are the major reason that teenage unemployment rises in June and falls in September.

Structural Unemployment

Some individuals lack significant marketable skills, a barrier that makes finding work an ordeal in even the best of times.

Structural unemployment occurs when a worker's skills fail to match the requirements of virtually any job opening.

Why are people who are structurally unemployed usually jobless for long periods? First, structural change displaces some workers. For example, technological innovation may make certain skills obsolete. Many typesetters and specialists in cut-and-paste layout work lost their jobs with the advent of computerized typesetting and desktop publishing. In the past decade, corporate restructuring left many middle-aged middle managers jobless for extended periods. Second, some people, including many high school dropouts and most exconvicts, have acquired few, if any, marketable job skills through either education or previous employment. Firms may find it unprofitable to hire and train workers if expected training costs outweigh benefits to the firm. This is especially a problem if employees frequently find better jobs after being trained.

Cyclical Unemployment

Employment and output both rise during economic booms and decline during downturns.

Cyclical unemployment coincides with downturns in business cycles.

Marginal firms are especially vulnerable to recessions, pushing up unemployment rates. Figure 6 shows that joblessness has varied enormously over the past century. These swings are dominated by cyclical unemployment, a major target of macroeconomic policy.

Unless your family or friends are affected directly, unemployment may seem fairly abstract. Not all groups of workers are affected in the same way by a cyclical downturn. Table 2 shows unemployment rates for specific groups during selected periods of high and low employment. Historically, cyclical unemployment bore most heavily on manufacturing and construction workers. Until recently, professional and technical workers were less severely affected. However, during the recession of 1990–1991, professional, technical, and middle management personnel were hit far more heavily than in prior recessions.

Induced Unemployment

Finally, certain government policies may induce unemployment.

> **Induced unemployment** is a consequence of government policies that create "wedges" so that wages are not at their equilibrium values.

Minimum-wage laws, for example, overprice the labor of unskilled and inexperienced workers and limit job opportunities. Laws requiring wages at the union scale on government contracts also hinder full employment: they leave workers unemployed who would be willing to work for less on government contracts. And *unemployment compensation* provides incentives for people who sincerely desire work to turn down some job offers in hopes that they will find the perfect position if they keep looking.

• **Unemployment Compensation** Payment of unemployment compensation in the U.S. is usually limited to 26 weeks. After 26 weeks of payments to be jobless, unemployed Americans are largely on their own. However, in the depths of most recent recessions, Congress has extended eligibility for payment of unemployment compensation to 52 weeks, or even longer.

Unemployment compensation does buffer the harm to unemployed individuals, but when it reduces the personal relative costs of being jobless, it simultaneously reduces the relative benefits from accepting an offer of a position the individual views as less than ideal. The pre-

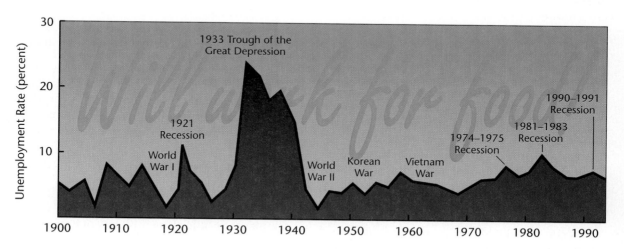

Sources: 1900–1928 derived from S. Lebergott, *Manpower and Economic Growth* (NY: McGraw-Hall, 1974): 1929–1993 derived from the Bureau of Labor Statistics and *Economic Report of the President,* various issues, 1970–1994.

The unemployment rate has varied considerably over time. Unemployment reached a peak in 1933 when roughly one in four workers was out of work. Unemployment rates dropped to 1.2%, an all-time low, during World War II.

FIGURE 6   The Rate of Unemployment, 1900–1993

TABLE 2   Unemployment Patterns during Periods of Prosperity and Recession

	1973 Peak	1975 Trough	1981 Peak	1983 Trough	1988 Peak	1992 Trough
Total unemployment (all occupations)	4.9	8.5	7.6	9.8	5.2	7.3
Professional and technical	2.2	3.2	2.8	3.3	2.2	3.8
Government	2.7	4.1	4.7	4.9	2.7	3.5
Service	5.8	8.6	8.9	10.6	4.8	6.5
Blue-collar	6.2	14.7	12.2	17.7	9.1	11.0
Manufacturing	4.4	10.9	8.3	12.3	5.1	7.8
Construction	8.9	18.0	15.6	20.0	10.0	16.7

Source: U.S. Bureau of Labor Statistics, *Employment and Earnings,* January 1994.

dictable result is that people spend more time looking for ideal positions and turning down jobs that are less than perfect. This drags out the processes of search unemployment.

The harsh reality is that many workers are forced to move down a notch when they lose one job and must find another. Some analysts argue that generosity to the unemployed often backfires; higher relative rates of unemployment compensation make it easier for unemployed people to cling to unrealistic expectations and to remain out of work longer. And, of course, it biases official unemployment statistics upward because cheaters who don't truly want to work are counted as jobless.

Accounting for Joblessness

More than one type of unemployment may account for some joblessness. For example, a golf pro in Michigan who lacked other skills might find a job easily each May, but be both seasonally and structurally unemployed in the dead of winter. Simple frictional unemployment and seasonal unemployment are normal byproducts of economic activity. These two types of unemployment pose relatively mild social problems when compared with structural, cyclical, or induced unemployment. Nevertheless, different government programs are broadly aimed at different types of unemployment:

1. State employment offices match job applicants with vacancies to reduce transaction

costs that boost frictional and seasonal unemployment.

2. Government retraining programs are intended to provide marketable skills to the structurally unemployed, and firms that hire the hard-core unemployed receive tax subsidies.

3. Occasional reforms to unemployment compensation systems (e.g., tighter monitoring to prevent cheating) are aimed at reducing induced unemployment. A lower minimum-wage rate that applies to trainees is aimed at reducing unemployment among teenagers.

4. Policymakers attempt to reduce cyclical unemployment by trying to dampen the frequency, intensity, and duration of economic downturns.

Curing cyclical unemployment is a primary focus of macroeconomic policy, but broad prosperity tends to ease unemployment of all types, as echoed in the adage "A rising tide lifts all boats."

THE DURATION OF UNEMPLOYMENT

The effects on official unemployment statistics are identical if 52 workers each lose a week of work or if one worker is jobless for a year, but the suffering associated with long-term unemployment is probably disproportionately higher. As time elapses, the allocative and disciplinary benefits from a lengthened duration of unemployment tend to decline, while marginal personal and social costs rise. After unemployment compensation payments run out, families must borrow or spend past savings to meet their expenses; but credit is tough to come by if you are jobless, and savings may already have been depleted.

Families that rely on regular paychecks may endure minor discomfort if a primary breadwinner is jobless for a short period, but extended unemployment is likely to be disastrous. The self-esteem of breadwinners often suffers most. It is especially hard for people who identify with their jobs to go from being, say, annual $100,000 plus managers to being $30,000 functionaries.

Unfortunately, as shown in Panel A of Figure 7, cyclical downturns prolong periods of unemployment for workers who lose their positions. Over the most recent recession, those who found new jobs within 5 weeks declined from

50% to roughly 35% of the total unemployment pool. At the same time the percentage of the unemployed who were jobless over 6 months doubled from 10% to 20%.

A recent tendency for greater cyclical unemployment among white-collar workers is compounded by the duration typical of their unemployment. Growing numbers of laid-off midlevel professionals endure a year or two of unemployment before finally landing jobs and, even then, too frequently, at pay cuts of 50% or more. One hurdle that confronts some suddenly-unemployed midlevel professionals is that many are deemed overqualified for vacancies that many of them, being desperate, would happily accept (see Focus 3).

Panel B of Figure 7 shows that loss of a job is not the sole reason for unemployment. In fact, only half of the currently unemployed were laid-

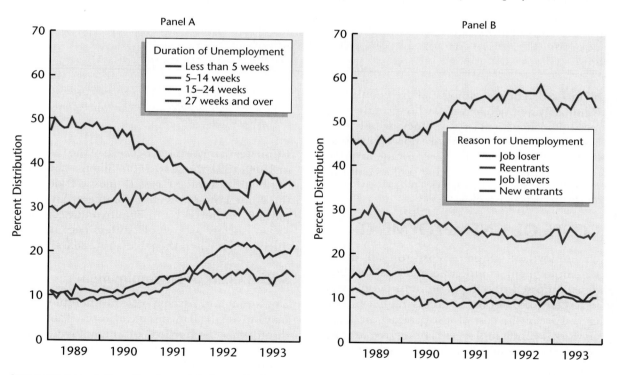

Source: Joint Economic Committee, *Economic Indicators,* March, 1994.

As the economy enters a recession the percentage of those unemployed who find jobs within 5 weeks declines (and vice versa). As a recession becomes prolonged, the percentage of people unemployed for more than 6 months grows (Panel A). Not all people who are unemployed lost jobs. Many of the unemployed are new entrants to the labor force and other are just now reentering the labor force or have voluntarily left their last job (Panel B).

FIGURE 7   The Duration of and Reasons for Unemployment

Overqualified for the Job?

Why would good managers ever pass up opportunities to hire people with better qualifications than are required for a position? One reason is that some managers may fear that they are hiring people who, ultimately, might replace them. (Would you hire someone likely to replace you in the chain of command or compete with you for a promotion, thus becoming your boss?)

Perhaps an even more powerful explanation is that overqualified people are viewed as likely to move on to other, higher-paid positions as soon as one becomes available. Few new workers immediately operate at peak productiv-ity; it takes time to become familiar with all the particulars of almost any job. If overqualified workers are viewed as less likely to stay, then employers may reasonably fear that they will not recover their costs from training a worker before the worker moves on. Thus, even superbly qualified people who are desperate and who would be willing to accept big pay cuts immediately may go jobless for very long periods.

People who lose positions be-cause of corporate downsizing are not alone in being unable to find slots because they are overquali-fied. During recessions, many firms sharply pare back budgets for recruiting new hires from college campuses. And jobs below what a college graduate had hoped for but much above burger-flipper can be unavailable because of the "overqualified" label. During the 1990–1991 recession, many recent graduates seemed trapped in unsatisfying temporary jobs (e.g., as servers in restaurants). Only when conditions gradually improved during 1992–1994 did these educated but inexperienced workers begin to trickle into the entry-level career-track positions they had expected to find a year or two earlier.

off or fired. The remaining half are people who voluntarily quit (job leavers), who recently reen-tered the labor force (e.g., mothers who left the labor force temporarily and are now reentering), or those entering the labor force for the first time (new entrants, e.g., graduating seniors entering the full-time work force for the first time).

COSTS OF UNEMPLOYMENT

Unemployment imposes costs on all of us. Unemployment compensation eases the bur-dens of missed paychecks on most people who lose their jobs, but the resulting higher payroll taxes spread the cost of lost production across all workers and employers. The aggregate costs of unemployment fall into two categories: lost income and social costs.

Losses of Aggregate Income

The production lost because of unemployment is not trivial.

*The **lost-income costs** of unemployment consist of the value of the output the unemployed could have produced.*

Estimates of income lost because of the recession of 1990–1991 range to $500 billion—about 8% of potential annual Gross Domestic Product in the United States. Even if the unemployed are partially buffered by unemployment compen-sation, society as a whole suffers because pro-duction falls when the jobless rate soars.

Social Costs of Unemployment

The social and psychic costs of unemployment may outweigh all the financial losses. Table 2 in-dicates that the burdens of unemployment are not spread evenly, but dry statistics cloud our understanding that real people stand behind these numbers. Consider the memories of a woman who was a college student during the Great Depression:

When I attended Berkeley in 1936 so many of the kids had actually lost their fathers. They had wandered off

in disgrace because they couldn't support their fami-
lies. Other fathers had killed themselves, so the family
could have the insurance. Families had totally broken
down. Each father took it as his personal failure . . .
so they killed themselves. It was still the Depression.
There were kids who didn't have a place to sleep, hud-
dling under bridges on the campus. I had a scholar-
ship, but there were times when I didn't have food. The
meals were often three candy bars.[3]

The self-confidence of workers who view their jobs as central to their lives may be crushed by extended unemployment. Joblessness also wreaks havoc with family structures. Families may exhaust their assets and go deeply in debt. Plans for college can go up in smoke. Teenagers suffer especially high unemployment rates, and some acquire criminal records. Table 3 provides estimates of some human costs of unemployment. The social and psychic costs of long-term unemployment are major reasons the Employment Act of 1946 emphasized promoting full employment.

Trauma from unemployment has been partially alleviated by higher unemployment compensation benefits and partly by having more than one breadwinner in many families. In 1960, both spouses worked full-time in only one-quarter of all families. More than half now have two wage earners; in 1993, in more than two-thirds of households where the husband was unemployed, another family member had a full-time job.

BENEFITS FROM UNEMPLOYMENT

The bad press unemployment receives largely derives from its economic, social, and psychic costs, while its allocative and disciplinary benefits go largely unpublicized.

Allocative Benefits

Frictional unemployment yields allocative benefits by matching workers and jobs. Finding a new

---

[3]Source: Studs Terkel, *Working: People Talk About What They Do All Day & How They Feel About What They Do* (New York: Pantheon Books, 1974).

TABLE 3   **Estimated Incidence of Some Social Traumas Caused by a 1% Increase in Unemployment Rates Over a 6-Year Period**

Social Trauma	Incidence of Trauma
Total mortality	**48,325**
Caucasian males	16,194
Caucasian females	21,662
non-Caucasian males	5,017
non-Caucasian females	5,452
cardiovascular mortality	26,518
cirrhosis of liver mortality	1,205
homicides	849
Mental hospital admissions	**5,538**
males	4,007
females	1,531
State prison admissions	**4,375**

Source: M. Brenner, "Influence of the Social Environment on Psychology: The Historical Perspective," in *Stress and Mental Disorder*, ed. J. Barrett (New York: Raven Press, 1979). Reprinted by permission. Updated to 1993 population by the authors.

job tends to be easier if you are not working full-time. At the same time, pools of idle labor allow firms to screen more potential employees than if unemployment were zero. The process of firms seeking suitable help while the unemployed seek jobs represents investment in labor market information. Lower transaction costs enhance economic efficiency. Unemployment also prompts some workers to return to school or to acquire skills through on-the-job apprenticeships.

Some critics cite unemployment as an evil unique to capitalism. Unemployment was unacceptable when the tenets of Marxism ruled Eastern Europe, but guarantees of jobs at all times for all citizens resulted in overstaffing and artificial work for many. For example, restroom attendants who sell tickets and toilet paper have been fixtures in Eastern European railway stations for generations, but their pay typically exceeds their receipts. (Siberia once beckoned Soviet citizens who objected to meaningless work.) Under central planning, quotas set for managers of state-run factories rarely specified costs; meeting production quotas was all that mattered. One result was that, under the old system, factory managers often stockpiled workers.

Recent reforms now force managers to try to minimize all costs, and massive layoffs in Russia and Eastern Europe during 1990–1993 seem to signal growing acceptance that unemployment can improve allocation by shifting resources to more valuable uses. Predictably, however, there has been a backlash. Many people in previously socialist countries resist reforms because of the widespread unemployment accompanying conversion from obsolete factory systems to modern industrialization. This modernization should, however, ultimately boost production and income for almost everyone.

Disciplinary Benefits

We all know people who fail to pull their own weight, embellishing their own contributions and making unwarranted demands for wages, vacations, and other perks. Co-workers often describe them as deadwood. Some economists view possible layoffs as curbs to undue demands for wages and fringe benefits. Threats of unemployment are also powerful work incentives for people who respond better to sticks than to carrots. These *disciplinary benefits* accrue, in the forms of lower costs and prices, to firms (and consumers) when there is slack in the labor market and threats of layoffs loom.

Evidence that the costs of unemployment generally outweigh its benefits includes the emphasis policymakers devote to curing it. Excessive unemployment has often sounded the death knell at the polls for political incumbents. Unemployment statistics based on surveys only crudely measure real (conceptual) unemployment, but they help gauge the success of government policy. And differentiating between types of unemployment helps in tailoring policies to attack the types that are especially troublesome—structural, cyclical, and induced.

One lesson from this chapter is that achieving the goals of macroeconomic policy—*full employment, price level stability, and economic growth*—may be extremely difficult. This lesson will be reinforced in the coming chapters.

CHAPTER REVIEW: KEY POINTS

1. **Voluntary unemployment** exists when people could find work quickly, but choose to look for what they view as better pay or working conditions. **Involuntary unemployment** occurs when people lack jobs but are willing and able to work at wages consistent with their skills.

2. Some government definitions (which may only loosely conform to economic concepts):
   a. The **labor force (LF)** consists of all *employed (E)* or *unemployed (U)* civilians over age 16 plus members of the Armed Forces stationed in the United States. Thus, $LF = E + U$.
   b. A **labor force participation rate (LFPR)** is the proportion in the labor force from a specific group. For the total labor force, the $LFPR = LF/Population$ over age 16.
   c. The **employment-population ratio** is total employment relative to the population over age 16.
   d. The **unemployment rate** is the unemployed as a percentage of the labor force or, U/LF.

3. **Wage stickiness** describes downward wage adjustments that occur only slowly and tends to prolong unemployment. Wages tend to be *sticky* because of minimum wage laws, union contracts, and policies firms use to reduce turnover among career employees.

4. Part-time workers who would like to work full-time are officially categorized as employed, but they also experience *part-time unemployment*.

5. The **contingency work force** includes part-time and temporary employees plus many business service providers and many of the self-employed. Growing numbers of workers who would like career positions are lumped together in the contingency work force.

6. Unemployed people so discouraged about job prospects that they do not look for work go uncounted in unemployment statistics. Some people who are not truly out of work indicate that they are to collect *unemployment compensation*. Thus, unemployment data may either understate the true unemployment rate because of **discouraged workers** and partial unemployment, or overstate it because of **dishonest nonworkers**.

7. **Frictional unemployment** arises because of transaction costs associated with normal entry and exit from the labor market, voluntary job changes, or layoffs or firings. Both workers and firms invest in information by searching for jobs or screening applicants until their expected marginal benefits no longer exceed their expected marginal costs.

8. **Seasonal unemployment** arises from the annually recurring influences of weather, vacations, and the like.

9. **Structural unemployment** results from mismatches between workers and jobs because of changes in the skill requirements of job openings or because individuals lack marketable skills.

10. **Cyclical unemployment** results from recessions.

11. Government policies that reduce work incentives or that prevent workers from securing employment (e.g., minimum-wage laws) cause **induced unemployment**.

12. Unemployment is not distributed equally across all groups. Workers in manufacturing and construction have been hit harder by cyclical unemployment during recessions than employees in most other lines of work, but this tendency seems to be weakening, with rising rates of cyclical unemployment among service workers and professional and technical personnel and midlevel managers.

13. Unemployment causes both economic and social costs. Society as a whole suffers because of the **lost income and output** that the unemployed could have produced. Individuals and their families also suffer psychologically when they are unemployed for long periods. Personal losses are, however, partly buffered by such programs as unemployment compensation.

14. The primary benefits of unemployment derive from (*a*) better matches between workers and jobs, and (*b*) discipline—some people work hard only because they fear loss of their jobs.

QUESTIONS FOR THOUGHT AND DISCUSSION

1. Which of the following individuals would be counted as unemployed by the Bureau of Labor Statistics? Which would be considered unemployed by an economist? Why do these lists differ?

   a. A Ph.D. in anthropology who works full-time as a cab driver while devoting three hours daily to searching for a job as a researcher or an assistant professor.

   b. After quitting work as a cab driver, the anthropologist remodels her home six days a week, devoting only Monday mornings to looking for work as an anthropologist.

c. An eighth-grader who temporarily loses her job delivering papers when the printer's union at the local newspaper goes on strike.

d. A chef who chops off two fingers the day before the Les Gourmands restaurant closes forever draws disability pay while vacationing before looking for another job.

e. A novelist who has not written a page in months because he can't think of a good plot for his next book.

f. A building contractor who employs a crew of 30 workers, all of whom are idle while awaiting a big job that starts in three weeks.

2. What improvements to official data on unemployment rates would make them better (negative) indicators of social welfare?

3. In 1990, the U.S. population was 251,394,000, of whom 188,049,000 were age 16 or over. The labor force including the Armed Forces was 126,424,000, the civilian labor force was 124,787,000, and civilian employment was 117,914,000. Compute the following:
   a. Employment/population ratio.
   b. Labor force participation rate for ages 16 and over.
   c. Total unemployment rate (including the military).

d. Civilian unemployment rate (ignore the military).

Why is the total unemployment rate lower than that for civilians?

4. Some critics believe that unemployment statistics tremendously underestimate unemployment because so many potential workers have become discouraged. Others argue that the published unemployment rate "measures with considerable lack of reliability the number of people in the labor force of this country who, if the pay were right and the hours were right, might be available for a little work once in a while." Which position do you think is correct? Why?

5. In October of 1982, the Reagan Administration faced political embarrassment: the unemployment rate had soared into the double-digit range (10.1%) for the first time since the 1930s. The White House implemented a proposal advocated by numerous previous presidents to base unemployment rates on the total (civilian plus military) labor force instead of on the civilian labor force alone. Our military force is between 2 million and 3 million people. What effect did this change have on published unemployment rates? Why did several previous presidents favor this change?

Chapter 7

Inflation

Whip inflation now.

President Gerald Ford, 1975
(Lost reelection bid, 1976)

Inflation is Public Enemy #1.

President Jimmy Carter, 1976
(Lost reelection bid, 1980)

Inflation is the cruelest tax.

President Ronald Reagan, 1982
(Reelected, 1984)

Inflation is another vital macroeconomic issue. Savers intent on buying new homes, paying for their education, or retiring in comfort can have their plans shattered by inflation (increases in most nominal prices). Rapid inflation obscures the meaning of nominal prices, making even simple exchanges confusing and uncertain. Fortunately for most Americans, the severe inflation experienced at times in some countries has been rare in the United States, although moderate inflation has been a nagging problem for decades.

Governmental attempts to combat inflation have an ancient lineage. The earliest recorded anti-inflation policies were price controls imposed by Egyptian pharaohs 4,000 years ago. In the United States, a battle against inflation begun during the 1960s escalated into the early 1980s, but inflation rates rose from 3.1% in 1967 to 13.6% in 1980. Finally, monetary growth was slashed during 1981–1982 to cure double-digit inflation. This shock therapy to growth of Aggregate Demand plunged the economy into its deepest slump (1981–1983) since the Great Depression, but by 1986, the economy had largely recovered, while inflation fell below 2%. Nevertheless, through the mid-1990s, mild inflation persisted, with average prices rising 2% to 4% annually.

The drop in U.S. national income in response to anti-inflationary policies parallels international adjustments. Russia's battle against inflation from 1990 to 1994, for example, imposed hardships on most Russians, threatening the presidency of Boris Yeltsin. Is defusing inflation worth the concomitant losses of employment and income? Such questions about costs and benefits are unanswerable without knowledge of what inflation is and how it is measured.

THE CONCEPT OF INFLATION

Most people view any price hikes as inflationary, but macroeconomics is concerned primarily with changes in the *average* level of absolute prices—changes that reflect inflation or deflation.

> **Inflation** *occurs when the average level of prices rises; the average price level falls during* **deflation**.

Price increases for a single good may not be inflationary. For example, a rise in the price of football tickets is not inflationary if offset by price cuts for long-distance phone calls or video rentals. Only increases in the average price level constitute inflation.[1]

PRICE INDEX NUMBERS

If the prices for housing, seafood, and leather jackets rise while prices for sweaters, frisbees, and gasoline fall, have we experienced inflation or deflation? Price indices allow systematic answers to such questions.

> *An* **index** *is a series of numbers that summarize what has happened over time to prices (inflation or deflation), productivity, labor markets, construction, or some aggregation of other items.*

An index is calculated as

$$\frac{\text{value of variable in current period}}{\text{value of variable in base period}} \times 100$$

Index numbers compress, sharpen, and simplify information. Comprehending these specialized statistics, which appear regularly in the media, is vital for interpreting economic change.

If you wanted to develop an index of local job opportunities, you might count the help wanted ads reported monthly in your local newspaper. Suppose 38,510 ads appeared in your paper during April 1995, the month selected for a base period. {Note that the index equals 100 for the base month [(38,510/38,510) ×100 = 100].} If 47,230 ads appear in May 1995, your index of job opportunities (based on these ads) would be

$$\frac{47,230}{38,510} \times 100 = 122.6$$

This index indicates that local job openings during May 1995 were roughly 122.6% of those available during April 1995, so your estimate suggests that work opportunities grew 22.6%. Index numbers are easier ways to interpret change than trying to digest the original (raw) numbers. As your job opening index developed a track record, you might notice it rising each November and December, reflecting Christmas employment, and falling each spring. This phenomenon is *seasonality*, or changes that recur each year. Most indices are seasonally adjusted to make data more comparable over time.

Now that you understand how indices work, we will examine the three principal indices used to measure inflation: (*a*) the Consumer Price Index (CPI); (*b*) the Producer Price Index (PPI); and (*c*) the Gross Domestic Product deflator (GDP deflator).

Measuring Consumer Prices (CPI)

The *Consumer Price Index* estimates purchasing power by tracking the costs of a sample market basket that consists of over 650 products and services, including food, energy, shelter, apparel, transportation, medical care, utilities, and insurance.

> *The* **Consumer Price Index (CPI)** *is a statistical measure of changes across time in the prices of a basket of typical goods purchased by typical consumers.*

To update the CPI, each month the Bureau of Labor Statistics (BLS) samples prices of items in

---

[1] Some economists even reject this definition, arguing that inflation requires *continuous* and *prolonged* increases in the price level. However, it is often hard to distinguish *continuing* inflation from *one-shot* increases in average prices, because even one-shot general price hikes take time.

this representative market basket in nearly 100 different major markets.

The BLS also conducts annual surveys of the prices paid and spending patterns of thousands of households in over 1,000 marketing areas to calculate weights for the CPI's components. The components of the CPI are *weighted* to reflect relative importance. For example, if typical families spend twice as much on syrup as on oatmeal, the weight for syrup prices will be twice that of the weight for oatmeal prices. The base period is changed every few years because spending patterns change, which requires updating weights for various goods. For example, cellular phones were unknown 15 years ago. Their current popularity means that their prices should now be reflected in the CPI. In 1987, the BLS switched its base period from 1967 to the period 1982–1984. Figure 1 traces the history of average consumer prices as measured by the CPI since World War II.

How the CPI Is Used

The CPI is used to estimate changes in the purchasing power of money and as an escalator (cost-of-living adjustment) in some contracts calling for future payments. Unfortunately, problems are inherent in any economic index used to prescribe policy.

- **Moving from Nominal to Real Values** Most economic variables are presented in their current dollar, or nominal, values.

> *Nominal* or *monetary values* are the dollar amounts received or paid.

Nominal values lose comparability over time unless adjusted for inflation or deflation.

> *Real values* are nominal values adjusted for changes in the price level.

For example, suppose your nominal income this year is $20,000. How does its purchasing power compare with your $10,000 income of ten years ago? Are you better off or worse off? If all prices also doubled, it would take twice as much money now to buy the goods you bought ten years ago, and you would be no better off. The purchasing power of your real income (Y_{real}) is current income ($Y_{current}$) adjusted for inflation or deflation according to the formula[2]

$$Y_{real} = [Y_{current}] / [CPI / 100].$$

Using the preceding formula with a CPI of 200 for this year (the base index for ten years ago is

---

[2]Y is the standard macroeconomics notations for national income.

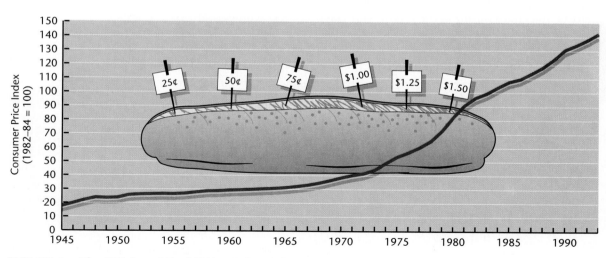

FIGURE 1   The CPI from World War II through 1993

100), your current real income is $10,000 ($20,000/2.00 = $10,000). Table 1 illustrates this conversion process for U.S. per capita income during selected years since 1929.

Just as we have adjusted nominal income to account for changes in the price level, we can adjust other nominal variables to see how relative prices are changing.

Deflating is the process of ensuring the comparability of nominal values by adjusting them for inflation.

The general formula for deflating any variable is

$$\text{real value} = \frac{\text{nominal value in dollars}}{\text{price level}/100}$$

For example, movie tickets rose from an average of $4 each in 1983 to an average of $6 in 1993. How much did real prices rise for movies? The CPI (based on 1983 prices) rose to 133. Thus, real 1993 movie prices were $6/1.33, or around $4.50 per ticket, after adjusting to the 1983 base. Similar calculations are used to deflate home prices, wages, or any other nominal variables.

A price index ideally estimates purchasing power lost per dollar of spending by typical people. But averages mean little if you are atypical. On a test, other students' average grades are less relevant to you than your own performance. You may fall far below the class average, or you may be the curve buster at the top of your class.

The CPI is a similar average and so may either overstate or understate the amount of inflation experienced by any given individual.

Inflation is especially harmful if the prices of goods you like rise faster than inflation, but you could actually gain during inflation if prices drop for the goods you buy most. For example, a pilot who toured the country in a personal jet could be clobbered by inflation propelled by higher fuel prices, while over the same period, a computer enthusiast gained from falling prices for computer hardware, software, and supplies. Inflation also affects people less to the extent that they easily substitute goods for which nominal prices change at different rates. For example, if you are indifferent to the choice between Coke and Pepsi, increases in Pepsi prices damage you far less than they do fans of Pepsi.

• **CPI as an Income or Payment Escalator** Many monetary payments are directly tied to the CPI. For example, if a union wage contract has an escalator clause, wages rise by roughly the same percentage that the CPI climbs. Escalator clauses that buffer purchasing power from inflation are included in union contracts covering roughly 8 million workers. Many pension plans, various transfer payment programs, and the income brackets in the U.S. income tax system are also closely linked to the CPI. However, as Focus 1 indicates, rigidly tying payments to the CPI may overcompensate for real inflation.

TABLE 1 Converting Nominal Income (Before Taxes) to Real Annual Income

Year	Aggregate Money Income ($billions)	Population (millions)	Nominal Per Capita Income (current $)	CPI (1982–84 = 100)	Real Per Capita Income (constant $)
1929	$ 84.3	121.8	$ 692	15.5	$ 446
1933	46.3	124.8	371	11.6	3,190
1960	409.4	180.7	2,266	29.6	7,650
1970	831.8	204.9	4,060	38.8	10,460
1980	2,258.5	222.3	10,160	82.4	12,310
1990	4,645.6	251.4	18,479	130.7	14,130
1993	5,610.0	257.9	21,753	139.8	15,560

Source: *Statistical Abstract 1993; Economic Reports of the President,* 1980–1994.

Is the CPI Biased as a Payment Escalator?

If the CPI precisely doubles, do typical consumers lose unless their money incomes at least double? Contrary to most people's intuition, the answer is no.

Not every price increases 5% if the CPI jumps 5%. Some monetary prices would rise faster and some slower when weighted *averages* of prices rise 5%. *Relative* prices rise for goods for which money prices rise faster than average, but the relative price actually falls for any good for which the money price does not rise as fast as average. For example, if average prices rise 5% while monetary prices for color TVs go up only 1%, the relative cost of a TV has fallen roughly 4% (compared to the prices of most goods).

The law of demand is a key for predicting how people respond to such changes in relative prices. Consumers will buy less of goods for which prices rise faster than average (i.e., those with increased *relative* prices) and more of goods for which monetary prices fail to

keep pace with the CPI (i.e., those whose relative prices have fallen). But how do consumer responses to such changes in relative prices affect the CPI's accuracy as a payment escalator?

An increase in monetary income precisely equaling the CPI would ensure that typical consumers could buy exactly the same bundles of goods as they purchased prior to the increase in the price level. But would they? No. The new set of relative prices would guide them to select different bundles which these individuals must prefer to the old (still affordable) ones they would now forgo. Therefore, typical consumers would gain more satisfaction— and thus, subjectively, more real income—if each rise in the CPI triggered precisely proportional escalation of their monetary incomes.

The lesson here is that payment escalation exactly equal to the percentage change in the CPI more than offsets any losses from infla-

tion. The payees would gain. But escalator clauses are intended only to ensure payees no losses from inflation; they are not intended to systematically improve the lot of typical payees. In recognition of these consumer adjustments, most escalator clauses are now activated only with a lag to offset this potential gain, or they are some fixed proportion of the CPI change, for example, 80%.

Congress has begun adjusting the CPI downward as a cost-of-living escalator for Social Security and other federal transfer payments. However, income tax rate structures use the unadjusted CPI to escalate the income brackets to which specific tax rates apply*. Thus, most taxpayers now gain from inflation because effective real tax rates are reduced when adjustments for a changed CPI are made.

*Recall (from Chapter 4) that U.S. income taxes are somewhat progressive: a higher income activates higher marginal tax rates on incremental income.

• **CPI as an Economic Indicator**   Every president since George Washington has pledged policies to secure price level stability, but with mixed results. Average prices have fallen at times (e.g., 1865–1890 and 1929–1933), but, more often, we have experienced at least mild inflation. Since World War II, the price level has risen persistently, so typical Americans now pay more attention to the Consumer Price Index than in earlier periods, and it has become a yardstick for evaluating macroeconomic policy.

Problems with the CPI

Estimating changes in consumer prices poses conceptual problems for the Bureau of Labor Statistics. How can the BLS adjust the CPI to accurately reflect changes in (a) consumption patterns, (b) the availability of new products, (c) new qualities in older goods, and (d) the prices of major assets such as homes, which some families bought earlier at lower prices, while others must pay higher current prices to buy now?

The CPI is thoroughly revised about once a decade. Between revisions, the fixed nature assumed for the "representative market basket" fails to reflect changes in typical buying patterns, reducing the CPI's accuracy. Inflation tends to be overstated because consumers purchase more goods whose prices rise most slowly and cut back on items where prices rise most rapidly. (See Focus 1.) For example, between 1972 and

1980, average energy prices rose 218%, but consumer outlays for energy only rose 140%.

The BLS now conducts annual Consumer Expenditure Surveys in attempts to keep pace with changing consumption patterns. This allows phased updating, partially offsetting biases in the CPI caused by the rigidly fixed market-basket approach.

Changes in quality may also distort price indices. Quality changes in products should not, by themselves, change the CPI, which measures the costs of purchasing a market basket that ideally yields a constant level of consumer satisfaction. The CPI overstates inflation if the BLS ignores the fact that price hikes sometimes merely reflect quality improvements. Suppose, for example, that 1996 movies are superior to films released in 1995. If ticket prices rise primarily because higher quality costs more, then the CPI might erroneously signal inflation. Ideally, dollar measures of how much consumers subjectively value quality improvements should be deducted from any price increases. Similarly, deteriorating quality may cause inflation to be understated. Inflation occurs even though money prices stay constant if, say, fast food becomes less tasty because soybeans are substituted for ground beef in burgers.

Direct measures of the value of quality changes are impossible, so the BLS uses an indirect method; it estimates the costs of quality changes. When figures are available, cost differentials between new and old features are treated as proxies for real values of quality changes. This poses severe problems. For example, do the costs of improving pollution-control devices represent improved automobile quality? Or are we actually just buying cleaner air?

Another problem in measuring inflation is that some asset owners gain from higher prices. For example, if inflationary pressures boost both wages and housing prices, current homeowners with fixed mortgage payments would not write bigger checks for their housing services. In fact, after adjusting for inflation, their real mortgage payments fall. For decades, the BLS measured housing costs by average monthly payments on *new* home mortgages, not by the rental value of typical housing services. As a result, when mortgage interest rates rose or fell, altering typical monthly payments, the BLS treated these changes as if all families bought new houses each month. The newer approach of the BLS is to use rental values as the cost of shelter. This helps the CPI to more truly reflect inflation for American households. Despite all these problems, the CPI is still a reasonable estimate of changes in average consumer prices.

Other Price Indices

The CPI only tracks changes in prices consumers pay. Other prices are also important.

• **Producer Price Index** The *Producer Price Index (PPI)* covers nonretail markets, averaging price changes for over 2,800 primary products and such intermediate goods as flour, steel, and office supplies. Most prices summarized by this index are the wholesale selling prices of representative producers, but some prices come from specialized markets such as commodity exchanges. The prices used for imported products (e.g., coffee beans) are the prices paid by the original importer (e.g., Folger's). Your reaction may be, "Why should I care about this concept? I only consume. I'm not a producer." Be aware however, that the PPI often signals the direction consumer prices will take.

• **The GDP Deflator** The *GDP deflator* is used to deflate the nominal value of our Gross Domestic Product. (GDP is the total market value of all goods produced in an economy in a year. GDP accounting is the subject of our next chapter.) The GDP deflator is largely based on other price indices. For example, each component of consumer spending is adjusted using appropriate data from the Consumer Price Index. Business spending for capital equipment or raw materials is deflated with appropriate parts of the Producer Price Index. Parts of other indices are used to deflate the prices of items not included in the CPI or the PPI, such as government services, construction, and agricultural outputs.

THE HISTORY OF U.S. INFLATION

Few Americans can remember when the price level fell. Average prices fell by roughly one-third between 1929 and 1933, while wages dropped by one-fourth, so wages after adjusting for deflation actually *rose*. Workers might seem to have gained, but remember that by 1933 the unemployment rate was almost 25%. There have been other periods when we experienced deflation, as you can see in Figure 2. For example, prices fell on average by roughly 40% between 1870 and 1895.

During the 1960s and 1970s, Americans gradually became accustomed to annual inflation ranging from 6% to 14%. By the 1990s, most of us viewed 2% to 4% inflation as price-level stability, rates that would have outraged Americans of an earlier era. To some extent, what you are accustomed to determines what you consider moderate or excessive inflation. Many South Americans view inflation rates of 40% to 50% as no big deal. Inflation in Argentina, Bolivia, and Brazil raged at annual rates as high as 400% to 800% at times between 1950 and 1993.

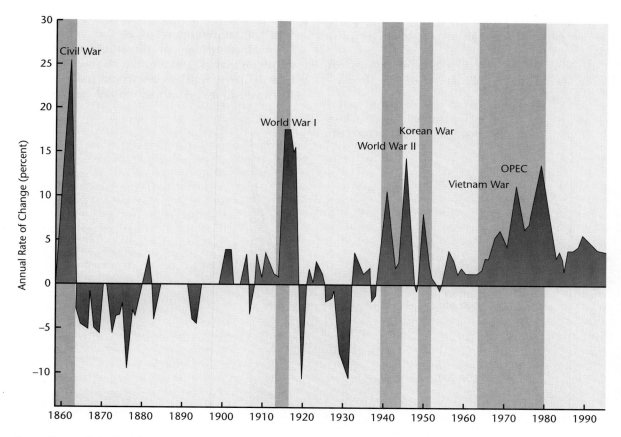

Source: Bureau of Labor Statistics, 1994.

This figure highlights the various inflationary and deflationary periods exerienced by the United States since 1860. The majority of these inflationary periods have occurred during extended military hostilities. Although the 1970s and early 1980s were relatively peaceful, the price level crept up briskly.

FIGURE 2   Inflation Since 1860

TYPES OF INFLATION

Now that we have seen how inflation is measured, let's turn to analyzing the different types of inflation. Inflation can be classified by how rapidly average prices rise, or by whether people expect it. Other distinctions pinpoint its causes. This section addresses all three approaches.

Creeping or Galloping Inflation vs. Hyperinflation

The price level may rise for a number of reasons and at different rates over time.

Creeping inflation occurs when average prices rise at fairly low rates.

Inflation has persisted at creeping rates for decades in the United States, but it "galloped" briefly in the 1970s.

Galloping inflation occurs if average prices rise at double-digit annual rates.

People in other countries have been even less fortunate. Most economists accept the definition of hyperinflation offered by Philip Cagan, a specialist in this area.

Hyperinflation occurs when average prices rise more than 50% per month.

Hyperinflations have occurred at rates that can only be described as astronomical. A kilogram of bread cost less than 1 deutsche mark in 1919, and 9 deutsche marks would buy an American dollar. Between the onset of World War I and 1923, average prices in Germany rose 1,422,900 million percent. By the end of 1923, $1 exchanged for an incredible 4.2 trillion deutsche marks, and a one-inch stack of 5 million deutsche mark notes would buy one egg. But even more remarkable inflations have oc-

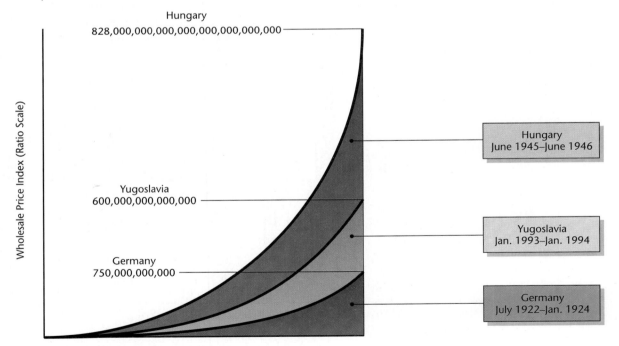

Sources: For China: Shun-Hsin Chou, *The Chinese Inflation: 1936–1949* (New York: Columbia University Press, 1973), p. 261. For Germany: Fritz K. Ringer, *The German Inflation of 1923* (New York: Oxford University Press, 1969), p. 69. For Hungary: B. Nogaro, "Hungary's Monetary Crisis," *American Economic Review*, XXXVIII (1948), pp. 526–542.

FIGURE 3   Selected Episodes of Hyperinflation: China, Germany, and Yugoslavia

curred. Hungary experienced inflation of 828 octillion (828 followed by 27 zeros!) percent between 1945 and 1946. Today, Yugoslavia is fighting the second most severe hyperinflation in history. Its 600 trillion percent inflation in 1993 was brought on by economic disintegration and UN sanctions for its role in the Bosnian conflict. Figure 3 illustrates these three twentieth-century hyperinflations.

Interestingly, studies by Philip Cagan indicate that a monetary system can still function as long as inflation stays below 50% *monthly*. Any time inflation looms on the horizon, however, bond markets become shaky, interest rates rise, and investment falters. Creeping inflation clearly poses fewer problems than hyperinflation for consumers, investors, and for macroeconomic policymakers. During episodes of hyperinflation, money becomes a hot potato that people spend as fast as they can in attempts to beat expected price hikes. But they quickly lose faith in money. When this happens, transaction costs skyrocket—barter takes over and goods and resources are traded directly for other goods or resources, without money as an economic lubricant.

Very rapid inflation usually signals an economy experiencing severe trauma. Wars, coups, or natural disasters may set the stage for galloping inflation or hyperinflation. Excessive inflation is also the norm for economies in transition, as illustrated in Focus 2.

Anticipated vs. Unexpected Inflation

A second way to categorize inflation or deflation is by how accurately people anticipate changes in the price level. Unexpected changes in average prices do far more harm than anticipated ones. Hedging is one way people try to buffer against expected losses of purchasing power.

Attempts to avoid possible losses from foreseeable possibilities are **hedges**.

For example, if you became convinced that virtually all prices will soon rise, you might hedge by buying a new car immediately or by making guaranteed reservations a year in advance for a resort vacation. Even stocks of canned food can be used to hedge against severe inflation.

Speculation based on inflationary expectations is potentially remunerative, but very risky. Buying real estate on credit before an inflationary boom, for example, can yield handsome real rates of return. (Are you familiar with the rule: Buy low and sell high?) But overly generous forecasts can be as damaging as projections that underanticipate changes in the price level. For example, investors who speculated that California real estate prices would continue on an upward trend that had lasted from 1946 into the 1980s were often bankrupted when housing prices plummeted in the early 1990s.

The lesson here is that the rate of inflation may be less harmful than its volatility. Price-level stability is desirable because consumers and investors can avoid unnecessary costs associated with hedging and speculating. A stable price level allows consumers to focus on buying the most satisfying goods and investors to concentrate on capital expenditures that will help firms best serve the needs of consumers, instead of strategies to avoid inflation or to profit from it.

Demand-Side Inflation

We can use the Aggregate Demand–Aggregate Supply model introduced in Chapter 5 to help identify different sources and types of inflation. When a given price rises, then (a) demand increased, (b) supply decreased, or (c) some combination of (a) and (b) occurred. This pattern offers parallels for the economy as a whole.

Demand-pull (demand-side) inflation *occurs when average prices rise because Aggregate Demand grows excessively relative to Aggregate Supply.*

When Aggregate Demand expands from AD_0 to AD_1 in Figure 4, the price level rises from P_0 to P_1. Inflation is sustained only if Aggregate Demand continues to rise.

Economies in Transition:
Inflation and Structural Change

Traditional ways of doing things are under siege everywhere central planning is being replaced by supply and demand. Change is costly, and such costs are often manifested by inflation during major political and economic upheavals. Price levels were destabilized throughout the early 1990s in Russia, China, Yugoslavia, and a host of other countries where market forces are displacing command economic systems.

During 1993, the Russian ruble, once pegged (artificially high) at an exchange rate of about $1.40 per ruble, tumbled to less than $0.001, or more than 1,000 rubles per dollar. As you might expect, prices skyrocketed for items most Russians deem to be necessities. At times, average price increases approached the 50% per-month hyperinflation threshold.

Bread, which had been subsidized under central planning in the USSR at about 5 cents per loaf (.04 rubles), quickly exceeded 1,000 rubles per kilo. Food staples, once plentiful for Russians who settled for monotonous diets after long waits in queues, disappeared from the store shelves. Armies of gangsters emerged, no longer afraid of the harsh punishments

once meted out in the USSR police state. Black markets flourished, with tourists from more stable economies getting incredible bargains—as long as payment was in dollars, francs, pounds, or yen.

Recent inflation in China has been more moderate, in part because China's leaders have decentralized economic decision-making over time. A first stage was gradual elimination of low prices set by central planners for most agricultural goods. The set prices had acted as price ceilings would have in a market economy, resulting in some food shortages and imports of food into China during the 1970s and early 1980s. As many food prices were freed to seek their own levels, the cost of food rose in urban areas, but China shifted from being a net importer of rice to being a net exporter. In the countryside, waves of peasants abandoned farming and swarmed into urban centers, attracted by the higher wages offered by modernized industries and by new opportunities to start their own small businesses.

Economic decentralization has contributed mightily to Chinese economic growth, now estimated at nearly 10% annually. But this

growth has been marred by 15% to 20% inflation rates, as the prices of housing, food, clothes, and other amenities have risen in urban areas.

Throughout this drive for modernization, ushered in under Deng Xiaoping, the Chinese leadership has tried to maintain tightly centralized political control. Time will reveal, however, whether dictatorship of the party can be sustained in the long run, once economic decisions are decentralized.

Variations on these inflation stories have unfolded in Vietnam and former Soviet states and satellites. One early stage in any major economic transition towards capitalistic markets seems to be a burst of inflation. Another common problem is widespread corruption, as officials demand—and get—bribes from would-be entrepreneurs and assorted hustlers who must secure import and export licenses and more general access to transportation, information and government officials, and the right to do business. With the passage of time, however, these economies show signs of settling down as the price system takes over and production takes off.

Economists are nearly unanimous in believing that inflation occurs when our demands for goods grow faster than our capacity to produce them. Indeed, a substantial minority of economists insist that this is the only realistic explanation for sustained inflation. Excessive demands ripple through a fully employed economy when the money supply grows too rapidly or government spends far more than it collects in taxes.

Supply-Side Inflation

Creeping inflations in many industrialized economies during the 1960s and 1970s at least partially originated from supply-side shocks.

Supply-side inflation results when Aggregate Supply shrinks (e.g., because of rising resource prices or technological reversals), causing the price level to rise and aggregate output to fall.

FIGURE 4   Demand-Side Inflation

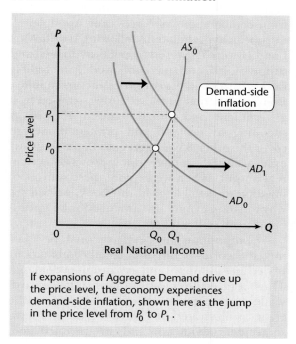

If expansions of Aggregate Demand drive up the price level, the economy experiences demand-side inflation, shown here as the jump in the price level from P_0 to P_1.

Figure 5 illustrates a supply-side shock as a shift in Aggregate Supply from AS_0 to AS_1. Runaway energy costs, worldwide drought, monopolistic greed, and disputes between labor unions and management are only a few of the culprits that some people identify as causal factors. OPEC oil price hikes during the 1970s were clearly severe shocks to the supply side. Supply-side shocks can be grouped into the broad categories of cost-push and administered-price explanations for inflation.

• **Cost-Push Inflation**   Exorbitant union wage hikes are often fingered as inflationary. This is one example of a *cost-push theory* of inflation. Powerful unions presumably demand wage hikes not warranted by increased worker productivity. Rising labor costs are then passed forward to consumers as pushed-up prices. This explanation pinpoints unions as the villains causing inflation. Blaming unions is especially popular among some politicians and business leaders. Other cost-push theo-

ries point to rising oil prices or to increases in the prices of imported goods or raw materials.

• **Administered-Price Inflation**   Some economists turn the mechanics of the union-based, cost-push inflation explanation upside down. According to the *administered-price theory*, firms with market power may be reluctant to raise prices because they fear adverse publicity, antitrust actions, or similar threats to their dominance in a market. They use hikes in wages or other resource costs as excuses to raise prices, generally by more than their higher costs would justify. Huge firms' failures to resist excessive wage demands, it is argued, tend to reinforce the momentum of inflation.

Mixed Theories of Inflation

Disputes about whether inflation is caused only by rising Aggregate Demand or only by shrinking Aggregate Supply parallel debates about whether the top or bottom blade of a pair of scissors cuts a

Inflation may originate from the supply side of the economy; when the Aggregate Supply curve shifts from AS_0 to AS_1, the price level rises from P_0 to P_1.

Figure 5   Supply-Side Inflation

piece of paper. An accurate portrait of any episode of inflation usually requires considering influences from both sides. Composition-shift and expectational theories blend demand-side and supply-side pressures.

- **Composition-Shift Inflation** The foundation of *composition-shift inflation theory* is the assumption that prices rise more easily than they fall. Thus, if demand rises in one sector of the economy, prices rise. But if there are offsetting declines in demands in other sectors, prices do not fall, at least in the short run. Instead, as sales shrink, firms reduce output and lay off workers. Thus, inflationary pressures emerge as the composition of demands and supplies changes. Growing sectors will typically experience increases in prices, while declining sectors suffer from stagnation and unemployment rather than long-term price cuts.

- **Expectational Inflation** Inflationary expectations may cause *expectational inflation* because prevalent forecasts are at least partially self-fulfilling—we create our own future realities by what we anticipate. Thus, producers who expect inflation build inventories by boosting output while cutting back on current sales. Why sell now when prices will soon be higher? Current sales are reduced by immediate price hikes and temporary decreases in supplies.

If at the same time, buyers expect inflation, they will try to accumulate their own inventories of durable goods. This bolsters their current demands, as they attempt to beat the higher prices expected later. Thus, inflationary expectations quickly cause price hikes because they reduce supplies and increase demands. These adjustments explain why inflation may develop incredible momentum. Inflation causes expectations of inflation, which stimulates more inflation, and so forth. You may have heard people refer to the "wage-price inflationary spiral" or to the "vicious circle of inflation." Inflationary expectations are important in explaining why inflation is so difficult to suppress.

The preceding theories of inflation are not mutually exclusive; many inflations emerge from combinations of forces. For example, all European hyperinflations following World Wars I and II were triggered by political turmoil and supply-side disturbances followed by incredibly rapid growth in these countries' money supplies. Bolivian inflation in the 1980s was caused by a government policy that financed 15% of its spending by taxation and printed money to cover the other 85%. Aggregate Demand grows excessively if the money supply grows faster than real output. When we explore these sources of inflation in detail later in this book, we will see why inflation cannot be sustained for long without growth of the money supply.

Composition-shift, expectational, or other mixed theories of inflation entail combinations of declines in supply and expansion of demand. Thus, Aggregate Supply curves shift leftward, while Aggregate Demand curves shift to the right, as illustrated in Figure 6. You now have some ideas about how indices are calculated, how various types of inflation rise, and how the forces at work in an inflationary process shift Aggregate Demands and Aggregate Supplies. Let's examine the effect of inflation on social welfare.

INFLATION'S COSTS AND BENEFITS

Surprisingly, some people win from inflation, while others lose. Losses from inflation are of two major types. First, inflation may reduce the efficiency of production and distribution. In either case, there will be declines in standards of living. These are the *real-income costs of inflation*. Second, inflation fractures the implicit and explicit agreements that bind people together. These are the *social costs of inflation*.

Real-Income Costs of Inflation

Inflation increases transaction costs and reduces real income (*a*) by making the information about market conditions summarized in monetary

FIGURE 6   Aggregate Demands and Supplies in a Mixed Inflation

Aggregate Demand increases during a mixed inflation (a movement from AD_0 to AD_1), imposing pressure for higher prices and outputs. Aggregate Supply, however, decreases (e.g., from AS_0 to AS_1), generating pressure for higher prices but less output. Thus, without more information, we cannot ascertain whether the national output grows or falls, but we can be sure that the price level rises.

prices less certain and (*b*) by unnecessarily shifting resources into the repricing of goods. Real income is also reduced because inflation distorts economic decisions.

• **Inflated Transaction Costs** Information about prices collected through expenditures of time and effort by producers, resource suppliers, and consumers becomes obsolete more quickly during inflation. Have you ever visited a store intending to buy a certain item, only to discover that you can no longer afford it because its price has risen? Workers are caught in a similar squeeze when they learn that price hikes have made it impossible for them to cover all the purchases they planned when they agreed to a wage offered by an employer. *Transaction costs* increase because perceptions about prices and purchasing power turn out to be mistaken far more frequently during inflationary periods than when average prices are stable.

Another way inflation increases transaction costs is that resources that could have been used productively elsewhere are used to reprice goods. Some repricing occurs at all times because relative prices change even when price levels are stable. During an inflationary period,

however, it is not unusual to find that most items in your grocery cart have been marked up since they were first put on the shelf. Restaurant menus and airline ticket schedules must be reprinted, and candy and cold drink machines must be adjusted to accept new denominations of coins. Where government regulates prices (e.g., utility rates or bus fares), considerable time and effort may be absorbed in redesigning rate schedules. Such increases in information cost are called the *menu costs* of inflation.

• **Distortion Costs** Another major cost of inflation emerges from feelings of uncertainty among savers and investors. Saving and investing reflects faith in the future. Uncertainty caused by inflation stifles investment and saving, which then hampers growth of Aggregate Supply. Funds that would normally flow into new capital may be diverted into real estate or inventories, so that growth and technological advances sputter well below the levels needed for a healthy economy. Firms also mark up price margins to compensate for increased risks. If so, over the long run, inflation causes Aggregate Supply to wither.

Relative prices are distorted if inflation artificially causes prices to rise at different rates; inefficient decisions about production and consumption result. For example, many people incurred huge mortgages in the early 1980s that required monthly payments they could afford only if double-digit inflation continued. An epidemic of foreclosures swept the country during 1984–1991 when inflation slowed down. Many buyers might have waited were it not for their fear that "if we don't buy now, we won't ever be able to afford a home." Inefficiencies in decision making caused by inflation are termed *distortion costs*.

Social Costs of Inflation

Inflation stimulates strife between buyers (who want low prices maintained) and sellers (who want prices raised to reflect rising production costs). Conflicts among consumers, producers, and regulatory agencies are accentuated during inflationary episodes. Ignoring menu and distortion costs for a moment, inflation is roughly what mathematicians call a *zero sum game*. For every loser during inflation (someone who must pay more for a given good), there is a winner (someone who receives a greater price for the things sold).

You gain during inflation if the prices of things you sell go up faster than the prices of things you buy. Some people lose because their incomes do not keep pace with the average prices of the goods they buy. Why all the furor over inflation if the gains and losses are roughly in balance? Income redistributions from inflation are a major source of inflation's social costs. Even though losses to some are offset by gains to others, the process seems capricious and erodes the trust we have in each other.

A basic problem is that inflation is often blamed for unfavorable events that would have arisen because of shifts in *uninflated* demands and supplies. Most of us feel that increases in our paychecks are much-deserved rewards for hard work. Have you ever considered that your raise is an increase in the price of your services and is seen as inflation by purchasers of the goods you produce? If your neighbor's pay rises

faster than your own, supply and demand may be at work, not inflation.

Even if our nominal income keeps pace with inflation, it erodes the value of money we have saved. A past irritant was that progressivity in our federal income tax system allowed inflation to bump us into higher tax brackets, a process called *bracket creep*. Federal income tax rates were indexed to inflation in 1985, reducing bracket creep, but it remains a problem where state or local governments use progressive taxes.

On the other hand, the prices of physical assets such as land and housing often rise even more rapidly than the rate of inflation. Homeowners gain during inflation; prospective home buyers lose. Borrowers are an important group of gainers from inflation. Homeowners with huge mortgages find repaying loans increasingly easy if inflation pushes up nominal income. (Would you like to borrow $1,000,000 today if inflation was going to be 1,000,000% next year—before the loan was due?) Of course, borrowers' gains are almost exactly offset by losses in the real wealth of lenders.

Government, business firms, farmers, and young families tend to be net debtors and often gain from unexpected inflation. The federal debt now exceeds $4 trillion. Holders of U.S. Treasury bonds are the losers in this exchange of wealth. Established households and mature people anticipating retirement are usually savers and lose from inflation. (The ultimate lenders are people with bank deposits, not bankers.) A related cost of inflation is that this redistributional effect of rewarding borrowing and penalizing saving provides substantial incentives to use credit, but going even deeper in debt than we already are is probably a bad idea for most of us.

Still another consideration is that some people live on fixed incomes: their pensions or wage contracts are not adjusted for changes in the cost of living. The growing numbers of contracts containing escalator clauses illustrates how people adjust to inflation over time. Even so, there are people whose incomes are at least partially fixed; those living on life insurance annuities or who long ago contracted for long-term fixed-dollar payments to cover them in their old age are examples. Inflation harms many senior citizens to the extent that portions of their incomes are fixed.

Redistributions caused by inflation are commonly seen as arbitrary and capricious, but many social ills blamed on it actually result from other forces. You may have seen news programs about how low-income people suffer most from inflation, a charge refuted by most studies of this problem. The difficulties faced by the poor result from poverty, not inflation per se. Joseph Minarik analyzed census data and concluded that the sustained but moderate inflation of the 1970s harmed people at the top proportionally far more than people at the lower end of the income spectrum.[3]

The income redistribution aspects of inflation generally do not affect the real level of national production, which Adam Smith (in 1776) rightly termed the *Wealth of Nations*. Rather, the redistributive properties of inflation are part of the larger problem of achieving and maintaining an equitable distribution of our real national income.

Benefits of Inflation

A little inflationary pressure may ease needed changes in relative prices. This is especially true if price reductions are resisted more vigorously than price increases. For example, in the 1970s the demand for college professors fell due to declines in enrollment, but the supply of profs grew. Market pressures to reduce professors' real wages were accommodated fairly easily by allowing their salaries' purchasing power to shrink through inflation. During this period, the rate of inflation grew faster than nominal salaries and, thus, real salaries fell. This process would have been far more traumatic if colleges had been forced to negotiate lower money wages for faculty, which might have been necessary had the price level been stable.

---

[3]Joseph J. Minarik, "Who Wins, Who Losses from Inflation," *The Brookings Bulletin* 15, no. 1 (1980); 6.

Inflation's effects on capital accumulation and economic growth may also be positive at times. If managers believe that equipment costs will rise in the near future, firms may invest more in capital equipment, boosting Aggregate Supply in the short run. Such planning can backfire, however; investment decisions made prematurely because of inflationary expectations can wipe out some investors.

A third possible benefit is that inflation may ease expanding government spending relative to private spending. Politicians may prefer to use inflation to finance more government spending instead of relying on an unpopular tax system—spending can grow without paying for it directly via taxes. For example, inflationary pressures were allowed to build during World War II. Tax hikes sufficient to finance the war without inflation might have posed severe disincentives for production. Of course, many people would argue that under most circumstances, inflationary growth of government is a cost, not a benefit, of inflation. This issue will be treated in more detail in future chapters.

The Discomfort Index

Arthur Okun, chairman of President Lyndon Johnson's Council of Economic Advisors, developed an index intended to summarize the general state of the economy.

> The economic **discomfort index** equals the inflation rate plus the overall unemployment rate.

In 1976, Jimmy Carter renamed this the *misery index* and used it to brand President Ford's economic policies as failures. Ronald Reagan then resurrected the misery index to condemn economic performance during President Carter's administration. The index was also featured in the 1984 political campaign.

The index for four-year presidential terms (averaged to smooth short-run fluctuations) since 1950 is presented in Table 2. This index showed remarkable stability during the 1950s and 1960s but took a big jump during the 1970s

TABLE 2   Average Discomfort Indices and Presidential Administrations, 1949–1994

Term	President	Average Percentage Inflation Rate	Average Percentage Unemployment Rate	Discomfort Index
1949–52	Truman	2.8	4.4	7.2
1953–56	Eisenhower	1.4	4.2	5.6
1957–60	Eisenhower	1.7	5.5	7.2
1961–64	Kennedy-Johnson	1.2	5.8	7.0
1965–68	Johnson	3.2	3.9	7.1
1969–72	Nixon	4.6	5.0	9.6
1973–76	Nixon-Ford	8.2	6.7	14.9
1977–80	Carter	10.6	6.5	17.1
1981–84	Reagan	5.2	8.6	13.8
1985–88	Reagan	3.4	6.4	9.8
1989–92	Bush	4.3	6.3	10.6
1993–94	Clinton	3.1	5.9	9.0

Source: *Economic Report of the President,* 1994.

and early 1980s. By 1990, however, the discomfort index had returned to levels accepted as normal before 1970.

Macroeconomic policies focus on the goals of full employment, price-level stability, and economic growth. Implementing appropriate policies requires relatively accurate measures of unemployment and inflation. You should keep the various costs and benefits of unemployment and inflation, as well as their data limitations, in mind while you study the material in the next few chapters.

CHAPTER REVIEW: KEY POINTS

1. **Inflation** occurs when the average level of prices increases; **deflation** entails declines in the average level of prices.

2. Index numbers are used to compare particular variables over time. The **Consumer Price Index (CPI)** measures average price changes for a given bundle of consumer goods over time. The CPI is based on typical consumer patterns for approximately 80% of the urban population.

3. The CPI is used extensively as an **escalator clause** (cost-of-living adjustment) in many contracts. It is also an **economic indicator** and is used to convert **nominal values** to **real values**. (Nominal values are synonymous with monetary values.)

4. **Deflating** nominal variables means dividing their monetary values by (1% of) a price index.

5. Among the major difficulties in computing the CPI are the problems inherent in adjusting the index for (*a*) new products, (*b*) changes in the qualities of existing products, (*c*) changes in the composition of consumer expenditures, and (*d*) already owned consumer durables such as housing.

6. The **Producer Price Index (PPI)** measures changes in the prices of goods in other than retail markets. The **GDP Deflator** adjusts GDP for changes in prices. It is composed of relevant portions of the CPI and the PPI, plus some additional prices covered by neither.

7. **Creeping inflation** occurs relatively slowly; **galloping inflation** occurs when average prices begin moving at double-digit annual rates. **Hyperinflation** entails average price hikes exceeding 50% monthly. Inflation is generally less harmful if it is anticipated than if it is a surprise to people.

8. Inflation increases transaction costs by making price information obsolete faster, and it causes resources that could be used productively elsewhere to be used for repricing. These are the *menu costs* of inflation.

9. Inflation also distorts relative prices and economic decision-making, and depresses incentives to save. Capital accumulation may or may not be hampered by inflation, depending on business expectations and the availability of funds for investment. These are the *distortion costs* of inflation.

10. There are **social costs of inflation**, too, because people feel greater uncertainty during inflationary periods. People living on fixed incomes are hurt by inflation, but many transfer payments and wage contracts now have escalator clauses that adjust payments for price-level changes. Borrowers tend to gain from unexpected inflation, while the ultimate lenders (e.g., savers with bank deposits) lose. When inflation boosts income, meeting a fixed mortgage payment becomes easier, so heavily mortgaged homeowners tend to gain.

11. The **discomfort (misery) index** is the sum of the inflation rate and the unemployment rate. It averaged 6% to 7% during the 1950s and 1960s. During the late 1970s and early 1980s, the index ranged from 13% to more than 20%. By 1988, economic growth had pushed the index below 10%. It rose slightly during the recession of 1991–1992, but then continued to slip downward slowly.

QUESTIONS FOR THOUGHT AND DISCUSSION

1. Many payments are tied to the CPI through escalator clauses to adjust for inflation. Are such formal adjustments necessary for payments tied to sales prices, such as percentage commissions or percentage sales taxes?

2. What characteristics make certain people more vulnerable than others to inflation? What characteristics tend to be true of people who tend to gain from inflation?

3. How would increases in net exports affect the rate of domestic inflation? Does growth of imports increase or decrease domestic inflation? Why?

4. Average U.S. inflation rates have been lower in the 1990s than in the 1970s or 1980s, but higher than the inflation rates typical of the 1960s. Why were fewer Americans as bothered by inflation in the 1990s as most were in the 1960s?

Growth

Macroeconomic

Unemployment

AS

Aggregate demand

Aggregate supply

Inflatio

AD

Macroeconomic equilibrium

Chapter 8

Measuring Economic Performance and Growth

Wise national policies, prudent wage demands, and smart investments all depend on macroeconomic performance. Each month, the Department of Commerce updates its estimates of unemployment and inflation; new estimates for *Gross Domestic Product (GDP)* are issued quarterly. Politicians, business decision-makers, union leaders, and Wall Street gurus then pore over these data the way fortunetellers study tarot cards. You now know something about unemployment and inflation, but GDP may seem a bit abstract. What is GDP? And why should anyone care about it?

The answer lies in linkages between Gross Domestic Product, which is an estimate of national output and income, and *economic growth*, a central concern of macroeconomics. Economic growth (as measured by changes in GDP) can cure excessive unemployment and dampen inflationary pressure. After completing this chapter, you should understand what GDP estimates represent and be aware of some problems with National Income accounting, which was developed roughly 60 years ago by Simon Kuznets (see his biography).

GROSS DOMESTIC PRODUCT (GDP)

Gross Domestic Product is the principal measuring rod for an economy's output. The Department of Commerce computes GDP primarily by compiling accounting data.

> ***Gross Domestic Product (GDP)*** *is the total market value of goods and services produced within a country during some period, usually one year.[1]*

Our Gross Domestic Product includes the value of all goods produced inside the United States, without regard for where the producing individuals or organizations are headquartered. Thus, incomes of all foreign individuals who work in the United States and all profits from the U.S. operations of foreign-owned corpora-

---

[1]Other conceptual definitions of GDP exist, but each has flaws. For example, some describe GDP as the total market value of all final goods produced annually. This definition works only if intermediate goods held as inventories at the end of the accounting year are viewed as final goods.

BIOGRAPHY

Simon Kuznets: Father of National Income Accounting

Russian-born but American-educated, Simon Kuznets (1901–1985) earned his Ph.D. from Columbia University in 1926 and began an association with the National Bureau of Economic Research that spanned a half-century. Kuznets developed and refined most measurements that underpin National Income accounting. Although the concept of National Income could be traced to François Quesnay, an eighteenth-century Frenchman, consistent aggregate measures of most aspects of economic life remained either crude or nonexistent prior to Kuznets's work.

Kuznets pioneered techniques to sum expenditures by different classes of purchases over different classes of goods. Thus, he provided systematic foundations for statistical studies of the relationships among income, consumption, and investment and well deserved the title "Father of National Income Accounting." Without his work, quantitative evaluation of the Keynesian revolution in economic thought would have been impossible. This realization prompted one economist to declare that "we live in the age of Keynes and Kuznets." For his monumental achievements in empirical economics, Kuznets won a Nobel Prize in 1971.

His almost single-handed construction of the National Income accounts made Kuznets aware of GDP's deficiencies as a measure of well-being. Recognizing that GDP ignores working conditions (e.g., stress and strain) and most nonmarket activities, Kuznets rejected reliance on National Income data as sole indicators of economic performance. Nevertheless, GDP is generally accepted today by economists, businesspeople, and politicians as the best barometer available for assessing a country's economic performance and growth.

---

tions are included in U.S. GDP.[2] The remainder of this chapter focuses on GDP, how it is measured, and shortcomings in measurement.

GDP as an Economic Indicator

Measuring GDP is a first step in tracking economic activity over time. Gauging the level of economic activity entails deflating GDP to adjust for inflation. Official estimates of GDP are

---

[2]The Gross *National* Product accounting system used prior to 1991 reverses this approach by including all outputs American entities produce, regardless of the location of production. For example, U.S. G*N*P includes parts of the foreign operations of U.S. corporations. By way of contrast, U.S. G*D*P ignores the incomes of Americans working abroad and the foreign operations of U.S. firms, while counting incomes of foreigners working here and the U.S. operations of foreign firms. If you encounter historical G*N*P data, just remember that U.S. G*N*P and U.S. G*D*P have differed little across time, typically less than 1%.

reported in *nominal* (dollar) amounts. Thus, these data series must be *deflated* (divided by [the GDP deflator/100]) to make them truly comparable across time. This yields estimates of real GDP that indicate the effectiveness of government policies. Forecasts of GDP also help government decision-makers time corrective policies. Good business managers consider macroeconomic forecasts when developing their plans for production, employment, and investments in new plants and equipment.

GDP and Economic Well-Being

Real Gross Domestic Production also provides a crude gauge of national well-being. Income and employment are tied to aggregate output, so individual incomes and spending tend to swing with macroeconomic activity. Dividing real GDP by population yields a rough measure of the average well-being of individuals. Per capita real GDP indicates how well-off average Americans are now relative to earlier times or to typical people in other countries and helps us compare growth rates among countries.

Usage of real GDP to measure production sometimes conflicts with GDP as measure of economic well-being. Trade-offs between measuring production and measuring well-being are invariably resolved in favor of accurate measurement of production. This is why we include such things as inventory accumulation and exports in estimated GDP. Some numbers included in GDP to measure total economic production distort attempts to gauge welfare. For example, in 1993, the U.S. spent 5.5% of its GDP on national defense. Did this make us better-off than citizens of countries that avoided such massive defense spending? Typical European countries spent about 2% of their GDPs on defense in 1993. As you will see in a moment, other complications also confound international comparisons of per capita GDP.

MEASURING GDP

Gross Domestic Product is measured in two basic ways: (*a*) the *expenditure approach* and (*b*) the *income approach*. Figure 1 illustrates these approaches with a version of the circular flow model introduced in Chapter 2. This shows that everything bought (expenditures) is sold by someone who receives income from the sale.

Ideally, both methods would yield identical numbers because spending on output flows as income to resource owners. Unfortunately, most of the data available are recorded for accounting purposes, so the figures used to calculate GDP are only roughly suited for economic

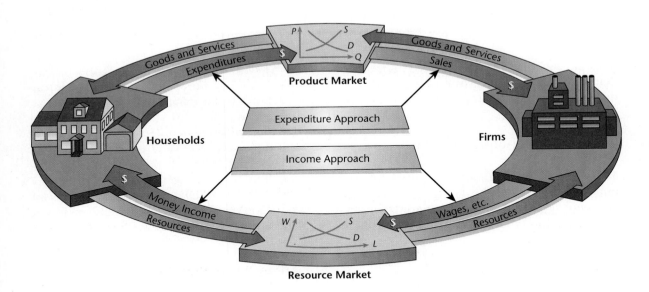

This simple circular flow model illustrates the two major approaches to GDP accounting: All goods are traded in the product market, and total expenditures equal the total value of output. Similarly, income is paid to owners of resources, and summing all such payments provides an estimate of GDP. Note that all expenditures necessarily equal all the payments made to resource owners to produce the output. That is, what is bought must have been sold, and vice versa. (Note: Clockwise arrows show money flows; counterclockwise arrows show flows of goods and resources.)

FIGURE 1   The Circular Flow and National Income Accounting

FIGURE 2 Expenditure and Income Approaches to GDP

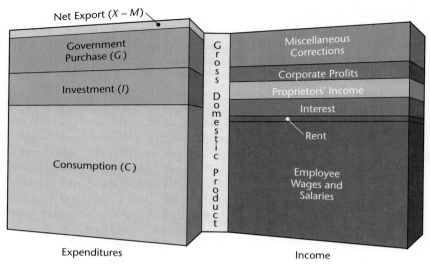

Gross Domestic Product can be estimated using either the expenditure approach or the income approach. As this figure illustrates, the sum of incomes paid to resource owners approximately equals total spending in the economy.
Note: Net exports have been negative for more than a decade.

analysis. Figure 2 displays the proportional makeup of GDP by major types of income and expenditures.

The Expenditure Approach

Measuring GDP by the expenditure approach leads us to the final buyers of all U.S. output.

> *Aggregate Expenditures are the sum of (a) consumer spending, (b) business investment, (c) government purchases, and (d) net spending by foreigners.*

This summation echoes the sources of Aggregate Demand described in a previous chapter. Figure 2 shows the division of the national pie into consumption (C), investment (I), government purchases (G), and net exports [i.e., exports – imports $(X - M)$].[3]

---

[3]The foreign sector appears to affect GDP only negligibly in part because imports offset exports in determining Aggregate Demand. However, this focus on components of Aggregate Demand as a foundation for compiling GDP makes it easy to overlook the tremendous contribution to Aggregate Supply derived through gains from specialization and trade according to comparative advantage.

• **Personal Consumption Expenditures (C)**
Household outlays include spending on non-durable goods (food and clothing), durable goods (appliances and cars), and services (e.g., medical care or haircuts).

> *Personal consumption expenditures (C) are the values of all commodities and services that households and individuals buy.*

This category is familiar because we all engage in consumption every day.

• **Business Investment (I)** Remember that investment, as economists use the term, does not refer to the flows of money or documents that we term financial investment.

> *Economic investment (I) refers to acquisition of new physical capital.*

Business spending for new capital is called **Gross Private Domestic Investment**, or **GPDI**. *Gross* means that all purchases of new buildings, equipment, and the like are included. Whether investment replaces obsolete or worn-out capital does not matter. *Private* means that government investment is excluded. *Domestic* means that the new capital is bought from U.S. producers. We exclude foreign investments by American firms, but investment by foreign companies in the United States is part of our GPDI.

The major components of investment spending are:

1. All new construction, including housing.
2. All final purchases of new equipment (e.g., machinery and tools).
3. Changes in business inventories.

New production facilities, apartment buildings, and office space clearly fit the definition of investment, but why not treat residential construction as consumer spending? One reason is that housing can be built for rental purposes. In addition, the useful life of housing is much longer than most consumer goods. Consequently, housing is regarded as a capital good, and all new construction is included in investment. On the other hand, the rental value of owner-occupied housing is considered consumption; a home produces shelter year after year.

The second item, capital equipment, expands the productive capacity of firms and, thus, is clearly investment. But what about stocks and bonds? Securities are financial rather than economic investments. Purchases of new stocks and bonds may facilitate business spending on real capital, but security transactions merely transfer purchasing power from buyers of stock to sellers without directly boosting productive capacity. Thus, purely financial transactions are not economic investment.

Inventory growth is also investment, while declines are disinvestment. Business inventories include (a) raw materials or intermediate goods bought for use as productive inputs and (b) finished goods held in stock to meet customers' demands. Customers quickly switch to other firms if your firm fails to deliver promptly. Adjustments for inventory changes are needed because we use sales data to estimate production. If inventory growth were ignored, GDP would understate total production. Inventory growth adds to investment, while shrinkage reduces in-

vestment. Goods held in business inventories should be counted in GDP in the year produced, not the year sold. Inventories vary from year to year, so changes in inventories must be estimated to consistently measure total production and our national income.

- **Government Purchases (G)** We consume commodities and services both as private individuals and collectively, through government. Government may buy goods in finished form from private firms, or it may pay for intermediate (unfinished) goods or basic resources to produce the final goods and services it provides. The most important resource government buys is its employees' labor.

Government purchases of goods and services (*G*), ranging from pay for police officers to fire hydrants to cancer research, are then provided at zero or minimal prices to their users. Many goods and services that government purchases and then provides are not sold in markets, so their value cannot be known with precision. Thus, all government goods enter the GDP accounts at the prices government pays for them—for GDP accounting purposes, government is assumed to add nothing to the value of the labor and other resources it uses.

Note that government purchases do not include transfer payments (e.g., Social Security or federal payments for disaster relief) that merely shift funds from one set of households to another set. Because transfer payments do not require production, they affect consumption and, consequently, Aggregate Demand only when recipients spend the funds received from government.

- **Net Exports (X – M)** Net exports are defined as exports (*X*) minus imports (*M*).

Exports are goods manufactured domestically and bought by foreigners.

We clearly must include exports in GDP to measure the value of all production in a year. But do imports reflect American production? The obvious answer is no.

Imports are goods produced in foreign countries and consumed or invested in the United States.

A Hyundai purchased in the United States is part of Korean production (and adds to Korean consumption when the owners of resources that produce the car spend their pay). When Americans buy a Hyundai, the price paid to Korean producers must be subtracted from U.S. consumption or it will appear that the car was produced in the United States. Similarly, if Swiss machinery is installed in an American factory, the purchase appears in the U.S. investment category, but it should be subtracted from U.S. GDP. Thus, in the expenditures approach to calculating GDP, imports are subtracted from exports to estimate the net effect of foreign trade on our economy.

To summarize: Using the expenditure approach, Gross Domestic Product is the sum of consumer spending (*C*), business investment (*I*), government spending for goods and services (*G*), and net exports (*X* – *M*):

$$C + I + G + (X - M) = GDP$$

Table 1 shows these expenditures.

The Income Approach

All spending ultimately translates into income. Thus, national output calculated by the expenditure approach must equal National Income.

National Income (NI) is computed by summing all payments to resource owners—wages, rents, interest, and profits.

Although National Income conceptually sums workers' wages for labor, interest paid to capital owners, landowners' rents, and entrepreneurial profits, the limitations of accounting data cause NI to be measured as the sum of five slightly different categories: (*a*) wages and salaries, (*b*) noncorporate proprietors' income, (*c*) corporate profits before taxes, (*d*) rental income, and (*e*) interest. Table 2 presents proportions and trends in these income payments for selected years.

• **Wages and Salaries**   This category covers not only money wages but also all employees' fringe benefits (e.g., bonuses, stock options, health insurance, paid vacations, and firms' contributions to Social Security). Table 2 shows that wages and salaries increasingly dominate U.S. National Income. The share of wages has risen from less than half of National Income in 1900 to roughly three-fourths today.

• **Proprietors' Income**   National Income accountants split accounting profit into two categories: proprietors' incomes and corporate profits. Proprietors' incomes are received by sole proprietors, partnerships, certain profes-

TABLE 1   Gross Domestic Product: The Expenditure Approach

Component		Billions of 1993 Dollars
Personal consumption expenditures	(C)	$ 4,418.2
Gross private domestic investment	(I)	882.5
Government purchases of goods and services	(G)	1,160.8
Net exports of goods and services	(X – M)*	–65.2
Gross Domestic Product		**$ 6,396.3**

*This negative number reflects a deficit in the 1993 U.S. balance of trade. Since 1982, we have consistently imported more than we exported.

Note: Rounding may cause minor inconsistencies.

Source: Economic Report of the President, 1994.

sional associations, and unincorporated farms. Included in farm income is an estimate of the value of food grown and consumed on farms—and or from home gardens. Although not marketed, this clearly represents production.

Much of this income category represents wages, interest, or rent that proprietors would have earned if they had not operated their own firms. Isolating this category according to purely economic concepts to identify opportunity costs is impossible, however, given the limitations of accounting data. Thus, we consider proprietors' income as "profit," but only for purposes of GDP accounting.

Proprietors' shares of National Income were falling until recently, declining from 17.5% in 1929 to only 7.8% in 1980. Wages grew in part when small family farmers were attracted by relatively more remunerative industrial jobs. A recent rebound in proprietors' shares may reflect resurgent entrepreneurship,—or it may merely track growing tendencies for firms to rely less on career employees and more on independent contractors, many of whom may only reluctantly be self-employed.

• **Corporate Profit** Corporations use their accounting profit in three ways. First, they must pay corporate income taxes. Second, they may pay stockholders dividends from their after-tax income. Finally, remaining profits are kept in the firm as working capital or to finance either internal expansion or external acquisitions (*mergers* and *takeovers*). Economists call profit kept by firms *undistributed corporate profits*; to accountants, they are retained earnings. Much of the category called corporate profit actually represents the interest forgone had stockholders bought bonds instead of stock. Again, because isolating pure economic profit from opportunity costs is not feasible, the convention is to lump all corporate profits with proprietors' income in the accounting term "profit."

Proprietors' income has fallen as a percentage of National Income, so you might expect growth in the share accruing to corporations. A glance at Table 2, however, reveals a trend for corporate profit to shrink relative to National Income. What accounts for the rise in the share of wages and erratic declines in both corporate and proprietors' incomes? A partial answer lies in the fact that government outlays as a percentage of total output rose markedly during this century. Most government-provided services require substantial labor, so the share of wages and salaries has grown steadily.

• **Rental Income** Accounting rents are usually derived from the leasing of real property (such as land, houses, offices), but they can be obtained from renting any asset (e.g., videotapes or U-Haul trailers). Determining what part conforms to economic rent as a payment solely for

TABLE 2 The National Income Approach to GDP (Selected Years, 1929–1993)

Category	1929 $ B	1929 %	1933 $ B	1933 %	1953 $ B	1953 %	1973 $ B	1973 %	1993 $ B	1993 %
Wages and Salaries	51.1	58.9	29.5	73.1	209.1	68.6	812.8	72.6	3,534.3	74.9
Proprietor Income	15.2	17.5	5.9	14.6	40.5	13.3	116.5	10.4	397.4	8.4
Corporate Profits	10.5	12.0	1.2	3.0	39.6	13.0	116.4	10.4	374.1	7.9
Rental Income	5.4	6.2	2.0	5.1	12.7	4.2	17.3	1.5	6.4	0.1
Interest Income	4.7	5.4	4.1	10.2	2.8	0.9	56.5	5.0	407.3	8.6
National Income	86.8	100	40.3	100	304.7	100	1,119.5	100	4,719.6	100

Notes: Rounding may cause minor inconsistencies. Rapid tax write-offs of depreciation increasingly understate rental shares.
Source: U.S. Department of Commerce, *Economic Reports of the President*, 1970–94 and *Survey of Current Business*, January 1994.

the use of land is impossible, so again we use accounting classifications. As you see in Table 2, rental income is now the smallest accounting category in National Income.

• **Interest** Interest is also rather self-explanatory—payments made for the use of borrowed capital (usually, financial capital). Interest payments are made by borrowers to banks or to holders of bonds, or by banks to their depositors. (Banks act primarily as specialized intermediaries. A bank arranges loans of its depositors' funds to borrowers. Thus, depositors—not banks—are the ultimate lenders.) National Income accounting conventions treat interest paid to holders of government bonds as a transfer payment and exclude it from the interest component of National Income. If interest on government bonds were included, interest would have been roughly one-seventh of National Income in 1993.

RECONCILING GDP AND NI

Gross Private Domestic Investment (GPDI) overstates growth of the nation's stock of capital because some capital wears out each year.

> *Accountants refer to the decline in value of capital because of wear and tear or obsolescence as* **depreciation**.

But actual depreciation data reflect rapid accounting write-offs to exploit advantageous tax treatments. The overstated "depreciation" computed by accountants is termed the *capital consumption allowance* by economists, but no better data are available.

Subtracting depreciation from Gross Private Domestic Investment yields *Net Private Domestic Investment*, an estimate of annual growth in a nation's capital. All else being equal, depreciation reduces capital owners' wealth. Thus, one step in reconciling GDP and NI entails subtracting depreciation from GDP to compute *Net Domestic Product (NDP)*. Conceptually, NDP estimates how much we could consume in a given year while maintaining a constant stock of capital throughout that year.

Net Domestic Product (NDP) is the net value of an economy's annual output after adjusting for depreciation.

Failure to consider depreciation would cause overstatement of the net value of production. In a sense, depreciation represents a "death rate of capital" that must be subtracted from the "birth rate of capital" (GPDI) to arrive at net capital formation.

Another major adjustment is required to reconcile GDP and National Income. The funds paid for goods and the funds firms receive are not equal. Sales and excise taxes, collectively known as *indirect business taxes*, drive wedges between what consumers or investors spend and sellers' net receipts. For example, sales taxes must be subtracted from a buyer's payment for a new car before income can be distributed to auto workers or manufacturers. Consequently, indirect business taxes must be subtracted from Net Domestic Product.[4] We reconcile GDP and National Income only after making these and other miscellaneous adjustments, as summarized in Table 3.

The Value-Added Technique

If National Income accountants relied primarily on income tax returns, calculating GDP would entail summing all declared incomes and then adding indirect business taxes and depreciation. But this strategy depends on honest tax returns, and even the latest figures available would be relatively out-of-date because (*a*) tax returns filed on April 15 are for the preceding year, and (*b*) it takes time for the IRS to compile and interpret the returns. For these reasons and more, National Income is calculated primarily as a double check on GDP figures.

An alternative is to collect all sales figures for a year. Most firms are subject to taxes reported monthly to government agencies, so sales

---

[4]Another adjustment entails adding foreign payments to resource owners based in the United States and subtracting payments of resource payments to owners based outside the United States. On balance, these adjustments are relatively small for the United States.

TABLE 3 Reconciling Income and Expenditure Approaches to GDP

	Billions of Dollars
Expenditure Approach	
Gross Domestic Product (GDP for 1993)	$6,327.1
minus: capital consumption allowance (depreciation)	–663.2
equals: Net Domestic Product (NDP)	5663.9
minus: indirect business taxes (IBT) and misc.	–559.9
equals: **National Income (NI)**	**$5,104.0**
Income Approach	
Wages and salaries	$3,750.6
plus: proprietors' income (business, professional farm)	439.4
plus: corporate profits before taxes	458.1
plus: rental income	12.7
plus: interest	443.2
equals: **National Income (NI)**	**$5,104.0**

Note: Rounding may cause minor inconsistencies.
Sources: Department of Commerce and *Economic Report of the President*, 1994 and *Survey of Current Business*, January 1994.

data are available on a regular basis. But what then? Merely summing all sales revenues entails *double counting*. For example, if USX's steel sales are added to Ford's sales, we count USX's output twice: when steel is sold to Ford and again when Ford sells new cars and trucks.

To avoid double counting, National Income accountants use the value-added technique.

*A firm's **value added** is computed by subtracting from its sales revenue any purchases of intermediate goods from other firms.*

This leaves only the value of the firm's own production: its value added.[5] National income accountants then sum the value added by each firm. Summing domestic values added by all firms yields reasonably accurate GDP figures, after adjusting for such things as inventory changes, the imputed (estimated) rental values of owner-occupied housing, and the imputed

values of food grown and consumed on the farm—from your home garden.

MOVING FROM GDP TO DISPOSABLE PERSONAL INCOME

National Income (NI), GDP, Net Domestic Product (NDP), Personal Income (PI), and Disposable Personal Income (DPI) tend to move together. Therefore, in future chapters we often use a single economic model to explain how all these data are determined. Nevertheless, understanding how they differ helps illustrate how macroeconomics is linked to everyday life. You already know that capital consumption allowances (depreciation) are subtracted from GDP to compute Net Domestic Product (NDP), and that subtracting indirect business taxes (e.g., sales taxes) from NDP yields all income earned by suppliers of productive resources, or National Income (NI). More adjustments are needed, however, before arriving at household income before taxes (Personal Income) and the after-tax income households actually have left to spend (Disposable Personal Income).

---

[5]Most foreign nations rely heavily on taxes on values added by business firms. Many American economists favor replacement of U.S. corporate income taxes by value-added taxes, an idea that is regularly resurrected in Congress as one way to efficiently reduce federal budget deficits.

From NI to Personal Income (PI)

National Income includes wages, interest, rent, proprietors' income, and corporate profit. Firms often serve as tax collection points; in fact, some people never see parts of the income attributed to them. For example, corporate taxes must be paid before stockholders have claims on corporate income; these taxes must be subtracted from National Income. Dividends are parts of stockholders' Personal Income, but corporate retained earnings (undistributed corporate profit) must also be subtracted from National Income. Moreover, all employers are legally obligated to match employees' Social Security contributions. National Income accounts subtract all Social Security taxes from NI on this journey toward Personal Income.

Personal Income (PI) is the money income received by households before they pay their personal taxes.

In addition to household income earned but not received, two forms of income are received but not earned. A growing share of our National Income is devoted to government transfer payments (e.g., welfare payments). Many firms also engage in charitable activities. Funds transferred through either government or business to private individuals must be added to National Income. At this point, we finally arrive at the total amount of personal income households receive.

From PI to Disposable Personal Income (DPI)

You might think that Personal Income is the amount available for personal consumption and saving, but direct taxes on individuals must be paid from Personal Income.

Disposable Personal Income (DPI) is income households can choose to consume or save after subtracting income taxes from Personal Income.

Table 4 details the breakdown from GDP to DPI for selected years.

TABLE 4   Gross Domestic Product and Related Data (billions of dollars)

		1929	1950	1993
Gross Domestic Product (GDP)		$103.1	$284.8	$6,327.1
minus:	capital consumption allowance (depreciation)	−7.9	−18.3	−663.2
equals:	Net Domestic Product (NDP)	95.2	266.5	5,663.9
minus:	indirect business taxes and misc.	−3.4	−14.1	−559.9
equals:	National Income (NI)	91.8	252.4	5,104.0
minus:	corporate profits with inventory adjustments	−10.5	−37.7	−458.1
	contributions for social insurance	−0.2	−6.9	−585.1
	net interest	−4.7	−3.0	−443.2
plus:	government transfer payments	0.9	14.3	383.7
	personal interest income	2.5	7.2	693.1
	dividends	6.8	8.8	157.8
	business transfer payments	0.6	0.8	21.8
equals:	Personal Income (PI)	86.2	235.0	5.374.0
minus:	personal taxes	−2.6	−20.7	−681.0
equals:	Disposable Personal Income (DPI)	88.6	215.2	4,692.2
minus:	consumer interest and personal transfers of foreigners	−6.9	−2.8	−123.7
minus:	consumption expenditures	−77.2	−191.0	−4,359.9
equals:	personal saving (S)	4.5	21.4	208.7

Note: Rounding may cause minor inconsistencies.

Source: U.S. Department of Commerce, *Economic Report of the President*, 1994 and *Survey of Current Business*, January 1994.

LIMITATIONS OF GDP ACCOUNTING

How well do estimates of GDP and National Income measure economic performance? These accounts, though well suited for some purposes, have limitations that fall into four broad categories: (a) inaccuracy, (b) incompleteness, (c) misclassification, and (d) ambiguity.

Inaccuracy

> There is a tendency toward specious accuracy, a pretense that things have been counted more precisely than they can be. . . . The classic case is, of course, the story in which a man, asked about the age of a river, states that it is 3,000,021 years old. Asked how he could give such accurate information, the answer was that twenty-one years ago the river's age was given as three million years.
>
> Oskar Morgenstern
> *"Qui Numerare Incipit Errore Incipit"*

Just how accurate must GDP accounts be to be useful to planners and forecasters? Estimation errors are clearly biased. For example, many people systematically understate the incomes reported on their tax forms. Statisticians commonly assume that measurement errors are offsetting, but we have a bridge to sell anyone who believes that as many people overreport income as underreport it. Underreporting biases estimates of GDP downwards, especially for countries in which tax avoidance (legal) and tax evasion (illegal) are significant.

Another problem is that most accounts are reported to the exact dollar. For example, per capita income for Utah was reported as $12,893. Would it be just as useful (and less misleading) to learn that per capita income in Utah was roughly $13,000? Statistics need be no more precise than their use dictates, nor should data be reported in a way that creates a false sense of certainty.

Incompleteness: Nonmarket Transactions

GDP is the value of all production so it should cover all outputs. National accounts focus on market transactions because dollar sales figures are reasonably available, but not all productive activity is marketed. Some nonmarket activities are included in GDP because crude estimates of their values are available (e.g., estimated rents for owner-occupied housing and estimates for food consumed by its producers). But the values of homemakers' services are excluded from GDP; any estimates would be almost pure guesses. This leads to the ludicrous situation where hiring someone to clean your home increases GDP, but the same work done by a family member does not enter our GDP accounts. The same is true of homemade haircuts and other do-it-yourself projects.

Only crude estimates are available for unrecorded activities such as cash or barter transactions, so the government excluded these estimates until 1986 (see Focus 1). Illegal activities have traditionally been treated as socially unproductive, so they are excluded from GDP. But should legalization of gambling or marijuana lead to growth in measured GDP even if people's behavior doesn't change? Under current accounting practices, it would. Such problems mean that comparisons of GDP over time or among countries must be tempered by recognition that GDP accounts are affected by the relative importance of do-it-yourself production and barter and by differences in laws and regulations.

Misclassification

Some GDP items seem misclassified. For example, individual spending on education is treated as personal consumption. Football games, parties, and some frivolous courses may qualify as consumption activities. But time and effort spent studying that will increase your future productivity should be classified as investment, not consumption. (Should your body's deterioration as you age be considered "depreciation"?) Government investments in flood control, research and development, transportation networks, and so on are treated similarly. These investments are reported as government spending instead of investment. Classification in this way tends to understate the extent to which present consumption is diverted to activities that enhance our future productivity, output, growth, and well-being.

Ambiguity: Government Output

The government seldom directly charges prices for its services to final users, so the value of government output is somewhat ambiguous. Critics who view most government spending as waste might advocate discounting its purchases to more accurately measure the value of total GDP. On the other hand, people who view government as a bargain might think that GDP would be more accurate if government spending were assigned a premium. Consequently, National Income accountants use the best estimate available, out-of-pocket government spending: primarily, wages paid to government workers.

Ambiguity: International Comparisons

The cliché "You can't compare apples and oranges" is often echoed in debate. Economists view such tasks as easier than this adage suggests; money prices provide a common denominator. But such comparisons get tougher when different types of money are used to do the pricing.

• **The Exchange Rate Approach**   Currencies (different types of money) of most countries are traded in international financial markets 24 hours each day at exchange rates driven primarily by international supplies and demands of these currencies.

> An **exchange rate** is the relative price of one currency in terms of another.

Exchange rates are quoted in the financial sections of most newspapers. An exchange rate for the German deutsche mark (DM) of 2.00 per dollar, for example, would mean that each DM is worth $0.50, and that $1 will buy 2DM.

The easiest approach for comparing GDP between countries is to use exchange rates for conversion to a common denominator. Thus, if German per capita GDP is 20,000DM and the exchange rate is 2DM per dollar, then 20,000DM = $10,000 per capita income in Germany, when converted into dollars. The exchange rate approach has been used for decades, primarily because of its computational convenience. Unfortunately, this approach often yields very misleading results, as described in Focus 2.

If the international economy and all domestic economies were perfectly competitive, exchange rates would adjust so that the price of any single good or resource or service would be identical everywhere in the world. In other words, if transaction costs were zero, price deviations for any given good would be zero, a concept known as the *law of one price.*

> The **law of one price** assumes that transaction costs are zero and concludes that only one price can exist at any given moment for identical items.

Absent transaction costs, a haircut in Bombay would cost the same, after converting Indian rupees for U.S. dollars, as the same haircut in Baltimore. The same would be true of computer disks or heads of lettuce. The real cost of living would be the same everywhere, after adjusting for such amenities as weather and scenic beauty.

In the real world, however, transaction costs are not zero, markets are imperfectly competitive, governments intervene to set exchange rates artificially, and quotas and tariffs hinder free flows of goods and resources across international borders. Consequently, international exchange rates for currencies often fail to reflect the relative costs of living in different countries.

• **The Purchasing Power Parity (PPP) Approach** Growing recognition of flaws in the exchange rate approach have led researchers to adjust GDPs according to relative costs of living. If such basic goods as food, clothing, and shelter cost much more (after exchange rate conversion) in one country (say, Japan) than in another (say, Brazil), then the well-being of the Brazilians relative to the Japanese is understated by the exchange rate approach, while Japanese well-being is relatively overstated.

The Underground Economy

We all know tax cheats who understate their income. Cosmetologists who report only half their tips, plumbers who give cash customers a break, and gamblers who keep no records are all engaged in the *underground economy.* Estimates of its size range from a conservative 3% to an astounding 20% of GDP, which means that underground participants may now cheat the U.S. Treasury out of as much as $300 billion in taxes annually.

Figure 3 presents one set of estimates of the size of the underground economy. Although researchers disagree on its size, one piece of evidence that the subterranean economy is increasingly significant is that the demand for the cash component in our money supply has grown sharply in recent decades. Large bills are the payment of choice in much of the underground economy.

Why is this happening? Part of the answer is that many Americans view high tax brackets as powerful incentives to cheat. This problem is compounded by the shrinking probability of an Internal Revenue Service audit. About 3% of all tax returns were audited in the 1960s; the proportion is now around 1.5%. In addition, tax evasion has become respectable in the eyes of some, who excuse their behavior with the argument that "everybody does it."

Cataloging all the ways people have found to cheat on their taxes would generate a book as thick as a New York phone directory. Legitimate businesspeople may not report cash income, or they may understate income by taking excessive tax deductions. If you claim new bedroom drapes as a business expense, you are involved in the underground economy. Barter is perfectly legal but it is a

major avenue for tax evasion. When a dentist trades a root canal for brickwork on a backyard fireplace, both the dentist and the bricklayer should report as income the value they received.

Nearly 70% of the underground economy consists of income that, if reported, would be legitimate; 30% or so of the funds flowing through untaxed channels are derived from criminal activities. Bank robbers, shoplifters, drug dealers, prostitutes, and loan sharks understandably try to minimize contacts with the IRS. Failure to pay legitimate taxes imposes higher rates on those of us who scrupulously pay our taxes.

Growth of self-employment in almost all economies during the past decade may signal a groundswell in entrepreneurial instincts, but it also stimulates unreported transactions in nations ranging from the United States to Sweden

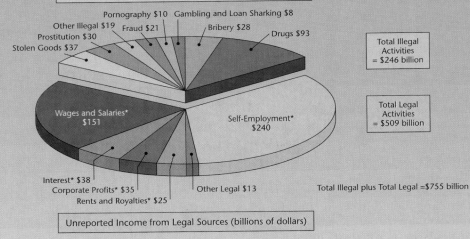

Unreported Income from Illegal Sources (billions of dollars)

Pornography $10   Gambling and Loan Sharking $8
Other Illegal $19   Fraud $21
Prostitution $30   Bribery $28
Stolen Goods $37   Drugs $93

Wages and Salaries* $151

Self-Employment* $240

Interest* $38
Corporate Profits* $35
Rents and Royalties* $25   Other Legal $13

Unreported Income from Legal Sources (billions of dollars)

Total Illegal Activities = $246 billion

Total Legal Activities = $509 billion

Total Illegal plus Total Legal = $755 billion

* Partly included in recorded GDP accounts.

Sources: Carl R. Simon and Ann D. Witte, *Beating the System: The Underground Economy* (Boston: Auburn House Publishing Co., 1981); updated by authors.

FIGURE 3   Sources of Underground Income, 1993

to Taiwan.* Tax evasion is far easier for the self-employed than for most other people.

What does the underground economy portend for economic statistics and public policy? For one thing, U.S. GDP growth may be understated to the extent that unreported income has grown in importance nationally. In 1986, the Department of Commerce began adjusting the GDP accounts to try to account for misreporting on tax returns. These adjustments totaled roughly $280 billion for 1993.

Another consideration is that unemployment statistics may be overstated (or labor force participation understated) if underground activity is not taken into account. Still another is that if poor people participate in cash or barter transactions proportionally more than high-income individuals, the degree of income inequality and the need for welfare programs may be overstated. Conversely, if high-dollar, white-collar crime is rampant, income may be even less evenly distributed than we think. This list of reasons for estimating the magnitudes and structures of underground transactions could be extended considerably.

We can wish that compliance with tax laws were more widespread among Americans, but, at the same time, we can be grateful that we do not suffer from the underreporting that appears common in parts of Europe. As Figure 4 shows, the underground economy is estimated to run as high as one-third of Italian GDP, or 30% of GDP in Greece.**

* "The Shadow Economy: Grossly Deceptive Product," *The Economist,* 19 September 1987, pp. 25–28.
** "Lies, Damned Lies, and Italy's GDP," *The Economist,* 27 February 1988, pp. 4–9.

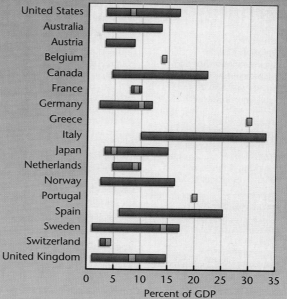

Sources: "The Black Economy: Ghostbusters," *The Economist,* Aug. 14, 1993, p. 55, and Carol Carson, "The Underground Economy," *Survey of Current Business,* May 1984, p. 33.

The red color bars indicate the lowest and highest estimates fo the underground economy as a percentage of a country's GDP. Obviously, research conclusions differ enormously, reflecting problems in securing and interpreting these data. Yellow identifies results from studies for 1992 GDP.

FIGURE 4 Estimates of the Underground Economy in Selected Countries

*The **purchasing power parity (PPP) approach** adjusts exchange rate conversions for differences in costs of living before comparing GDPs between countries.*

Table 6 illustrates the shifts in relative magnitudes that occur when per capita GDPs are adjusted by the PPP approach. Chinese per capita GDP, for example, is much greater after adjustments for purchasing power parity than if exchange rates alone are used for conversion.

Conversion according to purchasing power parity is still in its infancy, largely because data to measure consumer price indices are very crude, at best, in many developing nations. The importance of refining such statistical measures is attested to by the fact that, using the PPP technique, many analysts now forecast the possibility that, if its recent 10% annual growth rates continue, the Chinese economy, now second in the world (as shown in Figure 5), may surpass that of the United States to become the world's largest early in the next century. (A 10% growth rate, compounded, doubles an economy in a bit more than 7 years.) Because the exchange rate approach reflects an artificially low exchange

International Comparisons of Per Capita GDP

Could anyone survive for a year on less than typical American families spend on Thanksgiving dinners? In the 1980s, Chinese per capita annual income was regularly reported, based on market exchange rates, as $50. It seems unlikely that average Ethiopians, with reported per capita incomes of $130, were nearly three times more prosperous than the Chinese. Data such as those displayed in Table 5 are too often presented uncritically.

Table 5 International Per Capita GDPs (1991 dollars estimates based on exchange rates)	
China	$370
Columbia	1,260
Egypt	610
Ethiopia	120
India	330
Japan	26,930
Kenya	340
Mexico	3,030
Russia	3,220
Switzerland	33,610
United States	22,240

World Bank, *World Development Report 1993, Investing in Health* (Oxford University Press, 1993).

Per capita GDP may grossly distort snapshots of standards of living in different countries. We should recognize, first, that the underground economy and do-it-yourself production per capita tend to be negatively related to per capita GDP, being relatively less important in industrialized nations that rely heavily on specialization. Colombia's highly publicized underground economy, for example, is disregarded in computing Colombian GDP.

Meals cooked from a family's garden or from foraging are largely ignored in GDP estimates for primitive economies. A discarded shirt has zero value until it is scavenged from a garbage dump in Calcutta. Although such salvage does not enter India's accounting GDP, value was produced, so it should be. Similarly, hovels newly constructed of crushed tin cans on the outskirts of Cairo are not treated as investment in Egypt's GDP accounts, but should be.

Second, international misstatements of income and output abound. National incomes are probably understated in the United States and much of Western Europe because the data bases account only crudely for legal tax avoidance or illegal evasion. On the other hand, dictators often inflate GDP to feed their egos. Contrary to many estimates, scholars have recently concluded that per capita real GDP in the former USSR never exceeded that of Mexico; Kremlin bosses routinely exaggerated the USSR's performance. Underrepresentation may arise if foreign aid is based on statistics for impoverished nations. The leader of a less developed country may intentionally mislead aid providers in hopes of getting more aid.

Third, costs of living differ markedly: the *exchange rate* problem. Hamburgers cost roughly $16 in Tokyo, and hotel rooms in Zurich are 600% more than comparable rooms in Lima. Converting foreign GDP figures into U.S. dollars at prevailing exchange rates creates the ludicrous situation where a decline in the dollar in international currency markets causes estimates of foreign GDPs to rise proportionally, while a rising dollar causes estimates of foreign GDPs to plummet.

Finally, income is only one dimension of the quality of life, which is also affected by such things as weather and scenery, political liberty, job opportunities, access to medical care and education, and personal security (e.g., low crime rates and the absence of civil war).

The message here is that international comparisons of per capita income should be greeted with more than a grain of salt. Nevertheless, the data leave little room for doubt that most people in Ethiopia or India endure destitute lives relative to the prosperity enjoyed by most people living in advanced economies.

rate for Chinese currency relative to other currencies, such forecasts are contradicted when using the traditional exchange rate approach; the current Chinese GDP is much less when adjusted by exchange rates than when adjustments are made under the PPP approach.

GDP accounts were created to measure economic performance. These accounts may be misleading when used to weigh well-being in various countries, especially if the relative amounts of self-production, barter, or the underground economy vary much among countries, or if their relative costs of living are out of synch with the relative values of their respective exchange rates. Nuances in GDP accounting and the qualifiers created by the problems we've

TABLE 6   Exchange Rates vs. Purchasing Power Parity Adjustments to GDPs in Developing Countries

1992	$GDP per capita market exchange rates	$GDP per capita purchasing power parity	Total GDP, $P or purchasing power parity (billions of dollars)
China	370	2,460	2,870
India	275	1,255	1,105
Brazil	2,525	4,940	770
Mexico	3,700	6,590	590
Indonesia	650	2,770	510
South Korea	6,790	8,635	380
Thailand	1,780	5,580	320
Pakistan	400	2,075	240
Argentina	6,870	15,950	190
Nigeria	275	1,560	190
Egypt	655	3,350	180
Philippines	820	2,400	155
Malaysia	2,980	7,110	130

Disparate per capita GDPs between developed and developing economies tend to be far more pronounced when exchange rates are used for conversions than if purchasing power parity is taken into account. These differences exist because costs of living in less developed countries are far less than the exchange rates of their currencies would suggest; that is, exchange rates for currencies from less developed nations tend to be undervalued.

Sources: *World Economic Outlook 1993*, International Monetary Fund, FIU; World Bank; OECD. as reported in "Chinese Puzzles," *The Economist*, 15 May 1993, p. 83.

described cause some critics to assert that these aggregate data are worthless. It may be that parts of our measures of GDP and some of its relatives are a bit like the following example.

Imagine that all your classmates were transported back in time to around 1803. Each is assigned by President Thomas Jefferson to travel to various parts of North America and then to return to Washington, D.C., with estimates of distances between points. To standardize measurements, everyone is to pace the distances. People walking to New York or Boston would crosscheck each other, ensuring reasonable estimates for such short distances. But stride lengths differ, some people might wander in circles, and others might guess at the distance while riding in wagons. Still others might not even go to faraway destinations but would fill in travel vouchers as if they had. The figures turned in to President Jefferson might resemble parts of GDP accounting—far from perfect, but still better than no data at all.

GDP and Social Welfare

If per capita GDP rose by 1% last month, this need not imply that your personal quality of life improved by 1%. Your income and GDP growth may be correlated, but the relationship is far from perfect. For example, GDP would fall if you took a year off from work for a world tour. You might gain subjectively, but GDP accounts would not reflect your enjoyment of added travel and leisure. The GDP accounts ignore the value of leisure.

• **"Green" GDP and the Measure of Economic Welfare (MEW)**   The GDP accounting system also fails to deduct for negative aspects of economic growth, particularly environmental degradation. Greater outlays on product packaging boost measured GDP, but the accounting process fails to deduct the accompanying destruction of national forests and increased trash.

FIGURE 5 The World's Largest Economies in 1992 (trillions of dollars of GDP)

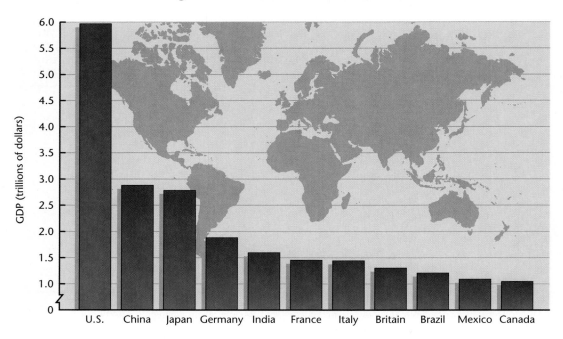

Source: *World Economic Outlook,* International Monetary Fund, 1993, as summarized in "Chinese Puzzles," *The Economist,* May 15, 1993, p. 83
The GDPs of many developing countries are closer to those of developed nations when purchasing power parity is used to adjust exchange rates than when exchange rates are not adjusted.

GDP does include the costs of removing litter and of increased medical care caused by pollution or auto accidents, but would we be better-off if a nuclear meltdown necessitated a billion-dollar cleanup? Hardly!

Some critics favor development of an index that emphasizes well-being instead of economic production. In 1993, the Clinton administration briefly considered keeping track of *green GDP*, which would correct GDP figures for harm from pollution, use of such nonrenewable resources as oil or iron ore, and restoration or destruction of such renewable natural resources as old growth forests. Economists William Nordhaus and James Tobin once adjusted GDP to account for certain deficiencies, arriving at an index they called a *measure of economic welfare*.

The **measure of economic welfare (MEW)** deducts items that do not contribute to economic welfare and adds beneficial items not now counted in GDP.

Major items they deducted from GDP included (*a*) spending that does not add to a better life (e.g., commuting costs and national defense) and (*b*) losses associated with pollution, urban congestion, and so on. Their major additions were (*a*) more inclusive estimates for unmarketed outputs (e.g., do-it-yourself projects) and (*b*) the value of increased leisure.

The controversial MEW estimates by Nordhaus and Tobin suggest that individual welfare seldom keeps pace with the growth of per capita GDP, but the data available are far too rough to yield definitive results. Despite the many difficulties associated with accurately measuring GDP and its components, it remains our best measure of economic growth and aggregate economic activity. Figure 6 traces changes in real

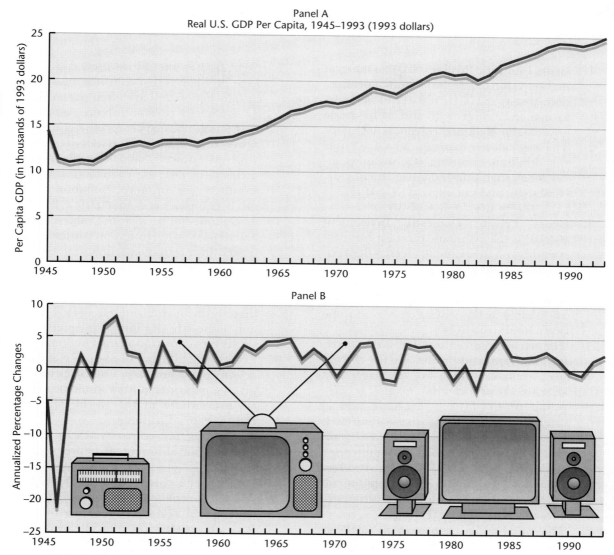

Panel A
Real U.S. GDP Per Capita, 1945–1993 (1993 dollars)

Panel B

Source: U.S. Dept. of Commerce, *Business Conditions Digest,* various issues, and *Economic Report of the President,* 1970—1994.

Per capita GDP equals nominal GDP divided by population. These data must be divided by the CPI to make the data—real per capita GDP—comparable across time. Panel A loosely reflects growth in the material welfare of Americans across this century, measured in 1993 dollars. Panel B shows that this growth has not been smooth.

FIGURE 6   Percentage Rates of Change in Real Per Capita U.S. GDP, 1950–1993

per capita GDP over the years. In the discussions of macroeconomic theory and policy that follow, we will constantly refer to GDP (both real and nominal) and the rates of unemployment and inflation. You should, however, keep in mind the limitations of all these estimates as described in this part of the book.

CHAPTER REVIEW: KEY POINTS

1. **Gross Domestic Product (GDP)** is the total market value of a nation's annual production. Measures of GDP trace economic performance and growth and help guide government policy and business decisions.

2. The *expenditures approach* to GDP sums consumption spending (*C*), business investment spending (*I*), government purchases (*G*), and net exports (*X* − *M*):
$$GDP = C + I + G + (X–M)$$

3. **Gross Private Domestic Investment (GPDI)** is the economic term for business spending on new capital. GPDI – depreciation = net investment.

4. *Government purchases (G)* do not include transfer (e.g., welfare) payments, which are treated as flows of income from some households to others.

5. The *income approach* to GDP sums wages, interest, rent, and profits. We use the figures available, which are (*a*) wages and salaries, (*b*) proprietors' income, (*c*) corporate profits, (*d*) rental income, and (*e*) interest. The sum of these figures is **National Income** (NI). Addition of indirect business taxes, which is not anyone's income, yields **Net Domestic Product** (NDP). The capital consumption allowance, "**depreciation**," is the difference between GDP and NDP.

6. The **value-added approach** to GDP accounting sums the sales of all firms and subtracts their purchases of intermediate products, which are goods bought by one firm from another for further processing. Failure to exclude purchases of intermediate goods from GDP figures would result in substantial *double counting* of production.

7. GDP figures should be used cautiously. One problem is that they may be systematically biased and are often presented in an artificially precise fashion. Another is that most nonmarket production is ignored (e.g., homemakers' services, do-it-yourself projects, and the like). GDP accounts include as production many disproducts (for instance, pollution abatement equipment is added to GDP, but environmental decay is not subtracted).

8. Currencies from different countries are traded in international financial markets at **exchange rates** (relative prices) set primarily by market forces, although governments affect exchange rates both directly (by buying and selling currencies) and indirectly (by imposing quotas and tariffs on goods traded internationally).

9. According to the **law of one price**, if transaction costs were zero, relative prices for given goods or resources would be identical everywhere in the world, after exchange rate adjustments.

10. **Purchasing power parity (PPP)** reflects cost-of-living differentials between countries.

11. International comparisons of GDP are especially problematic because countries differ in the relative importance of do-it-yourself production and the extent of barter and the underground economy. Ideally, per capita incomes should be adjusted for the relative purchasing power parity of currencies in different countries, but most comparisons are based on exchange rates between currencies because such data are much more readily available.

QUESTIONS FOR THOUGHT AND DISCUSSION

1. What would be the effect on GDP accounting if marijuana, prostitution, and gambling were legalized nationwide? What do you think would happen to economic well-being? Why?

2. Suppose all homeowners in America agreed to move into their next-door neighbor's house and pay that neighbor's rent. What would happen to GDP? Would your answer be the same if GDP estimates did not include an estimate of the rental value of owner-occupied housing? How would it differ?

3. Suppose one-fourth of all young women workers take a maternity leave and then, after their children are born, decide to stay home permanently. What would happen to our GDP accounts? As we defined GDP conceptually, what would happen to actual GDP relative to measured GDP? To measured GDP relative to economic welfare?

4. Why is NDP a more appropriate measure of true economic productivity than GDP? As they are currently constructed, which do you think is the best measure of economic welfare on a per capita basis: (a) GDP, (b) NDP, (c) NI, (d) PI, (e) DPI, or (f) consumption? Why is this category preferable to the others?

Net exports

Investment

Consumption

Price level

Inflationary gap

Recessionary gap

$Y=C+I+G+(X-M)$

45°

0

Part 3

Foundations of Macroeconomic Theory

Theories of gravity and celestial mechanics developed by Isaac Newton (1642–1727) imply that interactions in the cosmos follow a natural harmony. Adam Smith, in his *Wealth of Nations* (1776), extended Newton's ideas into the realm of economics with the theory that the invisible hand of self-interested behavior creates a natural harmony in the marketplace. Smith's views led to laissez-faire policy prescriptions compatible with the hostility toward powerful government expressed in the American Declaration of Independence, which also appeared in 1776.

Several generations of economists expanded Smith's ideas about macroeconomics into *classical theory*, which we explore in the beginning of Chapter 9. The political climate and the invisible hand approach, which concludes that simple market economies quickly gravitate toward full employment, merged to shape an American economy that, with some exceptions, was dominated by a free-market perspective until the worldwide Great Depression of the 1930s. Between roughly 1790 and 1930, however, most economies in Europe and North America steadily became more industrialized, and they were increasingly dominated by giant firms. Conventional economic theory adapted relatively slowly to this evolution beyond reliance on agriculture and local forms of simple manufacturing.

Recurrent booms and busts did little to shake most economists' faith in laissez-faire policies until the 1930s, when the Keynesian Revolution was launched in the middle of the Great Depression. *Keynesian theory* is examined in Chapters 9 and 10 and is blended with Keynesian *fiscal policy* in Chapter 11, where more classical approaches to fiscal policy are also surveyed. Keynesian theory suggests that only proper manipulation of the government budget (taxing and spending) can ensure reasonable macroeconomic stability in a market economy. Predictably, classical views suggest a more passive role as appropriate for government.

In Part 4 of this book, we will explore the important role of *money* from the perspectives of both classical and Keynesian macroeconomics. Then, in Part 5, Keynesian and classical analyses will be combined in a more sophisticated way to provide even more piercing insights into macroeconomic problems and how they might be resolved.

Net exports Investment Consumption

Chapter 9

Classical Macroeconomics and Keynesian Aggregate Expenditures

Classical and Keynesian theories are at the core of the major alternative approaches to modern macroeconomics. Classical economics focuses on how automatic adjustments in microeconomic markets ensure macroeconomic stability in the long run, pinpointing increases to Aggregate Supply as the key to resolving problems posed by scarcity. Its conclusions tend to support laissez-faire government policies. Keynesian theory, on the other hand, suggests that shocks to Aggregate Demand may destabilize an economy for prolonged periods, concluding that stimulative government policies are appropriate cures for excessive unemployment.

This chapter opens with an overview of classical reasoning. Then, in this and the next two chapters, we develop the Keynesian model one step at a time. In the next chapter, we will explore interactions between Aggregate Expenditures and National Output and scrutinize macroeconomic adjustments toward equilibrium. Then we will examine the role of government in stabilizing a market economy from the alternative perspectives of both Keynesian theory and the new classical macro-

economics. Understanding the anatomy of Aggregate Expenditures is a necessary first step, so this is our focus for much of this chapter.

CLASSICAL THEORY

Classical economics is a synthesis of theories put forth by numerous individuals from Adam Smith's time (the late 1700s) to the present. Central to classical theory is the idea that market economies automatically adjust to a full employment equilibrium as long as prices, wages, and interest rates are flexible.

> ***Classical economics*** concludes that, without government intervention, Aggregate Supplies and Aggregate Demands adjust naturally to offset pressures for long-term unemployment or substantial economic inefficiency.

Thus, classical macroeconomics predicts that any negative effects of business cycles will be overcome by market forces automatically.

Classical reasoning hinges on stabilizing mechanisms that resemble the biological processes contributing to *homeostasis*. For example, you begin to sweat if your temperature rises above 98.6°F. Your body cools as your perspiration evaporates. Low temperatures cause you to shiver and your teeth to chatter; movement of your muscle tissues then generates heat, raising your temperature toward 98.6°. Just as homeostasis is automatically restored, classical economics suggests that a market economy with flexible prices, wages, and interest rates automatically moves toward full employment and economic health. Behind the classical perception of a self-equilibrating economy is an idea known as Say's Law.

Say's Law

Jean Baptiste Say, a nineteenth-century French economist, believed that the very act of production creates an equivalent amount of demand.

> **Say's Law** asserts that *"Supply creates its own demand."*

This law pivots on the notion that people work, not for the sake of work itself, but only to obtain income to spend on goods they want. People produce (supply) fish sticks or roller blades only so they can buy (demand) food, cars, and other goods that make life more enjoyable. Similarly, investors do not seek income per se. Rather, they seek what their income will buy. Thus, the act of producing requires resources to be hired and paid, which in turn leads to resource owner's incomes being spent on other goods.

Say acknowledged the possibility of sporadic gluts of some goods but, reasoning that surpluses in any market must be offset by shortages in others, concluded that economy-wide gluts for most goods cannot occur. Surpluses or shortages in specific markets are remedied because surpluses drive down prices and production in the long run, while both rise to cure shortages. For example, a pinto bean surplus depresses bean prices, which, in turn, will reduce bean production. Thus, surpluses are quickly and automatically eliminated in a market system.

• **The Challenge of Underconsumption** Critics of Say's Law point out that people seldom spend all they earn, so saving might result in inadequate Aggregate Demand. If consumers spend less than all their income, some production may not be bought and firms' inventories will rise, causing disemployment when firms adjust to deficient demand. The classical rebuttal is that, in a pure market economy, all consumer saving is invested by business.

Early classical reasoning asserted that people save only to facilitate higher future consumption. In a monetary economy, saving is translated into funds available for loans. Stocks and bonds are merely financial investments that represent saving. According to classical reasoning, interest payments encourage consumers to forgo current consumption. Thus, the rate of saving is positively related to the interest rate, as shown in Figure 1.

The other side of the saving–investment market is business demands for loans for new capital. Lower interest rates stimulate more rapid investment. This occurs, in part, because of diminishing returns to capital. After adjusting for risk, firms rank potential investments by expected rates of return, from those with the highest expected returns to those with the lowest. Individual firms then borrow funds to invest in activities for which expected rates of return exceed the interest rate they must pay. In summary, saving is positively related to interest rates, as shown in Figure 1, while investment is negatively related to interest rates.

Flexible Wages, Prices, and Interest Rates

Flexible interest rates tend to equalize the amounts of saving and investment. If interest rates were below i_e in Figure 1, pressure would build for interest rates to rise as firms sought more financing for investment than savers willingly provided. Conversely, at interest rates above i_e firms would not borrow all the funds offered by savers. Surplus saving would induce some savers (through the intermediation of banks) to lower

FIGURE 1 The Classical Capital Market

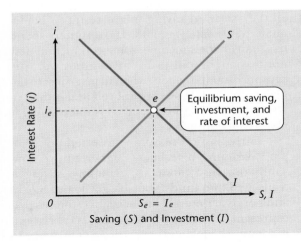

Classical economists argued that flexible interest rates would equate saving and investment in the capital market. Savers elect to postpone current consumption, and interest is their reward. Bigger rewards (higher interest rates) encourage more saving. The rate of return curve, on the other hand, reflects the declining marginal benefits to investors as annual investment rises. Business would demand more loans for investment purposes at lower interest rates. Thus, flexible interest rates equate saving and investment at point e, where $S_e = I_e$ when the interest rate is i_e.

their interest rates to borrowers. Competition would then force other savers (or intermediaries) to lower rates as well. It follows that interest rates respond to changes in the demands and supplies of loanable funds in ways that balance investment and aggregate saving. Any deficiency in demands from consumers caused by saving would be offset by business demands for loanable funds to channel into new investments in physical capital.

Classical economists went a step farther, arguing that *flexible wages and prices* ensure full employment even if interest rate adjustments in capital markets fail to do so. Wages and prices are like thermostat readings. If saving exceeds investment, then Aggregate Supply exceeds Aggregate Demand. If people are saving more, they are thus consuming less, and this deficiency of demand presses prices down when unwanted inventories accumulate, resulting in layoffs and creating temporary surpluses in labor markets. As wages and prices fall, the quantities of goods and labor demanded will rise, restoring the economy to full employment. On the other hand, any excess of Aggregate Demand over Aggregate Supply would cause the thermostat of price adjustments to generate wage hikes and price increases.

Notice that much of classical economics merely applies supply and demand analysis to macroeconomics. Suppose firms will hire only

80 million people at the $10 hourly wage shown in Figure 2, but 100 million people want jobs at $10 hourly. Will 20 million workers suffer prolonged unemployment? Classical reasoning answers "No," arguing that when this labor surplus lowers average wages to $8 per hour, all 90 million people willing to work for $8 hourly will find jobs. What about the other 10 million? Unwilling to work at an $8 wage, they would drop out of the work force.

Thus, flexible wages and prices are another safety valve in a market system. In the classical view, people lacking jobs are voluntarily unemployed because they prefer leisure to working at equilibrium wages. Jobs are always open for people willing to work at sufficiently low wages. Thus, classical economists use intuition and logic to conclude that involuntary unemployment is impossible and joblessness is not a social problem; it is an individual choice.[1]

• **Classical Theory and the Price Level** Say's Law, coupled with flexible interest rates, prices, and wages would, according to classical theory,

---

[1]Recall from Chapter 1 that logical structure alone does not validate a model. Economists may disagree about which logical models are best. A good model must explain real-world behavior. Classical logic offers one view, but, as you will see, embedded in the logical structure of the Keynesian model is the possibility of protracted involuntary unemployment.

FIGURE 2 Unemployment: The Classical View

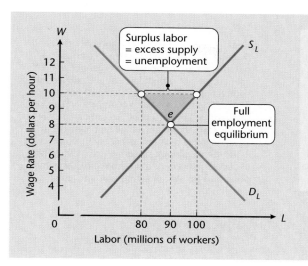

Surplus labor = excess supply = unemployment

Full employment equilibrium

W — Wage Rate (dollars per hour)

L — Labor (millions of workers)

S_L

D_L

Unemployment occurs, according to classical reasoning, primarily because wages are too high. The economy will self-correct for this problem when workers bid wages down to get jobs. This is what has happened at point *e*. The 90 million people who are willing to work have found employment at an hourly wage of $8.

Such adjustments fail to occur only if wages are downwardly sticky because of unions or legal minimum wages. Without legal wage floors, most who are unemployed must be so voluntarily, according to classical reasoning, and they could cure their lack of work by accepting lower pay.

keep workers fully employed. Essentially, classical reasoning views the Aggregate Supply curve as vertical at full employment. Figure 3 illustrates this concept by its initial equilibrium at point *a*, with national output of Q_f and a price level of P_0.

Suppose private spending fell because desires to save rose (the underconsumption problem described earlier); Aggregate Demand would shrink from AD_0 to AD_1. Excess supplies then yield a recession with swollen inventories, layoffs, and lower output (point *b*). According to classical theory, falling interest rates, prices, and wages ensure quick recovery to point *c*, restoring full employment at a lower price level (P_1). Reversed pressures (Aggregate Demand rises to AD_2) can induce a brief inflationary "boom" path like *ade* to full employment at Q_f with higher price level P_2. Although short-run deviations from full employment are possible, market economies rapidly self-correct through price-level changes without government intervention, confirming the laissez-faire political climate of earlier times.

In summary, classical economics depends on Say's Law and flexible interest rates, prices, and wages to ensure full employment. Classical analysis also teaches that the price level is di-

rectly related to Aggregate Demand, which in turn depends strictly on the money supply. Thus, classical reasoning supports a stable money supply as the key to price-level stability, precluding significant inflation or deflation. (How the price level and the money supply are related is detailed in the next part of this book.)

The Great Depression: Classical Theory at Bay

Until the Great Depression, classical economists steadfastly believed that market economies automatically gravitate toward full employment. Then the stock market crashed. Dana Thomas recalled October 29, 1929, or "Black Tuesday," with the following story:

The newspapers recounted the plight of a jury that before the crash had been sworn in for the trial of a former State Banking Superintendent indicted on charges of bribery. Several jurors had heavy commitments in the stock market. They were under strict orders from the judge not to read newspapers or engage in any conversation with outsiders. Nevertheless, news of the debacle in Wall Street had leaked into them and they pleaded with court attendants to let them contact their

FIGURE 3 Aggregate Supply and Classical Theory

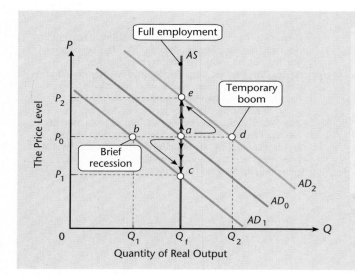

Unexpected expansions of Aggregate Demand (from AD_0 to AD_2) may create a temporary—but inflationary—boom (movement of the economy along a path like *ade.*) Unexpected contractions of Aggregate Demand (from AD_0 to AD_1) might cause a temporary recession (movement like path *abc*). According to classical reasoning, however, full employment is always quickly restored, primarily through adjustments of wages and the price level. The expected paths would go more directly from point *a* to point *c*, or from point *a* to point *e*.

brokers to find out how they stood. But there was nothing that could be done. One juror, while he sat in a sweat listening to courtroom testimony, lost $80,000.[2]

The ranks of the jobless grew from 3% to roughly 25% of the labor force between 1929 and 1933, while investment collapsed despite record low interest rates of around 1.5%. Many people were willing to work for almost nothing, but the job opportunities promised by classical theory seemed a mirage. The September 1932 issue of *Fortune* noted:

Dull mornings last winter the sheriff of Miami, Florida, used to fill a truck with homeless men and run them up to the county line. Where the sheriff of Fort Lauderdale used to meet them and load them into a second truck and run them up to his county line. Where the sheriff of Saint Lucie's would meet them and load them into a third truck and run them up to his county line. Where the sheriff of Brevard County would not meet them. And whence they would trickle back down the roads to Miami. To repeat.

---

[2]Dana L. Thomas, *The Plungers and the Peacocks* (New York: Putnam, 1967), p. 211.

The classical view that the people described in this passage were "voluntarily unemployed" seems callous and unrealistic. They were willing to work for considerably less than prevailing wages but were unable to find jobs.

Classical macroeconomics stressed the stability of a market system and had as its central goals (*a*) expansion of Aggregate Supply—our productive capacity, and (*b*) limiting growth of Aggregate Demand to muzzle inflation. According to Say's Law, *supply creates its own demand*, so classical theory predicts that rampant unemployment will be rare, and certainly cannot persist. Thus, most economists were baffled by the momentum and depth of the Great Depression. Reassessment of economic theory seemed in order.

The paradox for classical theory presented by the Great Depression set the stage for development of a theory to explain involuntary unemployment. The first major economist to challenge the classical stress on Aggregate Supply was John Maynard Keynes. (See his biography.) His *The General Theory of Employment, Interest, and Money* (1936) turned Say's Law upside down. Keynesian theory concludes that "demand creates its own supply."

BIOGRAPHY

John Maynard Keynes: Father of Modern Macroeconomics

Statesman and financier Bernard Baruch once squelched an economist's badgering by asking, "If you're so smart, why aren't you rich?" John Maynard Keynes (1883–1946) would not have been daunted by such a question. A keen observer of human affairs, Keynes amassed a private fortune by speculating in commodities, foreign currencies, and stock market securities. He was equally successful in the social, political, and academic arenas.

Keynes married a world-famous Russian ballerina and was a gay and shining light in the illustrious Bloomsbury group, England's foremost intellectual set. He served as a treasury official and represented the British government in economic negotiations following both World Wars. Nevertheless, he will be remembered longest as a leading figure in economics. Only the works of Smith and Marx rival Keynesian theories and policies in their impact on economic thought and practice in the twentieth century.

Much of modern macroeconomics is based on Keynes's 1936 treatise, *The General Theory of Employment, Interest, and Money*, his reaction to contradictions between classical economic theory and the worldwide Great Depression. This work challenged the conventional view that *aggregate equilibrium* is synonymous with *full employment*. Keynes reconstructed economic theory to explain persistent and high unemployment throughout market-oriented economies. He concluded that, far from being inconsistent with aggregate equilibrium, unemployment might be a consequence of it.

In brief, Keynes argued that a capitalist economy might experience high unemployment as a semipermanent situation, absent some external force to reduce it. For practical and political reasons, he thought that this external force must come from government and should take the form of large expenditures on public works projects capable of mobilizing idle labor. Therefore, Keynes turned away from the laissez-faire tradition that held almost any government economic intervention to be misguided.

Keynes's 1936 prediction that doses of government spending could revive dormant economies was borne out by rapid output growth during World War II, when massive defense contracts drove U.S. unemployment rates below 2%. Some Marxist critics perceive that era as evidence that market economies are doomed, with wars providing only temporary relief from inevitable stagnation leading to the demise of capitalism. According to Keynesian theory, however, economic vitality requires only adequate Aggregate Demand, and government spending can always bolster Aggregate Demand. War is unnecessary. Military outlays are only one possibility; government spending could as readily be directed towards infrastructure (e.g., schools and transportation systems)—or grandiose pork barrel projects, for that matter.

Despite the growth spurred by World War II, policymakers did not immediately embrace Keynesian theory. There is generally a long lag between ideas and actions. In the 1960s, the Kennedy Administration ushered in the first formal U.S. experiments with Keynesian policies. Keynesianism cut across party lines and continued to dominate economic policy until the 1980 election of Ronald Reagan.

Two decades of activist Keynesian policies yielded mixed results. Because the specter of deep depression largely gave way to persistent inflation in the 1960s and 1970s, Keynesian economics has been under fire from many quarters. Former President Reagan's supply-side economic policies were intended to turn back the Keynesian clock in favor of classical remedies, at least, rhetorically. Many observers attributed the recovery of 1983 to 1989 to powerful Keynesian policies—tax cuts, expanded government outlays, and huge deficits.

The Clinton administration's policies are supported by a more Keynesian analysis, but, as you will see in coming chapters, macroeconomic policy is increasingly eclectic, drawing ideas about equally from classical economics and from John Maynard Keynes—arguably the greatest economist of the twentieth century, but indisputably the most influential.

The Keynesian focus yields a model of *depression* with a punch line sharply at odds with the optimistic classical conclusion of full employment in the long run. Keynesian analysis indicates that high unemployment may plague a market economy in a short-run equilibrium that may persist for so long that the long run becomes almost irrelevant. To some degree, the widespread acceptance of Keynes's model in more prosperous times stems from its appealing policy prescriptions to remedy a depression: lower taxes and increased government spending.

THE KEYNESIAN FOCUS ON AGGREGATE DEMAND

Keynes's major concern was ensuring that Aggregate Demand is adequate for full employ-

ment of all resources. Keynes and his early followers demoted expansion of productive capacity and maintenance of price-level stability to secondary goals, to be pursued only *after* an economy reaches full employment, where, as classical theory suggests, Aggregate Supply is vertical (see Panel A of Figure 4). Keynes argued that although classical theory might apply in a fully employed economy, Aggregate Demand alone determines output and employment in the midst of a depression because Aggregate Supply in this range would be relatively flat.

Keynes's reasons for ignoring the price level and focusing primarily on Aggregate Demand can be seen in Panel B of Figure 4, which shows real GDP and the price level during the Great Depression. Real output began to grow after the depression bottomed out in 1933. This recovery followed when Aggregate

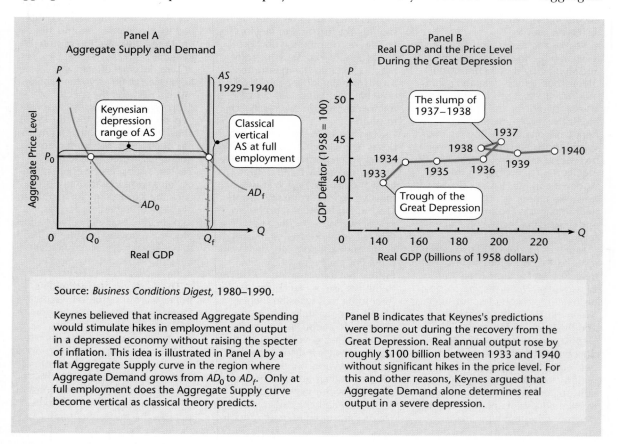

Source: *Business Conditions Digest*, 1980–1990.

Keynes believed that increased Aggregate Spending would stimulate hikes in employment and output in a depressed economy without raising the specter of inflation. This idea is illustrated in Panel A by a flat Aggregate Supply curve in the region where Aggregate Demand grows from AD_0 to AD_f. Only at full employment does the Aggregate Supply curve become vertical as classical theory predicts.

Panel B indicates that Keynes's predictions were borne out during the recovery from the Great Depression. Real annual output rose by roughly $100 billion between 1933 and 1940 without significant hikes in the price level. For this and other reasons, Keynes argued that Aggregate Demand alone determines real output in a severe depression.

FIGURE 4   The Keynesian Focus on Aggregate Demand

Demand grew without triggering major hikes in the price level.

In essence, Keynes assumed that idle productive capacity during depressed times allows production and income to stretch to accommodate growth in Aggregate Demand without spawning much inflationary pressure, as reflected in Panel A of Figure 4. Real output grew by more than 60% during the seven years after the depression reached its trough, while the price level rose less than 12%. Keynes' perception that Aggregate Supply is effectively horizontal in a depression let him focus on Aggregate Expenditures while ignoring changes in the price level.

Keynesian Aggregate Expenditures

The model of Aggregate Expenditures built in the remainder of this chapter largely follows Keynes's lead, but this framework is also now used, in modified form, by many modern economists who have been most influenced by the classical school of economic thought.

> *Aggregate Expenditures (AE), also known as Aggregate Spending, is the total value of annual spending on domestic production. An **Aggregate Expenditure curve** is the relationship between total spending and national income.*

Spending generally rises when income grows, so there is a positive relationship between Aggregate Expenditures and income.

• **Components of Aggregate Spending** You have learned that both Aggregate Demand and Gross Domestic Product (GDP) consist of spending for consumer goods (C), capital investment by private firms (I), government purchases of goods and services (G), and net exports ($X - M$). These categories also fit the structure of Aggregate Expenditures. A glance at Figure 5 shows that consumption absorbs almost two-thirds of GDP, with private investment and government spending constituting most of the rest. Exports are part of Aggregate Expenditures, while imports

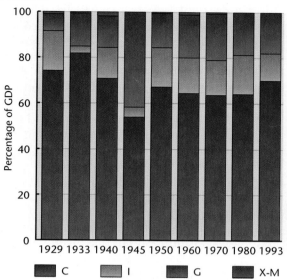

FIGURE 5   Components of Gross Domestic Product

Source: *Economic Report of the President, 1994.*

The four major components of GDP from the vantage point of Aggregate Expenditures are consumption, investment, net exports, and government spending. Consumer spending has been fairly stable at roughly two-thirds of the total. Investment and government spending constitute the bulk of the remainder. Net exports are a relatively minor proportion of this total.

add to the goods and services available; hence, imports contribute to Aggregate Supply. However, because Keynes viewed imports as replacing sales of domestic production, only the net influence of foreign trade ($X - M$) is considered in constructing Aggregate Expenditures.

CONSUMPTION AND SAVING

What determines total consumer spending? You may be able to identify other things that influence your family's spending, but the single most important factor is probably your family's current income. In his *General Theory* (1936), John Maynard Keynes asserted:

> *The fundamental psychological law, upon which we are entitled to depend with great confidence both a priori from our knowledge of human nature and from the detailed facts of experience is that men are disposed, as a rule and on the average, to increase their consumption as their income increases, but not by as much as the increase in their income. (p. 96)*

This insight, which now seems obvious, forever altered the thrust of macroeconomic reasoning. Classical economists had recognized that consumer spending is affected by income, but their belief that National Income automatically moves to a full employment level caused them to emphasize Aggregate Supply and economic growth. Consequently, they were much more interested in how interest rates cause income to be split between consumption and saving than in how consumption and income are related.

• **Consumption and Saving Schedules** Classical theory emphasizes interest as a reward for saving. Higher interest rates foster higher saving and lower consumption out of a given income. Keynes's *fundamental psychological law of consumption* barely hints at the very different orientation of Keynesian analysis. Figure 6 provides evidence to support Keynes's intuition.

The 45° line in Figure 6 reflects points mapped if consumption exactly equaled disposable income. (Any variable plotted against an equal variable, or itself, yields a 45° line.) If consumption points for all years landed on this reference line, then consumption would always equal disposable income. How can after-tax (disposable) income be used? By definition, anything not consumed is saved ($S = Y_d - C$). Thus, this 45° line is labeled $Y_d = C + S$; disposable income is absorbed by what you consume and save.

Saving is not limited to funds you store in financial institutions during some period.

> **Saving** is unconsumed income, or the change in total wealth over some period.

Wealth is the *stock of savings* accumulated during past saving periods. (Recall that saving is a flow variable.) But wealth is eroded when consumption exceeds disposable income.

> **Dissaving** occurs when people spend more on consumption than their income. It is financed by borrowing, or by spending past savings.

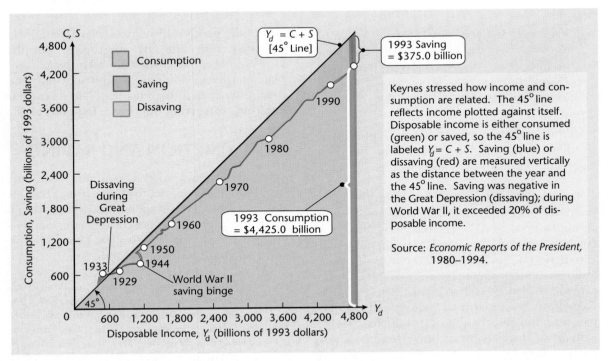

FIGURE 6   Income and Consumption in the United States, 1929—1993

Notice that saving was relatively high during World War II, but many families spent more than their incomes during the Great Depression and their wealth declined.

Aggregate consumption and saving absorb fairly stable shares of disposable income. Until recently, saving averaged roughly 7% of disposable income except during World War II and the Great Depression. Although rates of saving slipped a bit in the past decade or so, consumption has consistently been the most stable component of Aggregate Expenditures.

Consumption occurs when goods are used up in satisfying our wants and falls into five main categories: food, housing, clothing, transportation, and medical expenses. Low-income families often *dissave* by spending more than their income. As gross incomes rise, growing shares of income are allocated to taxes, transportation and housing services, and various luxuries. Figure 6 indicates how consumption is related to aggregate disposable income.

Autonomous and Induced Consumption and Saving

Keynes asserted that as income grows, so does planned consumption, but by less than income. People must consume something to live, however, even if they have zero income. This part of consumption is independent of income.

Autonomous consumption (C_a) is consumer spending unrelated to income.

You will encounter the term "autonomous" several times in the simple Keynesian model. Any autonomous variable is assumed to be independent of income.

People spend more on consumer goods if they receive more income.

Induced consumption occurs only because people have income to spend.

Thus, consumption includes both autonomous and induced elements. The bulk of consumption in a prosperous economy is induced; autonomous consumption accounts for most of consumption behavior only at very low levels of disposable income.

Consider Table 1. At zero income, autonomous consumption requires dissaving equal to spending, which is $4,000 in this example. Thus, autonomous saving equals –$4,000. Where planned consumption exceeds low levels of disposable income, there is planned dissaving. In Table 1, dissaving occurs at all income levels below $20,000. Saving is zero at the break-even point, which occurs when both income and planned consumption equal $20,000 in this example. Planned saving is positive for incomes exceeding $20,000.

Data from Table 1 underpin Figure 7. Autonomous consumption causes the intercept in Panel A to equal $4,000; induced consumption equals the vertical rise in consumption as income grows. The vertical distance between the 45° reference line (in blue) and the consumption line (red) is saving or dissaving. Panel B

TABLE 1   Representative Annual Consumption and Saving Schedules

(1) Annual Disposable Income	(2) Annual Planned Consumption	(3) Annual Planned Saving (1) – (2)	(4) Marginal Propensity to Consume ($\Delta 2$) ÷ ($\Delta 1$)	(5) Marginal Propensity to Save ($\Delta 3$) ÷ ($\Delta 1$)
0	$ 4,000	$ –4,000	—	—
$ 5,000	8,000	–3,000	0.8	0.2
10,000	12,000	–2,000	0.8	0.2
15,000	16,000	–1,000	0.8	0.2
20,000	20,000	0	0.8	0.2
25,000	24,000	1,000	0.8	0.2
30,000	28,000	2,000	0.8	0.2

FIGURE 7   Income, Consumption, and Saving

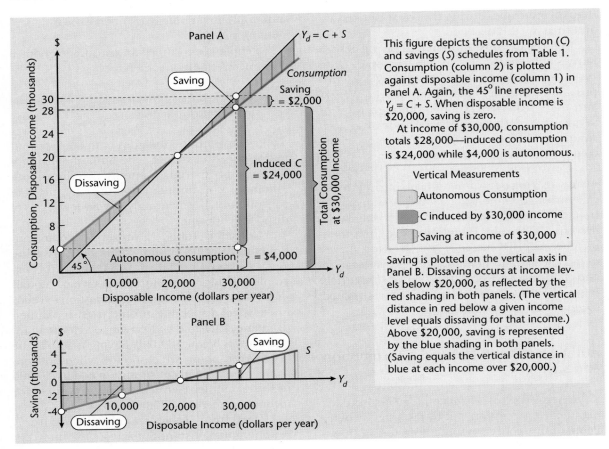

This figure depicts the consumption (C) and savings (S) schedules from Table 1. Consumption (column 2) is plotted against disposable income (column 1) in Panel A. Again, the 45° line represents $Y_d = C + S$. When disposable income is $20,000, saving is zero.

At income of $30,000, consumption totals $28,000—induced consumption is $24,000 while $4,000 is autonomous.

Vertical Measurements	
	Autonomous Consumption
	C induced by $30,000 income
	Saving at income of $30,000

Saving is plotted on the vertical axis in Panel B. Dissaving occurs at income levels below $20,000, as reflected by the red shading in both panels. (The vertical distance in red below a given income level equals dissaving for that income.) Above $20,000, saving is represented by the blue shading in both panels. (Saving equals the vertical distance in blue at each income over $20,000.)

plots the amount of planned saving left after planned consumption from Panel A. For example, if disposable income is $25,000, saving is $1,000.

Marginal Propensities to Consume and Save

Keynes asserted that consumption and saving grow as income grows but by less than income rises. Historically, Americans have saved an average of 7% or so of their disposable income. It is easier for policymakers to affect disposable income a little (through, e.g., taxes) than to directly control total income. What people will do with a bit more or less income is crucial.

*The **marginal propensity to consume (mpc)** is the relative change in consumption induced by a small change in disposable income.*

Throughout this book, we use Δ (the Greek letter delta) to represent a change in a variable. Arithmetically, the mpc is defined as

$$mpc = \frac{\text{change in planned consumption}}{\text{change in disposable income}} = \frac{\Delta C}{\Delta Y_d}$$

The marginal propensity to consume in Table 1 is 0.8. For each dollar increase (or decrease) in disposable income, consumption rises (or falls) 80 cents ($0.80). For example, when disposable income rises from $15,000 to $20,000 (by $5,000), planned consumption rises from $16,000 to $20,000 (by $4,000). Thus, the mar-

FIGURE 8 Marginal Propensity to Consume (mpc) and Marginal Propensity to Save (mps)

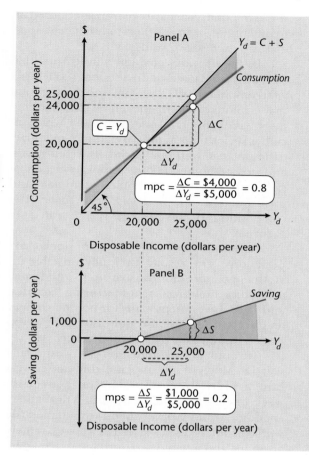

This figure depicts the marginal propensity to consume (mpc) and the marginal propensity to save (mps) and is based on the data in Table 1. The mpc is defined as the proportional change in planned consumption in response to a given change in disposable income, and it equals the slope of the consumption schedule. If, for example, disposable income increases from $10,000 to $12,500, planned consumption rises from $10,000 to $12,000. Thus, the mpc equals $2000/$2500, or 0.8.

The marginal propensity to save, or mps, is the proportional change in planned saving in response to a given change in disposable income. It equals the slope of the saving function. In Panel B, when disposable income increases from $10,000 to $12,500, planned saving increases by $500, so this mps equals 0.2 ($500/$2500).

ginal propensity to consume is $4,000/$5,000 = 0.8.

A geometric treatment of the mpc is shown in Panel A of Figure 8. Recall that slope is computed as *rise over run*. The change in planned consumption is measured by the vertical increase (*rise*) on the graph of consumption and is labeled ΔC. The change in disposable income is measured along the horizontal axis (*run*) and is labeled ΔY_d. Thus, the slope of the consumption function is $\Delta C/\Delta Y_d$, which is the mpc.

What do people do with an extra dollar of income if they don't spend it? They save it.

> The **marginal propensity to save (mps)** is the relative change in saving induced by a small change in disposable income.

Arithmetically,

$$mps = \frac{\text{change in planned saving}}{\text{change in disposable income}} = \frac{\Delta S}{\Delta Y_d}$$

For example, in Table 1, as disposable income rises from $15,000 to $20,000, planned saving increases by $1,000 and the mps equals $1,000/$5,000, or 0.2.

You may already see that the sum of the mpc and the mps equals 1; any change in disposable income is divided between changes in consumption and saving.[3] A graphic representation of the mps is shown in Panel B of Figure 8.

---

[3] From $C + S = Y_d$ it follows that any change in disposable income (ΔY_d) must yield changes in consumption (ΔC) or changes in saving (ΔS). Thus, $\Delta C + \Delta S = \Delta Y_d$. Dividing both sides of this equation by ΔY_d yields $\Delta C/\Delta Y_d + \Delta S/\Delta Y_d = \Delta Y_d/\Delta Y_d = 1$, so mpc + mps = 1.

Other Determinants of Consumption

The consumption function in Figure 8 portrays consumption expenditures. In our simple model, the sole determinant of induced consumer spending is disposable income (Y_d). We previously identified five other types of variables that largely determine autonomous consumption. These include (*a*) wealth and expectations about future income, (*b*) customary standards of living, (*c*) household sizes and age structures, (*d*) household balance sheets and stocks of consumer goods, and (*e*) consumer expectations about the prices and availability of products. When any of these five influences change, autonomous consumption changes; the entire consumption–income relationship shifts up or down. These "shift variables" tend to change fairly slowly, however, so the historic relationship between consumption and disposable income has been relatively stable.

Consumption spending accounts for about two-thirds of Aggregate Expenditures. Three other components must be added to consumption to reach Aggregate Expenditures: investment, government spending, and net exports. We turn now to a discussion of investment and its determinants. Then we briefly consider government spending and look at the foreign component of Aggregate Expenditures.

INVESTMENT

While consumption is the most stable component of GDP and Aggregate Expenditures, investment is relatively the least stable. According to Keynesian theory, the volatility of investment, precipitated in part by the "animal spirits" (herd instincts) of investors, may be the root cause of most business cycles.

Types of Investment

Economic investment entails buying new physical capital (buildings, machinery, tools, equipment, inventories, and the like) for future use in producing other goods and services. Some financial investments facilitate economic investment (for instance, purchases of newly issued stocks or bonds, which are merely specialized instruments for saving); others may not (e.g., speculative purchases of land).

In the previous chapter, you learned that Gross Private Domestic Investment (GPDI) is a vital component of Gross Domestic Product, and that economic investment can be classified into three basic groups: (*a*) *new construction*, which includes such things as office buildings, manufacturing plants, warehouses, hotels, retail stores, and private homes; (*b*) *new machinery and equipment*, including tools and office equipment and furnishings; and (*c*) *inventory accumulation*. The composition of investment is illustrated in Figure 9.

Investors frequently develop similar expectations. The result? Cyclically unstable investment patterns for construction—residential and office buildings, manufacturing facilities, and such. Investment plans for new machinery and equipment are also quite sensitive to expected ups and downs in economic activity.

Inventory accumulation is especially volatile. Much of it is unplanned because firms cannot precisely predict sales on a week-to-week, or even a year-to-year, basis. A firm's merchandise could arrive almost simultaneously with customers if sales forecasts were extremely accurate, and inventory requirements would be minuscule. Firms try to time inventories by sales forecasts (by the "just-in-time" delivery systems management gurus began pitching in the 1990s), but sales are often out of synch with even the best laid plans.

Failures of sales to go according to plan make inventory accumulation especially unstable, as shown in Figure 10. Firms unintentionally invest in new inventories if sales fall below business forecasts, but inventories shrink and there is unplanned disinvestment if sales are unexpectedly high. Inventories that unexpectedly dwindle signal firms to hire more resources and boost orders to suppliers, while unexpected inventory growth is a signal to lay off workers and slash orders. In the next chapter, you will see how these inventory adjustments set forces in motion to balance aggregate spending and output.

FIGURE 9   The Composition of Gross Private Domestic Investment

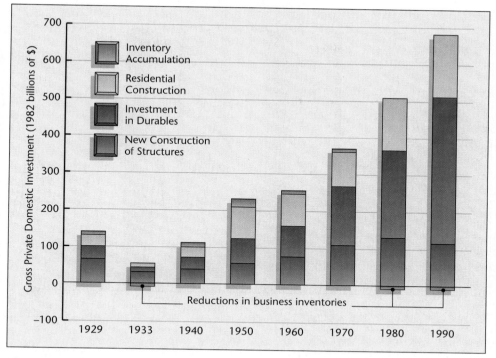

Source: *Economic Report of the President,* 1994.

Investment spending is the least stable component of GDP, and inventory accumulation is the most volatile form of investment.

Expected Returns from Investment

Investments will be made if they are expected to generate a rate of return at least as great as the market rate of interest.

> The **rate of return** is the annual percentage of earnings from an investment after all opportunity costs or, more analytically, the annual percentage by which assets will grow if the profits from an investment are continually reinvested.

Thus, rates of return are compounded annually, much like interest rates paid on checking accounts. We will discuss factors that influence expected returns from investment before delving into some intricacies of the costs of investment.

● **Expectations About the Business Environment**
New capital goods are expected to generate extra output that, when sold, will yield extra rev-

enue. Confidence about future demand is necessary before firms make investments to produce more output. When consumer spending is expected to grow and existing capital is already pressed to capacity, streams of new investment will rise. Conversely, if demand is expected to be weak, or if existing production facilities have substantial excess capacity, businesses will not invest much.

Long lags exist between placements of orders for new investment goods and achieving the capacity the investments make possible. Acquiring facilities to house new or expanded operations also takes time. Still another lag arises between production from new capital and final sales of the output. Throughout these processes, time is absorbed trying to comply with a maze of legal regulations. All these lags necessitate forecasting consumer demand far into the future, but uncertainties in all long-range projections make firms leery of many investments.

FIGURE 10 Changes in Business Inventories (billions of 1987 dollars)

Source: *Exonomic Report of the President,* 1994.

Inventory changes are by far the most volatile component of investment, which, in turn, is the most erratic part of the GDP. Inventories decline sharply when business sales unexpectedly boom or when business firms become very pessimistic in forecasting future sales. Inventories mushroom when firms anticipate sharp increases in sales or when customers unexpectedly quit buying.

Imperfect forecasts of a firm's sales are only one source of business risk. Expected changes in government policies may either encourage or squelch investment. For example, several Colorado mountain towns experienced flurries of investments in casinos and tourist traps when voters were expected to pass a 1990 referendum to legalize gambling at certain sites. (They passed it.) But if stiffer restrictions on foreign trade loomed on the horizon, firms that relied heavily on exports or imports might postpone investment plans indefinitely.

Business expectations can be contagious. If most other investors become pessimistic (bearish), might it be wise for you to reconsider your riskier ventures? If they become optimistic (bullish), might you be more apt to plunge? Waves of bullishness or bearishness partially account for investment volatility, but alternative explanations abound.

● **Technological Innovations**   Many firms and government agencies engage in extensive research and development (R&D). Technological advances permit new or better goods or less costly production methods for existing products. Investment to implement technological breakthroughs tends to be clustered over time because new technologies often arrive erratically and in waves.

Some economists ascribe much of investment volatility to the bunching of technological advances. For example, massive investment continues to flow into electronics–an ongoing computerized revolution is reshaping flows of information and how most of us work. The dynamics of this industry have enriched growing numbers of fast-moving entrepreneurs, including hardware manufacturers and software developers. This software covers word processing (rendering typewriters largely obsolete and inducing carpal tunnel syndrome in millions), electronic games (improving the hand-eye coordination of millions of kids), spreadsheets (displacing bookkeepers), and tax programs (reducing sweat around April 15th each year). Along the way, hardware ancillaries proliferate (e.g., CD ROMs, fax modems, hard drives, laser printers, and so forth).

The next decade portends continued bursts of technology. On the horizon: multimedia systems offering new modes of entertainment and more efficient and interesting approaches to education, smart TVs to facilitate shopping and to provide channel surfers with thousands of options each evening, and information highways accessible to schools, firms, and households.

• Stocks of Capital Relative to Total Production

Just as consumption is affected by the durables households already own relative to their incomes, the stock of physical capital relative to GDP influences investment. Strong investment incentives emerge when near-peak business activity presses against capital capacity. On the other hand, purchases of new capital fall when economic activity slips, idling substantial amounts of capital.

THE EQUILIBRIUM RATE OF INVESTMENT

Firms will buy machinery, construct buildings, or try to build inventories whenever they expect the gross returns on these investments to exceed all opportunity costs.

Diminishing Returns to Investment

Investment, like other economic activities, is subject to the law of diminishing returns. Suppose most forecasts reflect substantial optimism. Many investors are probably aware of a few sure-fire investments that might be expected to yield rates of return (r) of, say, 30% to 40%; examples might include a new "Doc-in-a-Box" health-care franchise or a plant to manufacture exercise pills minimizing the "no pain, no gain"

approach to physical exertion. Once these investments were made, only less profitable investments would be available—a recycling plant or a laundromat might be expected to yield annual returns of 20% to 30%.

After these investments, still less profitable investments would be the only options—renovation of a seedy motel or opening a used-book store might be anticipated to return 10% to 20% on investment. We are now near rock bottom—a shovel-sharpening shop or greasy-spoon franchise might generate near-zero rates of return, plus or minus 10%.

In summary, for a given mood among investors, the greater the level of economic investment, the lower the expected rate of return on additional investment. Typical rates of return are negatively related to the level of investment in part because the most profitable investments are the first undertaken. Changes in expectations shift the investment demand curve. Figure 11 shows expected rate of return schedules when investors are optimistic and when they are pessimistic.

Costs of Investment

Our analysis has focused on the demand side for investment goods, but the supply side also plays an important role in determining how much investment occurs. Investment decisions depend, in part, on costs for new capital. Rate of return functions like those in Figure 11 rise (shift to the right) when the prices of equipment and other capital fall, and shrink (move leftward) when these costs rise. Suppose prosperity spurs demands for new capital. Construction costs and equipment prices will rise. Thus, the positive slope of the supply curve for new capital helps buffer against overly optimistic surges in investment demand.

Now suppose fear of a recession reduces demand for new capital. Suppliers of capital goods may accumulate excess inventories. The positive slope of the supply curve for new capital goods implies that, as demand shrinks, the prices of machinery and new buildings will fall as capital suppliers liquidate their inventories. (The collapse of a regional boom often leaves millions of

FIGURE 11 The Negative Relationship between Expected Rates of Return and Investment

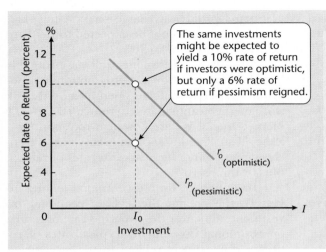

The same investments might be expected to yield a 10% rate of return if investors were optimistic, but only a 6% rate of return if pessimism reigned.

The quantity of investment and the rate of return are negatively related for each given outlook for business. Investments expected to be most profitable will be made first, and, as more projects are undertaken, only then will those only expected to be less profitable (lower rates of return) be included. As economic forecasts change, the entire curve (relationship) will shift (e.g., from r_o, the rates of return optimistic investors might expect, to r_p, the expected rate of return curve if they became pessimistic).

square feet of new office buildings empty, especially if construction companies speculatively built new space without firm offers from buyers.) Thus, the positive slopes of supply curves for capital goods also help limit the volatility of investment.

• **Taxes and Subsidies**   Taxes on investment income are another cost consideration. For example, higher corporate income taxes lower the (after-tax) rate of return curve. Investment tax credits or government funding of research and development, on the other hand, may boost demands for investment.

• **Interest Rates**   Interest is among the most important costs from investors' perspectives. When interest rates rise, investors' opportunity costs rise. If investors have funds, they might make loans instead of buying investment goods. If most investors borrow to invest, then a hike in interest rates makes investment less attractive. Interest rates (i) and rates of return (r) are both expressed as annual percentages, making it possible to put both on the vertical axis of Figure 12. Changes in interest rates involve movements *along* rate of return curves, while other types of changes (e.g., new taxes) *shift* these curves.

Ignoring transaction costs and risk for simplicity's sake, investment occurs as long as the expected rate of return is at least as great as the interest rate. Suppose you expect an 8.5% rate of return from some investment and can borrow at 8% interest. If you fail to make such an investment, then someone else will go after this profit. It is just like trading 8 cents for 8.5 cents. How many times will you go for a deal like this? Infinitely repeating this process would make you infinitely rich. Thus, any investment expected to yield a rate of return exceeding the interest rate can profitably be undertaken. Those yielding returns lower than interest rates will not be profitable and will not be made. This is why investment will be $150 billion in Figure 12 if the interest rate is 8% and the expected rate of return is reflected in curve r_p.

In summary, the expected rate of return schedule rises (shifts to the right) when GDP grows and investors become optimistic or when capital prices decline. Investor pessimism or higher capital prices shrink expected rates of return and investment. Interest rate changes induce movements along a rate of return curve: for a given expected rate of return, higher interest rates discourage investment, but falling interest rates foster investment and economic growth.

Inaccurate sales forecasts unexpectedly change inventories. When this is coupled with

FIGURE 12 How Interest Rates and Expected Rates of Return Affect Investment

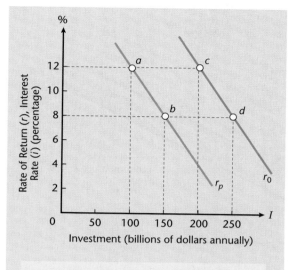

The interest rate is a major opportunity cost of investing. If the expected rate of return curve is r_p and interest rates fall from 12% to 8%, investment rises from $100 billion to $150 billion. Similarly, if interest rates are stable at 8% when, reflecting growing optimism, the expected return function shifts from r_p to r_o, investment rises from $150 billion to $250 billion.

the effects of herdlike changes in investors' expectations and wide swings in interest rates, it is no wonder investment is volatile. The example in Figure 12 suggests that annual investment would grow from $100 billion (point *a*) to $150 billion (point *b*) if the interest rate fell from 12% to 8% when investors were initially pessimistic (movement along the r_p curve).

A similar decline in interest rates would boost investment from $200 billion to $250 billion annually if investors are more optimistic (moving along the r_o curve from point *c* to point *d*). For every interest rate, shifts from optimistic to pessimistic outlooks (shifts between the curves), or vice versa, alter annual investment by $100 billion. Thus, in this example, swings in investors' moods and interest rates may either double—or halve—investment. The real-world volatility of investment is probably attributable

to changes both in expectations and in interest rates.

Investment and Aggregate Expenditures

We know that investment is affected by the level of National Income because the state of the economy significantly shapes investors' expectations. Business profits are bolstered by economic growth, which gives corporations greater opportunities to retain earnings for investment purposes. We will treat investment as autonomous, however, because we want the Keynesian model we are building here to be as simple as possible.

> **Autonomous investment** *is investment that is assumed independent of income in simple Keynesian models.*

Figure 13 shows autonomous investment (I_a) as determined by expected rates of return and market interest rates. It also shows how this "externally determined" investment affects Aggregate Expenditures. Investment is treated as external because it is assumed independent of income. In Panel A, an interest rate of 8% yields autonomous investment of $100 billion. In Panel B, the $100 billion of autonomous investment is added vertically to the consumption curve to obtain the private sector Aggregate Expenditures curve ($AE = C + I_a$).

Optimism joined with low interest rates creates high levels of autonomous investment. Pessimism or high interest rates cause autonomous investment to be very low. In fact, as we elaborate in future chapters, Keynesians believe that during severe economic downturns pessimism may so overwhelm even very low interest rates that investment will be trivial.

GOVERNMENT PURCHASES

Government purchases include roads, education, police and fire protection, school lunch programs, and Medicare payments. Cash transfer payments only translate into Aggregate

FIGURE 13 Aggregate Expenditure for the Private Sector (Households + Business)

In Panel A, investment is determined by the intersection of the rate of return (r) curve and the level of interest rates (i). If the interest rate were 8%, autonomous investment (I_a) would be $100 billion (point a, Panel A). Vertically adding this level of investment to the consumption line (C) in Panel B yields the Aggregate Expenditure curve labeled $AE = C + I_a$. Notice that the Aggregate Expenditure curve equals consumption plus investment ($AE = C + I_a$) if the economy consists only of households and firms. Finally, note that the 45° reference line is equal to $Y_d = C + S$.

Expenditures when recipients spend these funds on consumer goods, so these outlays are not included in government purchases. To help keep our analysis of Aggregate Expenditures simple, we will treat government purchases as independent of income.

Autonomous government purchases (G_a) are government purchases of goods and resources assumed to be independent of income in simple Keynesian models.

Although government expenditures appear loosely related to National Income, they are affected even more by the state of international relations (e.g., military buildups or peace treaties). Moreover, most government spending

has considerable momentum regardless of the health of the economy. Outlays for public health, highways, and education, for example, seem impervious to swings in the economy.

THE FOREIGN SECTOR

Exports (X) reflect foreign demands that increase Aggregate Expenditures for U.S. outputs. Imports (M) are goods produced by foreigners but available for use by American consumers, investors, or government. In fact, the accounting categories of consumption, investment, and government spending include many goods produced abroad. Although imports add to the Aggregate Supply available to

Americans, Keynesian analysis treats them as reducing Aggregate Expenditures on domestically produced goods because imports presumably replace some purchases of domestic output. Consequently, the Keynesian convention is to look only at the net effect of the foreign sector on Aggregate Expenditures, so $AE = C + I + G + (X - M)$.

National Income clearly affects imports. When times are prosperous domestically, we import more Saabs and Minolta cameras, and booming industrial production and vacations require more foreign oil. On the other hand, our exports depend primarily on foreign economic conditions, which may be in the doldrums even if the U.S. economy is prosperous. International economic interdependence is, however, accurately characterized by the cliché "When America sneezes, the rest of the world catches a cold." The net effect of international trade on our Aggregate Expenditures, however, is relatively small. Exports and imports each *average* around 10% of GDP, so net exports ($X - M$) are usually a very small percentage of GDP.

Sophisticated Keynesian models explicitly consider interdependencies between nations, but, for the purposes of the simpler Keynesian model of Aggregate Expenditures being constructed here, net exports are treated as independent of income.

> ***Autonomous net exports ($X_a - M_a$)*** *are the differences between exports and imports that are treated as independent of income in simple Keynesian models.*

Keep in the back of your mind, however, that the classical emphasis on Aggregate Supply probably addresses the importance of trade more realistically than does the simple Keynesian model, especially during prosperous times. International trade augments both the purchasing power of National Income and the value of our domestic output through:

1. Specialization according to comparative advantage.
2. Dissemination of new technology (e.g., communications networks have made TV

news almost instantaneously available throughout the world).
3. Competition to (*a*) *improve quality* (e.g., cars and electronics), (*b*) *reduce prices* (e.g., the textile industry), and (*c*) *cut production costs* (e.g., Mexican *maquilladero* plants assemble Korean TVs for distribution at lower prices in the United States).
4. Provision of certain goods that otherwise might not be available (e.g., coffee and chrome).

We address the growing importance of international trade and finance repeatedly through this book. Nevertheless, net exports are treated as independent of income in the simple demand-oriented Keynesian model under construction in this chapter.

AGGREGATE EXPENDITURES

Consumers account for the bulk of purchases of domestic output ($C = C_a + mpc \cdot Y$), but some output is bought by investors (I_a), some is purchased by government (G_a), and the rest is exported to foreigners ($X_a - M_a$). In the Keynesian model used in the next two chapters, we assume that income is the major influence on consumption, while private investment, net exports, and government spending are not affected by income.

Aggregate Expenditures (AE) sum all these types of spending.

$$AE = C + I + G + (X - M)$$

Rearranging terms to reflect differences between the autonomous spending and the induced spending (mpc $\cdot Y$) components of AE yields[4]

$$AE = C_a + (mpc \cdot Y) + I_a + G^a + (X_a - M_a P)$$

By the mid-1990s, U.S. Gross Domestic Product approached $7 trillion annually, or

---

[4]You soon will see that autonomous spending has the same effect on national income regardless of its source, so all types of autonomous spending (A) can be summed to simplify our analysis ($A = C_a + I_a + G_a + X_a - M_a$). The only type of spending affected by income is induced consumption (mpc $\cdot Y_a$). Thus, in the simplest linear Keynesian models, Aggregate Expenditures equal autonomous spending (A) plus consumption that is induced (mpc $\cdot Y_d$) by disposable income: $AE = A + mpc \cdot Y_a$.

$7,000 billion. Suppose that (a) autonomous investment (I_a) is $600 billion, (b) autonomous net exports ($X_a - M_a$) equal $100 billion, (c) autonomous government purchases (G_a) equal $900 billion, (d) autonomous consumption (C_a) is $1,900 billion, and (e) the marginal propensity to consume (mpc) is 0.5. Figure 14 depicts the resulting relationship between National Income (Y) and Aggregate Expenditures. The autonomous components (A) of Aggregate Expenditures sum to $3,500 billion, which corresponds to point A in Figure 14 [$A = C_a + I_a + G_a + (X_a - M_a)$ = $3,500 billion]. We must also consider induced consumption, which equals the mpc times income, or 0.5(Y). Thus, total Aggregate Expenditures rises by one-half of any increase in income as income rises, and vice versa. Note that at point e, income is $7 trillion.

In this chapter, our characterization of the simple Keynesian and classical approaches to macroeconomic theory as at opposite ends of the spectrum seems to reinforce a stereotype that economists seldom agree about anything. However, although the basic Keynesian model constructed here assumes a fixed price level, this framework underpins most serious models now used to forecast real growth (changes in the quantity of GDP). In mathematical form, appending equations to the basic Keynesian model permits simultaneous forecasts of economic growth and changes in the price level.

Virtually all modern economists find variants of this model useful. Regardless of which school of thought a given economist finds most appealing, a consensus seems to be emerging about certain theoretical issues. Most modern economists now recognize that

1. The overall health of any economy depends on both Aggregate Supply (the classical perspective) and Aggregate Demand (the Keynesian emphasis).

2. Macroeconomic adjustments entail both changes in wages and prices (classical) and quantity adjustments (Keynesian) whereby output and employment vary.

3. Consumption and saving are influenced by both interest rates (classical) and income (Keynesian).

FIGURE 14   Aggregate Expenditures (Private + Public + Foreign Sectors)

4. The structure of incentives embedded in relative wages and prices affects macroeconomic performance (classical theory and modern Keynesian structural macroeconomics).

Growing agreement about certain basic parts of theory does not extend to a consensus about which macroeconomic policies properly flow from this theory. Major differences among economists continue to swirl around the relative importance of Aggregate Supply and Aggregate Demand and the relative speeds of price and quantity adjustments—topics explored in more detail later in this book, along with more areas of agreement and disagreement among schools of economic thought. Most of all, disagreement revolves around proper economic roles for government—the relative efficiency of the marketplace versus government—and about whether macroeconomic policy should be actively adjusted when economic conditions change or only passively.

A major goal in this chapter has been to ensure familiarity with all categories of spending; $[C + I + G + (X - M)]$ are summed vertically to arrive at Aggregate Expenditures in what is sometimes called the *Keynesian cross* model. In the next chapter, this model is extended to explore how equilibrium National Income is influenced by Aggregate Expenditures.

CHAPTER REVIEW: KEY POINTS

1. **Classical theory** is a conglomeration of the thoughts of many economic thinkers dating back to Adam Smith. It stresses the efficiency and resilience of a market economy.

2. Classical economics is based in part on **Say's Law**: *Supply creates its own demand.* Coupled with assumptions that wages, prices, and interest rates are all perfectly flexible, Say's Law quickly drives a market economy toward full employment. All unemployment is considered voluntary, simply a refusal to work at the equilibrium wage. The protracted unemployment of the early 1930s diluted acceptance of classical theory and led to the development of the fundamentally different **Keynesian theory**.

3. Keynesian analysis focuses on Aggregate Demand. During the Great Depression, much of the economy's productive capacity was idle. During a slow recovery from 1933 to 1940, real output expanded by more than 60% with only slight increases in the price level. Keynesian economics assumes Aggregate Supply to be flat in a depressed economy so that the price level can be ignored; it is primarily concerned with maintaining Aggregate Demand consistent with full employment.

4. **Aggregate Expenditures (AE)** encompass total spending on domestic output during a year. Aggregate Expenditures has four components: (*a*) personal consumption expenditures (*C*), (*b*) Gross Private Domestic Investment (*I*), (*c*) government purchases of goods and services (*G*), and (*d*) net exports of goods and services (*X – M*).

$$AE = C + I + G + (X - M).$$

5. The single most important determinant of consumer spending is disposable income through its influence on **induced consumption**. Consumer spending is related directly to disposable income and is a stable component of Aggregate Expenditures. Other important determinants of consumption and saving include (*a*) wealth and expectations of future income, (*b*) customary living standards, (*c*) the sizes and age composition of typical households, (*d*) consumer goods on hand and household balance sheets, and (*e*) consumer expectations about prices and product availability. These determine the level of **autonomous consumption** (C_a), which is consumer spending unrelated to income.

6. The **marginal propensity to consume (mpc)** is the change in planned consumption arising from a given small change in disposable income; it specifies how much of an additional dollar of income will be consumed. Similarly, the **marginal propensity to save (mps)** is how much of an additional dollar in income will be saved, so mpc + mps = 1.

7. Capital investment refers to purchases of new output that can be used in the future to produce other goods and services. The three major components of investment are (*a*) new business and residential structures, (*b*) machinery and equipment, and (*c*) inventory accumulation.

8. Investment is the least stable component of Aggregate Expenditures, fluctuating widely over the course of a business cycle. The most volatile component of investment is *inventory accumulation*.

9. The primary factors determining the quantity of investment are (*a*) expected returns from investment, (*b*) market interest rates, (*c*) expectations about the business environment, (*d*) rates of technological change and innovation, (*e*) the level of existing stocks of business capital relative to total production, and (*f*) the costs of capital goods. All else being equal, changes in items (*c*) through (*f*) shift rate of return curves, while changes in interest rates cause movements along an expected rate of return curve. In simple Keynesian models, investment is treated as *autonomous* (I_a), or independent of income.

10. While government spending is probably influenced by changes in income, it is even more strongly affected by the state of international relations and domestic politics. Thus government spending as a component of Aggregate Expenditures is also treated as autonomous.

11. Exports and imports are reasonably balanced, so **net exports** ($X - M$) make a comparatively small contribution to Aggregate Expenditures. Simple Keynesian models treat net exports as autonomous.

QUESTIONS FOR THOUGHT AND DISCUSSION

1. The simple Keynesian model treats investment, government spending, and net exports as autonomous. How are each of these types of spending actually influenced by National Income? Why do we treat them as autonomous if all are influenced by income in fairly consistent ways?

2. Are classical economists correct in asserting that all unemployment is voluntary? Can you conceive of circumstances under which people willing to work for the wages paid other people with similar skills and experience would be involuntarily unemployed?

3. Classical economics relies on "invisible hand" mechanisms to ensure full employment.
   a. What adjustments in a capital market might help avoid the underconsumption problem?
   b. What adjustments in output markets eliminate gluts of goods?
   c. How do labor markets adjust to eliminate unemployment?

4. The vertical Aggregate Supply curve compatible with classical economics implies that Aggregate Demand only determines the price level. Keynesians insist that the Aggregate Supply curve is almost horizontal during a depression, so that changes in Aggregate Demand affect output and employment, but not the price level. What differences in assumptions about human behavior account for the different perspectives of classical economics and Keynesian economics?

5. Saving was negative for the economy as a whole during part of the Great Depression of the 1930s. How did this occur? What were the long-term effects of this negative rate of saving?

Net exports

Consumption

Investment

Inflationary gap

$Y=C+I+G+(X-M)$

45°

0

Recessionary gap

Price level

Chapter 10

Macroeconomic Equilibrium

Equilibrium in individual markets requires quantities demanded of specific goods to equal the quantities supplied at prevailing prices. All forces must, on balance, be offsetting, with no net pressure for prices or outputs to change. A macroeconomic equilibrium is similar—all pressures must balance—but the precise nature and duration of a macroequilibrium are matters of debate.

Classical theory concludes that, under laissez-faire policies, a market economy will hover close to full employment in the long run, with automatic adjustments quickly overcoming any macroeconomic shocks. Drawing from the evidence of the Great Depression, Keynes dismissed the pressures classical writers counted on to swiftly restore economies to full employment as either unbearably slow and weak or, worse, nonexistent. Keynes quipped that, "In the long run, we are all dead," and compared continuous economic disruptions to an ocean's waves: waiting for a long-run classical equilibrium is like waiting for the ocean to become flat. Consequently, Keynes focused on the problems of a short-run macroequilibrium, describing how substantial idle capital and unemployed labor could plague an economy for long periods.

Keynes's view that widespread joblessness might persist in a short-run macroequilibrium requires scrutiny. How plans for purchases by consumers, investors, government, and foreigners are summed to form an Aggregate Expenditures curve was explored in Chapter 9. For simplicity, our model in this chapter initially focuses solely on private sector activities. Then, in Chapter 11, government spending and taxes are brought into the picture as tools policymakers might wield to battle excessive unemployment or inflation.

AGGREGATE EXPENDITURES AND EQUILIBRIUM

We will initially ignore international trade, taxes, depreciation, transfer payments, government expenditures, and undistributed corpo-

TABLE 1 Levels of Income Employment and Output*

(1) Employment (millions of workers)	(2) National Output of Income	(3) Planned Consumption	(4) Planned Saving	(5) Planned Investment	(6) Unplanned Inventory Changes	(7) Aggregate Expenditures (3) + (5)	
100	$5,000	$5,100	$–100	$300	$–400	$5,400	pressure for income to rise
105	5,500	5,500	0	300	–300	5,800	
110	6,000	5,900	100	300	–200	6,200	
115	6,500	6,300	200	300	–100	6,600	▼
120	**7,000**	**6,700**	**300**	**300**	**0**	**7,000**	**equilibrium**
125	7,500	7,100	400	300	100	7,400	▲
130	8,000	7,500	500	300	200	7,800	pressure for income to fall
135	8,500	7,900	600	300	300	8,200	

*In billions of dollars.

rate profits.[1] This simplifying assumption blurs distinctions between GDP, NDP, and disposable income, permitting use of the term "income" (Y) to refer to all three. The values of net income and output are also equal, with profit acting as a balancing item.

Labor is required to produce output that, if sold, translates into National Income and maintains jobs. Thus, employment rises if National Income grows. Higher employment usually implies less unemployment. However, if output is unsalable at prices that cover costs, some firms will cut back or even shut down, and some workers will lose their jobs. Thus, more labor is idled as an economy becomes stagnant, whereas economic growth usually reduces unemployment rates. Aggregate Expenditures and National Output thus interact to yield a macroequilibrium.

National Output

Typical relationships among income, employment, and output are summarized in Table 1. Column 1 shows the employment needed to produce the levels of National Output (column

[1]Models of *closed, private economies* address only domestic spending by consumers and investors, ignoring government and the foreign sector. Government and international trade are taken into account in *open-economy macro models.* Before a model of a mixed, open economy is introduced, however, you need to gain familiarity with the mechanics of private sector macroeconomic relationships.

2) firms are willing to offer at current prices if they are confident it will be sold. You might think of the National Output schedule as reflecting a Keynesian Aggregate Supply curve because firms willingly produce whatever is demanded. For example, firms will employ 120 million workers and produce $7,000 billion (or $7 trillion) in output and income only if they expect sale of this output for $7 trillion. Remember, "demand creates its own supply" in Keynesian analysis.

Aggregate Expenditures

Aggregate Expenditure is the sum of all plans for consumer spending, investment, government purchases, and net foreign spending. However, basic Keynesian models of closed, private economies simplify analysis by ignoring government and the foreign sector, so column 7 in Table 1 reflects Aggregate Expenditures (AE) as the sum only of planned consumption (column 3) and planned investment (column 5); $AE = C + I$ summarizes the levels of planned Aggregate Expenditures for each level of output and income.

Keynesian Equilibrium

National Output is graphed as a 45° ray from the origin in Figure 1 because, in Keynesian the-

FIGURE 1 Keynesian Equilibrium

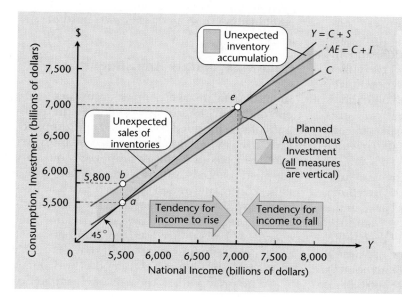

Equilibrium income (point e) is found where National Output ($Y = C + S$) just equals Aggregate Expenditures. Any disequilibrium would entail pressure to move the economy back to the $7,000 billion income level. If income were below $7,000 billion, Aggregate Expenditures would exceed National Output, so shrinking inventories would create expansionary pressure, boosting employment and output: the economy would move upward to point e. If output exceeds AE, inventories swell because sales are less than firms forecast. Production cutbacks and layoffs will then restore the economy to equilibrium at point e.

ory, Aggregate Supply (output) adjusts passively to Aggregate Demand (expenditures).[2]

> **Keynesian equilibrium** *is achieved when Aggregate Output and Income (on the horizontal axis) precisely equals planned Aggregate Expenditures (on the vertical axis).*

Keynesian macroeconomic equilibrium occurs when this Aggregate Expenditures curve intersects the 45° line. Following convention, Y (on the horizontal axis) denotes real National Income and is measured against planned Aggregate Expenditures (on the vertical axis).

Classical theory concludes that deviations from full employment represent disequilibria that are, at most, short-run phenomena quickly remedied by Say's Law and flexible interest rates, wages, and prices. Keynesian perceptions of a short-run disequilibrium have a different focus.

> **Disequilibrium** *occurs whenever plans for Aggregate Expenditures differ from Aggregate Output and Income.*

_____
[2]Recall that any variable plotted against an equal variable is on a 45° line.

How is equilibrium restored? Classical reasoning suggests that *supply creates its own demand*: price adjustments automatically adapt real Aggregate Spending to accommodate full employment levels of output. Keynesians respond that *demand creates its own supply*: supply passively adjusts to demand. In this context, *spending* and *demand* are synonymous.

Let's put Keynesian adjustment processes under the microscope—in a disequilibrium, Aggregate Expenditures determine output and employment. Table 1 lists eight levels of National Output and planned Aggregate Expenditures. At what level will equilibrium be achieved? Consider employment of 105 million workers with National Output equal to $5,500 billion (point a). Planned Aggregate Expenditure equals $5,800 billion (point b), and so exceeds the $5,500 billion in National Output. What adjustments will rebalance National Output and Aggregate Expenditures?

In this situation, most firms will not maintain inventories adequate for their customers' demands. As inventories evaporate (the vertical distance between AE and the 45° reference line), firms will respond by expanding employment and output. This stimulates income. Suppose employment grows from 105 to 110 million. Even employment of 110 million workers poses a problem: Aggregate Expenditures, now $6,200 billion, still exceed National Output, now $6,000 billion. Employment, output, and income will continue to climb until 120 million people are working. Aggregate Expenditures and National Output both equal $7,000 billion at this employment level. Any further pressures to expand output are offset by pressures to contract output—firms steadily maintain inventories that meet customers' demands.

Pressures to restore equilibrium are summarized in Figure 1. Unplanned inventory changes equal the vertical distances between the Aggregate Expenditures curve $(C + I)$ and the 45° National Output line $(C + S)$. For example, at output of only $5,500 billion (point a), planned Aggregate Expenditure is $5,800 billion (point b). Excess Aggregate Spending ($b - a = $300 billion) shrinks inventories, generating expansionary pressure that pushes the economy rightward from both a and b up the 45° National Output line to equilibrium at point e ($7,000 billion).

What happens if National Output exceeds planned AE? Suppose most firms were overly optimistic in forecasting consumer and investor demands and produced $7,500 billion worth of goods and services. Inventories of unsold goods would become bloated. Businesses cannot precisely regulate inventories because customers may buy either more or less than firms expect. In this case, firms would reduce inventories and output by cutting back production, necessitating employee layoffs. As output fell to point e in Figure 1, business inventories would shrink to the planned levels. This economy settles at an equilibrium income of $7,000 billion.

Both Table 1 and Figure 1 indicate that National Income will expand when output is less than $7,000 billion because spending exceeds production. When income or output exceeds $7,000 billion, income falls because production exceeds spending. Only when National Output is exactly $7,000 billion are all decision-makers content to continue operating at existing levels of production, consumption, and investment. All forces are balanced, and given the Keynesian assumptions that wages and prices are sticky, or downwardly rigid, net pressures for the economy to shrink or grow from this short-run equilibrium are weak or even nonexistent.

Price vs. Quantity Adjustments

In individual markets, price adjustments are part of the cure for disparities between the quantities of specific goods demanded and supplied. Price rises in individual markets if quantity demanded exceeds quantity supplied; if quantity supplied exceeds quantity demanded, price falls. You may wonder why such price adjustments are absent in Keynesian depression models. The reason is that Keynesians assume that *quantity adjustments* predominate in situations of excess capacity and high unemployment; the Aggregate Supply curve is treated as horizontal.

The price level is constant in a simple depression model because capacity is assumed not to be a crucial constraint; expanding output when many workers are idle does not require higher wage or price incentives. Classical analysis presumes severe capacity constraints because market economies are thought to hover close to full employment. Thus, the classical Aggregate Supply curve is vertical, and the classical model relies on *price-level adjustments* to buffer against shocks to Aggregate Demand. This part of the book focuses on the simple Keynesian model, with detailed treatments of price movements being postponed until later chapters.

A KEYNESIAN SAVING = INVESTMENT EQUILIBRIUM

Investigating how investment and saving are related provides another view of how National Income and Output are determined. Inspection of Table 1 and Figure 1 reveals that a stable equilibrium requires planned levels of saving and investment to be equal.

*Actual and planned saving and investment are all equal $(S = I)$ in a **macroequilibrium** in a private economy without government or foreign trade.*

Households' saving plans and firms' investment plans must both be realized for equilibrium to occur, regardless of whether the model used is Keynesian or classical.

Planned Saving and Investment

Columns 4 and 5 from Table 1 are graphed in Figure 2. In our simple model, firms plan to invest $300 billion regardless of national income, while consumers' saving is tied to income. Suppose income were $8,500 billion. Consumers would try to save $600 billion (point *f* in Figure 2), but investment plans absorb only $300 billion (point *g*). What will be the result?

Saving is the act of not consuming. Because income saved is money not spent, saving is a withdrawal of funds from the system.

> ***Withdrawals*** *occur when income is not spent on domestic output.*

In addition to saving, withdrawals include taxes (income paid to the government) and imports (most foreign income is spent in the recipients' own countries). Because spending is perceived to drive a capitalist system, withdrawals tend to stifle income creation in this simple Keynesian model.

Injections are the reverse of withdrawals; they reflect new sources of spending.

> *Autonomous spending (regardless of source) represents an **injection** into the Keynesian spending stream.*

We will discuss the effects of injections on National Income after we consider the consequences of such forms of withdrawals as household saving.

Excess saving causes unwanted inventories to pile up; output exceeds sales because withdrawals create excess supplies of most goods. Firms will find total consumer and business spending ($C + I$) insufficient to clear new output from the market. Production and employment will fall because firms do not desire these investments in inventory. Income drops as the economy moves back from points *f* and *g* toward equilibrium at point *e*, where planned saving and planned investment are equal. Planned and realized saving and investment are all equated, and income stops falling as equilibrium is approached.

These adjustments reverse direction if output is below the $7,000 billion equilibrium level. For example, when National Output is $6,500 bil-

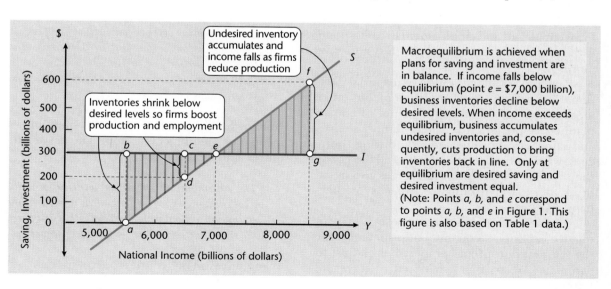

Macroequilibrium is achieved when plans for saving and investment are in balance. If income falls below equilibrium (point *e* = $7,000 billion), business inventories decline below desired levels. When income exceeds equilibrium, business accumulates undesired inventories and, consequently, cuts production to bring inventories back in line. Only at equilibrium are desired saving and desired investment equal.
(Note: Points *a, b,* and *e* correspond to points *a, b,* and *e* in Figure 1. This figure is also based on Table 1 data.)

FIGURE 2   Equilibrium Saving and Investment

lion, consumers desire to save $200 billion and spend $6,300 billion, while firms plan to invest $300 billion; Aggregate Expenditures ($C + I$) equal $6,600 billion. The $100 billion shortfall of goods to accommodate buyers shrinks inventories, which fall by an unplanned $100 billion in each period. Production then expands to restore inventories to desired levels. Income rises to $7,000 billion (from c and d in Figure 2 to point e) before inventories become stable; planned saving and investment both equal $300 billion at point e. Thus, equilibrium requires planned saving to equal planned investment ($S = I$).

Balancing Planned and Actual Saving and Investment

Inventory fluctuations, whether planned or unexpected by managers, ensure the constant equality of actual saving and investment. Remember that investment includes both planned and unplanned elements, where unplanned investment equals changes in inventories. Unanticipated inventory changes also help align investors' plans with those of savers by serving as business barometers. Unexpectedly brisk sales are great news for business, but inventories then unintentionally shrink. Firms adjust by boosting output. However, when weak sales fail to match forecasts, inventories swell and firms cut output and employment to correspond with households' plans to spend less and save more.

Inventory changes guide managerial decisions about output and employment, but other mechanisms also aid in equilibrium to equate planned saving and investment. Empty shelves and rainchecks become common during shortages, when consumers cannot buy all the goods they demand. Queues and shortages also signal firms to expand productive capacity or, perhaps, to raise prices.

Keynesian models presuppose idle productive capacity, so quantity adjustments clear the market; output and employment adjust to eliminate disparities between Aggregate Expenditures and National Output. Classical reasoning posits full employment, with all mar-

kets clearing through wage and price adjustments. Both theories agree, however, that only when planned investment exactly equals planned saving will a private economy attain equilibrium. When households' plans to save and firms' plans to invest are both realized, sales precisely sustain equilibrium output with no net pressure for growth or stagnation. How differing conditions may foster quantity adjustments instead of price adjustments is treated toward the end of this chapter.

THE MULTIPLIER EFFECT

If investment were zero in Table 1, Aggregate Expenditures would consist only of consumption (C) and equilibrium income would be $5,500 billion (point a in Figures 1 and 2). When autonomous investment of $300 billion is injected, however, its effect is multiplied so that equilibrium income rises to $7,000 billion (points e in both figures). The total change in income that ultimately results from this investment is five times the initial increase in spending!

You may wonder how a relatively small injection of investment ($300 billion) so powerfully expands income (by $1,500 billion). Multiplier processes provide the answer.

> The **multiplier effect** occurs when one person's spending becomes someone else's income, and some of the second person's income is subsequently spent, becoming the income of a third person, and so on.

But at what income level does this spending → income → spending cycle stop? The answer requires a bit of arithmetic.

> The **autonomous spending multiplier** is the total change in income generated, divided by the change in autonomous spending that triggered the spending → income → spending sequence.

When investment is the source of new autonomous spending, this autonomous spending multiplier equals the ratio $\Delta Y/\Delta I$.

Our example to this point assumes a marginal propensity to consume (mpc) of 0.8. Suppose we begin with zero investment. According to Table 1, equilibrium income would be $5,500 billion, because only at that level does planned saving also equal zero. Now suppose firms decide to invest $100 billion in new capital goods. The workers and owners of firms that produce this new capital receive $100 billion in additional income.

How will these workers and proprietors respond to this extra $100 billion in income? Their mpc is 0.8 in their roles as consumers, so $80 billion of this new income will be spent on consumer goods, and saving grows $20 billion. When these producers spend the $80 billion,

this second round of spending adds $80 billion to Aggregate Expenditures; National Output must rise by $80 billion, which becomes new income to the firms providing these consumer goods and to their employees. In turn, they will spend 80% of the $80 billion, or $64 billion, in income to their suppliers, and so on throughout the system.

The cumulative effect of this round-by-round spending is illustrated in Figure 3, assuming the mpc to be 0.8 so that the mps is 0.2. The multiplier in this case is 5. That the multiplier is the reciprocal of the mps is no coincidence ($1/mps = 1/0.2 = 5$). In fact, any change in *injections* (e.g., either additional autonomous consumption or new investment) divided by the

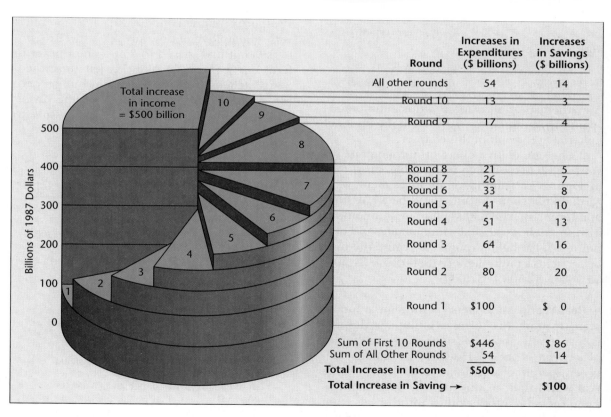

Round	Increases in Expenditures ($ billions)	Increases in Savings ($ billions)
All other rounds	54	14
Round 10	13	3
Round 9	17	4
Round 8	21	5
Round 7	26	7
Round 6	33	8
Round 5	41	10
Round 4	51	13
Round 3	64	16
Round 2	80	20
Round 1	$100	$ 0
Sum of First 10 Rounds	$446	$ 86
Sum of All Other Rounds	54	14
Total Increase in Income	$500	
Total Increase in Saving →		$100

An additional $100 billion in spending in Round 1 (shown at the bottom "stair") is subject to a spending→income→spending multiplier process, ultimately generating a total increase in income of $500 billion when the mpc = 0.8. Each increase in spending in each round, when multiplied by the mpc, is the increase in spending for the subsequent round. When the sum of this infinite series is calculated, aggregate income grows by $500 billion from this initial new injection of $100 billion.

Note: Data after Round 3 are rounded to the nearest billion.

FIGURE 3   The Multiplier Effect

marginal propensity to save yields the total multiplied effect on National Output and Income.

The only form of withdrawal in our simplified model is saving, so the multiplier is 1/mps. (A higher mps yields a faster rate of withdrawal and a smaller multiplier.) Alternatively, the multiplier is the change in income divided by the change in autonomous injections, so[3]

$$\frac{\Delta Y}{\Delta I} = \frac{1}{mps} = \frac{1}{1 - mpc}$$

If we consider withdrawals other than saving,

$$\begin{array}{l} \text{autonomous} \\ \text{spending} \\ \text{multiplier} \end{array} = \frac{1}{\begin{array}{c}\text{withdrawal fraction} \\ \text{per spending round}\end{array}}$$

$$= \frac{1}{1 - \text{fraction respent}}$$

and

$$\begin{array}{l}\text{total changes} \\ \text{in income}\end{array} = \begin{array}{l}\text{amount of} \\ \text{injection} \times \text{multiplier.}\end{array}$$

A mathematical derivation of this autonomous spending multiplier is provided in the optional material at the end of this chapter.

The cumulative effect of autonomous investment based on data from Table 1 is shown in Figure 4. If autonomous investment were zero, equilibrium output would be $5,500 billion (point a). The $300 billion in autonomous investment boosts equilibrium income and output to $7,000 billion (point e) because the mpc of 0.8 yields a multiplier of 5 ($300 × 5 = $1,500; $5,500 + $1,500 = $7,000).

• **Real-World Multipliers**   Our simple model seems to imply an enormous multiplier; the mps is, historically, about 7%, suggesting a multiplier of between 14 and 15. However, the linkages between spending rounds are much looser in the real world than in this model. More sophisticated models consider other withdrawals from the spending → income → spending sequence.

Withdrawals include taxes (roughly 30%) and other leakages such as imports, a case where the funds we spend go into the hands of foreign

suppliers. Moreover, the full multiplier effect is felt only after all spending rounds have been completed. Realistically, only the first few rounds of spending occur in the same year as any new injection. For all these reasons and more, statistical estimates of the value of the autonomous spending multiplier place its maximum real value at around 2, even during the Great Depression, when conditions were optimal for the multiplier to have its largest possible value.

The Great Depression: The Multiplier in Action

Brother, can you spare a dime?

A hit song from the 1930s

Prosperity reigned in the Roaring Twenties, with unemployment of only 3.2% in 1929, but by 1933, it had soared to 25%—one worker in four was jobless. No one was left unscathed. Soup kitchens could not feed all the hungry people, and Wall Street windows became diving platforms for those who preferred suicide to

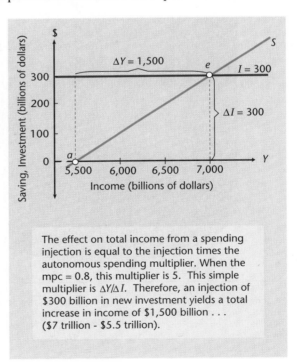

The effect on total income from a spending injection is equal to the injection times the autonomous spending multiplier. When the mpc = 0.8, this multiplier is 5. This simple multiplier is ΔY/ΔI. Therefore, an injection of $300 billion in new investment yields a total increase in income of $1,500 billion . . . ($7 trillion - $5.5 trillion).

FIGURE 4   The Total Effect of the Multiplier

---

[3]The mpc + mps = 1, so the mps = *1* − mpc and the multiplier may also be written as 1/(1 − mpc).

bankruptcy. Most U.S. financial institutions teetered on the brink, threatening to collapse like rows of dominoes. Unemployment compensation and Social Security had not yet been enacted to replace temporarily lost incomes. Economically, Americans had never faced harder times. This dismal plunge into the Great Depression from 1929 to 1933 is summarized in Figure 5, a Keynesian portrayal that seems fairly straightforward by today's standards, but which would have been a revelation in the early 1930s.

Data for the four components of Aggregate Expenditures ($C, I, G, X - M$) reveal that changes in net foreign spending and government purchases were quite small and largely offset each other during this period. Keynesians viewed the collapse of investment (ΔI in Figure 5) between 1929 and 1933 as the root cause of the erosion of Aggregate Expenditure—investment fell from $173.3 billion to only $28.3 billion. This $145 billion decline in investment was echoed by a $263 billion drop in income (from $848.1 billion in 1929 to $585.4 billion in 1933). Remember that the multiplier is the change in income divided by the change in injections, which in this case is roughly $\Delta Y/\Delta I$. Thus, our highly simplified Keynesian model suggests a multiplier during the Great Depression of 1.81 ($-263/-145 = 1.81$).

Government policies to combat instability have been refined considerably in the past 60

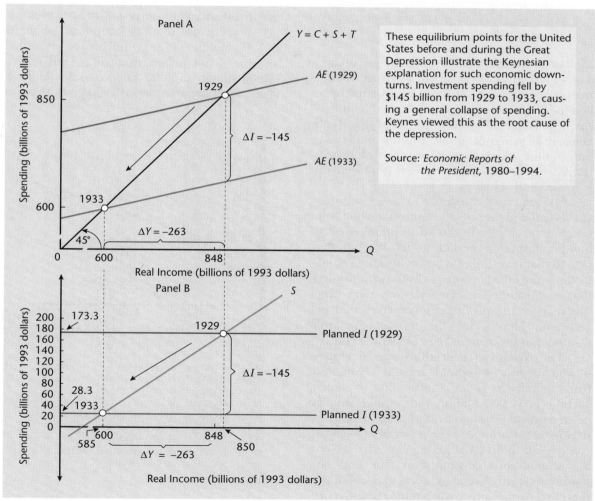

These equilibrium points for the United States before and during the Great Depression illustrate the Keynesian explanation for such economic downturns. Investment spending fell by $145 billion from 1929 to 1933, causing a general collapse of spending. Keynes viewed this as the root cause of the depression.

Source: *Economic Reports of the President, 1980–1994.*

FIGURE 5   Saving, Investment, and Income During the Great Depression

years. Most economists doubt that such a deep collapse will ever recur. How might government have flattened the Great Depression or made it shorter? In the next few chapters, we will examine tools the government now uses to combat both recessions and inflations.

The Paradox of Thrift

What happens if we as a society try to save more? Classical analysis suggests that saving promotes investment and growth, but a potential *paradox of thrift* may pose a problem.

> *Keynesian theory suggests that attempts to save more may cause income to fall so much that actual saving shrinks, a problem known as the* **paradox of thrift***.*

Most of us consider thrift a virtue. Ben Franklin's adage "A penny saved is a penny earned" haunts many of our psyches, and we think we might be better-off if we saved more. The term "paradox" correctly reflects, however, the belief that Ben's adage may be inappropriate for the overall economy at times. Basic Keynesian analysis indicates that if we all try to save more, we may all wind up worse off and actually save less.

Showing how the desire to save more may cause actual saving to fall requires a slight, but temporary, change in the assumptions used to build a simple Keynesian model. We have assumed that investment is autonomous, or unaffected by income. A more realistic assumption is that as income rises, firms become more optimistic about the profit prospects from new investment. Hence, for the moment we will assume that investment rises as income rises.

The paradox of thrift is illustrated in Figure 6, which shows households initially saving and firms initially investing $300 billion. National Income is $7,000 billion, with equilibrium at point *a* on curves S_0 and *I*. Suppose consumers decide to consume less (save more) at each income level, shifting the saving curve from S_0 to S_1. Autonomous consumption falls and autonomous saving becomes less negative, but the marginal propensity to save (mps) remains constant at 20%. People now want to set aside $400

billion (point *b*) if National Income stays at $7,000 billion. But what happens as the economy adjusts to this increased desire to save?

Consumption falls when households try to save more. Firms will counter declining sales and swelling inventories by cutting production, employment, and investment. Employment and income both fall from the original equilibrium of $7,000 billion (point *a*) to a new equilibrium at $6,000 billion (point *c*). Notice that saving actually declines $100 billion, to a $200 billion level. Why? Because actual saving and investment and planned saving and investment must all be equal in equilibrium. At point *c*, income is now only $6,000 billion; at this lower income level consumers want to save only $200 billion and investors want to invest only $200 billion.

Observe also that consumption, originally $6,700 billion ($7,000 billion in National Income −$300 billion in saving), will fall to $5,800 billion ($6,000 billion −$200 billion). Thus, the paradox of thrift suggests that in-

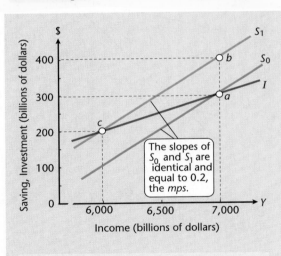

The slopes of S_0 and S_1 are identical and equal to 0.2, the *mps*.

If consumers try to save an extra $100 billion at every income level (raising autonomous saving), the consumption curve (not shown in this figure) shifts down and the corresponding saving curve S_0 shifts up to S_1. Unless the investment schedule simultaneously increases, income will fall from $7,000 billion to $6,000 billion (from point *a* to point *c*), and saving and investment will both fall from $300 billion to $200 billion.

FIGURE 6 **The Paradox of Thrift**

Does Saving Stimulate Growth or Drag it Down?

The answer, as for so many questions about economic issues, is "It depends." But on what does "It" depend? It turns out that whether increased desires to save facilitate prosperity or usher in economic collapse depends on why consumers want to save more: expectations about job prospects or rates of return on investments, or their general sense of where an economy is going.

Suppose deep-seated pessimism about job prospects for family breadwinners is generally matched by bearish (negative) expectations among potential business investors. If widespread economic malaise is the origin of increased desires to save, then the paradox of thrift raises its ugly head, and increased desires to save can push an economy toward the doldrums. On the other hand, suppose increased desires to save originate from greater optimism because, say, more people expect to live longer and want big retirement nest eggs to make their golden years of retirement more enjoyable. Interest rates will fall, and the prospect of servicing longer-term consumer needs (e.g., recreation, retirement communities, and

health care) will both redirect and stimulate investment and growth.

Complex considerations link expectations—whether optimistic or pessimistic—with rates of saving and investment, both planned and realized. How optimism or pessimism affects saving, and, consequently, economic growth, depends on the sources of people's expectations. Pessimism created by fear of a depression may stimulate planned saving and make manifest a Keynesian paradox of thrift, driving down both actual saving and actual investment.

But suppose long-range weather forecasts of worldwide drought fostered pessimism and fear of famine. Would plans for saving and investment be stimulated or depressed? In this case, increased concerns about survival might stimulate saving for a (non?)-rainy day, accompanied by booming investment in new equipment and seed to help cultivate drought-resistant crops. Thus, this type of pessimism may enhance prospects for economic growth.

Now, suppose that all astronomers simultaneously predict with 100% probability a collision two years from today between our

Earth and an asteroid the size of Mars. The resulting pessimism would probably trigger binges of consumption: Eat, drink, and be merry, for tomorrow you may die. Plans for saving and investment would both be likely to fall to zero shortly after the news was announced. And such plans would invariably be realized.

Now consider a case where people (college students?) live in deprivation but expect some factor not tied to their current income or saving to soon bring prosperity (e.g., getting a great job, winning a lottery, or being liberated from dictatorship by the army of a wealthy and generous democracy that will extend aid to your underdeveloped country). In such cases, optimistic expectations may squelch any plans for current saving and investment—in a short time, things will get better because of the external factor.

The point here is that how expectations affect plans for saving and investment is situational. Each set of circumstances requires a careful and case-specific analysis for a sense of the long-run effects on saving and investment, and ultimately, on economic growth.

creased desires to save may shrink actual saving and investment, with income and consumption also falling, leaving people with lower standards of living. This Keynesian line of reasoning certainly raises questions for those of us who think that more saving is always good for the economy. Unfortunately, increased saving may be a typical household response at the worst possible time, when an economy begins to slip into a recession. If families fear that breadwinners will lose their jobs, they may begin saving a little more each payday, trying to build nest eggs to cover expenses should income tumble. If grow-

ing numbers of households adopt this strategy, momentum for a recession will build.

The paradox of saving is probably irrelevant in an economy operating close to its capacity. Classical theory suggests that increased desires to save drive down interest rates, which stimulates investment and economic growth. The economic climate determines whether saving is more likely to depress income—a Keynesian possibility—or if greater willingness to save facilitates economic growth, as classical reasoning implies. This paradox is explored in Focus 1.

The Investment Accelerator

The multiplier process relies on the fact that any increase in autonomous spending creates income, which generates further consumer spending, creating more income, and so on. New investment may also be triggered by increased spending.

> An **investment accelerator** *exerts pressure for accelerated income growth when rising consumption and income stimulate new capital investment.*

New autonomous spending causes investment to accelerate, so that Aggregate Expenditure is both *multiplied* by induced consumption and *accelerated* by induced investment. Thus, a change in autonomous spending may increase income by even more than the multiplier effect alone. (More sophisticated Keynesian models than any considered in this book explain how interactions between investment accelerators and multiplier processes may destabilize Aggregate Expenditures.) The effects on National Income of interactions between the multiplier and accelerator are traced in Figure 7.

EQUILIBRIUM BELOW POTENTIAL GDP

We now turn to the most important conclusion of Keynesian analysis. Keynes was the first prominent mainstream economist to argue (*a*) that demand creates its own supply and (*b*) that sticky adjustments of wages, prices, and interest rates might stall an economy in a semipermanent, short-run equilibrium at less than full employment. Keynes's ideas departed sharply from those of classical economists, who counted on flexible prices, wages, and interest rates to quickly counter any deviations from full employment. The severity of the Great Depression signaled that invisible hand mechanisms may operate only slowly at times. High cyclical unemployment showed few signs of automatic cure prior to World War II.

Potential GDP

Potential GDP and full-employment GDP (or income) are rough synonyms.

> **Potential GDP** *is an estimate of what the economy could produce at high rates of utilization of our available resources, especially full employment of labor.*

Estimates of potential GDP reflect trends in productivity, the size and composition of the labor force, and other influences on our capacity to produce. Estimates of the ratio of actual GDP to potential GDP for 1929 to 1993 are illustrated in Figure 8.

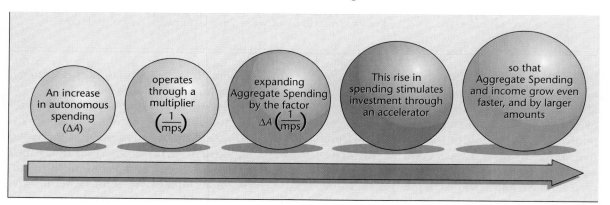

Investment is stimulated by a change in autonomous spending (ΔA) through the accelerator principle. This change in autonomous spending magnifies Aggregate Expenditures even more than is suggested by the multiplier process, but it also makes Aggregate Spending extremely volatile.

FIGURE 7 Integrating an Investment Accelerator into a Keynesian System

FIGURE 8   The Ratio of Actual GDP to Potential GDP, 1929—1993

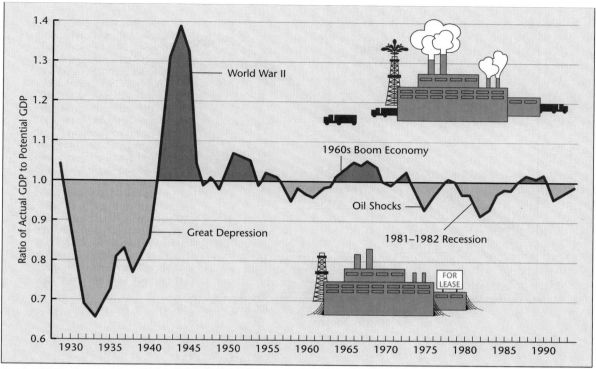

Sources: *Economic Report of the President,* 1994; Robert J. Gordon, *Macroeconomics* (New York: Harper Collins, 1993). Updated by authors.

Actual and potential GDP can diverge substantially. Since World War II their differences have been relatively minor. Nevertheless, recessions remain costly whether measured by lost income or by social trauma.

Potential GDP is not an absolute limit on productive capacity in the same way a production possibilities frontier is. For example, potential GDP might be exceeded through slavery, or if people who would normally choose not to work took temporary jobs to support a national defense effort (e.g., women during World War II), or if frictional unemployment artificially fell because many jobless workers accepted positions that, because of inflation, ultimately paid less than they expected. Ideally, potential GDP reflects only activities that are informed and voluntary, a point addressed in more depth later in this book.

The GDP Gap

Figure 8 illustrates that National Output can fall far below potential GDP.

> The **GDP gap** is the difference between potential and actual GDP.

In the simple Keynesian model from Table 1, now graphed in Figure 9, equilibrium income is $7 trillion at point a, where expenditure curve AE_0 intersects the 45° $Y = C + S$ line. If potential GDP at full employment is $7.5 trillion, then a GDP gap of $500 billion exists. Would market pressures quickly move the economy above its original $7 trillion equilibrium? The Keynesian response is No. How might this $500 billion GDP gap be filled to achieve full-employment income and output of $7.5 trillion? The Keynesian answer is to boost Aggregate Expenditure from AE_0 to AE_1. But by how much must autonomous spending be increased?

The Recessionary Gap

Given that the multiplier in our example is 5 $(1/0.2 = 1/mps)$, an increase in autonomous investment spending of $100 billion will raise

FIGURE 9 Recessionary and Inflationary Gaps

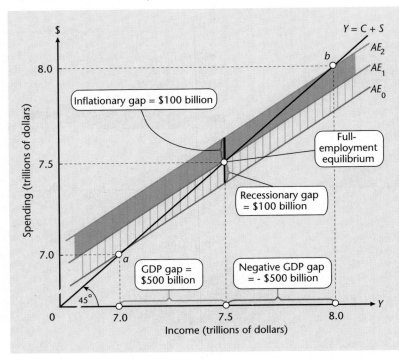

If full-employment income is $7.5 trillion but Aggregate Expenditures are only AE_0, the equilibrium at point a ($7 trillion) falls below full employment. A *GDP gap* of $500 billion exists. Given our multiplier of 5, the *recessionary gap* is $100 billion (the *vertical* rise in autonomous spending needed for a full employment equilibrium).

If Aggregate Expenditures were AE_2, excessive autonomous spending would yield an *inflationary gap* of $100 billion, with a negative GDP gap of - $500 billion. Although equilibrium (point b) is $8 trillion, the economy could not produce this much extra real output, so the price level would rise by 8/7.5.

Only at Aggregate Expenditures of AE_1 will full employment and a stable price level be compatible.

Aggregate Expenditures and output by $500 billion, filling the GDP gap so that full employment is achieved.

> The **recessionary gap** *measures the amount by which autonomous spending falls short of that needed to bring equilibrium income to full employment.*

The recessionary gap is measured along the vertical axis in Figure 9. Thus, the recessionary gap is defined by any shortfall in autonomous spending, not by the amount by which equilibrium income falls short of full-employment income (measured along the horizontal axis).

$$\text{GDP gap} = \text{recessionary gap} \times \text{multiplier}$$

Any shortfall in equilibrium income is a GDP gap and equals the recessionary gap times the autonomous spending multiplier.

The Inflationary Gap

What happens if autonomous spending is excessive?

> An **inflationary gap** *is the amount by which autonomous spending exceeds that needed to achieve full-employment equilibrium.*

The inflationary gap is the vertical distance between AE_1 and AE_2 in Figure 9, which equals $100 billion. Equilibrium at point b yields $8 trillion in income, but only $7.5 trillion can be produced at full employment, so this added demand drives prices upward because of increased competition among potential buyers. (Inflation is likely to be 6.7%; 8/7.5 = 1.067.)

AGGREGATE DEMAND AND AGGREGATE EXPENDITURES

Positive relationships between Aggregate Expenditure curves (*AE*) and Aggregate Demand curves (*AD*) seem intuitive: if an Aggregate Demand curve increases (shifts to the right), it seems the Aggregate Expenditure curve should also rise (shift upward). And vice versa. This intuition is usually correct. For example, if consumers splurge, anticipating a boom that will improve job security, both Aggregate Expenditure and Aggregate Demand rise. Similarly, if new tariffs alarm investors who fear that a global trade war will slam doors to our exports and reduce supplies of imported resources, both Aggregate Demand and Aggregate Expenditures fall.

Price Levels and Aggregate Expenditures

These relationships are not, however, always so straightforward. Recall that a price cut for a specific good, say, olives, does not increase demand; it increases the quantity of olives demanded—a move along the original demand curve for olives. A similar logic applies along an Aggregate Demand curve when the price level changes; the amount of domestic output demanded changes, but the Aggregate Demand curve itself does not shift. Although Aggregate Demand curves incorporate price-level changes, each Aggregate Expenditure curve is based on the Keynesian assumption of a constant price level. A bit of algebra should help in dissecting the connections shown in Figure 10 between the price level, Aggregate Demand, and Aggregate Expenditure curves.

National Income (Y), a monetary value, equals the product of the price level (P) and the level of real output (Q). Thus, $Y = P \times Q$ and, as long as the price level is constant, National Income (Y) and real output (Q) are identical and conform to the Keynesian approach. When the price level varies along an Aggregate Demand curve, however, classical price adjustments come into play. But how do changes in the price level affect Keynesian Aggregate Expenditure curves?

• **Price Levels and Autonomous Spending** Each Aggregate Expenditure curve in Panel A of Figure 10 assumes a specific price level. However, if the price level falls, autonomous spending will rise because consumers and in-

vestors can—and will—buy more goods or resources. Naturally, autonomous spending falls if the price level rises, all else being equal.

• **Deriving Aggregate Demand from Aggregate Expenditure Curves** Aggregate Expenditure $AE_{(P\,=\,100)}$ in Panel A of Figure 10 yields equilibrium income of $7.5 trillion (point a), with a corresponding point a on the Aggregate Demand curve in Panel B. If the price level (P) falls from $P = 100$ to $P = 92.8$, autonomous spending grows, boosting Aggregate Expenditure to $AE_{(P\,=\,92.8)}$; this new equilibrium is at $8 trillion (point b). Symmetrically, equilibrium moves to point c in both panels if the price level rises to $P = 108.3$. Connecting equilibrium points in Panel B for each possible price level and the AE curve associated with it in Panel A yields the Aggregate Demand curve, illustrating the close ties between Aggregate Expenditure curves and the Aggregate Demand curve. Thus, varying the price level in a Keynesian model allows derivation of a negatively sloped Aggregate Demand curve.

Shifts in Aggregate Demand Curves

Changes in the price level will shift the Aggregate Expenditure curve, but spending can change for other reasons, including changes in consumer confidence or in the business climate. If the price level is constant and Aggregate Expenditure changes, the Aggregate Demand curve also shifts, as illustrated in Figure 11.

Aggregate Demand curve AD_0 is associated with Aggregate Expenditure AE_0. Equilibrium income is $7 trillion at a price level of 100 (point a). Improved business optimism, for example, could increase autonomous spending to AE_1, yielding a new full-employment equilibrium of $7.5 trillion (point b). Thus, increased autonomous spending of $100 billion yields additional income of $500 billion (the change in autonomous spending times the multiplier) at the existing price level ($P = 100$), and AD_1 is the new Aggregate Demand curve associated with this higher level of Aggregate Expenditure, AE_1.

FIGURE 10 Aggregate Expenditures and Aggregate Demand

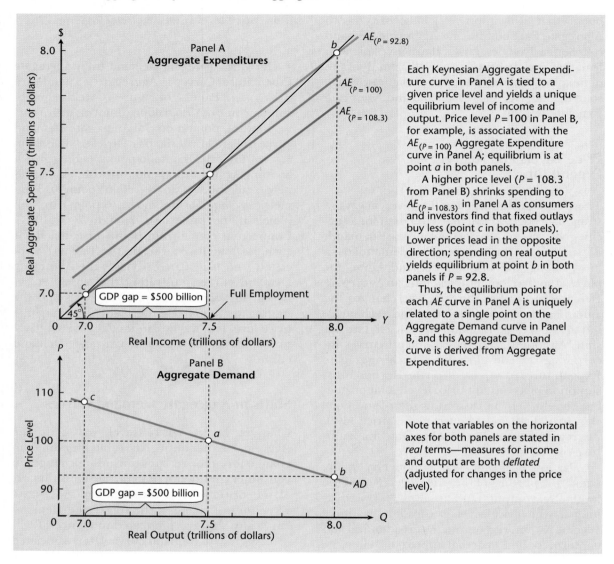

Each Keynesian Aggregate Expenditure curve in Panel A is tied to a given price level and yields a unique equilibrium level of income and output. Price level $P=100$ in Panel B, for example, is associated with the $AE_{(P=100)}$ Aggregate Expenditure curve in Panel A; equilibrium is at point a in both panels.

A higher price level ($P=108.3$ from Panel B) shrinks spending to $AE_{(P=108.3)}$ in Panel A as consumers and investors find that fixed outlays buy less (point c in both panels). Lower prices lead in the opposite direction; spending on real output yields equilibrium at point b in both panels if $P=92.8$.

Thus, the equilibrium point for each AE curve in Panel A is uniquely related to a single point on the Aggregate Demand curve in Panel B, and this Aggregate Demand curve is derived from Aggregate Expenditures.

Note that variables on the horizontal axes for both panels are stated in *real* terms—measures for income and output are both *deflated* (adjusted for changes in the price level).

In summary, if the price level is stable, changes in autonomous spending shift the Aggregate Demand curve horizontally by the amount of autonomous spending times the multiplier. Now we will consider how recessionary and inflationary gaps can be closed.

Aggregate Demand and GDP Gaps

Real income and output (Q) cannot exceed the $7.5 trillion full-employment level (point b) in Figure 11. Therefore, if equilibrium income rises to $8 trillion ($AE_2$ in Figure 11), the price level must rise. Equilibration requires that $8 trillion = $P \times 7.5 trillion, so the price level will rise to 8/7.5, or roughly 1.067 (point c). (A price index would rise from 100 to 106.7.) Thus, this $100 billion inflationary gap will inflate the price level by almost 7%. Preventing this inflationary adjustment to excessive Aggregate Expenditure entails cutting the autonomous spending of either consumers, investors, government, or

FIGURE 11 Shifting Aggregate Demand to Close GDP Gaps

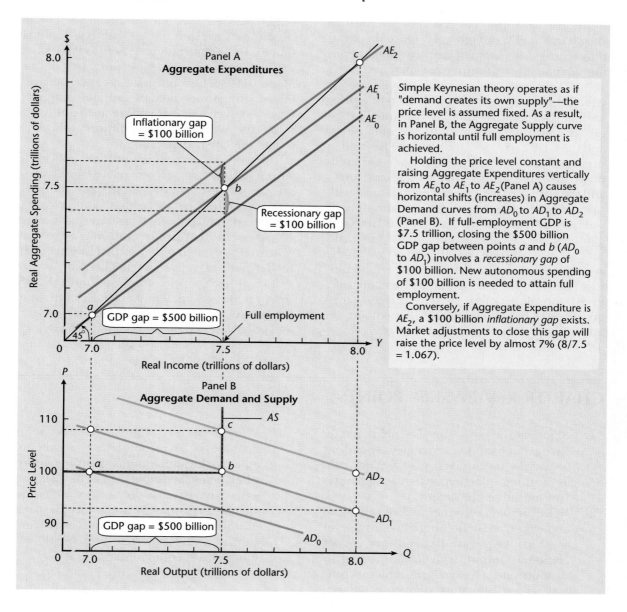

Simple Keynesian theory operates as if "demand creates its own supply"—the price level is assumed fixed. As a result, in Panel B, the Aggregate Supply curve is horizontal until full employment is achieved.

Holding the price level constant and raising Aggregate Expenditures vertically from AE_0 to AE_1 to AE_2 (Panel A) causes horizontal shifts (increases) in Aggregate Demand curves from AD_0 to AD_1 to AD_2 (Panel B). If full-employment GDP is $7.5 trillion, closing the $500 billion GDP gap between points a and b (AD_0 to AD_1) involves a *recessionary gap* of $100 billion. New autonomous spending of $100 billion is needed to attain full employment.

Conversely, if Aggregate Expenditure is AE_2, a $100 billion *inflationary gap* exists. Market adjustments to close this gap will raise the price level by almost 7% (8/7.5 = 1.067).

foreigners. Some methods government might use to combat these inflationary pressures are presented in Chapter 11.

Keynesian analysis largely focuses on achieving full employment in an economy operating below its potential; inflation that might emerge from excessive Aggregate Demand is generally ignored. The price level is sensitive, however, to total spending by both consumers and investors, and vice versa. Let us see why.

Simple Keynesian theory views production decisions as being based strictly on expected sales; prices are assumed fixed. This is implicit in the idea that demand creates its own supply. Thus, the Aggregate Supply curve compatible with Keynesian analysis of a recession is horizontal until full employment is reached. Then, paralleling a classical Aggregate Supply curve, the Aggregate Supply curve becomes vertical, as shown in Panel B of Figure 11. Once the economy reaches full employment, growth in spending ultimately yields pure price increases.

If Aggregate Demand is AD_0 in Figure 11, equilibrium output will be $7 trillion at a price level of 100 (point a). There is substantial excess capacity and unemployment in this equilibrium, and the GDP gap = $500 billion. The Keynesian prescription is to increase Aggregate Expenditure so that Aggregate Demand increases to AD_1, and the economy achieves full employment with price-level stability at point b. Expanding output from $7 trillion to $7.5 trillion to fill the GDP gap can be accomplished by boosting autonomous spending by the amount of the recessionary gap. But if Aggregate Expenditure rises so much that Aggregate Demand shifts to AD_2 an inflationary gap is created, triggering price inflation of nearly 7% (to point c in Panel B).

The central topic in Chapter 11 is how fiscal policy (government spending and taxing) might be used to eliminate inflationary or recessionary gaps and move GDP to a noninflationary full employment. When Keynes wrote *The General Theory of Employment, Interest, and Money* in 1936, he was primarily concerned with filling a huge recessionary gap and suggested massive government spending as the best way to bolster Aggregate Expenditures sufficiently to end the Great Depression.

A word of caution is in order. Policies to shrink inflationary or recessionary gaps depend on accurate estimates of these gaps and then timely action. The incredible difficulties encountered when policymakers try to achieve full employment and price-level stability have been obscured by oversimplification in our Keynesian model in the current chapter. This analysis provides a foundation for understanding slightly more complex models and possible solutions to the broader range of macroeconomic problems and stabilization policies treated in Chapter 11.

CHAPTER REVIEW: KEY POINTS

1. Keynesian theory suggests that erratic changes in **business investment spending** (especially inventories) play a major role in causing fluctuations in Aggregate Income and employment.

2. In Keynesian analysis, equilibrium income and employment occur at the output level at which **Aggregate Expenditure equals National Output**, with firms wanting to produce and sell exactly the amounts consumers and investors want to purchase. Any deviation from Keynesian equilibrium sets forces in motion to drive the economy toward a new equilibrium.

3. When planned saving equals planned investment ($S = I$), a private and closed economy will be in **macroequilibrium**. Actual saving and investment are equal at all times because inventory adjustments and similar mechanisms ensure this balance.

4. When *autonomous spending* in the economy increases by $1, income rises by an amount equal to the **autonomous spending multiplier** times the original $1. The *multiplier effect* exists because the original $1 in new spending becomes $1 in new income, parts of which are then spent by successive consumers and businesses. The simple autonomous spending multiplier is

$$\frac{\Delta Y}{\Delta A} = \frac{1}{\text{mps}} = \frac{1}{1 - \text{mpc}}$$

where ΔA represents some form of autonomous spending. More generally, the multiplier equals 1/(withdrawal fraction per spending round).

5. Investment spending plummeted from 1929 to 1933. This sharply reduced equilibrium income and may have been the primary cause of the Great Depression.

6. The **paradox of thrift** appears to be an important challenge to our conventional wisdom. If more consumers decide to increase their saving, then income, consumption, investment, and saving may all decline.

7. **Potential GDP** is an estimate of the output the economy could produce at full employment. The **GDP gap** is the difference between potential and actual GDP.

8. The **recessionary gap** is the amount by which autonomous spending falls short of that required to achieve a full-employment level of income; it is measured on the vertical axis. An **inflationary gap** is the amount by which autonomous spending exceeds what is necessary for a full-employment equilibrium and exerts upward pressure on the price level.

9. Aggregate Expenditure curves are constructed for a given (fixed) price level. If the price level rises, Aggregate Expenditures fall, and vice versa. This leads to a unique relationship that allows us to derive an Aggregate Demand curve from specific levels of Aggregate Expenditures at various price levels.

10. If the price level is constant, higher autonomous spending increases Aggregate Demand by shifting the Aggregate Demand curve to the right, and vice versa.

11. Keynes thought that raising Aggregate Demand would boost output during a depression without raising the price level. Simple Keynesian theory suggests that the Aggregate Supply curve is horizontal up to the point of full employment. Once full-employment GDP is reached, classical reasoning reigns: the Aggregate Supply curve is vertical, and increases in Aggregate Demand cannot generate extra output. In a fully employed economy, additions to Aggregate Demand simply bid up prices and result in inflation.

QUESTIONS FOR THOUGHT AND DISCUSSION

1. What alternatives are available to a retailer whose inventories are growing because sales are not as large as planned? Will the alternative retailers typically select be important in determining National Income? How? How will the strategies chosen by retailers with excess inventories vary over the business cycle? Why is this important?

2. What are the similarities and the differences between equilibrium for Aggregate Expenditure and National Output curves and equilibrium for Aggregate Demand and Supply when the price level is a consideration? How do these macroeconomic equilibria compare with the equilibria in markets for individual goods and services?

3. In the simple Keynesian model presented in this chapter, the only form of injection considered is autonomous investment and the only withdrawal is saving. What are other possible injections? Other withdrawals? How might exports and imports be incorporated to make this model a more complete picture of the way the world really works?

4. Do you think prices will fall in response to declines in Aggregate Demand, as classical economists suggest? Or will quantities decline, as Keynesians believe? What bearing does your answer have for designing policies to combat inflationary pressures? If the economy has considerable excess capacity, will expanding Aggregate Expenditures cause output to grow, or will the price level simply rise?

OPTIONAL MATERIAL: GRAPHICAL TECHNIQUES IN ECONOMICS

A more rigorous treatment of our model will help you understand why income changes by some multiple of any change in autonomous spending. [We use delta (Δ) to signify change. Thus, ΔY is read "change in income."] How much will total income change (ΔY) as a result of a given change in, say, autonomous investment spending (ΔI)? This ratio ($\Delta Y/\Delta I$) is known as the *autonomous spending multiplier*.

We assume that consumption is related to income and that changes in income will cause consumption to change by a value equal to the mpc times the change in income. We know that

$$Y = C + I \tag{1}$$

(output is either consumed or invested), so

$$\Delta Y = \Delta C + I \tag{2}$$

(Changes in output reflect changes in consumption or investment.)

If consumption spending is related to income by the mpc, then

$$\Delta C = \text{mpc} \cdot \Delta Y \tag{3}$$

(This is the change in induced consumption.)

The change in consumption is equal to the change in income times the proportion of the change you intend to spend.

Substituting equation 3 into equation 2 yields

$$\Delta C = \text{mpc} \cdot \Delta Y = \Delta I \tag{4}$$

Now we need to move all income (ΔY) terms to one side by subtracting mpc $\cdot \Delta Y$ from each side of equation 4, so

$$\Delta C - \text{mpc} \cdot \Delta Y = \Delta I \tag{5}$$

Factoring the ΔY terms on the left side of equation 5 leaves

$$\Delta Y \cdot \text{mpc} = \Delta I \tag{6}$$

Dividing both sides by (1 — mpc) yields

$$\Delta Y = \Delta C \cdot \left(\frac{1}{1 - \text{mpc}}\right) \tag{7}$$

The term 1/1 — mpc is the autonomous spending multiplier. Because mpc + mps = 1, then mps = 1 — mpc. Thus, another way to write the autonomous spending multiplier is 1/mps.

We have used investment to show how hikes in autonomous spending yield increases in income via the multiplier. Mathematically identical effects occur if autonomous consumption, government spending, or exports are raised. Economists often use A to stand for all forms of autonomous spending when writing formulas for multipliers. Thus, the following are all equivalent ways to write the autonomous spending multiplier:

$$\frac{\Delta Y}{\Delta A} = \frac{1}{\text{mps}} = \frac{1}{1 - \text{mpc}} \tag{8}$$

If the marginal propensity to consume is 0.8, the autonomous spending multiplier will be 5, because $1/(1 - 0.8) = 1/0.2 = 5$. Calculate multipliers for alternative values for mpc (e.g., 9/10, 6/7, 5/6, 4/5, 3/4, 2/3, and 3/5). Observe what happens to multipliers as mpc rises and mps falls. Naturally, reversed multiplier effects follow cuts in autonomous spending. Some multipliers that are appropriate for government purchases and taxes are treated in the optional material following the next chapter.

Net exports
Consumption
Investment
Inflationary gap
Recessionary gap
Price level
=C+I+G+(X–M)
45°
0

Taxation and government spending have dominated political debates about such issues as equity and efficiency for centuries, but the rates and structures of taxes and spending may also be vital for attaining macroeconomic stability. Keynesian theory concludes that excessive unemployment may persist in a short-run macroequilibrium, but that this is not inevitable. Keynesians traditionally viewed fiscal policy as a tool to fine-tune Aggregate Expenditures and protect people from turbulent swings in their well-being.

> **Fiscal policy** *entails the use of government spending and tax policies to stimulate or contract macroeconomic activity.*

Policymakers of the 1960s and 1970s relied heavily on Keynesian analysis to justify stimulative tax cuts and expanded government spending. Predictably, the Keynesian deemphasis of Aggregate Supply and rejection of classical laissez-faire policies did not go unchallenged. The *new classical macroeconomics* has rejuvenated classical analysis; in contrast to the activist role for government counseled by most earlier Keynesians, it supports only a passive governmental role in regulating Aggregate Demand.

One offshoot of new classical macroeconomics, *supply-side economics*, was the guiding force behind significant cuts in tax rates in the early 1980s. Supply-siders argued that high tax rates discourage productive effort so much that reducing tax rates would increase Aggregate Supply, National Income, and tax revenues. In the early 1990s, Presidents Bush and Clinton, when trying to reign in record federal budget deficits, each partially reversed President Reagan's supply-side policies by raising income tax rates, primarily on upper-income Americans.

Our initial task in this chapter is to incorporate government spending and taxing into our simple Keynesian model of a closed, private economy.[1] Then we will examine how policymakers might adjust taxes and government spending to smooth cyclical swings in Aggregate

---

[1]Recall that models of closed, private economies ignore government and international trade.

Demand and, consequently, in output, income, and employment. Finally, we will examine objections from new classical economists to the traditional Keynesian approach, and the differences in policy recommendations that emerge from these competing schools of economic thought.

FISCAL POLICY: THE DEMAND SIDE

The simple Keynesian model developed in Chapter 10 ignored government. A slightly more sophisticated model requires explicit consideration of government taxing and spending.

> *The federal government operates a **balanced budget** when its tax revenues equal its outlays of funds, a **budget deficit** when its outlays exceed revenues, and a **budget surplus** if tax revenues exceed outlays.*

Changes in taxes and government outlays fall into two categories: discretionary and automatic. We will initially consider how federal policymakers can exercise discretion when they change tax laws or the level of government outlays.

> ***Discretionary fiscal policy** involves deliberate legislative changes in government outlays or taxes to adjust Aggregate Demand (AD) and stabilize the economy.*

How do Keynesians view the effects of fiscal policy on planned Aggregate Expenditures? Let's begin by assuming, for simplicity, that (a) government spending (G) is autonomous and shifts neither the planned consumption nor the planned investment schedules, (b) investment (I) is also autonomous—at a constant level independent of income—and (c) taxes (T) are also autonomous. These restrictive assumptions will be relaxed a bit after you gain familiarity with our expanded model.

Discretionary Spending and Equilibrium

The numerical Keynesian model built in Chapter 10 is expanded in Table 1 to consider government. These data are graphed in Figure 1. Without government, the private sector yields equilibrium spending and income of $7 trillion (point a). But this leaves a GDP gap of $500 billion if full employment income is $7.5 trillion. Keynesian analysis perceives any forces pushing the economy toward full employment as weak, so there is a recessionary gap of $100 billion that will not be remedied quickly through private action.

Our multiplier of 5 (the mpc = 0.8) means that $100 billion in extra autonomous spending will close the $500 billion GDP gap. One way to

TABLE 1   Curing a Recessionary Gap with the Keynesian Remedy of Government Spending*

	Private Sector Only						Addition of Government Sector		
(1)	(2)	(3)	(4)	(5)	(6)	(7)	(8)	(9)	(10)
Employ-ment (millions)	*National Output (Y)	*Planned Consumption (C)	*Planned Saving (S)	*Planned Investment (I)	Aggregate Expenditure without government	Pressures on Income and Output (AE_0)	Government (G)	Aggregate Expenditure with government (AE_1)	Pressures on Income and Output
100	$5,000	$5,100	$–100	$300	$5,400	pressure for income to rise	$100	$5,500	pressure to income for rise
105	5,500	5,500	0	300	5,800		100	5,900	
110	6,000	5,900	100	300	6,200		100	6,300	
115	6,500	6,300	200	300	6,600	▼	100	6,700	▼
120	**7,000**	**6,700**	**300**	**300**	**7,000**	equilibrium	**100**	**7,100**	equilibrium
125	**7,500**	**7,100**	**400**	**300**	**7,400**	▲	**100**	**7,500**	▲
130	8,000	7,500	500	300	7,800	pressure for income to fall	100	7,900	pressure for income to fall
135	8,500	7,900	600	300	8,100		100	8,100	

*In billions of dollars.

FIGURE 1 Using Fiscal Policy to Achieve Full-Employment Equilibrium Income

Equilibrium without government spending is $7 trillion (point *a*), leaving a *GDP gap* of $500 billion. The economy gravitates to full employment if government spends $100 billion: Aggregate Spending grows from $AE_0 = C + I$ to $AE_1 = C + I + G$. The $100 billion in new government spending is subject to the multiplier just as private autonomous spending is, so the *recessionary gap* is filled. Thus, the $100 billion times the multiplier (which is 5 because the mpc = 0.8) closes the GDP gap and restores full employment at $7.5 trillion.

reach potential GDP would be to fill the recessionary gap with $100 billion in government spending (column 8 in Table 1). When Aggregate Expenditure shifts from AE_0 to AE_1 in Figure 1 because government spending rises from zero to $100 billion, equilibrium moves from point *a* to full employment at point *b*.

Spending multipliers were originally described in terms of investment ($\Delta Y/\Delta I$), but all injections and withdrawals, whether government or private, are subject to the multiplier principle. Government spending is merely a form of injection, so, dollar for dollar, it stimulates Aggregate Expenditure as powerfully as new investment. For example, federal contracts generate new income for contractors and their employees. Some of their new income is saved, but most will be spent. This spending then becomes new income for those from whom they buy, which is then spent or saved. And so on.[2]

The effect of government purchases can be described in a manner parallel to the planned saving = planned investment approach outlined in Chapter 10. Saving and taxes are both withdrawals, while investment and government purchases are both injections. *Planned injections must equal planned withdrawals at equilibrium.*[3]

Figure 2 illustrates the planned injections = planned withdrawals approach, which parallels the savings = investment model developed when only private spending was considered. Introduction of $100 billion in new government spending boosts total injections ($I + G = $300 billion + $100 billion = $400 billion). Planned saving ($300 billion in planned withdrawals) at the initial equilibrium of $7 trillion is now less than planned investment plus new government spending ($400 billion in total planned injections), so output rises until injections equal withdrawals. Thus, the new equilibrium requires output to rise to $7.5 trillion.

Taxes and Equilibrium

We now know how raising government spending affects equilibrium. Introducing taxes (T) into our model takes us another step closer to

---

[2]You may wonder how the government can spend more without raising taxes. One possibility is by borrowing funds through sales of U.S. Treasury bonds. Alternatively, budget deficits can be financed by printing more money. The specific mechanisms used by the Federal Reserve System (the agency empowered to print and regulate money) are addressed in Chapter 13. The process of printing money to cover a deficit is a bit more circuitous than we suggest here. The ability to print money certainly distinguishes the federal government from the rest of us.

[3]Algebraically, since $C + I + G = C + S + T = Y$, then $I + G = S + T$ is an equilibrium condition.

FIGURE 2 Injections = Withdrawals Approach to Equilibrium

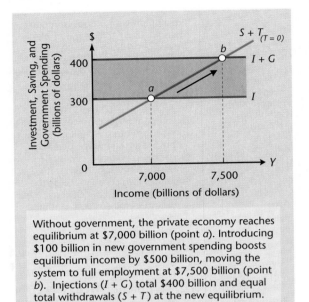

Without government, the private economy reaches equilibrium at $7,000 billion (point a). Introducing $100 billion in new government spending boosts equilibrium income by $500 billion, moving the system to full employment at $7,500 billion (point b). Injections ($I + G$) total $400 billion and equal total withdrawals ($S + T$) at the new equilibrium. Note that, in this example, since $T = 0$, $S = I + G$.

reality. The autonomous tax multiplier can be expressed much like the autonomous expenditures multiplier.

> The **autonomous tax multiplier** is the proportional change in income caused by a given change in autonomous taxes and is written as $\Delta Y / \Delta T_a$.

Taxes, like saving, are withdrawals that pull down spending and income. Thus, the autonomous tax multiplier is a negative number.

Suppose people began spending almost as fast as they received income. Table 2 reflects this change in behavior by showing planned consumption (column 3) at $500 billion higher and planned saving at $500 billion lower (column 4) for each income level than in Table 1.

Private sector activity alone yields an equilibrium (where column 2 equals column 6) of $9.5 trillion in income, so Aggregate Expenditure is $2 trillion too high for price-level

stability at the $7.5 trillion level of full-employment output. This negative GDP gap ($7.5 trillion – $9.5 trillion = –$2 trillion) combines with the autonomous spending multiplier of 5 (mpc = 0.8) to yield an inflationary gap of $400 billion, which means that autonomous spending is $400 billion too high. Alternatively, autonomous saving is $400 billion too low (distance bc in Figure 3). This model lacks government spending, so boosting tax withdrawals is the only way government can reduce Aggregate Expenditures.

Consumer decisions about spending depend on disposable income (Y_d) instead of Aggregate Income (Y) because households alone ultimately bear all tax burdens. Consider how new autonomous taxes of $500 billion will affect Aggregate Expenditures. Subtracting these taxes (column 8) from National Income (column 2) yields disposable income ($Y - T = Y_d$), shown in column 9 of Table 2. Note that the relationship between disposable income and consumption is identical to the one between income and consumption from Table 1, when we ignored taxes.

How much of this $500 billion in taxes will come from consumption and how much from saving? With an mpc of 80% and an mps of 20%, consumption will initially fall 0.8 times the $500 billion in taxes, for a total of $400 billion. This shifts consumption in the Aggregate Expenditure schedule down by $400 billion for every level of gross (pretax) income, while the saving schedule falls $100 billion at all income levels.

The new saving curve S_t (saving after taxes are imposed) is exactly $100 billion lower (on the vertical axis) than the original saving curve S in Figure 3. (Remember, a drop in saving is shown as a shift of the saving curve to the right because consumers will now save less at each income level.) From the perspective of the the injections = withdrawals approach, withdrawals in the form of after-tax saving are shown as S_t. Taxes of $500 billion are also withdrawals, so the total withdrawal function = $S_t + T$. In Figure 3, this is exactly $500 billion above S_t (distance cd in Figure 3); thus, it is $400 billion above the original S curve for each income level.

On the other side of the ledger, investment of $300 billion is still the only injection in this

TABLE 2 Curing an Inflationary Gap with Taxes*

(1) Employment (millions)	(2) National Output & Income Y	(3) Planned Consumption C	(4) Planned Saving S	(5) Planned Investment I	(6) Spending Without Taxes	(7) Net Pressure on Output	(8) Taxes T	(9) Y_t	(10) C_t	(11) S_t	(12) Aggregate Expenditure	(13) Net Pressure on Output
110	$6000	$6400	$-400	$300	$6700		$500	$5500	$6000	$-500	$6300	pressure for income to rise
115	6,500	6,800	-300	300	7,100	pressure for income	500	6,000	6,400	-400	6,700	
120	7,000	7,200	-200	300	7,500		500	6,500	6,800	-300	7,100	
125	**7,500**	7,600	-100	300	7,900	pressure for income to rise	**500**	**7,000**	**7,200**	**-200**	7,500	equilibrium
130	8,000	8,000	0	300	8,300		500	7,500	7,600	-100	7,900	
135	8,500	8,400	100	300	8,700	▼	500	8,000	8,000	0	8,300	pressure for income to fall
140	9,000	8,800	200	300	9,100		500	8,500	8,400	100	8,700	
145	**9,500**	9,200	300	300	**9,500** equilibrium		500	9,000	8,800	200	9,100	

*in billions of dollars.

economy. Equilibrium requires total withdrawals to equal total injections, so $S_t + T = I$ at point *a* in Figure 3. Equilibrium National Income (determined now by Aggregate Expenditure of $C_t + I$, where C_t reflects after-tax consumption) falls from $9.5 trillion to $7.5 trillion. The autonomous tax multiplier ($\Delta Y/\Delta T_a$) equals –$2,000 billion/$500 billion, so it is –4. Private saving is –$200 billion in this equilibrium; so tax withdrawals of $500 billion precisely offset dissaving ($200 billion) plus the investment injection of $300 billion to ensure full employment without inflation.

- **The Tax Multiplier** In our example, the autonomous spending multiplier ($\Delta Y/\Delta A$, where *A* = the sum of all forms of autonomous spending) is 5, because the marginal propensity to consume is 0.8. But the autonomous tax multiplier ($\Delta Y/\Delta T_a$) was just calculated as –4 in this case. Notice the relationship: one minus the autonomous spending multiplier equals the tax multiplier

$$1 - (1/\text{mps}) = \Delta Y/\Delta T_a$$
$$1 - 5 \quad = \quad -4$$

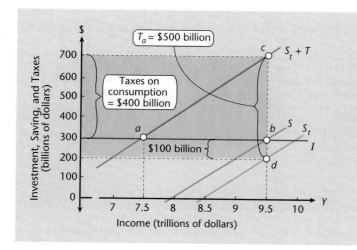

Government spending is ignored in this simple model, and taxes are assumed to affect only spending behavior, not productive effort. Taxes reduce saving by the autonomous tax times the mpc, or 0.2($500 billion), for a total reduction of $100 billion in autonomous saving. However, net withdrawals rise by $400 billion at each income level: $\Delta S + \Delta T_a =$ -$100 billion + $500 billion. Thus, through the multiplier process, equilibrium income falls from $9.5 billion to $7.5 billion, so inflationary pressure subsides because of tax withdrawals. The tax multiplier $\Delta Y/\Delta T_a$ is -4 in this case. (-$2,000 billion/$500 billion = -4.)

FIGURE 3 Eliminating Inflationary Pressure with Taxes (Injections = Withdrawals Approach)

The autonomous tax multiplier is the negative value of one less than the spending multiplier.[4]

An example of why this is so is shown in Table 3.

Table 3 traces the effects on spending of $100 billion increases in government purchases and taxes, both individually and together, through a few rounds of transactions, assuming that the mpc = 0.8. In column 1, 80% of each extra dollar of income is spent and becomes someone else's income. Thus, a new injection of $100 billion in government spending (Round 1) means that $80 billion in consumer spending is induced in the second round. The people whose incomes rise by this $80 billion then spend $64 billion, which becomes other people's extra income. And so on. The autonomous spending multiplier is 5, indicated at the bottom of column 1.

The effect of new autonomous taxes of $100 billion on spending is shown in column 2. Note that in Round 1, this tax does not affect gross (pre-tax) incomes; the $100 billion tax hike may be viewed by taxpayers as a cut in disposable income, but National Income is not affected initially. Only after the drop in disposable income lowers consumer spending would output be reduced if all else (including government spending) were constant. Thus, government purchases affect Aggregate Expenditure in Round 1; new taxes do not. Subsequent rounds cancel, so the autonomous tax multiplier is negative and equals one minus the spending multiplier.

- **The Balanced-Budget Multiplier** Table 3 has a startling conclusion. If both government spending (column 1) and autonomous taxes (column 2) rise $100 billion, equilibrium income, on balance, grows exactly $100 billion (end of column 3). Thus, a basic Keynesian balanced-budget multiplier is exactly one.[5]

> *The **balanced-budget multiplier** indicates that identical increases in autonomous spending and in autonomous taxes will yield an identical increase in equilibrium income, so it always equals 1.*

[4]A more general form of this simple tax multiplier is −mpc/mps: We know that mpc + mps = 1 Substituting this into part of 1 − (1/ mps), we get 1 − [(mpc + mps)/mps]. Factoring, we have 1 − [(mpc/mps) + (mps/mps)], which simplifies to 1 − (mpc/mps) − 1, which equals (−mpc/mps).

[5]A bit of math shows why the balanced-budget multiplier in this simple Keynesian model equals one: the spending multiplier (1/mps) plus the tax multiplier (−mpc/mps) equals (1 − mpc)/mps. But 1 − mpc = mps, so (1 − mpc)/mps equals 1.

TABLE 3   Round-by-Round Effects of $100 Billion Increases in Spending, Taxing, and the Balanced Budget*

Effect	(1) $100 Billion in Extra Government Spending	(2) $100 Billion in Extra Autonomous Taxes	(3) $100 Billion in Extra Taxes and Purchases
Round 1: initial effect of change on income	$100	0	$100
Round 2: induced spending	80	$ -80	0
Round 3: induced spending	64	-64	0
Round 4 through all subsequent rounds	256	-256	0
Total Change	$500	$-400	$100
MULTIPLIER (mpc = 0.8)	5	-4	1

*In billions of dollars.

Note: Each $1 increase in government purchases creates $1 in new income in Round 1, but each $1 in new taxes does not influence first-round income. In Round 2, each $1 in new government purchases has caused the person whose income was increased to spend $0.80, but this is offset by the reduced spending of $0.80 caused by each $1 in new taxes. Moreover, the effects of the new spending and taxing offset each other in all subsequent rounds. Thus, only Round 1 spending has any net effect on income, and the balanced-budget multiplier equals one.

The conclusion is that equal increases (or decreases) in government spending and taxes will raise (or lower) equilibrium National Income by an identical amount. Table 3 should help you discern the fiscal mechanisms at work when either spending or taxing is changed. The autonomous spending and tax multipliers and the balanced-budget multiplier are described in more detail in the optional material at the end of this chapter.

Let us summarize the discretionary fiscal policies Keynesians traditionally prescribe to cure specific economic ills. Inflationary pressures can be relieved through tax hikes, cuts in government outlays, or a mix of both. Tax increases or cuts in government spending drive federal budgets toward surplus or reduce deficits. If excessive unemployment is the major problem, then tax cuts or increased government outlays temporarily move the budget into a deficit (or reduce a surplus) and expand output, employment, and income.

AUTOMATIC STABILIZERS

Keynesians view budget deficits as the right medicine to cure a recession and surpluses as remedies for inflation. Most politicians enjoy granting the tax cuts and new spending projects Keynesians prescribe for recession—such measures are popular with voters. But raising taxes and slashing budgets to fight inflation are poison for incumbents when reelection time rolls around. New laws to create surpluses during business expansions that might erupt into inflation are, fortunately, not always necessary. Certain features of our tax system and some government spending programs automatically push budgets toward surpluses during booms of the business cycle and into deficit during cyclical downturns.

Discretionary variations in spending and taxes require congressional action, but they are not the only fiscal instruments available to help us achieve full employment and price-level stability. Keynesians count on certain built-in mechanisms in the economy to dampen swings in Aggregate Expenditure and economic activity. Until now, we have unrealistically assumed

that neither taxes nor government spending depend on income. The fact that both are sensitive to changes in National Income gives our economy some automatic resilience.

Automatic stabilizers are tax structures and government spending programs that cause budget deficits to grow automatically during recessions or surpluses to grow when expansion is rapid.

Automatic stabilizers are sometimes called nondiscretionary fiscal policy because no overt government action is required.

Automatic Tax Adjustments

Personal and corporate income tax revenues are both closely tied to income. When prosperity boosts National Income, federal revenues from progressive corporate and personal income taxes rise more than proportionally. Corporate profit is the most sensitive of all incomes to swings in economic activity. A 10% decline in National Income might totally wipe out corporate profit, while 10% growth may cause aggregate profit to double or even triple, as illustrated in Figure 4. Thus, tax revenue from corporate income is highly cyclical.

Progressive personal income tax rates are the main reason why tax collections rise or fall proportionally faster than income. This process acts as an automatic stabilizer during inflationary episodes because as income rises, tax collections rise even faster, accelerating withdrawals from the economy and dampening inflationary growth of nominal income. This effect is now partially offset because Congress indexed personal income tax *brackets* (the ranges across which particular tax rates apply) to inflation beginning in 1985.[6] When a recession begins, tax revenues tumble even faster than gross income falls, swelling budget deficits.

---

[6]The Tax Reform of 1986 reduced the progressivity of income tax rates, but some of the previous sharp progressivity was restored by the Clinton administration in 1993. Overall, flattening of tax rates diminishes the potential power of automatic stabilizer aspects of our tax structure.

FIGURE 4   Corporate Tax Revenue and Employment

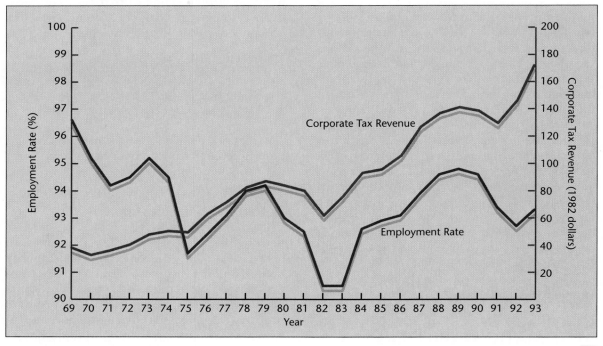

Source: *Economic Report of the President,* 1994.

This figure illustrates the effects of automatic tax adjustments when unemployment increases as the economy enters a recession. A downturn in economic activity reduces employment, which causes corporate profits to decline (or their rates of growth to decline). As a result, corporate tax revenues decline substantially. The opposite chain of events follows when the economy recovers and employment expands.

Automatic Changes in Government Outlays

Transfer payments rise during recessions, thus helping stabilize consumption, and ultimately, Aggregate Expenditure. More people are eligible for welfare payments during hard times. People retire earlier during recessions and later during booms. Consequently, Social Security payments help buffer the economy against both downturns and inflationary expansions.

Unemployment compensation is another automatic stabilizer because workers' incomes do not drop to zero when they are laid off. Consumption by unemployed workers' families would plummet during widespread layoffs without unemployment compensation, and cyclic downturns would be worse than they are. The Great Depression would probably have been much less severe had modern automatic stabilizers been in effect.

Falling tax collections and rising transfer payments during downturns help consumers maintain their customary spending levels. Facilitating consumption helps buffer any declines in National Income. Just how powerful are automatic stabilizers? Although inadequate to completely offset strong pressures for a recession, they do slow abrupt changes in the economy, giving policymakers more time to formulate discretionary policy. Some studies suggest that recent recessions would have been from one-third to one-half more severe in the absence of automatic stabilizers. But automatic stabilizers may be a mixed blessing.

• **Fiscal Drag**   When potential income is growing rapidly, our built-in stabilizers may retard actual economic growth, a problem Keynesians refer to as *fiscal drag*.

Fiscal drag *may hinder the natural growth of GDP because rising income boosts tax revenue and may shrink outlays for transfer programs.*

Suppose all resources are fully employed and the budget is balanced. Technological advance, capital accumulation, and labor-force growth all contribute to growth of potential GDP. If tax rates are not lowered, economic growth boosts tax revenues; a budget surplus may even emerge if government outlays are stable. This potential surplus hinders growth in disposable income and Aggregate Expenditure; withdrawals grow but injections do not. This may retard economic growth, so increasing government spending or lowering tax rates may unshackle the economy. Both approaches are politically popular. Most of us can think of areas where we would like more government spending or where we would like our taxes cut.

CYCLICAL VS. STRUCTURAL DEFICITS

Budget surpluses or deficits have been treated as inconsequential in themselves to this point, having importance only to the extent that they affect Aggregate Expenditure. After decades of successively higher record federal deficits, a proposed constitutional amendment that the federal budget be balanced annually receives lots of popular support, but some serious pitfalls may be embedded in this appealing notion. Imbalance in the federal budget may be more a symptom of economic distress than a result of discretionary policy. For example, deficits swell during recessions because tax revenues fall and government outlays rise. Conversely, automatic stabilizers theoretically could create budgetary surpluses if unsustainable and inflationary growth mushroomed.

Should taxes be raised and government spending cut during a recession to eliminate a deficit? The preceding analysis suggests not. If inflation looms, should we cut taxes or raise spending to eliminate a surplus? Again, Keynesians conclude that either would be unwise. Federal deficits or surpluses are affected by the level of GDP as well as by discretionary fiscal policy, so the appropriateness of fiscal policy is not obvious solely from the evidence of actual deficits or surpluses. Economists now differentiate between *structural* and *cyclical* deficits.

A **structural deficit (or surplus)** *is an estimate of the budget deficit (or surplus) that tax and spending structures would yield if the economy achieved its potential.*

During a recession, estimating the structural deficit entails adding to the actual deficit extra tax revenues that would be collected if full employment were achieved and deducting the outlays on unemployment benefits and other transfer payments caused by cyclical unemployment.

A **cyclical deficit** *occurs when falling income during a recession shrinks tax revenues while increasing transfer payments. Prosperity, on the other hand, could yield a* **cyclical surplus**.

Whenever the economy deteriorates, the cyclical budget deficit worsens, and vice versa.

Transfer payments can be treated as negative taxes (*negative* because the government pays people), which decline in importance as National Income rises. Figure 5 illustrates various possible relationships between *net taxes* (tax revenues minus transfer payments) and government purchases for three alternative tax structures. Note that the tax functions are all positively sloped; net taxes rise as income rises. We will assume that noninflationary full-employment income is $7.5 trillion and that government purchases (G) are independent of income.

Excessive tax rates may limit Aggregate Expenditure to levels inadequate for full employment. This fiscal-drag case occurs with tax structure T_0 and Aggregate Expenditure AE_0, which together yield equilibrium at point *a* in Panel A of Figure 5. Tax rates are high, so the structural deficit at full employment (point *b*) is really a surplus to the tune of $100 billion in this example; however, the cyclical deficit at the $7 trillion equilibrium income (point *a*) is $50 bil-

FIGURE 5 The Structural Deficit and the Cyclical Deficit

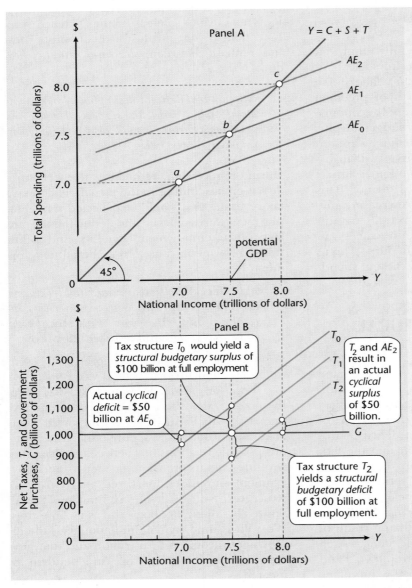

The *stuctural deficit* is the deficit that would exist at full employment, given the existing mix of government spending and tax rate structures. The *cyclical deficit* grows when economic circumstances prevent full employment. This figure illustrates relationships between net taxes (taxes minus transfer payments) and government spending for three alternative tax structures.

Tax structure T_0 is associated with Aggregate Expenditures AE_0, and a *structural surplus* prevents full employment, but at the equilibrium income of $7 trillion, the spending/tax structure yields a $50 billion *cyclical deficit*.

Budget-tax combinations T_2 and G are associated with Aggregate Expenditures of AE_2 and represent a considerably more expansionary budget mix. At full employment, this budget-tax mix would result in a *structural deficit* of $100 billion.

Tax schedule T_1 is associated with Aggregate Expenditures AE_1 and balances the budget at full employment, with zero structural deficit.

NOTE: Subscripts link tax structures (T) from Panel B with the resulting Aggregate Expenditure function (AE) in Panel A.

---

lion. Thus, an excessive structural surplus can create a cyclical deficit.

Contrast this with the budgetary mix of G and tax structure T_2. Simultaneous inflationary pressures and cyclical budgetary surpluses coexist if Aggregate Expenditure is AE_2 and the tax schedule is T_2; at equilibrium point c, a cyclical surplus of $50 billion is realized. This budget combination yields a structural deficit of $100 billion at full employment (ignoring inflationary pressure). This structural deficit is much more expansionary than that represented by G and T_0. Finally, a combination that balances the structural budget is represented by tax schedule T_1, which yields Aggregate Expenditure AE_1. Cyclical deficits result below full employment, while surpluses are generated above full employment.

Suppose low tax rates bloat Aggregate Expenditures. A substantial cyclical budget surplus exists if the Aggregate Expenditure curve is AE_2 and the tax curve is T_2. If perpetually balanced budgets were legally mandated, we would cut taxes and raise spending—bad policies certain to worsen inflationary pressure. Policies of either raising tax rates or cutting spending may cure inflation by enlarging any current budget surplus to dampen Aggregate Expenditure.

During inflation, however, proposals that "government costs, in addition to other prices, need to be raised," are anathema to voters. But beneficiaries of public programs, including those whose incomes depend on government contracts, lobby against budget cuts that threaten their standards of living. Even politicians who constantly attack big government fear a backlash from voters whose pet programs are cut. In fact, political opposition to spending cuts or tax hikes is so intense that we need not worry about simultaneous inflation and actual surpluses.

The reverse situation is a budget structure with a structural surplus but a cyclical deficit because tax rates are so high that the economy is stuck well below full employment; fiscal drag is quite powerful. Some analysts have suggested that the sluggish American economy of the late 1950s and of the early 1980s suffered from this malady.

The critical point is that huge cyclical deficits do not imply an expansionary tilt to fiscal policy, nor are large cyclical surpluses evidence of contractionary policies. Mounting federal deficits in recent years have been a mix of (a) *cyclical deficits* driven by high unemployment that subsided only slowly after peaking during the recessions of 1981 to 1983 and 1990 to 1991 and (b) huge *structural deficits*, sparked in part by large tax cuts and by unrelenting growth of government outlays. Recent estimates place the structural deficit at nearly two-thirds of the actual deficit and growing.[7]

---

[7]W. Beeman, J. Dreyer, and P. van de Water, "Dimensions of the Deficit Problem," in *Essays in Contemporary Economic Problems, 1985: The Economy in Deficit*, ed. P. Cagan (Washington, D.C.: American Enterprise Institute, 1985). Beeman et al. also argue that relatively slow productivity growth contributed to rising structural deficits over the past two decades.

In summary, the actual deficit is determined by the fiscal mix of the federal budget and the state of the economy. Expansionary fiscal policy creates structural deficits, and recession triggers cyclical deficits. Deficits may arise because high tax rates produce an anemic economy. Congress can only set tax rates; it cannot dictate the resulting tax revenues.

CLASSICAL ECONOMICS AND FISCAL POLICY

Classical theory tends to support policies that are relatively laissez-faire. Most classical theorists are skeptical about the efficiency of big government and fear that government outlays may crowd out more valuable forms of private investment and consumption. Requiring a balanced budget—higher tax revenues to cover higher outlays—may curb politicians' impulses to spend.

Another wing of the new classical school, *supply-side economics*, spearheaded a tax-cutting mentality in the early 1980s and has been as much a political agenda as a mode of analysis. High tax rates are alleged to (a) inspire widespread tax evasion and tax avoidance, (b) intensify lobbying for tax loopholes, and (c) smother productivity.

Does Taxation Have a Natural Limit?

An advisor to an Egyptian pharaoh is credited with first observing that high tax rates may hinder incentives to work and investment, reducing actual tax revenues. Joseph Schumpeter, while serving as Finance Minister in Austria during the 1920s, proposed an economic "law" that taxpayer resistance precluded any government from collecting taxes of more than 27% or so of people's income. He may have been close to being right.

• **The Laffer Curve**   Arthur Laffer, a celebrated supply-sider, explained this concept to a journalist at a Washington, D.C., restaurant and sketched on a napkin what has become known as the Laffer curve.

*The **Laffer curve**: Very low tax rates might be raised to yield higher tax revenue, but raising tax rates excessively eventually drives tax revenues down when taxpayers decide either (a) that the extra effort necessary to generate extra taxable income is not worth it or (b) that cheating the tax system is okay.*

If Uncle Sam's bite is too fierce, many taxpayers will prefer leisure over additional work and will consume immediately from income instead of saving and investing. And tax evasion may divert more activities into the underground economy. A modified Laffer curve is shown in Figure 6.

Supply-siders argue that high tax rates are disincentives to produce, so that income shrinks as tax rates climb. This means that the same tax revenues might be generated by both a high tax rate and a low one.

Marginal tax rates are the percentage taxes on small amounts of extra income.

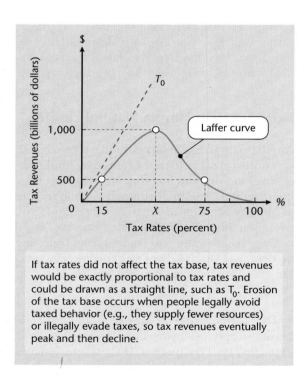

If tax rates did not affect the tax base, tax revenues would be exactly proportional to tax rates and could be drawn as a straight line, such as T₀. Erosion of the tax base occurs when people legally avoid taxed behavior (e.g., they supply fewer resources) or illegally evade taxes, so tax revenues eventually peak and then decline.

FIGURE 6   The Laffer Curve

In Figure 6, marginal tax rates that average either 15% or 75% yield tax revenues of $500 billion, while marginal tax rates that average X percent yields $1 trillion to the tax collector. Any increase in marginal tax rates over X percent actually shrinks tax collections.

How will people react if high marginal tax rates reduce the gains from working, saving, and investing? Potential workers may adjust to high tax rates with more nonmarket activities, such as do-it-yourself projects. Potential savers and investors will realize less interest income if marginal tax rates are high, so they will consume more currently, forgoing future consumption.

Evidence of this sort of behavior was provided when wealthy people in Britain splurged on furs, Rolls-Royces, and other luxuries in the 1970s when marginal income tax rates peaked at 99%. Investing was not worthwhile because of rapid inflation and the staggering tax rates on investment income. The British economy stagnated in the 1960s and 1970s, while areas of London where high society gathered abounded with conspicuous consumption of luxury goods.

Some analysts argue that the United States operates close to the peak of the Laffer curve and favor reducing tax rates to ease disincentives against work and investment. They fear that tax hikes to slice recent deficits may restrict economic growth and squelch tax revenues. Ronald Reagan, a major convert to supply-side economics, persuaded Congress to cut marginal tax rates by an average of 25% between 1981 and 1983. Results? Between 1980 and 1994, the economy grew by 134%, while federal tax revenues grew 145%. But budget deficits grew because politicians failed to control federal outlays, which expanded 152%.

Notice that Keynesians may accept the general form of the Laffer curve while perceiving different behavior as its basic cause. New classical economists blame declines in tax revenues as tax rates rise on reduced incentives to comply with tax laws and to supply goods and services. Keynesians perceive high tax rates and fiscal drag as smothering Aggregate Expenditure. Admitting that high tax rates also inhibit supply incentives, Keynesians still perceive macroeconomic problems as originating primarily from the demand side, while new classical economists see high tax rate disincentives as more powerful on the supply side. Predictably, concerns about both efficiency and equity become more pronounced when the issue of tax structures is raised.

Tax Revenue and Progressive Marginal Tax Rates

Social reformers have long advocated progressive taxes to flatten the distribution of income. (Recall that a progressive tax is one for which higher marginal tax rates fall on higher incomes.) Many economists in the classical camp, however, argue that sharply progressive tax rates (*a*) cannot accomplish this goal and (*b*) diminish and distort productive activity.

After passage of the Sixteenth Amendment in 1913, relatively low tax rates were initially levied on only the top 2% or so of income recipients. Income tax rates climbed over the next 30 years and were applied more broadly. By the end of World War II, top marginal tax rates on personal income had peaked at 91%, and corporate incomes faced marginal rates exceeding 70%, at least on paper. But few Americans were in the top brackets, and almost none paid rates anywhere close to the legal maximum. A deluge of loopholes—tax exemptions, deductions, credits, rapid depletion and depreciation allowances—made the top rates a farce, so complicating the tax code that even experts often felt as lost as lab rats in an endless maze.

Relative prosperity in the United States for the past 50 years or so has bumped increasing numbers of voters into higher real income brackets. The most successful rebellions against high tax rates have come from voters who describe themselves as middle-class. From the 1950s into the 1980s, sporadic tax cuts and tax reforms have erratically flattened marginal income tax rates. Between 1986 and 1991, nearly all tax loopholes were closed, and the number of marginal tax brackets on personal income fell from 15 (ranging from 11% to 50%) to 4: 15%, 28%, 31%, and 33%. Unfortunately, these reforms did little to simplify our tax laws.

The 1993 Budget Reduction Act raised marginal tax rates on high-income individuals.

The number of tax brackets expanded to five: 15%, 28%, 31%, 36%, and 39.6%. Critics question whether more tax revenue is collected from "the rich" through high marginal tax rates or lower ones. Opponents of increased progressivity cite evidence that flattening tax rates increased the share of total taxes borne by upper-income taxpayers in the 1980s and early 1990s, as shown in Panel A of Figure 7. Between 1981 and 1988, the share of income taxes paid by the top 2% of income recipients rose by 50%, from roughly 18% to almost 27%.

More evidence that increased progressivity may be counterproductive is provided in Panel B, which traces federal tax revenues and federal revenues from individual income taxes as percentages of GDP. The relationships are comparatively constant. Tax structures have been flatter in some periods and steeper in others. Nevertheless, roughly 29% of GDP has been collected in total taxes, with roughly 10% being collected in income taxes on individuals, regardless of how progressive tax rates were at any point in time. Critics of progressivity echo Schumpeter's law, which suggests that people ultimately find ways to beat any tax system intended to collect more than about 27% of their income. Choosing not to make much income is one such technique.

What appears to be true for the United States, however, may not hold worldwide. As Figure 8 illustrates, tax revenue as a percent of GDP varies from nearly 50% in Sweden to the 20% to 30% range in Australia, Japan, and the United States. The effective tax rates in the former Soviet Union (hidden in the form of low wages and high prices set by the government) were higher than any shown in Figure 8. The collapse of the USSR and mounting pressures for tax cuts in the countries where taxes are heaviest may be evidence that it may take a long time for tax burdens to fall to an equilibrium consistent with Schumpeter's law—if it is truly universal.

Government Purchases and Transfers: New Classical View

Keynesians view government purchases as direct sources of Aggregate Expenditures and transfer payments as quickly translated by re-

FIGURE 7 Tax Revenues and the Progressivity of Tax Rates

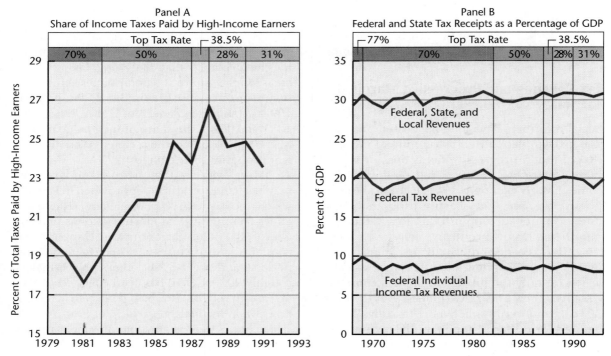

Panel A traces the shares of total tax revenues borne by taxpayers near the top of the U.S. income distribution. Their shares of total tax payments have risen when tax rates have been flattened. Tax revenues as percentages of GDP appear almost impervious to the degree of progressivity, as shown in Panel B. Declines in taxes as percentages of GDP across recent decades have tended to reflect economic downturns, while increases in this tax/GDP ratio generally reflect periods of recovery from recession. Any relationship between government's tax take and the degree of progressivity is hard to discern from these data. These results suggest that policies to "soak the rich" may be most effective when high income individuals are not discouraged by high tax rates from working hard and investing wisely.

cipients into new consumer spending. Advocates of the new classical economics sense that this focus on demand is shortsighted and worry about the incentive effects of government programs. Their reasoning goes like this: Modern government provides school lunch programs, public parks and highways, medical care for the poor and the aged, subsidized housing and transportation, and a host of other goods. There is less incentive to sacrifice our time by working and less net gain from investing if the government guarantees us a reasonably comfortable life by providing many necessities.

Transfer programs are viewed as problems for two reasons. First, incentives to work and invest are reduced for those who work and invest and who then pay taxes that government channels to others. Second, those who receive trans-

fer payments also suffer disincentives against work or saving. (Would you work as hard if you were forced to give your neighbors 50% of your income? Would your neighbors?) According to some new classical economists, extensive government purchases and generous transfer payments trap low-income individuals in a rut—a psychology of dependence takes hold, discouraging work effort and deterring attempts to improve their economic status. Much of welfare reform proposed by the Clinton administration is designed to control this cycle of poverty by helping low-income individuals get back on their feet. The emphasis is on limits to the duration of government support, job training, a baseline health-care system, and such services as daycare for the children of poor parents who work.

FIGURE 8   Tax Burdens on the International Scene

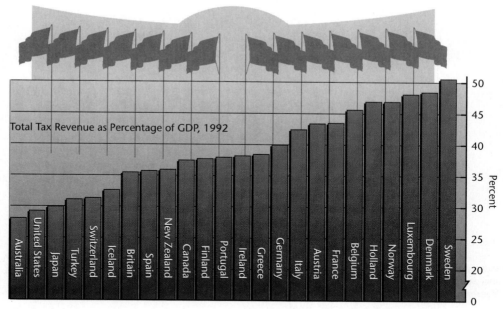

Tax burdens (as measured by taxes as a percent of GDP) have been rising in most industrialized countries for decades. Americans complain about being heavily taxed, but, as you can see, they get off much easier, on average, than people in many other countries.

In conclusion, new classical economics would redirect fiscal policymakers to (*a*) set non-intrusive economic policies that permit markets to make long-run adjustments and (*b*) limit tax rates and government outlays because of disincentives that dampen Aggregate Supply. Keynesians, in contrast, have traditionally focused on cures for short-run problems and stressed activist fiscal policy as a tool to adjust Aggregate Demand. Specific differences between these schools of thought are summarized in Figure 9.

FISCAL POLICY IN ACTION

For half a century, Keynesians have emphasized changes in tax rates and spending by government as cures for macroeconomic problems. The conventional wisdom before the Keynesian revolution was that taxation and spending should be adjusted to balance the actual budget at all times. Then the economy would automat-

ically adjust to a noninflationary full-employment equilibrium. A problem with putting this idea into practice is that higher tax rates may yield lower tax revenues, and vice versa, because tax rate structures influence our major tax base: income. Failure to understand this led President Hoover and the Congress to raise tax rates in 1932, exacerbating the economic collapse of 1929 to 1933.

The Tax Increase of 1932

Keynesians and new classical economists agree that a fetish for balancing the budget was one reason why the economy, following what should have been a minor recession in 1929, continued tumbling downward until 1933. Their explanation for the intensity and duration of the Great Depression is that President Hoover and the Congress reacted to a minor, recession-caused deficit (like the \$50 billion for AE_0 and T_0 in Figure 5) by raising tax rates. This further depressed National Income and tax revenues,

FIGURE 9 Traditional Keynesian vs. New Classical Views of Fiscal Policy

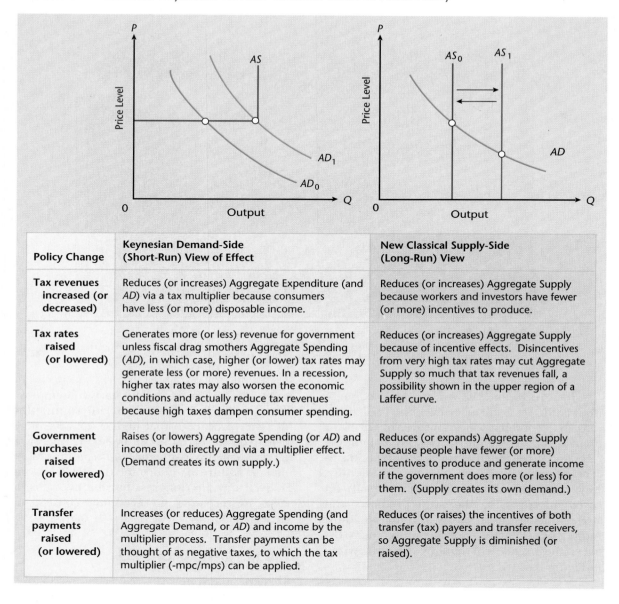

Policy Change	Keynesian Demand-Side (Short-Run) View of Effect	New Classical Supply-Side (Long-Run) View
Tax revenues increased (or decreased)	Reduces (or increases) Aggregate Expenditure (and AD) via a tax multiplier because consumers have less (or more) disposable income.	Reduces (or increases) Aggregate Supply because workers and investors have fewer (or more) incentives to produce.
Tax rates raised (or lowered)	Generates more (or less) revenue for government unless fiscal drag smothers Aggregate Spending (AD), in which case, higher (or lower) tax rates may generate less (or more) revenues. In a recession, higher tax rates may also worsen the economic conditions and actually reduce tax revenues because high taxes dampen consumer spending.	Reduces (or increases) Aggregate Supply because of incentive effects. Disincentives from very high tax rates may cut Aggregate Supply so much that tax revenues fall, a possibility shown in the upper region of a Laffer curve.
Government purchases raised (or lowered)	Raises (or lowers) Aggregate Spending (or AD) and income both directly and via a multiplier effect. (Demand creates its own supply.)	Reduces (or expands) Aggregate Supply because people have fewer (or more) incentives to produce and generate income if the government does more (or less) for them. (Supply creates its own demand.)
Transfer payments raised (or lowered)	Increases (or reduces) Aggregate Spending (and Aggregate Demand, or AD) and income by the multiplier process. Transfer payments can be thought of as negative taxes, to which the tax multiplier (-mpc/mps) can be applied.	Reduces (or raises) the incentives of both transfer (tax) payers and transfer receivers, so Aggregate Supply is diminished (or raised).

which resulted in attempts to balance the budget through still higher tax rates, and so on.

Figure 10 presents the actual relationships between expenditures and net tax revenues (after subtracting transfers) to real Gross Domestic Product for 1929 to 1933. The superimposed curves show government spending and taxes before and after the tax rate increase of 1932. This tax increase was designed to generate roughly one-third more revenue in fiscal 1932 than in 1931. Policymakers failed to realize how severely higher tax rates could depress GDP. (Real GDP quickly fell by roughly 20%.) Keynesians interpret Figure 10 as evidence that massive withdrawals of funds arising from these higher tax rates inhibited Aggregate Demand

FIGURE 10   The Tax Increase of 1932

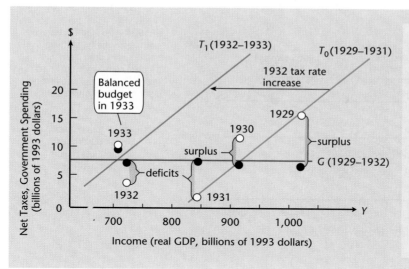

Actual government purchases and net taxes (taxes minus transfers) are shown for the years from 1929 through 1933, using a Keynesian framework to scrutinize the tax hike of 1932. A modest deficit in 1931 persuaded Congress and President Hoover to increase tax rates in an attempt to balance the budget. The unfortunate result was a leftward shift in the net tax function and a decline in equilibrium income. That the budget balanced by 1933 was cold comfort.

Note: ● = government purchases;
       ○ = taxes minus transfers.

and added to the severity of the Great Depression. Some new classical economists see this as proof that, even in the 1930s, high tax rates stifled Aggregate Supply.

The Tax Cut of 1964–1965

Keynesians recommend tax rate cuts or increased government purchases when a recession causes even a slight cyclical budget deficit.[8] The idea that cutting tax rates might stimulate Aggregate Demand *and* National Income *and* tax revenues first gained wide acceptance in the 1960s. President Kennedy's economic advisors viewed the 1950s as a lethargic period hampered by high tax rates that created fiscal drag. They argued that cuts in tax rates would stimulate growth, reduce poverty and unemployment, and generate higher tax revenues.

A massive tax cut enacted during the Johnson administration supported these pre-

dictions. Keynesian (demand-side) reasoning was used to sell these tax cuts politically, although some supply-side arguments were also used. A 1964–1965 tax cut broadly reduced tax rates. Personal income tax rates dropped from brackets of 18% to 91% to brackets of 14% to 70%. Taxes on corporate income were cut from 52% to 48%. The results of this experiment with broad cuts in tax rates are shown in Figure 11. The economy, and hence the tax base, expanded so rapidly that the 1964 deficit actually gave way to a small surplus in 1965. New classical economists naturally interpret this success as evidence that the economy was on the wrong side of the Laffer curve and that tax revenue was stimulated as Aggregate Supply grew.

These examples provide evidence that putting fiscal policy to work is more complex than our simple theory suggests. Whether changes in tax rates will reduce budget deficits depends on the state of the economy and the initial level of tax rates. The Kennedy-Johnson round of tax cuts suggests that if the economy is poised for growth, tax cuts may simultaneously stimulate growth and reduce deficits. Another possibility is that cuts in tax rates may stimulate economic growth while budget deficits explode, as President Reagan discovered in the 1980s.

---

[8]In the example illustrated back in Figure 5, cutting tax rates from T_0 to T_1 raises Aggregate Expenditure to AE_1 tax revenues increase to $1 trillion at an income level of $7.5 trillion, and the federal budget is balanced. Notice that tax collections actually increase in response to cuts in tax

FIGURE 11   The 1964–1965 Tax Cut

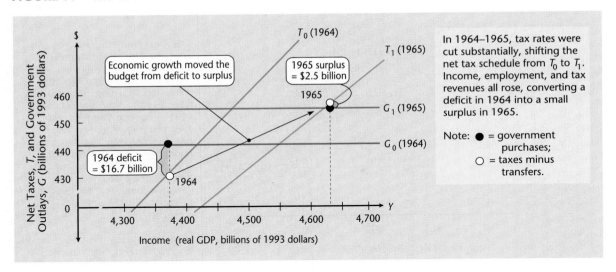

In 1964–1965, tax rates were cut substantially, shifting the net tax schedule from T_0 to T_1. Income, employment, and tax revenues all rose, converting a deficit in 1964 into a small surplus in 1965.

Recent Budget Deficits

The American economy followed a rocky path through the 1970s, with budget deficits at new record levels almost each year. (Our most recent budget surplus was experienced in fiscal year 1968–1969.) By the 1980s, dismay about the growth of federal spending had become epidemic. President Reagan had campaigned on a platform to slash tax rates and a multitude of government programs. It proved, however, far harder to restrain spending growth than to cut tax rates.[9] A major reason was that the Reagan administration wanted to expand military budgets and cut domestic spending, while many in Congress were determined to increase domestic spending and opposed bigger defense budgets. Both sides won on their spending priorities, but both lost in attempts to halt types of spending they opposed. Consequently, annual deficits exploded from the $80 billion range of the late 1970s into the $250 billion to $350 billion range in the 1990s.

---

[9]R. Eisner and P. Pieper, "A New View of the Federal Debt and Budget Deficits," *American Economic Review*, March 1984, pp. 11–29, and testimony before the Joint Economic Committee of Congress on January 16, 1986.

• **The Tax Cuts of 1981–1983**   During the 1970s, the supply-side wing of new classical macroeconomics gained the ears of prominent politicians who blamed Keynesian fiscal policies for rising deficits, rapid inflation, and high unemployment. President Reagan sought, and the Congress passed, a 25% tax cut in 1981, phased in over three years. At the same time, eligibility for transfer payments was tightened, and the growth of nonmilitary government spending was cut slightly. Advocates of these policies hoped to stimulate Aggregate Supply so much that inflation and unemployment would fall quickly. They also hoped that tax revenues would be so responsive to economic growth that budget deficits would abate.

This approach yielded income far below the optimistic predictions that had accompanied supply-side rhetoric. Restrictive monetary policy from 1981 to 1983 did reduce inflation, but unemployment rose and the economy only slowly recovered from the deep recession of 1981 to 1983. Annual federal budget deficits seemed stuck around the $300 billion mark. Figure 12 illustrates that the 1981–1983 tax cuts may have increased the structural deficit by shifting the net tax function downward and to the right.

FIGURE 12 The 1981–1983 Tax Cuts and the Structural Deficit

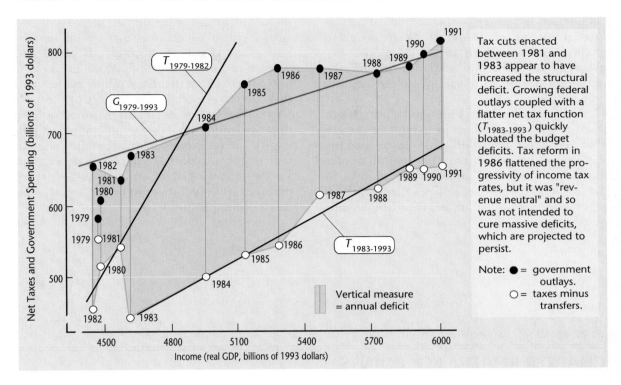

Tax cuts enacted between 1981 and 1983 appear to have increased the structural deficit. Growing federal outlays coupled with a flatter net tax function ($T_{1983-1993}$) quickly bloated the budget deficits. Tax reform in 1986 flattened the progressivity of income tax rates, but it was "revenue neutral" and so was not intended to cure massive deficits, which are projected to persist.

Note: ● = government outlays.
○ = taxes minus transfers.

• Deficit Reduction Plans in the 1990s Deficits have been political issues since long before the Civil War. A balanced budget amendment has been in the hopper for decades. Congress passed the Gramm-Rudman Act of 1986, in hopes that a legal target date for a balanced budget would limit the growth of federal spending. However, circumstances (e.g., recession during 1990–1991 and spending on the Gulf War) activated clauses that largely rendered the law moot. Congress enacted additional Deficit Reduction laws in 1990 and, again, in 1993, perhaps foreshadowing a chain of repeated attempts to legally mandate a balanced budget. Someday, one of these laws may be successful.

Despite campaign promises of "No new taxes," President Bush sharply departed from the supply-side philosophy of the 1980s, succumbing to political pressure to raise taxes in 1990. His Deficit Reduction plan was intended to reduce cumulative federal deficits by $500 billion by 1995. Higher federal taxes were levied on income, gasoline, cigarettes, alcoholic beverages, luxury goods, and airline tickets. Nevertheless, tax revenues failed to grow because of an economic slowdown—a classic example of a cyclical deficit. The deficit for 1991 was almost $350 billion—roughly $1,400 in new federal debt for every American piled up in just one year.

An eerily similar Deficit Reduction Act was passed shortly after Bill Clinton took office. Again, tax hikes (this time, primarily in the form of higher marginal taxes for upper-income Americans) were keys to the plan, along with major cuts in defense spending. And again, the goal was to reduce the cumulative deficit by roughly $500 billion over a five year period. But unlike the blockage of President Bush's plans by the recession of 1990 to 1991, President

Clinton's plan may prove at least partially successful if the economy continues to rebound. The lesson here may be that structural deficits (under the control of federal policymakers) and cyclical deficits (which depend on economic trends) both come into play to determine the economic health of the nation and the fortunes of politicians.

This chapter has examined government spending and tax policies from both Keynesian and new classical perspectives. Our stress on the differences between these schools of thought is intended to help you understand how government spending and tax policies may influence unemployment, inflation, and rates of economic growth. Keep in mind, however, that nearly all economists now agree about large parts of economic theory. For example, there is broad agreement that incentives shape economic behavior and that both Aggregate Demand and Aggregate Supply are important. Economists also tend to agree that fiscal policy matters and that monetary policy—the subject of the next part of this book—also matters. After we have discussed more about money and monetary policy, we will reexamine in greater depth the potential problems posed by persistent deficits and a growing national debt, and the perspectives of different schools of thought on these and other macroeconomic problems.

CHAPTER REVIEW: KEY POINTS

1. **Keynesian fiscal policy** is the use of federal spending and tax policies to stimulate or contract Aggregate Spending and economic activity to offset cyclical fluctuations. Classical (supply-side) fiscal policies rely on low tax rates and minimal government spending to allow Aggregate Supply to grow.

2. **Discretionary fiscal policy** consists of deliberate changes in federal government spending and taxation for stabilization purposes. Without congressional action, *automatic stabilizers* such as corporate and personal income taxes and various transfer programs cause changes in spending and taxation as economic conditions change.

3. Increases in *government spending* increase Aggregate Expenditure and National Income through the multiplier process in the same way as changes in investment or autonomous consumer spending.

4. Changes in *net tax revenues* (tax revenues minus transfer payments) affect Aggregate Expenditures differently than changes in government spending do. Changes in net taxes directly affect disposable income and, therefore, saving. These effects are transmitted into spending through the **autonomous tax multiplier** $[\Delta Y/\Delta T_a = 1 - (1/mps)]$, which is weaker than the spending multiplier.

5. In a Keynesian model of a depression, the **balanced-budget multiplier** equals one; equal increases (or decreases) in government spending and taxes will increase (or decrease) Aggregate Expenditures and equilibrium income by an equal amount.

This result follows from the fact that the autonomous tax multiplier is one minus the autonomous spending multiplier.

6. **Automatic stabilizers** tend to cushion the economy. When income falls, automatic stabilizers keep the level of disposable income from falling as rapidly as income does. Our progressive income tax causes tax collections to fall proportionally faster when income is falling and to increase proportionally faster when income is rising.

7. Built-in stabilizers can pose the problem of **fiscal drag**. When potential income is rising, automatic stabilizers brake the economy and slow the rate of growth.

8. The **structural deficit** is an estimate of the deficit that would be generated at full employment under existing tax and expenditure structures. This is a way to estimate the expansionary or contractionary influence of any tax and expenditure mix.

9. The **cyclical deficit** is attributable to business conditions. As unemployment grows, the cyclical deficit grows, and vice versa.

10. The **Laffer curve** indicates that high tax rates may impose such large disincentives to productive effort that Aggregate Supply and tax revenues are both restricted.

11. **Marginal tax rates** are the percentage taxes applied to small gains in additional income.

QUESTIONS FOR THOUGHT AND DISCUSSION

1. Do you think a more progressive tax structure than currently exists would be fairer? More efficient? How does greater progressivity in income tax rates serve as an automatic stabilizer? How might progressivity inhibit economic growth and worsen government deficits?

2. Professional football teams sometimes trade their future draft choices for veteran players. In what sense is this like government financing current purchases through deficits? What are the crucial differences for future production, if any, between the two situations?

3. Explain the sense in which federal taxes determine how much each of us will help control inflation. If you could print money, would you ever try to remove any from circulation as long as there were trees and green ink? Why? Then why does the federal government bother to collect taxes?

4. What are the similarities and differences between taxes and saving? Are these differences important for the purposes of determining National Income? Why or why not?

5. Suppose that the most revenue that can be generated from taxes on income is $1 trillion. Draw a Laffer curve indicating the amounts of tax revenues that would be generated by marginal income tax rates of 0%, 100%, and the X percentage rate that you think would be most likely to generate the $1 trillion maximum. What tax rate did you select for X?

OPTIONAL MATERIAL: MORE MATHEMATICS OF KEYNESIAN MULTIPLIERS

This overview of tax, balanced-budget, and autonomous-spending multipliers should provide insights into what elected officials may be trying to do the next time they weigh a policy change.

The Autonomous Spending and Tax Multipliers

All spending injections—regardless of whether from more government spending, more investment, more autonomous consumption, or more exports—are perfect substitutes in their impact on equilibrium income. A recessionary gap can be erased (or an inflationary gap created) through new autonomous spending subject to the autonomous spending multiplier.

Alternatively, tax cuts can trigger economic growth. The autonomous tax multiplier equals one minus the autonomous spending multiplier. Algebraically, income is the sum of consumption, investment, government spending, and net exports: $Y = C + I + G + (X - M)$. Suppose all taxes (T_a), investment (I_a), government purchases (G_a), net exports ($X_a - M_a$), and part of consumption, (C_a) are autonomous and that $mpc(Y - T_a)$ is induced consumption. The mpc is based on disposable income, so

$$Y = C_a + mpc\left(Y - T_a\right) + I_a + G_a + \left(X_a - M_a\right)$$

We define total autonomous spending as $A = C_a + I_a + G_a + (X_a - M_a)$. This leaves $Y = A + mpc(Y - T_a)$, or $Y = A + mpcY - mpcT_a$. Subtracting $mpcY$ from both sides leaves $Y - mpcY = A - mpcT_a$. Factoring Y from the left side yields $Y(1 - mpc) = A - mpcT_a$, and then dividing both sides by $1 - mpc$ gives

$$Y = A\left(\frac{1}{1 - mpc}\right) + T_a\left(\frac{-mpc}{1 - mpc}\right)$$

English translation: Aggregate income (Y) equals autonomous spending [$C_a + I_a + G_a + (X_a - M_a) = A$] times the autonomous spending multiplier [$1/(1 - mpc)$], plus the level of taxes (T_a) times the autonomous tax multiplier [$-mpc/(1 - mpc)$]. [The autonomous tax multiplier can be rewritten ($-mpc/mps$).] Thus, if the spending multiplier is 5, the tax multiplier is –4; if the spending multiplier is 4, the tax multiplier is –3; and so on.

The Balanced-Budget Multiplier

In our simple Keynesian model, all else being equal, any change in National Income can be traced to changes in autonomous spending or taxes:

$$\Delta Y = \Delta A\left(\frac{1}{1 - mpc}\right) + \Delta T_a\left(\frac{-mpc}{1 - mpc}\right)$$

If the mpc equals 0.8, the spending multiplier equals 5 and the tax multiplier equals –4. Thus, $\Delta Y = \Delta A(5) + \Delta T_a(-4)$. If government spending and taxes each grow by $20 billion, income also rises by $20 billion: $20 billion × (5) *plus* $20 billion × (–4) *equals* $20 billion.

We can generalize: Equal changes in autonomous government spending and taxes cause income to change in the same direction and by the same amount. The applicable multiplier, termed the *balanced-budget multiplier*, always equals one because it reflects the numerical sum of the autonomous spending and tax multipliers:

$$\left(\frac{1}{1 - \text{mpc}} \right) + \left(\frac{-\text{mpc}}{1 - \text{mpc}} \right) = \left(\frac{1 - \text{mpc}}{1 - \text{mpc}} \right) = 1$$

Reviewing Table 3 in the body of this chapter should help convince you why, if both government purchases and taxes are increased by $1, then equilibrium income will rise by exactly $1.

More realistic assumptions than those we have used underpin the sophisticated econometric models used to forecast national economic activity. For example, how income affects taxes, investment, and government outlays is recognized. Although serious forecasting models are mathematically more complex than those considered here, the approaches are similar: assumptions about the behavior of various economic agents are used to predict National Income and Output.

Money

Bank

Interest rates

M_{s0}

M_{s1}

FED

Discount rate

M1

Reserve requirement

M_d

Part 4

The Financial System

Modern macroeconomics has extended insights from both Keynesian and classical economics. Despite growing consensus about parts of basic theory, some major issues remain unresolved.

First and foremost is the question of how actively government should try to control business cycles. Most economists who favor passive government policies draw inspiration from the laissez-faire conclusions of classical economics. In contrast, the new Keynesians are less convinced that market forces can quickly resolve all macroeconomic problems and a bit less skeptical about the efficiency and corrective power of an activist role for government in neutralizing business cycles. Nevertheless, the growing consensus seems to be that government action to control radical swings in economic activity is appropriate, but only when a business cycle is extreme. New classical economists are less vehement than were their predecessors that all countercyclical activity by government is counterproductive, while failed attempts to fine-tune the economy in the 1960s and 1970s left most new Keynesians somewhat gun-shy about recommending discretionary policy to smooth every blip on the economic horizon.

A second, related issue centers on underpinnings for Aggregate Demand. Keynesians isolate income as the major influence on Aggregate Demand. New classical economists ranging from supply-siders to modern monetarists identify the amount of money available as the major influence on Aggregate Demand.

You need to know more about monetary economics to appreciate areas of agreement and disagreement between the new Keynesians and the new classical economists. What money is, what services it performs, and how money is created are the questions addressed in Chapter 12. Then, Chapter 13 provides an overview of the Federal Reserve System and the tools it uses to determine the money supply and to regulate our financial system.

Chapter 14 looks at the demand for money and how the supply and demand for money jointly determine the price level, the rate of inflation, Aggregate Output, and the rate of interest. In addition to looking at the burdens and benefits of budget deficits and public debt, Chapter 15 traces linkages between monetary policy and the federal budget and addresses the international consequences of persistent budget deficits.

In Part 3 of this book, we discussed how government taxing and spending policies might interact with private spending (consumption, investment, and net exports) to alter Aggregate Demand and, ultimately, National Output. This part addresses money as a social convention, discusses the purposes of financial institutions, and explains how government's monetary policies affect Aggregate Demand. In Part 5, we develop these themes more completely to delve deeper into recent macroeconomic problems.

Chapter 12
Money and Banking

The love of money as a possession—as distinguished from the love of money as a means to the enjoyment of the realities of life—will be recognized for what it is, a somewhat disgusting morbidity, one of those semi-criminal, semi-pathological propensities which one hands over with a shudder to the specialists in mental disease.

John Maynard Keynes

Any list of inventions that shaped modern civilization would include the wheel, the wedge, and *money*. Suppose an anthropologist from Venus visited Earth. Venusians might be puzzled by why Earthlings work, invest, lie, cheat, steal, or commit murder for beads, bits of metal, dirty paper, or bookkeeping entries in computers in buildings called "banks." The role of money might seem inexplicable—unless Venus also had a monetary system. And, of course, it would.

Our first task in this chapter is to explain why societies everywhere use money to facilitate specialization and exchange. After an overview of the economic functions of money, we survey different types of money and the components of our money supply. Finally, we explore the processes of money creation and destruction.

BARTER: EXCHANGE WITHOUT MONEY

Some pundits foresee a cashless society in which all transactions will be executed via computer. But can you imagine a society without money? Our ancestors used some form of money at least as early as the seventh century B.C., but we know that our earliest ancestors had no money. Only a few small, isolated tribes managed to enter the twentieth century without a monetary system.

If you lived in a society without money, you would be limited to producing or stealing everything you used—or you could engage in barter.

> **Barter** *occurs when people directly exchange their goods for someone else's goods.*

Under barter, you must find someone who has what you want and who wants what you have to trade. This requirement is called the *double co-*

incidence of wants. Even a double coincidence of wants, however, does not ensure that even most beneficial exchanges will be consummated. If you had a spare pony and wanted a loaf of bread, and met a baker loaded with bread who wanted a pony, you still might not strike a bargain—making change would be nearly impossible.

The basic problem is that barter systems fail to generate efficient amounts of information about potentially beneficial agreements. Transactions are infrequent because information is extremely costly. Consequently, specialization of labor and trade according to comparative advantage tend to be minimal. Most people are largely self-sufficient producers-consumers, so standards of living are primitive. Small wonder that money is rated with the wheel as an invention crucial to the development of the modern world.

WHAT IS MONEY?

I measure everything I do by the size of a silver dollar. If it don't come up to that standard then I know it's no good.

Thomas A. Edison

What money is may seem obvious, but how would you respond if asked how much money you have? You could count only the cash in your purse or pocket. More likely, you would extend this to "money" held in checking accounts or savings accounts. You might include the total value of any U.S. Savings Bonds or corporate stocks or bonds you own. But why stop there? Most of your possessions are worth money. How about the values of your other assets: a car, clothes, books, a Ping-Pong table, or other things you own. Just how much money do you have? Ambiguities in this question arise from failure to differentiate between wealth and money.

*Your **wealth** is the difference between the value of your assets and the value of your liabilities.*

In addition to being an asset itself, money has the unique characteristic of being the unit by which other assets or liabilities are measured.

FUNCTIONS OF MONEY

A descriptive definition of money emerges from certain functions it performs:

__Money__ is (a) a medium of exchange, (b) a measure of value or unit of account, (c) a store of value, and (d) a standard of deferred payment.

Memorizing this list might help you on an exam, but learning what each part of this description implies will help you understand the essence of money. You may even be able to anticipate operational definitions of money used by modern analysts.

Medium of Exchange

Money makes the world go around.

Unknown

The necessity of a double coincidence of wants under barter is finessed by money.

*Money performs as a **medium of exchange** when it is used to execute transactions.*

This is the most important and most easily understood function of money. If you sell assets (for example, labor services), you normally expect cash or a check, although you may be willing to trade your assets for other assets. To acquire something from someone else, you generally expect to shell out cash or a check, although you might use a credit card or take out a loan. *Credit* is simply an extension of money.

The prominent economist Robert Clower characterizes monetary economies as societies in which "money is traded for goods, and goods are traded for money, but goods are not traded for goods." His statement requires a slight qualifier: goods *seldom* trade for goods in a monetary economy, but barter organizations that spring up to avoid or evade taxes use bookkeeping "credits" that are actually a form of money. A plumber who trades credits from fixing your pipes for a pet pygmy pig is using these credits as money.

Measure of Value

Money is an elastic yardstick.

Unknown

If we did not have money to measure relative prices, the values of bearskin rugs might be stated in terms of bath brushes or Butterfingers, which in turn might be stated relative to shirts or shoelaces.

> *Money serves as a **measure of value** or standard unit of account when used as a common denominator to rank the relative prices of goods.*

Use of money as a standard unit of account reduces the information needed to make sound market decisions. Measuring the values of all goods in terms of all other goods would be extremely tedious, involving enormous transaction costs, because the relative prices between goods increase faster than the number of goods considered.

For example, suppose apples (*a*) and burritos (*b*) are the only two goods in an economy. In this case, there is only one relative price to consider. If you know how many apples must be traded to get a burrito, you automatically know how many burritos must be traded for an apple. Introducing a third good, carrots (*c*), complicates things. You still need to know rates of exchange between apples and burritos, but it is now also necessary to know the price of carrots in terms of both burritos and apples. Three relative prices are now important: P_a/P_b, P_a/P_c, and P_b/P_c. Adding a fourth good, doughnuts (*d*), yields six relative prices. Table 1 will help you grasp why the number of relative prices expands faster than the number of goods exchanged.

The formula for determining the number of basic relative prices in an *n*-good economy (where *n* equals the number of goods) is $[n(n-1)]/2$. The formula becomes $[4(4-1)]/2 = 6$ prices in the case of four goods. For 100 goods, relative prices jump to 4,950 in number. Imagine how complex pricing would be in a barter system where millions of different goods were traded. Thus, using money as a unit of account greases the wheels of exchange by reducing information costs. Small groups can rely less on self-production because monetary exchange substantially boosts the value of total output. People depend on monetary prices as guides that signal them to specialize in producing goods in which they have comparative advantages.

TABLE 1 Relative Prices in a Four Good Economy

Good Used to Price	Good to Be Priced			
	apples	burritos	carrots	doughnuts
apples	$\frac{P_a}{P_a} = 1$	$\frac{P_b}{P_a}$	$\frac{P_c}{P_a}$	$\frac{P_d}{P_a}$
burritos	$\frac{P_a}{P_a}$	$\frac{P_b}{P_b} = 1$	$\frac{P_c}{P_b}$	$\frac{P_d}{P_b}$
carrots	$\frac{P_a}{P_c}$	$\frac{P_b}{P_c}$	$\frac{P_c}{P_c} = 1$	$\frac{P_d}{P_c}$
doughnuts	$\frac{P_a}{P_d}$	$\frac{P_b}{P_d}$	$\frac{P_c}{P_d}$	$\frac{P_d}{P_d} = 1$

Each good is priced in terms of every other good in this four-good economy. Follow, the horizontal "apples" row to the vertical "burritos" column. That ratio, P_b/P_a is the price of burritos in terms of apples. Suppose it takes 4 apples to buy 1 burrito. Then the price of 1 apple is 1/4 burrito. Notice that the ratios P_a/P_a, P_b/P_b, P_c/P_c and P_d/P_d. These elements identify items priced in terms of themselves (1 apple/1 apple = 1) and so can be ignored. Moreover, each price below this diagonal is the reciprocal of a price above it. Information is duplicated, so the prices below the diagonal also can be ignored.

Store of Value

Money . . . lulls our disquietude.

John Maynard Keynes

People hold money not only for transactions they anticipate, but also because money is normally a relatively riskless way to hold wealth.

> *Money performs as a **store of value** when people hold it as an asset because it is relatively less risky or because they view the transaction costs of conversion into other assets as too high.*

You can hold money without paying brokerage fees, but you would probably incur such fees if you bought stocks, bonds, capital equipment, or real estate. The values of these other assets also tend to be more volatile than the purchasing power of money. There is some risk, however, because money loses value during inflation (but bonds, for example, do also).

Another way risk enters the picture emerges from *diversification*. The values of diverse assets are unlikely to be affected in the same ways by the same things. For example, if you own both a new car dealership and a junkyard, a recession may kill new car sales while your junkyard does quite well. You learned earlier that the purchasing power of a dollar is $1/P$, where P is (1/100th of) the price level; doubling the price level cuts the value of a dollar in half. Since World War II, inflation has steadily pushed up the price level. Even so, the old saying "Don't put all of your eggs in one basket" suggests that it can be wise for people to include some money in their portfolios of assets. Since then, money has played an integral role in the development of modern portfolio theory, which is a vital part of modern financial analysis in American business.

Standard of Deferred Payment

> *Money is a contract with parties unknown for the future delivery of pleasures undecided upon.*
>
> David Bazelon, *The Paper Economy* (1965)

Money as a standard of deferred payment is implicit in the other three functions of money, but it is worth discussing to illustrate the relationship between time and money.

> *Money performs as a* **standard of deferred payment** *by allowing intertemporal contracts.*

Money is a link between the past, present, and future.

Prior to the depression-era writings of John Maynard Keynes, orthodox economists rejected the notion that you might want money for other than reasonably immediate purchases.

Many forms of production require time for completion and would not be done without a contract specifying future monetary payments. Military or construction contracts are examples. Such repetitive exchanges as labor contracts are also conducted much more efficiently if only one contract is used for many present and future transactions. Still other deals require immediate delivery of a good with delayed payment for the buyer's convenience. For example, you may be borrowing to finance your education. When you sign a credit contract, you agree to make later payment of the funds you borrow—plus interest. All these contracts are measured in money.

Liquidity and Money

A vital characteristic of any asset is its liquidity, which depends on the costs incurred in converting it into cash. Many people think that liquidity is defined only by the time required for conversion, but almost any asset can be converted into cash almost immediately. If you are willing to sell your stereo system for $10, I will buy it right now. *Time required to sell, certainty about price*, and the *quality of information* are crucial aspects of asset liquidity, which hinges on transaction costs.

> *Liquidity is negatively related to the transaction costs incurred in the purchase or sale of an asset.*

One way to rank an asset's liquidity is to estimate the percentage you would lose if you had to sell it immediately. Houses are relatively illiquid. You usually pay realtor fees and other transaction costs when you sell one home and buy another. In contrast, most savings accounts are highly liquid. You can close one savings account at your bank and open another, losing almost no interest or principal in the process—just your time.

TYPES OF MONEY

An incredible variety of items have served as money at various times and places, but all can be classified as either commodity money or fiat money.

Commodity money *is valuable apart from what it will buy.*

Gold, for example, is useful in jewelry or dentistry, even when it is not used for money. But some money is useless except when treated as money.

Fiat money *has value only because of its use as money.*

Certain pieces of paper of which you would probably like more (e.g., $100 bills) are examples of fiat money. Use of fiat money is ultimately based on faith—faith in its purchasing power, in its general acceptability, and in the stability of the government that issues it.

Commodity Monies

Rubber balls once served as money in Amazonian jungles. Members of the African Masai tribe once measured their wealth in cattle but had no money per se. Early in our history, beads, stone spearheads, and arrowheads were used as money on every inhabited continent. On the Pacific island of Yap, sculptured stones weighing up to three tons are still used as money, as indicated in Focus 1.

What caused these forms of money to fall into disuse? Several characteristics are necessary for use of any commodity as money over a long period:

1. Acceptability.
2. Durability.
3. Divisibility.
4. Homogeneity (uniformity or standardization).
5. Portability (high value-to-weight and value-to-volume ratios).
6. Relative stability of supply.
7. Optimal scarcity (and hard to counterfeit).

These attributes are reasonably self-explanatory. Pet snakes, for example, could never gain wide acceptability. Ice cream lacks durability (it melts). Diamonds are too heteroge-

neous—there are fine diamonds, and then there are those sold by shifty-eyed rascals in back alleys. Elephants are not reliably portable, nor are they divisible. (If divided, they are not durable.) The wheat supply is too volatile—a bumper crop would cause money's value to plummet. Economic activity would be linked too tightly to good or bad harvests. *Optimal scarcity* means that any commodity used as money cannot be too common, nor can it be counterfeited easily. Bricks or two-by-fours are insufficiently scarce.

Historically, the commodities that best combine the characteristics for use as money are rare metals, especially gold and silver. Standardization was achieved by making coins of these precious metals and stamping face values on them. The earliest known metal coins date back to imperial Rome in the sixth century B.C.

When the world relied almost exclusively on gold and silver coins for money, feudal royalty often found their treasuries inadequate for the palaces, ornate finery, and large armies and navies they thought were due them. A common solution was to wage war to capture foreign treasure. This strategy was seldom successful. (War is a *negative-sum game*, which means that the total losses to all participants outweigh the gains to the "winners," if any.) An alternative for heads of state was to debase the coinage so that profits from seigniorage rolled in.

*The profit government makes when it coins or prints currencies whose face values exceed their commodity values is known as **seigniorage**.*

Early government mints stretched relatively pure gold and silver coins by melting them down and adding generous portions of nickel, copper, zinc, or lead before restamping coins. (Similar ideas have inspired people to put soybeans and sawdust into hamburgers.) One consequence of debasement is that it limits private profits from melting coins down whenever face values are less than the value of the gold or silver the coins contain. Focus 2 explores yet another result of debasement.

Inflationary pressure that may arise from debasement is a major reason some advocates of laissez-faire capitalism vehemently oppose gov-

Yap Money: Solid as a Rock?

Micronesia, an archipelago in the South Pacific, is a U.S. trust territory in which dollars pay for most purchases from outsiders (e.g., at local stores that sell imported clothing, food, or cars). On the tiny Micronesian island of Yap, however, carved limestone wheels ranging in diameter from 31 inches to 12 feet have been used to consummate transactions for over 15 centuries. Exchanges involving such traditional things as dowry rights or land still turn on payments using these ancient stone sculptures.

Some of the larger stones have shared ownership, accounted for either mentally or by marking off the shares different families own. During World War I, Yap was briefly occupied by Germany. When the locals refused to pay "taxes," German officials painted parts of some stones to identify them as German property. Yapese "taxpayers" quickly ransomed these "coins" by surrendering parts of their harvests of coconuts, copra, and fish.

The stones have some advantages over conventional money. Most have long histories well known to all the locals, and each is

somewhat unique, so theft is rare. The Yap money supply is easily the most stable anywhere in the world; despite demands from foreign collectors and museums, about 6,600 of the stones remain on the island. But there are disadvantages. Conventional bankers are unwilling to deal with the stones, so stone money cannot earn interest.

Chipped or cracked stones that can be repaired are sculpted into smaller, less valuable pieces of money. An irreparably broken stone, however, loses all value, so most sit propped up alongside the owners' homes or in rows at the local "bank" for decades, or even centuries, although they can be moved when ownership changes hands by putting logs through their center holes and lifting or rolling them. Once, while being ported between islands, a giant stone slipped over the side of an outrigger canoe into deep water. Nevertheless, it continued to count in trades for decades, but at a discount. People knew its location and that it was intact; that they could not put their hands on it was almost irrelevant. Mental accounting kept track of its owner-

ship, much as ownership of the gold bars formerly used by the United States in its international transactions was once transferred, unseen, while remaining deep in the vaults at Fort Knox.

Outsiders might view the Yapese as naively relying on a primitive system to keep track of money, but is our banking system really so different? After all, most Americans keep the bulk of our money in banks, stored as electronic blips in a computer. We never really see much of our money, nor does it truly exist in a physical sense.

|← 12 feet across →|

ernment discretion in printing money. Many "gold bugs" favor a return to a gold standard in which every dollar would be backed by a dollar's worth of gold. The amount of money in circulation would then be controlled by the forces of supply and demand. Gold bugs are willing to accept the inefficiency of producing money through mining and then burying gold or silver in a place like Fort Knox; they view this costly process as worthwhile because it limits government's control over the money supply.

Paper money dates back to the Ming dynasty in China (1368–1399). Until recently, many paper

monies could have been classified as pseudo-commodity money because governments would convert the paper money into specified amounts of gold or silver on demand. The United States was the last country to abandon the gold and silver standards; it was not until 1933 that this country went off the gold standard domestically. From 1933 until 1974, foreign bankers and governments could proffer $35 in bills and get an ounce of gold from the United States Treasury, but it was illegal for American citizens to hold gold coins or ingots. U.S. dollars were, however, redeemable for silver until the late 1960s.

Gresham's Law

In the 1950s, it was very common to use silver coins minted 40 to 60 years earlier. What happened to all the gold and silver coins minted in the United States prior to 1964? Sir Thomas Gresham, a sixteenth-century financial adviser to Queen Elizabeth, may have had the answer. He observed that debased coins remained in circulation while relatively pure coins disappeared rapidly after debasement. This led him to state a famous economic doctrine that has stood the test of time: "bad money drives out good." This idea is known as Gresham's Law. People will spend coins that contain far less valuable metal than their face values and hoard (save) coins that contain metal worth close to or more than the coins' face values. This explains why almost all our current dimes, quarters, half-dollars, and "silver" dollars are relatively recently minted cupronickel sandwiches.

Fiat Money

Some Americans still believe that currency is backed by gold in Fort Knox.

*Paper money and coins are collectively called **currency**.*

Recall that fiat money has value only because it is money. Take a close look at a dollar. You will see "Federal Reserve Note" above George Washington's picture, but nothing about the worth of the bill in gold or silver. Now look at any "silver" coin. These coins are sandwiches of cupronickel (not silver) around copper; face values of coins are about 15 to 40 times the total value of the metal. What makes these bits of metal and paper valuable if they are not backed by gold or silver? One hint lies to the left of George's picture: (THIS NOTE IS LEGAL TENDER FOR ALL DEBTS, PUBLIC AND PRIVATE.) The government declares that pieces of paper printed by the Federal Reserve System and bits of metal from the U. S. Mint are money by fiat. (*Fiat* can be interpreted as "because we command.")

Now that you know that our money has no gold or silver backing, should your behavior change in any way? No. Even if you are convinced that the government commits fraud by issuing coins and bills, you can buy just about anything for which you have the money, so you will continue to try to get money in the same ways as previously. The real foundation for fiat money is the *faith* we have that it can be used to buy goods and services. In other words, our money is "backed" by pizzas, theater tickets, and haircuts—and also by government's ability and willingness to maintain money at a relatively stable value by controlling the money supply.

Major advantages of fiat money are that (*a*) its supply can be controlled fairly precisely by government; (*b*) it is much less costly to produce than commodity money, making its use relatively efficient; and (*c*) if monetary policymakers do a good job, fiat money has all the qualities required of a good commodity money. The major disadvantage of fiat money is that if irresponsible monetary policymakers run the printing presses too fast, they wreak havoc on the financial system and the economy in general—a point we will revisit in future chapters.

THE SUPPLY OF MONEY

The purchasing power of money and the cost of credit (interest rates) are determined by supply and demand in much the same manner that prices are determined for shoe polish or fudge. In the remainder of this chapter, we describe the assets that make up the U.S. money supply and examine the role of financial institutions in determining the money supply. This sets the stage for analyzing how the demand and supply of money jointly determine the price level, the rate of inflation, and the rate of interest.

The functions of money hint at operational definitions of the money supply: money is a medium of exchange, a measure of value, a store of value, and a standard of deferred payment. Be aware, however, that just as no measure of unemployment precisely fits the economic concept of unemployment, no measure of the money supply conforms perfectly to money as a concept.

Narrowly Defined Money (M1)

Currency (coins and paper bills) is the most easily identified component of the money supply because it may be used (*a*) for virtually all transactions, (*b*) to price goods and services, and (*c*) as an asset. Demand deposits are the other major assets that perform all monetary functions.

> *Demand deposits are funds in checking accounts in commercial banks, savings and loans, or credit unions.*

These funds are legally required to be available *on demand*, normally by check, debit card, or through automatic teller machines (ATMs). Together, currency and demand deposits (plus such minor accounts as travelers' checks) are the narrowly defined money supply known as *M1*:

> **M1** = currency + demand deposits in financial institutions

We do need to qualify this a bit. Only currency held by the nonbanking public is included in the money supply. We would be double counting if both the currency you deposit in your checking account and your demand deposits were counted. Deposits of the federal government are also ignored because, via the Federal Reserve System, it can print money at will. Moreover, because federal spending is not limited by money the government has on hand, inclusion of federal deposits would not aid us in predicting Aggregate Expenditures when using money supply data.

"But," you might object, "credit cards can pay for almost anything. And how about my savings account?" Sadly, a credit card is simply an easy way into debt; credit cards are not stores of value, so they are not money. Standard savings accounts also fail the test because spending savings account "money" requires prior conversion into cash or a demand deposit. Try presenting a savings passbook to pay for your next meal out—you will be washing dishes in no time!

Banks and such *thrift institutions* as savings and loan associations (S&Ls) and credit unions now offer some checking account services (e.g., NOW accounts) that pay interest to depositors. Recent changes in federal law have transformed most "thrifts" into banks and some of their deposits into checking accounts.[1] Throughout this book, we usually mean all banklike institutions when we say "banks" and include all checkable accounts when we refer to "checks."

Demand deposits and currency are the only major assets that are both mediums of exchange and widely accepted as money. We admit that parking meters do not accept checks, that few cab drivers will change a $100 bill for a $3 fare, and that few banks would settle a $100,000 mortgage if you rolled up with a dump truck filled with 10 million loose pennies. But checks and currency can be used for most transactions much more easily than can other assets.

Near-Money (M2, M3, and L)

Some economists do count certain highly liquid assets, such as savings accounts (*time deposits*), as part of the money supply. The economists who use broader definitions of the money supply than M1 believe that people's spending levels are more predictable by monetary data if we include the liquid assets that are highly interchangeable with currency and demand deposits.

One broader definition is *M2*, which adds such assets as noninstitutional money market

---

[1] In retrospect, not all of the deregulation of financial institutions during the 1980s was especially clever. For example, S&Ls were largely freed to speculate in real estate, but their depositors were guaranteed against loss by the FSLIC, a federal agency. The unfortunate but predictable result (elaborated in the next chapter) was that many S&Ls were incompetently or fraudulently managed, and taxpayers are taking it on the nose to the tune of roughly $200 billion.

funds and savings in commercial banks and thrift institutions to M1:

$$\textbf{M2} = \text{M1} + \text{miscellaneous short-term time deposits}$$

$$= \text{currency} + \text{demand deposits} + \text{small time deposits}$$

Other monetary theorists expand the definition of money to *M3*, which includes such items as large time deposits and institutional money market mutual funds:

$$\textbf{M3} = \text{M2} + \text{institutional money market mutual funds} + \text{large time deposits}$$

There is one even broader official definition of the money supply, *L*, which adds such liquid assets as short-term government bonds and commercial paper to M3. Exactly which definition of the money supply is most useful depends on how it will be used. Throughout this book, when we say "money," we mean *currency plus any funds available by writing checks (M1)*. How various measures of the money supply have grown is shown in Figure 1.

All these measures of the money supply have grown substantially over the years, as have our GDP and the cost of living, as measured by the consumer price index (CPI). How should these positive correlations be interpreted? Does monetary growth cause inflation? Does it cause GDP to grow, or does economic growth cause the money supply to expand? How does monetary growth affect the total output of goods, and vice versa? These questions are at the heart of a continuing controversy between monetarists and Keynesians, and they are examined in the next few chapters.

M1 Sum of currency, demand deposits, travelers checks, and other checkable deposits (OCDs)

M2 M1 plus overnight RPs and Eurodollars, MMMF balances (general purpose and broker/dealer), MMDAs, and savings and small time deposits

M3 M2 plus large time deposits, term RPs, term Eurodollars, and institution-only MMMF balances

L M3 plus other liquid assets

Source: *Economic Report of the President,* 1994, *Federal Reserve Bulletin,* 1994

The money supply is composed of various aggregates, depending on how broadly you define it. *M1* is the narrowest definition, while *L* is the most expansive.

FIGURE 1   Measures of the Money Supply

BANKS AND THE CREATION OF MONEY

Where does money come from? We know that U.S. currency is printed by the Federal Reserve System (bills) or minted by the Treasury (coins). But demand deposits (checking accounts) are the largest component of our money supply. Currency is little more than convenience money, less than 30% of M1. How do demand deposits originate?

The Origin of Fractional Reserve Banking

Several centuries ago, money consisted primarily of gold coins. Wealthy people found the amounts of gold they accumulated quite heavy. (Gold is only semiportable.) An even bigger drawback is that thieves love gold; stolen gold pieces (or modern coins for that matter) are rarely identifiable. Looking around for safe places to store their wealth, people in medieval Europe thought of goldsmiths. Goldsmiths made jewelry, gold statues, and other precious goods. Most also had some excess space in their heavily guarded vaults.

Most goldsmiths were willing to store valuables for a small fee and issued receipts for the gold deposited with them. Buyers found it convenient to exchange these receipts instead of physically getting the gold, and sellers were happy to take the receipts because they knew they could redeem them for gold whenever they wished. This was the beginning of checking accounts—the receipts issued by the goldsmiths were primitive demand deposits.

Goldsmiths observed that they stored nearly all of a community's coins and that the gold in their vaults fluctuated little. When a buyer paid for a purchase with a gold receipt, sellers typically were content to leave the gold in the vault. After all, receipts could be used for purchases as readily as gold. One depositor's withdrawal was just another customer's deposit. The goldsmiths began lending some of the gold on deposit to borrowers who would pay interest. In fact, they seldom physically relinquished much gold—just like depositors, most borrowers preferred receipts to the actual gold. This was the origin of modern fractional reserve banking.

Demand Deposit Expansion

People sometimes physically withdrew gold, so the total value of receipts that could be written as loans was limited. Goldsmiths kept reserves in their vaults to meet withdrawals of deposits.

> Banks keep **reserves** on hand to meet withdrawals by depositors (or legal requirements).

Suppose a goldsmith observed that, although deposits and withdrawals were sporadic, the amount of gold in the vault varied less than 10% annually. How much might a prudent goldsmith loan from a given deposit of gold?

For simplicity, consider a monopolist who owns the only local vault. (We look at a multibank world in a bit). This goldsmith cautiously stops lending when the value of receipts (demand deposits) issued is five times larger than the gold on deposit. That is, reserves equal 20% of deposits—twice the observed variation in deposits (10%) and solid insurance against excessive deposits being withdrawn simultaneously.

> **Fractional reserve banking** legally permits financial institutions to hold less than 100% of their deposits as currency in their vaults.

We also assume the goldsmith already has many deposits and loans outstanding prior to the transactions we will consider and views "the bank" as "fully loaned up" (reserves equal 20% of earlier deposits).[2] Finally, we initially assume that no one actually withdraws any gold during the period considered; receipts for gold are perfectly acceptable as money.

---

[2]When we introduce the Federal Reserve System in the next chapter, you will learn that banks legally must keep certain proportions of deposits in reserves: The money creation process is analytically unaffected by whether reserves are held in the interest of prudence or because the Fed requires banks to do so.

Suppose Allen, a gold miner, deposits $1,000 worth of newly mined gold in Goldsmith's bank. This deposit and issuance of a receipt are written in the bank's "T account" shown in Table 2. T-account statements represent partial balance sheets for the bank. The left-hand and right-hand entries must balance and reflect only changes in the accounts following the new $1,000 deposit. The $1,000 recorded on the right side (credit) represents a liability or debt of the bank: Goldsmith owes Allen $1,000 on demand. The left side (debit) shows an increase of $1,000 in the bank's reserves, which is Goldsmith's new asset.

TABLE 2   Initial Deposit of $1000 in a New Account in Goldsmith's Bank

Assets (Debits)	Liabilities (Credits)
+$1,000 Reserves (Gold) $ 200 Planned reserves (*RR*) $ 800 Excess reserves (*XR*)	+$1,000 (Demand Deposit—Allen)

When Bob, a local customer, wants to borrow, Goldsmith is happy to lend him as much as $800. How did we arrive at $800? Goldsmith calculates: 20% times $1,000 equals $200, which is planned for reserves (*RR*). Actual reserves of $1,000 minus $200 in planned reserves equals $800 in excess reserves (*XR*) available for the loan. When Bob borrows the full $800, the bank deposits $800 to Bob's account, and the bank's accounts change as shown in the T account of Table 3. When you borrow money from a bank, the standard practice is to credit your account instead of handing you cash. The bank's assets are increased by an $800 IOU from Bob; its new liability is Bob's demand deposit for $800.

TABLE 3   First-Round Lending: Changes in Accounts in Goldsmith's Bank

Assets (Debits)	Liabilities (Credits)
+$800 (IOU—Bob)	+$800 (Demand Deposit—Bob)

Suppose Bob writes Carol a check for $800—he did intend to spend the money he borrowed. Table 4 shows the bank's view of this exchange. Bob's $800 demand deposit simply becomes Carol's demand deposit. In fact, because all deposits stay in this bank, we can ignore further transactions between the bank's customers. Such transactions are irrelevant for the bank's asset–liability position and for the amount of money in circulation. Notice that the $1,000 in gold reserves now backs $1,800 in demand deposit money. This may sound like a magician's trick, but it is the way banks operate.

TABLE 4   A Transaction Between Two of Goldsmith's Depositors

Assets (Debits)	Liabilities (Credits)
(No change)	−$800 (Demand Deposit—Bob) +$800 (Demand Deposit—Carol)

When Deirdre wants to borrow money, Goldsmith can still lend up to $640, because actual reserves of [$1,000 − 0.20($1,000 + $800)] = $640 in excess reserves available to lend her. Alternatively, 80% of Carol's deposit (0.80 × $800) is $640. Her IOU and the loan that is deposited to Deirdre's account are shown in the T account in Table 5.

TABLE 5   Second-Round Lending: Changes in Accounts in Goldsmith's Bank

Assets (Debits)	Liabilities (Credits)
+$640 (IOU—Deirdre)	+$640 (Demand Deposit—Deirdre)

When Ed comes in to borrow money, Goldsmith offers a loan of as much as $512 because $1,000 − [0.20($1,000 + $800 + $640)] = $512. Again, 80% of Deirdre's $640 deposit is $512 and is available to loan. Table 6 depicts this loan and demand deposit (DD).

TABLE 6   Third-Round Lending: Changes in Accounts in Goldsmith's Bank

Assets (Debits)	Liabilities (Credits)
+$512 (IOU—Ed)	+$512 (Demand Deposit—Ed)

At this point, the $1,000 the bank holds as reserves supports $2,952 in demand deposits ($1,000 + $800 + $640 + $512). How much longer can this process continue? The answer is that the bank can make more loans as long as 20% of all demand deposits is less than the $1,000 held in reserve. To spare you further agony, all possible subsequent loans and demand deposits (DDs) are summarized in Table 7.

TABLE 7   All Remaining Rounds Lending: Changes in Accounts in Goldsmith's Bank

Assets (Debits)	Liabilities (Credits)
+$2,048 (IOU—All others)	+$2,048 (Demand Deposit—All others)

How did we know how large this entry would be? Well, the bank will continue to make loans until 0.20(DD) = $1,000. If both sides of this equation are multiplied by five, we get DD = 5($1,000) = $5,000. The $1,000 held in bank reserves will support up to $5,000 in DDs, regardless of whether these DDs are based on loans or not. In fact, the original $1,000 in new money deposited by Allen allowed the creation of an additional $4,000 in demand deposits generated as loans. Table 8 summarizes all these transactions.

It is not absolutely necessary for Goldsmith as a monopoly banker, to go through all these lending rounds. After experimenting a bit, Goldsmith would learn that Allen's $1,000 deposit could be translated directly into a $4,000 loan to Bob. We have gone through each step of this loan-money creation process because of its relevance for a multiple-bank financial system.

The Potential Money Multiplier (m_p)

Notice that the multiplier by which the money supply is expanded (5) is the reciprocal of the percentage Goldsmith plans as reserves against demand deposits (1/5 or 0.20).

The **potential money multiplier** ($m_p = 1/rr$) indicates the total demand deposits that can be generated from a new deposit of $1 in a banking system that is "fully loaned up," if people keep all their currency in the bank (no one keeps any cash on hand).

TABLE 8 Summary of Transactions at Goldsmith's Bank

Assets (Debits)	Liabilities (Credits)
1 +$1,000, Reserves	+$1,000 (Demand Deposit—Allen)
2 +800 (IOU—Bob)	+ 800 (Demand Deposit—Bob)
3 No change	− 800 (Demand Deposit—Bob)
	+ 800 (Demand Deposit—Carol)
4 +640 (IOU—Deirdre)	+ 640 (Demand Deposit—Deirdre)
5 +512 (IOU—Ed)	+ 512 (Demand Deposit—Ed)
6 +2,048 (IOU—All others)	+ 2,048 (Demand Deposit—All others)
Total +$5,000	+$5,000 (Total new Demand Deposits)
($1,000 gold reserves)	
($4,000 IOUs)	

The arithmetic parallels that used for spending multipliers. The autonomous spending multiplier is $1/mps$ (the marginal propensity to save), while the potential money multiplier is $1/rr$, where rr is the reserve ratio or percentage of demand deposits (DDs) held as reserves.[3]

The Actual Money Multiplier (m_a)

In reality, banks are seldom fully loaned up, and people hold some "convenience" currency to cover small transactions. These leakages from the deposit→loan→deposit stream hold the actual money multiplier far below its potential value. Let us see why.

Any reserves banks hold in excess of their planned (or legally required) amounts are available for loans. These excess reserves (XR) can be expressed as a proportion of a bank's total deposits: $XR/DD = xr$. Thus, the actual money multiplier (m_a) could be as high as $1/(rr + xr)$, but only if no other drains limit the money multiplier. But people keep some money as cash, and firms hold some currency. These currency drains from the banking system are a major reason the actual money multiplier never reaches its potential value. The Federal Reserve Bank of

St. Louis estimates the historical average real money multiplier at 2.6.

The real world multiplier can be written as a complex formula accounting for all forms of cash withdrawal from the banking system.[4] The point to remember is that cash withdrawals keep the actual money multiplier (m_a) from ever reaching its potential value ($1/rr = m_p > m_a$).

> The **actual money multiplier** (m_a) expresses the relationship between the money supply and currency in circulation or in bank vaults.

The simplest algebraic expression of the actual multiplier (m_a) is

$$m_a = MS/MB$$

where MS is the money supply and MB is the currency that legally can serve as reserves in banks. MB is known as the *monetary base*, or *high-powered money*; it is the base on which the money multiplier operates in the money creation process (much as autonomous spending is the base for total spending in a Keynesian model).

---

[3]If we denote total planned reserves as RR, the proof is simple: because $rr \times DD = RR$, then $DD = (1/rr) \times (RR)$.

[4]For example, an intermediate formula is $m_a = 1/(rr + xr + \text{other leakages})$, where other leakages include such things as cash held by the public or transfers of currency to foreign banks. Expanded algebraic versions of the actual money multiplier treat currency separately from funds used as reserves by various type of financial institutions, which are decomposed into different types of accounts.

*The **monetary base** equals currency in the hands of the nonbanking public plus all bank reserves.*

Failure to distinguish the monetary base from the money supply is a common error. Notice that a precise relationship between the monetary base and the money supply is embedded in the preceding equation for the actual money multiplier:

$$MS = m_a \times MB$$

Thus, the money supply equals the actual money multiplier times the monetary base.

• **A Multibank Model** When a community has many banks, each bank expects most checks written by its customers to be deposited in the banks of the payees. Does this mean that the total amount of deposits in any single bank is likely to be highly volatile? Not really. Banks find that, even though customers' individual accounts vary tremendously over the month, the average daily amount in a given account is fairly stable on a month-to-month basis over the year. This occurs because most people have reasonably stable patterns of income and spending and seldom let their accounts drop below some comfortable minimum value.

Flows of deposits among banks do not affect the total amounts of reserves in the banking system but will cause individual banks to hold slightly higher percentages of excess reserves (*xr*) than would be held by a monopoly banker. This reduces the size of the real-world money multiplier. Other than this, the process of money creation follows the pattern outlined in the preceding section, which assumed a monopoly bank.

Let us look at an example in which IBM sells a $1 million computer system to an oil firm in Venezuela. The payment is from a Venezuelan bank and so represents new money to the U.S. banking system. IBM deposits this $1 million in new money in the First National Bank, which enables First National to create $800,000 by giving USX (formerly U.S. Steel) a loan. The two entries in First National's accounts are shown in Table 9. USX took the loan to buy smelting equipment; it writes a check for $800,000 to American Smelting. But American Smelting banks with the PennState Bank. When PennState takes American Smelting's deposit of USX's check and demands $800,000 from First National, First National loses $800,000 in reserves and reduces USX's account by $800,000. This is shown as entry 2b in Table 9. Notice that First National still has USX's IOU for $800,000 plus $200,000 on reserve in the event that IBM wants to withdraw some money.

When American Smelting deposits USX's check and PennState collects from First

TABLE 9   Transaction with Another Bank Account in First National Bank

Assets (Debits)	Liabilities (Credits)
1 +$1,000,000 Reserves	+$1,000,000 (Demand Deposit—IBM)
2a +800,000 (IOU—USX)	+800,000 (Demand Deposit—USX)
2b −800,000 Reserves	−800,000 (Demand Deposit—USX)
Reserve Position after Transaction	
Assets (Debits)	**Liabilities (Credits)**
1 $ 200,000 Reserves	+$1,000,000 (Demand Deposit—IBM)
2a 800,000 Loan (IOU—USX)	
Total $ 1,000,000	$1,000,000 (Total Demand Deposit)

TABLE 10   Second-Round Transaction Accounts in PennState National Bank

Assets (Debits)	Liabilities (Credits)
1 +$ 800,000 Reserves	+$ 800,000 (DD—American Smelting)
2 +640,000 (IOU—Security Life)	+640,000 (DDt—Security Life)
3 −640,000 Reserves	−640,000 (DD—Security Life)

Reserve Position after Transaction

Assets (Debits)	Liabilities (Credits)
$ 160,000 Reserves (Cash)	$ 640,000 (Demand Deposit—American Smelting)
640,000 Loan (IOU—Sony)	
Total $ 800,000	$ 800,000 (Total Demand Deposit)

National, PennState's accounts change per entry 1 in Table 10. PennState can loan $640,000 to Security Life Insurance if it regards anything greater than 20 percent as excessive reserves, shown as entry 2. (First National had to turn down Security Life's application—it had no excess reserves to spare.) If Security Life writes a check to Xerox, which banks with New York's City Bank, PennState loses $640,000 reserves and Security Life's account falls to its original balance (entry 3). But PennState still has $160,000 in reserves plus Security Life's IOU for $640,000.

City Bank's accounts now change as in entry 1 of Table 11. It can lend Sony $512,000 (neither First National nor PennState has excess reserves available). When Sony takes the loan, City Bank makes entry 2 in its books. The multiple expansion process can be continued from customer to customer as reserves flow between banks until an additional total of $4,000,000 in newly created money in the form of demand deposits is generated through loans. The money creation process for an entire banking system parallels that for a single monopoly bank.

TABLE 11   Third-Round Transaction Accounts in City Bank of New York

Assets (Debits)	Liabilities (Credits)
1 +$ 640,000 Reserves	+$ 640,000 (Demand Deposit—Xerox)
2a +512,000 (IOU—Sony)	+512,000 (Demand Deposit—Sony)
2b −512,000 Reserves	−512,000 (Demand Deposit—Sony)

Reserve Position after Transaction

Assets (Debits)	Liabilities (Credits)
1 $ 128,000 Reserves (Cash)	+$ 640,000 (Demand Deposit—Xerox)
2a 512,000 Loan (IOU—Sony)	
Total $ 640,000	$ 640,000 (Total Demand Deposit)

You may have a nagging feeling that something is wrong because new money seems to have appeared out of thin air. If so, you are not alone in being a bit mystified by bankers' juggling acts. Still, the fractional reserve process of money creation is ancient and is widely accepted as compatible with sound banking practices.

You may be concerned that there is not enough money in bank vaults to meet withdrawals of deposits. Suppose IBM tries to withdraw its $1,000,000 from First National. Will this system fall like a house of cards? One part of the answer is that we have only covered the changes in bank accounts as $1 million in new reserves was used to create an original demand deposit of $1 million and an additional $4 million in demand deposits based on loans. The reserves backing other deposits in First National are available to cover IBM's withdrawal. Another option is that First National might sell USX's $800,000 IOU to another bank. This is effectively what has happened if you have ever borrowed money from one lender for, say, a car and then received a request that you pay a different lender. Your paper IOU was sold (or *factored*, as it is known in banking circles).

The Money Destruction Process

The reverse of the money creation process is money destruction. IBM can usually withdraw its $1,000,000 from First National without a problem because most banks hold adequate excess reserves. Suppose IBM withdraws its $1,000,000 and keeps it in the corporate vault. First National will feel uncomfortably short of reserves, to the tune of $800,000. Remember, First National was holding $200,000 in reserves against the $1,000,000 deposit, so it loses $800,000 in reserves that backed other accounts ($1,000,000 − $200,000 = $800,000).

When USX's $800,000 loan is due, First National will not renew the loan, nor will First National make new loans when USX repays its loan. USX's repayment must come from existing bank reserves. Ultimately, PennState Bank will reduce outstanding loans by Security Life's $640,000, City Bank will reduce loans by Sony's

$512,000, and so on. IBM's withdrawal of $1,000,000 from the banking system's reserves will cause a $4,000,000 drop in demand deposit money, originally created by expansionary lending. IBM's $1,000,000 demand deposit will also be lost, so demand deposits will drop by a total of $5,000,000. However, IBM will have $1,000,000 in currency, which was not included in the money supply while it was held as bank reserves. Thus, there is a net $4,000,000 reduction in the money supply caused by IBM's decision to hoard $1,000,000 in its own vault.

Banks holding 20% reserves should operate acceptably unless they rapidly lose 20% or more of their deposits. If this happens, are such banks insolvent? No. When only a few banks run short of reserves, other financial institutions will buy (at a discount) the IOUs from loans these banks have made. Alternatively, banks with inadequate reserves can usually borrow funds from institutions that have excess reserves available.

> Banks lend to, and borrow from each other through a private banking network called the **federal funds market**.

These interbank lending mechanisms normally enable banks that have inadequate reserves to replenish their reserves and honor all their demand deposit liabilities.

Unfortunately, there have been times when reserves in the financial system as a whole were inadequate, and there were a lot more loans for sale than there were buyers. The "runs" on banks and financial panics that resulted finally caused the Congress to establish a "banker's bank" (the Federal Reserve System, which is the subject of Chapter 13) with the enactment of the Federal Reserve Act of 1913. Before we investigate government regulation of the banking system, we need to survey other types of financial institutions.

FINANCIAL INSTITUTIONS

Major types of financial institutions include credit unions and savings and loan associations, which act as banks when they make loans based on accounts that are, effectively, demand deposits. Insurance companies and stock exchanges also facilitate efficient allocations of capital in a market economy. Important economic roles performed by financial institutions include (a) channeling funds from savers to investors, (b) providing secure places for savers to keep their deposits, and (c) facilitating flows and payments of funds (most payments are made through checking accounts).

Financial Intermediation

Channeling savings to investors is the single most important macroeconomic function of our financial system. Households allocate their after-tax incomes between consumption and saving. Rather than let your savings sit idle, you are probably willing to let other people use them if they pay you interest so that you ultimately receive more than they borrow. Financial institutions find borrowers willing to pay higher interest rates than must be paid to savers.

> *Financial intermediation occurs when financial institutions make the savings of households whose incomes exceed their spending available to investors, or to other households that wish to spend more on consumer goods than their incomes allow.*

Differences between interest paid by borrowers and that paid to savers generate income to the owners of financial institutions. Imagine how chaotic it would be if all savers had to seek out their own borrowers, and vice versa. Transaction costs might be insurmountable. How could borrowers find savers willing to entrust them with loans? If you were a saver, how would you locate people who wanted to borrow? How would you screen loan applicants to ensure a high probability of repayment?

Financial institutions specialize in evaluating the credit worthiness of loan applicants, and then they monitor borrowers. By spreading the risk of default across large numbers of loans, financial intermediaries are able to pay interest rates that will attract deposits from savers.

The Diversity of Financial Institutions

Different financial institutions use different methods to secure the savings of individuals, which then can be either loaned or invested directly. Since people have different ideas about the best way to save (or borrow) and firms differ in the types of debt they are willing to incur, it seems natural that various types of financial intermediaries have developed to meet these diverse needs. A second reason for the diversity of financial institutions is the mix of federal and state laws and regulation governing them. Because of major banking deregulation that began in 1980, many of these institutions are growing less distinct.

- **Commercial Banks** Full-service *commercial banks* provide more services to their depositors than simple maintenance of checking and savings accounts. Most banks offer a variety of personal and commercial loan services, issue bank credit cards such as MasterCard and Visa, and have trust departments available to administer wills and estates.

- **Thrift Institutions** Saving and loan associations, mutual savings banks, and credit unions are all called *thrift institutions*. The major difference between thrift institutions and commercial banks used to be that commercial banks offered checking accounts while thrift institutions could not. However, a major revision of our banking laws in 1980 made it possible for thrift institutions to offer accounts that are almost identical to bank checking accounts.

Most of the loans made by savings and loan associations and mutual savings banks are used to finance housing, although S&Ls are broadening the types of loans they make. Membership in a credit union is normally limited to the employees of a particular firm or members of a particular labor union or profession, although in some rural areas a geographic boundary determines eligibility for membership. Credit unions offer their members loans for many consumer purchases, including housing.

- **Insurance Companies**   Many people will bet a small amount of money on the outcome of the flip of a coin. However, only a few high rollers are willing to bet thousands of dollars with no better than even odds of winning. Most of us want the probable outcome of risky activities to favor us substantially, or we just don't want to play.

> **Risk aversion** occurs when people are willing to pay a premium to avoid risk.

Most of us are willing to pay money to avoid some of the financial consequences of taking risks, so **insurance companies** can sell us a guarantee against risk for a fee that is large enough to cover their claims and operating costs and still permit a profit. No one can predict whose house will burn down next, yours or your neighbor's. Thus, all insurance policy buyers make small contributions toward a fund that can be used to compensate the person whose house goes up in flames.

Insurance companies can provide this service and expect to make profits as long as the fee (premium) is greater than the amount they might have to pay, multiplied by the probability of payment. Vast amounts of money are paid to insurance companies as premiums for life, auto, and health insurance, or as contributions to pension funds, many of which are administered by insurance companies. These funds are made available for loans to business firms or are invested directly by the insurance companies.

- **Securities Markets**   Brokers who buy and sell financial securities also provide financial intermediation.

> **Securities** include paper assets such as stocks and bonds. A **bond** is simply an IOU issued by a corporation or government agency that pays interest to the lender. A **share of stock** is a claim to partial ownership of a corporation.

TABLE 12   Financial Intermediaries

| | Commercial Banks | Thrift Institutions | | Credit Unions | Insurance Companies | Securities Markets |
| | | **Savings and Loans** | | | | |
		Mutual Savings Banks				

Primary sources of funds (liabilities)	Deposits
	  Checking accounts
	  Savings accounts
		Deposits
		  Shares (savings)
		  Checking accounts
		  Other
				Deposits
				  Shares
				  Checking accounts
					Insurance policies	Securities dealers act primarily as intermediaries and hold few deposits

Primary uses of funds (assets)	Business loans
	Consumer loans
	  Automobiles
	  Home equity loans
	  Furniture and
	    appliances
	  Education
	  Personal
		Home mortgages
		  Home equity
		    loans and
		    Improvements
				Consumer loans
				  Autos, etc.
					Business loans
					  Real estate
					  Direct financial
					    investment
						Stockbrokers and investment bankers charge brokerage fees for getting savers (purchasers) together with the business firms that do the direct economic investment with the funds made available

Notes	Banks "create" money by crediting your account, when they extend a loan to you	Major function is to finance housing, although business construction is an increasingly importantactivity		Focus on consumer loans for members only	Insurance company premiums exceed their expected payouts, people buy insurance because they are risk averse	

Most corporations and government agencies do not solicit you directly for funds that you might be willing to lend. Instead, they typically leave this specialized sort of solicitation to brokers, who communicate offers to buy or sell securities through stock exchanges. Although the New York Stock Exchange (also known as Wall Street) is the best known, there are a number of smaller regional stock exchanges.

Table 12 summarizes the different roles played by important financial intermediaries. Be aware, however, that differences among these institutions are increasingly blurred because of deregulation. These trends are somewhat controversial because lessening of regulation may have helped set the stage for a wave of financial collapse (e.g., 1980s savings and loan boondoggles). This deregulation was accompanied by a shift of regulatory authority from numerous smaller regulatory agencies into the hands of the world's most influential financial regulator: our central bank, the Federal Reserve System, which is the topic of Chapter 13.

CHAPTER REVIEW: KEY POINTS

1. **Barter** requires a *double coincidence of wants*—trade can occur only if each party has what the other wants and if divisibility poses no problems.

2. **Money** ensures this double coincidence of wants; the seller will accept money because of what it will buy, while the buyer is willing to exchange money (and, thus, all else it will buy) for the good or service in question.

3. Money facilitates specialization and exchange by decreasing transaction costs. The more sophisticated the financial system, the greater the level of production and consumption and the higher the standard of living.

4. Money is a **medium of exchange**. It is used for most transactions in monetary economies.

5. Money is a **measure of value**. Used as a standard unit of account, it is the common denominator for pricing goods and services.

6. Money is a **store of value**. It is among the most nominally secure of all assets people can use to hold their wealth.

7. Money is a **standard of deferred payment**. Serving as a link between the past, present, and future, it is used as a measure of credit to execute contracts calling for future payments.

8. **Liquidity** is negatively related to the transaction costs incurred in exchanges of assets. *Time, certainty regarding price*, and the *quality of information in a market* are all dimensions of liquidity. Assets are liquid if transaction costs are low, *illiquid* if transaction costs are high.

9. **Commodity monies** (precious metals, stones, or arrowheads) have values that are independent of what they will buy. **Fiat money** (paper currency) is valuable only because it is money; its use is based on *faith*.

10. The profit governments make from printing money or stamping coins is called **seigniorage**.

11. According to Gresham's Law, *bad money drives out good*.

12. The very narrowly defined money supply (**M1**) is the total of (*a*) **currency** (coins and bills) in the hands of the nonbanking public plus (*b*) **demand deposits** (checking accounts of private individuals, firms, and nonfederal government units in financial institutions).

13. Some highly liquid assets are viewed as *near-monies* and are included in broader definitions of the **money supply** (**M2** and **M3**) by monetary analysts who believe the spending of the public can be predicted better if these assets are included. Examples of such highly liquid assets

include short-term *time deposits* (savings accounts) or *certificates of deposit* (CDs). The assets included in money supplies defined more broadly than M1 are judgmental, because these assets are not mediums of exchange.

14. Banks "*create*" money through loan-based expansions of demand deposits (checking account money). They make loans based on currency they hold as **reserves**, and these loans take the form of new demand deposit money.

15. Banks hold reserves that are far less than their deposit liabilities. The larger the proportion of deposits held as either excess or required reserves, the smaller are the money multiplier and resulting money supply, given some fixed total amount of reserves.

16. The **potential money multiplier** (m_p) equals $1/rr$, where rr is the banking system's planned or legally required reserves as a percentage of deposits. The *actual money multiplier* is much smaller because (*a*) households and firms hold currency that could be used as a base for the money creation process were this currency held in bank vaults as reserves against deposits, and (*b*) banks hold excess reserves to meet withdrawals of deposits.

17. The actual money multiplier (m_a) equals MS/MB, where MS is the money supply and MB is the **monetary base**, or *high-powered money*. Naturally, $MS = m_a MB$.

18. *Financial institutions* facilitate flows and payments of funds and provide secure places for savers' deposits. Their most important economic function is to channel funds from savers to financial investors and other borrowers through a process called **financial intermediation**. Commercial banks, savings and loan associations, mutual savings banks, credit unions, insurance companies, and stock exchanges are all financial intermediaries.

QUESTIONS FOR THOUGHT AND DISCUSSION

1. If the Obsidian Bank receives a deposit of $50,000 and the required reserve ratio equals 0.25 for all banks, what is the maximum amount of money Obsidian can loan? What does the potential money multiplier equal? How much additional money could be created by the entire banking system from the $50,000 deposit?

2. Money is (*a*) a medium of exchange, (*b*) a unit of account or measure of value, (*c*) a store of value, and (*d*) a standard of deferred payment. There are items that perform some, but not all, of these functions. Which functions do credit cards (Visa, MasterCard, Discover) serve? Which are not served? How about savings deposits? Gold or silver? Stocks and bonds?

3. How important is the degree of liquidity in determining which assets qualify as money? List the following items according to their degree of liquidity, from least liquid to most liquid: (*a*) dollar bill, (*b*) U.S. government bond, (*c*) house, (*d*) car, (*e*) pedigreed dog, (*f*) television set, (*g*) savings account, and (*h*) human skills.

4. What financial barriers might confront people who live in different societies with different monetary systems and who wish to trade with one another? Would it be advantageous if the entire world used a common currency? What do you think are some of the reasons we do not have a world currency?

5. In 1933, Adolph Hitler decreed that the old German deutsche mark was worthless and could be exchanged at a fixed rate for new reichsmarks. The British redeemed their old currency in the late 1960s, replacing it with a "metric" currency. What circumstances might make it appropriate to completely withdraw one currency from circulation and replace it with a new currency?

Chapter 13

Central Banking: The Federal Reserve System

Whoever controls the volume of money . . . is absolute master of all industry and commerce.

President James A. Garfield

Efficient financial institutions are vital for macroeconomic performance. Money binds together individual markets for goods and resources. A country's central bank is charged with ensuring the efficiency and stability of the financial sector.

> The **central bank** of a country: (a) controls the volume of money in circulation, (b) performs the government's banking functions, (c) regulates banks and other financial institutions, and (d) serves as a "banker's bank"—holding deposits from commercial banks and making loans to them as needed.

The **Federal Reserve System (Fed)** is the United States' central bank, and it may be the most powerful and independent of all U.S. government agencies. During hearings on Fed policies, one senator compared getting a straight answer out of the chairman of the Fed's Board of Governors to "nailing a chocolate cream pie to a wall."

The structure of the Fed and the tools it uses to control the money supply and shape financial conditions are examined in this chapter. We also survey different types of financial institutions, the major goals of financial regulators, and the consequences of certain policies intended to alter macroeconomic activity.

THE PURPOSES OF FINANCIAL REGULATIONS

Financial institutions are not lenders per se, but merely act as intermediaries between savers and borrowers. Nervous depositors sometimes try to withdraw all their savings simultaneously, but this is not always possible. With fractional reserve banking, a bank's assets (loans outstanding) are not collectible until the date due, but liabilities (e.g., checking deposits) are typically payable on demand. A related problem occurs when inept or dishonest officers of financial institutions misuse the funds we entrust to them.

Financial intermediation can be volatile. Savings and loans toppled like rows of dominoes amid widespread charges of fraud in the 1980s. It is not surprising that financial institutions are regulated more tightly than any other industry except, perhaps, secret weapons research or atomic energy. Thus, major goals for a central bank include (a) protection of depositors' savings, (b) macroeconomic stability, and (c) promotion of efficiency.

In this context, efficiency requires minimizing the costs of financial intermediation, or the bankers' "spread" (i.e., differences between the costs of loans to borrowers and the interest incomes received by depositors—the ultimate lenders). This is the financial equivalent of the principle that efficiency requires producing all services at the lowest possible opportunity cost. Unfortunately, protecting people's savings and ensuring economic stability can conflict with financial efficiency.

• **Early Central Banks** Many of this nation's founders feared that a central bank would concentrate economic and political power in the hands of a few. Alexander Hamilton's persuasive skills were stretched to the limit to establish the first Bank of the United States shortly after the U.S. Constitution was ratified. This central bank replaced a system in which the federal government, 13 states, and many private banks issued different currencies. The phrase "not worth a continental" crept into our language after money issued by the Continental Congress became worthless. The dollar became sound only when the Bank honored federal debts incurred during the Revolutionary War.

The Bank of the United States was privately owned and operated, but it was also the government's bank because it (a) stored tax revenues, (b) paid the government's obligations, and (c) arranged loans to and from the government. The Bank was unpopular with most westerners and agricultural interests, who felt it served only the rich "eastern establishment." The death of Hamilton and ascendance of his political rival, Thomas Jefferson, led in 1811 to the end of our first experiment with central banking.

The Second Bank of the United States, chartered in 1816, was operated by Nicholas Biddle, a member of a prominent Philadelphia family. Despite some initial success, President Andrew Jackson vetoed the act to recharter it. In 1836, the original charter expired. Nicholas Biddle was disgraced in a minor financial scandal, and the bank's collapse precipitated the financial crash of 1837. For the next 75 years, the American economy experienced substantial but erratic growth without a central bank.

THE FEDERAL RESERVE SYSTEM

The U.S. economy prospered from the American Revolution until the Great Depression despite financial crises roughly every 20 to 25 years. Most financial panics ushered in periods of stagnation. A wave of bank failures in 1906 and 1907 led to establishment of a third central bank, the Federal Reserve System, in 1913. Among the Fed's objectives is to act as a "lender of last resort." This means the Fed lends money to inherently sound banks so they can survive bank runs when financial panics drive armies of depositors to demand withdrawals.

The seven members of the Fed's **Board of Governors** are appointed to staggered 14-year terms because Congress feared the central bank might become highly politicized. Each president and Congress has limited power over the Fed because they appoint only one new member of the Board of Governors every other year. Board members were traditionally bankers, causing some people to question how diligent they are as public watchdogs. Recent presidents have drawn increasing numbers of governors from the general public, including more than a few economists.

The Fed (in concert with the Comptroller of the Currency, the Federal Deposit Insurance Corporation, and various state government agencies) audits banks to guard against fraud and enforces a set of complex regulations. Among its other services to the banking community, the Fed processes checks drawn on one bank and deposited elsewhere. The Fed's key role, however, is to conduct monetary policy. Before we examine monetary policymaking, you need to know a bit more about the structure of the Fed.

Federal Reserve Bank Districts

The 12 regional districts of the Federal Reserve System are depicted in Figure 1. Each district has a primary bank and one or more branch offices. Check any dollar bills you have on hand; many bills travel far from their points of issue.

Federal Reserve Banks and their branches do not serve the general public directly. These "bankers' banks" help member banks clear checks drawn on other banks, make loans to bankers, and try to facilitate efficiency in our economy's financial sector. The Fed operates under the fiction that it is "privately owned" by federally chartered private banks, but it is actually an arm of government created by Congress. Its decisions have the force of law, and all returns on its financial investments exceeding 6% annually must be paid to the U.S. Treasury.

• **Member Banks** Roughly 13,000 privately owned banks or other intermediaries that issue checking accounts (e.g., S&Ls) now operate in the United States, of which fewer than half are national banks chartered by the Comptroller of the Currency. *National banks* must be members of the Federal Reserve System; *state banks* (chartered by individual states) may, upon approval, qualify as *member banks*. The Fed now sets legal reserve requirements on deposits in *all* banklike financial institutions, so it has considerable direct power over most of our financial system.

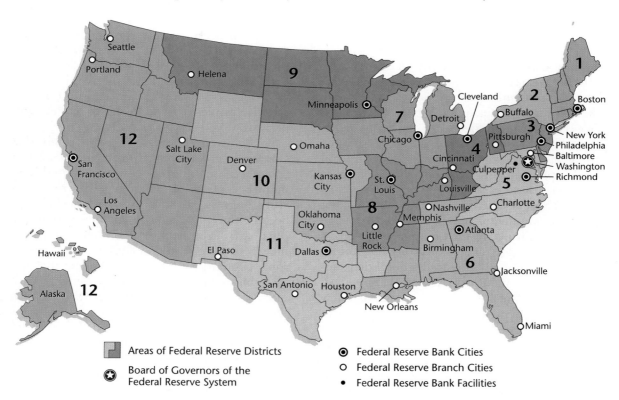

Source: *Federal Reserve Bulletin.*
The Federal Reserve System consists of 12 districts. Each district has a Federal Reserve Bank, and most also have Branch Banks.

FIGURE 1   Federal Reserve Branch Banks

Organization of the Fed

The Chairman of the Federal Reserve System is supposedly only a "first among equals." Like the Supreme Court's chief justice, he nominally has only one vote but, in fact, exercises a disproportionate amount of power. Of course, effectiveness in controlling monetary policy depends on the chair's personality, the effectiveness of the Federal Reserve staff, and on the dynamics of relationships among the various governors.

Congress established the Fed as a pseudo-private organization to shield it from political chicanery that could distort its regulatory and stabilization policies. As a "private" organization, Fed member banks elect six of the nine directors of each District Bank; the other three are appointed by the Board of Governors. The Board of Directors of District Banks elect District Bank presidents. But real policymaking power is exercised by the *Federal Open Market Committee (FOMC)*—all seven members of the Board of Governors plus the president of the New York District Bank. Four other District Bank presidents rotate on the committee. The FOMC has enormous control over our entire financial system through its conduct of monetary policy. Committee members' long terms of office and votes (7 of 11) give the real clout within the FOMC to the Board of Governors, especially the chairman, as indicated in Figure 2.

Economists focus on incentives. Should our central bank maximize profits? Should monetary policymakers be subjected to political pressures in our democracy? Before we tackle these problems, let us see why the answers to these questions are so important.

TOOLS OF THE FED

The Federal Reserve System's major tools to control the money supply and broad financial conditions are (*a*) reserve requirements, (*b*) open-market operations, and (*c*) discounting operations. Secondary tools of the Fed include controls over stock market credit and moral suasion ("jawboning"). Day in and day out, the Fed actively uses open-market operations to implement its ever-changing policies. Reserve requirements and discounting operations are important, though generally less frequently used, instruments of monetary policy.

Reserve Requirements

A bank's reserves can be kept in its vaults or on deposit at Federal Reserve banks.

*The Federal Reserve System sets the **reserve-requirement ratio (rr)**, a legal floor on the percentage of a bank's deposits that must be held in reserves.*

Banks cannot survive for long if reserves sink to the legal minimum; they need excess reserves to accommodate any outflows of funds. Otherwise, they could not meet any demands for withdrawals of demand deposits (DDs) without being in trouble with the Fed.

bank reserves = required reserves (rr x DD) + excess reserves (XR)

Note that all reserves available to meet the Fed's reserve requirements are *bank reserves*, which include both *excess reserves* and *required reserves*. The overall banking system usually operates with very few excess reserves, however, because banks lend and borrow money from each other daily through the privately operated *federal funds market*.

• **Electronic Banking and Real Money** On average, people today handle much less cash relative to their income than was typical in earlier times. Electronic deposits of paychecks and payments of bills are increasingly common, automatic teller machines (ATMs) are sprouting like weeds as ready sources of cash, and credit cards have replaced cash for many purchases. Therefore, a rising proportion of our money is stored in banks. But do banks keep much "real money" in their vaults? If *real money* is interpreted as meaning bills and coins, the answer is "not much." Banks keep enough currency on hand to meet their depositors' demands for cash withdrawals, and that is about it.

FIGURE 2 The Federal Reserve System's Roles in the Financial Sector

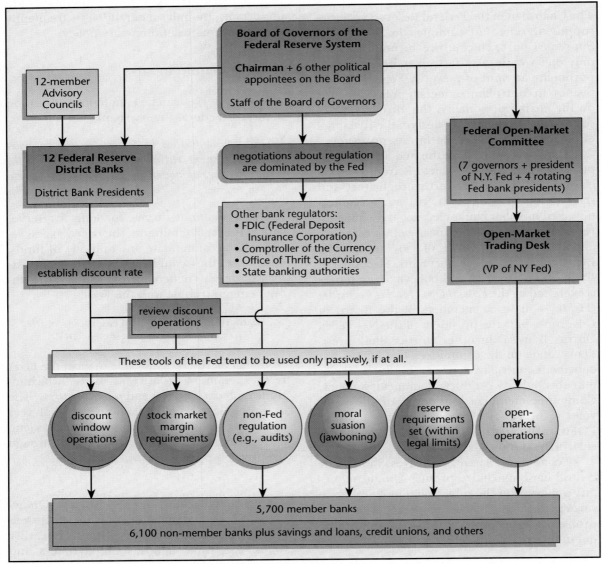

This figure may look a bit like a formal organization chart, but it actually illustrates the Fed's pivotal role in the conduct of monetary policy. Other government agencies help stabilize and shape financial activity by, for example, (a) chartering banks and other financial intermediaries, (b) auditing their books, or (c) steering flows of financial investments (into, e.g., low-income housing), but the Fed's broad powers make it the dominant player in regulating financial intermediaries and controlling the money supply.

A typical bank now holds deposits of well over $50 million. Where do they store all these funds? You learned in the previous chapter that banks in a fractional reserve system hold only a portion of their deposits as reserves. However, no bank would ever hold tens of millions of dollars in cash—there is no sense in tempting thieves. Consequently, banks deposit most of their reserves with Federal Reserve Branch or District Banks.

Even these Fed banks do not hold many deposits in the form of cash; keeping track of inventories of tons and tons of the green stuff would be a monumental problem. You know that your bank account is simply a few electronic impulses stored in the bank's computer. The Fed does the same thing with reserves banks keep on deposit at Branch or District Banks—it is all in the computer. Roughly two-thirds of the nation's money supply now exists only in computers.

● **Reserve Requirements and the Money Multiplier** One way the Fed adjusts the money supply is by changing the reserve-requirement ratio (rr). If the Fed *increases* the reserve-requirement ratio, then the potential money multiplier, $1/rr$ falls. The smaller potential money multiplier (m_p) means the total reserves in the banking system will support only smaller potential totals of loan-based demand deposits. Conversely, a *decrease* in the reserve-requirement ratio enables banks to increase the money supply through expansion of demand-deposit-based loans.

Most banks try to hold roughly the same percentage of excess reserves against demand deposits no matter what happens to the reserve-requirement ratio. Why? Because fluctuations of bank deposits depend on people's behavior, not on the Fed's reserve requirements. Notice that the reserve-requirement ratio does not influence the total amount of reserves in the banking system. Instead, it affects the potential multiplier, m_p. Naturally, whenever the m_p changes, the actual money multiplier (m_a) moves in the same direction.

The amounts of excess reserves held by banks are *negatively* related to the expected profitability of lending any excess reserves, but *positively* related to the expected costs of acquiring reserves should borrowing be necessary to meet the Fed's reserve requirements. In other words, the percentage of deposits held as excess reserves will be *negatively related* to the *difference* between (*a*) the interest rates banks can charge borrowers and (*b*) the interest rates banks themselves must pay to borrow reserves from other banks or the Fed.

The reserve-requirement ratio (rr) is the Fed's most powerful tool. Suppose that the rr were increased from 1/6 (16.7%) to 1/5 (20%), a change of 3.3 points. The potential money supply would fall by 1/6 (m_p falls from 6 to 5). Curiously, this powerful tool is seldom used. Reserve-requirement ratios have been changed only about 30 times since the Great Depression because the very power of such changes makes it difficult to predict the magnitude of their effect. A second tool of the Fed, open-market operations, is the best tool available for the day-to-day conduct of monetary policy. It permits more subtle changes in the money supply.

Open-Market Operations (OMO)

The Fed's most important tool, open-market operations, links monetary policy with the bonds issued by the U.S. Treasury to finance federal budget deficits.

> ***Open-market operations (OMO)*** *entail buying and selling U.S. Treasury securities and are used to increase or decrease the size of the monetary base.*

The monetary base (MB) is defined as total currency held by the nonbanking public plus reserves held by banks: MB = currency + bank reserves. Thus, the monetary base is the foundation for our money supply because the money creation process builds from reserves in the banking system.

The Federal Open Market Committee (FOMC) adjusts the size of the monetary base through *open-market* purchases or sales of U.S. Treasury securities. To increase the money supply by expanding the monetary base, the FOMC's "open-market desk" buys Treasury bonds, primarily from banks, but also from private individuals or nonbank firms. The FOMC sells bonds to reduce the monetary base. Funds the Fed pays to nonbank sellers are invariably deposited in banks, however, so they end up as bank reserves. Similarly, private buyers of bonds withdraw funds from banks to pay for their purchases. Thus, regardless of with whom the Fed deals, the effects on total bank reserves and the money supply are similar.

When the Fed buys bonds, bank reserves are increased and the banking system will increase loan-based demand deposits in accord with the money creation process discussed previously. You may wonder where the Fed gets the money to buy the bonds. The answer is that the Fed can print new currency, or it can simply credit the reserve accounts of the private banks via computer at one of the Federal Reserve District Banks.

T-account entries for an expansionary open-market transaction are shown in Table 1. When the Fed buys $1,000 in Treasury bonds from Bank A, the Federal Reserve Bank credits reserves held for Bank A by $1,000; the Fed's assets are debited by $1,000 in Treasury bonds; Bank A's assets change from $1,000 in Treasury bonds to $1,000 in new reserves. Bank A views the sale of the bond to the Fed just as it would a payback of a loan by a private borrower. Note, however, that this "payoff" creates new reserves for the banking system as a whole, while repayment of a private loan does not. These new reserves can then be loaned to private borrowers, creating new demand deposit money via the expansionary money multiplier process.

In Chapter 12, you learned that a decline in the monetary base underpinning the money supply precipitates a "money destruction" process. If the Fed wants to shrink the money supply, it can sell bonds to commercial banks. This reduction of the monetary base sops up excess reserves and may even threaten to cut into banks' required reserves. The amount of loan-based demand deposits falls as banks try to rebuild their reserves, turning down applications for new loans or renewals of old ones. The *money destruction* process following a Fed sale of Treasury bonds precisely reverses the money creation process. If the positive numbers in Table 1 were negative, and vice versa, the table would illustrate a contractionary open-market operation.

You may wonder how the Fed can persuade banks or individuals to sell bonds when the FOMC conducts expansionary open-market operations. A bidding process is used; the sellers are those willing to offer desired amounts of bonds at the lowest prices. No matter how high the prices are, the Fed buys the bonds, as Focus 1 illustrates. When the Fed wants to withdraw reserves from the banking system to reduce the money supply, it sells some Treasury bonds from its portfolio. The Fed takes the highest bids for bonds it sells, no matter how low the bids are.

Actually, the open-market desk of the FOMC both buys and sells bonds every business day, primarily to adjust the maturity dates of the bonds it holds, but also, occasionally, to mask the direction of its policies.

1. If the Fed buys more bonds than it sells, total bank reserves are increased and the money creation process leads to monetary growth.
2. If the Fed sells more bonds than it buys, reserves are reduced and the money destruction process causes the money supply to shrink.

Open-market operations ultimately affect the money supply *only* through changes in the amounts of reserves in the banking system, *not* through changes in the money multiplier. The maximum possible value of the multiplier (m_p) is determined by the reserve-requirement ratio (rr). The Fed's discounting operations, however, affect both the size of the monetary base (MB) and the value of the actual money multiplier (m_a).

TABLE 1   T-Account Changes for a Typical Open-Market Transaction

Federal Reserve Bank	
Assets	**Liabilities**
+$1,000 Treasury bonds	+$1,000 Reserves held for Bank A
Member Bank A	
Assets	**Liabilities**
−$1,000 Treasury bonds +$1,000 Loanable reserves	No change

The Go-Around:
An Expansionary Open-Market Operation

The time is 4:40 PM on a Wednesday in mid-November. The place is the Federal Reserve Bank of New York's trading room on the eighth floor. The manager of the Open Market Account reaffirms with trading officers an earlier decision to buy about $3 billion of Treasury bills. The banking system clearly needs additional reserves to meet increased public demands for currency and deposits as holiday shopping crests near the end of the quarter. After a brief discussion, the manager authorizes the operation.

The officer-in-charge at the trading desk turns to the Fed's securities traders, who sit before phone consoles linked to dealers in U.S. government securities. "We're asking for offerings of all bills for regular delivery," she says, which means delivery and payment will take place the next day, on Thursday. Each trader has vertical strips on which offerings will be recorded from dealers. Ed, one of the group, presses a button on his phone, sounding a buzzer on the console of a government securities dealer. "Jane," Ed says, "we want offerings of bills for regular delivery."

Jane replies, "I'll be right back." She turns and yells, "The Fed is in,

asking for all bills for delivery tomorrow." Information screens around the world flash the news, and salespeople begin ringing customers to see if they want to offer any bills. Meanwhile, Jane checks with the trading manager of her firm to see how aggressively she should price the firm's own securities.

Twenty minutes later Jane rings back. "Ed, I can offer $15 million in bills maturing February 9 at 5.20%, $40 million March 13 bills at 5.42, $25 million March 20s at 5.44, and another 25 at 5.46. I'll sell $75 million July 13s at 6.12 and another 100 at 6.09. I can offer $20 million September 21s at 6.25 and 50 October 16s at 6.28. All for delivery tomorrow."

Ed reads back each offering to double check, then says, "Can I have those firms?" "Sure." Each trader quickly records offerings on the preprinted strips. The officer-in-charge arrays individual dealer strips on an inclined board atop a stand-up counter. A quick tally shows that dealers have offered $13.3 billion of bills for regular delivery, that is, on Thursday.

The officer and a colleague compare interest rates across the different maturities, targeting those with high yields (and thus,

low prices) in relation to adjoining issues. She circles any special bargains with a red pencil, and other offers with yields on or above a yield curve she draws mentally through heavily offered issues. Her associate keeps a running tab of the amounts being bought. When the desired volume has been circled and crosschecked, individual strips are returned to the traders, who quickly ring up dealers. Ed says, "Jane, we'll take the $25 million March 20s at 5.44, the 75 July 13s at 10.12, and the 50 October 16s at 6.28 for regular delivery. A total of $150 million. No thanks on the rest."

Less than an hour after launching the operation, all follow-up calls have been completed. The Trading Desk has bought $3,009 million of Treasury bills. Only the paperwork remains. The traders write up tickets authorizing the accounting section to instruct the Reserve Bank's Government Bond Department to receive and pay for the bills the Fed has purchased.

Original source: Paul Meek, *Open Market Operations* (New York: Federal Reserve Bank of New York, 1985). Condensed and updated by the authors. Reprinted (after editing) by permission of the Federal Reserve Bank of New York.

Discounting Operations

The Fed is a bankers' bank. When banks lack sufficient reserves to meet reserve requirements or want more excess reserves, they can borrow funds from the *discount windows* of the Fed's District or Branch Banks. Loans from the Fed become a part of a bank's reserves, increasing the monetary base and, consequently, the money supply.

*The interest rate the Fed charges bankers is called the **discount rate (d)**.*

Most bank borrowing from the Fed is to cover temporary deficiencies. Whether banks will have deficient reserves, however, depends strongly on the discount rate. Whenever the discount rate (d) is substantially less than market interest rates (i), the monetary base grows; the

Fed extends credit (reserves) to banks, which allows bankers to expand their loans and demand deposits. When the discount rate the bank pays is below the interest rate it charges on loans, it is a bit like trading nickels for dimes.

On the other hand, a discount rate that greatly exceeds market rates of interest penalizes bankers forced to borrow from the Fed because of unforeseen withdrawals. Banks consequently try to avoid any need to borrow by holding greater excess reserves (although they often avoid borrowing from a District Bank by borrowing through the federal funds market). Thus the actual multiplier m_a shrinks as the differences between the discount rate and the market interest rate grows.

All else being equal,

1. When the discount rate is raised, banks borrow less, reducing total reserves or limiting their increase. Banks also lend less, so excess reserves in individual banks grow while the actual money multiplier and money supply decline.
2. When the Fed decreases the discount rate, banks borrow more from the Fed and cut holdings of excess reserves; this increases the actual money multiplier and money supply.

The Fed's Secondary Tools

Although the reserve-requirement ratio, open-market operations, and the discount rate are the major tools at the Fed's disposal, other devices in the Fed's toolbox help it control financial markets and economic activity:

1. The Fed sets *margin requirements* to control stock market credit.
2. The Fed uses *moral suasion* (it "jawbones"), which means it rages at people or institutions who do things it does not like.

Until the 1980s, the Fed could also (*a*) regulate credit to consumers and business firms during wars or crises, and (*b*) set the maximum interest rates payable to depositors. Congress rescinded both these Fed powers during a wave of deregulation.

• **Margin Requirements** Many people blamed overspeculation caused by buying on margin for

the stock market crash of 1929 and the Great Depression. In the 1920s, stock could be purchased with down payments of as little as 10%.

*The Fed sets the **margin requirement** (the percentage down payment required) for purchases of corporate financial securities.*

Many 1920s' investors used almost all their assets for the 10% margin payments on stock. When the stock market crashed, these investors were required to make up the losses. Since they only had 10% of the original value of the stock invested, these additional payments were impossible for many. When they could not produce the additional funds, they were wiped out. In the aftermath of 1929, the Federal Reserve System was granted power to regulate *margin requirements*, which have hovered around 50% for decades. Presumably, higher margin requirements squelch speculation, and lower margin requirements stimulate speculation.

Evidence is sparse, however, that margin requirements influence stock prices very much. Indeed, a powerful theory suggests that prudent financial investors will offset any speculative bubble caused by stock buyers overly enthused by low margin requirements. Suppose financial investors expected a 10% return on stocks but a 12% return on equally risky real estate. Funds would flow into real estate from the stock market. The stock market would fall a bit, and real estate prices would rise until the returns were equalized at, say, 11%.

These sorts of adjustments will cure even minor overspeculation in stocks. If low margin requirements prompt speculation that boosts stock prices slightly, the expected returns (e.g., dividends) per dollar invested in stocks decline. This makes real estate or other investments comparatively more attractive to prudent investors, so money will flow from the stock market until the returns from all investments are equated. Overspeculation in stocks because of low margin requirements is, thus, eliminated automatically.

• **Moral Suasion** Self-restraints on increases in prices or union wages are commonly advocated by presidents trying to contain inflation. In 1992, President Bush hammered credit card companies for "high" interest rates that inhibited growth out of the recession that ultimately may have cost him reelection. Little evidence exists, however, that his vocal displeasure did much to lower credit card interest rates.

Moral suasion *is oratory or the threat of tighter regulation used when policymakers want people or institutions to act against their individual interests (or to see their interests in a different light).*

The Fed occasionally has tried to jawbone banks into expanding or contracting credit, but economists tend to be somewhat skeptical that appeals to the public interest are effective. On the other hand, President Clinton's appeal to drug companies to reduce rates of price increases for prescription drugs has had some apparent effect. Local gas companies often ask people to reduce thermostats during cold snaps to preserve supplies, and people often comply.

The Fed's moral suasion may have some effect, however, because it is backed up by the power to audit and otherwise harass banks. A major problem is that moral suasion is less predictable than virtually any other tool. Although once common, in recent years the Federal Reserve System has seldom exhorted bankers to do much that is contrary to their own interests.

Which Tools Are Used?

The Federal Reserve System strongly influences the money supply, but it lacks precise and direct control. The Fed could not, for example, track bills that might have dissolved if you ever forgot to empty your pockets before putting clothes through a washing machine. Nor can it precisely dictate the loans banks make. We indicated earlier that the money supply (*MS*) is the product of the money multiplier (m_a) and the monetary base (*MB*):

$$MS = m_a \times MB$$

The Fed can actively change the discount rate or reserve-requirement ratios to try to manipulate the value of the actual money multiplier and thereby change the money supply. Alternatively, it can use open-market operations (and, to a lesser extent, discount operations) to

vary the monetary base in attempts to alter the money supply. Table 2 summarizes how tools of the Fed affect the money supply by altering the behavior of banks and the public.

If the Fed does not independently determine the money supply, what other groups have influence, and how? The Fed does tightly control the monetary base through open-market operations. The public can affect the money multiplier through its holding of cash. As private stores of cash grow, currency available for bank reserves shrinks; the actual money multiplier and the money supply fall because the money expansion process only applies to currency in bank vaults or reserves at the Fed. Banks also may unintentionally alter the actual money multiplier by varying their percentages of excess reserves: the greater the excess reserves held by banks, the smaller will be the actual money multiplier and the money supply.

If private activities can alter the actual money multiplier and thwart the desire of the Fed to change the money supply, then which tools most effectively accomplish the Fed's goals? Any versatile do-it-yourselfer accumulates some tools that rust because they are seldom, if ever, used. This analogy applies to moral suasion and to changes in stock market margin requirements, which are used only rarely. Reserve-requirement ratios are seldom varied, and then only slightly. They are too powerful to be very useful.

The discount rate has been pegged slightly above interest rates in the federal fund market for almost 30 years. This prompts banks to borrow from each other through the privately operated federal funds market and discourages borrowing from the Fed. The discount rate is usually changed two or three times a year to reflect changes in interest rates in the federal funds market. Changes in the discount rate normally are not intended to affect the money supply directly, because the Fed wants the actual money multiplier to be constant. Thus, discount rate changes are intended to stabilize the percentage of deposits held as excess reserves.

Open-market operations are the best tool to control the money supply by directly altering the reserves in the banking system. In the long run, open-market operations do not affect the

TABLE 2 Fed Tools and Their Effects

Tool Used	Potential Money Multiplier ($m_p = 1/rr$)	Excess Reserves Ratio ($xr = XR/DD$)	Actual Money Multiplier ($m_a = MS/MB$)	Monetary Base (MB)	Currency in the Hands of the Nonbanking Public	Bank Reserves	Loans, Demand Deposits and Money Supply (MI)
Reserve requirement ratios (rr)							
Raise rr	lower	no change	lower	no change	no change	no change	lower
Lower	higher	no change	higher	no change	no change	no change	higher
Open-market operations							
Buys bonds	no change	no change	no change	higher	higher	higher	higher
Sells bonds	no change	no change	no change	lower	lower	lower	lower
Discounting operations							
Lower rate	no change	lower	higher	higher	higher	higher	higher
Raise rate	no change	higher	lower	lower	lower	lower	lower
Moral suasion	no change	ambiguous	ambiguous	no change	no change	no change	ambiguous
Stock market margin requirements	Lower margin requirements presumably cause more stock market speculation, while higher margins presumably discourage speculation. There is, however, little statistical support for this proposition and a powerful theory that refutes it.						

Note: Unless interest rates paid on deposits change, households and firms are assumed to keep stable proportions of their money holdings in the forms of cash and demand deposits respectively.

money multiplier. Active changes in reserve-requirement ratios or the discount rate operate primarily through changes in the actual money multiplier, but these sorts of manipulations have yielded erratic and unsatisfactory results when used. Open-market operations are now the Fed's most-used tool.

FINANCIAL INSTITUTIONS IN TRANSITION

Markets are becoming more interconnected. Financial instruments are becoming more complex: Distinctions between banks and other financial intermediaries are blurring; integration of economies and financial markets is increasing.[1]

Alan Greenspan (1993)
Chairman of the Federal Reserve System

A maze of state and federal laws historically limited competition among bankers. Rural banks once depended primarily on local customers and nearby farmers, while banks in big cities catered to their own neighborhoods. The expansion of interstate trade generated pressure

---

[1]A. Greenspan, "No Single Regulator for Banks," *Wall Street Journal* 15 Dec. 1993, p. A14.

TABLE 3   Foreign Exchange Rates—Key Gross-Currency Exchange Rules for Major Countries

	Dollar	Pound	SFranc	Guilder	Peso	Yen	Lira	D-Mark	FFranc	CdnDollar
Canada	1.3576	2.0221	.94199	.70306	.41772	.01285	.00080	.78976	.23229	
France	5.8445	8.705	4.0553	3.0267	1.79831	.05532	.00346	3.3999		4.3050
Germany	1.7190	2.5605	1.1928	.89021	.52892	.01627	.00102		.29412	1.2662
Italy	1687.0	2512.8	1170.55	873.64	519.08			981.38	288.65	1242.6
Japan	105.65	157.37	73.307	54.713	32.508		.06263	61.460	18.077	77.82
Mexico	3.2500	4.8409	2.2551	1.6831		.03076	.00193	1.8906	.5561	2.3939
Netherlands	1.9310	2.8762	1.3399		.59415	.01828	.00114	1.1233	.33040	1.4224
Switzerland	1.4412	2.1467		.74635	.44345	.01364	.00085	.83839	.24659	1.0616
U.K.	.67137		.46584	.34768	.20657	.00635	.00040	.39056	.11487	.49452
U.S.		1.4895	.69387	.51787	.30769	.00947	.00059	.58173	.17110	.73650

Source: *Dow Jones Telerate, Inc.*

These tables showing cross-currency exchange rates appear in the *Wall Street Journal* and other major newspapers almost every day. Note that, paralleling Table 1 in Chapter 12, the numbers below the blank diagonal are reciprocals of numbers above the diagonal. For example, the U.S. dollar's exchange rate for the Canadian dollar is shown in row 1, column 1, while the Canadian dollar's exchange rate for the U.S. dollar is in the last row, last column.

for legal reforms to allow banks to merge and to establish branches. Thus, banking is increasingly concentrated in the hands of bigger banks, many of which are owned by bank holding companies that operate what are effectively branch banks located across state lines. However, pressure for financial reform continues, largely because of growth in international competition.

The growth of international trade is apparent in our diets, the clothes we wear, and the cars we drive. Internationalization of financial markets is proceeding at an even faster clip.

Annual GDP in the United States is roughly $7 trillion, and *annual* gross world product is about $35 trillion, but *every day*, almost $1 trillion in foreign currencies is traded in foreign exchange markets.

Exchange rates (the relative prices of different currencies) for some of the world's more important currencies are shown in Table 3. Arbitrage and speculation to ensure that exchange rates are virtually identical in all countries underpin the bulk of these vast international flows of funds. Some of these flows, however, reallocate economic investment from countries with net saving into countries where investments in physical capital appear more profitable.

The accelerating speed at which money changes hands in international money markets has been accompanied by dramatic changes in in-

ternational banking. In 1970, all of the world's 10 largest banks were headquartered in the United States. Erratic inflation, the dollar's loss of dominance in world money markets, the growth of other economies, and a host of other factors have created pressures for change. Today, the United States holds only 20% or so of the world's banking giants. Although the dollar remains the world's most important medium of exchange, other currencies have now become more important in world money markets.

Major deregulation intended to increase competitiveness in financial markets was enacted in 1980, but many reforms were phased in gradually. Deregulation enabled many banks to become virtual "money supermarkets," but it also opened the doors for expanded lending activity by such firms as General Electric, Sears, Ford, and AT&T. Although financial transactions continue to expand rapidly, banks' shares of total lending in the United States fell from roughly 40% in 1960 to about 28% in 1993. Even greater losses of competitive advantage were experienced by savings and loans and credit unions. Banks and similar institutions must be flexible to survive and serve the public in our changing financial environment, but, as Focus 2 indicates, the specific forms taken in some deregulation that were intended to increase financial competitiveness may have contributed to recent problems in the financial sector.

The Collapse of Savings and Loans

... the weak, meek and ignorant are always good targets.   Lincoln S&L memo to bond salespeople

Half of all savings and loan associations (S&Ls) folded during the 1980s, at a cost to taxpayers expected to mount to from $200 billion to $400 billion by the year 2010, as illustrated in Figure 3. The S&L mess was precipitated by a series of events, including fraud and mismanagement.

Figure 3   The Costs of the Savings and Loan Bailout

Until the 1970s, most S&Ls were conservative and safe havens for savers who sought slightly higher interest rates than those paid by banks. Competition was restricted in two major ways. First, new banks or S&Ls could open only if the prospective founders convinced regulators that a community had unserved needs for more financial services. Second, legal ceilings limited the interest rates depositors could be paid. The security of S&Ls was also enhanced by federal programs that guaranteed mortgages to encourage home ownership by families.

Erratic inflation and interest rates in the 1970s sowed the seeds for the S&L mess. Most S&L assets (mortgages) were long term and at relatively low interest—20- to 40-year mortgages at 5% to 8% annually were common—but depositors could withdraw their savings with little prior notice. Rising interest rates on other finan-

cial assets caused massive outflows of deposits from S&Ls (a process termed *disintermediation*), but the S&Ls could not force homeowners to pay off their mortgages before the payments were due. S&Ls suffered severe losses and their capital-to-asset ratios (the ratio of stockholder capital in the S&L to total assets) plummeted. Few new mortgage loans were available, and mortgage interest rates soared.

This squeeze on home financing added to other pressures for reform. The Depository Institutions Deregulation and Monetary Control Act (1980) allowed investments other than home mortgages and raised the cap on insured accounts from $40,000 to $100,000. But few S&Ls were equipped for more vigorous competition, and many sank into deeper trouble. Just as sharks and pirates are attracted by sinking ships, financial sharks quickly circled weak S&Ls.

Many S&Ls began to underwrite more risky, but potentially more profitable, investments that included commercial real estate (shopping malls, condominiums, and office buildings), raw land, and junk bonds (risky, high-yielding bonds, issued to finance highly speculative mergers). As interest rates dropped during the 1980s, S&L profits rose; the spread between cost of funds and returns on investments became positive, and the industry appeared to be weathering the storm. But this "boomlet" was doomed.

First, anti-inflationary monetary policies took hold, weakening real estate markets that had been pumped up because many investors had viewed real estate as good hedges against inflation.

Second, the Tax Reform Act of 1986 slashed the highest tax brackets by half and plugged tax break loopholes that favored holding of commercial real estate. The results were a dumping of real estate and nationwide price declines averaging 20% to 40%.

Roughly three-fourths of S&L assets were in mortgages at pre-collapse values, so S&L balance sheets nosedived as real estate foreclosures grew. By the late 1980s, S&L insolvencies had depleted funds in the Federal S&L Insurance Corporation (FSLIC). Bowing to political pressures, Congress agreed to finance a bailout, and it established the Resolution Trust Corporation (RTC) to dispose of the real estate and other assets it collected in foreclosures. Problems with these thrift institutions caused Congress to move the bulk of the power previously exercised by the Federal Home Loan Bank, the FSLIC, and the Federal Credit Union Administration into a new Office of Thrift Supervision.

The S&L house of cards was flattened by multiple forces. First, the S&Ls short-term liabilities (deposits) and their long-term earning assets were an unstable mix. When short-term interest rates rose, the interest paid to savers exceeded the interest S&Ls earned on their existing portfolios of loans.

Second, the *moral hazards* inherent in the deposit insurance system compounded S&Ls' losses. Depositors felt safe because of FSLIC insurance and cared little about whether an S&L was prudently managed. (People are more careful if assets are not insured.) Deregulation attracted numerous sharks who speculated aggressively and embezzled depositors'

THE FED'S INDEPENDENCE UNDER ATTACK

The Great Depression of the 1930s obliterated faith in monetary policy. The Keynesian Revolution (from 1936 into the 1960s) convinced most economists of that era that fiscal policy is the best way to stabilize the economy. In the 1970s, however, monetary policy made a strong comeback; few economists now believe that "money doesn't matter."

A gradual reaffirmation of the importance of monetary policy began in the early 1960s. Keynesians roundly condemned the Board of Governors for following "slow-grow" monetary policies that partially offset the expansionary fiscal policies adopted by Presidents Kennedy and Johnson. In the 1970s, "stop-and-go" monetary policies were partially blamed for stagflation and the reemergence of the business cycle. Then the Fed's restrictive monetary policies were blamed for a severe slump in business activity during 1981 to 1983. (Most observers conceded, however, that these policies dampened inflation and eventually reduced interest rates.) More recently, the Fed was also identified as a culprit for prolonging the recession of 1990 to 1991.

Focus 3 provides insights into why the Fed has been accused of following erratic policies that destabilize the economy. A congressional resolution prescribes that the Fed should limit monetary growth to a range of from 2% to 6% annually and should announce its targets for growth well in advance so that businesses and financial institutions can adjust. (This proposal is closely related to the view that rules, not discretion, should govern demand-management policies. Reasons for monetary growth rules are described in more detail in later chapters.)

Proposals to Reform the Fed

Renewed recognition of the power of monetary policy has generated pressure for the Fed to be politically accountable. Many regulatory agencies are seen as controlled by the industries they are supposed to oversee. The Fed is often accused of being a captive of banking interests and of following monetary policies that benefit bankers without regard for the public interest. The Fed has mounted a multifaceted defense of its independence and discretion over policy. The fear of politicizing policy is a central issue. The Fed argues that it should be free to follow what it perceives to be the best monetary policies possible, not policies based on political considerations.

What incentives do the governors of the Fed have to follow policies most beneficial for the economic well-being of the American people? Banks that "invest" in the Fed are limited to 6% rates of return, and political checks on Fed governors are weak. The Fed responds that its officers and administrators are public-spirited people who simply want the satisfaction of knowing that they are doing the best job they can for the American public. This answer satisfies few economists, who believe that the most powerful of human motivations is self-interest. However, subjecting the Fed to political pressure is not a very appealing alternative to relying on the Fed management's interest in the public welfare. Nevertheless, critics charge that the Fed is too powerful to be consistent with

Stop-and-Go Fed Policies

For decades, the U.S. economy has been plagued by faltering growth, variations in the dollar's exchange rate, and swings in rates of unemployment and inflation. Monetary growth has also been erratic. Are these facts connected? One group of new classical economists, the monetarists, cite inconsistent growth of the money supply as the basic cause of all these problems.*

Such external shocks as the Vietnam War, conflict in the Persian Gulf, and OPEC oil price hikes may also partially explain cyclical swings, but most monetarists view attempts at economic fine-tuning as doomed. Indeed,

many observers lay full blame for a deep recession from 1981 to 1983 and for a milder one from 1990 to 1992 at the Federal Reserve's doorstep.

Uneven but growing inflation marked the 1970s. Inflation has not reached double-digit rates since 1980 and has lost its rank as "Public Enemy #1" in the minds of most people, but it continues at annual rates of 3% to 4% in the 1990s—rates that would have been intolerable in the 1950s and 1960s. Paul Volcker, chair of the Fed during the late 1970s and early 1980s, viewed curbing the growth rate of the money supply as the key to halting inflation.

In 1979, the Fed announced that it would target M1 and control its rate of growth. Since then, monetary growth and GDP growth continue to be on a roller coaster: up for a few quarters and then down for the next few. The Fed announces targets, but then adjusts them when economic conditions seem to warrant different targets.**

Figure 4 indicates that slowing growth of the money supply is a painful process. Economists have reached a consensus that the Fed's "disinflation" strategies, adopted to squelch the double-digit inflation of the 1970s, triggered the downturn of 1981 to 1983. No consensus exists, however, as to whether

FIGURE 4   Rate of Change in M1 and GDP

In the early 1980s, the Fed announced it would target and control the rate of growth of the money supply. Since then, both M2 and GDP have risen for a few quarters, then fallen the next few. Targeting the money supply has been challenging for the Fed, but as this figure shows, changes in M2 and GDP are relatively closely correlated.

the benefits of slower inflation outweighed the losses of employment and output because of the recession. The drop in the rate of monetary growth between 1979 and 1980 was so abrupt that, although inflation decelerated, the economy went into a deep slump. Severe monetary restrictiveness was then temporarily abandoned to facilitate economic recovery. Between 1986 and 1994, however, the Fed held monetary growth under a tight reign.

The Recession of 1990–1991

Discerning a pattern in the Fed's policies during the early 1990s requires more detective work. Most economists view low interest rates as critical for balanced investment and economic growth. The Fed lowered its discount rate 25 times from 1989 to 1993. Federal deficits during the early 1990s were at record levels, so expanding the monetary base should have been easy: the Fed could simply absorb (monetize) substantial chunks of new federal debt by buying Treasury bonds. Then, readily available bank reserves would swell the money supply—after bankers made loans to investors. But this predicted chain of events failed to unfold.

The Fed regularly announces targets for monetary growth in the moderate range (2% to 6%), with precise targets depending on economic conditions. However, Figure 4 indicates that while unemployment rates hovered between 6% and 8% during the recession of 1990–1992, the money supply (M2) fell below the Fed's targeted growth rates.

This slow growth represented a sharp departure from most economic recoveries since World War II, when the real (inflation-adjusted) money supply grew at an average annual rate of 7%.*** Among possible explanations for sluggish monetary growth are the following:

1. The Fed bought too few Treasury bonds through its open markets operations, so the monetary base expanded too slowly.
2. Despite increased availability of bank reserves, banks, fearing widespread defaults, were reluctant to lend, and pessimistic investors were reluctant to borrow during this recession.
3. Foreign financial investors responded to lower U.S. interest rates by transfering their funds to countries where interest rates were higher, reducing the funds available for lending by U.S. financial intermediaries.

More refined information and better detective work is needed before we can identify which factors best account for slow monetary growth in the midst of recession. One thing, however, is certain. Irate voters tend to adopt throw-the-rascals-out attitudes when the economy is in the doldrums. In 1992, more incumbent senators and members of congress retired or were defeated than in any other election in the preceding four decades, and Bill Clinton replaced George Bush in the White House.

* Monetarists' views are explored in more depth in the next few chapters.
** Milton Friedman, a leading monetarist, compares the Fed to a farmer who used his barn door for target practice. "A visitor was astounded to find that each of the numerous targets on the door had a bullet hole precisely in the center of the bull's-eye. He later discovered the secret of such remarkable accuracy. Unobserved, he saw the farmer first shoot at the door and then paint the target." Friedman contends that the Fed "simply repaints the target" repeatedly. Source: "The Fed Hasn't Changed Its Ways," *The Wall Street Journal,* 20 August, 1985.
*** Mike McNamee, "Memo to Democrats: Read Alan's Lips" *Business Week,* 3 August, 1992, p. 22. Data: *Federal Reserve Bulletin,* August 1993; and *Survey of Current Business,* July 1992; and Paul W. McCracken, "Why Things Aren't Getting Better" *The Wall Street Journal,* 23 July, 1992, p. A12.

democratic government, and the tools in its armory, too diverse. These charges echo the fears of the founding fathers who resisted Alexander Hamilton's desires for a central bank.

One possible reform entails separating monetary policy from the regulation of financial institutions. In 1993, the Clinton administration proposed continuation of the Fed's control over monetary policy, but regulation of financial intermediaries would be unified under the umbrella of a super federal agency. Among other powers, this consolidated agency would assume the bulk of the auditing functions currently performed by (*a*) the Fed, (*b*) the Federal Deposit Insurance Corporation, (*c*) the Comptroller of the Currency, (*d*) the Office of Thrift Supervision, and (*e*) various agencies of state government. In addition, this unified agency would charter new banks and thrift institutions and review and approve any proposed mergers of banks or S&Ls. But this is only one of many proposals for reforms of financial regulation. Will the role of the Fed change? Should it? If so, how? Only time will tell.

We have discussed the most regulated major American industry in this chapter. These regulations, which grew rapidly during the Great Depression, stem from recognition that controlling monetary aggregates is necessary to control aggregate economic activity. The Fed uses three main tools to alter the money supply: reserve requirements, open-market operations, and discounting operations. The effectiveness of monetary policy in controlling inflation or averting a recession is the focal point of the next chapter.

CHAPTER REVIEW: KEY POINTS

1. Because fractional reserve banking makes it impossible for all banks to pay all demand deposits simultaneously, government action may help resolve monetary crises. The **central bank** of a country (a) controls the volume of money in circulation, (b) performs the government's banking functions, (c) serves as a "banker's bank," and (d) regulates banks and other financial institutions. The central bank of the United States is the **Federal Reserve System**, or **Fed**.

2. The Federal Reserve System's most powerful but least used primary tool is its power to change the **reserve requirement ratio** (rr). Increases in rr reduce the money multiplier and money supply, and vice versa.

3. The most useful tool of the Fed is **open-market operations (OMO)**. After all adjustments, open-market operations affect the monetary base, not the money multiplier. When the Fed sells government bonds, bank reserves are reduced and the money supply declines. Fed purchases of bonds increase bank reserves and the money supply.

4. The **discount rate** (d) is the interest rate the Fed charges member banks. When the discount rate is low relative to market interest rates, banks hold few excess reserves and will borrow funds from the Fed. Consequently, the money supply increases. High discount rates relative to market interest rates cause banks to borrow less from the Fed and provide incentives for larger holdings of excess reserves. The actual money multiplier and total bank reserves fall, and the money supply falls.

5. The Fed's other tools include **margin requirements** to limit stock market credit and **moral suasion** or *jawboning*.

QUESTIONS FOR THOUGHT AND DISCUSSION

1. What effect will a million-dollar bank robbery have on the M1 money supply? (Remember that M1 is cash in the public's hands plus demand deposits.)

2. Until 1980, the reserve-requirement ratios for state-chartered banks were generally lower than the ratios required for national banks. How might this partially explain the growth in state banks relative to national banks during the preceding 60 years? What effects would this have on the Fed's ability to control the money supply? On pressures for the Fed to reduce reserve requirement ratios for national banks? How might you test to see whether your answers to these questions are correct?

3. Banks have been forbidden to establish branches across state borders, and many states absolutely forbid branch banking. Bank holding companies have finessed those laws in some places, and there is now substantial political pressure to relax these laws. President Bush proposed legalizing nationwide interstate branch banking in 1991. What potential gains and losses do you perceive from allowing nationwide branch banking?

4. Should opening a financial institution be more complicated than starting a business as a florist? What special controls, if any, should the government exercise over financial institutions?

5. Given that most bank deposits are insured for up to $100,000 by the Federal Deposit Insurance Corporation (FDIC), do reserve requirements add to the safety of depositors? If not, what is the purpose of requiring banks to hold reserves?

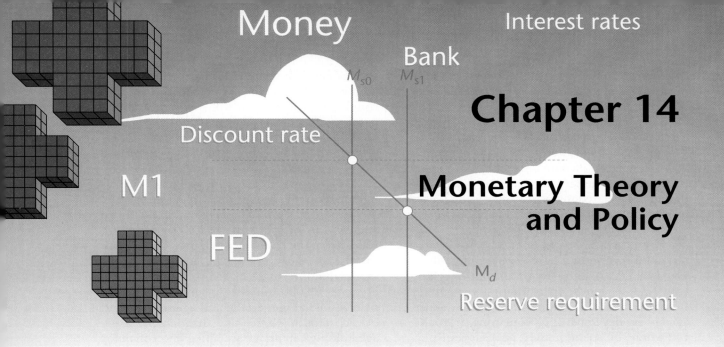

Chapter 14

Monetary Theory and Policy

[The possession of money] in quantity can be a blessing to the virtuous individual, but a curse to masses afflicted by gluttony. Prudent coiners of a society's money gain for their country a stable prosperity, but profligate masters of money can visit ruin on their nation and all of its neighbors.

Daniel Webster (attributed)

You would gain if all the money you possess were doubled. But how critical is the total quantity of money in circulation? If everyone's money were doubled, would you benefit? Would most people? Controversy raged over such issues even before the conquistadors triggered inflation by shipping tons of stolen gold from the New World to sixteenth-century Spain. The depression era work of John Maynard Keynes rekindled these debates, which are still far from resolved.

Just as markets for goods are in equilibrium only if the quantities supplied and demanded are equal, the quantities of money supplied and demanded must be equal to balance financial markets. In this chapter, you will learn how monetary equilibrium affects national income, the price level, investment, and the interest rate.

Equilibration processes are sketched from classical, Keynesian, and monetarist perspectives. Most modern economists borrow eclectically from all three of these schools of thought, with few fully subscribing to all the positions we ascribe to a particular "brand" of theory. Exposure to all three camps, however, should help you understand the range of how most economists now view money as affecting human behavior. Differences in adjustment processes determine (*a*) whether monetary policy or fiscal policy is more potent and (*b*) how actively government should try to dampen business cycles, or whether passive policies that rely heavily on market forces are more likely to yield a prosperous stability.

THE DEMAND FOR MONEY

I have all the money I need for the rest of my life— provided I die by 4 o'clock this afternoon.

Henny Youngman

As with "What is money?" the answer to "Do you have enough money?" seems obvious. Your behavior, however, indicates that at times you have too much money, so you spend it; at other times you try to acquire more money because you have too little. Ambiguity arises because many people use *money*, *income*, and *wealth* interchangeably. You might easily justify answering no if asked if you had enough income or wealth. But money is identical to neither income nor wealth, although it is related to both. Money is the device used to buy goods and by which we measure our incomes, wealth, and the prices we pay.

Most people spend in fairly predictable ways and receive money at regular intervals. If you try to secure more money income by selling your time or goods, or by saving more money from your income, you have temporary shortages of money relative to your time or goods. But when you spend money, you see your purchases as more desirable than their monetary costs; relative to these goods, you have temporary surpluses of money.

Individual demands for money are fairly complex. It would be fruitless to break up our demand for cars into "vacation," "work," "commuter," or "shopping" motives. Some economists, however, find it useful to compartmentalize reasons we hold money instead of consuming more or investing in other assets. The functions money performs were addressed previously: money is a medium of exchange, a unit of account, a store of value, and a standard of deferred payment. One trivial way to explain your demand for money is to say that you desire money for the functions it performs. You can gain more insight into how money works by looking at three basic motives for holding money: the *transactions*, *precautionary*, and *asset demands* for money.

Transactions Demands

Before the Great Depression, traditional classical reasoning focused on spending plans as the sole rational motive for holding money.

> The **transactions demand for money** arises because people anticipate spending it.

This is usually the dominant reason for holding money. You can predict many if not most trans-

actions fairly accurately. You know how much your monthly rent and car payment will be and roughly how much you will spend on utilities, gasoline, and meals. You probably also have a good idea about how much money you will receive in the near future. Most workers receive their paychecks regularly: daily, weekly, biweekly, or monthly. Students may receive money monthly or once or twice a semester.

Predictable transactions flows of money to and from an individual paid $2,000 monthly are reflected in the blue line in Figure 1. The vertical rise of the area shaded in green shows money-holding patterns for someone with an identical $2,000 monthly income, but who is paid $1,000 at the middle and again at the end of each month. Notice that this person's average holdings of money are much lower than for the individual paid monthly. We have shown more rapid declines in money holdings right after a payday than toward the end of the pay period. You are typical if you write a lot of

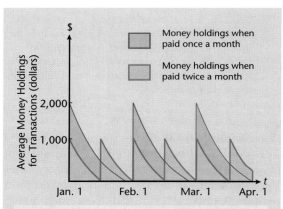

Transaction patterns with money cause most of us to have far less money on hand at the end of a pay period than at the beginning. Most people pay their major bills right after payday, with spending shrinking to a trickle until the next paycheck. Consequently, people paid more frequently tend to hold less money than people with the same total income, but who wait longer between paychecks. For example, a worker paid $1,000 twice a month will hold only half the average money balances held by one paid $2,000 once each month.

FIGURE 1   Transactions Balances

checks right after you get paid, and then find yourself almost broke before you are paid again.

Precautionary Demands

Even people who hold enough money to cover their planned spending feel uncomfortable with no extra money in reserve. There always seem to be little—and sometimes big—emergencies that require money. For example, you may have the hard luck of a flat tire or lost textbooks, or you may be pleasantly surprised to find a tape you want on special in a store at your local mall. People hold precautionary balances of money on hand to meet unexpected expenditures.

> The **precautionary demand for money** arises because people know that unanticipated spending is required at times.

The major difference between the transactions and precautionary demands for money lies in the degree of predictability about future spending. Both motives, however, suggest that your average of money balances held will be positively related to your income; you probably hold more money now than when you were ten years old, and far less than you will hold when you put your student days behind you and find a good job. Figure 2 stacks the precautionary demand for money on top of the transactions demand to show how the total of these two demands is related to income. One of Keynes's innovations in monetary theory is the idea of the precautionary motive. While earlier classical writers ignored this motive in their writings on money, they would have had little difficulty accepting this idea because, like transactions balances, precautionary balances of money are closely related to income.

Asset Demands

Keynes's major innovation in monetary theory is the concept of an asset demand for money, an idea that clashes with early classical theory.

FIGURE 2   Nominal Income, Precautionary Balances, and the Demand for Money

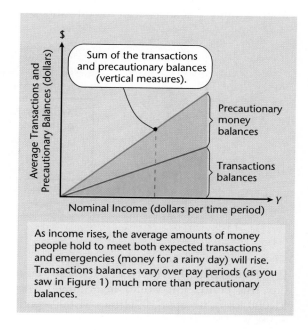

As income rises, the average amounts of money people hold to meet both expected transactions and emergencies (money for a rainy day) will rise. Transactions balances vary over pay periods (as you saw in Figure 1) much more than precautionary balances.

> The **asset demand for money** arises because people sometimes want to hold part of their wealth in the form of money.

Early classical theorists argued that no one will hold money as an asset because they could earn interest on stocks or bonds if they made these financial investments instead. Keynesians argue that a desire to hold some wealth in the form of money originates from (*a*) expectations that the prices of stocks or bonds will fall in the near future, (*b*) reluctance to hold only assets that tend to swing widely in value, or (*c*) a belief that transaction costs are higher than any expected return from investments in stocks or bonds.

• Speculative Balances   Suppose you intend to buy stocks, bonds, or real estate out of funds you have saved.

> People hold **speculative money balances** if they expect the prices of alternative assets to fall in the near future.

If you expect the prices of these financial investments to fall in the near future, you will postpone their purchase until prices are down, holding money as an asset in the interim.

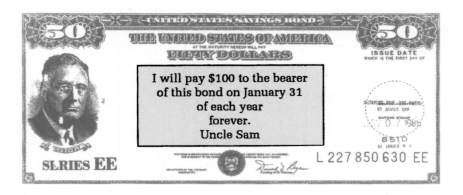

If it required a 10% return to persuade you to buy this bond, you would be willing to pay $1,000 for it, because 10% times $1,000 equals $100, which is the annual payment. If you required a 20% return on your financial investment, the bond would be worth only $500 to you: 0.20($500) = $100. Thus, higher interest rates imply lower bond prices (20% > 10% and $500 < $1,000).

A general formula for this type of bond (called a *perpetuity*) is

$$present\ value\ =\ \frac{annual\ payment}{interest\ rate}$$

Rising interest rates reduce bond prices (the present value of the bond), and falling interest rates drive bond prices up. If you and other potential bond buyers believe that interest rates will rise soon, you will speculate against bonds and hold money while waiting for bond prices to fall.

• **Risk Avoidance** Keynes emphasized the speculative aspect of the asset demand for money. Other economists have developed other reasons why people may hold money as an asset. Assets yielding relatively high average rates of return tend to be relatively risky. Most people are *risk averse*, so they buy various kinds of

• **Bond Prices and Interest Rates** Suppose you were offered a chance to buy a government bond that offered the following terms:

insurance. We invest only if the assets we buy with money are expected to yield returns that compensate us for our reduced liquidity (less money held) *and* the increased risk of loss.

Newspapers occasionally profile eccentrics who seemed destitute, but who left their heirs hoards of cash hidden in mattresses. Risk-averse people will hold money when expected rates of return from other assets are viewed as too low to overcome their riskiness. Consider, for example, two financial investments: (*a*) $10,000 in cash, with a zero return or (*b*) $10,000 worth of ZYX stock, which has a 96% probability of yielding a 6% rate of return, but a 4% chance of losing the $10,000. Buying ZYX stock is probabilistically more valuable than holding the cash (0.96 × $10,600 = $10,176 > $10,000), but many people would hold the cash in preference to risking the 4% probability of losing the entire $10,000.

• **Costs of Illiquidity** Money is the most liquid of all assets. If you have so little wealth that the costs of investing overshadow any potential gains, you will hold money instead of investing. For example, if you have only $50 to invest and expect a $50 share of stock to generate a $5 profit, it is better to hold money if the stockbroker's fee is more than $5.

All these reasons for people to hold money as an asset lead to the conclusion that money holdings are negatively related to the interest rate. Transactions demands are related to time, as suggested in Figure 1. But neither precautionary nor asset demands for money are systematically related to time. It is impossible to compartmentalize chunks of money precisely, but the transactions, precautionary, and asset motives are reasonable explanations for why most of us keep positive balances of money handy. Typical total money holdings for a person paid $2,000 once a month are depicted in Figure 3.

The Costs of Holding Money

As with other goods, the quantity of money demanded will depend on its opportunity cost. Most goods or resources can be bought with money, so it might seem difficult to specify the sacrifice associated with money holdings. These sacrifices, however, take the form of either interest forgone from income-earning assets not held (the Keynesian view) or forgone consumer goods and services (the classical view).

• **The Classical View** The amount of consumption you sacrifice by holding a dollar falls as the cost of living rises. For example, if the price of a candy bar jumps from $0.50 to $1, then the candy you sacrifice to hold $1 drops from two bars to only one bar. You previously learned that comparing nominal values (e.g., dollars) requires deflating for inflation, that is, dividing the nominal value by the price level. Thus, the real subjective value of a dollar in exchange for consumer goods from the vantage point of a typical consumer is roughly the reciprocal of the price level ($1/P$). If the price level rises, you must hold more dollars to consummate given amounts of "real" transactions. This implies a negative relationship between the quantity of money demanded and the reciprocal of the price level, as shown in Panel A of Figure 4. This cost of holding money is at the root of traditional classical monetary theory.

But relationships between the cost of living and the quantity of money demanded are not quite this simple. Suppose we experienced inflation for a substantial period and that you expected it to continue. Fearing a decline in value of money, you would want to *reduce* your dollar holdings and purchase more goods. (Dollars buy more today than you expect them to in the future). Consequently, *new* classical theory posits a negative relationship between expected inflation and the demand for money. We will explore this relationship more in a moment.

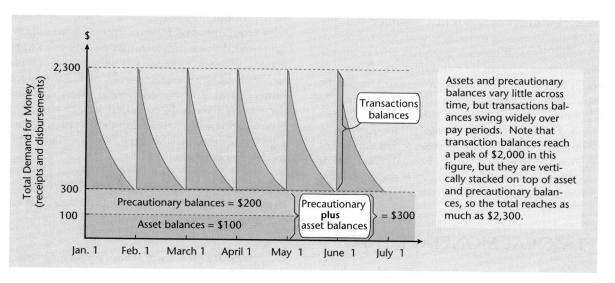

FIGURE 3   Typical Patterns of Money Holdings

FIGURE 4 Classical vs. Keynesian Views of the Cost of Holding Money

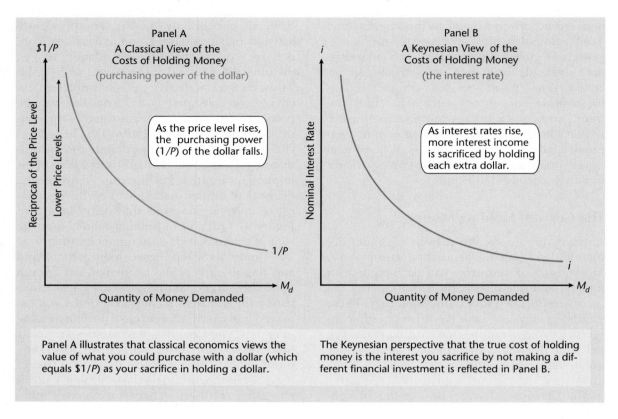

Panel A

A Classical View of the Costs of Holding Money
(purchasing power of the dollar)

$1/P

Reciprocal of the Price Level

Lower Price Levels

As the price level rises, the purchasing power (1/P) of the dollar falls.

1/P

Quantity of Money Demanded

M_d

Panel B

A Keynesian View of the Costs of Holding Money
(the interest rate)

i

Nominal Interest Rate

As interest rates rise, more interest income is sacrificed by holding each extra dollar.

i

Quantity of Money Demanded

M_d

Panel A illustrates that classical economics views the value of what you could purchase with a dollar (which equals $1/P$) as your sacrifice in holding a dollar.

The Keynesian perspective that the true cost of holding money is the interest you sacrifice by not making a different financial investment is reflected in Panel B.

• **The Keynesian View** Keynesians perceive the interest rate as the cost of holding money, because they view stocks or bonds that pay interest as the closest alternatives to money as an asset. You receive no interest on cash holdings and relatively low interest rates on demand deposits. If interest rates are relatively high on nonmonetary assets, you are more likely to hold your wealth in stocks or bonds than if interest rates are low, when money is a more attractive asset. This Keynesian emphasis on interest rates (reflected in Panel B of Figure 4) differs from the traditional classical view that the costs of holding money are the goods that might be enjoyed were the money spent.

CLASSICAL MONETARY THEORY

Before Adam Smith cleared the air with his *Wealth of Nations* in 1776, most nations' policies were grounded in *mercantilism*, a doctrine that failed to differentiate money from wealth. Gold and silver were thought to be real wealth, so European countries often engaged in wars and colonial expansion to find these precious metals. Losers in wars of conquest were forced to pay winners out of their national treasuries. Aztec gold and Inca silver poured into Europe. Monarchs often debased their currencies to finance Old World wars and New World colonies. Whether debasement or foreign conquest enriched the royal coffers, the money in circulation grew.

The British philosopher David Hume (1711–1776) was among the early economic thinkers who noted that rapid monetary growth triggers inflation.

Quantity theories of money *identify the money supply as the primary determinant of nominal spending and, ultimately, the price level.*

Quantity theories of money were first formalized about a century ago by economists at Cambridge University and by Irving Fisher of Yale University. Fisher's analysis began with the equation of exchange.

The Equation of Exchange

Gross Domestic Product can be written as PQ because GDP has price level (P) and real output (Q) components. But how is the money supply related to GDP? Economists approach this question by computing how many times, on average, money changes hands annually for purchases of final output. For example, GDP in 1994 was roughly $7 trillion and the money supply (M1) averaged about $1 trillion, so the average dollar was used roughly seven times for purchases of output produced in 1994.

> The average number of times a unit of money is used annually is called the **income velocity (V)** of money.

Velocity is computed by dividing GDP by the money supply: $V = PQ/M$. Multiplying both sides of $V = PQ/M$ by M yields $MV = PQ$, a result called *the equation of exchange*.

> The **equation of exchange** is written
>
> $$M \times V = P \times Q$$

This equation is definitionally true given our computation of velocity[1] and is interpreted as the quantity of money times its velocity is equal to the price level times real output, which equals GDP. Note that this equation suggests that the *velocity* of money is just as important as the *quantity* of money in circulation.

A rough corollary is that *the percentage change in the money supply* plus *the percentage change in velocity* equals *the percentage change in the price level* plus *the percentage change in real output*:[2]

$$\frac{\Delta M}{M} + \frac{\Delta V}{V} = \frac{\Delta P}{P} + \frac{\Delta Q}{Q}$$

Focus on the right side of this equation. Does it make sense that if the price of, say, tea bags rose 1% and you cut your purchases 2%, your spending on tea would fall about 1%. Intuitively, the percentage change in price plus the percentage change in quantity roughly equals the percentage change in spending. Reexamine the equation. Suppose output grew 3%, velocity did not change, and the money supply rose 7%. Average prices would rise 4% (7% + 0% = 4% + 3%). Learning these relationships will help you comprehend arguments between classical monetary theorists and their detractors.

The Crude Quantity Theory of Money

From certain assumptions about the variables in the equation of exchange (M, V, P, and Q), classical economists (including Fisher) conclude that, in equilibrium, the price level (P) is exactly proportional to the money supply (M). Let us see how they arrived at this conclusion.

• **Constancy of Velocity**   Classical economic reasoning views the income velocity (V) of money as determined solely by institutional factors, such as the organizational structure and efficiency of banking and credit, and by people's habitual patterns of spending money after receiving income. Velocity is thought to be constant, $(\overline{V})$, at least in the short run, because changes tend to occur slowly (*a*) in financial technologies (e.g., the ways checks clear or loans are

---

[1]Irving Fisher, whose biography appears in Chapter 17, focused his version of the equation of exchange on total transactions (T) in an economy rather than real National Income (Q). Transactions differ from GDP because of (*a*) sales of things not produced in the relevant year, such as used goods or land, (*b*) transactions involving intermediate goods, which would be double counted compared to the income version of the equation, and (*c*) purely financial transactions, such as purchases of stocks, bonds, or foreign currencies. Thus, Fisher's equation of exchange is $MV = PT$ rather than the $MV = PQ$, and his V stands for *transactions velocity* instead of income velocity.

[2]For math purists only, this is roughly equivalent to taking the time derivative of the equation of exchange in its natural logs and ignoring the cross partials.

granted or repaid) and (b) in the inflows and outflows of individuals' money (people's spending habits and their frequencies of receipts of incomes).[3] Thus, we see a central assumption of the classical quantity theory: $\Delta\overline{V}/V = 0$. Focus 1 reveals, however, that assuming constant velocity would be unrealistic for international monetary data in recent years. Nor would this assumption fit U.S. data for different measures of the money supply; between 1970 and 1993, for example, velocity for M1 increased by roughly 40%, while velocity for M2 was relatively constant and velocity for M3 fell by roughly 15%.

But why does classical economics view velocity (V) as unaffected by the price level (P), the level of real output (Q), or the money supply (M)? An answer lies in why people demand money. Classical macroeconomics assumes that people want to hold money only to consummate transactions and that people's spendings are fixed proportions of their incomes. The transactions motive is basically classical. Since National Income is roughly equal to GDP (or P × Q), then the demand for money M_d (a transactions demand) can be written

$$M_d = \overline{k}PQ$$

where $\overline{k}$ is a constant proportion of income held in monetary balances.[4] For example, if each family held one-fifth of its average income of $10,000 in the form of money, then the average quantity of money each family would demand would be $M_d = 0.20(\$10,000) = \$2,000$. The quantity of money demanded in the economy would be $2,000 times the number of families.

• **Constancy of Real Output** Classical theory also assumes that real output (Q) does not depend on the other variables (M, V, and P) in the equation of exchange. Classical economists believe the natural state of the economy is full employment, so real output is influenced solely by the state of technology and by resource availability. Full employment is ensured by Say's Law if prices, wages, and interest rates are perfectly flexible. Moreover, both technology and the amounts of resources available are thought to change slowly, if at all, in the short run. Thus, real output (Q) is assumed to be approximately constant, and $\Delta Q/Q = 0$. This may seem like a very strong assertion, but the intuitive appeal of the idea that real output is independent of the quantity of money (M), its velocity (V), or the price level (P), is convincing both to classical monetary theorists and to new classical economists who have updated the classical tradition.

The idea that the amount of paper currency or coins issued by the government has virtually no effect on the economy's productive capacity seems reasonable. Similarly, the velocity of money should not influence capacity. But what about the price level? After all, the law of supply suggests that the quantities of individual goods and services supplied will be greater the higher the market prices are. Shouldn't the nation's output increase if the price level rises? Classical economists say **no**. Here is why.

• **A Crude Monetary Theory of the Price Level** Suppose your income and the values of all your assets exactly double. (That's the good news.) Now suppose that the prices of everything you buy and all your debts also precisely double. (That's the bad news.) Should your behavior change in any way? Your intuition should suggest not. Using similar logic, classical economists conclude that, in the long run, neither real output nor any other aspect of "real" economic behavior is affected by changes in the price level. Economic behavior is shaped by relative prices, not the absolute price level.

Recall that the percentage changes in the money supply and velocity roughly equal the percentage changes in the price level and real output. If velocity is constant and output is stable at a full employment level in the short run, then

$$\Delta\overline{V}/V = \Delta\overline{Q}/Q = 0$$

---

[3]Bars over variables indicate constancy.

[4]We know that the equation of exchange relates the supply of money to National Income through velocity: $MV = PQ$. Let us divide both sides by V: $M = PQ/V$. Because the quantities of money supplied and demanded must be equal in equilibrium ($M_s = M_d$), $\overline{k}$ must equal $1/\overline{V}$, both $\overline{k}$ and $\overline{V}$ being constants. As a result, classical monetarists discerned a fixed relationship between $\overline{k}$ (the proportion of annual income people want to hold as money) and $\overline{V}$ (the velocity of money).

Velocity on the International Scene

The quantity theory of money concludes that velocity is constant and that faster monetary growth must foster more rapid inflation. But what happens if the public desires more money as the money supply expands? Velocity falls, confounding monetarist forecasts of inflation.

Velocity did fall in the 1980s for most measures of money supplies for developed nations, as illustrated in Figure 5. Slowdowns in velocity dampened pressures from rapid monetary growth. But why did velocity fall? One reason is that financial deregulation in the United States and elsewhere caused an avalanche of new financial instruments. People shifted funds into the interest-bearing accounts that now constitute larger parts of most monetary aggregates and paid their bills more slowly to maintain bigger checking account balances.

A related issue is that innovative financial instruments increase liquidity in the world and, consequently, change the definitions appropriate for money supplies. For example, Michael Milken almost single-handedly invented the *junk bond* market to facilitate mergers in the 1980s. (He was ultimately jailed for violations of U.S. security laws.) Assorted forms of junk bonds, the spread of ATMs and credit cards, and blurred boundaries between savings accounts and demand deposits are only a few examples of recent technologies that affect velocity.

Most monetarists concede that their forecasting models broke down over the past decade or so, but argue that after people fully adjust to deregulation, velocity will regain its relative stability, restoring the classical relationship between monetary growth rates and inflation. However, whether velocity ever stabilizes depends in part on rates of innovation in financial technologies. And financial technologies are changing rapidly in our increasingly globalized economy because of huge potential profits from arbitrage, speculation, and international investment. Every day almost $1 trillion worth of U.S. and foreign currencies are traded in world markets. With gross world product of only about $30 trillion to $40 trillion annually, this means that the *transactions velocity of money* in international financial markets is approaching warp speed. It seems improbable that acceleration of the income velocity of money in any open economy will lag far behind.

FIGURE 5 The Velocity of Money (Selected Countries)

Source: *The Economist*, July 27, 1985. Updates by the authors. Reprinted by permission.

The income velocity of money equals nominal GDP divided by the money supply. The measure of the money supply used for the United States is M3; for Britain, M3; for Japan, M2+CDs; and for West Germany, Central Bank Money (CBM).

Classical economists are left with a fixed relationship between the money supply (M) and the price level (P). In equilibrium, the rate of inflation exactly equals the percentage growth rate of the money supply:

$$\Delta M/M = \Delta P/P.$$

Thus, any acceleration of monetary growth would not affect real output, just inflation.

The Classical View of Investment

Firms buy machinery, construct buildings, or attempt to build up inventories whenever they expect the gross returns on these investments to exceed the total costs of acquiring them. Classical economists assume relatively stable and predictable economies, so they focus on the costs of acquiring investment goods; business investors' expectations of profits are assumed realized, and the costs of new capital goods are presumed stable.

Equilibrium investment occurs when the expected rate of return on investment equals the interest rate. Prices for capital equipment are fairly stable, so any changes in the costs of acquiring capital primarily result from changes in interest rates. [Investors are effectively trading dimes for dollars as long as the cost of borrowing (the interest rate) is less than the return from investments made possible by borrowing.] Naturally, people will not invest unless they expect a return at least as high as they would receive if they simply lent their own money out for the interest.

Classical theorists view investment as very sensitive to the interest rate and believe that large swings in investment follow minute changes in interest rates. The expected rate of return (r) curve in Figure 6 is relatively sensitive, or flat. In this example, a decline in interest of ½ point (from 8% to 7.5%) boosts investment by 60% [(80 − 50)/50 = 30/50 = 0.60]. Flexible interest rates and a highly sensitive investment (rate of return) schedule easily equate planned saving and investment. All saving is invested, stabilizing the economy at full employment.

FIGURE 6   The Classical View of Investment

Classical economists view investment as quite sensitive to even slight changes in interest rates and view business expectations about rates of return as reasonably stable and normally realized.

Classical Monetary Transmission

Classical monetary economists view linkages between the money supply and National Income as not only strong, but direct. This *classical monetary transmission mechanism* (how money enters the economy) is shown in Figure 7. Panel A reflects the effects of monetary changes on nominal income, and Panel B translates these changes into effects on real output.

Nominal income in Panel A is $6 trillion (point *a*) if the money supply is initially $1 trillion ($M_d$). Note that $\overline{Q}_f$ is the full employment level of output and $MV = PQ$, so $M = kPQ$, where $\bar{k} = 1/\overline{V}$. This figure initially assumes that $\overline{V} = 6$ and, thus, that $\bar{k} = 0.1666$, or almost 1%. This $6-trillion nominal income $\left(\overline{Y} = P_0\overline{Q}_f\right)$ is equal to 6 trillion units of real output (point *a* in Panel B) at an average price level P_0 of 100 $\left(M\overline{V} = P\overline{Q}_f \rightarrow 1 \times 6 = 1 \times 6\right)$. Money supply growth to $1.5 trillion ($M_1$) boosts nominal income to $9 trillion (point *b* in Panel A). Output is fixed at full employment $\left(\overline{Q}_f\right)$ and velocity is constant at 6, so introducing this extra money into the economy increases Aggregate

FIGURE 7 The Classical Monetary Transmission Mechanism and the Price Level

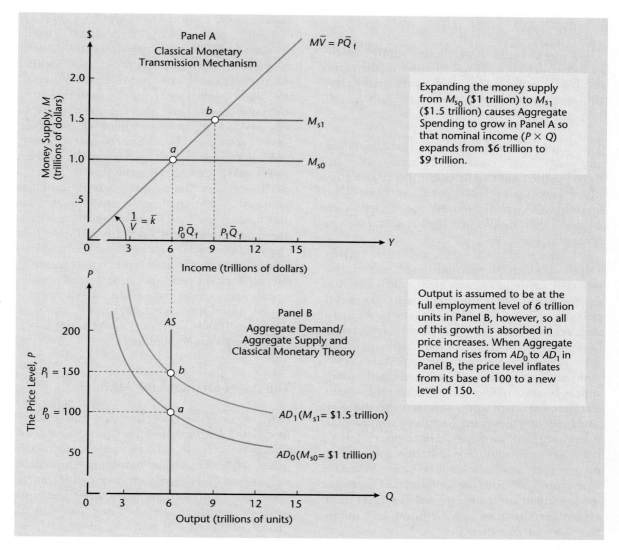

Expanding the money supply from M_{s0} ($1 trillion) to M_{s1} ($1.5 trillion) causes Aggregate Spending to grow in Panel A so that nominal income ($P \times Q$) expands from $6 trillion to $9 trillion.

Output is assumed to be at the full employment level of 6 trillion units in Panel B, however, so all of this growth is absorbed in price increases. When Aggregate Demand rises from AD_0 to AD_1 in Panel B, the price level inflates from its base of 100 to a new level of 150.

Demand from AD_0 to AD_1 which pushes the price level to 150 (point b in Panel B, where $M\bar{V} = P\bar{Q}_f \rightarrow 1.5 \times 6 = 9 = 1.5 \times 6$). Thus, in a classical world, monetary policy shifts Aggregate Demand up or down along a vertical Aggregate Supply curve with only price effects, not quantity effects.

• **Summary: The Crude Quantity Theory** Summarizing the traditional classical foundations of

the early *crude quantity theory of money*, we know that the equation of exchange is a truism because of the way velocity is computed: $MV = PQ$. It follows that

$$\frac{\Delta M}{M} + \frac{\Delta V}{V} = \frac{\Delta P}{P} + \frac{\Delta Q}{Q}$$

If velocity is assumed constant (written $\bar{V}$) and real output is fixed at a full employment level (written $\bar{Q}_f$), then $\Delta V/V = 0$, and $\Delta Q/Q = 0$.

Moreover,

$$\frac{\Delta M}{M} = \frac{\Delta P}{P}$$

Thus, any changes in the money supply will be reflected in proportional changes in the price level. This is the major result of the crude classical quantity theory of money:

$$M\overline{V} = P\overline{Q}_f$$

Another conclusion is that real output (or any other "real" economic behavior) is unaffected in the long run by either the money supply or the price level. These early versions of the quantity theory of money are clearly misnamed—they should be called *monetary theories of the price level*.

Classical theorists concluded by saying "Money is a veil." By this they meant that money, inflation, or deflation may temporarily disguise the real world, but in the long run, money affects only the price level and has virtually no effect on such real variables as production, employment, labor force participation, unemployment, or relative prices. Even though classical theorists vehemently opposed large expansions of the money supply because of fear that inflation temporarily distorts behavior, it is probably fair to say that classical monetary theory leads to the conclusion that, in the long run, "money does not matter." It does not affect production, consumption, investment, or any other "real" economic behavior. When we deal graphically with the demand and supply of money in later sections, we will resurrect these classical propositions to see how modern monetary theory treats them.

KEYNESIAN MONETARY THEORY

The brunt of Keynes's attack on the classical quantity theory of money was aimed at its conclusions that (a) velocity is constant and (b) full employment is the natural state of a market economy.

Early classical economists believed that money balances are held only for transactions purposes and that the transactions anyone engages in are roughly proportional to that individual's nominal income. Thus, planned money balances were assumed roughly proportional to nominal income. "Why," they asked, "would people want to hold money unless they intend to spend it? Virtually any other asset yields a positive rate of return—and money holdings do not. No one holds more money than they need for transactions. They hold income-earning assets instead of money whenever possible." Keynes responded by adding the precautionary and asset (speculative) motives to the transactions motive for holding money.

Remember that people adjust their money balances until what they demand equals what they have. If you have more money than you demand, you spend or invest more, reducing your money balances. If you demand more money than you presently hold, you acquire more by cutting back on your spending out of income, liquidating some of your assets, or selling more of your time. Keynes emphasized financial investments (stocks or bonds) as the major way to reduce one's money holdings.

The Asset Demand for Money

One major difference between the classical model and Keynes' model is that classical economists view the world as a reasonably certain place, while Keynesian reasoning emphasizes uncertainty and describes how our expectations about uncertain futures might affect the economy. Rising uncertainty is a major reason for growth of the asset demand for money.

Suppose you are working on an assembly line when the economy nose-dives. Many of your co-workers are laid off. You would probably start saving more because you could be the next one to find a pink slip in your pay envelope. As your savings mount, assets in the form of money balances grow. What happens to the velocity of money? *Velocity falls as saving increases.* Why not convert these funds into a stock or bond that pays interest or some positive rate of return? You must be kidding! The economy is in a tailspin—a recession may be under way. The crucial point here is that when people expect hard times, the velocity of money falls as people convert money from transactions balances to precautionary or asset balances. Conversely, money balances are increasingly held for transactions purposes when prosperity seems just around the corner. This causes velocity to rise.

Let us see what all this means within the context of the equation of exchange. Because the percentage changes in the money supply plus velocity are equal to the percentage changes in the price level plus the real level of output, a 5% decline in velocity (money supply assumed constant) will cause nominal GDP to fall by 5%. If prices do not fall fairly rapidly, output and employment will decline by about 5%. (One economic law seems to be that *if circumstances change and prices do not adjust, quantities will.*) The economy may settle in equilibrium at less than full employment.

Keynes and his followers assumed that price adjustments are *sticky* (slow), especially on the down side, and that people's expectations are volatile. This implies that the velocity of money may vary considerably over time and that the real economy may adjust only slowly, if at all, to these variations.

• The Liquidity Trap

Classical economists viewed the interest rate as an incentive for saving: you are rewarded for postponing consumption. Keynes's rebuttal was that interest is a reward for sacrificing liquidity. According to Keynes, how much you save is determined by your income and will be affected very little by interest rates. However, interest rates are important in deciding the form your saving takes. You will hold money unless offered some incentive to hold a less-liquid asset. Interest is such an inducement. Higher interest rates will induce you to relinquish money and hold more of your wealth in the form of illiquid assets.

Keynes believed that very high interest rates cause people to hold little, if any, money in asset balances; the demand for money consists almost exclusively of transactions and precautionary balances. But low interest rates result in large asset balances of money. Just as we horizontally sum individual demands for goods to arrive at market demands, we can sum the transactions, pre-

cautionary, and asset demands for money to obtain the total demand for money. This demand curve for money is shown in Figure 8.

Note that at a very low interest rate, the demand for money becomes flat. This part of the demand curve for money is called the *liquidity trap.*

> A **liquidity trap** occurs if people will absorb any extra money into idle balances because they are extremely pessimistic or risk averse, view transaction costs as prohibitive, or expect the prices of nonmonetary assets to fall in the near future.

It implies that if the money supply grew (say, from M_{s0} to M_{s1}), any extra money you received would not be spent, but hoarded, that is, absorbed into idle cash balances. Monetary growth would increase Aggregate Spending very little, if at all. Expectations about economic conditions might become so pessimistic that people would hoard every cent they could "for a rainy day," an instance of the liquidity trap. Alternatively,

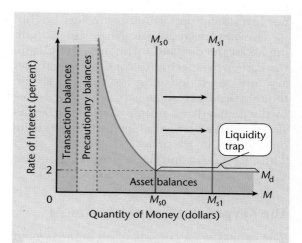

The Keynesian total demand for money is the horizontal sum of transactions, precautionary, and asset demands for money. Keynesian theory predicts a *liquidity trap* at very low interest rates in which growth of the money supply yields neither extra spending nor declines in interest rates. Extra money is merely absorbed through hoarding into idle cash balances in a liquidity trap.

FIGURE 8   Liquidity Preference and the Demand for Money

historically low interest rates might persuade nearly everyone that interest rates will soon rise. You would not want to hold bonds because rising interest rates would reduce bond prices and you would suffer a capital loss; you and many other investors would hold money while waiting for interest rates to rise and bond prices to fall.

Even though Keynes was writing during the Depression, he suggested that no economy had ever been in a perfect liquidity trap. At the trough of the Great Depression, however, the nominal interest rate hovered around 1.5% and there may have been a "near-liquidity" trap. Severe depressions may cause near-liquidity traps because (a) banks pile up huge excess reserves when nominal interest rates are very low because the returns from lending are small; (b) bankers fear that all loans are very risky, even those that normally would pose no problem of repayment; and (c) private individuals hoard their own funds, fearing that bank failures are probable and that neither their job prospects nor investment opportunities are very bright.

Keynes rejected classical theory in his thinking about the demand for money, broadening the earlier perspective to consider precautionary and asset demands for money. Keynes thought that interest rates are determined solely by the demand and supply of money. His classical predecessors viewed interest rates as being determined in the market for capital goods. Thus, Keynesian and classical economists differ sharply in their perceptions of investment.

The Keynesian View of Investment

The capital stock consists of all improvements that make natural resources more productive than they are in their raw states: equipment, buildings, inventories, and so forth. Net economic investment is the growth of the capital stock during a given period. Classical and Keynesian theories differ about how variations in the money supply affect investment. Over a business cycle, investment fluctuates proportionally more than either consumption or government purchases. Inventory accumulation is especially unstable.

Keynesians focus on investors' volatile moods: optimistic expectations of large returns generate high levels of investment, while pessimism stifles it. Both Keynesian and classical writers agree that greater investment eventually leads to lower rates of return. Keynesian analysis takes the position that the interest rate, which is the major opportunity cost of investment, is only one aspect of investment planning and is not the overwhelming influence posited by classical economists. This perspective emphasizes changes in investors' expectations as far more important in explaining changes in investment. Figure 9 shows why.

Suppose the initial investment curve is r_0 and that equilibrium investment is $70 billion (point a) at an 8% interest rate. Note that the rate of return curves are relatively steep in this Keynesian view of the world. A drop in the interest rate to 7.5% moves the equilibrium from point a to point b, causing investment to grow only slightly, from $70 billion to $80 billion.

Now suppose that investors become skeptical about future economic conditions so that the

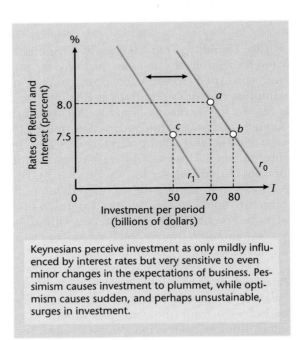

Keynesians perceive investment as only mildly influenced by interest rates but very sensitive to even minor changes in the expectations of business. Pessimism causes investment to plummet, while optimism causes sudden, and perhaps unsustainable, surges in investment.

FIGURE 9 The Keynesian Explanation of Volatile Investment

expected rate of return schedule shifts leftward from r_0 to r_1. Equilibrium shifts from point b to point c, and investment falls sharply to $50 billion. If investors' herdlike mentality (Keynes described them as possessed of "animal spirits") then caused them to begin bubbling with optimism, the schedule would shift rightward, moving equilibrium from c back to b, so that investment rises back to $80 billion. Keynesians argue that investment is not very responsive to small changes in interest rates but investment demand responds strongly to changing expectations.

To summarize, both Keynesian and classical economists agree that equilibrium investment requires the expected rate of return on investment to equal the rate of interest. However, Keynesians attribute cyclical swings of investment to changes in investors' expectations of future returns. They believe that investment is less influenced by changes in interest rates than it is by the unpredictable expectations of investors. Classical economists perceive investors' expectations about returns as quite stable and explain large variations in investment as responses to small changes in interest rates.

Keynesian Monetary Transmission

The demand and supply of money determine the nominal rate of interest in financial markets, as shown in Panel A of Figure 10. Keynesian theory suggests that during recessions, changes in the interest rate (Panel A) may cause small changes in the level of investment (Panel B), and thus in National Income (Panel C). However, the demand for money is thought to be especially sensitive to interest rate movements during economic downturns. Hence, interest rates may not decrease (or increase) very much as the money supply is increased (or decreased). Even if expansionary monetary policies do reduce interest rates a bit, Keynesians believe that investment is relatively insensitive to the interest rate, and so income is affected little, if at all, by monetary policies.

Keynesians argue that changes in the money supply do not affect consumer spending directly, but only indirectly through a money → interest

rate → investment → income sequence. Even then, the effects of monetary policy are thought to be slight and erratic, because the linkages are perceived to be weak. This view of the chain of events emanating from a change in the money supply is called the **Keynesian monetary transmission mechanism**. If the money supply is increased from $800 billion to $1,000 billion (a 25% increase) in Panel A of Figure 10, the interest rate falls from 8% to 7% and investment grows slightly from $200 billion to $220 billion (a 10% increase). Total output grows via the multiplier effect from $6 trillion to $6.06 trillion (only a 1% increase). This suggests that monetary policy will be weak compared to fiscal policy. Note that Panel D reflects the Keynesian view of a slack economy (Aggregate Supply is horizontal up to the full employment level of output); monetary expansion induces only quantity adjustments, and the price level is unaffected.

Keynesian Analysis of Depressions and Inflations

Classical and Keynesian predictions differ most during a depression. Classical economists advocate laissez-faire policies because they believe the natural long-run state of the economy to be a full employment equilibrium. If pressed, however, most would assert that expansionary monetary policies increase Aggregate Spending enough to rapidly cure any depression. Classical reasoning also suggests that restrictive monetary policies are the only lasting remedy for inflation.

Most Keynesians agree that monetary restraint dampens inflationary pressures but disagree with the view that monetary expansion is powerful in curing a depression. During a depression, pessimism reigns and interest rates tend to plummet. Consequently, Keynesians suggest that an economy in recession will not recover quickly in response to expansionary monetary policies, because any extra money people receive is seldom spent but is hoarded. This is another way of saying that the velocity of money falls to offset monetary growth. Keynesians compare money to a string—you can pull on it to restrain inflation, but trying to push the economy

FIGURE 10   The Keynesian Transmission Mechanism: Money, Interest Rates, and National Income

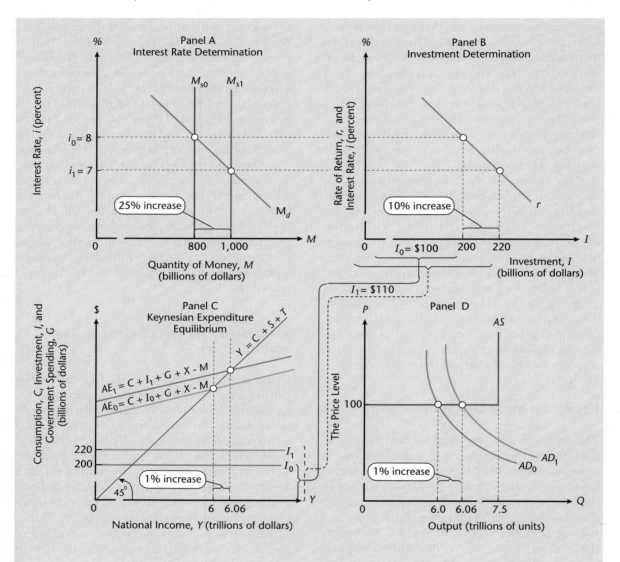

According to Keynesians, expansionary monetary policy operates by reducing interest rates slightly (Panel A), stimulating investment only slightly (Panel B). Through the multiplier process, the new autonomous investment increases income (Panel C). In Panel D, expansionary monetary policy increases Aggregate Demand from AD_0 to AD_1, boosting national ouptut from 6 trillion to 6.06 trillion units. The increase in Aggregate Demand results in only minor changes in output and no changes in the price level. Thus, Keynesians view monetary policy as having only minimal impact.

out of the doldrums through expansionary monetary policy is like "pushing on a string." Expansionary monetary policy is viewed as stringlike both because banks may not lend out their reserves if their view of the economic hori-

zon is pessimistic and because people may simply hoard rather than spend most of any extra money that comes their way.

Early Keynesians recommended massive government spending and tax cuts to cure recessions quickly. They emphasized fiscal policy because of a widespread (though mistaken) belief that central banks throughout the world attempted to push their respective nations out of the Great Depression with expansionary monetary policies. Only long after the depression did researchers discover that although the U.S. monetary base rose slightly between 1929 and 1933, the money multiplier shrank and the money supply fell sharply. Remember that good information is costly; the economic data of the time were awful.

MONETARISM

The Keynesian Revolution stirred a counter-revolution by *monetarists*, who recognize some holes in older versions of classical theory but reject any need for massive government intervention to stabilize an economy. Their counterattack, led by Milton Friedman, began with a reformulation of the demand for money.

The Demand for Money Revisited

Monetarists concede that money might be demanded for reasons other than anticipated transactions, but see no reason to compartmentalize the demand for money as Keynesians have. Instead, they have identified certain variables that influence the amounts of money demanded. Milton Friedman has arrived at the most widely accepted formulation of the *new quantity theory of money*. Friedman distinguishes the nominal money people hold from their "real" money holdings. *Real money* is the purchasing power of the money a person holds. It can be computed by dividing the face values of money assets by the price level (M/P). As the price level rises, the face amount of money needed to buy a particular bundle of goods rises proportionally.

Determinants of the Demand for Money

According to Friedman, the variables (besides the price level) that will be *positively* related to the quantity of money demanded are (*a*) peo-ple's total real wealth (including the value of their labor), (*b*) the interest rate, if any, paid on money holdings, and (*c*) the illiquidity of nonmonetary assets. He also identifies some variables as *negatively* related to the real (purchasing power) amounts of money people will hold: (*a*) the interest rate on bonds, (*b*) the rate of return on physical capital, and (*c*) the expected rate of inflation.

- **Wealth (or Permanent Income)** Classical economists (and Keynesians, to a lesser extent) relate the demand for money to current income. Friedman suggests that expected lifetime income better explains both consumption patterns and money holdings. Take two 25-year-olds, one, a recent college graduate in accounting and the other, a manager of a convenience store. Each has a current annual income of $24,000. The consumption level of the young accountant is likely to be higher than that of the convenience store manager because higher expected lifetime income increases the prospects of borrowing money; thus, the accountant will hold more money for transactions purposes.

- **The Interest Rate on Money** You do not receive interest on cash you hold and only relatively low interest on your demand deposits. Banks do, however, offer free checking accounts and other incentives for depositors who keep certain minimum balances in their accounts. Most people would probably maintain higher checking account balances if the interest rates paid to depositors were increased.

- **The Illiquidity of Nonmonetary Assets** Most college students are not poor, they are just broke. That is, they have highly marketable skills. Another way of saying this is that they hold wealth in the form of human capital but lack many other assets. According to Friedman, if most of your assets are very illiquid, you will hold more money than will people who have similar amounts of wealth but whose major assets are

BIOGRAPHY

Milton Friedman: The Rebirth of Monetarism

Milton Friedman (b. 1912) is among the most publicly visible of modern economists. He has won respect from both his followers and those economists who disagree strongly with his views. Few significant honors in economics have not come Friedman's way. He was president of the American Economic Association in 1967 and in 1976 received the Nobel Prize in economics. Looking very much like everyone's "favorite uncle," Friedman often disarms his adversaries with a wink and a gentle smile, but those who have argued with him find him a formidable debater. He is able to express complicated ideas in simple terms understandable by those untrained in formal economic theory. This makes him popular with the media and keeps Friedman in touch with a wide audience.

Friedman has been a vital force in attacking the orthodoxy of the Keynesian economics. He has done this in a way that combines his argumentative talents with solid, empirical research and a desire not merely to tear down existing economic theory but to restructure it. Friedman's most notable research has involved monetary theory, but, as with all master economists, his thoughts have touched many areas of economics. In the monetary field, Friedman has reconstructed the quantity theory of money, reemphasized the importance and significance of monetary policy, questioned the Keynesian interpretation of the Great Depression, and developed his own prescriptions for preventing future economic catastrophe.

Friedman has also made major contributions in such areas as risk and insurance (answering why people simultaneously gamble and buy insurance) and has developed a theory of consumption based on wealth, as opposed to the Keynesian view that consumption depends only on current income.

Along the way, he has attempted to restate the classical liberal philosophy of Adam Smith in terms pertinent to the modern era. (Friedman's admiration of Adam Smith is virtually unbounded: he wears a necktie patterned with cameos of Smith during public appearances.) Friedman has offered many ideas about replacing the influence of government with market solutions. For example, he argues that government should give vouchers (grants) to parents so that all children can attend schools tailored to their individual needs. He also argues that cash grants to poor people make more sense than such programs as food stamps because these grants would both leave more choices in the hands of the poor and require fewer tax dollars.

Friedman's restatement of the quantity theory of money is important because it made the theory statistically testable, something the old theory was not. His restatement is essentially a theory of the demand for money, whereas the original version was a theory of the price level. Friedman's analyses of the statistical evidence indicate that the demand for money is stable over the long run, and he concludes that large changes in the supply of money cause undesirable fluctuations in employment and in the price level. His disenchantment with fiscal policy is due in large measure to the fact that government deficits are most often financed by inflationary expansions of the supply of money and credit. Finally, Friedman has been critical of the performance of the Board of Governors of the Federal Reserve System. He sees the Fed as either following the wrong policy (trying to control interest rates instead of the money supply) or yielding to political pressure rather than sound economic logic.

---

more liquid. His reasoning is that some liquidity is desired to meet emergencies, and people with substantial human capital may not be able to liquidate their major assets (themselves) very easily. Selling yourself into bondage or slavery is illegal, and finding a job takes time. Consequently, Friedman expects that you will probably hold more cash than similarly "wealthy" people who are not in college. (We remember that when we were students, we were flat broke most of the time.)

• **Interest Rates on Bonds and Rates of Return on Investment** The major alternatives to holding money are spending it on consumer goods *or* buying it on stocks, bonds, or capital goods. Monetarists stress the value of consumption as the opportunity cost of holding money (1/*P*), but they also recognize either direct investment or purchases of stocks or bonds as possibilities. If such activities are your best alternatives to holding money, then the prices you pay for holding money are the interest (*i*) that could be received from a bond or the rate of return (*r*) you might expect from buying stocks or investing directly in physical capital.

Friedman accepts a negative relationship between the interest rate or rate of return on capital and the quantity of money demanded, but, in support of earlier classical reasoning, his studies conclude that the demand for money is relatively insensitive to the interest rate. He absolutely rejects any hint that a liquidity trap has ever existed.

• **Expected Rates of Inflation**   The idea that gaining wealth requires you to "buy low and sell high" implies that if you expect inflation, then you should get rid of your money while it has a high value and buy durable assets instead. During inflation, money becomes a hot potato, because expectations of inflation cause people to reduce their money holdings. The greater the expected inflation, the more rapid the velocity of money.

The Stability of the Demand for Money

Monetarists are willing to accept the idea that the demand for money is influenced by variables other than income, but they view these relationships as very stable. Moreover, they believe that most variables that influence the demand for money are relatively constant because they are the outcomes of an inherently stable market system. Table 1 summarizes variables that influence the amounts of money people will want to hold. Monetarists believe that the bulk of any instability in a market economy arises because of erratic government policy; the Federal Reserve System is the main villain in their scenario. Before investigating why the Fed is perceived as the culprit, we need to examine the monetarist monetary transmission mechanism.

TABLE 1   Variables Affecting the Nominal Demand for Money

Positively

1. Income
2. Wealth
3. Cost of living (CPI)
4. Uncertainty about future income and expenses
5. Expected hikes in interest rates
6. Expected declines in the prices of bonds, stocks, or real estate

Negatively

1. Interest rate (*i*)
2. Rate of return on capital (*r*)
3. Expected inflation
4. Frequency of receipt of income

The Monetarist Monetary Transmission Mechanism

Monetarists, like their classical predecessors, believe that linkages between the money supply and nominal National Income are strong and direct. Monetarists perceive the demand for money as stable, so an expansion in the money supply is viewed as generating surpluses of money in the hands of consumers and investors. These surpluses of money, when spent, quickly increase Aggregate Demand.

Classical economics stresses Aggregate Supply, viewing Aggregate Demand as adjusting quickly and automatically when supply conditions change. (Supply creates its own demand.) Recognizing the importance of Aggregate Demand in the short run because the economy may falter occasionally, most monetarists believe that growth of the money supply can boost spending and drive a slumping economy toward full employment. Much like classical theorists, monetarists perceive the market system as inherently stable and think that the economy will seldom deviate for long from full employment.

Monetarists consequently predict that, in the long run, growth in the money supply will be translated strictly into higher prices, even if monetary expansion occurs during a recession. Expansionary macroeconomic policies will, however, induce greater output more quickly in the midst of a recession. In other words, the Aggregate Supply curve described by Keynesians may accurately represent a recessionary economy, but only in the very short run. This view of the world is portrayed in Figure 11.

Suppose the money supply is initially at $800 billion and the price level is 100. The economy is temporarily producing at point a, which is 1.5 trillion units of real GDP below capacity, because full employment income is 7.5 trillion units. If the money supply and Aggregate Demand were held constant, then prices and wages would eventually fall to a long-run equilibrium at point b. Full employment would be realized when the price level fell to 80. If the money supply were expanded to $1 trillion, Aggregate Demand would grow and full employment output of 7.5 trillion units would be realized more rapidly (point c). However, the price level is higher in this long-run equilibrium, being maintained at 100.

Most monetarists oppose active monetary policy to combat recessions. They view long-run adjustments as fairly rapid, believing instead that deflation will quickly restore an economy to full employment. An even greater fear is that discretionary monetary policy might overshoot, converting recession into inflation. This is shown in Figure 11 by too rapid growth of Aggregate Demand when the money supply is increased to $1.2 trillion. In this case, the consequence of policy to combat recession is a 20% percent increase in the price level (point d). According to this monetarist line of thinking, overly aggressive monetary expansion can eliminate recession and unemployment more quickly than do-nothing policies, but only at the risk of sparking inflation.

SUMMARY: CLASSICAL, KEYNESIAN, AND MONETARIST THEORIES

The monetary theories of classical economists, Keynesians, and monetarists are outlined in Figure 12. The major differences in these traditional schools of thought are found in (a) the nature of the demand for money, (b) the nature of the investment relationship, (c) the monetary transmission mechanism, and (d) assumptions about the velocity of money.

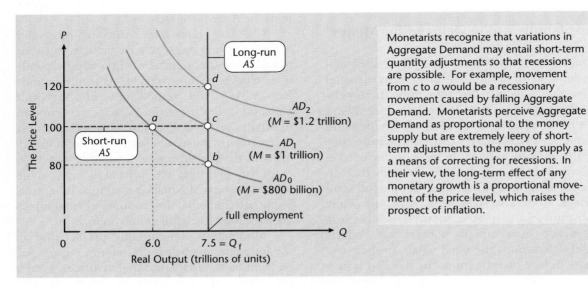

Monetarists recognize that variations in Aggregate Demand may entail short-term quantity adjustments so that recessions are possible. For example, movement from c to a would be a recessionary movement caused by falling Aggregate Demand. Monetarists perceive Aggregate Demand as proportional to the money supply but are extremely leery of short-term adjustments to the money supply as a means of correcting for recessions. In their view, the long-term effect of any monetary growth is a proportional movement of the price level, which raises the prospect of inflation.

FIGURE 11   Monetarist Views of Expansionary Monetary Policy

Differing assumptions about money creation and the effectiveness of monetary policy split Keynesians and monetarists. Many monetarist models ignore institutional mechanisms used to create money (e.g., that the Fed might buy government bonds from banks, thereby increasing excess reserves, which are multiplied into new loan-based demand deposits). Remember, however, that the Fed directly controls the monetary base, not the money supply. Monetarists often simply assume that increases in the monetary base translate into money in the hands of the consuming, investing public. A common monetarist analogy is that a helicopter dumps money into the economy. They then argue, not unreasonably, that if people receive sufficient new money, they will feel wealthier, quit worrying about bad times, and spend it. The result is economic growth and reduced unemployment. This part of the monetarist scenario dispenses with theoretical black holes like liquidity traps.

Modern Keynesians describe not only consumer–investor liquidity traps, but bank liquidity traps as well. Here is their story. Suppose a recession is underway with interest rates at all-time lows. The Fed buys government bonds from banks, increasing the monetary base. Will the banks' new excess reserves translate into more borrowing, demand deposits, and spending? (This is necessary for the monetarist transmission mechanism to work.) Keynesians think not.

If you were a banker in a depressed economy, would you want to cut already low interest rates in order to attract new borrowers, many of whom, given the economic climate, look like potential deadbeats? Would the small cuts in interest that are feasible be sufficiently attractive to prudent borrowers to induce them to apply for new loans? Keynesians (and today, nearly all economists) answer no to both questions. They argue that the banks will simply accumulate more and more vault cash if the Fed tries to counter recessionary tendencies through open-market operations. This is just another aspect of the argument that money (and monetary policy) is a string that is useless for pushing the economy out of the doldrums.

MONETARY POLICY VS. FISCAL POLICY

Classical economics and supply-side approaches lead to the conclusion that Aggregate Demand matters little, if at all, in the long run. Keynesians and monetarists alike, however, focus on Aggregate Demand. Monetarists and contemporary Keynesians clearly have different views on some things, but this should not cloud their areas of agreement. Their differences lie in different views about (a) how important monetary policy is relative to fiscal policy, not that one alone matters to the exclusion of the other, and (b) how quickly and effectively government policies can adjust to reverse momentum towards an excessively inflationary expansion or into a recession.

Relative Effectiveness Arguments

Keynesians and monetarists agree that money matters but differ as to *how much* it matters. Keynesians argue that monetary growth will not raise spending or cut interest rates very much in a slump. Figure 13 shows why. Keynesians view investment as relatively insensitive to interest rates, depending instead primarily upon business expectations. This suggests that slight drops in interest rates when the money supply grows (Panel A) will affect investment and output very little (Panel B). Fiscal policy, on the other hand, is extremely powerful in a slump. Adding government purchases to investment in Panel B boosts autonomous spending and, via the multiplier, massively raises national production and income.

Monetarists see the demand for money as relatively insensitive to interest rates but perceive investment as highly dependent on interest. Even a small increase in the money supply drives interest rates down sharply in the monetarist view (Panel A in Figure 14), which in turn strongly stimulates investment (Panel B). Monetarists also see expansionary monetary policy as bolstering consumer spending, both because extra money burns holes in people's pockets and because lower interest rates make

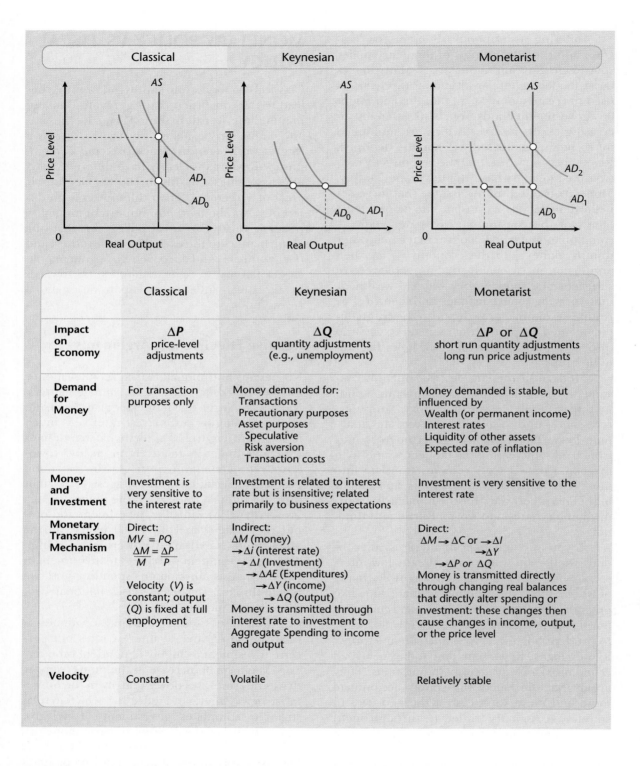

	Classical	Keynesian	Monetarist
Impact on Economy	ΔP price-level adjustments	ΔQ quantity adjustments (e.g., unemployment)	ΔP or ΔQ short run quantity adjustments long run price adjustments

Demand for Money	For transaction purposes only	Money demanded for:
		  Transactions
		  Precautionary purposes
		  Asset purposes
		    Speculative
		    Risk aversion
		    Transaction costs
			Money demanded is stable, but influenced by
			  Wealth (or permanent income)
			  Interest rates
			  Liquidity of other assets
			  Expected rate of inflation

Money and Investment	Investment is very sensitive to the interest rate	Investment is related to interest rate but is insensitive; related primarily to business expectations	Investment is very sensitive to the interest rate

Monetary Transmission Mechanism	Direct:
	$MV = PQ$
	$\dfrac{\Delta M}{M} = \dfrac{\Delta P}{P}$
	
	Velocity (V) is constant; output (Q) is fixed at full employment
		Indirect:
		ΔM (money)
		$\rightarrow \Delta i$ (interest rate)
		  $\rightarrow \Delta I$ (Investment)
		    $\rightarrow \Delta AE$ (Expenditures)
		      $\rightarrow \Delta Y$ (income)
		        $\rightarrow \Delta Q$ (output)
		Money is transmitted through interest rate to investment to Aggregate Spending to income and output
			Direct:
			$\Delta M \rightarrow \Delta C$ or $\rightarrow \Delta I$
			  $\rightarrow \Delta Y$
			    $\rightarrow \Delta P$ or ΔQ
			Money is transmitted directly through changing real balances that directly alter spending or investment: these changes then cause changes in income, output, or the price level

Velocity	Constant	Volatile	Relatively stable

Figure 12   Major Differences Between Classical, Keynesian, and Monetarist Monetary Theories

FIGURE 13   Monetary vs. Fiscal Policy: The Keynesian View

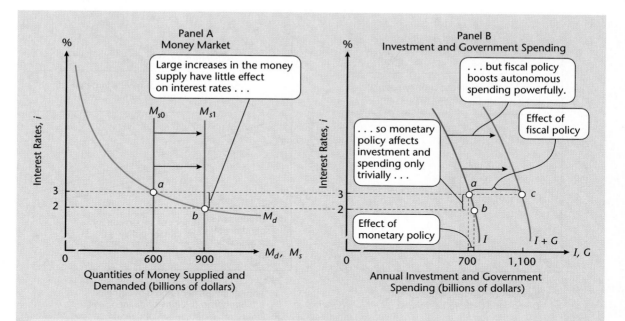

An expansion of the money supply from $600 billion to $900 billion reduces interest rates from only 3% to 2% in a Keynesian slump (Panel A). This small decline in interest rates only raises investment by $50 billion in Panel B because investment is insensitive to interest rates in the Keynesian view. Fiscal policy, on the other hand, is very effective in the Keynesian slump, because dollar for dollar it is just as powerful as new investment in inducing further income through the multiplier process. New government spending of $400 billion ($c-a$) in Panel B expands autonomous spending far more powerfully than does the 50% monetary growth depicted in Panel A.

buying on credit easier and cheaper. Thus, monetarists view money as a powerful tool.

Fiscal policy has only a negligible effect, according to monetarist reasoning, because new government spending does not raise injections ($I + G$) nearly as much as does even a small decline in interest rates. Moreover, monetarists object that government spending may *crowd out* investment. Careful study of Figures 13 and 14 will enable you to understand the fundamental reasons why Keynesians advocate fiscal policy to regulate Aggregate Spending, while monetarists prefer monetary policy.

Keynesians and monetarists agree that when an economy is at full employment, growth of Aggregate Demand raises the price level. Both would agree that, when an economy is in a severe slump, increases in Aggregate Demand will restore full employment. They would, how-

ever, disagree on the appropriate way to expand Aggregate Demand. Monetarists favor expansionary monetary policy to increase private consumption and investment, while Keynesians view that approach as ineffective because of widespread pessimism on the parts of workers, consumers, and business firms. Keynesians, therefore, favor expansionary fiscal policy.

Rules vs. Discretionary Policies

Most economists who draw ideas heavily from the classical school believe that designing discretionary monetary and fiscal policies to buffer business cycles is an impossible task. They favor doing away with all discretion in policymaking and adopting stable and permanent monetary and fiscal rules. These critics believe that the

FIGURE 14 Monetary vs. Fiscal Policy: The Monetarist View

Panel A illustrates the monetarist contention that a slight increase in the money supply (M_{s0} to M_{s1}) will reduce interest rates dramatically (from 9% to 5.5%) because the demand for money (M_d) is relatively insensitive to interest rate changes. Marked declines in interest rates resulting from the extra $100 billion in money cause investment to soar by $1.5 trillion (in Panel B), stimulating autonomous spending far more than even a massive dose ($400 billion) of new government spending.

market system is inherently stable and that severe swings in business activity inevitably follow ill-advised discretionary policies. One mechanism to eliminate discretion in monetary policymaking is a monetary growth rule.

*A **monetary growth rule** would dictate that the money supply be increased at a rate compatible with historical growth of GDP, say 3% annually.*

Suppose you are driving a high-powered car on a fairly straight highway that is banked slightly along the edges to keep you on the road. Unfortunately, someone has blackened the front and side windows—you cannot see where you are or what lies ahead. To make matters worse, your gas pedal sticks at times, the steer-

ing wheel is loose, and your brakes alternate between pure mush and grabbing so sharply that you skid. You can vaguely see where you have been through a fogged-over rearview mirror. What is your best strategy?

If you press the gas pedal too hard, you may go so fast that the curbs at the edge of the road will fail to keep you on course. If you try to steer, you may guide yourself over the side. Your best strategy will be to carefully adjust the accelerator to maintain a slow but steady speed and let the car steer itself away from the road's edges.

The economists who blame cyclical swings on erratic monetary or fiscal policies perceive macroeconomic policymakers as being in our economy's driver's seat. Attempts to fine-tune the economy through discretionary policies are viewed as the fumblings of people who barely deserve learners' permits playing with the controls of an Indianapolis 500 racecar. They tend to oversteer and to jump back and forth from the accelerator to the brake. The resulting stop-and-go economic pattern might resemble your path when you were learning to drive, and, unlike policymakers, you knew what you were passing and could see what lay ahead. We also hope that the steering, braking, and acceleration of the car you drove responded more precisely than the cumbersome tools available to monetary and fiscal policymakers.

In addition to a monetary growth rule, most economists opposed to discretion in policymaking advocate certain fiscal rules:

1. Government spending should be set at the amounts of government goods and services that the public would demand if the economy were at full employment; no make-work projects should be permitted.
2. Tax rates should then be structured so that the federal budget would be roughly in balance if the economy were at full employment.

Although monetarists perceive some problems emerging from improper spending and tax policies (e.g., Hoover's tax hike in 1930–1932, Johnson's simultaneous wars on poverty and in Vietnam, and the enormous budget deficits of the Reagan years), they cast central bankers (the Fed) as the major villains in their explanations of cyclical chaos in market economies.

The Culpability of the Fed

Monetarists view the market system as largely self-stabilizing and predictable; they perceive erratic government policies as the leading cause of business cycles. Monetarists believe that rapid inflation is explained by excessive monetary growth, which results in "too much money chasing too few goods." Alternatively, severe deflations, recessions, or depressions result when the money supply grows too slowly (or even falls), resulting in "too little money chasing too many goods." Government can prevent macroeconomic convulsions by simply holding the rate of growth of the money supply roughly in line with our (slow growing) capacity to produce.

This sounds fairly easy. Why has government not learned these simple monetary facts of life and followed policies to achieve a stable price level and facilitate smooth economic growth? The monetarist answer to this question is that no one is able to predict precisely what will happen to our productive capacity in the near future. Moreover, instituting policies and having them take effect requires time. (We discuss the problems posed by time lags in a later chapter.) Monetarists also believe that the Fed tries too hard to control the economy. Finally, political considerations too often dominate sound policymaking. The solution, according to many monetarists, is to follow a rule of expanding the money supply at a fixed annual rate in the 2% to 4% range compatible with historical growth of our productive capacity.

The Failure of Discretionary Fine-Tuning

From the 1940s through the 1960s, most economists viewed the Great Depression as evidence that only Keynesian engineering can ensure a prosperous and stable economy. Keynesians recommended discretionary changes in taxes and spending as the proper fiscal tools. Other economists argue that the Fed can keep the economy on track by expanding or contracting the money supply as needed. Fiscal and monetary policies both have been frequently changed to try to fine-tune the economy by balancing Aggregate Demand with Aggregate Supply.

Tax rates were cut and the money supply was expanded to stimulate a previously sluggish economy during the early 1960s. Then, monetary restraint was applied in 1966 to curb mounting inflationary pressures. A temporary tax surcharge was imposed in 1969. The money supply grew rapidly in the early 1970s, screeched to a halt causing a short collapse during 1975–1976, accelerated from 1977 to 1979, and then slowed sharply in the early 1980s. Cuts in tax rates from 1981 to 1983 were coupled with a monetary slowdown to reduce inflation while expanding output, but resulted in rapidly rising government deficits.

Keynes believed that central banks tried to follow expansionary policies but failed to cure the Great Depression. This is, in part, why Keynes and his followers sought to replace passive monetary policy with activist fiscal policies. Milton Friedman and other monetarists question the widely held belief that the Great Depression occurred despite expansionary monetary policies. Collecting and reviewing monetary data for the United States for the past century, they discovered that the money supply fell considerably just before and during the Depression. Their interpretation is that the Federal Reserve System caused the Depression because (perhaps unwittingly) it followed contractionary policies.

In fact, most monetarists believe that improper monetary policy is the major cause of business cycles: when the money supply grows too slowly, economic downturns and stagnation soon follow; when the money supply mushrooms, increases in the price level are inevitable.

These difficulties are the major reasons for monetarists' advocacy of stable monetary growth rates. Table 2 summarizes crucial differences between fiscal and monetary policies according to the traditional theories of Keynesian, monetarist, and classical macroeconomics.

Classical theory, with its emphasis on Aggregate Supply, provides some insights, but not a complete picture, of macroeconomic problems encountered in most modern economies (e.g., sustained high rates of unemployment). Nor does Keynesian theory, with its stress on variations in Aggregate Demand in a world beset by depression, systematically address such problems as naggingly high unemployment accompanied by persistent creeping inflation. Even monetarism, which treats Aggregate Supply from a classical perspective while recognizing the relevance of Aggregate Demand in the short run, has failed to explain economic events of recent years.

You may have the sense that these theories are so disparate that the prospects for economists

TABLE 2   Alternative Views of Monetary and Fiscal Policies

Traditional Keynesians	The Classical Tradition	
	Monetarists	Supply-Siders
1. Fiscal policy is very powerful.	1. Fiscal policy is relatively unimportant due to *crowding out*.	1. High tax rates and vast government spending both reduce the incentives for people to be productive.
2. Monetary policy is not very powerful or important in economic slumps.	2. Erratic monetary policy is the major cause of business cycles. Money is important at all times.	2. Erratic fiscal policy confuses investors and workers, reducing incentives forproductivity. Erratic monetary policy diverts resources from production into hedges against inflation or deflation.
3. Monetary policy affects spending through changes in interest rates and investments.	3. Monetary policy affects spending in all markets simultaneously ($MV = PQ$)	3. Money is a veil.
4. Discretionary policies are necessary to offset the economy's necessary instability.	4. Smooth growth of the money supply is crucial. Rules should replace discretion in policy. The economy is inherently stable.	4. Steady monetary policy enhances the quality of information about economic decisions.
5. Velocity is erratic; it rises during inflation but falls sharply during recessions.	5. Velocity is relatively stable.	5. Velocity is stable if monetary policy is stable.
6. During deep depressions, fear causes velocity to plummet, resulting in *liquidity traps*.	6. Liquidity traps are highly implausible and have never actually occurred.	6. Liquidity traps are irrelevant to the real world.

ever reaching any consensus are practically nil. From the 1940s through the 1980s, the policies of the Federal Reserve System meandered back and forth between Keynesian, classical, and monetarist recipes, with results that, predictably, were mixed. Several things have become fairly clear, however. One is that frequent changes in both monetary and fiscal policy have confounded economic stability as often as they have helped dampen business cycles; extremely active fine-tuning does not work. Another is that all of these traditional theories have left a legacy, filling in pieces of the puzzle of how a mixed economy with substantial networks of both markets and government actually works.

NEW CLASSICAL ECONOMICS AND NEW KEYNESIAN ECONOMICS

Most economists today interpret economic behavior through lenses that blend recent insights with pieces assembled from a range of traditional theories they find appealing. Regardless of whether economists are aligned more closely with new classical theory or new Keynesian theory, they tend to agree on more than was true in earlier debates—this may be a sign of slowly emerging consensus on a number of issues. But areas of disagreement remain.

The positions of these two groups (detailed in the remaining macroeconomic parts of this book) are outlined in Table 3. Notice that issues about Aggregate Demand are far more settled than issues about Aggregate Supply. Differences among new classical economists and new Keynesian economists hinge primarily on differing theoretical views about the relative speeds of price adjustments versus quantity adjustments in response to changes in the economic climate. How fast these adjustments occur depends on the competitiveness of markets, on various institutional factors (e.g., the extent of unionization and legal structures), and on workers' attitudes towards wage cuts.

TABLE 3   New Classical Macroeconomists and New Keynesians: Emerging Consensus?

Issue	New Classical	New Keynesian
Aggregate Supply		
Market Structures	Markets are extremely competitive and clear quickly	The vigor of competition varies widely across markets
Wage and Price Adjustments	Extremely quick—markets clear rapidly	Imperfect competition makes prices sticky; institutional rigidities make wages sticky
Unemployment	All unemployment except that caused by minimum wage laws is voluntary	Institutional wage stickiness may cause prolonged involuntary unemployment
Aggregate Demand		
Monetary Policy	Changes Aggregate Demand	Changes Aggregate Demand
Velocity of Money	No consensus	May be destabilized by legal or technological changes, or by changes in expectations
Inflation	Supply shocks may drive up the price level, but sustained inflation is primarily monetary	Supply shocks may drive up the price level, but sustained inflation is primarily monetary
Fiscal Policy	Alters incentives and AS; unpredictable effects on AD because relative prices change	Changes both AD and AS, but institutional rigidities preclude effective fine-tuning
Rules vs. Discretion	Rules are more stabilizing because markets will adjust	Discretionary policy making is appropriate in extreme cases

Wage-price stickiness, which sounds extremely abstract, has profound implications for whether discretionary monetary or fiscal policies can improve macroeconomic stability, or whether we would all be better off, on average, if markets were allowed to adjust without active government policies. The new Keynesians focus on explanations for wage-price stickiness. If wages and prices are extremely sticky, major macroeconomic problems may be cured more rapidly if the government acts. The new classical economics, on the other hand, assumes that markets clear through almost instantaneous price adjustments, and that active policymaking is likely to be dysfunctional.

We will look at various ways to finance government activity in the next chapter; monetary and fiscal policies are linked through the government budget equation. We will also examine the effects of the growth of government debt caused by persistent federal deficits. Then, in subsequent chapters, we will examine pressing macroeconomic issues from the perspectives of theorists who favor active policies when the economy faces major problems versus the views of theorists who prefer more passive policies based closer to a laissez-faire philosophy.

CHAPTER REVIEW: KEY POINTS

1. You increase your *spending* when you have "too much" money; your rate of *saving* rises when you have "too little" money.

2. People hold money for predictable spending (**transactions demands**) with a cushion for uncertain outlays or income receipts (**precautionary demands**). People also have **asset demands** for money because (*a*) money is relatively riskless, (*b*) transaction costs associated with less-liquid assets may exceed expected returns, or (*c*) people speculate by holding money when they expect the prices of alternative assets (e.g., stocks, bonds, or real estate) to fall.

3. According to classical monetary theory, the sole rational motive for holding money is to *consummate transactions*.

4. Interest rates and bond prices are *inversely related*. Bond prices fall if interest rates rise, and vice versa.

5. The costs of holding nominal amounts of money are (*a*) *the reciprocal of the price level* (1/*P*) if the choice is between saving money or buying consumer goods, or (*b*) *the interest rate*, if money is viewed as an asset substitutable for some highly liquid income-generating asset, say a bond. *Inflation* also imposes costs on holdings of money.

6. The **income velocity** (*V*) *of money* equals GDP (*PQ*) divided by the money supply (*M*).

7. The **equation of exchange**, a truism, is written $MV = PQ$. Therefore, the percentage change in the money supply plus the percentage change in velocity roughly equals the percentage change in the price level plus the percentage change in real output:

$$\frac{\Delta M}{M} + \frac{\Delta V}{V} = \frac{\Delta P}{P} + \frac{\Delta Q}{Q}$$

8. Classical economics assumes that *velocity* (*V*) and *output* (*Q*) are reasonably constant and independent of the money supply (*M*) and the price level (*P*). Classical economists believe that changes in the money supply result in proportional changes in the price level and expressed this belief in early versions of the quantity theory of money. The *quantity theory of money* is more accurately *a monetary theory of the price level*.

9. Keynes's attack on the quantity theory disputes the assumptions that (*a*) the natural state of the economy is full employment, (*b*) the velocity of money is inherently stable,

and (c) the only rational motive for holding money is for transactions purposes.

10. Monetarists perceive a direct link between the money supply and National Income. Because the demand for money is relatively stable, growth of the money supply puts excess money balances in the hands of consumers and investors who, in turn, spend this surplus money on goods and services. Monetary growth may expand output in the short run, but monetarists conclude that, in the long run, higher prices will result.

11. The difficulties confronting monetary and fiscal policymakers have caused many economists to favor putting the economy on automatic pilot. The advocates of replacing *discretionary policy* with **monetary growth rules** would replace the Federal Open Market Committee with a couple of reliable but unimaginative clerks. Their job would be to increase the money supply by a fixed, small (3%?) increase annually, and the federal budget would be set to balance at full employment.

QUESTIONS FOR THOUGHT AND DISCUSSION

1. Do you think most people want to balance illiquid assets against highly liquid assets, such as money? Why? How does your line of reasoning lead to the demand for money? Does your answer suggest that the demand for money will be sensitive to interest rates? To the cost of living? How, and why or why not?

2. Describe the differences between Keynesian and monetarist monetary transmission mechanisms. Why are these differences important? In what way does Keynesian fiscal policy short-circuit the difficulties they perceive in transforming new money into new spending?

3. As people expect more inflation, they may begin treating money as a hot potato; average money holdings may fall, with the result that velocity increases. On the other hand, increased inflation may generate more uncertainty, which may cause people to increase their money holdings. People who anticipate higher inflation and want to accumulate a given real amount of saving before retirement, but who are leery of most financial investments, may try to build their holdings of money. On average, do you think the inflation of the past 20 years has caused real money balances per capita to rise or fall? How would you test this hypothesis? To what extent can inflation be considered a tax on money balances?

4. Keynesian theory suggests that the relevant substitutes for money are securities, while monetarists argue for a broader range of substitutes that include consumer and investment goods. How important is this difference in explaining the impact of money on economic activity? Why?

5. Suppose a rule of 3% annual monetary growth were imposed. How long should policymakers doggedly follow such a policy if inflation soared to more than 20% or unemployment hovered around 15%?

Money

Interest rates

Discount rate

M_{s0} M_{s1}

Bank

M1

FED

M_d

Reserve requirement

Chapter 15

Budget Deficits and Public Debt

Unemployment, inflation, and economic growth obviously bear on the quality of our lives, but few Americans can identify how federal budget deficits and public debt affect them personally. Nevertheless, many people are upset because our federal budget has been awash in red ink.

> The **budget deficit** *is the annual difference between federal outlays and receipts* $(G - T)$.

The sum of annual deficits during the 1980s exceeded the totals piled up by all presidents from George Washington through Jimmy Carter.

> **National (public) debt** *results from cumulated federal deficits.*

National debt has roughly quadrupled since 1980 and will surpass $5 trillion by the end of 1995.

Critics of huge federal deficits and astronomical public debt argue that organizations that spend more than their receipts are doomed, asserting that the federal government should be run "more like a business" or at least balance its budget like most state and local governments. A pattern is developing. Between 1985 and 1994, three major "budget reduction laws" were enacted, each intended to eliminate federal deficits "within five years." In each case, the budget laws passed for the next year or two amended the act, postponing the day of reckoning. Then, when it became obvious that the budget target in the particular act was out of reach, eleventh-hour negotiations culminated in passage of yet another piece of legislation. Are huge budget deficits really cause for concern? Or are deficits and the debt just political issues used to bash incumbent officeholders around election time?

In this chapter a number of issues surrounding deficits and national debt are addressed. How can the federal government finance persistent deficits for decades? What consequences follow binges of deficit spending? When, if ever, is a deficit desirable? Have linkages between budget deficits and deficits in our international trade caused us to sell U.S. resources to foreigners wholesale? Must future generations of Americans pay for our free-spending ways?

RECENT GROWTH OF DEFICITS AND DEBT

Federal deficits are increasingly common and surpluses, increasingly rare, despite biannual pledges from political candidates that they will balance the budget. Figure 1 traces the recent history of deficits and total interest-bearing public debt. The federal budget has been in deficit 90% of the time since World War II; our most recent surplus occurred in 1969.

Political battles over the budget usually pivot on spending priorities instead of curbing the deficit. Whose programs will be sacrificed? For example, Presidents Ford and Reagan both sought to build up national defense and urged

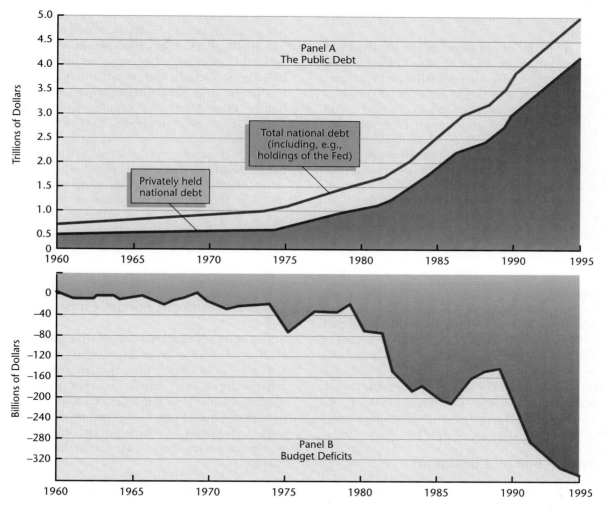

Source: *Economic Report of the President*, 1994.

Budget deficits from the 1950s through the 1970s were considered enormous at the time, but they have been swamped (even after adjustments for inflation) by more recent deficits. National debt has almost quadrupled since 1980.

FIGURE 1 **Budget Deficits and the Public Debt**

cuts in transfer programs to reduce deficits. Congress, however, resisted cuts in transfer payments. The result? Record deficits and soaring debt because both defense and transfer spending grew. The demise of the Cold War in the early 1990s gave President Clinton latitude to slash the defense budget, but sharp cutbacks in real defense spending did little to reverse the deficit. Instead, most of the so-called "peace dividend" was used to expand the federal government's role in battling crime, providing medical insurance, and building technological infrastructure (e.g., subsidies for an "information highway").

The continuing growth of public debt worries many people. In 1992, Ross Perot garnered almost 20% of the presidential vote by harping primarily on the single issue of government deficits. Our previous analysis, however, suggests that deficit spending may facilitate recovery from a recession. Almost all modern economists are convinced that Herbert Hoover and the Congress erred when they raised taxes to balance the fiscal 1933 budget—the economy quickly sank to the lowest point of the Great Depression. We will now examine how deficits can be financed and the different budget constraints facing the private and public sectors.

PRIVATE VS. PUBLIC FINANCE

What mechanisms enable individuals and governments to run deficits? How can governments run persistent deficits? Many people draw incorrect analogies between government finance and business or household budgeting because they do not understand the different spending constraints facing the private and the public sectors.

Private Budget Constraints

The availability of funds limits spending by households, proprietors, and partnerships. Funds are made available through (a) sales of current assets, (b) current income (including inheritance or gifts), or (c) borrowing against assets or expected future income. You know how

tightly credit is rationed to fund private spending if you have ever exceeded your credit limit. Even young people with great potential future income have problems borrowing. (This is one reason the government guarantees most student loans.) Sole proprietorships and partnerships face similar spending constraints, but big corporations tend to have fewer problems acquiring funds.

• **Corporations**   The idea that corporations regularly balance their budgets is false. Most corporate giants become more indebted with each passing decade, but they also have more revenue and hold more assets. Big corporations establish huge lines of credit with major financial intermediaries, and they also borrow by issuing bonds. Their bonds are usually more salable than IOUs from households, proprietorships, or partnerships, because most large corporations are superior credit risks. Corporations have an additional source of purchasing power available: they can sell stock to finance spending. The ability to sell bonds and to offer ownership shares (stock) gives corporations more flexibility and power than other firms in securing funds to cover operating expenses or for new investments in plant and equipment.

Local Government Budget Constraints

States, counties, cities, school districts, and other local government units face slightly different spending constraints. Like proprietorships or partnerships, they finance current spending with revenues from selling goods and services or some of their assets. Like corporations, they may issue bonds to obtain purchasing power, but government does not sell ownership shares (stock).

• **Taxes**   Another major difference between the private sector and government is that government can enact *taxes* to finance spending, which gives it enormous power to acquire resources. But even the power to tax allows only limited command over resources. Overly optimistic revenue projections or excessive spending by local governments sometimes results in loan defaults. Some hobbyists collect defunct municipal bonds the way others collect stamps. They know that few of these bonds will ever be redeemed; rarity and appearance alone determine their values.

Lotteries now augment revenues in many states, with proceeds (half of ticket revenues) usually being earmarked for parks or schools. Advocates favor lotteries as "voluntary taxes," but critics oppose them as regressive—poor people buy disproportionate numbers of tickets, despite incredible odds against striking it rich. (Las Vegas slot machines have much better payoff ratios.) Moreover, lotteries provide only tiny shares of total revenues to states that offer them.

• **Regulation or Confiscation** Government also channels resource allocations through *regulation* or *confiscation*. For example, regulations force car owners to buy emission-controlling exhaust systems and limit firms' pollution levels. Through such regulations, the government buys a cleaner environment for all of us, and we pay for it without explicit tax increases. You may think that government in the United States does not use direct confiscation. The right of *eminent domain*, however, is used by all levels of government to secure land for such things as highway rights-of-way or areas for dams or parks. When government exercises eminent domain those forced to sell their property are paid a government-determined "fair market value." Although the military draft is not used at present, it is another example of government confiscating resources.

The Federal Budget Constraint

A national government has another major tool at hand: it can print additional *monetary base* to pay for its outlays. (Recall that the monetary base equals currency plus all reserves in the banking system.) In many countries, the central bank covers government outlays by issuing bonds, collecting taxes, or creating additional monetary base. In the United States, financing a deficit ($G - T$) with monetary base is a more indirect process because, in an accounting sense, our Treasury "borrows" money from the Fed, which actually creates the additional monetary base.

The Treasury first issues new bonds to cover a federal deficit. The Fed then buys the bonds through expansionary open-market operations. Bank reserves grow and are transformed into new money through the money multiplier process. Bonds bought by the Fed are considered, for accounting purposes, to be part of national debt. It is nonsense, however, to suggest that total debt is larger because one government agency (Treasury) owes another (the Fed). Thus, in what follows, we ignore Treasury bonds held by the Fed when we count the national debt.

In summary, government can secure resources to provide goods and services through (*a*) sales of current assets or outputs; (*b*) loans from U.S. citizens and firms, foreign citizens or governments, or commercial banks; (*c*) taxation; (*d*) confiscation; or (*e*) expansion of the monetary base (currency in circulation plus bank reserves).

Confiscation can be regarded as taxation in kind, so central government outlays are characterized by a government budget constraint.

The **government budget constraint** *identifies financing options open to the federal government:*

$$G = T + \Delta B + \Delta MB$$

where G = total governmental outlays, T = total governmental revenues from taxes, charges, and sales, ΔB = change in the national debt, and ΔMB = change in the monetary base. Consequently, the federal deficit can also be expressed as

$$G - T = \Delta B + \Delta MB$$

In plain English, this equation means that if the federal government spends more than it collects ($G - T > 0$), it must either borrow ($\Delta B > 0$) or create (print) the monetary base difference ($\Delta MB > 0$). The money expansion process applies to any growth of the monetary base, as described earlier. If the government collects more than it spends ($G - T < 0$), it can either retire some existing debt ($\Delta B < 0$) or retire some money it has previously created ($\Delta MB < 0$). Budget deficits cause growth in the national debt or in the money supply, while government surpluses make it possible to pay off some of the national debt or remove some money from circulation or both. Borrowing money or selling current assets to secure purchasing power are common to both private and government decision-makers. But private citizens cannot legally tax, confiscate, or create (print) more monetary base.

When thinking about the national debt, few people take into account that wealthier people or organizations usually owe far more than poorer ones. For example, you probably owe more now than when you were ten years old. Similarly, each of the world's 1,000 largest industrial corporations probably owes more than any recent start-up company. Most analysts conclude that if the federal government had a garage sale to sell all federally owned parks, equipment, highways, and buildings, it could easily retire all its debt. In Figure 2, we trace the debt of U.S. households, businesses, and government entities as percentages of U.S. GDP. Notice that private debt has often grown, relative to national income, as fast or faster than federal debt, but that federal debt, which had been on a downward path relative to GDP from World War II into the 1970s, has climbed steadily in more recent years.

Are there limits to a government's command over resources? The ultimate limit is peo-

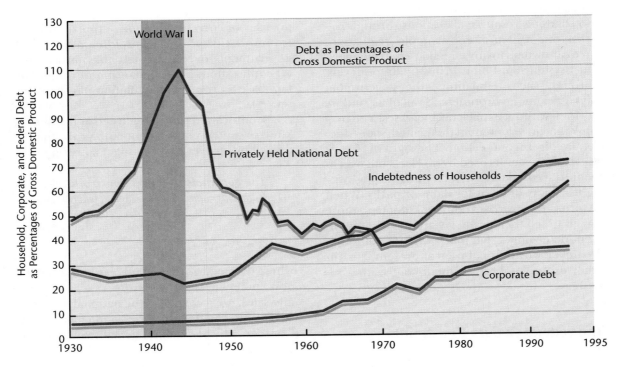

Source: *Economics Report of the President, 1994*

National debt as a percentage of U.S. GDP peaked during World War II, declined until 1975, and has been rising since then. Household debt has also been rising across the decades, it surpassed privately-held federal debt in the 1960s now exceeds 70 percent of our GDP. Corporate debt is also rising, in part because of funding required to finance recurrent waves of corporate mergers.

FIGURE 2   Private and Public Debt as Percentages of U.S. Gross Domestic Product

ple's faith that government will survive, honor its contracts, and maintain the money it issues at reasonably stable values. The worthlessness of bonds issued by Russian czars, Chinese warlords, and other dictators overthrown by military coups or revolutions attests that this faith is not always justified. Fiscal mismanagement has been the problem as frequently as political oppression or widespread corruption.

FUNCTIONAL FINANCE VS. BALANCED BUDGETS

Should the budget be balanced at all times or only over the business cycle? Or is balancing the budget irrelevant? Each of these positions finds some disciples among politicians, economists, and the public at large. Let's examine the logic of whether balancing the budget really matters.

Balancing Budgets Annually

Many people who want less government also favor continually balancing the budget for political reasons. Their rationale is that more of a laissez-faire approach will unchain market forces and stimulate economic growth, and a "balanced budget" amendment to the Constitution would limit the ability of Congress to spend and would reduce the economic role of government. Even if you favor tighter limits on government, however, you should recognize that a balanced-budget amendment might open a Pandora's box. We could find ourselves faced with Herbert Hoover's dilemma: curing deficits may worsen unemployment and stymie economic growth. If GDP began falling, tax revenues would fall. At the same time, rising unemployment would mandate more outlays for such transfer payments as unemployment compensation.

Raising tax rates would shrink both Aggregate Supply and Aggregate Demand and could actually reduce tax revenues. Attempts to slash government spending might even shrink GDP so much that tax revenues would fall even more than any spending cuts, worsening the deficit. Few economists are convinced that fiscal

policy has zero effect on National Income, and even fewer favor rigidly balanced budgets. Focus 1 describes a recent revival of an ancient argument that total government spending matters, but how the budget is financed is irrelevant.

Budget Balancing Over Business Cycles

A more sophisticated view admits that annually balanced budgets may foster instability. This proposal is to balance the budget *over the business cycle*. Its advocates realize that we should not raise taxes or cut spending to cover cyclical deficits caused by recessions, or liquidate inflation-caused surpluses through tax cuts or hikes in spending. This group contends that cyclical deficits should be offset by surpluses collected during prosperity. Thus, over a complete business cycle, there would be no net growth in national debt.

Keynesians have typically criticized this approach by arguing that prosperity may not last long enough or be strong enough to generate surpluses sufficient to offset deficits, especially if recessions tend to be either extended or especially severe. Our economy might equilibrate around a lower average level of income than might otherwise be sustainable.

Functional Finance

Keynesian economists traditionally favored activist fiscal policies, arguing that we should try to balance *the economy* at full employment, and that balancing or not balancing the budget is irrelevant per se. In this view, injections (investment plus government spending plus exports) need to be set to equal withdrawals (saving plus taxes plus imports) at a high rate of capacity utilization. A budget mix that yields full employment is best; taxes and government outlays never need to balance precisely.[1]

---

[1]Abba P. Lerner, "Functional Finance and the Federal Debt," in *A Nation in Debt: Economists Debate the Federal Budget Deficit*, Richard Fink and Jack High Washington, D.C. American Enterprise Institute, (1987).

Ricardian Equivalence and Inflationary Finance

Debates about how to finance government date back for centuries. The great classical economist David Ricardo (1772–1823) analyzed public debt and deficits as if people regarded public debt as equivalent to private debt. The Ricardian equivalence theorem as he elaborated it stated

When for the expenses of a year's war, twenty millions are raised by means of a loan, it is the twenty millions which are withdrawn from the productive capital of the nation . . . . Government might at once have required the twenty millions in the shape of taxes; in which case it would not have been necessary to raise annual taxes to the amount of a million. This, however, would not have changed the nature of the transaction. An individual instead of being called upon to pay £100 per annum, might have been obliged to pay £2000 once and for all. *

Recently, Robert Barro,** has resurrected Ricardo's view point that public debt and taxes are equivalent. According to Barro, if government borrows more today (issues bonds), taxpayers realize that higher future taxes will be required to pay interest on the debt and eventually repay it, so our current saving rates should rise as we bank funds to pay these future tax bills.

Barro's version of Ricardian equivalence essentially treats the burden of paying for government spending as unaffected by the mode of finance; citizens adjust to taxes, public debt, or new monetary base as mechanisms that simply transfer parts of gross private saving to use by the public sector.

Ultimately, nominal variables such as the price level or the monetary rate of saving or interest will reflect how government budgets are financed, but real macroeconomic variables—employment, output, and National Income—would be unaffected.

An intriguing historical footnote is that before he confronted the dilemma posed by the Great Depression with his *General Theory*, John Maynard Keynes's views on the irrelevance of the mode by which government finances its spending appeared quite classical, differing little from those of Ricardo—or Barro. In 1923, Keynes observed that

It is common to speak as though, when a government pays its way by inflation, the people of the country avoid taxation. We have seen this is not so. What is raised by printing notes is just as much taken from the public as is beer-duty or income-tax. What a government spends the public pays for. There is no such thing as an uncovered deficit. But in some countries it seems possible to please and content the public, for a time at least, by giving them, in return for the taxes they pay, finely engraved acknowledgments on water-marked paper. The income tax receipts which we in England receive from the surveyor, we throw into the wastepaper basket; in Germany they call them bank-notes and put them into their pocketbooks; in France they are termed Rentes and are locked up in the family safe. ***

According to these classical perspectives, we gain nothing by piling up public debt or issuing monetary base instead of financing government through taxes. We might as well balance the budget annually. Naturally, Keynes's views on this issue changed sharply when, in the 1930s, he tried to address the challenge of economies plagued by idle capital and unemployed labor.

One important assumption of Barro's model is that taxpayers have an infinite time horizon because they are concerned about the effects of present debt on their children and future generations. This seems questionable. Moreover, predictions based on Ricardian equivalence have not been borne out. Tax cuts and swelling deficits did not stimulate higher saving rates in the 1980s. In fact, saving rates fell. Rising saving during 1985–1990 might seem to support Barro, but his model is inconsistent with such lags. This increased saving is, however, consistent with Keynesian theory (rising income during the 1983–1989 recovery stimulated saving) or with demographic changes (baby boomers are outgrowing the high consumption period of young family formation and are beginning to save for retirement).

* D. Ricardo, "Principles of Political Economy and Taxation," *Works and Correspondence*, vol. 1 (1807, Cambridge: Cambridge University Press, 1951).
** R. Barro, "Are Government Bonds Net Wealth?" *Journal of Political Economy*, December 1974.
*** J.M. Keynes, *Monetary Reform* (New York: Harcourt General, 1924), pp. 68–69.

*The **functional finance** approach to the government budget emphasizes that taxes are only one way to finance government outlays. How best to pay for government depends on which policies are least costly under existing economic conditions.*

Taxation to cover new government spending is the least expansionary mode and is most appropriate when the economy is close to full employment. If the Treasury borrows to cover a deficit, the people who buy government bonds may reduce their spending. Investors also tend to be squeezed, because Treasury bonds absorb private saving and drive up interest rates. Nevertheless, bond financing is usually considered more expansionary than taxation as a way to finance government outlays.

The most expansionary method of all is to create more monetary base to cover a deficit. But this path can be explosive. During 1991–1993, Yugoslavia (comprising only Montenegro and Serbia, after Bosnia and Croatia each declared independence in 1990) tried to finance almost all government spending via the printing press. The resulting hyperinflation mounted to 1,000,000% per month, threatening to eclipse the all-time record set by Hungary from 1945 to 1946.

CROWDING OUT

What the government gives it must first take away.

John S. Coleman

Keynesians believe that increased government purchases can stimulate a depressed economy. New classical economists disagree, arguing that government spending tends to **crowd out** private economic activity. They point out that *gross private saving* (total output minus private consumption) is absorbed by government purchases regardless of whether government taxes (*T*), borrows (ΔB), or inflates the money supply (ΔMB). Nevertheless, how government is financed strongly affects the impact of government purchases. The Fed is the government's banker and, with the Treasury, determines how deficits and surpluses are financed. This reso-

lution is crucial in determining levels for prices, interest rates, trade balances, and National Income and Output.

Crowding out and paying for government are closely related.

***Crowding out** is the idea that increases in government purchases inevitably cause reductions in private consumption or investment.[2]*

Government outlays may crowd out private activities through (*a*) less leisure for workers, (*b*) reduced consumer purchasing power (caused by inflation or tax hikes), or (*c*) lower profits for investors (because of higher interest rates). Keep in mind, however, that it is possible that the goods government provides may be more valuable than the activity crowded out.

Government's Costs when Resources Are Idle

The alternatives individuals lose when government acquires more resources determine who really pays for government. Suppose that our economy is in a depression with massive unemployment of land, labor, and capital. Government might boost output by drafting (confiscating) idle resources, or it could secure money to pay for them through taxes, growth of the monetary base, or borrowing. If these resources would have been completely unproductive in the absence of government action, the opportunity costs of the extra output are zero; the additional government services would not cost anyone anything.

The production possibilities frontier in Figure 3 allows us to examine an increase in government spending and the resulting induced consumption. If many resources are idle and the economy is initially at point *a*, raising government spending from G_0 to G_1 closes the reces-

---

[2]Early "crowding-out" hypotheses focused only on how government deficits drive interest rates up and, consequently, reduce investments. Our treatment follows a more recent convention that crowding out encompasses all reduction in private activities caused when government programs grow.

FIGURE 3 The Costs of Government: Crowding Out

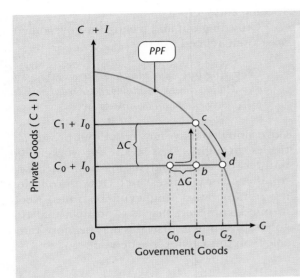

The general problem of how government spending can *crowd out* private activity is illustrated in this figure. Beginning from a point of considerable unemployment (*a*), government can increase spending from G_0 to G_1; new consumption equal to $C_1 - C_0$ will be induced through the multiplier. The opportunity costs of such increases are the value of the private uses to which that ΔG would have been put, including the leisure foregone by the newly employed. Once the economy has achieved full employment (point *c*), increased government spending to G_2 (point *d*) necessarily causes a reduction in private spending from C_1 to C_0. Critics of the growth of government view expanded government as an inefficient block to investment that would foster healthy long-run economic growth.

sionary gap in this idealized case. Consumption induced through the Keynesian multiplier process will drive total consumption from C_0 to C_1. This completes closure of the GDP gap, so the path to full employment is $a \to b \to c$.

This seems to be an exception to the *TIN-STAAFL* rule that "There is no such thing as a free lunch." It is not. Few resources are ever totally without valuable uses "in the absence of government action." For example, idle labor produces leisure; most of us prefer no work to work with no pay. To induce idle labor to work voluntarily, government must pay a wage that offsets the value of the leisure lost in producing the extra output; increases in employment come at the cost of forgone leisure.

Government might use direct confiscation to impose on the owners of idle resources the full cost of providing extra government goods; drafting unemployed labor for armies of conservation workers or highway repair crews would be examples. If tax revenues are used to pay the owners of the newly employed resources, the burden falls largely on taxpayers. If government creates money to pay for these resources, then the higher incomes of the owners of previously idle resources may be partially offset by inflationary reductions in the purchasing power of other citizens.

Suppose the government issues bonds to buy the resources used to produce extra government goods. The consequences are illustrated in Figure 4. When more Treasury bonds are issued, raising the supply of bonds from S_0 to S_1 (in Panel A), bond prices fall. The falling price of bonds causes interest rates to climb from i_0 to i_1 (from point *a* to point *b* in Panel B). Successful borrowers pay higher interest rates and some private investment is crowded out. This dampens the growth in Aggregate Demand, which rises only from AD_0 to AD_1—not to AD_2—in Panel C, as would occur without crowding out.

Borrowers and potential borrowers pay the short-run burden of more government spending when a budget deficit is financed by sales of new government bonds. Figure 5 illustrates how real interest rates jumped with the record deficits of the late 1970s and early 1980s and then fell when deficits declined temporarily in the late 1980s. In the longer run, consumers will pay higher prices because investment shrinks, adding less to the stock of capital. With less capital growth, real wages and output will not rise as fast.

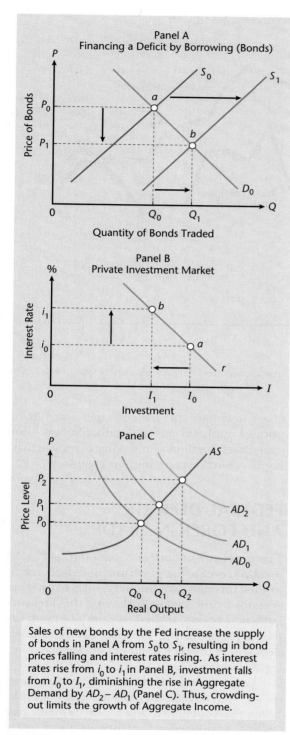

Panel A
Financing a Deficit by Borrowing (Bonds)

Panel B
Private Investment Market

Panel C

Sales of new bonds by the Fed increase the supply of bonds in Panel A from S_0 to S_1, resulting in bond prices falling and interest rates rising. As interest rates rise from i_0 to i_1 in Panel B, investment falls from I_0 to I_1, diminishing the rise in Aggregate Demand by $AD_2 - AD_1$ (Panel C). Thus, crowding-out limits the growth of Aggregate Income.

FIGURE 4 The Crowding-Out Effect: Investment

When the economy is at less than full employment, the degree of crowding out depends in part on the interest sensitivity of demands for loans by investors and consumers. During severe recessions, induced Keynesian growth of income can overwhelm any losses in purchasing power caused by crowding out. However, crowding out always restricts the power of the Keynesian multiplier process to boost real income, especially in a fully employed economy.

Government's Costs During Full Employment

We have assumed that some resources were idle when government purchases grew. Expanded government spending is a standard Keynesian prescription when the economy is in a slump. Who pays for government growth if the economy is fully employed? When all resources are efficiently and fully employed, any increase in government purchases necessitates declines in either private consumption, investment, or net exports. Refer back to Figure 3. If the economy began at point c, boosting government purchases from G_1 to G_2 would move the economy to point d and shrink the sum of private spending (consumption and investment) from $C_1 + I_0$ to $C_0 + I_0$.

Government causes crowding out through tax hikes, confiscation, inflation, or higher interest rates. Excessive reliance on any single mechanism may cause political turmoil and significantly reduce some resource owners' incentives to be productive; therefore, government commonly chooses a mix of these ways to cover new government spending.

For example, President Johnson realized that the voting public would reject tax increases to pay for both the war in Vietnam and the war on poverty in the late 1960s. In spite of advice from his Council of Economic Advisors that tax increases were necessary to avoid inflationary pressures, President Johnson chose to run budgetary deficits. What choices were available? Because $G - T = \Delta B + \Delta MB$, the alternatives were either to borrow the money or print it.

FIGURE 5 Real Interest Rates and Budget Deficits as Percentages of GDP

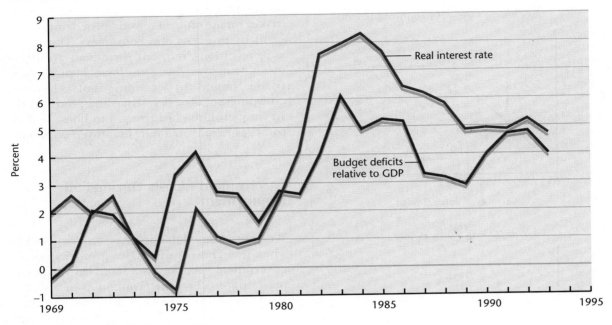

Source: *Economic Report of the President,* 1994.

When budget deficits have grown relative to our GDP, real interest rates (money rates of interest adjusted for inflation) have also tended to rise.

The Treasury initially covered the deficits by issuing new bonds. A large proportion of the loanable funds available would have been absorbed if these bonds had been purchased solely by the public; interest rates would have soared, leaving little money available for private investment. The Federal Reserve Board elected to buy many of the new bonds issued by the Treasury. This expanded the monetary base and caused the money supply to rise, preventing the full brunt of financing the Vietnam War from falling exclusively on private investment. Inflation caused prices and nominal income to swell, so total tax revenues increased.

The overall result was that crowding out spread the costs of the war on poverty and the Vietnam War across four groups: (*a*) investors, who paid higher interest rates; (*b*) consumers, who paid higher prices; (*c*) taxpayers, who paid higher taxes; and (*d*) Selective Service draftees—being drafted was a form of confiscation of labor (and lives) to pay for the Vietnam War. This example correctly suggests that the mix of policies

government uses to finance its spending has important implications for the distribution of income; each method of reducing private activity imposes burdens on different groups.

FEDERAL DEFICITS AND FOREIGN TRADE

The government budget equation ($G - T = \Delta B + \Delta MB$) reveals that government deficits can be funded through expansionary open-market operations by the Fed or by having the Treasury issue new bonds. If the Fed does not monetize the deficit by buying Treasury bonds, national debt that is privately held by Americans or foreigners grows.

Government spending not covered by taxes ($G - T > 0$) represents production not used by households but unavailable for investment. This "saving" may be voluntary (private purchases of Treasury bonds) or involuntary (new money creates inflationary pressure that has been called "the cruelest tax"). This private but uninvested saving may be made available to government by domestic entities or by foreigners.

Trade Deficits

Foreigners make parts of their gross saving (production minus consumption) available by exporting more to us than we export to them; we experience a trade deficit in which imports exceed exports. To see how foreign trade and budget deficits are related, remember that in a macroeconomic equilibrium all injections ($G + I + X$) must be balanced by total withdrawals ($S + T + M$). Thus,

$$G + I + X = S + T + M$$

Thus, if we rearrange terms and include the foreign sector into the government budget equation, it can be expressed as

$$G - T = (S - I) + (M - X) = \Delta B + \Delta MB$$

where S = domestic savings, I = domestic investment, M = imports, and X = exports.

Explicitly considering the international sector in the government budget constraint suggests that federal deficits must equal the domestic savings surplus (saving minus investment) plus the trade deficit (imports minus exports). For example, in 1980 the budget deficit was $60.1 billion, the savings surplus was $45.4 billion, and the United States ran a trade deficit of $14.7 billion [60.1 = (45.4) + (14.7)]. By 1993, the budget deficit had grown to $225.8 billion and the domestic savings surplus had grown to $160.1 billion, balanced by a trade deficit of $65.7 billion [225.8 = 160.1 + 65.7].

Thus, federal deficits can be financed by increasing domestic saving or by borrowing foreigners' savings. Alternatively, the deficit can be financed by a reduction in domestic investment or a reduction in our exports of goods and services. In effect, a trade deficit represents net funds that the United States borrows from abroad. Finally, note that for a given budget deficit, increased domestic investment (saving held constant) must ultimately be financed by a worsening trade deficit.

In summary, with aggregate levels of saving fixed, rising budget deficits will inevitably result in growing trade deficits or a reduction in domestic investment. Figure 6 illustrates the unpleasant arithmetic of budget and trade deficits, which specialists in international finance term the *absorption problem*. As budget deficits mushroomed in the 1980s, trade deficits widened as well. The persistent budget deficits of the 1980s were paralleled by mounting trade deficits, which will probably not be resolved until our federal budget deficit shrinks.

Some people, alarmed by huge U.S. deficits in international trade, have proposed high tariff walls and restrictive import quotas. This might prevent a flood of imports from competing with U.S. output, but the expanded government budget deficit $G - T = (S - I) + (M - X)$ reveals that protectionist policies would also shift the brunt of the budget deficit into greater crowding out of private investment. Thus, the only options to borrowing from abroad ($M - X$) are (a) to cut government outlays, (b) to increase taxes, (c) to increase domestic saving rates, or (d) to suffer lower rates of domestic investment. The other options are so unlikely that the brunt of reduced loans from foreigners would be losses of capital accumulation in the United States. The Laffer curve (described earlier) depicts one possible constraint on government's ability to slash a budget deficit by raising taxes. Reducing the budget deficit through spending cuts is also very difficult because large parts of federal outlays are mandated by law.

THE PUBLIC DEBT

You may have heard someone say that the United States is on the verge of bankruptcy. Critics who cite growth of public debt as a sign of impending collapse and urge government to operate more like a business just aren't paying attention. Although the federal debt is enormous and growing, private debt has grown even faster. Part of this is household debt, primarily for home mortgages, but much private debt is corporate. Although substantial corporate debt is accounted for by merger activity, successful

FIGURE 6 Budget Deficits and Trade Deficits

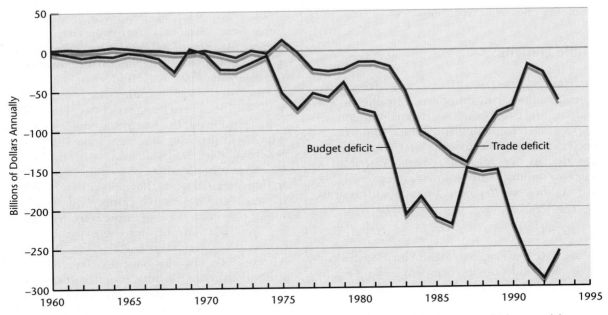

Large shares of the massive federal budget deficits of the past decade have been financed by foreigners who have used the dollars they have received from our trade deficits to buy U.S. government bonds, corporate securities, and real estate. Thus, U.S. trade deficits have paralleled our budget deficits.

corporations not involved in mergers also invariably owe more with each passing decade. Doomsayers fail to consider (*a*) the ability of government to tax and to create money to cover budget deficits or to pay off the national debt, (*b*) the basic differences between internal and external debts, and (*c*) the relative versus absolute size of the debt.

External vs. Internal Debt

The major difference between private and public debt is that all private debt is held externally—the borrowers owe other people—whereas public debt is primarily held internally—we owe most of our *national debt* to Americans. That is, we owe it to ourselves. (Do you own any U.S. Savings Bonds?)

> **External debt** *is owed to outsiders;* **internal debt** *is owed to those who, at least in part, are obligated to pay the debt.*

Borrowing from internal sources does not change the total current amount that may be spent. When our government issues new bonds, the purchasing power temporarily surrendered by U.S. bond buyers just offsets the government's gain in purchasing power. People in the United States as a whole neither gain nor lose immediately through such transactions, although the uses of these funds may affect future American purchasing power. If borrowed funds are used for a government investment in, say, a hydroelectric dam, then real future income may be increased, because more and cheaper electricity may be available over the productive life of the facility.

On the other hand, if government borrows to pay for such current operating costs as police protection or transfer payments, funds may be diverted from private investments and future purchasing power may fall. For example, if a war is financed by bonds, lower rates of domestic capital formation may hinder standards of living for generations. Just as borrowing funds internally does not change total current purchasing power, repayment of internal debt does not simultaneously affect total American purchasing power. People who cash their bonds receive purchasing power exactly equal to losses of purchasing power to taxpayers or the government.

When private households or firms borrow externally, they immediately gain purchasing power that lenders temporarily sacrifice. Similarly, when the government sells bonds to foreign governments or investors, the United States as a whole temporarily gains purchasing power. But unless external lenders permit repeated refinancing, external borrowing entails eventual external repayment. If the borrowed funds were used for investment goods that were sufficiently productive to cover the principal borrowed plus interest charges, the borrowers still would be ahead after repayment. If, on the other hand, the loans were used to finance consumption, then repayment to external lenders could entail net losses of purchasing power. This case requires curtailing future consumption because higher consumption is enjoyed today.

Table 1 indicates that the proportion of the national debt held by foreigners grew markedly after 1970. Before 1975, foreign holdings of U.S. government debt were negligible. As real interest rates rose, foreigners bought greater quantities of our debt. When foreigners buy U.S. bonds, we experience gains in purchasing power. Future generations of Americans may lose purchasing power if foreigners decide to hold fewer U.S. bonds and redeem their bond-holdings. Future generations also bear the burden of paying the interest on externally held debt.

Figure 7 illustrates how real interest rates, inflation, and deficits as a percentage of Gross Domestic Product compare among developed nations. This figure indexes all countries to the United States (U.S. = 100). Big budget deficits are usually associated with high real rates of interest. Relatively high U.S. real interest rates partially explain why Japanese investors were major buyers of U.S. government bonds, corporate bonds, companies, and real estate during the 1980s.

Interest on Public Debt

Until recently, national debt held by the public was declining as a proportion of GDP (see Figure 8). Beginning in the early 1970s, rising deficits and relatively high interest rates caused total public debt and interest payments—as a percentage of GDP—to grow. Interest rates fell in 1986, slowing the upward trend in interest as a percentage of GDP as old debt was *rolled over* and new debt was financed at lower real rates.

> **Debt rollover** *occurs if, when a bond issue comes due, the debt is refinanced.*

Government and corporations typically go deeper into debt as time passes. (Most corporations also roll over their debts.) However, investors who buy government bonds must have confidence in the stability and taxing power of the government.

Politically unstable countries find it difficult to borrow, because investors fear that the current government may fall or disavow the debt. New regimes commonly disavow the debt of overthrown governments, rendering it worthless. For example, owners of bonds issued by czarist Russia, post–World War I Germany, and many South American countries experienced this misfortune. The discounts at which the

TABLE 1   Percentage of U.S. Public Debt Held by Foreigners

Year	%
1939	0.5
1946	0.8
1965	5.2
1970	5.3
1975	11.5
1980	16.3
1985	16.9
1990	18.3
1993	19.8

Sources: *Federal Reserve Bulletin*, May 1994; and *Economic Report of the President*, 1994.

FIGURE 7   International Comparisons of Interest Rates, Deficits, and Inflation (1990)

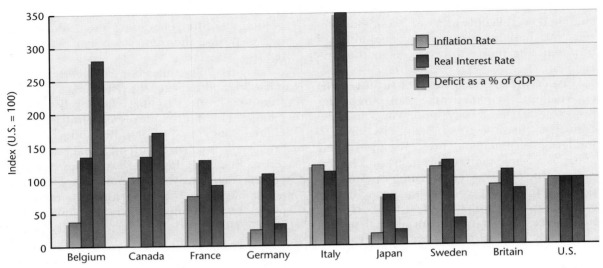

Relative to many other countries, U.S. federal deficits as a percentage of Gross Domestic Product, the rate of domestic inflation, and real interest rates (monetary interest adjusted for inflation) were not out of line in 1990. Note, however, the consistently superior position of the Japanese economy.

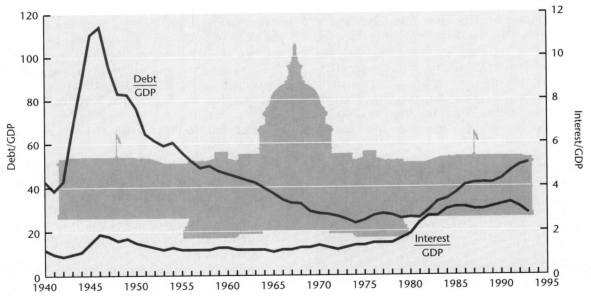

Source: *Economic Report of the President,* 1994.

The public debt as a percentage of GDP declined until the mid-1970s. Right after World War II, the public debt exceeded GDP; today, the ratio is nearly 50%. When greater public debt has been financed, interest rates have risen. New debt and old debt that was rolled over have to be floated at these higher rates of interest. The result is that interest paid on public debt as a percentage of GDP rose during the early 1980s. Since the mid-1980s, however, interest rates have fallen, and as debt was refinanced, interest costs as a percentage of GDP leveled off.

FIGURE 8   Federal Debt Held by the Public and Interest on the Debt as a Percentage of GDP

debts of some countries are sold are shown in Table 2. The amount of the discount is roughly proportional to the difficulties faced when one of these countries tries to borrow or to refinance (roll over) its debt. Debt can be floated almost perpetually, however, as long as the government of a country is reasonably stable and maintains its credit (pays its interest payments).

An often-ignored aspect of federal debt is that the Fed acquires large chunks of national debt when it buys bonds during expansionary open-market operations. Other government agencies also buy bonds when they run surpluses. Accountants count these agencies' bond-holdings as national debt, but this is a lot like saying that your right pocket owes your left pocket if you shift spare change from one pocket to another.

If taxes are raised to pay interest on federal debt, incentives to work and invest may wither. In 1993, the interest cost of the national debt was nearly $200 billion, or nearly 14% of all federal outlays. When the federal government finances a huge deficit by selling debt securities, real interest rates climb or remain high, and considerable private borrowing for investment may be crowded out. The exact effect will depend on the state of the economy and private saving rates. If the economy is especially sluggish, increased deficits may not crowd out investment. If saving rates rise, large deficits may not raise interest rates. However, in general, large deficits push up interest rates. The end result is that future generations may inherit a smaller capital stock and, hence, reduced production possibilities—one real burden of the public debt.

Burdens on Future Generations

Does national debt burden future generations? As we discussed previously, if newly incurred debt diverts funds from investment to satisfy present consumption, then future generations lose the investment income that might have been generated. But future generations do not lose because of national debt per se. Rather, they lose because the current generation opts for more consumption and less investment out of today's income. For example, when a family borrows to finance a vacation rather than borrowing to pay for a college education, different generations within the household benefit.

Future generations may bear higher taxes to pay interest on the national debt. Of course, members of future generations also receive the interest payments as bondholders, so the burden evens out as long as the national debt is held internally—that is, as long as we owe it to ourselves. Future generations can lose, however, if foreigners decide to reduce their holdings of U.S. bonds. It is not obvious that they will, or that the national debt will ever be retired, or that it would be desirable for us to retire it.

Must the National Debt Be Repaid?

What would happen if we retired the national debt? Would the government be ruined? Suppose government raised income taxes enormously to repay the outstanding debt. People who hold the existing public debt tend to be individuals in high-income categories, so they would be paying a lot of the higher taxes and then, when they redeemed the bonds, they would receive the payments—a transfer to themselves. Alternatively, the value of all Treasury bonds could be taxed 100%. Goodbye national debt. (This is not a likely option.)

TABLE 2   Discount Debt

Country	Bid price May 1988	Bid price Sept. 1991
Argentina	28.0	40.3
Bolivia	10.5	11.0
Brazil	55.0	39.0
Chile	61.0	89.0
Mexico	53.5	59.6
Nicaragua	2.0	6.0
Nigeria	29.0	42.7
Peru	4.0	13.0
Philippines	50.0	57.3
Venezuela	55.0	67.3

Source: Reprinted by permission of Bear, Stearns & Co. Inc. Recent secondary market price quotes for debt of various countries, in cents on the dollar.

Some critics of national debt policies argue that if the government can issue unlimited debt, it will continually overspend. These critics argue that Congress often mistreats the ability to issue debt and is unwilling to exercise fiscal restraint. Persistent increases in both government debt and spending tend to support their line of argument. It may be easier to increase the national debt (and the debt ceiling) than to say no to projects supported by powerful special-interest groups.

Some Benefits of Public Debt

National debt would not exist if it did not have a benefit side. (This is true even if the only benefit is that alternatives for financing federal deficits were worse.) Stabilization policy depends heavily on the ability of the federal government to deficit spend and pay for this spending with bonds. Annually balancing the budget could prove disastrous during recessionary periods. Additionally, the national debt provides a relatively risk-free asset (government bonds) for individuals who need to protect their financial capital. (Of course, there is the risk of inflation.) You should realize by now that manipulation of the public debt is crucial for the most effective instrument of monetary policy: open-market operations. The Fed buys bonds from banks when it wants to expand the money supply and sells bonds to restrict the money supply.

One recent development is the potentially explosive growth of surpluses in the Social Security Trust Fund. These surpluses legally must be invested in federal debt and, as Focus 2 indicates, may make growth of our national debt a moot issue.

Remeasuring Public Debt and Budget Deficits

The deficit and debt statistics reported earlier in Figure 1 reflect a federal budget that began moving severely out of balance in the early 1970s. However, growing numbers of economists dispute these figures. They suggest that we would have been better off had we totally ignored these data instead of adopting incorrect policies based on these numbers.[3]

Correcting alleged flaws in budget deficit and debt data requires (a) converting the nominal budget and the public debt to real values, (b) adjusting public debt for interest rate changes (converting the value of the debt from par value to market value), and (c) revising the budget so that reported values conform to generally accepted accounting principles.

For the same reasons that nominal GDP is adjusted for inflation to yield real GDP, the nominal budget deficit and public debt should be deflated to reflect changes in the price level. Real national debt remains constant if it doubles while the price level also doubles. In the same way that inflation wipes out the value of money, it also reduces the value of the national debt.

Similarly, if interest rates rise, all bond prices fall, and the national debt issued previously becomes less burdensome. The reported public debt is the par value of government bonds in the hands of the public or foreigners. *Par value* means that if a government bond was issued for $100,000 in 1980, the public debt grew by $100,000. Public debt statistics are not adjusted to reflect changing market values if interest rates later change so that the market value of this bond changes. The par value of a bond remains constant, but the market value of the debt changes as interest rates fluctuate. Consequently, to measure national debt accurately, published government statistics should be adjusted for changes in interest rates.

Finally, the government has a large stock of tangible assets, including land, buildings, and equipment. Annually adjusting our public debt data in the same way as corporations would to obtain net worth tells a different story. Figure 10 shows the budget deficit and public debt adjusted for inflation, its market values, and changing values of assets and liabilities since 1960. An interesting note is that there are years in which the government reported a deficit and this adjusted budget indicates a surplus.

---

[3]Robert Eisner, *How Real Is the Federal Deficit?* (New York: The Free Press, 1986).

Will Social Security Absorb Our National Debt?

The 1940s ushered in an era in which federal budget surpluses have been tiny, rare, and cumulatively swamped by deficits that have driven a rising national debt. Explosive growth of government debt has been dwarfed by growth of private debt, with U.S. saving rates being relatively low compared to many other industrialized countries.

In part, private saving rates were depressed by family formation among baby boomers, many of whom borrowed heavily to acquire the houses and other amenities that have become the norm for those who pursue the American dream. By the 1980s, private domestic saving fell far short of the funds needed for adequate domestic investment and to finance record federal deficits. As we have indicated, the result was that U.S. federal deficits were covered by imports that allowed foreigners to invest heavily in the United States.

Many people are concerned that our deficits have effectively "sold our country to foreigners at cut-rate prices." Others worry that some future day of reckoning will usher in financial catastrophe and economic collapse. Are there natural economic limits to the size of our national debt? Do any natural forces exist to offset our national momentum toward infinite debt? One force that soon may relieve swollen deficits and rising debt is projected growth of the Social Security Trust Fund.

The Social Security system ran large deficits from the 1970s into the early 1980s. Deficits accumulated during this era, when each retiree was supported by about four active workers, threaten to bankrupt the Social Security Trust Fund when post—World War II baby boomers finally begin retiring in 2010. Demographers pre-

dicted that by 2030, each retiree would be backed up by only about two active workers. A "blue ribbon" panel was appointed to find a solution to this problem.

This panel based its recommendations on relatively pessimistic forecasts about unemployment rates and rates of economic growth; it wanted to ensure that another crisis would not arise from temporary Band-Aid solutions to the problem. The resulting 1983 reform of the Federal Insurance Contribution Act (FICA) more than doubled the FICA tax. Consequently, FICA revenues exceeded Social Security benefit payments by a healthy $155 billion in 1992, with even heftier surpluses on the horizon.

Social Security surpluses are legally required to be placed in "reserves" that are based on "investments" in long-term U.S.

Treasury bonds. This seems, on the surface, to be both prudent policy and a good way to ensure a healthy market for government securities. Figure 9 reflects Social Security Administration long-term forecasts of its expected outlays (benefit payments), income (FICA tax revenues), and reserves (holdings of U.S. Treasury bonds). The Social Security Trust Fund Reserve, based on expected cumulative surpluses, is anticipated to mount to roughly $12 *trillion* by 2030. A wave of baby boomer retirements should begin around 2008, however, and last until about 2030. Reserves will gradually be dissipated until, by 2050, they are completely exhausted.

The enormity of the financial flows into and out of the Social Security Trust Fund will require major macroeconomic adjustments based on careful planning. The

FIGURE 9   Long-Term Forecasts for Social Security Outlays, Income, and Reserves

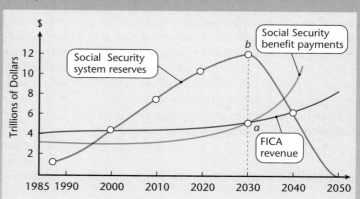

Source: Social Security Administration estimates (1988), updated by authors.
Note: When FICA revenue exceeds benefit payments (up to point *a*), total FICA reserves grow (until point *b*). Thereafter, payments exceed revenue, so FICA reserves decline.

$12 trillion in total reserves expected by 2030, for example, is about 10 times as large as the level of privately held federal debt in 1990.

One effect of the imminent surge of FICA revenues may be a powerful reversal of federal deficits and national debt. Every dollar of surplus in the Social Security system will slash the federal deficit by a dollar. If the Social Security system's surpluses are, as is expected, larger than the rest of the U.S. Treasury's deficits, then the federal government will run a net surplus. Anticipated surpluses will undoubtedly absorb all outstanding national debt by the upcoming turn of the century.

In a sense, public saving (through the Social Security Administration) may become so enormous that real interest rates in private financial markets will plummet. This should facilitate both domestic investment by U.S. companies and substantial investment abroad. If these developments occur as expected, the United States, which moved from being the world's largest creditor nation in the 1980 to being its greatest debtor by 1986, could easily revert to being the world's largest supplier of investment funds.

The Social Security surpluses expected over the next 40 years are, in a sense, a nest egg that could, if invested properly, support our retirement system permanently. A major issue is how should these funds be invested? Even if our national debt were to double by 2000, it would only amount to $8 trillion, and total reserve funds are expected to mount to $12 trillion. As you might expect, answers from all over the political spectrum have been offered to the question of how these retirement funds should be used.

Some critics argue that the expected Social Security surpluses justify huge current expenditures to fix our roads, enrich our educational system, or cure poverty everywhere. Others want to defend Social Security from any spending binge. Rep. Andrew Jacobs of the House Social Security Subcommittee has characterized this task as, "It'll be like walking through a bad neighborhood with a diamond ring."

Others assert that this public saving (Social Security) is just a distortive shift away from what should be decisions by private individuals. According to this line of reasoning, FICA taxes should be slashed so that private individuals can choose their own retirement plans. A variant of this approach would be to allow individuals to specify for themselves the types of investments into which their taxes will be placed. This approach has been described as "privatization."

Baby boomers flooded our educational system in the 1950s and 1960s and invaded the labor market in the 1970s and 1980s. The depressed saving rate of the 1970s and 1980s reflected their attempts to borrow huge amounts so that they could buy their way into the good life. It is predictable that the aging and then retirement of this bubble of humanity will have profound social and economic consequences. A burst of saving (albeit public saving) for retirement by this group will probably transform persistent federal deficits into surpluses and national debt into national credit. The precise ways in which this occurs will be determined by how macroeconomic policymakers choose to cope with the issues we have addressed in this chapter.

The reported "official" deficit may provide misleading signals for macroeconomic policy. In years when policymakers think there is a deficit and the budget is really in surplus, contractionary measures to balance a budget would be counterproductive. Even after the adjustments are made, however, there is clearly a striking move toward a government in deficit in recent years. But how much should we be alarmed by these trends?

International Comparisons of Debt

While U.S. policymakers struggle against budget deficits, how do our levels of debt and deficits compare to those of other industrialized countries? Until the mid-1970s, national debt as a percentage of U.S. GDP was declining. Figure 11 shows budget deficits, gross public debt, and household savings rates as percentages of Gross Domestic Product (GDP) for 13 developed countries in 1990. The lines across the figure are averages for these 13 countries. Most ran deficits and most had large public debts in proportion to their GDPs. The United States currently has an average deficit, a below average debt ratio, and a below average saving rate. U.S. debt and deficits are large absolutely, but don't appear disastrous relative to those in many other developed countries.

One area worthy of major concern is the net international investment position of the United States. Figure 12 traces our path as we deteriorated from the world's largest net international investor in 1981 to its biggest net debtor by 1990. This deterioration is partially explained by recent federal deficits, which have been financed in part by foreign investment in the United States. We have continued to be the world's largest debtor into the mid-1990s.

FIGURE 10   Reported and Adjusted Values of the Budget Deficit

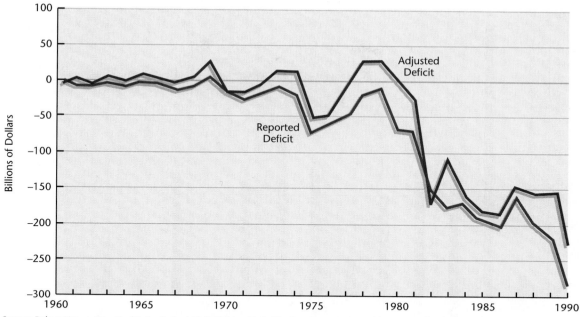

Source: Robert Eisner, *How Real Is the Federal Deficit?* (New York: The Free Press, 1986), Table B.12 (updated by authors).

Robert Eisner has dragged the antiquated accounting system used by the federal government for its budgeting into closer conformity with modern corporate accounting standards. His estimates suggest that recent federal deficits have not been as terrible as the offical data indicate.

THE ABILITY TO CONTROL GOVERNMENT SPENDING

Virtually every president in the past 30 years has promised to curtail "wasteful" government spending, but all found cutting the federal budget an overwhelming task. Doing so quickly seems almost impossible.

> ***Relatively uncontrollable outlays*** *cannot be changed without changes in major federal laws. They are often beyond administrative control and involve contractual obligations of government.*

Many enormous items in the federal budget are continuing programs that Congress is legally obligated to fund. For example, Social Security payments are legally guaranteed to recipients, commitments for Medicare funding were made by the Congress years ago, and con-

tracts for most transportation or defense systems take years to complete. Moreover, the government's legal obligations to provide public assistance, to operate the Post Office, to regulate pollution and industrial safety—the list seems to go on forever—are long-term commitments that simply cannot be abandoned quickly. Estimates by the Conference Board, a research organization, indicate that roughly 60% of all outlays were relatively uncontrollable in the 1960s. That proportion has now grown to over 75%.

Panel A of Figure 13 shows the growth of real federal outlays and tax revenue. Despite political rhetoric about reducing the size of government, real outlays have grown steadily. Where has this growth in expenditures originated? Panel B shows the composition of federal expenditures. The major increases in spending shares since 1970 have been in interest on the public debt and transfer payments. Major declines as shares of total outlays have

FIGURE 11   International Comparisons of Deficits, Debt, and Household Saving Rates

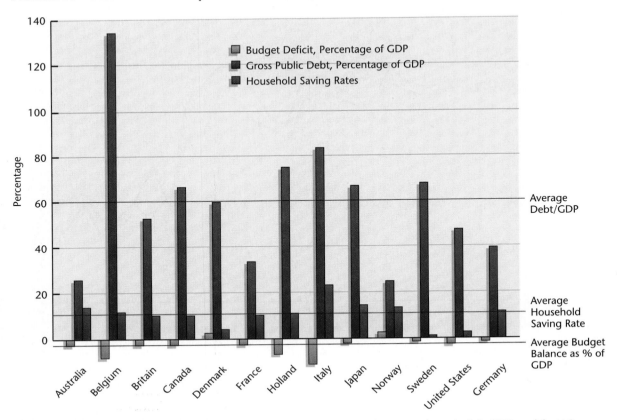

The U.S. budget deficit as a percentage of GDP was about average relative to international standards in 1993, and the U.S. public debt was relatively lower than in most countries, but Americans typically save smaller shares of their personal income than do average people elsewhere. Source: *Statistical Abstract of the United States, 1993.*

been in purchases of goods and services (both military and nonmilitary).

• **Gramm-Rudman Balanced-Budget Act**   In 1985, Congress adopted a new strategy in an attempt to control soaring deficits: the Gramm-Rudman Deficit Reduction Act set specific deficit reduction targets. If these targets were not met, across-the-board spending cuts were mandated. In effect, Congress was like a dieter who puts a lock on the refrigerator and gives the key to someone else. Many parts of the budget were excluded from these sweeping cuts, however, including most categories labeled relatively uncontrollable. Cold comfort, indeed, for those who wanted to reduce the size of government!

The Gramm-Rudman Act set limits to the size of the federal deficit beginning in 1986. In each of the five fiscal years following 1986, the targeted federal deficit was to be reduced, until it reached zero in 1991. If Congress and the president were unable to reach agreement, then automatic selective spending cuts were to take effect. Despite the political fanfare and rhetoric that accompanied this law, federal deficits did not reach zero by 1991. In fact, they grew. The Gramm-Rudman's Act inability to achieve stated targets stemmed from the fact that projected deficits for each coming year understated the actual deficits that resulted. Congress also pushed up deficits by adding funding to the budget after the October 15 deadline for automatic spending cuts. Each new budget act that failed to con-

FIGURE 12   The Net International Investment Position of the United States

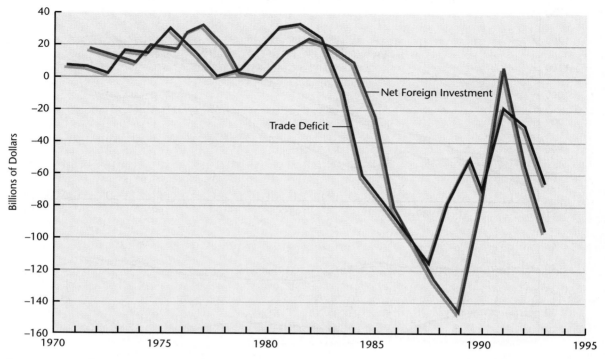

Between 1982 and 1990, the United States went from being the world's biggest creditor nation to being its biggest debtor, in large part because big chunks of persistent record federal deficits were financed by foreigners who bought U.S. Treasury bonds. That process seems to have reversed in the most recent past. Source: *Economic Report of the President,* 1994.

form to the Gramm-Rudman Act was worded to amend Gramm-Rudman, so the net effect of this approach was not especially meaningful.

- **The Deficit Reduction Act of 1990**   The failure to achieve the Gramm-Rudman objective of eliminating budget deficits culminated in passage of the Deficit Reduction Law of 1990. This law mandated tax increases and spending cuts, and it attempted to cap federal spending to further reduce the federal deficit. Higher taxes on income, gasoline, liquor, cigarettes, and luxury goods (jewelry, furs, boats, etc.) were forecast to raise $165 *billion* over a five-year period (these excise taxes combined raised less than $100 *million* by 1993). Spending cuts were targeted for farm subsidies, student loans, and Medicare reimbursements to doctors and hospitals.

Increased federal savings were also forecast as arising from reduced military spending and lower interest payments on the public debt. Previously, the Gramm-Rudman Act specified yearly deficit targets; under the new law the focus was controlling federal spending, not cutting the deficit, which means the deficit was allowed to grow as long as the increase was not attributable to increased federal outlays.

It might appear that the government tied its hands behind its back and would be unable to allocate funds for emergencies, but this was not the case. Funding for the savings and loan bailout, Persian Gulf hostilities, and any emergencies (e.g., disaster relief) fell outside of the spending targets. Uncle Sam prohibited the right hand from writing checks over a certain amount, but the left hand could still sign at any time.

FIGURE 13 Real Federal Revenue and Outlays and the Composition of Federal Outlays

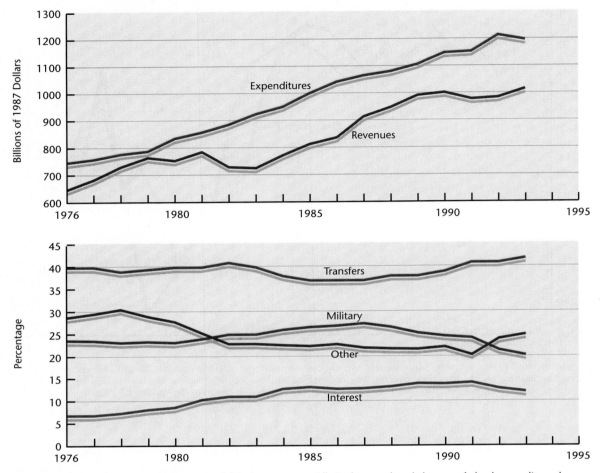

Deficits have been enormous and the national debt has grown rapidly in the past decade because federal expenditures have grown much faster than federal tax revenues (Panel A). Growing shares of government outlays are absorbed by transfer payments and interest rates on the national debt (Panel B), while the military budget, which had been declining relative to other types of spending from 1963 through 1977, recovered somewhat during the 1980s. Source: *Economic Report of the President,* 1994.

Predictably, the 1990 Deficit Reduction Law failed to achieve its goals. The recession of 1990 to 1991 held tax revenues far below forecasts, and federal outlays were swollen by a surge of transfer payments. At the same time, federal spending ballooned because of the Persian Gulf War. Deficit reduction, like dieting, appears easier to formulate than to put into practice.

• **The Deficit Reduction Act of 1993** President Clinton's election predictably ushered in a Deficit Reduction Act of 1993, but Table 3 re-veals that the basic approach differs little from that of its predecessor. Nevertheless, growth of the economy from 1992 onward holds the prospect that this act's stated goal of reducing the deficit by a total of $500 billion between 1993 and 1998 may be attainable—unless another recession disrupts attainment of revenue projections, or if health-care reform, welfare reform, and the re-building of infrastructure proposed by President Clinton prove more costly than expected. If proposed programs cost much more than expected, deficits may resume an upward path.

TABLE 3   A Comparison of the 1990 and 1993 Deficit Reduction Acts

Category	1990	1993

Income Tax Rates	Top rate increased from 28% to 31%	Top rates increased:
		    Single Income > $115,000; Rate increased from 31% to 35%
		    Married Income >$140,000: Rate increased from 31% to 35%
		    Income >$250,000; Rate increased from 31% to 39.6%

Minimum Tax Rate	Rate increased from 21% to 24%	Rate Increased:
		    Income < $175,000; Rate increased from 24% to 26%
		    Income >$175,000; Rate increased to 28% on excess.

Limits on Deductions	Set **temporary** limits on deductions (would expire in 1995): $300 in deductions eliminated for every $10,000 in income.	Limits became **permanent**
Medicare Payroll Tax	Extended the 1.45% (2.9% for self employed) payroll tax to be paid on income from $55,000 to $125,000.	Limit eliminated: all earned income subject to Medicare tax.

Excise Taxes	a. Gasoline tax increased $.05 per gallon
	b. Cigarette tax increased $.04 per pack
	c. Liquor tax increased $1.00 per 100 proof gallon.
	d. Beer tax increased $.16 per six pack
	e. Wine tax increased $.21 per gallon
	f. Airline passenger tax increased from 8% to 10%
	g. 10% excise tax added to:
	    Cars (P>$30,000)
	    Boats (P>$100,000)
	    Jewelry (P>$5,000)
	    Furs (P>$100,000)
	    Planes (P>$250,000)
		a. Gasoline tax increased $.043 per gallon
		b. Gasoline tax ($.025 per gallon) to expire in 1995, extended 4 years.
		c. Eliminated the 10% excise tax on: boats, jewelry, furs and planes
		d. Indexes the $30,000 price for cars to inflation.

Corporate Income Tax		Top rate increased from 34% to 35%

Corporate Tax Deductions		Deductions reduced or eliminated (effectively a tax increase):
		    Moving expenses—reduced
		    Business meals—reduced from 80% deductible to 50% deductible
		    Club dues—eliminated
		    Executive compensation—salaries over $1,000,000 not deductible
		    Pension expenses—reduced deductibility
		    Charitable contributions—paperwork requirements increased
		    Lobby expenses—eliminated
		    Securities dealers—transactions taxes increased
		    Real estate depreciation—extended from 31.5 years to 39 years

Tax Credits - Working Poor	Increased Tax Credit by $5 billion over 5 years	Increased Tax Credit by $21 billion over 5 years
Medicare	Increased annual premiums Increased deductible to $100 Reduced payments to hospitals and doctors $43 billion over 5 years.	
Agriculture Subsidies	Reduced by $13 billion over 5 years	
Estate Taxes		Increased rate for estates > $2.5 million from 50% to 53% Increased rate for estates > $3 million from 50% to 55%

What can we conclude about the current state of deficits and the public debt in the United States? Clearly debt, no matter how it's measured, has been growing over the past decade. Any deficit must be financed with bonds or new monetary base, and, as we have seen, persistent deficits have predictable impacts on our international accounts.

To the extent that added debt is used for public investment, future generations may gain, but they will bear the burden if debt and deficits are used to finance consumption for the current generation. Large deficits and debts can increase real interest rates that may soak up additional government resources in the future. Reducing government spending is quite difficult because so many federal outlays are uncontrollable.

Finally, our national debt and deficits compare favorably to other developed countries. All in all, the growing debt and continuing deficits in our country are a cause for concern and need to be addressed over the long haul, but they do not appear to be the crisis that so many politicians and pundits would have us believe.

CHAPTER REVIEW: KEY POINTS

1. The **budget deficit** equals annual government outlays minus receipts. The **public debt** is total federal indebtedness resulting from current and past deficits.

2. **Balancing the budget annually** might result in incorrect fiscal actions to combat either inflation or recession. Some have suggested balancing the budget **over the business cycle**. This would entail running deficits during recessions and surpluses over the boom. Unfortunately, business cycles are not symmetric, and the budget may not be easy to balance over the cycle without hampering prosperity. Advocates of **functional finance** believe the size of the public debt to be unimportant, suggesting that we ignore balancing the budget and focus on balancing the economy instead.

3. The federal government can finance **public spending** by collecting taxes (T), creating additional monetary base (ΔMB), selling government securities (ΔB), or confiscation. All of these techniques are drains on *gross private saving* (production minus private consumption) that can crowd out private economic activities. The notion called **Ricardian equivalence** suggests that whether government spending is financed by taxes or borrowing is irrelevant.

4. The **crowding-out hypothesis** states that increases in government purchases inevitably reduce private consumption, investment, or leisure.

5. Federal deficits can be financed by increasing domestic saving, by securing the savings of foreigners, or by reducing domestic investment or exports. All else held constant, a growing budget deficit will cause a growing trade deficit.

6. Some government spending (now estimated at three-fourths) is **uncontrollable**. These programs are long range or are committed by law each and every year. Reducing these outlays is virtually impossible.

7. A major difference between private and public debt is that *private debt* is entirely owned by persons **external** to the issuing institution, while the bulk of *public debt* is **internal**, being owed to ourselves. Private debt has grown faster than public debt since the early 1950s and is currently almost twice as large.

8. The **real burden** *of the national debt* stems from the federal government **crowding out** private investment as it drives interest rates up when it competes with the private sector for loanable funds. As a result, future generations may inherit a smaller capital stock and a smaller production possibilities frontier.

9. Among the major benefits of the public debt are its use as a *stabilization instrument* and as a *risk-free asset* for savers.

QUESTIONS FOR THOUGHT AND DISCUSSION

1. What are the potential advantages and disadvantages of amending the Constitution to require that federal outlays and receipts be balanced each time the earth circles the sun?

2. The Japanese government contends that persistent U.S. trade deficits with Japan reflect our persistent federal budget deficits, not Japanese trade policy. They argue that U.S. trade deficits will disappear as soon as we start balancing our federal budget. Is the Japanese argument essentially correct? Why?

3. Government spending can be financed by taxation, by borrowing, or by creating additional monetary base. Rank these from least expansionary to most expansionary and explain your ranking system.

4. What mechanisms cause the Federal Reserve System to experience pressure to expand the money supply when the Treasury runs a huge deficit? When the Fed yields to this pressure, does this add or detract from the goal of achieving macroeconomic stability? Why?

5. Why do foreigners willingly hold Treasury bonds that represent so much of our national debt? Is it desirable from our vantage point for them to do so? What are the long-term consequences of these loans?

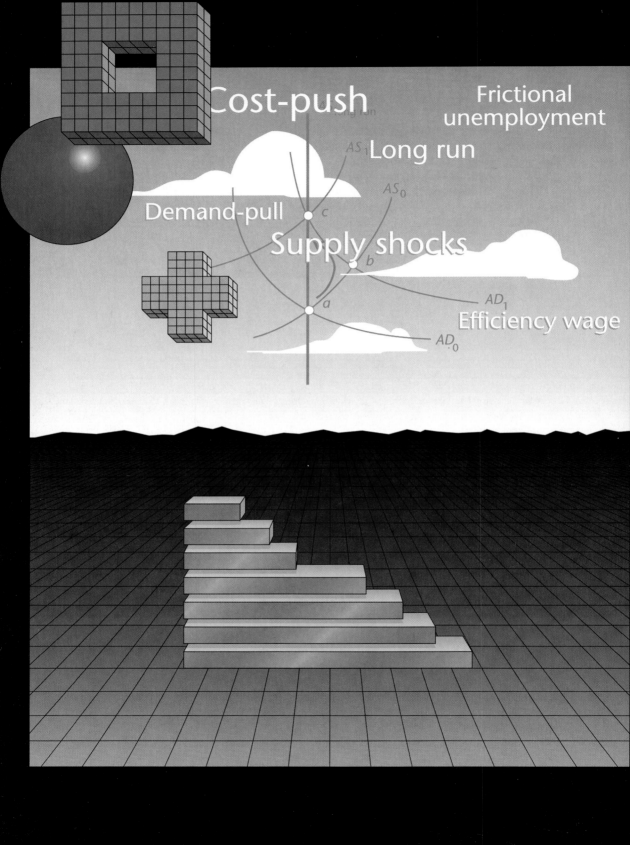

Part 5

Challenges to Macroeconomic Policymaking

Different circumstances may call for very different monetary and fiscal policies. Today, few economists believe that macroeconomic problems are easily resolved or that even careful blends of policy can properly fine-tune an economy. Chapter 16 begins by summarizing how various policies will shift Aggregate Demand (AD) and Aggregate Supply (AS) curves. Then we address the issue of the flexibility or stickiness of wages and prices, which is critical for the extent and duration of unemployment. Finally, historical changes in monetary and fiscal policies and the resulting shifts in AD and AS curves are used to interpret the prosperous 1960s, the stagflation of the 1970s, the erratic 1980s, the recession that opened the 1990s, and the recovery that began in 1992.

Should government actively use monetary and fiscal policies to pursue full employment, price-level stability, and economic growth? Or should it rely primarily on market forces? This basic issue is addressed in Chapter 17. On one side are policy activists, who urge frequent adjustments to fiscal and monetary tools; on the other are policy passivists, who favor a more laissez-faire approach—markets should be allowed to adjust to shocks within an environment of relatively constant and predictable policies.

We open Chapter 17 by describing how Aggregate Demand and Aggregate Supply may interact to yield a *Phillips curve*, a Keynesian notion that policymakers face a trade-off between unemployment and inflation. New classical macroeconomics offers several challenges to this theory, including (*a*) *natural rate theory*, which asserts that, in the long run, discretionary policy cannot alter employment, real interest rates, or economic growth; (*b*) the theory of *rational expectations*, which implies that, even in the short run, private adjustments to discretionary policy may thwart its effectiveness; and (*c*) *real business cycle* theory, which suggests that all activist policies impede automatic market adjustments to Aggregate Supply shocks.

The debate about proper macroeconomic policy continues in Chapter 18. Opponents of activist policies cite imperfect information, improper timing, incorrect "doses" of policy, and political incumbents' desires for reelection as flaws inherent in discretionary policymaking. Most new classical analysts favor stable macroeconomic policies, including *monetary growth rules*, according to which the money supply would grow at a fixed rate each year. At the other extreme are analysts who view markets as unstable and macroeconomic policies as insufficiently potent, by themselves, to push a market economy along a stable growth path.

This part of the book concludes with Chapter 19, where we examine the challenge of achieving long-run *economic growth and development*. Even prosperous, developed nations judge political leaders by their success in achieving economic growth. More severe hurdles to improved standards of living are confronted in countries plagued by inadequate natural resources, explosive population growth, and insufficient capital.

Cost-push

Frictional unemployment

Demand-pull

Chapter 16

Supply shocks

Microfoundations of Macroeconomic Policy

Efficiency wage

Long run

The macroeconomic goals of high employment, a stable price level, and healthy economic growth are intertwined, but historical data seem to reveal few systematic connections between these variables. The U.S. economy has experienced growth when average prices were rising—and when average prices were falling. Similarly, inflationary episodes have been accompanied by low unemployment rates—and by widespread unemployment. Unraveling this jumble of data entails examining relative shifts in Aggregate Demand and Aggregate Supply.

In this chapter, we take a closer look at the microfoundations of Aggregate Demand and Aggregate Supply for insights into how government policies can be used to shift these curves. Then we turn our attention to labor markets and examine how sticky wages may cause high rates of involuntary unemployment to persist. Finally, we examine the underlying features of demand-side and supply-side inflation and put them into a historical context.

THE AGGREGATE DEMAND CURVE

Now that you know why the relative shifts of Aggregate Demand and Aggregate Supply matter, let's reexamine the foundations for these curves.

> The **Aggregate Demand** curve reflects a negative relationship between the price level (P) and the quantity demanded (Q) of National Output.

We will take a moment to review why Aggregate Expenditures on our domestic production tend to be sensitive to the price level and why Aggregate Demand curves are negatively sloped.

Slope of the Aggregate Demand Curve

All else being equal, planned spending on U.S. production falls when the domestic price level rises because of

1. The *interest rate effect*, whereby higher interest rates reduce planned investment,

Aggregate Expenditures, and, ultimately, output.

2. The *wealth effect*, whereby the purchasing power of assets stated in money terms falls, causing declines in wealth, and, consequently, in spending.

3. The *foreign sector substitution effect*, whereby consumers substitute goods produced elsewhere for American-made goods, while investors find that the profitability of foreign investment has risen relative to that for investment in the United States.

These mechanisms were introduced in Chapter 5. You now have more foundations for understanding each effect. When the price level rises, each mechanism operates to reduce the Aggregate Expenditures schedule, which results in a leftward movement along the Aggregate Demand curve. For simplicity, we will temporarily assume that all domestic prices, including wages and rents, increase by exactly the same proportion.

• **Interest Rate Effects**   A major reason for the negative slope of the Aggregate Demand curve is the effect that higher prices have on the chain reaction from interest rates to investment to Aggregate Spending and then to income and output. (These adjustments closely parallel the Keynesian monetary transmission mechanism introduced earlier.)

When prices rise, the real purchasing power of a fixed money supply (M/P) falls. Consider Panel A in Figure 1. The nominal money supply is assumed constant at M_{s0}. An increase in the price level from P_0 to P_1 shifts the real supply of money from M_{s0}/P_0 to M_{s0}/P_1. Equilibrium interest rates rise from i_0 (point a) to i_1 (point b) because of this decline in the real money supply. Rising interest rates move equilibrium from point a to point b in Panel B. Thus planned investment falls from I_0 to I_1 because higher interest rates drive up the costs of investment.

This reduction in planned investment drives the Aggregate Expenditures schedule in Panel C down from AE_0 to AE_1 reducing real National Income from Y_0 (point a) to Y_1 (point

b). Finally, this lower National Income at higher prices means that, in Panel D, real output must fall from Q_0 (point a) to Q_1 (point b). Duplicating this same process for every possible price level yields the negatively sloped Aggregate Demand in Panel D. Thus, higher interest rates that result from higher prices crowd out investment and, in addition, squeeze both consumer credit and government spending at the state and local levels (especially that which is bond financed). In summary, higher interest rates reduce all these sources of Aggregate Spending.

• **The Wealth Effect**   Suppose the price level were to fall sharply. To the extent that your wealth would rise because of the increased purchasing power of your assets held as money, you could buy more goods and would spend more. Conversely, even if your monetary income kept up with the price level during inflation, you would still lose to the extent that your wealth was stored as bonds, as cash, or in bank accounts, so you would reduce your spending.

A related adjustment occurs because most of us want to maintain fairly stable amounts of liquid assets relative to our income. Thus, even if your income rises as fast as the price level, you may temporarily reduce the proportion of income you consume to restore the purchasing power of your liquid assets through a short-term higher rate of saving. Because consumption declines as the price level climbs (due to the wealth effect), Aggregate Spending also falls in a manner similar to that described for the interest rate–investment adjustments in Figure 1.

• **Foreign Sector Substitution Effect**   We import goods when foreigners can produce them at lower cost and export goods when American production costs are lower than those in other countries. If the prices of U.S. goods rise, you will buy more imported goods than previously because they will be relatively cheaper. At the same time, foreign consumers will reduce their purchases of now higher-priced American goods. Thus, inflation causes imports to increase and exports to decrease, resulting in reduced

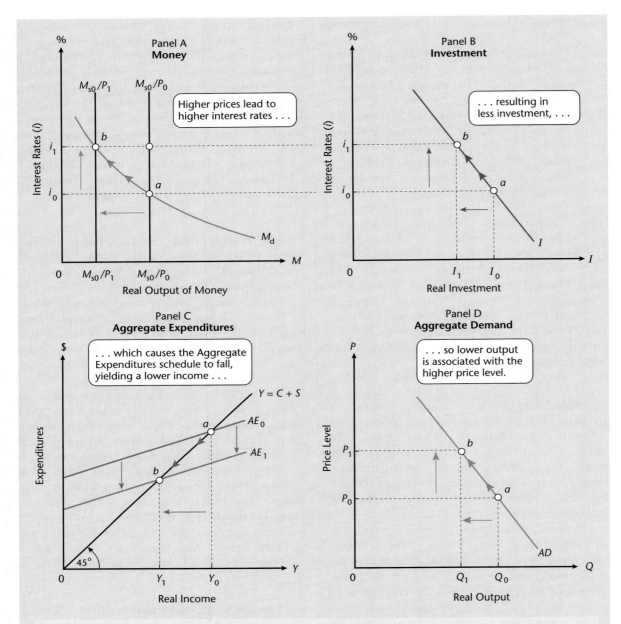

FIGURE 1   Interest Rates, Investment, and the Aggregate Demand Curve

Aggregate Expenditures and National Income and Output.

Increases in American prices are usually accompanied by higher U.S. costs of production. Higher wages and increased costs for U.S. land and machinery make it profitable for investors (both foreign and domestic) to substitute foreign investment for investment in the United States, reinforcing the decline in Aggregate Expenditures as the price level rises from P_0 to P_1 in Figure 1. Over the last three decades many U.S. manufacturers have expanded operations in Mexico, Taiwan, and other low-wage countries.

To summarize, higher price levels are associated with lower quantities along Aggregate Demand curves because (a) higher interest rates reduce investment and purchases of consumer durables, (b) real values fall for financial assets stated in monetary terms, (c) imports grow and exports fall, and (d) domestic investment declines while foreign investment flourishes.

Shifts in Aggregate Demand

Any changes in planned Aggregate Expenditures (vertical shifts in Keynesian cross diagrams) that do not originate from changes in the price level cause horizontal shifts of the Aggregate Demand curve. Thus, spending plans ultimately determine the magnitude of Aggregate Demand. Shifts of the Aggregate Demand curve are caused by changes in monetary or fiscal policies or by changes in planned consumption, investment, or foreign spending. How expanded spending plans shift Aggregate Demand to the right is shown in Panel B of Figure 2. Plans to spend more originate in tax cuts, increases in government purchases or transfer payments, or more optimistic expectations by consumers and investors. Expansionary monetary policies such as open-market purchases of bonds or reductions in either reserve requirements or the discount rate also increase Aggregate Demand. Conversely, when the government pursues contractionary monetary or fiscal policies, the Aggregate Demand curve shifts to the left. This is shown as the movement from AD_0 to AD_1 in Panel A of Figure 2.

THE AGGREGATE SUPPLY CURVE

Classical theory relies on market adjustments to changes in individual supplies and demands to keep an economy close to full employment. Thus, it predicts a vertical long-run Aggregate Supply curve. Keynesian theory deals with a depressed economy—so many resources are idle that Aggregate Supply is horizontal in the short run. An intermediate position is that Aggregate Supply is positively sloped.

*In the short run, the **Aggregate Supply curve** reflects a positive relationship between the price level and the real quantity of National Output.*

This short-run positive relationship occurs primarily because production costs (e.g., wages) are sticky relative to output prices when demand changes. Increases to Aggregate Demand cause movements of the *AD* curve up along the Aggregate Supply curve in which prices rise more quickly than wages, so higher profit per unit induces more output. Declines in Aggregate Demand reverse these movements along the Aggregate Supply curve: prices fall more quickly than costs, so profits decline and firms reduce production.

If output is below Q_0 on the Aggregate Supply curve shown in Figure 3 and much capacity is idle, then output can increase in the short run without significant hikes in the price level. But when the classical prediction of full employment is approached, even small increases in output above Q_f necessitate large increases in the price level. Between output levels Q_0 and Q_1 moderate growth in output results in relatively smaller price hikes.

National Output and the Work Force

Increases in the total demand for labor generate pressure for more employment and output and for hikes in wages and prices as well. Conversely, declines in the economy-wide demand for labor create pressure for lower employment, output, wages, and prices. There are,

FIGURE 2 Events that Shift the Aggregate Demand Curve

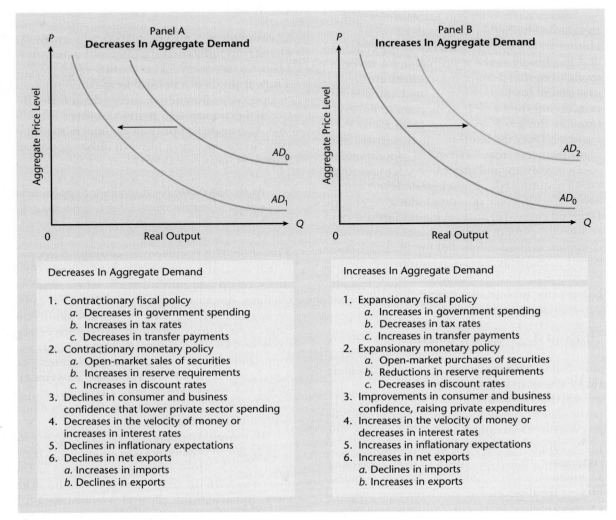

Panel A
Decreases In Aggregate Demand

Aggregate Price Level / Real Output

AD_0
AD_1

Panel B
Increases In Aggregate Demand

Aggregate Price Level / Real Output

AD_2
AD_0

Decreases In Aggregate Demand

1. Contractionary fiscal policy
   a. Decreases in government spending
   b. Increases in tax rates
   c. Decreases in transfer payments
2. Contractionary monetary policy
   a. Open-market sales of securities
   b. Increases in reserve requirements
   c. Increases in discount rates
3. Declines in consumer and business confidence that lower private sector spending
4. Decreases in the velocity of money or increases in interest rates
5. Declines in inflationary expectations
6. Declines in net exports
   a. Increases in imports
   b. Declines in exports

Increases In Aggregate Demand

1. Expansionary fiscal policy
   a. Increases in government spending
   b. Decreases in tax rates
   c. Increases in transfer payments
2. Expansionary monetary policy
   a. Open-market purchases of securities
   b. Reductions in reserve requirements
   c. Decreases in discount rates
3. Improvements in consumer and business confidence, raising private expenditures
4. Increases in the velocity of money or decreases in interest rates
5. Increases in inflationary expectations
6. Increases in net exports
   a. Declines in imports
   b. Increases in exports

however, differences between short-run and long-run adjustments. Understanding Aggregate Supply requires an appreciation of these differences.

Labor Markets: The Short Run

Keynesian models emphasize short-run adjustments. Suppose Aggregate Demand grew slightly during a severe depression like that of the 1930s. Keynes believed that high unemployment permits firms to fill all vacant positions at the going wage, so the relevant part of the ag-

gregate labor-supply curve is assumed to be flat, while extensive idle capital limits diminishing returns as a problem. Thus, if the demand for labor grows during a depression, employment and output rise, but wages and prices may not. Consequently, Keynesian analysis assumes a horizontal Aggregate Supply curve (see the Keynesian depression range in Figure 3). Remember that from Keynes' point of view, Say's Law was backward and should have read "Demand creates its own supply."

Keynes' assumptions about depressed labor markets are drawn from the 1930s experience of a prolonged depression. Labor's supply curve

FIGURE 3 The Aggregate Supply

As is true for typical market supply curves, the Aggregate Supply curve is positively sloped. Thus, increases in Aggregate Demand along a stable Aggregate Supply curve normally entail increases in the price level and national output.

normally has a positive slope because drawing more workers into the labor force requires higher wages; rising wages also enable unemployed workers to more rapidly find jobs they perceive as suitable. As firms pay higher wages to attract additional employees, wages rise for all workers. This results in a moderately positive slope in the Aggregate Supply curve in its intermediate range in Figure 3.

Workers know that higher prices lower their real wages, but there is a lag between a given inflationary decline in real wages and labor's recognition of this loss. Workers may temporarily be "fooled" by hikes in money wages that are less than inflation, so more labor services may be offered even if real wages decline. This is shown in Figure 4. Initially, Q_0 workers are hired at a wage of $10.00 per hour [at point a where $D_{L(P=100)}$ and $S_{L\ (P=100)}$ cross]. Since the price level is 100, real wages (w/P) are also $10.00 ($10.00/1.00 = $10.00).

Firms hire more labor to produce more output if they perceive increased profit opportunities; output prices that rise faster than nominal wages. Rising prices ($P = 120$) generate additional demands for labor equal to $D_{L(P=120)}$, so employment grows to Q_1 and wages rise to $11.00 per hour. In the short run, workers fail to revise their expectations about changes in the price level and are fooled because they believe the original price level will prevail. Notice that real wages (w/P) have actually fallen to $9.17 per hour ($11.00/1.20 = $9.17). Workers may suffer from *inflation illusion* in the very short run, but their misconceptions are unlikely to persist.

• **Labor Markets: The Longer Run** The long-run orientation of classical reasoning represents the polar extreme from Keynesian analysis. New classical economics assumes that workers react to changes in real wages almost instantly, keeping the economy close to full employment. At the very least, there can be no involuntary unemployment.

Workers try to base decisions about work on real wages, not on nominal money wages—what their earnings will buy, not the money itself. In the longer run, workers recognize that price hikes reduce their real wages (w/P) and react by reducing the real supply of labor. This is shown as a reduction in labor supply to $S_{L\ (P=120)}$ in Figure 4. This restores the labor market to long-run equilibrium at point c, where Q_0 workers are employed at a real wage of $10.00 ($12.00/1.20 = $10.00).

To summarize, suppose Aggregate Demand grows in an economy that is close to full employment. Higher money wages may temporarily lure more workers into the labor force if they expect the price level to remain constant. Once workers recognize that prices have risen, they demand commensurate raises. This yields the almost vertical long-run Aggregate Supply curve shown as the classical range in Figure 3.

In reality, workers react slowly to changes in real earnings. A couple of reasons help explain why individual workers may be more easily "fooled" by inflation than are the firms that

FIGURE 4 Labor Markets and Changes in Inflation Rates

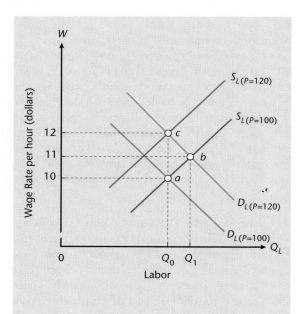

Workers know that higher prices lower their real wages, but there is often a lag between inflation and labor's recognition of this loss. Rising prices ($P = 120$) increase the demand for labor, so employment moves from the original equilibrium point a to point b. Initially, more labor is supplied at $11 per hour. Eventually, however, workers realize that this higher nominal wage is less than the original real wage $10, and labor supply shifts to $S_{L(P=120)}$. The new equilibrium is point c, where employment declines to Q_0 and real wages return to $10 ($12/1.20 = $10).

Thus, the real wage paid a worker from the vantage point of the firm is w/p_i. Workers, on the other hand, must forecast the prices of all goods they expect to buy (e.g., the CPI) before they can estimate the future purchasing power of their monetary wages. The real wage from the point of view of a typical worker equals w/CPI, where CPI is the price level. Thus, firms may need less information about future prices (only p_i) to make profitable decisions than workers need (forecasts of most prices in the CPI) as a guide for personally beneficial decisions.

Finally, in reality, when real wages drop, the options open to most workers are limited. Quitting and looking for a new position involves significant transaction costs including the search, interview, lost wages, and possible uprooting of family for a move to another region of the country. Labor immobility and high information and transaction costs may mean that labor isn't "fooled" but can only adjust in the longer term.

As a result, firms have better access to information about inflation, while actually needing less information than workers do to react to changes in the price level. Workers also respond relatively slowly because (a) most long-term union contracts set nominal wages for the length of these agreements, (b) both employers and employees often implicitly agree to contracts where wages are adjusted only at scheduled intervals, and (c) changing jobs often entails considerable costs in search time and lost income.

Shifts in Aggregate Supply

The Aggregate Supply curve shifts when technology changes or when resource availability or costs change. Technological advances boost Aggregate Supply, while disruptions in resource markets, higher tax rates, or inefficient new government regulations are among negative shocks to Aggregate Supply.

• **Shocks Operating Through the Labor Market** The notion that enhanced incentives to supply resources would boost Aggregate Supply was at the heart of the 25% cut in tax rates during 1981 to 1983 and was also partially

employ them. First, a major decision by a big firm may put millions of dollars on the line, while individual workers have only their salary at risk. Thus, firms devote more resources to forecasts of inflation. Second, a firm only needs to estimate how much extra revenue will be generated if extra workers are hired to know how much of a monetary wage (w) it can profitably afford to pay. This calculation requires only estimates of the worker's physical productivity and a forecast of the price (p_i) at which the firm will be able to sell its own product.

responsible for attempts to cut growth in government transfer payments. The Reagan administration felt that this strategy would boost Aggregate Supply more than these tax cuts increased Aggregate Demand, so that substantial growth would more than offset any emerging inflationary pressure. Naturally, higher marginal tax rates would reduce the effective supply of labor and, consequently, Aggregate Supply.

A second type of labor market disturbance would occur if the power of unions grew and they commanded higher wages. Wage hikes raise production costs and push up prices, shrinking Aggregate Supply. This potential problem has diminished in importance over the last two decades as union membership as a percent of the workforce has declined not only in the United States but worldwide.

More recently, the restructuring of American industry has led to serious changes in most labor markets. Global competition, rapidly changing technology, expanded labor legislation, and a broader legal liability of firms for various labor issues have resulted in corporate downsizing and more intensive use of a contingency labor force. The wholesale trimming of employees in many companies has led some to argue that many corporate employees who managed to keep their jobs are now overworked.

Another problem area would be any rise in the inflation rate workers expect. Inflationary expectations continuously shift labor supply curves leftward as workers try to protect the purchasing power of their earnings. Naturally, decreases in inflationary expectations or in union power will shift the labor supply and Aggregate Supply curves toward the right. Finally, people's preferences between work and leisure obviously affect Aggregate Supply.

• **Incomes Policies** Some analysts think that incomes policies may moderate inflationary expectations. The term *"incomes policy"* refers to measures intended to curb inflation without altering monetary or fiscal policies. These methods include moral suasion, wage-and-price guidelines or controls, and wage–price freezes

of the type imposed in 1971. President Nixon hoped the freeze would reduce expected inflation and halt continuous shrinkage of Aggregate Supply. Ideally, it might have increased the supplies of labor and output, shown as the shift of the Aggregate Supply curve from AS_0 to AS_2 in Panel B of Figure 5.

Unfortunately, incomes policies may perversely affect inflationary expectations and Aggregate Supply. If workers and firms share a belief that prices will soar soon after controls are lifted, they may withhold production from the market now in hopes of realizing higher wages or prices later. For example, suppose you face the following choice: you can (*a*) work during a period when wages are frozen and save money to cover your college expenses or (*b*) borrow to go to college during a freeze and then repay the loan from funds you earn after the lid is removed from wage hikes. You (and many other people) might delay working until after the freeze. Incomes policies also hinder necessary relative price adjustments; in Chapter 18 we detail how the resulting distortions in economic behavior retard Aggregate Supply.

• **Other Shocks Affecting Productive Capacity** New regulations that hamper production shift the Aggregate Supply curve to the left (a movement from AS_0 to AS_1 in Panel A of Figure 5), but elimination of inefficient regulation shifts the curve rightward. From the mid-1970s onward, deregulation and privatization of parts of our economy have been aimed at removing inefficiency and boosting Aggregate Supply.

Technological advances expand Aggregate Supply, while external shocks that raise costs for imports or resources will shrink Aggregate Supply. Shocks to the U.S. economy occurred when OPEC coalesced in 1973 and world oil prices quadrupled shortly thereafter. Most industrialized countries endured painful leftward shifts in their Aggregate Supply curves. Rightward shifts occur when new resources are found. For example, Great Britain discovered oil in the North Sea, and exploitation of huge pools of Mexican oil during the late 1970s

Decreases in Aggregate Supply	Increases in Aggregate Supply
Originating in the Labor Market	
1. Declines in labor force 2. Increased preference for leisure by labor 3. Increased union power yielding higher wages 4. Increased inflationary expectations by labor 5. Enhanced Social Security or unemployment compensation and other welfare programs 6. Increases in marginal tax rates on wages	1. Increases in labor force 2. Increased preference for work by labor 3. Reduced bargaining strength of organized labor 4. Reduced inflationary expectations by labor 5. Reductions in available welfare payments 6. Decreases in marginal tax rates on wages
Affecting Production Capability	

1. New regulations that impede efficiency
2. Shocks that increase resource costs (e.g., OPEC embargo and increased oil prices)
3. Tax changes that reduce capital accumulation
4. Any events that reduce the economy's overall rate of productivity increase
5. Increased monopoly power
6. Depletion of natural resources
7. Barriers against imports
	1. Reducing unnecessary government regulations
	2. New regulations that enhance efficiency
	3. Discoveries that increase the amounts and decrease the costs of important resources
	4. Technological advances
	5. Tax changes that encourage capital accumulation and improved productivity
	   a. Reductions in capital gains taxes
	   b. Investment tax credits
	   c. Research and development funding
	6. Policies that reduce monopolistic practices
	7. Increase in imports

FIGURE 5   Events that Shift the Aggregate Supply Curve

helped Mexico. Gluts of oil on world markets and the relative instability of OPEC drove prices down; energy costs fell from the mid-1980s onward, boosting our Aggregate Supply to the right.

Influences that shift Aggregate Supply are listed in Figure 5. Understanding macroeconomic movements requires a good grasp of these concepts. We will now survey some recent theories developed by **new Keynesian economists** to explain why wages are sticky, causing involuntary unemployment to persist during some periods.

UNEMPLOYMENT

Excessive unemployment reduces output and income, erodes human capital, and imposes widespread suffering. Classical analysis suggests that in the longer-term, the economy will equilibrate at full employment. In contrast, traditional Keynesian analysis indicates that adjustments to Aggregate Demand can restore full employment even in the shorter term. But as Figure 6 illustrates, in recent years unemployment has been not only persistent, but

Average unemployment

Unemployment exceeding 26 weeks as a percentage of total unemployment

Source: *Bureau of Labor Statistics, 1994.*

Average U.S. unemployment rates have risen over the past five decades. Long term unemployment (that where a worker is jobless for an extended period) has also followed an upward trend.

FIGURE 6   The Upward Trend in Unemployment Rates

growing. And increasing numbers of workers are left jobless for increasingly long periods.

The traditional Keynesian model, as we have seen, explains unemployment as a consequence of inadequate Aggregate Demand and **sticky wages**. Labor markets, according to Keynes, may not clear. For example, workers are often not willing to accept a reduction in their money wages, setting a floor on wages and preventing the market from clearing. Thus the price of labor may not adjust so that the quantity demanded equals the quantity supplied. Modern Keynesians (or **new Keynesians**, as they are called) have developed richer theoretical microfoundations to explain why labor markets sometimes fail to clear, which can lead to persistent involuntary unemployment. Within this ongoing area of research, explanations for failures of labor markets to clear can be grouped under *labor contract* considerations, *efficiency wage* theories, and *dual labor markets* (insiders and outsiders). Before we look at the U.S. record on unemployment, we will examine each of these microeconomic foundations for new Keynesian analysis.

Labor Contracts

Unlike wheat, corn, or soybeans, labor is not traded on spot markets. (Almost no workers are employed one hour at a time, with constant recontracting.) Transaction costs are significant in most labor negotiations. Individuals negotiate either directly or through unions with firms about wage rates and the conditions of their employment. The high costs of information and mobility (moving between jobs or hiring new employees) are the major reason that most employment relationships take on a long-term nature. Even though most workers today can expect to have five to seven jobs over the course of their careers, this still means that the average job is held six or seven years.

Such long-term relationships imply that wages and working conditions are usually negotiated only periodically; once a year is typical. Union contracts usually extend from two to three years, with wage rates being negotiated in nominal terms and often with escalator clauses to adjust wages for inflation. Even where union agreements are not in effect, federal or state laws or both, often require that overtime pay rises as the hours of work increase beyond some point.

These **labor contracts**, whether written (*explicit*) or unwritten (*implicit*), mean that wages and benefits are set for lengthy periods and adjust in a lagged fashion to changes in economic conditions. Thus, when the economy turns downward, wages fall only slowly to create job openings for the unemployed. Another reason many firms reduce their wage offers only slowly during recessions is found in the notion of efficiency wages.

Efficiency Wages

The existence of substantial and sustained unemployment clashes with standard theories of competitive markets. According to classical theories of competitive labor markets, wage cuts would quickly and automatically eliminate unemployment (surpluses of labor). But the new Keynesians are skeptical that this is how the real world actually works.

The supply and demand for labor shown in Figure 7 yield an equilibrium of q_L and employment at wage w_L under standard assumptions. A worker who failed to perform conscientiously (a problem known as *shirking*) could be fired. However, if this labor market were competitive, this worker would almost immediately find another job at wage w_L. Thus, the threat of being fired would be ineffective as a disincentive against loafing or dishonesty.

Employers are aware that shirking must be offset by other incentives. One strategy is for the firm to engage in *reputation building*. A reputation for seldom laying off workers, even when business is slack, may attract topnotch workers without requiring wage premiums. In such cases, shirking, if discovered, would cause a worker to forfeit job security. On the other hand, a reputation as an unreliable and harsh employer may stimulate shirking, and the firm may be forced to expend more resources monitoring employee performance.

Another tactic to curb shirking is for firms to pay more than prevailing market wages. A

FIGURE 7   Efficiency Wages and Equilibrium Unemployment

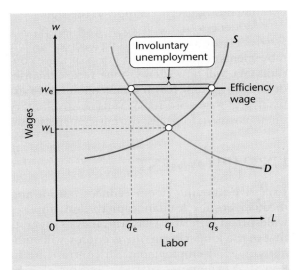

Efficiency wages are set above market equilibrium to increase the costs of dismissal and reduce shirking by employees. Efficiency wages, if paid by all employers, increase the costs of being fired by creating a pool of unemployed, $q_s - q_e$; this increases costs for dismissed employees. Such attempts by employers to reduce shirking are one of several explanations for involuntary unemployment in labor markets.

firm may start new employees at a low wage but, after satisfactory performance, quickly raise their wages to a premium level. These workers would lose their premium wages if fired and would be less likely to be able to duplicate their current salaries and benefits.

> ***Efficiency wages*** *are wages that exceed market-clearing wages and are intended (a) to raise the costs to employees of being dismissed, thereby reducing shirking, and (b) to retain key people during a recession because it is difficult to replace them once they are hired by competing firms.*[1]

This may seem paradoxical because, if all firms pay wages that exceed the market-clearing

------

[1]Luring old employees back or finding adequate replacements during the upturn is difficult and costly.

wage, dismissal would not harm employees. Figure 7 suggests, however, that high efficiency wages (W_c) to control shirking reduce employment to q_e. Unemployment equals $q_s - q_e$ in this type of equilibrium, because q_s workers are willing to work at wage w_e. Dismissed employees will be at least temporarily unemployed, raising their cost of shirking. Similarly, employers find it difficult to skim the best workers from the labor pool while only paying a market-clearing wage. Thus, involuntary unemployment may be partially explained by employers' attempts to offset shirking and to reduce turnover costs (workers quitting) by paying premium wages. Global competition and corporate downsizing are making it more difficult for firms to continue to pay premium wages to all workers. Once unemployed, workers may also face a dual labor market.

Dual Labor Markets

The concept of **dual labor markets** involves segmenting the national labor market in two sectors: (*a*) a primary nonmarket-clearing sector paying efficiency wages (*insiders*) and (*b*) a secondary sector where the market clears, but which is much more competitive (*outsiders*). Almost all workers want to work in the primary sector because wages and benefits are higher.

In Figure 8, this primary sector is shown in Panel A and the secondary market is shown in Panel B. For simplicity, the total labor force at any moment is assumed fixed. High wages (w_1) are paid to L_1 workers in the primary sector. Any vacant primary positions are quickly snapped up by eager workers who want high pay and job security. Although, from workers' perspectives, there are shortages of high paying jobs in the primary sector, it is nearly always possible to find lower paying and less desirable jobs (burger flipper?) in the secondary labor market, shown in Panel B. The secondary market's demand for labor is shown as D_{L2} and begins at wage w_1 (point *a*). The residual labor supply is S_{L2}, and this market clears at point *b*, an equilibrium wage of w_2. Total employment is $L_1 + L_2$, and unemployment equals $L_f - L_2$ in Panel B. These workers represent a curious blend of both voluntary and involuntary unemployment: they continue to apply for positions in the primary sector, but are unwilling to take a job in the secondary sector.

Examples of workers for whom the dual labor market theory provides an explanation for

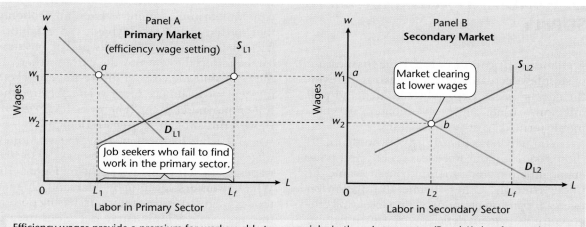

Panel A
Primary Market
(efficiency wage setting)

Job seekers who fail to find work in the primary sector.

Labor in Primary Sector

Panel B
Secondary Market

Market clearing at lower wages

Labor in Secondary Sector

Efficiency wages provide a premium for workers able to secure jobs in the primary sector (Panel A), but few workers can land these positions. Anyone willing to work at low wages finds employment quickly in the secondary market (Panel B), but people unwilling to work for wage w_2 remain jobless.

FIGURE 8   Unemployment in a Dual Labor Market

unemployment would include engineers or middle managers who lost career positions at firms in declining industries. These workers would be very reluctant to take jobs as, for example, order takers at drive-through windows in fast-food restaurants.

Recent corporate downsizing has pushed many workers previously in the primary sector into secondary labor markets. Former career employees often exhaust their unemployment benefits while attempting to secure new jobs in the primary sector. A growing number of these workers now comprise the contingent labor force we described in Chapter 6: part-time and temporary employees, the self-employed, and consultants who offer business services.

Long-term labor contracts (whether implicit or explicit), efficiency wages, and dual labor markets all provide microfoundations to help explain wage stickiness and unemployment in an Aggregate Demand–Aggregate Supply framework. We now turn to the issue of how changes in Aggregate Supply and Aggregate Demand affect the rates of unemployment and inflation.

SHOCKS TO AGGREGATE DEMAND AND AGGREGATE SUPPLY

Equilibrium prices rise only if demands increase or supplies decrease. Inflation that originates on the *demand side* is referred to as "demand-pull inflation," while *supply-side* inflation is commonly termed "cost-push inflation."

You may have heard people complain, "If those *@!% unions were less greedy and powerful, inflation and unemployment would be under control." Others blame all inflation on overly expansionary monetary policies. Still others cite government deficits as causing inflation: "Inflation would disappear if the federal budget ever balanced." Then there are those who blame business profiteering, wars, or foreigners for our problems. What have been the basic sources of U.S. inflation in the last few decades?

And why is unemployment often so persistent? We will explore the expected equilibrium paths during both supply-side and demand-side inflation to begin to answer these intertwined questions. Then we can compare these results with recent history.

Demand-Side Inflation

Growth of Aggregate Demand in an economy operating below capacity increases employment, output, income, and, perhaps, the price level. End of the Keynesian story. But suppose an economy is in a noninflationary equilibrium at full employment, such as that labeled point *a* in Figure 9: full-employment GDP equals Q_f and the price level is P_0. "Full employment" allows for frictional unemployment caused by flows of workers between jobs and in and out of the work force. Labor supplies initially reflect no expectations of inflation, which, along with other institutional characteristics (unemployment compensation rates, labor laws, and so on) and aggregate productive capacity, yield the Aggregate Supply curve AS_0.

Now assume that Aggregate Demand rises from AD_0 to AD_1 because government spending grows, moving the economy toward a new short-run equilibrium at point *b*. Even an economy that started at full employment can expand if frictional unemployment falls and if business can be induced to employ the extra workers. If they can shift the costs of hiring these workers forward to consumers, firms will hire beyond the full-employment point. The price level rises to P_1 with this swollen Aggregate Demand.

But what happens to real wages? Money wages do not rise as quickly as prices, so real wages (w/P) fall. This is shown in Figure 10. When workers eventually demand higher money wages to restore their purchasing power, the Aggregate Supply curve decreases toward AS_1, (in Figure 9). Along the equilibrium path between points *b* and *c*, labor finds that, although it earns higher money wages, these wages are partially eroded by continuing inflation. How long will this process continue? Labor repeat-

FIGURE 9   Demand-Side Inflation: The Counterclockwise Path

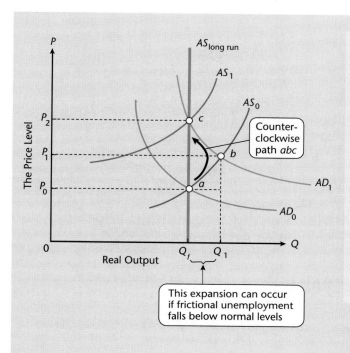

Frictional unemployment, a normal by-product of economic activity, is reflected by the difference between Q_1, which assumes that everyone who wants to work is employed, and Q_f, which allows for frictional unemployment. Frictional unemployment may artificially fall below normal levels ($Q_1 - Q_f$) if expansions of Aggregate Demand temporarily fool some frictionally unemployed workers into taking jobs that pay low real wages (movement from a to b). In the long run, however, workers will adjust their wage demands to reflect higher prices and unemployment will rise back to normal levels (movement from b to c).

Thus, if cyclical unemployment is negligible, expanding Aggregate Demand may temporarily reduce frictional unemployment, but this decline is artificial; so the ultimate effect of expansionary policy is to increase the price level, and the economy follows the counterclockwise path shown in this figure.

Counter-clockwise path abc

This expansion can occur if frictional unemployment falls below normal levels

edly reacts to price hikes by demanding higher wages until equilibrium at point c is reached. At this point, real wages have regained their original values, the economy is back at full employment, and the aggregate price level equals P_2—precisely labor's new expectations about the price level.

> Price-level increases initiated when the Aggregate Demand curve expands (shifts to the right) are called **demand-side** (or demand-pull) **inflation**.

Prices continue to rise when labor's inflationary expectations adjust and so might be thought of as supply-side inflation, but this is simply the second phase of a demand-side cycle; the original inflationary impetus came from increased demand. The forces that set this inflationary spiral in motion shift the Aggregate Demand curve to the right. Notice that as labor reacts to the inflationary spiral, the economy's

equilibrium path runs from point a to b to c, following a *counterclockwise path*.

We indicated earlier that a Keynesian inflationary gap such as that reflected by $Q_1 - Q_f$ in Figure 9 creates inflationary pressure. In a sense, this is a negative GDP gap. *Overfull employment* can occur if frictional unemployment is artificially driven down by expansions of Aggregate Demand. Automatic pressures ultimately reduce output back to full employment levels. The economy illustrated in Figure 9 first moves from a to point b. When workers eventually realize that they have been fooled, the labor supply falls, returning the system to full employment at point c, but at a higher price level. Recall that (*a*) we initially assumed full employment, with allowances for normal frictional unemployment, and (*b*) if the economy is initially plagued by excess capacity, only the first phase of this cycle needs to occur—growing demand can yield much more output with only slightly higher prices.

FIGURE 10 Changes in Real Wages and Inflation

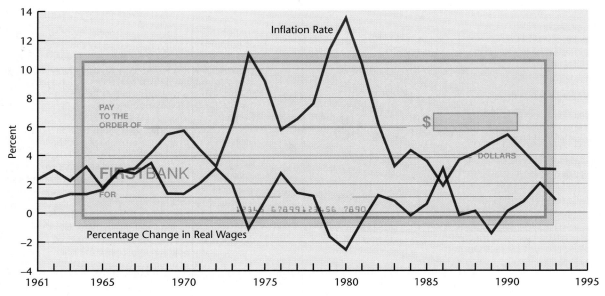

Source: *Economic Report of the President,* 1994.

Rises in money wages lag price changes so that real wages typically fall when the rate of inflation rises. Conversely, when inflation declines, real wages tend to rise. Real wages in this figure include both wages and benefits.

Supply-Side Inflation

The double whammy of high unemployment and rapid inflation was once thought quite unlikely. Policymakers believed that low unemployment rates might spark rapid inflation, and vice versa, but faith in Keynesian policies to fine-tune Aggregate Demand to yield healthy growth and a reasonably stable price level was commonplace. A major reason neither conventional classical nor Keynesian theories offer much insight into why high rates of inflation and unemployment might occur simultaneously is that, from the 1940s into the 1970s, both schools of thought largely ignored shifts in Aggregate Supply.

Economists of a classical persuasion traditionally cited shifts in Aggregate Demand to explain inflation because the Aggregate Supply curve was assumed to be vertical and stable. Keynesian theory also viewed Aggregate Supply as stable, but treated it as horizontal during a recession. Thus, Keynesians focused on shocks to Aggregate Demand as disrupting output and

employment. The resulting debate over whether shifts in Aggregate Demand ultimately yield price-level adjustments (the classical position) or adjustments to employment and the output level (the Keynesian position) caused economists to neglect shocks to Aggregate Supply.

The world economy was bombarded by supply shocks during the 1970s, however, creating problems that seemed enigmatic to most economists. High unemployment and inflation first occurred simultaneously in 1974 through 1975, giving rise to the term "stagflation," a contraction of stagnation and inflation.

> ***Stagflation*** *entails simultaneous high unemployment and rapid inflation.*

This malady proved persistent. Inflation and unemployment were both above historical norms for almost a decade. Attempts to reduce inflation from the double-digit range during 1979 to 1981 partially succeeded by 1982 but briefly drove civilian unemployment above 10%.

OPEC price hikes were the most notable supply shocks to the U.S. economy in the 1970s, but other types of shocks are clear possibilities. Suppose workers began viewing leisure more favorably and work less favorably and that hard bargaining by unions became the norm in key industries. The effect of a major energy price increase is shown in Figure 11. Higher energy costs shift Aggregate Supply to the left. Suppose the original equilibrium is at point d. As Aggregate Supply shrinks from AS_0 to AS_1 equilibrium moves from point d to e. Firms will demand less labor because higher energy prices can only partially be passed on to consumers in the form of higher product prices. Unless something boosts Aggregate Demand, less real output is demanded at the new price level P_1 and real output and employment fall to Q_1. For incumbent politicians, this is the worst of all worlds: rising prices and unemployment, and declining real incomes and output.

As the economy moves to point e, politicians may worry about voters' reactions to a recession. Why this can be a concern is indicated in Focus 1. Policymakers may also perceive a duty to maintain full employment under the Employment Act of 1946 and the Humphrey-Hawkins Full-Employment and Balanced Growth Act of 1978. Political pressure will mount to launch expansionary policies in response to any movement from point d to point e. If, on the other hand, policymakers view inflation as an evil that must be tamed and try to restore the price level to P_0 by decreasing Aggregate Demand to AD_2, the economy will move from point d to point g, further decreasing National Output and exacerbating unemployment.

Alternatives to achieving full employment by expanding Aggregate Demand would be policies to restore Aggregate Supply from AS_1 to AS_0. More output and employment would be generated at lower prices. The supply-side policies we listed in Figure 5 are aimed at increasing our productive capacity, a task not accomplished overnight, so the federal government has historically tended to be demand-management oriented. Nevertheless, the supply-side policies adopted in the early 1980s were avowedly a reaction against Keynesian policy-

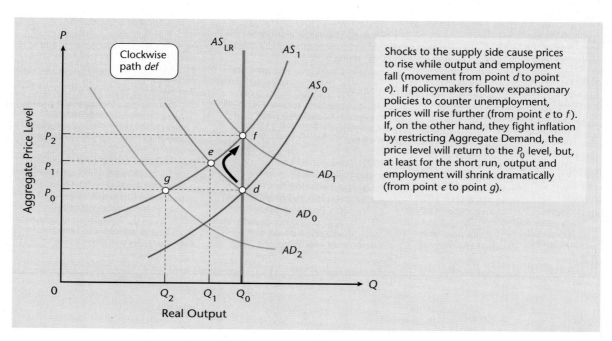

Shocks to the supply side cause prices to rise while output and employment fall (movement from point d to point e). If policymakers follow expansionary policies to counter unemployment, prices will rise further (from point e to f). If, on the other hand, they fight inflation by restricting Aggregate Demand, the price level will return to the P_0 level, but, at least for the short run, output and employment will shrink dramatically (from point e to point g).

FIGURE 11   Supply-Side Inflation: The Clockwise Path

Macroeconomics and Presidential Elections

Commentators criticize many political campaigns as resembling beauty contests: looks, personality, and images created by public relations specialists (spin-doctors) are viewed as dominating recent political contests. But there is a growing body of evidence that economic circumstances have powerful effects on the outcomes of major elections.

Prosperity favors political incumbents and, apparently, the candidates of the party of the previous president. Economist Ray Fair has developed a simple statistical equation based on simple macroeconomic variables—unemployment and growth of per capita real income—that "picked" the winner in all but three presidential elections held between 1948 and 1994 (and his equation predicted those three elections to be close).

Republican President Hoover did not stand a chance of reelection in 1932; the Great Depression that began late in 1929 (the year he took office) continued to worsen until 1933. Democrat President Franklin D. Roosevelt's reelection in 1936 occurred during recovery, as did his reelection in 1940; the economy had faltered again in 1937 but recovered from 1938 through 1946. World War II yielded high levels of patriotic fervor and economic prosperity, ensuring Roosevelt's reelection for a fourth term in 1944. President Truman was reelected in November 1948, the month a business cycle reached its peak. Republican Dwight Eisenhower (a popular hero from World War II) defied the odds in

besting Adlai Stevenson in 1952 when the economy was expanding, but his victory in 1956 occurred in the middle of an economic recovery from a 1954 recession (the economy weakened again in 1957).

Richard Nixon blamed a minor recession in 1960 for his narrow loss to Democrat John F. Kennedy. President Lyndon Johnson was reelected by a landslide in 1964, in the middle of the longest economic recovery since World War II. His vice president, Hubert Humphrey, lost a close election to Richard Nixon in 1968 despite a relatively strong U.S. economy. Fair's equation picked Humphrey as the winner by a slim margin. (Humphrey's loss may have reflected dismay about Johnson's conduct of the unpopular Vietnam War). President Nixon was determined to win by a landslide in 1972; per capita income soared in that election year, and his wish (along with the wishes of most other incumbents) was granted.

Gerald Ford (who became president after Nixon resigned amid the Watergate scandal) lost his 1976 bid for reelection to Jimmy Carter; the economy was still weak from the "energy crisis" and a severe recession in 1975. The economy recovered somewhat from 1976 to 1978, but double-digit inflation and growing unemployment in 1979 and 1980 doomed President Carter to his loss to Ronald Reagan.

President Reagan's goal of stimulating rapid economic growth through incentive-based supply-side policies was frustrated when

the Fed followed disinflationary policies in the early 1980s; the period 1982 to 1983 was the deepest economic downturn that the United States had experienced since the Great Depression. However, a strong recovery that began in 1983 swept President Reagan into another four-year term.

This recovery continued through the 1988 election, which pitted George Bush against Michael Dukakis. Between 1983 and 1988, unemployment fell steadily, finally reaching 5.5%, the lowest rate in nearly two decades. Inflation, which had been at double-digit rates in 1981, had stabilized by 1988 to a rate that most people perceived as tolerable. Economic growth continued on a path of moderate recovery. With the economy looking up, George Bush's victory in the 1988 election was no surprise.

This analysis suggests that President Bush may have lost reelection in 1992 because of the recession of 1990 to 1992. Fair's equation predicted a very narrow victory for Bush, but the upturn that began in late 1991 was shallow and widely described as a "jobless recovery". Only after Bill Clinton had taken office were corrected data found to indicate that growth during 1992 was faster than the data available at election time had indicated. Cold comfort, indeed, for Bush, who had joined with Ronald Reagan in stripping resources from data collection agencies (e.g., the Bureau of Labor Statistics) in attempts to help balance the federal budget.

making and were explicitly intended to expand Aggregate Supply.

However, President Reagan's supply-side package looked a lot like Keynesian policies to stimulate Aggregate Demand: tax rates were cut,[2] and government outlays (military and domestic) grew, echoing policies launched 20 years earlier by the Kennedy administration as Keynesian policy. The results were also similar. Budget deficits were much larger in the 1980s than in the 1960s, but otherwise, the expansions of 1961 to 1968 and 1983 to 1989 looked like twins.

Stimulating Aggregate Demand is a relatively quick and easy process; government cuts tax rates or boosts its spending or transfer payments, or the Fed increases monetary growth. The government commonly counters shrinkage of Aggregate Supply by increasing Aggregate Demand, shown by a shift from AD_0 to AD_1 in Figure 11. With demand management, the economy will move along the equilibrium path described by the arrow from point e to f. Full employment is ultimately restored, but at a higher price level. Notice that the long-term equilibrium path for supply-side inflation is from point d to e to f, a *clockwise pattern*. (Remember that, in contrast, a demand-side inflationary cycle follows a counterclockwise pattern.)

Supply-side inflation is initiated when the Aggregate Supply curve shifts to the left and the price level rises as output falls.

A few qualifications are worth noting. First, shifts in the Aggregate Supply curve from AS_0 to AS_1 originate in a multitude of ways summarized previously under Figure 5. Second, the federal government need not increase government spending to shift the Aggregate Demand curve from AD_0 to AD_1. For example, the Fed might stimulate rapid monetary growth in attempts to push the economy out of a recession.

---

[2]Supply-siders argue that supply-side tax cuts of 1981 to 1983 were largely offset by a less publicized jump in Social Security taxes in 1982. According to supply-side logic, this huge increase in payroll taxes may have significantly harmed incentives for labor effort.

The U.S. Economic Record[3]

You are now prepared to examine recent U.S. experiences with inflation, unemployment, and patterns of growth. We just showed that demand-side inflations equilibrate in a counterclockwise fashion, while supply-side inflations cause the economy to follow a clockwise pattern.

- **Inflation in the 1960s and 1970s** The inflations of the 1960s and 1970s are graphed in Figure 12. The most significant difference between this and previous graphs is that we have altered the axes slightly to accommodate the data. The GDP deflator is still measured on the vertical axes, but each period starts out at a base of 100. We also have converted the horizontal axis to real GDP divided by potential GDP to adjust for growth in our productive capacity. Potential GDP grows because of such things as technological advances, capital accumulation, or growth of the labor force.

The demand-pull inflation of the 1960s resulted primarily from increased government spending for domestic programs, the space program, the escalation of the Vietnam conflict, stimulation from the 1964 tax cut, and rising monetary growth. As you can see in Panel A, the equilibrium process followed a counterclockwise path.

Contrast the 1960s inflation with that of the mid-1970s, which may have been triggered by rising prices for OPEC oil and other imported goods. A second major external shock was a worldwide agricultural drought, leading to price hikes in the United States as mountains of U.S. farm output found its way into the world market. The Arab oil embargo reinforced inflationary pressures during this period. Many economists also include the 1971 to 1973 price controls as a shock to the supply side. Panel B of Figure 12 shows that the system equilibrated in a clockwise fashion, although price controls disguised inflationary pressure during 1971 to

---

[3]See the pioneering work in Robert J. Gordon's *Macroeconomics*, 6th ed. (New York: HarperCollins, 1993) for an extended version of the approach in this section.

FIGURE 12   Supply-Side and Demand-Side Inflations in the United States, 1962—1979

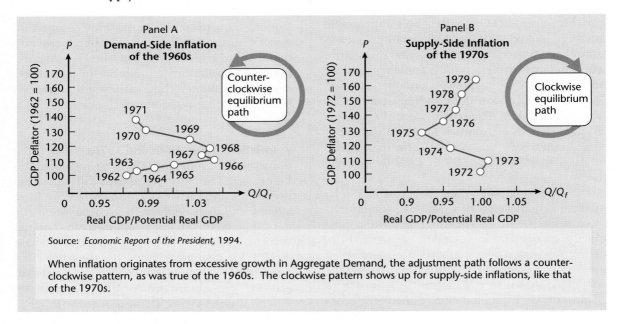

Source: *Economic Report of the President*, 1994.

When inflation originates from excessive growth in Aggregate Demand, the adjustment path follows a counter-clockwise pattern, as was true of the 1960s. The clockwise pattern shows up for supply-side inflations, like that of the 1970s.

1973. This figure indicates that inflation in the 1970s derived primarily from supply-side or cost-push, pressures.

• **The Contrast Between the 1930s and the 1970s**   Declines in either Aggregate Supply or Aggregate Demand tend to increase unemployment. Two clear episodes of these types of shift in AD and AS are shown in Figure 13. Aggregate Demand and Aggregate Supply curves are superimposed over data for the Great Depression in Panel A and for the commodity price shocks of 1973 in Panel B. Employment and unemployment rates have been substituted for real output on the horizontal axes to present a better picture of what happens to both employment and unemployment when either Aggregate Supply shrinks or Aggregate Demand falls.

During the Great Depression, investment collapsed, reducing Aggregate Demand from AD_0 to AD_1 in Panel A. Unemployment rates rose from 3.2% to 24.9%. In a similar fashion, commodity price shocks in 1973 (e.g., OPEC's) reduced Aggregate Supply from AS_0 to AS_1 in Panel B. This increased the unemployment rate from 4.8% to 8.3%.

• **Disinflation in the 1980s**   Restrictive monetary policies intended to suppress an inflationary hangover from the 1970s precipitated a severe slump during 1981 to 1983, but inflation continued at high rates. Interest rates jumped to record highs in 1979 and again in 1981. Tighter monetary policies than had been followed in over a decade finally caused both inflation and interest rates to begin drifting down in 1982. One side effect, however, was that, during 1983, the civilian unemployment rate briefly reached double digits. Some economists viewed the 1981 to 1983 slump as the castor oil required to cure earlier policy excesses.

Figure 14 uses our Aggregate Demand and Aggregate Supply framework to illustrate these general movements. Several years of growing demand and high inflation had enflamed inflationary expectations, shrinking the Aggregate Supply curve. This is shown as the shift from AS_0 to AS_1 in Panel A. To slow this inflationary spiral, the Fed tightened the screws during 1981 and 1982, shifting Aggregate Demand from AD_0 to AD_1. This dampened inflationary expectations and, coupled with tax cuts that kicked in during 1982 and 1983, helped stabilize the

FIGURE 13   Unemployment Following Shocks to Aggregate Demand and Aggregate Supply

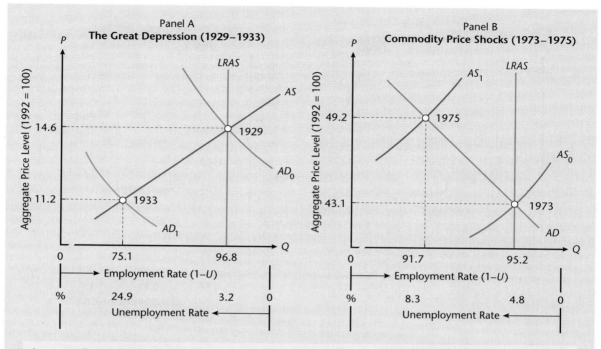

Aggregate Demand collapsed during the Great Depression (Panel A), and output, the price level, and employment all declined, while unemployment rose to record levels. By way of contrast, the precipitous decline in Aggregate Supply in the 1970s raised the price level, while output fell relative to its potential, as the unemployment rate rose to a high for the post–World War II period.

Aggregate Supply curve at AS_1. The resumption of mildly expansionary fiscal and monetary policies in 1983 allowed Aggregate Demand to drift back toward AD_0. The net result was *disinflation* and falling real output between points *a* and *b* (1980 to 1983 in Panel B) and then steady growth along AS_1 (points *c* and *d*) with significantly lower inflation (1983 to 1989 in Panel B).

The clockwise equilibration path is reflected in the actual equilibrium path for the economy illustrated in Panel B of Figure 14. The path of the economy between 1979 and 1983 indicates that Aggregate Supply continued to shrink because tight monetary policies decompressed inflation, but only by precipitating a severe recession. Economic growth between 1983 and 1989 points to movement along a flatter and more stable Aggregate Supply curve (*AS* in panel A).

Decompressing inflation is usually costly. In the early 1980s, the economy slipped below its earlier growth path. Cumulative losses of real income were estimated at roughly $3 trillion, due largely to policies intended to quell any possibility of a resurgence of accelerating inflation.

Disinflation *is a significant reduction in the rate of inflation.*

Many people who expected continued inflation had plunged into real estate and other inflation hedges, so disinflation left them stuck paying high real rates of interest. When the real burdens of their mortgages were not eased by inflation, many of these investors were devastated. Homes that had sold for $75,000 in 1975 were typically over $100,000 by 1980. Disinflation burst the bubble of asset prices swollen by infla-

FIGURE 14 Recovery in the 1980s and the Slump of 1990—1991

Source: *Economic Report of the President*, 1994.

Panel A illustrates the disinflation process after the sustained buildup of an inflationary spiral. Leftward shifts of the Aggregate Supply curve (due to rising inflationary expectations) are combined with reduced Aggregate Demand to produce a recession and quell inflation. Disinflation occurs between points *a* and *b*. Without policies to dampen Aggregate Demand, the economy would have experienced substantially more inflation each year. However, there is a severe drop in output, as per the U.S. experience between 1981 and 1983. Once the inflationary psychology dissipates, rising Aggregate Demand allows growth with less inflation. Panel B shows actual values for the U.S. economy during the 1980s. Note the slump of 1990 to 1991 (path *cde* in Panel A).

tionary expectations. Real estate foreclosures soared. Similar misfortune befell farmers and many rural banks. Farmers who had borrowed to purchase high-priced land faced bankruptcy when both farm incomes and land values plummeted.

Firms had grown accustomed to price hikes as cures for all sorts of problems, and workers had fully adjusted their expectations and wage demands to sustained inflation. When disinflation smothered price increases as a cure-all, firms had to find other ways to boost sales and profits. During disinflation, productivity growth and new products are keys to business success because prices cannot be raised. New products typically yield higher profits and facilitate growth. Another common solution of firms to problems posed by disinflation is to cut labor costs. Firms tend to bargain harder, and workers, sensing reduced inflation, tend to be more receptive to smaller wage increases.

Pressures to raise productivity during disinflation alter firms' investment patterns. First, more investment is directed toward productivity-enhancing plant and equipment, and less is aimed at expanding capacity. Second, more investment is financed internally as firms try to limit their debt burdens. Finally, acquisition binges that some firms undertake during inflationary periods are reversed when debt consolidation pressures them to sell subsidiaries.

During 1983 to 1990, the United States enjoyed its most sustained expansion since World War II, but a slump greeted 1990. The Fed had responded to a mild resurgence of inflation in 1989 with restrictive policies. Then, in 1990, Congress tried to reduce the federal budget deficit through increases in excise taxes, and a 5% income tax surcharge (making the marginal income tax rate 33%) was levied on families with taxable incomes exceeding $50,000 annually. The result of these attempts to curb budget deficits and dampen inflation can be seen in the shallow downturn reflected in the data for 1990 and 1991 in Figure 14.

The economy continued to recover during 1992 through 1994. Both inflation and unemployment continued to fall. Congress and President Clinton agreed to a new Deficit Reduction Act that, coupled with the present recovery, appears destined to result in lower deficits. But many problems persist. Significant changes are taking place in the workplace.

• **Corporate Restructuring in the 1990s**   Most business cycles are at least somewhat unique. The recession and recovery of the early 1990s was no exception. This is shown in Figure 15. Panel A contrasts employment patterns during the 1991 to 1994 recovery with those during the 1981 to 1982 business cycle and with the average pattern for other cycles during 1969 to 1982. Employment grew faster during previous recoveries than during the most recent one. By seven quarters after the trough of the earlier business cycles, employment surpassed that of the previous peak by 5% to 6%. In the 1992 to 1994 recovery, over the same time frame, the U.S. economy barely exceeded previous peak employment. In a similar fashion, Panel B shows how the Job Opportunity Barometer (JOB)[4] has performed over this latest business cycle. As Panel B shows, this index continued to decline following the trough of March 1991.

-----

[4]JOB is a composite index based on several measures of labor market conditions, including real average weekly earnings, the unemployment rate, involuntary part-time employment, the duration of unemployment, an index of help-wanted advertising, and a measure of temporary employment.

Source: Federal Reserve Bank of Cleveland, *Economic Trends,* January 1994.

FIGURE 15   **Employment and Job Opportunities in Recent Business Cycles**

One reason for the upward trend in hard-core unemployment (workers without jobs for more than 26 weeks, shown in Figure 6) during the 1980s and 1990s is a revolution in corporate management over the past decade or so. More merger activity occurred between 1981 and 1987 than during any comparable period of American history. Many of these mergers came on the heels of a relaxation of antitrust guidelines by the Reagan administration, and much of this consolidation was intended to make U.S. industry more competitive in our increasingly internationalized economy. After a brief slowdown in merger activity in the late 1980s, this latest wave of mergers came on strong again in the 1990s.

One goal of corporate managers engulfed by this merger mania was *downsizing* to make the surviving firm lean and mean—and profitable. One obvious strategy is to release redundant personnel. When two firms merge, the combined firm has one more president (CEO) than it needs. And one more chief financial officer (CFO). And so on. Many companies are also striving to become "horizontal" instead of "vertical." Fewer, but bigger, companies are trying to do more work with fewer bodies—especially, expensive bodies. Thus, more top managers directly supervise more workers, with many middle managers being shown the door in the process.

Computer networks have made it easier for managers to directly monitor increasing numbers of subordinates who work in offices. Improved transportation and communication networks (e.g., fax machines, modems, and voice-mail systems) have expanded the customer base a salesperson can service. Thus, technological advances have disrupted the career plans of many white-collar workers who might once have thought that only assembly-line jobs were threatened by automation. The result? Millions of skilled workers and professionals who signed on with a major corporation in the 1950s, and 1960s, and 1970s have learned that the big pension and the proverbial gold watch awaiting the end of 40 years of service are a mirage.

The more specialized the expertise of a worker, the greater will be the wage typically earned by that worker. But, unfortunately, greater expertise and expectations of premium wages carry a cost. If you have a lot of expertise, much of which is especially applicable only to your current long-time employer, then losing your job often means protracted unemployment.

A related problem is that, for workers in their 40s or 50s, firms with vacancies may be reluctant to pay the premium wages to which ex–middle managers had become accustomed. Many workers who wind up being displaced in the course of corporate downsizing require longer periods before they locate work than would less experienced workers for whom large wage premiums would be unrealistic goals. And many of these displaced career employees ultimately must settle for lower wages and less satisfying work than they once enjoyed.

The changing environment of worker–employer relationships may seem bleak, especially for college students on the verge of spending a long time in the work force. Allow us to offer a possible antidote to all of this gloom and doom. Although job security may be falling, our average standards of living continue to improve. By almost all material measures, each succeeding generation of Americans is increasingly prosperous. And this prosperity is being spread worldwide. Relative to our grandparents, people today are better educated and have more square footage of housing, a more varied diet, better health care, more forms of entertainment, better access to transportation, and technological wizardry that was once only in the realm of science fiction. This means that most people do succeed in finding work, or we would be unable to afford this lifestyle. The keys to success in our changing world appear to be flexibility and high productivity—things that, to some extent, remain under the control of the individual.

This chapter has addressed how macroeconomic change can be interpreted with the tools of Aggregate Demand and Aggregate Supply. Formulating policies to stimulate growth and counter inflation and unemployment is facilitated if we understand the effects of relative shifts in Aggregate Demand curves and Aggregate Supply curves. Nevertheless, proper policymaking remains a formidable challenge because experts fall into several camps and often disagree about (a) how to interpret the current state of the economy and (b) how particular policies are likely to operate. In the next two chapters, we will examine several of the dilemmas and limitations facing policymakers as they attempt to stabilize the economy.

CHAPTER REVIEW: KEY POINTS

1. Most economists, whether classically oriented or Keynesian, now agree that, in the long run, Aggregate Supply curves are vertical. However, the new Keynesians contend that **wage and price stickiness** can make the short run Aggregate Supply curve positively sloped for lengthy periods, and thus, short run targets may be most appropriate for macroeconomic policymaking.

2. Long-term **labor contracts** (whether *implicit* or *explicit*), **efficiency wages**, and **dual labor markets** all provide microfoundations to help explain wage stickiness and involuntary unemployment in an Aggregate Demand—Aggregate Supply framework.

3. Decreases in the Aggregate Supply curve cause **supply-side inflation** and declines in real incomes and output. Excessive increases in the Aggregate Demand curve cause *demand-side inflation*, which initially is accompanied by increased incomes and output.

4. If Aggregate Demand grows excessively in a fully employed economy, the first phase of a demand-pull cycle entails rising prices, outputs, employment, and incomes. In the second phase, supply-side adjustments to demand-originated disturbances cause prices to continue to rise, but total employment, production, and income fall. Demand-side inflation induces a *counterclockwise* adjustment path of inflation versus real output. If the economy starts at less than full employment, only the first phase necessarily occurs when Aggregate Demand increases.

5. **Supply-side inflation** generates a *clockwise* adjustment pattern. During the first phase of a supply-side (cost-push) cycle, prices rise while real output and incomes fall. If the government attempts to correct for the resulting inflationary recession by increasing Aggregate Demand, the second phase occurs: prices continue to rise, but real output and incomes rise as well.

6. **Stagflation**, a contraction of the terms stagnation and inflation, is the simultaneous occurrence of high rates of both unemployment and inflation.

7. Mild but increasing demand-side inflation accompanied the prosperity of the 1960s. From the mid-1970s into the early 1980s, stagflation took over with a vengeance. Whether this stagflation was the supply-adjustment phase of the earlier demand-pull cycle or originated solely from supply-related shocks cannot be established conclusively. It seems likely, however, that even if the economy had been stable when the supply shocks listed previously emerged, considerable supply-side inflation would have plagued the U.S. economy from 1973 to 1980.

8. **Disinflation** is a significant reduction in the rate of inflation. Most people adjust their behavior if they expect inflation. Their expectations cause disinflation to entail losses in real income before it restores the economy to a relatively stable growth path. Thus, the 1981 to 1983 recession was especially severe.

9. In recent decades, accelerating technological advances and the globalization of economic activity have increased the speed of structural economic change. A massive wave of corporate mergers in the 1980s and 1990s has lead to significant corporate *downsizing*, with reduced job security for many workers who had intended to be career employees at large firms.

QUESTIONS FOR THOUGHT AND DISCUSSION

1. How does the internationalization of economic activity affect Aggregate Demand for the United States? How does it affect Aggregate Supply? Negotiations for the North American Free Trade Agreement (NAFTA) and the General Agreement on Tariffs and Trade (GATT) were largely concluded by 1994 and open the door for freer trade. How has NAFTA and GATT affected employment in the United States? What effect have these agreements had on the average rate of inflation in the United States? On our rate of real economic growth?

2. What social and economic forces might underpin the upward trend in the average rate of unemployment across recent decades?

3. The average rate of inflation by decade rose from the 1950s through the 1970s. Why has inflation been less of a problem in the United States over the past decade or so? Is this abatement of inflation related to the upward trend in average unemployment rates? If so, how?

4. What are the differences between deflation and disinflation? List five worldwide events that might spark a new round of stagflation.

5. Draw a set of Aggregate Demand and Aggregate Supply curves and label them AD_0 and AS_0, respectively. Now illustrate the first step in demand-side inflation and label any new curves with a subscript 1. What might have caused this first step in demand-side inflation? (You should be able to list six broad possibilities.) Now illustrate the second step in demand-side inflation and label any new curves with the appropriate subscript. What causes this second step to take place? What path does demand-side inflation take?

Cost-push

Frictional unemployment

Chapter 17

Demand-pull

Active vs. Passive Policymaking

Supply shocks

Efficiency wage

Long run

Economic growth may be squelched if policy-makers limit Aggregate Demand to combat inflation, but trying to stimulate growth and reduce unemployment rates by boosting Aggregate Demand can spark inflation. Elected officials face a dilemma because sluggish growth, inflation, and high unemployment are all unpopular with voters. Another dilemma is that traditional Keynesians advocate active policies to counter major economic shocks, while those of a classical persuasion favor relying on market adjustments and view erratic government policies as causes, not cures, for instability. Should policymakers actively try to counter macroeconomic shocks, or should they count on market adjustments to automatically stabilize the economy?

This chapter addresses trade-offs between inflation and unemployment. Most complete business cycles involve elements of both demand-side and supply-side inflation. How employment, output, and inflation are related is critical. National income is positively related to employment and tends to be negatively related to unemployment. Another issue addressed is

why inflation and interest rates seem positively related. Finally, we introduce theories—*real business cycles, efficient markets*, and *rational expectations*—that support the view of new classical macroeconomists that government should provide a stable environment of sound, but passive, policies within which markets can adjust to any destabilizing shocks.

TRADE-OFFS BETWEEN UNEMPLOYMENT AND INFLATION

We all, or nearly all, consent,
when wages rise by ten percent,
it leaves the choice before the nation,
of unemployment or inflation.

Kenneth Boulding

Our general Aggregate Demand—Aggregate Supply framework hints at a possible negative relationship between unemployment and inflation: boosting Aggregate Demand raises real output and employment when substantial productive capacity is idle, but ever greater upward pressures on prices and wages emerge as excess capacity disappears. Are such trade-offs between unemployment and inflation (if they truly ever exist) strictly short-run phenomena, or do they persist into the long-run? These issues are critical for sound macroeconomic policymaking.

More than three decades ago, A. W. Phillips plotted unemployment data for Great Britain during the preceding century against corresponding data for wage inflation. Curves that seem to fit such data have become known as *Phillips curves*.

> The **Phillips curve** *portrays an inverse statistical relationship between the rate of inflation and the unemployment rate.*

Phillips's work focused on wage inflation, but later researchers addressed apparent trade-offs between unemployment and price inflation. For example, reducing inflation to zero might require unemployment of 8%, while pressing unemployment below 5% might require 6% annual inflation.

• **Productivity and Inflation** A fairly tight relationship links nominal wage inflation, price inflation, and productivity:

$$\dot{p} = \dot{w} - \lambda$$

where $\dot{p}$ is the percentage rate of inflation, $\dot{w}$ is the percentage change in wages, and λ is the percentage change in productivity.

For example, if workers produce 5% more this year than last, then wages can rise 5% before firms feel pressure to maintain profit margins by raising prices. This relationship is illustrated in Figure 1 where a Phillips curve is superimposed over U.S. data for the 1960s. An annual rate of productivity gain (λ) of 2% (based on rough historical averages) is assumed and is reflected by shifting the scale for price inflation $(\dot{p})$ down by 2% relative to wage inflation $(\dot{w})$. Thus, 4% wage hikes combined with 2% productivity gains only impose pressures for prices to rise 2%. But if productivity gains are nil and workers successfully demand higher wages, the likely result is price inflation.

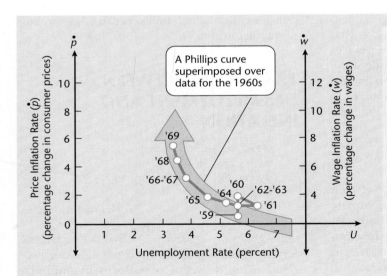

Phillips curves suggest that if Aggregate Demand is high and rising steadily, inflation will be substantial but unemployment will be low. On the other hand, consistently low Aggregate Demand yields little inflation but more unemployment. Wages may increase faster than prices if productivity rises. Overall, movements during 1959 to 1969 reflected the expansionary fiscal and monetary policies of this era.

Note: Productivity is assumed to have grown by 2% annually, so the two vertical axes are calibrated differently.

Source: *Economic Report of the President,* 1994.

FIGURE 1   A Phillips Curve for the 1960s (U.S. Data)

• The 1960s: An American Phillips Curve?
According to the Keynesian theory that dominated economic thought by 1960, Aggregate Supply should be relatively stable. Thus, a stable Phillips curve would allow Aggregate Demand to be fine-tuned to yield the least harmful mix of unemployment and inflation. The dilemma seemed clear: if high inflation is associated with low unemployment, and vice versa, then the Phillips curve is a "menu" of the trade-off facing policymakers who try to minimize our economic woes.[1]

The Phillips curve in Figure 1 was thought roughly reflective of the choices facing U.S. policymakers. At a target of zero price inflation, workers would suffer roughly 6% to 8% unemployment. Unemployment rates as low as 3% to 4% were thought feasible only with inflation of 4% to 6%. Policymakers would have preferred less of

each, but Phillips curve analysis suggested that this was impossible.

Shifts in Aggregate Demand: A Stable Trade-Off?

National Output and Income are closely tied to employment. In turn, a close negative relationship exists between employment and unemployment: higher employment generally means lower unemployment, and vice versa. But changes in the size or composition of the labor force may obscure this relationship. For example, rapidly rising labor-force participation rates might precipitate higher frictional unemployment even if real output and employment grew.

An Aggregate Supply curve is a positive relationship between national output and the price level, while a typical Phillips curve depicts an inverse correlation between unemployment and inflation. Thus, Phillips curves roughly mirror Aggregate Supply curves, as shown in Figure 2. Points $a, b, \ldots, g$ in Panel A roughly correspond

---

[1]Recall (from Chapter 7) that the misery index is the sum of the rates of unemployment and inflation. Sluggish growth, interest rates that depress investment, or imbalances of international trade are among other difficulties that also signal macroeconomic distress.

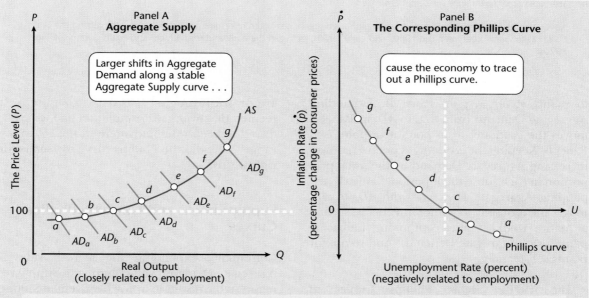

Ever larger sustained increases in Aggregate Demand in Panel A along a stable Aggregate Supply curve would trace out a series of equilibria like $a, b, \ldots, g$ as employment and output both increased. Unemployment rates would fall during these movements, but prices would rise, tracing a pattern roughly like $a, b, \ldots, g$ along the stable Phillips curve in Panel B. Notice that the price level would be stable at point c in both panels.

FIGURE 2 Aggregate Supply and the Phillips Curve

FIGURE 3   The Shifting Phillips Curve Relationship

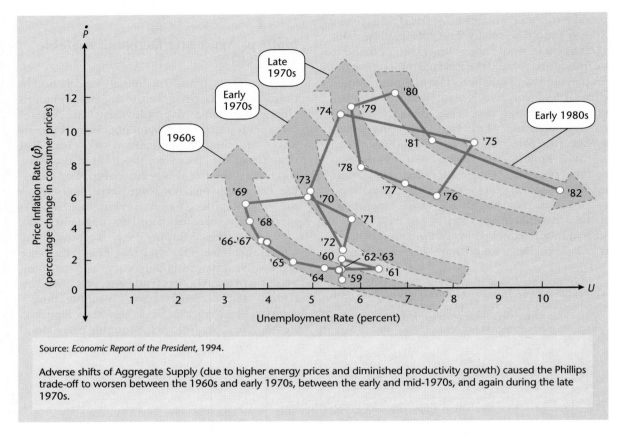

Source: *Economic Report of the President*, 1994.

Adverse shifts of Aggregate Supply (due to higher energy prices and diminished productivity growth) caused the Phillips trade-off to worsen between the 1960s and early 1970s, between the early and mid-1970s, and again during the late 1970s.

to points *a, b,. . . , g* in Panel B. Expanding Aggregate Demand from AD_a to AD_b in Panel A moves the economy from point *a* to point *b* in Panel B. Keeping the economy at point *b* requires increasing Aggregate Demand by the same proportion in each subsequent period. Similarly, expanding Aggregate Demand from AD_a to AD_c moves the economy to point *c* in Panel B; staying at point *c* would require continuous similar expansions of Aggregate Demand.[2] And so on, for points *d, e, f,* and *g*.

• **The 1970s: Stable Phillips Curves at Bay?**   The idea that the Phillips curve was stable unraveled in the 1970s. Four Phillips curves

---

[2]Readers familiar with differential equations will recognize this as a description of moving from static analysis of price-level changes to a more dynamic analysis of sustained inflation.

are drawn through 1970s data in Figure 3. It seemed that ever greater inflation had to be endured to keep unemployment in the 5% to 6% range. Why did the Phillips curve worsen (shift rightward)?

Supply Shocks and Unstable Phillips Curves

Continually expanding the growth rate of Aggregate Demand while Aggregate Supply remains stable results in upward movements along a stable Phillips curve, as in Figure 2. The 1960s seemed to provide evidence of a roughly stable Phillips curve, but bouts of stagflation in the 1970s betrayed the naiveté of this view. Shocks to Aggregate Supply apparently worsened the short-run trade-off between unemployment and

FIGURE 4 Shifting the Phillips Curve

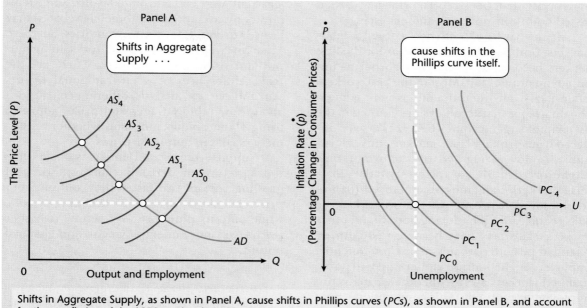

Shifts in Aggregate Supply, as shown in Panel A, cause shifts in Phillips curves (PCs), as shown in Panel B, and account for the stagflation of the 1970s and early 1980s.

inflation, as shown in Figure 4. Suppose Aggregate Supply began to shrink, declining from AS_0 to AS_1 to AS_2 and so on, in Panel A. Output and employment fall while the price level rises (stagflation), confronting policymakers with ever harsher short-run options—curves PC_0, PC_1, PC_2 and so on, in Panel B. As Phillips curves deteriorate, achieving a given low unemployment rate entails ever more rapid inflation.

Since its discovery, the Phillips curve has been in the eye of a stormy controversy. Keynesians initially heralded Phillips's discovery of a negative statistical relationship between unemployment and inflation as presenting policymakers with a stable trade-off. But economists of a classical bent dismiss the Phillips curve as a short-run artifact and hold that policymakers who try to swap inflation for lower unemployment will soon find the relationship illusory. Their **natural rate theories** suggest that, in the long run, macroeconomic policies affect only absolute prices, not such real variables as unemployment, output, or interest rates. We need to explore these differing interpretations of why

Phillips curves may shift so that an economy experiences stagflation, as the United States did in the 1970s.

KEYNESIAN PHILLIPS CURVES

Keynesians initially explained the existence of the Phillips curve as caused by *bottlenecks* encountered as an economy moved ever closer to full employment. After it became apparent that trade-offs between unemployment and inflation might be unstable, a *structural shock theory* was developed to show why Phillips curves might shift. We describe both approaches in this section.

The Keynesian Structuralist Approach

An early Keynesian explanation for the Phillips curves—the **structuralist approach**—goes like this: as unemployment falls and full employment is approached, it becomes increasingly costly to produce extra output. One reason is that as more and more industries operate nearer their capacities, firms increasingly encounter bottlenecks that boost costs, which are then passed on to consumers as higher prices.

Major structural bottlenecks occur in labor markets. Competition among firms for the best workers becomes increasingly vigorous as unemployment rates fall. Most of the best workers retain jobs even when unemployment is high. The dual labor market analysis presented in the last chapter suggests that when workers are displaced from primary labor markets (due, for example, to downsizing and restructuring), they may be forced into less attractive secondary markets. Workers remaining unemployed (or underemployed) in prosperous times often lack the skills required for jobs during hard times; other workers' skills may have become rusty during extended periods of joblessness. Consequently, employers begin offering higher wages to pirate qualified workers away from other firms as unemployment rates fall. This competition drives up costs, prices, and so on.

Structural Shocks and Wage-Price Stickiness

More sophisticated Keynesian explanations for Phillips curves' shapes hinge on two key ideas: (a) shocks to market demands and supplies continually bombard all economies and (b) wages and prices are assumed downwardly sticky.[3] That is, wages and prices rise more easily than they fall (as discussed in Chapter 6). At any moment in time the structure of demands—both private and public—is in flux. These are shocks to the economy. As new products are developed or national priorities change, the demands for some goods rise while those for others fall.

Output growth in sectors where demand grows is limited in the short run by the capital and trained labor readily available. Thus, wage and price hikes are the primary adjustments to stronger demand. In sectors where demand shrinks, the norm is production cutbacks and

---

[3]This theory of "stochastic macroequilibration" is elaborated in James Tobin, "Inflation and Unemployment," *The American Economic Review* 62, no. 1 (March 1972): 1–18.

layoffs, not price reductions. Workers accept wage cuts only reluctantly, so firms find it easier to cut wage costs through layoffs. Some temporary price cuts (e.g., automobile rebates) may be used to liquidate excess inventories, but these price cuts will be accompanied by declining output and rising unemployment. These are the major differences between traditional Keynesian and classical analysis: different conclusions about how rapidly wages and prices adjust to bring about equilibrium, and whether adjustment occurs in output or prices.

Suppose Aggregate Demand is stable while the structure of demand changes. Prices in growing sectors rise faster than outputs, but prices fall slowly if at all in declining sectors, while outputs plummet. Net result? A higher price level, more unemployment, and less total output.

> *Structural shocks* cause Aggregate Supply to fall temporarily because of friction encountered in moving resources from declining to growing sectors.

How this Keynesian analysis is consistent with Phillips curves is shown in Figure 5.

At our initial equilibrium at points a in both panels, the price level is stable at 100. Assume that Aggregate Demand remains at AD_0 but that its structure changes, jarring resource markets. Aggregate Supply shrinks from AS_0 to AS_1, and equilibrium moves from point a to point b. Given downward wage-price stickiness in declining markets, structural changes raise the price level. If policymakers try to maintain output at Q_f and unemployment at U_f, expansionary policies will increase Aggregate Demand from AD_0 to AD_2; the economy shifts from point b to point c in both panels of Figure 5. Thus, adapting policies to hold unemployment at U_f yields annual inflation of 3% if structural changes of the same magnitudes and frequencies continually recur.

This result suggests that continuous changes in the structure of economic activity create a natural *inflationary bias* in the economy. Policymakers might slash Aggregate Demand to AD_1 (point d in Panel A) to suppress natural in-

FIGURE 5 Full Employment Output, Shocks, and the Rate of Inflation: The Modern Keynesian Approach

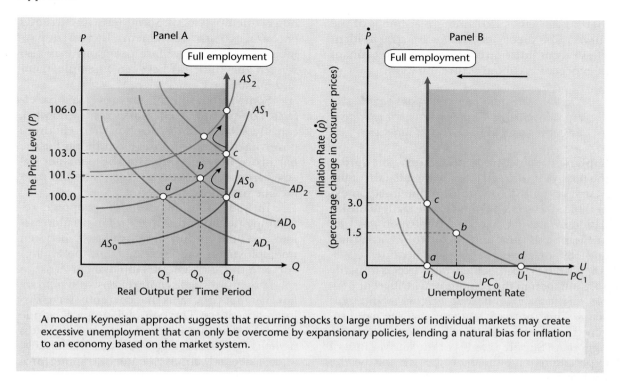

A modern Keynesian approach suggests that recurring shocks to large numbers of individual markets may create excessive unemployment that can only be overcome by expansionary policies, lending a natural bias for inflation to an economy based on the market system.

flation, but unemployment would then rise to U_1 in Panel B. Thus, policymakers can reduce either the unemployment or the inflation caused by structural economic changes, but not both. Less inflation means fewer jobs, and vice versa.

A Keynesian Theory of Stagflation

Classical theory discounts the possibility of lasting Phillips curves and emphasizes the stabilizing qualities of automatic market adjustments. Erratic government policy is cited as a major source of macroeconomic shocks. On the other hand, Keynesian structuralist and shock theories help rationalize the existence of Phillips curves. But how well do these competing approaches illuminate the rocky path the U.S. economy has followed in the past three decades?

Keynesians considered multiple disruptions as important in disrupting Aggregate Supplies and Phillips curves in the 1970s, classifying shocks under five broad headings: (*a*) inflationary expectations, (*b*) external shocks, (*c*) labor market disturbances, (*d*) structural changes in product markets, and (*e*) disruptions emerging in the public sector. Let us examine each, remembering that Aggregate Supply and the Phillips relationship can shift in either direction.

• **Adaptive Inflationary Expectations** Any event that reduces Aggregate Supply induces supply-side inflation and worsens the trade-off between unemployment and inflation (shifts the Phillips curve to the right). Keynesians recognize that inflationary expectations negatively affect Aggregate Supply. (In fact, A. W. Phillips'

1958 analysis of trade-offs between unemployment and inflation included statistical adjustments for past inflation and several other factors that he viewed as explaining placement of the curve.) The theory of *adaptive expectations* identifies recent inflation as the major determinant of expectations about future inflation.

*The theory of **adaptive expectations** suggests that expectations about future inflation are typically a weighted average of past rates of inflation.*

Suppose most people expected inflation during the next year to equal (1) half the inflation of the past year, plus (2) one-third of the inflation experienced a year ago, plus (3) one-sixth of the inflation from two years back. If inflation was 14% in the past 12 months, 9% for the year earlier, and 18% three years ago, then, because 14/2 + 9/3 + 18/6 = 13, people would expect roughly 13% inflation in the coming year. Different people might assign different weights to different years. This approach suggests that the more severe the recent history of inflation, the faster Aggregate Supply recedes to the left because of expectations and the more severe will be the trade-off between unemployment and inflation.

• **Shocks to the System**   During 1974 through 1981, recurrent oil price hikes boosted firms' energy costs, reducing Aggregate Supply and eroding the Phillips curve. This is shown in Figure 5. Wars and bad weather or other natural disasters have similar effects. On the other hand, discoveries of new resources, technological advances, prolonged periods of economic stability, or reductions in international tensions may improve the Phillips trade-off.

• **Labor Market Changes**   Incentive structures that affect work effort also help explain the Phillips curve's location. Unemployment compensation, for example, affects many workers' labor–leisure choices. Higher unemployment compensation payments will encourage greater unemployment, intensifying inflationary pressure. Unemployment compensation (*a*) encourages temporary layoffs by firms because it eases hardships on firms' workers when orders for output drop and (*b*) extends the average duration of unemployment. Social Security currently encourages early retirement. Increased payments under most welfare programs may also worsen the trade-off between unemployment and inflation.

Some recent reforms may reverse these effects. For example, welfare recipients who work can use subsidized daycare for their children; government now supports job training for the hard-core unemployed; and the penalties exacted from Social Security recipients who earn income have been reduced.

In 1994, President Clinton proposed revamping the unemployment compensation system to help reduce the trade-off between unemployment and inflation (shift the Phillips curve to the left). The Reemployment Act consolidates into a single comprehensive system six government programs that currently serve dislocated workers. This consolidation will, at one location, permit workers to apply for jobless benefits, get counseling and assess their skills, and, if needed, apply to enter retraining programs. The plan is to streamline the current process and prepare displaced workers for a changing economy that demands that new employees be flexible and useful.

All these reforms may soften trade-offs between inflation and unemployment by increasing work effort and Aggregate Supply. Policies to foster mobility and match idle workers and job openings also improve the Phillips trade-off, as will programs to reduce discrimination so that productivity becomes the primary criterion for employment.

These changes in labor policy are directed at counteracting worker displacement caused by global competition and corporate restructuring. Dual labor market analysis suggests that competition for primary sector jobs paying higher efficiency wages may intensify. Enhancing individuals' productivity will increase their chances of becoming reemployed and retaining their positions in the long run.

Demographic changes also affect how unemployment and inflation are related. Post–

World War II baby boomers flooded labor markets from 1962 to 1980. But younger workers tend to bounce from job to job and are unemployed more often, worsening the Phillips relationship. As this group ages, the maturation of much of the work force should reduce the severity of this trade-off. Women's labor force participation rates grew markedly from the 1950s onward. Even though this influx of labor bolstered Aggregate Supply, it also may have worsened the Phillips curve because women's unemployment rates are typically higher than those of males.

Collective bargaining may also affect the Phillips curve. If growth of unions' power enables them to obtain contracts with inflationary wage hikes, or if strike activities intensify, the trade-off between inflation and unemployment will deteriorate. As trade union membership as a percentage of the labor force has declined, the effect of unions on unemployment and inflation has noticeably weakened.

• **Structural Changes in Product Markets**   One explanation for the shape and existence of Phillips curves is drawn from continuous changes in the structure of demands for goods, combined with wage and price stickiness and a policy of trying to maintain full employment. The menu of choices between unemployment and inflation worsens if external shocks become stronger or if structural changes occur more rapidly. If consumers' preferences or investors' perceptions of the economic outlook change markedly, the structure of output may also change drastically. Of course, this trade-off is more favorable the slower or less extreme these changes are during a given interval.

Changes in laws governing foreign trade become more important as our economy becomes more internationally oriented. Hikes in tariffs or cuts in import quotas raise the prices of imported goods and can certainly worsen the dilemma posed by the Phillips curve. Competition is also reduced. Similarly, growth of domestic monopoly power and the resulting drives for greater profits will worsen the inflation–unemployment trade-off.

• **Public Sector Changes**   Just as shocks to the structure of private demands can shift the Phillips curve, so can disruptions to the composition of public sector demands for goods and resources. Changes in tax structures, subsidies, and transfer payments also affect the trade-off. Major revisions of such regulations as those policed by the Occupational Safety and Health Administration, minimum-wage laws, environmental protection, leasing policies for mineral exploration on public lands, or changes in property rights structures may all shift the Phillips curve relationship. The direction of the shift depends on whether a particular regulatory change enhances or encumbers economic efficiency.

For modern Keynesians, an explanation for the stagflation of the 1970s goes something like this: rising inflationary expectations and disruptions associated with the Vietnam War caused the first deterioration in the Phillips curve in the early 1970s. The increase in world oil prices in 1974 caused the second shift. More oil price hikes in 1979 and 1981, coupled with worldwide crop failures, caused further erosion of the Phillips curve in the early 1980s. And relative cessation of shocks to the economy later in the 1980s ultimately improved the Phillips curve trade-off.

THE NEW CLASSICAL NATURAL RATE THEORY

New classical economists predictably disagree with Keynesian interpretations of recent history. **Natural rate theory**, a strand of new classical economics, rejects the idea that macroeconomic policy ultimately affects any "real" variable. Thus, these theorists perceive no permanent connection between unemployment and inflation. They reason that money is a veil in the short run, but that in the long run, such nominal things as the absolute price level are determined by the money supply and will be unrelated to any aspect of real behavior, such as unemployment or relative prices. Natural rate theory concludes that any negatively sloped Phillips curve is transitory and that Aggregate Supply will shift persistently only because of changing inflationary expectations.

The Natural Rate of Unemployment

Is zero unemployment a worthy goal? Yes, of course, seems an easy answer. But keeping the unemployment rate at zero would require people dissatisfied with their jobs to stick with them until they found new ones, or they would be unemployed. Moreover, firms would be pressured to immediately hire anyone who applied for work. And if you were not in the labor force and then decided to look for work, you would be forced to take the first job offered—otherwise you would be unemployed. Zero unemployment is not as attractive a goal as it sounds.

Natural rate analysis concludes that nearly all unemployment is voluntary, the sole exceptions being unskilled people who are unemployed because minimum-wage laws prevent employers from hiring these workers at the low wages commensurate with their productivity. Natural rate theorists view all other unemployment as the result of friction: it takes people time to find what they regard as suitable employment, and while they are looking for work, they are unemployed by choice. Individuals can presumably get jobs almost instantly if they are willing to take the wage they are worth to the first employer willing to hire them. Frictional unemployment can be viewed as a cost of investment in labor market information and mobility. Table 1 presents estimates of the natural rate of frictional unemployment for several developed economies.

According to natural rate theory, expansionary macroeconomic policy reduces frictional unemployment only because workers are fooled by unanticipated inflation into thinking that the higher wages offered by firms represent real increases in the purchasing power of their earnings. Anyone who is unemployed can get a seemingly suitable, high-paying job quickly during expansionary periods, when the pool of frictionally unemployed workers is small. In the natural rate view, these artificial declines in frictional unemployment reflect cyclical overemployment that is a consequence of inadequate investment in labor market information. But why do employers offer higher wages when expansionary policies are followed? Expansionary

TABLE 1 Unemployment (Frictional) Rates Required to Keep Inflation Stable (%)

	1971–1975	1981–1983
United States	6	6 $1/2$
Japan	1	2
West Germany	1 $1/2$	8
France	3 $1/2$	8
Britain	4	9
Italy	7	6 $1/2$
Canada	7	7 $1/2$
Holland	4	10 $1/2$

Sources: OECD, Layard and Nickell, 1984, from *The Economist*, 14 May 1988, p. 69. Reprinted by permission.

The rate of unemployment required to keep inflation in check moved up sharply throughout much of the industrialized world after 1970. Whether this reflected higher inflationary expectations or structural changes that boosted frictional unemployment is debatable.

policies cause business firms to forecast booming sales that will enable them to raise the prices of their products. After workers recognize that their wages do not buy as much as expected because prices are also rising, many will become dissatisfied and quit to look for more lucrative work.

The eventual result is that frictional unemployment will rise back to its natural rate when workers cease being fooled. The natural rate of unemployment is the rate that exists before expansionary policy is initiated; it is achieved when all transactors have accurate expectations about inflation. If expansionary policies are continued, workers will learn to expect inflation and will demand wages that rise continuously to compensate for inflation. This means that Aggregate Supply will shrink continuously.

Wage Adjustments to Inflation

A starting point for the natural rate explanation for Phillips curves is to assume a macroeconomic equilibrium with no inflation, as at points *a* in both panels in Figure 6. The price index is 100 (point *a* in Panel A), and the unemployment rate is consistent with potential real output (point *a* in Panel B). Inflation is initially zero, and the

FIGURE 6   Equilibrium Output and the Rate of Inflation (Natural Rate Approach)

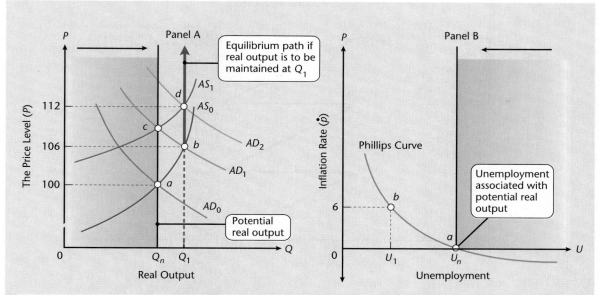

Natural rate theory suggests that attempts to maintain unemployment below its normal, frictional rate require continuous expansions of Aggregate Demand, raising the possibility of accelerating inflation.

natural rate of unemployment, U_n, is between, say, 5% and 7%. The shaded parts of Figure 6 represent output and unemployment below and above the natural rate, respectively.

Now assume that overly expansionary monetary policy drives Aggregate Demand up to AD_1. Real output will rise to Q_1 (point *b*), but the adjustment process entails 6% inflation, and the price level rises from 100 to 106. We suggested earlier that this equilibrium cannot be sustained for long. Workers will find their real wages falling, triggering attempts to catch up. As they do so, the Aggregate Supply curve shrinks to AS_1 and the economy moves toward point *c* in Panel A. If policymakers try to maintain output at Q_1 and unemployment at U_1 by shifting Aggregate Demand to AD_1 another inflationary round equal to roughly 6% is unleashed as the economy moves to equilibrium at point *d* in Panel A. The equilibrium path for the economy is denoted by the arrow: policymakers must continually create 6% inflation to maintain unemployment at U_1.

Our model to this point naively supposes that workers always expect inflation to be zero, only seeking wage adjustments after the price level has risen. Policymakers are confronted with additional problems if workers begin to anticipate inflation.

The Long-Run Phillips Curve

Natural rate theory suggests that Phillips curves do not present policymakers with stable frontiers along which inflation can be traded off against unemployment.

Natural rate theory *maintains that each Phillips curve is associated with a particular rate of expected inflation. If workers foresee higher rates of inflation, the Phillips curve worsens by shifting outward.*

Panel A of Figure 7 illustrates how this occurs. Suppose that the economy is at point *a* ini-

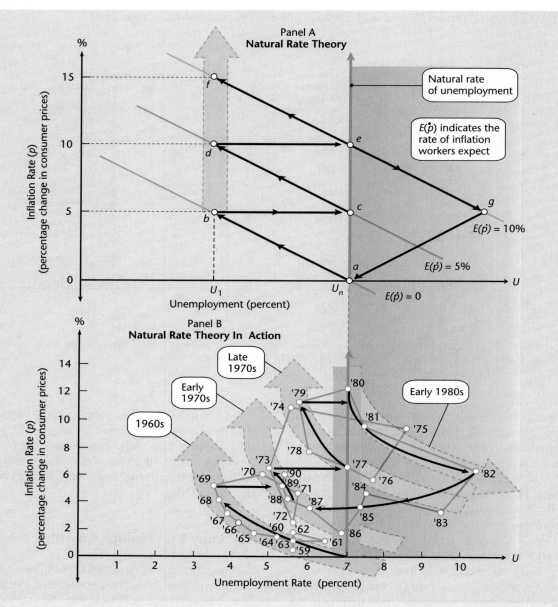

Panel A
Natural Rate Theory

Natural rate of unemployment

$E(\dot{p})$ indicates the rate of inflation workers expect

$E(\dot{p}) = 10\%$

$E(\dot{p}) = 5\%$

$E(\dot{p}) = 0$

Unemployment (percent)

Panel B
Natural Rate Theory In Action

Late 1970s

Early 1970s

1960s

Early 1980s

Unemployment Rate (percent)

Source: *Economic Report of the President,* 1994

Natural rate theory suggests that unemployment will be less than the natural rate (U_n) only if workers expect less inflation than occurs and that it will be more than the natural rate if workers expect more inflation than results from macroeconomic policy. In the long run, workers will adjust perfectly to any changes in price levels so that normal, frictional unemployment will be maintained, which is totally independent of the price level or inflation. Notice that the Phillips curve improved substantially from 1982 into the 1990s, perhaps as a consequence of a substantial decline in expected inflation.

FIGURE 7   National Rate Theory and the Shifting Phillips Curve

tially; there is frictional unemployment equal to U_n with zero inflation and zero inflation expected; $E(\dot{p})$ indicates the inflation rate that workers expect. What happens if policymakers view unemployment of U_n as unacceptably high and follow expansionary policies? Growth of Aggregate Demand yields increased sales, so firms offer higher wages to attract new workers to accommodate the higher demands for their products. Workers who are frictionally unemployed will have little difficulty finding what they perceive as good, high-paying jobs. Thus, expansionary policies push the economy along the Phillips curve from point a toward point b.

The fly in this ointment is that higher demands for goods are seen as opportunities to raise prices. As workers learn to expect 5% price hikes, the Phillips curve shifts rightward and the economy moves to point c at the old natural rate of unemployment U_n. This occurs because workers will demand wage increases of 10%–5% to cover past inflation plus 5% for expected inflation. But firms forecast only 5% growth in nominal demands for their outputs and will refuse to meet workers' demands for 10% wage hikes. Frictional unemployment rises as workers hit the pavement looking for better jobs.

If policymakers again view unemployment (U_n) as unacceptably high, they might follow even more expansionary policies. If so, the economy initially will move from point c to d, but then ultimately to e, as workers again cease being fooled. All that policymakers will have achieved is 10% inflation with no long-term reduction in unemployment. If policymakers were undaunted by their failures, they might even proceed to f.

If they had learned their lesson, however, they would find moving directly and quickly back from e to a almost impossible. The buildup of inflationary momentum may force policymakers to engineer a recession to point g to dampen inflationary expectations. An extended recession may be required before the economy will return to point a. Similar adjustments may explain why a severe recession occurred in 1981 to 1983 when deflationary monetary policies brought inflation under control. Panel B of Figure 7 shows data for 1960 through 1990, suggesting that natural rate theory explains the experience of recent decades reasonably well.

Pure natural rate theorists view rising expectations of inflation as the only explanation for any worsening of any short-term relationship between inflation and unemployment. There is a family of short-run Phillips curves; each depends on different expectations of inflation by labor. Unemployment will gravitate back to its natural rate in the long run. Thus, no long-run trade-off exists between inflation and unemployment. In Figure 7, the long-run Phillips curve is the vertical path *ace*. According to natural rate theory, if policymakers try to hold unemployment below the natural rate, the short-run Phillips curve trade-off worsens. Accelerating bouts of inflation (up the vertical arrow in Panel A) are inevitable until policymakers accept the futility of trying to hold unemployment below its natural rate.

THE NATURAL RATE OF INTEREST

Natural rate theory also views attempts to achieve lower interest rates than are consistent with individuals' decisions as ultimately self-defeating. We will now examine why the natural real rate hypothesis identifies the interest rate as an inappropriate target for monetary authorities.

The Natural Real Rate of Interest Hypothesis

When people discuss "the" interest rate, they usually mean the annual monetary premium paid for the use of money. Interest rates vary almost as much as wage rates or other prices. The different interest rates paid by borrowers to lenders reflect, among other considerations, risk, length of time to maturity of the note or bond, the availability of credit, and legal constraints. For simplicity, however, we will assume that there is only one interest rate for borrowing. Economists refer to these percentage monetary premiums as *nominal rates* of interest.

*The **real rate of interest** is the annual percentage of purchasing power paid by a borrower to a lender for the use of money.*

Estimating realized real rates of interest (r) is simple: the nominal interest rate (i) minus the percentage rate of inflation ($\dot{p}$) yields the percentage purchasing power premium, or real interest rate (r), paid over the life of a note or bond:

$$r = i - \dot{p} \qquad \text{(real interest)}$$

For example, if nominal interest is 8% and the price level rises 10% annually, the real rate of interest is roughly —2% so lenders lose 2% of purchasing power each year.

Workers who expect inflation will bargain for higher nominal wages in order to protect their real wages. Naturally, people whose incomes are based on interest react similarly. The natural rate hypothesis suggests that borrowers and lenders adjust nominal interest to expected inflation $E(\dot{p})$ so that the willingness of borrowers to pay purchasing power premiums (desired real interest, r_d) exactly equals the purchasing power premiums lenders require for the use of money. Thus, when a note or bond is issued,

$$i = r_d + E(\dot{p}) \qquad \text{(nominal cost of borrowing)}$$

If inflation is expected, lenders try to charge higher nominal interest to ensure that they will not lose purchasing power, but why will borrowers be willing to pay such "high" interest rates? To understand this essential point, consider the housing market during the late 1970s, during which housing prices increased by from 10% to 30% annually in some regions.

Suppose that you expect housing prices in your area to increase by 15% annually. To keep it simple, we will assume that you can borrow money at a nominal interest rate of 10%. If you ultimately repay the loan with dollars that have depreciated in value by 15% annually, this situation is similar to being paid 5% of the price of your house annually to live in your own home. Negative real rent sounds pretty good to most of us, which explains, in part, why housing prices have boomed in some areas in recent years.

The **natural rate theory of real interest** suggests that the desired real rate of interest (r_d) reflects (a) purchasing power premiums needed to induce savers to delay gratification (most of us value having a good today more than having the same good tomorrow), (b) premiums needed to induce people to hold wealth in less liquid forms, and (c) the expected productivity of new capital, which yields extra goods in the future. The real interest rate is the percentage of extra goods that can be enjoyed if consumption is delayed so that extra capital is available for production.

Keynes and Fisher Effects

According to the natural rate hypothesis, expansionary monetary policy might temporarily reduce nominal interest rates, but in the long run, expansionary policies drive nominal interest rates up, not down. Figure 8 shows why by relating the supply and demand for loanable funds to nominal interest rates. The supply and demand for loanable funds is linked closely to the market for money discussed earlier. Changes in real interest rates will shift these supplies and demands.

Suppose monetary policymakers view a nominal interest rate of 6% (at point a, the intersection of D_0 and S_0) as too high: they perceive it as inhibiting investment and spending. If they follow expansionary open-market operations, the supply of loanable funds initially rises to S_1 and the nominal interest rate falls to 4% (point b). This temporary fall in nominal interest rates caused by expansionary policies will yield even larger declines in real interest rates because natural rate theory predicts that overly expansionary policies cause inflation.

*The **Keynes effect** predicts declines in interest rates following expansionary monetary policy, and vice versa.*

If expansionary policies trigger annual inflation of 4%, the real rate of interest is zero. Borrowers eventually will boost real demands for funds to, say, D_1 because borrowing seems

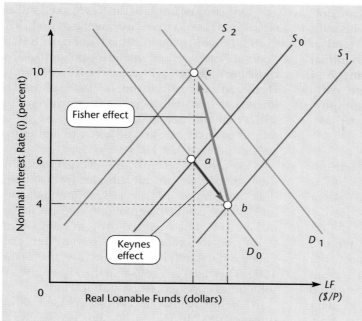

The natural rate of real interest theory suggests that an expansion of the money supply may temporarily increase the supply of loanable funds and drive nominal interest rates down via the Keynes effect, but if inflation results and comes to be expected, the Fisher effect may cause nominal interest rates to rise above the inflation level. These effects operate in exactly opposite directions when contractionary policies are followed. The lesson here (paralleling that for the natural rate of unemployment) is that policymakers' attempts to artificially reduce interest rates are ultimately doomed to failure.

Panel B
The Keynes and Fisher Effects in Action

Sources: *Moody's Bond Record, Business Conditions Digest,* and *Economic Reports of the President,* 1980–1994.

Expansionary monetary policies in 1978 drove real interest rates down via the *Keynes effect* as inflation exceeded nominal interest in 1979. Nominal interest rates rose to compensate for unexpected inflation during 1980–1982, even though inflation was falling; this was the *Fisher effect* in action.

FIGURE 8   Keynes and Fisher Effects in the Market for Real Loanable Funds

so cheap: loans are repaid in depreciated dollars. Lenders will reduce supplies to S_2 because they gained no real purchasing power at a zero real interest rate. In the long run, the nominal interest rate rises to 10% (point c in Panel A of Figure 8). Irving Fisher, a prominent early American monetary theorist (see his biography) was the first to systematically address adjustments of this type.

*The **Fisher effect** predicts upward adjustments in nominal interest rates as borrowers and lenders compensate for expected inflation and downward shifts if deflation is expected.*

Contractionary monetary policies tend to reduce the availability of credit in the short run; thus, in such cases the Keynes effect drives nominal interest rates up. After borrowers and lenders have learned to expect the deflationary pressures resulting from contractionary policies, however, the Fisher effect brings nominal interest rates down.

One clear example of the Keynes and Fisher effects in action occurred during the period 1978 to 1982, as illustrated in Panel B of Figure 8. The Federal Reserve eased monetary policy in 1978, reducing real rates of interest (the Keynes effect). During most of 1978 through 1980, real rates of interest were actually negative or nearly zero. By 1981, real and nominal interest rates began to soar as financial markets adjusted to higher expected inflation (the Fisher effect).

Even more recently, however, inflation in the United States steadily subsided from double-digit rates during 1983 to 1989, but nominal interest rates remained persistently high, as shown in Figure 9. The eventual drop in nominal interest rates to conform to these lower rates of inflation did not fully occur until between 1990 and 1994. This delay suggests that the Fisher effect is sometimes experienced only after a long lag.

Unemployment rates also trickled down during 1983 through 1993, but erratically, as shown in Figure 9. Thus, in the long run, natural rate theory has some predictive power about how

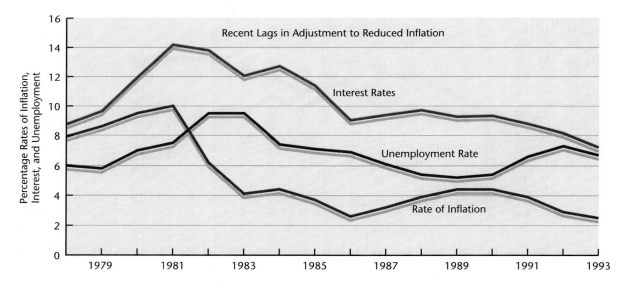

Source: *Economic Report of the President,* 1994

There was a relatively long delay between diminishing inflation during the 1980s and the subsequent drop in interest rates predicted by the Fisher effect. Simple natural rate theory suggests that unemployment probably exceeded its natural rate during the early 1980s, when a recession followed on the heels of a sharp reduction of monetary growth. The consequent decline in the rate of inflation, which had been growing from the 1960s through the 1970s, only slowly reduced inflationary expectations (the Phillips curve improved during the late 1980s).

FIGURE 9   Recent Lags in Adjustments to Reduced Inflation

BIOGRAPHY

Irving Fisher: The Birth of Modern Monetary Theory

Irving Fisher (1867–1947), the premier American economist of the early twentieth century, was a pioneer in applying mathematical tools to economic theory. His objective was not only to develop theories with great explanatory power, but to develop them in operational terms. A cofounder of the Econometric Society, Fisher tried to base his theories on measurable variables that permitted his hypotheses to be tested.

Fisher's best-known works address the theories of money, capital, and interest. His equation of exchange is typical of his meticulous approach. Fisher began with an accounting identity: $MV + M'V' = PT$, where M is the quantity of currency, V is the velocity of currency in circulation, M' is the quantity of demand deposit dollars, V', the velocity of demand deposits, P is the price level, and T is total transactions in the economy.* In this equation M, P, and T are directly observable and measurable. Hence, the equation can be solved for V, and Fisher's hypothesis that V and V' are stable can be tested. The equation of exchange remains central in resolving disputes about macroeconomic theory and policy disputes.

Two of Fisher's major works, *The Purchasing Power of Money* and *The Theory of Interest* stressed the need for stable monetary policies. In the latter of these books, Fisher also distinguished nominal from real rates of interest. The nominal rate consists of the real rate, based on the real productivity of new capital investments, plus a premium for anticipated inflation on the part of lenders. The nominal rate, then, is the rate of interest stated in contracts for loans or purchases. The premium for expected inflation generates the Fisher effect: $i = r_d + E(\dot{p})$.

In addition to teaching and research, Fisher was a successful inventor who patented scores of devices. Among other items, he invented a folding chair and the Rolodex (wheels used in most offices today to hold business cards and addresses). Income from his inventions enabled him to invest. He was very interested in public health issues and put time and money into the temperance movement, and he invested heavily in health food companies.

Few of the reform movements Fisher supported ultimately achieved their goals. For example, the constitutional amendment that prohibited alcoholic beverages was repealed after it ushered in an era of lawlessness. Some health food firms he invested in—Kellogg's and Post—now produce such sugary cereals as Coco-Puffs and Sugar Pops, which says something about where the profit motive can lead even the most well-intentioned of reforms.

Nevertheless, Fisher was an active participant in the social and economic debates of his time. His life was one of accomplished scholarship and useful invention. Fisher's ideas live on. Growing numbers of modern economists now echo his call for monetary stability.

*Modern quantity theorists simplify Fisher's equation to $MV = PT$ by summing the two forms of money. Today, however, most economists use some variant of the $MV = PQ$ formula introduced in Chapter 14.

---

unemployment, inflation, and interest rates are related. Critics point out, however, that long delays before interest rates and unemployment equilibrate to their natural rates mean that natural rate theory predicts macroeconomic movement little better than a theory that "what goes up must come down," and vice versa. In economics, as in many areas, timing is everything.

Overall, natural rate analysis suggests that active policy is futile in the long run; it cannot permanently reduce either real interest rates or unemployment. The advocates of a *fixed monetary growth* rule believe that discretionary policies work temporarily only if people suffer from *money illusion*. Even transient declines in unemployment and interest are harmful because they thwart people's desires; everyone eventually compensates for having been fooled by policymakers. But can people be fooled consistently? A recent theory answers no.

NEW CLASSICAL MACROECONOMICS

You can fool some of the people all of the time, and all of the people some of the time, but you can't fool all of the people all of the time.

Abe Lincoln

You can fool some of the people all of the time, and all of the people some of the time, and them's pretty good odds.

Brett Maverick (a TV and movie Western)

Another challenge to demand-management policies has been issued by new classical macroeconomists who doubt that activist macroeconomic policies will work consistently, if at all. Their predictions are based on theories about competitive markets.

COMPETITIVE MARKETS

The theory of competitive markets is predicated on a number of assumptions. The most important of these for analyzing macroeconomic policy are

1. Market participants have perfect information about all potential transactions.
2. Transportation costs are zero, so all goods and resources can move freely and instantaneously between markets.
3. Buyers try to maximize their satisfactions; sellers, their profits; and workers, their net well-being.
4. All prices are perfectly flexible.

A perfectly competitive economy will operate efficiently at all times because any profit opportunities or opportunities for workers or consumers to improve their welfare will be exploited instantly. The problem posed for activist policymaking is that Keynesian policies work only if an economy is inefficiently operating inside its production possibilities frontier. If the economy is efficient and at its capacity, active policymaking generates only price adjustments (inflation or deflation), not quantity adjustments (changes in output and employment).

Equally critical is the fact that fiscal and monetary policies will have different effects in the short run than in the long run only if people are ignorant either about the thrust of policies or their long-run effects. We discussed in the previous section how expansionary or contractionary policies might have different effects in the short run than in the long run. Let us see why perfectly efficient competitive markets might cause long-run adjustments to occur instantly when demand-management policies are used.

Efficient Markets

Efficient markets theories suggest that activist policymakers try to fool people in the fashion of riverboat gamblers, but these policies do not work because Lincoln was a better observer of human nature than was the scriptwriter who contributed Maverick's famous line. In fact, these new classical theorists go beyond Lincoln, asserting that you can't fool all of the people *any* of the time because markets operate efficiently if substantial information about profit opportunities is widely available.

*The **efficient markets** theory assumes vigorous competition for any ideas or information that might prove profitable. Competition causes any predictable abnormal gain from an investment to be exploited almost instantly.*

Profits that might reasonably be expected from some activity will draw alert profit seekers like garbage trucks draw flies. Thus, easily anticipated economic profits will evaporate because of competition. When an attractive investment becomes public knowledge, the cost of investing will be bid up so that only normal returns can be realized. Only above normal profits that reasonable people would not anticipate remain as possibilities. Thus, extraordinarily high returns from an investment are largely a matter of luck.

Rational Expectations

A close relative of efficient markets theory is the theory of rational expectations. If people's expectations are formed rationally, they will learn to identify the variables that shape the circumstances affecting their lives.

> *The theory of **rational expectations** suggests that after policymakers pursue either expansionary or contractionary policies a few times, people learn to predict both likely changes in policies and the effects of such changes. Consumers and investors will then offset predictable policies, preventing them from having any real effect.*

Accordingly, adherents of the rational expectations approach believe that policy goals cannot be achieved, even in the short run, unless the effects of demand-management policies come as complete surprises to the public. Rational expectations theorists believe that predictable policies cannot consistently fool the public. This is a modern extension of the idea that inflation illusion is never permanent.

Natural rate theory is an important cornerstone for rational expectations theory. The concepts of natural rates of interest and unemployment are starting points in exploring the view that demand-management policy is impotent even in the short run. Consider Figure 10. Suppose a heavy short-run dose of expansionary monetary policy shifts Aggregate Demand from AD_0 to AD_1 boosting prices and real output to P_1 and Q_1, respectively (point b). This drives down unemployment rates and both nominal and real interest rates. When people eventually begin to anticipate inflation, then output, unemployment, and the real interest rate return to their original values while prices and nominal interest rates rise (point c). After this cycle occurs once or twice, most people learn to anticipate it and try to take advantage of their ability to predict the future.

Suppose you are one of those who have observed this cycle and begin following the Fed's policies closely. If increases in the prices of bonds and declines in interest rates invariably follow expansionary monetary policies within a few weeks, then you should make some money if you buy bonds the instant that monetary expansion begins. Since you will be holding bonds when interest rates fall, the increase in bond prices should profit you immensely. (Recall the inverse

FIGURE 10 Rational Expectations, Equilibrium Output, and the Price Level

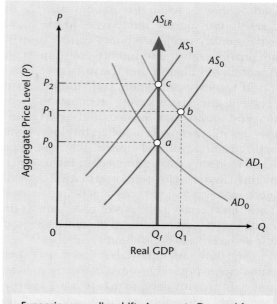

Expansionary policy shifts Aggregate Demand from AD_0 to AD_1. As both output and the price level rise, people begin to anticipate inflation and take steps to offset the effects of inflationary federal policymaking. Simple natural rate theory would predict a path like $a \longrightarrow b \longrightarrow c$, while rational expectationists would expect a move directly from $a \longrightarrow c$ as people instantly adjusted to the expansion.

relationship between bond prices and interest rates.) As you and other "money watchers" try to put this strategy into practice, the demand for bonds, and hence, their prices, would begin to rise just as soon as expansionary monetary policies are adopted. The short-run lag between expansionary policies and the declining interest rate will collapse to zero: the adjustment becomes instantaneous. In Figure 10, as individuals anticipate the effects of policy, the economy will move directly from point a to point c and Aggregate Output will not change.

This is not, however, the end of the story. In the long run, nominal interest rates presumably rise to reflect inflationary expectations. Therefore, you and all the other Fed watchers will want to sell all your bonds before interest rates increase. Because the short run is now extremely short, the time to sell bonds is the instant you discern an expansionary policy. Because you will only be one among many unloading bonds when the money supply increases, the almost immediate result of an expansionary monetary policy will be to drive bond prices down and interest rates up in anticipation of inflation. But the story goes on.

If you expect inflation, you (and just about everyone else who is paying attention) will want to spend your money on goods and services while they are still cheap. (Remember, buy low.) If you manage a firm, you will immediately raise prices when monetary expansion begins; higher prices might help you build inventories that will be worth more money if you just wait a bit before you sell. Thus, inflationary policies will cause almost immediate increases in nominal demands for goods and reductions in their nominal supplies.

For those unemployed, inflationary expectations adjust quickly to expansionary policies, and they are unwilling to accept a job at lower real wages. Therefore, unemployment will not fall below the natural rate as a consequence of expansionary policy. The end of this rational expectations story is that unless the government disguises its policies, an expansionary policy will almost instantly drive up the price level and nominal interest rates, with little or no effect on employment and output. A reversal of this story can be told for contractionary policies (see Focus 1).

Note that one essential difference between the simple natural rate theory and rational expectations theory is the speed with which accurate expectations are assumed to be realized. Simple natural rate analysis would predict a path like $a \rightarrow b \rightarrow c$ in Figure 10, while rational expectationists would expect a direct movement from point a to point c, with no temporary increases in output and employment.

• **Limitations of Rational Expectations Theory**
Just how realistic is rational expectations theory? Most of the population may ignore monetary and fiscal policies, but major economic institutions carefully study government policies in the hopes of predicting future economic activity so they can get the jump on their competition or buffer themselves from hardship. Examples include banks, major corporations, unions, trade groups, and foreign governments. These groups do have substantial resources that can be shifted rapidly whenever the direction of policy seems likely to change. For example, price hikes are common adjustments whenever the imposition of wage and price controls appears imminent.

Other factors, however, may limit the potential impact of rational expectations. First, rational expectations analysis assumes that people are able to accurately forecast government policymaking when it often seems the government is unable to do this itself. Information about government policies is unavoidably expensive and imprecise. As a result, many people remain rationally ignorant. Critics contend that, in the short run at least, government policy may push employment, prices, and interest rates away from their natural levels.

Second, this theory assumes that many people understand how the economy will adjust to particular policies. Economic forecasters who have studied the economy for years often disagree on paths of economic adjustment. The idea that anyone can systematically forecast the effects of policy with precision is extremely dubious. One reason is that public policy may alter the structure of output. For example, the Clinton administration increased domestic outlays while slashing defense spending, changing the structures of incentives and aggregate output. Most economists now agree that economic structures strongly affect aggregate performance (e.g., as in much of East Europe today). Similarly, expansionary monetary policy may reduce interest rates in the short run, resulting in rising investment that may alter the long-run production possibilities for the economy.

Finally, rational expectations theory assumes that wages and prices are perfectly flexible and adjust instantaneously to market forces. Union contracts, efficiency wages, certain laws and regulations, long-term business contracts, and numerous other obstacles all keep wages and prices from adjusting immediately to changes in Aggregate Demand and Aggregate Supply. It takes time for private investors and households to (*a*) recognize that policies and situations have

Rational Expectations and Hyperinflation

[Rational expectationists] are optimistic that inflation can be wiped out with little pain if only the government makes credible its determination to do so.

Paul Samuelson

Hyperinflation—inflation of at least 50% per month—tends to devastate monetary systems so that barter takes over. Most modern analyses of inflationary spirals suggest that halting inflation requires protracted high unemployment; presumably, the more rapid the inflation, the more severe the adjustment. Surprisingly, several hyperinflations have been stopped almost overnight with minimal increased unemployment.

Figure 11 traces major hyperinflations in Austria, Hungary, Poland, and Germany after World War I. In each country, the abrupt halt in inflation was as spectacular as the rise itself. How did policy-makers gain control of their monetary systems to end hyperinflation? The answer lies in the events preceding the hyperinflation and the actions taken to end it. Paul Samuelson's observation (above) provides a clue to the solution, but first let's examine the causes.

After World War I, Austria, Germany, Hungary, and Poland all faced severe hardships and financed massive budget deficits by printing fiat money; all except Poland owed sizable war reparations. Their currencies depreciated at alarming rates, and inflation had a momentum that appeared unstoppable. But in Thomas Sargent's view,

inflation only seems to have a momentum of its own; it is actually the long-term government policy of persistently running large deficits and creating money at high rates that imparts the momentum to the inflation rate.*

One rational expectations perspective is that stopping inflation, especially hyperinflation, requires more than just temporary adjustments in monetary and fiscal policy; the entire policy regime must be altered. Government finance must change in a credible way so that the public believes that government is committed to eliminating the abuses that caused hyperinflation. Such measures ended hyperinflation in all four countries.

First, all four governments created independent central banks that were prohibited from issuing unsecured credit. Second, all four committed to relatively balanced budgets and agreed to cover government debt strictly through bond financing. Finally, the debtor countries renegotiated war reparations. Thus, by altering the rules of the game, these governments literally stopped hyperinflation in its tracks.

Argentina recently went through a similar experience. Throughout the 1970s and early 1980s, inflation in Argentina rose until it exceeded 500% per year. In 1985, a new government instituted austerity measures, a new currency, and the will to stop hyperinflation. By early 1986, relative normalcy had returned to Argentina. It appears that policies that worked after World War I in Europe continue to work today. A similar cold-turkey approach to the problem of government finance may offer the only sure cure for hyperinflations now raging in countries ranging from the former Yugoslavia to Russia to Brazil.

*Thomas J. Sargent, *Rational Expectations and Inflation* (New York: HarperCollins, 1986). This book discusses how several major hyperinflations were ended.

FIGURE 11   The Ends of Four Major Hyperinflations

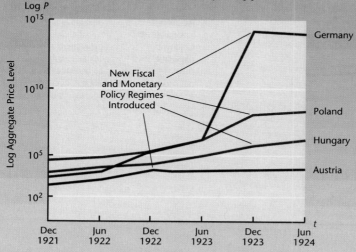

changed, (b) implement plans to reflect new circumstances, and (c) have their new plans take affect. Government policymakers face parallel recognition, administrative, and impact lags. (These policy lags are discussed in more depth in the next chapter.) All of these reasons cause critics of this version of new classical macroeconomics to believe that short-run macroeconomic movements can loosely be controlled by appropriate policies.

Real Business Cycles

Most economists, whether Keynesian or classically oriented, traditionally viewed business cycles as temporary departures from some long-run trend of economic growth. For more than 60 years, these deviations were viewed as resulting primarily from erratic changes in Aggregate Demand. This focus on Aggregate Demand helps explain why orthodox Keynesians typically argue that fiscal policy offers a cure for business cycles, while most new classical economists favor a stable monetary growth rule, viewing fiscal policy as both counterproductive and ineffective.

Concentration on Aggregate Demand is viewed as misdirected by **real business cycle** analysts. This group, a subset of new classical macroeconomists, disputes the assumed transitory nature of business cycles and differs with the traditional view that erratic Aggregate Demand is responsible for changes in economic activity. Real business cycle analysts contend that most fluctuations in real GNP are permanent, not temporary. These economists also contend that shocks to Aggregate Supply are the principal causes of business cycles.

Shocks to the system, according to the theory of real business cycles, are often random and include such events as the introduction of new production techniques (e.g., Henry Ford's assembly line or the Japanese "team" concept), introduction of new products (the steam engine, lasers, and microchips), changes in climatic conditions (freezes, floods, or droughts), new discoveries of basic resources (oil fields in Mexico and Alaska), price shocks for important raw materials (oil price hikes in the 1970s), or widespread changes in lifestyles.

For example, consider the negative shock shown in Figure 12. Assume that the shock (e.g.,

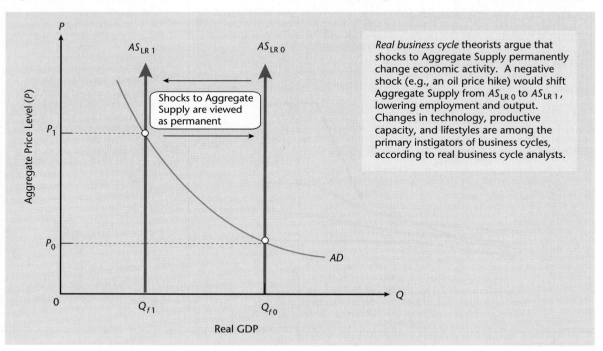

Real business cycle theorists argue that shocks to Aggregate Supply permanently change economic activity. A negative shock (e.g., an oil price hike) would shift Aggregate Supply from $AS_{LR\,0}$ to $AS_{LR\,1}$, lowering employment and output. Changes in technology, productive capacity, and lifestyles are among the primary instigators of business cycles, according to real business cycle analysts.

Shocks to Aggregate Supply are viewed as permanent

FIGURE 12   Real Business Cycles

an oil price increase) reduces the economy's productive capacity, thereby reducing labor productivity. This reduces the demand for labor so less labor is hired, reducing employment and output. Graphically, the Aggregate Supply curve shifts leftward from AS_{LR0} to AS_{LR1}, and real GDP falls from Q_{LR0} to Q_{LR1}. Notice that this shift is permanent unless something pushes Aggregate Supply back to AS_{LR0}.

The policy conclusions of this analysis echo those generated by other new classical models: government should follow passive policies. If government actively responds to a supply shock with expansionary policies, the end result will merely be increases in the price level. If contractionary policies are pursued in hopes of suppressing cost-push inflationary pressure, the result will be deeper price adjustments than would occur if government policy had remained passive.

Most economists largely reject the real business cycle model for several reasons. First, its advocates have had difficulty in showing that periodic supply shocks have been sufficiently strong to explain cycles that have averaged roughly four years in duration. Second, proponents of real business cycle theory have been unable to connect particular technological events (or shocks) to subsequent business cycles (the lone exception is the 1973–1974 oil price shock). Finally, this theory suggests that negative Aggregate Supply shocks reduce productivity and the demand for labor, thereby reducing real wages. The empirical record of business cycles and wages does not support this chain of events. Nevertheless, this theory has sharpened our focus on linkages between short-term business fluctuations and long-term economic growth.

By now, your head may be spinning with all of the different perspectives of economists about macroeconomics. In Figure 13, we summarize the relative positions of various groups of economists ranging from those who would favor macroeconomic fine-tuning to the different strands of the new classical macroeconomics, which are all critical of activist macroeconomic policy. Keep in mind, however, that the differences between different schools of thought are less extreme than was true 20 or 30 years ago, and that few economists can be pigeonholed precisely into any of

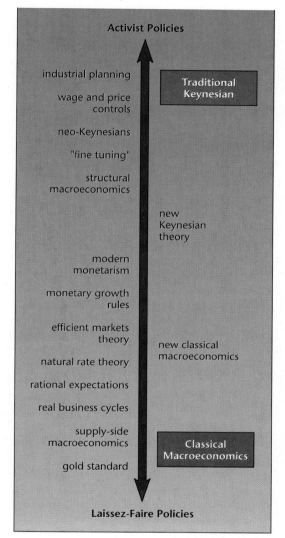

FIGURE 13   A Continuum of Economists' Views About Policy

these schools of thought. Most economists recognize that the world is far more complex than can be summarized by any single theory and borrow bits and pieces of theory that are in accord with their individual views of how the world works.

To this point in the book, we have addressed monetary and fiscal policy instruments and a few of their limitations. In the next chapter, we tackle other objections to discretionary macroeconomic policies and introduce some alternative approaches to policy.

CHAPTER REVIEW: KEY POINTS

1. The **Phillips curve** depicts a trade-off for policymakers between unemployment and inflation. Lower unemployment rates presumably might be purchased through higher inflation or vice versa; it is up to policymakers to choose the least harmful mix of evils. The Phillips curve appeared to be relatively stable through the 1960s, but it shifted sharply in the 1970s and early 1980s so that much higher rates of unemployment appeared necessary to dampen inflationary pressures. The reasons for the instability of the Phillips curve are the subject of a continuing debate within the economics profession.

2. Modern Keynesian analysis suggests that several factors in addition to inflationary expectations can cause stagflation and instability in the Phillips curve. Wages and prices are assumed **sticky**, especially in a downward direction. Unexpected shocks to the supply side, rapid structural changes in demand or output, changes in labor institutions that affect incentives for work, and changes in public regulatory policies all are capable of shifting the Phillips curve. The Keynesian **structuralist approach** emphasizes production bottlenecks as foundations for the Phillips curve.

3. The theory of **adaptive expectations** suggests that people base their expectations of inflation on a weighted average of inflation in recent years.

4. The **natural rate theory** of the instability in the Phillips trade-off focuses on worker expectations of inflation. As labor begins to anticipate inflation, greater increases in wages are required for a given level of real output. Thus, accelerating inflation is required if policymakers desire to hold unemployment below its natural rate, but even this policy will not work forever.

5. **Real interest rates** (r) are the puchasing power premiums paid for the use of money. **Nominal interest rates** (i) are the monetary premiums paid for the use of money. These rates roughly differ by the rate of inflation: $r = i - \dot{p}$.

6. The **natural rate theory of real interest** hypothesizes that nominal interest rates will be adjusted to reflect the desired real interest rate (r_d) plus the expected rate of inflation: $i = r_d + E(\dot{p})$.

7. If interest rate targets or unemployment rate objectives are set below their natural rates, expansionary policies may ultimately cause nominal interest rates to rise, not fall. Natural rate theorists believe that only temporary reductions in interest rates or unemployment can be obtained through expansionary policies and, even in the short run, only by fooling lenders or workers.

8. The **Keynes effect** predicts that monetary growth will decrease interest rates, and vice versa. The **Fisher effect** is the upward adjustment of nominal interest rates when transactors begin expecting inflation.

9. The **new classical macroeconomics** is based on the model of perfect competition, or **efficient markets**, which suggests that even in the short run, macroeconomic policy only works when the economy is operating inefficiently and that inefficiency does not occur in a market system.

10. The theory of **rational expectations** suggests that people eventually figure out how a given change in policy affects the economy and learn to predict how policymakers react to swings in economic activity. Thereafter, people will focus on what policymakers are doing and make adjustments that prevent the policies from accomplishing their objectives.

11. **Real business cycle theory** views shocks to Aggregate Supply as permanent and suggests that attempts by macroeconomic policymakers to fine-tune the economy are either self-defeating or harmful.

QUESTIONS FOR THOUGHT AND DISCUSSION

1. Some economists argue that the Smoot-Hawley tariff enacted in 1930 was a major cause of the collapse in the stock market and the resulting Great Depression. Rational expectations analysis suggests that the impact of future events will be rapidly capitalized into stock prices. One political sage recently suggested that recent balanced budget acts point to a new fiscal policy regime, accounting for the stock market's record performance from 1992 to 1994. What argument can you make that lower budget deficits would benefit the stock market? Are there other factors that might account for the stock market's sustained rise from 1992 to 1994?

2. After full adjustment for the Fisher effect, what will be the nominal interest rate in the following situations?

   a. $r_d = 8\%$, $E(\dot{p}) = 8\%$

   b. $r_d = 5\%$, $E(\dot{p}) = -3\%$

   c. $r_d = 6\%$, $E(\dot{p}) = 18\%$

3. If indexation is used for such retirement programs as Social Security, should pensions be adjusted using average changes in take-home salaries so that retirees share in the gains and losses of workers, or should cost-of-living adjustments be used to ensure pensioners a constant purchasing power income? What are the advantages and disadvantages of each approach?

4. Keynes argued during the Great Depression that the way to put unemployed workers back on payrolls and get machinery humming again was to increase the demand for goods and services by putting more money in people's pockets. His main argument emphasized insufficient Aggregate Demand. If Aggregate Demand were increased, the economy would climb out of any recession or depression. Many economists believe that the Keynesian method for resolving the problems of recession may not produce the desired results in an era of stagflation. Why do most economists now believe that Keynesian demand management is effective only for problems like those of a depression era and cannot remedy the multitude of problems facing the economy today?

Cost-push

Frictional
unemployment

Demand-pull

Supply shocks

Long run

Efficiency wage

Chapter 18

Limitations of Stabilization Policy

Whether active or passive policies are more likely to moderate business cycles splits modern economists into two camps: new Keynesians, who tend to favor active countercyclical policy if circumstances suggest that severe macroeconomic problems will take a long time to resolve, and new classical economists, who generally oppose activist policies. If policies operate in predictable ways, as most early Keynesians believed, then stabilization would be reasonably straightforward: ascertain any trade-offs between price-level stability, employment, and economic growth so that goals can be set realistically, and then translate these goals into appropriate fiscal and monetary policies. Goals may involve hard choices, but failures to achieve reasonable macrostability can be traced to policymakers who are just "too dumb" to apply a few simple economic principles.

Adam Smith's preferred blend of laissez-faire policies and invisible-hand market solutions is mirrored in several modern schools of thought, including the *Austrian* school, a group of thinkers typified by Ludwig von Mises and Friedrich Hayek. (See their biography.) These groups, which include the new classical economists, contend that discretionary policy causes more macroeconomic problems than it cures. Various (and sometimes contradictory) reasons are offered for opposing discretionary policymaking. Some critics view activist policies as extremely harmful; others view them as largely useless minor irritants.

Many modern monetarists, for example, cite potentially erratic and damaging effects from active policies as reasons for favoring a stable monetary growth rule. Other new classical economists believe the reactions to policy by private individuals and firms often stifle seemingly desirable effects of countercyclical measures, so activist policies are seen as largely futile.

In this chapter, you will learn more about obstacles to designing and implementing proper discretionary policies. Frankly, macroeconomic policymaking is as much an art as it is a science. Common difficulties facing policymakers include problems of timing and imperfect information, imperfect monetary and fiscal policymaking institutions, and imperfect politicians who tailor policies to maximize their

BIOGRAPHY

Ludwig von Mises and Friedrich A. Hayek: Austrian Economics

The Austrian school of economics dates back to early in the 19th century, when Carl Menger and Eugen Bohm-Bawerk laid foundations for modern theories of demand. Austrians rejected earlier emphasis on "objective" costs (e.g., labor theories of value accepted by Smith and Ricardo) as underpinning market dynamics. Prices, they said, were ultimately subjective: things are worth what people think they are worth. The foremost disciples of this approach in the 20th century were Ludwig von Mises (1881–1973) and Friedrich A. Hayek (1899–1992), who stressed how our perceptions broadly shape the entire spectrum of economic activities.

Born in Austria, von Mises taught at the University of Vienna before fleeing to America to escape Hitler's invasion. As a youth he was fond of tennis, but when someone noted that he was not very good at it, he replied, "The fate of the ball does not interest me very much." Human creativity and its consequences were his passions. Von Mises chose not to be limited to a narrowly defined economics. He attempted, instead, to survey the full range of human action, focusing on the supremacy of the individual as a purposeful decision-maker who constantly adjusts prices, production, and consumption in order to live better and to enjoy maximum freedom. In a free marketplace, *economic calculation* provides prices and profits as signals that motivate firms to mesh production with consumers' demands. But in a government-directed economy,

agencies have no measure comparable to profits by which to evaluate their operations.

Von Mises also rejected the Keynesian notion that business cycles can be cured by countercyclical policy. Such an idea ignores the fact that politicians have a strong propensity to spend in good times as well as bad. Von Mises viewed government managers as always fumbling in the dark because they cannot possibly know all the data needed to make "correct" macroeconomic adjustments. He concluded that *budget management* is likely to set off a chain reaction of, first, inflation, then price controls, and, ultimately, economic stagnation.

Friedrich Hayek, another giant of Austrian economics, became a Nobel laureate in 1974. Hayek argued that government control is, inevitably, the enemy of freedom and denounced the growth of government as *The Road to Serfdom* (the title of his best-selling book).

Hayek decried constructivism above all else, calling it "the pretense of knowledge" and "the illusion of human omnipotence." *Constructivism* is the idea that enlightened leaders can steer a society in desirable directions. Theocratic theories and the concept of a revolutionary elite (developed by Vladimir I. Lenin, an early Russian revolutionary who led the Soviet Communist Party to power), epitomize the constructivist vision. Hayek, however, believed that culture and civilization are not consequences of deliberate human design but are instead the products of the survival of society's successful

groups. Hence, civilization depends on rules of behavior, not on goals.

Here are some examples of constructivism in action: in the 1980s and 1990s, Iraq's dictator, Saddam Hussein, wanted to unify Arabs to zealously follow the precepts of Islam as he interpreted them. His regime killed tens of thousands of Iranians, Kurds, and Iraqis in attempts to reconstruct society to his design. Hitler, too, was a constructivist, as were the Soviet Union's Joseph Stalin and China's Mao Zedong.

Hayek viewed Keynesianism as a less virulent strain of the constructivism disease. Keynes's message is seductive: government can manipulate total spending to control the twin problems of unemployment and unstable prices. Keynes's comforting message has not been lost on many politicians, who no longer consider themselves to be helpless before the convulsions of a business cycle or limited in what they can deliver voters. Keynesian analysis looks like an instruction manual for running the economy as a well-oiled machine.

The trouble, said Hayek, is that societies are more like organisms than machines. Our interactions are so complex that they cannot be manipulated as many Keynesians suppose. In vain attempts to maintain very low unemployment, government may feel compelled to spend faster and faster, so that prices rise faster and faster as well. This kind of artificial stimulant, said Hayek, distorts the price signals that indicate individuals' desires and genuine scarcities.

prospects for reelection. These problems severely limit the effectiveness of discretionary policymaking and stand as arguments for following macro policy rules.

LAGS, DOSES, AND STABILIZATION

Stabilization policy suffers from fits and starts because of lags in recognition, administration, and impact. Suppose discretionary monetary and fiscal policies are equally powerful and have equally harmful side effects. Because of the different timing lags that characterize them, there is still a question of whether monetary or fiscal policy is preferable.

Recognition Lags

Our perceptions of the present are clouded, and our predictions about the future emerge only from more or less educated guesswork.

> *The time required for policymakers to realize that macroeconomic conditions have changed is the* **recognition lag**.

Monetary and fiscal policymakers are equally affected. It takes time and effort to gather, process, and interpret data so we have some feel for macroeconomic trends. Even then, the data may be sketchy, contradictory, or misleading. Of course, if half of all workers were laid off tomorrow, policymakers would know by next week that we (and they) were in deep trouble. But our economy is sluggish, making it difficult for policymakers to determine exactly how hard and in which direction to steer.

Administrative Lags

After a macroeconomic change is identified, it still takes time to institute proper policies.

> *The time required to implement new policies is called the* **administrative lag**.

If recession seemed to be on the horizon, monetary policymakers could print money and buy bonds (open-market operations), or they might lower the discount rate or reserve requirements. Reversed measures would be appropriate if inflationary pressure were picking up steam. Changes in monetary policy can be implemented quickly by the Fed's Open Market Committee (FOMC). Consequently, administrative lags pose only trivial problems for monetary policymaking.

Fiscal policymaking, however, confronts major administrative lags, because discretionary changes in taxation or government outlays require legal changes. New legislation can take years, so minor crises may become catastrophic before (*a*) new laws are drafted, (*b*) congressional committees finish wrestling with questions about whose taxes to cut or raise or whose pork-barrel legislation to pass or kill, (*c*) both the House and Senate pass some compromise bill, (*d*) the president signs the bill, and, finally, (*e*) any legal challenges clear the courts.

The longer administrative lag for fiscal policy might suggest a preference for monetary policy. Some advocates of fiscal policy, however, suggest that this lag could be finessed if the president were granted discretionary power to raise or lower tax rates within narrow limits, say, 10%. Alternatively, the president might be given the power of a line-item veto or discretion to impound funds for certain public works projects to help balance the budget or fight inflation, or to authorize preselected projects if recession threatens. One major hurdle is the reluctance of Congress and the voters to grant any president this much new power.

Impact Lags

It also takes time for any change in policy to affect the economy.

> *The time required for new policies to affect the economy is the* **impact lag**.

Our $7 trillion economy can develop a lot of momentum; changing its direction through fiscal and monetary policies might be compared to using a rowboat oar to steer an ocean liner against a strong tide.

Even after legislation is passed, changes in most government outlays have long impact lags because it takes time for old government contracts to lapse or for new contracts to be awarded and then begun. The personal income tax system, however, is the major fiscal policy tool for altering consumer spending via the multiplier process. Consumers quickly learn about changing tax rates because their paychecks almost immediately reflect higher or lower withholdings. People rapidly translate tax cuts that increase their take-home pay into new cars, video cassette recorders, clothes, or more frequent chocolate chip ice cream cones. Adjusting to tax increases may be painful, but most consumers do so fairly rapidly because they must. The impact lag for fiscal policy may be long for changes in government purchases, but it is comparatively short when tax rates are changed.

In contrast, the impact lags of monetary policy may be relatively long and variable. When expansionary open-market operations are used, banks' excess reserves quickly grow. But bankers may hoard these funds if their confidence is down so that the lending → spending → lending sequence is squelched. Nevertheless, the loanable funds available generally rise and interest rates drop. While consumers may view this as an inducement to buy more durable goods, a decline in interest rates does not generally have nearly as large or immediate an effect on consumer spending as does a healthy cut in tax rates.

Lower interest rates will boost business investment, but investors may take time to respond. Decisions about new capacity involve extensive deliberations in the big firms that do the bulk of investment in our economy. Corporate planning is so complex that most major investments require heavy commitments of funds years before additional capacity comes on line. This extended investment process is countercyclical in itself because changes in economic activity may have little effect on these decisions in the short run. The impact of monetary expansion on consumption and investment spending is positive, but it may be both slow and

erratic. While estimates of the effect of monetary policy on spending place the beginnings of the new spending at as soon as two or three months, the full effects of monetary expansion or contraction appear to take up to seven years.

Discretionary monetary policy has parallels in an automatic baseball-pitching machine that randomly selects its pitches. The first pitch a batter faces may take five minutes to float over home plate belt-high, while the second pitch whistles by low and outside. (If all pitches were identical, batters' problems would be over.) Just as the batter tires of waiting for the third pitch and starts across home plate for the dugout, the ball suddenly arrives. This analogy suggests that a variable lag is just as dangerous as a long lag. Baseball pitchers purposely vary their speed or placement to frustrate batters. The variable impact lags of discretionary monetary policy are unintentional, but they similarly frustrate decision-making in the private sector.

Thus, although fiscal policy has a longer administrative lag than monetary policy does, this may be offset by a shorter impact lag and the more certain outcome of revisions in tax rates. According to critics of discretionary fiscal policy, prolonged discussions of the need for tax reform or higher tax rates to control ballooning deficits have introduced greater uncertainty into investment decisions. And the long and variable impact lag of monetary policy is a major shortcoming of discretionary policy in the eyes of proponents of monetary growth rules. Table 1 summarizes lags, effects, and the primary uses of major fiscal and monetary policies. The table provides a glimpse at the complexity involved in choosing a policy mix.

Destabilizing Effects of Policy Lags

Critics contend that recognition, administrative, and impact lags make fine-tuned macro policies an oxymoron. Suppose that the economy is self-stabilizing but that it does have a natural cyclical pattern as shown in Figure 1. The story of the effect of these lags may go like this.

Suppose the economy begins to heat up at the beginning of 1996. Policymakers recognize

TABLE 1 A Summary of Appropriate Lags, Timing of Major Effects, and Uses of Selected Specific Fiscal and Monetary Policy

Policy	Administrative Lag	Impact Lag	Major Effects	Major Use
Fiscal Policies				
Change in taxes	L	S	LR	Stimulate or curb private spending
Change in investment tax credits	L	L	LR	Stimulate investment, capital formation, and economic growth
Change in government purchases	L	L	SR	Countercyclical fiscal policy, pork barrel, and so forth
Change in regulations	L	S	LR	Increase regulation to curb abuses and "cutthroat" competition; reduce regulations to improve efficiency in the market
Changes in composition of government purchases	L	S	LR	Change the distribution of government spending—guns versus butter
Monetary Policies				
Change in discount rate	S	L	SR	Encourage or discourage borrowing (signals to market)
Change in reserve requirements	S	L	LR	Change the potential money multiplier
Open-market operations	S	L	SR	Week-to-week control of the money supply and interest

The recognition lag is equally long for both types of policymaking. The letter L stands for a relatively long lag, while S means that the lag is relatively short. The major effects of policies occur roughly in the short run, SR (1–3 years), or they occur in the long run, LR (4 years and over).

the emergence of inflationary pressures by the end of the first quarter of 1996 (point *a*) and implement contractionary policies by midyear. The braking effect of the engineered reduction in Aggregate Demand begins just as the economy would have begun to cool down by itself (point *b*). The effect of this seemingly correct policy is to cause a deeper recession than would have occurred normally in the latter half of 1997 (point *c*). Lags lead to a timing problem, worsening the cycle.

The recognition, administrative, and impact lags consume nine months before proper policies to expand activity are felt in the econ-

omy—again, just as self-correction mechanisms would have ended the recession. Mistiming means that expansionary policies are too powerful and that the inflationary pressure of mid-1998 is accelerated (point *d*). And so on.

Figure 1 portrays the worsening of a business cycle by correct, but poorly timed, policies. This example suggests that active countercyclical policy may be self-defeating, actually making the business cycle worse than it would be with a fixed monetary growth rule and fixed tax and government outlay structures. For instance, you can stabilize "waves" in a water bed if you push down on a wave at just the right time and with

FIGURE 1 The Business Cycle with Poorly Timed Policies

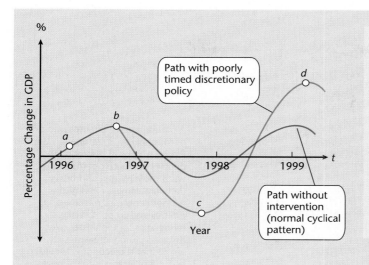

Path with poorly timed discretionary policy

Path without intervention (normal cyclical pattern)

Year

You can stabilize "waves" in an unbaffled water bed by pushing down on waves at just the right time and with just the right pressure, but if your timing or pressure is off, the waves may be amplified. Similarly, incorrect policies may make business cycles more severe. If new classical macroeconomists are correct, cycles self-correct quickly without discretionary changes in monetary or fiscal policy. Fluctuations may pose problems for proper timing of macroeconomic policy because of lags in (*a*) recognition, (*b*) administration, and (*c*) impact. It is even more possible that macroeconomic self-corrections may begin before all these lags have elapsed.

just the right pressure, but if your timing or pressure is off, you may synchronize with the waves and amplify them substantially. In a similar fashion, mistimed or incorrect policies may create chaos out of minor economic fluctuations.

Overdosing or Undermedicating a Sick Economy

Inflationary and recessionary gaps are, respectively, the decreases or increases in autonomous spending needed to decompress inflationary pressure or to push the economy out of a recession by filling the GDP gap. Unfortunately, these gaps cannot be measured precisely—we never know the exact limits of our productive capacity, nor do we know the precise sizes of autonomous spending or tax multipliers. Monetary policymakers are plagued with similar ignorance about capacity, and the values of either the money multiplier or its velocity may vary. [Recall that velocity (*V*) helps us measure how a stock of money is translated into spending: $V = PQ/M$.] Another problem for monetary authorities is that the growth rates of M1, M2, and M3 may vary substantially. Which of these should policymakers try to control? Of course,

this also confounds setting a monetary growth rule.

These difficulties make it nearly impossible for policymakers to know how much stimulus to inject or withdraw. At times, as with Franklin Roosevelt's first two administrations, discretionary policies may be "too little, too late," and the Great Depression (1933–1939), dragged on and on. In the eyes of critics who advocate putting the economy on automatic pilot, policymakers more commonly administer too much medicine. Lags in discretionary policies make it easy to overdose the economy so that recessions lead into periods of hyperactivity and inflation.

Alternatively, excessive doses of sedatives may cause an overstimulated economy to crash into a deep depression. Opponents of fine-tuning cite the economic nosedives of 1974–1975 and 1981–1983 as evidence of the harm done by abrupt reductions in monetary growth after extended inflationary growth. In situations where occasional aspirin would cure our economic headaches, the Fed may administer uppers and downers in a cyclical fashion. The result is that the economy follows a snakelike stop-go path, with demand-side inflationary cycles causing supply-side cycles, causing demand-side cycles, and so on, as shown in Figure 2.

FIGURE 2 The Economy's Snakelike Path

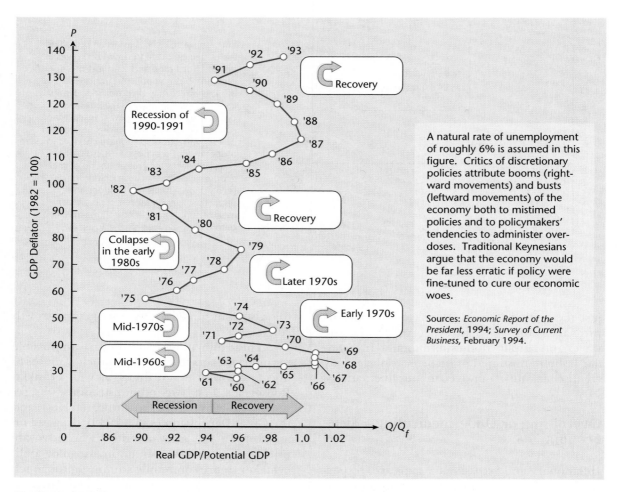

A natural rate of unemployment of roughly 6% is assumed in this figure. Critics of discretionary policies attribute booms (rightward movements) and busts (leftward movements) of the economy both to mistimed policies and to policymakers' tendencies to administer overdoses. Traditional Keynesians argue that the economy would be far less erratic if policy were fine-tuned to cure our economic woes.

Sources: *Economic Report of the President*, 1994; *Survey of Current Business*, February 1994.

INSULATION AGAINST MONETARY POLICYMAKING

Some modern Keynesians are skeptical that countercyclical monetary policy can be consistently effective. Their objection is based on a belief that technological changes in financial institutions are induced by *tight money* or *easy money* policies.

> **Financial insulation** *occurs when organizations develop new technologies that allow them to use money more efficiently so that more transactions can be supported from a given amount of monetary base.*

Among other effects, financial insulation tends to raise the income velocity of money (V). Here is one example of ways the financial system adjusts to tight money policies and, in the process, reduces the power of the Fed's monetary tools.

Suppose monetary authorities try to combat inflationary pressures with contractionary policies. Excess reserves throughout the banking system fall, and credit availability throughout the economy is diminished. Especially when interest rates are high, any single bank's profits are enhanced if it finds new ways to support more loans from given total reserves.

In the 1960s, bank officials learned how to conserve on reserves by pooling their excess reserves. If one bank needed funds temporarily to meet its reserve requirements, it would borrow some of the excess reserves of another bank at a lower interest rate than the Fed charged at the discount window. The *federal funds market* (a market for excess reserves) that grew out of this effort is now available to bankers across the country. Because of this financial insulation, banks can literally lend or borrow millions of dollars for as little as one or two days at comparatively low interest rates. And few banks now hold more than 1% in excess reserves.

Many institutions learn how to shield themselves from tight credit conditions. For example, high nominal interest rates cause many firms to delay payments to suppliers while trying to push their own customers to make payments faster. Financial intermediaries, major corporations, accountants, and stockbrokers, among others, develop new techniques (e.g., new credit instruments) for minimizing money balances when a credit crunch hits. This is a creative response of the financial system. Discoveries of ways

to dampen the effects of contractionary policy increase both velocity and the money multiplier and reduce the power of the Fed. The Fed's tools do not work as well when banks take steps to insulate themselves from the effects of Fed policies.

• Money, Prices, and Financial Insulation
Figure 3 illustrates how financial institutions may adjust to counter monetary policy. The growth rates of M1 (lagged eight quarters), real GDP, and the GDP deflator are graphed. Both real GDP and the GDP deflator track M1 growth during the 1970s. Beginning in 1982, price changes and M1 growth uncharacteristically diverged while real GDP continued on track. More recently, high rates of money growth have not translated into price increases because velocity has fallen. Many factors may account for velocity's decline, including financial inventiveness, monetary deregulation, disinflation, and declining interest rates. One fact stands out: basic

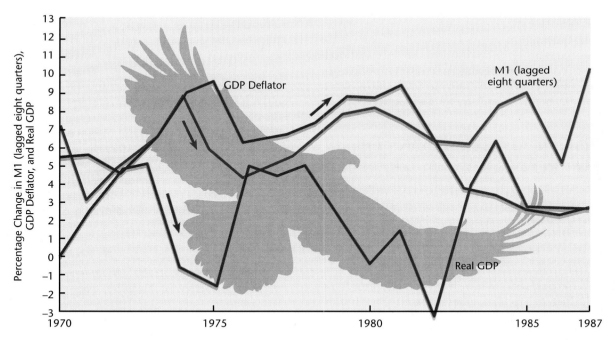

Source: *Economic Report of the President,* 1994.

Real GDP and GDP deflator generally tracked the rate of growth of M1 until the 1980s. During the 1980s, the velocity of money fell due to financial inventiveness, monetary deregulation, disinflation, and declining interest rates.

FIGURE 3   Growth Rates of M1 (Lagged Eight Quarters), GDP Deflator, and Real GDP

departures from past relationships make implementing monetary policy more difficult.[1]

Discretionary monetary policy can be compared to a pesticide, with firms being a variety of insects. Just as initial doses of a new pesticide wipe out a lot of bugs, contractionary monetary policies may reduce the availability of credit, causing marginal firms to succumb. And just as the insects that survive repeated doses of the pesticide become immune to it after a few generations, the firms that have learned to adjust to credit crunches become immune to contractionary monetary policies. Moreover, these surviving firms have a profitable advantage: many competitors will have collapsed during periods of tight money. Thus, adjustments by financial institutions to Fed policies further limit the power of discretionary monetary policies.

The internationalization of capital markets has also weakened the power of both monetary and fiscal policymakers in recent years. Many economists view as increasingly moot all debates about whether management of Aggregate Demand is more or less important than policies to stimulate Aggregate Supply. Their perspective, outlined in Focus 1, is that spillovers from the increasing globalization of international markets swamp the macroeconomic policies of any single country in determining that country's prospects for prosperity or stagnation.

POLITICAL DIMENSIONS OF MACRO POLICY

Every recovery is hailed by an incumbent president as the result of his own wise policies, while every recession is condemned by him as the result of the mistaken policies of his predecessor.

Gardner Ackley (Ackley's Law)

We have described how macro policy should be conducted if policymakers, for all their limitations, were selfless people interested only in the welfare of the entire populace. But macroeconomic policymakers are either politicians or their appointees. Might policies be affected by political goals? Both Keynesian and monetarist theories suggest that, in the short run, expansionary policies can be used to move the economy toward full employment, and policymakers can also use contractionary policies to combat inflationary pressures.

Political Business Cycles

Macro policy is sometimes compared to alcohol. Alcohol can be medicinal; a little can loosen you up and allow you to have more fun. At least in the short run, expansionary policies stimulate employment, investment, and new sales for business firms. Everything looks rosy. But just as a mild buzz is often followed by a hangover, a binge of expansionary policies may be followed by a period of drying out. Unemployment and inflation soar, and business activity slumps.

The idea that political tactics can be destabilizing is reasonably straightforward. Incumbent politicians seeking reelection may hope for spillovers into the ballot box from short-lived preelection upswings that follow tax cuts and a shot of new government spending. If monetary authorities are in cahoots with incumbents, they can help out with a chaser of expansionary monetary policy. Incumbents do well in elections during prosperity but are turned out of office in droves when the economy sours. After the election, inflation emerging from politically motivated expansionary policies can be dealt with by a strong dose of tax hikes, cuts in government pork-barrel projects, and monetary restraint. Thus, democracies may be plagued by political business cycles.

Political business cycles may occur if incumbent policymakers try to manipulate macroeconomic policies to enhance their reelection prospects.

Politicians who adopt policies to influence voting patterns obviously hope that voters have short memories. Several studies indicate that incumbents' success in retaining their offices is closely related to how fast disposable income

---

[1]For a detailed discussion of these issues, see J. A. Cacy, "Recent M1 Growth and Its Implications," *Economic Review*, Federal Reserve Bank of Kansas City, December 1985, pp. 18–23.

Internationalization and Macroeconomic Policy

Year after year, international trade accounts for growing shares of GDP in most countries throughout the world. Even the rapid growth of trade, however, seems slow when compared with growth rates for flows of funds between countries. International flows of funds were roughly 6,000% greater than international flows of goods and services during the late 1980s, and this ratio has accelerated into the 1990s. Almost $1 trillion worth of funds flow through international capital markets each day.

Only small shares of these flows of financial capital between countries are used to pay for imbalances of international trade. Instead, they reflect the internationalization of markets for capital. More than 95% of all international flows of money involve (a) arbitrage to make the exchange rates of different currencies equivalent in different markets or (b) speculation in anticipation that exchange rates will change in the near future.

Nevertheless, financial capital flows toward investments that are expected to be the most profitable without regard for national borders. A deposit in a new bank account in Delaware, for example, may be transformed into investment in new manufacturing facili-

ties in South Africa, Bangladesh, or Poland within a few days. Similarly, a transnational corporation headquartered in Australia but seeking funds to finance the hostile takeover of a silicon-chip manufacturer in Hong Kong may find that a broker in Berlin can offer funds at the lowest rate of interest.

The increasing mobility of financial (and ultimately, economic) capital improves the efficiency of economic activity throughout the world. An important side effect is that this mobility reduces the power of domestic monetary and fiscal policymakers everywhere to execute macroeconomic policies that are independent of global developments.

Suppose, for example, that the Fed were concerned about inflation. If the Fed tried to tighten U.S. credit markets by selling U.S. Treasury bonds through open-market operations, this might temporarily exert upward pressures on domestic interest rates. However, the higher U.S. interest rates would quickly attract, say, Japanese savers, who might buy more U.S. Treasury bonds in hopes that interest rates in the United States will soon fall. The net result is that the Fed's contractionary policies could be largely offset by inflows of foreign finan-

cial capital. Similarly, expansionary open-market operations (Fed purchases of U.S. bonds) might be offset by outflows of financial capital from the United States.

Fiscal policy has also been weakened by the globalization of markets. Suppose a tax cut was initiated to stimulate the economy. The resulting increase in our National Income would be diminished because our higher income would cause us to import more, so that some of the expansionary impetus would be experienced in countries from which we import. Regional economic integration (e.g., the European Community, or the North American Free Trade Agreement between the U.S., Canada, and Mexico) further dilutes the independent power of a country's macroeconomic policymakers, because prosperity or stagnation is diffused through the economies of the country's trading partners.

The internationalization of financial markets ultimately diminishes the power of discretionary policy. Advocates of passive economic policies cite the increasing futility of discretionary policy as one more reason why permanent policies should be established that allow markets to adjust to any economic shocks.

grows during the year immediately preceding elections.

With these incentives for politicians to pursue policies leading to booms prior to elections and then to slowdowns immediately after the voting, what does the U.S. record show? Table 2 shows that between 1952 and 1990, our real disposable income typically grew at higher-than-average rates during election years than during off-election years. The relationship is not

perfect, but disposable income usually grew faster in presidential election years.

We dealt with the issue of the Fed's independence in Chapter 14. Recall that the Fed contends that it can do a better job if it is independent from political pressures. Figure 4, which relates monetary growth to recent presidential election years, shows that monetary growth has generally been higher than average immediately before presidential elections. These monetary expan-

TABLE 2 Annual Percentage Change in Real Disposable Personal Income

President(s)	Election Years	Off-Election Years
Eisenhower (1953–1956)	2.7	1.0
Eisenhower (1957–1960)	5.9	1.1
Kennedy/Johnson (1961–1964)	4.1	4.2
Johnson (1965–1968)	3.3	4.9
Nixon (1969–1972)	4.1	4.0
Nixon/Ford (1973–1976)	3.7	–0.08
Carter (1977–1980)	2.0	4.4
Reagan (1981–1984)	3.1	0.08
Reagan (1985–1988)	7.3	2.1
Bush (1989–1992)	2.0	1.8
Clinton (1993–1994)	—	4.0
Average	4.0	2.5

Source: *Economic Report of the President,* 1994.

sions yielded mixed results, however: the incumbent party's candidate lost five of the nine presidential elections from 1960 to 1994.

Political business cycles are not unique to the United States. Among the most striking foreign examples is the case of Israel. There were six major elections during the period 1952 to 1973. In every instance, the period immediately preceding an Israeli election was more prosperous than the period immediately after the election. After reviewing 1961 to 1972 data for 90 elections in 27 countries, one political scientist found that for 19 of the 27 countries, "real disposable income accelerated in 77% of election years compared with 46% of years without election."[2]

[2]E. Tufte, *Political Control of the Economy* (Princeton, NJ: Princeton University Press, 1978), p. 11.

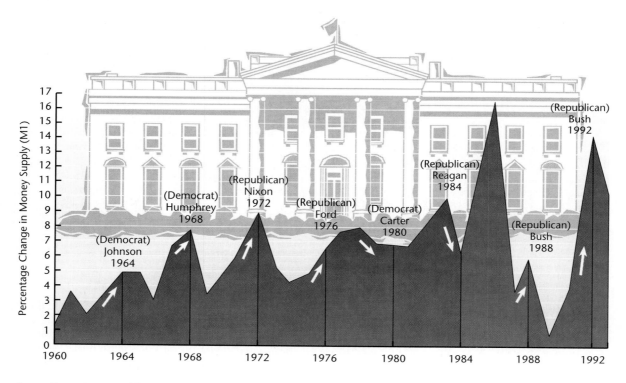

Source: *Economic Report of the President,* 1994.

In the past three decades, monetary growth has been higher than average immediately before presidential elections. (*Note:* The incumbent party and its candidate are shown for election years.)

FIGURE 4 Elections and Monetary Growth

In 1943, the Polish economist Michael Kalecki suggested that, after World War II, cycles caused by business instability would be supplanted by political business cycles in modern democracies. The evidence seems to support his contention that when politicians have a working knowledge of fiscal and monetary tools, they try to use these tools for their own ends.

Has Keynesian Theory Induced Government Growth?

A final criticism of activist policies is that as politicians use these tools, the government sector will grow larger relative to the private sector. Opponents of large government have lost most battles in the past 50 years; government's role has expanded in most of the world's democracies. Many of these critics identify Keynesian fiscal policy as the culprit.

Keynesian theory originated amid attempts to end a massive worldwide depression caused by inadequate demand during the 1930s. The Keynesian prescription? Spend your way into prosperity; ignore budget deficits and fight unemployment by boosting government spending and cutting taxes. Although largely ignored, the Keynesian cure for inflation is a healthy budget surplus. Nevertheless, as we indicated in our chapter Deficits and Public Debt, greater total U.S. deficits were sustained during the inflationary period from 1970 to 1980 than in the previous 200 years. And the deficits of the 1980s then tripled the size of our national debt.

Many conservative politicians and economists continued into the 1960s to preach the old-time religion of cyclically balanced budgets, but the Keynesian approach gained increasing acceptance from 1936 into the 1970s. Critics of Keynesian policies have argued that government spending inevitably mushrooms once politicians learn that governmentally provided goods and services need not be paid for by politically unpopular tax increases.

Immense deficits eventually produced the Gramm-Rudman Act (1985), an attempt by Congress to force itself to bite the bullet. It accomplished little, so Congress passed Deficit Reduction Acts in 1990 and again in 1993. Eliminating programs and cutting budgets has proven a hard task for both the administration and Congress. Critics see a national debt exceeding $5 trillion, a federal budget exceeding $1.6 trillion, and persistent record deficits as evidence that Keynesian theory promotes governmental growth.

Since World War II, government spending and transfer payments as percentages of GDP have grown substantially in most democratic countries, as shown in Figure 5. This growth may be the result of the respectability of Keynesian policies. Until recently, deficits were not viewed with much alarm, even during inflationary periods. To the extent that deficits cause inflation, inflation should be viewed as a hidden tax. But if poorly informed voters blame government-generated inflation on unions or businesses, then politicians are encouraged to hand out "free lunches"–popular new government programs without unpopular tax hikes. Many voters are very aware of the direct benefits of deficit-financed special-interest spending but fail to recognize the inflation indirectly caused by such deficits.

During depressions, the deficits caused by higher government spending and lower taxes have beneficial effects: output and employment grow–but government also grows. Government outlays are seldom cut during inflationary periods, and proposals to raise taxes are political suicide. Few politicians are willing to be accused of "raising the price of government" by raising tax rates. The net result is that government grows during economic downturns but does not shrink during inflationary periods, as proper fiscal policy would dictate. According to critics of Keynesian policies, this occurs because the inflationary effects of high and rising government spending are disguised.

In summary, macroeconomic policies may be misused by politicians who cut taxes and increase government spending (a) shortly before elections, anticipating a short-lived prosperity that will aid them in reelection and (b) during economic slumps, without offsetting increases in taxes or cuts in government spending during prosperity or inflation. The former leads to po-

FIGURE 5   The International Growth of Government

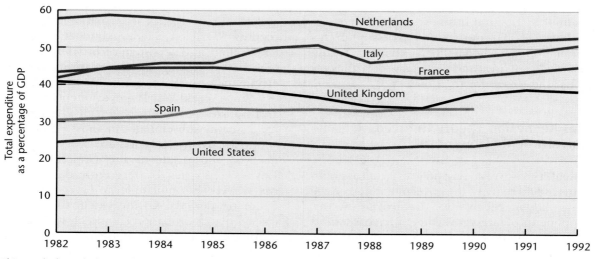

This graph shows little growth of government in the past decade, but the longer term trend is substantial growth.

litical business cycles; the latter, to expansion of the government and declining reliance on the private acts of individual households and firms.

ARE RECESSIONS ENGINEERED TO DECOMPRESS INFLATION?

The argument that political considerations upwardly bias the growth of government might suggest that incumbent politicians will do almost anything to avoid a recession. At times, however, inflationary pressure may overwhelm politicians' preferences.

Curbing Aggregate Demand can lessen inflation. A mild recession might defuse inflationary pressure caused by excessive demand, but severe depressions may emerge if contractionary demand-management policies are used to combat severe supply-side inflation. If, as Figure 6 illustrates, Aggregate Supply is shifting leftward from AS_0 to AS_1 equilibrium output will fall to Q_1. But if contractionary demand-management policies are used to keep prices stable, a severe recession (or worse) will result as output falls to Q_2. Mild supply-side inflations already bear the seeds of recession.

Recessions to Discipline Labor

Labor markets tighten during economic booms caused by excessive demand, so firms must hustle to fill their labor needs. Wages begin to rise, flattening profits. Hence, prices are pushed up because many firms seem to mark up costs by a fixed percentage to set their prices, a method known as *cost-plus* (or *mark-up*) *pricing*. Labor unions become more militant, strikes for higher pay and benefits proliferate, and labor productivity falls as more workers with lower skill levels find jobs during prosperity. Labor cost per unit of output rises as this occurs, intensifying upward pressures on prices.

Some observers argue that extended prosperity may necessitate a recession to dampen inflationary expectations and "discipline labor" so that workers will work harder and accept less. Only a bout of high unemployment will bring workers' expectations about wages, fringe benefits, and other job conditions into line with the real value of their production and firms' desires for higher profits. This is a minority view, unpalatable to most economists and policymakers, but the idea contains some kernels of truth.

Among the major benefits of recessions are the opportunities afforded firms to clear out

FIGURE 6 Dampening Supply-Side Inflation with Contractionary Demand-Management Policies

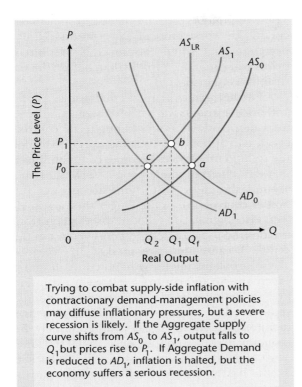

Trying to combat supply-side inflation with contractionary demand-management policies may diffuse inflationary pressures, but a severe recession is likely. If the Aggregate Supply curve shifts from AS_0 to AS_1, output falls to Q_1 but prices rise to P_1. If Aggregate Demand is reduced to AD_1, inflation is halted, but the economy suffers a serious recession.

deadwood and to boost labor productivity. Workers know that finding other jobs is more difficult during recessions and that substantial disposable income may be lost if they quit their present jobs. Therefore, they work harder and complain less. The natural long-run result of a recession is that profits rise and owners and managers of firms are again happy. The recurrence of this process led one radical economist, David Gordon, to entitle an article, "Recession Is Capitalism as Usual."

Policymakers' Abhorrence of Recessions

Engineering a recession to defuse inflation reflects desperation by nervous policymakers. Excessive unemployment makes voters irate

and can lead to changes of the guard at the White House and in Congress. Business downturns create pressures for expansionary policies that may rekindle inflationary pressures. Some radical economists view recession as capitalism's way of restoring labor market equilibrium, but policies that predictably result in recessions are pursued only reluctantly. To some degree, however, the slumps of 1969 to 1970, 1973 to 1975, 1981 to 1983, and 1990 to 1991 all resulted from such policies.

INCOMES POLICIES TO COMBAT INFLATION

Monetary and fiscal policies have been our government's favorite macroeconomic tools, followed closely by more direct forms of economic regulation.

Incomes policies include such strategies as wage and price controls, wage and price guideposts or guidelines, and presidential jawboning.

Incomes policies are designed to reduce inflationary pressures without actually changing government spending, taxing, or monetary policy. If successful, both unemployment and inflation will be less severe. A wage and price freeze is the most restrictive form of incomes policy, followed by wage and price controls, guidelines and guideposts, and, finally, jawboning.

Seven of the eleven presidents following Herbert Hoover used some form of incomes policy. Wartime wage and price controls were abandoned at the end of World War II. For roughly five years, there were no explicit controls, but the onset of the Korean War prompted President Truman to reinstate some curbs. Both sets of wartime restraints were mandatory, having the force of law. The Eisenhower era, from 1953 to 1961, was free of controls.

Guideposts were introduced under President Kennedy in 1962 and stiffened by President Johnson, who accompanied these efforts with considerable jawboning. These voluntary guideposts lost their bite as inflationary pressures mounted in the late 1960s, when both domestic spending and outlays for the Vietnam conflict escalated. President Nixon instituted full-fledged price controls, beginning with a 90-day price freeze in August 1971. In 1979, President Carter resorted to jawboning (with threatened losses of government contracts) in an attempt to make his "voluntary" wage and price guidelines more effective.

Evaluation of Incomes Policies

Incomes policies, like many other government policies, have both friends and foes. Supporters of wage-price policies point principally to their impression that market shares in many important markets in the United States are so concentrated that pricing decisions made within these "monopolistic" industries are not in the public interest. Properly administered controls presumably will make the behavior of these firms more compatible with the interests of society. Monopolistic attempts to expand profits are thought to cause price hikes that translate into supply-side inflation.

Unions or firms that dominate a market may unilaterally raise prices, fueling inflationary pressures. Many primary product industries (steel, oil, and lumber, among others) exhibit these characteristics, so their price increases tend to ripple through the economy. Proponents also argue that when the major underlying cause of continuing inflation is the inflationary expectations of workers and firms, controls can reduce both these expectations and the basic rate of inflation.

Opponents cite the 1971 to 1973 wage and price controls for evidence that controls do not work. The evidence is diagrammed in Figure 7. The rate of inflation was actually declining just prior to President Nixon's announcement of a wage-price freeze in 1971. Throughout the freeze and during Phase II, when wage and price increases were strictly controlled, the inflation rate began soaring. Inflation continued even after controls were lifted in 1973, and it took a severe recession in 1975 to 1976 to temporarily slow the inflationary spiral. Figure 7 also shows that President Carter's guidelines

had little effect on inflation in the late 1970s.

Critics have pointed to this evidence to counter the view that controls reduce the inflationary expectations of workers and businesses. These opponents contend that controls actually create the worst kind of expectation–the expectation that when the controls are lifted, prices will rise more rapidly than before the restraints were instituted.

Further, critics maintain that artificial wage and price restraints warp market signals and lead to widespread shortages. Long-term controls breed corruption in government as bribery for the right to raise prices becomes common. Black markets emerge when people seek shortcuts around shortages. Distortions are greater the tighter controls are or the longer they are in effect. Price signals to reallocate production from less desired to more desired items get lost in the shuffle because they are masked by controls. These problems might be handled by granting exceptions to the controls, but each exception precipitates numerous applications for other exceptions. The complexity of regulations and monitoring tends to escalate, and eventually the economy may be strangled by terminal red tape.

Guideline or guidepost policies unbacked by any legal muscle rely on appeals to patriotism. The battle is already lost if unions and the top managers of vital industries do not respond to the call. Most presidents have recognized this fact and have coupled voluntary controls with moral suasion, or *jawboning*. Business and labor leaders are invited to the White House for little chats about antitrust investigations, public admonition, or various forms of regulatory harassment. Such confrontations with business and labor seldom achieve more than surface compliance and public relations rhetoric. Firms commonly learn to announce even higher price hikes than they desire so that, when faced with political heat, they can roll back the prices a bit. In this way, business leaders and politicians can each claim victory.

A crucial question about incomes policies is whether such schemes, without appropriately restrictive monetary and fiscal policies, would actually solve the inflationary dilemma. An incomes policy could be seen as a panacea by pol-

FIGURE 7 Inflation During the 1971—1981 Wage-Price Controls/Guidelines

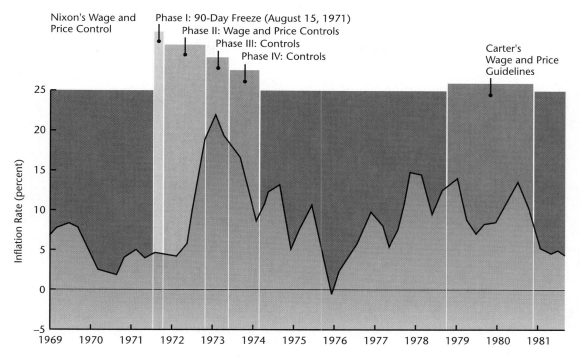

Source: *Business Conditions Digest,* January 1986.

Inflation actually increased during President Nixon's four phases of wage and price controls, and intensified, erratically, throughout the 1970s.

icymakers, who might then feel free to follow expansionary monetary or fiscal policy if that suited their whims. Incomes policies are, at best, temporarily effective when expansionary monetary and fiscal policies are pursued; incomes policies will fail to hold the economy together for any longer than the very short run.

A BRIEF EVALUATION OF POLICY RULES VS. DISCRETION

Many of the ideas in this chapter address the shortcomings of discretionary policy. Advocates of stable macroeconomic policy rules continue to mount powerful and often persuasive arguments that discretionary policies do not work as intended. But their assertions are at times contradictory. Can discretionary policies be perverse because of inefficiencies caused by lags,

incorrect doses, improper targets, or venal politicians, and simultaneously impotent because markets operate efficiently or because of rational expectations? In combination, these arguments are logically inconsistent.

Advocates of discretionary policies also offer persuasive arguments, many of which were presented in Chapters 10 through 16. At times, discretionary policies have performed as advertised. The economic boom following the 1964 tax cut is one example of successful discretionary policy. On the other hand, abysmal policy failures during the 1970s are testimony to the folly of fighting supply-side disturbances with demand-management techniques.

Whether discretionary policies or rules work better depends in part on the circumstances and on the people who control policies. However, the central questions remain: (*a*) Is the economy inherently stable, or is the market

TABLE 3   A Summary of Theories About Demand-Management Policies

	Critical Assumptions	Discretionary Monetary Policy	Discretionary Fiscal Policy	Monetary Growth Rules
Classical (Pre-Keynesian) (Policy is useless.)	Flexible wages, prices, and interest rates ensure full employment. *Supply creates its own demand.*	Only the price level is affected, and then in precise proportion to the money supply.	Irrelevant except to the extent that the size of government relative to the private sector is changed.	Might prevent price-level declines in a growing economy, but largely irrelevant. Money is a veil, not affecting real variables.
Keynesian (Policy works.)	Wages and prices are downwardly sticky but upwardly flexible. Interest rates will not fall below the level of interest in the liquidity trap. *Demand creates its own supply.*	Ineffectual in a liquidity trap. Only influences Aggregate Demand through any decreases in interest rates, causing increases in autonomous investment, which expands demand through the multiplier process.	Immediately increases Aggregate Demand via the multiplier process.	Irrelevant except to the extent that the interest rate is affected, and hence investment and Aggregate Demand are are also affected.
Post-Keynesian monetarists (Policy works, but is probably harmful.)	Keynesian analysis may to be correct for the very short run in its Aggregate Demand orientation, but classical assumptions are correct for the long run. Velocity and the demand for money are stable.	Nominal GDP will be proportional to the money supply. Discretionary policy causes business cycles. The depression was a consequence of contractionary policies; inflation is the result of overly expansionary policies.	Affects the size of government relative to the private sector and may pose problems because of political pressures to print money to cover government deficits. Otherwise, irrelevant for macroeconomics, although crowding out may be a severe problem if government spending grows. Modern supply-siders also argue that potential GDP is shrunk because of disincentives when tax rates are high.	Permits the private sector to anticipate policy and facilitates noninflationary growth without raising the possibility of contractionary policies causing severe recessions. A monetary growth rule will eliminate swings in real output because of changes in policies. Prices will rise only slightly if economic growth exceeds monetary growth.
Natural rate theory (Policy is only temporarily effective, but it is also harmful.)	There are natural rates of frictional unemployment and natural real rates of interest. Differences between natural rates and actual rates occur only when people inaccurately forecast changes in price levels.	Unemployment and real interest rates will decline below their natural rates only if people are fooled by overly expansionary policies. This can happen only in the short run; in the long run, everyone catches on.		
New classical macroeconomics (Policy does not work.)	Markets are efficient. Rational expectations theory suggests that inflationary expectations will reflect predictable changes in policies quickly.	People will not be fooled by predictable policies, even in the short run, so expansionary policies will be immediately translated into high prices and higher nominal interest rates.		

system unstable? (*b*) Can changes in spending, taxes, and monetary policies lend greater stability to a market economy, or are erratic government policies major sources of business cycles and instability? These questions cannot be answered definitively.

Just as generals are sometimes accused of always fighting the last war, economic policymakers in the 1970s used the demand-management tools that were developed to solve the demand-side problems of earlier decades. Table 3 summarizes various theories about demand-management policies and should help in organizing your thoughts about these issues.

Although the supply-side policies of the 1980s yielded mixed results, healthy economic growth depends primarily on growth of Aggregate Supply, which expands a society's production possibilities frontier. Demand-side policy plays a less important role in economic growth and development. The next chapter focuses on aspects of Aggregate Supply that enhance economic growth and development.

CHAPTER REVIEW: KEY POINTS

1. Macroeconomic policymaking is at least as much an art as it is a science. A multitude of problems preclude perfect analysis and policy.

2. A **recognition lag** occurs because it takes time to get even a modestly accurate picture of changes in the state of the economy. An **administrative** (implementation) **lag** exists because it takes time to get the tax and monetary machinery in gear even when policymakers' plans are made. An **impact lag** confounds the proper timing of policy; the economy budges only stubbornly to the prods of the policymakers' tools. These lags, which may be long and variable, may cause discretionary policy to be more destabilizing than stabilizing.

3. Lack of precise knowledge about recessionary gaps, inflationary gaps, and GDP gaps, as well as uncertainty about multipliers and velocity, means that estimating the correct doses of monetary and fiscal medicine is extremely difficult.

4. Some modern Keynesians challenge the long-term effectiveness of monetary policy, arguing that adjustments in financial technologies will ultimately **insulate financial institutions** and make monetary tools inoperative.

5. Incumbents' prospects for return to office improve as per capita disposable income grows immediately prior to elections. There is some evidence that policymakers try to manipulate Aggregate Demand to enhance their positions in the eyes of voters, which induces **political business cycles**.

6. Some critics of Keynesian fiscal policies also suggest that the government grows relative to the private sector because policymakers increase spending and cut taxes during downturns, but neither cut spending nor restore taxes during periods of prosperity or inflation.

7. *Intentional recessions* can decompress accumulated inflationary pressures and inflationary expectations. However, recessions tend to be very hard on political incumbents, so many politicians favor incomes policies of various sorts.

8. **Incomes policies** (mandatory wage-price freezes or controls, voluntary guidelines, or jawboning) muzzle the effectiveness of the price system, creating shortages and widespread misallocations of resources.

9. The more involved a country is in international trade and finance, the less will be the impact of any given monetary or fiscal policy because the effects are diffused by foreign markets.

QUESTIONS FOR THOUGHT AND DISCUSSION

1. Evaluate the proposal of granting the president discretionary power to raise or lower taxes 10% in order to overcome the administration lag that plagues fiscal policy. If there are substantial differences between this proposal and the power the Fed now has over the money supply, what are they? If such a presidential power were enacted, would the president or the Fed have more discretionary power to control economic activity? Why?

2. If you were the president and were intent on serving four more years, what actions would you take to ensure a booming economic climate around election time? What might be the longer-term consequences of your policies?

3. How might critics of discretionary policy try to reconcile the apparent contradictions between their charges that the effects of policy are (*a*) impredictable because of unstable and long lags (signs of inefficiency) and (*b*) offset because the economy is inherently efficient (e.g., rational expectations theory)? Do these contradictions in theory significantly undercut the arguments of those who advocate the replacement of discretionary policy by fixed policy rules? Why or why not?

4. Interest rates skyrocketed in late 1979, with the prime rate exceeding 20%, but they then plummeted even more rapidly than they had risen. Interest rates then soared again in 1981 but dropped afterward. From today's perspective, which parts of these violent fluctuations represented the Keynes effect, and which parts the Fisher effect?

Chapter 19

Economic Growth and Development

Identifying changes in the human condition that facilitate economic progress has challenged economists and social philosophers for centuries. Economic growth and development is a universal goal; most people expect higher standards of living than their parents enjoyed and hope for even greater prosperity for their children. Before the Industrial Revolution, however, each generation lived much as their immediate ancestors had.

Figure 1 suggests that the greatest economic growth in the near future may likely occur in the Far East and South America. Americans gain from healthy economic growth abroad because trade now links the prospects of people everywhere. For example, sluggish conditions outside our borders weaken demands for our exports. Symmetrically, when the United States rebounds from a recession, the world economy tends to recover as well. Prosperity abroad generates another benefit, due to increasing recognition that military conflict tends to impose losses on all combatants: flourishing nations are less likely to engage in military adventures—they have too much to lose.

From the 1920s into the 1960s, communist countries and countries based primarily on the market system competed intensely to see which would grow faster. The ongoing privatization of formerly communist economies attests to the relative power of the market system as an engine for economic progress. Historically, economic growth (at least our own) was regarded as unambiguously good. More recently, mounting concern about the environment and recognition that the world's resources are finite have caused many to ask, "Economic growth for what?"

ECONOMIC GROWTH

Most of us applaud trends that enrich our lives, but is economic growth invariably good? If a population explosion expanded the work force and caused GDP to grow, it might simultaneously reduce average standards of living. Do we want maximum income? Maximum income per capita? And what about the pollution that often accompanies economic growth and the way

FIGURE 1 Worldwide Economic Growth Projections

*Eastern Europe comprises Bulgaria, Czech Republic, Hungary, Poland, Romania, and Slovakia.
**Southeast Asia comprises Hong Kong, Malaysia, Singapore, South Korea, Taiwan, and Thailand.

Source: *New York Times,* January 3, 1994.

Economic growth projections for selected regions and countries for 1994 show exploding growth in Asia while most of the rest of the world struggles to ignite a recovery or to keep one going.

growth uses up stores of such nonrenewable resources as petrochemicals or valuable minerals?

How Are Economic Growth and Development Related?

People become bigger as they emerge from the shelter of the womb and proceed through infancy and childhood into adulthood. But infants differ from adults both quantitatively and qualitatively. Similarly, economies tend to mature as they grow and vice versa. Economic growth usually refers to expanded output—*quantitative* dimensions of change—while economic development refers to *qualitative* advances.

> ***Economic growth*** *enables more goods to be produced;* ***economic development*** *entails improvements in the quality of life, in the qualities of goods available, or in how production is organized.*

Describing economic progress requires both concepts. Focus 1 discusses the Rule of 72, which is a handy technique for getting a sense of how quickly quantifiable variables can grow.

Aggregate Demand, Aggregate Supply, and Economic Growth

Macroeconomic theories covered earlier identify boosting Aggregate Demand during recessions as a way to push Gross Domestic Product toward its potential. All the forces that underpin Aggregate Demand and Aggregate Supply help determine actual GDP in the short run, but in the long run, potential GDP is governed by Aggregate Supply alone. Stimulating Aggregate Demand is like administering food and medicine to a malnourished child. Just as a starving child we feed and medicate may remain developmentally impaired, so, too, short-run doses of Aggregate Demand alone

Growth and the Rule of 72

Many people are mystified by concerns about whether the economy grows at rates of 2%, 3%, 4%, or whatever the small number happens to be. Policymakers and economists worry about these small numbers because each 1% of growth represents extra production of roughly $70 billion worth of 1995 U.S. GDP—hardly small change. Because continuous growth is compounded over the years, each 1% difference in the annual growth rate would mean a total difference of over $800 billion in production between 1995

and 2005—more than $3,000 for every man, woman, and child in the United States.

Growth is a cumulative process analogous to compound interest. If you are paid 10% interest on $100 compounded annually, then at the end of the first year your $100 stake is worth $110. At the end of two years you have interest on both the principal plus the accumulated interest, so your original $100 is now $121: [(1.10 x ($100 + $10) = $121. And so on. The rule of 72 simplifies calculations that require compounding.

*The **Rule of 72** is a rule of thumb whereby the time required for any variable to double is calculated by dividing its percentage rate of growth into 72.*

This rule works because growth or decline is compounded. Thus, if the annual interest rate is 10%, financial investments will double in about 7.2 years, not 10 years. A country's population will double in 36 years if population growth is 2% annually, but it will require only 18 years to double at a 4% annual rate of increase.

cannot ensure healthy economic growth. Economic growth as an area of study addresses the long-run enlargement of Aggregate Supply and, thus, potential real GDP. In this chapter, we largely ignore adjustments to Aggregate Demand and assume that monetary and fiscal policies are set to accommodate economic growth—that is, any expansion of Aggregate Supply.

SOURCES OF ECONOMIC GROWTH

What makes the value of potential real GDP grow? Value can increase in either of two ways: (*a*) physical output can be expanded or (*b*) given outputs can become more valuable in exchange. The value in exchange of given physical outputs can rise via expanded trade according to comparative advantage, a concept discussed in Chapter 2. Potential physical output can be expanded via (*a*) increases or improvements in land—the natural resource base, (*b*) increases in the size of the population and the labor force, or in its quality, (*c*) capital accumulation, or (*d*)

technological advances. Let us examine aspects of all these sources of growth.

Land and Natural Resources

Few resources in any category (land, labor, capital, or entrepreneurship) are truly homogeneous and, thus, identically productive. Climate, the fertility of land, and the flora and fauna native to an area vary greatly around the world. Siberian tundra, for example, is quite different from rain forests in the Amazon. In some places, economic growth follows the discovery and exploitation of valuable resources—veins of minerals or pools of oil, for example. Growth also might be stimulated by more efficient use of existing land or land reclamation. However, international competition has driven down the real prices for most raw materials in recent decades, with new technologies playing increasingly important roles in international markets. These trends usually make a nation's natural resource base a weak reed upon which to hang a development strategy.

Population and Labor Force Changes

Population growth alone may not yield economic growth because the labor force drawn from a given population can vary. We will treat this relationship first and then describe the interactions between population and National Income.

• **Population and the Work Force**   Population growth expands the size of the potential work force. All else being equal, if the work force increases proportionally as population grows, per capita GDP (one measure of standards of living) will decline. Why? Additional labor reduces the capital and land per worker, so labor productivity and per capita GDP will decline. This is one more example of the law of diminishing returns rearing its ugly head.

Consider Figure 2. Production possibilities frontier PPF_1 is based on assumptions that 100 workers, 100 machines, and 1,000 acres of land can produce any combination ranging from 100 computers to 100 units of food. Suppose agriculture uses capital and land relatively more intensively, while labor is used more intensively in computer production. If all resources were exactly doubled, potential output should double. Feasible outputs are shown as the combinations along PPF_2 which is a radial expansion of (that is, it approximately parallels) PPF_1

Now suppose we held capital at 100 machines and land at 1,000 acres, but doubled labor to 200 workers. The production possibilities frontier expands from PPF_1 to PPF_3: maximum food output only grows to 160 units, and only 190 computers can be produced. The PPF does not expand to PPF_2 as labor doubles because we have not doubled land and capital inputs. Similarly, if labor were quadrupled to 400 units, diminishing returns would prevent the potential outputs of computers or food from also quadrupling. Using 400 workers, 100 machines, and 1,000 acres of land yields PPF_4 with maximums of only 205 units of food or 275 computers per month.

In a densely populated country such as India, needs for more housing, roads, and

FIGURE 2   Increasing Population and Diminishing Returns

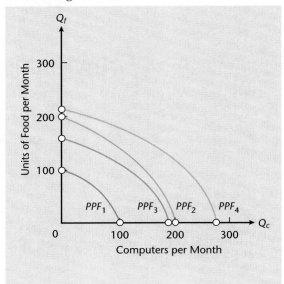

Unless all resources increase by the same proportion, the production possibilities frontier will expand unevenly and less than proportionally. PPF_2 represents a doubling of all resources and output is twice that of PPF_1, whereas PPF_3 and PPF_4 represent a doubling and quadrupling of labor, respectively, resulting in proportionally smaller increases in output. This unevenness means that population growth will tend to push standards of living down.

schools could cause standards of living to fall even if the labor force grew faster than population. Extra workers add to total output in all but the most heavily populated regions, however, so per capita GDP normally rises with increases in the ratio of the work force to a given population.

The labor force as a percentage of the population is the *labor force participation rate*. Certain social customs and mores help determine labor force participation. For example, the Protestant work ethic creates expectations that push almost 80% of all American males between the ages of 25 and 55 into the work force. Wage rates are also clearly important. High wage rates raise the cost of not working and encourage labor force participation.

Another important determinant of the work force relative to population is the rate of population growth. Variations in population growth rates may cause a society to have high proportions of young and dependent members during one decade and large numbers of old and dependent members six or seven decades later. Of course, this is only one of many possibilities.

Suppose birth rates have been falling for some time. Labor force participation rates will first rise as the number of children falls and more women are free to enter the labor force if custom permits. Then the work force will gradually decline relative to population as fewer young people enter the work force and the number of retirees rises relative to population. Finally, labor force participation will stabilize. (Can you outline some short- and long-term economic effects of the post–World War II baby boom, followed by the baby-bust of the 1970s and 1980s?)

• Population Growth and Subsistence

We indicated in Chapter 5 that some early economists viewed population growth as irresistibly depressing life toward a subsistence level. Technological advances or long periods of favorable weather for agriculture would merely result in higher wages, then population growth, and, ultimately, the misery of an even larger number of people. Reverend Thomas Malthus was the most prominent of these early theorists. In 1798, he wrote:

> I think I may fairly make two postulata. First, that food is necessary to the existence of man. Secondly, that the passion between the sexes is necessary, and will remain nearly in its present state. . . . These two laws ever since we have had any knowledge of mankind, appear to have been fixed laws of our nature. . . . Assuming, then my postulata as granted, I say that the power of population is indefinitely greater than the power in the earth to produce subsistence. . . . Population, when unchecked, increases in a geometrical ratio. . . . Subsistence only increases in an arithmetical ratio. A slight acquaintance with numbers will show the immensity of the first power in comparison of the second.[1]

---

[1]T. Malthus, *Essay on the Principle of Population*, 1st ed. (London: 1798), privately published.

Malthus meant that food output might grow in a sequence like 1, 2, 3, 4, 5, 6, ... But given enough food, space, and other necessities, human population would grow in a sequence like 1, 2, 4, 8, 16, 32, . . . (much like rabbits). Population would be kept in check, however, by disease, starvation, or war, to grow only at the same pace as food: 1, 2, 3, 4, ...

This grim theory led the historian Thomas Carlyle to label economics "the dismal science," a tag line some critics use to this day. Bare subsistence seemed inevitable to Malthus. His theory that population will constantly press against resources depends on limits he classified as *positive* (things that increase deaths) or *preventive* (things that reduce births). All these limits were seen as deriving from limited food supplies. In this way, Malthus hypothesized a physiological standard of living to regulate population, with starvation as the ultimate check.

The second edition of Malthus's *Essay on the Principle of Population* (1807) allowed habits to influence the minimal standard of living, a notion intended to explain how the laboring classes in several countries during Malthus's era lived considerably above subsistence. He nevertheless felt that almost insurmountable barriers block permanent improvement of the lot of the working classes. According to Malthus, improved conditions ultimately do not improve the average quality of life. Instead, more people will be alive, but only at subsistence levels. Malthus preached that only through sexual continence could we avoid his grim predictions, but he was so pessimistic about the prospects for worldwide chastity that, to him, a razor's edge existence for the bulk of humanity seemed inevitable.

Malthusian population theory, influential and popular for much of the nineteenth century, lost favor when scholars recognized that Malthus had underestimated the power of technological change. Modern critics of Malthus's theory point out that humans, unlike rabbits, possess the ability to innovate, altering the carrying capacity of their environment. The most pertinent technological advances include several efficient birth control techniques plus machinery and knowledge that have allowed food supplies to grow rapidly during the past century.

Prophets of doom have systematically been too pessimistic about technological advances. For example, some forecaster in 1895 might have predicted that the United States would "never sustain 250 million people because there wouldn't be enough land to pasture all the horses." Our imaginations tend to be limited by the here and now, prisoners of current technologies. Thus far, optimists who believe that technological advances will permit adequate food, clothing, and shelter for a steadily increasing world population have been correct. Little evidence supports the view that growing proportions of the world's population are doomed to a razor's edge existence.

The idea that equilibrium occurs at subsistence seems irrelevant in advanced nations. Many impoverished nations, however, maintain tradition-bound economies that lack technical progress, retarding economic growth. Explosive population growth in many developing regions regularly reawakens interest in Malthus's ideas. Widespread misery and hardship in parts of Africa, Asia, and South America seem to at least partially confirm long-term forecasts made almost 200 years ago by Malthus and his cohorts. Many emerging nations combine the worst of both worlds: the high birth rates typical of agrarian economies and the low death rates of industrialized nations.

How have most people in Western Europe, Japan, and North America escaped this fate? Their production and incomes have grown faster than their populations, which in some nations have recently seemed at a standstill. But why has population growth in highly developed societies not responded to economic growth, driving per capita income down to subsistence levels? A partial answer lies in medical advances and the availability of low-cost, effective birth control devices—a development that Malthus would have regarded as immoral. Medical improvements greatly raised the probability that children would survive to adulthood, reducing the need to have large families. In most advanced societies, children seem to be regarded as "inferior goods." That is, as per capita income rises, there is a tendency to substitute a higher standard of living and more leisure for more children, despite the fact that more children can be afforded at the higher income levels.

More critically, rapid technological advances and the accumulation of both physical and human capital have caused income in developed nations to grow more rapidly than population. Hence, although war has been all too common, few nations have had to endure the starvation and plagues that Malthus viewed as the other natural checks on population. In fact, as Table 1 indicates, population in many developed countries tends to be relatively stable or even declining, while primitive and less developed nations continue to experience explosive population growth.

SAVING, INVESTMENT, AND CAPITAL FORMATION

One path for increasing both potential real output and per capita income is expansion of the quality or quantities of the resources with which we work, primarily in the form of new capital. However, this route to the good life is not always smooth. Figure 3 shows that if we choose to con-

TABLE 1 Percentage Annual Population Growth for Selected Countries (Average Rates for 1980–1990)

Developed Countries		Less Developed Countries	
Country	Percent	Country	Percent
Austria	0.0	Algeria	3.0
Belgium	0.0	Bangladesh	2.8
Canada	1.0	Brazil	2.5
Czech Republic	0.3	China	1.3
France	0.5	Ecuador	2.9
Germany	-0.1	Ghana	3.6
Italy	0.2	Honduras	3.5
Japan	0.6	India	2.1
Norway	0.3	Iran	3.6
Sweden	0.1	Jordan	3.5
U.S.A.	1.0	Mexico	2.2
Russia	0.9	Pakistan	2.9
		Uganda	3.1
		Zambia	3.7
Average	0.3		2.9

Source: U.S. Department of Commerce, Bureau of the Census, *Statistical Abstract of the United States*, 1993.

FIGURE 3 The Effects of Consumption/Savings Choices on Economic Growth

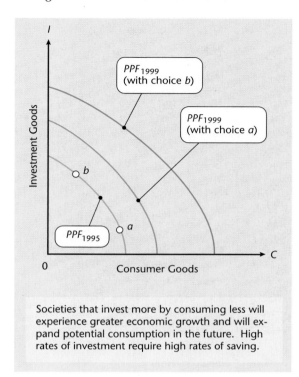

Societies that invest more by consuming less will experience greater economic growth and will expand potential consumption in the future. High rates of investment require high rates of saving.

sume much and invest little of our National Income (point *a* on *PPF*$_{1995}$), economic growth will proceed slowly. On the other hand, if our society chooses to sacrifice substantial potential consumption (point *b*), we can produce and consume at higher levels in the future because of the extra capital accumulation that lower current consumption permits.

Figure 4 shows how growth rates of investment and per capita GDP are related. Higher rates of gross domestic investment seem to be directly related to economic growth. While other factors are important, investment is critical to expanding output.

The share of National Output devoted to capital goods instead of consumer goods may reflect only individual decisions, or it may result from governmental action. When this decision is left to individuals, there is *voluntary saving*. When governments follow policies that force consumption down to allow capital accumulation, the process is *involuntary saving*.

Voluntary Saving

The act of saving can be viewed as a decision to delay consumption. Just what factors influence the choice between consuming now and postponing consumption so that we can enjoy more later? Although there are a number of considerations, two major influences on individuals consumption versus saving choices are the interest rates paid to savers and the level of income. A third important influence may be the distribution of income.

• **Interest Rates** The Keynesian Revolution ushered in a deemphasis on interest rates as primary determinants of saving, suggesting instead that income governs decisions to save. However, there has been a resurgence in the classical belief that the interest rate paid savers is critical for decisions about saving and investment. The argument runs along the following lines.

Increases in the interest rate paid to savers (who are the ultimate lenders) raise the relative price of consumption today versus consumption tomorrow. Thus, higher interest rates cause people to postpone consumption. Higher interest rates also discourage people who are marginal borrowers and who would use their borrowings for consumer purchases. This means that the quantity of funds supplied to investors will grow as interest rates rise, facilitating investment.

Must higher interest rates paid to savers discourage investment? Not necessarily. After-tax interest income is the concern of savers, and high after-tax rates of return are the goals of investors. A variety of government policies can be manipulated so that the net interest rates received by savers rise, while interest costs to investors fall. Most presidents have supported some preferential tax treatment on investment income. There is, however, an ongoing debate among economists over the effectiveness of such tax preferences.

In Figure 5, initial equilibrium for investment (curve I_0) and saving (S_0) results in savers receiving and investors paying a taxable 8% interest rate on $50 billion in loanable funds. Tax breaks for both savers and investors could boost

FIGURE 4 The Relationship Between Investment Growth Rates and Changes in GDP Per Capita (Selected Countries)

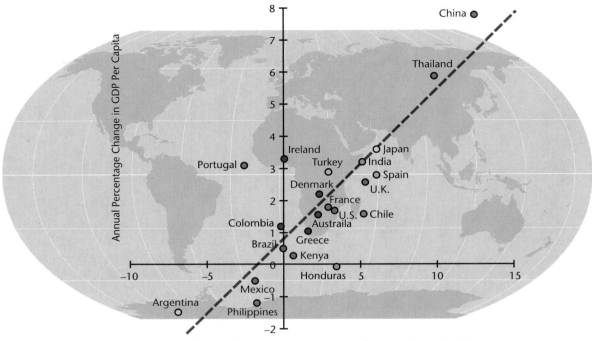

Source: World Bank, *World Development Report 1992: Investing in Health* (Oxford: Oxford University Press), 1993.
This figure compares the growth rates of Gross Domestic Investment with growth rates in per capita GDP for 22 countries, developed and developing. The data suggests there is a solid positive correlation between investment and economic growth.

the demand for investment goods to I_1 while increasing saving from S_0 to S_1—if savers view an untaxed 6% interest rate (on S_1) as equal to a taxed 10% (on S_0). If interest is exempted from taxes and taxes on capital gains are cut, investors have $90 billion available to invest at annual interest costs to them of 8%.

Other policies to increase both after-tax interest paid to savers and after-tax rates of return to investors include cuts in marginal tax rates, rapid depreciation allowances, investment tax credits, or expanded eligibility for Individual Retirement Accounts (IRAs). Direct government subsidies to investors could also automatically reward savers as the demand for investment grew. But critics of these policies argue that such incentives often distort investment incentives and may channel funds to less productive sectors.

Legislation recently proposed in the Congress would replace income taxes with taxes on consumption; savings would be deducted from taxable income under this proposal. Taxes on consumption rather than income would stimulate saving and facilitate investment.

• **Income** In a Keynesian model, income (Y) largely determines saving (S). The relationship between the average propensity to save (S/Y) and income is one barrier that can limit growth in impoverished countries. If you are poor, you may be forced to either consume at low levels forever or to slash already low consumption now as a way to finance investments with future payoffs. Investing in your education entailed a similar choice; you probably could consume much

FIGURE 5 Saving, Investment, and Interest Rates

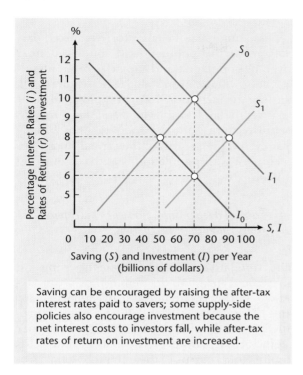

Saving (S) and Investment (I) per Year
(billions of dollars)

Saving can be encouraged by raising the after-tax interest rates paid to savers; some supply-side policies also encourage investment because the net interest costs to investors fall, while after-tax rates of return on investment are increased.

more now if you were not in school. This saving versus consumption dilemma is less of a hardship for wealthy people and countries. Widespread poverty, on the other hand, inhibits saving and capital accumulation.

• **Inequality** Impoverished countries tend to have less-equal income distributions than more developed nations. One way to accumulate capital is to rely on high saving rates by the wealthy and to hope that current deprivation of the masses will pay off in higher incomes for future generations. This idea is called the *trickle-down theory*. However, the wealthy may not save in ways that foster domestic growth. Instead, they might buy foreign stocks or bonds or consume imported luxury goods. Foes of income redistribution programs often assert that saving and investment will fall if money is transferred from the rich to the poor. They argue that recent declines in American saving relative to GDP are consequences of rapid expansion of social programs.

Involuntary Saving

Governments do have some alternatives to voluntary saving if, for whatever reasons, they view voluntary saving and investment as inadequate for the desired growth rate. The trick is to divert more of total output into the production of new capital goods by forcing consumption down.

• **Central Planning and Forced Saving** The Marxist term *surplus value* refers to gaps between what workers are paid and the average value of their total output. Marxists contend that capitalists exploit workers by seizing surplus values. It is ironic that Marxist societies have been extraordinarily exploitative. Government sets wages and prices in a centrally planned economy. Under Soviet five-year plans initiated in 1929 and used until 1990, low wages were set relative to individual output, while prices for most nonessential consumer goods were kept artificially high. Holding consumption far below production forced people to "save." The USSR rapidly attained the status of a world power.

Forced saving is intended to foster rapid growth, but we now know that growth in the USSR was actually slower than in most countries that rely most heavily on private saving and investment. The apparent evolution (based largely on bloated statistics) of the Soviet Union from sleeping giant to world power from 1930 to 1970 persuaded leaders of many underdeveloped countries to adopt the Soviet model. The result? Their countries suffered a double whammy: slow growth *and* the inefficiency inherent in central planning. A low wage–high price strategy under central planning is just one way a government can acquire resources to use for capital accumulation. "Land reform" programs are another: large estates are consolidated into collective farms or allocated to peasants. Revolutionary governments also nationalize the factories or financial assets of deposed elites as sources of "social" capital accumulation.

The transition of Eastern Europe from central planning toward heavier reliance on market forces has resulted initially in less forced saving with high unemployment and reduced productivity. Central planning used coercion to enforce productivity, but these pressures eventually faced diminishing returns: productivity, incomes, and standards of living collapsed. Moving to a market-oriented economy may require decades to develop the social institutions of private property and other market mechanisms. The turmoil of transition delays possible benefits from capitalist markets. Although forced-saving strategies in Eastern Europe had mixed results, other ways to force higher saving exist in democratic, market-oriented economies: inflation and taxation.

• **Inflation** A government can issue contracts for schools, highways, or industrial facilities and then pay its contractors with freshly printed money. If the economy is initially at full employment, inflation will crowd out private consumption. This has been a popular strategy to force saving, most notably in South America. For example, from the 1950s through the 1970s, Brazil experienced high rates of real economic growth despite high inflation. The Brazilian economy faltered, however, in the 1980s, in part because its enormous foreign debt was stated in terms of foreign, not Brazilian, currency. A series of governments have alternatively tried to stimulate the Brazilian economy and to halt the momentum of past inflationary policies, but, through 1994, Brazil continued to be plagued by a mix of recession and hyperinflation.

• **Taxation** High tax rates may also be used to reduce private purchasing power and consumption and to increase government investment. But the Laffer curve identifies a danger that very high tax rates may result in such severe disincentives for work effort and private investment that GDP falls so much that tax revenues shrink.

Capital Widening and Deepening

The rate at which the capital stock grows is crucial for economic growth and determines the relative capital-labor mix in the economy.

Capital widening occurs if the capital stock grows, but only at or below the percentage growth rate of the labor force.

Let us assume that the labor force is a fixed percentage of the population. Capital widening (even if, population and capital grow at identical rates) will not even stabilize per capita GDP, because the increased doses of capital and labor relative to land result in *diminishing returns*. Because land resources cannot grow, it is likely that even if the growth of the capital stock does keep pace with population, standards of living will fall.

Capital deepening occurs when the capital stock grows faster than population.

The cumulative effect of high rates of saving and investment (capital deepening) over an extended period is a higher ratio of capital to labor (the K/L ratio). This tends to raise labor productivity and yields higher levels of real per capita income. However, the fixity of land yields diminishing returns in the enhanced labor productivity that occurs as the capital stock grows. Thus, the higher a country's capital-to-labor ratio, the harder it is to use new **capital formation** as a source of additional economic growth.

Growth rates recently slowed for the "four tigers," Hong Kong, Taiwan, Singapore, and South Korea, where double-digit growth had been based on the simple formula of labor-intensive exports. But wage rates climbed faster than productivity as these economies grew. Slower growth caused policymakers in all four countries to try to expand their capital-to-labor ratios by channeling investment into capital-intensive, high-tech industries during 1985 through 1993. Singapore and South Korea tried tax breaks, credits for private groups, public works projects, and higher wage floors to discourage labor-intensive investment. The results were disappointing. Capital deepening failed to generate growth rates exceeding those in Hong Kong and Taiwan, whose governments decided to do nothing to make one industry more attractive than another.

The preceding analysis suggests that even though rich countries with high capital-to-labor ratios may find it easier than poor countries to finance capital accumulation through saving, capital deepening is less likely to foster growth in rich countries than in poor ones. It is crucial, however, that saving be channeled to the most productive investments—a task that seems to be done better by financial markets than by government planners. Nevertheless, many analysts who recognize that U.S. growth rates may have been lower than those experienced in parts of Western Europe and along the Pacific Rim (Taiwan, South Korea, Singapore, Hong Kong, Japan, and parts of China) predict that growth rates elsewhere in the world will slow down as other countries attain our levels of per capita GDP.

In summary, saving to facilitate capital formation can be voluntary, or governments can use various tactics to compel greater saving. Voluntary saving is encouraged by attractive interest rates and high per capita income. Centrally planned economies can force consumption below production, thus creating forced savings. Several Pacific Rim countries have recently discovered that as a country's capital-to-labor ratio grows, the generation of further growth through capital deepening faces diminishing returns.

Finally, critics of the traditional capital formation → development sequence point out that more capital may not help for several reasons. First, housing construction typically absorbs a sizable chunk of total investment (roughly 30% in the United States from 1980 to 1990). This spending, critics argue, should be classified as spending on consumer durables. Second, much investment is often public investment for social or political reasons, and rates of return may be quite low. Investment that yields excess capacity and underutilization of plants and equipment is especially useless. For example, the British steel industry spent huge sums on plant modernization in the 1970s. But their new plants were consistently underutilized and therefore added little to National Income. (After Prime Minister Thatcher sold these plants to private owners in the 1980s, the British steel industry recovered somewhat.) These critics

argue that real long-term economic growth is the result of technological advances, changes in habits, and advances in education. We will now examine one widely accepted ingredient of growth: technological change.

Technological Advances

Given amounts of resources, if used efficiently, will produce specific levels of output over a stated time interval. At a later time it may be possible to produce more output with the same resources. This is not magic.

> *Technological change* is the process that permits us to produce more from a given resource bundle, or the same output with fewer resources.

Subcategories of technological change include (*a*) greater efficiency in market processes, (*b*) improved knowledge about how to combine resources, (*c*) totally new production processes, (*d*) improvements in the qualities of human and nonhuman resources, and (*e*) new inventions and innovations (the creation of new products). The idea of *progress* is inextricably tied to technological advances.

Technological change can be viewed in two ways. In one sense it is embodied in new forms of capital; in another, technical changes or innovations encourage substantial investment and thus increase the capital stock. The emergence of money, electricity, automobiles, supermarkets, and computer chips are examples. Joseph Schumpeter saw major technological breakthroughs as avenues for increased profits for capitalists and as the major source of progress for society. Potential roles for government in fostering technological advances are discussed in Focus 2.

Technological change can be stimulated by research and development. Innovative entrepreneurs such as Thomas Edison, Alexander Graham Bell, and Henry Ford were responsible for much of the early technological progress in the United States. Government can foster technological advances by directly funding research and development projects or through tax incentives to innovators. Less developed countries may stimulate growth and progress by importing

Can Government Stimulate Technology?

A few creative people invent things just because they like to tinker, but most inventors want to make a living from their endeavors. Marketing any new good or innovating a new technology for an existing good is both risky and costly. Firms that market innovative products or technologies tend to be controlled by profit-seeking owners. Thus, bigger incentives (in the form of potentially higher income) may prompt more rapid innovation.

Why should government attempt to foster innovation? Primarily because the potential gain to society generally exceeds the potential private gain (profit) to the innovator. For example, a cure for cancer, however profitable, could not generate profit for its discoverer as large as the benefits to society from such a discovery.

Consequently, the government grants patents for some types of inventions. In the United States, a patent gives its holder a limited monopoly on the innovation for a period of 17 years and can be renewed once. Competitors are legally barred from making and selling precise duplicates of the good or manufacturing process. But some competitors may infringe on important patents—especially in countries with weak patent enforcement. And other competitors quickly try to clone successful ideas, skirting infringement by producing close—but not precise—substitutes for the innovation. This competition reduces prices and may spur further innovations by copycats, but it is also a disincentive for major inventions, especially those requiring heavy doses of expensive research and development.

Another possible shortcoming of our patent system is that ideas per se are not patentable. Suppose you

awoke tomorrow morning with an incredible idea that required $100,00 for conversion into a commercial product. If potential competitors who saw your product could then immediately "reverse engineer" your idea for $50,000 and implement it into a nonidentical but equivalent product, would you spend time and money developing it? No way! Ideas that cannot be translated into a reasonably unique product are unlikely to be pursued if cloning of the product's function is simple.

Finally, such intellectual properties as computer software are only weakly guarded by copyright laws originally intended to protect the rights of writers and composers. (Pirated software is even more common than the pirating of music tapes and CDs.) Court cases have established that software with a similar "look and feel" does not necessarily violate an original developer's rights. For example, Apple Computer has repeatedly sued on the grounds that Microsoft's Windows program mimics the Apple Macintosh interface. And Intel has sued the AMD Corporation for allegedly duplicating codes embedded in its 486 computer chip. However, the courts rarely have found for the plaintiffs in such cases.

What can government do? Recent international treaties have been negotiated (the Uruguay round of the General Agreement on Tariffs and Trade, or GATT) to make copyright and patent protection more uniform globally. With the aim of stimulating innovation, Congress has reformed some laws to better protect developers of intellectual property. But there is a trade-off: tighter protection may stymie other innovators who want to improve patented products and

processes in especially dynamic industries (e.g., microprocessors, and multimedia software for communications, entertainment, and education).

Subsidies for science education and tax breaks for private spending on research and development (R&D) are other ways to encourage new technology. Or government can directly fund basic R&D intended to broadly expand human knowledge, but focused on ideas and concepts unlikely to be patentable. Most of such government funding is now awarded to non-profit institutions and universities. However, researchers often lack the inclination or incentive to translate their basic research findings into practical products or processes—or to transmit this knowledge to those who would do so. This is why regulatory strings are gradually being loosened to allow their institutions, or the researchers themselves, to spin off for-profit enterprises or to license their practical findings to business firms.

Some observers want government to identify particular firms or target industries that seem most likely to develop new products or production technologies. Tax breaks, federal subsidies, and protection from import competition are among the strategies that have been advocated to foster growth in target industries. But critics fear that this approach would merely generate intense lobbying for classification as a target industry. (Wool growers and beekeepers secured subsidies for their outputs as "vital to the national defense" during the Cold War in the 1950s, and they still receive subsidies in the mid-1990s.)

new technologies. Another possibility is to import capital goods from more advanced countries.

The sources of U.S. economic growth are shown in Table 2 for the past six decades. Edward Denison and Dale Jorgenson both found that roughly 40% of our long-term economic growth is tied to greater quantity and quality of the labor force. The remainder is related to capital growth and improved technologies that enhance productivity.

One interesting point shown in Table 2 is the reduction in growth between 1973 and the early 1980s. During this period, labor and capital as a source of economic growth continued at roughly the same pace as previously, but the growth of productivity actually was negative.

Several reasons have been offered to explain the slowdown in productivity growth. First, the OPEC price increases in 1973 resulted in a sharp reduction in energy usage by American business. This reduced the amount business could produce with existing capital and labor, thereby reducing productivity.

Second, beginning in the early 1970s, America placed added emphasis on a cleaner environment and workplace safety. Extensive regulations aimed at improving both areas significantly reduced productivity as investment was channeled from producing goods to improving environmental emissions and reducing workplace accidents.

Third, some economists have argued that the rate of technological progress may have reached diminished returns. They argue that the early postwar years were unusual in that the depression and World War II prevented business from exploiting many technological breakthroughs. A burst in innovation followed World War II, gradually slowing down as time passed. Others have pointed out that we cannot expect innovation to proceed at a steady pace. Innovation and invention arrive in clumps, possibly feeding on each other. Today, research and development on genetics and microchips may result in another burst of innovation.

A slightly different method of securing technology is followed by countries that send some of their most promising young people to more advanced countries to study at colleges and universities. This is one popular way to build the foundations for economic growth.

Social Foundations: The Infrastructure

The path to economic growth in some societies rests on rich lodes of natural resources. The world beats paths to the doors of oil-rich sheikdoms and

TABLE 2   Sources of Economic Growth

	Denison 1929–82		Jorgenson 1947–85		Denison 1973–82		Jorgenson 1973–79	
	Annual Percent	Percent of Total	Annual Percent	Percent of Total	Annual Percent	Percent of Total	Annual Percent	Percent of Total
Labor	1.34	46	1.12	34	1.13	73	1.39	66
Capital	0.56	19	1.45	44	0.69	45	1.40	66
Productivity	1.02	35	0.75	22	–0.27	–17	–0.67	–32
Total Capital & Productivity	1.58	54	2.20	66	0.42	28	0.73	34
Total Economic Growth	2.92	100	3.28	100	1.55	100	2.12	100

Sources: Edward F. Denison, *Trends in American Economic Growth*, 1929–1982, (Washington, D.C.: The Brookings Institution, 1985), Table 8.1, p. 111; and Dale W. Jorgenson, "Productivity and Economic Growth," Harvard Institute of Economic Research discussion paper no. 1487, June 1990, Table 1. These issues are discussed in detail in Andrew B. Abel and Ben S. Bernanke, *Macroeconomics* (Reading, MA: Addison-Wesley Publishing Company, 1992), pp. 282–291.

mineral-rich countries, strewing left and right money that can be used as developmental seed money. Other primitive economies have tougher rows to hoe—they must build the foundations of economic development carefully.

*The **social overhead capital** or **infrastructure** of a country includes institutions such as a modern legal system to enforce contracts and property rights, a well-organized financial system, efficient communication and transportation networks, and a well-educated and disciplined work force.*

Economic prosperity requires a sophisticated financial system. If the financial system is not well organized, existing firms and industries must rely on internally generated funds (retained earnings) or on foreign sources to finance capital expansion. The same is true for other types of social overhead capital such as communication and transportation networks. Many firms need channels to sell their products nationwide or worldwide because, over some range of output, average production costs fall as output increases for virtually all production processes. Primitive communication and transport systems can prevent firms from exploiting these declining costs.

Finally, no country can experience significant industrialization without a skilled labor force. This requires the availability of a wide range of educational opportunities so that people can hone their skills in accord with their innate abilities, as well as reasonable access to health care. Thus, a nation must set high priorities in the areas of health and education if its economy is to sustain a high level of growth. Edward Denison, attributes nearly 20% of U.S. growth between 1929 and 1982 to improved education.[2]

For all of these reasons, the Clinton administration targeted four main areas to increase American economic growth. First, it proposed a reemployment act that brought job training, job placement, and jobless benefit programs under one roof. Second, the administra-

tion lent its support to the development of an information superhighway to expand and enhance communications throughout our economy. Third, President Clinton made health care reform with universal access a top priority. Finally, the Clinton administration pressed forward to pass the North American Free Trade Agreement (NAFTA), negotiated an expanded General Agreement on Trade and Tariffs (GATT) agreement, and has pressured other countries (most notably Japan) to open its markets to American manufacturers.

DEVELOPMENT AND THE UNFOLDING OF HISTORY

Many historians and social philosophers have attempted to chart the progress of civilizations in broader terms than we have been discussing. Economic events often play central roles on the stage of history. Are there long-term patterns of growth and development common to the economic advances of all societies? Many observers believe so. Does growth ultimately bring stagnation? Most of us hope not, but some students of civilization believe it does.

Economic Development According to Marx

One of the most influential thinkers of the last century was Karl Marx, who suggested an unabated course of progress and development. (Optimists about the prospects for humankind are increasingly convinced that he was wrong about the specifics.) Marx's prognosis was that every society goes through six major stages of history, culminating in an ideal state.

1. *Prehistory*. Prior to the dawn of civilization, humankind consisted largely of self-sufficient but nomadic hunter-gatherers. Gradually, these random groups evolved into
2. *Primitive culture*. Extended families and tribes emerged during this period. Agriculture began to bind small groups to

---

[2]Edward F. Denison, *Trends in American Economic Growth, 1929–1982* (Washington, D.C.: The Brookings Institution, 1985), p. 30.

BIOGRAPHY

Karl Marx: Revolutionary Socialism

Marx was a genius . . . the rest of us were talented at best.

Friedrich Engels

The ideas of Karl Marx (1818–1883) have had a larger impact on the twentieth century than those of virtually any other social philosopher, indelibly marking several academic disciplines including philosophy, psychology, history, and economics. Nevertheless, his major work, *Das Kapital*, must be seen for what he meant it to be: a critique of capitalism. Although Marx's was clearly the dominant contribution, virtually all his work was done in collaboration with his friend, Friedrich Engels. Curiously, Engels lived comfortably on his income from owning and managing a factory.

Scholars disagree on the extent to which events in Marx's life colored his thoughts on society, but two characteristics of his personality and experience are prominent. One is that adversity often came his way. For example, although Marx earned a Ph.D. in philosophy from the University of Jena, no university would hire him. His inflammatory rhetoric and alliances with radicals deprived him of a

stable income and led to his expulsion from Germany. Exile was to play an important role in his life. Later, Marx was also expelled by the governments of Belgium and France.

His family finally settled in England, which was far too tolerant of individual freedom to expel him. Marx sporadically eked out a living as a journalist, serving a short stint as a foreign correspondent to the *New York Herald-Tribune*. (Would the course of history have been altered if the newspaper had ever given him a raise?) Had it not been for occasional doles from Engels, the entire Marx household might have starved. As it was, they were destitute.

Another aspect of Marx's personality was ambivalence, which may have originated with his parents' conversion to Christianity from Judaism, more for social convenience than from conviction. During adulthood, his dual commitments to political action and scholarly understanding were often in conflict. Marx's scholarly passions frequently interfered with his political activism, while his political zeal crept into his writing.

Consequently, partisan outbursts and scathing condemnations of class interests permeated all his scholarly works.

Despite his internal turmoil, or perhaps because of it, Marx left a lasting mark on the world. His ambitious attempt to synthesize all social knowledge since Aristotle was intended to extend understanding of the conditions of human development so that the movement to higher stages of development might be accelerated. His vision of this ultimate society, dimly sketched, was that of a communist system based on rational planning, cooperative production, and equality of distribution. Above all, it was to be a society freed from all political and bureaucratic hierarchies.

Those societies that we call Marxist today score very poorly on this last point, but for Marx the "withering away of the state" was critical. Perhaps the tendency of his followers to compromise on this matter was what led Marx to allegedly declare on his deathbed, "I am not a Marxist."

---

specific territories, but animal herding and hunting continued to be important. As claims to exclusive territories became more extensive, some families were more successful than others in establishing their rights to land, resulting in a system known as

3. *Feudalism.* The offspring of successful warlords became wealthy landholders, who were titled but most of whom owed their

ability to protect their turf to a king. Kings typically extracted "protection" tributes from lesser wealthy landowners; however, the actual production on the manors held by these minor lords was done by peasants, who owned no land and paid a share of their crops to the titled landowners. (The sharecropping system continues to this day in many regions.) This chain of exploitation governed the social and economic behavior of all members of society from the highest-born prince to the humblest peasant. Industrialization and the gradual evolution of shopkeepers into powerful merchants slowly eroded the powers of feudal royalty, although some merchants and feudal lords became industrial magnates during the transition to

4. *Capitalism*. The Industrial Revolution and growth in commerce were facilitated by urbanization. Dispossessed peasants streamed into the cities. They owned no resources except their own labor because their income was held at subsistence levels. According to Marx, capitalists accumulated enormous wealth during this period through the expropriation of a surplus value equal to the difference between the total value of production and the subsistence wages paid to workers. In Marxist jargon, all rents, interest payments, and profits are surplus values. Marx predicted that ever-growing disparities between the wealth of capitalists and the impoverishment of labor would generate class conflict and the triumph of a workers' revolution. The successful revolution would lead to a transition period called the

5. *Dictatorship of the proletariat*. During this period, all basic industries and productive resources would be nationalized, which means that revolutionary governments would seize them from capitalists and hold them in trust for the workers, or proletariat. Each worker would receive compensation only for his or her own production to ensure an absence of capitalistic exploitation. There would be a highly progressive income tax and a confiscatory inheritance tax. Gradually, all material wants would be satisfied, and the need for government would fade, leading to the ultimate state of

6. *Communism*, or *socialism*. In this highest stage of economic development, basic human needs and wants would be met according to the Marxist principle, "From each according to his ability to produce, to each according to need." And everyone would live happily ever after.

Turmoil and the overthrow of Marxist dictators in Eastern Europe and the increasing adoption of market-based development strategies indicate that Marx's theories, however plausible in the minds of many people, simply did not work.

Stages of Economic Growth

There have been many non-Marxist theories of the stages of economic development. Among the most noteworthy is one offered by Walt W. Rostow, who is concerned with transitions from a primitive economy to a fully developed and mature industrial economy. Rostow identifies certain stages on the path of growth and development to economic maturity:

1. *Traditional society*. Traditional societies are based on agrarian economies that employ primitive technology.
2. *Preconditions for growth*. The traditional economy begins to change, with rapid increases in agricultural productivity. Growing agricultural surpluses free workers for industry and allow investment in capital goods. At this point, entrepreneurship begins to blossom.
3. *Takeoff*. High saving rates during this period permit rapid expansion of productive capacity.
4. *Drive to maturity*. Output and income from industrialization grow rapidly.
5. *High mass consumption*. During this stage, services become very important, and consumer goods are widely available for all members of society.

Marxist and non-Marxist models are similarly abstract in failing to provide clear guidelines for initiating and then sustaining economic development. Many less developed countries seem caught in an almost insurmountable maze of problems.

Nevertheless, less developed countries are increasingly adopting decentralized markets as the surest mechanisms to achieve healthy growth. Decentralization, the privatization of

Economic Development and Political Freedom

For the past century or so, the most prosperous nations on earth have also been among the most democratic; people in England, the United States, and in recent decades, Japan and much of Western Europe have enjoyed political freedom denied most people elsewhere. Many analysts, including such prominent advocates of capitalism as Milton Friedman, contend that prosperity, the market system, and political democracy go hand in hand: political freedom promotes capitalism, the market system promotes prosperity, and prosperity promotes freedom, in an endless loop.

In the past two decades, however, rapid growth has occurred in many countries that have been far from democratic: Singapore, South Korea, Indonesia, Chile, and, most notably, China (since 1980) have grown at incredible rates. Some recent studies by, among others, Robert Barro, have found negative correlations between political freedom in less developed nations and their respective growth rates. Should we conclude, as authors of some studies have, that political freedom may actually be a barrier to growth and that some cultures program people so that a majority may favor a dictatorship if it offers economic security and prosperity? For example, does a tradition of Confucianism and their recent experience with Maoist Marxism predispose the people of China to

blend the market system they are adopting with a political dictatorship?

The notion that political freedom may inhibit growth goes something like this: a country ruled by a dictatorship can grow rapidly by compelling people to work, and their efforts will not be diverted into concerns about politics and elections, or redistributions of income, for example. Democratic reforms in less developed nations, on the other hand, too often spin out of control into disagreements, and sometimes civil wars, over the issue of political governance. Russian nationalists, for example, limited the ability of the government of Boris Yeltsin to focus on economic reform during 1991 to 1994. Similarly, India, the world's most populous democracy, has been embroiled in conflicts between Hindus, Muslims, Tamils, and Sikhs since India became independent from Britain in 1946.

According to this perspective, a dictatorship can focus on the task of economic growth by minimizing battles about which ethnic or religious group will control the government. If the group in power has a clear vision that private markets will work, it can unilaterally restructure regulations to favor private business interests and cut deals with foreign firms, thereby creating a favorable environment for growth. China, for example, has enjoyed double-digit annual

growth, primarily because Deng Xiaoping has not relinquished the power of the Communist Party in China. Instead, the policies of the Communist Party became more favorable to markets. This is in contrast to the experience of the former USSR, where the emphasis on political reform under Premier Gorbachev during 1985 to 1991 led to the breakdown of the Soviet Union and may have delayed the process of economic reform.

The advocates of the more conventional view that political democracy is vital for a market system, and vice versa, respond that, indeed, you can force enslaved people to work very hard for short periods, but this strategy cannot sustain economic development in the long run. People who are free will be more interested in their personal economic prospects than people who are not free. Moreover, free markets can set the groundwork for political freedom. A dictatorship may set the forces of development in motion, but after people feel that their access to food, clothing, and shelter are secure, they will demand political freedom. In a sense, political freedom, like environmental quality, may be related to income: the higher per capita income is, the more insistent people are that government be democratic and that the environment be relatively clean.

major industries, and deregulation are seen as keys for development in countries ranging from South America to Eastern Europe to Mexico to India. There is continuing debate, however, about how capitalist-style economic freedom

and political democracy are related. Does economic freedom promote the adoption of democratic institutions? Does political freedom facilitate economic growth, or does it inhibit growth? Focus 3 examines these issues.

PROBLEMS OF DEVELOPING NATIONS

Some underdeveloped countries may be caught in what has been called the *trap of underdevelopment*. For these countries, the prospects for curing poverty appear dismal, with most families living on the razor's edge of subsistence. The trap of underdevelopment is illustrated in Figure 6.

The Trap of Underdevelopment

Less developed countries typically experience high rates of population growth that result in low per capita income. Meager incomes leave families so little extra that saving per worker is

very low, resulting in low national capital-to-labor ratios. Further, low-income families spend most of their earnings on rather primitive products. Finally, low saving rates and little capital per worker cause productivity to be stagnant. This again translates into poor wages and, thus, low per capita income. No matter where you begin in Figure 6, the story is the same. How do countries escape from this vicious circle of poverty?

Breaking the Bonds of Underdevelopment

Impediments to development include (*a*) explosive population growth and lack of education and job skills, (*b*) little capital per worker, (*c*)

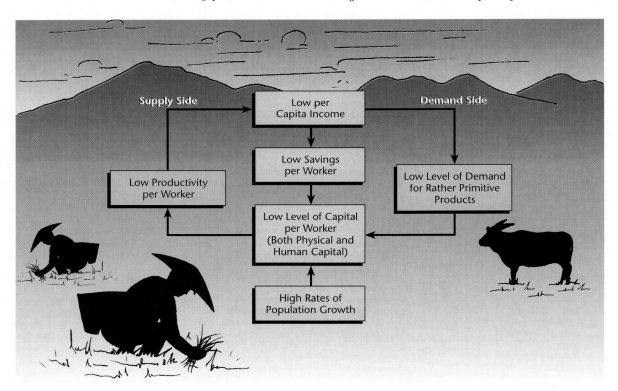

In many less developed countries, high rates of population growth lead to little physical or human capital per worker, which results in low productivity and income, which leads to low levels of saving and Aggregate Demand. This in turn leads to little capital per worker, and so on. Such a cycle makes it extremely difficult for primitive economies to escape the trap of underdevelopment and achieve economic growth.

FIGURE 6 The Trap of Underdevelopment

primitive technology, (d) cultural norms that are hostile to commercial ventures, (e) few domestic natural resources, and (f) unstable political systems. How can countries suffering from such barriers break the bonds of underdevelopment?

Economic development does not happen overnight, but less developed countries (LDCs) can do several things to facilitate development. They can eliminate government impediments to business activity, encourage the adoption of modern agricultural technology, improve the country's infrastructure so that the labor force can use modern agricultural and industrial technologies efficiently, and institute policies to reduce population growth and increase saving.

This is a tall order for any country. Consider the task of reducing population growth. "Free" birth control programs are barely more successful than exhorting people to abstain from sex. Many people in underdeveloped lands view children as old-age insurance and measure their own success by how many of their children attain adulthood. Better medical care or increases in National Income are quickly translated into population growth. For example, a population explosion followed major discoveries of oil and other natural resources in Mexico. Some countries consider population growth to be such a dire problem that they resort to involuntary programs. Indira Gandhi's government in India lost power for a period in the 1970s when her younger son, Sanjay, directed the army to grab men off the streets in rural areas and sterilize them. In 1981, China passed laws limiting rural couples to two children, while urban couples were prohibited from having more than one child. Press releases periodically reveal that thousands of infant girls have been killed by Chinese parents who want male children. This is further evidence that government policies may have unforeseen and undesirable (or even tragic) side effects and that devising policies to accomplish growth and development may be an overwhelming task.

The effect of policies that can trigger development is diagrammed in Figure 7—reducing population growth, increasing capital per worker, and implementing improved technology all produce self-reinforcing benefits. As per capita incomes rise, saving per worker and consumer demands for new and improved products also rise. As more capital per worker is acquired, worker productivity will rise, resulting in greater wages and income. The circle begins again, this time for the better. It can be quite difficult, however, for any country to begin the development process on its own. Start-up capital often comes from foreign, more highly developed countries.

Is There Really a Trap of Underdevelopment?

The vicious circle of underdevelopment suggests that breaking the bonds of poverty requires domestic sacrifices supplemented by aid from abroad. Growth may depend on the rate of capital formation (investment), which in turn is a function of saving, which is determined by income. Low income levels prevent the saving necessary for sufficient investment to fuel economic growth. Critics of the trap of underdevelopment thesis point out that it is refuted by the very existence of developed countries. These countries all started out poor with low levels of capital; if the vicious circle of poverty thesis were true, developed countries would not exist today.

For example, in the early 1800s Hong Kong was a barren rock; by 1900 it was a substantial port. Hong Kong has little land and may be the most densely populated country on earth. It has few natural resources and must import most of its raw materials. Today, Hong Kong is a major manufacturing, trading, and banking center. In fact, the Hong Kong experience is so successful that India is in the process of turning its Andaman Islands in the Bay of Bengal into a free port and huge export processing zone. And deregulation of the Indian economy is making India a rival to China, the world's most important developing economy. Critics ask, "How can all of this be true if the trap of underdevelopment thesis is true?"

Critics of this thesis further argue that development is based on factors other than natural resources, capital accumulation, and reduced population growth. They argue that

FIGURE 7 Breaking the Bonds of Underdevelopment

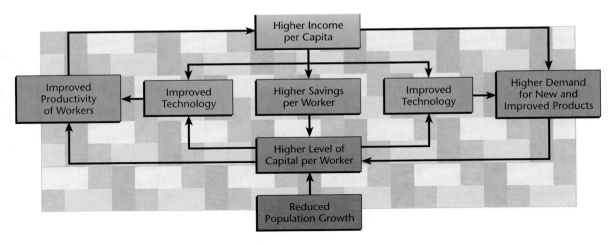

Facilitating advancement in developing nations may require reducing population growth, improving technology, and increasing the saving rate—all very difficult tasks.

successful development hinges on such factors as human aptitudes and attitudes, social and political institutions, external contacts, market opportunities, and natural resources (to a lesser extent). Development is not just a matter of capital accumulation and saving; it is vitally related to individual entrepreneurs being able to perceive opportunities and then take advantage of them. Growth is, of course, conditioned by the opportunities offered by the environment—natural resources and social institutions—but the pace and pattern of growth will depend on the quality of an economy's entrepreneurial talent.

These critics point to Hong Kong, Taiwan, and Singapore as counterexamples to the traditional capital accumulation theory of growth and development. Only when free trade and unrestricted entrepreneurial activity are available as springboards to economic growth will injections of foreign capital be helpful because, as P. T. Bauer has noted, "A society which cannot develop without external gifts is altogether unlikely to do so with them."

How Developed Countries Can Aid Less Developed Nations

The case for foreign aid is regarded as axiomatic, so that either progress or lack of progress can be used to argue for more aid. Progress is evidence of success, and lack of progress is evidence that more must be done.

P. T. Bauer

Many people perceive the most pressing needs of developing nations to be enormous injections of capital, introduction of new technology, and substantial education and job training programs. Developed nations are often in a good position to provide physical capital because many have an abundance and their investors are looking for profitable places to invest. Similarly, the educational systems of developed countries can train technically qualified people for developing industries. Moreover, industrialized countries can provide technology to raise the productivity of workers in less developed countries.

The Role of International Credit

International capital flows permit countries with more attractive investment opportunities than their domestic savings can finance to obtain resources from countries with excess saving. Countries experiencing temporary economic problems might borrow from world capital markets rather than suffer sharp contractionary policies that restrict consumption and investment. Countries such as Hong Kong, Taiwan, Malaysia, and Israel, to name a few, have gained from foreign capital infusions. From World War II until the 1980s, the United States was a net supplier of capital to the rest of the world, primarily through direct investment by private firms in foreign countries. Before World War I, the United States financed domestic investments with loans from Great Britain and other European countries.

From 1981 through the present, enormous U.S. federal budget deficits were partially financed by balance of trade deficits. This net inflow to the United States drains funds that might have financed development in less developed countries. Although the federal deficit set records, exceeding $300 billion at times, swelling Social Security revenues should soon reverse the U.S. demand for foreign capital. (The U.S. balance of trade deficit declined during 1987 to 1993.) In general, however, international capital flows move into countries with good growth and profit opportunities.

New capital may also be provided in the form of foreign aid: either grants or loans. The United States has provided billions of dollars in aid each year, administered through the Agency for International Development (AID). Another source of funds for less developed countries is the World Bank, funded by highly developed member nations, which arranges huge loans for social investments such as dams, education, communications, and transportation systems. Most investment flows between countries, however, are private and are channeled through multinational corporations. These companies must perceive substantial potential profits before they invest, and they seek opportunities where there are abundant natural resources, a ready (and cheap) labor force, and a stable political climate.

One problem that arises when development is financed by long-term loans from more mature economies is that, to maintain an acceptable credit rating, a less developed country must make regular payments. A worldwide recession such as the 1981 to 1983 slump reveals how much financial juggling this can entail. Hundreds of billions of dollars in development loans were due for repayment to major American banks. These banks had primarily loaned out the deposits of OPEC countries, and many of the OPEC countries wanted to withdraw funds because of declining oil revenues. The worldwide recession, high nominal and real interest rates, the strengthening of the U.S. dollar until 1985, and the fall in the prices of many commodities exported by developing countries put incredible strains on debtor countries' ability to service their external debts. Some analysts warned that the entire international financial system teetered on the brink of collapse. However, refinancing or rescheduling of the debt payments, collapsing oil prices, and a gradual economic recovery into the 1990s reduced the financial pressures on many developing nations that do not rely primarily on oil revenues.

Many have argued that developed countries have a moral responsibility to aid less developed countries in their search for the good life. However, the world's industrialized nations are not totally philanthropic in contributing to the growth and development of less developed countries. Facing diminishing returns to more capital within their own borders, these countries seek outlets for their internally generated technological advances and capital growth, sources of raw materials and cheap labor, and markets for their finished products. Viewing our world as a self-enclosed "Spaceship Earth" emphasizes the international scope of our interdependencies. As the entire world matures economically, disparities in living standards between countries should decrease. For whatever reason, most observers believe that the fortunes of the developed nations and their less developed neighbors are inextricably intertwined.

CHAPTER REVIEW: KEY POINTS

1. **Economic growth** refers to quantitative changes in the capacity to produce goods and services in a country. It occurs through expanding capital or labor resources, discoveries of new sources of raw materials, or development of more productive technologies. **Economic development** refers to improving the qualitative aspects of economic growth, including changes in the quality of life.

2. The **Rule of 72** is a rule of thumb for estimating how long it takes for a variable to double in value given some percentage growth rate. Simply divide 72 by the growth rate. For example, if growth in GDP is occurring at 6% per year, GDP will double in approximately 12 years (72/6 = 12).

3. *Diminishing returns* because of the fixity of land cause output to grow more slowly even if labor and capital increase in fixed proportions.

4. Reverend Thomas Malthus and other nineteenth-century economists were convinced that population growth is almost uncontrollable and theorized that equilibrium is attained only when bare subsistence is common to all.

5. *Population growth* tends to slow as a country develops. The least developed countries of the world tend to have the highest rates of population growth.

6. **Capital formation** requires high saving rates. If *voluntary saving* is used to finance development, greater incomes, higher interest rates paid to savers, and (perhaps) less equal income distributions will lead to higher rates of investment. Governments may use *involuntary saving* to free investment resources through confiscation, taxation, or inflation.

7. **Capital widening** occurs when the capital stock and labor force grow at the same rates. **Capital deepening** requires the capital stock to grow faster than the labor force.

8. **Technological advances** occur when given amounts of resources acquire greater productive capacity.

9. Rapid development requires a strong **social infrastructure**: education, communications, transportation, and other networks that facilitate production.

10. The **trap of underdevelopment** hypothesis suggests that some countries are so poor that only external aid will permit significant growth. Critics of this theory argue that aid is unnecessary and unwise. These critics favor substantial deregulation that will allow entrepreneurs to exploit opportunities in world markets as a surer path for development.

QUESTIONS FOR THOUGHT AND DISCUSSION

1. Despite relatively low saving rates in the United States, we have typically grown faster than many countries with higher rates of saving (e.g., England). What does this say about the importance of the structure of investment relative to its level?

2. If all taxes on saving were eliminated, the average U.S. saver's return would be increased by roughly 30%. Increased incentives to save would add $30 to $40 billion to annual savings. Would such a policy increase productivity? Long-term growth?

The real earnings of workers? Would it reduce inflation? Reduce unemployment? Would different groups gain in the short run than would in the long run? Is such a policy politically feasible?

3. If you were the leader of an impoverished and densely populated country, what policies might you adopt to foster economic growth and development? To what extent would you encourage private entrepreneurs and for which kinds of projects? What role should your government play in developing social infrastructure?

4. Why do many highly trained people from developing nations seek employment in advanced countries? Why are these highly educated people apparently more productive and highly paid in these advanced countries than they are in their home countries?

5. P. T. Bauer, a critic of foreign aid, has argued that "development depends on personal and social factors, not on handouts." He further asserts that "foreign aid means at most some capital is cheaper than if it had been raised independently at market rates." His argument refutes the notion that foreign aid is indispensable for progress. Do you agree with him? Why or why not?

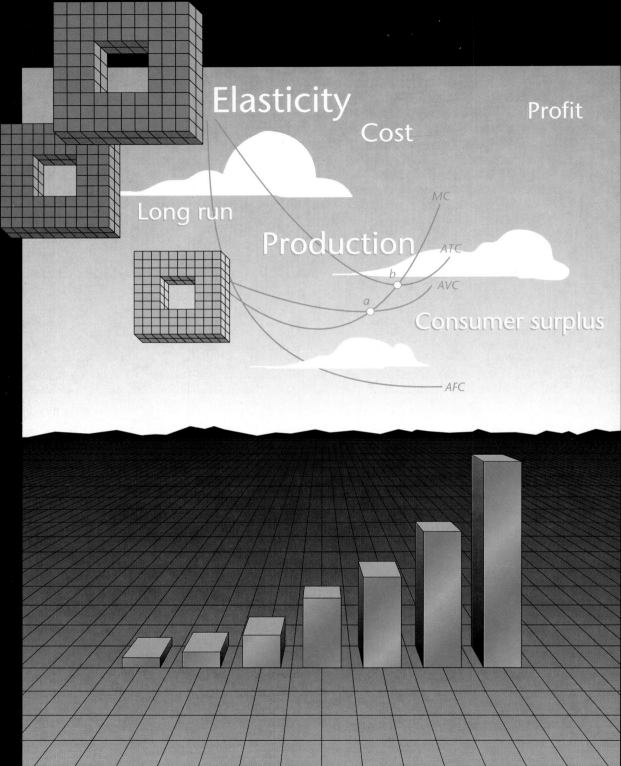

Part 6

Core Concepts in Microeconomics

We will concentrate on decisions in households and business firms for the next eight chapters and then investigate the micro role of government. You now know how useful supply and demand are in analyzing problems ranging from yam prices to affordable housing. Until now, we have relied heavily on your intuition to explain the slopes of supply and demand curves. This part of the book allows you to explore in depth just why supply curves slope upward, while demand curves slope down.

The first chapter in this part introduces *elasticity*, which allows a more precise use of supply and demand analysis to predict how market prices and quantities change. In the next chapter, we analyze *consumer choice* and develop the underpinnings of consumer demand curves. The third chapter explores the nature of *business firms*. Finally, the last chapter in this part delves into *production*, that is, how inputs are transformed into outputs, and how technology shapes a firm's *production costs*. You need to understand these foundations to understand firms' decisions in the next part, firms decide which goods to produce and what prices to charge by weighing consumer demands against production costs.

Elasticity
Cost
Profit

Chapter 20

Long run

Production

ATC

b

AVC

a

Elasticity

Consumer surplus

AFC

Predictions about the costs and benefits of alternatives are vital for informed choices. Firms know they will sell less output if they raise prices because buyers' demand curves slope downward, but how much less? Buyers who offer higher prices expect more to be available because supply curves are positively sloped, but how much more? *Elasticity* addresses questions of this type and can help guide decisions.

ELASTICITY AND RESPONSIVENESS

The concept of elasticity provides a systematic way to estimate how one variable responds to changes in some other variable.

> **Elasticity** *measures the proportional responsiveness of one variable with respect to changes in another.*

If X influences Y, then the elasticity of Y with respect to X equals

$$\frac{\Delta Y}{Y} \Big/ \frac{\Delta X}{X}$$

The responsiveness of quantity (Q) to price (P) allows us to calculate the responsiveness of total revenue (TR) to price, because $TR = P \times Q$. Thus, elasticity helps us predict changes in a firm's revenues, but other uses abound. For example, firms substitute capital for labor if capital costs fall relative to wages. How much substitution occurs as resource prices change? Experience shapes our expectations, but how is past inflation translated into people's inflationary expectations? Understanding how to calculate elasticity for these examples is unimportant for now, but remember that elasticity is useful whenever variables are systematically related.

Suppose you are the chief executive officer (CEO) of United Bullmoose Enterprises (UBE) and are irritated because profit is less than you think possible. UBE's chief economist assures you that all demand curves are negatively sloped, so if you raise the price of plastic mooseheads (UBE's big novelty seller), annual sales will slip below the million you currently sell. Total production costs will fall, but will sales revenues rise, fall, or remain constant? Suppose producing each moosehead costs $10. Raising the price from $20 to $25 might be disastrous if you lost half your customers, but if only 50,000 of UBE's million annual moosehead sales were lost, profits would rise by $4.25 million. (Why?)[1] How should UBE deal with this dilemma?

THE PRICE ELASTICITY OF DEMAND

The problem you are wrestling with is the price elasticity of the demand for moose heads.

> *Price elasticity of demand is a measure of the proportional change in units purchased when price is changed by a given small proportion.*

If both changes are quite small, this roughly equals the percentage change in quantity divided by the percentage change in price. Price elasticity can be written

$$e_d \cong \frac{\text{Percentage Change in } Q_d}{\text{Percentage Change in } P}$$

$$= \frac{\%\Delta Q_d}{\%\Delta P}$$

$$= \frac{\text{Change in } Q_d}{Q_d} \bigg/ \frac{\text{Change in } P}{P}$$

$$= \frac{\Delta Q_d}{Q_d} \bigg/ \frac{\Delta P}{P}$$

$$= \frac{\Delta Q_d}{\Delta P} \cdot \frac{P}{Q_d}$$

Calculations of the price elasticity of demand always yield negative numbers because if price is increased, quantity demanded falls, and vice versa. To simplify things, economists conventionally use the *absolute value* of price elasticity.

The Problem of Bases and Percentages

Suppose the price of plastic moose heads is cut from $20 to $12, and annual sales surge from 1

million units to 5 million. Price elasticity (e_d) is 10 using the percentage formula:

$$e_d \cong \frac{\%\Delta Q_d}{\%\Delta P} = \frac{(5-1)/1}{(12-20)/20} = \frac{400\%}{-40\%}$$

$$= -10 \left(\text{Absolute value} = 10 \right)$$

Watch what happens if we turn this example around. Sales shrink from 5 million to 1 million moose heads if prices rise from $12 to $20, and the percentage formula yields

$$e_d \cong \frac{\%\Delta Q_d}{\%\Delta P} = \frac{(1-5)}{5} \bigg/ \frac{(20-12)}{12} = \frac{-80\%}{66.7\%}$$

$$= -1.2 \left(\text{Absolute value} = 1.2 \right)$$

Divergent elasticity estimates in this example (10 if price is cut, 1.2 if price is raised) demonstrate that calculations using the percentage formula depend on whether prices rise or fall.[2] We need to discuss this inconsistency before we provide a cure for it.

The basic problem results from a standard practice in math courses of using initial values as bases to calculate percentage changes. Percentage changes computed this way may create substantial ambiguity. For example, suppose the annual profit of a subsidiary, United Bullmoose Oil, climbs from $200 million to $1 billion. The media report the 400% jump and imply that UBE's profits are somehow responsible for inflation. The next year, profit drops to $150 million, and the media dutifully report an 85% decline. Readers are likely to think that UBE is still way ahead because a 400% gain seems to overpower an 85% decline, but it does not: $200 million → $1,000 million → $150 million. UBE had one very good year, but its profit is now less than it was initially.

• **Using Midpoints as Bases** Elasticity estimates computed by standard percentage changes may be only trivially inconsistent if

---

[1] After the price hike, sales revenue ($P \times Q$) is equal to $950,000 \times $25 = $23,750,000$, while costs are $9,500,000 ($950,000 \times 10). This yields profit of $14,250,000. The original profit was $10,000,000 [($1,000,000 \times 20) − ($1,000,000 \times 10)].

[2] The percentage change formula that uses original values for bases yields point elasticity estimates.

prices and quantities change very little, but inconsistency poses major problems when prices or quantities change drastically. Such problems with percentages as normally computed have led economists to compute **arc elasticity** using as bases the midpoints of changes in prices and quantities:

$$e_d = \frac{Q_n - Q_o}{(Q_n + Q_o)/2} \bigg/ \frac{P_n - P_o}{(P_n + P_o)/2}$$

The subscript o refers to the original price and quantity, and the subscript n refers to the new price and quantity.[3] Naturally, the 2s in both denominators can be canceled out, but we use them here to provide consistency and to remind you that we are using midpoints.

Returning to our example of prices of $12 and $20 for plastic mooseheads generating sales of 5 million and 1 million units, respectively, we now get the same absolute value elasticity estimate of 2.67, regardless of whether the price is raised or lowered:

$$e_d = \frac{1 - 5}{(1 + 5)/2} \bigg/ \frac{20 - 12}{(20 + 12)/2}$$

$$= \frac{-(4/3)}{8/16} = -2.67 = |2.67|$$

and

$$e_d = \frac{5 - 1}{(1 + 5)/2} \bigg/ \frac{12 - 20}{(20 + 12)/2}$$

$$= \frac{4/3}{-(8/16)} = -2.67 = |2.67|$$

These elasticity coefficients suggest that for each 1% change in price, the quantity demanded changes by roughly 2.67%. Thus, using midpoint bases to calculate price elasticity clears up ambiguities created by using standard percentages.

---

[3] The formula for elasticity can be manipulated in ways that some students find easier to calculate. One example is e_d = (Change in Q/Change in P) × (Sum of P/Sum of Q).

Ranges of Elasticity

Price elasticity of demand is a measure of the responsiveness of quantity demanded to given small changes in price.

> Demand is **price inelastic** if the absolute value of the elasticity coefficient, $|e_d|$, is less than 1.0.

Price changes are proportionally greater than the resulting quantity changes for goods with inelastic demands. Goods with an inelastic demand are products where the amounts you demand are substantially immune to price changes. Inelastically demanded products range from lifesaving drugs and treatments, to energy and gasoline, to salt and pepper. For example, if the price of dog food doubled, would people put their pets on half rations? No. Most people view their pets and, consequently, pet food as one item that is relatively insensitive to price changes. (But in the longer run, they might switch to cats or smaller dogs.) Note that we are talking about dog food here, not a particular brand of dog food. If the price of one brand of dog food rose, people might substitute another brand, therefore the elasticity for any brand of dog food is higher than for dog food as a product.

Demand curve D_0 in Figure 1 is relatively inelastic at a price of $2. When price rises from $2 to $2.50, quantity demanded only falls from 100 to 98—not much of a change (e_d = 1/11, or roughly 0.09). Compare this to demand curve D_1 in the same figure, where a change in price from $2 to $2.50 results in quantity demanded falling from 100 to 40. Quantity demanded is very responsive to a change in price (e_d = 27/7, or roughly 3.86). Thus, D_1 depicts a product with a relatively *elastic* demand at a price of $2.

> Demand is **price elastic** if the absolute value of the elasticity coefficient exceeds 1.0.

Many consumers are willing to forgo elastically demanded goods if their prices rise significantly, a sign that a product may have numerous close substitutes. Goods that have nu-

FIGURE 1 Demand Curves with Different Elasticities

In this figure, the demand curve D_1 is more elastic at prices between $2.00 and $2.50 than is the demand curve D_0. Given the same price change, the reduction in quantity demanded is much greater for D_1 then for D_0, and therefore, D_1 is more elastic than D_0 between $2.00 and $2.50.

merous substitutes and exhibit relatively elastic demand curves include Saabs, Häagen-Dazs ice cream, and Wendy's hamburgers. Note that the demand for any specific brand will be more elastic than the overall demand for the product itself. For example, the demand for Pepsi is more elastic than the demand for cola. In a similar vein, national performing arts demand in local summer theater performances is relatively unresponsive to price changes, while the demand for a specific local play, opera, or ballet is likely to be more sensitive to price changes because many substitutes (movies, sporting events, and other local recreational activities) are available.[4]

• **Slope and Elasticity** Slope as an indicator of how one variable responds to changes in another suffers from a major disadvantage: units

[4]For a thorough discussion of this issue, see Marianne Felton, "On the Assumed Inelasticity of Demand for the Performing Arts," *Journal of Cultural Economics*, June 1992.

of measurement affect slope. For example, a demand curve for which coffee prices are stated in dollars has 1/100th the slope of the same demand curve when prices are stated in pennies. And that same demand curve would have 1/2,000th the slope if quantity were measured in tons of coffee instead of pounds.

The superiority of elasticity as an indicator of relative responsiveness is that only proportions matter; elasticity is *dimensionless*, which means that units of measure do not bias results. The price elasticity of the demand for coffee is the same regardless of whether prices are stated in cents, dollars, or yen, and it is not affected by whether weight is stated in pounds, tons, or kilograms.

Elasticity and Total Revenue

Price elasticities of demand are guides to what will happen to *total revenue* (the dollar sales of firms) if prices change slightly. Total revenue equals the price charged times the quantity sold ($TR = P \times Q$). For example, a hamburger stand will generate $1 million in total revenue if it sells a million burgers at $1 apiece or one burger at $1 million. Naturally, firms' total revenues must equal total spending by consumers.

When quantity rises because prices fall, offsetting effects make the direction of change in total revenue uncertain. Because $TR = P \times Q$, how much price or quantity changes will determine whether total revenue rises or falls (since they move in opposite directions). If we know, however, that demand is inelastic, then, when prices fall, the increase in quantity will be relatively less than the decrease in price and total revenue will fall. Conversely, if demand is elastic and price falls, then revenue rises because quantity grows relatively far more than price falls. The opposite story holds when prices rise. Inelastic demands mean that quantities decrease little relative to the increase in price, so total revenue rises. Elastic demands, on the other hand, yield declines in quantity that are large relative to any price hike. Let's look at two extreme cases to illustrate how total revenue and price elasticity are related.

FIGURE 2   A Demand Curve Confronting an Individual Soybeam Farmer (Perfectly Elastic Demand)

A horizontal demand curve has infinite price elasticity ($e_d = \infty$). Because total revenue equals $P \times Q$ and the price does not change with output, total revenue is exactly proportional to output.

• **Elastic Demands**   Firms producing products that are perfect substitutes in buyers' eyes confront horizontal demand curves, as illustrated in Figure 2. Attempts by one firm to raise the price even slightly above the market price will chase all potential buyers to other firms.

Perfectly elastic demand curves have price elasticities of infinity and are horizontal.[5]

For example, one soybean farmer's crop is the same as another's. Even the largest soybean farmers produce only a tiny share of total world supplies, so no single farm's output has a distinguishable impact on world soybean prices. This means that any attempt by the farmer represented in Figure 2 to price soybeans above $10 per bushel will generate zero sales. The farmer can sell all the farm can produce at $10 and so would never charge less than $10. Since price will not vary from $10 per bushel, the farm's total revenue is exactly proportional to its *out-*

put. If the farm initially produces 1,000 bushels of soybeans annually and then expands output by 20% to 1,200 bushels, revenue also increases by 20%, rising from $10,000 to $12,000.

If demand is relatively elastic, then price changes trigger proportionally larger adjustments in quantity. Consequently, if $e_d > 1$ but not perfectly elastic, then total revenue will fall when prices are raised and grow if prices drop.

• **Inelastic Demands**   The other extreme case would occur if a demand curve were vertical, as in Figure 3.

Perfectly inelastic demand curves would have zero elasticity and be vertical.

If such cases ever existed, the firm's total revenue would be exactly proportional to the *price* charged.

Perfectly inelastic demand curves are nonsensical; one is shown here only to help you un-

Vertical demand curves have a price elasticity of zero ($e_d = 0$). Although such perfectly inelastic demand curves are impossible, this figure shows that the total revenue will be exactly proportional to price. Nevertheless, this example is useful because it represents the opposite end of the spectrum from the perfectly elastic demand shown in the previous figure.

FIGURE 3   A Hypothetical Perfectly Inelastic Demand

---

[5]For those who are mathematically inclined, as the slope of the demand curve approaches zero, the elasticity of demand approaches infinity.

derstand elasticity. Zero price elasticity implies not only a total lack of substitutes for the good, but also that consumers could and would pay any price to receive a specific quantity of it. Any such good would be essential for life, but our limited budgets would make it impossible to afford.

You might think that the prices of insulin for diabetics or dialysis for people with defective kidneys would not affect the quantities demanded by patients who need them. The cruel facts are that if the prices of these medical necessities were raised, more diabetics would try to control their disease with diet therapy. If prices were raised sufficiently, poorer patients would die and the quantities of insulin or dialysis demanded would fall. Every year people die because they cannot afford expensive, specialized medical treatment.

If demand is relatively inelastic, then price changes trigger proportionally smaller adjustments in quantity. Consequently, if $e_d < 1$ but not perfectly inelastic, then total revenue will fall when prices fall, but rise if the price is increased.

• **Unitary Elasticity of Demand** An interesting intermediate case occurs when total spending on a good does not vary with the price charged. An example was provided by a farmer who observed that revenues from peach sales were about the same regardless of whether a flood or hurricane wiped out most of a peach crop or there was a bumper harvest. If 1% declines in peach harvests boost peach prices 1%, total spending on peaches is virtually unchanged and the price elasticity of demand equals one.

> A **unitarily elastic demand** curve occurs when the elasticity coefficient equals one, so total revenue from the good is unaffected by a change in price.

Total spending on a good for which demand is unitarily elastic does not vary with the price charged. For example, a unitarily elastic demands occur when people budget a certain amount of money for, say, magazines and will not deviate from that outlay regardless of price. A representative unitary elastic demand curve is shown in Figure 4.

FIGURE 4   A Demand Curve with Unitary Elasticity

Total revenue ($P \times Q$) is unaffected by changes in price and quantity if demand is unitarily elastic. Unitarily elastic curves ($e_d = 1$) are rectangular hyperbolas, which have the characteristic that all rectangles drawn from the curve to the axes have exactly the same geometric area ($P \times Q$). You will see more rectangular hyperbolas as we proceed further in economics.

If the price elasticity of demand for a product is greater than zero but less than one, the demand curve is *relatively inelastic*. Economists sometimes shorten this to *inelastic*. If the price elasticity is greater than one but less than infinity, the demand for the product is *relatively elastic*, or *elastic*.

A firm facing a demand curve with price elasticity of one or less always finds it profitable to raise the product's price because revenue will rise, and as output and units sold fall, total production costs will decline. (Profit must increase if revenues grow and total costs fall.) As the price is increased, growing numbers of consumers will buy substitutes for the good; those who cannot substitute ultimately will be forced to do without.

Price elasticities of demand are obviously important to firms because they indicate what will happen to sales revenues when prices are

TABLE 1   Price Changes, Elasticities, and Total Revenues

Price Elasticity of Demand	How Total Revenues Change	
	Price Increases	Price Decreases
Perfectly inelastic ($e_d = 0$)	TR increases	TR decreases
Inelastic ($0 < e_d < 1$)	TR increases	TR decreases
Unitarily elastic ($e_d = 1$)	No change in TR	No change in TR
Elastic ($\infty > e_d > 1$)	TR decreases	TR increases
Perfectly elastic ($e_d = \infty$)	TR falls to zero	TR decreases

raised or lowered. Price elasticities of demand are also important to consumers because they reflect how desperately buyers want particular goods and how the composition of consumer budgets will change as relative prices change. Table 1 summarizes how the firm's total revenue (and consumers' total spending) for a good changes as prices change.

Elasticity Along a Demand Curve

Constant elasticities of demand are rare. You might think the linear demand curve in Panel A of Figure 5 would have a constant price elasticity. Not so. The rectangle drawn at point *a* represents the highest revenue available on this demand curve; $P \times Q$ is maximized. Any price deviation from $10 lowers revenue, as shown in Panel B and its table. This demand curve is price elastic above point *a*, as price hikes reduce revenue: e_d exceeds one. Symmetrically, price cuts below $10 shrink revenue, so below point *a* the demand curve is price inelastic: e_d is less than one. At point *a*, demand is unitarily elastic: e_d equals one. The conclusion is that price elasticities of demand tend to rise as higher and higher prices are charged.[6]

---

[6]As we discussed earlier, elasticity is equal to $\Delta Q_d / \Delta P \cdot P/Q_d$. Note that the left-hand side of this term is the slope of the demand curve and the right-hand side is the ratio of price to quantity demanded for each point on the demand curve. For a straight-line demand curve, slope is constant, but as you move up and down the demand curve, the ratio P/Q_d will change. Thus, elasticity and slope are not the same thing. Specifically, when price is high and quantity is low, the ratio P/Q_d will be large and demand will be elastic. Alternatively, when price is low and quantity demanded is large, the ratio P/Q_d will be small and elasticity will be low (inelastic).

Determinants of Elasticity of Demand

As we have seen, demand curves rarely have constant elasticities along the full range of possible prices and quantities, but Table 2 presents some estimates of price elasticities of demand for several goods within the price ranges you would roughly expect for each good. For any product, several factors determine whether demands for that good is relatively inelastic or elastic. Major determinants of elasticities of demand include

1. the number, quality, and availability of substitutes for a good
2. the proportion an item absorbs from a typical budget
3. the length of time considered

- **Substitutes**   The number of substitutes available is the dominant influence on price elasticities of demand. Rising prices drive consumers toward substitutes; falling prices are incentives to find more uses for a good. For example, the demand for Campbell's pork and beans is very price elastic because slight price hikes will cause consumers to switch to other brands, and slight price cuts will raise Campbell's sales at the expense of competing brands. On the other hand, as Table 2 illustrates the demand for tobacco, health services, and short-run residential utility service is relatively inelastic because few substitutes are available.

- **Budget Proportion**   Price changes for items absorbing little of your income may go unnoticed (maraschino cherries, for example), but

FIGURE 5   Varying Price Elasticities along a Linear Demand Curve

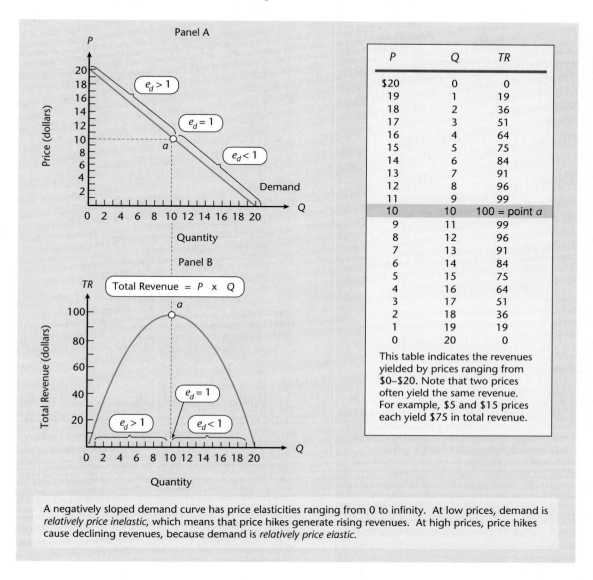

P	Q	TR
$20	0	0
19	1	19
18	2	36
17	3	51
16	4	64
15	5	75
14	6	84
13	7	91
12	8	96
11	9	99
10	10	100 = point a
9	11	99
8	12	96
7	13	91
6	14	84
5	15	75
4	16	64
3	17	51
2	18	36
1	19	19
0	20	0

This table indicates the revenues yielded by prices ranging from $0–$20. Note that two prices often yield the same revenue. For example, $5 and $15 prices each yield $75 in total revenue.

A negatively sloped demand curve has price elasticities ranging from 0 to infinity. At low prices, demand is *relatively price inelastic*, which means that price hikes generate rising revenues. At high prices, price hikes cause declining revenues, because demand is *relatively price elastic*.

you will probably adjust quickly to changes in the prices of more important items (e.g., clothes or gasoline).

• **Time**   Another important determinant of price elasticity is the period allowed for adjustments to price changes. Elasticity generally rises as longer intervals are considered, because as time elapses, more substitutes become feasible (see Figure 6). Elasticities are measured for a specified period for this reason. For example, Table 2 indicates that the demand for gasoline is relatively inelastic in the short run, but relatively elastic in the long run.

A gasoline price hike might reduce purchases only trivially in the very short run (say, a week or two) and only slightly more in the short run (say, six months to a year). People will gradually modify their driving habits to save gas and,

TABLE 2 Price Elasticities of Demand for Selected Goods and Services

Good or Service	Price Elasticity of Demand
Automobiles	1.35
Beer	1.13
Housing	1.00
Alcohol	0.92
Tobacco	0.33
Major league baseball	0.23
Health services	
Small copayment (< 25%)	0.10–0.17
Large copayment (> 25%)	0.14–0.22
Gasoline (transportation only)	
Short run	0.1–0.3
Long run	1.50
Electricity	
Long-run total usage	0.88
Short-run residential	0.13

Sources: Data for automobiles from G. Chow, *Demand for Automobiles in the United States* (Amsterdam: North-Holland Publishing Company, 1957); for beer, T. Hogarty and K. Elzinga, "The Demand for Beer," *The Review of Economics and Statistics*, May 1972; for housing, R. Muth, "The Demand for Non-Farm Housing," *The Demand for Durable Goods*, ed. A. Harberger (Chicago: University of Chicago Press, 1960); for alcohol, H. Houthakker and L. Taylor, *Consumer Demand in the United States*, 2d ed. (Cambridge: Harvard University Press, 1970); for tobacco, B. Gordon Watkins III, "The Tobacco Program: An Econometric Analysis of Its Benefits to Farmers," *The American Economist*, 1990; for baseball, Bruce R. Domazlicky and Peter M. Kerr, "Baseball Attendance and the Designated Hitter," *The American Economist*, 1990; for health services, W. Manning et al., "Health Insurance and the Demand for Medical Care: Evidence from a Randomized Experiment," *American Economic Review*, 1987 and E. Keeler, et al., *The Demand for Episodes of Treatment in the Health Insurance Experiment* (Santa Monica, CA: The Rand Corporation, Report R-3454-HHS, 1988); for gasoline and electricity, J. Griffin, *Energy Conservation in the OECD, 1980–2000* (Cambridge, MA: Ballinger, 1979).

thus, will demand a little less. Carpooling is one possibility. But in the longer run (say, two to five years), gas price hikes induce people to buy smaller cars, get tune-ups more regularly, or rely more on mass transit. Some may even move closer to work, shopping, and so on. Longer periods allow consumers to make more adjustments in gas consumption in response to any given price change.

FIGURE 6 Time and Price Elasticity of Demand

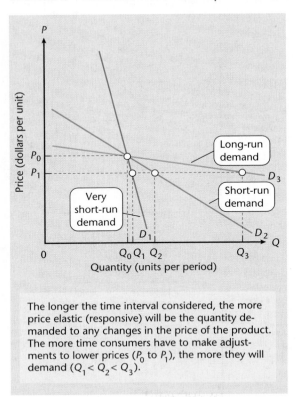

The longer the time interval considered, the more price elastic (responsive) will be the quantity demanded to any changes in the price of the product. The more time consumers have to make adjustments to lower prices (P_0 to P_1), the more they will demand ($Q_1 < Q_2 < Q_3$).

Another interesting influence of time on demand is that some goods require substantial time for consumption. Time limits your enjoyment of food. (Your stomach has a limited capacity; eating one burger a week is possible, averaging one per minute is not.) You can only wear one hat at a time. Vacations are expensive not only because of the money you spend but also because of income sacrificed when you do not work. Airline tickets typically have higher monetary prices than touring by car, but air travel is increasingly popular because of the time it saves.

Other Elasticities of Demand

Before addressing such issues as how elasticities determine who bears the burdens of taxes, we will look at other major types of elasticities.

• **Income Elasticity of Demand** Rich people do not just buy more goods; the things they buy also differ from the purchases of poor people.

The ***income elasticity of demand*** *for a good measures the proportional change in the quantity demanded resulting from a given small proportional change in income.*

You might think of income elasticity as the ratio of percentage changes in the amount of a good demanded relative to income, but, for reasons that parallel the rationale for midpoint-based computation of price elasticities, we actually compute income elasticity as

$$e_y = \frac{\%\Delta Q}{\%\Delta Y} = \frac{Q_n - Q_o}{\left(Q_n + Q_o\right)/2} \bigg/ \frac{Y_n - Y_o}{\left(Y_n + Y_o\right)/2}$$

The letter Y stands for income, and, again, subscript n refers to new values, subscript o represents original values, and both 2s could be dropped from the denominators without affecting this calculation.

Such luxuries as scuba lessons or limousines are highly income elastic because each 1% rise in income increases the amounts sold by over 1%. If income grows 1% and the amount of a good sold rises slightly, but by less than 1%, demand is income inelastic. Rising incomes stimulate purchases of all **normal goods** (income elasticities are positive).[7] Purchases of **inferior goods** decline as income rises, and their income elasticities are negative. Lard, pinto beans, and used tires are examples. Income elasticities of demand for some broad product categories are displayed in Table 3.

Business decisions often pivot on forecasts and income elasticities. How might a recession affect sales, for example? Income elasticities are critical for planning in such industries as oil and gasoline, used auto parts, specialty foods, and retailing. Would the operator of a travel agency be exuberant about forecasts of an economic boom and depressed if a recession hit? Clearly yes, if the demand for travel is income elastic. Knowledge about income elasticity helps firms plan production, employment, and investment.

---

[7]Sometimes data for the prices or quantities of goods are not available, but sales data ($P \times Q$) are. In such cases, economists approximate income elasticities by (Percentage change in expenditures/Percentage change in income). If the result exceeds (or is less than) one, demand is presumed to be income elastic (or inelastic).

- **Cross Price Elasticity of Demand** Cross elasticities of demand are also important information about consumer behavior.

*The **cross price elasticity of demand** estimates the proportional change in the quantity of one good demanded when the price of another related good is changed.*

Formally, cross price elasticity is calculated by

$$e_{xz} = \frac{\%\Delta Q_x}{\%\Delta P_z} = \frac{Q_{xn} - Q_{xo}}{\left(Q_{xn} + Q_{xo}\right)/2} \bigg/ \frac{P_{zn} - P_{zo}}{\left(P_{zn} + P_{zo}\right)/2}$$

where Q_{xo} (old) and Q_{xn} (new) are good x purchases before and after price changes for good z (P_{zo} and P_{zn}, respectively). Again, the 2s could be dropped from the equation.

TABLE 3   Income Elasticities of Demand for Selected Goods and Services

Good or Service	Income Elasticity of Demand
Automobiles	3.00
Major league baseball	1.30
Housing	1.15
Beer	0.93
Charitable donations (households)	0.70
Corporate contributions	0.85
Medical services	0.2–0.36
Dental services	0.8–2.0

Sources: Data for automobiles, G. Chow, *Demand for Automobiles in the United States* (Amsterdam: North-Holland Publishing Company, 1957); for housing, R. Muth, *Cities and Housing: The Spatial Pattern of Urban Residential Land Use* (Chicago: the University of Chicago Press, 1969); for beer, T. Hogarty and K. Elzinga, "The Demand for Beer," *Review of Economics and Statistics*, May 1972; for charitable donations, M. Feldstein and A. Taylor, "The Income Tax and Charitable Contributions," *Econometrica*, November 1976; for medical services, J. Newhouse and C. Phelps, "New Estimates of Price and Income Elasticities of Medical Care Services," *The Role of Health Insurance in the Health Services Sector*, ed. R. Rosett (New York: National Bureau of Economic Research, 1976); see also, E. Keeler, *et. al.*, *The Demand for Episodes of Treatment in the Health Insurance Experiment* (Santa Monica, CA: The Rand Corporation, Report R-3454-HHS, 1988); for corporate contributions, P. Navarro, "The Income Elasticity of Corporate Contributions," *Quarterly Review of Economics and Business*, Winter 1988; for baseball, B. Domazlicky and P. Kerr, "Baseball Attendance and the Designated Hitter," *The American Economist*, 1990; for dental services, Sherman Folland et al., *The Economics of Health and Health Care* (New York: Macmillan Publishing Company, 1993).

Consider the sales of American cars (brand *X*) after U.S. import restrictions drive up the prices of Japanese cars (brand *Z*). If all else were constant, we would expect American car sales to grow when imported cars became higher priced. Thus, we would expect a positive relationship between the prices of imported cars and the quantities of American cars sold domestically; the cross price elasticity of demand (e_{xz}) should be positive. When cross price elasticities of demand are *positive*, the items in question are **substitute goods**. Other sets of substitutes are artificial turf and natural grass, beans and rice, and vans and travel trailers. In fact, broad competition for consumers' dollars causes most goods to be at least weak substitutes for each other.

Sets of goods for which cross price elasticity of demand is *negative* are **complementary goods**. For example, as prices for calculators and electronic toys have fallen, the demand for alkaline batteries has jumped markedly. Other examples of complementary goods include ham and eggs, cameras and film, suits and ties, and pretzels and beer.

THE PRICE ELASTICITY OF SUPPLY

Price elasticities of supply are typically positive because supply curves slope up.

> The **price elasticity of supply** measures the responsiveness of quantity supplied to changes in price.[8]

The formula for this elasticity is the same as for computing price elasticities of demand:

$$e_s = \frac{Q_n - Q_o}{\left(Q_n + Q_o\right)/2} \bigg/ \frac{P_n - P_o}{\left(P_n + P_o\right)/2}$$

If extending the supply curve of a good would result in an intersection with the vertical (price) axis, the amount of the good supplied is highly responsive to its price. In a case such as S_2 in Figure 7, the elasticity of supply exceeds one and the supply curve is *relatively elastic*. If a supply curve is horizontal, such as S_∞ in Figure 7, then the elasticity of supply is infinity and supply is *perfectly price elastic*. Buyers can demand any amounts of these goods without affecting the price at all. Examples of goods having perfectly elastic supplies include such things as a family's groceries; no matter how many cans of tuna your family personally consumes, your purchases will not affect the price you pay. Thus, the supply of tuna to you is perfectly elastic, even though the market supply of tuna is positively sloped. Similarly, any small bakery that buys flour in bulk is faced with a perfectly elastic supply of flour. In these and similar cases, individual demands determine the amounts people buy, but not the prices they pay.

If extending the supply curve would result in intersection with the quantity axis, the amount of a good supplied is comparatively unresponsive to its price. A supply curve such as S_3 in Figure 7 is *relatively inelastic*. In the extreme situation where the quantity supplied is totally unresponsive to price, the supply curve is vertical (S_0 in Figure 7) and the price elasticity of supply is zero ($e_s = 0$). Examples of these *perfectly inelastic* supplies include land (the fixed amount available is unaffected by price) and other highly specialized items or resources; Rembrandt paintings, Stradivarius violins, and the comedy of Whoopi Goldberg are each unique. When supplies are fixed, demand alone determines a good's price or person's wage, but the quantity exchanged is not related to the price paid.

You may have noticed that perfectly inelastic supplies look just like perfectly inelastic demands and that perfectly elastic demands and supplies also appear to be identical. How about *unitarily elastic supply* curves ($e_s = 1$)? Do they resemble unitarily elastic demand curves? Not at all. For e_s to equal one, the quantity supplied must change in fixed proportion with price. All supply curves that are straight lines through the origin have this characteristic (supply curve S_1 in Figure 7).

---

[8]Note for the mathematically adept: as the slope of a supply curve approaches zero, the elasticity of supply approaches infinity.

FIGURE 7 Elasticity Ranges For Supply Curves

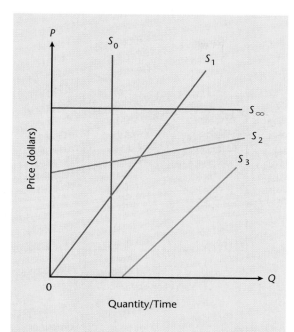

Quantity/Time

Supply curves that intersect the price axis (S_2) are *relatively elastic* ($e_s > 1$). Horizontal supply curves (S_∞) are *perfectly price elastic* ($e_s = \infty$). In such cases total revenues or spending will be exactly proportional to the quantity demanded. If the amount supplied is comparatively unresponsive to price (S_3), supply is *relatively inelastic* and, if extended, intersects the quanitiy axis. A vertical supply curve (S_0) is *perfectly price inelastic* ($e_s = 0$) and intersects the quantity axis. Although rare, such supplies do exist. Land sites are an example. In such cases, total spending (revenue) is exactly proportional to price. All supply curves that are straight lines from the origin (S_1) are *unitarily elastic* ($e_s = 1$).

FIGURE 8 Time and Price Elasticity of Supply

The longer firms have to adjust supplies, the more price elastic supplies are in response to price changes.

Supply Elasticities and Time

Time spans influence supply. Longer periods obviously enable firms to make more of a good available. Less obviously, supplies respond more strongly to price changes as time elapses because the ranges of feasible adjustment grow. For example, if eggplant prices rise, vegetable growers can increase their crops very little in only a month or two. A year or so, however, enables a farmer to acquire more seed and plow and fertilize more acreage. Thus, the price elasticity of supply is also positively related to the time interval considered. (In fact, all economic elasticities tend to be positively related to time.) Figure 8 summarizes these effects of time on supply.

ELASTICITY AND TAX BURDENS

In any year, tax reform seems to be one of the top domestic issues facing the United States. The phrase "tax reform" is just empty rhetoric unless we know who bears the burden of various taxes. Elasticity plays a major role in answering the question of who bears the tax burden.

Tax Incidence

The *legal incidence of a tax* falls on the individual or firm responsible for writing the check for taxes to government.

> The ***economic incidence*** *of taxation (or **tax burden**) falls on the person who suffers reduced purchasing power because of the tax.*

Tax burdens can be avoided by the party bearing the legal incidence through *tax shifting*. A tax passed on to the consumer in the form of higher prices is *forward shifted*. Taxes are *backward shifted* if tax burdens are transferred to workers in the form of lower take-home wages or to other resource suppliers in the form of lower factor payments.

Taxing a good drives a wedge between the price paid by buyers and the net price received by sellers. The government is a third party to the transaction causing the price paid by the buyer to exceed the price received by the seller. The tax burden tends to be shared between buyers and sellers.

Equilibrium in Figure 9 occurs at point *d* without taxes, and 16 million video tapes are sold monthly for $7 each. Suppose a $2 tax per cassette is levied on manufacturers. Graphically, the market supply of tapes falls to S_1, since firms will now have to get $9 per tape to be willing to sell 16 million (point *c*) and must receive $8 per tape to be willing to part with 12 million (point *a*). Thus, the supply curve shifts vertically by $2 (distance $cd = ab$, the amount of the tax) at each quantity.

At the new equilibrium (point *a*), the quantities supplied and demanded must be equal, but the price paid by consumers and the price received by sellers differs by the $2 tax. Thus, at the new equilibrium, buyers pay $8 for each of 12 million video tapes per month, while, net of the $2 tax, suppliers receive $6 per tape.

The intersection of taxed supplies and demands helps to identify the proportions of taxes borne by buyers and sellers. In this simple case, each side bears $1 of the tax. Consumers now pay $8 per tape (instead of $7), and sellers only get $6 per video instead of the $7 that they had previously received. Different elasticities and slopes for the supply and demand curves will yield different proportional burdens. Note that the tax reduces incentives to produce video tapes as well as incentives to buy them. Part of the tax burden is borne by consumers in terms of higher prices, and part is borne by sellers (or their employees or resource suppliers) in terms of lower output, employment, and sales. This may create inefficiency and is one reason econ-

FIGURE 9   The Incidence of Taxation

Regardless of the legal incidence, the burdens of taxes are normally shared by buyers and sellers. A $2 tax collected from sellers results in supply shrinking from S_0 to S_1. Consumers experience a $1 increase in price (from $7 to $8). Sellers see their output fall from 16 million to 12 million per month and their net of tax sales price falls to $6 (point *b*). In this example, the tax burden is split evenly between buyers and sellers, but the tax may be quite unevenly split in other situations.

omists refer to tax wedges as creating *disincentive effects*.

A critical point is that, after adjusting for taxes, the quantity demanded at the total price paid by the buyer must equal the quantity supplied at the net price received by the seller; neither excess demands (*shortages*) nor excess supplies (*surpluses*) can exist. Considering extreme elasticities helps us develop general principles about tax burdens.

• **Inelastic Supply**   The supply of land to society as a whole is roughly perfectly inelastic. Rental prices paid for land reflect demands for land, and renters do not care whether their rent

FIGURE 10 The Burden of a Tax on Land (Perfectly Inelastic Supply)

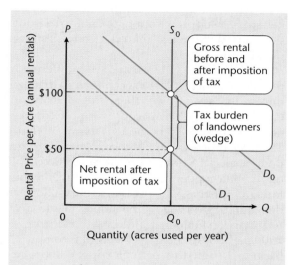

The full burden of a tax on anything that is perfectly inelastically supplied is borne by the current owner or seller. Attempts to forward-shift such taxes cause excess supplies and downward pressures on prices. (Note: The shift of the demand curve from D_0 to D_1 represents only that part of the demand curve that affects the net incomes of land owners. The full demand of buyers continues to be reflected by D_0, but half of the demand is absorbed as government revenue.)

FIGURE 11 The Burden of a Tax on Salt (Perfectly Inelastic Demand)

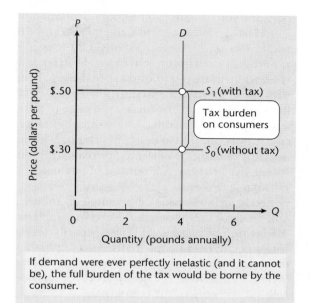

If demand were ever perfectly inelastic (and it cannot be), the full burden of the tax would be borne by the consumer.

is kept by the landlord or split between an owner and Uncle Sam. Figure 10 illustrates the effects of taxes on the demand and supply of land. The annual rent for land is $100 per acre when demand is D_0 and supply is S_0. (If landowners do not rent their land out, we might treat them as their own tenants; the opportunity cost of not renting is $100 per acre per year.)

Suppose that a 50% tax on land rents were imposed. If landlords tried to recoup the $50-per-acre tax by raising rents to above $100, there would be a surplus of rentable land. As landlords with vacant land tried to attract renters, the gross rental price of land would fall back to $100. The owners cannot avoid the $50 tax burden per acre by selling, because any buyer would base the value of land on the $50 net rent per

acre it yields, not the initial $100. From the standpoint of landowners, the demand for land has now fallen to D_1. Thus, land prices would be halved because of the 50% land rent tax; landowners bear both the legal and the economic incidence of the land tax because the supply of land is perfectly inelastic.[9]

- **Inelastic Demand** The demand for common table salt is among the least price elastic of all regular household purchases. Recognizing the inelasticity of this demand, the early Romans enacted a tax on salt to ensure that the tax burden fell on the consumer. Suppose your annual demand for salt is shown in Figure 11. Because spending on salt absorbs so little of your budget and because of an absence of substitutes, even a 300% or 400% increase in its price probably would not noticeably affect the amount you use on your eggs or the rest of your food. You will consume roughly four pounds of salt annually,

[9]An issue addressed later in this book is the single tax movement, whose advocates like the idea that landowners fully bear any tax on land.

whether salt is free, costs $0.30 a pound, $1 a pound, or whatever.

Initially, competition among salt producers permits you to buy almost any amount you would like without affecting the market price of $0.30 a pound. A new tax of $0.20 a pound would shift the supply curve to S_1 as firms now need $0.20 more per pound to break even. Even with these increased costs, suppliers can easily forward shift the tax by raising the price to $0.50 a pound, a price at which there is neither an excess supply nor excess demand. The conclusion is that if demand is perfectly inelastic, the consumer will bear the full burden of any taxes.

We stated earlier that demands are never perfectly inelastic. This salt example is intended only to show that if demand were very inelastic, the burden of a tax would fall primarily on the consumer. Would people reduce the salt in their diets if it rose to $100 per pound? Of course. Would salt be used on snowy roads or icy sidewalks at such prices? Of course not.

Elasticities of demand reflect buyers' desperation for goods because of the availability or lack of substitutes. Similarly, supply curves mirror the urgency of sellers' needs for customers because of the availability or the lack of good options for their resources. The more desperate buyers or sellers are or the smaller the proportion of their budgets devoted to the product or resource, the less elastic are their respective demands or supplies, and the more difficult it is for them to alter their behavior to avoid a tax. This makes it easier to stick them with the burdens of taxes.

Our analyses of land and salt show why governments are fond of taxes on inelastically demanded goods (tobacco, alcohol, and energy) or inelastically supplied resources (property): such taxes maximize government revenue because they have little effect on quantity consumed. Revenue projections, however, are sometimes way off. For example, nicotine patches now make revenue forecasts from cigarette taxes more tenuous because it is easier to quit. The story changes when elastic demands or supplies are taxed.

• **Elastic Demand** Arizona mines dominate U.S. copper production. Suppose Californians buy huge amounts of copper at a world price of $900 per ton after delivery costs, and that low transportation costs to California generate exceptional profits for Arizona mines. This would cause Arizonans to rely on the California market, so their supply of copper to California would slope upward (be less than perfectly elastic) as shown in Figure 12.

If individual Californians are indifferent to the choice between Arizona copper and that produced in, say, Chile, then the demand of Californians for Arizona copper is perfectly elastic at a price of $900 per ton, as shown in Figure 12. Now suppose the California legislature imposes a special $100 state tariff (read "tax") only on Arizona copper. Californians can readily buy foreign copper at $900 per ton, so the Californian demand curve facing Arizona mines falls from D_0 to D_1. Arizona miners wind up with net prices of $800 per ton. In this case, the tariff is completely backward shifted to Arizona copper mines' resource suppliers, whose wages, profits, rents, or receipts of interest must absorb this tax. Whenever demand for a good is perfectly elastic, suppliers bear the full burden of any taxes.

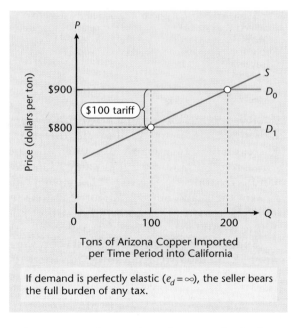

If demand is perfectly elastic ($e_d = \infty$), the seller bears the full burden of any tax.

FIGURE 12 **The Burden of a Hypothetical California Tariff on Arizona Copper (Perfectly Elastic Demand)**

Trade wars were precipitated by high state tariffs when states attempted to export their taxes to other states' citizens immediately after the American Revolution. This prompted authors of the U.S. Constitution to include a commerce clause, which reserves to the federal government the right to regulate interstate commerce. Consequently, the ability of individual states to export taxes is now quite limited.

• **Elastic Supply**   The long-run supply curve of the aluminum industry is thought to be roughly perfectly elastic because average production costs are constant, no matter how much or how little aluminum is produced. Many materials are substitutes for aluminum in some uses, but none are close substitutes in all uses. Thus, Figure 13 shows a perfectly elastic supply of aluminum and a less elastic demand for it.

Without taxation, 140 million tons of aluminum will be sold annually for $500 a ton.

If supply is perfectly elastic ($e_s = \infty$), consumers pay 100 percent of any taxes in the form of higher prices.

FIGURE 13   The Burden of a Tax on Aluminum (Perfectly Elastic Supply)

Suppose that a tax of $100 a ton were levied on aluminum producers. Supply shifts from S_0 to S_1, because the producers could not cover production costs unless they received at least $600 per ton from consumers, who cut back purchases to 120 million tons annually at this higher price. Notice that at $600 a ton, there are neither excess supplies nor excess demands. Production and consumption are both 120 million tons annually. The conclusion is that taxes will be 100% forward shifted if supplies are perfectly elastic.

Summary: Taxes and Elasticity

Taxes will be 100% forward shifted (borne by consumers) if either (a) demand is perfectly inelastic (e.g., salt) or (b) supply is perfectly elastic (e.g., aluminum). Taxes will be backward shifted completely (borne by suppliers) if either (a) supply is perfectly inelastic (e.g., land) or (b) demand is perfectly elastic (e.g., copper). You may believe that these extreme cases of elasticities are rare in the real world. Four chapters hence, you will learn that competitive markets can result in individual buyers confronting perfectly elastic supplies and in individual firms facing perfectly elastic demands for their products.

Few products have market demands and supplies that are either perfectly inelastic or perfectly elastic, but our examples do suggest a workable general principle: The greater the elasticity of market demand relative to the elasticity of market supply, the greater the backward shifting of any tax burden. The smaller the ratio (*elasticity of demand*)/(*elasticity of supply*), the greater the forward shifting of the tax burden.

Elasticity is vital for understanding the decisions of consumers and suppliers, and you will encounter numerous applications of elasticity in the coming chapters. If you feel befuddled at times when you encounter applications of elasticity, don't give up in despair. Refer back to this material to clarify terminology and then keep plugging forward.

CHAPTER REVIEW: KEY POINTS

1. The **price elasticity of demand** is a measure of the responsiveness of the amount demanded to small price changes and is defined as

$$e_d \cong \frac{\text{Percentage change in quantity demanded}}{\text{Percentage change in price}}$$

$$= \frac{\%\Delta Q_d}{\%\Delta P}$$

2. Problems result when calculating elasticity if initial prices and quantities are used as bases, so economists typically use *midpoint bases*. The price elasticity of demand is negative, but, for convenience, economists use absolute values to avoid the negative sign.

3. If price elasticity is less than one, then demand is relatively unresponsive to changes in price and is said to be **inelastic**. If elasticity is greater than one, the demand is very responsive to price changes and is **elastic**. Demand is **unitarily elastic** if the elasticity coefficient equals one.

4. Elasticity, price changes, and total revenues (i.e., expenditures) are related in the following manner: if demand is inelastic (or elastic) and price increases (or falls), total revenue will rise. If demand is elastic (or inelastic) and price rises (or falls), total revenue (i.e., expenditures) will fall. If demand is unitarily elastic ($e_d = 1$), total revenue will be unaffected by price changes.

5. The number and quality of substitutes, the proportion of the total budget spent, and the length of time considered are three important determinants of the elasticity of demand. Demand is more elastic the more substitutes are available, the more of the budget the item consumes, and the longer the time frame considered.

6. Along any negatively sloped linear demand curve, parts of the curve will be elastic, unitarily elastic, and, finally, inelastic. The price elasticity of demand rises as the price rises.

7. **Income elasticity of demand** is the proportional change in the amount of a good demanded divided by a given proportionate change in income. *Normal goods* have income elasticities above zero, while *inferior goods* have negative income elasticities.

8. **Cross price elasticity of demand** measures the responsiveness of the quantity demanded of one good to price changes in a related good. That is, price cross elasticity is the proportional change in the quantity of good *X* (e.g., Chevrolets) divided by a given proportional change in the price of good *Y* (e.g., Fords). If the cross elasticity of demand is positive (or *negative*), the goods are *substitutes* (or *complements*).

9. The **price elasticity of supply** measures the responsiveness of suppliers to changes in prices, and its definition parallels that for the price elasticity of demand: the proportional change in the amount supplied divided by a given proportional change in price. The price elasticity of supply is typically positive, reflecting the positive slope of the supply curve.

10. All economic elasticities tend to increase as the time interval considered becomes longer. Thus, long-run supplies and demands are more price elastic (and flatter) than short-run supplies and demands.

11. Individual firms (sellers) often face perfectly elastic demands and individual consumers (buyers) often face perfectly elastic supplies for products. Market demands and supplies, however, are almost never perfectly elastic.

12. The individual who actually loses purchasing power because of a tax is said to bear the tax's **economic incidence** (*tax burden*). This may be quite different from the individual who is legally responsible for the tax, who bears its *legal incidence*. When these individuals differ, the tax has been shifted. A tax can be *forward shifted* (to con-

sumers) or *backward shifted* (to labor or other resource owners).

13. If demand is perfectly inelastic or supply is perfectly elastic, a tax will be completely forward shifted. If supply is perfectly inelastic or demand is perfectly elastic, the tax will be completely backward shifted.

QUESTIONS FOR THOUGHT AND DISCUSSION

1. Prices for precious metals are set on worldwide commodity exchanges and are influenced by the values of major currencies, investors' inflationary expectations, and the state of international relations. These price changes clearly affect the quantities of gold and silver ingots sold, as well as the amounts of jewelry sold. Gold is also used extensively by dentists for bridges, inlays, and crowns. The *Wall Street Journal* reports that when gold prices jump from $415 to $875 per ounce, gold consumption by dentists falls from 706,000 ounces to 341,000 ounces. Compute the price elasticity of demand for gold as used by dentists for bridges, inlays, and crowns.

2. When you calculate cross elasticity of demand, what are you trying to determine? What does a negative coefficient signify? A positive coefficient?

3. Some sports fans support the home team regardless of how well the team does; others only buy tickets if the team is a winner. Demand grows as a team's record improves. Would you expect the price elasticity of demand to rise or fall as a result of a winning season? That is, would you expect season-ticket prices to rise more than proportionally relative to other tickets as a team's record improved, or less than proportionally? Is the elasticity of supply of tickets to sporting events zero, or is it positive over the long run? Why?

4. Suppose you are the state tax commissioner, and your state legislature decides to raise $120 million in annual tax revenues by imposing a $1 tax per case of beer. They have looked at the figures, and 10 million cases of beer are sold monthly at $3 per case in your state. If you were called to testify before the legislative tax committee, what would you have to say about their prospects for $120 million in new revenues? Suppose your estimate of the price elasticity of the demand for beer equals one. How high would the tax need to be to yield the desired revenues?

5. The British *Globe and Mail* reported that, in 1981, England drastically increased taxes on cigarettes:

    In an austere March budget, the conservative government slapped an extra 30 cents on the tax for a pack of 20. It followed with another increase in July, sending the tax up 30 percent [44 cents total increase in taxes] in six months and the average price of a pack to the equivalent of about $2.50.

    Taxes grew to absorb roughly 75% of the total price of a pack of cigarettes; one industry expert estimated that cigarette sales would decline to 107 billion from the 121.5 billion sold in 1980.

    a. Use the expert's forecast of industry sales to compute the price elasticity of demand for cigarettes. Is the demand for cigarettes relatively elastic or relatively inelastic? Does your answer conform to your intuition about the nature of the demand for cigarettes?

    b. How much added tax revenue could the British government expect to collect? How much sales revenue (after taxes) could the tobacco companies expect to lose?

    c. Approximately how much would the tobacco companies have had to increase prices to keep their after-tax revenues from falling?

Elasticity

Cost

Profit

Chapter 21

Long run

ATC

Consumer Choice

AVC

Production

Consumer surplus

AFC

Economics relies on some concepts of human behavior that are closely akin to psychology in explaining consumers' choices as they try to maximize their satisfactions, either individually or as family units. Scarcity forces people to choose. In this chapter, we consider how individuals choose rationally in attempts to maximize their satisfaction or economic welfare. You will see that marginal analysis provides a logical view of consumer choices, which sometimes superficially seem dominated by fads or whims. The consumer behavior we describe is also vital information for making business decisions, as you will discover while studying the next few chapters.

The major goal in this chapter is to explore some foundations of consumer behavior. We will extend the analysis of Chapter 3 to discover what lies behind demand curves and why they slope downward. We will begin by categorizing things that satisfy or displease people and distinguishing between commodities and services. The focus then turns to utility analysis, which offers an economic interpretation of rational consumer behavior. How substitution and in-

come effects translate into total price effects along a demand curve is also explored. Then we will examine the issue of consumer sovereignty versus consumer regulation. Optional material on indifference analysis concludes the chapter. All these concepts should provide many insights into your own behavior and the behavior of others in their everyday living and consuming.

COMMODITIES AND SERVICES

A *good* is anything that adds to our enjoyment of life; a *bad* detracts from our happiness. *Consumer goods* directly enhance satisfaction and include most ordinary objects of everyday use: food, clothing, cars, and so on. *Capital goods* include machines and other produced resources that benefit us less directly by generating consumer goods. Distinguishing these types of goods may require looking at use. For example, cars are consumer goods when used by households, but capital goods if used by firms. Huge surpluses may convert goods into bads; many home gardeners are inundated with more zucchini than they or their neighbors can eat, and much of it winds up in the trash.

Commodities are produced goods that can be owned; cowboy boots and garden hoses are examples. We can hire and enjoy *services* without necessarily buying the items or agents that produce them: tuition gives you access to classes, but you own neither your desk nor your instructor. Examples of other services are medical care and TV broadcasts.

It is important to note, however, that all goods are ultimately reducible to services. For example, different foods service various parts of our bodies. Bicycles transport us. Houses protect us from foul weather, and clothes warm and adorn us. Machines transform materials to create commodities that are enjoyed when they generate services. In fact, virtually every economic activity has value only to the extent that it generates useful services. Capital goods, land, and commodities simply embody streams of services.

Market systems allow ownership of most service-producing goods, but the government prohibits owning slaves, nuclear weapons, or certain illegal substances. Development of a consumer theory to explain how individuals select among service-producing goods begins with a look at the concept of utility.

UTILITY

Nineteenth-century economists were fascinated by utilitarianism, a school of thought founded by Jeremy Bentham, an eccentric English philosopher.

> **Utilitarianism** *is the idea that the pleasure or pain from any activity respectively adds or detracts from a person's utility, or satisfaction.*

Utilitarians proposed numerous social reforms in hopes of achieving their central goal, the greatest happiness for the greatest number. Utilitarians assumed that individual pleasure can be measured and then summed, each person being weighted equally, to calculate aggregate social welfare.

Imagine that people were born with forehead gauges that recorded satisfaction in utils, an imaginary measurement, much as your electric meter measures kilowatts. Over lunch your gauge registers the following: 1 burger = 73 utils; 17 french fries = 31 utils; a small cola = 24 utils; and a net gain = 128 utils. Measuring the subjective value of national income would be a snap: simply sum everyone's gains in total utility. A utilitarian goal would boil economic policy down to doing whatever was necessary to maximize the utility score.

The appealing goal of achieving the greatest happiness for the greatest number remains a basis for policies advocated by many politicians, but it raises some acute normative issues. The Russian author Fyodor Dostoyevski confounded utilitarians with his anguished question, "What if eternal happiness for the rest of humanity could be bought with the death by torture of an innocent babe?" Policies that unambiguously maximize social utility in an ethical manner could not be devised even if utilometers existed.

Utility analysis offers rich insights into human behavior. Although subjective gains from a dollar's worth of goods may vary considerably among individuals, the following section shows how we can approximate the relative satisfactions from various goods to a given individual by looking at utility in monetary terms.

Modern economics rejects direct utility measures because (*a*) most of us cannot specify our preferences more precisely than by a rank order (first, second, and so on) of possible bundles of goods, and (*b*) satisfaction is not scientifically comparable between individuals. There is no way to ascertain exactly how much anyone likes candy (or anything else) relative to someone else's enjoyment of candy. This led economists to develop *indifference analysis*, a more scientific technique explored at the end of the chapter.

Total and Marginal Utility

Suppose you enjoy quenching your thirst on hot days with fresh lemonade. If we measure utility in dollar terms, then the marginal utility of

BIOGRAPHY

Jeremy Bentham: The Birth of Utilitarianism

Jeremy Bentham (1748–1832), a lawyer, philosopher, and social reformer, was hardly an economist, although his influence on subsequent economic thought was immense. He admired the ideas of Adam Smith but rejected Smith's view that people's interests are smoothly reconciled through the invisible hand of competitive markets. Bentham focused on conflicts between private and public interests, especially as manifested in illegal activities. He saw Smith's "harmony of interests" as desirable, but not as a natural consequence of human behavior. Thus, Bentham devoted his long life to designing institutions that would facilitate the harmony of interests Smith took for granted.

Bentham tried to integrate law, economics, politics, and education into a unified science of behavior. His theory identified pleasure and pain as the forces controlling human actions. The goal of Bentham's hedonistic philosophy was the attainment of the greatest good, or *maximum utility*.

Bentham's most conspicuous successes were in law and judicial procedure. He applied the principles of utility and "felicific calcula-

tion" to crime and punishment, suggesting that the evil of a crime is proportionate to the number of people it harms. It follows, therefore, that punishment of crimes should not be based on mere motive, but on the amount of social pain caused by a felony. Properly speaking, Bentham viewed law and law enforcement from the economic perspective of incentives. He theorized that stiffer punishments would raise the cost of crime, compelling self-interested individuals to commit fewer misdeeds, and the public interest would be served.

Bentham was notably eccentric. His pet pig roamed freely through his mansion, and he once petitioned the London City Council for permission to line his driveway with mummified human cadavers, which he thought "far more aesthetic than flowers." At the age of 32, Bentham immodestly stated, "[I] dreamt the other night that I was a founder of a sect; of course a personage of great sanctity and importance. It was the sect of the utilitarians."

Despite his eccentricities, Bentham's dream proved prophetic. His ideas attracted a

loyal group of disciples (including the philosophers James Mill and his son, John Stuart Mill), and his proposals for social reforms were widely translated into action. Benthamite principles were among the intellectual wellsprings of many nineteenth-century social reforms. Possibly the secret of Bentham's success is that he instilled in his disciples not only specific ideals but also concrete plans to achieve them.

Bentham also dreamed of immortality. His sizable estate was left to the University of London on the condition that his body be embalmed in a certain way, stuffed and dressed in his own suit of clothes, and that it attend all meetings of the University's trustees. In this way, Bentham hoped to be present whenever utilitarian principles were discussed at his university. Bentham's wishes were carried out. (Minutes of all trustees' meetings record him as "present but not voting.") Over 160 years later, the dauntless utilitarian still resides in his glass closet in a corridor at University College, the University of London.

---

lemonade, MU_L, is roughly the amount you would willingly pay for an extra lemonade. For example, after three sets of tennis on a 90° afternoon, suppose you stroll into your town's only air-conditioned lemonade stand, where the server, an old friend, informs you that icy, fresh lemonade is now $1 per glass. Your throat parched, you decide that one glass is barely

worth $1. As you finish it and rise to leave, the ade-tender offers you a break: a second lemonade for only $0.85. "All right," you say, "just one more." After gulping it down, you are already off your stool when the ade-tender asks, "How about another for $0.60?" Sitting back down, you put money on the counter. After your third lemonade, she asks, "How about a fourth at the old price of $0.50?" Somewhat befuddled, you nod your head. The four lemonades have cost you $2.95 ($1.00 + $0.85 + $0.60 + $0.50), and your total utility is shown in Panel A of Figure 1. Notice that total utility is rising as you drink these additional lemonades.

After the fourth glass, you are ready to face the heat, but the ade-tender offers you still another glass, this one for only $0.25. You cannot pass up the bargain. Then she invites you to have a sixth lemonade on the house. It is 90° in the shade, so you assent. Feeling a bit waterlogged, you turn down the offer of a seventh, even though it is free. "Tell you what," she says, "will you drink it if I pay you $0.50?" Being an impoverished student, you agree. You also drink an eighth, for which you are paid $1. Ultimately, however, you approach your capacity. You

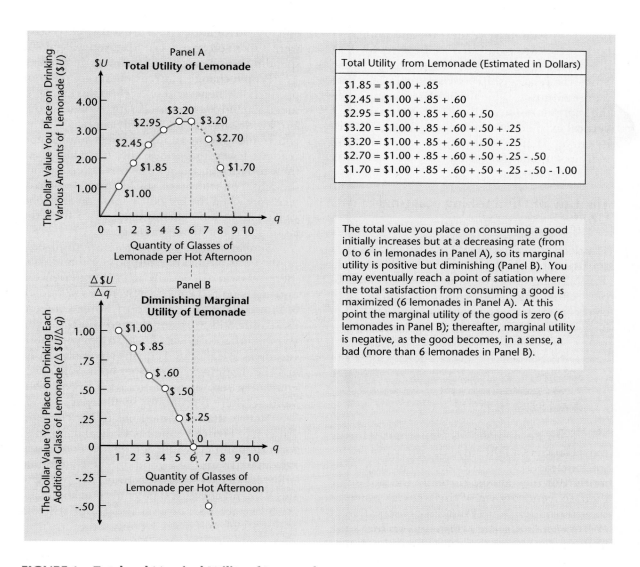

Total Utility from Lemonade (Estimated in Dollars)

$1.85 = $1.00 + .85
$2.45 = $1.00 + .85 + .60
$2.95 = $1.00 + .85 + .60 + .50
$3.20 = $1.00 + .85 + .60 + .50 + .25
$3.20 = $1.00 + .85 + .60 + .50 + .25
$2.70 = $1.00 + .85 + .60 + .50 + .25 - .50
$1.70 = $1.00 + .85 + .60 + .50 + .25 - .50 - 1.00

The total value you place on consuming a good initially increases but at a decreasing rate (from 0 to 6 in lemonades in Panel A), so its marginal utility is positive but diminishing (Panel B). You may eventually reach a point of satiation where the total satisfaction from consuming a good is maximized (6 lemonades in Panel A). At this point the marginal utility of the good is zero (6 lemonades in Panel B); thereafter, marginal utility is negative, as the good becomes, in a sense, a bad (more than 6 lemonades in Panel B).

FIGURE 1   Total and Marginal Utility of Lemonade

agree to drink the ninth for the $3 she offers, but only if you can wait a half-hour. Since it's now or never, you decide to pass. (You would drink the ninth for $25, but she will not offer that much.)

Marginal utilities from different goods reflect our subjective preferences.

> **Marginal utility (MU)** *is the gain in satisfaction derived through the consumption of one additional unit of a good.*

Panel B of Figure 1 shows how the marginal utilities in dollars are related to your total satisfaction from lemonade (Panel A). The points on both curves are connected as if the server had offered these deals by sips rather than glassfuls. Study the relationship between total utility and marginal utility. The accumulated area under the marginal utility curve (note the expanded vertical axis) equals the height of the total utility curve. That is, total utility is the sum of the marginal utilities for each lemonade you drank.

The Law of Diminishing Marginal Utility

The declining marginal utility from lemonade as you drink more and more during a given time interval occurs with virtually all goods and all people. Observing that similar reactions were common, classical economists generalized this behavior into

> The **law of diminishing marginal utility**: *The marginal utility from consuming equal units of a good eventually declines as the amount consumed increases.*

The word "eventually" is important. Horror movie fanciers might enjoy their first movie this week immensely and their second film even more. But they almost certainly will not enjoy their sixteenth movie of the week as much as their third. Benjamin Franklin's observation in *Poor Richard's Almanac,* "Fish and visitors stink in three days," says far more about the diminishing marginal utility of visitors than about the deterioration of fish.

CONSUMER EQUILIBRIUM AND DEMAND

Individuals try to maximize their satisfaction, and firms try to maximize their profits. These types of *optimization* require minimizing costs incurred in accomplishing any given task. The following concept governs all optimization processes: The *law of equal marginal advantage* requires equivalent goods or similar resources to be allocated in equally advantageous ways at the margin. Failure to conform to this principle is inefficient. For example, if the last dollar you spend on magazines fails to yield the added pleasure you would receive were it spent on an extra sundae, you will gain by spending less on magazines and more on sundaes.

People change patterns of consumption or production whenever resources (in this example, the command over resources represented by your last few dollars) are inefficiently allocated. Thus, you would gain by eating an extra sundae and reading fewer magazines and probably make these sorts of adjustments with very little conscious thought. You settle into a stable consumption pattern only when the last dollar spent on any good yields satisfaction equal to that gained from the last dollar spent on any other good.

Similar *marginal adjustments* span all economic decision-making. Suppose you and your identical twin are equally strong, experienced, and intelligent. If your twin produces $64 worth of mowed lawns in eight hours, while you generate only $48 worth of cleaned windows, you should shift into mowing lawns so that your labor resources are allocated equally advantageously, at $8 per hour instead of $6 per hour. Whenever equivalent resources are not used to equal advantage, there is economic inefficiency.

Notice that the marginal utility curve in Panel B of Figure 1 contains all the data needed for a demand curve for lemonade: consumers buy an extra unit of a good only if its marginal utility is not exceeded by its price. According to this demand curve, you buy only one lemonade at $1, two at $0.85, three at $0.60, four at $0.50, five at $0.25, and drink six only if they are free. This example illustrates how early economists explained negative slopes of demand curves by the law of diminishing marginal utility.

Maximizing Utility

We see that relative satisfactions from goods can be approximated by looking at utility in terms of money. We cannot scientifically ascertain whether one person gains more than someone else from an extra dollar of income or extra syrup on a waffle. We may be fairly sure, however, that the personal marginal utilities of each person from particular goods are roughly proportional to the goods' prices, because people adjust their spending patterns whenever relative prices and marginal utilities are not in balance.

Suppose that you allocate $12 from your weekly budget for ice cream, your favorite snack. Table 1 lists your total and marginal utilities from macadamia nut crunch and chocolate ice cream cones. How many of each will you buy at $1 apiece to maximize your satisfaction? Eating five chocolate and seven crunch cones maximizes your total satisfaction at 46 utils per week. No other $12 combination yields more utility.

Let's see how this purchasing pattern develops. Table 1 shows that your first macadamia nut cone generates 8 utils while your first chocolate cone yields only 5 utils. Thus, your first purchase will be a macadamia nut cone. What flavor would you buy second? Each cone is $1, and a second macadamia nut yields extra satisfaction of 7 utils. Your third choice will also be macadamia nut, which increases your satisfaction by 6 utils. Now, your fourth macadamia nut cone only yields 4 utils compared to 5 utils for your first chocolate cone. Thus, your fourth

TABLE 1 Total (TU) and Marginal (MU) Utilities for Ice Cream Cones (price = $1 per cone)

Macadamia Nut Crunch			Chocolate		
Quantity	TU	MU	Quantity	TU	MU
1	8	8	1	5	5
2	15	7	2	9	4
3	21	6	3	12	3
4	25	4	4	14	2
5	28	3	5	15	1
6	30	2	6	15	0
7	31	1			

cone will be chocolate. You will ultimately spend the $12 on seven macadamia nut and five chocolate cones per week. Notice that the decision for each purchase hinges on the flavor with the greatest marginal utility per dollar spent.

Balancing Marginal Utilities

In the example shown in Table 1, your purchasing pattern suggested that you would look at the next cone, whether chocolate or macadamia nut and determine which flavor provided you with the largest increase in utility.

> The **principle of equal marginal utilities per dollar:** *A consumer maximizes utility when the last dollar spent on any good generates the same satisfaction as the last dollar spent on every other good.*

Your purchasing pattern becomes stable only when the last dollar spent on ice cream yields the same satisfaction as the last dollar spent on lemonade, clothes, books, or housing.

Satisfaction from the last spending on a good is calculated by dividing its marginal utility by its price. For example, if the last chocolate cone was $1 and its marginal utility was 1, then $MU_{ch}/P_{ch} = 1/1 = 1$, and the marginal utility per dollar of the last cone was 1. Individuals are in equilibrium when

$$\frac{MU_a}{P_a} = \frac{MU_b}{P_b} = \ldots = \frac{MU_z}{P_z}$$

where $a, b, \ldots, z$ are the various goods purchased. In our ice cream cone example, the marginal utilities per dollar equaled one for both macadamia nut crunch and chocolate cones. By equating marginal utilities per dollar, utility is maximized. No other allocation of resources will result in higher satisfaction. A little introspection should confirm that your own spending pattern conforms to this principle of equal marginal utilities per dollar.

A corollary of the principle of equal marginal utilities per dollar is that consumer equilibrium requires that *marginal benefits from every*

Rational Ignorance and Artificial Intelligence

Research into **artificial intelligence (AI)** has traditionally relied on pure logic to create computer programs intended to mimic the thinking of rational people. After two decades of research, researchers are beginning to conclude that being logical and behaving rationally are not necessarily the same thing.

Logical thinking generally means that absolutely sound inferences require consistency with precisely specified sets of assumptions. Unfortunately, according to MIT professor Jon Doyle, "any set of beliefs and any sound inference is as good as any other. Logicism ignores the purpose of reasoning and the value of beliefs and reasoning to the reasoner."

To avoid this conundrum, Professor Doyle argues that economic notions of consumer rationality and choice offer a set of

tools that may help AI researchers design machines that are as rational as humans. As this chapter illustrates, the economic concept of consumer rationality involves

1. Consumer preferences.
2. Limited resources that entail costs; accomplishing any objective involves expenditures of time, money, and effort.
3. Maximization of some goal, generally utility.

Professor Doyle notes that economic analysis "provide[s] the proper framework for addressing the problem of how one should think, given that thinking requires effort and that success is uncertain." Computers, like people, must make trade-offs. For example, examining all possible moves in a chess game may be possible, depending on how long you are

willing to wait for an answer, but inefficient. People inherently seem to know that learning involves something other than memorization. Indiscriminate memorization simply leads to memory clogging for both people and computers.

In the future, rational learning and artificial intelligence should combine to better equip computers (which have only limited storage capacity) so that they can discern what information is important and what to ignore. Future computers ideally will mimic people's thinking processes in sensing when it is wise to be rationally ignorant.

Sources: John Doyle, "Rationality and Its Role in Reasoning," *Proceedings of the Eighth National Conference on Artificial Intelligence* (AAAI Press, 1990), pp. 1093–1100; and "When Logic Is Not Enough," *The Economist*, 23 August 1990, pp. 69–70.

---

good are proportional to their relative market prices. Market prices and the subjective demand prices discussed in Chapter 1 are different ways of viewing opportunity costs. Demand prices can be thought of as the ratios of the marginal utilities of various goods. Only if market prices do not exceed demand prices will you buy. In equilibrium, these subjective price ratios must equal the relative market prices for all the goods you choose to purchase. That is, $MU_a/MU_b = P_a/P_b$ for any two goods we choose to label a and b, respectively.[1] Focus 1 addresses the issue of whether economic assumptions about how people process information are reasonable.

---

[1]This statement is compatible with the principle of equal marginal utilities per dollar because in equilibrium, $MU_a/P_a = MU_b/P_b$; if each side of the equation is multiplied by P_b/MU_b and then simplified, the result is that $MU_a/MU_b = P_a/P_b$.

Price Adjustments and Marginal Utility

Let's use this format to describe how quantities demanded adjust as relative prices change. First, consider what would happen to your equilibrium purchases of ice cream cones (from Table 1) if a worldwide macadamia nut crop failure boosted the price of macadamia nut crunch to $2 per cone. Your utility schedules along with the new prices are shown in Table 2. You now buy only four macadamia nut crunch cones, and your consumption of chocolate cones drops to four per week. Marginal utilities per dollar now equal 2. Adjusting your spending pattern to various possible prices for macadamia nut ice cream traces out the demand curve shown in Figure 2.

To summarize, the higher-priced goods you buy uniformly generate more marginal utility

TABLE 2 Total (TU) and Marginal (MU) Utilities for Ice Cream Cones When the Price of Macadamia Nut Crunch Rises to $2 per Cone

Macadamia Nut Crunch				Chocolate			
Quantity	TU	MU	MU/P	Quantity	TU	MU	MU/P
1	8	8	4.0	1	5	5	5.0
2	15	7	3.5	2	9	4	4.0
3	21	6	3.0	3	12	3	3.0
4	25	4	2.0	4	14	2	2.0
5	28	3	1.5	5	15	1	1.0
6	30	2	1.0	6	15	0	0
7	31	1	0.5	7	14	−1	

than your lower-priced purchases: the more you pay for a good, the more it is worth to you at the margin. You are in equilibrium when the marginal utilities per dollar are equal for all goods. Ultimately, the last dollar you spend on any good yields the same satisfaction as the last dollar spent on any other good. Finally, if you choose not to spend all of your money, the satisfaction you gain from your saving or holding each dollar must equal the satisfaction you would gain from spending it on some other good.

Effects of Price Changes

You will buy less of any good that rises in price, substituting for it goods that decline in relative price. Another effect when the price of a good rises is that the purchasing power of your income shrinks. This drop in purchasing power reduces your total ability to buy consumer goods and services. How purchasing patterns respond when the prices of goods change can be decomposed into **substitution effects** and **income effects**.

When the price of macadamia nut ice cream cones rises from $1 to $2, the equilibrium quantity falls from 7 to 4 cones per week (based on the data in Table 2). As an exercise, calculate the price elasticity of demand for these cones for this price change.

FIGURE 2   The Demand for Macadamia Nut Ice Cream

• **Substitution Effects**   Substitution is the primary cause of negative slopes along demand curves.

> *The **substitution effect** is that portion of the change in quantity demanded due solely to a change in relative prices.*[2]

---

[2]Mathematically, the substitution effect of a change in the price of a good is always negative. This means that an increase in the price ($\Delta P > 0$) of some good (coffee, for example) will result in a substitution effect (toward tea?) that decreases the amount of coffee consumed ($\Delta Q < 0$). Thus, $\Delta Q / \Delta P$ is negative. Conversely, the substitution effect means that a decrease ($\Delta P < 0$) in the relative price of a good (say, ham) will cause increases ($\Delta Q > 0$) in the quantity consumed (and substitution away from beef). Again, $\Delta Q / \Delta P$ is negative.

Most goods have numerous possible uses. When the price of a good is reduced, it will be advantageous to devote the good to more of these uses.

For example, buses now provide low-priced transportation for many of us. Rides would be economical for far more people if fares were $0, and the homeless might sleep on warm buses instead of in cold alleys or under bridges. A $15 bus fare would induce most of us to walk, drive cars, or hire taxis. When ballpoint pens were introduced in the 1940s, they were refillable, cost about $25 each, and were a status symbol for busy executives. They now cost about a quarter, are used by almost everyone, and are discarded when the ink runs dry. Expensive ink pens are rare, and pencils are less commonly used than they would be if ballpoints still cost $25.

These examples suggest that we substitute some uses of some goods for similar uses of related goods as relative prices change. The critical point is that it is always advantageous to substitute away from goods that become relatively more costly and to expand uses for goods that become cheaper. Substitution effects are always negative and underpin the law of demand: *quantity demanded falls as price increases, and vice versa.*

The substitution effect is the change in purchasing patterns caused by changes in relative prices alone, artificially assuming constancy in total purchasing power. But rising prices, for example, will reduce the purchasing power of your income. We need to deal separately with how such changes in real income alter purchasing patterns.

• **Income Effects** The purchasing power of your dollars falls if prices rise, but a dollar buys more consumer goods if prices fall.

> **Income effects** *are adjustments people make because the purchasing power of a given income is altered when prices change.*

Suppose that a $400 tuition per semester hour absorbs so much of your budget that you initially take classes only part-time. If stellar performance elicited a 90% scholarship, you could afford everything you bought previously and might simply pocket the $360 per semester hour your scholarship now covers. Instead, you would probably enroll in more courses, in part because of substitution in response to this drop in the relative cost of tuition, but also because of the now greater purchasing power of your income. This income effect would allow enrollment in even more courses, or you might buy more books, a better calculator, nicer clothes, tastier food, or more frequent concert tickets.

The income effect may be negative, positive, or zero. All else being equal, when the price of a good rises, your purchasing power falls. For normal goods, the income effect is positive. For example, a decrease in the price of gasoline increases the purchasing power of your income. This alone results in higher levels of gas purchases. However, the income effect is negative for inferior goods such as lard, potatoes, lye soap, or black-eyed peas. For example, if your diet largely consists of potatoes because you are poor and they are cheap, your purchasing power increases if the price of potatoes falls and you can afford to buy tastier foods to secure your caloric needs. Even though you may buy more potatoes because of the substitution effect, the independent effect of your higher real income is to reduce potato consumption.

In summary, when prices fall, consumers substitute towards lower-priced goods and are able to buy more of all goods as their overall purchasing power grows. Falling prices generate these two benefits for consumers, but as we see next, market-set prices generate an additional benefit known as consumer surplus.

Consumer Surplus

We can look at individual demand curves for a specific good from two different perspectives:

1. Most of the time we see demand curves as answers to the question, "How much will be

bought at each possible price?" The quantity demanded depends on the price.

2. Alternatively, we might view demand curves as graphing answers to the question, "If people have certain amounts of good *X*, what is the most they would be willing to pay for an extra unit of *X*?"

This second perspective views price as depending on quantity. Both approaches yield the same demand curves.

The view that a good's marginal value depends on the amount available is a key to specifying in monetary terms the satisfaction gained from being able to buy at a single market price. Using our original lemonade example (see Figure 3), you paid $2.95 total for the first four glasses, but only $0.50 for the fourth (last) glass. But if lemonade sold for a flat price of $0.50 per glass, you would spend $2 to drink four lemonades, thereby gaining $0.95 worth of utility. This gain represents consumer surplus.

Consumer surplus *is the difference between the amounts people would willingly pay for various amounts of specific goods and the amounts they do pay at market prices.*

This is roughly the area below the demand curve but above the price line, assuming that income effects are trivial.

Even though consumer surplus cannot be measured quantitatively, this concept permits qualitative assessments of such things as the efficiency of some of the government policies addressed in a later chapter.

The Paradox of Value

Two hundred years ago, economists were stumped by an apparent paradox:

*The **paradox of value** addresses why absolute necessities such as water are valued (priced) so*

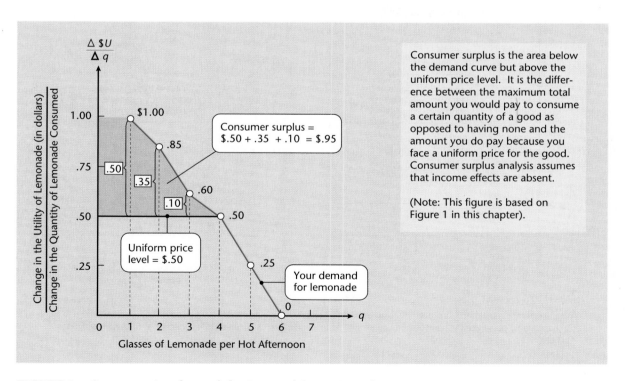

Consumer surplus is the area below the demand curve but above the uniform price level. It is the difference between the maximum total amount you would pay to consume a certain quantity of a good as opposed to having none and the amount you do pay because you face a uniform price for the good. Consumer surplus analysis assumes that income effects are absent.

(Note: This figure is based on Figure 1 in this chapter).

FIGURE 3   Consumer Surplus and the Demand for Lemonade

cheaply, while frivolities like diamonds are highly valued and command outrageous prices.

Questions about this paradox were used to stump Ph.D. candidates in economics for generations. It arises from difficulties in distinguishing between total utility and marginal utility.

Suppose that Panel A in Figure 4 depicts your family's demand for water. If you are typical, water is so cheap that you treat drinking water as if it were free: you drink water until an extra glass would actually detract from your well-being; the marginal utility is zero. However, because you know that your water bill (which averages $20 monthly) reflects total use, you are probably somewhat careful about watering your lawn, washing your car, fixing leaky faucets, running bath water, and so on.

But suppose you were offered an all-or-nothing choice: 100 gallons of water for $500

monthly or no water at all. (Many American families use 100,000 gallons or more a month.) If you could afford it, you would willingly pay at least $500 per month for water, limiting its use to drinking, preparing food, and sponge baths. Your lawn and plants would die, your car would go dirty, and washing machines and flush toilets would be forgotten luxuries. (Do you think this might explain why prospectors smell ripe after a few days of roaming the desert?) If you had to, you would pay considerably more for the 10,000 gallons of water you use each month than the $20 or so you do pay, so water yields an enormous consumer surplus.

The total utility of water is substantially higher than its marginal utility and price, while the total utility of diamonds is close to their marginal utility and price. The areas representing consumer surpluses in Figure 4 are shaded. This analysis should help you understand why diamonds, which are not nearly as necessary to life

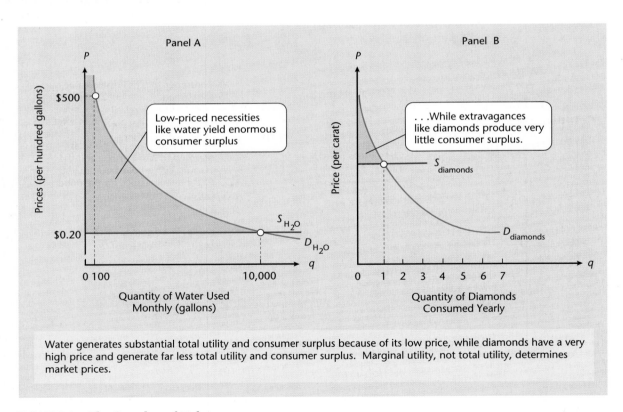

Panel A

Panel B

Low-priced necessities like water yield enormous consumer surplus

. . .While extravagances like diamonds produce very little consumer surplus.

Water generates substantial total utility and consumer surplus because of its low price, while diamonds have a very high price and generate far less total utility and consumer surplus. Marginal utility, not total utility, determines market prices.

FIGURE 4   The Paradox of Value

as water is, are valued and priced much higher than water. The total utility, marginal utility, and price of diamonds are nearly identical for those of us who own, at most, a few of the baubles. The lesson to be learned from the paradox of value is that marginal utility, not total utility, determines the value and market price of individual products.

INFORMATION AND RATIONAL CHOICE

Typical shoppers would view you as an annoying know-it-all if you asked if their consumption patterns caused their marginal utilities for the various goods they buy to be in fixed proportions to prices, implying equivalent MU/P for all items purchased. Suppose instead that you asked why they buy certain amounts of particular goods, or why they reject others. They might mumble that some items are "good buys," while referring to others as "overpriced" or "not worth it to me." Most of the time, people seem to behave as economic models of demand suggest, even if they don't understand the jargon economists use to describe their behavior.

Economists, however, are far from unanimity on whether people really act in very rational or calculating ways. Take a moment to read the biographical sketch of Thorstein Veblen, a founder of the institutionalist school of thought, which largely rejects the kind of reasoning we have described. One reason for skepticism is that many goods are much more complex than the simple abstractions considered by much of economic theory.

Goods as Bundles of Attributes

Consumer theory has been expanded recently to consider every good as embodying a variety of utility-relevant characteristics, or *attributes*. Cigarettes provide oral gratification and give smokers "something to do with my hands"; they are also carcinogenic, stimulate hostility from nonsmokers, and waste time. Sugar Smacks have a certain texture and taste and loads of calories. Rice and potatoes have very similar attrib-

utes and are thus substitutes; each is also quite complementary with steak.

The complex mixes of attributes embodied in most goods complicate many decisions. For example, even the best-trained doctors and pharmacists may be unaware of drug interactions that can leave tragedy in their wake. Nevertheless, we all must make decisions in an imperfect world rife with uncertainty.

Uncertainty and Imperfect Information

You can never be 100% certain of the attributes of a specific unit of any good, no matter how familiar. You may inadvertently buy a moldy loaf of your favorite bread or be injured by an exploding cigarette lighter. There is even less certainty about unfamiliar goods that are bought only once or twice in a lifetime. No one who undergoes surgery can ever be certain in advance about the outcome of an operation. Nor, for that matter, can any surgeon. Uncertainty exists because we have only imperfect information about the present and no crystal ball to predict the future.

Transaction costs would be minimal in a static world. Constant change drives up the costs of acquiring and updating information. Securing full information would be impossible, any attempt to do so would be prohibitively costly, and some information has only trivial value. The result is that decisions are made in an environment of rational ignorance.

Rational ignorance occurs because people seek information only as long as their expected benefit exceeds their expected cost. Thus, consumers choose to be rationally ignorant of much information.

For example, most goods are available at a wide range of monetary prices, and most people pay more than the lowest monetary prices at a given time. But searching until you were sure you were paying the least possible for a good would probably absorb time and effort worth more than any resulting monetary saving. Similarly, you might spend a lifetime trying to identify the perfect spouse for you from the population of single people. The costliness of search, however,

BIOGRAPHY

Thorstein B. Veblen: Status and the Leisure Class

The economic characterization of human behavior as the rational calculation of benefits and costs seemed ludicrous to Thorstein Veblen (1857–1929), one of the great iconoclasts and tragicomic figures of economics. Veblen was trained in philosophy but concentrated on economics because of what he perceived as deficiencies in economic analysis.

A first-generation American of Norwegian stock, Veblen viewed capitalism and the American scene as if he were a newcomer to the planet. He found the institutions and behavior of Americans more than a bit strange—exotic and bizarre are probably more appropriate terms. His intellectual work consists primarily of cultural analysis, the high-water mark of which is pungent criticism. A good example of his satire is contained in this attack on the marginal utility principle:

> *The hedonistic conception of man is that of a lightning calculator of pleasures and pains, who oscillates like a homogeneous globule of desire . . . under the impulse of stimuli that shift him about the area but leave him intact. . . . He is an isolated, definitive human datum, in stable equilibrium except for the buffets of the impinging forces that displace him in one direction or another. . . . When the force of the impact is spent, he comes to rest, a self-contained globule of desire as before.*

Veblen believed that human behavior is best analyzed as interactions of instincts and habits and that many social processes can be interpreted as results of cultural lags. In his doctrine of *conspicuous consumption* (status competition), Veblen explained how the desire to keep up with the Joneses motivates people to buy goods in a way that is culturally determined, not price determined. In a more general sense, Veblen insisted on studying the origin and nature of economic institutions. He was especially critical of the leisure class and businesspeople, whom he viewed as parasites. He argued that conventional economics fails to consider social and economic institutions, artificially reducing human nature to a matter of rational calculation.

As eccentric as Bentham, Veblen washed his dishes in a rain barrel and seldom bathed. Though grubby and quite homely, he lost several academic positions because he was a promiscuous and indiscreet womanizer, and he was still an assistant professor when he died at age 72.

Veblen's criticisms of economic theory were largely based on anti-rationalist premises and were certainly not the first of their kind. However, Veblen's savage humor and great erudition made him a formidable critic of the business system. He originated a distinctively American line of inquiry into economics, *institutionalism*, which continues to find proponents to this day.

---

probably accounts for findings that propinquity (nearness, or proximity, in place or time) is a major determinant of whom one marries. Broadening the options available in any decision-making situation can be costly and pose unforeseen problems.

The Bewildering Maze of Choices

Thousands of firms and products fade from the scene every year, but even more thousands are launched. Ever-widening ranges of choice become available as firms attempt to attract huge customer bases to their product lines. This is often held up as a major advantage of market systems; even eccentric tastes and preferences can be accommodated when almost innumerable different goods are available. Typical grocery stores now carry over 15,000 different items; together, the stores in a large shopping mall often offer five times as many.

One result of having many choices and constant flux in markets is that the additional information required for wise consumer decisions is costly.[3] Firms constantly modify products and packaging in hopes of getting noncustomers to sample their goods: "Try our new, improved. . . ." You might be irritated if you searched high and low for a familiar red box of your favorite cereal, concluded that the store was out, and then, on a later shopping trip, discovered that the maker had switched to a blue box.

Even more confusion arises when choices are wider. A gourmet may dither for hours over a lengthy menu at a posh restaurant. Some people spend days trying to find the perfect gift for a friend or the perfect suit for a job interview. Selecting goods would be simpler if fewer options were available. You may know people who would have few problems in finding a TV program to watch if fewer channels were available, but who cannot stop pushing the changer when a cable system offers 50 or 60 choices?

Russian émigrés to the United States often remark that the biggest culture shock is choosing from the millions of options our society offers. Might some people who dislike decision-making feel more comfortable in more regimented societies? For example, the arranged marriages common in traditional societies might reduce the anxiety many people experience when less rigid mating rituals prevail. Career choices might be far less traumatic for some people if they were simply assigned jobs. Social institutions exist, however, that lessen the need to choose. Private schools that require uniforms eliminate concerns about what a child will wear. A military career limits the scope of individual choice. At the extreme, few choices are required of prison inmates. Indeed, some convicts become so institutionalized that they cannot bear life outside prison walls.

Most of us, however, enjoy the wide range of options in a market system, and view the cars, houses, or clothes we purchase as expressions of our individuality. We are accustomed to the inconvenience and confusion of shopping or sorting out the activities we want to do. We almost

intuitively develop techniques to make reasonable judgments in an environment of rational ignorance.

An even greater problem for any type of decision-making is that *rational ignorance* may yield decisions that seem wrong in retrospect. People try to maximize their satisfaction by balancing expected marginal benefits (e.g., marginal utilities or marginal revenues) against expected marginal costs. Some expectations may prove too pessimistic; a dreaded blind date may turn out to be the person you've dreamed about. If people form their expectations reasonably, however, the probability of a pleasant surprise should, on average, be balanced by the probability of a disappointing outcome. This partially explains hangovers, high divorce rates, food poisoning, the spread of AIDS, fatal accidents, and why some people suffering serious illness may be stuck with incompetent quacks and die for lack of information about specialists who might have cured their disease.[4]

Quality and Prices

Why does anyone ever leave a tip after eating at a restaurant? Why, when shopping may entail driving longer distances, do so many people buy at high-priced stores even if the same brands and items are available at discount stores closer to the customers' homes? These examples superficially seem to contradict the economic assumption that, after adjusting for transaction costs, people always try to pay the lowest possible prices for any good or resource. Habit plays a role in some cases, but desires for superior service and attempts to avoid unpleasant surprises are also important.

That the price people are willing to pay is positively related to the perceived quality of a good or resource is not a secret. Plump red tomatoes sell for higher prices than mushy ones.

---

[3]Product differentiation may also drive up production costs, and hence, market prices—a process we describe later in this book.

[4]Some of these examples are drawn from Gary Galles' "The Best Choice May Be the Wrong One," in *Great Ideas for Teaching Economics*, 6th ed., ed. Ralph T. Byrns and Gerald W. Stone (New York: HarperCollins, 1995).

Renting a room in Aspen during peak ski season costs more than renting that same room in May. But quality differentials in such cases are not a key to answering our questions about tips and premium prices.

Economists analyzing close substitutes that differ primarily in quality usually treat the markets as related, but separate. For example, race horses and nags are assumed to be sold in separate markets. A subtle point is that people will pay higher prices as implicit insurance policies intended to ensure quality and avoid mistakes caused by uncertainty and imperfect information. This inverts the notion that higher quality induces higher prices. Instead, the idea is that higher prices induce higher quality: sellers who receive bribes in the form of premium prices are expected to alter their behavior in ways that satisfy the buyer. This is different from paying a higher price for existing quality.

Thus, the prospect of a tip presumably secures faster service at a restaurant, especially one where you are a regular customer. Premium prices at swanky stores presumably secure better service and easier refund policies when products prove unsatisfactory.

In many instances, prices exceeding the minimums necessary reflect attempts to ensure that suppliers help buyers avoid mistakes in contending with uncertainty and imperfect information. But what happens when information available to firms and their customers differ? The next section examines these markets with asymmetric information.

ASYMMETRIC INFORMATION

Transactors (buyers and sellers) seldom have equal knowledge.

Asymmetric information occurs when people have different levels of knowledge about a bargaining situation.

At times, knowledge asymmetries are not a problem. For example, a stereo dealer may have vast technical knowledge about woofers, tweeters, distortion, and so on, when all you care about is whether a stereo has a great sound.

Economists categorize problems of asymmetric information into two major groups: *moral hazard*, where an inadequately monitored party to a contract takes a hidden action that violates the other party's interests, and *adverse selection*, where, before a contract is finalized, one party conceals information that would make the contract unacceptable to the other. Moral hazard is present, for example, if a cashier skims cash paid for meals at a restaurant, or if a seller later decides to renege on a guarantee. Adverse selection, on the other hand, is at fault if only high-risk drivers buy car insurance, or if a firm buys merchandise on credit knowing that it will file for bankruptcy before paying. We will deal with inefficiencies arising from moral hazard before exploring problems of adverse selection.

Moral Hazard

Transactions for future performance create moral hazards that can frustrate expectations about costs and benefits. Inability to perfectly forecast and control future behavior is the key problem. For example, if you paid for knee surgery in advance, might a surgeon do sloppier work than if you will pay only if the knee responds satisfactorily? On the other hand, after your knee is repaired, might you delay payment and haggle over the surgeon's charges?

A moral hazard occurs when one party to a contract can unexpectedly raise the costs or lower the benefits of the other party, who cannot perfectly monitor or control the first party's actions.

Moral hazards arise because choices tend to reflect personal costs and benefits; the effects on others are, at most, secondary considerations. No contract for future performance can cover every possibility, so most transactions rely heavily on good faith efforts. But time tends to blur promises to diligently consider the interests of the other party to a bargain.

Suppose your instructor agreed to enter As in the grade book right now for every student who promises to work hard this semester.

Would most students follow through and study diligently? Could ignoring the effects on other people cause athletes with guaranteed contracts to engage in riskier outside activities (e.g., skiing or hang-gliding)? Is moral hazard present when parents provide credit cards for emergencies to college students? Might drivers who always removed ignition keys after parking their uninsured cars tend to forget to lock them up if insurance covers losses from theft or vandalism? This is why insurance companies offer huge discounts for policies with high deductibles!

Opportunistic behavior after an arrangement is made is most severe if parties to a contract do not anticipate its renewal. Moral hazard is less important if both parties expect future agreements. Unexpectedly imposing costs or reducing the benefits of the other party causes it to rely less on good faith when a subsequent contract is negotiated. This reluctance will increase the bargaining costs of both parties. (We return to this point in a moment while discussing problems in used car markets.) If either party does not expect repeat business, a related problem known as adverse selection can be severe.

Adverse Selection

Estimates of expected costs and benefits from a contract tend to be unbiased if each party shares fully all the information available before reaching a final agreement. Frequently, however, one side may conceal or distort information to strengthen its bargaining position. This can verge on fraud. For example, someone who already took a course might sell you an old text, knowing that the instructor is requiring use of a newer edition.

> **Adverse selection** *occurs when one bargaining party ultimately suffers unexpected disadvantages because the other party conceals information prior to a contract.*

You may have heard of pensioners who have been bilked of their life savings by con artists; confidence games are extreme examples of the problem of adverse selection. Operators of fly-by-night businesses often guarantee faulty goods, knowing that the guarantees are worthless. Some deadbeats try to build up records of paying small bills so that they can secure credit that will allow them to run up indebtedness that they never intend to pay.

The problem of adverse selection is a major reason for laws that forbid fraud, and a common rule of law is that ambiguity in a contract will be interpreted against the party who wrote the agreement.

The Market for Lemons

Used car markets exemplify classic problems posed by asymmetric information.[5] Consider a simple model of information in used car markets. Suppose sellers with perfect information sell cars to one-time buyers with limited information. Buyers may know the proportion of lemons and good cars, but cannot distinguish lemons from cream puffs. Adverse selection allows sellers of lemons to misrepresent their cars. Because buyers cannot ascertain quality in this model, both lemons and good cars sell for the same price!

Lemons will be overpriced while cream puffs are undervalued. But owners of good cars will not want to sell at these reduced prices, while owners of lemons are delighted to sell. The result of this oversimplified model is that only lemons are offered for sale, or a market fails to exist. The lesson here is that when quality is unknown to the buyer, equilibrium prices fall and fewer transactions occur, even though further gains from exchange could be realized. However, since markets for used cars thrive in most communities, what has this model ignored?

The answer is that alternative mechanisms have developed around this market to partially resolve problems of asymmetric information. Drivers who fear buying lemons in the open market may buy only from close friends, who presumably hope to maintain amicable rela-

---

[5]This problem was originally discussed in George A. Akerlof, "The Market for 'Lemons': Quality Uncertainty and the Market Mechanism," *Quarterly Journal of Economics*, 1970, pp. 488–500.

tionships. Publications such as *Consumer Reports* provide data on quality and frequency of repair for most vehicles. Firms such as Lemon-Aide emerge: experts who will, for roughly $75, assess quality and look for hidden defects for potential buyers. Guarantees also help, but only if they are enforceable.

Federal law now requires mileage certificates on all cars, and some states have enacted defect disclosure laws intended to protect consumers from unscrupulous dealers. Some economists argue, however, that since most auto dealers have continuing relationships with their communities, such laws may be unnecessary.

Adverse selection and moral hazard are most significant in markets dominated by one-time transactions. There are, however, many other circumstances when society skews market outcomes by providing added protection to consumers.

Consumer Policy

Can consumers make appropriate choices for themselves? *Caveat emptor* (let the buyer beware) is an ancient legal doctrine that buyers are the best judges of whether they receive full value and so should bear the consequences of their own decisions. But the doctrine of *caveat venditor* (let the seller beware) also has a long history, reflected in prohibitions against fraud and in imposing legal liability on sellers for damages if dangers lurk in a product. Society increasingly holds firms responsible for product safety and reliability. Naturally, these regulatory costs are passed forward as higher prices, forcing us to buy built-in insurance policies on some goods we purchase.

The strongest trend, however, is toward government edicts that either prohibit or mandate certain activities. A century ago, one could

legally purchase any available drug. Today, many drugs are absolutely banned (LSD and heroin are examples); others require doctors' prescriptions. And producing automobiles without safety and antipollution equipment is forbidden.

We know that people's ideas cannot be pigeonholed precisely, but those who favor market solutions over government regulation tend to have faith in people's abilities to choose for themselves. They reason that if consumers lack information, government can either provide the information or leave it to organizations such as Consumers Union. On the other side of the fence sit those who distrust the market system to provide safe and environmentally clean products. These people point to the increasingly sophisticated nature of products and have little faith in the ability of the typical person to choose given the volume and depth of information necessary to make informed product choices.

The positions you take on such issues depend on whether you view individuals themselves or government experts to be in a better position to judge a person's well-being given the complexity and sophistication of modern products. Both groups will suffer from uncertainty and rational ignorance. Should using air bags be mandatory? Should AIDS patients be denied access to potentially beneficial drugs until the Food and Drug Administration has approved them? Should hang-gliding be prohibited? These and similar questions about the role of government regulation are addressed in a later chapter.

Some consumer issues and the basis of demand theory have been our focus in this chapter; in the next, you will study firms' goals and objectives and, then, firms' production and costs. These foundations of demand and supply will be blended in the next part of this book to explain pricing and output decisions by firms under a variety of market situations.

CHAPTER REVIEW: KEY POINTS

1. **Utilitarianism** proposes that the best society is the one that provides the greatest happiness for the greatest number of people.

2. **Marginal utility** is the extra satisfaction gained from consuming a bit more of a good. The **law of diminishing marginal utility** states that the marginal utility of any good eventually declines as the amount consumed increases.

3. Measured in dollars, the declining portion of a marginal utility curve translates into a demand curve.

4. Maximum consumer satisfaction (*consumer equilibrium*) requires that the last dollar spent on any good yield the same gain in satisfaction as the last dollar spent on any other good: $MU_a/P_a = MU_b/P_b = \ldots = MU_z/P_z$. This is known as the **principle of equal marginal utilities per dollar**.

5. **Substitution effects** are changes in consumer purchasing patterns that emerge if relative prices change, artificially assuming that the purchasing power of income is constant.

6. **Income effects** are changes in buying patterns that occur solely because the purchasing power of one's monetary income changes when the prices of individual goods rise or fall.

7. **Consumer surplus** is the area above the price line and below the demand curve. It is a consumer's gain from buying at a uniform price instead of paying prices equal to the marginal utility of each unit.

8. The **paradox of value** is resolved by recognizing that necessities may yield more total utility than luxuries, but that people adjust their purchases so that prices reflect marginal utility.

9. We are seldom certain about the *attributes* of any unit of a good. Information is costly and its marginal benefits may be trivial. Thus, our decisions are based on less than full information; we are **rationally ignorant** because we pursue information only as long as its expected benefit exceeds its expected cost.

10. Market prices commonly are positively related to quality, but higher prices than necessary often reflect attempts to alter suppliers' behavior so that higher quality is delivered to buyers. These bribes are intended to help us avoid unpleasant surprises arising from making decisions in an imperfect world.

11. **Moral hazard** results when some arrangement provides incentives for one party to engage in inefficient behavior that raises costs or reduces benefits to the other party. **Adverse selection** occurs when one party to a bargain has superior information when the bargain is struck, resulting in unexpected losses to the other party.

QUESTIONS FOR THOUGHT AND DISCUSSION

1. Leisure is a good. When wages increase, the cost of leisure rises because you sacrifice more if you don't work. Thus, the substitution effect of a wage hike reduces leisure. How does the income effect of an increased wage rate affect decisions about work if leisure is an inferior good? If it is a normal good? If it is a luxury good?

2. Why do marginal utilities diminish more rapidly as consumption of a good is increased during short periods (e.g., a day) as opposed to longer periods (e.g., a year)?

3. The law of equal marginal utilities per dollar suggests that the last dollar spent on any good yields the same gain in satisfaction as the last dollar spent on any other

good. Do your spending patterns conform to this idea? Are there ever barriers that prevent people from achieving this equilibrium for consumption?

4. Some reliable companies state that their policy is "satisfaction guaranteed or your money will be cheerfully refunded." Are there some goods for which such guarantees by retailers do not alleviate a need for government regulation? If so, what are they?

5. List the attributes that distinguish goods whose provision we can leave to the marketplace from those for which government regulation is required? What criteria might be appropriate to differentiate between people who should be allowed to make their own choices from people who need to be looked after? Society does allow some people to make some choices denied to others. Can you name some instances?

OPTIONAL MATERIAL: GRAPHICAL TECHNIQUES IN ECONOMICS

The impossibility of measuring utility by more objective units than in imaginary utils vexed economists until early in this century. Economists developed a new approach, *indifference analysis*, which finally allowed them to sidestep this difficulty. This modern approach to consumer choice begins with a look at individual budget constraints.

Budget Lines

Just as production possibilities frontiers limit society's ability to produce and consume, each individual family is constrained by its income in choosing among consumption alternatives. A consumer's budget line is usually straight because the purchasing pattern a family chooses seldom affects market prices.

> A **budget line** (or constraint) depicts the choices available to a consumer who faces constant prices and who has a given income.

Figure 5 shows budget lines for two levels of income using the assumption that asparagus (A) and a proxy for all other goods, called shmoo (B), each cost $1 per pound. Any point in the AB space represents a specific combination of asparagus and shmoo and would require a certain level of income.

We can write the family's budget constraint as equal to

$$Y = P_aA + P_bB$$

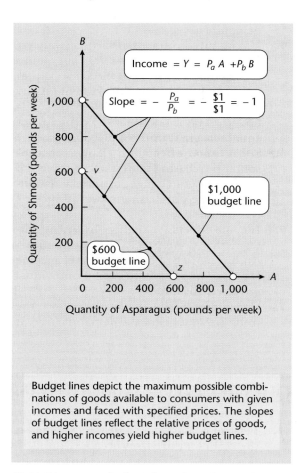

Budget lines depict the maximum possible combinations of goods available to consumers with given incomes and faced with specified prices. The slopes of budget lines reflect the relative prices of goods, and higher incomes yield higher budget lines.

FIGURE 5 Typical Budget Lines for Two Levels of Income

where P_a and P_b are the prices of asparagus and shmoo, respectively, and all family income (Y) is spent on either asparagus (A) or shmoo (B). Because income is limited, asparagus can be traded for shmoos as long as the family stays within its income constraint. Subtracting P_aA from each side yields

$$P_bB = Y - P_aA$$

Finally, we can solve for the amounts of B, given certain purchases of A, if we divide this equation by P_b:

$$B = \frac{Y}{P_b} - \frac{P_a}{P_b} A$$

This equation defines the budget line for the family in Figure 5.

Because both asparagus and shmoo cost $1 per pound ($P_a = P_b$), point v represents the situation where the family has $600 per week, all of which is spent on shmoo. Note that $Y/P_b = $600/$1 = 600$ pounds of shmoo. Point z represents just the opposite: all income is spent on asparagus, nothing is spent on shmoo.

The slope of the budget line equals $-P_a/P_b$, which equals -1, because shmoo and asparagus are priced identically. Thus, as income changes, the family's budget line moves in or out, but as long as the ratio of the two prices remains the same, the slope of the budget line will not change.

The budget line pivots if asparagus prices double to $2 a pound. A consumer with a $600 weekly income could now buy a maximum of only 300 pounds of asparagus, but could still buy as much as 600 pounds of shmoo. Alternatively, if the price of asparagus fell to $0.50 a pound, up to 1,200 pounds of asparagus might be purchased from a $600 income. Budget lines reflecting various possible prices for asparagus, with the price of shmoo still at $1 a pound and with a $600 weekly budget, are shown in Figure 6.

Indifference Curves

Consider two arbitrarily selected combinations of shmoo and asparagus, shown as bundle x and

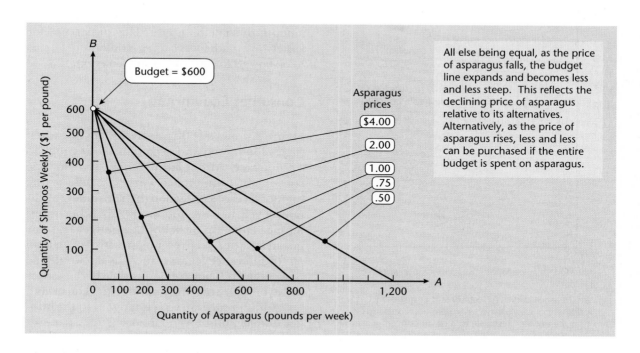

FIGURE 6   Budget Lines for $600 Income with Various Prices for Asparagus

bundle y in Figure 7. Indifference analysis assumes that you always prefer more of each good to less, and that you either (a) prefer bundle x to y, (b) prefer y to x, or (c) are indifferent between bundle x and bundle y. Clearly you prefer x to y because x has the same amount of asparagus but more shmoo. Now let us create a new bundle z by adding small amounts of asparagus or shmoo, or both, to combination y until you are indifferent between x and the new bundle z. These bundles are shown in Figure 7.

We have connected the points representing the combinations where you are indifferent between x, z, and similarly desirable bundles.

> **Indifference curves** *reflect a consumer's preferences and connect all bundles of goods between which the consumer is indifferent.*

Indifference curves have certain properties:

1. Every possible combination of goods is on some indifference curve.

Indifference curves reflect consumer tastes and preferences and connect combinations of goods that are equally desirable to a given consumer.

FIGURE 7   Typical Indifference Curves

2. Indifference curves are negatively sloped because you must get more of one good to maintain your level of satisfaction when you give up some of the other good.
3. Indifference curves that are further from the origin are preferable because they represent larger bundles of goods.
4. Indifference curves never intersect.
5. The slope of an indifference curve reflects the *relative* subjective benefits (marginal utilities) of the goods, $-MU_a/MU_b$.
6. Indifference curves are convex (bowed in toward the origin).

The first five of these properties should be fairly obvious. The sixth is based on diminishing *relative* marginal utilities. In this context, this means that consumers prefer variety to monotony. The following example asks you to use your intuition to show why.

Suppose steak is your favorite meat but you almost despise chicken. What would happen if your meat intake were restricted to steak for a solid year? We would bet that you would sacrifice a few steaks for a box of the Colonel's best. The more you have of a single thing, the more you are willing to give some of it up to have a larger amount of something else. This preference for variety over sameness causes indifference curves to be bowed toward the origin (convex).

Consumer Equilibrium

Figure 8 shows a $600 weekly budget line when prices for shmoo and asparagus both equal $1 a pound and various indifference curves for one consumer. Indifference curve I_2 reflects the highest level of satisfaction this consumer can attain, given her income level. Any other indifference curve on or below this budget line (for instance, I_0 or I_1) represents less satisfaction than I_2. Indifference curves such as I_3 would be preferable to I_2 but are not feasible because they lie beyond the consumer's budgetary constraint.

Indifference curve I_2 is tangent to the budget line at point z. The amounts of asparagus and shmoo associated with point z (A_0 and B_0) represent this consumer's best choices for consumption, given current prices and income.

FIGURE 8 A Consumer's Equilibrium

Consumer satisfaction is maximized by purchasing the bundle of goods where the highest possible indifference curve is just tangent to the budget line. Any other affordable bundle is less satisfying; any more desirable bundle (than z, in this case) cannot be afforded.

Notice that at point z the slopes of the budget line and indifference curve I_2 are equal. This means that relative market prices (the slope of the budget line) equal relative marginal utilities (the slope of the indifference curve).

Thus the slope of indifference curve I_2 at point z is $(-MU_a)/MU_b$ and the slope of the budget line at point z is $(-P_a/P_b)$. Because both are equal at point z,

$$\frac{-MU_a}{MU_b} = \frac{-P_a}{P_b}$$

or

$$\frac{MU_a}{P_a} = \frac{MU_b}{P_b}$$

Notice that indifference curve analysis yields the same condition for consumer equilibrium as the principle of equal marginal utilities per dollar, but we need not assume that consumers have utilometers that accurately measure utility for each product.

Deriving Individual Demand Curves

We will keep this person's income at $600 weekly and look at changes in the consumer's equilibrium as the price of asparagus varies. This permits us to extract the information necessary to graph a demand curve for asparagus.

Panel A of Figure 9 superimposes a set of indifference curves on the budget lines from Figure 6 for a person with $600 weekly income who faces various possible monetary prices for asparagus. We have connected the equilibria for these different prices of asparagus with a *price–consumption curve*. Each point on this curve corresponds to a different price for asparagus on the corresponding $600 budget line. At these points of tangency, indifference curves reflect consumer preferences, while budget lines reflect income constraints. Each tangency point represents maximum satisfaction given the constraints of this consumer's income and the relative market prices of the two goods. We can find the quantity of asparagus associated with each price by dropping a line from the price–consumption line to the horizontal (asparagus) axis. Voilà! We have the information needed to build a demand schedule and draw a demand curve, as in Panel B of Figure 9. Points a through e in the two panels correspond.

Income and Substitution Effects

You will substitute a good that falls in price for goods that rise in relative price. Additionally, when a good falls in price, the purchasing power of your income grows. These separate substitution effects and income effects can be graphically decomposed with indifference analysis.

In Figure 10, we initially assume that the price of asparagus is $2 per pound and our consumer is in equilibrium buying 100 pounds per

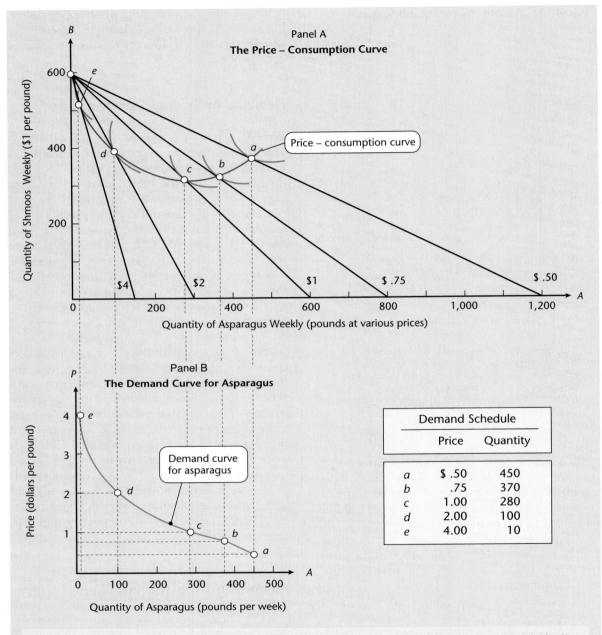

Panel A
The Price – Consumption Curve

Price – consumption curve

Panel B
The Demand Curve for Asparagus

Demand curve for asparagus

Demand Schedule		
	Price	Quantity
a	$ .50	450
b	.75	370
c	1.00	280
d	2.00	100
e	4.00	10

The price-consumption curve is traced out by the successive tangencies between indifference curves and the budget lines representing alternative prices for asparagus. In Panel A, points a through e show declining consumption of asparagus as its price rises. Points a through e from the price-consumption curve in Panel A translate into points a through e on the demand curve in Panel B.

FIGURE 9   Consumer Equilibria and the Price–Consumption Curve

FIGURE 10   Income and Substitution Effects

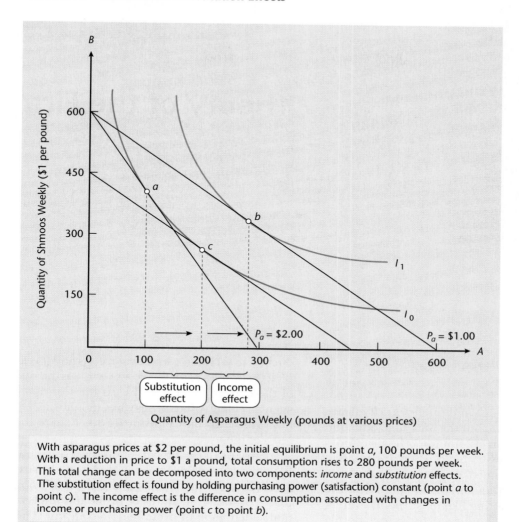

With asparagus prices at $2 per pound, the initial equilibrium is point *a*, 100 pounds per week. With a reduction in price to $1 a pound, total consumption rises to 280 pounds per week. This total change can be decomposed into two components: *income* and *substitution* effects. The substitution effect is found by holding purchasing power (satisfaction) constant (point *a* to point *c*). The income effect is the difference in consumption associated with changes in income or purchasing power (point *c* to point *b*).

week (point *a*). If the price of asparagus falls to $1 per pound, the new equilibrium is 280 pounds per week (point *b*). To split this total change into both income and substitution effects, we ask the following question: how much would she have purchased if the price fell but real income (satisfaction) remained constant?

We find this by plotting a new budget line that has the lower price for asparagus (parallel to the budget line where $P_a = \$1$). This budget line is tangent to indifference curve I_0 (keeping real income and satisfaction constant) at point *c*. This

budget line reflects the change in relative prices and is parallel to the budget line tangent to point *b*. Thus, with no change in purchasing power, this consumer increases her purchases of asparagus to 200 pounds per week (point *c*) when the price drops to $1 per pound (the substitution effect equals 100 pounds). The remaining 80 pound increase in consumption is due to increased purchasing power (income) resulting from the price decline. The total change (180 pounds) thus equals the sum of the substitution effect (100 pounds) and the income effect (80 pounds).

Chapter 22

Theory of the Firm

The business of America is business.

Calvin Coolidge

Home-cooked meals and public education are types of production, but the bulk of production occurs in private firms, not households or government. Almost every building on a busy street houses a firm, from bakeries to car dealerships to insurance agencies and on and on. Firms are everywhere, sprouting like mushrooms even in nations that were, until recently, rather hostile to private enterprise. Why does private business increasingly dominate production? Productive efficiency is the major reason.

Firms' roles as centers for production and as channels for the distribution of goods were introduced in Part 1. This chapter provides an overview of the international business environment, starting with an exploration of what production means to consumers and some important aspects of the production process. We then examine reasons for firms to exist. Individuals and families don't personally produce all the goods they want, because self-sufficiency would be incredibly inefficient. Firms coordinate team production to (*a*) reduce transaction costs and (*b*) exploit economies of scale. We also address the role of the entrepreneur and discuss the principal–agent problem, which arises when monitoring behavior is costly and individuals don't share the goals of their employers.

Surveys of legal forms of business organizations and of how firms are financed lead to an examination of business goals, and to the conclusion that accounting measures of profit and the economic definition of profit seldom conform. This raises the following question: is the standard assumption that firms try to maximize economic profit consistent with the differing goals of decision-makers within many firms? This chapter concludes by addressing criticisms of giant modern corporations and providing some evidence about the changing nature of business competition.

MODERN BUSINESS

Households and government generate some goods, but production—from prescription medicines to hot tubs to hot pizza delivered to your

FIGURE 1 The Changing Distribution of Employment by Firms and Government

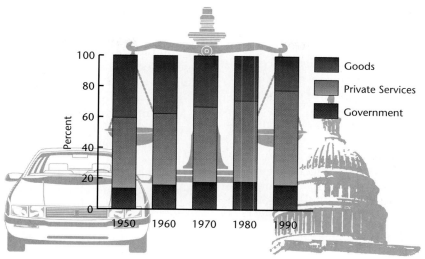

Source: *Economic Report of the President*, 1993.

Over the last four decades, the United States has shifted from producing goods to services. Since manufacturing has historically been a fertile source of rapidly rising productivity, some of our more recent lagging productivity growth has been tied to this shift in employment.

door—is concentrated in firms. Painting contractors, the New York Yankees, and Honda are all business firms.

> **Firms** *are specialized organizations that buy resources from households and other firms to produce goods or services for sale to customers.*

Firms range in size from an itinerant fruit vendor, who ekes out a meager living by selling apples out of the back of a pickup, to such multinational corporations as Exxon, with billions of dollars in annual sales being generated by tens of thousands of employees operating out of hundreds of manufacturing facilities and offices spread around the globe.

Activities once operated by government are increasingly being privatized throughout the world. In the early 1990s, for example, 6,000 retail shops formerly controlled by what was then the Czechoslovakian government were sold to private owners. Western Europe, Mexico, and many South American countries are also experimenting with privatization. A recent study by the World Bank examined a dozen major privatizations in

Britain, Chile, Malaysia, and Mexico.[1] The study concluded that nearly all of these privatizations produced net gains through higher investment, improved pricing to consumers, managerial innovation, and efficiencies created by industrial downsizing and reducing the size of their work force. In the United States, privatization includes a trend toward local government contracts with private firms to operate municipal hospitals, garbage collection, prisons, and bus systems.

As Figure 1 shows, today more than 80% of U.S. employment flows through private firms. But in the last four decades the proportion of employment in the goods-producing sector has fallen from 40% to nearly 20% today. This decline in goods producing has seen a parallel rise in the service sector, both private and public. Government employment now accounts for nearly 17% of all employment, exceeding that of manufacturing. Any private firm, regardless of its size, relies on production of goods and services that can be sold.

---

[1]A. Galal et. al., "Welfare Consequences of Selling Public Enterprises," *World Bank*, 1993.

Production

Resources that enter a production process are known as *inputs*; the transformed materials and services are *outputs*. Inputs include machine or labor hours, physical space (e.g., acres used yearly), raw materials, and partially processed (*intermediate*) products bought from other firms. A firm's output may be purchased by consumers, other firms, or government.

Natural forces or accidents may make things more valuable for human use. For example, geothermal heat and pressure convert coal into diamonds, and the life processes of generations of flora and fauna make soil more fertile. Relying exclusively on nature or luck would, however, sustain only a minuscule human population, most of whom would live a razor's edge existence. People's productive activities are the major contributions to enhanced value of goods and services.

Production transforms inputs into outputs (products or services) that are more valuable in form, place, possession, or time.

"More valuable" means that the goods ultimately generate greater consumer utility.

Output occurs when materials and services change their form, are available at different places and times, and are possessed by those who value them the most. Altering *form* entails reshaping materials: crude oil is less valuable than gasoline. Augmenting *place* utilities requires movement: a lobster is worth more in a restaurant's glass tank than in the ocean. *Possession* utilities arise by shifting ownership from people who value goods less to people who value them more: realtors match home buyers who are moving into an area with sellers who are moving out. *Time* utilities are created when goods are made available when they are wanted most: speculators buy newly harvested wheat and store it to sell when wheat output is nil. Firms make goods more valuable in form, place, or time, or they transfer ownership to people who value them more highly.

The Short Run and the Long Run

People often talk about short-run versus long-run consequences of events. For example, in the short run, winning a pie-eating contest may give you a bellyache. Repeatedly win pie-eating tournaments and, in the long run, you will need a bigger car. You may enjoy partying in the short run, but in the long run, your grades will suffer. Short and long runs in economics refer to the completeness of adjustment rather than to time periods per se. Relatively fewer options are available to firms in the short run.

*The **short run** is a period during which the amount of at least one resource is fixed and firms can neither enter nor exit a market.*

Because at least one factor (resource) is fixed in the short run and exit is prohibited, firms will face some costs that cannot be avoided (are fixed) even if the firm produces no output at all. In the long run, however, a firm can completely adjust the amounts of all resources and can either enter or leave industries.

*The **long run** is a period of sufficient duration for all feasible resource adjustments to any event to be completed, including entry into and exit from the market.*

The specific time intervals required for different firms to achieve long-run adjustment differ markedly. Some firms can liquidate all their assets in days; others may require years. Small restaurants can close within days, but building a chemical plant can take decades. Seven years elapsed between the time General Motors decided to build the Tennessee Saturn plant and when the first car came off the line. Capital requirements and the extent of regulation are only two of many influences on how long it can take to enter or exit an industry.

Plants, Firms, and Industries

Firms operate one or more *plants*, which are production facilities ranging in size from the case a tattoo artist uses to carry ink and needles to a million acres of ranch land. Firms that operate more than one plant are *multiplant* firms. Wal-Mart is a multiplant retail firm, and R.R. Donnelley & Sons, a large printing firm, has printing (manufacturing) facilities in various locations around the globe. Firms that produce several types of goods are called *diversified* firms. Giant, multiproduct firms that operate plants in several industries are called *conglomerates*. For example, General Motors produces cars, trucks, military electronics and hardware, and appliances, and it is also heavily involved in consumer loans. In fact, most large corporations in the world are conglomerates.

An *industry* is composed of all firms competing in the same market. Examples of industries include tires, tobacco, or clothing.

> *Horizontally integrated firms are those operating at a number of sites using similar methods to produce the same goods and services.*

Thus, Toyota produces the same cars in Japan and California, and McDonald's golden arches grace the scenery from Berlin to the Grand Canyon to Singapore. Other firms often have different divisions that represent various production levels within an industry.

> *Vertically integrated firms are those who operate at different production levels within an industry.*

Most steel producers are vertically integrated, operating mines, smelting plants, mills for producing rolled steel, and fabrication plants. Similarly, most large oil companies are vertically integrated with oil field recovery, refining, transporting, and retailing operations.

It might seem easy to identify the firms that make up an industry, but consider motor vehicles. Are limousines and golf carts reasonable substitutes? Should trucks and vans be included? Motorcycles? Is lumping all these goods in a single industry appropriate? Another problem in identifying an industry is that conglomerates are often major players in several industries and nonconglomerates may be vertically integrated.

WHY DO FIRMS EXIST?

No single household could produce even a respectable fraction of the array of goods most consumers take for granted, from brass beds to yogurt to films and TV programs to world tours. Businesses have huge comparative advantages over households in coordinating resources to generate vast amounts of output at low costs. Thus, firms exist because they are efficient. But firms can produce existing goods more efficiently or innovate new goods only if entrepreneurs recognize opportunities in the marketplace and then act.

The unique role defining an *entrepreneur* is the establishment of a firm that, with luck, generates profit; other qualities entrepreneurs share are explored in Focus 1. Entrepreneurs prosper by establishing firms that efficiently coordinate specialized resources. To succeed, a firm's production and management teams must (a) reduce transaction costs and (b) exploit economies of scale and scope.

Reducing Transaction Costs

Transaction costs shrink consumers' purchasing power and resource suppliers' incomes. Enormous transaction costs would be incurred in trying to coordinate a single formal dinner by hiring resources instead of buying products from specialized firms; information, mobility, and negotiation processes are far from instantaneous, perfect, and costless. Imagine how difficult it would be to build a home, or to make all the parts and then assemble a car, if all workers were independent subcontractors rather than employees.

You learned in Chapter 4 that intermediaries reduce transaction costs. Virtually all firms are intermediaries, in the sense that the materials they process to make more valuable products are secured from other firms. For example, a chicken ranch that sells eggs to the supermarket where you buy groceries can be viewed as merely altering the form of the chicken feed it bought from a supplier. Thus, chicken ranches are intermediaries that, like all firms, could not survive without reducing transaction costs for their customers.

Shopping malls are in the business of renting space to retail firms. This reduces transaction costs for both retailers and consumers. Malls help slash transaction costs by massing large numbers of sim-

So You Want to Be an Entrepreneur?

Work provides many people with the primary meaning for their lives. Surveys indicate that most students want interesting, secure, and remunerative careers. Many also seek jobs that reward hard work with rapid advancement or that contribute to social well-being. Finding the right job entails a little job hopping. Today, fewer people spend most of their working lives employed by the government or one large firm and more are turning to self-employment and entrepreneurship to find the right mix between work and their desired lifestyle.

Entrepreneurs often march to the beat of their own drummers. Many seemed misfits early in their careers, losing a series of jobs because they were not team players. Most equated compromise with losing and would do almost anything to get their own way. People with personalities that conflict with large organizations often express desires to "be my own boss," but relatively few who go off on their own enjoy much success. Indeed, most who eventually succeed do so only after a series of failures. Overstating how devastat-

ing bankruptcy can be is difficult, especially for entrepreneurs who stake their dreams on the success of failure of an enterprise.

Several characteristics seem to separate highly successful entrepreneurs from most small proprietors or heads of giant corporations:

1. *Vision and timing.* Entrepreneurs see opportunities where others see only problems. Being in the right place at the right time is often a key. Different people interpret the same complex facts differently. Successful entrepreneurs tend to organize information so that solutions seem obvious. Their solutions may improve quality in existing goods, cut production costs, or develop new products and introduce them to the market place.
2. *Conviction and action.* Entrepreneurs act when they perceive a problem. Other people may see solutions, but fear of losing regular paychecks prevents them from pursuing their ideas. Entrepreneurs tend to have powerful egos; they want

to leave their mark on the world.
3. *Bearing of risk and uncertainty.* Successful entrepreneurs typically have such faith in their plans that they are willing to risk all their time and capital (and, where possible, other people's time and capital), rejecting the financial security most people seek.
4. *Workaholism.* Most people want high income from a job that allows leisure every evening and on weekends and regular vacations. A 40-hour, 9 to-5 job is not a goal of most successful entrepreneurs, some of whom put in 100+ hours per week for decades.

Entrepreneurs imagine alternative uses of resources, and by organizing resources to match their visions, they alter the course of history. If this brief discussion has not squelched any desire you might have to be an entrepreneur, then you need to watch for opportunities to provide things that people want, be willing to absorb risk, and work extraordinarily hard. Then pray for luck.

---

ilar outlets that allow shoppers to see what is available without traveling extensively between stores and to compare prices and quality. The variety of goods available in modern supermarkets provides another example of how a firm can cluster goods to minimize the transaction costs of customers.

Economies of Scale and Scope

Specialization and the division of labor are at the heart of modern production. People once relied

almost exclusively on production within families or clans. Today, a few types of production remain relatively solitary pursuits, such as writing novels or customizing computer software, and relatively few resources are required to successfully operate such small organizations as magazine stands or mortuaries. But only huge organizations can efficiently produce and market steel, gasoline, or oil tankers. Specialized technology often requires teamwork by thousands of workers using billions of dollars' worth of capital.

Economies of scale in production or distribution occur when average costs decline in the long run as a firm expands its productive and distributive capacity.

When production processes use vast amounts of capital and armies of employees, the *managerial coordination* of production teams becomes as specialized a function as engineering or piloting a jumbo jet. Production can be coordinated by professional managers (who are employees of corporations or government agencies) or by entrepreneurs.

Even when economies of scale are not significant, large or multiplant firms sometimes lower their costs by producing multiple products.

Economies of scope occur when a firm realizes lower costs by producing or distributing multiple products which utilize the same technologies or marketing and distribution networks.

It is cheaper to produce beef and leather simultaneously than to have one group of ranches raising cattle to supply only leather and another group to supply only beef.

Large firms establish marketing, distribution, and service networks. Closely related products can share these networks, reducing the overall cost of providing them to consumers. For example, when 3M developed Post-its, they were able to advertise and distribute them much as they had done with their other office products. Casio found that, as the market for calculators grew, average costs for liquid crystal displays (LCDs) fell dramatically. These production economies (and profit opportunities) led Casio to enter the market for watches that used LCDs.

One hurdle to efficient production is that a firm's goals may not be well served by the resource suppliers whose productive activities require coordination. Such conflicts are important determinants of the best legal form for a business.

LEGAL FORMS OF BUSINESS

Businesses are operated as sole proprietorships, partnerships, or corporations. Table 1 indicates that over 70% of all U.S. firms are proprietorships, but they account for only 6% of total sales in the United States. At the other extreme, about one firm in five is incorporated, but corporations generate 90% of all revenues. Over the last two decades, both partnerships and corporations

TABLE 1   Number of Firms, Sales, and Profits by Type of Company and Percent of Total

	Year	Sole Proprietor	Partnership	Corporation	Totals
Number of Firms (thousands)	1970	5,770 (69)	936 (11)	1,665 (20)	8,371
	1980	8,932 (69)	1,380 (11)	2,711 (21)	13,023
	1990	14,298 (73)	1,635 (8)	3,628 (19)	19,561
Total Sales (billions)	1970	199 (10)	92 (5)	1,706 (85)	1,997
	1980	411 (6)	286 (4)	6,172 (90)	6,869
	1990	693 (6)	465 (4)	10,440 (90)	11,598
Profits (billions)	1970	31 (29)	10 (9)	66 (62)	107
	1980	55 (18)	8 (3)	239 (79)	302
	1990	133 (25)	14 (3)	389 (73)	536

Source: *Statistical Abstract of the United States,* 1993.
Numbers in parentheses are the percent distributions.

have fallen as a percent of the total number of business firms, and partnership profits as a percent of total profits have dropped by two-thirds while corporate profits as a percent have risen. Sole proprietorship sales as a percent of total have fallen by 40% but sole proprietor profits have remained constant as a percent of the total.

The message seems to be that a first step toward success is to incorporate. Then why do nearly 14 million or so sole proprietorships exist? The answer comes from an examination of the strengths and weaknesses of each type of organization.

Sole Proprietorships

Establishing a sole proprietorship often requires little more than declaring, "I am in business."

> A **sole proprietorship** is a firm owned and operated by one individual.

Major advantages are a proprietorship's relative (*a*) ease of organization, (*b*) flexibility, (*c*) control by the owner, and (*d*) freedom from government regulation.

Sole proprietors, however, suffer from some major drawbacks. Size is limited by the proprietor's initial wealth and credit standing and by business profits over time. Capital accumulation tends to be a slow process. Proprietors normally perform most management functions, and such firms lack permanence:—they cannot outlive their owners.

The greatest disadvantage, however, is a proprietor's unlimited liability, that is, legal obligations to pay for debts or damages. Nearly all a proprietor owns, including personal assets (e.g., savings and cars), may be sold to pay a firm's debts if it fails or is held liable for damages in a lawsuit. More is at risk than an owner's investment, although insurance can guard against the financial risks of some legal hazards.

Partnerships

Pooled resources in a partnership can expand the resource base that limits sole proprietorships.

> **Partnerships** are businesses formed by two or more people combining their resources.

Partnerships are easy to establish, relatively simple to control, allow some specialized management, and are subject to relatively few regulations. Many doctors, for example, operate in partnerships. This permits them to share office expenses and reduces the need for every doctor to be on-call to patients 24 hours a day and 7 days a week.

A major problem arises because partnership debts are joint and each partner incurs unlimited personal liability for a firm's debts. A dishonest or incompetent partner can cost you all you own since you are responsible not only for your own actions, but the actions of your partner as well. Shared ownership can also create discord about policies, decreasing personal control—a vital issue for many entrepreneurs. Other drawbacks are that resources for growth tend to remain quite limited, and partnerships automatically dissolve upon the withdrawal or death of any partner.

Corporations

The loss of entrepreneurial control that occurs when a sole proprietor takes on partners escalates tremendously when even more people (e.g., stockholders, professional managers, and government) come into the picture because an entrepreneur decides to incorporate. Incorporating a firm requires submitting a charter to a state government outlining the intended line of business and specifying how the firm will be financed and governed.

> **Corporations** are firms sanctioned by state laws and considered legal entities separate and distinct from their owners.

Once corporations are formed, numerous special taxes and regulations hinder their operations.

Then why are firms ever incorporated? A major reason is that corporations excel at raising financial capital because they can sell *common stocks* (ownership shares) and *bonds* (corporate IOUs). Combined with undistributed profits, these funds facilitate acquisition of economic capital. Another major corporate advantage is the **limited liability** of stockholders, which means that owners of a corporation cannot lose more than they paid for stock. Other assets of individual stockholders are not jeopardized if the firm fails. Without limited liability, few individuals could (or would) invest in stock of modern corporations.

Other advantages include potential stability and permanence; corporations do not shut down when a stockholder dies. A final advantage is that corporations can hire highly specialized management. However, large corporations are often controlled by their top managers because stock is so widely spread that individual stockholders have little influence on business policies. This yields potential gains for corporate managers but poses major disadvantages for stockholders.

The divorce of ownership from managerial control opens up opportunities for fraud, so strict accounting and reporting requirements govern corporate life and add to business costs. Because corporations are viewed as fruitful sources of tax revenue, some of corporate income is subject to *double taxation*: corporations pay taxes on their incomes, and then, if some after-tax income is distributed to stockholders, these *dividends* are taxed again at the individual's personal income tax rate. Table 2 summarizes the attributes of the three major forms of business organization.

Other Forms of Enterprise

Proprietorships, partnerships, and corporations dominate production, but other types of organizations exist. *Producer cooperatives* share profits from marketing such things as handicrafts or farm outputs. *Consumer cooperatives* share savings achieved by buying in quantity. Cooperatives are flourishing in China and Eastern Europe, primarily because many Chinese and Eastern Europeans, while

TABLE 2   Summary of Legal Forms of Business Organization

Form of Business	Advantages	Disadvantages
Sole Proprietorship	1. Easy to organize 2. Simple to control 3. Offers freedom of operation 4. Not subject to much government regulation	1. Difficult to acquire funds (capital) for expansion 2. Lacks permanence 3. Subject to unlimited liability 4. Makes owner perform all management functions
Partnership	1. Easy to organize 2. Makes greater specialization of management possible 3. Makes securing financial resources easier than in sole proprietorship (pooling of funds) 4. Subject to limited regulation	1. Prone to disagreements by division of ownership 2. Ends automatically with death or withdrawal of one partner 3. Subject to unlimited liability 4. Subject to limited financial resources
Corporation	1. Capable of raising large amounts of capital through sale of stocks and bonds (but bank loans dominate financing) 2. Limits liability of stockholders 3. Stable and permanent, a legal entity (person) all its own 4. Allows employment of specialized management personnel	1. Subject to considerable government regulation 2. Burdened by heavy taxes and organizing costs 3. Subject to double taxation of corporate income and dividends 4. Separates ownership and control (principal–agent problems)

recognizing the shortcomings of state enterprises, don't yet feel ready to launch purely private business firms. Cooperatives may be an intermediate step on the road toward capitalism.

Nonprofit corporations operate most hospitals, private schools, public radio and TV stations, and charities (standard corporations are run for profit—a purpose inconsistent with the goals of most people who operate charities). *Closely held corporations* and *limited partnerships* are intended to secure tax advantages and limited liability for family-owned businesses or partnerships. Many doctors, dentists, and lawyers who would normally be considered as sole proprietors operate as *professional corporations*. These professional corporations are treated as corporations for tax purposes but do not allow for unlimited liability. Society has determined that the services of these individuals would be the subject of serious incentive problems if their liability to their clients (patients) were limited.

Still other minor organizational forms abound, varying in their specifics by the state laws governing them. Determining how a firm will be legally organized is only one step for an entrepreneur. Securing business funding is another hurdle in establishing a firm.

FINANCING BUSINESS OPERATIONS

Production is necessary before goods can be sold to generate revenue. The lag between incurring production costs and receiving revenue means that some great ideas for a business are never put into action.

Financial Intermediation

Few families have sufficient wealth to launch fledgling enterprises on even a moderate scale without some external financing. Economic growth in a healthy economy requires financial intermediation.

Financial intermediaries *channel people's savings to investors in economic capital.*

Financial intermediaries include commercial banks, insurance companies, and stockbrokers. This process of moving private saving through markets for financial capital to investors in economic capital is shown in a circular flow model in Figure 2, which illustrates that the ultimate capital suppliers in our economy are savers.

The relatively small amount that individual families save precludes them from devoting sufficient resources to secure information to ensure wise financial investment decisions. High transaction costs are incurred in identifying which financial investments are likely to be reasonably secure and capable of generating solid returns to savers. Consequently, although owners of unincorporated firms often sink all their savings into their firms, only a minority of other families buys stocks and bonds directly.

Most families' saving takes the form of after-tax deposits in financial institutions such as banks, mutual funds, or other firms that specialize in trimming transaction costs and exploiting economies of scale while executing financial contracts and processing financial information. Thus, external financing for business operations flows primarily through these huge financial intermediaries.

Self-Financing and Retained Earnings

We have indicated that the initial size of a sole proprietorship or partnership is limited by the personal credit ratings and resources of the owners. Many small corporations are similarly limited to the resources of those who start them. Most proprietorships or partnerships that succeed build up slowly because growth depends on income from the business. Corporate growth may also be financed by *retained earnings*, that is, after-tax income that is not distributed as dividends to stockholders. Unless an established and prosperous firm aggressively tries to absorb substantial numbers of other firms through merger, much of its growth tends to be internally financed.

The prospect that internal financing may be adequate for growth at some future time is cold comfort for aggressive entrepreneurs in the throes of launching an enterprise. Some small firms are able to grow rapidly by preparing per-

FIGURE 2 Financial Intermediation in a Circular Flow Model

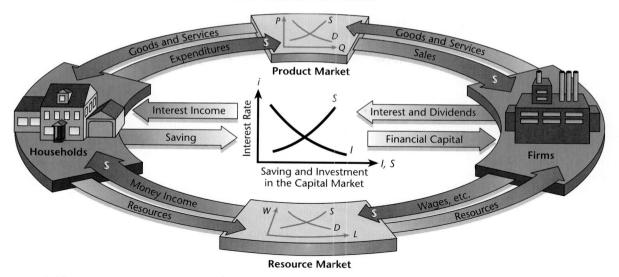

Household saving is channeled to investors in economic capital through financial intermediaries. More direct forms of investment are precluded for most families by high transaction costs, which include such costs as stockbrokers' fees and the costs of negotiating contracts.

suasive business plans that improve access to financial capital. The right to issue stocks and bonds facilitates this access if a firm is incorporated.

Common Stock

Issuing common stock is one way corporations may secure financing for economic capital.

> **Common stock** *provides holders with shares of ownership in a corporation.*

The shares of corporate profits distributed to stockholders are called *dividends*; stockholders may also realize *capital gains* (or *losses*) if the market values of their stocks rise (or fall).

The *initial offering* of a stock raises funds for business firms, but most stock transactions occur in the *secondary market*, in which stockholders rather than firms transfer stocks to other financial investors. Although the total value of common stock in nonfinancial corporations is about $6 trillion today, less than 0.2% of this value is for stock in companies in business less than five years.

Financial investors require adequate returns to compensate them for risk. The probability that a new firm will fail in its first year is high. While there exists a flourishing market for new stock offerings with high potential rewards, high risks keep most relatively uninformed investors from purchasing these issues.

Small savers know that small stockholders have much less control than a firm's officers have. But those who establish and control a new corporation have less incentive to perform diligently than they would if they owned the corporation outright. Small savers tend to opt for more security and lower returns than they are likely to get from stock ownership; the prospects of high returns from new stocks are very speculative.

Corporate Bonds

Bonds (corporate IOUs) are assets for their holders but liabilities for the corporations that issue them. Bonds are also transacted primarily in secondary markets. Only the initial sale of a bond generates funds for the firm that issues it.

Bondholders have legal rights to receive interest payments as long as the firm operates. High probabilities of default (nonpayment) by start-up companies, however, leave only large, well-established corporations with much access to funding through bond sales.

Loans from Financial Intermediaries

Most people keep the bulk of their savings in commercial banks, which dominate financial intermediation processes in the United States. Although *venture capital* firms do specialize in funding new firms that develop promising business plans, most loans are made to huge, well-established firms. Even financial specialists tend to be amazed when they actually look at the numbers and discover that highly publicized sales of stocks and bonds account for only 1/25th as much of the recent financing of corporate activities as bank loans, which receive relatively little attention.[2]

You now have some notions about how firms are legally organized and financed and why society relies primarily on firms for production. We need to address the other side of explanations for the existence of firms—their purposes from the vantage points of those who own and operate them.

BUSINESS GOALS

Adam Smith's 1776 assertion that people pursue their own interests translates, for the purposes of consumer theory, into the idea that people try to maximize their utility, or satisfaction. People in business want to generate income for themselves, and most also want to produce goods and services of which they can be proud. But maximizing utility may be inconsistent with maximizing tangible income (the power to purchase goods). For example, most people could increase tangible income by working two jobs or by enduring harsher job conditions. Instead, most ultimately prefer more leisure and more enjoyable work to higher tangible income. In this section, after exploring the meaning of economic profit, we will examine whether maximizing a firm's profit is consistent with maximizing the personal satisfactions of professional managers and other key employees.

Profit Maximization

Such slogans as "buy low, sell high" or "never give a sucker an even break" echo people's expecta-

tions that firms try to maximize their profits. **Profit maximization** is the standard economic assumption used to analyze the behavior of firms.

> *Profit is a firm's total revenue minus its total cost; loss is incurred when revenue fails to cover costs. Profits are positive, while losses are negative.*

Although, economists and bookkeepers define profits and losses similarly, economic profits and accounting profits often differ. Different definitions of costs explain this inconsistency.

- **Economic vs. Accounting Costs**   You know that the value of the best alternative forgone is the economic cost of anything from lard to romance. All costs, whether monetary or nonmonetary are opportunity costs. One way to break down economic (opportunity) costs of production is to view them as either explicit or implicit costs.

> *Explicit costs require outlays of money.*

For example, wages paid to employees, rent payments, and utility bills are all explicit costs.

> *Implicit costs are the opportunity costs of resources the firm's owner makes available for production with no direct cash outlays.*

Examples include the value of an entrepreneur's labor and the interest that could be earned were the owners' assets (including the values of stock in corporations) not tied up in the business. Both implicit and explicit costs bear heavily on rational business decisions.

> *Economic costs of production include both explicit and implicit costs.*

On the other hand, bookkeeping tends to focus on monetary costs. Bookkeeping is a mechanical exercise focused only on explicit costs; it primarily records flows of funds and provides a base for computing taxes. Accounting requires evaluation of data for decision-making, a purpose not well served by some standard bookkeeping practices for cost accounting or tax accounting. Fortunately, standards for managerial accounting increasingly conform to the economic view of cost. Let us look at some problems that emerge when implicit costs are ignored.

---

[2]Frederic S. Mishkin, *The Economics of Money, Banking, and Financial Markets*, 4th ed. (New York: HarperCollins, 1995).

- **Profit** Economists include explicit and implicit costs when they think of total (opportunity) cost, while bookkeepers commonly fail to include in total cost many implicit costs incurred by the owners of a firm.

> *Economic profit* occurs only when a firm's revenue exceeds all costs, including explicit and implicit costs.

Here is an example of how economic profits and accounting profits differ. Imagine that two years after receiving your college degree your annual salary as an assistant store manager is $28,000, you own a building that rents for $10,000 yearly, and your financial assets generate $3,000 per year in interest. On New Year's Day, after deciding to be your own boss, you quit your job, evict your tenants, and use your financial assets to establish a pogo-stick shop.

At the end of the year, your books tell the following story:

Total Sales Revenue		$130,000
Cost of pogo sticks	$85,000	
Employees' wages	20,000	
Utilities	5,000	
Taxes	5,000	
Advertising expenses	10,000	
Total (Explicit) Costs		–125,000
(subtract from revenue)		

"Congratulations," your bookkeeper pipes up, "you made a

Net (Accounting) Profit of		5,000!"

"Hold it just a moment," you say, "I have studied economics. You forgot to subtract my *implicit costs*. Being in this business caused me to lose as income

Salary	–28,000	
Rent	–10,000	
Interest	–3,000	
Total Implicit Costs		–41,000

"Therefore, I've had an economic profit that's negative, a *loss* of –36,000

This harebrained business is a loser!"

If, however, you enjoy operating the pogo-stick shop more than your best alternative (assistant store manager), your higher job satisfaction is called psychic income. *Psychic income* is an implicit revenue that refers to non-monetary satisfaction gained from an activity. Bookkeeping profit typically overstates economic profit because bookkeepers fail to subtract implicit costs, which tend to be significant, while implicit benefits are usually small.

The explicit cost data used to compute accounting profit for tax purposes are more accessible than the additional implicit cost data needed to estimate economic profits or losses. Thus, taxes and national income accounts are based on accounting data. Business decisions tend to be rational, however, and so are most frequently based on expected economic costs and profits.

Accountants typically recognize that conventional bookkeeping costs and profits are inadequate; after calculating taxable profits, they subtract estimates of implicit costs from bookkeeping profit. This type of managerial accounting provides a better picture of a firm's track record.

Normal Profits as Production Costs

One lesson from this discussion is that implicit costs should be considered in production costs. If a firm's accounting profit is less than that normally received by firms with comparable levels of investment and risks, in the long run its owners will move their resources into ventures where profits at least cover implicit costs. Chronic economic losses ultimately force a firm to shut down.

Economic profits and losses will be zero in the long run in competitive markets because profits attract new sellers like picnics attract ants; persistent losses (negative profits) drive firms from the market. Economic profits or losses persist only when entry and exit from an industry are constrained. Profits spur competition and growth of market supply, while losses signal that society wants resources shifted elsewhere. Economists simplify the discussion of cost by including implicit costs, therefore when economic profits are zero, the firm is earning a normal return (positive accounting profits enough to cover implicit costs). We will return to this issue again in the next chapter.

Other Business Goals

Executives' career ambitions and desires for job security sometimes conflict with maximizing corporate profit (the bottom line). Some analysts contend that firms try to maximize sales revenues (the top line in annual reports), hoping that growth of sales revenues will be interpreted as success by the stock market. Others argue that, after ensuring satisfactory profits that keep stockholders at bay, top managers try to follow socially responsible policies. Their contention, based on psychological theories, is that few people work for money alone; most of us want to feel that our contribution to society's welfare is positive. Many modern managers consider the interests of the firm's other *stakeholders*, including employees, the communities in which they operate, and customers. Today, various court decisions and regulations have significantly reduced managerial discretion in the areas of plant closure, personnel relations, waste disposal, and product marketing.

In several books, economist John Kenneth Galbraith takes a different tack, arguing that top managers attempt to secure high incomes and job security for members of their own social class, other administrators and professional employees whom he characterizes as the *technostructure*. Managers and members of this technostructure may have goals incompatible with those of stockholders, creating problems for modern corporations.

PROBLEMS FACING BUSINESS ORGANIZATIONS

Maximizing a sole proprietor's utility is equivalent to maximizing his or her economic profit, but only after weighing all psychic benefits and costs, including losses of leisure. Do corporate managers necessarily try to maximize stockholders' profits? Executives are, after all, people who can be expected to maximize their own interests.

Separation of Ownership and Control

Some economists contend that unless most stockholders become restless, managers pursue goals other than maximum profits. Bookkeeping practices that are not identical between firms sometimes obscure comparisons. What evidence can managers offer that stockholders' gains are being maximized? Stock prices reflect expectations about a firm's profits. But accounting profits in *annual reports* (corporate documents that legally must be published each year) seldom conform closely to a firm's economic profits.

Just as taxpayers try to maximize take-home pay by taking every possible deduction to minimize taxable income, some bookkeeping practices reduce accounting profit while increasing after-tax economic profits. For example, if an accountant uses a schedule established by the Internal Revenue Service that sets depreciation allowances (a tax-deductible cost) in excess of actual depreciation, a firm's taxes on income are reduced or delayed, increasing its economic profit. But the lower taxable income reported in the firm's annual report may alarm stockholders. If the bottom line on annual reports is sometimes misleading, how can chief executive officers (CEOs) signal their competence to stockholders?

The Principal–Agent Problem

Firms face major obstacles when coordinating the productive efforts of groups of employees with disparate goals and objectives. Specialization and the complexity of everyday life lead to countless situations where one party, a **principal**, contracts with another, an **agent**, in expectation that the agent will serve the principal's interest.

Large firms operate primarily through agents, which include most of their employees. Pay incentives are one aspect of contracts by which people try to alter the behavior of others. Some contracts between principals and agents are verbal and informal. You are a principal, for example, if a friend agrees to fill your gas tank if she can keep the change from the $20 you hand her. Her agreement makes her your agent.

> The **principal–agent problem** arises when the agent pursues personal goals that conflict with the principal's contractual rights.

Your friend, for example, might keep more change from the $20 by not completely filling your tank, or she might buy cheap gas after you specified premium unleaded.

Conflicts between the legal rights of a firm (the principal) and the goals of its employees (one group of its agents) can cause inefficiency. A firm's costs will be inefficiently high if, for example, it hires a purchasing agent who solicits bribes from suppliers who then sell intermediate goods to the firm at inflated prices. Consequently, monitoring resource suppliers' performance is a major task in coordinating production.

Principal–agent problems may arise when maximizing a firm's profit conflicts with the self-interests of business decision-makers. For example, the desires of business executives for such things as plusher offices, longer vacations, first-class travel, sycophantic subordinates, or higher personal salaries clearly raise costs and shrink profits.

Just as most people would rather get goods free than pay for them, many workers want to minimize their effort but still be paid. The principal–agent problem of *shirking* occurs when workers fail to perform properly. Shirking occurs, for example, if a security guard naps during a night shift, or when a professional athlete with a guaranteed contract reports to training camp flabby and poorly conditioned. Shirking also occurs if, say, a raw materials supplier tries to charge for more than it delivers.

An employer can avoid possible principal–agent shirking problems by directly supervising employees. But supervision is often difficult and costly. This is why many employers have adopted incentive compensation systems such as stock options for executives, commissions and bonuses for sales people, and incentive-based performance contracts for multiyear, multimillion dollar professional athletes. In addition to these problems, firms face complex competitive pressures from the marketplace.

Market Pressures and Evolution

Economists typically find the profit maximization goal persuasive because competition for lucrative managerial slots pressures top managers to try to maximize profits. Most economists also reject the idea that accounting information systematically misleads stockholders. Some people might be fooled, but the enormous profits at stake cause experts to scrutinize annual reports so that corporate information is efficiently processed.

Nevertheless, mistakes are fairly common. Many executives survive despite gaffes that cost their firms enormous profits. For example, critics charge that Ross Johnson, the CEO of RJR Nabisco (the result of the largest merger in history), wasted tremendous amounts of funds on his personal comfort and generally mismanaged the firm's assets. On the other hand, managers often forgo options that would generate solid profits. For example, dozens of publishers turned down the opportunity to publish *In Search of Excellence*, by Tom Peters and Robert H. Waterman, Jr. The book ultimately sold millions of copies.

A key to success as an executive is to be relatively more efficient (or less inefficient) than your competitors. Bankruptcy of the firm or stockholder revolts occasionally dislodge top managers who consistently fail to maximize their firm's profits, but the most powerful pressures for efficiency in corporate giants probably emerge from the market for corporate control. A firm that does not perform at least as well as average at maximizing profit will have assets that are worth more than the total value of the corporation's stock. Such firms are natural targets for hostile takeovers, the acquisition of one firm by a group of owners and managers who think they can do a better job.

John Kenneth Galbraith is one critic who rejects economic theories that stress competitive markets and the goal of profit maximization. Galbraith argues that giant corporations (*a*) dominate economic activity because small competitive firms cannot afford the modern technologies required for efficient economies of scale and scope, (*b*) are controlled by corporate managers who seek maximum power and pay for themselves instead of maximum profits for stockholders, (*c*) tend to corrupt government policies to help consolidate managerial power and achieve managers' goals rather than the public interest, and (*d*) use extensive advertising to avoid meaningful competition.

What evidence supports Galbraith's claims? First, corporations do account for a dominate share of U.S. business revenues and control large shares of our national resources. There is an erratic long-term trend towards even greater concentration in the ownership of total manufacturing assets, which contributes to corporate giantism. Some giant firms substantially exceed the sizes of the governments of medium-sized countries, as shown in Figure 3. According to Galbraith, our only hope for a just society is for modern corporate managers to become more socially responsible, but he is somewhat pessimistic about the prospects for such changes of heart.

A competitive market system rewards those who serve consumers and society, while forcing inefficient firms to adapt or exit the market. Many firms vie for consumers' patronage in competitive markets. Will society derive the same benefits if a few firms dominate a market? Most people think not. Modern economic life often seems far removed from competitive models of the economy. There is, however, evidence that markets serve consumers reasonably well and that size alone does not insulate firms from competitive pressures. Giants compete with giants.

Such once dominant retailers as Sears, Montgomery Ward, and J. C. Penney have lost ground to firms like Wal-Mart, Venture, and Target. And what happened to the giant railroads of a century ago? Most disappeared or were absorbed into Amtrak, a government-subsidized money loser.

After Ford Motor Company lost millions of dollars when it launched the ill-fated Edsel in the 1950s, it more than recouped these losses when it developed the Mustang and Explorer, cars that passed the market test. A shaky economy and competition from foreign automakers imposed billions of dollars in losses on U.S. automakers in the late 1970s. Chrysler teetered on the brink of bankruptcy but recovered when Henry Ford II fired Lee Iacocca, the father of the Mustang, and he became the chief executive officer at Chrysler. He immediately authorized $500 million in development funding for the minivan introduced

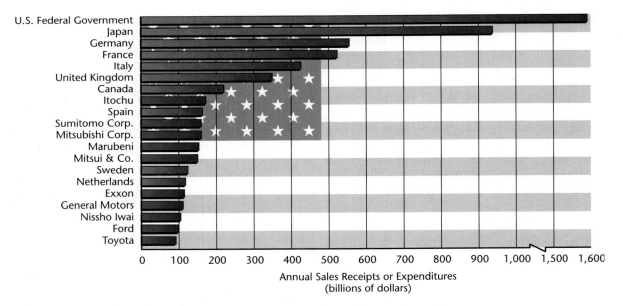

Source: "The Global 1000?", *Business Week,* July 12, 1993 and *Statistical Abstract of the United States, 1993.*
The 20 largest organizations are not all governments. Nearly half, in fact, are private organizations—automakers being the most numerous.

FIGURE 3   Twenty of the Largest Organizations in the World, by Annual Receipts or Expenditures, Billions of Dollars

Reengineering: Take a Clean Sheet of Paper

As the cost of communication and computing plunges, scores of companies, to be competitive, are reinventing themselves. After years of pouring millions of dollars into information technology, firms recognize that this technology is giving them an unprecedented opportunity to take out a clean sheet of paper and redesign their companies.

Operations that were once done sequentially by several people are now consolidated under one person with instant access to the necessary information to satisfy customer needs. By combining these tasks into a single job, one insurance company found it could offer customers a formal policy quote within one hour, a process that had previously required several days.

Shuffling papers between specialists caused another insurance firm to take 22 days to approve policies even though each policy was only worked on for a total of 17 minutes. The revolution in information technology has rendered sequential task routing obsolete. Now everyone in firms has more or less instant access to all relevant information for decision-making. This permits one employee to take charge and have the authority to solve a customer's problem. The goal is to improve customer satisfaction and, by reducing bureaucracy, to keep from bouncing the customer between departments.

Finally, high-speed data communications is permitting new relationships between firms. Manufacturers are beginning to shift the responsibility for inventory control to intermediate suppliers. A similar relationship exists between Wal-Mart and many of its suppliers. For example, Wal-Mart is permitting Proctor & Gamble to manage the stocks of their products at all stores. The economies gained make Wal-Mart more competitive and permit them to offer a greater variety of products at lower costs.*

*See "Reinventing Companies," *The Economist*, 12 October 1991, pp. 67–68; and "Take a Clean Sheet of Paper," *The Economist*, 1 May 1993, pp. 67–68.

---

in the mid 1980s. Today, Chrysler is profitable and sells nearly half of all new minivans bought in America. All automakers recovered in the late 1980s when they marketed more fuel efficient and reliable cars.

Interindustry competition has become increasingly important. Xerox once had a near monopoly on copying equipment but now competes with IBM and a host of Japanese firms. IBM had a stranglehold on the computer market in the 1960s, but now must compete with Apple, Radio Shack, Control Data, NEC, DEC, Xerox, Compaq, AT&T, and hundreds of small electronics firms. Today, the market value of the software giant, Microsoft, exceeds that of IBM. Interestingly, Microsoft's principle asset (its computer program code) is intellectual property and Microsoft does not own any manufacturing facilities of any consequence.

Giants often emerge from nowhere when entrepreneurs perceive a void in the marketplace or a better way to organize their operations (see Focus 2). Steve Jobs, a 17-year-old high school student, and Steve Wozniak, a 22-year-old college dropout, launched Apple Computers from their garage in 1978 for under $500, creating a billion-dollar firm within four years after they marketed the first low-cost personal computer. It is hard to overstate how risky business can be. A boom in personal computer sales and software in the early 1980s made overnight millionaires of hundreds of young programmer workaholics in the Silicon Valley, an area just south of San Francisco. Gluts on the market quickly appeared, however, and hundreds of firms collapsed during the late 1980s as consumers demanded more sophisticated software. Today's integrated software is designed, programmed, and tested by huge teams employed by large software firms. Most of the small entrepreneurial effort is devoted to shareware (i.e., programs distributed from bulletin boards to users who pay small registration fees if they find the programs useful).

Examples of dynamic competition are almost innumerable. Some firms that have, relatively, lost or gained a lot in the past few years are listed in Figure 4, which indicates how the corporate pecking order changes over time.

The key point is that high profits attract aggressive competition, both foreign and domestic, so consumers' needs are met in a reasonably efficient fashion. Many people remain unhappy with market outcomes, however, and increasingly turn to government to resolve economic problems. Health-care reform is just one recent example. Income distributions that result from the market system are often perceived as unfair. And what about national defense or such problems as pollution and excessive unemployment? We will explore these and similar questions later in the book when we examine areas in which government plays an active role in our society.

Underpinnings for consumer demands were discussed in the previous chapter, but supply has been addressed only intuitively. In the next chapter, we explore how production relationships link inputs and outputs to determine costs and shape managerial decisions about how much to produce and which technology to use. Then, in the next few chapters, we investigate how competition for consumers' dollars differs in intensity across industries and interacts with production costs to determine prices, output, and consumer purchases.

Ten Largest Companies by Market Value (billions of dollars)

	Company	Market Value
1.	Nippon Telegraph & Telephone	140.52
2.	American Telephone & Telegraph	82.4
3.	Royal Dutch Shell Group	81.6
4.	Exxon	81.4
5.	General Electric	79.3
6.	Mitsubishi Bank	73.6
7.	Sumitomo Bank	66.0
8.	WalMart Stores	64.1
9.	Industrial Bank of Japan	63.2
10.	Sanwa Bank	61.2

Turnover Among Top Ten	
Entered the Top Ten	**Left the Top Ten**
Mitsubishi Bank	Coca-Cola
Sumitomo Bank	Philip Morris
Industrial Bank of Japan	Merck
Sanwa Bank	IBM

Top Ten Emerging Companies	
Company	**Country**
Telefonos De Mexico (Telmex)	Mexico
Korea Electric Power	Korea
Cathay Life Insurance	Taiwan
Telebras	Brazil
Grupo Financiero Banacci	Mexico
Cifra	Mexico
China Steel	Taiwan
Grupo Televisa	Mexico
First Commercial Bank	Taiwan
Hua Nan Bank	Taiwan

Source: "The Global 1000", *Business Week*, July 12, 1993.

FIGURE 4   The Ten Largest, Top Ten Emerging Companies and Turnover among the Top 10 Global Corporations

CHAPTER REVIEW: KEY POINTS

1. **Production** increases the value of goods in their *form, place, possession*, or *time*.

2. The *short run* is a period in which at least one resource and one cost are fixed. In the *long run* all resources can be varied, but technology is assumed constant. These periods, therefore, are not defined by time, but rather by the nature of the adjustment process. Firms can enter or leave an industry in the long run because all resources are variable.

3. Firms exist primarily to coordinate production teams that will (*a*) reduce transaction costs and (*b*) exploit economies of scale and scope. **Economies of scale** exist when average production costs decline as the level of output rises. **Economies of scope** occur when firms realize lower costs by producing or distributing multiple products.

4. Four out of five firms are either **sole proprietorships** or **partnerships**, but **corporations** account for more than 90% of all goods and services sold and receive roughly two-thirds of all profits in the United States. Compared to corporations, however, sole proprietorships and partnerships are more easily formed and less subject to government regulation. The major advantages of corporations are the *limited liabilities* of stockholders and better access to markets for financial capital.

5. **Financial intermediaries** channel household saving into the hands of investors in economic capital and include such organizations as banks, mutual funds, insurance companies, and stock brokerage houses. Banks are the most important intermediaries, accounting for the bulk of the financing of business organizations.

6. *Economic costs* include both explicit and implicit costs. **Explicit costs** involve outlays of money for goods or resources. **Implicit costs** are the opportunity costs of resources provided by a firm's owner. Payments for rent, electricity, and wages are explicit costs, while the values of the owner's labor and capital are implicit costs.

7. Bookkeeping rarely considers implicit costs, while both implicit and explicit costs are included in economic costs. Consequently, **accounting profits** often overstate the economic profitability of an enterprise because the opportunity costs of owner-provided resources are ignored. Normal accounting profits are an economic cost of production, and the economists simplify this by noting that when **economic profits** are zero, the firm is earning a normal return (i.e., positive accounting profits are sufficient to cover implicit costs).

8. A **principal** is a party with contractual rights for performance of certain tasks by an **agent**. The **principal–agent problem** arises when the principal cannot adequately monitor the behavior of the agent, and the personal motives of the agent conflict with the objectives of the principal.

9. An erratic trend towards increased concentration of economic power in America has continued for more than a century. Corporate goals of making profits are under attack by people who believe that modern corporations are too powerful, both politically and economically. These critics argue that big business should be *socially responsible*.

10. Even though control of much of modern economic life is concentrated in the hands of those who control giant corporations, changing technology, changing market shares, and the growth of various imports are evidence that the processes of competition are still reasonably vigorous.

QUESTIONS FOR THOUGHT AND DISCUSSION

1. How might a principal–agent problem arise in each of the following cases where you can identify a principal and an agent? (Hint: Be sure that a contract exists before answering.)
   a. A corporate giant hires a new chief executive officer.
   b. You buy 90% of the stock in a small company that your best friend is starting; she will manage the day-to-day operations.
   c. You consign an old junker to a used car dealer to sell for you.
   d. A parent tells a child to do a chore.
   e. A purchasing specialist contracts for paper to print this text for the publisher.

2. Which of the following would be more likely to be reflected in explicit costs, and which would be more likely to be implicit costs? Why?
   a. The time and effort of the president of a corporation.
   b. Interest on funds placed in corporate bonds.
   c. The time and effort of an entrepreneur.
   d. Interest that funds placed in corporate stocks could earn.

3. What types of implicit costs will tend to be relatively more important as a percentage of total costs for a small proprietorship than for a typical giant corporation? What implicit costs do you think might be relatively more important for the corporation? Overall, for which type of organization do you think implicit costs would be relatively more significant?

4. Corporations have traditionally been private institutions that generate profits, create jobs, and accumulate capital, pursuits that Milton Friedman, Nobel Prize winner in economics, thinks they should continue to concentrate upon to promote economic efficiency. Friedman feels that corporations should ignore the social responsibility that critics of corporate policies would foist upon them because he sees the job of promoting social goals as belonging to government, not corporate management. These critics, however, want to make corporations accountable to the American public. How might corporations be forced to develop social consciences? Would profits and stock prices be lower? Who would bear the burden of the changes critics have advocated? Would society benefit? What are the arguments for and against these proposals to make corporations quasipublic institutions?

5. Suppose you were the chief executive officer of a major corporation. Would your primary goal be to maximize profits for stockholders or to maximize your own income including a high salary, friendly subordinates, plush offices, private airplanes, and other perks? What does your answer suggest about the compatibility of maximum corporate profits and the separation of ownership from control? What does this imply for economic efficiency?

Elasticity
Cost
Profit
Long run

Chapter 23

Production and Costs

Production

Consumer surplus

In this chapter, we explore how production links inputs and outputs to determine costs and shape managerial decisions about how much to produce and which technology to use. This chapter is important because an understanding of how costs vary with output is important in order for us to be able to predict how firms will respond to price changes.

Our descriptions of production and cost may often make it seem as though business decisions are as mechanical as following a recipe: hire a few workers, buy machinery and raw materials, then heat iron ore to 3,000°F. Voilà! Steel. But the world of business is never so simple. Entrepreneurs and managers often face enormous uncertainty while making decisions that can put millions of dollars at risk. Anyone who has implemented a new technology or written a computer program knows from experience that everything new takes twice as long as planned (no matter how conservative the plan) and that countless bugs, glitches, and bad breaks will be encountered along the way.

The idealized relationships presented in this chapter characterize production processes

that use mature technologies, but these concepts may seem very abstract at times because we often ignore specifics to highlight more important relationships. Nevertheless, you need a starting point to understand the complexities of everyday business decision-making. Production and costs are detailed in this chapter. We begin by surveying economic facets of typical production processes. This leads to a discussion of various production costs in both the short run and the long run and, finally, to a brief overview of the mysteries of technological change.

PRODUCTION FUNCTIONS

A firm can vary all productive resources in the long run, but at least one resource is fixed in the short run. Linkages between inputs and outputs are formalized in production functions.

> **Production functions** *summarize relationships between combinations of inputs and the maximum outputs that each combination can produce.*

Output = f(inputs) is an example of a production function and is read as "output is a function *f* of inputs." The function *f* summarizes how current technology translates various combinations of inputs into specific amounts of output. In this context, technology encompasses current knowledge about production techniques, as well as such things as government regulations, weather, and the laws of physics and chemistry.

Production functions are commonly written $q = f(K, L)$, where *q* equals output, *K* equals capital services, and *L* equals labor services used per production period. (For simplicity, land and entrepreneurship are ignored for now.) Suppose that production engineers indicate that 1,000 swimsuits can be sewn daily using 600 machine hours (75 sewing machines per 8-hour shift) and 800 labor hours (100 workers each 8-hour shift). The function *f* summarizes a production relationship of this type. Technological advances boosting productivity 50% would require switching from the *f* production function to, say, *g*. Now, $q = g(K, L)$, and 600 machine hours plus 800 labor hours yield 1,500 swimsuits. Complete production functions identify output possibilities in the long run, when a firm can vary all resources. In the short run, however, at least one resource is fixed.

PRODUCTION IN THE SHORT RUN

Imagine that five years after you finish your degree you are in the sand-and-gravel business. Most firms can vary labor more easily than any other basic resource. Thus, to keep things simple for now, suppose that you control the amount of labor hired in the short run, while all other resources are constant because you have long-term leases on fixed amounts of capital equipment (trucks and bulldozers) and land.

If no one works in your business, production and revenue obviously will both be zero. Working alone, you might excavate and sell 10 tons of earth material daily. Suppose that you hire an assistant and find that output expands to 22 tons daily. In this case, production more than doubled while labor inputs only doubled.

Does this mean your assistant is the better worker? Not at all. Working alone, you must run the truck, handle all marketing, operate the bulldozer, keep the books—the list goes on and on. The cliché "chief cook and bottlewasher" fits too closely for comfort. After hiring an assistant, you can drive the truck while your helper excavates, keep the books while your employee runs the bulldozer, and so on.

You are able to produce much more as a team than as separate individuals because of gains from the division of labor. As you hire even more workers, you might find that specialization enables output to continue to rise more than proportionally for the first few extra workers. Eventually, however, the gains from specialization will be overwhelmed as the law of diminishing marginal returns comes into play, and each extra worker adds less than the preceding worker did to total production. The law of diminishing marginal returns is a specific application of the more general law of diminishing returns described in Chapter 1.

Marginal and Average Physical Products of Labor

Suppose that your work force is becoming so specialized that you decide to apply some concepts you learned in college. The data in columns 1 and 2 of Table 1 relate production and various levels of labor inputs, holding other resources constant. This data represents the total product curve. Note that total product curves and production functions are not the same things. A production function allows all inputs to vary, while the total product curve assumes that only one input changes. We are using labor as the variable input, but had we held labor constant and varied capital (or land), the analysis would be quite similar, although the specific curves would differ.

If you know total output for each level of labor hired (columns 1 and 2), output per worker is calculated by dividing total output (*q*) by labor (*L*).

*The **average physical product of labor (APP_L)** equals total output divided by labor (q/L).*

TABLE 1   Total Output and the Average and Marginal Physical Products of Labor (Sand-and-Gravel Operation)

(1) Labor (workers per 8-hr shift) (L)	(2) Output (tons of sand and gravel removed daily) (q)	(3) APP_L Average Physical Product of Labor, (q/L)	(4) MPP_L Marginal Physical Product of Labor, ($\Delta q / \Delta L$)
0	0	0	0
1	10	10.00	10
2	22	11.00	12
3	36	12.00	14
4	52	13.00	16
5	70	14.00	18
6	86	14.33	16
7	100	14.28	14
8	112	14.00	12
9	122	13.55	10
10	130	13.00	8
11	137	12.45	7
12	143	11.92	6
13	148	11.38	5
14	152	10.85	4
15	155	10.33	3
16	157	9.81	2
17	158	9.29	1
18	158	8.78	0
19	157	8.26	−1

These figures are entered in column 3 of the table. You will also want to know how much each extra worker adds to total output.

> *The **marginal physical product of labor (MPP_L)** is the additional output produced by an additional unit of labor, computed by dividing the change in total output (Δq) by the change in labor (ΔL): $\Delta q / \Delta L$.*

Hiring decisions intended to maximize profit hinge on labor's marginal physical product. Extra workers will not be hired unless the extra revenue from their marginal physical products would exceed the extra costs of hiring them. Only workers generating at least as much revenue as it costs to hire them will be employed, a decision we detail in Chapter 28. In most cases, each worker's productivity (the MPP_L) will be higher as the amounts of other resources used rise; a worker operating a bulldozer on a dry riverbed will produce more sand and gravel than a shovel wielder digging on a city lot.

The MPP_L is calculated by looking at small changes in labor hired and the resulting changes in output. With large numbers of workers (as at a steel mill), a given change in the amount of labor (ΔL) is divided into the resulting change in output (Δq) to approximate the MPP_L. One worker equals ΔL for a small firm like your operation. Labor's marginal physical products ($\Delta q / \Delta L$) for your firm are listed in column 4 of Table 1.

The **total product curve** graphed in Panel A of Figure 1 (from columns 1 and 2 of Table 1) for your sand-and-gravel operation relates production and various levels of labor inputs, holding other resources constant. Panel B shows the corresponding marginal and average physical products of labor.

FIGURE 1 The Total, Marginal, and Average Physical Products of Labor (Sand-and-Gravel Example)

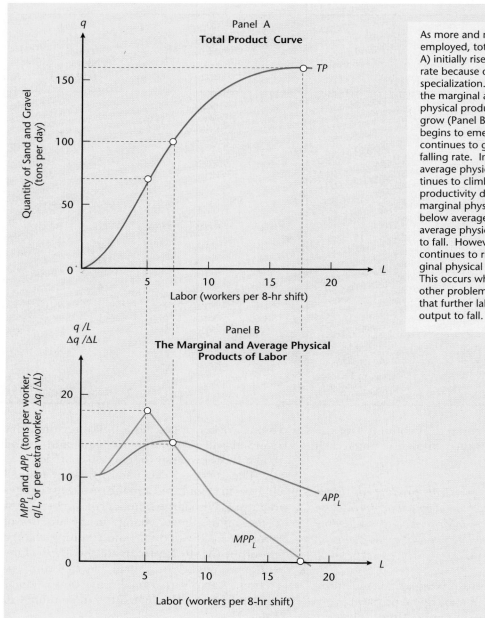

As more and more labor is employed, total output (Panel A) initially rises at an increasing rate because of gains from specialization. In this range, the marginal and average physical products of labor both grow (Panel B). As congestion begins to emerge, total output continues to grow, but at a falling rate. In this range, average physical product continues to climb, but marginal productivity diminishes. Once marginal physical product falls below average physical product, average physical product begins to fall. However, total output continues to rise until the marginal physical product is zero. This occurs when congestion or other problems are so severe that further labor inputs cause output to fall.

The Short-Run Law of Diminishing Marginal Returns

A problem of congestion emerges as your organization grows. Your dump trucks' passenger compartments become crowded and more time is wasted at the excavation site waiting to load trucks that arrived earlier. A second challenge emerges from coordinating increased work effort: ensuring that the left hand knows what the right hand is doing, limiting coffee breaks to 15 minutes, and so on. Table 1 and Figure 1 indicate that congestion and loss of coordination eventually become so severe that the seventeenth worker adds only one ton of material per day, the eighteenth's contribution is nil, and hiring the nineteenth worker actually yields a drop in output.

The decline in extra output as extra workers are employed might seem a consequence of hiring better workers first and then hiring mediocre or inferior workers. This is unnecessary to explain diminishing marginal returns. In fact, we might assume that all workers were clones from a robot factory. Every worker is then the last or marginal worker, because if you fired any one of them, you would have one less employee. As more and more workers are added to a fixed amount of resources such as capital, land, and supervision, workers' marginal physical products tend to diminish regardless of the qualities of the individual workers.

> The **law of diminishing marginal returns** occurs when equal increases of variable resources are successively added to some fixed resource; marginal physical products eventually decline.

The fixity of at least one resource in the short run makes diminishing marginal returns unavoidable: not all resources can be varied proportionally, so capital and land per worker fall as more workers are hired, inevitably leading to diminishing additions of output as extra labor is hired. This basic economic law is without exception. Were it not for diminishing returns, enough food might be grown in a flowerpot to feed the world.

Table 1 and Figure 1 reflect the outputs produced if various numbers of workers put in 8-hour days. Gains from specialization enable each of the first five workers to add more than the preceding worker to total output, but the forces that compel marginal productivity to diminish overwhelm any gains from further specialization for the sixth and subsequent workers. While total output continues to increase, it increases at a declining rate, until the eighteenth worker adds nothing to total output.

SHORT-RUN PRODUCTION COSTS

Production is tightly linked to the costs that shape business decisions. Now that we have sketched out production, we turn to the process that translates the total, average, and marginal physical products of labor into production costs. Production costs are divided into *fixed costs* and *variable costs*. All production costs fall within these two categories, so total costs (*TC*) equal total fixed costs (*TFC*) plus total variable costs (*TVC*), or

$$TC = TFC + TVC$$

Business people commonly refer to fixed costs as *overhead*, while variable costs are often called *direct costs* or *operating costs*.

Fixed Costs

History is bunk.	*Sunk costs are sunk.*
Henry Ford	*Anonymous*

At least one resource is fixed in the short run, which implies that some short-run costs are also fixed. These fixed costs were incurred previously, so they are also known as *historical* or *sunk costs*.

> **Fixed costs** are the sum of all short-run costs that are not related to the level of output.

For your sand-and-gravel operation, fixed costs would include such things as business licenses, rent you are obligated by a lease to pay, principal and interest on leases for trucks or other equipment, utility hookup charges, and franchise fees. You might be required to make payments during each period, but fixed costs are unaffected by your firm's output.

• **Fixed Costs and Decision-Making** Suppose you bought a deluxe mountain bike and were dismayed when its price was slashed two weeks later. Then a broken leg persuaded you to sell the bicycle to cover your unexpected medical bills. Least relevant to the price you should charge would be (*a*) the price you paid, (*b*) the current sales price, (*c*) storage costs, (*d*) expected enjoyment from riding after you get out of your cast, or (e) the current prices of similar used bikes?

If you chose answer (a) to this question, you intuitively understand the irrelevancy of fixed (or sunk) cost for rational decision-making. Many people are astounded when told that fixed costs have no bearing on rational decisions about how much to produce, how much to charge for your output, and so on.

Fixed costs are meaningful only to the extent that, like history or archaeology, we can learn from them. Since they are fixed, there is a sense in which no alternative exists, so the *opportunity costs of fixed resources are zero*, at least in the short run. Therefore, only costs that vary with output should affect production decisions in the short run.

Variable Costs

Such expenses as labor costs, gasoline, truck maintenance, and office supplies will be positively related to the amount of business your sand-and-gravel operation does.

> *Variable costs* are costs incurred when a firm produces, which vary with the level of production.

Any costs incurred only when a firm produces are variable costs. Consider the data for your business in Table 2 and Figure 2. Labor is the only variable resource in the short run, and we will assume that you can hire all you need at $50 each per 8-hour shift (the supply of work-

TABLE 2   Total Output, Total Costs, and Fixed and Variable Costs (Sand-and-Gravel Example)

(1) Labor (workers per 8-hr shift) (L)	(2) Output (tons of sand and gravel removed daily) (q)	(3) Wages per worker (8 hr daily) (w)	(4) Total Variable Cost ($w \times L$) (TVC)	(5) Total Fixed Cost (TFC)	(6) Total Costs (TC = TVC + TFC)
0	0	$50	$0	$100	$100
1	10	50	50	100	150
2	22	50	100	100	200
3	36	50	150	100	250
4	52	50	200	100	300
5	70	50	250	100	350
6	86	50	300	100	400
7	100	50	350	100	450
8	112	50	400	100	500
9	122	50	450	100	550
10	130	50	500	100	600
11	137	50	550	100	650
12	143	50	600	100	700
13	148	50	650	100	750
14	152	50	700	100	800
15	155	50	750	100	850
16	157	50	800	100	900
17	158	50	850	100	950
18	158	50	900	100	1000
19	157	50	950	100	1050

FIGURE 2 Total Costs, Total Fixed Costs, and Total Variable Costs (Sand-and-Gravel Example)

Total cost (*TC*) and total variable cost (*TVC*) curves are "parallel" because their difference is total fixed cost (*TFC*), which is constant, no matter how much or how little is produced. Both *TC* and *TVC* rise slowly at first, because total product (from Figure 1) initially increases at an increasing rate. Then, as total product continues to rise, but at a decreasing rate, *TC* and *TVC* rise at increasing rates.

ers is perfectly elastic). All other resources and costs are assumed constant, and total fixed cost is assumed to be $100 per day.

The total product curve (*TP*) in Figure 1 shows the amounts of labor (*L*) required to produce varying levels of output. When we multiply the horizontal (labor) axis of Figure 1 by the wage rate (*w*), it becomes the total wage bill (*w* × *L*) incurred for each level of labor you might hire. (Basic relationships are unchanged when any function is multiplied by a constant.) Wages are the only variable costs of production, so this wage bill equals total variable cost (*TVC* is column 4 in Table 2). Thus, the relationship between the quantity of output and total variable costs is the *TVC* curve in Figure 2.

When total fixed costs (*TFC*) are added vertically to the *TVC* (wage bill) curve, we have a picture of how your total costs (*TC*) vary with output. Total fixed costs are unaffected by production (a constant $100). We need to explore costs a bit more, however, before we launch into decision-making.

Note that Figure 2 turned sideways roughly mirrors Panel A in Figure 1. Variable costs re-

flect wages to labor, and labor employed determines the amount of output, so there is a natural, tight link between total cost, production, and the amount of labor hired. Now we will explore other costs that are closely related to labor's average and marginal products.

Average Costs

Some definitions will enable us to examine costs more completely. *Average total cost (ATC)* is total cost incurred per unit of output and is sometimes termed *unit cost*, or simplified to *average cost*.

> ***Average total costs*** equal total costs divided by output (*TC/q*).

Total costs are composed of fixed and variable costs, so average total cost (*ATC*) equals average fixed cost (*AFC*) plus average variable cost (*AVC*). After the cost data for excavating various amounts of earth have been collected, computing each type of average cost only requires dividing each by the output level.

TABLE 3 Average Total Costs, Average Fixed Costs, Average Variable Costs, and Marginal Cost

(1) (L) Labor (Workers per 8-hr shift)	(2) (q) Output (Tons of sand and gravel removed daily)	(3) (TVC) Total Variable Cost $(w \times L)$	(4) (TFC) Total Fixed Cost	(5) (AVC) Average Variable Cost (3)/(2)	(6) (AFC) Average Fixed Cost (4)/(2)	(7) (ATC) Average Total Cost (5) + (6)	(8) (MC) Marginal Cost (¢3)/(¢2)
0	0	$ 0	$100	$—	$—	$—	$—
1	10	50	100	5.00	10.00	15.00	5.00
2	22	100	100	4.54	4.55	9.09	4.17
3	36	150	100	4.17	2.78	6.95	3.57
4	52	200	100	3.85	1.92	5.77	3.13
5	70	250	100	3.57	1.43	5.00	2.78
6	86	300	100	3.49	1.16	4.65	3.13
7	100	350	100	3.50	1.00	4.50	3.57
8	112	400	100	3.57	0.89	4.46	4.17
9	122	450	100	3.69	0.82	4.51	5.00
10	130	500	100	3.85	0.77	4.62	6.25
11	137	550	100	4.01	0.73	4.74	7.14
12	143	600	100	4.20	0.70	4.90	8.33
13	148	650	100	4.39	0.68	5.07	10.00
14	152	700	100	4.60	0.66	5.26	12.50
15	155	750	100	4.84	0.65	5.49	16.67
16	157	800	100	5.10	0.64	5.74	25.00
17	158	850	100	5.38	0.63	6.01	50.00
18	158	900	100	5.69	0.63	6.32	—
19	157	950	100	6.05	0.64	6.69	—

Average fixed cost (AFC) *is the fixed cost per unit of output (TFC/q).*

Average variable cost (AVC) *is the variable cost per unit (TVC/q).*[1]

Table 3 lists these costs for your sand-and-gravel operation. Let's explore all these averages in more detail to see how they are typically related to production.

• **Average Fixed Costs** Just because total fixed costs do not vary with output does not make an *AFC* curve horizontal. *AFC = TFC/q*, where *TFC*

is constant. Figure 3 shows how the *AFC* is related to the output of your operation, calculated in column 6 of Table 3. Total fixed costs are constant, so, as output increases, fixed costs per unit of output decline, a process that many managers describe as spreading overhead through high volume.[2]

• **Average Variable Costs** Managers can control variable costs by changing the level of output. As output grows, the *AVC* initially tends to

---

[1]Dividing both sides of *TC = TFC + TVC* by output (*q*) yields (*TC/q*) = (*TFC/q*) + (*TVC/q*), and thus, *ATC = AFC + AVC*.

[2]Notice that if we arbitrarily select any two points on the *AFC* curve (say, *a* and *b*), the rectangles formed by dropping horizontal and vertical lines to the axes have identical areas ($100). (Since *AFC = TFC/q*, multiplication of *AFC* by *q* yields *TFC*: (*TFC/q*) × *q = TFC*, which is constant.) Thus, the *AFC* curve is a rectangular hyperbola. Recall that unitary elastic demand curves are also rectangular hyperbolas.

FIGURE 3 Average Fixed Costs

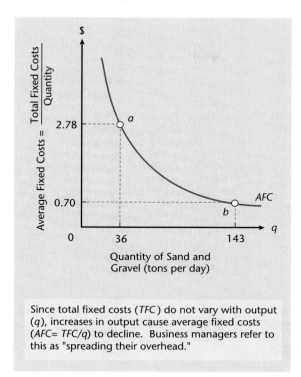

Since total fixed costs (*TFC*) do not vary with output (*q*), increases in output cause average fixed costs (*AFC*= *TFC/q*) to decline. Business managers refer to this as "spreading their overhead."

fall. But eventually, diminishing marginal returns will drive up average variable costs. Seeing why this occurs requires understanding a bit about marginal cost, which is the most important cost concept of all for business decision-making.

Marginal Costs

The extra production costs incurred are vital for decisions about changing output levels.

> **Marginal cost (MC)** *is the change in total cost associated with producing an additional unit of output.*

Since $TC = TFC + TVC$, any change in total cost reflects changes in variable costs; fixed cost does not depend on the output level.[3] Thus, producing an extra unit of output incurs marginal cost that equals either (*a*) the change in the total cost

---

[3]Proof: Dividing $\Delta TC = \Delta TFC + \Delta TVC$ by a small change in output (Δq) reveals that $MC = (\Delta TC/\Delta q) = (\Delta TFC/\Delta q) + (\Delta TVC/\Delta q)$. But output does not affect fixed costs, so $\Delta TFC/\Delta q = 0$ and $MC = (\Delta TC/\Delta q) = (\Delta TVC/\Delta q)$.

or (*b*) the change in the total variable cost. Marginal cost for your firm is listed in column 8 of Table 3.

Figure 4 shows how average variable cost (*AVC*) and marginal cost (*MC*) change as you process various amounts of earth. Why are these curves U-shaped? Recall that the marginal physical product of labor (MPP_L) initially rose as you hired more labor but then fell when diminishing marginal returns were encountered. This means that the labor costs of additional output (its *MC*, in this case) initially decline, but diminishing returns ultimately cause marginal costs to rise as additional workers add less and less to total output. Similarly, the average physical product of labor (APP_L) initially rose, but then declined as more workers were employed, caus-

The average variable cost (*AVC*) curve falls when marginal cost (*MC*) is below it, and rises when *MC* exceeds *AVC*. Average variable cost is at its minimum when *AVC* = *MC*. Both curves are U-shaped because, initially, gains from specialization push *AVC* and *MC* down. But eventually, as output is expanded, diminishing returns are encountered and the *MC* and *AVC* curves both rise.

FIGURE 4   Marginal Cost and Average Variable Cost

FIGURE 5   Short-Run Costs of Production

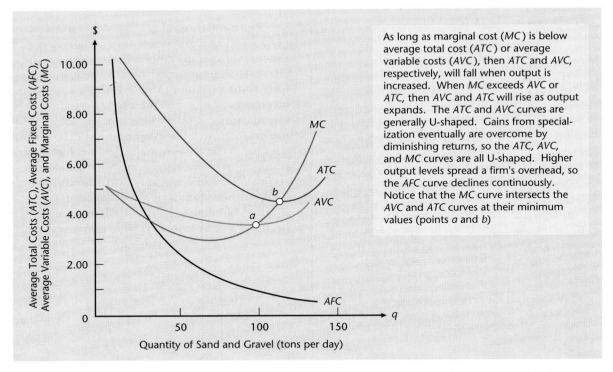

As long as marginal cost (*MC*) is below average total cost (*ATC*) or average variable costs (*AVC*), then *ATC* and *AVC*, respectively, will fall when output is increased. When *MC* exceeds *AVC* or *ATC*, then *AVC* and *ATC* will rise as output expands. The *ATC* and *AVC* curves are generally U-shaped. Gains from special-ization eventually are overcome by diminishing returns, so the *ATC*, *AVC*, and *MC* curves are all U-shaped. Higher output levels spread a firm's overhead, so the *AFC* curve declines continuously. Notice that the *MC* curve intersects the *AVC* and *ATC* curves at their minimum values (points *a* and *b*)

ing the U shape of average variable cost curves. These relationships between production levels and costs will be detailed in a moment.

• **Graphically Summing Average Costs** In Figure 5 we tack an average fixed cost (*AFC*) curve onto a graph with typical U-shaped mar-ginal cost (*MC*) and average variable cost (*AVC*) curves. Summing vertically the *AVC* and *AFC* as-sociated with each output level yields the aver-age total cost (*ATC*) curve shown. Notice that as output increases, differences between the *AVC* and *ATC* curves shrink. The *ATC* and *AVC* con-verge, because their vertical differences equal *AFC*, which falls as output rises. We now take a quick look at how costs relate to production.

Relating Costs to Production

It is no coincidence that total product and total costs are closely related, and that Figure 2 when turned sideways has a shape similar to Panel A of Figure 1. In a similar fashion, average variable

costs are closely related to average physical prod-uct, and marginal costs are related to marginal physical product. Let's see why.

Suppose, for a moment, that you start a sec-ond operation with no fixed costs and hire one worker for $10 per hour to convert trash into trinkets sold at tourist traps. (Labor is your only expense because trash is free.) If this worker converts trash into two trinkets per hour, aver-age variable cost is $5 per trinket ($10 wage/2 trinkets = $5 per trinket). Thus, average phys-ical product is related to average variable cost by the formula $AVC = w/APP_L$ when labor is the only variable cost.[4] If a second $10-per-hour

---

[4]To derive this relationship a little more formally, re-call the simplifying assumption for your sand-and-gravel firm that all nonlabor resources were fixed. Therefore, total variable cost (*TVC*) equals the wage bill ($w \times L$), and aver-age variable costs ($AVC = TVC/q$) equal wL/q. Since the av-erage physical product of labor (APP_L) is q/L, if we invert APP_L [it is then $1/(q/L) = L/q$] and multiply by the wage (a constant, w), we have calculated the average variable costs of production [$w/(q/L) = w/APP_L$]. Algebraically, $AVC = (TVC/q) = (wL/q) = w(L/q) = w(1/APP_L) = (w/APP_L)$.

TABLE 4   Relating Production and Costs (Sand-and-Gravel Example)

(1) L	(2) q	(3) (q/L) APP_L	(4) ($\Delta q/\Delta L$) MPP_L	(5) w	(6) (w/APP_L) AVC	(7) (w/MPP_L) MC	(8) AFC	(9) ATC
0	0	—	—	$50	$—	$—	$—	$—
1	10	10.00	10	50	5.00	5.00	10.00	15.00
2	22	11.00	12	50	4.54	4.17	4.55	9.09
3	36	12.00	14	50	4.17	3.57	2.78	6.95
4	52	13.00	16	50	3.85	3.13	1.92	5.77
5	70	14.00	18	50	3.57	2.78	1.43	5.00
6	86	14.33	16	50	3.49	3.13	1.16	4.65
7	100	14.28	14	50	3.50	3.57	1.00	4.50
8	112	14.00	12	50	3.57	4.17	0.89	4.46
9	122	13.55	10	50	3.69	5.00	0.82	4.51
10	130	13.00	8	50	3.85	6.25	0.77	4.62
11	137	12.45	7	50	4.01	7.14	0.73	4.74
12	143	11.92	6	50	4.20	8.33	0.70	4.90
13	148	11.38	5	50	4.39	10.00	0.68	5.07
14	152	10.85	4	50	4.60	12.50	0.66	5.26
15	155	10.33	3	50	4.84	16.67	0.65	5.49
16	157	9.81	2	50	5.10	25.00	0.64	5.74
17	158	9.29	1	50	5.38	50.00	0.63	6.01

worker increases total hourly output to three trinkets, that worker's marginal product is one trinket, but it raised labor costs by $10. Thus, that trinket's marginal cost is $10 and, when wages are the only variable cost, marginal physical product is related to marginal cost by $MC = w/MPP_L$.[5]

Let's return to the sand-and-gravel operation. Table 4 replicates labor's total, average, and marginal physical products from Table 1. Average variable costs (w/APP_L) and marginal costs (w/MPP_L) based on these data are reported in columns 6 and 7, respectively, and average fixed costs (column 8) are computed by divid-

ing fixed costs by output levels. Summing AFC and AVC then yields the ATC of production (column 9).

• **Average Product and Average Variable Cost**
Figure 6 shows that when six workers are on the job (points b, Panels A and B), average product is at its maximum (14.33 tons) and average variable cost is at its minimum value ($3.49). Workers receive a constant wage, so we can calculate labor costs when AVC (which is wL/q) is at its lowest. Symmetrically, from this wage bill, you can infer the hiring of labor when average variable cost is minimized. This result is shown as the shaded values in Table 4.

Let us get away from technical descriptions for a moment and look at the intuitive result of this analysis. If the amount produced per worker (APP_L) is at its highest value (point b in Panel A), then the amount spent on labor per unit of output (AVC) logically must be at its lowest value (point b in Panel B).

---

[5]Only labor costs change as your sand-and-gravel operation processes more tons of earth, so marginal costs ($MC = \Delta TC/\Delta q$) are simply the changes in the total wage bill associated with higher production $MC = \Delta(wL)/\Delta q$. The wage rate is constant, so $MC = \Delta(wL)/\Delta q = w\Delta L/\Delta q$. Since the marginal physical product of labor (MPP_L) equals $\Delta q/\Delta L$, we can invert the MPP_L, multiply by w, and arrive at the marginal cost of production. Again the algebraic sequence is $MC = (\Delta TVC/\Delta q) = (\Delta(wL)/\Delta q) = w\Delta L/\Delta q = w(1/MPP_L) = (w/MPP_L)$.

FIGURE 6   The Relationships Between APP_L, MPP_L, AVC, and MC

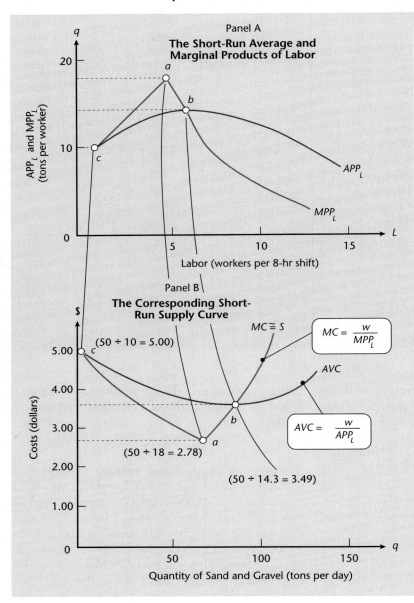

Panel A
The Short-Run Average and Marginal Products of Labor

APP$_L$ and MPP$_L$ (tons per worker)

Labor (workers per 8-hr shift)

APP_L

MPP_L

Panel B
The Corresponding Short-Run Supply Curve

$ (dollars)

Costs (dollars)

$MC \cong S$

$$MC = \frac{w}{MPP_L}$$

AVC

$$AVC = \frac{w}{APP_L}$$

$(50 \div 10 = 5.00)$

$(50 \div 18 = 2.78)$

$(50 \div 14.3 = 3.49)$

Quantity of Sand and Gravel (tons per day)

For simplicity we assume that only labor (*L*) can be varied in the short run. Thus, all marginal costs and variable costs are associated with the wage bill (*wL*). When the marginal physical product of labor (MPP_L) is at its maximum (point *a* in Panel A), the last worker hired added the most output, so the marginal cost (*MC*) of the last unit produced is at its minimum (point *a* in Panel B). Similarly, when the average physical product of labor (APP_L) is at its maximum (point *b* in Panel A), the average amount of labor used (hence, the average amount of wage cost) per unit of output is at a minimum, so average variable cost (*AVC*) is also at its minimum (point *b* in Panel B).

• **Marginal Product and Marginal Cost** Labor's marginal physical product at your firm is drawn in Panel A of Figure 6; the corresponding marginal cost curve is in Panel B. These curves parallel the data in Table 4, and thus are reflections of each other. Marginal product is maximized (18 tons daily) and marginal cost is minimized ($2.78) if five workers

are hired (shown as the shaded areas in Table 4). Clearly, if the last worker hired produced the most (maximum MPP_L at point *a* in Panel A), then the last few tons of gravel processed cost the least (minimum *MC* at point *a* in Panel B).

The relationship between production and costs is critical for the supply decisions of firms. Of course, production costs are only one dimension of a firm's decision matrix. The other side is demand. In the next few chapters, demand-originated constraints on firms facing various degrees of competition will be dealt with at length.

To simplify the analysis of short-run production and costs, only labor has been allowed to vary, but our results would be qualitatively similar if we allowed all resources but one to vary. The approach to long-run production costs is slightly different because all of a firm's resources are variable. Technology is assumed constant in the long run, however, in part because most resources may be varied more quickly than technology is likely to change, and in part because technological changes tend to be somewhat unpredictable, a topic we will deal with later in this chapter.

COSTS IN THE LONG RUN

The long run allows a firm to completely adjust all resources and costs. Fixed costs eventually become variable because no resource is fixed in the long run. Just when do fixed costs become variable? In the long run, you might sell previously fixed resources to other firms and rid yourself of obligations to meet fixed payments. The original obligation, however, remains a sunk cost; you cannot change history. Alternatively, you might obligate your firm to pay for more machinery, another short-run fixed cost. Until your name is on the dotted line for a new building or machine or to renew a franchise or lease, these expenses are variable costs. Then they become fixed costs, but only for the short run.

In the long run, a firm may enter or leave an industry and either expand or contract the scope of any operation. More land, buildings, or new machinery can be acquired. Alternatively, property holdings can be reduced through sale or by allowing leases to lapse; old equipment can either be sold or depreciated and scrapped.

Least Cost Production

Profit-maximizing managers can alter their resource mix in the long run to achieve productive efficiency so that production costs for any given amount of output are minimized. Equivalently, they try to maximize the output produced for a given total cost. Efficiency requires conformity with the law of equal marginal advantage, which, applied to consumer behavior, yields the principle of equal marginal utilities per dollar. This law applies in a parallel way to production.

> The **principle of equal marginal productivities per dollar:** *Marginal physical products of resources must be proportional to their prices.*

This application of the law of equal advantage to production means that

$$\frac{MPP_L}{w} = \frac{MPP_K}{i} = \frac{MPP_N}{n} = \cdots$$

where MPP_K equals the marginal physical product of capital, MPP_N equals the marginal physical product of land, i equals the interest rate, and n equals the rental rate for land. To see why this equation works, suppose that the last \$1 paid in wages generated 1 ton of sand while the last \$1 you spent on capital yielded 2 tons of sand. You would gain an extra ton of sand to sell if you shifted \$1 away from labor towards capital.

Similar gains of output (or reductions in cost) are possible any time the marginal productivities of resources are not proportional to resource prices.

> **Least cost production** *in the long run entails adjustments until this principle of equal marginal productivities per dollar is met.*

This principle suggests that relatively higher wages induce a firm to *substitute* capital for labor. This has occurred in the auto industry in recent years as high labor costs have caused an army of industrial robots to invade the assembly line. Symmetrically, higher capital costs induce substitution toward labor. When interest rates are high, investment in new capital falls, and labor is substituted for capital.

You should not get the impression, however, that resources are only substitutes for one another. Resources may also be *complements* in production. Labor productivity, for example, tends to be positively related to the capital and land with which labor has to work. Increases in nonlabor resources tend to raise labor's total, average, and marginal physical products. The close short-run relationships between production and costs (total, average, and marginal products and costs) suggest that in the long run, average and marginal costs will be influenced by all the resources used.

Long-Run Average Costs

Plants of different sizes can be built in the long run, so a unique set of short-run cost curves exists for each possible plant size. Possible changes in the short-run marginal costs and average total costs of a garment manufacturer with (a) 100, (b) 200, or (c) 300 sewing machines are highlighted in Figure 7. Under these short-run cost curves, we have placed an *envelope curve*, which reflects the plant sizes associated with the average costs of producing each level of output. This envelope is the long-run average cost (*LRATC*) curve for the firm.

> A **long-run average total cost (LRATC)** *curve reflects the plant size that allows the minimum possible short-run average costs to produce each possible level of output.*

Notice that this envelope curve is not tangent to the minimum point on each *SRATC* curve. Only a plant in which 200 machines are used to produce 4,000 garments per day (point *a*) yields the absolute minimum long-run average cost of production. At this point, the envelope curve is tangent to the minimum point of the *SRATC* curve. To the left of this point all short-run cost curves are tangent to the *LRATC* curve on the left side of their respective minimums. To the right of point *a*, tangencies with the envelope curve are at the right sides of the short-run curves.

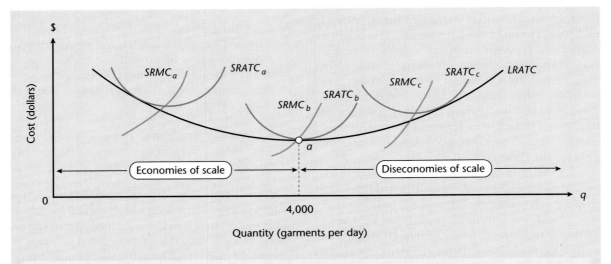

Short-run costs depend on the fixed amounts of capital and land used in concert with labor, which, for convenience, we assume is the only variable resource. The long run average total cost (*LRATC*) curve is an *envelope* of short-run average total cost (*SRATC*) curves. Economies of scale occur if expanding land and capital reduce average costs. Diseconomies of scale are present when average costs rise as capacity grows.

FIGURE 7   The Long-Run Average Cost Curve

Economies and Diseconomies of Scale

Notice that the long run average cost (*LRATC*) curve in Figure 7 falls as output rises and then increases as output rises further.

> **Economies of scale** *exist when long-run average costs decline as output rises.*

> **Diseconomies of scale** *occur in the range where long-run average costs rise with increases in output.*

When diseconomies are encountered, reducing the scale of operations allows production at lower average costs.

It might seem that if all resources were expanded by some fixed proportion, output must expand by that same proportion. Gains from specialization, however, may expand output more than proportionally as the scale of operation grows from some small level. These advantages give rise to economies of scale, causing average production costs to fall.

On the other end of the spectrum, diseconomies of scale emerge because of limitations to efficient management. Giant firms encounter diseconomies of scale because managerial control decays as layers are added to any hierarchy. The information that must be digested and acted on snowballs, so coordinating the activities of ever larger groups becomes an ever more formidable task. Another problem is that vertical hierarchies require decision-making at many different levels. The principal–agent problem becomes pervasive because monitoring performance is increasingly difficult; not all these decision-makers will focus on doing everything with maximum efficiency to realize maximum profits. Organizations may become so large and clumsy that, like dinosaurs, extinction is a real possibility.

To counteract this problem, large bureaucratic firms have recently begun to reengineer. Rapid advances in microcomputing power coupled with plummeting prices have permitted large firms to reorganize their operations, extending economics and improving service (see Focus 2 in the previous chapter).

Between the cases of decreasing and increasing economies of scale is the case of constant returns to scale. Constant returns to scale means that average total cost is constant (flat) and marginal cost equals average total cost. Over some range of output, firms can simply add a plant with essentially the same unit costs as the previous plant. For example, franchising firms often find this to be the case.

Economies of Scope

Even if a firm is too small to enjoy economies of scale in any individual product market, it can achieve economies by producing components that are used in several products. For example, petroleum refineries crack petroleum into many different products including gasoline, diesel, home heating oil, and other petroleum distillates. By producing many products, average production costs at a refinery are reduced. In essence, producing good *A* reduces the cost of producing good *B*. These economies of scope (or joint production) can result in significant cost reductions.

> **Economies of scope** *occur when one firm produces or distributes several different products that share the same production facility or inputs.*

Most gas stations have now become convenience stores that provide gas, food, and car-washing services. Nearly all chemical plants use petroleum as a basic input to produce paint, plastics, fertilizers, and many other final products. Many software firms develop generic drivers or subroutines that they use over and over to produce numerous games and books on disk.

Economies of scope, however, eventually face the same managerial control problems common to economies of scale. Adding the complexity of different products can make these problems harder since they involve coordination of managers responsible for many different products.

Measuring Long-Run Average Costs

Any firm that fails to exploit economies of scale will have higher average costs than those of competing firms that do; firms that are too small for efficient operation must either grow or fail. Many people think that bigger firms can almost always produce at lower costs than smaller firms. While it is true that a firm must be large enough to exploit all feasible economies of scale, bigger plants may encounter diseconomies of scale and be forced to reduce the scope of their operations or sink.

Studies of Portugal's decline as a world power from 1400 to 1600 indicate that its wooden sailing ships were too large for the prevailing technology. A large part of the Portuguese fleet sank in bad weather, in part because of huge cargos. In the 1970s, the U.K. and France's Concorde passenger jets suffered such great cost disadvantages that their government sponsors took financial baths. Today's space shuttle is showing similar signs of suffering cost disadvantages to unmanned rocket satellite launching. How large is the optimal convenience store or gas station? How about atomic

power plants or oil refineries? In the 1930s, the world's largest auto assembly plant was Ford's River Rouge plant. It was never fully used, and today much of it has been torn down. It was simply too large to be efficient.

The ranges where economies or diseconomies of scale are actually encountered vary substantially among industries. Engineering estimates and the few statistical studies of cost functions that are available indicate that there typically are substantial ranges of output for which average costs are roughly constant, as depicted in the middle of the *LRATC* curve in Figure 8.

An idea known as the *survival principle* suggests that clustering within an industry of firms or plants of a particular size is conclusive evidence about the efficient scale of operations. Some economists have tried to apply this principle to specific industries as a way of measuring the minimum points of long-run average

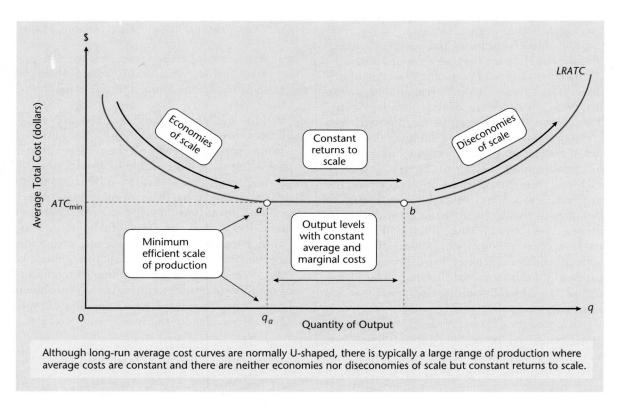

Although long-run average cost curves are normally U-shaped, there is typically a large range of production where average costs are constant and there are neither economies nor diseconomies of scale but constant returns to scale.

FIGURE 8   Typical "Real World" Average Cost Curves

cost curves. Critics, however, argue that survival depends on a multitude of factors (luck, monopoly power, business acumen, growth or decline of an industry, and so on) and, thus, that some inefficient firms may survive, while some efficient firms fail.

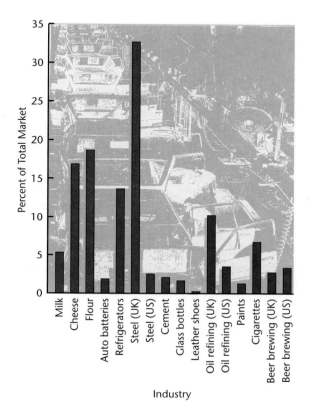

Sources: F.M. Scherer and D. Ross, *Industrial Market Structure and Economic Performance* (Princeton, N.J.: Houghton Mifflin), 1990; Dennis Carlton and Jeffrey Perloff, *Modern Industrial Organization* (New York: HarperCollins), 1990; William S. Comanor and Thomas A. Wilson, *Advertising and Market Power* (Cambridge, Mass.: Harvard University Press), 1974; Stephen Davies, "Minimum Efficient Size and Seller Concentration: An Empirical Problem," *The Journal of Industrial Economics,* March 1980, pp. 287—297; Gary L. Shoesmith, "Economies of Scale and Scope in Petroleum Refining," *Applied Economics,* 1988, pp. 1643—1652; and Craig MacPhee, "The Economies of Scale Revisited: Comparing Census Costs, Engineering Estimates, and the Survivor Technique," *Quarterly Journal of Business & Economics,* Spring 1990, pp. 43—67.

The minimum efficient scale (*MES*) is the smallest size plant (point *a* Figure 7) that has long-run average total cost near its minimum. *MES* is usually reported as a percent of total industry output and is used as an explanation of industrial concentration. The larger MES is, the fewer efficient firms a market can support.

FIGURE 9 Minimum Efficient Scale (MES) for Selected Industries 1974—1990

Minimum efficient scale (MES) plants are the smallest that will produce output at minimum average total cost.

Minimum efficient scale (output q_a corresponding to point *a* at the beginning of the flat portion in Figure 8) has been estimated for various industries using accounting data, engineering estimates, and the survival technique. Typically, *MES* is reported as a percent of the total market. Figure 9 presents some estimates of *MES* for selected industries here and abroad. Measuring long run cost curves is unavoidably imprecise, but the concept is still useful in analyzing industry adjustments to changes in demands, resource prices, or other events.

In summary, economies of scale encourage size. If the minimum efficient scale of production in an industry requires huge firms, then fewer firms will inhabit that industry. (This raises questions about government policies to control excessive market power, issues that are addressed in later chapters.) On the other hand, significant diseconomies of scale tend to reward compact firms so that many competitors inhabit an industry.

Firms and industries grow in response to widespread perceptions of profit opportunities or wither when economic losses are expected to persist. Long-run adjustments allow firms to enter an industry and grow infinitely or to shrink to zero and leave an industry; a firm can perfectly adjust its size by purchasing more or fewer resources, but, by assumption, we hold technology constant. We need to consider the possibility, however, that research and development may respond strongly to profit opportunities.

TECHNOLOGICAL CHANGE

Much human progress arises from incremental improvements in the methods available to satisfy our wants.

Technological change increases output from a given set of resources or allows distribution of previously unknown goods.

Technological change takes two basic forms: (*a*) improvements to nonhuman resources or

(b) new knowledge about how to combine resources. New capital equipment that cuts production costs or a new strain of seed that boosts crop yields are examples of technological advances in nonhuman resources. New plowing methods that conserve topsoil or medical procedures that reduce a transplant patient's recovery time would be examples of new knowledge that represents technological progress.

Major technological breakthroughs tend to arrive in waves that influence numerous industries or forms of production. Advances in microprocessing and optical networks have already begun to revolutionize the way we obtain, absorb, and process information. Predicting the direction of such sweeping technological advances is impossible. In a few instances, however, profit incentives within a specific industry cause the direction of technological change to be reasonably predictable.

Consider, for example, adjustments to higher energy costs. Most industries had adapted to low-cost, abundant energy sources during the period from 1900 to 1973. Oil drove much of our technology. Then oil prices quadrupled between 1974 and 1975. Car buyers' demands for better gas mileage were echoed in many industries when firms scurried to find energy-efficient technologies. Electronic fuel injection replaced carburetors, roughly doubling average gas mileage. New types of insulation were developed, as were production processes that recycled heat or used less of it. Similar adjustments are taking place today as added taxes on energy increase the relative cost of many energy sources.

Profit opportunities may induce new technologies that change outputs and production techniques or improve resources, and ultimately drive down costs. Some technological changes occur as quickly as a creative mind can solve a new problem. At other times, refining a technology is never-ending. It is also uncertain whether giant or small enterprises are systematically favored by technological advance. Some new technologies enhance economies of scale and scope; others work best when an operation is small. We can be sure, however, that technological advances make options available that reduce average production costs.

The technology for producing semiconductors is expected to increase the cost of an efficient production plant from roughly $250 million today to nearly $2 billion by the turn of the century. Such high costs, risks, and volumes of production are causing firms to forge worldwide alliances to produce microchips for the future.

In other areas, technology has reduced the costs of communications and air cargo. This has permitted many firms to hold trivial inventories in retail shops. Benetton, for example, analyzes daily sales data from retail stores all over the world and then selectively produces and ships what is needed to restock stores using overnight delivery. Gone are the days of large backroom inventories: what's on the rack is what's available on any given day.

Production based on immediate retail needs requires more flexibility in both production equipment and employees. Manufacturing plants must be designed so that lines can be shifted to produce different products quickly and efficiently. Similarly, workers must master wide variety of skills and be flexible as the line changes. This revolution in production is changing employment careers as firms recognize that workers must be more skilled and have more responsibility.[6]

Edward Dennison[7] has estimated the sources of long-term U.S. economic growth. His estimates show that, second only to growth in the labor force, technological change has accounted for over 20% of long-term economic growth and over half of our productivity gains during the last half-century.

Predicting the precise duration and effect of technological change is impossible, so we usually consider only the long-run adjustments of entry into and exit from an industry, or the shrinkage or growth of a firm. We will examine economic responses to changing circumstances in the next few chapters.

---

[6]See P. Milgrom and J. Roberts, *Economics, Organization and Management* (Englewood Cliffs, N.J.: Prentice-Hall, 1992), pp. 586–88.

[7]Edward Dennison, "Contributions to 1929–82 Growth Rates," *Trends in American Economic Growth, 1929–82,* (Washington D.C.: The Brookings Institution, 1985).

CHAPTER REVIEW: KEY POINTS

1. A **production function** expresses a relationship between inputs and output. Production transforms goods to make them more valuable in form, place, time, or possession. A *total product curve* shows how output is affected as the amount of only one input changes.

2. The **short run** is a period in which at least one resource and one cost are fixed. In the **long run** all resources can be varied, but technology is assumed constant. These periods, therefore, are not defined by time, but rather by the nature of the adjustment process.

3. The **average physical product of labor** (APP_L) equals q/L. The **marginal physical product of labor** (MPP_L) equals $\Delta q/\Delta L$ and is the output generated by an additional unit of labor.

4. According to the **law of diminishing marginal returns**, when increasing amounts of a variable resource are applied to a fixed resource, although the marginal physical product of the variable factor may initially rise, beyond some point its marginal product inevitably falls.

5. A firm's total costs can be separated into *fixed* (or *overhead*) *costs* and *variable* (or *operating*) *costs*. **Fixed costs** do not vary with output, do not alter rational decisions, and are referred to as *sunk costs*. Leases, utility hookup charges, opportunity costs of an owner's resources, and other overhead expenses are fixed costs in the short run. Wages paid to employees, bills for raw materials, and other costs that change when output is changed are **variable costs**.

6. When total fixed costs and total variable costs are each divided by output, **average fixed costs** (*AFC*) and **average variable costs** (*AVC*) are obtained, respectively. Summing the two yields **average total cost** (*ATC*). **Marginal cost** (*MC*) is defined as the additional cost of producing one more unit of a good and equals $\Delta TC/\Delta q$.

7. Firms can enter or leave an industry in the long run because all resources are variable. The *long-run average total cost (LRATC) curve* is an *envelope curve* under all short-run average total cost curves (different-sized plants). It shows the minimum long-run average costs for each output level. Long-run average total cost curves typically have **economies of scale** (*LRATC* falling) over some portion of the curve, but eventually exhibit **diseconomies of scale** (*LRATC* rising). **Economies of scope** (joint production or distribution) can result in significant cost reductions even for small firms that produce or distribute several products.

8. Measuring long-run costs is a complex problem. One method is to examine the size (and cost structure) of firms that have been successful and have survived in an industry over a long period of time. Other methods include using both accounting and engineering data to estimate the *LRATC* curve. Economists have estimated **minimum efficient scale** (*MES*), the smallest plant that can be operated at minimum *LRATC*. *MES* is typically reported as a percent of industry output.

9. **Technological change** increases output from given resources. New technology develops from new knowledge or improved nonhuman resources and results in new products or lower costs. Technological improvements account for much of our long-term economic growth and rising productivity.

QUESTIONS FOR THOUGHT AND DISCUSSION

1. Which of the following tend to be fixed costs, and which are probably variable costs? Why does the time period considered matter for each case?
   a. Silk purchased by a Parisian haute couture dress designer.
   b. The guaranteed salary of baseball star Andres Galaraga.
   c. A $100,000 contract signed by a couple to buy a home.
   d. A magazine subscription for a doctor's office.
   e. Student loans taken out to pay a student's tuition.
   f. Payments to migrant workers for harvesting ripe plums.

2. Describe the forces that, as more and more labor is hired, cause output to rise at an increasing rate and then at a decreasing rate, and that may ultimately cause output to fall as more labor is employed. How do these forces affect marginal and average costs in a similarly systematic fashion? Why? Can you think of any production processes that would not operate in accord with these general principles? What are they?

3. Suppose that you offered to buy pizza and cold drinks to bribe your friends to help you move into a new apartment and were deluged with offers of help. What problems would you encounter if too few actually showed up? How would this affect your average cost per box or stick of furniture moved? What are some possible fixed factors that would decrease the efficiency of your move and drive up its cost if too many helpers volunteered? How would this raise the cost of your move? How many big strong friends

do you think would be the ideal number to accomplish this task?

4. The average productivity of labor rises as long as labor's marginal productivity exceeds the average. We call this range of production Zone 1. Do you think firms would knowingly choose to operate in Zone 1, where hiring additional workers raises average productivity? Why or why not? Would firms ever operate in Zone 2, the range of output where the marginal returns from labor were positive but diminishing? Would they operate in Zone 3, where the marginal physical productivity of labor is negative? In what zone will firms operate? (A colleague once described another professor as a "Zone 3 personality." What do you suppose was meant by this remark? Have you ever worked with such a person?) Draw a typical total product curve and include average and marginal physical products. Identify these production zones. (Note: Firms always try to operate in one of these zones, but most firms will close down rather than operate in the other two.)

5. Can you construct a total product curve for "knowledge of economics," with your study time as the variable (labor) input? How might this curve shift with variations in time with tutors, reference books, reading the *Wall Street Journal*, studying only when you are too tired to party, and so on? At what point would the law of diminishing marginal returns come into play? Should you cease studying at the onset of diminishing returns? You may have heard people suggest that " when you reach the point of diminishing returns, it's time to quit." Are they using this term correctly?

OPTIONAL MATERIAL: ISOQUANTS AND PRODUCTION

How the resource mix is varied in the long run to maximize a firm's profit was touched on in our discussion of the principle of equal marginal pro-

ductivities per dollar. Now we will address these long-run adjustments using slightly more sophisticated tools.

Isoquants

Producing any given amount of output can be accomplished with numerous combinations of inputs. For example, suppose you own a firm that packages and sells Birdhouse gourd seeds to home gardeners who grow houses for their feathered friends. You estimate that you can wholesale 10,000 cases of packaged seeds at $2 per case over the course of a season. Five of the many different possible combinations of capital (machines) and labor (workers) that will accomplish the job are listed in Table 5. These combinations run the gamut from a few machines with many workers hand-counting and stuffing the packages to production processes using numerous automated machines and very few workers to load seeds and watch the machines work. As you might expect, the process you would eventually gravitate to will be the one with the lowest cost. The last column of Table 5 depicts the total costs of packaging 10,000 cases of seeds if labor and capital each cost $1,000 per unit. To minimize the costs of producing 10,000 packages, you would employ three machines and three workers. The information in Table 5 is graphed in Figure 10; a smoothly curved line connects the five combinations from Table 5. This curve represents all possible mixtures of labor and capital that can produce 10,000 cases and is referred to as an *isoquant*.

Isoquants are similar to the consumer indifference curves discussed in the optional material at the end of an earlier chapter, but with one major difference. Isoquants show constant levels of output, which is measurable; indifference curves show constant levels of satisfaction, which cannot be measured with precision. Just as the slope of an in-difference curve reflects the relative subjective desirability of the two goods considered ($-MU_a/MU_b$), isoquants reflect the relative marginal productivities of the two resources ($-MPP_L/MPP_K$).

Let us take a moment to examine what happens to the marginal products of labor and capital relative to each other when we substitute labor for capital or vice versa. When we change from production process c to production process b (move from point c to point b in Figure 10), we give up one unit of capital; to keep production constant, we must hire two units of labor, which suggests that the third machine does the work of two workers. When we move from point b to point a (giving up another machine), how many workers must be hired to keep production constant? The answer is four, suggesting that the productivity of four workers is required to replace that lost from the second machine. As we substitute more and more labor for capital (move down and to the right on the isoquant in Figure 10), ever-increasing amounts of labor are necessary to keep production constant. Alternatively, the marginal product of labor declines relative to that of capital. The opposite is true when capital is substituted for labor (movements to the left on the isoquant). Thus, the law of diminishing marginal productivity is reflected in the shapes of isoquants, which are convex (bowed in) from the origin.

Isocost Curves

Superimposed on the isoquant for 10,000 cases of seeds in Figure 10 is a set of isocost curves. *Isocosts* represent different levels of expenditures by your firm for various combinations of labor and capital when the price of labor is $1,000 per unit and the

TABLE 5 The Various Combinations of Labor and Capital that Will Package 10,000 Cases of Birdhouse Gourd Seeds

Point	Units of Capital (K)	Units of Labor (L)	Output: Cases of Gourd Seeds (q)	Total Cost if w = $1,000, r = $1,000 (TC)
a	1	9	10,000	$10,000
b	2	5	10,000	7,000
c	3	3	10,000	6,000
d	5	2	10,000	7,000
e	9	1	10,000	10,000

FIGURE 10 Isoquant (Equal Output) Curve for Birdhouse Gourd Seeds

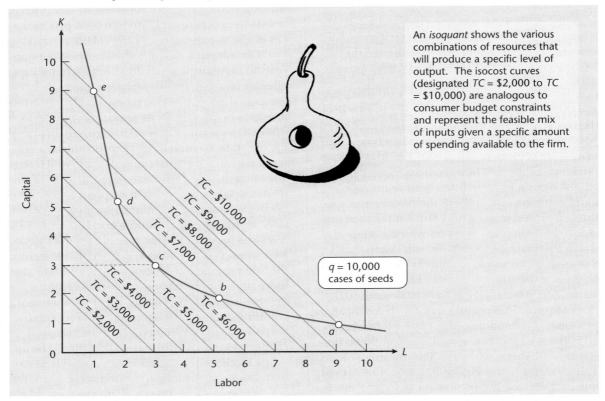

An *isoquant* shows the various combinations of resources that will produce a specific level of output. The isocost curves (designated $TC = \$2,000$ to $TC = \$10,000$) are analogous to consumer budget constraints and represent the feasible mix of inputs given a specific amount of spending available to the firm.

price of capital is $1,000 per unit. These isocosts are close relatives of the consumer budget lines described in the optional material in an earlier chapter.

Just as the slope of the budget line in consumer indifference curve analysis reflects the prices of the two goods considered ($-P_a/P_b$), the slopes of isocosts reflect the prices of the resources considered ($-w/k$, where w is the wage rate and k is the unit cost of capital). Notice that production process a ($L = 9, K = 1$) yields total costs of $10,000, which lies on the $TC = \$10,000$ isocost curve. As Figure 10 illustrates, 10,000 cases of seeds can be packaged at a minimum cost of $6,000 using three workers and three machines (point c). Graphically, costs are minimized for a given level of output where the isocost curve is just tangent to the isoquant, for an output level of 10,000 packages. At this point, $MPP_L/MPP_K = w/k$.

This is similar to the tangency between consumer indifference curves and budget lines in which maximum satisfaction is attained for a given

budget. Recall (from the preceding chapter) that this point conformed to the principle of equal marginal utilities per dollar: $MU_a/P_a = MU_b/P_b$ or $MU_a/MU_b = P_a/P_b$. Thus, in accord with the principle of equal marginal productivities per dollar, our result that $MPP_L/w = MPP_K/k$ or $MPP_L/MPP_K = w/k$, means that minimizing costs requires the marginal payments to resource owners to be in accord with the resource's contribution to production.

One final note: Just as there are numerous isocost curves that represent different levels of cost, there are also numerous isoquants for production levels other than 10,000 packages. We have simplified the analysis by assuming that you expected 10,000 packages of seeds per season to be the most profitable level of output.

Diminishing Marginal Product

The analysis in this chapter assumes that the typical production process eventually is subject to

FIGURE 11 Diminishing Returns and Isoquants

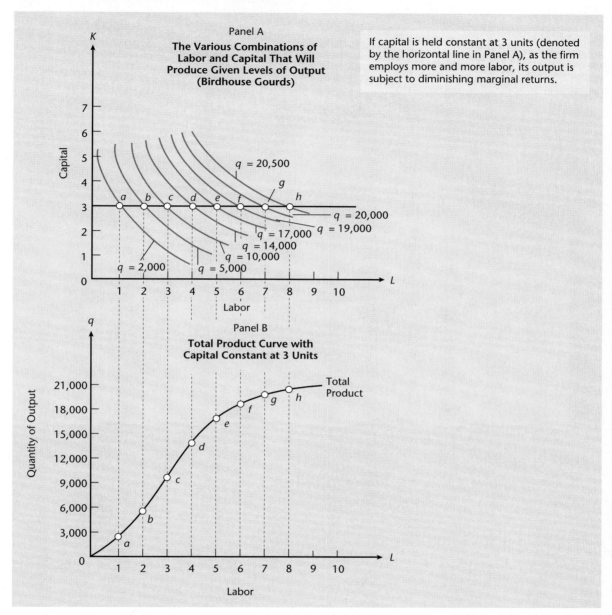

Panel A

The Various Combinations of Labor and Capital That Will Produce Given Levels of Output (Birdhouse Gourds)

If capital is held constant at 3 units (denoted by the horizontal line in Panel A), as the firm employs more and more labor, its output is subject to diminishing marginal returns.

q = 20,500
q = 20,000
q = 19,000
q = 17,000
q = 14,000
q = 10,000
q = 5,000
q = 2,000

Panel B

Total Product Curve with Capital Constant at 3 Units

Total Product

diminishing returns to the variable input. The same principle applies to production analysis using isoquants. Figure 11 illustrates the diminishing marginal physical product of labor when the amounts of other resources are held constant. In Panel A of Figure 11, capital is held constant at 3 units. Points *a* through *h* represent the amounts of labor needed to produce output

levels ranging from 2,000 to 20,500 units. In Panel B, the total product curve is derived from Panel A when capital is fixed at 3 units and shows diminishing returns of labor. As we add more and more labor to a fixed stock of capital, the increased output from hiring additional labor eventually falls.

Part 7

Product Markets

Vigorous competition is the norm for most landscapers, retailers, and homebuilders. Other firms only broadly compete for customers: your local phone company may vie with bookstores or travel agents for shares of your budget. Some firms specialize in such standard goods as lumber; others focus on such unique goods as organ transplants. A tiny town may support only one gas station, while high capital costs create monopolies in bigger markets: one giant firm, COMSAT, operates most communications satellites. Our economy encompasses many types of competition. The purpose of this part is to explore the consequences of the many forms of competition among business firms. We analyze the range of market organizations between pure competition and monopoly.

The first chapter examines pure competition and the role firms play as price takers and quantity adjusters. Then, in the second chapter, problems caused by monopolies are contrasted with the results of pure competition. Having discussed these extremes, we then survey monopolistic competition, oligopoly, game theory and strategic behavior. The last chapter concludes this part with discussions of antitrust policies and the regulation of business. Government antitrust actions and regulations are attempts to direct market allocations of resources and incomes in ways thought to be more economically efficient or socially preferable.

Oligopoly | Competition

Chapter 24

The Competitive Ideal

Monopoly

Asymmetric information

Game theory

High school students taking SATs recognize that their real competition for college scholarships and admissions is all the high school students taking SATs all across the country; competition from their immediate acquaintances is almost irrelevant. Similarly, most farmers do not consciously compete with nearby farms because they recognize that each is so small relative to the world market that no single farm produces enough to affect prices for agricultural outputs. Impersonal competition that is fierce but diffused is the focus of this chapter. To put these these vigorously competitive markets into a broader perspective, you need a sense of the full range of possible market structures for products.

MARKET STRUCTURES

The range of market structures in Table 1 identifies several factors that define the intensity of competition within an industry. These factors include (*a*) the number of firms in the industry, (*b*) the nature of the product itself, (*c*) the sig-

nificance of entry barriers, and (*d*) the extent to which individual firms can control prices.

Market structures range from pure competition (many firms) to monopoly (one firm). In between these extremes are monopolistic competition and oligopoly. Your intuition probably suggests that the price charged when many firms offer a product is probably lower than in a monopoly market where one firm sells all of a product. The costs of entering or leaving an industry is another consideration. Again, your intuition should suggest that ease of entry should help hold market prices down.

As you can see, the advantage of market-structure analysis is that simply by knowing a few characteristics of a market, you can predict how firms will price their products. Market structure analysis helps you isolate these few, most important factors that determine firm behavior.

The model of pure competition presented in this chapter focuses on an idealized market structure containing so many small competitors that any single firm's behavior is irrelevant to its competitors. Firms in this model lack any dis-

TABLE 1   The Range of Market Structures

Monopoly	Oligopoly	Monopolistic Competition	Pure Competition
1. One firm industry 2. No close substitutes for product 3. Substantial and effective barriers to entry 4. Potential long-run profit 5. Substantial market power and control over price	1. Few firms 2. Decision-making is mutually interdependent 3. Major barriers to entry 4. Potential long-run profit 5. Shared market power and control over price	1. Numerous potential buyers and sellers 2. Differentiated products 3. No entry or exit barriers 4. No profit in long run 5. Diffused market power and little control over price	1. Numerous potential buyers and sellers 2. Homogeneous products 3. No entry or exit barriers 4. No profit in long run 5. Diffused market power and no control over price
◄──── Highly Concentrated Markets		Less Concentration ────►	

Market structures depend on the number of firms in the industry, the extent of product differentiation, the existence or absence of long-run barriers to entry or exit, and the ability of firms to determine prices. Economists traditionally based predictions about an industry's conduct and performance on the industry's structure, a tendency characterized as the Structure→Conduct→Performance (*S-C-P*) paradigm.

cretion about pricing in this competitive climate and must be efficient merely to survive. The next section opens with requirements for a purely competitive market structure. Short-run pricing and output decisions are then explored, followed by a look at the importance of competitive entry and exit. We then evaluate these to set a benchmark for efficiency for use when evaluating other markets.

THE WORLD OF PURE COMPETITION

The consequences of competition for the pricing and output decisions of firms are most easily established in the model of **pure competition**,[1] which requires that

1. Potential buyers and sellers are numerous and each is so small relative to the market that individual decisions about purchases or

---

[1] A theory called "perfect competition" is more restrictive than the theory of pure competition. It adds perfect (instantaneous and costless) information about goods and resources and perfect (costless) mobility of goods and resources in the long run to the assumptions that underpin the purely competitive model. Nevertheless, the basic conclusions of these models are quite similar.

output do not noticeably affect market demand or supply, nor, consequently, do individual decisions affect the market price.
2. Firms in the industry produce a *homogeneous* (standardized) good.
3. Barriers to entry or exit are insignificant in the long run; new firms are free to enter the industry if doing so appears profitable or exit if they anticipate losses.

Generic office supplies, most agricultural products, and a few other relatively homogeneous goods are produced in highly competitive markets. Each buyer or seller is too insignificant to single-handedly affect the total demand or supply of the good, leaving competitive buyers and sellers as *quantity adjusting price takers*; they have no choice but to accept the price set in the market.

> ***Price takers*** *are buyers or sellers who are so small relative to a market that the effects of their transactions are inconsequential for market prices.*

Thus, individual competitive buyers view the supply curves facing them as perfectly elastic (horizontal) at the current market price. Similarly, competitive sellers perceive the demand curves they face as horizontal at the market price.

FIGURE 1 Demand Curves for a Competitive Firm and a Competitive Industry

Although the market demand for gold is far from elastic (Panel A), the demand curve facing each mine operator is horizontal, or perfectly elastic (Panel B). Competition forces small firms producing undifferentiated products to be price takers.

Competition vs. Rivalry

Competition usually connotes rivalry. We all grow up competing for grades, merit badges, positions on teams, and dates. Iowa farmers broadly compete with other farmers from all around the globe. How are prices set for their corn, wheat, or pigs? Do farmers argue that their products are superior and so should command a premium price? Clearly not. Nor do they offer coupons or instant winner bingo to compete for buyers.

Competitive price setting occurs for basic farm products (from eggs to sugar to orange juice concentrate), raw materials (coal or crude oil), primary products (steel or lumber), and precious metals (gold or silver) roughly 240 business days each year at commodity exchanges in major cities around the globe.[2] Market prices

are set for hundreds of commodities in an auction environment by the bids and offers of thousands of buyers and sellers or their broker representatives.

Commodity exchanges seem chaotic to visitors. Commodities are traded in a climate approaching pure competition, primarily by public outcry. Wild-eyed traders angle various numbers of fingers overhead and scream bids and offers on a huge, crowded trading floor. The din rivals that during the opening kickoff at the Super Bowl. No single buyer or seller can sway prices as bids and offers are accepted or rejected. A trader may buy cotton for a Tokyo customer one minute and sell Georgia peanuts the next, but most traders are narrowly specialized. Small farmers often sell their entire crop at the going market price in a single transaction. Farmers are examples of price takers.

If you struck gold at your sand-and-gravel site, you could sell all the gold you mined at the going market price ($600), as shown in Figure 1.

[2]The Chicago Board of Trade is the world's biggest commodity exchange.

The demand curve facing each purely competitive mine is a horizontal line (d) at the market price (P_e = \$600). Trying to charge a price above P_e would result in no sales, while cutting price below P_e would not increase the ability to sell gold: all your output can be sold at the going price. Thus, purely competitive firms decide what amounts of output to produce and sell at current prices. Even firms mining hundreds of claims using millions of dollars worth of equipment can sell gold only at the going price. This is why pure competitors, including farmers, are price takers.

Purely competitive firms compete in one dimension: technically efficient production. They try to minimize costs while producing the level of output that maximizes profit. We will present some recipes that a firm must follow to select the output that maximizes profit, but be aware that this also requires decisions about which resources and technologies to use. Real-world decisions usually involve coping with less information than economists assume firms have when they build the purely competitive model.

• **Rivalry** The stress on quantity decisions by pure competitors contrasts sharply with competition among carmakers, for example. It is difficult and costly for a new firm to enter the auto market. Cars are not standardized, and the pricing and output decisions of any of the big three U.S. automakers or their foreign counterparts clearly affect the sales of other producers. Advertising, styling, and aggressive marketing are as important as pricing strategy. These firms are rivals, but unlike purely competitive firms, they do not compete solely on the basis of efficient production of output at a market-determined price.

Freedom of entry and exit is vital for competition to be effective over time.

> ***Freedom of entry and exit*** *means, in the long run, firms can enter an industry with no cost disadvantages relative to established firms, and established firms can costlessly transfer resources to other industries.*

For example, few barriers limit entry and exit into agriculture. Prosperity invariably at-tracts more resources into farming. Prices and profits then fall, decreasing incentives for further entry. On the other hand, bad times in farming are signals that too many resources are in agriculture, and some farmers will shift their resources to industries that seem more prosperous.

The model of pure competition underpins supply and demand analysis, which provides fairly reliable predictions about how certain events will affect prices and outputs. Few industries match all the assumptions of pure competition, but remember that a model should be no more complex than is required for the purpose at hand; models are judged by predictive accuracy, not by realism of assumptions. Pure competition also sets the normative yardstick for efficiency used to judge other market structures. Although pure competition may be rare, rapid growth of international trade has made many markets much more competitive in recent years.

SHORT-RUN COMPETITIVE PRICING AND OUTPUT

All firms are assumed to maximize profit (the excess of revenues over costs), a process that can be described in several ways. The simplest explanation of short run profit maximization is the total revenue minus total cost ($TR - TC$) approach.

Total Revenue – Total Cost Approach

A pure competitor is a price taker, so how much to produce (quantity adjustment) is its major decision.[3] Will producing and selling as much as possible maximize profits? The example outlined in Table 2 leads us to the answer. Suppose you can mine weekly gold output levels ranging from nothing to 12 ounces and that the market dictates a price of \$600 per ounce. Whether you

---

[3]There are choices about what technology to use, what kind and how much labor to employ, and so on. For simplicity, we lump all these as parts of the output decision, postponing our study of resource markets until later chapters.

TABLE 2   Cost Data for a Competitive Gold Miner

(1) Weekly Output in Ounces (*q*)	(2) Price per Ounce (*P*)	(3) Weekly Total Revenue (*TR*)	(4) Weekly Total Cost (*TC*)	(5) Weekly Profit (3) – (4) (π)
0	$600	$ 0	$ 570	$ –570
1	600	600	810	–210
2	600	1,200	1,000	200
3	600	1,800	1,240	560
4	600	2,400	1,530	870
5	600	3,000	1,920	1,080
6	600	3,600	2,410	1,190
7	600	4,200	3,000	1,200
8	600	4,800	3,690	1,110
9	600	5,400	4,480	920
10	600	6,000	5,370	630
11	600	6,600	6,360	240
12	600	7,200	7,450	–250

sell one ounce of gold or 12 ounces, each ounce currently sells for $600. The total revenue curve in Panel A of Figure 2 shows how revenue grows as output rises; its slope is constant at $600 per ounce of gold. If fixed costs are $570 weekly, the production costs associated with each output level are shown in column 4 of Table 2 and graphed in Panel A as *TC*.

Subtracting total costs from total revenue is a straightforward way to calculate profit. You can mine the amount where this difference, profit (π), is the largest. Look at column 5 in Table 2; producing 7 ounces of gold yields maximum profit of $1,200. In Panel A of Figure 2, profit is maximized where the vertical distance between total revenue and total costs is greatest; in Panel B, profit is maximized where the vertical distance between the profit curve and the horizontal axis is greatest. The profit-maximizing output in this example occurs at 7 ounces.

Notice that two break-even levels of output are shown in Panel A of Figure 2.

> ***Break-even*** *or **normal profit points** occur where total revenue = total cost; economic profit is zero.*

These points are critical for decisions about entering risky lines of business. You would natu-rally like any risky activity to potentially break-even at low levels of output and sales. One lesson here is that there are two aspects of profit maximization, regardless of market structure. First consider the demand side (total revenue and price), then the supply side (production costs). Each side affects profit-maximizing output or pricing decisions, or both.

Total revenue minus total cost is easily understood. A more fruitful approach for operational decisions, however, is the *marginal cost equals marginal revenue* (*MC* = *MR*) approach. The total revenue minus total cost (*TR* – *TC* = π) and marginal revenue equals marginal cost (*MR* = *MC*) approaches yield mathematically identical results, but they arrive at profit maximization by different routes and provide different insights.

Marginal Revenue = Marginal Cost Approach

We discussed marginal cost in the preceding chapter. We need to analyze marginal revenue before discussing how firms link these concepts to set output at its most profitable level.

• **Marginal Revenue**   Marginal cost is the increase in total cost incurred by producing one

FIGURE 2 *TR – TC* Approach to Finding Maximum Profits

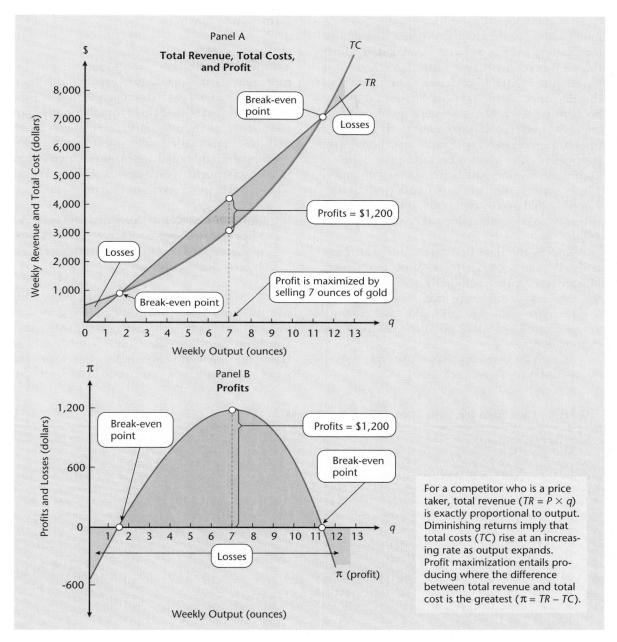

Panel A
Total Revenue, Total Costs, and Profit

TC

TR

Break-even point

Losses

Profits = $1,200

Losses

Break-even point

Profit is maximized by selling 7 ounces of gold

Weekly Revenue and Total Cost (dollars)

Weekly Output (ounces)

Panel B
Profits

Break-even point

Profits = $1,200

Break-even point

Losses

π (profit)

Profits and Losses (dollars)

Weekly Output (ounces)

For a competitor who is a price taker, total revenue ($TR = P \times q$) is exactly proportional to output. Diminishing returns imply that total costs (*TC*) rise at an increasing rate as output expands. Profit maximization entails producing where the difference between total revenue and total cost is the greatest ($\pi = TR - TC$).

more unit of output. Marginal revenue is defined in a similar fashion:

> **Marginal revenue** *is the increase in total revenue from selling one more unit.*

For a purely competitive firm, marginal revenue equals price ($MR = P$). Consider your gold mine. The price of gold is set in the international commodity market for precious metals centered in New York, London, and Zurich, so mining firms are price takers. If the going rate for gold is $600 per ounce, a firm's marginal revenue is $600 per ounce sold, regardless of how many ounces individual firms sell. Remember that each gold mine is too insignificant to affect the total market price or output. Return for a moment to Figure 1. Each mine operator views the demand curve faced as horizontal at the $600 price. Each firm's perception of demand curves as perfectly elastic means that each mine operator expects total revenues to be exactly proportional to output, because price is fixed and total revenue equals price times quantity. Thus, because the price is unaffected by the amounts sold by any firm, each ounce of gold is expected to generate marginal revenue equal to $600.

Review the data in Table 2. Column 2 reveals the market price to be $600 per ounce. Marginal revenue is the change in total revenue from the sale of one more unit, so as we go from 5 ounces to 6 ounces of gold sold, total revenue jumps from $3,000 to $3,600 weekly for a net change of $600.

Marginal revenue equals the price (MR = P) of the commodity in competitive markets.

Our next order of business is determining how competitive firms use this price and cost information to maximize profits.

● **Profit Maximization**   Suppose you have information about the marginal cost and the price of each unit of output. How much should be produced and sold? One rule of thumb for any firm (regardless of industry structure) might be to make any small adjustment (including the production of an additional unit of output) that brings in at least as much in revenues as it absorbs in costs. This translates into economic jargon as the

Marginal revenue = marginal cost rule: All profit-maximizing firms produce and sell an extra unit of output only if marginal revenue is at least as great as marginal cost.

Your revenue from selling one more unit of gold (from Table 3) is graphed in Figure 3 as the demand curve d ($P = MR = \$600$). Marginal cost from your cost data (column 7 in Table 3) is graphed as the MC curve in Figure 3. Consider what happens when you produce and sell the

TABLE 3   Cost Data for Your Competitive Gold Mine

(1) Weekly Output in Ounces (q)	(2) Total Fixed Cost (TFC)	(3) Total Variable Cost (TVC)	(4) Total Cost (TFC + TVC) (TC)	(5) Average Variable Cost (TVC/q) (AVC)	(6) Average Total Cost (TC/q) (ATC)	(7) Marginal Cost (ΔTC/Δq) (MC)	(8) Price Equals Marginal Revenue (P = MR)	(9) Total Revenue (TR = Pq)	(10) Profit (π)
0	$570	$ 0	$ 570	$ 0	$—	$—	$600	$ 0	$–570
1	570	240	810	240.00	810.00	240	600	600	–210
2	570	430	1,000	215.00	500.00	190	600	1,200	200
3	570	670	1,240	223.33	413.33	240	600	1,800	560
4	570	960	1,530	240.00	382.50	290	600	2,400	870
5	570	1,350	1,920	270.00	380.00	390	600	3,000	1,080
6	570	1,840	2,410	306.67	401.67	490	600	3,600	1,190
7	570	2,430	3,000	347.14	428.58	590	600	4,200	1,200
8	570	3,120	3,690	390.00	461.25	690	600	4,800	1,110
9	570	3,910	4,480	434.44	497.78	790	600	5,400	920
10	570	4,800	5,370	480.00	537.00	890	600	6,000	630
11	570	5,790	6,360	526.33	578.19	990	600	6,600	240
12	570	6,880	7,450	573.33	620.83	1,090	600	7,200	–250

FIGURE 3 *MR = MC* Approach to Finding Maximum Profits

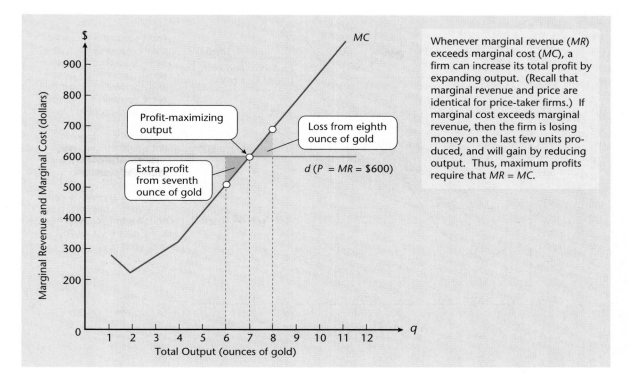

Whenever marginal revenue (*MR*) exceeds marginal cost (*MC*), a firm can increase its total profit by expanding output. (Recall that marginal revenue and price are identical for price-taker firms.) If marginal cost exceeds marginal revenue, then the firm is losing money on the last few units produced, and will gain by reducing output. Thus, maximum profits require that *MR = MC*.

seventh ounce of gold. The extra revenue to your firm is $600, but the seventh ounce of gold only costs $590 to produce. Thus, extra profit from the sale of this seventh unit is $10. In fact, you will increase total profit by the blue triangle below the demand curve as you increase output from 6 to 7 ounces.

What would happen to profit if you produced the eighth ounce? You would receive only $600 for it, but its production costs would be $690. You will lose $90 on the eighth ounce if you produce and sell it. Your profit will fall by the area of the reddish triangle above the demand curve as output rises from 7 to 8 ounces.

Conclusion? Price and marginal revenue are identical in pure competition, so a profit-maximizing pure competitor produces where marginal cost equals price: $P = MR = MC$, which in this example occurs at 7 ounces. This analysis leads to profit-maximization rule that holds for firms ranging from pure competition to pure monopoly: *All profit-maximizing firms produce and*

sell until marginal cost just equals the marginal revenue (MR = MC) derived from the sale of the good.

Marginal revenue and marginal cost data for your gold mine (from Table 3) are graphed in Figure 4, along with average total cost. The marginal revenue equals marginal cost approach reveals that 7 ounces is still the profit-maximizing output level (point *e*). The *TR – TC* approach provides one way to compute total profit. Total revenue equals price times quantity; for 7 ounces of gold at $600 per ounce, this is $4,200.

Geometrically, this is the area 0*ceg* in Figure 4. But how much is total cost? Since average total cost for 7 ounces is $428.58 for each ounce (point *a*), the total cost for all 7 ounces is $3,000 ($428.58 × 7 = $3,000). The area 0*bag* geometrically represents total cost (average cost times quantity). Thus, total weekly profit is $1,200 ($4,200 – $3,000), which is the blue area *bcea* in Figure 4.

An alternative way to compute total profit is to multiply average profit per unit times out-

FIGURE 4   Measuring Short-Run Profits

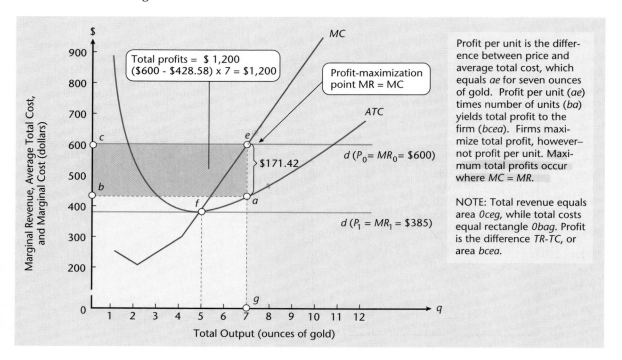

Profit per unit is the difference between price and average total cost, which equals *ae* for seven ounces of gold. Profit per unit (*ae*) times number of units (*ba*) yields total profit to the firm (*bcea*). Firms maximize total profit, however– not profit per unit. Maximum total profits occur where $MC = MR$.

NOTE: Total revenue equals area *0ceg*, while total costs equal rectangle *0bag*. Profit is the difference $TR-TC$, or area *bcea*.

---

put. Price minus average total cost $(P - ATC)$ equals average profit per unit, so average profit per unit when 7 ounces are produced is the distance *ae* in Figure 4, which is $171.42 ($600 – $428.58). Thus, total weekly profit is still $1,200 ($171.42 × 7, the shaded area *bcea*, which also equals $TR - TC$). Whether we maximize total revenue minus total cost or use the marginal revenue equals marginal cost approach, the mathematical solution is the same for the firm's profit-maximizing decision.

Figure 4 also shows what happens if the price of gold falls sharply. At roughly $385 per ounce, marginal revenue equals marginal cost at point *f*, or an output level of roughly 5 ounces. Average total cost, however, is in the $380 range, so the firm barely breaks even at a $385 price per ounce of gold. The lowest break-even or normal profit price in a competitive industry occurs when the demand curve facing each individual firm (the price line) is tangent to the minimum point of the firm's average total cost curve. Remember that zero economic profit

means the firm generates positive accounting profits just sufficient to keep the firm's owners satisfied. Typical firms will neither incur economic losses nor enjoy economic profits at such a price, so there will be no net tendency for the industry to shrink or grow because of entry and exit. In a moment you will see that this breakeven situation characterizes firms in purely competitive industries in long-run equilibrium.

Measuring profits may seem a precise process, but decisions must be made even though managers never perfectly predict the profit yielded by any decision. What matters is the direction of change: will profit rise or fall if a firm adopts a certain policy? Expected marginal benefits and costs are crucial for all types of decisions. For example, when public policy decisions are made about tax structures, incentive systems, or various regulations, the same kinds of questions arise: if a specific policy were altered, in what direction would social welfare, net consumer satisfaction, or business profits change? If decision-makers know this, they can adjust toward optimal policies.

• **Loss Minimization and Plant Shutdown** Alas, business is not always profitable. One of two choices must be made if sales revenues cannot cover all costs. The firm will experience losses if it elects to produce and sell output. If the firm shuts down, however, it incurs losses equal to fixed costs. Which decision will yield the smaller loss?

Suppose the demand for gold collapses, dropping its price to $300 per ounce, as reflected in Figure 5. Should you mine any gold? Our rule that a firm maximizes profit or minimizes loss by equating marginal revenue and marginal cost seems to indicate that optimal weekly output in this instance is 4 ounces (point *e*). At this level of output, total revenue (area 0*aeh*, or $1,200) fails to cover total costs (area 0*bch*, or $1,530), yielding a loss (area *abce*, or $330 weekly). The result is the same if we apply an average revenue minus average cost approach to this situation. In Figure 5, average revenue (price) is $300 at point *a*, while average

total cost is $382.50 at point *b*. Thus, the average loss per unit of output of $82.50 times 4 ounces yields a total loss of $330 (the reddish area *abce* in Figure 5).

Suppose you closed the mine to avoid selling gold below its average total cost. Losses would equal fixed costs: the entire $570, or area *gbcf*, in our example. Remember that fixed costs are incurred whether or not any output is produced. These include such expenses as rent payments, utility charges (for minimum service), administrative overhead, and insurance. Fixed (sunk) costs are not current opportunity costs because they cannot be avoided; the alternatives they once represented were lost in the past. Thus, exiting this competitive industry is virtually costless in the long run.

Variable costs are a firm's opportunity costs of production. Average variable costs of $240 (point *f* in Figure 5) are incurred in wages, materials, and other expenses when 4 ounces of

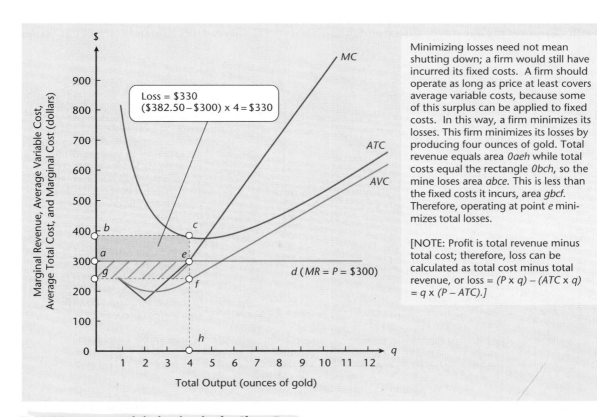

Minimizing losses need not mean shutting down; a firm would still have incurred its fixed costs. A firm should operate as long as price at least covers average variable costs, because some of this surplus can be applied to fixed costs. In this way, a firm minimizes its losses. This firm minimizes its losses by producing four ounces of gold. Total revenue equals area 0*aeh* while total costs equal the rectangle 0*bch*, so the mine loses area *abce*. This is less than the fixed costs it incurs, area *gbcf*. Therefore, operating at point *e* minimizes total losses.

[NOTE: Profit is total revenue minus total cost; therefore, loss can be calculated as total cost minus total revenue, or loss = (*P* × *q*) − (*ATC* × *q*) = *q* × (*P* − *ATC*).]

FIGURE 5   Loss Minimization in the Short Run

gold are mined. Consequently, average variable costs will be covered as long as the mine can sell gold for more than $240 per ounce. As the mine operator, you might allocate the difference between price ($300) and average variable costs ($240) to a fund to cover fixed costs. Even if all fixed costs were not covered, some could be; a loss of $330 is better than a loss equal to fixed costs of $570. Note that the critical costs to cover are variable costs, not fixed costs. As the saying goes, sunk costs are *sunk*.

When will it pay the firm to shut down? The answer is that a firm will be ahead by closing its doors if the price of a good fails to cover its average variable costs. This is shown in Figure 6. You should close the mine if the price of gold falls below $215 per ounce, which is the minimum value of the average variable cost curve (point *e*). At a price of $215, the mine just recoups its variable costs from the sale of 2 ounces of gold weekly because variable costs are $215 per unit for labor, materials, and so forth. Consequently, total losses are $570 (area *abce*) whether 2 ounces of gold are produced and then

sold for $215 or not; nothing is contributed to fixed costs from the production and sale of these units.

What happens if gold falls below $215 per ounce, to, say, $200? If the mine produced 2 ounces of gold, in addition to $570 in fixed costs, you will lose at least $15 more per ounce, yielding total losses of $600 [$570 + ($15 × 2)]. Operating at all would not minimize your losses. If the price falls below $215, temporarily abandon the mine. Thus, a $215 price corresponds to the mine's *shutdown point*. It is the lowest price that will induce you to operate, and you will try never to mine less than 2 ounces of gold.

> ***Shutdown point***: *Profit-maximizing (and loss-minimizing) firms shut down when the market price falls below the minimum point of the average variable cost curve.*

Take a moment to compare Figures 4, 5, and 6. Note that profit can be realized if the demand curve (price line) facing a firm intersects its *ATC* curve. Unfortunately, short-run losses

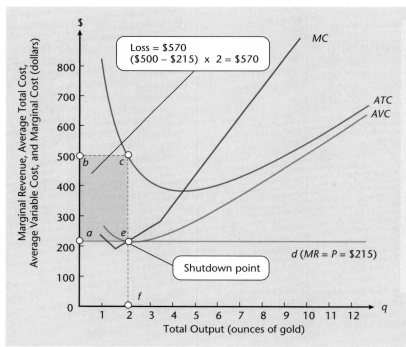

The short-run shutdown point is at a price of $215 per ounce and an output of two ounces per week. At any price below $215, the firm's losses would be larger if it continues to produce. At prices below $215, variable costs of production will not be covered. Thus, at prices below $215, the firm will close its doors to minimize losses.

NOTE: Total revenue equals area *0aef*, but total costs equal rectangle *0bcf*. Thus, at a $215 price, regardless of whether the mine produces 2 ounces of gold or shuts down, losses equal fixed costs—area *abce*.

Source: Tables 1 and 2.

FIGURE 6   Short-Run Shutdown Point

are inevitable if the firm's *ATC* curve lies above the demand curve at all output levels. In a moment, you will see that if the demand curve is exactly tangent to the *ATC* curve, the best the firm can do is earn normal profits. Figure 7 summarizes the short-run operating rules for purely competitive firms.

Short-Run Supply

Our analysis so far suggests that the first question every profit-maximizing firm confronts, regardless of market structure, is whether to operate in a market. If the demand curve it faces has any segment that is above its average variable cost curve (which, among other costs, must reflect the values foregone from alternative types of production), then it will operate in that market. If operation in a market is profit-maximizing (or loss minimizing), then a second question addresses how much to produce; the answer is that profit is maximized when marginal cost equals marginal revenue. We now examine the nature of the short-run firm and industry supply curves.

• **Short-Run Supply Curves of Purely Competitive Firms** You may have deduced that a competitive firm's marginal cost curve is also its short-run supply curve as long as price exceeds the minimum point of the average variable cost curve. These points on a marginal cost curve reflect the profit-maximizing outputs corresponding to various market prices for the good. If price falls below minimum average variable costs (*AVC*), marginal costs and marginal revenue become irrelevant; the firm's best move is to close its plant and suffer losses equal to fixed costs. However, whenever the price exceeds the shutdown point (the minimum *AVC*), the firm minimizes losses or maximizes profit by supplying the amount of output where $P = MR = MC$. This is a firm's short-run supply response.

> *A pure competitor's **short-run supply curve** is the segment of the marginal cost curve that lies above the minimum point of the firm's average variable cost curve.*

This is shown in Figure 8. When price and marginal revenue equal P_0, this firm supplies only

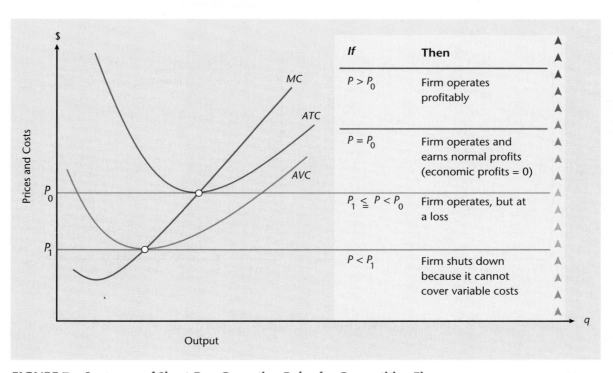

FIGURE 7 **Summary of Short-Run Operating Rules for Competitive Firms**

FIGURE 8 The Firm's Short-Run Supply Curve

A competitive firm's short-run supply curve is its marginal cost curve, as long as the point where the price equals marginal cost occurs above the minimum of the average variable cost curve ($P = MC > AVC$). If price cannot cover average variable cost, then the firm will shut down ($q = 0$).

q_0. As the price rises, the firm increases the amount it supplies to maximize profit or minimize loss by equating that price with marginal costs, so if price increases to P_1 and P_2, the firm will supply q_1 and q_2, respectively. Now let us see how individual firm's supply curves are combined to form an industry supply curve.

• **The Short-Run Industry Supply Curve**   A competitive industry contains numerous firms, so there is a predictably tight relationship between the industry supply curve and firm supply curves. Consider, for simplicity, an industry comprised of two firms with individual supply curves as shown in Panel A of Figure 9. When the market price is $1, the first firm will supply 10 units and the second firm will supply 30 units. Together, they supply 40 units at the $1 price, as plotted in Panel B. Recall from Chapter 3 that this process is called *horizontal summation*.

> The **short-run industry supply curve** is the horizontal sum of the supply curves of all firms in a purely competitive industry.

Horizontal summation of the supply curves of individual firms (Panel A) yields the industry supply curve (Panel B).

FIGURE 9   The Industry Supply Curve

We simply add the quantities produced by each firm at each possible price to arrive at the industry short-run supply curve. You can verify this graphically by adding together the quantities that each firm will turn out at various prices, and you will see that these total quantities supplied conform to those plotted in Panel B.

We have now related individual and market supplies. The output decisions of individual firms, when summed, determine the market supply schedule. This market supply, in concert with consumers' demands for a good, determines the market-clearing price. An industry is in equilibrium when firms supply all they are willing to at the going price and consumers can buy all they desire at that price. All firms maximize profit by producing where $MR = MC$. Firms minimize losses by shutting down if price fails to cover AVC.

• **Supply Responses and Time** All decisionmakers gain flexibility as the time horizon ex-

pands. Industry responses to shifts in demand depend in part on how long firms have to adjust. Alfred Marshall, the eminent British economist introduced in Chapter 3, designed a systematic way for economists to treat time conceptually. Responses are classified as occurring in the *market* (immediate) *period*, the *short run* (*SR*), or the *long run* (*LR*). The more time an industry has to adapt to changes in demands, the greater are quantity adjustments and the smaller are price adjustments. Thus, the market elasticity of supply is positively related to the time allowed for an industry to adjust. In the market period, supply is purely inelastic because we assume, for simplicity, that neither resources nor inventories can be adjusted. Supplies are somewhat elastic in the short run and even more elastic in the long run.

This relationship is shown in Figure 10. Suppose the original demand for gold is D_0, where price is $600 and quantity sold is Q_0. If demand rises to D_1, gold would rise to $850 per ounce during the market period to reflect min-

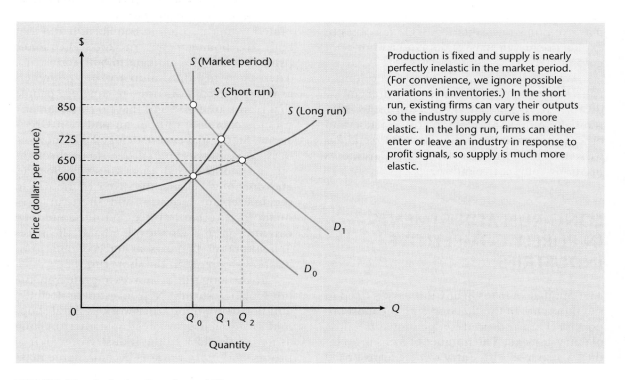

Production is fixed and supply is nearly perfectly inelastic in the market period. (For convenience, we ignore possible variations in inventories.) In the short run, existing firms can vary their outputs so the industry supply curve is more elastic. In the long run, firms can either enter or leave an industry in response to profit signals, so supply is much more elastic.

FIGURE 10 Industry Supply and Time

ing firms' temporary inability to boost output. If the higher demand persists, mines might boost output by paying overtime wages, hiring new workers, or through other short-run devices. This rise in quantity supplied by existing firms yields a short-run price of $725, which is below the price of $850 per ounce immediately after demand rose to D_1. But prospectors will ultimately find more gold; as owners of new mines respond to higher profits, supplies will rise further, reducing the long-run equilibrium price to $650.

The range of potential adjustments in an industry expands when firms have more time to adapt. In the long run, quantities adjust more and price adjusts less for a given change in demand than in the market period or the short run. Firms cannot modify output in a single market period to minimize losses or to exploit new profit opportunities when demands change.

Firms can only partially adjust in the short run, because at least one resource is fixed. Only in the long run are all resources variable so that firms can enter or leave markets as their owners choose. Given sufficient time, technology may even improve as miners seek new ways to exploit the higher market demand and price of gold.

What role does profit play in the longer run? What happens if new firms enter an industry? If technological breakthroughs substantially reduce production costs? These and other issues are examined in the next section as we step from short-run to long-run adjustments in purely competitive industries.

LONG-RUN ADJUSTMENTS IN PURELY COMPETITIVE INDUSTRIES

The number of firms in any industry is fixed in the short run, but in the long run, the most important characteristic of competition is freedom of entry and exit. The number of firms in an industry may rise with entry of new firms or fall as existing firms fail or move into different product lines. Economic profit attracts new firms to an industry, while economic losses signal owners to liquidate existing firms or to look for new product lines. Entry into prospering industries and exit from those that are faltering is basic to the smooth operation of a market economy and to accommodating consumers' priorities.

Economic Profits as Market Signals

Economic profits are a surplus after all implicit and explicit costs of production are subtracted from total revenue. Thus, average total costs include allowances for the opportunity costs of the entrepreneurial talents and capital a firm uses, among other things. Normal economic returns to these resources must be earned. Economic losses push a firm's owners into moving their resources into other activities. On the other hand, if revenues exceed all costs, a firm may try to expand in an attempt to capture as much economic profit as possible. In a sense, however, economic profit ultimately self-destructs by attracting new competitors into the industry.

Suppose the markets for statues and for potted plants are both in equilibrium and that both are homogeneous products. Economic profits are zero for all firms in both industries. Then the demand for indoor plants plummets as interior decorators unite to convince people that plants are passé and that no corner in any room is complete without an imitation Greek statue. Statue makers are deluged with new orders, while florists and garden shops throughout the country watch their sales wilt. Specials and discounts become the order of the day in the houseplant industry, and short-run economic losses occur as prices, outputs, and total revenues decline. On the other hand, the prices and outputs of statuary soar and economic profits are widespread in the short run.

In the long run, resources migrate from the houseplant industry. New investment declines, and florists train for other work as floral shops fold. Investment gravitates into statuary making as new firms flock to the industry in search of profits, and more workers become statue makers. Thus, over the long run, competition eliminates both economic losses in the plant industry and economic profits in statuary; plant prices recover from their depressed state, and statue prices fall from their short-run peaks. At the final equilibrium along the long-run supply curves for each industry, firms realize only normal (zero) economic profits, and all opportunity costs are covered by revenues.

Let us discuss market adjustments in more detail. The long run allows all resources (including capital) to enter or leave an industry. New firms move into growing industries, while existing firms wither or die in declining industries. Thus, we expect resources to flow from less profitable toward more profitable industries. Entry and exit from highly competitive industries can be accomplished with ease. Many hit-and-run competitors jump into profitable markets and leave as soon as other markets appear more profitable. This hit-and-run pattern is socially beneficial because it ensures that even erratic consumer demands are accommodated quickly.

The Process of Competition

Social gains from competition depend heavily on freedom to enter or exit markets as firms seek profit or try to avoid loss. If typical firms make zero economic profits, then (all else being equal) there will be no long-run changes in the number of firms in the industry, the amount of output supplied, or the price of the good. Recall that normal returns to capital owners and entrepreneurial talent are economic costs to the firm. *Zero economic profits* mean that all costs are covered, that is, the firm's resources cannot be used more advantageously elsewhere.

> ***Zero, or normal, economic profit*** *is a long-run equilibrium condition for firms in a competitive industry. The output, price, and number of firms in the industry will all be stable.*

To summarize, in a long-run equilibrium, no pure competitor will want to

1. change its output, because price equals marginal cost ($P = MC$).

2. change its plant size, because short-run average total cost equals long-run average total cost ($SRATC = LRATC$).

3. enter or leave the industry, because price equals long-run average total cost ($P = LRATC$).

But if most firms in an industry experience economic profits, competitive pressures tend to eliminate these profits over time, because prices will fall or costs will increase. Conversely, economic losses tend to cause prices to climb or costs to decline, or both.

• **Price Changes Eliminate Economic Profits or Losses** If firms in an industry earn positive economic profits, existing firms try to capture greater profits by expanding capacity and output. Entrepreneurs outside the industry also have incentives to enter these markets in the long run. Both types of adjustments increase an industry's output, reducing prices because consumers will increase their purchases only if prices decline.

On the other hand, if most firms in an industry experience economic losses, then some will cut their production, and in the long run, the firms with the highest opportunity costs (best alternative uses of their resources) will leave the industry. Thus, the long-run effects of economic losses are that the industry's supply will decline and prices will rise.

• **How Profits or Losses Affect Costs** Competition will grow for the resources used by a profitable industry. If supplies are perfectly elastic for all resources used by an industry, production can expand without driving up average production costs. Resource costs will rise as production in an industry rises, however, to the extent that some resources are especially suited for certain industries and not others. For example, what do you think happens to the costs of acquiring oil drilling rights as the price of oil balloons? What happens to the prices of agricultural land when food prices soar? Costs rise to reduce profits in both cases.

The following is another example of how rising costs eliminate profits: if your firm enjoyed extremely high profits because it hired an exceptionally efficient management team, might some competitor try to hire members of this team? What would happen to their salaries?

The market forces that raise costs in an industry in which most firms make economic profits also lowers costs in instances where most firms incur losses. Both average costs and marginal costs rise in profitable industries and shrink when economic losses are the norm. To simplify the analysis in the following discussion, we focus only on price (not cost) adjustments. Remember, however, that changes in either prices or costs will eliminate economic profits or losses in competitive markets in the long run. Moreover, we assume in the following discussion that prices adjust smoothly toward long-run equilibrium. You should recognize that some firms may overreact in unison to economic profits or losses, so that prices may swing somewhat before ultimately converging on their equilibrium values.

Long-Run Equilibrium in a Purely Competitive Industry

Firms operate close to capacity in highly profitable industries, but if business conditions go sour, they slash production. Consider the industry shown in Figure 11. This industry is in short-run equilibrium before the entry of new firms. Industry demand and supply are D_0 and S_0, respectively, and industry output equals Q_0; each firm produces an output of q_0, where $P_0 = MR = MC$. Typical firms in this industry make short-run economic profits equal to the blue area, causing firms to willingly incur higher than minimal per unit costs as they produce extra output to exploit profit opportunities.

Pure competition allows easy entry, so this is a short-run situation, because external entrepreneurs will seek shares of these profits. New firms will swell industry supply to S_1, with a higher output, Q_1, and a lower equilibrium price, P_1. But observe what happens to each individual firm. As prices decline, each firm ad-

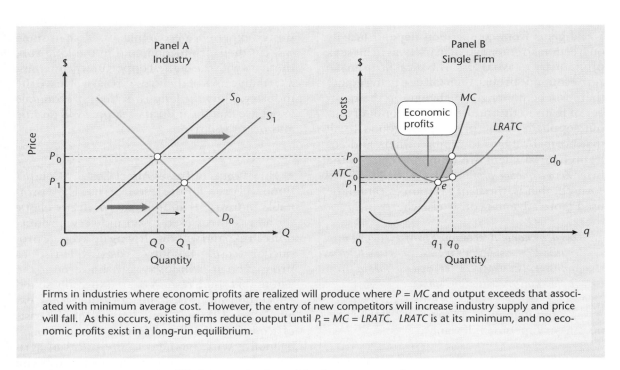

Firms in industries where economic profits are realized will produce where $P = MC$ and output exceeds that associated with minimum average cost. However, the entry of new competitors will increase industry supply and price will fall. As this occurs, existing firms reduce output until $P_1 = MC = LRATC$. $LRATC$ is at its minimum, and no economic profits exist in a long-run equilibrium.

FIGURE 11   Long-Run Equilibrium Beginning with Short-Run Profits

justs to a new profit-maximization output (q_1) below the original level (q_0). Our industry consequently now contains more firms, but the absence of profit leaves each producing less than before.

What happened to profit? Each firm previously in the industry was earning positive profits. Entry reduces prices and the amounts that each firm produces. Economic profits shrink to normal levels (zero economic profits) because the price falls to the minimum of long-run average total costs (*LRATC*, point *e*). Remember that the resources a firm's owners provide have opportunity costs that are included in average total costs. Accounting profits are not zero in the industry; they are simply at normal levels—just high enough so that the owners earn as much in this industry as in their next best option.

You may wonder whether symmetric exit adjustments occur in unprofitable situations. Such adjustments are illustrated in Figure 12, which shows individual firms initially encoun-

tering short-run losses. Price is originally at P_0, which is below average total cost (ATC_0) but above average variable costs (not shown in the figure), because firms are continuing to operate. Losses are equal to the reddish area. The least efficient firms incur the largest losses and will fold or move into a different activity. Industry supply will shrink as these firms leave the industry, so the price will rise and losses will be eliminated. Profits might temporarily reappear if enough firms leave, curtailing the exodus of firms. Ultimately, however, price rises to P_1 and profits return to normal levels (point *e*). Notice that this is just the opposite of the adjustment process described in the profitable situation just considered. Industry output falls, but individual firm's output grows as the price recovers to normal levels when some firms exit the industry.

At the ends of periods with economic losses or profits, why does profit settle at normal levels (zero economic profits)? A moment's reflec-

If most firms in an industry suffer economic losses, they will restrict production below the minimum point of their *LRATC* curves. As some firms leave the industry, the market supply falls and the price rises. As the price rises, existing firms will expand their production to the level of output where long-run average cost is minimized. At this point, $P_1 = MC = LRATC$, and neither economic profits nor economic losses are experienced.

FIGURE 12   Long-Run Equilibrium Beginning with Short-Run Losses

tion should provide the answer. Competitive theory presumes that entry and exit are virtually costless, so the logical stopping point occurs when each firm in the industry earns only normal profits. All opportunity costs are covered, so the owners of existing firms know of no opportunities for their resources that are more profitable, nor do entrepreneurs outside the industry perceive profit opportunities in the industry. Only then will there be no net incentives for firms to enter or leave the industry.

Another important result of long-run competitive adjustments is that all firms in the industry are forced to adopt the most efficient technology available. This is shown in Figure 13. Long-run pressures will force the price of the product to P_{LR} because pure competition forces each firm to the lowest point on the $LRATC$ curve. Any firm not adopting the technology and amounts of capital that yield the lowest minimum short-run average total cost ($SRATC$) curve will earn less than normal profits and will founder in the long run. No firm stays in any industry if it

suffers sustained economic losses. Since $P = MC = ATC$ in the long run, the ultimate equilibrium point is the lowest point on the $LRATC$ curve, which is also the lowest point on the relevant $SRATC$ curve. This means that outputs in competitive markets will be produced at the lowest possible long-run average total cost. Hence, competition yields both technical and allocative economic efficiency. As you will see in a later section, this result has profound implications for maintaining competition in a free market economy.

Long-Run Industry Supply Curves

Now that you know a bit about competitive adjustment processes, we can examine the long-run supply curve for the entire purely competitive industry. Horizontal summation of existing firms' short-run supply curves yields the short-run industry supply curve. The *long-run industry supply curve* reflects the effects on output as entry and exit occur in response to changes in demand. The industry is in long-run equilibrium only after all desired entries and exits have occurred so that active firms realize only normal profits.

Changing demands, technologies, and products cause erratic swings in many industries. The economy continually gropes toward equilibrium, but full equilibrium may never be attained in most industries. Even so, short-run and long-run equilibria remain valuable concepts because of their analytical convenience and their predictive power. Without these notions, we have analytical mush; there are no reference points from which to compare other periods or to predict the eventual trends of outputs and prices. Long-run industry supply curves can take three general forms: (*a*) constant costs, (*b*) increasing costs, and (*c*) decreasing costs. We will examine each of these.

• **Constant Cost Industries** The long-run supply (*LRS*) curve of a constant cost industry is illustrated in Figure 14.

> In a **constant cost industry**, average production costs are unaffected if the market demand shifts and the number of firms in the industry changes.

In the long run, a firm in a competitive industry produces where $P = MR = MC = SRATC = LRATC$, and the size of the plant will minimize the average costs of production. Neither economic profits nor economic losses will be realized, but normal profits will compensate owners for the resources they provide.

FIGURE 13 Long-Run Equilibrium for the Competitive Firm

FIGURE 14   Long-Run Supply (Constant Cost Industry)

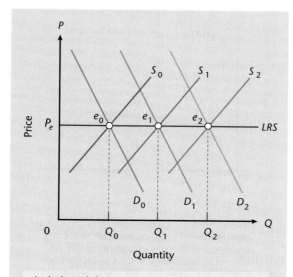

An industry's long-run supply curve is perfectly elastic (horizontal) if the resource costs of individual firms are unaffected by the number of firms in the industry. Industries that use only small percentages of highly specialized resources in an economy will operate under constant costs.

As demand grows from D_0 to D_1 to D_2, long-run responses are increases in short-run supplies from S_0 to S_1 and S_2, respectively, as the number of firms in the industry grows proportionally with demand. As entry occurs, long-run average costs are the same for new entrants as they are for established firms. All cost curves for individual firms are identical; the number of firms in the industry adjusts proportionally as demand changes. Thus, the long-run supply curve for a constant cost industry is perfectly elastic. An industry can expand with constant equilibrium price and costs only if technology and the costs of the resources it uses are not affected.[4]

---

[4]Were all industries subject to constant cost, the production possibilities frontier would be a straight line. You might review the material in Chapter 2 if you are unsure why this is true.

• **Increasing Cost Industries**   Industries deviate from the constant cost model for several reasons. The requirement that input prices not rise as an industry's output rises is especially difficult if an industry relies on limited supplies of specialized resources; larger amounts of these resources can be made available only at ever higher costs. This characterizes increasing cost industries.

> In an **increasing cost industry**, average production costs rise as market demand and the number of firms in the industry grow.

In an increasing cost industry, growth of market demand pulls up resource costs, and the average total cost and marginal cost curves for each firm in the industry rise. Thus, demand growth shifts up the long-run break-even points for each firm as minimal long-run average total costs rise, as shown in Figure 15.

If industry demand grows from D_0 to D_1, the industry expands as new firms enter.

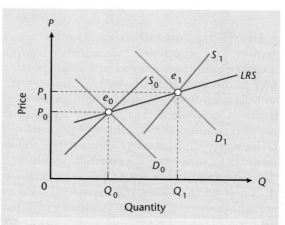

The long-run supply curve of an increasing cost industry will be positively sloped because the prices of the specialized resources it uses will rise as industry output expands. This effect will be stronger the larger the industry is relative to national output and the more specialized the resources are. This effect is common and yields production possibilities frontiers that are "bowed out" from below, as described in Chapter 2.

FIGURE 15   Long-Run Supply for an Increasing Cost Industry

Competition for resources drives the short-run supply curve to S_1 and the equilibrium price to P_1. Rising equilibrium costs and prices yield a positively sloped long-run supply (LRS) curve. Higher prices to cover the higher resource costs allow provision of greater quantities to the market. Moreover, these rising costs cause fewer firms to enter the industry than would enter constant cost industries experiencing similar growth of demand.

Regardless of the extent of competition, most industries are characterized by increasing costs in the long run. For example, our domestic oil industry faces increasing costs in attempts to boost petroleum production. Most readily accessible crude oil has been depleted. Higher oil prices induce landowners to charge more for drilling rights. Future oil supplies will be drawn from deeper wells or high-cost locations (offshore drilling or Alaska). Alternatively, Americans may try other energy sources, most of which are much more costly than oil. This is also true for fine furniture as quality hardwood forests are depleted.

- **Decreasing Cost Industries** One industry's growth may stimulate efficiencies in complementary industries. For example, mass production in the auto industry early in this century stimulated a flock of support industries: tires, batteries, gasoline and oil, and so on. As these support industries grew and implemented new technology, their average cost curves shifted downward, supplying intermediate products to the auto industry at lower prices. Car prices dropped. In the 1980s, the expansion (and increased power) of personal computers led to a growing market for sophisticated software. As the installed base of personal computers exploded, software power grew while prices fell.

> In a **decreasing cost industry**, average production costs fall as market demand and the number of firms in the industry grow.

Thus, in a decreasing cost industry, growing demand yields lower equilibrium prices as an industry's output expands, as shown in Figure 16.

FIGURE 16 Long-Run Supply for a Decreasing Cost Industry

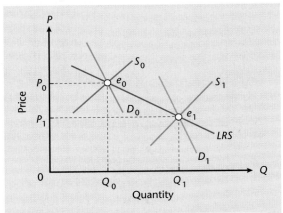

Decreasing cost industries generate negatively sloped long-run supply curves, and are quite rare, because decreasing costs must rely on substantial economies of scale or on positive externalities within the industry or in support industries that supply intermediate goods. In fact, many economists argue that this is only a theoretical possibility, never encountered in the actual world of production. The concepts of constant, increasing, or decreasing costs apply only for the long run. Decreasing cost industries seem more plausible, however, if we consider the possibility of technological advances.

In rare circumstances, a few industries might experience decreasing costs, but most industries eventually encounter increasing costs, so growing demand yields higher prices in the long run. The possibility that technological advances may be spurred by the search for profits, however, means that some industries may experience decreasing costs in the very long run. This seems to be true of many high-tech products today.

EVALUATING COMPETITIVE MARKETS

Some important points in this chapter are useful in evaluating competition:

1. Pure competition is characterized by freedom of entry and exit by firms that are *price takers* and *quantity adjusters*.

2. A pure competitor maximizes profit or minimizes loss by producing the level of output that equates price, marginal revenue, and marginal cost ($P = MR = MC$).

3. In the long run, pure competitors use the most efficient technology available, and $MC = P$.[5] This will also be the minimum point on the $LRATC$ curve, because the long-run dynamics of entry and exit drive economic profits to zero regardless of whether the industry is characterized by constant, increasing, or decreasing costs.

In the long run,

$$P = MR = MC = SRATC = LRATC$$

and profits will be at normal levels, or zero economic profit.

Economic Efficiency

In a purely competitive market, firms employ resources until the marginal cost of the last unit of a good equals its price. In the absence of external costs (e.g., pollution) or external benefits (e.g., education, inoculations), the opportunity cost to society of these resources equals the marginal cost of the resources to producers. If there are no externalities (discussed in depth in a later chapter), these resource costs equal their **marginal social costs** (**MSC**), that is, the value to society of the resources used to produce one more unit of a good. Competition through freedom of entry and exit ensures that this is at the lowest possible average cost and that there is no waste in production. A purely competitive economy is an efficient economy, both allocatively and technically. One aspect of economic efficiency is that all goods must be produced at their lowest possible opportunity cost (technical efficiency). Competition meets this requirement by ensuring production at minimal $LRATC$. Allocative efficiency requires the mix of goods produced to match consumer preferences.

_____
[5]Technical differences between short-run and long-run marginal costs are not considered here. Courses in intermediate microeconomics deal with these differences.

Here again, competition meets the criterion because consumers get the products they want at the least opportunity cost.

Social Welfare

Positive economics cannot directly address the fairest way to divide the pie. However, if we assume that the proper distribution of income is a normative problem best settled in the political arena and that the resulting outcome is acceptable, then the competitive market system is not only efficient, it also maximizes social welfare. Here is why.

Your demand curve for any good is based on the marginal benefits (utility) that you would receive from consuming various possible amounts of the good, as we discussed in our consumer choice chapter. Our assumptions imply that the marginal utility you receive from consuming is also the marginal benefit society receives. That is, your gain is also society's gain because you are a member of society. When we sum all consumer demands, we derive the market demand curve for an industry's product, which is also the _marginal social benefit_ (_MSB_) to all of society from having a bit more of the good.

With consumer benefits and producer costs in mind, we can refer to the industry supply and demand curves, respectively, as the marginal social cost (_MSC_) and marginal social benefit (_MSB_) curves. When a purely competitive industry is in long-run equilibrium, _marginal social cost equals marginal social benefit_ ($MSC = MSB$). The industry is producing where the marginal social benefit from the last unit produced is just equal to the marginal social cost of the resources needed to produce that unit of product. This concept is illustrated in Figure 17.

The $MSB = MSC$ condition is optimal from society's point of view. Since the opportunity costs of resources represent alternatives for all of society, we want our resources to be used as efficiently as possible. If production were inefficient, then it would be possible for some people to gain without imposing losses on others.

Consider output level Q_0 in Figure 17. The social benefit from a bit more output than Q_0 is P_0 (point b), which greatly exceeds the marginal cost (P_1) of the resources required to produce a

FIGURE 17   Economic Efficiency and Competition

If there are no externalities in production or consumption, then purely competitive markets generate efficient solutions. If, in addition, the distribution of income is deemed equitable, the competitive market equilibrium maximizes social welfare. The competitive industry produces output Q_e at a price of P_e (point e); at this price–output combination, $MSB = MSC$.

little more of the good (point a), so society as a whole could gain if more resources were used to produce more of this good. And in a purely competitive industry, they will be. If Q_0 were initially produced and sold at price P_0, existing firms would enjoy economic profit. This would cause the industry to grow until equilibrium output Q_e is reached at a price and (average and marginal) production cost of P_e (point e). The adjustment process is just reversed if industry output exceeds Q_e. Purely competitive markets tend to squeeze the last bit of gain possible from the resources available.

Some economists who believe strongly in competition as an effective and desirable allocative mechanism are convinced that the model of pure competition grossly understates the virtues of the market system. Their views are sketched in Focus 1.

Decentralized Decisions and Freedom

Most advocates of the market system point to the economic efficiency of competition as its major virtue, but prize even more the absence of any need for a central economic authority. The ideas of Adam Smith and other early advocates of capitalism were forged during a period of revolt against the dictates of monarchs of their era. Isaac Newton had observed movements of the planets and stars and concluded that natural forces generate a stable and orderly universe. Smith perceived that the invisible hand of the marketplace had similarly beneficial effects and that the iron fist of government was exercised far too often. In a truly competitive market system, each household and firm make decisions that, in large measure, affect only themselves. This diffusion of power limits the power of some individuals over other individuals. According to proponents of relying on the marketplace rather than government, this diffusion of coercive power allows the maximum possible personal freedom for everyone.

Leon Walras elaborated with mathematical precision Smith's ideas about how people's wants are accommodated in a competitive market system, and Vilfredo Pareto developed a concept of economic welfare that still dominates economic analysis. Pareto also proved that a purely competitive equilibrium is efficient and that other equilibria fail to maximize social welfare. Efficiency and the absence of centralized coercion are major reasons why purely competitive markets are the ideal against which we measure industrial performance. From society's point of view, it might seem desirable that all industries be competitive so that Adam Smith's invisible hand would yield the results we have described. Competition and access to markets may, however, be very limited if technology dictates that large firms, relative to market demand, will be most efficient.

Some Shortcomings of Market Economies

Many industries are far from competitive—in some, competition may be impractical. For ex-

Dynamic Entrepreneurs vs. Competition: The Austrian School

The model of competition is largely rejected by the Austrian school of thought. (*Austrian* refers to the national origin of this school's founders, but its ideas now have advocates around the globe.) Here is an Austrian perspective on competition.

How firms using the same technology adjust output of a homogeneous good is described accurately by models of competition, but this is a trivial aspect of real competition. Traditional analyses fail to address a major source of disequilibrium: the entrepreneur. What matters is how competition affects human progress. Why are the foods we eat more varied than those available in an earlier era? Why don't hand-cranked autos still clog our highways? The answer to these and thousands of similar questions, according to Austrians, is that entrepreneurial innovations are the competitive mechanisms that drive the growth and decline of industries and civilizations.

Entrepreneurs innovate new technologies that create better and cheaper products and force older firms to adapt or perish. The key to entrepreneurial success is finding creative ways to serve human wants by implementing new technologies or marketing new goods better, faster, and at less cost. This can mean producing existing goods at lower costs or enhancing their quality, or it may mean creating markets for entirely new goods.

The U.S. Post Office, for example, was an uncontested government monopoly until United Parcel Service (UPS) was launched by entrepreneurs who thought that people would pay handsomely to have packages delivered faster and more conveniently. UPS prospered when shippers found it faster and more cost efficient to have packages delivered by this private firm. Then the founder of Federal Express put competitive heat on both UPS and the Post Office after he successfully tested the market demand for overnight delivery.

This dynamic form of competition creates new industries and destabilizes old ones. Thus, competition as a source of disequilibrium is more important in the Austrian view than the equilibrating entry and exit of firms conventional theory stresses. Austrians share conventional notions about pressures for competitors to adopt cost-saving technology or to mimic successful product lines. Extending our previous example, the overnight delivery market created by Federal Express has been invaded by UPS, the Postal Service, Airborne Express, DHL, Emery and fax machine manufacturers, and others. Conventional theory stresses the effects of this second wave of competition; the Austrian school emphasizes the initial entry by UPS and Federal Express.

Austrian economists offer countless examples of competition as a robust process, not as a stagnant set of equilibrium conditions specified by competitive models: Gutenberg destroyed handwritten book publishing with his movable type; Thomas Edison's electric light changed our way of life; Henry Ford's assembly line made cars available for the masses. More recently, two young engineers working out of a garage launched Apple Computer and marketed the first personal computers. The original designers of computerized spreadsheets have changed the way accountants work. Members of the Austrian school stress the dynamic competition among entrepreneurs rather than the imitative behavior of firms now scrutinized in the competitive models.

Austrians also charge that competition assumes large numbers of similar firms to be vital for vigorous competition. The stress on numerous competitors is blamed for bizarre antitrust laws and business regulations that strangle much truly competitive behavior among entrepreneurs. The number of competitors is far less important, in this view, than the qualities of goods and the rate of technological advance in an industry.

---

ample, competition among electric utilities would probably create inefficiencies because of the type of technology used. (People don't want multiple electric lines down their streets.) In other cases, lack of competition is a consequence of illegal collusion or government policies to protect other goals (patents, medical licensing to protect the public health, and so on).

Even if the economy were quite competitive, there might still be problems of fraud, information asymmetries, inequity in the distributions of income and wealth, or externalities that the mar-

BIOGRAPHY

Leon Walras and Vilfredo Pareto: General Equilibrium and Welfare Analysis

Leon Walras (1834–1910) designed a general system of analytical principles for economic theory. Walras tackled the complex problem of the interdependence of all sectors of the economy and represented this complexity in a system of simultaneous equations.

Walras was descended from a Dutch journeyman tailor who migrated to the south of France in 1749. His father was a classmate of Antoine Augustin Cournot (discussed in the next chapter) in Paris and, like Cournot, was a school administrator. The young Walras learned from Cournot the meaning of functional relations between variables. However, concerns about the limits of Cournot's demand curve for a single good led Walras to seek a wider framework within which to express the demand for a good as a function not only of its own price, but of a host of prices of related goods. This was the point of departure for his *general equilibrium model* of an economy.

Most economic writers before Walras followed the lead of Alfred Marshall and employed a convention in dealing with particular markets called *partial equilibrium analysis*. This convention calls for ignoring some determinants of demand and supply in order to concentrate on the more direct causes of equilibrium price and quantity. Walras departed from this practice by recognizing the interdependencies that exist between markets because the process of price determination occurs in all markets simultaneously. To isolate one market for study without regard to the others was no more appropriate, in Walras's view, than studying the position of the earth in the solar system without regard to other planets. His *architectonics*, consequently, was an elaborate but highly abstract system of mathematical equations that painstakingly detailed the economic conditions for simultaneous equilibrium in every economic market.

Walras's general equilibrium approach to economics did not win favor with the reigning academic hierarchy in France, forcing him to take a teaching position in Switzerland at the University of Lausanne, where he remained until he was replaced in 1893 by Vilfredo Pareto.

Pareto (1848–1923), born of a Genovese father and French mother, was trained as an engineer. At 45 years of age, he accepted the chair at Lausanne. Pareto's system of thought and his vision of social processes differed from Walras's, but Pareto cast his pure theory of economics in much the same mold, extending and refining Walras's general equilibrium system. Moreover, Pareto did what Walras had not been able to do: he founded a school of thought. His disciples cooperated in theoretical research, cultivated personal contacts, and defended one another in controversy. The school, reflecting Pareto's own heritage, was primarily Italian.

Two of Pareto's contributions to economics are especially noteworthy. First, he identified a situation of maximum efficiency for a society as one in which it is impossible to increase the happiness of one individual without decreasing that of someone else. Today, all the conditions specifying economic efficiency are referred to as "Pareto optimal."

Second, Pareto proved that a state of maximum efficiency and social welfare is identical with equilibrium under pure competition. This led him to conclude that the problems in reaching a position of maximum efficiency, as well as their solutions, were the same for a collectivist economy as for an economy founded on private property.

Pareto's chief objective was to develop general equilibrium models covering the whole spectrum of social phenomena. Both he and Walras were aware that their equations could not be solved due to the lack of data and the large number of variables involved. Nevertheless, theirs was a great achievement from the standpoint of logical clarity, and the impact of their thoughts on modern economic theory ranks them both among the dozen most influential economists of all time.

ket would not resolve in ways society deems appropriate. Moreover, certain goods will not be provided optimally by a private market system. Atomic bombs, police services, and legal decisions are examples of items no society would want sold to the highest bidder.

Some economists also argue that because research and development have such important spillover benefits to the entire economy and often require bigness, such efforts might be less than optimal if left to small, competitive firms. Finally, there are questions about what social restrictions, if any, should be imposed on trade between people in different countries. The tools you have learned to use in the last few chapters will help you examine the outcomes of private market behavior and assess corrective government policies for these specific problems.

CHAPTER REVIEW: KEY POINTS

1. Freedom of **entry and exit** is the hallmark of **competition**. A *purely competitive* market comprises numerous potential buyers and sellers of a homogeneous product, none of whom controls its price. All buyers and sellers are sufficiently small relative to the market that none is a *price maker*.

2. A purely competitive buyer faces a perfectly elastic supply curve, while purely competitive sellers face perfectly elastic demand curves. All pure competitors are **price takers** or *quantity adjusters*.

3. A purely competitive firm **maximizes profits** by producing output up to the point where *total revenues minus total costs (TR – TC)* is maximized, which also occurs when *marginal revenue equals marginal cost (MR = MC)*. Price must be greater than the minimum of the average variable cost curve, however, which is the **shutdown point**. Because competitive firms face perfectly elastic demands, price and marginal revenue are identical.

4. A purely competitive firm's **short-run supply curve** is its marginal cost curve above the minimum of its average variable costs. Horizontally summing the marginal costs from existing firms yields the *short-run industry supply curve*.

5. Firms cannot adjust output in the *market period*, so total supply is perfectly inelastic. In the *short run (SR)*, existing firms in an industry can vary output, but at least one resource is fixed and entry and exit cannot occur. Total supply is at least somewhat elastic. Supply is much more elastic in the *long run (LR)*, because all factors of production are variable and firms may enter or leave the industry.

6. Competition erases *economic profits* through entry of new firms in the long run, and economic losses are eradicated by exit from the industry. Thus, competitive firms receive exactly enough revenue over the long run to pay the opportunity costs of resources used and realize only **zero**, or **normal, economic profit**.

7. Short-run economic profits are ultimately eliminated because output will be expanded by new firms in a competitive industry, or increased competition for profitable inputs will drive up resource costs. The long-run adjustments that eliminate short-run losses follow precisely reversed patterns.

8. In the long run, pure competitors are forced by competitive pressures to adopt the most efficient (least costly) plant size and technologies. They operate at output levels where

$$P = MR = MC = SRATC = LRATC$$

9. In **constant cost industries**, the minimum *LRATC* is unaffected by how many firms are in the industry. Costs rise for each firm as firms enter **increasing cost industries**

and decline for **decreasing cost industries**. Thus, the *long-run industry supply curve* is positively sloped for increasing cost industries, horizontal for constant cost industries, and negatively sloped for decreasing cost industries.

10. A purely competitive market is efficient in the sense that goods desired by consumers (society) are produced at the lowest possible opportunity cost. Every feasible bit of net gain is squeezed from the resources available; **marginal social benefits** and **marginal social costs** are equated by the competitive forces of supply and demand ($MSB = MSC$), assuming the absence of externalities. This will be socially optimal and maximize social welfare if the distribution of income is deemed equitable. Markets do not require decision-making power to be vested in a central authority. This permits substantial personal freedom and the absence of coercion.

QUESTIONS FOR THOUGHT AND DISCUSSION

1. Suppose your firm has a contract requiring delivery of 1,000 video cameras for $1,000 each, and your average total cost is $800 per camera. Why would it be an error to fill a special rush order for one more at a price of $1,500 if producing the extra camera would boost your average total cost to $801? How much would your profit fall if you filled this special order?

2. Are there any differences between the pure competition described in this chapter and the *cutthroat* competition despised by many business executives?

3. The stock market is viewed by some critics of capitalism as the epitome of monopoly or market power. Are most people who buy or sell stock price makers or price takers? Do you think stock and commodity markets basically meet the requirements for purely competitive markets? Why or why not?

4. Is a big city economy more competitive than one in a small town? How? Do you think your grocer has monopoly or market power? How much? Can you cite recent market entry and exit among firms located within 5 miles of your home? What industries have been involved? Do you know of any giant firms that have emerged, almost from oblivion, in the past five years? Any that have failed? Is our economy basically competitive or noncompetitive?

5. State governments in Maine, Hawaii, and Wisconsin have passed laws regulating plant closings. Most require a 90-day prenotification, and some specify exit fees and the severance pay required for each worker displaced. Proponents of these laws argue that limits on plant closings minimize regional disruption. Notification allows workers time to find alternative employment and communities time to attract new firms. Opponents charge that such limits make it more difficult for firms to respond to changing market conditions. These limits, they argue, seriously diminish the social benefits of vigorous competition. Do you think government should protect jobs and local income security with restrictions on plant closings or relocations? Why or why not?

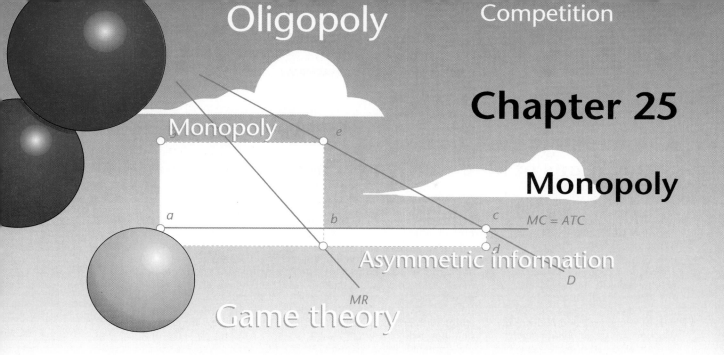

Different people view monopoly very differently. To some, it evokes memories of a game involving Boardwalk, Park Place, and the B&O Railroad, in which the ultimate winner has all the property and money. Some firms see a monopoly position as desirable and try to eliminate all their competitors. Monopoly power sometimes seems sinister. Some people blame such evils as poverty and inflation on concentrated economic power. Orthodox Marxists perceive monopoly capitalism as a natural extension of a market system and as the final stage before capitalism succumbs to a communist revolution.

The theory of pure, unregulated monopoly is the focus of this chapter, even though pure monopolies are rare and most of these are overseen by government regulators. Just as we set 0° Celsius and 100° Celsius as benchmarks for measuring temperature, monopoly and competition (from the previous chapter) set relative benchmarks for assessing economic performance. Output and pricing decisions tend to differ substantially between firms having considerable market power and those without such power. Thus, economists traditionally have as-

sumed that market structure drives an industry's conduct (e.g., the extent of advertising or the erection of barriers to entry) and its performance (e.g., pricing, profitability in the long run, and the speed with which it innovates new technologies). As you learned in the previous chapter, this is now known as the *Structure → Conduct → Performance* paradigm.

The first systematic analysis of monopoly was pursued more than a century ago by a French economist, Antoine Augustin Cournot. One central concern of Cournot, and of economists today, is the inefficiency that may result from monopoly. This inefficiency provides a rationale for regulation to control economic concentration.

MONOPOLY MARKETS

Monopolies raise the specter of concentrated power, economic inefficiency, and an inequitable income distribution. But what exactly is a monopoly?

*A **monopoly** is a firm that is the lone producer of a good for which there are no close substitutes.*

BIOGRAPHY

Antoine Augustin Cournot: Foundations of Modern Game Theory

The life of Antoine Augustin Cournot (1801–1877) was testimony to Andrew Carnegie's assertion, "It does not pay to pioneer." The value of Cournot's work was recognized only after his death. His life was characterized by anonymity and tragedy. This genius of economics and philosophy was born into a family of French farmers who had tilled the same land for almost 300 years. He spent most of his life as a school superintendent, and even that job was secured only through the influence of his friend Siméon Denis Poisson, the famous French physicist and statistician. Cournot is remembered best in his homeland as a philosopher; in the English-speaking world he is hailed as a brilliant pioneer in economics.

Only Cournot's first and most influential book was translated into English. It fairly bristles with originality, among other lasting contributions, Cournot (a) formally introduced demand and supply curves, (b) mathematically derived the marginal revenue equals marginal cost rule for profit maximization, and (c) specified equilibrium conditions for monopolists, inter-dependent oligopolists, and firms operating under pure competition.

Cournot's analysis of monopolistic profit maximization contains the kernel of his theory of the firm. As an example, Cournot considered a monopolist who could costlessly supply water from a mineral spring with uniquely healthful qualities. Sale of a single liter of water might bring an extremely high price, but Cournot demonstrated that a monopoly will not charge the highest price the market will bear. Rather, it will adjust its price to maximize total receipts; because costs are zero, this is equivalent to maximizing profit.

Cournot demonstrated that this is accomplished when marginal revenue (derived from the demand curve) equals marginal cost ($MR = MC$). Cournot's procedure is now commonplace, but before 1838 there was no formal theory of profit maximization. Virtually every fundamental axiom in the economic theory of the firm stems from Cournot's trailblazing analysis.

Cournot's demeanor was solitary and melancholy, traits that influenced his writing. His austere books abound with facts and rigor-ous mathematical proofs. He confessed to a fellow French economist that he was unpopular with his publishers because none of his books sold enough to be profitable until years after their publication. Unfortunately, his most productive years were absorbed by his duties as a school administrator.

Recognition of the profundity of Cournot's work was obstructed by his contemporaries' discomfort with mathematics, a problem made worse because gradual deterioration of his eyesight impaired the accuracy of Cournot's mathematical notation. For their part, the prejudice and shortsightedness of other economists blinded them to his advances in theory, which remained largely unappreciated until more than two decades after his death. Today, however, his contributions are heralded as the inspiration for mathematical game theory, which many economists view as the most promising approach now available for describing *strategic interaction*, whether between firms, poker players, military tacticians, or international diplomats.

High barriers to preclude entry by potential competitors are essential for a successful monopoly to be maintained across time.

Public utilities are probably the purest forms of monopoly in the United States, but even they face some competition. A local electric power company competes with solar cells or petroleum-based, electricity-generating systems, but these options to conventional electricity are insufficiently close to threaten power companies' retention of customers. Professional baseball, the National Football League, and the National Basketball Association operate somewhat like shared monopolies, with team owners jointly setting policies to govern such things as limits on player compensation. But even these organizations must compete for fans with college and high school teams, so these are not pure monopolies.

Internationally, the DeBeers group of South Africa has controlled roughly 90% of world diamond output for almost a century. When, in the mid-1980s, the former Soviet Union's entry into international markets threatened DeBeers' monopoly power as a supplier of gem quality stones, the former USSR and DeBeers reached an agreement that effectively maintained DeBeers' market power. More recently, however, Russia's economic woes and its need for hard currency induced a hiccup in diamond markets as Russia considered voiding the prior agreement (scheduled to expire in the mid-1990s anyway) and offering its half-dozen living-room-sized vaults of prime gem stones to the market. The DeBeers monopoly on diamonds, historically the single best example of pure monopoly power, may no longer exist by the end of this decade.

The definition of monopoly raises several issues. How does a firm become a monopoly? Monopolies in some goods may enrich firms' owners at the expense of the rest of society, but does a monopoly position guarantee riches? How does a monopoly prevent entry into an industry by other firms? How close can substitutes be before a firm loses its status as a monopoly?

You know of many goods for which there is only one producer or seller, but these firms are not necessarily monopolists. For example, HarperCollins has an exclusive right to publish this text. Is our publisher a monopolist? No, because there are several close, albeit imperfect, substitutes for this text. Not only is a monopolist the only seller of a given product, but the good itself must lack close substitutes.

Consider the market for cameras producing instant snapshots. Polaroid is now the only producer of cameras that provide finished pictures in 60 seconds or less. Are regular cameras really close substitutes for instant picture cameras? Should the appropriate market for ascertaining whether Polaroid has a monopoly be the market for the instant picture camera rather than for cameras as a whole? Today's one-hour film processing machines clearly compete with Polaroid's monopoly, but if you consider the closeness of substitutes, our publisher's exclusive right to sell this book is clearly inferior to Polaroid's monopoly on instant cameras.

Market Power

Recall that a purely competitive firm faces a horizontal demand curve and can sell all it produces at the going market price. Therefore, a pure competitor's marginal revenue (its revenue from selling an extra unit of output) equals the market price. Pure competitors are price takers and can only select the *quantities* they will produce and sell. Price taking behavior is fundamental in constructing a standard supply curve.

Many firms that supply goods with close but imperfect substitutes are not true monopolists, but they possess *market power* because they have some discretion about pricing. Any firm with market power is a *price maker*.

> **Market power** is a firm's ability to alter the price of its output because of inadequate competition or a lack of perfect substitutes for its products.

Constructing a standard supply curve poses a problem whenever firms possess market power. Suppose you asked the CEO of such a firm how much output her firm would produce and sell at a price of say, $10. At $15? At $20? You would not get very far before she would say "Whoa! Your question presumes that prices are set externally, but my firm sets the prices we charge. You can't just come in and dictate prices. Under capitalism, firms get to set prices." And she would be right, within limits.

The existence of some control on the supply side allows any firm with market power to select a *price and output combination* from the market demand curve. Each feasible price generates a maximum amount such a firm can sell. Alternatively, such firms might choose an output level and then charge the maximum price that causes that quantity to be sold. This discretion over price distinguishes pricing when firms have market power from pricing established in purely competitive markets, where each firm can choose only the quantity it will sell. What price maximizes a firm's profits? Is it the price the most desperate buyer is willing to pay? That which maximizes total revenue? Or that which maximizes the output sold? None of these answers is correct. Then what price will a firm with market power charge?

MONOPOLY PRICING AND OUTPUT

Because it is the sole source of a good without close substitutes, a pure monopolist faces the entire market demand curve, which slopes down: prices are inversely related to quantity demanded. Any firm with market power must lower its price to sell more if it can charge only one price at a time. Differences between the marginal revenues for pure competitors and for firms with market power are illustrated in Figure 1.

Most monopolists can sell extra output only by cutting the price for all units sold. For example, if Polaroid wanted to sell more cameras next year, it could not just lower its price to the few extra customers who required discounts to buy over the next year; Polaroid would be forced to lower the price of its camera to virtually all customers. Thus, marginal revenue will equal the price a monopolist receives from selling an extra unit minus the revenue lost because prices must be reduced on all other units sold.

The demand curve D facing the monopolist in Panel B of Figure 1 is based on the data in the figure. The market demand curve is D because the monopolist controls the industry. Total revenue (TR) equals price per unit (P) times the amount sold (Q) and is listed in column 3. If the firm set its price at $9, 3 million units would be sold annually and total revenue would be $27 million. The firm would sell 4 million by lowering its price to $8, and annual total revenue would rise from $27 million to $32 million, for an extra $5 million. Why would total revenue fail to rise by $8 million, the full price of the million units sold? The answer is that the firm received $8 for each of the extra 1 million units sold, but it lost $1 per unit on the first 3 million units sold, resulting in an average increase in total revenue of only $5 for each of the last million units sold (8 – 3 = 5).

Marginal revenues are listed in column 4 of the table included in Figure 1. Marginal revenue equals $\Delta TR/\Delta Q$ and is labeled MR. Notice that when quantity sold exceeds 6 million units and price is reduced below $6, marginal revenue is actually negative. This means that total revenue falls when the price is lowered and extra units are sold.

- **Revenue and Elasticity** Recall (from the "Elasticity" chapter) that there are close relationships between elasticity, price, and total revenue. For example, if expanding output requires such large price cuts that total revenue falls, the demand curve is price inelastic and marginal revenue is negative. How demand, marginal revenue, price, total revenue, and price elasticity are related is graphed in Figure 2, which reflects the data used in Panel B of Figure 1.

When quantity is less than 6 million units and the price exceeds $6, demand is price elastic and the price cuts required to sell more output are proportionately less than the increases in output. Thus, when output expands and prices are lowered, total revenue rises; so demand is elastic, because marginal revenue is positive at prices above $6. Conversely, total revenues fall as the price is reduced below $6, and demand is inelastic; the inelastic range of a demand curve is associated with negative marginal revenue. If small price changes do not alter total revenue, marginal revenue is zero and demand is in a unitary elastic range. Let's see how marginal revenue affects the short-run price–quantity combination a profit-maximizing monopolist selects from the demand curve.

- **Profit-Maximizing Price and Output** Any profit-maximizing firm produces and sells additional output as long as each extra unit adds to total revenue at least as much as it adds to total cost, that is, the firm will continue to produce and sell as long as marginal revenue is greater than or equal to marginal cost ($MR \geq MC$).

The revenue data in our previous example are augmented in Figure 3 by cost data in Table 1. This firm will produce and sell 4 million units at a price of $8 each, receiving total revenue of $32 million. Average total costs are $6 per unit, so $24 million is absorbed in total costs, leaving a total profit of $8 million—the blue rectangle *abec*, which equals price ($8) minus average total

Panel A
Pure Competition

P = MR = Revenue gained from sale of extra units

$d = P = MR$
$\varepsilon = \infty$

Price per Unit (dollars)

Annual Quantity (thousands)

Hypothetical Data for a Firm in Competition			
(1) P	(2) q (thousands)	(3) TR (thousands)	(4) MR
$8	0	$0	—
8	1	8	$8
8	2	16	8
8	3	24	8
8	4	32	8
8	5	40	8
8	6	48	8
8	7	56	8
8	8	64	8
8	9	72	8
8	10	80	8
8	11	88	8

Panel B
Monopolist

Revenue lost

Revenue gained

Price per Unit (dollars)

Annual Quantity (millions)

⬛ − ⬜ = Marginal revenue from 4th million

Hypothetical Data for a Monopolist			
(1) P	(2) Q (millions)	(3) TR (millions)	(4) MR ($\Delta TR/\Delta Q$)
$12	0	$0	—
11	1	11	$11
10	2	20	9
9	3	27	7
8	4	32	5
7	5	35	3
6	6	36	1
5	7	35	-1
4	8	32	-3
3	9	27	-5
2	10	20	-7
1	11	11	-9

The revenue a pure competitor gains by selling an additional unit equals the price of the output ($MR = P$) because demand for the firm's product is perfectly elastic (Panel A). A firm with market power must reduce price to sell extra output, so marginal revenue is always less than price ($P > MR$). In Panel B, a monopolist can sell 3 million units at $9 each ($27 million) or 4 million units at $8 each ($32 million). Thus, the fourth million adds only $5 per unit, on average, in revenue ($32 million - $27 million = $5 million).

FIGURE 1   Marginal Revenue for Competition and Monopoly

FIGURE 2 Relationship Between Demand, Marginal Revenue, Total Revenue, and Elasticity (e_d)

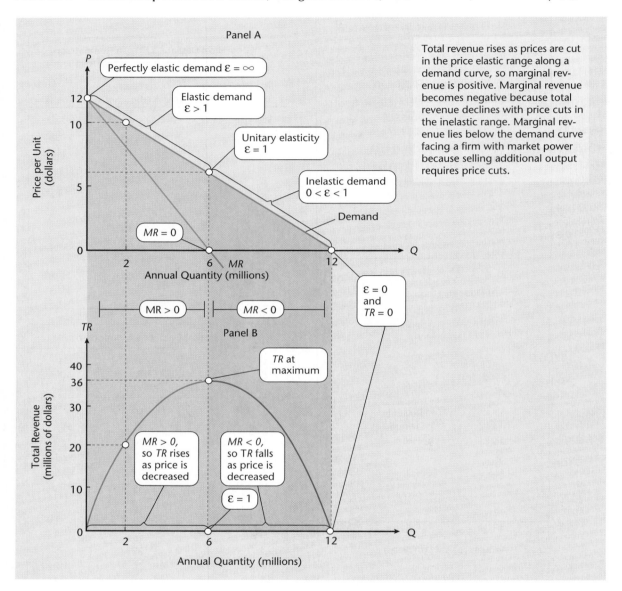

Panel A

Perfectly elastic demand $\varepsilon = \infty$

Elastic demand $\varepsilon > 1$

Unitary elasticity $\varepsilon = 1$

Inelastic demand $0 < \varepsilon < 1$

Demand

$MR = 0$

MR

Annual Quantity (millions)

$MR > 0$ $MR < 0$

$\varepsilon = 0$ and $TR = 0$

Panel B

TR at maximum

$MR > 0$, so TR rises as price is decreased

$MR < 0$, so TR falls as price is decreased

$\varepsilon = 1$

Annual Quantity (millions)

Total revenue rises as prices are cut in the price elastic range along a demand curve, so marginal revenue is positive. Marginal revenue becomes negative because total revenue declines with price cuts in the inelastic range. Marginal revenue lies below the demand curve facing a firm with market power because selling additional output requires price cuts.

cost ($6) times the number of units sold (4 million) = $8 million.

Why does the firm sell 4 million units? Why not 3 million or 5 million? Profit maximization requires any firm to produce and sell an extra unit any time the funds brought in from an extra sale (MR) at least covers its cost (MC). If only 3 million units were sold, this monopolist would

forgo profits of $500,000 (column 8 in the table: $8 million – $7.5 million = $500,000). If 5 million units were sold, the last million would add costs that exceeded extra revenues by $2.5 million. In general, to maximize profit a firm would

1. increase output whenever $MR > MC$
2. decrease output whenever $MR < MC$

FIGURE 3   Profit Maximization and the Monopolist

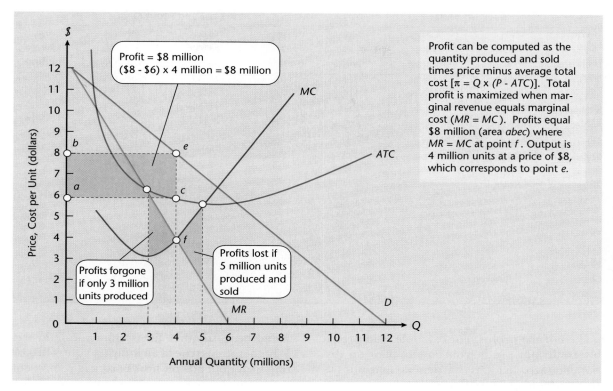

Profit can be computed as the quantity produced and sold times price minus average total cost [$\pi = Q \times (P - ATC)$]. Total profit is maximized when marginal revenue equals marginal cost ($MR = MC$). Profits equal $8 million (area $abec$) where $MR = MC$ at point f. Output is 4 million units at a price of $8, which corresponds to point e.

As is always the case, profit maximization requires a firm to produce extra output until $MR = MC$, which occurs at point f in Figure 3.

• Loss-Minimizing Price and Output   A common myth is that monopoly is always profitable. Monopolists can control the prices they charge for their products, so it seems natural that they will earn economic profits. Figure 4 depicts an instance where a monopolist would suffer losses if the good were produced. For example, surveys indicate that many people would like a trip on a space shuttle. Even for a monopolist, the current costs of such tours remain prohibitive relative to current demand. In the future, however, such tours may become possible.

There are literally thousands of patented products for which demand is insufficient to justify production. The cost structures for these products are so high that no feasible price–output combination would allow a monopolist to

The $MR = MC$ rule minimizes the losses of any firm, including a monopoly, as long as variable costs are covered by revenues.

FIGURE 4   Loss-Minimizing Output for a Monopolist

TABLE 1 Profit Maximization and the Monopolist

Revenue Data				Cost and Profit Data			
(1) Q (millions)	(2) P	(3) TR (millions)	(4) MR	(5) TC (millions)	(6) ATC	(7) MC ($\Delta TC/\Delta Q$)	(8) Profit (millions)
0	$12	$0	—	$8.0	—	—	$–8.0
1	11	11	11	12.5	12.50	4.50	–1.5
2	10	20	9	16.0	8.00	3.50	4.0
3	9	27	7	19.5	6.50	3.50	7.5
4	8	32	5	24.0	6.00	4.50	8.0
5	7	35	3	29.5	5.90	5.50	5.5
6	6	36	1	36.0	6.00	6.50	0
7	5	35	–1	43.5	6.21	7.50	–8.5
8	4	32	–3	52.0	6.50	8.50	–20.0
9	3	27	–5	61.5	6.83	9.50	–34.5
10	2	20	–7	72.0	7.20	10.50	–52.0
11	1	11	–9	83.5	7.59	11.50	–72.5
12	0	0	–11	96.0	8.00	12.50	–96.0

make normal profits. For example, you probably could not profit from monopolies on disposable razor blade resharpeners, machines to reweave runs in pantyhose, or winders for string collectors. Demands would be trivial relative to costs. To protect against this problem, a shop in Toronto called "The New Product Store" exhibits and test markets inventors' gimmicks for a fee.

Even if a monopolized good initially passes the market test, rising costs or shrinking demand may cause failure. In the short run, if P_e exceeds average variable costs, the firm shown in Figure 4 would continue to produce despite losses. But what about the long run? This monopolist has two options: leave the industry and put its capital to more profitable use, or try to bolster demand sufficiently to lift its operations into the black, perhaps through aggressive marketing. No firm will tolerate persistent losses; in the long run, any firm will move its resources into more lucrative lines of business.

• **A Long Run for Monopolists?** In competitive markets, short-run economic profits are elimi-

nated because other firms enter the industry. Whether this is true of an industry controlled by one firm depends on how hard it is to prevent new firms from entering the market to exploit profit opportunities. If new competitors can be prevented from entering the industry, the monopolist may adjust its productive capacity along its long-run average cost curve to most profitably accommodate permanent changes in demand, as shown in Panel A of Figure 5.

Alternatively, protection from the discipline of competition may allow a monopoly to operate inefficiently. Why not hire your relatives and friends at higher salaries than their productivity justifies if a monopoly position ensures you a high income anyway? Why bother to work hard or to control costs? And why worry about quality and consumer satisfaction? Any customers who are going to buy the monopolized product must buy from your firm. If a monopolist chooses the good life, X-inefficiency may absorb much of potential monopoly profit by driving up fixed costs, as shown in Panel B of Figure 5.

*Excessive costs incurred because a firm is not hard pressed by competitors is **X-inefficiency**.*

FIGURE 5 Long-Run Adjustments by Monopoly Firms

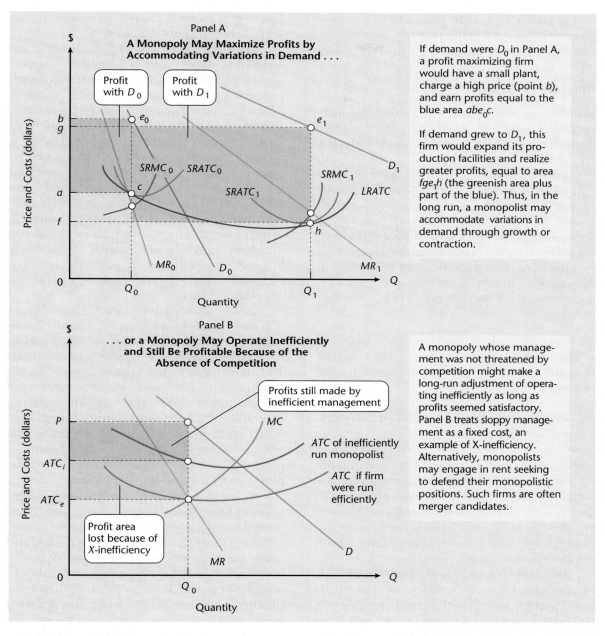

Panel A
A Monopoly May Maximize Profits by Accommodating Variations in Demand . . .

Profit with D_0

Profit with D_1

$SRMC_0$ $SRATC_0$

$SRATC_1$

$SRMC_1$

$LRATC$

MR_0 D_0

MR_1 D_1

Price and Costs (dollars)

Quantity

Q_0 Q_1

If demand were D_0 in Panel A, a profit maximizing firm would have a small plant, charge a high price (point b), and earn profits equal to the blue area abe_0c.

If demand grew to D_1, this firm would expand its production facilities and realize greater profits, equal to area fge_1h (the greenish area plus part of the blue). Thus, in the long run, a monopolist may accommodate variations in demand through growth or contraction.

Panel B
. . . or a Monopoly May Operate Inefficiently and Still Be Profitable Because of the Absence of Competition

Profits still made by inefficient management

MC

ATC of inefficiently run monopolist

ATC if firm were run efficiently

Profit area lost because of X-inefficiency

MR

D

Price and Costs (dollars)

Quantity

P ATC_i ATC_e

Q_0

A monopoly whose management was not threatened by competition might make a long-run adjustment of operating inefficiently as long as profits seemed satisfactory. Panel B treats sloppy management as a fixed cost, an example of X-inefficiency. Alternatively, monopolists may engage in rent seeking to defend their monopolistic positions. Such firms are often merger candidates.

Some monopolies also engage in *rent seeking* by strategically incurring expenses to defend their monopoly positions. Examples include wasteful outlays for advertising, political lobbying, unnecessary excess capacity, or litigation to intimidate potential entrants: a threatened suit alleging patent infringement may bar entry of an entrepreneur with a new twist on an established product, but who lacks resources to fight a lawsuit.

Of course, inefficient monopolies are natural targets for takeover by corporate raiders who intend to manage the firm more efficiently, allowing the previous owners to loaf on the beach. These two prospects—long-term economic profits or a rich, comfortable life—are good reasons for a monopolist to fear market entry by new competitors.

Barriers to Entry

Maintaining profitability when a firm has market power requires restricting the entry of other firms that would like to move into the industry.

> **Barriers to entry** *are obstacles that make it less profitable or more difficult for new firms to enter an industry.*

Some barriers to entry arise from government regulations, others result from the strategies of existing firms, and still others are technological or natural. A monopolized industry is not a requirement; entry barriers exist in a broad range of market structures.

• **Regulatory Barriers** Some barriers erected by regulations are largely beyond the control of existing firms.

> **Regulatory barriers** *to entry are erected by government policies.*

For example, compulsory auto safety standards increase per unit costs, posing obstacles for potential entrants to the car market who want to produce cheap cars. Other regulatory barriers are strongly supported by existing firms in the industry and may result from intensive lobbying by these special interest groups.

Legal barriers include government bans on competition. Laws that prohibit most competition for profitable first-class mail carrying are strongly supported by postal unions and firms with contracts with the U.S. Postal Service. For example, its competitors cannot deliver to mailboxes. Without this constraint, competition for first-class mail delivery might parallel that for parcel-post deliveries from United Parcel Service and other package handlers. But even these statutes fail to discourage some entrepreneurs. Several delivery firms now hang mail in plastic bags on the doorknobs of recipients, and Emery and Federal Express offer one-day delivery between many major cities.

Regulatory barriers include patents and copyrights. Patent and copyright monopolies may be justified as incentives for technological research and development and for cultural enrichment. Many inventors count on profits from a patent monopoly to justify risky inventive efforts. However, patents and copyrights are licenses for monopoly; patents bar competitive production for 17 years and may be renewed. For example, patents protect Polaroid's monopoly in the market for instant picture cameras. In 1986, Polaroid was awarded hundreds of millions of dollars in a suit because Kodak had infringed on Polaroid's patents. More often, however, the pirating of patented or copyrighted products is conducted secretly, as discussed in Focus 1.

Today, growing numbers of firms no longer wait the two to four years required for the Patent Office to award them a monopoly. Increasingly, competition decides who gets market share. Patents, when awarded, are often treated as just another tradable commodity, to be exchanged for royalties or the right to use other patents. Product life cycles in some industries (e.g., consumer electronics) have shrunk to roughly two years; waiting for a costly and problematic patent award can jeopardize an enterprise, putting it far behind its competition.

As a consequence, copyrights are quickly becoming the modern shortcut around the cumbersome patent process. Copyrights protect more narrowly than patents but are a fast and cheap way to protect a specific expression of an idea while waiting for the patent process to protect the idea itself. With today's high-tech competition, a constant flow of innovative products is more profitable than waiting for future royalties from patent.

Government licensing restrictions ostensibly protect consumers from fraud or shoddy practices but may actually be disguised entry barriers. For example, giving a friend advice about how to beat a traffic ticket might get you cited for practicing law without a license. Some doctors recently

Patents, Trademarks, Copyrights, and Piracy

Monopoly rights for inventors are reserved by patents, business identities are guarded by trademarks, and intellectual properties such as music, films, and writing are protected by copyright laws.

Patented inventions like the telephone and the electric light have revolutionized our lives and enriched their inventors. Public and private research and development in the United States alone now employs over a million scientists and technicians, with annual outlays exceeding $200 billion. Research funding is pouring into faster computer microchips and the information highway, a sophisticated array of consumer goods, and rapid advances in production technologies. The U.S. Patent Office recently began granting patents for gene splicing techniques that have yielded new agricultural products, pharmaceuticals, and strains of laboratory mice. This line of research is expected eventually to yield cures for diseases ranging from diabetes to multiple sclerosis.

Trademarks also generate market power. More than politeness causes your order for a "coke" in a restaurant to prompt the question, "Is Pepsi OK?" The Coca Cola Company fears that its trademark label will go the way of "kleenex,"

"xerox," and "aspirin," which were all protected brand names at one time. Any trademark that becomes widely used to refer to a product generically may lose its legal exclusivity. Consequently, Coca Cola prosecutes those who misuse its brand name. Fortunes are often spent to imprint a brand name in the public's consciousness and then to protect a product's image; such firms as Gucci, Cartier, and Chanel each spend over $1 million a year on brand-name security alone.

In addition to books, recordings, and computer software, copyrights protect product designs. Software developers have formed an organization to fight unauthorized duplication, and record producers use ASCAP and BMI to serve as efficient clearinghouses to reduce transaction costs between artists and thousands of business. ASCAP and BMI pressure businesses to license music for commercial purposes by employing agents to see if businesses play background music to entertain customers. If, for example, a restaurant plays tapes to create an atmosphere for diners, the owner is asked to purchase a license to play the music. A lawsuit immediately follows any refusal. The law is clear: playing music for commercial purposes without a license is illegal. ASCAP and BMI

prorate their revenue to the music's copyright holders.

Counterfeit goods weaken the incentives patents, copyrights, and trademarks provide inventors, designers, and artists. Pirated copies of recordings rob musicians of millions in royalties annually. Imitations of brand-name goods are often inferior in quality. Brittle "high-strength" fasteners and other bogus parts have endangered civilian and military aircraft. In 1990, the Justice Department seized over 18 tons of counterfeit auto parts. The U.S. Department of Commerce estimates that almost a million American jobs are lost to foreign-made *knockoffs*, the industry's term for counterfeited goods.

Increasingly globalized markets made it obvious that intellectual properties are not uniformly protected around the world. Piracy depreciates the market power derived from patents, trademarks, and copyrights. The growth of piracy and counterfeiting was the impetus behind inclusion of improved worldwide protection of intellectual property rights in the Uruguay Round of the General Agreement on Tariffs and Trade (GATT).

advocated making it illegal for clerks in jewelry stores to pierce ears. Doctors and lawyers respectively may argue that such laws protect patients and clients but they also help ensure customers for licensed professionals.

Elaborate regulations often bar smaller firms from competing effectively. For example, some evidence exists that tighter regulation by the Food and Drug Administration in 1962 following the thalidomide disaster of 1962 reduced R&D spending by big pharmaceutical companies and drove

most small drug firms completely out of that market. Even worthwhile regulations may generate social costs by squelching potential competition.

• **Strategic Barriers** Monopolists are ingenious in trying to keep competitors out of a market. For example, a monopolist might try to corner the market for a natural resource that was a key ingredient in a production process, hoping to stymie all potential competitors. But nonmonopolists are also adept at developing policies to make life harder for potential entrants.

> ***Strategic barriers*** *raise the costs of entry and result from the policies of existing firms in an industry.*

Some strategic barriers are legally permissible (e.g., annual style changes or extensive national advertising) but others violate U.S. antitrust laws (e.g., establishing exclusive marketing territories or pooling patents may bar entry by new firms). Strategic behavior and antitrust laws are detailed in the next two chapters.

• **Natural Barriers**   Barriers may also emerge from the cost structures inherent in some types of production.

> ***Natural barriers*** *to entry arise when economies of scale are substantial relative to market demand and severely limit the number of firms in an industry.*

That is, minimum efficient scales of production are huge. (The *MES* concept was introduced in the chapter "Production and Costs.") Allocative efficiency requires one firm to fully service the market in extreme cases where the *MES* is 100%.

> *A **natural monopoly** emerges if economies of scale permit only one firm to achieve the lowest possible average cost while serving a specific market.*

For example, a single natural gas company can efficiently service a given area. If 20 gas companies serviced your neighborhood and consumers did not collude to use gas from only one company, how often would the roads be torn up to install new pipelines? How many pipes would run down every alley? How many firms might you need to contact before planting a tree? Installing a storm sewer system would be a nightmare.

Figure 6 illustrates how a *natural monopoly* arises from a production process with a high *MES*. An unregulated monopoly could charge P_3 for Q_2 amount of output, reaping profits equal to the shaded area. This production process is characterized by high fixed costs and relatively low variable costs. Economies of scale are tremendous because average costs decline when overhead costs are spread across large amounts of output.

Why does competition degenerate to monopoly in such markets? Suppose four firms were breaking even by producing Q_0 at price P_3, where $Q_0 = Q_2/4$. Each would try to wrest customers from competitors because the marginal revenue from servicing new buyers would ex-

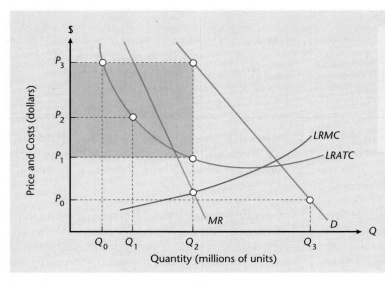

Competitive processes in markets where economies of scale cause average costs to decline across the full range of market demand will ultimately evolve into a *natural monopoly*. Economies of scale are so significant that local natural monopolies are almost inevitable for electricity, natural gas, water and sewer facilities, and local telephone service.

FIGURE 6   A Natural Monopoly Market

ceed marginal cost. But as industry output grows, the price falls faster than average costs fall. Suppose, for example, that each firm doubled output. Price will be P_0 at industry output Q_3 ($Q_3 = Q_1 \times 4$). If all firms are the same size (Q_1), average total cost will be P_2 and every firm will lose $P_2 - P_0$ per unit. Three firms must eventually exit this market, leaving the fourth to collect the full monopoly profit (the shaded area in Figure 6).

Such natural monopolies as utility companies are regulated in attempts to transfer benefits from economies of scale to consumers. Unregulated natural monopolies could reap immense profits and, as you will see in a moment, tend to be allocatively inefficient. In the "Antitrust and Regulation" chapter, we consider illegal barriers to competition from artificial attempts to monopolize, and we investigate potential regulatory benefits when technology makes monopoly a natural outcome of the market.

PRICE DISCRIMINATION

Market power implies some control over price. We have shown how a monopoly that charges only one price maximizes profit. If a monopolist can separate buyers into submarkets and has control over price, different groups can be charged different prices.

> *Price discrimination* occurs when a good is sold at different prices that do not reflect differences in production costs.

We previously defined consumer surplus as the difference between the amounts people would willingly pay for various amounts of specific goods and the amounts they do pay at market prices. Price discrimination allows some of the monetary value of consumer surplus to be transferred from consumers to the producer.

Have you sat next to people who paid less than you did for tickets to see a film? Theaters often have different prices for children, students, adults, and senior citizens. Does it cost a

theater more to seat a 32-year-old at a given show than to seat a senior citizen? Clearly not. Doctors often argue that they render charity by charging their richer patients more than their poorer patients pay for the same service. (Might they charge whatever the market will bear in both cases?) Airline ticket prices vary widely for roughly the same service (depending on early reservations and special promotions). And the family in front of you in a grocery checkout line may pay much less for the same food than you do if it uses coupons and you don't. These are all examples of price discrimination.

Why do firms charge different customers different prices? Is price discrimination socially beneficial or harmful? And what conditions make price discrimination possible?

Requirements for Price Discrimination

Price discrimination requires a firm to have market power. The firm need not be a monopoly. Any seller that is a price maker rather than a price taker possesses market power. This occurs whenever the demand curve facing an enterprise has negative slope. In this sense, your local florist has market power even if it is not a monopolist.[1]

A second requirement for price discrimination is that buyers with different demand elasticities be separable into submarkets. Different demand elasticities may arise from differences in incomes, preferences, locations, and so on. Once groups of customers are separated, a firm must be able to prevent *arbitrage*, when buyers who pay a lower price must be deterred from selling to people charged a higher price. Price discrimination abounds in medical treatment

---

[1]Pure competitors cannot charge different prices for a homogeneous product because the demand curves they confront are horizontal. If one pure competitor raised its price, all customers would simply go elsewhere and their business would be lost to the firm. A competitive firm could (if it were altruistic) sell its product at below the prevailing market price to a given group, but it would lose some of its normal profits in the process.

Arbitrage and Price Discrimination

In *Cartels in Action*,* George Stocking and Myron Watkins reported a classic case of arbitrage:

Rohm & Haas of Philadelphia and DuPont [were] the only American producers of methyl-methacrylate plastics. They marketed methyl-methacrylate, in the form of molding powders, for a variety of industrial uses at $0.85 a pound. To licensed dental laboratories they supplied, at more than $22 a pound, prepared mixtures consisting of methyl-methacrylate powder (polymer) and liquid (monomer), both essential to the manufacture of dentures. At the same time they refused to sell the monomer in any other form to any other buyer. In this way they apparently planned to force the dental trade to rely exclusively upon them for supplies. The enormous price spread attracted "bootleggers" who found that they could "crack" the commercial powders back to the liquid, and sell the polymer and monomer together at a profit to the dental trade. To combat this practice, at the suggestion of a licensee, Rohm & Haas considered adulterating the cheap commercial powders so that, for use in dentures, they would come under the ban of the Food and Drug Administration. The licensee suggested that:

A millionth of one percent of arsenic or lead might cause them to confiscate every bootleg unit in the country. There ought to be a trace of something that would make them rear up.

Although Rohm & Haas thought this was a "very fine" suggestion, there is no evidence that they put it into effect.

*George Stocking and Myron Watkins, *Cartels in Action* (New York: Twentieth Century Fund, 1946), pp. 402–404. Reprinted by permission.

---

because arbitrage is impossible. One patient cannot sell another a liver transplant or an inoculation against mumps. Focus 2 reports an interesting example of arbitrage. Price discrimination schemes fail when arbitrage cannot be prevented.

In summary, price discrimination raises the prices some groups pay, while it reduces prices for other groups. (Without price discrimination, both groups would pay a common price somewhere in the middle.) Price discrimination requires a firm to have market power and it must be able to (*a*) separate groups into submarkets with different price elasticities of demand and (*b*) prevent low-price users from selling to high-price users. We will now examine how two types of price discrimination affect monopoly profits.

Profits from Price Discrimination

Different customers are charged different prices only if this increases a firm's profits. In the extreme case, a firm practicing **perfect price dis-crimination** extracts from all consumers their demand prices for every unit of a good it sells. These demand prices are the maximum payments each individual would willingly make rather than do without.

This case is illustrated in Figure 7, where we consider a monopolist marketing a cure for baldness. To keep the graph simple, we assume that fixed costs are zero while marginal costs are constant at $200 per bottle.[2] If it set a single profit-maximizing price, this monopolist would charge $500 per bottle of tonic and sell 6,000 units. Total profit would be $1,800,000 [($500 − $200) × 6,000 = $1,800,000]. But this firm can profit from price discrimination. For the firm to fully extract its customers' consumer surpluses, it must sell the first few bottles for between $800 and $799, the next few for between $799 and $798, and so on, until the last bottle is sold for only a fraction over $200.

---

[2]Note that whenever marginal costs are constant, they also equal average variable costs. If fixed costs are zero, then $MC = AVC = ATC$.

FIGURE 7 Monopoly Profits and Perfect Price Discrimination

Perfect price discrimination allows the patent medicine monopolist to charge everything consumers are willing to pay to have hair rather than do without it. All potential consumer surpluses are converted into revenues for the perfectly price-discriminating firm.

Perfect price discrimination allows this firm to appropriate all consumer surplus above a price of $200. This form of price discrimination allows the tonic bottler to boost profit from the $1,800,000 (the rectangular area) associated with normal monopoly pricing to $3,600,000 (the area of the entire shaded triangle above marginal costs).[3] Perfect price discrimination would enable a monopolist to truly charge everything the market will bear. But no firm can determine the precise maximum each individual is willing to pay for each unit of a good. At best, a firm might segment the public into a few distinct groups for whom arbitrage is impossible and whose elasticities of demand differ.

---

[3]Notice that the area of the two triangles equals the area of the rectangle. Thus, profit doubles from $1.8 million to $3.6 million.

How even imperfect market segmentation can be profitable is shown in Figure 8, which illustrates demands for two groups of consumers. Fixed costs are zero and marginal cost is a constant $2. This firm charges $5 per unit in Market A, and profit is $18,000; the lower price ($3.75) in Market B yields a profit of $12,250. Total profit is $30,250. If this firm charged a single monopoly price, it would sell 13,000 units at $4.25 and make a total profit of $29,250. Price discrimination generates $1,000 per month in excess of regular monopoly profits.

This second form of price discrimination includes grocery coupons, frequent flyer bonuses, and student or senior citizen discounts for bus rides or films. Other types of price discrimination are more subtle. Residential phone lines cost less than business lines and long-distance rates historically generated higher profit rates than did local services. These gaps greatly exceeded cost differentials prior to reorganization of the AT&T system in 1983.

We need to point out why some apparent price discrimination is illusory. It may seem price discriminatory that parking lots charge lower monthly rates than weekly rates, which are lower than daily, which, in turn, are lower than hourly rates. But wage costs for parking attendants fall as parking moves from short term to long term. Similarly, quantity discounts to major buyers of goods commonly reflect lower transaction costs. Lower rates for weekend parking or off-peak long-distance calls also reflect lower opportunity costs and not mere differences in the desperation of buyers. Weekend parking or off-peak-hour phone calls are not the same goods as spaces or calls during busier hours. Price discrimination is not present when differences in opportunity costs are reflected in the prices of similar goods.

COMPETITIVE VS. MONOPOLIZED MARKETS

We showed in the previous chapter that pure competition yields efficient prices and outputs. Prices are higher when firms exercise market power, and output is less than would be pro-

FIGURE 8 Group Price Discrimination and Firm Profitability

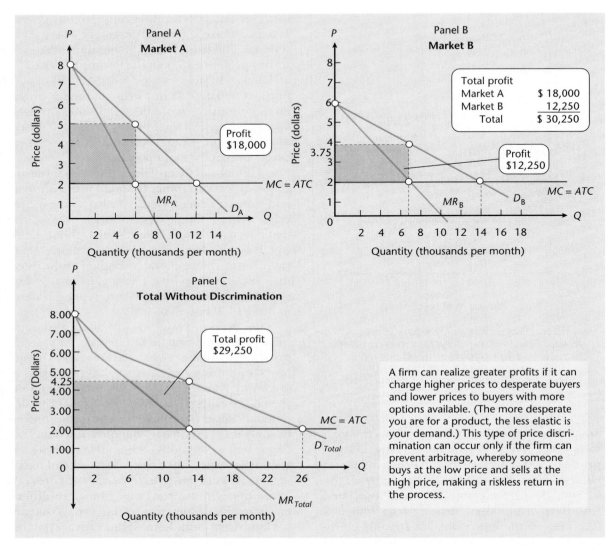

A firm can realize greater profits if it can charge higher prices to desperate buyers and lower prices to buyers with more options available. (The more desperate you are for a product, the less elastic is your demand.) This type of price discrimination can occur only if the firm can prevent arbitrage, whereby someone buys at the low price and sells at the high price, making a riskless return in the process.

duced were the industry competitive. Is the exercise of market power, therefore, allocatively inefficient? The answer is almost invariably yes. Market power may also cause what many people perceive as inequity in the distribution of income.

Differences in Prices and Outputs

A purely competitive equilibrium is shown in Panel A of Figure 9. At point a, industry output equals Q_c and price equals P_c. A purely competi-

tive market supply curve is the sum of the marginal cost curves (above $AVCs$) of all firms in an industry. Contrast these results with those for an unregulated, nondiscriminating monopolist, described in Panel B of the figure. Industry demand for the good is identical, and the monopolist's marginal cost curve is assumed to be the same as that which collectively characterizes firms in the competitive industry. Equilibrium price and output will be P_m and Q_m, respectively. This higher price when market power exists often prompts complaints about price gouging from buyers; the

FIGURE 9   Pure Competition vs. Nondiscriminating Monopoly

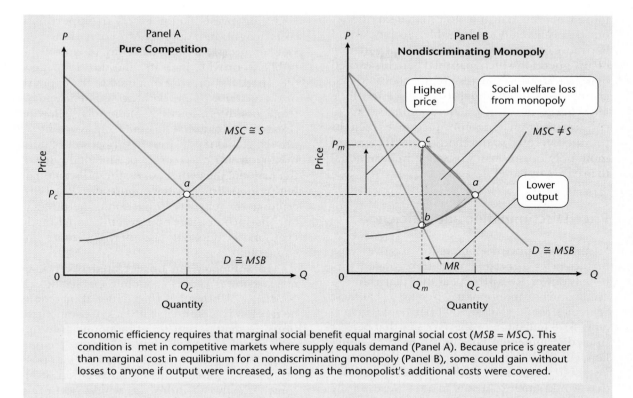

Economic efficiency requires that marginal social benefit equal marginal social cost (*MSB = MSC*). This condition is met in competitive markets where supply equals demand (Panel A). Because price is greater than marginal cost in equilibrium for a nondiscriminating monopoly (Panel B), some could gain without losses to anyone if output were increased, as long as the monopolist's additional costs were covered.

monopoly price is higher while the output is lower than for a competitive industry.

Note that in Panel B, the monopolist's marginal cost curve is not the market supply curve. Price is not a given for firms with market power. Since a monopolist can select a price that maximizes profit, its marginal cost curve is *not* a supply curve. We have denoted this as $MSC \neq S$. In fact, the quantities supplied by any firm with market power cannot be ascertained from price alone; such firms first want to know how desperate buyers are (how elastic their demand curves are) before selecting both price and production. There is no supply curve per se.

The Inefficiency of Monopoly

In the preceding chapter, we showed that the demand curve for any industry's good is roughly society's marginal benefit curve for that good.

Thus, the marginal social benefit of the good is roughly its price ($P \cong MSB$). Pure competition forces each manufacturer to use the least costly production technology, so the marginal social costs of production are reflected in competitive supplies. This is shown in the competitive panel of Figure 9 with the notation that marginal social cost approximates supply ($MSC \cong S$). The purely competitive market equilibrium at point *a* equates society's marginal (opportunity) cost of producing this good with the marginal benefits, as $MSB \cong P = MC \cong MSC$. Maximum benefits from available resources are realized only if the price equals the cost for the last unit produced and sold ($P = MC$). This is the reason purely competitive markets set standards for efficiency by which all other market structures are judged.

At the equilibrium for a nondiscriminating monopoly, price (marginal social benefit) exceeds marginal social cost; society would gain more from extra units of the good than their extra output costs. That is, $P > MSC$. This might seem desirable at first glance (Doesn't society get more from the marginal unit than it sacrifices?) but this is actually undesirable. Society would like more of its resources devoted to production of any good for which marginal benefits exceed marginal costs. Resources are not allocated efficiently because monopolists produce too little and charge too much. The potential gains to consumers from extra production exceed its production costs, so the allocative inefficiency of monopoly causes losses of social welfare equal to area *abc* in Panel B.[4]

Price Discrimination and Efficiency

Surprisingly, price discrimination may overcome inefficiencies associated with unregulated monopoly power. Recall from Figure 7 that a nondiscriminating monopolist selling baldness remedies would charge $500 per bottle, generating $1.8 million in profits. We saw that perfect price discrimination boosted profit to $3.6 million, but the $200 price charged for the last bottle would be identical to the constant unit price that would emerge if this market were purely competitive. In addition, the marginal social costs and benefits will both equal the price of that last unit. Thus, price discrimination can lead to the economic efficiency associated with pure competition. Price discrimination, however, is typically far from perfect (even at the margin). Moreover, under pure competition, most of the net social benefits of the marketplace are in the form of consumer surpluses, but these benefits are appropriated by owners of firms with market power if they can price discriminate.

---

[4]This excess burden of monopoly is sometimes referred to as a *welfare loss triangle*.

Monopoly and Inequity

Charging prices far in excess of opportunity costs delights monopolists. Most of us, however, view monopoly pricing as a way to rip off the public to provide high incomes for a few people. Huge incomes are obtained at the expense of the general public because (*a*) inefficiencies from nondiscriminating monopoly behavior prevent real national income from reaching its potential, and (*b*) the purchasing power of non-monopoly incomes is eroded. The total value of the national pie withers so that nondiscriminating monopolists can have more pie. Price discrimination may overcome some inefficiency, but the income distribution tends to be made even more unequal and perhaps more inequitable.

In summary, an unregulated exercise of market power causes economic inefficiency ($P > MC$), which implies that national income is held below its potential. The lack of competitive pressure may permit some monopolists to operate in a slack and wasteful fashion, worsening the problem. Moreover, market power may pose problems of inequity in the distribution of income. Ideally, all industries would be purely competitive. Unfortunately, this is impossible because certain technologies embody enormous economies of scale and lead to natural monopolies, or certain firms are able to erect significant barriers to entry.

Natural monopolies are typically regulated in an attempt to ensure optimal and efficient operation. The government uses antitrust laws to try to make other industries behave as if they were competitive, or it may split some industries into smaller firms to ensure competition. In the next chapter we examine monopolistic competition and oligopoly, the part of the spectrum between monopoly and competition.

CHAPTER REVIEW: KEY POINTS

1. An unregulated **monopoly** controls the output and price of a good for which no close substitutes exist.

2. Few monopolies are unregulated, but all firms with any ability to control prices have **market power**. Models of pure monopoly provide insights into the behavior of the many firms with this power.

3. **Barriers to entry** help firms maintain market power. **Regulatory barriers** are established by government policies and include such things as patents or licenses. **Strategic barriers** include excessive model changes or advertising. **Natural barriers** result from extreme economies of scale, where average costs decline over a large range of output relative to market demand. A **natural monopoly** occurs if one firm can achieve the minimum efficient scale (*MES*) of production only when producing for the entire market.

4. A nondiscriminating monopolist's *marginal revenue* is less than its price. **Marginal revenue** equals the price the monopolist receives from the sale of the additional unit minus the revenue lost because prices must be reduced on all other units sold. Market power causes the marginal revenue curve to lie below the demand curve.

5. The demand for a good is elastic when output is below the quantity where marginal revenue is zero. Demand is unitarily elastic when marginal revenue is zero. Demand is inelastic for outputs above the point where marginal revenue is zero.

6. A monopolist maximizes profit (or minimizes loss) by selling that output where marginal revenue equals marginal cost. The price charged corresponds to the maximum price from the demand curve at this $MR = MC$ output level.

7. Monopolists' profit-maximizing (or loss-minimizing) output levels do not normally occur at the minimum points on average total cost curves. Equilibrium output levels can be less or more than that which minimizes average total cost.

8. If a monopolist is able to maintain its monopoly position in the long run, then pricing, output, and economic profit will reflect variations in demand. A monopolist may also choose inefficient, but comfortable, policies, a problem known as **X-inefficiency**.

9. **Price discrimination** entails sales of essentially the same good at different prices when these differences are not justified by variations in costs. Price discrimination occurs in airline fares, theater ticket prices, charges for medical and dental services, and many other areas.

10. Effective price discrimination requires a firm to have some market power and the ability to separate customers into groups with different price elasticities of demand. It must also prevent *arbitrage*, the selling of the good to high-price customers by low-price customers.

11. Price discrimination boosts a firm's total profit. *Perfect price discrimination* allows a firm to reap as profit all the consumer surplus that could be derived from the product.

12. A nondiscriminating monopoly is less allocatively efficient from society's point of view than are competitive industries. A monopolist typically produces less than would be produced if the industry were purely competitive and sells at a higher price. Price discrimination may reduce this inefficiency, but it intensifies issues of inequity in the distribution of income.

QUESTIONS FOR THOUGHT AND DISCUSSION

1. Rank these firms according to the extent of their market power (control over price).
   a. A grocery store in the suburbs of Atlanta, GA.
   b. The daily newspaper in Peoria, IL.
   c. A public golf course in Phoenix, AZ.
   d. Pacific Gas and Electric in Seattle.
   e. The biggest wheat farm in the United States.
   f. A New York taxicab owner.
2. How is the price elasticity of the demand a firm faces related to the extent of its market power?

3. Why is it easier for a surgeon to price discriminate than it is for a company that makes patent medicines?
4. Give two examples for each of the three basic types of entry barriers.
5. How do theaters gain by offering discounts to students and senior citizens? How are the price elasticities of demand for theater tickets different for typical students and seniors than for other population groups?

Imperfect Competition and Strategic Behavior

Competition throughout the world economy is being invigorated by international trade. IBM, Cray, and Compaq, for example, now face rivalry from European and Japanese computer manufacturers. At the same time, concerns about concentrated economic power are heightened by an ongoing wave of enormous mergers that began to gather momentum in the 1980s. Over 90% of the largest mergers of all time have occurred since 1980.

The bulk of our output now flows through the largest 200 American firms, which control roughly two-thirds of U.S. manufacturing assets. These giants are in industries that lie between the extremes of competition and monopoly. None is a price taker; all have substantial market power.

- **Oligopoly** Many major industries are dominated by a few huge firms, which individually lack the control possessed by unregulated monopolists; they must consider other firms' reactions in setting prices, production, and marketing strategy.

Oligopolies are industries dominated by a few firms whose decisions are strategically linked; barriers to entry tend to be significant.

Models of pure competition and monopoly provide insights into oligopolistic behavior, but neither pure competitors nor monopolists base their decisions on the expected reactions of other firms. Thus, theories of oligopoly cannot just blend theories of competition and monopoly.

Oligopoly models must account for interdependence in decision-making. That is, each individual firm weighs its potential rivals' reactions when it chooses a business strategy. Theories of oligopoly abound because the dynamics of interdependence differ markedly from one industry to another. Just as proper play in poker depends as much on how well you read your opponents as it does on the cards you are dealt, oligopolists' strategies depend on their individual positions relative to those of current competitors and potential rivals.

Until recently, most specialists in industrial organizations thought that a general model should be developed to cover the behavior of all firms that operate in oligopoly markets. Most economists have concluded that this is not possible. One modern approach to analyzing oligopoly involves modeling strategic behavior.

Strategic behavior *entails ascertaining what other people or firms are likely to do in a specific situation and then pursuing tactics that maximize your gains or minimize your losses.*

Thus, no single model is sufficiently general to cover all oligopoly markets and strategic behavior.

• **Monopolistic Competition** Oligopoly is closer to monopoly than to pure competition. Ease of entry and exit in monopolistically competitive markets forces firms into a slightly more competitive mode.

Monopolistic competition *requires easy entry and exit into industries in which many potential suppliers compete vigorously with makers of close, but not perfect, substitutes for their brand-name products.*

Monopolistic competitors do not base decisions on the anticipated individual reactions of their many competitors, so they are not mutually interdependent in the way oligopolists are. Product differentiation (e.g., packaging, advertising, or styling), however, gives them some control over prices.

Few models of firm behavior occupied the vast middle ground between pure competition and monopoly until the 1930s, when the works of Joan Robinson and E. H. Chamberlin made it clear that most earlier models left huge gaps.[1] The continuum from competition to monopolistic competition through oligopoly to monopoly is not smooth, and where an industry fits may change over time. For example, 40 years ago automaking was clearly an oligopoly; General Motors, Ford, and Chrysler sold roughly 95% of all cars in the United States. Rambler, Jeep, Hudson, Studebaker, and Packard sold the other 5% but these firms have died or been absorbed into the Big Three. However, competition from BMW, Fiat, Honda, Hyundai, Nissan, Toyota, Volkswagen, and other foreign carmakers has moved this oligopolistic industry a bit closer to the monopolistically competitive mode.

This chapter begins by examining the issue of product differentiation. Then we present monopolistic competition and two classic oligopoly models: cartel behavior and the kinked demand curve. Finally, we will explore recent developments in the theory of strategic behavior. Which theory of market structure best fits a particular industry may be difficult to determine, but each model can be useful in analyzing some policies of specific firms.

PRODUCT DIFFERENTIATION

The model of pure competition assumes that numerous firms produce identical products. Homogeneous outputs are the norm in farming and a few other industries, but most firm's products are at least somewhat differentiated.

Product differentiation *is the process of altering goods that serve a similar purpose so that they differ in minor (either real or imagined) ways.*

Some firms differentiate within their product lines. For example, GM produces Chevrolets, Buicks, Pontiacs, Oldsmobiles, and Cadillacs. Others concentrate on differentiating their products from those of competitors; ABC, CBS, NBC, and the Fox Network compete for advertisers' dollars by broadcasting slightly differentiated soap operas, sit-coms, sporting events, and news programs, while the Cable News Network (CNN) offers continuous news coverage, ESPN specializes in sports, and MTV and VH-1 offer music videos.

Product differentiation can provide society with a beneficial mix of goods and may signal

---

[1]A century earlier, A. A. Cournot (his biography is in the previous chapter) blazed a path for theories of strategic interactions among firms, but his work was written in French and was largely ignored by English-speaking economists before the 1930s.

BIOGRAPHY

Joan Robinson and E. H. Chamberlin: Bringing Realism to Theories of Market Structure

Until Edward Hastings Chamberlin (1899–1967) attempted to fuse the theories of monopoly and competition, the case of many sellers offering differentiated products had been overlooked. Earlier mainstream economists concentrated on the theory of pure competition, which assumes many sellers of homogeneous products. Chamberlin instead saw close competitors in nearly every market trying to gain market power by differentiating their products. For example, firms often allege the superiority of their products over others.

Chamberlin revised his Harvard Ph.D. dissertation and published *The Theory of Monopolistic Competition* in 1933. His was among the few dissertations to ever profoundly alter economic theory. The central feature of his analysis is that it portrays the demand curves facing firms with differentiated products as being negatively sloped.

In other words, firms that compete on the basis of product differences could raise prices without losing all their customers, but they would sell less output. This fact mirrors elements of monopoly. However, competition tends to lower this negatively sloped demand curve to a point of tangency with the firm's average total cost curve, so that no monopoly profits are realized in the long run. Chamberlin's theory was combined with Joan Robinson's ideas to spark numerous studies of industrial markets in the 1940s and 1950s. These analytical feats have provided useful insights into numerous market situations. In Robinson's phrase, she and Chamberlin introduced a "box of tools" sharper and more generally applicable than those that preceded their works.

I don't know much math, so I have to think.

Joan Robinson

The iconoclastic British economist Joan Robinson (1903–1983) was a combatant in virtually every major controversy in economic theory and policy between 1930 and 1983. However, her foes joined her friends in admiring the innovative quality of her ideas and research. She married E. A. G. Robinson (another distinguished British economist) after completing her formal studies in economics and was among the small group of Cambridge University economists who aided John Maynard Keynes in launching the Keynesian Revolution.

An avowed radical and Marxist, she blended the insights of Keynes, Marx, and neoclassical reasoning in a manner uniquely her own. Robinson bridged capital theory, the theories of value and distribution, macroeconomics, and the economics of policymaking, but her most noteworthy contributions were in the area of imperfect competition. At almost exactly the same time that Chamberlin issued his theory of monopolistic competition from Cambridge, Massachusetts, Joan Robinson launched a parallel theory from Cambridge, England, in *The Economics of Imperfect Competition*.

Robinson's imperfect competition, however, stresses oligopolistic interdependence and views competition and monopoly as mutually exclusive, while Chamberlin identified modern business as a blending of the two. Robinson refined the theory of price discrimination, introduced the concept of *monopsony power* (that is, the ability of powerful buyers to control prices), and separated average revenue (demand) and marginal revenue curves.

competition in process. Homogeneity, on the other hand, may result from orders by some central authority. For example, covered wagons in Western movies are all quite similar because the film industry created an image and has them built to order. Few pioneers loaded their belongings into picturesque prairie schooners while migrating to the Old West. They rode, instead, in the motley assortment of wagons then available; two men reportedly moved their gear from St. Louis to Denver in a wheelbarrow in 1867.

Nevertheless, many firms accentuate product differences to try to make us value their products more than those from rival firms. You may think that gasoline is gasoline, but big oil companies expect advertising to alter customers' perceptions. Are Tide, All, Cheer, and Dash meaningfully different? Soap makers spend millions to persuade us that they are. Ford, GM, Chrysler, and numerous foreign producers all sell autos that provide the same basic transportation services. Despite their many similarities, most of us prefer certain cars based on advertising, styling, the frequency of repair, or our past experience.

• **Advertising** Some critics believe that marketing puffery often persuades consumers to buy useless items or creates a distorted image that a particular brand of product is unique. Product differences can be real or illusory. Differentiation only requires that consumers perceive differences. An example of a differentiated product that is physically homogeneous is liquid bleach. All standard liquid bleach is chemically identical, but most people buy such advertised brands as Clorox instead of cheaper generic substitutes. Why? Because marketing programs create imaginary differences among brands.

Meaningless differences are also found in aspirin-based pain relievers that ads claim contain "the ingredient that doctors recommend most." We seldom hear that the ingredient is aspirin and that generic brands are as potent as Bayer. Some folks seem convinced that the more you pay, the more it's worth. Of course, product differentiation may also be real. Some goods truly are superior.

Can you remember the worst advertisement you ever saw or heard? If so, the advertiser partially accomplished its goal by making an unforgettable impression. Different types of ads usually target different groups of consumers. An ad you view as obnoxious may be thought amusing or informative by most members of a targeted group. How firms gain from marketing differentiated products is obvious. Pure competitors are price takers that sell identical products. Firms try to use product differentiation to boost the demands for their goods and shrink their price elasticities. Successful dif-

ferentiation provides a firm with market power; they become price makers. This enables the firm to sell more product even if it raises the price.

In Figure 1, we show how differentiation gives firms some control over price. Without this control, firms can adjust only output levels to maximize profits: the demand curve facing a pure competitor is perfectly elastic. Successful product differentiation expands the demand curve and makes it less elastic. One critical result is that each marginal revenue curve now lies below the demand curve facing the firm, much like that for the monopolist described in the previous chapter. Consequently, product differentiation allows prices to vary considerably among goods that are close substitutes.

Demands facing monopolistic competitors are much more elastic than the industry (monopoly) demand because there are close substitutes for each firm's products. Still, these firms can hike prices and not lose all their customers. Some of us will continue to eat Wheaties even if the price rises a bit, but if General Mills were to boost the price too much relative to other cereal prices, our breakfast habits would change to reflect our fading loyalty.

MONOPOLISTIC COMPETITION

Monopolistic competition resembles pure competition in allowing easy entry or exit but differs because each firm produces a differentiated good. Monopolistically competitive industries have

1. Large numbers of potential buyers and suppliers.
2. Differentiated products that are close substitutes.
3. Easy entry or exit in the long run.

Successful product differentiation creates market power by expanding the demand curve the firm faces and decreasing its price elasticity; this can allow a monopolistic competitor to act a little like a monopolist. Each monopolistic competitor has some control over price. But, as we shall see, like pure competitors, monopolistic

FIGURE 1 Production Differentiation and Firm Demand

Numerous perfect substitutes exist for the output of a purely competitive firm, so demand is perfectly elastic (d_c). The absence of perfect substitutes makes the demand for the output of a monopolistic competitor less than perfectly elastic. Even this small amount of market power pushes the marginal revenue curve for a monopolistic competitor below the price for its output. The fewness of competitors similarly affords market power to oligopolists, so the demand curves they face exceed their marginal revenue curves.

FIGURE 2 Short-Run Profitable Equilibrium for a Monopolistic Competitor

The MR = MC cost rule (point a) for maximum profits applies to all firms, including those in monopolistically competitive industries. These firms can make economic profits in the short run.

competitors earn only normal profit in the long run because entry by potential competitors is easy.

Short-Run Pricing and Output

A monopolistic competitor's profit-maximizing short-run price and output combination is shown at point a in Figure 2; output q_0 is sold at price P_0. Regardless of market structure, all firms maximize profit by producing where marginal revenue equals marginal cost. In the short run, this successful firm's economic profit equals the shaded area.

Monopolistic competitors may suffer short-run losses; profits would be impossible if a

firm's average total cost curve were always above the demand curve. Like all firms, a monopolistic competitor would minimize losses by selling that output where marginal revenue equals marginal cost, as long as the price it could set (average revenue) exceeded average variable costs.

Long-Run Adjustments

Monopolistic competitors differentiate products to exploit short-run profit opportunities, and they would like their profits to persist. These hopes are usually frustrated because typical monopolistic competitors earn only normal profits in the long run; the long-run industry adjustments parallel those for pure competition. Entry of new firms seeking profits cannot be prevented, which may increase production costs. Profits are also dissipated because prices fall when new competitors expand output and take customers from existing firms.

This shrinks the demand for a successful firm's products. When new firms enter the market, the demand curves of established firms shift leftward and become more elastic, ultimately leaving all firms in an equilibrium of the sort shown in Figure 3. Marginal revenue equals marginal cost at point a, and the long-run average total cost ($LRATC$) curve is just tangent to the demand curve at point b. This tangency allows the firm to sell its output at a price just equal to average cost ($P_e = ATC_e$), yielding only normal profits in the long run. Product differentiation allows the prices of comparable goods to vary in monopolistic competition, but only within a narrow range.

Resource Allocation and Efficiency

Pure competition is allocatively efficient because marginal social benefit equals marginal social cost ($P = MSC$), and it is productively efficient because average costs are minimized. In Figure 3, demand would be d_c for a pure competitor; the equilibrium at point c entails more produc-

tion, which is sold at a lower price ($P_c = \min LRATC_{min} = MC$), and more output than would be produced by a monopolistic competitor. Note that, even though both perfect and monopolistic competitors only realize normal profit in the long run, the monopolistically competitive price is higher (P_e), and each firm sells less (q_e).

*The failure of firms that have market power to produce that output which minimizes average total costs is known as the **excess capacity theorem**.*

This analysis suggests that monopolistic competition is both allocatively and productively inefficient. Product differentiation often entails little real value. *Allocative inefficiency* (failure to produce the mix of goods consumers want most) is present if price exceeds marginal social costs ($P > MSC$). Persuasive advertising (the use of slogans and imagery to stimulate psychological impulses to buy) is frequently the culprit.

Even though monopolistic competitors reap only normal long-run profits, monopolistic competition creates *productive inefficiency*: costs are not minimized. A pure competitor would produce for P_c per unit; advertising and

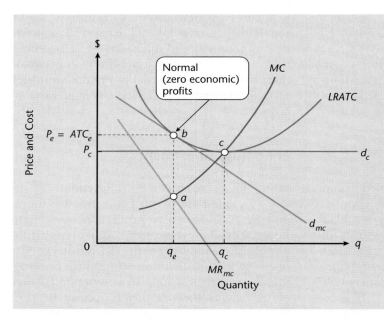

In the long run, entry and exit from the industry will prevent the monopolistically competitive firm from experiencing either economic profits or losses. Economic profits would be possible if the demand curve exceeded average total costs over any range of output; economic losses would be unavoidable if the average total cost was above demand at all output levels. Thus, competition yields an equilibrium where demand is just tangent to the long-run average total cost curve (point b) and the price equals long-run average total cost ($P = LRATC$). For pure competitors in the long run, $P = MR = MC = LRATC_{min}$, so there is economic efficiency. The long-run equilibrium for the monopolistically competitive firm is such that $P > MR$ and $MR = MC$. Even though $P = LRATC$, $P > MC$ suggests that there is allocative inefficiency. Moreover, average costs are not minimized, so there is productive inefficiency.

FIGURE 3   Monopolistic Competition: Long-Run Equilibrium and Efficiency

other costs of artificial differentiation drive up a monopolistic competitor's minimum to P_e, which is above the minimum average total cost in Figure 3. Monopolistic competition misallocates resources because costs, and thus prices, are higher and each firm's output is less.

Some economists contend that any minor inefficiency is more than offset by the greater range of choices available. Is product differentiation desirable because consumers gain a greater range of choice, or is most differentiation an artificial and worthless consequence of misleading advertising? Your answer to this question, which may easily vary from one industry to the next, indicates whether or not you think monopolistic competition provides an offset to its allocative and productive inefficiency. If you view product diversity as worthless and are unwilling to suffer from this type of inefficiency, one solution is to buy generic goods whenever possible.

OLIGOPOLY

Less competitive than monopolistic competition, oligopolies lie closer to monopolies in the spectrum of market structures.

Mutual Interdependence

If entry is restricted and a few firms dominate an industry, each firm recognizes that any action it takes will be countered by others. For example, Chrysler's extended warranties were quickly matched by many carmakers. Then Chrysler equipped all its cars with air bags in 1989, and other automakers briskly followed suit. Any hit TV show or software program quickly spawns clones. Just as musicians mimic other successful musicians, any successful competitive technique is rapidly imitated by other firms as they try to expand their own market shares.

A market shared by two firms is certainly an oligopoly, but would 10 or 20 sellers still be considered few? The answer is not clear-cut. What matters is whether a handful of large *interde-pendent* firms consciously dominate an industry. If firms' decisions anticipate rivals' strategies, the industry is concentrated and oligopolistic.

> *Mutual interdependence* exists when firms consider their rivals' reactions while adjusting prices, outputs, or product lines.

Consciousness of rivals' expected reactions to policy changes arises primarily from the fewness of firms in an oligopoly. Success often depends on assessing rivals' responses. Failure to predict rivals' reactions may result in bad news on the bottom line of an oligopolist's annual report.

The Origins of Oligopoly

Some oligopolies began as monopolies, gradually becoming oligopolistic after new firms struggled to become established. Others emerged out of a competitive environment after big firms vanquished or absorbed their rivals. The major causes of oligopoly are mergers and barriers to entry.

• **Economies of Scale** Technical efficiency sometimes requires enormous plants and massive equipment, which can act as major barriers to entry. Economies of scale cause an industry to gravitate into a natural monopoly when only a single firm of considerable size relative to market demand is able to produce at a low cost. An industry tends toward the oligopoly mold if economies of scale are less formidable.

An offshoot of technological advance in the last century was pressure for ever larger plants (e.g., steel, railroads). Substantial entry barriers may exist if new technology (e.g., robotics) mandates huge operations. Existing firms with established product lines may be able to activate new technologies so rapidly that new firms cannot get a toehold in the industry. It is possible, however, for large amounts of old capital to be an anchor that keeps established firms from keeping pace with upstarts that adopt the latest technology. For example, U.S. steel producers have had problems in recent decades because most American steel plants are ancient, while their competitors in Japan, Korea, and Germany operate modern equipment in newer facilities.

Recent technological advances have probably been relatively less favorable to huge firms than to smaller ones. For example, cable TV has diluted the oligopolistic power of major networks (ABC, CBS, and NBC), and recent entries in computers have gained on established giants like IBM. Some disadvantages of large firms may have been partially offset by computerization and improved communications, but in the 1980s and 1990s, U.S. employment growth has been most rapid in smaller firms. Increasing numbers of people now work at home, being linked to their employers primarily through computer modems, fax machines, and cellular phones. This trend probably favors small operations over large ones.

• **Strategic Barriers** Strategic barriers may also impede entry. For example, firms may pool research and development efforts while excluding outsiders, or frequently change models, or advertise excessively. Product differentiation is often a major entry barrier. Extravagant marketing may intimidate potential entrants with tight budgets; trying to combat established competitors' marketing outlays raises the minimum efficient scale of production for new entrants. Alternatively, an oligopoly may market numerous versions of a basic good (e.g., cereals, cigarettes, or over-the-counter drugs) or offer retailers huge discounts for preferential shelf space (Coke and Pepsi), leaving little space in retail outlets for potential rivals.

• **Regulatory Barriers** Another strategy to bar entry occurs when mature industries and their unions lobby to erect legal import quotas and tariff walls against foreign competition. Textiles, apparel, automobiles, agriculture, and steel are all industries with protection from foreign competition. Established industries often succeed in having laws tailored as hidden entry barriers.

This is an international game. For example, mandatory safety standards make it more costly to ship vehicles between countries. Curiously, some Japanese cars cannot be imported into the United States for reasons of safety, while most American autos must be retooled before export to meet Japanese safety standards.

• **Mergers** Oligopolies also arise through merger because combining two firms may be a less rocky path for growth than using retained earnings, selling new stock, or borrowing. However, recent *takeovers* by corporate raiders highlight certain pitfalls of merger as a path for growth: (*a*) top managers of takeover targets fear for their own job security, and (*b*) communities often become embroiled in merger battles when a target firm is a major employer that provides a town's economic lifeblood. Laws and court decisions making it harder for firms to close plants and aimed at inhibiting corporate takeovers have recently begun to appear on the landscape.

Oligopolistic Decision-Making

Interactions in extended families (parents, grandparents, aunts, uncles, siblings, cousins, in-laws, etc.) range from cooperation to violence, reflecting the vagaries of the personalities involved and coalitions among family members. Similar interdependence complicates analysis of oligopolies because how firms interact depends on cost structures, the number of competitors, the nature of outputs, and the personalities and perceptions of top managers.

Different models can be used to describe patterns of cooperation and rivalry when a few firms dominate an industry. If firms compete aggressively, their pricing and output may mimic that for competitive firms so that profits are negligible. Consequently, oligopolists often try to cooperate by boosting prices and limiting outputs; this benefits these firms at the expense of the general public. Such oligopolistic scheming is generally either *collusive* (formal conspiracies) or *noncollusive* (informal, but consciously cooperative).

One obvious collusive strategy is for oligopolists to try to unite and share both the market and monopoly profits. This is known as forming a *cartel*. Noncollusive pricing may emerge naturally if each firm acts cooperatively because each realizes that others will offset any strategy aimed at enlarging market share and profit.

In this section, we investigate only two classic oligopoly models. The kinked demand model is noncollusive, while cartels depend on collusion. More complex oligopolistic interactions are described in our sections on game theory and strategic behavior.

• **The Kinked Demand Curve**   Prices in highly concentrated industries were once thought to be unresponsive to changes in costs or demands. The *kinked demand curve model* of oligopoly pricing sought to explain stickiness of oligopolistic prices as a natural result of noncollusive behavior.[2]

> The **kinked demand curve model** assumes that firms maintain their current price if any one firm raises its price, but all firms match any price reduction by any single firm.

How these assumptions affect pricing strategy is shown in Figure 4. At point a, the price is currently P_e and q_e units of the good are sold by each firm in this oligopoly. Demand curve D_0 represents the highly elastic demand facing a firm if other firms ignored its price changes. If the firm were alone in lowering its price, its sales revenues would soar (a movement along D_0 to the right of q_e). If this firm were to raise its price and the others did not follow, however, its sales would plummet (movement along D_0 to the left of q_e) because consumers will shift to competitors' products.

If rivals match all price changes, however, demand curve D_1 reflects the firm's less elastic options. If it slashes prices and all other firms

do the same, the firm's sales grow only slightly. The firm's sales fall little if both it and its rivals boost prices. Along D_1 the firm loses few sales to other firms because their relative prices are constant. All firms merely gain or lose sales based on the elasticity of the industry's total demand. The respective marginal revenue curves for D_0 and D_1 are labeled MR_0 and MR_1.

This model's assumptions imply that only part of each curve is relevant: price cuts will be matched by rivals, but price hikes will not. Thus, the demand curve facing a firm is the thicker part of the D_0 curve for outputs less than q_e and the thicker portion of D_1 for outputs above q_e. Matching segments are emphasized similarly for marginal revenue curves. Note that this marginal revenue curve has a gap at output q_e between points b and c, corresponding to the kink in demand, hence the name "kinked demand curve."

This kink and the gap in the marginal revenue curve are critical. In Figure 4 profit maximizers produce where marginal revenue equals marginal cost, so q_e output is sold at price P_e as long as the marginal cost curve stays between MC_0 and MC_1. Thus, this model explains why prices might be sticky in oligopolistic industries even if costs change. Marginal cost can rise from point c to point b without affecting the price.

Kinked demand models seem reasonable, but critics point to some flaws. First, price rigidity may be no more frequent in oligopolies than other industries.[3] Concentrated industries appear to quickly pass along cost increases as they occur. After all, advertising, quality, and new product development may raise costs without significantly expanding market demand. If only one firm's profit is squeezed, it may be forced to maintain its current price. But if profits for all firms in an oligopoly shrink, all might follow a price hike; this yields a new kink at the higher price.

Second, kinked demand models fail to explain (a) why entry does not occur, (b) how oligopoly emerges, (c) how the equilibrium price,

---

[2]In his 1982 Nobel Prize acceptance address, George Stigler discouraged the use of kinked demand curves because of insufficient empirical support for sticky prices predicted by the model. Nevertheless, the kinked demand curve model helps highlight how oligopolistic interdependencies operate.

[3]This was the finding of George Stigler, reported in "The Kinky Oligopoly Demand Curve and Rigid Prices," *Journal of Political Economy*, October 1947, pp. 432–449.

FIGURE 4 Kinked Demand Curve Oligopoly Model

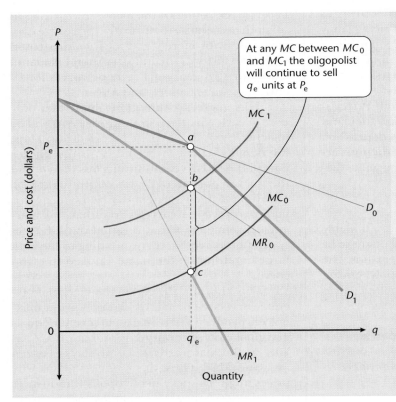

At any MC between MC_0 and MC_1 the oligopolist will continue to sell q_e units at P_e

If an oligopolist's competitors are likely to match any price reductions but ignore price increases, then the demand facing each firm is comparatively inelastic with respect to price cuts but is highly elastic in response to price hikes. Only the thicker portions of the demand and marginal revenue curves shown are relevent for such firms. Prices are sticky if oligopolistic firms face kinked demand curves. Even if costs change substantially, such firms will not alter their prices because they fear that none of their competitors will follow price hikes but all will match price cuts.

P_e is initially established, or (d) how prices change. These problems have caused the model to be used sparingly by researchers. Nevertheless, the kinked demand model has the virtue of simplicity in conveying the flavor of strategic business reactions and rivalry.

• **Cartels** Few Americans knew the term "cartel" before 1973 or 1974, when OPEC (Organization of Petroleum Exporting Countries), the best known cartel, became a household word.

> A **cartel** is an organization through which members jointly make decisions about prices and production.

Cartels usually require outright collusion, although in a sufficiently concentrated industry (two or three firms), tacit (unspoken) collusion is possible. Collusive price fixing for most manu-

factured products is illegal in the United States, but it is permitted in many international markets.

Cartels operate primarily in natural resource markets and, at various times, have controlled international markets for such basic materials as copper, tin, bauxite (aluminum ore), diamonds, chrome, phosphate, petroleum, coffee, and bananas. Most successful cartels are coordinated by the governments of major producing countries. Cartels formerly existed for sugar, rubber, nitrates, steel, radium, magnesium, and electric lights. Why do cartels seem to come and go? How do cartels set prices and production?

A successful cartel requires control over the bulk of output by a small group of cartel members. Cartels cannot maintain high prices if many fringe competitors are not members. A small group is more likely than a large group to agree about pricing and output strategies, because the members of any group have different goals and objectives.

The good must also be fairly homogeneous; numerous differentiated substitutes would require agreements on an extensive array of prices. After a cartel price is established, sales territories or production quotas must be set. Doing this for multiple goods and prices would be a formidable task. Mature technology is also a key for cartel success. If technology advances rapidly, constant changes in costs make it difficult for members to agree on prices. Moreover, the incentive to cheat on a cartel arrangement may be overwhelming if a firm discovers a new way to cut production costs.

Cartels will be more successful the less elastic the market demand for the good. A cartel can simultaneously raise prices and boost total revenue if its market demand curve is relatively price inelastic. Less elastic demand also lessens problems of excess capacity as prices are increased. Finally, some method is needed to monitor member compliance and prevent cheating.

• **Cartel Pricing Policies** A cartel's members jointly decide what price to charge and how much to sell. Most cartels try to produce and price as a monopolist would. This joint-profit maximization approach is diagrammed in Panel A of Figure 5. The cartel sets price at P_0 ($MR =$

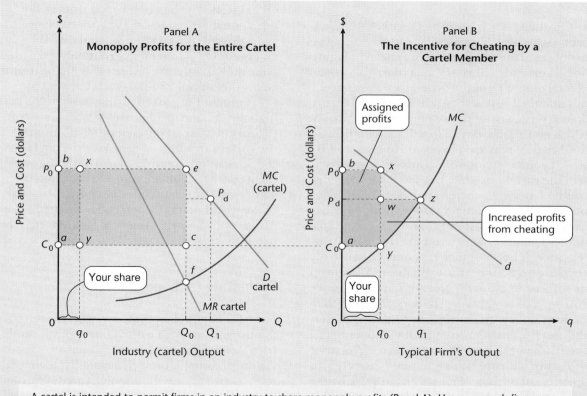

A cartel is intended to permit firms in an industry to share monopoly profits (Panel A). However, each firm can increase its own profits by offering secret price concessions to other firms' customers. Thus, there is a powerful incentive for cartel members to cheat, and cartels tend to be unstable. When governments help establish or perpetuate cartels, however, any cheating is easier to control, so moderately stable cartels may result. Note that Panel B represents an individual member; output (q_0) is a fraction of total output (Q_0), a fact reflected by the scales on the x axes. Since we imply that only one member is cheating, $0q_0 + Q_0 Q_1$ in Panel A equals $0q_1$ in Panel B, because $0q_0$ (Panel A) $= 0q_0$ (Panel B) and $Q_0 Q_1$ (Panel A) $= q_0 q_1$ (Panel B).

FIGURE 5   Cartels and the Incentive to Cheat

MC for the cartel at point f) and restricts its members' combined output to Q_0. This yields the largest possible total profit (the shaded area $abec$), but a crucial issue remains: sharing the cartel's output and profit among its members.

How to allocate production depends on the product and the market. In some cases, exclusive territories are assigned: each firm agrees to service only its own territory. Where this approach is unworkable, output quotas may be established for each firm. OPEC uses this approach; every member country agrees to limit its crude oil sales to the quota set by the cartel leadership. These agreements are, however, routinely broken.

• **Cheating** Each cartel member has strong incentives to cheat. Suppose that you are one of five members of the cartel shown in Panel A of Figure 5 and currently sell your equal share ($q_0 = Q_0/5$) of total output Q_0 at the cartel price P_0. Your firm's marginal cost is shown in Panel B of Figure 5. At q_0 output, your profits equal $abxy$ in Panel B, which also equals $abxy$ in Panel A after adjusting for differences in scale between Panels A and B.

If you persuade your competitors to maintain the cartel price (P_0) but secretly offer a discounted price P_d to selected customers, your profits will grow from pirating some of the other cartel members' customers and servicing some of the demand that is unmet at the higher cartel price. The marginal revenue to you from cheating exceeds your marginal cost. Your profits will rise because (*a*) you are not giving price cuts to your assigned customers, (*b*) your competitors do not give price cuts to the customers they retain, and (*c*) you can sell to more buyers: the customers who will not buy at a cartel price of P_0, but who are willing to pay P_d for $Q_1 - Q_0$ amounts of output. Your profits will rise by the area ywz in Panel B, which is the difference between your marginal cost of producing extra output $q_1 - q_0$ and the price P_d you receive for each extra unit of production.

• **Instability** Cheating on a cartel agreement can be profitable, but only if it is undetected. Cartels collapse if widespread cheating is un-

covered; most members will cut prices and behave in a fairly competitive fashion, with the result that the profits that originally motivated formation of the cartel vanish. The fact that undetected cheating offers the prospect of great profits is one of the greatest threats to the stability of a cartel. Cheating is only one hazard to cartel stability. There are incentives to try to retain customer loyalty by granting price concessions where sales to individual buyers are large and infrequent. Huge economies of scale and high fixed costs may create irresistible pressure to slash prices during periods of slack demand so that overhead costs can be spread across larger output and sales. For example, cracks in OPEC's effectiveness appeared during the international recession of 1981 to 1983; worldwide consumption shrank, and an oil glut emerged. OPEC members routinely exceeded their quotas, offering crude oil at big discounts below the official $34-per-barrel price.

Perhaps the greatest threat to a cartel is that high prices and profits will attract new competitors or spur development of substitutes for the cartel's products. From World War II into the 1970s, for example, the Brazilian government restricted coffee exports to bolster its price. The result? Brazilian coffee lost much of its share of the world market when coffee plantations in Africa and Central America were started by profit seekers.

Evaluating Oligopoly

How do oligopolies compare with more competitive industries? Firms in oligopolistic industries exercise considerable market power, yielding economic inefficiency similar to that described earlier for monopoly. In equilibrium, the marginal social benefit (price) of their products exceeds the marginal social cost. Compared with purely or even monopolistically competitive industries, output will tend to be lower and at higher prices to consumers.

If oligopoly arises from economies of scale, however, it is possible that consumers pay lower prices than they would were the market more competitive. Furthermore, if research and development (R&D) leading to technological advances requires massive outlays, small competitive firms may be unable to finance adequate innovation. Some economists suggest that society gains over the long run when short-run profits reaped by oligopolistic firms are plowed back into the development of newer and better products.

Evidence on the effects of oligopolies is mixed. Economies of scale are clearly responsible for the oligopolistic nature of some industries. In other instances, however, satisfactory economies of scale can be realized by smaller firms, and oligopoly is sustained by legal or strategic entry barriers. Finally, the evidence does not support the idea that large firms are especially responsible for new inventions and technological advances in our economy. If anything, it appears that the desire for increased market power has been the driving force behind the creation of most oligopolies.

Successful collusion requires a stable environment, but unless cartels have the legal support of government, stability is unlikely. When products are significantly differentiated, or resource costs are volatile, or demands are fickle, or entry is easy, or competitors are numerous, or technology advances rapidly, or policing a cartel agreement is excessively costly, then the quiet cooperation that oligopolists would like may be replaced by strategic behavior as intense as championship chess and as hostile as war.

GAME THEORY

Business leaders and, indeed, people in general, differ greatly in what they are able to accomplish with given amounts of resources. Consequently, small armies led by brilliant military strategists sometimes defeat large armies commanded by unimaginative generals. Skilled poker players may be consistent winners even if, on average, they are dealt poor cards, while mediocre players usually walk away from a game as losers despite average or better cards. And one firm may fail miserably, while an apparently similar firm prospers. Luck is sometimes a decisive factor, but even more frequently, correctly forecasting the behavior of your friends or rivals and then developing an effective strategy is the key to success or failure.

Economists who consider strategic behavior[4] stress that (a) a single firm's actions may affect industrial concentration, (b) dynamic decisions (decisions made over time) are invariably rational, and (c) differential information shapes firm behavior and market structure.

This first point leads to the idea that, either individually or jointly, firms often pursue strategies to bar entry into their industry; potential competition often determines incumbent firms' current pricing and output policies. For example, banks located close to each other may unite to oppose the chartering of a new bank, citing the low interest rates they charge, lack of need for another bank, their willingness and ability to accommodate all creditworthy applicants for loans, and their service to the community.

The second point is that firms, like all economic agents, make sequential rational decisions over time. What you will do in a particular situation depends on what you learned from experience after making decisions in similar situations. Firms consider the previous reactions of their rivals when planning a business strategy. Dynamic game theory models of rational decisions extend the boundaries of earlier theory.

The third point recognizes that bargaining parties may have different information about potential transactions that often affect incentives and decisions. For example, a firm's manager may know that a huge layoff is scheduled as soon as a contract is completed but may try to keep workers from looking for other jobs through false reassurances that the firm has a pending new contract to be fulfilled. This type of *knowledge asymmetry* is common. Traditional models that treat information as free and perfect, or that assume that all transactors share the same information base, typically yield different conclusions than models that recognize asymmetric information.

The 1994 Nobel Memorial Prize in Economics was awarded to John Nash, John

---

[4]G. Bonanno and D. Brandolini, *Industrial Structure in the New Industrial Economics* (Oxford, U.K.: Clarendon Press, 1990). See also Alexis Jacquemin, *The New Industrial Organization: Market Forces and Strategic Behavior* (Cambridge, MA: The MIT Press, 1987).

Harsanyi, and Reinhard Selten for their pioneering work in game theory and strategic bargaining.

Our next step is to describe game theory and look at a simple *prisoners' dilemma* model where both players move simultaneously. We then introduce a dynamic product standards game that illustrates the frequent benefits of being able to move first.

Strategy in Game Theory

The absence of overt or tacit collusion leads to rivalrous behavior that business leaders think of as competition. Pure competition is an impersonal process in which firms adjust outputs to a market-determined price. Oligopolists who compete in a noncooperative fashion have more weapons at their disposal, including adjustments of prices, outputs, product lines and capacity, advertising, and their rates of technological innovation. This diversity of possible strategies among oligopolists led to the development of game theory in 1944 by the mathematician John von Neumann and the economist Oskar Morgenstern.

> **Game theory** *is the study of strategic interactions among interdependent decision-makers.*

Game theory has been extended beyond oligopolistic behavior and is now applied to such areas as poker, courtship, athletic competition, collective bargaining, and national defense. A game requires pairing the costs and benefits of all possible strategies adopted by one player with all possible strategies adopted by an opponent. The payoff to each player depends on the strategies of other players, but players can select only their own strategy, not the strategies of other players. Then each set of possible outcomes is analyzed to ascertain an equilibrium, which occurs when every player optimizes, after adjusting for the likely strategies of other players.

Winners' gains exactly offset losses to losers in such *zero-sum games* as poker. Most examples of game theory in economics are *non-zero-sum games*. Gains typically exceed losses in *positive-*

sum games; exchange according to comparative advantage is an example. When two countries produce and trade products according to comparative advantage (described in Chapter 2), citizens of both countries gain as more total goods are consumed. Violence is generally a *negative-sum game*; victims of a mugging may suffer bodily damage in addition to monetary loss, while the mugger only gains the money. Net gains may be either positive or negative in some non-zero-sum games depending on the strategies of the players. For example, all firms in a market can profit if all charge the same high price, but if all charge a low price, all their profits are low.

Prisoners' Dilemma

A classic noncooperative game known as the *prisoners' dilemma* is often applied to cases of business rivalry, and helps explain why cartel arrangements break down. Suppose that two armed robbers (Able and Charley) are jailed separately and cannot communicate. Each is told that if neither confesses, both will serve a year in prison. If only one confesses and helps to convict the other, the squealer will go free while the silent party will serve ten years. If both confess, however, both will be sentenced to four-year terms.

Figure 6 shows a *payoff matrix* describing each robber's options and payoffs. For example, if both hold out (don't confess), each spends a year in jail $(-1, -1)$. Similarly, their terms are for four years $(-4, -4)$ if both confess. What should each player do?

Equilibrium in this prisoners' dilemma occurs if both players follow their dominant strategies. A strategy is dominant if, no matter what strategy your opponents select, your payoff is maximized (or a negative payoff is minimized).

> *A **dominant strategy** is a player's best response to any strategy other players might pick.*

Consider Able's dominant strategy. No matter which strategy Charley picks, Able gains by confessing, because he goes free if Charley holds out (compared to a year in jail if he, Able,

FIGURE 6   Payoff Matrix for the Prisoners' Dilemma

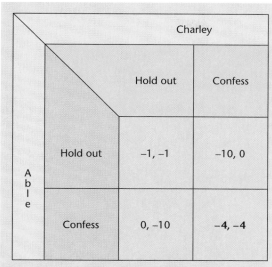

Sentences of Able, Charley

In this game, Able and Charley cannot communicate and face these payoffs. If one party confesses and the other does not, the confessor goes free and the other party spends 10 years in jail. If both are silent, they both go to jail for 1 year; if both confess, they each spend 4 years behind bars. The result is that both will confess and spend 4 years in jail – no other choice is a dominant strategy for either player. The dilemma results from the payoffs shown and the fact that they cannot communicate. In this case, confess-confess is a Nash equilibrium because "confess" is each player's dominant strategy.

holds out), while saving six years if Charley confesses (ten years – four years). In fact, both Able and Charley have dominant strategies: confess. Consequently, *confess-confess* is a dominant strategy equilibrium, because it is each player's dominant strategy. The dilemma facing prisoners is that they are unable to cooperate so that each gets the shorter sentence: one year each in the case of Able and Charley. Refuting the "honor among thieves" stereotype, almost all prisoners succumb and rat on their colleagues.

How does the prisoners' dilemma apply to oligopoly? Consider a cartel that sets output ceilings for each member. Every member will enjoy reasonable profit if no firm cheats by exceeding its quota, but a lone cheater will gain even more profit. If cheating is rampant (and it will be if players follow dominant strategies), all members' profits suffer. The power of the prisoners' dilemma game is reflected in the collapse of OPEC. The dilemma OPEC members faced ultimately brought down energy prices. The prisoners' dilemma model also applies in such areas as bids at an auction, the nuclear arms race, and strikes by unions when collective bargaining breaks down.

Cooperation in Game Theory

One obvious question is, "Why don't both prisoners agree not to confess? Then, each spends only a year in jail." Since one robber could potentially go free by confessing when the other doesn't, whether communication beforehand would matter would depend on whether agreements to hold out are binding. Although both might agree not to rat on the other, both eventually confess unless each can enforce their agreement on the other. If, however, agreements are binding, the results of the game differ.

> ***Cooperative games*** *permit players to make binding agreements, and players may form coalitions.* ***Noncooperative games*** *permit neither binding commitments nor coalitions.*

The prisoners' dilemma makes it clear that binding commitments change a game's equilibrium by changing the payoff matrix. For example, if Charley would murder Able if Able confessed and Able knows it, then Able's costs of confessing rise dramatically. This changes the payoffs, so the game is now different. How can players ensure that commitments are binding? Violence is a possibility, but agreements may also be made binding through such mechanisms as legally enforceable contracts, government regulations, or side payments (bribes) from one party to another.

Examples of cooperative games include (*a*) international trade; (*b*) collective bargaining, in which firms and unions bargain over employment conditions; and (*c*) plea bargaining between prosecutors and defense attorneys. Cooperative games break down, however, if a party can gain by violating what was supposed to be a binding agreement. The prisoners' dilemma, hostile corporate takeovers, or pure competition are all examples of noncooperative games.

Moving First

The sequence of moves is unimportant in a simple prisoners' dilemma. No matter which prisoner chooses first, Able always confesses because he knows that if he is silent, he will spend ten years in jail if Charley follows dominant strategy, rather than four years if he (Able) confesses. But the sequence of moves is important in many games. For example, a chess player who starts with the white pieces has the first move, an advantage over an equally talented player who uses the black pieces.

   Consider the case of IBM and Compaq in Figure 7. Both manufacturers must select either small (3.5″) or large (5.25″) disk drives as standard for their own computers, and both gain by using the same sizes. Their payoffs illustrate why making the initial decision, or *first move*, can be highly profitable for firms. If IBM (assume it goes first) installs 3.5″ disk drives, so will Compaq. If Compaq selected first, it would select 5.25″ drives and IBM would install large drives to maximize its profit (payoff). The first firm to introduce its standard clearly sets the industry standard. Each of these equilibria is also an example of a Nash equilibrium.[5]

> A **Nash equilibrium** is a strategy combination where no player has a net incentive to change unless other players change.

   In the final equilibrium, either both will use 3.5″ or both will use 5.25″ drives; each firm will avoid losses by sticking with its now profitable

---

[5]This section is based on Eric Rasmusen, *Games and Information: An Introduction to Game Theory* (Oxford, U.K.: Basil Blackwell, 1989).

FIGURE 7   The First Mover Advantage

Payoffs to (Compaq, IBM)

The ability to set industry standards for disk drives depends on the payoffs and the ability to move first. Both manufacturers gain if they select the same size drives for their computers. If IBM moves first it will select small drives, while Compaq will select large if it can move first. Both small-small and large-large are Nash equilibria – neither firm has an incentive to change after one equilibrium (set of strategies) has been selected. In this game, the outcome depends on which firm moves first.

strategy. In the prisoners' dilemma, there was only one Nash equilibrium (confess-confess), but there are two in this case. The final equilibrium turns on which player moves first. Many games have multiple Nash equilibria, and game theorists have developed sophisticated decision rules (beyond the scope of our inquiry) to determine which outcomes are most likely.

Dynamic Games

Real life games are seldom one-shot events like the prisoners' dilemma but involve a sequence of choices over time. Consider the prisoners' dilemma repeated for a number of periods. How can we determine what would be a player's best set of choices over time?[6]

Both Able and Charley would like to cooperate and be silent, but without the ability to enforce agreements, both would ultimately confess. Both also know that in the last repetition of the game, both confessed, so each might as well confess in the next to last period, and so on, until both confess in round one! Thus, both Able and Charley will serve $4 \times n$ (the number of periods in the game) years in jail.

Dynamic (repeated) games lead to more sophisticated strategies than do one-shot games. These more sophisticated strategies can result in higher overall payoffs over time (or less jail time in the prisoners' dilemma). Two possibilities for infinitely repeated games are a *grim* strategy and *tit for tat*.

• **Grim Strategy** The opposite of being first is to wait for an opponent's first move. Although most boxing trainers urge their boxers to be first, some boxers are natural counterpunchers who wait until their opponents make the first move. Similarly, many people may try to gather information in uncertain situations by letting the opponent move first. For example, people who are negotiating with a used car dealer often gain by refusing to answer the salesperson's question, "How much are you willing to pay for this car?," insisting instead that the dealership state a rock-bottom price as a starting point for haggling.

Following a noncommittal policy is known as a *grim strategy*.

> A **grim strategy** *entails refusal to commit to a position until the other player commits to a position.*

Since some move is required in the first round, a prisoner following a grim strategy will begin in a cooperative (silent) mode. Prisoners who stick to grim strategies remain silent until the other person confesses but then confess in each

subsequent round. If both steadfastly follow grim strategies, both receive minimum sentences. A grim strategy is at fault when two timid people, both of whom might like a deeper relationship, are each afraid to say, "I love you." Their romance is doomed if neither makes a first move.

• **Tit for Tat** Extensive experiments suggest that, in repetitive games, most people ultimately tailor their interactions to their opponents' previous choices. Instead of sticking to a strategy based on how your opponent first commits, you might begin in a cooperative mode, but then repeatedly echo whatever your opponent did in the previous period.

> A **tit-for-tat strategy** *begins cooperatively. Thereafter, in any period, tit for tat entails echoing what the opponent did in the previous period.*

Tit for tat in everyday life means responding in kind to people's behavior. Whether they treat you well or badly, you treat them in precisely the same fashion. Tit for tat may not result in a stable equilibrium. For example, if one player begins tit for tat cooperatively, but another starts in a noncooperative mode, the players will infinitely flip-flop for as long as the game continues.

Asymmetric Payoffs

Game theorists have explored ways to avoid the ratting disaster in a prisoners' dilemma. *Reputation building* convinces opponents that past behavior is a good predictor of future behavior. Since the past entails only sunk costs, why wouldn't each party in a repeated prisoners' dilemma let bygones be bygones and make the best decision in each round? Firms, governments, and individuals often nurture reputations for toughness or hard bargaining. *Asymmetric payoffs* between parties are one possible motive for reputation building.

> In an **asymmetric payoff**, *the payoffs from cooperation for at least one party are higher than the payoffs to some other players.*

---

[6]We ignore the effect of time on the value of outcomes; that is, a discount rate of zero is assumed. This simplification seldom affects the outcomes of games.

One example of asymmetric payoffs (Figure 8) involves consumers who decide to purchase only from sellers with clean environmental records. These consumers boycott polluters' products. The (0, 0) payoff connotes consumers' refusals to deal with sellers who have ever polluted.

A reputation as a nonpolluter will ensure long-run returns, so nonpollution as a strategy means that consumers will continue to purchase products. Buyers only pick boycott as a defensive action when sellers cheat (save on pollution control costs) and pollute. While pollute-boycott is a Nash equilibrium, it is not a dominant strategy (the only outcome) as confessing is in the prisoners' dilemma. Reputation can be important in many models, including, for example, an oligopolist that builds a reputation for matching price cuts of opponents but not price increases, or *entry deterrence* decisions, in which a potential new entrant must judge the willingness of incumbent firms to fight market entry.

STRATEGIC BEHAVIOR IN BUSINESS

Much of this part of the book has addressed traditional theories of industrial organization. Central to this conventional approach is the idea that the existing *market structure* (e.g., many or few firms) inevitably leads to specific types of *conduct* by firms (e.g., pricing policies or mergers), which, in turn, yield an industry's *performance* (e.g., its efficiency in allocating resources and the profitability of the firms in it). Recently, however, some economists have begun to question the rigidity of linkages between an industry's structure, its conduct, and its performance.

Contestable Markets

No firm with market power enjoys long-run economic profits unless competitors are precluded from entry. The theory of *contestable markets* pivots on the idea that competitive vigor is less related to the number of firms currently in an industry than to the ease of market access by other firms if prospects for economic profit exist.[7]

> ***Contestable markets theory*** *suggests that easy market entry can force even firms that are the sole current sellers of goods to produce the same output levels and set the same prices as would competitive firms.*

Conventional market structure analysis assumes that the number of firms in an industry determines the extent of market power and, thus, the prices charged for output. Contestable markets theory turns this assumption on its head, argu-

	Consumers	
Seller	**Buy**	**Boycott**
Nonpolluting	3, 3	0, 0
Pollute	4, –2	**0, 0**

Payoffs to (Sellers, Consumers)

Some consumers will boycott the outputs of polluting firms – the 0,0 payoff is the choice of consumers who boycott if the firm pollutes even once. Boycotts are strictly defensive – consumers prefer to buy. Pollute-boycott is one Nash equilibrium, but it is inferior to another possible equilibrium. If consumers and firms communicate, and if short-term effectiveness of increased pollution control is not excessively costly to the firm, the nonpollute-buy Nash equilibrium will be the most likely outcome; firms will cultivate reputations for "clean" production to maintain long-run viability.

FIGURE 8   An Asymmetric Payoff Matrix

[7]The theory of contestable markets is described in W. Baumol, J. Panzar, and R. Willig, *Contestable Markets and the Theory of Industry Structure* (New York: Harcourt Brace Jovanovich, 1982).

ing that the prices buyers are willing to pay for given amounts of goods determine the numbers of firms in an industry if outsiders are relatively free to enter the market. Even if a firm is the sole supplier in a market, that firm is forced to behave as if it were in competition if the market is "contestable." This theory identifies the absence of barriers to entry and exit as the motor that drives the allocative and productive efficiency of vigorous competition.

Critics argue that many significant barriers are natural (technological) and others result from the conscious strategies of incumbent firms. Building excess capacity is one way firms try to deter entry. Unused excess capacity may not harm existing rivals. If used, however, it may drive some incumbent firms to exit. One example would be building a new plant that raised industry output until all existing rivals suffered losses. Such a new plant (whether used or not) would clearly deter potential new entrants. Excess capacity might be one prong of a *predatory strategy*.

Predatory Behavior

Predation is intended to drive rivals from the market. Predatory tactics include low prices, expanded output, aggressive advertising, the cloning of rivals' products, rapid technological innovation, redesigns of existing products to make them incompatible with rivals' products, or monopolizing access to essential resources.

Predatory behavior *occurs when a firm attempts to drive rivals from the industry and deter entry.*

After rivals exit, the predator firm presumably will raise prices to levels consistent with its market power. Predation is often hard to distinguish from normal competition and, thus, is difficult to prosecute in the courts. Firms may use predation to expand market shares while lowering expected rates of profit to other incumbents or potential rivals.

Predatory behavior is forbidden by U.S. antitrust laws and has been discussed for a century; John D. Rockefeller (founder of the original Standard Oil Company) was charged with predatorially monopolizing oil. Standard acquired a 90% market share of the petroleum business between 1870 and 1899. (No proof was ever offered, however, that prices were raised following the demise of competitors. Standard Oil may simply have been the least cost producer of oil.)

Monopoly profits attract potential entrants. Consider the monopoly shown in Figure 9. A ri-

Predatory pricing occurs when one firm lowers price (to P_P in this case) to drive rivals from the industry. This incumbent firm is prepared to incur losses equal to the red-shaded area *facd* because of the expectation that, with a future monopoly price of P_m, future economic profits (area *ageb*) will more than recoup these losses.

FIGURE 9   Predatory Pricing

val's entry would raise industry output, so prices and profits would fall. During a period of predation, an incumbent intent on regaining its monopoly will, for example, set a predatory price of P_p and try to service industry demand Q_p while incurring losses equal to the shaded area *facd*. After its rival withdrew from the industry, the monopoly would reinstate price P_m.

Note that the predatory firm loses substantially more than its rival does; the incumbent must accommodate all demand, while its rival is free to cut output to cut its losses. Presumably, the predatory firm expects to more than offset this loss after reestablishing its monopoly position. One problem for this model is that boosting prices after rivals are driven from the market may be self-defeating because new entry would again be stimulated. Consequently, aggressive firms will try to adopt policies that deter entry or induce exit at the least cost. Some economists have concluded that firms will select strategies whose costs do not rise with market share, strategies that involve fixed expenditures. Examples include research and development (R&D) spending, institutional advertising intended to promote the brand name, and manipulation of regulatory policies.

Consider a predator and a rival who produce identical goods with constant marginal costs, selling output for price P_0 in Figure 10. Suppose the predator offers a superior innovation (demand rises to D_1) with higher cost, MC_1, which buyers value at P_1, where $P_1 > MC_1$. One strategy is to price the innovation below P_1 but above MC_1; the rival sells nothing because buyers value the superior product by more than the price difference ($ac > ab$). The rival eventually exits, enabling the predator to price monopolistically.

Predators may manipulate pricing, timing, and innovation in ways almost impossible to make illegal. Low prices, for example, may signal potential competitors that entry would be a mistake. Dominant firms can also redesign product lines with components incompatible with rival products.

Another tactic is product preannouncement. By announcing plans to enhance its product line soon, an incumbent may bar entry and make it harder for rivals to sell. Software is characterized by substantial demand-side economies, so users often become locked into a given program; a sufficiently large user base can block sales of rival products. New entrants find it hard to gain a niche in these markets, despite the obsolete nature of many programs and the advances made by other software developers. Microsoft, by previewing Windows 95

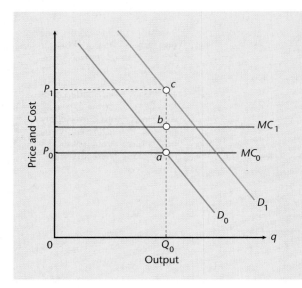

Some economists argue that predatory behavior can occur from product innovation or by redesigns that make existing products incompatible with rival products. In this instance, the dominant (predator) firm introduces a new or revised product that has market demand of D_1, and the product is valued by consumers at P_1. Since rivals' products are inferior, a price below P_1 will potentially drive rivals from the industry, enabling the predator to raise prices. Economists have developed game theory scenarios that use (*a*) rapid technological innovation, (*b*) duplicative products intended to absorb shelf space in stores and prevent access by competitors, and (*c*) advertising as predatory weapons. The major problem with these nonprice predatory models is our inability to distinguish predatory from normal competitive behavior.

FIGURE 10   Nonprice Behavior to Deter Entry

in September 1994 (to be released in 1995), may have used this strategy to mitigate the success of IBM's OS/2 Warp operating system released in October 1994.

Predatory pricing works especially well if a firm (or a cartel) has significant cost advantages. For example, Wal-Mart was convicted in an Arkansas court of predatorily pricing some prescription pharmaceuticals below cost, driving several local drug stores out of business.

Alternatively, OPEC, for example, set prices that significantly exceeded the marginal costs of oil for all OPEC member countries during the years 1974 to 1980. U.S. oil companies, assuming that oil prices would continue to climb, invested tremendous resources into developing relatively high-cost sources of domestic oil. When world oil prices plummeted in the early 1980s, many high-cost oil projects (e.g., conversion of oil shale in the Rocky Mountains) were abandoned, and U.S. oil companies absorbed enormous losses.

When oil prices subsequently rose, few oil companies even considered reopening their high-cost U.S. projects. They recognized that OPEC could simply cut prices to levels that would impose further losses on high-cost operations. Thus, even if the current price would support a project, it was not pursued because of the potential for OPEC to undercut the price. The dynamics of this semipredatory situation also fit under the umbrella of *limit pricing* models.

Limit Pricing

The vigor of competition is largely determined by outsiders' ability to enter a market. A classic model of strategic behavior is limit pricing. The *limit pricing model* postulates an incumbent firm and potential entrants with the same cost curves (this simplifies the analysis). Further, new entrants can expect to capture only that part of the market not satisfied by the incumbent. Thus, the new entrant believes that total industry output after entry will equal the incumbent's current output plus its own.

The average total cost curve and industry demand facing incumbents and potential entrants are shown in both panels of Figure 11. In Panel A, the incumbent has set a price of $8 and sells 200,000 units. If another firm enters, and the incumbent firm continues to produce 200,000 units, total output will rise and industry prices will fall. As Panel A shows, the demand curve facing a new entrant will be $D_{New\ Entrant}$ (the difference between industry demand and incumbent sales at each price), and the only equilibrium for this market will be 300,000 units sold at $5 (the incumbent sells 200,000 units and the entrant sells 100,000).

Consequently, as Panel B shows, the incumbent firm can deter entry by setting a price slightly below $8 because any potential entrant would expect losses upon entry. At any price below $8 (e.g., $7 in Panel B), the residual demand of the new entrants would be below their average total cost curves, imposing losses to the new entrants. Notice that the limit price is not the monopoly price, but an incumbent firm can earn long-run economic profits with this strategy.

Sunk Costs as Entry Barriers

Economists express several reservations about this version of a limit price. First, why should potential entrants believe an incumbent will maintain old output levels after entry of a competitor? Both firms might gain if industry output were reduced. Second, if both have the same cost curves, what distinguishes potential entrants from incumbents? And if entrants have superior financial resources, why couldn't they force an incumbent to exit?

Developments in game theory have added a rich array of strategic possibilities to limit pricing models. Our earlier discussion of game theory demonstrated that the ability to make binding commitments makes a threat more credible. Just how can an incumbent firm make its threat to continue producing 200,000 units seem credible?

One way to see the answer is to envision two armies trying to occupy an island connected by bridges from opposite sides, as shown in Figure 12. Each army will let the other have the island rather than fight. (Fighting is very costly!) If Army 1 immediately burns its bridge, Army 2

FIGURE 11 Limit Pricing

Panel A

If incumbent sets price at or above $8, new firms can enter and earn profits. . .

Panel B

but at a price of $7, new firms will incur losses and not enter.

Losses if new firms try to enter the market

$D_{Incumbent}$

ATC

$D_{New\ Entrant}$

Output (thousands)

Price and Costs

If economies of scale are important, firms in an industry following a limit pricing strategy would not realize profits over the long haul if prices were set to maximize short-run profits. New entrants, as shown in Panel A, might still be able to cover their average costs given the "residual" demands available to them. (The residual demand curve represents the demand remaining after existing firms have serviced their current customers.) If, as shown in Panel B, the industry establishes a price a bit below this level (less than $8), the residual demand available to potential entrants is inadequate to support a new firm.

will allow Army 1 to occupy the island since Army 1 now only has one option left: to fight. This analogy suggests than an incumbent firm can commit to a large output by acquiring considerable excess capacity, signaling to any potential rivals that huge increases in output will punish any firm rash enough to enter the market.

Economists have recently begun to explore the role that sunk costs play in entry decisions.[8] An irreversible capital decision may effectively deter entry when capital depreciates slowly and when no used market for such capital exists. This

capacity to rapidly expand output, plunging the industry into a price war, may deter entry.

A reconsideration of limit pricing models is based on information asymmetry.[9] Incumbents do not charge low prices because of high capacity; low prices are used to signal potential entrants that demand is insufficient to sustain another firm or that the incumbent has low production costs. Some firms use low prices to acquire market share to learn the intricacies of a

[8]John Sutton, "Endogenous Sunk Costs and Industrial Structure," in G. Bonanno and D. Brandolini, *Industrial Structure in the New Industrial Economics* (Oxford, U.K.: Clarendon Press, 1990), 22–37.

[9]P. Milgrom and J. Roberts, "Limit Pricing and Entry Under Incomplete Information: An Equilibrium Analysis," *Econometrica*, 1982, pp. 443–460. Also see P. Milgrom and J. Roberts, "Information Asymmetries, Strategic Behavior and Industrial Organization," *American Economic Review Papers and Proceedings*, 1987, pp. 184–193.

FIGURE 12   Burning Bridges and Sunk Costs

If Army 1 burns the bridge behind it, Army 2 will retreat from this island, because its leaders know that Army 1 now has no option but fighting, and Army 2 would rather give up the island than fight. (Hernando Cortez burned his ships after arriving in Mexico, intent on motivating his Conquistadors to conquer the Aztec empire.) Similarly, a firm heavily committed to an industry because of costly excess capacity may persuade potential rivals to look for greener pastures in other markets.

particular product line or business. This learning-by-doing approach can drive average costs down as experience is gained, providing firms with competitive advantages well into the future.

Accommodation

Some economists have concluded that the costs to firms of limit pricing or predation far outweigh *accommodation* of entry. Several game theory models indicate that nonprice techniques or buying rivals at premium prices avoid predation costs or allow greater profits than occur under limit pricing. Alternatively, entry may simply be accommodated without a fight, depending on the payoffs. For example, if a small, cheap hotel were built in a resort area, an existing resort might use the small hotel to handle overflow customers. The more the small hotel focused on specialized customers, the less threatening it would be to the resort and the greater the likelihood of accommodation.

Modern economists view prices, capacity, and innovation as weapons competitors use to acquire or maintain competitive advantages in specific markets. Competitive advantages extend beyond product markets, so this analysis is increasingly used to investigate resource markets and firms' financial decisions.

Most advocates of this newer approach recognize that conventional market structure analysis provides some valid insights into how firms behave. Instead of totally scrapping the traditional approach, their research is intended to refine its insights and to correct what they perceive as its errors in charting a direction for government policy, especially antitrust laws. In the next chapter, we consider government attempts to curb market power through either antitrust laws or direct regulation.

CHAPTER REVIEW: KEY POINTS

1. **Monopolistic competition** occurs when entry into an industry is easy and there are large numbers of suppliers of differentiated products. Demands facing monopolistic competitors are negatively sloped but still highly elastic.

2. **Product differentiation** refers to differences that consumers perceive between close substitutes, which can be real or imagined. These perceptions are created by such things as advertising and promotion or by differences in the actual goods. Product differentiation is intended to expand the demand for a firm's output and to make demand less elastic.

3. Monopolistically competitive firms produce and sell levels of output that equate marginal revenue and marginal cost. The price is then determined by demand. This is similar to monopoly, but the level of short-run profits derived from market power is generally lower, when numerous other firms sell close substitutes.

4. Entry is relatively easy in monopolistic competition, so profits fall to normal levels in the long run. However, equilibrium output will be less and prices will be higher under monopolistic competition than in competitive markets.

5. An **oligopoly** is an industry comprising a few sellers who recognize their *mutual interdependence*.

6. *Economies of scale* are among the causes of oligopolies. Some goods require substantial plants and equipment, so efficient production requires servicing a considerable portion of total industry demand. *Mergers* also facilitate the creation of oligopolies by joining competitors into single firms. Finally, oligopolies may exist because of other types of *entry barriers* that deter new firms from entering the industry.

7. There are numerous oligopoly models, but they break down into two major categories: **collusive** and **noncollusive**. The noncollusive **kinked demand curve** model assumes that if one firm raises its prices, other firms will ignore the increase, while other firms in the industry will match any price cuts. The result is a demand curve for the firm that is *kinked* at the current equilibrium price. This irregularity leads to a discontinuity (gap) in the marginal revenue curve. Consequently, changes in costs may not lead to changes in prices. This theory forecasts sticky prices in oligopolistic industries, but price stickiness is not confirmed empirically. Kinked demand curve models also fail to explain how the original equilibrium price is established, how prices change, or how entry by new rivals is deterred.

8. A **cartel** is an organization established to facilitate collusion by firms in an industry. It sets price and output ceilings for all its members. Cartels must be concentrated in the hands of a few firms that control significant proportions of an industry's output. The product needs to be reasonably homogeneous because agreements regarding heterogeneous products would be complex and difficult to enforce.

9. Cartels try to *maximize joint profits* and then allocate territories or industry output quotas. The stability of any cartel is threatened by the profits potentially available through undetected price cuts, or *cheating*.

10. Industry output will be less and prices will be higher under oligopoly than in pure or monopolistic competition.

11. **Strategic behavior** entails ascertaining what other people are likely to do in a specific situation and then following tactics that maximize your gain or minimize any harm to you.

12. **Game theory** is the study of strategic interactions among interdependent decision-makers, including those in oligopoly markets. *Payoff matrices* are constructed to examine how transactors minimize their losses or maximize their gains, given the most likely decisions of other players in a game.

13. In a **prisoners' dilemma**, the *dominant strategy* (a player's best response, no matter what strategy is pursued by the player's rivals) of each party results in inefficiency. *Cooperation* would allow both to gain, but lack of cooperation is the dominant strategy.

14. **Dynamic games** involve sequences of choices over time and result in a wide array of possible strategies. A *grim strategy* entails cooperating until your opponent fails to do so and then clobbering the opponent in every subsequent round. A *tit-for-tat strategy* responds in kind to whatever your opponent did in the previous round.

15. **Predatory behavior** involves activity by firms to drive rivals from the market or to deter entry. Once rivals disappear, predators can set prices consistent with their market power. A problem with this model is that reentry would normally occur when the high price is resumed, unless the predator firm has significant cost advantages so that potential rivals expect reentry to prompt lower prices once again.

17. **Limit pricing** is a strategy intended to inhibit market entry. Limit pricing techniques include low prices that make it unprofitable for new entrants or that signal that the market is insufficient for a new entrant. Low prices also convey the message that the incumbent firm is a low-cost (efficient) firm.

QUESTIONS FOR THOUGHT AND DISCUSSION

1. One oligopoly model suggests that firms will attempt to capture as large a market share as possible by locating in the center of the market. This model suggests that people will not be served if they want substantially different products than the majority of people want. According to the developer of this model, Harold Hotelling, this accounts for such things as parallel programming by television networks, the middle-of-the-road images sought by politicians, the homogeneity of apple cider, the similarities between Protestant churches, and the phenomenon of four gas stations at the corners of busy intersections, among other things. How do you think his view that there is too little product differentiation stacks up against the view that monopolistic competition causes too much artificial product differentiation?

2. Name some of the conditions that would make it easier for a cartel to be successful. How likely are these conditions to be met? How might the firms comprising an oligopoly coordinate their activities without forming an illegal cartel? (Note: cartels are illegal under American Antitrust law discussed in the next chapter.)

3. In the 1950s, teenagers sometimes played a game called "chicken." Drivers initially half a mile apart would drive their cars at each other at high speed. The first driver who turned to avoid a crash was castigated as a "chicken." What do you think was the most common result of this game? How does this game resemble the nuclear weapons race that once plagued relationships between the United States and the former Soviet Union?

4. What evidence might you look for to discover whether some concentrated industry was contestable and vulnerable to competition?

5. Most capitalistic economies have an infinite horizon, with the possible exception of Hong Kong, which will be returned to China in 1997. Does the prisoners' dilemma explain Hong Kong's current brain drain as skilled labor emigrates to other nations? What would you try to do if you owned a trading firm in Hong Kong with mobile assets?

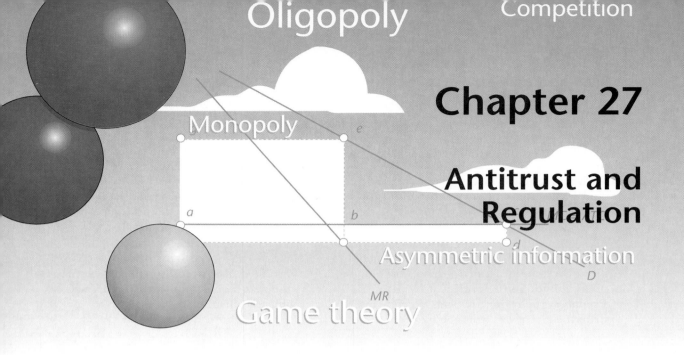

Chapter 27

Antitrust and Regulation

People of the same trade seldom meet together, even for merriment and diversion, but the conversation ends in a conspiracy against the public, or in some contrivance to raise prices.

Adam Smith, *The Wealth of Nations*, 1776

Political pressures for corrective action arise from the inefficiencies and perceived inequities of excessive market power—topics described in the preceding three chapters. Government's options to combat abuses of market power include (*a*) antitrust laws, (*b*) regulation, and (*c*) nationalization (governmental operation of important industries). However, critics charge that public officials often abuse market power at least as much as private firms and are too often legally protected from competition. Dismay with how nationalized industries operate has unleashed a broad trend toward *privatization*; state enterprises are being converted into private firms from China to Russia to Mexico to South Africa. Our focus in this chapter is government's primary policy options: antitrust laws and regulation.

THE STRUCTURE–CONDUCT–PERFORMANCE PARADIGM

Traditional market structure analysis (described in the previous three chapters) appears deceptively simple: begin by ascertaining the structure of the industry in which a firm operates. (Is it competitive, monopolistic, monopolistically competitive, or oligopolistic?) This *market structure* is assumed to rigidly determine each firm's *conduct* (output decisions and pricing behavior), which yields an industry's overall *performance* (e.g., its efficiency and profitability). This approach, called the *structure-conduct-performance* paradigm (*S-C-P* theory), is outlined in Figure 1.

Traditional S-C-P theory dictates three steps in analyzing an industry. First, it emphasizes properly categorizing an industry's market structure according to (*a*) the number of active competitors, (*b*) barriers to entry and exit, and (*c*) the extent of product differentiation. Second, conventional models conclude that certain pricing and output decisions (conduct) predictably arise from market power or its absence. (Sparse competition, barriers to entry, or product het-

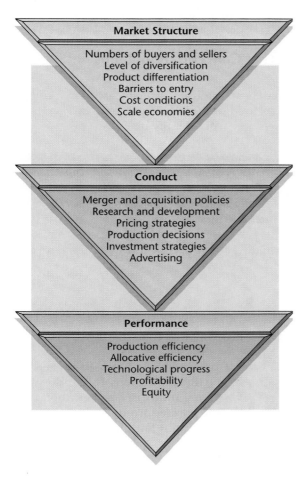

FIGURE 1 Market Structure

Market Structure

Numbers of buyers and sellers
Level of diversification
Product differentiation
Barriers to entry
Cost conditions
Scale economies

Conduct

Merger and acquisition policies
Research and development
Pricing strategies
Production decisions
Investment strategies
Advertising

Performance

Production efficiency
Allocative efficiency
Technological progress
Profitability
Equity

This traditional structure-conduct-performance model of industrial organization is increasingly challenged by analysts who charge that it ignores (a) too many factors influencing behavior that are specific to an industry or its dominant firms, and (b) asymmetries of information that put transactors on different negotiating stances than would occur if all information were shared. This S-C-P approach is also indicted for overemphasis on the number of firms in an industry and scant attention to dynamic aspects of competition, including ease of entry and exit.

erogeneity create market power.) Finally, this theory suggests that the equilibrium price of any imperfectly competitive firm invariably exceeds marginal social cost; too little of the good is produced, creating allocative and productive inefficiencies.

Movement along the continuum of market structures from monopoly toward pure competition appears to yield more efficient resource allocations. Consequently, the structure-conduct-performance approach suggests that government policy to cure problems of industrial organization is straightforward: outlaw monopolies or near monopolies where possible, while tightly regulating market power that arises from economies of scale.

Thus, the S-C-P approach indicates that competition is the most efficient structure for an industry, and unregulated monopoly, the least. According to the theory of contestable markets, however, business tactics are not determined by structure alone. But antitrust policy is intended to diffuse market power, as is much of the economic regulation of business. Before we consider antitrust and regulatory policies in depth, we will examine the current structure of U.S. industry and discuss some implications for the economic performance of the hundreds of thousands of firms in our economy.

MEASURING MARKET POWER

Dynamics within specific industries vary widely, but on average, according to the S-C-P paradigm, performance verges on that of a monopoly as an industry's biggest firms gain larger market shares. *Size* is often equated with *market power*, but big industries may contain many huge firms, none of which has much market power. For example, the U.S. oil industry contains almost 17,000 oil producing companies, of which a dozen or so generate sales exceeding $1 billion. Even Exxon, the largest oil company, markets only about 11% of U.S. petroleum sales, or less than 5% of world production. Firms often achieve size because of economies of scale, superior technology, or managerial talent, but competition among giants appears increasingly vigorous.

The Lerner Index of Monopoly Power

The structure-conduct-performance approach has led to attempts to quantitatively estimate the market power concentrated in the hands of a few firms in an industry. Our analysis of monopoly suggests that market power creates a gap between marginal cost and price. This led economist Abba Lerner to propose the **Lerner index of monopoly power (LMP)**, which is

$$LMP = \frac{price - marginal\ cost}{price}$$

The LMP is zero for pure competitors because price equals marginal cost. Marginal cost and price in Figure 2 are both $30 at competitive output q_c (point a); LMP = (30 – 30)/30 = 0. The exercise of market power increases the Lerner index because the equilibrium gap between price and marginal cost rises. Monopoly output and price in Figure 2 are q_m and $50, respectively (point b), so LMP = (50 – 30)/50 = 0.40. While a rising LMP may reflect growing market power, the marginal cost data required to calculate this index are not generally available, re-

quiring economists to turn to other measures of monopoly power.

Market Concentration Ratios

Data are sporadically available (with a five-year delay) to compute industry concentration ratios, which may help identify market power.

> ***Concentration ratios*** *are the percentage of total industry sales, assets, employment, value added, or output accounted for by an industry's biggest four or eight firms, although any number of firms could be used.*

Formally, four-firm concentration ratios are defined as

$$CR_4 = \sum_{i=1}^{4} S_i$$

where S_i is the market share of the ith firm and $S_1 > S_2 > S_3 > S_4$.

Table 1 presents recent four-firm concentration ratios (CRs) for various U.S. industries in 1987. Changing industry concentration can generally be interpreted from data for changes in concentration ratios and for the number of firms in the industry. For example, market power among firms producing electronic computing equipment has fallen sharply. Not only has its concentration ratio fallen, but the computer industry had five times as many firms in 1987 as in 1967. This undoubtedly reflects technological advances that are still taking place in computers.

The Herfindahl-Hirschman Index

Traditional theory suggests that concentrated industries are more likely to sustain economic profits. The Federal Trade Commission has concluded, however, that a single firm's market share is quite often the best predictor of its profits, regardless of concentration in the industry as a whole. The Federal Trade Commission sug-

The Lerner Index of Monopoly Power (LMP) is equal to *(P - MC)/P*. The LMP for a pure competitor (output q_c at point a) would equal 0, or [(30 - 30)/30 = 0]. But LMP > 0 for any firm with market power. For example, the monopolist in this figure selling q_m units at $50 would have an LMP of 0.40, or [(50 - 30)/50 = 0.40].

FIGURE 2   The Lerner Index of Monopoly Power (LMP)

TABLE 1 Concentration Ratios: Share of Value of Shipments Accounted for by the 4, 8, 20, and 50 Largest Companies in Each Manufacturing Group, 1987

SIC code	Major Group	Companies (numbers)	Total Sales (million dollars)	Value of Shipments (Sales) Concentration Ratios Percent Accounted for by 4 largest Companies	8 largest Companies	20 largest Companies	50 largest Companies	Herfindahl-Hirschman Index for 50 largest Companies
	All Industries	310,341	2,475,901.0	9	12	18	27	36
20	Food and kindred products	15,692	329,725.4	11	18	32	47	68
21	Tobacco products	98	20,757.1	82	94	99	99	2,345
22	Textile mill products	4,982	62,786.4	15	25	38	52	113
23	Apparel and other textile products	21,301	84,242.6	10	14	20	29	36
24	Lumber and wood products	32,014	69,746.7	11	16	23	31	45
25	Furniture and Fixtures	10,775	37,461.0	10	15	26	36	47
26	Paper and allied products	4,215	108,988.7	18	30	52	68	172
27	Printing and publishing	57,376	136,195.6	7	13	23	34	34
28	Chemical and allied products	8,313	229,546.1	14	21	34	53	97
29	Petroleum and coal products	1,320	130,414.0	30	49	72	69	375
30	Rubber and miscellaneous plastics products	12,149	86,634.3	9	13	21	31	46
31	Leather and leather products	1,965	9,082.4	13	21	36	55	95
32	Stone, clay and glass products	12,682	61,476.6	11	18	30	41	62
33	Primary metal industries	5,400	120,248.2	17	26	41	55	121
34	Fabricated metal products	32,470	147,366.1	9	13	18	26	33
35	Industrial machinery and equipment	48,900	217,669.9	13	17	26	37	70
36	Electronic and other electric equipment	13,523	171,286.4	19	27	39	52	129
37	Transportation equipment	9,158	332,935.7	52	64	76	85	1,044
38	Instruments and related products	8,962	107,324.8	19	28	44	60	150
39	Miscellaneous manufacturing industries	16,062	32,012.0	6	10	16	25	19

Source: U.S. Department of Commerce, Bureau of the Census, 1987 Census of Manufacturers, *Concentration Ratios in Manufacturing*, 1992.

gests that, on the average, each 10% rise in market share yields a 2% increase in profitability.

This evidence shifted the attention of the Justice Department's Antitrust Division to the **Herfindahl-Hirschman Index** (HHI), which estimates concentration by emphasizing the firms with the largest market shares, as measured by the following formula:

$$HHI = \sum_{i=1}^{n} s_i^2$$

where S_i is the market share of the ith firm. The HHI places the greatest weight on the largest firms by squaring market shares.

Notice the stress on an industry's biggest firms squaring mark. The lone firm in a monopolized industry would have a market share $S_1 = 100\%$, and the HHI $= 100^2 = 10,000$. If, on the other hand, 100 firms each control 1% of sales, then the HHI would be 100. Thus, the HHI falls as the number of firms in an industry rises or as firms' sizes become more uniform. Consider a market where four firms have 20% each and 20 firms have 1% each, and a second market where one firm has 77% and 23 firms each have 1%. Four-firm concentration ratios in both industries would be 80%, but the HHI paints a different picture; 1,620 and 5,952, respectively. HHIs capture differences in concentration hidden by concentration ratios alone. Note that HHIs are also listed back in Table 1.

Difficulties in Categorizing Industries

A major deficiency of all measures of concentration is ambiguity in identifying an industry's boundaries. Firms are supposedly classified into industry groups whose products are easily substituted by consumers, but distinguishing between close and distant substitutes is difficult. One solution might be to examine the cross elasticities of demand between products. Unfortunately, the data required to estimate cross elasticities are rarely available.

Alone, even information on substitutability by consumers might be inadequate to define an industry; production substitutability must be considered as well. Markets are *contestable* if a number of firms use roughly the same types of plant and equipment to manufacture different products and if switching from one product line to another is easy. For example, the technology for photocopying might allow Xerox to shift easily into computer production, or such camera makers as Kodak or Polaroid might easily shift into manufacturing copying machines. Defendants in antitrust cases increasingly use contestability to rebut legal charges. Firms that can easily cross industry boundaries should be grouped as potential competitors.

Although Standard Industry Classification (SIC) codes attempt to classify industries, many SIC codes are overly inclusive. For example, patented products with no close substitutes may be lumped with goods that are only roughly similar. For years, photocopying machines (dominated by Xerox) were categorized with other copying equipment. Are ditto machines, mimeographs, and printing presses really close substitutes for Xerox equipment?

Perhaps the major defects of SIC codes for domestic markets is their handling of imports. Concentration is overstated if imports of close substitutes are ignored. Even recognizing such difficulties, however, concentration ratios and HHIs provide crude snapshots of shared market power.

MERGERS AND MARKET POWER

Concentration increases when major competitors merge, whether measured by concentration ratios or a Herfindahl-Hirschman Index. The economic inefficiency associated with market power gained through merger may be socially undesirable if the firms are among the leaders of a concentrated industry. On the other hand, merger of small firms into one viable competitor in a concentrated industry can be socially beneficial if the merged firm is more efficient and more able to compete with established giants. Ideally, public policy would prohibit all harmful mergers, but only those that are harmful.

One obvious motive for a merger is to eliminate a competitor and consolidate market power. A second motive may be to exploit cost savings arising from economies of information, marketing, advertising, production, or financing, or to pool complementary technologies or patents. For example, most large book publishers have recently sought alliances with multimedia firms.

Major Merger Movements

Four major waves of mergers have swept our economy in the last century. Each torrent of mergers arose out of the economic conditions and the legal climate of the times.

• **The First Wave: Horizontal Mergers**   John D. Rockefeller, Andrew Carnegie, Cornelius Vanderbilt, J. P. Morgan, and other tycoons engineered much of the first wave of mergers around the turn of the last century, aggressively trying to consolidate oil, steel, railroads, sugar, finance, and other industries. Corporate holding companies known as *trusts* permitted these men to gain control of vast amounts of capital. History is filled with colorful stories about their chicanery in trying to acquire the assets of competitors.

The vast majority of mergers and acquisitions during this period were *horizontal mergers*; absorbing direct competitors can be a shortcut in attaining market dominance. Such giants as U.S. Steel, General Electric, and Standard Oil were formed. Abuse of the resulting market power was apparently routine. Perceived offenses by these major companies fomented a general outcry for restrictions on trusts, leading to the passage of the Sherman Antitrust Act in 1890, which attempted to forbid major horizontal mergers. Ironically, the courts continued to allow numerous horizontal mergers until loopholes were tightened by the Clayton Act of 1914.

• **The Second Wave: Vertical Mergers**   A second irony is that the second merger wave followed passage of the Clayton Act, ending only after the Great Depression wilted corporate profits. Acquisitions during this period were primarily *vertical*, which entails gaining control over various stages of production from raw materials to finished manufacturing. Firms desiring to grow via merger were channeled toward vertical mergers, because horizontal mergers were squelched by bans on "monopolization or attempts to monopolize." Horizontal mergers during this period were relatively trivial compared to the boom of monopolization that occurred during the first great merger wave.

• **The Third Wave: Conglomerates**   The stock market crash of 1929 vaporized prospects for promotional profits, and slack demands for output during the Great Depression curtailed

mergers based on economies of scale. Figure 3 shows that the merger rate fell drastically and remained low until the third big wave appeared late in the 1950s, again, paradoxically, on the heels of major antitrust legislation, the Celler-Kefauver Antimerger Act of 1950. This third wave lasted into the early 1970s. The bulk of the mergers during this period were *conglomerate mergers*, which combine firms from unrelated industries. For example, DuPont's (a chemical company) 1982 acquisition of Conoco Oil was a conglomerate merger.

• **The Fourth Wave: Corporate Raiders**   Merger activity was subdued through the 1970s, but the perception that the Reagan administration was sympathetic to corporate raiders renewed interest in mergers. Antitrust guidelines announced in 1982 fostered conglomerate mergers and also allowed horizontal or vertical mergers that would have been challenged by earlier administrations. During the 1980s over 31,000 mergers and acquisitions with a total value of $1.34 trillion were consummated. Table 2 lists the largest U.S. mergers in history.

The late 1980s and early 1990s witnessed both mergers and their flip side, *voluntary restructuring*—the jettisoning of bad acquisitions. Nearly 30% of all acquisition activity in the 1980s (roughly 10,000 deals) involved selloffs of corporate assets. Today, many firms are scaling back to do what they do best.

Is Concentration Increasing?

The evidence on whether industrial concentration is increasing is mixed. Most economists cite figures like those in Table 1 to argue that, on average, domestic concentration ratios for most industries changed little over the last two decades. Relative stability of our industrial structure is supported by data for concentration ratios. Note that although the number of firms in many industries has increased, many giant firms have apparently retained their market shares.

Critics often argue that market power within particular industries is less important than the in-

FIGURE 3 Waves of Mergers and Acquisitions over the Past Century

Sources: Data for 1895—1968 from F.M. Scherer, *Industrial Market Structure and Economic Performance* (Chicago: Rand McNally & Company, 1980), p. 120. Scherer cites the following sources for the data: Ralph L. Nelson, *Merger Movements in American Industry, 1895—1956* (Princeton: Princeton University Press, 1959), p. 37; U.S. House of Representatives, Select Committee on Small Business, Staff Report, *Mergers and Superconcentration* (Washington, D.C., 1962), pp. 10, 266; and U.Í. Federal Trade Commission, *Current Trends in Merger Activity, 1968* (Washington, D.C., March 1969). Data for 1963—1984 from *Economic Report of the President*, 1985. Data for 1986—87 from *Mergers and Acquisitions*, Vol. 22, April 1988.

creasing concentration of economic power accomplished primarily through mergers. Conglomerate mergers have allowed the largest American firms to steadily acquire a growing share of all U.S. manufacturing assets over the past half century. Figure 4 indicates that the top 200 firms (0.1% of all U.S. manufacturing corporations) control three-quarters of all manufacturing assets, and this percentage has crept up slowly over the last half-century as manufacturing has declined in importance in our economy.

Is Big Bad?

Major debates also surround the issue of whether bigness and badness are synonymous in the case of a conglomerate. Virtually all giant firms operate in several industries, and nearly all operate across national boundaries. Thus, although concentration within specific industries may be relatively stable, giant multinationals are increasingly important players on the international scene. In addition to their huge shares of manufacturing assets (capital), these giants also account for growing proportions of employment, sales, and profits.

Giant conglomerates may not have as much market power as big firms that operate in only one industry, but they do have substantial economic clout and may exercise their power in the political arena. Multinational firms are of special concern because of their interests in international politics, but even giants are not immune to market forces.

Regulatory barriers to entry or restrictions on imports facilitate concentration, but significant economies of scale can make concentration

TABLE 2 The Largest Mergers and Acquisitions in U.S. History

Firm Acquired	Acquiring Firm	$Billion	Year
1. RJR–Nabisco	Kohlbert, Kravis & Roberts	24.9	1988
2. Warner Communications	Time	13.9	1989
3. Gulf Oil	Chevron	13.3	1984
4. Kraft	Philip Morris	11.5	1988
5. Squibb	Bristol Meyers	11.5	1989
6. Getty Oil	Texaco	10.1	1984
7. Conoco	DuPont	8.0	1981
8. Standard Oil of Ohio	British Petroleum	7.9	1987*
9. Federated Dept. Stores	Campeau	7.4	1988
10. Marathon Oil	USX (U.S. Steel)	6.5	1981
11. Contel	GTE	6.2	1990
12. Beatrice Food	Kohlberg, Kravis & Roberts	6.2	1986
13. RCA	General Electric	6.2	1986
14. Superior Oil	Mobil Oil	5.7	1984
15. Pillsbury	Grand Metropolitan	5.7	1988
16. General Foods	Philip Morris	5.6	1986
17. Safeway Stores	Kohlberg, Kravis & Roberts	5.3	1986
18. Farmers Groups	BAT Industries	5.2	1988
19. Southern Pacific	Santa Fe RR	5.2	1983
20. Southland	JT Acquisitions	5.1	1987

Source: *Fortune*, various issues, 1980–1991.
*For 45% percent share that British Petroleum did not already own.

unavoidable in some industries. High capital costs erect substantial entry barriers if profits are uncertain. Where economies of scale are substantial, high fixed costs combined with low marginal costs cause average costs to fall across a wide range of output. In the short run, average variable costs may reach their minimum (the shutdown point) at extremely low prices and high output levels. These economies of scale incite cutthroat competition during periods of slack demand. A price war often shrinks the number of firms in an industry when losers go bankrupt. Price wars also generate pressures for collusive price-fixing agreements or for cries from the industry for government bailouts and protective regulations and controls.

Some defenders of modern corporate giantism argue that size is a tribute to the success of entrepreneurs and managers in serving consumers' needs in exceptionally efficient ways. Large corporations may also be a consequence of capital-intensive and highly complex modern technology. Other defenders contend that large enterprises are necessary to comply with the maze of federal, state, and local regulations governing modern business practice. Small firms have difficulty acquiring the capital needed to sustain these endeavors.

Public Policies Toward Business

Government policies about industrial structure have been directed along two broad lines. The first, regulation, has existed since the adoption of the U.S. Constitution: article I, section 8 (the "Commerce Clause") gives Congress the power "to regulate Commerce with foreign Nations, and among the several States. . . ." Any federal law might be considered regulation, but the term usually entails some government body setting rules for a market about prices, outputs, or operating and managerial procedures. In such

FIGURE 4 Proportion of Manufacturing Assets Held by the 100 and 200 Largest U.S. Corporations, 1950—1993

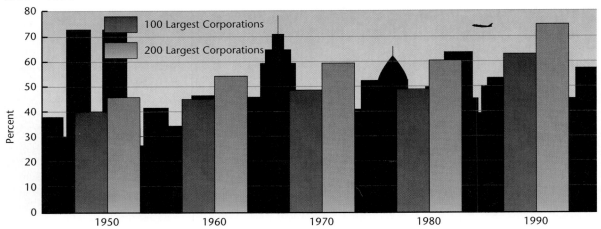

Source: *Statistical Abstract of the United States,* 1993.

situations, government substitutes regulation for the forces of competition.

Antitrust is the second broad approach to dealing with industry structure. Several laws have amended the Sherman Antitrust Act of 1890. The antitrust approach ideally restructures industry to conform closely to the assumptions of pure competition. Mergers that would lead to unwarranted concentration would be prohibited. Where this is not possible, law and regulation ideally force an industry's performance to mimic the competitive ideal.

ANTITRUST POLICY

The previous three chapters set the stage for a discussion of antitrust policies. The rationale for vigorous antitrust actions to counter the effects of excessive market power is fairly simple. Pure competitors adjust output until the last unit sold provides benefits just equal to production costs. That is, marginal social benefits equal marginal social costs ($MSB = MSC$), so that the market operates in an economically efficient manner.

When firms exercise market power, the price of the last unit sold tends to exceed both its cost and the competitive price. Economic inefficiency is a problem when the price (marginal social benefit) charged by a firm exceeds marginal social cost. Therefore, competitive markets tend to be more allocatively efficient than those controlled by firms with market power. Moreover, consistent monopoly profit may result in concentrations of wealth and economic power that are incompatible with most social and political ideas of equity.

This analysis may seem straightforward, but as the preceding analysis suggested, major disagreements exist about whether large firms or noncompetitive strategies are inherently bad. One legal point of view is that monopoly is bad per se. The idea of a benevolent monopoly is discarded in favor of the argument that abuse invariably flows from substantial market power. A natural conclusion from this point of view is to stamp out market power through forced *divestiture*, the breaking up of large corporations into numerous independent small companies.

For example, in the early 1980s, in a settlement of a long-standing antitrust case, AT&T was forced to divest itself of all its local operating companies. At the same time, the government dropped its massive antitrust case against IBM. Today, AT&T and all of the regional Baby Bells are earning record profits, but IBM is on its knees. Some economists argue that the vigorous competition injected into the telephone market has made each spinoff of the old AT&T stronger and more competitive. The opposite, they argue, led to a bloated, complacent, and vulnerable IBM.

Public policy has generally presumed that market power should be curtailed. This presumption is based primarily on theories presented in the last few chapters. The stated goals of antitrust policy are to outlaw monopolization of markets and to prohibit specific misconduct associated with market power. We need a brief overview of our major antitrust laws before evaluating the success of antitrust in the United States.

The Antitrust Laws

The thrust of each of the four major U.S. antitrust laws is to limit market power or to prohibit undesirable business practices. All were enacted in response to perceived business abuses, beginning with allegations against Standard Oil and the railroads late in the last century. In response to strong political support for a constitutional amendment to outlaw monopolies, the Sherman Antitrust Act was enacted in 1890.

• **The Sherman Act**   The two major provisions of the Sherman Antitrust Act (as subsequently revised) are

> **Section 1:** *Every contract, combination in the form of trust or otherwise, or conspiracy, in restraint of trade or commerce among the several States, or with foreign nations, is hereby declared to be illegal.*

> **Section 2:** *Every person who shall monopolize, or attempt to monopolize, or combine or conspire with any other person or persons, to monopolize any part of the trade or commerce . . . shall be deemed guilty of a felony. . . .*

Both sections then go on to spell out penalties for violation of the law. The act stipulates that corporations may be fined up to $1 million; individuals may be fined up to $100,000, or they can be imprisoned for up to three years, or both, at the discretion of the court.

Section 2 has been especially hard to enforce. Identifying a specific market to prove monopolization requires scrutiny of both the market (and its geographic characteristics?) and the nature of the product (substitutability from the vantage points of both consumers and other potential producers). Once such questions are settled, the court must determine what constitutes a monopoly. Must a firm control 100% of a market to be guilty of monopolization? Should a 90% market share be illegal? 80%? 70%?

Section 2 also prohibits attempts to monopolize. What conduct is intended to produce a monopoly? It seems strange from today's perspective, but early court cases often prosecuted union strikers as violators of the Sherman Act. These cases and other ambiguities in the Sherman Act led to passage of more specific antitrust laws.

• **The Clayton Act**   The Sherman Act was amended by the Clayton Act in 1914, which spelled out particular offenses more precisely and introduced into law the phrase "where the effect [of various practices] may be to substantially lessen competition or tend to create a monopoly."

According to the Clayton Act,

> **Section 2:** *It shall be unlawful for any person engaged in commerce . . . to discriminate in price between different purchasers of commodities of like grade and quality. . . .*

The courts have enumerated many specific standards for enforcement of the price discrimination section (section 2). For example, price discrimination is permitted if a defendant can show that it does not reduce competition (e.g., discounts for students and senior citizens to movies and supersaver fares on airlines). Moreover, price discrimination is permitted for intangible properties or services (e.g., medical care) or where differences in costs (e.g., transportation) account for different prices.

• **The Federal Trade Commission Act**   The Clayton Act was reinforced by the Federal Trade Commission (FTC) Act of 1914, which created a commission, the FTC, to investigate and challenge any "unfair methods of competition. . . , and unfair or deceptive acts or practices in or affecting commerce." The act did not define "unfair practices," leaving the interpretation of the statute and the determination of what practices are unfair or deceptive up to the FTC, subject to review by the courts. The courts have severely restricted the scope of the FTC. Curtailing business fraud and such deceptive practices as false and misleading advertising has been one area where it has been reasonably effective. The FTC's vigor in challenging perceived unfair business practices ebbs and flows with the political tides, but the FTC remains a watchdog guarding consumer interests.

• **The Robinson-Patman Act** Section 2 of the Clayton Act was amended by the Robinson-Patman Act in 1936 in the midst of the Great Depression. This act was designed to limit price discrimination in the form of special promotional allowances. Discounts were permitted only where justified by differences in costs or when introduced as good faith efforts to meet competition. Because quantity discounts have been attacked under the Robinson-Patman Act, many economists criticize the law as a protector of small firms from competition rather than a guarantor of competition. Huge differences exist between protect-

ing competitors from failure and promoting competition. The basic contents of the four major acts are summarized in Table 3.

Exemptions from Antitrust Laws

The Sherman Antitrust Act made every "combination . . . in restraint of trade" illegal. As this act was interpreted by the courts, political pressures and economic realities arose that have virtually exempted several important groups from antitrust prosecution, including agricultural cooperatives, sports organizations, industry export associations, insurance companies, labor unions, and closely regulated industries.

National policy favors the right of workers to unionize and bargain collectively. The Sherman Antitrust Act, however, was originally used to stifle union activity. Sections 6 and 20 of the Clayton Act largely exempted collective bargaining by workers from antitrust actions.

Curiously, the courts have almost totally exempted professional baseball and have provided specialized exemptions for other amateur and professional sports organizations from antitrust actions on the strange doctrine that they are not

TABLE 3   Summary of Antitrust Laws

Statute and Year of Enactment	Major Provisions
Sherman Antitrust Act (1890)	Prohibits contracts, combinations, and conspiracies in restraint of trade, and forbids monopolization or attempts to monopolize.
Clayton Act (1914)	Prohibits certain forms of price discrimination, contracts that prevent buyers from dealing with sellers' competitors, acquisition of one corporation's shares by another if the effect will be to substantially lessen competition, and interlocking directorates between competing corporations.
Federal Trade Commission Act (1914)	Established the FTC to investigate unfair and deceptive business practices.
Robinson-Patman Act (1936)	Amended the Clayton Act (section 2) to prohibit discounts and other special price concessions. Price discrimination is permissible only where it is 1. based on differences in cost. 2. a good faith effort to meet competition. 3. based on differences in marketability of product.

in interstate commerce because sporting events are "entertainment, not business." Thus, the NFL, NBA, NCAA, AAU, and a variety of other associations in our multibillion-dollar sports industry are reasonably free to collude against their employees, potentially competitive organizations, or each other. These exemptions are, however, increasingly under attack in the courts and Congress.

Normally, the more tightly regulated an industry is, the greater is its exemption from antitrust laws. For example, public utilities and cable television monopolies are seldom challenged, because their rights to monopolize are recognized and their rate structures are regulated. Because regulatory agencies presumably express the public interest, exemption from antitrust laws seems sensible to allow the public to realize any gains from cooperation among regulated firms.

ANTITRUST IN PRACTICE

Current antitrust enforcement is based on the Sherman Act, as amended, but sections 1 and 2 are rather broadly written. What are the meanings of "monopolize" and "attempt to monopolize"? What behavior is permitted, and what is prohibited? And how will oligopolists be treated? How will firms know if they can merge without the threat of prosecution?

Monopolization and Market Power

A literal interpretation of section 1 of the Sherman Act would ban most major transactions. The Sherman Act is vague about what is legal and what is not, leaving that decision to the courts. Nor does section 2 clearly define "monopoly." To make matters worse, the courts historically have been a bit schizophrenic in interpreting the Sherman Act.

• **The Rule of Reason** In two early cases involving Standard Oil and the American Tobacco Company, the Supreme Court ruled that trusts

(monopolies) could either be "good" or "bad" and suggested that the Sherman Act only outlaws "bad" restraints on trade.

> The **rule of reason** approach attempted to distinguish good trusts from bad trusts, using such criteria as whether they set their prices to yield supernormal profits or attempted to run competitors out of business.

Both Standard Oil and American Tobacco were judged "bad" trusts and were subjected to divestiture: they were split into several firms.

Certain anticompetitive practices (refusals to deal and tie-in sales, defined in next section) were permitted if a firm proved that its conduct fit logically with other practices permitted by law. Whether a practice was held to be "reasonable" depended on such things as the percentage of the market affected, expected duration of the practice, and the relative strengths of the parties involved.

• **The Per Se Doctrine** In the 1945 case of *U.S. v. Aluminum Co. of America* (*Alcoa*), the Supreme Court applied the *per se doctrine* to interpret antitrust laws. The Court reasoned that the Sherman Act does not condone "good" trusts and forbid "bad" trusts; it prohibits all monopolization and restraints on trade. Whether a firm abused its power or obtained its monopoly by reasonable methods was irrelevant. The existence of monopoly was sufficient. In this case, Alcoa was forced to sell some assets to other producers to enhance competition in the aluminum industry.

> The **per se doctrine** asserts that certain contracts or combinations seem inherently so contrary to competition that they are illegal per se.

The government needs only to show that such agreements were reached; whether competition has been harmed is immaterial. Per se violations include (*a*) price-fixing agreements, (*b*) schemes to split customers into territories, (*c*) agreements between competitors to refuse to deal with certain suppliers or customers, and (d) tie-in sales, where a dominant seller forces a buyer to purchase peripheral products in order to purchase the desired good.

After the per se approach was adopted, the courts also began trying to address what constitutes a monopoly by looking at such factors as the number, size, and strength of the firms in the market; the nature of the technology; and any economies of scale.

Merger Policy

Some antitrust efforts are intended to squelch market power in its infancy. Strong antimerger policies were the rule during the 1960s and 1970s but were relaxed in the 1980s. The Justice Department currently requires premerger notification by firms. This forces big firms to wait 30 to 50 days after notifying the government before consummating any merger. During the waiting period, the Department of Justice can evaluate the legality of proposed mergers, and it can immediately sue to block mergers it opposes. This approach helps avoid the mess often encountered in the dissolution of a company that has already been merged.

The Justice Department under the Reagan administration announced merger guidelines to improve the predictability of federal merger policy. After noting that numerical standards must be tempered by judgment, the department categorized mergers according to (a) the level of the Herfindahl-Hirschman index in the industry and (b) the change in the index that would occur because of the merger. The Justice Department also considers such factors as (a) whether one of the merging firms is a dominant leader in the industry, (b) ease of entry into the market, and (c) ease and profitability of collusion.

Horizontal mergers that might have generated economies of scale or other benefits were once prevented by rigid enforcement of antimerger laws. More recently, the Department of Justice has taken the position that, "although they sometimes harm competition, mergers generally play an important role in a free en-

terprise economy. They can penalize ineffective management and facilitate the efficient flow of investment capital and the redeployment of existing productive assets." While challenging competitively harmful mergers, the department sought to avoid unnecessary interference with that larger universe of mergers that are either competitively beneficial or neutral.[1]

But new high-tech industries and rapidly changing technologies are making old-style merger evaluation difficult. In the past, gauging a merger's competitive impact when, for example, two cigarette or appliance manufacturers merged was relatively straightforward. Concentration ratios and Herfindahl-Hirschman calculations are decidedly more problematic when mergers involve developing technologies and emerging markets.

Trends in Antitrust

Market structures often differ so much from the model of pure competition that some economists and policymakers advocate vigorous antitrust initiatives. Antitrust laws have been on the books for more than a century, however, with little perceptible effect on our industrial structure. Indeed, as we showed in Figure 3, huge merger waves closely followed every major antitrust act. A few corporate giants of past years have been dismembered by antitrust actions (Standard Oil, American Tobacco, AT&T, and Alcoa), but most (GM, DuPont, General Electric, IBM, etc.) have escaped the chopping block of antitrust largely intact.

Most antitrust litigation is initiated by small companies with complaints about low prices charged by competitors. For example, local pharmacies in Arkansas successfully sued Wal-Mart in 1994. Most antitrust battles turn on narrow interpretations of legal technicalities, with the courts frequently trying to protect competitors instead of competition. Nobel Prize winner, George Stigler, after reviewing international data, found little evidence that market concen-

---

[1]Merger guidelines issued by the U.S. Department of Justice, 14 June 1982.

BIOGRAPHY

George Stigler: The Changing View of Regulation

The politicians who invited George Stigler (1911–1993) to a White House dinner after he was awarded a Nobel Prize in 1982 were dismayed when Stigler, during a press conference, described the economy as in a depression. His friends were not surprised. Stigler's record of advocating laissez-faire policies is matched by a reputation for being a straight shooter who calls them as he sees them.

The University of Chicago's "school" of economic thought has been known for its opposition to activist government policies throughout this century. Tall and lanky George Stigler shared stewardship over this tradition with his short, fellow Nobel Prize–winning friend, Milton Friedman, for almost half a century. Friedman is best known for his work in macroeconomics and monetary theory, while Stigler has been a pioneer in the study of modern microeconomics.

Stigler's research has been testimony to the notion that genius often consists of an ability to see old ideas in new ways. He received his Ph.D. in 1938 from the University of Chicago and spent most of his career there, with oc-casional side tours to Minnesota, Columbia, and the London School of Economics. He has extended the frontiers of economic study in many areas, including industrial organization, the economics of information, and the sources and effects of government regulation. A hallmark of his work has been rigorous hypothesis testing to ascertain which economic theories seem supported by real-world data.

Stigler fundamentally disagrees with those who view the market system as inherently defective because few markets conform to the assumptions of pure or perfect competition. Stigler has found that industries characterized by monopolistic competition or oligopoly act much more competitively, with respect to price, than most models of imperfect competition predict. In particular, he rejects the sticky prices assumed in the kinked demand curve model. Empirical work that found no relationship between price stickiness and market structure led him to urge the abandonment of kinked demand models.

Stigler was among the first to consider information as an economic good that consumers and firms alike pursue until its marginal benefits and marginal costs are equal. Stigler's seminal 1961 article fueled an explosion of research effort that helped launch the economics of information as a major subdiscipline of economics. He was also the first major modern economist to perceive that regulation is often instigated by the regulated. His extended studies of antitrust policies and regulation have made him extremely skeptical that much government economic activity is in the public interest.

Another focus of his interest has been the sociology of economics as a field of study. His essays on the development of economic theory and methodology are a staple of economists' reading lists. When Stigler challenged his grandson to name Adam Smith's best friend, the youngster is said to have responded, "You, Grandpa." (Most likely correct answer: David Hume.) Nevertheless, the boy's answer accurately reflected George Stigler's lasting enthusiasm for the ideas of the eighteenth-century Scottish moral philosopher and economist.

---

tration differs between countries that have strong antitrust laws and those that do not.

The magnitude of antitrust action depends primarily on the political climate. Teddy Roosevelt gained a reputation as a "trustbuster" at the turn of the century, but attacking market power has been on a back burner in most recent administrations. However, there are some signs that the Clinton administration is more of a stickler about certain mergers that would probably have gone unchallenged a decade ago. Nevertheless, the reasons for vigorous antitrust policies may have diminished over time. Our economy is increasingly open, so foreign producers make most of our domestic markets highly competitive. Indeed, many economists now contend that the most effective antitrust laws are free trade agreements that smash barriers protecting corporate giants from foreign competition.

The Antitrust Division under President Clinton is attempting to balance a position that leans toward traditional populist trustbusting while recognizing that mergers in the healthcare, defense, and some high-tech industries may be beneficial. The continuing trend toward ever greater concentration of assets in the hands of the few hundred largest American companies, however, is very discomforting to people disturbed by the potential political aspects of concentrations of economic power. They consider it unfortunate that antitrust policies leave conglomerate mergers relatively untouched. We now turn to regulation, the second government option to deal with concentrated economic power.

REGULATION

That life grows ever more complex is a cliché. Complex societies are also regulated societies. At one time, you could count on your fingers the regulations governing most American industries. Today, you might need to count all the appendages on all the residents of a medium-sized city.

Business regulation is a massive task for government regulators, for the firms they oversee, and for a cast of thousands of lawyers and consultants from both sides. Concerns about pollution and the environment, discrimination, consumer and occupational safety and health, and a host of other social, economic, and political problems all contribute to the rising tide of business regulation. But business activity is not alone in being regulated. Consumer protection laws usually affect firms most directly, but regulations also limit consumers' options. Laws mandate school attendance until your midteens, prohibit self-prescription of penicillin or pot, require stopping at red lights, forbid walking your dog without a leash and a scoop, and so forth and so on.

Observers influenced by laissez-faire thinking charge that misguided regulation tramples our freedom and suffocates American business. Instead of providing a chicken for every pot, government's finger is in every pie. Excessive regulation is blamed for reducing supplies and driving up production costs. This group blames unnecessary red tape that stifles productivity for recent lags in our international competitiveness. Critics of the laissez-faire approach, on the other hand, advocate expanded regulation because they view competitive forces as weak. Moreover, they view unregulated markets as rife with misinformation, inequity, and instability.

In this section, we will examine (a) the nature and extent of regulation, (b) an economic justification for some regulations, and (c) a brief evaluation of regulation.

The Growth of Government Regulation

Victims of a raw deal often react with, "There ought to be a law." This is one reason why hundreds of federal, state, and local agencies now regulate business. Public utilities, for example, were engulfed by a wave of regulation that swept through most states during 1912 through 1917. Figure 5 surveys the growth in the number of major federal regulatory agencies but only hints at regulatory growth in the 1960s and 1970s. Each of these regulators rapidly acquired more and more personnel throughout this period. State and local governments joined in the rush to regulate; the *Federal Register*, which lists new federal regulations, mushroomed from a few hundred pages annually to thousands of pages each month.

The Great Depression shattered support for moderate laissez-faire capitalism like a blow from a sledgehammer. Many new regulations in the 1930s were intended to smooth disruptions from business cycles and increased government controls over pricing and other practices in banking, public utilities, securities transactions, and labor contracts; farmers were supported, mortgage loans were guaranteed, and our welfare system was expanded.

FIGURE 5   Numbers of Major New Federal Regulatory Agencies

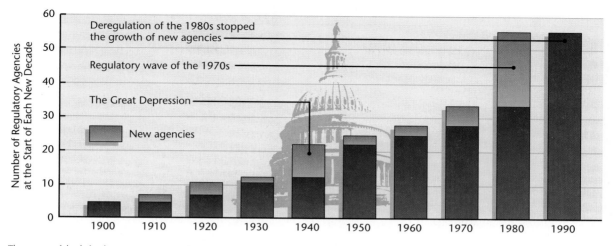

The power of the federal government to regulate commerce is established in the Constitution. This power was exercised little before the 1930s, but the 1960s and 1970s were an era of regulatory growth.

The 1940s and 1950s were dormant decades for regulation, but a new wave erupted in the 1960s and 1970s. The doubling of new regulatory agencies shown in Figure 5 paradoxically occurred during a period when real disposable personal income rose by over 40%—one of the more prosperous periods in our history. What stimulated this regulatory burst? One theory of regulatory growth is that sophisticated technology makes the simple rules of the past obsolete. The prominent social scientist, Kenneth Boulding (1912–1993), argued that just as an astronaut in a space capsule must follow a far stricter regimen than a cowboy on the prairie, so, too, must a space-age economy be controlled more tightly than the simpler economy of an earlier era.

Is it possible to reverse the upward trend of regulation? Perhaps, but most proposals to deregulate business encounter fierce opposition. It seems paradoxical that, on a case-by-case basis, most individual regulations are fervently supported by large groups of people (including executives in regulated industries), despite public opinion polls suggesting that most people perceive regulation to be excessive. Surprisingly, regulated industries spearhead much of the resistance to deregulation. For example, con-

sumer groups and the liquor industry joined to vigorously resist proposals to thoroughly deregulate alcoholic beverage production. The support of regulated firms for regulation is evidence that it often acts as a barrier to entry against potential competitors.

Before we can judge whether our society is overregulated, we need a sense of how profoundly regulation shapes the U.S. economy. The IRS, FAA, FTC, FDA, EPA, and SEC are only part of the alphabet soup of well-known federal regulators. Table 4 lists some major federal regulatory agencies and describes their functions.

THEORIES OF REGULATION

Some people view market systems as rife with fraud, discrimination, dangerous working conditions, overpaid executives, and other maladies. In previous chapters, you saw how monopoly power, strategic behavior, and imperfect information may cause economic inefficiency. Regulation is one possible remedy for some of these market failures. The three main theories of regulation are (*a*) public interest, (*b*) industry interest, and (*c*) public choice.

TABLE 4   Some Major Federal Regulatory Agencies

Agency	Areas of Concern and Major Regulatory Function(s)
Product Markets	
Antitrust Division of the Justice Dept.	Promotes competition by enforcing federal antitrust laws.
Federal Communications Commission	Regulates broadcasting, telephone, and other communication services.
Federal Maritime Commission	Regulates foreign and domestic ocean commerce.
Federal Trade Commission	Protects consumers from unfair trade practices, false advertising and overly restrictive licensing.
Interstate Commerce Commission	Regulates interstate surface transportation, including trucking, railroads, and water carriers.
Labor Markets	
Equal Employment Opportunity Commission	Investigates complaints of discrimination based on race, religion, sex, or age in hiring, promotion, firing, wages, testing, and all other conditions of employment.
National Labor Relations Board	Regulates and enforces collective bargaining agreements between companies and unions, and certifies elections of bargaining representatives.
Financial Markets	
Commodity Futures Trading Commission	Regulates futures trading on eleven U.S. futures exchanges.
Comptroller of the Currency	Supervises operations of over 4,700 national banks.
Federal Deposit Insurance Corporation	Examines, insures, and regulates banks.
Federal Home Loan Bank Board	Supervises and regulates savings institutions that specialize in financing of residential real estate.
Federal Reserve Board	Regulates banks and all financial institutions that offer draftable (checking) accounts.
Securities & Exchange Commission	Regulates all public securities markets to promote full disclosure.
Energy and Environment	
Corps of Engineers	Oversees construction along rivers, harbors, and waterways.
Environmental Protection Agency	Develops and enforces environmental standards for air, water, toxic waste, and noise.
Department of Energy	Oversees national energy policy.
Nuclear Regulatory Commission	Licenses and regulates civilian nuclear power facilities to protect public health and safety and the environment.
Health and Safety	
Consumer Product Safety Commission	Requires reporting of product defects and redesign and labeling to reduce unreasonable risks of injury from consumer products.
Federal Aviation Administration	Regulates aviation industry.
Food & Drug Administration	Protects against impure and unsafe foods, drugs, cosmetics, and other potential hazards.
Occupational Safety & Health Administration	Regulates workplace safety and health conditions.
National Highway Traffic Safety Administration	Regulates motor vehicle safety through safety standards, uniform national speed limit, and protects consumers from vehicles with reset odometers.

Source: U.S. Office of the Federal Register, *The United States Government Manual 1993–1994.*

The Public Interest Theory of Business Regulation

The public interest theory of regulation centers on potential market failure; examples include problems emerging from excessive monopoly power, asymmetric information, strategic behavior, and externalities. The idea that imperfect information adversely affects market solutions is used most to rationalize laws regulating consumer protection and labor markets.

> The **public interest theory of regulation** is the idea that people need protection from business abuses or other market failures. This theory assumes that regulation serves the public's interest by restricting harmful business activities.

Using antitrust policy to lessen monopoly power by breaking up huge firms may inefficiently raise costs. If the minimum efficient scale of production (*MES*) is high relative to market demand, then at most only a few firms can achieve the lowest possible production costs.

Government provides highways, but most other natural monopolies (industries with such extensive economies of scale that only one firm can operate efficiently) are privately owned (e.g., electricity generation, railroads, cable TV, and the distribution of natural gas).

• **Natural Monopolies** Requiring competition among small firms inefficiently denies the public the lower costs and prices available through economies of scale. But how can policymakers prevent natural monopolies from limiting output and raising prices?

The dilemma a natural monopoly poses is diagrammed in Figure 6, which shows how economies of scale may allow only one firm to operate efficiently. If two firms each produced Q_m average total costs for each firm would be AC_m. Since $2Q_m = Q_0$, limited demand drops the prices (P_0 at point *a*) these two firms could charge below AC_m. Having two or more firms is unsustainable, because each would lose money until only one survived. If consumers bought

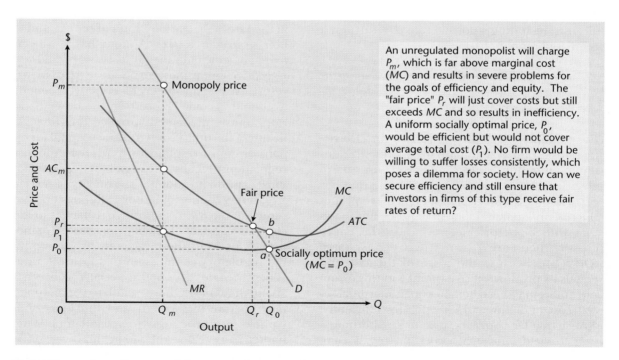

An unregulated monopolist will charge P_m, which is far above marginal cost (*MC*) and results in severe problems for the goals of efficiency and equity. The "fair price" P_r will just cover costs but still exceeds *MC* and so results in inefficiency. A uniform socially optimal price, P_0, would be efficient but would not cover average total cost (P_1). No firm would be willing to suffer losses consistently, which poses a dilemma for society. How can we secure efficiency and still ensure that investors in firms of this type receive fair rates of return?

FIGURE 6   The Dilemma of the Natural Monopolist

from an unregulated monopoly, however, output would be limited to Q_m and sold at price P_m possibly exceeding the price associated with some competition. Price exceeds marginal cost in this monopoly solution, so there is economic inefficiency.

The public interest is served best if only one firm exploits these economies of scale and then prices appropriately. A regulated uniform price restricted to a "fair price," P_r, would yield normal profits, and consumers would pay less than the unregulated price P_m. However, socially optimal pricing and output requires that $P = MC$. Could a regulator reasonably require that the last unit Q_0 be sold at price P_0 so that efficiency is realized? If a price of P_0 is charged for each unit of output, the firm's revenue equals area OP_0aQ_0 which is inadequate to cover total costs equaling area OP_1bQ_0. No firm would be willing to stay in business if regulations forced such constant losses. Fortunately, a form of price discrimination provides a way out of this quandary.

• **Block Pricing**   Block pricing techniques can efficiently generate sufficient revenues to cover all costs, including a normal rate of return for a regulated monopolist.

*In a **block pricing** system the more you use of the regulated monopolist's product, the lower the price for extra units.*

For example, block pricing is used for electricity rates. You pay a hookup fee and then a minimum monthly charge. As you use more electricity, your total bill rises but the rate per extra kilowatt-hour declines. Figure 7 replicates the cost and demand data in Figure 6 but shows that with block pricing, revenues (the entire crosshatched area) can cover costs (area (OP_2eQ_0)). Because the price of the last unit equals its production cost (point b in this example), marginal social benefit equals marginal social cost and this market operates efficiently. Notice that block pricing uses price discrimination to yield efficiency. Block pricing is commonly used for public utilities (natural gas, electricity, and telephone services), for railroads

and other forms of regulated transportation, and for pipelines.

• **Rate Making in Practice**   In practice, utility regulation is a complex process that absorbs the efforts of thousands of people. *Rate making* (setting utility prices) requires the agency to select a base period for calculations (usually the preceding year). All the firm's operating costs, including depreciation and taxes, are then summed. A reasonable accounting profit, derived by multiplying the rate base by the percentage rate of profit allowed, is added to operating costs.

*The **rate base** is the value of capital to which the profit rate applies. The regulator ideally adjusts **rate structures** so that total revenue covers all operating costs, including a normal profit.*

Desires for minimal rates must be weighed against allowing normal rates of return. This trade-off invariably provokes disagreements about (*a*) appropriate values for items allowed in the rate base, (*b*) "fair" rates of return, and (*c*) how to structure rates. A utility has few incentives for efficiency if all "costs" are allowed. Executive limousines, corporate retreats in lush resort areas, and generous employee benefits would all become "costs." On the other hand, rates must adequately protect the financial health of the utility for it to attract capital for expansion or to respond to new environmental regulations. Finally, the regulatory commission must continually monitor the quality of service.

Utility commissions normally target rates of return in the 8% to 12% range. Changes in fuel costs, demand, or efficiency can cause sustained deviations from the target return, prompting the regulatory commission to adjust the rates. When people are not especially concerned about their utility bills, regulated monopolies may operate inefficiently and still squeeze favorable rate structures from regulators. When higher costs arouse the public, however, utility companies may be unable to charge rates high enough to cover costs.

FIGURE 7 How Block Pricing Permits Revenues to Cover Costs and Facilitates Efficiency ($MSB = MSC$)

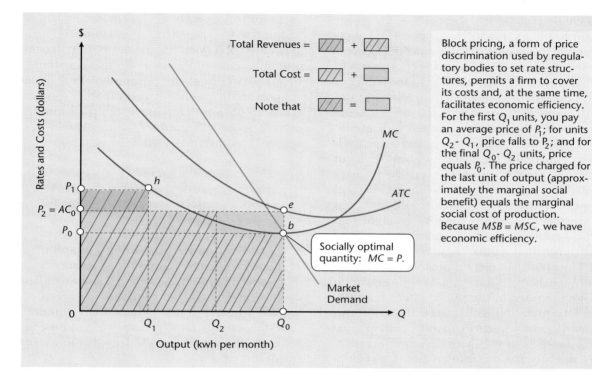

Total Revenues = ▨ + ▨

Total Cost = ▨ + ▢

Note that ▨ = ▢

Socially optimal quantity: $MC = P$.

Block pricing, a form of price discrimination used by regulatory bodies to set rate structures, permits a firm to cover its costs and, at the same time, facilitates economic efficiency. For the first Q_1 units, you pay an average price of P_1; for units $Q_2 - Q_1$, price falls to P_2; and for the final $Q_0 - Q_2$ units, price equals P_0. The price charged for the last unit of output (approximately the marginal social benefit) equals the marginal social cost of production. Because $MSB = MSC$, we have economic efficiency.

• **Externalities and Direct Regulation** Benefits or costs to a party not directly involved in an activity are *externalities*. Some forms of auto safety equipment convey externalities. Others do not. Seat belts and air bags, for example, protect only a car's occupants and could be sold just like wheel covers, stereos, and so on. Drivers and their passengers are the primary beneficiaries of this equipment. It directly protects the individual buying it, and externalities are negligible.[2]

Shock-absorbing bumpers, on the other hand, generate externalities. The buyer gains, but other drivers do as well. Damages are reduced when a car with a shock-absorbing bumper collides with other cars. External benefits are bestowed on passengers of cars with reg-

ular bumpers, but payments for such external benefits are impossible to collect. Thus, private purchases of shock-absorbing bumpers will be less than socially optimal, so carmakers are now required to provide such bumpers. This is an example of a positive externality in which regulation governs the form of a good. Compulsory education and inoculations against communicable diseases also entail positive externalities.

Negative externalities spread costs beyond the transaction in question. If a firm discharges waste into a stream, people who use the stream for recreation pay part of the costs, even if they never buy the product. No firm will adequately control its waste voluntarily if cleaning up imposes costs not borne by its competitors. Competitors will undercut price premiums that cover the higher costs of nonpolluting firms. Government intervention may be necessary to compensate for these third-party costs. Direct regulation generally limits some forms of pollution and forbids

---

[2]This argument ignores the effect on insurance rates of added injuries to occupants who do not wear protective restraints, and it also assumes that harm to passengers consists only of medical costs.

other, more dangerous pollutants. We leave a detailed discussion of environmental policies to a later chapter.

In summary, rationales for government intervention in business activities emerge from several sources. Some regulations are responses to economies of scale in production or the nature of the product itself. Some regulation arises from an industry's ability to promote its self-interest; some also serves the bureaucrats charged with administering the law, who gain power and larger budgets by expanding the scope and complexity of regulation. Finally, externalities are the primary rationale for environmental protection. Each of these explanations seems to fit specific cases, but the overseeing of business is only part of the regulatory landscape. Your activities are also shaped by governmental regulation.

The public interest rationale for regulation went unchallenged for years. When regulation has not operated in the public interest, a standard interpretation is that these imperfections are simply consequences of imperfect people doing their jobs as regulators in imperfect ways. Only recently has this explanation for regulatory peccadilloes been questioned.

Industry Interest Theory of Regulation

The state—the machinery and power of the state—is a potential resource or threat to every industry in the society. With its power to prohibit or compel, to take or give money, the state can and does selectively help or hurt a vast number of industries.[3]

George J. Stigler

The public interest rationale for regulation prevailed until the early 1970s, when George Stigler fundamentally changed the way many economists view much of economic regulation. After decades of studying the American economy, Stigler identified numerous instances where regulation failed to guard public interests. If the public interest approach were correct, we would

expect regulation primarily in highly concentrated industries (to regulate monopoly power) or in industries with significant economies of scale or scope. But many regulations in such areas as taxi service, air transportation, trucking, and some professional licensing arrangements (barbering, for example) find little support in the public interest rationale. Stigler asked an obvious question: If the public interests are not being served, whose are? His answer turned previous theory on its head.

The **industry interest theory of regulation** asserts that regulation is often tailored to serve the interests of regulated industries instead of those of the general public.

The Constitution gives Congress power "to regulate commerce among the several states." The government can tax, compel resource allocations, or change the economic decisions of households and firms without their consent. The state can use these great powers to raise or lower profitability in any industry through four major mechanisms:

1. Direct subsidies to the industry, special tax breaks or punitive taxes, or advantageous or harmful operating regulations.
2. Restriction or encouragement of entry or exit (e.g., barriers on imports).
3. Subsidies, taxes, or limitations on complementary or substitute products.
4. Direct price-fixing policies (price floors or ceilings).

All four mechanisms have altered profitability in many industries. The merchant marine (U.S. oceanic shipping) is heavily subsidized, as is medical care for the elderly (Medicare). Entry restrictions were effective in the airline industry, where the Civil Aeronautics Board (CAB) did not license a single new entrant during the 40 years after its establishment in 1938. Another example is regulation of trucking by the Interstate Commerce Commission (ICC). In the 1960s and 1970s, applications for new truck lines averaged over 5,000 annually, while the number of firms in operation contin-

---

[3]George J. Stigler, "The Theory of Economic Regulation," *The Bell Journal of Economic & Management Science*, Spring 1971.

ually shrank.[4] Law and medicine, too, are professions that benefit from restrictions on entry. (For example, competition from nurse practitioners, chiropractors, and paralegals is limited.) Restrictions on the number of taxicabs that can operate in New York have resulted in a $100,000 current value of taxi medallions (permits), driving up the costs to would-be drivers and, consequently, the costs of taxi fares.[5]

Government policies also affect an industry's substitutes and complements. Laws banning the use of yellow food dyes that allowed margarine to mimic the appearance of butter were enacted in the 1950s, when the dairy industry fought to hold its market for butter. Today, direct price fixing is found in milk and cheese price supports and in many farm and tobacco subsidy programs. (Agricultural price floors were addressed in Chapter 4.) Truckers vigorously supported improvements (subsidies) to interstate highways and, naturally, railroads opposed their development.

Construction unions have successfully opposed reforms to local building codes that block labor-saving technology. The consequence is that many building codes require outdated, labor-intensive construction techniques that drive costs up but provide employment for union workers. Some economists have argued that these building codes contributed to homelessness by reducing the availability of low-cost housing.

Few of these regulations are in the public interest. Some advocates of regulation blame incompetent managers for failing to guard the public interest. Others argue that agencies are often "captured" by the regulated industry. Regulators need expertise, and what better source for expertise to help solve problems than from within the industry? Constant contact with industry experts frequently persuades regulators of industry positions. This helps explain why regulations often favor the industry rather than the public and why many states now fund consumer advocacy agencies.

One notable exception to the success of industry interest regulation is the International Whaling Commission. Initially established to further the interests of the whaling industry and the nations involved in whaling, it appears to have now been "captured" by animal rights forces and now serves as the leading antiwhaling regulator and advocate.

George Stigler concluded that public interest theories fail to explain most regulations because they assume that business opposes regulation. Assuming instead that firms seek regulations to serve their own interests yields inferences vastly different from those based on public interest theories. His *industry interest* theory views government as the supplier of regulatory services to an industry. These services are paid for through lobbying or campaign contributions to policymakers who favor regulations the established firms want.

All firms seek monopoly power and abhor cutthroat competition; most would prefer to be part of a cartel. Cheating by members, however, causes unregulated cartels to disintegrate. One way to stabilize a cartel is through regulation of entry and prices. The major benefit of regulation to an industry is probably entry restriction.

Curiously, cartels are outlawed in some instances and implemented through law in others. Thus, railroads supported passage of the Interstate Commerce Act, early airlines favored establishment of the Civil Aeronautics Board, and so on. Regulated industries commonly mount major political offensives against proposed deregulation, but convictions of Teamster's Union officials in 1982 for trying to bribe a member of Congress to oppose trucking deregulation are evidence that firms are not the only beneficiaries of regulation.

Occupational licensing is a barrier to entry for lawyers, medical doctors, barbers, plumbers, dog groomers, realtors, travel agents, and so on. You can be jailed or fined if you operate without a license. The call for licensing is often clothed in public interest rhetoric so that the public will not notice its pockets being picked. As higher earnings stimulate the supply of potential entrants into a profession, entry restrictions evolve that impose ever higher qualifications for new applicants. Higher

---

[4]Ibid.

[5]Donald Dewey, *The Antitrust Experiment in America* (New York: Columbia University Press, 1990), p. 15.

standards frequently bar would-be members of a profession who have credentials superior to those of grandfathered long-term practitioners. Of course, all this is done in the name of increasing professional quality for the public.

Public Choice Theory of Regulation

This perspective is closely akin to Stigler's theory. Public choice models frequently link special-interest laws and regulations with the interests of those who administer them.

> The **public choice theory of regulation** emphasizes that bureaucrats produce complex regulations so that their power and budgets will grow.

The public choice theory of regulation augments the industry interest approach by pointing out that regulatory bureaucrats also have personal interests. Regulation may be excessively complex, for example, because this increases personnel requirements, feeding into empire building by heads of government agencies. The power of bureaucrats is enhanced when broadly written laws grant regulators substantial discretion over the form of regulation. This elicits lobbying by regulated firms and provides a market for experts who switch jobs back and forth between an industry and its regulators.

Public choice theory combines with Stigler's industry interest theory to explain much of regulation. The voice of business is not the only input into regulatory processes, however, and in many cases, firms have conflicting interests. Real concerns about social well-being permeate both the political process and administrative agencies, and genuine public interest considerations may prevail.

PERSPECTIVES ON REGULATION

Critics argue that red tape drives up the cost of living, and that the costs of bureaucratic rules governing business escalate every year. Both *direct* and *indirect costs* must be considered to evaluate this argument.

Direct Costs of Regulation

The direct costs of regulation include the *administrative costs* of operating regulatory agencies and the *compliance costs* incurred by regulated entities.

> **Direct costs of regulation** include (a) administrative costs to the government (employee salaries, office supplies, and other overhead expenses) and (b) compliance costs incurred by regulated entities (primarily the private sector, but also by other governmental units that must comply with regulations).

Some recent studies have estimated some direct costs of federal regulation.[6] These researchers found that compliance costs were many times larger than administrative costs. Extrapolating their results to 1995, nearly $400 billion to $500 billion is now absorbed annually to meet federal regulations—roughly one-third of U.S. private investment, or nearly $2,000 per U.S. citizen. In 1994, a task force headed by Vice President Gore was charged with developing a plan to "reinvent government." Identifying ways to eliminate wasteful federal programs and inefficient red tape was a centerpiece in this study.

Indirect Costs of Regulation

Government budget outlays have swollen as public demands for regulatory programs have grown. The costs of government go far beyond the national budget, however, because even programs with laudable objectives may generate indirect costs through their effects on workers, consumers, and other participants on the economic stage.

---

[6]M. Weidenbaum and R. DeFina, *The Rising Cost of Government Regulation* (St. Louis: Center for the Study of American Business, 31 January 1981); and U.S. Office of Management and Budget, *Regulatory Program of the United States Government, April 1, 1990–March 31, 1991* (Washington, D.C.: U.S. Government Printing Office, 1990).

Indirect costs of regulation are undesirable changes in behavior in response to regulations and resemble the excess burdens of taxation.

Consider unemployment compensation. Many workers effectively receive paid vacations if they are laid off. Unemployment compensation is largely untaxed and is often as high as 80% of a worker's take-home wage. Thus, this program creates incentives for some people to work irregularly, sticking the burden on workers with stable jobs.

Taxes are also distortive. Many employee benefits are disguised as legitimate business expenses. Firms offer tax-free fringe benefits to their employees because, were these benefits paid in cash, employees' income taxes would rise. Thus, many employees select more extensive health and dental care coverage than they would if these benefits were taxable. Further, some employees drive company cars that are newer and grander than cars they would buy for themselves, and they eat more elaborate lunches than they would if they were paying their own tabs.

Indirect costs are incurred whenever people adjust to policies in ways not intended by policymakers. It may be that regulations are complex because many people find ways to avoid simpler rules. The complicated lives we lead while adjusting to a maze of bureaucratic rules are among the indirect costs of government. When all direct and indirect costs of all federal, state, and local regulations are considered, regulation probably absorbs 5% to 10% of our national income. But costs are only one side of the regulatory equation; a balanced view would require estimates of the benefits of government regulation or deregulation. Unfortunately, data are not available that would permit scientific estimates of the benefits of regulation.

There is a consensus that some regulation is necessary. But when has regulation gone too far? Recently, the Food and Drug Administration (FDA) killed the McCurdy Fish Company (a small, herring smokehouse in Maine). This closure resulted from regulations that required fish to be eviscerated before salting and smoking. The regulations grew out of problems with freshwater whitefish, and officials insisted that it made sense to apply the standards to all fish. Ocean herring, however, are small saltwater fish that are processed in a concentrated brine solution that kills potential toxins. Further, the regulations apply only to fish processed within the United States, allowing foreign suppliers to process herring in the same manner that closed McCurdy.[7]

These examples, several recent studies, and several presidential study groups all attest to the costliness of regulation, which is ultimately reflected in lower business profits, less income to workers, and higher rates of unemployment. In the neighborhood of $500 billion is devoted to regulatory activity. Big government may create problems just as enormous as those posed by big business or big labor.

Deregulation and Reregulation

Politicians often pledge to reduce government intervention in the private sector. The past two decades have ushered in substantial deregulation of trucking, airlines, banking, and a few other industries. Increased competition in these industries pushed prices down sharply. The economic pressures generated from airline deregulation led to many changes in the industry, including Continental Airlines' use of the federal bankruptcy statute to void its union contracts and the closure of many unprofitable airlines.

Regulation often involves a complex combination of price and entry restrictions that can lead to higher prices and less service. Moreover, the competition among regulated firms tends to ignore pricing and to be especially focused on advertising, product quality, or new product development. Regulation is often a compromise among conflicting public interests, industry interests, and bureaucratic objectives, which make the results of deregulation somewhat unpredictable. Deregulation of AT&T taught us that deregulating the provision of a good or service

---

[7]Brent Bowers, "FDA Regulatory Tide Swallows Up McCurdy Fish Co." *The Wall Street Journal*, 18 May 1993, p. B2.

often involves submarkets that may be quite different from each other. Deregulation that works well in one submarket may be less successful in another.

That deregulation may be disruptive is evidenced by the turmoil and declines in national income throughout much of Eastern Europe as tightly regimented economies begin uneasy transitions toward less regulation. On a slightly smaller scale, almost every form of deregulation entails a certain amount of costly confusion. This is especially true when only one side of balanced sets of regulations are eliminated.

The recent U.S. savings and loan crisis is an example. Deregulation advocates failed to consider the *moral hazards* that arise if financial institutions are given a wide latitude in loans while a government insurance program guarantees the first $100,000 of each account in insured institutions. The lesson of this calamity (which will ultimately cost American taxpayers a total estimated at between $120 billion and $200 billion) is not that this deregulation was a big mistake but, rather, that deregulation must be studied carefully so that such problems can be anticipated and remedied. The S&Ls that collapsed in the late 1980s probably would not have had as much money to loan if insurance on deposits had been eliminated for financial intermediaries that chose risky investment strategies and if this absence of insurance had been widely publicized.

Deregulation generally stimulates competition, a fact that many people find discomforting. For example, almost every major airline crash generates calls for reregulation of the airlines. This reaction ignores the fact that deregulation affected the Civil Aviation Board's command over rate structures and ability to limit competition, not the FAA's control over safety issues. In fact, a recent study by the FAA indicates that airline safety has actually improved since U.S. skyways were deregulated. The number of passenger fatalities per 100 million miles flown has dropped steadily since 1977. But critics point out that this safety record may prove illusory as the fleet ages because competition has reduced the funds available to purchase new aircraft. Competition in the airlines has reduced prices, putting pressure on both train and bus service. Competition, while good for consumers, is uncomfortable for many decision-makers in the airline industry who would like to see regulation reimposed.

One lesson is to be wary of advocates of regulation who try to persuade legislators that certain laws or rules are in the public interest. Self-interest is a strong incentive to develop arguments that may bamboozle the general public. Although many government activities do serve the public interest, the specifics of many of the government policies are similarly shaped by special-interest groups.

CHAPTER REVIEW: KEY POINTS

1. Market power exists whenever a firm can set the price of its output. (Market power and monopoly are not synonymous.) Market power builds a gap between price and marginal cost. The **Lerner index of monopoly power** (*LMP*) uses this fact to measure market power as $(P - MC)/P$. However, estimating MC with accounting data is almost impossible.

2. Market concentration ratios provide some evidence of monopolization or oligopolis-tic power. **Concentration ratios** are the percentages of total sales, output, or employment in an industry controlled by a small number of the largest firms in the industry.

3. The **Herfindahl-Hirschman Index** (*HHI*) is the sum of squared market shares ($\sum S_i^2$). Squaring places more emphasis on big firms. The Justice Department now uses the HHI as a guide to the permissibility of mergers.

4. Major difficulties are encountered in defining an industry. The existence of *close consumption substitutes* is one consideration; the ease with which potential competitors might enter an industry is another. The Department of Commerce lumps firms into Standard Industrial Classifications (SICs) to try to solve this problem, but with only mixed success.

5. **Horizontal mergers** (the absorption of competitors) dominated the first major wave of mergers in the United States from 1890 until 1914. The Clayton Act outlawed most horizontal mergers, so a wave of **vertical mergers** (mergers that unite suppliers of raw materials or intermediate goods with processors or other firms further along the production chain) lasting until the Great Depression increased economic concentration. Merger activity died during the Great Depression, but revived in the mid-1950s when companies that were very dissimilar were merged into **conglomerates**. Merger activities slowed down during the 1970s but reemerged strongly during the 1980s in a fourth wave that some people describe as "the golden age of dealmaking."

6. One reason for merging is to increase the scope of a firm's operations so that economies of scale in information, marketing, advertising, production, or financial management may be exploited. Another reason, by far the most important for policy, is that merger eliminates business rivals and facilitates *economic concentration* and *market power*. Increases in market power that result from merger may be reflected rapidly in higher prices for the merged companies' stock.

7. Big firms might be justified by enormous capital requirements or substantial economies of scale. In such cases, proper public policy may take the form of **regulation**. The major thrust of public policy where no such justifications for bigness exist has been to encourage competition through **antitrust actions**.

8. Agricultural cooperatives, athletic organizations, labor unions, export trade associations, insurance companies, and regulated industries are largely exempt from antitrust action.

9. In applying the **Sherman Antitrust Act**, the courts have historically taken two different approaches. The **rule of reason** approach prohibits bad monopolies and permits reasonable restraints on trade, while the **per se doctrine** forbids all monopolies regardless of conduct.

10. The bulk of the regulatory agencies in this country were created during three decades. The first great surge occurred during the 1930s, when policymakers attempted to soften the effects of the Great Depression and prevent future large swings in economic activity. Well over half of all regulatory agencies, however, came into existence in the 1960s and 1970s. It is not obvious why regulation increased so dramatically during a period of relative prosperity and high economic growth.

11. The **public interest** theory of regulation focuses on some possible failures of the price system, including poor information, fraud, externalities, and monopoly power.

12. A **natural monopoly** can exploit substantial economies of scale, rendering direct competition impractical. Society has turned to regulation, primarily in the form of price discriminatory rate structures (*block pricing*), to prevent natural monopolies from reaping enormous profits and to move them toward socially efficient levels of output.

13. Regulating public utilities is considerably more difficult than simple theory would suggest. Major problems arise in determining the *rate base*, a *fair rate of return*, and *allowable costs*. Regulatory agencies face a difficult task in balancing the interests of consumers and utility investors.

14. The **industry interest theory of regulation** expressed by George Stigler suggests that industries can gain from regulation and therefore demand regulation from the government. As Stigler noted, the state can, and often does, change the profitability of an industry through four main

mechanisms: (*a*) direct taxes or subsidies, (*b*) restrictions on entry, (*c*) impacts on an industry's complementary or substitute products, and (*d*) direct price-fixing policies.

15. **Public choice theory of regulation** attributes much of the complexity of modern regulation to empire building by the heads of government agencies.

16. **Direct costs of regulation** arise when a firm incurs costs to comply with laws and regulations. The **indirect costs of regulation** are incurred in attempts to avoid or reshape regulation. The cost of hiring lobbyists to influence regulation is an example. Together, these costs amount to 5% to 10% of U.S. Gross Domestic Product.

QUESTIONS FOR THOUGHT AND DISCUSSION

1. According to standard theory, the major economic problem posed by the exercise of market power is economic inefficiency. Studies that have attempted to measure the "welfare loss" caused by monopoly have, however, yielded tiny estimates of loss. No serious empirical study suggests that more than 1% to 2% of GDP is lost because of market power, with most estimates being much less than 1%.[8] Is antitrust action a waste of taxpayers' resources if these estimates are correct? Are there other socially important reasons to limit industrial concentration? If so, what are they?

2. When the Oakland Raiders moved to Los Angeles in 1982, they touched a vital nerve in the National Football League. This move, which was subsequently upheld by the courts, weakened the NFL's influence over the movement of franchises and threatened to undercut the pooling of network television revenues (60% of NFL income). The NFL is now lobbying Congress for a blanket antitrust exemption. Do you think professional sports should be exempt from antitrust laws? Should owners of professional teams be permitted to move their teams at their discretion? NFL critics argue that the league is more inter-

ested in limiting the number of teams and ensuring profits for the existing 30 owners. Do you agree?

3. Are the interests of the general public, the regulated industry, competing industries, or government regulators most obviously served by the following types of regulations? Which industries gain and which lose in each case?

   a. An AIDS vaccine is kept off the market for two years while the Food and Drug Administration tests it on animals to ascertain whether it is safe for humans.

   b. Gasoline must contain 15% fuel alcohol additives each winter in an attempt to reduce Denver's brown cloud of air pollution.

   c. Penalties on clerks in stores are raised if they sell beer to minors.

   d. Restaurants must be inspected every 180 days by the Department of Health.

   e. Installation of new, safer toilet seats is mandated for every facility serving the public or employing more than six workers.

   f. The heirs of smokers who ultimately died because of their addiction are able to collect damages from tobacco companies?

4. The Occupational Safety and Health Act (OSHA) requires that workplaces be made as safe as possible (or more so, according to some critics), with little or no regard for costs. How would you expect OSHA reg-

---

[8]The first such study (Arnold Harberger, "Monopoly and Resource Allocation," *American Economic Review* 44, (May 1954) pp. 77–87) estimated this loss at only one-tenth of one percent of our GDP. No subsequent reputable study has estimated a loss exceeding 1% of GDP.

ulations to affect prices for goods previously produced under hazardous conditions relative to the prices of those that have always been produced in safe work environments? What would you expect to happen to wages in previously hazardous industries? In previously safe industries? What will happen to real wages economy-wide? To health insurance rates? Should it matter for the purposes of OSHA regulation whether the risks of particular occupations are well known or not? If so, why?

5. Suppose you were a Food and Drug Administration (FDA) official charged with licensing new drugs. There are two types of errors to which you might fall prey: (a) you might license a harmful drug or (b) you might keep a very beneficial drug off the market. What do you think is the nature of the trade-off between these types of errors? Which of these two types of errors would you wish to minimize if your goal is (a) to maximize your prospects for job security or promotion, or (b) to maximize the public welfare? Are there natural checks in the marketplace if you make the first type of error? If you make the second type of error? What are the probable effects on research and development activities of pharmaceutical companies if you minimize the licensing of harmful drugs? If you minimize keeping good drugs off the market? In which direction do you think you would lean if you were a typical FDA official?

8
Resource Markets

Why are some people prosperous, while others are destitute? Land, labor, capital, and entrepreneurial talent are all needed to produce goods and services that people want. In the previous part of this book, we have examined how household demand interacts with production costs and market structures to determine prices and outputs. Our attention now turns to how similar interactions in resource markets affect the structure of resource payments and resource employment. This ultimately shapes the distribution of income and, at a more personal level, determines your own level of prosperity.

Most production costs are ultimately payments to resource suppliers. A competitive approach to resource markets, called *marginal productivity theory*, is developed in the next chapter. Firms' demands for labor depend on how much revenue each worker generates. This foundation for resource demands is blended with a theory of factor supplies to explain resource prices and allocations in competitive markets. We focus on competitive labor markets, but the forces of marginal productivity are exerted in competitive markets for all resources.

Demands and supplies for resources share many characteristics of markets for consumer goods. Just as markets for consumer goods range from purely competitive to monopolistic, resource markets range from situations of diffused power to markets with single sellers or buyers. The use of economic power to alter wage structures and employment by large firms and such organizations as unions and employer associations are the subject of the second chapter in this part. Unions traditionally try to use their economic clout to raise wages, while firms traditionally try to maximize profits by holding wages and other production costs in check.

In a static environment with little technological change, a large firm such as a textile mill in a small southern town may try to maximize profits by minimizing wages and other costs. Workers may react over time by combining into unions to bargain collectively for higher wages. However, in a growing economy with rapid technological change, this pessimistic view can be replaced with an optimistic view in which high profits go to creative firms with high-quality, leading-edge products, which are generated by paying high wages to attract the best workers. This more dynamic view of the economic process envisions an endless stream of innovations coming from people as the key, not a boring stream of the same old standardized items produced by machines, with people as mere robotized accessories. Investments in *human capital* are central to this dynamic process and keys to prosperity in an increasingly competitive world economy.

Discussions of how markets for land, capital, and entrepreneurship determine rates of rent, interest, and economic profit await you in the third chapter, which concludes with an overview of how marginal productivity operates to distribute total income among the owners of different resources. The last chapter in this part addresses the issues of poverty and government redistributions of income.

Chapter 28

Discrimination

Implicit
Contracts

Labor

Competitive
Labor Markets

Human cap

Wage $VMP = MRP$

S_L

...us buy and consume goods. This requires ' us (children and retirees may be ex- o generate income by selling resources: or, land, capital, or entrepreneurial tal- come is largely determined by the s and types of resources you control— ir prices. Technology and the vigor of ition largely determine how resources l and how well resource owners are com- d.

...mpetitive pressures in labor markets op- varying degree, in all resource markets. pter begins by exploring firms' demands r when both labor markets and output are highly competitive. Decisions about ment are our second area of concern; noices underpin labor supplies. *Human* ...*eory*, our next topic, explains how peo- e specialized skills to enhance their job unities. The resulting skill differentials in- both the demand side and the supply side markets, which in turn determine equi- wages and employment.

...ne people see current wage differentials

mediocre doctors make four times as much as master plumbers? Why do outstanding teachers make less than second-rate lawyers? How disparate are wages according to gender, race, and age? Reasons for such wage differentials are our final concerns in this chapter.

DERIVED DEMANDS FOR RESOURCES

Resource markets differ from markets for consumer goods primarily because resources usually satisfy human wants only indirectly, through production. Thus, people's *direct* demands for consumer goods create *derived demands* for resources, that is, demands based on the resources' productive contributions to final consumer goods. In a sense, resource supplies are also largely derived, in that resource owners seek income to purchase goods; a worker, for example, trades labor for income with which to buy food and shelter.

*Consumers' demands for goods yield **derived de-***

This is why job opportunities for computer programmers and electronics engineers expand when technology advances to make new types of goods available. Conversely, demands for teachers shrank when school enrollments dropped in the 1960s. Demands for teachers are now rebounding to accommodate the offspring of the 1950's baby boomers.

The demand for final goods is one dimension of the demand for labor; the other is labor productivity, which depends on workers' skills, technology, and the availability and prices of other resources. But how do profit-seeking firms translate these influences into a hiring decision? Recall that firms maximize profit by expanding output until marginal revenue equals marginal cost ($MR = MC$). A parallel condition specifies how this profit maximization is manifested in labor markets: firms hire additional labor to produce and sell more output until the last unit of labor adds as much to revenue as it adds to costs. This principle is the cornerstone for resource acquisitions in all resource markets.

THE DEMAND FOR LABOR

How do employers decide how many workers to hire? Would you employ someone for $8 per hour who could produce $10 worth of goods per day? Hardly. You would lose $54 for each 8-hour shift. But you would jump at the chance to hire a different worker who cost $8 hourly and generated $200 in daily output. Firms' demands for labor are related to worker productivity and the value of output.

Let's return to your Colorado gold mine and assume that labor is the only variable input; other influences on production are fixed. The law of diminishing marginal returns means that beyond some point, extra workers add less and less to total production. For simplicity, Table 1 ignores the possibility that specialization might initially yield increasing returns. The first miner hired generates 3 ounces of gold weekly. Employing a second raises total output to 5 ounces per week, for a gain of 2 ounces per week. This *marginal physical product of labor (MPP_L)* is listed in column 3 for up to 10 workers.

Marginal Revenue Product

Computing the marginal revenue product requires calculating the extra revenue from the gold each additional miner produces.

> **Marginal revenue product (MRP)** *is the extra sales revenue from the output generated by an extra resource unit:*

$$MRP_L = \frac{\Delta TR}{\Delta L} = \frac{\Delta TR}{\Delta q} \times \frac{\Delta q}{\Delta L} = MR \times MPP_L$$

Regardless of market structure, all firms base hiring decisions about all resources on each factor's MRP, which can be calculated as either $\Delta Pq \div \Delta L$ or $MR \times MPP_L$ (marginal revenue times marginal physical product of labor). A resource's MRP reflects its value to a firm, which is not always the same as its value to society as a whole.

Value of the Marginal Product

How socially valuable is a resource? We showed earlier that a good's price approximates its marginal social benefit ($P \cong MSB$).[1] Similarly, a resource's marginal social benefit is the value (as measured by price) of its marginal physical product, calculated as $P \times MPP$.

> *The social value of the output produced by an extra resource unit is known as the* **value of the marginal product (VMP)**.

In competition $P = MR$, so the marginal revenue product of labor ($MRP_L = MR \times MPP_L$) and the value of the marginal product are identical ($VMP_L = MRP_L$).

International markets set a competitive price for gold, which in Table 1 is assumed to be $500 per ounce (column 4). The value of the

---

[1]This statement assumes that resource endowments are deemed equitable and that externalities are absent. We discuss complications caused by externalities and inequity in later chapters.

TABLE 1 Data for Western Gold Mine

(1) Number of Workers L	(2) Total Oz. of Gold Produced per Week q	(3) Marginal Physical Product of Labor MPP_L	(4) Price of Gold per Oz. $P = MR$	(5) Value of the Marginal Product of Labor $VMP = MRP$
1	3.0	3.0	$500	$1,500
2	5.0	2.0	500	1,000
3	6.8	1.8	500	900
4	8.4	1.6	500	800
5	9.8	1.4	500	700
6	11.0	1.2	500	600
7	12.0	1.0	500	500
8	12.8	.8	500	400
9	13.4	.6	500	300
10	13.8	.4	500	200

Note: This table assumes that other factors are fixed and that gold is sold in a competitive market.

marginal product in column 5 is computed by multiplying columns 3 and 4. A pure competitor's demand for labor is based on the value of its marginal product. Note that VMP_L is influenced by both labor productivity (MPP_L) and the demand for the product (P). Labor's VMP_L curve in your gold mine is illustrated in Figure 1; this is your short-run demand curve for labor.

Shifts in Demands for Labor

Competitive demands for labor ($VMP_L = P \times MPP_L$) may shift in response to changes in (a) output prices, (b) prices of other resources, (c) technology, or (d) the inherent productivity of workers.

- **Output Prices**   Many people treat gold as insurance. Political unrest could boost international demands for gold. If gold's price rises to $1,000 per ounce, your demand for miners' labor (VMP_L) rises from D_0 to D_1 in Figure 2. The amount each miner produces is unaffected, but the value of each output level doubles because gold prices double. If waning interest in gold then drives its price down to $100 per ounce, your demand for miners shrinks to D_2.

- **Prices of Other Resources**   Changes in the prices of other resources, and consequently in their utilization, can also shift demands for labor. Resources are frequently complementary. For example, miners' productivity tends to rise if lower capital costs induce investment in new capital equipment. Replacing dull picks and shovels with newer tools allows miners to recover more gold. Rising marginal physical prod-

A competitive firm's short-run demand for labor is the value of the marginal product curve for labor (VMP_L). The VMP_L is equal to $P \times MPP_L$. Because in competitive product markets $P = MR$, $VMP_L = MRP_L$.
(Note: This figure is based on Table 1).

FIGURE 1   A Competitive Firm's Demand for Labor (Data for Western Gold Mine)

FIGURE 2 Shifts in the Demand for Labor

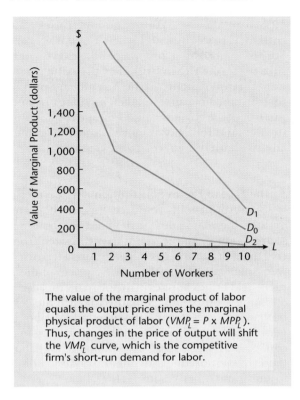

The value of the marginal product of labor equals the output price times the marginal physical product of labor ($VMP_L = P \times MPP_L$). Thus, changes in the price of output will shift the VMP_L curve, which is the competitive firm's short-run demand for labor.

ucts of labor would raise both their *VMPs* and your demand for labor. Similarly, higher capital costs and reductions in capital per worker might reduce your demand for miners' services.

In addition to their complementarity, however, resources are also substitutes for one another. For example, declines in capital costs or huge wage hikes could cause miners to be replaced by machinery. In the short run, higher wages cause a backward movement along a firm's demand curve for labor. In the longer run, higher wages can cause the firm's demand for labor to shift to the left because labor will be replaced by capital. For example, coal mining has been a declining industry for decades primarily because of aggressive wage hikes demanded by the United Mine Workers union.

• **Technological Change** Technological changes can directly raise demands for labor. You would hire more miners if newly invented machinery boosted each miner's productivity. But technological advances do not always raise demands for labor. Sophisticated new excavation equipment might replace some miners. The process of replacing human labor with machinery is known as *automation*. During the 1960s, some analysts feared that automation would lead to the structural unemployment of a growing pool of workers. In the long run, these fears have been largely proven groundless, in part because producing, repairing, and operating automatic machinery require labor. However, automation may cause temporary but traumatic dislocations of workers, even if falling demands for labor in some markets are offset by growing demands in other occupations.

Some forecasters predict that industrial robots will increasingly take over routine assembly line work, and that employment will shift primarily toward service industries. Many auto workers lost their assembly line jobs when robots were introduced in the early 1980s, compounding the high unemployment in Detroit and other motor cities caused by slack sales worldwide. In the long run, however, this automation may have saved more jobs than it destroyed. Without domestic automation, the growing comparative advantages of foreign automakers threatened the survival of the entire American auto industry and all its jobs.

A fundamental problem is that automated machinery increasingly replaces unskilled and semiskilled workers, with growth in employment opportunities and wages occurring primarily in high-skill occupations. Real wages fall and employment opportunities evaporate for people whose skills are negligible or whose skills are made obsolete by modernization. We will deal with these problems in more depth later in this part of the book, especially in our chapter on income distribution.

• **The Quality of Labor** Demands for labor rise when people work harder or acquire more productive skills. Education or on-the-job training can enhance labor productivity. Conversely, if miners began working less diligently, their *VMPs* and your demand for their labor would fall.

Elasticity of Demand for Labor

We have seen that the demand for labor is a derived demand and that employment varies inversely with the wage rate. But how much do wage changes affect employment?

*The responsiveness of the amount of labor demanded (ΔL) to a change in wages (Δw) is measured by the **elasticity of demand for labor**, roughly[2]*

$$e_L = \frac{\%\Delta L}{\%\Delta w}$$

The elasticity of demand for labor is directly related to (*a*) the elasticity of demand for output, (*b*) labor's share of total costs, (*c*) the ease of substitution between labor and other resources, and (*d*) the time allowed for adjustments to changes in wages.

• **Price Elasticity of Demand for Output** The more elastic the demand for a final output, the harder it is for a firm to raise prices to cover higher labor costs. For example, onion farmers individually could not pass on a raise to onion harvesters because the demand facing any single onion farm is perfectly elastic. A wage hike will lower the quantity of labor demanded substantially when higher wages cannot easily be passed forward to consumers because the demand for a good is very elastic. Alternatively, if falling wages cause production costs and prices to drop, sales and employment will rise; the greater the elasticity of demand for the product, the more sales and employment rise. Thus, the more elastic (or inelastic) the demand for the product, the more elastic (or inelastic) the demand for labor.

• **Labor's Share of Total Cost** The effect on employment of a given wage change depends on how significant a share of total costs is devoted to wages. For example, if wages are only 10% of total cost, a 20% wage hike raises total costs (and price) by roughly 2%. But if wages are 80% of total costs, a 20% wage hike exerts pressure for a 16% rise in price. For the same rise in wages, employment will be less affected in the first instance because smaller increases in output prices will cover the higher wage costs. Thus, the demand for labor is more elastic the greater labor's share of total cost, and vice versa.

• **The Ease of Factor Substitution** The easier it is to substitute one resource for another, the greater the elasticities of demand for both resources. For example, if it is easy to switch from coal to oil or natural gas in generating electricity, then small changes in the relative prices of these fuels yield huge changes in the primary fuel used, and utility companies' demands for each fuel will be very elastic. Similarly, the demand for labor is very elastic if workers are easily replaced by machines, and vice versa. The demand for labor tends to be more inelastic the more difficult it is to substitute other resources for labor.

• **Time** Longer periods allow firms to adjust more completely to changing wages. Resource substitutions are easier, and technological change also becomes more feasible. For example, soaring wage rates for coal miners during 1945 to 1965 stimulated automation and more efficient excavating techniques. Thus, the elasticity of demand for labor becomes larger when the time horizon expands to allow more latitude about both technologies and resources. Table 2 summarizes the effects of these four factors on the elasticity of demand for labor.

THE SUPPLY OF LABOR

You should now have some ideas about ways in which productivity and output prices shape resource demands, and about some determinants of the elasticities of resource demands. We have assumed that a firm can hire all the labor it wants

---

[2]Precise computation of e_L requires using midpoint-based formulas as described in the chapter on elasticity.

TABLE 2   Influences on the Elasticity of Demand for Labor

Demand for Labor Is	
More Elastic if	**Less Elastic if**
1. Output demand is relatively elastic. (Vegetables)	1. Output demand is relatively inelastic. (Cigarettes)
2. Wages are a large percentage of total cost. (Word processing)	2. Wages are a small percentage of total cost. (Computer chips)
3. Resource substitution is easy. (Robots in manufacturing)	3. It is difficult to substitute resources. (Nursing care)
4. Firms have more time to adjust to wage changes. (Long run)	4. Time for adjustment is severely limited. (Short run)

at a fixed wage, but demand is only one dimension of any resource market. Understanding labor markets requires us to examine supply as well.

*The **supply of labor** depicts the amounts of time people are willing to work per period at alternative wage rates.*

Labor supplies for individual markets and the economy as a whole are determined by

1. Population size and labor force participation rates.
2. Preferences of individuals about leisure versus income from work.
3. Rates and structures of wages.
4. *Human capital*, or the education, training, and skills of potential workers.

These influences on labor supplies are considered next.

Population and Labor Force Participation

Over 60% of our population over age 16 participates in the labor force, but labor force participation varies by several characteristics, including age and gender, as shown in Figure 3. People aged 20 to 54 years are, predictably, most likely to work for pay in the labor market.

*A **labor force participation rate** is the percentage of a given population that is in the work force, that is, has a job or is looking for one.*

Social dynamics influence participation rates. Only 35% of women over age 20 were in the work force in 1950. Today, 58% work for pay. Men's participation fell from 86% to roughly 76% over this same period. We need to examine some influences on individual labor supply decisions to explain trends of this type.

Labor vs. Leisure Choices

Suppose you are offered a job at $10 per hour and can set your own work schedule. Even if you are a full-time student, you might reduce your course load a bit to take advantage of such an offer. Assume that you decide to work 20 hours a week. If the offer were raised to $25 per hour, you might drop out of school altogether and work 40 or 50 hours per week. This means that your labor supply curve is positively sloped between hourly wages of $10 and $25, as shown by curve *ab* in Figure 4.

Let's really get outrageous. If you were offered $70 per hour, would you work more than 50 hours weekly? At a very high wage, you might feel that you were earning plenty by working only 20 hours weekly. Fourteen hundred dollars is a tidy sum, and if you work long hours, you might not have time to enjoy the fruits of your labor. Thus, in Figure 4 we show a *backward-bending* supply of labor for all wages above $25 per hour.

Why are individual labor supplies often negatively sloped at high wage rates? The key to answering this question is understanding that changes in wage rates alter the price of **leisure**—

FIGURE 3 Labor Force Participation Rate by Age and Gender

Gender and age are only two of the many variables that influence participation in the labor force. Others include education, spouse's income or other family income, race, and the number and age of children in the family. One of the most important changes taking place in labor markets is the downward drift of male labor force participation and the upward surge of women in the labor markets since 1960.

a good that is negatively related to the amount of labor supplied. You have less leisure time available the more you work.

Recall the income and substitution effects that we explored as separate aspects of people's responses to price changes for a good. The **substitution effect** of a higher wage reduces your consumption of leisure activities relative to work because the higher your wage, the more income you surrender when you take off from work. As your wage rises, you tend to work more and consume less leisure time because the opportunity cost of free time has risen. There is, however, an offsetting **income effect**: the demand for leisure, as for any normal good, rises with income. Thus, your higher income causes you to want to "buy" more leisure by working less.

The income and substitution effects of a wage change operate in opposite directions. At low wages, the substitution effect usually overwhelms the income effect because total income is so low. Thus, a higher wage rate leads to the provision of more work because people tend to substitute work (and the potential for greater consumption) for leisure. When the substitution effect dominates the income effect, the labor supply curve is positively sloped. When your wages and total income are very high, however, the income effect often overpowers the substitution effect in your labor decision. This results in a backward-bending supply curve for your labor similar to the curve *bc* in Figure 4.

This discussion treats work versus leisure decisions as if individual workers can fine-tune their choices down to the minute. In reality, however, full-time work normally absorbs 40 hours a week of scheduled work. Employed professionals tend to have more control over when

FIGURE 4 The Individual's Supply of Labor

As the wage rate rises, it becomes increasingly costly not to work; therefore, the *substitution effect* induces people to work and reduce leisure. On the other hand, higher wages make greater incomes possible, and this *income effect* will cause people to want more leisure time to enjoy their income. If the substitution effect is more powerful than the income effect, the supply of labor is positively sloped. This tends to be the case when wages are low. However, at high wage rates, the income effect may overpower the substitution effect, in which case the supply of labor is backward bending.

they work, but most wind up putting in a lot more hours than the folks on an assembly line, for example. If you are unwilling to work at least 40 hours weekly, in all likelihood your hourly wage will be much lower. The regimentation of scheduled full-time work is the price most people pay in order to hold permanent full-time jobs.

Wage Structures and Rates

A change in the wages of any member of a household may affect the labor supply decisions of other members. For example, if a primary worker's earnings fail to keep pace with inflation, other family members may enter the labor market to maintain the family's standard of living. Another possibility is that a big raise for a primary breadwinner may induce other members

to cut back their work effort as the family unit consumes more household services from other family members. If market wages rise for other household members, families may substitute in the opposite direction. Some economists argue that this effect is especially powerful if a family's entire income is subject to high tax rates. Focus 1 examines the effects of tax rates on labor supplies internationally.

Social roles, customs, and numerous other nonfinancial considerations also influence labor decisions. For example, the birth of a child may temporarily keep its mother at home. Desires for education or training also affect the timing and duration of individual participation in the labor force.

Education and skills also affect labor force participation because of the wages you can earn. Analyses of markets normally assume that each unit of the item considered is identical. Human labor, however, is far more varied than are long-stemmed roses, bulldozers, or acres of farmland. Some variations among people are innate and some are accidental, but many are cultivated to amplify differences in human productivity.

Human Capital

People are not born with the same potential intelligence or raw talent, but inherited differences are magnified or offset by acquired skills. Sharpening productive talents or acquiring new skills is called *investment in human capital*.

> **Human capital** represents improvements made to the labor embodied in human beings.

Most of us spend years in school or in on-the-job training preparing ourselves to be more productive. Attention to our general health or migrating to find more suitable jobs also involves investment in human capital. Self-improvement fanatics may spend most of their lives acquiring human capital. We bring to our training or education certain natural aptitudes and strengths. We invest in human capital in efforts to improve our abilities to perform certain tasks.

Women and Marginal Tax Rates: A Global View

Taxes, especially marginal income tax rates (the added income tax on additional income), inhibit people's willingness to put in additional hours or to work at all. Economists from around the world met recently to discuss how tax rates affect individual labor supplies. All economists applied the same research techniques to their respective countries to ascertain the extent to which income taxes have reduced labor supplies from families.

Table 3 suggests that the effect of progressive income tax rates on labor supplies was rather consistent across these countries. The magnitude of the negative effect of progressive income tax rates on the willingness of women to work is remarkable, and it became even more significant as the size of a woman's family expanded. These findings suggest that progressive income tax rates make it more difficult for society to achieve a balanced labor force composed equally of men and women, if that is a social goal. Today, U.S. marginal tax rates are a maximum of 39%, at least partially explaining a recent surge in labor force participation by women.

Table 3
Percentage Change in Labor Supplies Accounted for by Income Tax Rates by Gender

Country	Men	Women	Maximum Marginal Tax Rate
Sweden	−15.0	−29	58
France	0.0	−25	60
Italy	0.0	−20	72
United States	−2.6	−20	50

Source: "Special Issue on Taxation and Labor Supply in Industrial Countries," *The Journal of Human Resources*, Vol. 25, No. 3 (Summer 1990). Note: All studies used data from the early 1980s.

• **Investment in Education** Investing in new physical capital requires sacrifices of potential current consumption so that higher future consumption can be realized. Acquiring skills through education entails similar sacrifices. The time and money you sacrifice to attend college are examples.

College is partially a consumption experience for many students, offering football games, parties, and other social opportunities. Love of learning may also play a role, but most students perceive earning a degree as one step toward a higher income stream and access to "the good life." If you view your education primarily as an investment that should increase your future income, it is important to select your major carefully because some majors may merely make you a scholarly short-order cook.

Investments in human capital involve balancing higher lifetime earnings against the costs of acquiring valuable skills. As a college student, you must pay for tuition, books, and other out-of-pocket expenses, and less time is available for work. Moreover, your first job as a new graduate may not yield the wage you might have earned had you moved directly from high school into the labor market and acquired four years of work experience. After a few years on the job, however, your income will probably exceed that of most high school graduates who entered the labor market directly.

Figure 5 graphs typical out-of-pocket costs and income forgone against lifetime earnings from a college degree. The green line reflects a typical earnings profile for college graduates over their working lives, while the blue line indicates average earnings for high school graduates who do not go to college. Area *A* represents out-of-pocket expenses, *B* is forgone earnings, and *C* is the gross returns to average college graduates. As long as area *C* is sufficiently larger than *A* + *B* to cover a normal rate of return, you can gain by investing in more education. (We detail such calculations two chapters hence.)

FIGURE 5 Payoffs from Investments in Education

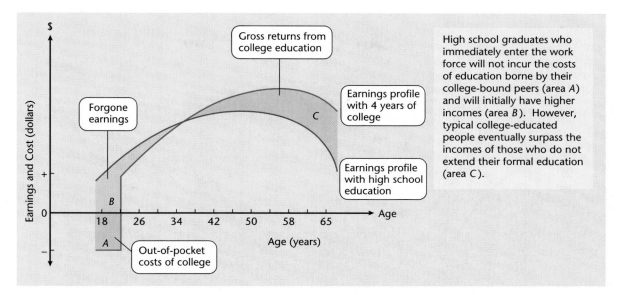

High school graduates who immediately enter the work force will not incur the costs of education borne by their college-bound peers (area *A*) and will initially have higher incomes (area *B*). However, typical college-educated people eventually surpass the incomes of those who do not extend their formal education (area *C*).

Your own prosperity depends on returns from your human capital, but society as a whole shares in both the costs (through taxes) and benefits of much education and training. Education tends to make life more pleasant for everyone. For example, we all benefit from widespread literacy. Can you imagine the gridlock if most drivers could not read traffic signs? We also gain by having well-educated voters. Finally, well-educated people generate higher incomes, pay more taxes, and commit relatively fewer crimes.

These sorts of positive externalities (described in Chapter 4) from educated people to society are effectively public goods, that is, collective benefits that justify some sharing of education costs through taxes. However, external gains to others decline as we become increasingly educated. Things learned in grade school make us semicivilized. High school civilizes us even more, on average if not in every case. But more benefits derived from college are personal, either in the form of consumption now or higher income later.

Marginal productivity theory suggests that you will receive more income to the extent that a degree makes you more productive. The onset of diminishing returns, however, implies that more education eventually yields successively

smaller additions to your lifetime income. These reflections are supported by the private rate of return estimates developed by numerous economists over the last few years. Rates of return decline as individuals become more educated. For example, the personal rate of return from completing the last year of high school (9 through 11 to 12 years) is roughly 18% while the average return from a college degree is now around 15%.

Figure 6 shows college/high school wage ratios for men and women during the past two decades. College/high school wage ratios reflect the average wage premium paid to people with college degrees compared to people with only high school diplomas. This wage premium is now 61% for men and 45% for women. Wage premiums fell during the 1970s, reflecting the rapid increase in college-educated baby boomers who outstripped the growth in demand for their services. Since 1980, wage ratios for all college-educated people have been expanding once again.

One cautionary note: these returns reflect only private earnings and do not include social benefits and personal gratification from extended education. For example, the public benefits from the works of Einstein, Keynes, or most

FIGURE 6 College/High School Wage Ratios 1973—1988

The dip in both series until 1980 reflected the surge of "baby-boomers" into the educated part of the work force. At this low point, average premiums from finishing college were only 30 percent above wages for workers who stopped attending school after graduating from high school. More recently, however, premiums for advanced education have grown, reflecting the competition relatively unskilled U.S. workers face from unskilled workers throughout our increasingly internationalized economy, and the premiums in the global economy for goods and services that require advanced skills. High levels of human capital are relatively less abundant in the world economy than in the United States.

Notice that prior to 1980, the premium incomes to college-educated women relative to other women was higher than that for college-educated men relative to other men, but that in recent years, a college degree generates relatively high premiums for male college graduates. To some extent, this may be an example of supply and demand at work. In the past, men were far more likely than women to get college degrees. Today, more than half of all baccalaureate degrees are awarded to women.

Nobel Prize winners probably could not have been produced by people with only high school educations.

Formal education is one type of human capital—it broadens both your horizons and your options, including job opportunities. It is also used as a device for the screening and signaling described below. Proficiency in some occupations is enhanced little by schooling, however, but grows immensely with experience and on-the-job training.

• **Work Experience** Economists distinguish between general and specific training.

General training increases a worker's marginal productivity equally for many firms.

For example, general training on a personal computer raises a worker's potential productivity with many firms, and acting lessons may open up many roles to an actor.

Specific training only increases the productivity of the worker where currently employed.

For example, completing written sales and order forms for a specific employer may have no benefit when you change jobs and your new employer has an entirely new (or computerized) system.

• **General Training** A firm will invest in human capital only if it expects to recoup at least a normal return on its investment. How can a firm that invests large sums to train technicians ensure that they will not quit before it recovers its investment? Other firms willingly pay the going wage for trained personnel. Firms are reluctant to bear the costs of general training, so trainees typically bear these costs by temporarily accepting wages below the values of their marginal products. Apprenticeship programs are prime examples: apprentices pay for their general training by accepting wages below those they would earn if employed by other firms in less-skilled jobs for which they were already trained.

Few firms offer much general training internally. The military uses a different approach. It guarantees general training but requires recruits to legally commit to several years of service. This partially explains why a military enlistment contract is far harder to break than, say, a teacher's contract, and why the military harshly penalizes deserters.

• **Specific Training** Although much of a technician's training is general, some portion normally represents specific training. Expertise gained when a technician works only on one firm's product often cannot be transferred to other companies; that training is specific to that employer. Firms can ignore competition for job-specific skills that lack value to other firms.

Firms consequently absorb the costs of specific training and share in the returns. Military weapons training or a utility meter reader's knowledge about the quickest route through a neighborhood are examples. A firm tries to pay specifically trained workers more than its competitors would, but less than the values of the workers' marginal products. These slight wage premiums reduce worker turnover and ensure that, on average, firms secure returns on their investments in specific training. Pension plans based on tenure at a firm are another strategy to reduce labor turnover.

Wage Structures and Labor Supplies

Even if all individual supplies of labor were backward bending, the supply of labor facing any firm or industry in the long run would still be perfectly elastic or positively sloped. The explanation for this seeming paradox is actually very simple.

Suppose Accounting Associates of Atlanta (AAA), a major accounting firm, raises its wage offers slightly. No matter how content accountants happen to be, some will overcome inertia and leave their current jobs to take AAA's offer. More pay for the same work sounds pretty good, and the higher the pay, the more numerous will be the accountants available to meet AAA's labor requirements. AAA, a lone firm, is clearly faced with a positively sloped supply curve of accountants, even if the total supply of current accountants is backward bending. But how about the supply of workers facing the accounting industry? If wages for all accountants doubled, might backward-bending supplies of labor for all current accountants mean that less accounting gets done? No!

One reason is that some workers not currently using their accounting skills would respond to higher pay by moving back into this line of work. Many young people seeking remunerative careers might also view accounting more favorably. These young people, plus experienced workers with skills closely related to accounting (e.g., bookkeepers or financial planners), would view the jump in accountants' wages as an incentive to retrain in that field. Pay for accountants rose sharply in the 1980s, and business colleges were flooded with accounting majors. Similar adjustments occur in any industry with growing needs for any type of labor. Higher wages are magnets that attract extra labor services in the long run (just as economic profits attract entry and competition).

In summary, individual supplies of labor are normally positively sloped, but may bend backward at relatively high wage rates. Even if individual labor supply curves are negatively sloped, however, the supplies of labor facing firms or industries will be positively related to wage rates. The demand for labor depends on labor productivity, technology, the demand for the final product, and the levels of other productive resources employed. We are now in a position to merge labor market supplies and demands to see how equilibrium wages and employment are determined.

LABOR MARKET EQUILIBRIUM

In a standard plot of some Horatio Alger stories popular earlier in this century, a poor young country bumpkin, comes to the sinful big city. Through righteous thoughts and modest exertion, he wins fame and fortune (a la Forest Gump). Unfortunately, righteousness, wishful thinking, or modest exertion seldom secure high incomes. Horatio Alger's legends may occasionally come true, but marginal productivity theory probably more accurately reflects how labor markets will affect your future well-being.

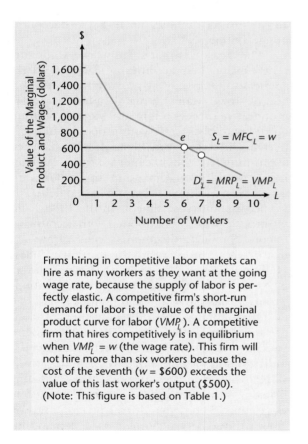

Firms hiring in competitive labor markets can hire as many workers as they want at the going wage rate, because the supply of labor is perfectly elastic. A competitive firm's short-run demand for labor is the value of the marginal product curve for labor (VMP_L). A competitive firm that hires competitively is in equilibrium when $VMP_L = w$ (the wage rate). This firm will not hire more than six workers because the cost of the seventh ($w = \$600$) exceeds the value of this last worker's output ($\$500$). (Note: This figure is based on Table 1.)

FIGURE 7   Profit Maximization and Employment for a Competitive Firm

Marginal Factor Cost

The number of workers hired to maximize profits depends on what you must pay them.

> ***Marginal factor cost (MFC)*** *is the extra cost incurred in hiring an additional unit of a resource.*

Marginal factor costs are identical to wage rates (w) in purely competitive labor markets. All payments for labor (e.g., salaries, employer shares of Social Security taxes, and such fringe benefits as health insurance and paid vacations) are considered *wages*.

Profit Maximization and Employment

The profit-maximizing rule for output decisions (expand until $MR = MC$) leads to the idea that more resources will be hired as long as the extra funds brought in by a resource (its MRP) are at least as great as the money taken away (its MFC). Thus, firms hire more of any input whenever $MRP \geq MFC$. For purely competitive firms operating in competitive labor markets, this translates into a rule: Hire until the VMP_L of the last worker employed equals that worker's marginal factor cost. Competitively set wage rates equal marginal factor costs so profit maximization for pure competition requires that $VMP_L = w$.

Our gold mining example detailed in Table 1 is reproduced in Figure 7. We assume that miners are interchangeably homogenous. Mining gold is hard, dirty work, so assume that a purely competitive labor market dictates that each miner be paid $600 weekly. At this wage, you hire six miners (point *e* in Figure 7), because the value of the marginal product of the sixth worker is also $600. You would not hire a seventh, because the extra $500 in revenue to you is less than the $600 cost of hiring. You would hire a seventh miner only if weekly wages were $500, an eighth miner at $400, and so on. But if wages rose to $700 weekly, the sixth miner, who generates only $600 in marginal revenue product, would be laid off.

FIGURE 8   Equilibrium in the Competitive Labor Market

The wages determined in competitive labor markets (Panel A) determine the amounts of labor employed by competitive firms (Panel B), which expand their hiring until the value of the marginal product equals the wage rate ($VMP_L = MRP_L = MFC_L = w_e$).

Wages and Employment

Figure 8 depicts the interaction of labor supplies and demands for both an individual firm and all firms hiring from a given labor market. The market demand for labor, D_L is only roughly the sum of individual firms' demands.[3] The market supply of labor, denoted S_L is precisely the horizontal sum of individual labor supplies. Interactions of labor supply and demand determine the equilibrium level of wages (w_e) and employment (L_e).

Equilibrium processes resemble those in purely competitive markets for goods. If current wages are below equilibrium, shortages of labor

---

[3]In deriving the market demand curves for consumer goods, we horizontally sum individual demands. In competitive factor markets, such summations of VMP curves are only a first approximation. Assume wages fell. Each firm in an industry would demand more labor and produce more output, but this added output could be sold only at lower prices. When the price of the good fell, each firm's VMP would shift to the left and less labor would be demanded, as you saw in the gold mine example. This effect reduces the market elasticity of the demand for labor, partially offsetting the employment effect of lower wages. Simple summation does not consider the effects of changes in factor costs on product prices. We leave an expanded discussion of this point to advanced classes.

create a tight job market, and employers will bid wages up in attempts to fill vacancies. During 1974 to 1984, wages rose sharply for anyone with expertise in petroleum or computers. Head hunters from employment agencies contacted some people every week or so to see if they were interested in changing jobs. Eventually, however, wages move toward equilibrium.

Wages above equilibrium create labor surpluses and unemployment. The unemployed will ultimately bid wages down as they try to secure jobs, but this can be a painful and time-consuming process. For example, the recession of 1990 to 1991 extended into 1994 in California, depressing both local economies and the incomes of workers.

Every firm that hires from a competitive labor market faces a labor supply curve that is horizontal at the existing market wage (w_e) and can hire as much labor as it wishes at that wage. Purely competitive firms hire only until the value of the marginal product of labor ($VMP_L = MRP_L$) equals marginal factor cost, which is the wage rate ($MFC_L = w$). In Figure 8, L_e workers are hired at a wage of w_e (point e in Panel A). Thus, the market clears when $VMP_L = MRP_L =$

$MFC_L = w_e$; anyone qualified and willing to work at the prevailing wage is employed, while firms hire exactly as much labor as they choose. Purely competitive markets for capital, land, or entrepreneurial skills, which are explored two chapters hence, operate in a similar fashion.

Labor Market Efficiency

Adam Smith's invisible hand receives high marks for efficiency in purely competitive product markets. If externalities are not a problem, the demand curve for any good reflects society's marginal benefits, and the supply curve for the good reflects society's marginal opportunity costs; resources are efficiently allocated where demands for goods meet supplies. These allocations reflect societal wants, given the prevailing structure of ownership rights to resources, which in turn largely determines the distribution of income.

Competitive resource markets are similarly efficient. The demand for labor reflects society's demands for the goods labor produces, because the VMP_L curve roughly portrays society's *marginal benefit* curve from employment. The labor supply curve facing an industry reflects the *marginal costs* to society of employing labor in that industry, because that labor might also be at leisure or employed in other industries. This is diagrammed in Figure 9.

Society receives what it pays for when competitive labor markets are in equilibrium (point *e*) because the marginal social benefits and marginal social costs of employment are equal. Suppose employment were only at L_0. The marginal social benefits from additional employment and production equal w_1 (point *a*), while marginal costs are only w_0 (point *b*). A net social gain equal to distance *ab* can be realized by shifting an additional unit of labor into this industry. Thus, employment level L_0 is below the socially optimal level of employment in this industry. Conversely, if employment were L_1 the net loss to society from employment of the last worker would be distance *cd*.

Society's resources are allocated efficiently only when marginal social benefits and costs are

FIGURE 9   Efficiency in Competitive Labor Markets

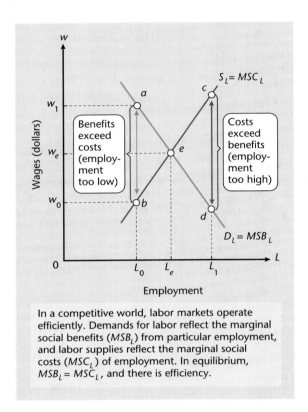

In a competitive world, labor markets operate efficiently. Demands for labor reflect the marginal social benefits (MSB_L) from particular employment, and labor supplies reflect the marginal social costs (MSC_L) of employment. In equilibrium, $MSB_L = MSC_L$, and there is efficiency.

equal, a result achieved in competitive labor markets because they are reflected, respectively, in the demands and supplies of labor. J. B. Clark, the first internationally prominent American economist, was the developer of the $VMP_L = w$ rule for efficiency in labor markets. His ideas still dominate analyses of resource markets.

STRATEGIC BEHAVIOR IN LABOR MARKETS

Firms routinely engage in strategic behavior in product markets. This behavior carries over to the labor market as firms attempt to reduce turnover of employees, identify the best employees to hire, and encourage employees to give their best effort.

BIOGRAPHY

J. B. Clark: Developing Marginal Productivity Theory

John Bates Clark (1847–1938) was the leading American economic theorist at the turn of the century. His position in American economics was similar to that of Alfred Marshall in British economics. Clark was an important innovator in economic theory even though he lacked the vigorous intellectual stimulation Marshall received at Cambridge.

Clark's complete writings were intended to restructure classical theories of value and distribution, but his most enduring contribution is found in the *marginal productivity theory of income distribution* set forth in *The Distribution of Wealth* (1899). Clark sought to prove that every unit of labor and capital is paid precisely the value it adds to total product—its marginal productivity. His model hinges on resource mobility, competition, and the law of diminishing returns.

Labor and capital are each interchangeable, according to Clark, so each worker or piece of capital is, in a sense, the last one. Clark reasoned that, although tasks within a firm differ in importance, if a worker engaged in an important task were removed, the remaining work would be reassigned so that

all essential tasks would be done, leaving the least important tasks undone. This means that no single unit of labor is more important than any other.

Firms operate in a region of their production functions where diminishing marginal returns cause each worker added to a work force to raise total output by a smaller amount than did the previous worker. The employer will hire more workers as long as the last one hired contributes at least as much to total revenue as the cost of employing that worker. Because every worker is the marginal worker, and because the *last* worker hired adds to the employer's gross income an amount equaling the wage rate in a competitive labor market, all workers are paid the values of their marginal products.

Properly understood, Clark's marginal productivity theory is a rebuttal to Marx's charge that competitive capitalism systematically robs labor because workers contribute more to total product than the wages they receive. Clark maintained, on the contrary, that the payment to capital is also determined by its marginal productivity and that there is no surplus

value expropriated from labor as alleged by Marx. Whatever amount of labor is employed, capital so shapes itself that each unit of equivalent labor is working with the same amount of capital. Thus, the product of every unit of capital is also equivalent to every other; when every unit is paid the value of its contribution to total product, there is no surplus to be expropriated. In short, each factor receives a payment determined by the product of its own final increment, and the reward to capital, no less than the reward to labor, is a necessary payment for its productivity.

Early economists were even more prone to take positions on normative issues than are economists today, many of whom pride themselves on their scientific objectivity (if such a thing is possible). Clark tried to use his positive findings to "prove" that payments of income according to contribution (marginal productivity) are inherently equitable. The fact that this idea is as controversial today as it was when Clark first pronounced and published his "proof" is testimony that normative issues cannot be resolved scientifically.

Implicit Labor Contracts

Employee turnover and quit rates are negatively related to wage premiums a firm pays employees with substantial specific training. Firms that invest heavily in specific training for employees have strong incentives to retain them. Paying

higher wages than other firms will offer is one way to reduce quit rates, but firms use many nonwage incentives as well (e.g., seniority rules and generous pension plans tied to longevity with a firm).

Most career employees do not pressure their employers for big raises during prosperous periods; in turn, these firms offer job security by not laying off such workers when business conditions soften. In such hidden handshakes between firms and career employees, formal contracts guaranteeing permanent employment are never signed.

*In an **implicit labor contract**, the worker informally agrees to extend loyalty to the firm in exchange for treatment as a career employee.*

Consultants have extolled the management style in Japan for decades; most giant firms prize loyalty and teamwork between managers and workers. Implicit contracts seem even more prevalent than in the United States. These consultants emphasize the need for U.S. firms to cultivate similar worker loyalty. Paradoxically, implicit contracts have been undercut in both countries because of (*a*) the recession of 1990 to 1992 (which lingered in Japan through 1994), (*b*) increasingly vigorous international competition, and (*c*) tidal waves of corporate mergers, with broad layoffs accompanying corporate downsizing.

This decline in implicit long-term labor contracts may have stimulated the swelling importance of contingent workers in the U.S. labor force. Contingent workers include part-time and temporary workers and many of the self-employed. Contingent workers are often older, and their shorter remaining work lives may exclude some of them from job openings that require substantial specific training. This is one example of how market outcomes may seem inequitable, and occasionally even cruel.

Figure 10 shows that contingent workers have grown from one-fourth of the labor force in the 1960s to nearly 35% today. Pools of semi-idle workers act like a grain surplus overhanging the wheat market, which may account for recent declines in real average weekly earnings as shown in Figure 10. Some economists attribute this swelling pool of contingent workers not only to vigorous international competition, but also to rising nonwage labor costs that are partially attributable to new Federal labor laws.

Recent corporate downsizing has profoundly affected employee loyalty. A recent study surveyed nearly 3,000 employees from some of

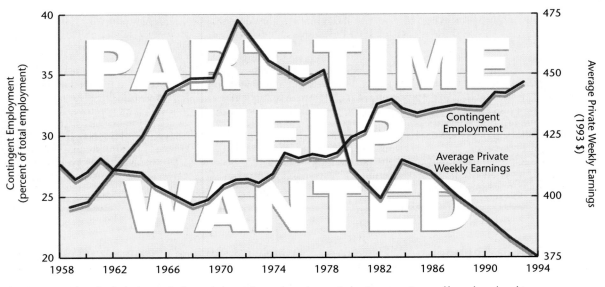

Contingent workers include the total of part-time employees, employees in business services, self-employed and temporary workers. These workers represent a pool of well trained workers that overhangs the labor market. As the proportion of contingent workers in the workforce grows, this may suppress wage increases and make implicit labor contracts less important.

FIGURE 10   The Contingent Labor Market and Average Real Weekly Earnings

Americas' largest corporations.[4] Many of these workers (42%) had experienced downsizing, 28% had seen managerial cutbacks, and one-fifth feared being fired or laid off in the near future.

The study painted a new picture of worker loyalty, how workers measure success, and the incentives employers can use to reduce turnover. Figure 11 and its table suggest that workers are quite concerned about personal satisfaction and how work affects their personal lives, and they are willing to switch employers to get what they want. (However, many workers are unwilling to switch jobs if this would mean losing coverage by health-care insurance—an issue addressed in our chapter on health care.) This study concluded that "workers are more loyal, more committed, more innovative, and more satisfied with their jobs when they have more of a say in how to do their jobs and have more control over the scheduling of their work hours."

Workers' desires for job security and satisfaction may be on the upswing, so that implicit contracts could be resurrected in a significant way and made more formal. The findings of this study raise a major question: is the growth in contingent workers due to corporate downsizing and rising labor costs from government mandates, or is it due to changing worker attitudes about the workplace? Are some workers trading security and higher earnings for the freedom and other benefits of part-time, temporary, or self-employment? Or are firms hiring contingent workers to avoid certain taxes, regulations, and rapidly rising health insurance rates for full-time employees? Many recent trends in labor markets are still too new for definitive answers.

Screening and Signaling

Employers (*principals*) and potential employees (*agents*) alike confront problems of adverse selection and moral hazard when negotiating. *Moral hazard* arises if workers *shirk*, or if firms fail to deliver on well-intentioned promises about job conditions after an employee is on board. *Adverse selection* is a problem if unem-

---

[4]E. Galinsky *et al.*, *The National Study of the Changing Workforce* (New York: Families and Work Institute, 1993).

ployed workers consciously exaggerate how diligently they will perform or if firms paint overly rosy pictures of dreary dead-end jobs. How can potential adverse selection be countered?

Employers often set minimal job requirements to *screen* applicants. Education, experience, government licensing, recommendation letters, and promotion from within are all screening devices. Such screens compel potential employees to acquire skills, experience, or education to meet the requirements for the job offered by the employer.

> **Screening** *occurs when a principal (employer) examines the qualifications of a potential agent (employee) before offering the agent a contract (a job).*

Alternatively, agents knowing their own abilities may attempt to convey this information to potential principals by obtaining education or certificates as signals observable by principals.

> **Signaling** *occurs when potential agents try to communicate special qualifications that will elicit the offer of a contract from a principal.*

Screening and signaling are attempts to finesse adverse selection. Just as lemons depress prices for all used cars, "lemon" workers would drive down all wages if screening and signaling were impossible. Unfortunately, screening stimulates résumé inflation and phony degrees from diploma mills. Even if employers closely check credentials, no barrier is ever 100% effective in screening out incompetence or dishonesty. Some critics also charge that overemphasis on formal credentials bars some workers from having appropriate access to some jobs.

Efficiency Wages

Signaling and screening devices are designed to reduce employer-employee conflicts that originate from asymmetric information in the hiring process. Once hired, the firm has a vested interest in getting the best from each employee. Asymmetric information is, however, still a problem. For example, loafing on the job may occur if

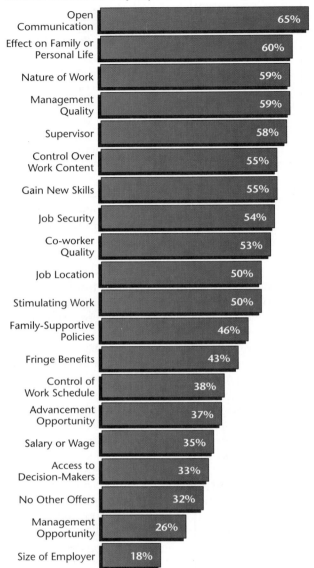

Reasons considered "very important" in deciding to take current job

Reason	%
Open Communication	65%
Effect on Family or Personal Life	60%
Nature of Work	59%
Management Quality	59%
Supervisor	58%
Control Over Work Content	55%
Gain New Skills	55%
Job Security	54%
Co-worker Quality	53%
Job Location	50%
Stimulating Work	50%
Family-Supportive Policies	46%
Fringe Benefits	43%
Control of Work Schedule	38%
Advancement Opportunity	37%
Salary or Wage	35%
Access to Decision-Makers	33%
No Other Offers	32%
Management Opportunity	26%
Size of Employer	18%

What Does Success Mean to You?	
Personal satisfaction from doing a good job	52%
Earning the respect or recognition of others	30%
Getting ahead or advancing in job or career	22%
Making a good income	21%
Feeling my work is important	12%
Having control over work content and schedule	6%

Source: E. Galinsky *et al., The National Study of the Changing Workforce* (New York: Families and Work Institute, 1993).

FIGURE 11   Reasons for Taking a Job and Measures of Success

firms cannot closely monitor performance; the chance to loaf while drawing a paycheck is a moral hazard. A firm, on the other hand, may convert inconveniences to itself into burdens on its workers if, for example, it tries to maintain morale by concealing the fact that bad investments have gutted employee pension plans.

The existence of substantial and sustained unemployment in some labor markets clashes with standard theories of competitive labor markets, because wage reductions should quickly and automatically eliminate unemployment (surpluses of labor). One explanation for the apparent paradox of involuntary unemployment focuses on how firms try to tailor employment decisions to offset moral hazards.

The supply and demand for labor shown in Figure 12 yields an equilibrium of L_L employment

FIGURE 12 Efficiency Wages and Equilibrium Unemployment

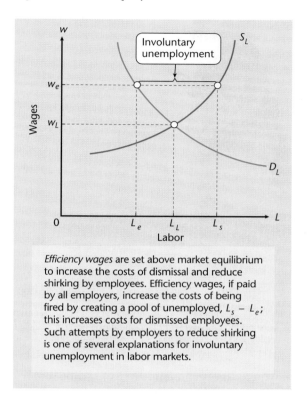

Efficiency wages are set above market equilibrium to increase the costs of dismissal and reduce shirking by employees. Efficiency wages, if paid by all employers, increase the costs of being fired by creating a pool of unemployed, $L_s - L_e$; this increases costs for dismissed employees. Such attempts by employers to reduce shirking is one of several explanations for involuntary unemployment in labor markets.

at wage w_L under standard assumptions. A worker not performing satisfactorily (shirking) could be fired, but if this labor market were purely competitive, this worker almost immediately finds another job at wage w_L. Thus, if all the assumptions of pure competition were met in a labor market, the threat to fire a worker is ineffective as a disincentive against loafing or dishonesty.

Employers are aware that such moral hazards must be offset by other incentives. One solution is for the firm to engage in *reputation building*. A reputation as a firm that seldom lays off workers, even when business is slack, may attract excellent workers without requiring payments of premium wages. In this case, shirking, if discovered, would cause a worker to forfeit job security. On the other hand, a reputation as an unreliable employer that mistreats workers may stimulate shirking by workers. In such cases, the firm may be forced to expend more resources monitoring employee performance.

Another solution to curb shirking is for an employer to pay wages above prevailing market wages. A firm may start new employees at a low wage but, after the newly hired worker performs well, quickly raise the pay to a premium level. These employees would lose their premium wages if fired and would be less likely to be able to duplicate the salary and benefits of their existing jobs.

Efficiency wages are wages higher than market-clearing wages and are intended to raise the costs of dismissal and reduce shirking by employees.

This may seem paradoxical because, if all firms pay wages that exceed the market-clearing wage, dismissal would not harm employees. Figure 12 suggests, however, that high efficiency wages (w_e) to control shirking reduce employment to L_e. Unemployment equals $L_s - L_e$ in this type of equilibrium, because L_s workers are willing to work at wage w_e. Dismissed employees will be at least temporarily unemployed, raising their costs of shirking. Similarly, employers find it difficult to skim the best workers from the labor pool while only paying a market-clearing wage. Thus, involuntary unemployment may be partially explained by the employers' attempts to offset moral hazards by paying premium wages. Just as lemons are eagerly sold in the used car market, disproportionate numbers of shirkers may inhabit the pool of unemployed workers.

WAGE DIFFERENTIALS

It is no secret that one key to a high-paying job is expertise in a hot field demanded by many employers. The types of expertise in greatest demand change constantly, in part because of the continuing growth of international trade. You should recognize, however, that factors other than human capital can influence pay differentials enormously. In 1776, Adam Smith observed that if similarly valuable human capital is required in two jobs, then, all else being equal, pay (including fringe benefits) will be lower for the job with working conditions that are more convenient, pleasant, slower paced, safer, more certain, or that require less responsibility. Figure 13 indicates how average pay varies across certain occupations.

FIGURE 13   Average Pay in Selected Jobs, 1993

Wage diferentials reflect differences (a) in people (e.g., human capital, personality, employment discrimination), and (b) in the desirability of different types of work. This figure suggests how human capital and willingness to endure demanding, unpleasant, or dangerous conditions blend to generate wage differentials across various occupations.

Some jobs are so inherently obnoxious or dangerous that premium pay is necessary to attract workers. Suppose you had the option of greeting restaurant customers for $10 per hour or emptying grease traps for a restaurant chain at the same wage. Most of us would obviously choose to greet diners. This typical reaction shrinks the supply of grease-trap cleaners and expands supplies of labor for more pleasant jobs. Similarly, most people will perform more dangerous work only if they view the extra compensation for risk as appropriate. Thus, trash collectors tend to draw higher pay than ditch diggers, and specialists at putting out oil-rig fires receive premium wages relative to roofers. Even before *perestroika*, Siberian coal miners drew twice the pay of typical factory workers.

Regional wage differences arise from higher costs of living (New York City versus Atlanta), harsher climate (North Slope, Alaska, versus Portland, Oregon), or less attractive scenery (Midland, Texas, versus Boulder, Colorado). Some occupations offer stable em-

ployment (government service), while others confront workers with seasonal layoffs or uncertain futures (construction). Secure employment yields lower wages (military enlistment versus steelwork on skyscrapers). And workers in occupations offering opportunities for tax evasion will be willing to accept lower official wages.

Some wage differentials arise from the condition of the firm or industry in which you are employed or from local prosperity. Bigger firms tend to pay better than smaller firms, as do growing and more profitable industries. Stagnant local economies, on the other hand, at least temporarily tend to depress all wages. These problems are cured, in part, by labor mobility. In the long run, workers flow out of stagnant firms, industries, and regions, moving toward jobs in more prosperous work environments.

Wage Differentials and Discrimination

The systematic earnings differentials displayed in Table 4 are sometimes cited as evidence that wage

TABLE 4   Median Annual Earnings by Race, Gender, and Age (1993)

	Median Weekly Earnings	Median Annual Earnings	Percent of All Workers' Earnings		Median Weekly Earnings	Median Annual Earnings	Percent of All Workers' Earnings
Men	529	27,508	112.8	**Occupations**			
16–24	291	15,132	62.0	Executive	665	34,580	141.8
25 over	578	30,056	123.2	Professional	698	36,296	148.8
				Technical	548	28,496	116.8
Women	399	20,748	85.1	Sales	467	24,284	99.6
16–24	274	14,248	58.4	Admin/Clerical	391	20,332	83.4
25 over	420	21,840	89.6	Service	286	14,872	61.0
				Mechanics	508	26,416	108.3
White	485	25,220	103.4	Construction	492	25,584	104.9
Men	555	28,860	118.3	Transportation	454	23,608	96.8
Woman	408	21,216	87.0	Farm/forest/fish	283	14,716	60.3
Black	367	19,084	78.3	**All Workers**	469	24,388	100.0
Men	401	20,852	85.5				
Women	337	17,524	71.9				
Hispanic	321	16,692	68.4				
Men	345	17,940	73.6				
Women	294	15,288	62.7				

Source: U.S. Bureau of Labor Statistics, Bulletin 2429; and *Employment and Earnings,* April 1994.

discrimination is too often exercised on the basis of race, gender, or age. Numerous studies indicate that appearance plays a role in how successfully people pursue careers. Differentials in human capital, willingness to endure unpleasant or dangerous job conditions, regional preferences, and circumstances peculiar to particular firms or industries also help explain occupational wage differentials. The pay differentials in Table 3 only partially reflect meaningful differences in occupational patterns, education, and training and experience. Wage gaps between those under and over 25 years of age are largely explained by different levels of experience. Experience cannot account, however, for most of the wage differences by race and gender.

Occupational Crowding

History is replete with cases where individuals were denied equal access to jobs or paid less than others. The very perception of discrimination exacts a toll on workers' attitudes and performance, regardless of whether their perceptions have an objective basis in fact.[5]

Women may suffer especially from wage discrimination because many employers view women's work decisions as secondary to their husbands' career moves. The prospect of job security for women may facilitate wage discrimination. The resulting potential for exploitation is a powerful argument for recent "equal pay for equal work" laws, which may promote equity without hindering efficiency.

Some people want this law extended to raise wages for careers into which most women were once channeled: nursing, teaching, and clerical work. They argue that these workers are underpaid because of occupational crowding.

Occupational crowding *occurs when women or members of other disadvantaged groups are pressured toward certain low-wage occupations.*

[5]Ibid, p. 26.

FIGURE 14   Discrimination and Wage Differentials (Salary Gaps)

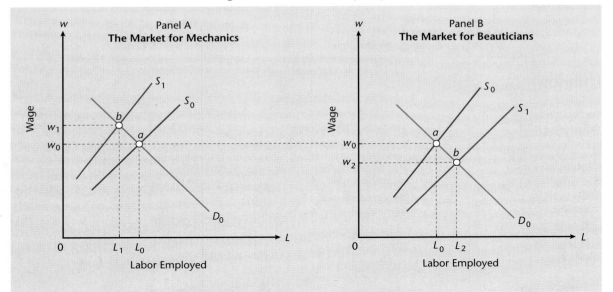

Excluding women from certain occupations (e.g., work as auto mechanics) reduces the supply of labor and boosts wages in these markets, as shown in Panel A. At the same time, however, labor supplies are swollen and wages are relatively depressed in the occupation into which women are channeled (e.g., cosmetology), as indicated in Panel B.

For example, nurses are typically far more educated and bear more responsibility than hospital janitors. Advocates of the *doctrine of comparable worth* are aghast that janitors tend to be paid more. Such apparent discrepancies in pay relative to the value of a job must be the result of sex discrimination, according to their reasoning. In fact, a recent study by the AFL-CIO concluded that "women's work pays best if it's done by a man."[6]

Figure 14 shows how occupational crowding can create pay differentials between men and women. Begin by assuming a lack of discrimination, that the vocations of auto mechanic and beautician require comparable training and effort, and that entry is unrestricted into either occupation. Both types of workers would earn wages of w_0 and each market would employ L_0 units of labor with roughly equal proportions of men and women (points a in both panels).

Suppose jobs as mechanics or similar work were now closed to women, while cosmetology and a few other jobs remain open to all. The supply of mechanics shrinks by almost half when women are excluded, while a few male beauticians retrain as mechanics when mechanics' wage rise. Most women previously working as mechanics will move into such jobs as beautician. Supply curves shift to S_1 in Figure 14, reflecting fewer mechanics and more beauticians. An occupational wage differential of $w_1 - w_2$ results.

Decomposing Wage Differentials

A recent study by the Bureau of the Census[7] found that, on average

1. Women are more likely to have career interruptions than men.

---

[6]*Salaried and Professional Women: Relevant Statistics*, compiled by the AFL-CIO's Department for Professional Employees, 1988.

[7]U.S. Bureau of the Census, "Male-Female Differences in Work Experience, Occupation, and Earnings: 1984," *Current Population Reports*, series P-70, no. 10 (Washington, D.C.: U.S. Government Printing Office, 1987).

TABLE 5 Accounting for Male-Female Wage Differentials

Proportion of Male-Female Earnings Differential Accounted for by Differences in the Mean Values of the Independent Variables (based on coefficients for males) Characteristics	Not High School Graduates	High School Graduates	College Graduates
Experience[1]	0.139	0.222	0.226
Schooling[2]	(NA)	0.008	0.127
Field of study	(NA)	(NA)	0.116
Skilled trades[3]	0.129	(NA)	(NA)
Occupational structure[4]	0.303	0.300	0.174
Other characteristics[5]	0.024	0.071	0.128
All characteristics	0.595	0.601	0.655
Residual	0.405	0.399	0.345

Source: U.S. Bureau of the Census, Current Population Reports, series P-70, no. 10, *Male-Female Differences in Work Experience, Occupation, and Earnings, 1984* (Washington, D.C.: U.S. Government Printing Office, 1987).

[1]Number of years with current employer, years in current occupation less years with current employer, years of work experience less years in current occupation, whether usually worked full time during work years, length of time between current and previous job.

[2]Type of high school program, number of math, science, and foreign language courses in high school, whether public or private high school (high school and college graduates); highest degree and field of study (college graduates).

[3]Whether in precision production, craft, or repair occupation.

[4]Percent of persons in occupation who are female.

[5]Marital status, type of geographic area, whether covered by a union contract, size of firm, class of worker, whether involuntarily left last job, race and Hispanic origin, disability and health status, presence of children.

2. Women tend to have fewer years on their current jobs than men.
3. Women graduates cluster in education and nursing-related fields.

Over half of male college graduates (57%) majored in law, medicine, dentistry, science, math, business, economics, or engineering, compared with only 28% of women.

Women workers averaged roughly 70% of the pay for men in 1990. What proportion of this difference is strictly gender related, and what proportion is explained by work interruptions, less experience and tenure on the current job, level of education and major, or other factors that might affect productivity? Table 5 provides the results from the Bureau of the Census study that adjusted the actual wage difference for various characteristics of individuals.

For college graduates, experience accounts for nearly one-fourth of the wage differential. Education and field of study account for another one-eighth, nearly all of which was due to choice of major. Occupational structure explains roughly one-sixth of the total pay differential. These data demonstrate that occupational crowding is central to the male-female wage gap. Finally, such characteristics as marital status, region, union or nonunion, race, and presence of children accounted for almost 13% of the pay gap between men and women. All these factors explained almost two-thirds of the total wage gap, with much of it accounted for by occupational crowding.

Comparable Worth

Equal pay for *comparable* work is now legally required in more than a dozen states, and bills are pending in Congress and several other state legislatures.[8] Even in states where comparable

---

[8]"Comparable Worth: It's Already Happening," *Business Week*, 29 April 1986, pp. 52–56.

worth is not the law, many firms are adopting job evaluation programs in quests for internal equity. The salary gap that comparable worth is expected to close varies by occupation and age.[9] But, as Table 4 shows, younger women now fare much better than older women. This is partially a reflection of better education and training, but it also reflects the growing number of young women majoring in business, computer science, law, medicine, and engineering.

Unequal access to remunerative jobs historically pushed women into fields with relatively low pay, but whether laws requiring equal pay for comparable work will achieve the goal of its advocates is debatable. The first problem in implementing this approach is ascertaining how much specific jobs should pay. Most markets to which this doctrine would apply are quite competitive, but we presumably cannot rely on market wage solutions. This means that government officials will need to consider the qualities of each job; skill requirements, how pleasant the work environment is, and the relative risks to workers are only a few of the many factors that would need to be considered. Weighing education and classroom teaching duties against hot, sweaty, and dangerous work on a construction crew, for example, is unavoidably subjective. The slow and costly process of unraveling such complex issues would be unlikely to satisfy many people.

Suppose all these problems were resolved. The basic problem remains that wages have been depressed by swollen supplies of nurses, teachers, and clerical workers. New laws raising wages above the equilibrium pay for holders of jobs that have historically been women's work will, unfortunately, have effects similar to those of a legal minimum wage. Firms would have strong incentives to find substitutes as higher salaries were legally mandated. For example, office work would become even more automated. Receptionist slots would be pared to the bone. Electronic filing systems would be simplified to reduce routine clerical work. Business correspondence would become more standardized to minimize the need for individualized letters, and firms would rely even more heavily on negotiations by telephone. Nurses would find more of their tasks taken over by orderlies or technicians. Schools would be pressured to contain costs by increasing student/teacher ratios. Many women currently employed in these occupations would lose their jobs, and there would be surpluses of secretaries, teachers, and nurses.

Likely consequences of wider adoption of the comparable worth approach would be higher unemployment rates among women and widening inequality in the relative earnings of women. Thus, this approach might be like some policies we described in Chapter 4: many members of the groups targeted for help may be harmed in unforeseen ways. Fortunately, this problem may cure itself as time elapses and women increasingly shun traditional women's careers to become doctors, lawyers, pilots, or engineers.

Effects of Wage Discrimination

Most studies of wage differentials between males and females and between blacks and whites come to similar conclusions: roughly one-third of these differentials arise from employment discrimination, with experience and occupational crowding apparently accounting for most of the rest.[10] These differentials generate forces that can be self-perpetuating. For example, groups suffering from lower wages have less incentive to invest in education or on-the-job training because the rate of return from this investment will tend to be less. This problem is exacerbated if only inferior schooling is available, a problem facing many black students. Inferior schools are infamous for channeling students into crowded, low-paying occupations.

Unfortunately, the doctrine of comparable worth is questionable as a cure for problems caused by occupational crowding. The best rem-

---

[9]"The Truth About The Salary Gap(s)," *Working Women*, January 1988, pp. 61–62.

[10]See O. B. Bodvarsson, "Using Reverse Regression to Estimate Salary Discrimination When the Wage-Setting Process is Costly," paper presented to the Southern Economic Association, November, 1990. Using detailed national data for 2,400 black and white men between the ages of 29 and 39, Bodvarsson found that discrimination was nonexistent in occupations where workers were paid commissions or on a piece rate basis. The same conclusion was reached for professional and technical workers.

edy for such problems may be better career counseling and improved access to education.

This chapter has focused on the effects of competition in labor markets, but many labor markets are far from competitive. Some imperfections originate in the private sector (e.g., unions), but some also emerge from government policies (e.g., limits on the employment of youngsters, health and safety regulations, and minimum-wage laws). The next chapter explores some consequences of inadequate competition in resource markets and government policies for the labor market.

CHAPTER REVIEW: KEY POINTS

1. The demand for any resource is related to the (a) amounts of other factors employed, (b) production technology used, and (c) demand for the product. Because the demand for labor (or any factor) hinges on the demand for final products, it is a **derived demand**.

2. **Marginal revenue product** (*MRP*) is the firm's revenues generated by hiring the marginal unit of some input which is equal to $MR \times MPP$. In pure competition, this is the same as **value of the marginal product** (*VMP*), which is equal to $P \times MPP$.

3. Increases (or decreases) in the demand for the product, labor productivity, or the amounts of other resources used will normally increase (or decrease) the *VMP* and demand for labor. Technological changes may either increase or decrease labor demands. *Automation* is the replacement of workers by new technologies.

4. The **elasticity of demand for labor** is directly related to (a) the *elasticity of demand for the final product*, (b) *labor's share of total costs* represented by the wage bill, (c) the ease of factor *substitution*, and (d) *the time for adjustment*.

5. The **supply of labor** depends on (a) wage rates and structures; (b) labor-force participation; (c) the number of hours people are willing to work; and (d) the education, training, and skills of workers.

6. Workers experience both **income** and **substitution effects** when wage rates change. Increased wages cause labor to substitute work for leisure, because work expands consumption opportunities and leisure is more costly. However, higher wages mean that for a given amount of labor effort, workers will earn more income, and, if leisure is a normal good, they will want to consume more leisure and work less. If the substitution effect is larger than the income effect, supplies are positively sloped. Backward-bending labor supplies result when income effects dominate substitution effects.

7. Labor quality improves through investments in **human capital**, which include formal education and on-the-job training. Education benefits both the individual and society at large. Training is classified as either general or specific; **general training** enhances a worker's productivity equally for many firms, while **specific training** only increases the worker's productivity for the current employer.

8. While the individual's labor supply curve may be backward bending, the supply of labor to any industry will always be positively sloped. Industry supplies and demands for labor establish the *equilibrium wage*, as each firm hires additional units of labor until the value of the marginal product equals the market wage rate.

9. Any resource will be employed up to the point where the additional revenue competitive firms receive (*VMP*) just equals the cost of an additional unit of the resource (*MFC*). In competitive labor markets, the *marginal factor cost (MFC)* equals the *wage rate(w)*, so pure competition in all markets means that $VMP_L = MRP_L = MFC_L = w$.

10. Competitive demand curves for labor represent the marginal benefits to society from additional employment, and supply curves reflect the marginal cost to society of using those resources. Employing labor to the point where $D_L = S_L$ is efficient because society's benefits from additional employment equal its costs. More or less employment than this yields inefficient resource allocations, because society gets more (or less) than it desires in an opportunity cost sense.

11. Workers and employers in large firms have often reached **implicit contracts** whereby the firm effectively guaranteed job security for career employees in exchange for the workers' loyalty.

12. Turnover and quit rates are negatively related to the levels of specific training workers have received and the wage premiums paid them. Firms that invest heavily in their employees have strong incentives to retain them and do so (*a*) by paying higher wages (**efficiency wages**) than other firms will offer and (*b*) through special rules based on seniority or pension provisions that reward longevity with the firm.

13. The most important determinants of **wage differentials** are (*a*) human capital, (*b*) working conditions and (*c*) occupational crowding. All else being equal, premium wages are paid to compensate workers who endure less pleasant jobs.

QUESTIONS FOR THOUGHT AND DISCUSSION

1. Marginal productivity theory suggests that people are paid according to the productive contributions of their resources, including labor. But such things as seniority rules clearly create situations where some people who are paid less are more productive than some people who are paid more. Do you think that the forces of marginal productivity generate a strong tendency for payment to be roughly proportional to contribution? Why or why not?

2. Some successful people like to brag that they started with nothing and owe "nothing to nobody." Marginal productivity theory suggests that technology and the amount of capital and the number of people we work with are powerful influences on our productivity and income. How are rugged individualists who believe they have done it on their own both supported and rebutted by marginal productivity theory?

3. Some 1930s radicals held that pay should be determined by how vital a job is to society. For example, people who maintain traffic lights or collect trash would be paid more than Hollywood stars or the promoters of such fads as Barney. Do you think this argument has merit? Why, or why not?

4. Some highly intelligent, well-educated people work very hard and receive little in return. Is a Ph.D. in music who practices constantly and becomes the world's 211th-best oboe player entitled to more pay than a waiter? Does capitalism undervalue artistry or esoteric knowledge? If so, how should we determine appropriate incomes for people whom the market system spurns?

5. Several studies, after adjusting for other individual characteristics, suggest that short men are paid less than tall men and that short men are less likely to be promoted. Other studies suggest that attractive people tend to receive higher pay and quicker promotions than do those who are considered either plain or ugly. Are these results consistent with marginal productivity theory? Do you think these studies are correct? If so, what do you think accounts for these and similar findings?

Entrepreneur   Monosony

Chapter 29

Discrimination

Implicit contracts

Labor

Imperfect Competition in Labor Markets

Human capital

Wage $VMP = MRP$

Product markets range from pure competition to monopoly. Resource markets run a similar gamut. Our description of competition in labor markets in the previous chapter only obliquely addresses certain practical questions about work and pay. For example, relative wages and access to certain jobs may depend less on willingness and ability to excel on the job than on such things as (*a*) connections (e.g., are you a union member, or is your golfing buddy an executive for your potential employer?), (*b*) credentials (e.g., job experience, recommendations, or college degrees), (*c*) personality characteristics only loosely related to productivity (e.g., how can a shy but determined applicant compete for a job against a less diligent but charming extrovert?), and (*d*) a potential employer's market power in either resource or output markets.

You will study three basic types of imperfections in resource markets in this chapter: (*a*) firms with market power that restrict output and thus demand fewer resources; (*b*) resource buyers with clout that reduce quantities demanded to depress resource prices; and (*c*) resource sellers with market power that boost resource prices

by restricting the quantity available. Labor markets are especially plagued by noncompetitive influences; government regulations abound, and powerful unions restrict supplies to drive wages up, while powerful employers flex their economic muscle to depress wages.

Our first concerns are problems posed from the demand side when employers exercise substantial market power, either as sellers of goods or as buyers of labor. Then we look at concentrated power from the supply side, among sellers of labor—primarily, labor unions. Finally, we survey the history and current status of American unionism.

MONOPOLISTS' DIMINISHED LABOR DEMANDS

You already know that firms with market power raise prices and restrict output to maximize profit. The result for resource markets is that fewer resources are employed than when markets are competitive.

Suppose gold output trickled off in your Colorado mine, but that you discovered a rich vein of tantalite ore. Tantalum is used to line tanks for liquids, as an alloy in tungsten carbide cutting tools, and in certain electronics applications. It is also quite rare, so assume that you gain substantial market power. Relevant portions of the demand for tantalum and your production function are listed in Table 1.

Tantalum output for various numbers of miners parallels that for gold production, but your market power means that the demand curve for tantalum slopes downward. For example (from columns 2 and 3 of Table 1), if you sell 50 pounds weekly, you can charge $90 per pound. Raising output to 110 pounds, however, requires a price cut to $50 per pound.

Market power depresses marginal revenue below price because added output is salable only if prices are cut for all units produced. You must now decide (1) what price to charge and how much to produce to maximize profits and (2) how many workers to hire to get the job done. The answer to question 1 automatically answers question 2 because it takes a specific number of workers to produce the most profitable level of output.

Any firm maximizes profit when the revenue generated by the last worker hired (MRP) equals the wage outlays incurred by hiring the last worker (MFC). If all markets are competitive, this translates into the rule that the value of the marginal product (VMP = MRP) equals the wage (MFC = w), so VMP = MRP = MFC = w. A rule that profit is maximized when VMP = w works only for competitors operating in competitive labor markets. The more general rule for maximum profits is that MRP = MFC. Market power causes the value of the marginal product to exceed the marginal revenue product and reduces the amount of labor hired.

Let's apply this approach to your mine. Column 3 of Table 1 shows that hiring more workers raises output but lowers tantalum prices. Marginal revenue from tantalum mined by extra workers (column 5) is below its price. Each extra miner adds MR × MPP = MRP to your dollar sales volume (column 7, the marginal revenue product of labor), but this is below the value of the marginal product (P × MPP in column 8). For example, the third miner raises tantalum output by 18 pounds (from 50 to 68 pounds per week), but its price falls from $90 to $80 per pound. The $10 price cut on the first 50 pounds of tantalum shrinks the revenue from hiring a third miner to only $940 (column 7) instead of the $1,440 (18 × $80) value of that third miner's marginal product (column 8).

Thus, because market power causes the price of output to exceed its marginal revenue, labor's value of the marginal product (VMP = P × MPP) is greater than its marginal revenue

TABLE 1 Data for Tantalum Production

Production Function						Demand for Labor		
(1)	(2)	(3)	(4)	(5)	(6)	(7)	(8)
Number of Workers L	Pounds of Tantalum Produced per Week q	Price of Tantalum per Pound P	Total Revenue TR $(P \times q)$	Marginal Revenue MR $(\Delta TR/\Delta q)$	Marginal Physical Product of Labor MPP_L $(\Delta q/\Delta L)$	Marginal Revenue Product of Labor MRP_L $(MR \times MPP_L)$	Value of the Marginal Product of Labor VMP_L $(P \times MPP_L)$
1	30	$100	$3,000	$100.00	30	$3,000	$3,000
2	50	90	4,500	75.00	20	1,500	1,800
3	68	80	5,440	55.22	18	940	1,440
4	84	70	5,880	27.50	16	440	1,120
5	98	60	5,880	0	14	0	840
6	110	50	5,500	−31.67	12	−380	600
7	120	40	4,800	−70.00	10	−700	400

product ($MRP = MR \times MPP$). The maximum profit rule requires that the marginal revenue product equals the marginal factor cost ($MRP = MFC$). Thus, profit is maximized for your tantalum mine when

$$VMP > MRP = MFC = w$$

The revenue the last worker adds (MRP) equals the cost of hiring (MFC), which in this case is the competitive wage rate w, but this wage rate is below the value of the marginal product. Your market power allows you to pay workers less than the marginal social value of their output and forces us to distinguish between the $VMPs$ and $MRPs$ of labor. $MRP = MR \times MPP$, so marginal revenue product also equals the change in total revenue realized by hiring one more unit of labor ($MRP = \Delta TR/\Delta L$). Both MRP and VMP (columns 7 and 8 from Table 1) are diagrammed in Figure 1.

Suppose that you now hire labor from a competitive market at $440 weekly. To equate the MRP with the $440 wage, you would hire four workers (point a). Note that at point a, $MRP = MFC$ ($MRP = \$440 = MFC$). The fifth worker adds nothing to total revenue ($MRP = 0$) but would cost $440 per week—clearly a losing proposition.

Monopolistic Exploitation

Resource suppliers who are paid less than the values of their marginal products are said to be *exploited*.[1]

> *If market power causes the value of the marginal product of labor to exceed the wage rate, the difference is known as **monopolistic exploitation**.*

The fourth worker's VMP is $1,120 (point b), which is far above the fourth worker's MRP and wage of $440. The difference between the VMP

---

[1]*Exploitation* sounds like a very judgmental term, but it is the standard language of this analysis. The early work in this area was done by Marxist economists. This does not invalidate their analysis, but it does explain this inflammatory terminology.

FIGURE 1 Equilibrium Employment for the Tantalum Monopolist

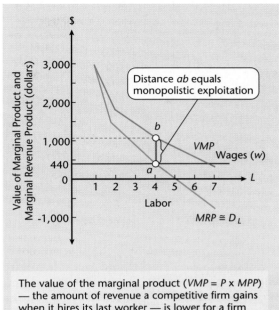

The value of the marginal product ($VMP = P \times MPP$) — the amount of revenue a competitive firm gains when it hires its last worker — is lower for a firm with market power, because $P > MR$. Hence, the marginal revenue product ($MR \times MPP$) is less than the value of the marginal product. Monopolistic exploitation is the difference between VMP and w (distance ab).
(Note: The VMP and MRP shown are drawn from Table 1.)

and w (line ab, or $680) is called *the rate of monopolistic exploitation of labor*.

MONOPSONY IN A LABOR MARKET

Another source of exploitation arises if firms exert economic clout as resource buyers. No single firm's hiring noticeably affects wages in competitive labor markets. For example, in large cities, prevailing wages for secretaries, clerks, and delivery people are unaffected by any one firm's hiring. Contrast such markets with those for small towns where a coal mine or textile mill dominates employment.

TABLE 2 Supply of Labor Data for a Firm with Monopsony Power

(1)	(2)	(3)	(4)
		Total Labor Cost	Marginal Factor (Labor) Cost
Labor	Weekly Wage	TC_L	MFC
L	w	$(w \times L)$	$(\Delta TC_L / \Delta L)$
1	$250	$250	$250
2	300	600	350
3	380	1,140	540
4	485	1,940	800
5	550	2,750	810
6	600	3,600	850
7	700	4,900	1,300
8	800	6,400	1,500

*A **monopsonist** is a sole buyer of a good or resource.*

A labor monopsonist is the sole employer in a specific labor market and faces the entire labor supply. Thus, its hiring decision determines the wage rate. A labor market in which a monopsonist pays all workers equally is outlined in Table 2. Hiring three workers requires the monopsonist to pay a wage rate of only $380 per week to this community's three most eager beavers.[2] Thus, employing four local workers forces the monopsonist to raise its wage offer to $485 to attract the next, slightly less eager beaver to work and necessitates a raise of $105 each to the preceding three workers.

The important result is that monopsony power raises marginal factor cost (*MFC*) above the wage rate. If this firm hires three workers at $380 per week, its labor costs are $1,140; these costs rise to $1,940 if the firm employs four workers at $485. Hiring a fourth worker without wage discrimination requires a wage increase to $485 per week to the original three workers, which boosts total labor costs by $800, not $485. Such wage increases cause the *MFC* to exceed the wage rate for each employment level. The *MFC* shown in column 4 of Table 2 is the change in total labor costs from hiring one extra worker. How does the

excess of this *MFC* over the wage rate affect this firm's hiring? Figure 2 shows the labor supply and its *MFC* to this monopsonist.

A monopsonist's marginal factor cost curve is above the labor supply curve, just as a monopolist's marginal revenue curve is below the demand curve it faces. The value of the marginal product from our gold mine of previous chapters is also shown, so Figure 2 depicts a monopsony selling a competitive output and $VMP = MRP$. This firm maximizes profit by hiring labor until the $MRP = MFC$ at $800 (point *c* in Figure 2) but only pays $485 each to the four workers willing to work for that weekly wage (point *d*). Thus, $VMP = MRP = MFC > w$.

Monopsonistic Exploitation

A labor monopsonist hires fewer workers and pays lower wages than a firm hiring in a competitive labor market. If this firm faced a $600

If the supply of labor facing a firm is positively sloped, then the wage increases that must be granted to all workers cause the marginal factor cost (*MFC*) curve to lie above the supply curve. This analysis ignores possible wage discrimination to simplify the analysis.

FIGURE 2 Equilibrium Wage and Employment for a Monopsonist

---

[2]To simplify this analysis, we temporarily assume that wage discrimination (a topic we address in a moment) is impossible.

wage from a competitive labor market, it would hire six workers (point *e*). Thus, the monopsonist pays workers less than a competitive employer would. Monopsony power enables it to hire four workers for a $485 wage (point *d*), far below the values of their marginal product of $800 (point *c*). The difference ($315, distance *cd*) is termed *monopsonistic exploitation* of labor.

> *Monopsonistic exploitation* occurs when a firm exercises its clout in hiring labor; it equals the difference between the value of the marginal product of labor (VMP) and its wage rate (w).

Few pure monopsonists exist, although huge firms located in small communities may dominate local labor markets and exercise substantial monopsony power. For example, residents in small towns may rely heavily for employment on lumber mills in the Northwest, or textile mills in the Southeast. A more common type of monopsonistic exploitation occurs when firms control individual employees sufficiently to wage discriminate. For many occupations (e.g., forensic scientists, teachers, and firefighters), governments (federal, state, and local) enjoy some monopsony power.

Wage Discrimination

Have you ever worked for a company that discouraged workers from sharing information about wages or salaries? Many firms that do not set standard pay scales treat salary information as confidential. This is a common practice when a firm practices *wage discrimination*.

> *Wage discrimination* occurs when workers receive different pay that is inconsistent with their individual marginal productivities.

This is possible only if a firm has some monopsony power, just as price discrimination for goods requires a firm to possess market power. This type of monopsony power may be exercised whenever any employee views a particular firm as offering special advantages such as location, job security, or opportunities for promotion.

Our discussion in the monopoly chapter showed that price discrimination may partially remedy the economic inefficiency created when firms exercise market power. Wage discrimination may similarly cure some of the inefficiency caused by monopsony power. For example, if the monopsonist shown in Table 2 and Figure 2 could perfectly wage discriminate, it would hire six workers (exactly the same as would a competitive firm) rather than the four it hires as a nondiscriminating monopsonist. However, it would respectively pay the first through sixth workers weekly wages of only $250, $300, $380, $485, $550, and $600—the total weekly wage bill would be only $2,565, instead of the $3,600 that would be paid weekly by a purely competitive employer. The $1,035 difference represents monopsonistic exploitation. Although this wage discrimination does facilitate efficiency, it is widely viewed as inequitable (more on this in a moment).

Employers who treat salary information as confidential argue that publicizing wage differentials just leads to bickering about which employee deserves what. Under this system, employees have little incentive to reveal their own pay but seek information about the pay of others. If you learned that someone made less than you did, you would probably be silent if their work was comparable to yours. If, however, someone with a comparable job made more than you, you might use the information to negotiate a raise. If you think about this for a moment, you will understand why many workers join employers in a conspiracy of silence when salary information is confidential. Although secrecy may reduce quibbling about salaries when pay scales are not standardized, the major advantage for employers is that confidentiality facilitates wage discrimination and monopsonistic exploitation. Many critics of capitalism identify competition and greed as the basic forces that underpin exploitation and wage discrimination. The problem, instead, is an absence of adequate competition, as we point out in Focus 1.

Minimum-Wage Laws and Monopsony Power

The effects of minimum-wage laws in competitive labor markets are summarized in Panel A of

Are Exploitation and Discrimination Caused by Capitalistic Greed?

Are too many greedy business owners too obsessed with maximizing profit? Relative to most white males, are other groups of workers typically underpaid, given their productivity? You may be surprised to learn that it is logically inconsistent to respond positively to both questions. To see why, let's begin by considering how profit seeking would affect situations where wages were less than workers' marginal revenue products.

Suppose you inherited a small fortune you wanted to turn into a large fortune, and you were convinced that some people are exploited by being paid less than their labor is worth. One strategy might be to place a want ad in the newspaper declaring, "If you are worth $12 hourly but are only paid $6 hourly, come work for *My Company*. I will pay you $7 an hour". If you avoided hiring workers paid the values of their marginal products, hiring instead only workers that you exploit to the tune of $5 hourly, your fortune should grow rapidly. But your success would incite mimicry, and you would soon see ads from competitors: "If *My Company* pays only $7 for $12 worth of your productivity, come to work for *Our Enterprise*. We'll pay you $8 per hour." But this would elicit even higher wage offers as competition to exploit profit opportunities grew. Ultimately, all the workers worth $12 an hour would be paid $12 an hour.

The conclusion that exploitation should be eliminated by aggressive competition by profit seekers seems to conflict with research findings that women and members of other disadvantaged groups make less than the pay of white males with comparable

education and experience. Only two logical reconciliations are possible. Either (*a*) all workers are paid what they are worth, on average, and wage gaps reflect differences in productivity, not bigotry, or (*b*) competition for profits is too weak to eliminate wage differentials not justified by productivity.

Some people use this analysis to argue that profit seeking is vigorous, ensuring that people are uniformly paid what their labor is worth and that wage gaps by gender, ethnicity, or race merely reflect differences in the willingness and ability of people from different groups to accomplish various jobs. For example, women are asserted to have more career interruptions because of family obligations and to be less committed to their careers, while typical members of most minority groups are asserted to have inferior educations and erratic work experience that has diminished their productivity.

A powerful counterargument suggests, however, that many people who make hiring decisions have agendas other than profit alone and that this creates wage structures not based on performance alone. Many white male executives, for example, surround themselves with sycophants with shared interests (e.g., golf, the stock market, gourmet meals, or office politics). Some might try to defend their hiring practices with statements such as, "Surveys prove that productivity suffers because female supervisors make both men and women uncomfortable," or, "I hired my friend's son because I've known him since he was a baby and have confidence that he will do a great job." Nevertheless, even if conscious prejudice seldom governs employment policies, the

results of hiring based on friendship or shared interests instead of capacity to do the job denies equal access to good jobs with high pay. This counterargument concludes that use of criteria for hiring and promotions other than potential performance alone prevents realization of the productive potential of nonwhites and females.

An irony is that white males are probably not enriched by discriminatory practices, which cause economic inefficiency if jobs are filled by white males who are not the best applicants. Many potential gains available through specialization according to comparative advantage are lost, and the total value of national output will be less than if performance alone governed employment practices.

How can such inefficiencies and inequities be overcome? Ideally, people who make employment decisions for firms would become more profit oriented—not less! Focusing on productivity instead of group affinity would undoubtedly decrease wage differentials based on race, ethnicity, and gender.

Affirmative action plans are a controversial option. Preferential hiring of women and members of minority groups is intended to broaden access to jobs but, however well intended, sometimes creates it own set of inefficiencies and inequities. These plans too often degenerate into quotas that are filled, in part, by eroding reasonable qualifications for the job. This escalates a backlash from some white males passed over for employment or promotions. In "Income Distribution," we discuss more of the pros and cons of some proposed remedies for discrimination in employment.

Figure 3. The prevailing wage is $4.25 before the minimum wage is introduced into this competitive market, and 68 units of labor are employed (point a). When a $5 minimum wage is imposed by law, employment falls to 58 (point b), and unemployment increases to 40 units of labor (98 – 58); more people want to work at the higher wage (point c).

The effect of a minimum wage may be quite different if firms exert monopsony power. Before enactment of a minimum wage in Panel B, fewer workers are employed (50) at a lower wage ($3.75) by the monopsonist (point g) than by a comparable competitive firm (point a). Introducing the minimum wage alters the monopsonist's MFC by forcing the firm to pay at least $5 per hour, at which it can hire up to 98 workers (point c). Average wages must rise to

attract more than 98 workers, so the firm's MFC curve becomes $ebcdf$, and profit-maximizing employment is 58 workers at $5 per hour (point b).

The result that minimum-wage laws may boost both employment and wages by monopsonistic firms is often cited as a benefit of these laws. Critics rebut this analysis with studies showing that the biggest effect of higher minimum wages is disemployment of inexperienced teenagers in competitive labor markets. Employment is also likely to fall if firms practiced systematic wage discrimination before passage of a minimum wage. (We showed how wage discrimination raises employment by monopsonists. Minimum-wage laws may eliminate this effect.) Thus, the consensus of opinion is that substantial increases in minimum wages probably foster unemployment.

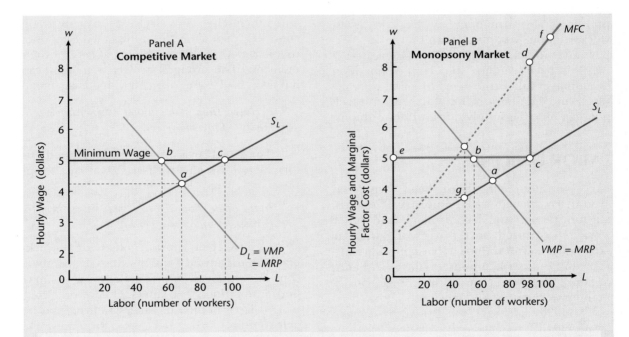

A minimum-wage law will cause unskilled workers to experience unemployment if the labor market is competitive, as shown in Panel A. Setting a minimum wage at $5 means that 40 individuals who want to work will be unable to find jobs (point c minus point b). It is theoretically possible, but unlikely, for a minimum wage to increase employment if there is substantial monopsony power in the labor market. In Panel B, a $5 minimum wage alters the monopsonist's MFC so that 8 new employees are hired; equilibrium employment moves from point g to point b.

FIGURE 3   Minimum-Wage Laws in Competitive and Monopsony Labor Markets

A Summary of Imperfect Competition by Employers

Translation of the $MRP = MFC$ rule into equilibrium wages and employment depends on a firm's product and labor markets, as summarized in Figure 4. When product and labor markets are both competitive (Panel A), the firm hires efficiently where $VMP = w$. Panel B shows that when a monopolistic seller hires from a competitive labor market, workers are paid less than the values of their marginal products, and fewer workers are hired than under competitive conditions. A monopsony labor market combined with a competitive product market is depicted in Panel C. Firms with monopsony power also hire fewer workers, at lower wages, than would pure competitors. Last, Panel D illustrates equilibrium employment and wages when a labor monopsonist has market power in the output market. Not surprisingly, a monopsonist who is also a monopolist hires the fewest workers at the lowest wages and is the most exploitative; the difference $VMP - w$ is greatest.

You have seen how imperfect competition by employers alters the demand for labor, wage rates, and equilibrium employment. We will now examine the supply side and labor unions.

LABOR UNIONS

Unions traditionally have been organized around a particular craft or industry. Plumbers, machinists, air traffic controllers, and other workers organized on the basis of particular skills rely on **craft unions** to bargain with management. **Industrial unions**, on the other hand, organize all the workers in such industries as mining, steel, autos, and rubber.

Until their merger, the *American Federation of Labor* (AFL) consisted only of craft unions and competed with the *Congress of Industrial Organizations* (CIO), which covered only industrial unions. Jurisdictional strikes often erupted when both attempted to organize the same workers. For example, conflicts in chemical plants between the CIO's Oil, Chemical, and Atomic Workers Union and AFL craft unions representing electricians or machinists sometimes became violent. A treaty between AFL and CIO unions was finally consummated with their 1955 merger into the AFL-CIO.

Today, jurisdictional fights exist primarily between AFL-CIO unions and such independents as the Longshoremen and Teamsters unions. These disputes focus on which union will represent given workers and what goals to pursue. Job security and higher wages involve trade-offs. For example, the United Mine Workers union traditionally sought huge wage hikes despite the resulting mass substitution of capital for labor and consequent disemployment of many union members. Other unions prize job security and so temper their demands for higher wages.

Union Security

Unions attempt to ensure job security for their members in part because union leaders seek security themselves. Special clauses in many union contracts are designed to strengthen the hands of union leaders as sole bargaining agents for their members. The strongest protection a union can have is a *closed shop* agreement with management.

*A **closed shop** makes union membership a prerequisite for employment.*

The Taft-Hartley Act of 1947 outlawed this form of union security. *Open shops* are at the opposite pole from closed shops.

*In an **open shop**, the firm employs workers regardless of union membership.*

Unions legally must negotiate for all workers in an organized firm, but dues or membership are optional. Thus, an open shop may permit nonunion free riders. Unions only control the labor of their members, so firms may be able to nullify strikes by using nonunion workers (called *scabs* by union members) extensively, yet nonunion workers receive the same benefits as union workers.

The *union shop* is similar to a closed shop.

***Union shop** employers may hire either union or nonunion labor, but new employees must join the union within a specified period to keep their jobs.*

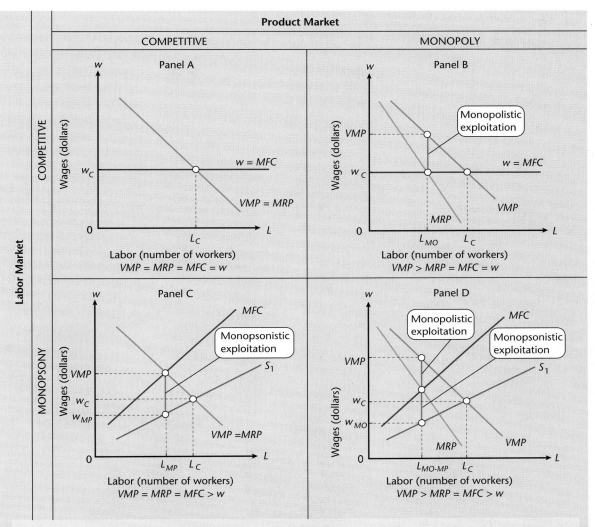

The marginal value of labor to society is the *VMP* curve; the marginal social cost of labor is the competitively determined wage (*w*). In a competitive world (Panel A), there is no exploitation of labor, and economic efficiency exists because the marginal benefit to society of a specific employment just equals marginal social cost (*VMP* = *w*, so *MSB* = *MSC*). Monopolistic exploitation (Panel B) is accompanied by inefficiency because VMP > MRP implies that the marginal social benefit exceeds the monopolist's marginal private benefit from hiring extra workers (*MSB* > *MPB*, so *MSB* > *MSC*). Monopsonistic exploitation (Panel C) is a situation where the monopsonists' marginal private costs are greater than the marginal social costs of employment (*MFC* > *MSC* = *w*), so again there is inefficiency. Panel D illustrates the case where the factors leading to inefficiency because of monopoly and monopsony power are combined.

FIGURE 4   Summary of Wage and Employment Equilibria

Under a union shop arrangement, union members can be expelled only for nonpayment of dues. This protects workers from being expelled (with loss of their jobs) for infractions such as disagreeing with the union leadership or violating union policies.

Besides abolishing closed shops, the Taft-Hartley Act allowed state **right-to-work laws**

FIGURE 5 Turning Points in American Labor History

1778–1940 Labor Struggles for the Right to Collectively Bargain

1778— NY printers demanded wage hikes, but their organization dissolved after raises were granted.

1786— Philadelphia printers gained a minimum weekly wage of $6 in the nation's earliest authenticated strike.

1806— The Philadelphia Cordwainers went bankrupt after members were found guilty of conspiring to strike.

1834— The National Trades Union formed the first national labor federation, but folded during the financial panic of 1837.

1842— In Commonwealth v. Hunt, the Massachusetts Court held labor unions to be legal organizations. Massachusetts and Connecticut laws prohibited children from working more than 10 hours a day.

1862— The "Molly Maguires," a secret society of Irish coal miners, were charged with acts of terrorism against mine bosses; 14 of their leaders were imprisoned and 10 were executed.

1869— The Knights of Labor gained 700,000 followers by winning railroad strikes and advocating the 8-hour day.

1884— A Bureau of Labor was formed in the Department of Interior, growing into the Department of Labor in 1913.

1886— One policeman was killed and several were wounded in the Chicago Haymarket riot, arousing public opinion against unionism and retarding a drive for the 8-hour day. The American Federation of Labor (AFL) was founded.

1890— The United Mine Workers first organized in Columbus, Ohio.

1894— The American Railway Union's strike against the Pullman Co. was defeated when Federal troops enforced injunctions. Eugene V. Debs and other leaders were imprisoned.

1908— The United Hatters' boycott of D.E. Loewe and Co. was held to be in restraint of trade under the Sherman Act.

1912— Massachusetts passed a minimum wage for women and minors.

1914— The Clayton Act limited use of injunctions in labor disputes and legalized union picketing.

1917— A copper miners' strike ended when an Arizona sheriff deported 1,200 "wobbly" (Industrial Workers of the World) strikers. Union efforts to organize workers signing "yellow-dog" contracts were held to be illegal.

1921— The Supreme Court held that nothing in the Clayton Act legalized secondary boycotts (Duplex v. Deering).

1933— Frances Perkins became Secretary of Labor, the first woman named to the Cabinet.

1935— The National Labor Relations (Wagner) Act established the right to organize unions. The Social Security Act was enacted. The Congress of Industrial Organizations (CIO) was formed.

1937— GM recognized the United Automobile Workers and U.S. Steel recognized the Steel Workers as bargaining agents.

1938— Fair Labor Standards Act

outlawing the union shop. Twenty-one states have passed such laws. Unions responded with **agency shop** agreements that require all employees to pay union dues. This arrangement has been defended as preventing nonunion workers from free riding; all workers represented by a union should share the costs of collective bargaining. Unions also exert control over workers through **checkoff provisions** in contracts, which require firms to deduct dues from paychecks. These provisions make it easier for unions to collect dues and retain members. The Taft-Hartley Act prohibits firms from deducting union dues unless authorized by a majority of workers, but roughly 80% of union contracts now have checkoff provisions.

Unions did not develop overnight. The path to modern collective bargaining was paved with

FIGURE 6   Turning Points in American Labor History

1941–1994 Labor Focuses on Social Reform

1946— The Employment Act of 1946 required policies promoting "maximum employment, production, and purchasing power."

1947— The Taft-Hartley Act forbade closed shops and secondary boycotts, and allowed states to pass "right-to-work" laws.

1949— An amendment to the Fair Labor Standards Act (1938) directly limited child labor for the first time.

1955— Merger of the American Federation of Labor and Congress of Industrial Organizations unified over 85 percent of all U.S. union members.

1959— The Landrum-Griffin Act made certain activities by labor or management illegal.

1962— Federal employees' unions were granted the right to bargain collectively with government agencies.

1963— The Equal Pay Act of 1963 prohibited wage differentials based on sex.

1964— The Civil Rights Act of 1964 barred job discrimination because of race, color, religion, sex, or national origin.

1965— "Medicare" first provided partial coverage for those over 65 for most medical expenses.

1968— The Age Discrimination in Employment Act made job discrimination against persons aged 40 to 65 illegal.

1970— The first strike in Post Office history virtually paralyzed mail service. The Occupational Safety and Health Act set safety and health standards for the nation's workplaces.

1974— The Social Security Act for the first time provided for automatic cost-of-living adjustments.

1975— Interns and residents backed by the AMA struck 22 NY hospitals.

1981— Air traffic controllers represented by PATCO illegally struck and most of these federal employees were fired.

1988— The United Automobile Workers and General Motors attempt a new form of labor-management relations known as "jointness" and industrial democracy.

1992— Americans with Disabilities Act is passed.

1993— Family Leave Act is passed.

---

strife between union organizers and business owners and managers who did not want to share power with labor. Many attempts to organize unions met with violence that verged on war on a small scale. Some of the chronology of the union movement is detailed in Figures 5 and 6. The next section examines the history of unions in this country.

The American Union Movement

A forerunner of modern unions was the Carpenters' Society of Philadelphia, established in 1724, which bargained for wage increases and organized charity work. An interesting note is that members who disclosed wages to non-members were fined.[3] During the early 1800s, numerous unions emerged and then faded away, but within a century, unions had become fixtures on the national scene.

Until the Great Depression, firms commonly fought union organizers with firings, violence, and **yellow-dog contracts**, by which workers agreed not to join any union. Employers also cir-

culated **blacklists** of union "troublemakers." Finally, unions faced considerable legal adversity. Judges sympathetic to business owners issued *injunctions* (or restraining orders) against numerous union acts, including strikes or boycotts. If a union violated an injunction, its leaders could be held in contempt of court and jailed.

In the Danbury Hatters' case in 1908, the Supreme Court declared unions to be in restraint of trade, violating the Sherman Antitrust Act.[4] The court ruled that a national boycott had cost the Lowe Hat Company $80,000 and applied the Sherman Act's triple damage clause to the United Hatters union. This case, more than any other, forced unions into the political arena. The Clayton Act (1914) largely shielded unions from antitrust prosecution for strikes and boycotts.

Union growth during the 1920s was hampered when firms aggressively labeled unions as un-American, and yellow-dog contracts were standard operating procedure. A series of violent strikes fostered antiunion sentiment. Demands for skilled workers from craft unions fell as mass production spread. Prosperity also aggravated

---

[3]William Miernyk, *The Economics of Labor and Collective Bargaining* (Lexington, MA: Heath, 1965), p. 14.

[4]Loewe v. Lawlor, 208 U.S. 274 (1908).

declines in union membership because booming wages and job security left industrial workers content.

The Great Depression softened the country's mood toward unionism. Believing they were on the brink of disaster, many workers collectively acted to buffer the chaos of the business cycle, and total union membership tripled between 1933 and 1940. Organizing drives were aided by passage of the Wagner Act in 1935. This prolabor legislation guaranteed the right to organize unions and made it an unfair labor practice for a firm to refuse to negotiate with a union supported by a majority of its workers.

Union membership as a percentage of the labor force continued to grow through the 1940s, but many aspects of the Wagner Act were perceived as biased in favor of unions. This dissatisfaction resulted in passage of the Taft-Hartley Act (1947), which outlawed *secondary boycotts* (refusals by union members of one firm to handle any intermediate products produced by other firms that were being struck) and *jurisdictional strikes* (where the only issue was which union would represent workers), and which also permitted states to pass right-to-work laws forbidding union shops.

Are Unions Passé?

Many antiunion people are obsessed that unions are increasingly powerful, but their influence is actually waning in the United States while rising in most other developed nations (Figure 7). Union membership as a percentage of the work force has fallen for three decades; fewer than one in seven American workers now belong to a union.

Some researchers argue that American unions were far too successful in winning wage increases during the 1960s and 1970s compared to their foreign counterparts. This hampered the ability of U.S. manufacturers to compete in world markets, prompting them to take harder lines against unions. Others argue that unions were too successful in obtaining social legislation. Past political success may have negated the historical role of unions. Examples include minimum-wage laws; laws outlawing job discrimination based on race, age, or disability; occupational safety and

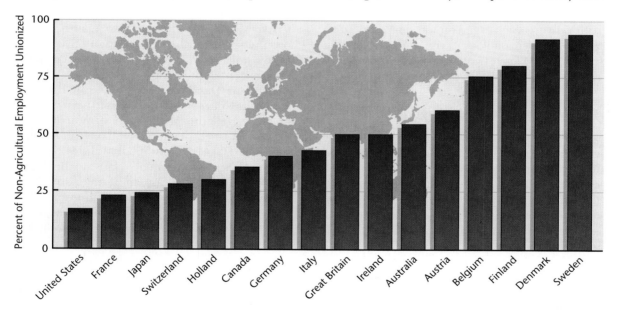

Source: Bureau of Labor Statistics, *Employment and Earnings,* January 1988 and *The Economist,* August 1990.

Total union membership in the United States has been falling in recent years and union membership as a percentage of the work force has been declining for over three decades. These trends in the United States are counter to those occurring in several other developed nations.

FIGURE 7 **Union Membership as a Percentage of the Nonfarm Work Force: Selected Countries, 1993**

health laws; social security; child labor laws; unemployment and worker's compensation; and, most recently, state laws and court decisions that restrict plant closures. All of these have reduced the arbitrary authority of management and increased job security—the original and, as many argue, most important function of unions. (But corporate downsizing in the 1990s may give the union movement renewed strength. Unions are increasingly focused on issues of job security and less focused on issues of pay.)

Finally, a major problem facing union organizers is the growing importance of service industries and white-collar workers. Neither group seems as ripe for union membership as were the industrial workers of an earlier era. With this brief history in mind, we now turn our attention to collective bargaining and union strategies to raise wages for their members.

UNIONS AND COLLECTIVE BARGAINING

Just as corporate managers represent stockholders interests, unions represent many workers' interests (with similar principal–agent problems) while negotiating work contracts. Major union contracts cover thousands of workers. The public hostility so frequent between firm managers and union leaders is often blended with private symbiosis; managers of firms and managers of unions often have more interests in common than either has with the groups they represent (stockholders and the union rank and file). Unions do provide a collective voice for workers and have helped curtail managerial abuses in many firms and industries. Most people, however, view increases in wages as the major role of a union.

Union Strategies to Raise Wages

Demands for labor are downward sloping, so, in the short run, wage hikes reduce the quantity of labor demanded and thus normally eliminate some jobs. Union negotiators must weigh this trade-off. If an industry is largely nonunion, demand for union labor may be relatively elastic, making unemployment a more likely prospect for union members when union wages are raised.

In the long run, firms will adjust to higher wage rates through automation, replacing union workers with machinery. Or, in some cases, firms will shut down if they cannot break even while paying union wage rates. These sorts of adjustments do not entail movements along a static demand curve in response to higher wage rates. Instead, the entire demand curve for labor shifts leftward.

Giant national unions try to protect their members' jobs by organizing entire industries. The growth of international trade is making this a formidable task for industries that must compete with foreign producers (e.g., auto makers). In cases of purely local labor markets (construction, for example), only local workers must be unionized to protect union jobs from nonunion competition. A union can choose from several strategies to raise wages once an industry is organized. Consider Figure 8. Without unionization, firms' demands for labor would be D_0 and the supply of labor, S_0, with resulting employment of L_e workers at a wage of w_e (point a).

- **Restricting the Labor Supply** A first union strategy might be to try to shrink labor for this industry by shifting the labor supply curve leftward to S_1, raising the union wage to w_u (point b). The union movement has supported policies such as child labor laws, restrictive immigration policies, compulsory retirement plans, laws to protect women from hard or hazardous work, and shorter work weeks. Most craft unions require lengthy apprenticeships to restrict competition from other workers. Some unions that dominate a particular labor market charge high initiation fees or simply limit new membership to shift the supply of union labor to the left.

- **Rationing Work** A union that controls all of an industry's work force might simply bargain for a wage of w_u. This creates a huge labor surplus and substantial unemployment or underemployment ($d - b$ in Figure 8). The union then uses a *hiring hall* to spread the work available to its members. Rules to allocate jobs range from first-come, first-served to strict seniority.

- **Stimulating the Demand for Union Labor** If the union can negotiate a wage of w_u and then

FIGURE 8   Various Union Strategies to Raise Wages

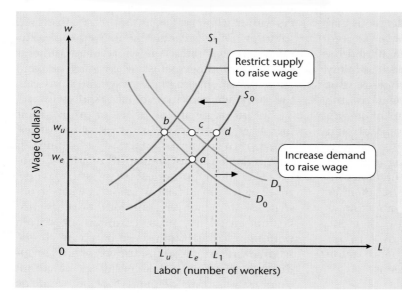

Unions can be instrumental in raising wages by either (*a*) reducing the supply of labor or (*b*) increasing the demand for labor. The effective supply of labor can be reduced by imposing barriers to entry into an occupation, such as a requirement of union membership, extensive experience, or professional licensing. The demand for labor can be enhanced by improving labor productivity, by increasing the demand for output or through contracts that require featherbedding.

raise the demand for its members' labor to D_1, they suffer only minor unemployment at point c (labor supply exceeds labor demand at wage rate w_u by $d - c$). Examples of this approach include using political clout to obtain local building codes that require labor-intensive construction technologies, or lobbying for quotas to limit foreign competition for union members' services or a limit on foreign imports of certain products (Japanese trucks and cars). Unions also work with management to increase worker productivity.

• **Featherbedding**   Featherbedding refers to work rules that artificially boost the number of workers required for certain tasks. Although forbidden by the Taft-Hartley Act, it has been a union strategy to bolster demands for labor in several industries: railroads, printing, and shipping (dockworkers). For example, long after coal engines were replaced by diesel, railroad unions insisted that trains carry firemen, who rode along even though there were no coal fires to tend.[5] For years, New York musicians had a union contract requiring standby orchestras for every event at which out-of-state musicians played.

---

[5]Some states had laws requiring firemen on each train. Such a requirement was a part of the Arizona State Constitution until 1964.

Bilateral Monopoly

Just as oligopolists act strategically to cope with interdependencies in setting prices and output, negotiations between unions and management at times resemble a card tournament—or war. Several models have been developed to characterize this process. One early model of collective bargaining is called *bilateral monopoly*.

> ***Bilateral monopoly*** *assumes that a union is the sole agent for a firm's labor [a monopoly on the labor (supply) side], while the firm is the sole employer of union labor [a monopsony on the hiring (demand) side].*

The monopsonist employer depicted in Figure 9 would prefer to hire L_e units of labor at a wage rate of w_f. The union, on the other hand, would want the L_e units of labor to be paid at least w_u. Given the marginal revenue product (*MRP*) curve shown, wage rate w_u is the maximum that the firm would be willing to pay for L_e units of labor.

The wage limits for bargaining range from w_u to w_f, but this model fails to predict exactly what the wage settlement will be. Moreover, we assumed that the union seeks the highest wage consistent with full employment of its L_e members. The powers that control a union may have other

FIGURE 9 Bilateral Monopoly in Labor Markets

The early bilateral monopoly model of collective bargaining assumed that employers with monopsony power must deal with unions with market power as suppliers of labor. When a buyer with monopsony power confronts a seller with market power, price and quantity are determined by which side is the better negotiator or has more power.

FIGURE 10 Hicks's Theory of Industrial Disputes

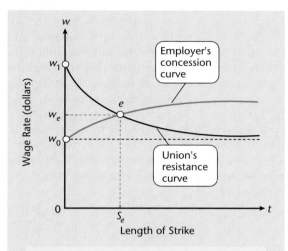

The onset of a strike (time 0) is a signal that union workers demand much higher wages than management is willing to pay. As time elapses, workers become willing to settle for less as their financial reserves evaporate, while management is increasingly willing to raise its offer as its inventories decline and stockholders and customers apply pressure to settle. Declining wage demands and rising wage offers intersect to signal the end of this particular strike at time S_e.

goals, such as maximum wages for workers with seniority or job security for union officials. For these reasons, the bilateral monopoly model is useful primarily in specifying some general limits to bargaining. About all we can say at this point is that the negotiated wage tends to be closer to the wage desired by the party (union or management) with the greatest power or bargaining savvy.

Bargaining and the Duration of Strikes

Bilateral monopoly models identify a range of wages within which union and management will agree but fail to specify a final wage. Moreover, these models ignore strikes. John Hicks, a Nobel Prize winner, developed a more robust model of collective bargaining, adapted in Figure 10.[6] The firm willingly offers a wage of w_0 without a

[6]J. R. Hicks, *The Theory of Wages* (London: Macmillan, 1932), Chapter 7.

strike, but the union initially insists on a wage of w_1, a difference so great that a strike begins at time zero (0).

Strikers ride financial and emotional roller coasters. After the euphoria of a brief vacation, reality begins knocking at workers' doors. Backlogged do-it-yourself projects are finished, and boredom sets in as a strike drags on. As unemployment checks and union benefits run out, strikers exhaust past savings and worry about their bills. These hardships press wage demands down along the union resistance curve in Figure 10 as time passes.

Over the same period, the firm's willingness to pay higher wages is traced out as the employer's concession curve. Few strikes are surprises, so most firms can meet predictable orders from stockpiled inventories. Managers often form skeletal work crews during a strike, but inventories evaporate and managers become exhausted; the operation grinds toward a halt, increasing firms' willingness to pay higher wages. The intersection of the employer's concession curve and the union resistance curve marks the end of this strike. The final wage settlement is at w_e and the expected duration of this strike is S_e. As you can see, this simple model offers considerable insight into labor negotiations. Notice, however, that if both sides recognize in advance that the final contract will be for wage w_e, a strike is unnecessary. Thus, many strikes may be accidental, reflecting miscalculations about the respective offers ultimately acceptable to each side.

Today, global competition and the high mobility of factories and capital make going out on strike a riskier proposition. Even for those unions only facing a domestic labor force, striking requires careful planning and execution because of growing numbers of part-time, temporary, and self-employed workers who might accept jobs as permanent replacement. A strike by professional football players in 1989 failed when NFL owners hired temporary replacement players. Teachers, too, are often vulnerable if school boards decide to replace strikers.

The short strike in late November of 1993 against American Airlines by the flight attendants union illustrates this point. American Airlines threatened to replace striking attendants with new hires (a legal option open to companies). Nearly a year earlier, American had obtained permission from the Federal Aviation Administration to reduce the training period for replacement workers from six weeks to ten days. Their training would be limited to safety issues, and they would be certified only for a single type of aircraft.

Recognizing the threat of potential replacements, the leadership of the flight attendants called the strike over the busy Thanksgiving holiday and limited the strike to 11 days! They would inflict about a $10 million–a–day loss on American but lose only a week's pay, while severely limiting American's use of permanent replacements. This strategic and highly successful use of a short work stoppage during an important commercial period may hint at future directions for union strategy.

We will now turn our attention to the effects of unions that extend beyond the unionized sectors of the economy.

ECONOMIC EFFECTS OF LABOR UNIONS

Unions . . . receive more credit and at the same time more blame than they deserve.

Gary Becker

In addition to concerns about the political power of large unions, opponents of unions worry about three possible economic effects of unions: (*a*) distorted wage structures, (*b*) inflationary pressure, and (*c*) disruption caused by strikes.

Union and Nonunion Wage Differentials

Most people believe that unions can raise their members' wages substantially over nonunion wages. Figure 11 shows how a **union-nonunion wage differential** can develop. Assume that markets for union (*U*) and nonunion (*NU*) workers are initially identical, with 20 million workers employed in each sector at a wage of w_e. Total employment equals 40 million. The markets for union and nonunion workers are illustrated in Panels A and B, respectively.

If negotiation raised union members' wages to w_1, 5 million (20 million – 15 million) union workers would be disemployed. After all, one cost of higher wages is less employment. As these workers abandon the job market or seek nonunion jobs, the supply of union labor falls to S_1. Nonunion wages drop when some of the 5 million disemployed union workers are absorbed. The nonunion wage would shrink to w_2 as the nonunion labor supply swells to S_2, amplifying the wage differential. Note that total employment falls a bit, because some people disemployed from the union sector will be unwilling to work at this depressed nonunion wage rate.

Two surveys by H. Gregg Lewis (in 1963 and 1986) summarized more than 200 studies of the relative wage effects of unions during the period 1920 to 1979. Lewis placed the average wage gap in the 15% to 20% range, varying from a depression-era high of almost 50% to a low of 2% fol-

FIGURE 11   Union and Nonunion Wage Differentials

Restricting the supply of labor may cause union wages to rise (Panel A), but flows of labor into the nonunion sector may cause nonunion wages to fall (Panel B).

lowing World War II.[7] Lewis's work suggests that wage gaps are greatest during economic downturns and least during periods of economic prosperity. He estimates that during 1967 through 1979, the average wage gap was 15%.

The recent erosion of unions, however, may mean that union-nonunion wage gaps have been falling. A recent study suggests that union-nonunion pay gaps fell roughly 4% during the 1980s.[8] Lewis noted that this wage gap varies substantially, however, and appears to be affected by geographic region, the type of job, and such characteristics of typical workers as marital status, race, health, and age. This gap widens as an industry becomes relatively more unionized and narrows when unemployment in an industry grows, or if most firms in an industry are larger, or when typical workers are relatively more educated.

Many people think that unions have boosted most workers' wages. Numerous his-

[7]H. G. Lewis, *Unionism and Relative Wages in the United States: An Empirical Inquiry* (1963) Chapter V, and *Union Relative Wage Effects: A Survey* (1986) (both from Chicago: The University of Chicago Press).

[8]K. E. Anderson, P. M. Doyle and A. E. Schwenk, "Measuring Union-Nonunion Earnings Differences," *Monthly Labor Review*, June 1990, pp. 26–38.

torical studies contradict this perception, finding that the extent of unionization does not affect labor's share in national income, neither in the United States nor in other countries. You should remember, also, that union wage premiums are created, in part, by depressing wages in nonunionized sectors of an economy. Also note that if wage structures are distorted by unions that have power in certain sectors, then output in those sectors will be less than the efficient amounts—a case of allocative inefficiency.

Unions and Inflation

Some opponents of unions rant that curing inflation requires controlling "those *@#$%&! unions." Inflation is blamed on unions on the theory that they artificially boost wages through collective bargaining or strikes. Firms then pass these higher costs forward by charging higher prices, inspiring unions to demand higher wages to offset members' losses due to inflation, and so on. This high-wage → higher-price → higher-wage spiral is thought by many to be the principal cause of inflation in the United States.

Critics of this analysis point out that unions represent only one worker in seven and argue that union wage hikes can only raise prices modestly. If union labor absorbs 20% of all production costs and unions negotiate 10% wage hikes, output prices need only rise by 2% on the average. Moreover, they might point to Figure 11 and argue that union wage hikes are partially offset by resulting cuts in nonunion wages. Blaming rapid inflation on unions is ludicrous in the eyes of these critics.

One rebuttal is that this analysis ignores union strength in such key industries as steel, automobiles, chemicals, all crucial inputs for other economic sectors. Higher wage costs and prices for major intermediate goods ripple through the economy as upward price pressures on all outputs. Moreover, union wages set standards for many nonunion firms, which match collective bargaining agreements to avoid unionization of their workers. Finally, if higher wages create massive unemployment and the federal government responds with expansionary macroeconomic policies, there is a classic supply-side inflation cycle. However, the growth of international trade unquestionably has reduced the power of unions to affect wage differentials or to influence the rate of inflation. Nevertheless, the debate surrounding the impact of union wage hikes on inflation will probably continue for as long as unions exist.

Losses from Strikes

Unions are blamed for innumerable economic woes. One question that arises is if unions represent only one worker in seven, how can they cause rapid inflation, economic chaos from strikes, and other social ills? Economists lack consensus about unions, but most believe their impact is exaggerated. Strikes and the closed-door collective bargaining process make juicy material for the media. Publicity often makes union organizing and bargaining look like bloody battles.

Source: Bureau of Labor Statistics, *Current Wage Developments,* February 1988.

Only a small percent of the work force is on strike during any given year, and most strikes are for short periods. Although the numbers of workers involved in strikes seem large, only less than one-tenth of one percent of labor time is lost because of strikes.

FIGURE 12 Major Work Stoppages in the United States 1960–1993: Number of Workers Involved (Millions—Left Scale) and Percent of Total Working Time Lost (Percent—Right Scale)

Collective bargaining is a frustrating process, but it works most of the time. Nearly 100,000 collective bargaining contracts are negotiated each year with less than 100 ending in a work stoppage. Furthermore, most strikes last less than two weeks and, as Figure 12 illustrates, a very small percentage of total working time (less than 0.1%) is typically lost to strikes. Although most strikes center on disagreements about wages, other major issues that cause strikes include (a) union organization and security, (b) work rules, (c) overtime questions, (d) safety, (e) interunion and intraunion matters (e.g., assignment of work between competing unions, or sympathy strikes), (f) job security disputes, and, more recently, (g) the comprehensiveness of health and pension benefits.

Strikes may have significant costs beyond the income lost by the strikers. Firms incur higher costs in getting their products to customers during strikes, and some sales may be lost because of inability to meet deadlines. After a strike is settled, most firms recoup losses through increased shipments, and all that is suffered is delay. But this is not always the case. Strikes by farm workers may leave crops rotting on the ground. Consumer goods, homes, and capital equipment go up in smoke when firefighters strike. Strikes that reduce supplies cause consumers to bear the costs as higher prices and lower consumption.

The public has traditionally opposed strikes by public employees, especially nurses, teachers, firefighters, and police officers. Laws usually forbid strikes by public employees and substitute binding arbitration as a means of resolving conflicts. Strikes do occur, but many groups of public employees now mix collective bargaining with old-fashioned politics to pressure elected officials into meeting their demands.

This chapter has explored the effects on wages and employment when concentrated economic power is wielded in labor markets by resource buyers (monopoly and monopsony power) or resource sellers (primarily unions). The markets for land, entrepreneurship, and capital examined in the next chapter tend to be far more competitive, but you may find a few cases where some of the analysis of this chapter seems to apply. As is more normally the case, markets for nonlabor resources tend to operate according to the marginal productivity theory introduced in the previous chapter, but each market does so in its own unique way.

CHAPTER REVIEW: KEY POINTS

1. The **marginal revenue product** (*MRP*) curve for a firm selling in an imperfectly competitive product market will be below the **value of the marginal product** (*VMP*) curve. All firms will hire labor until the marginal revenue product equals the *marginal factor cost (MFC)* of labor. Because *MRP* < *VMP*, employees of firms with market power are paid less than the values of their marginal products. This difference is called **monopolistic exploitation**.

2. A **monopsonist** is the sole buyer of a particular resource or good. Labor monopsonists face an entire market supply of labor. If all workers are paid equally, a monopsonist's marginal factor cost curve will lie above the labor supply curve it faces. Relative to competitors, labor monopsonists pay lower wages and hire fewer workers. In addition, labor will be paid less than the value of its marginal product, a difference referred to as **monopsonistic exploitation**.

3. When competitive conditions prevail in both resource and product markets, the firm hires labor until *VMP = MRP = MFC = w*. When monopoly prevails in the product market, but the monopoly firm hires labor under competitive conditions, labor is hired up to the point where *VMP > MRP = MFC = w*. Given a competitive product market and monopsony power in the labor

market, a firm will maximize profits by hiring labor until $VMP = MRP = MFC > w$. Finally, when a firm has both monopoly and monopsony power, labor is hired up to the point where $VMP > MRP = MFC > w$.

4. A minimum wage legally set above the equilibrium wage in competitive labor markets will raise unemployment. It is possible, but unlikely, that minimum wages might increase employment and wages simultaneously, but only where there is substantial monopsonistic exploitation of unskilled workers and wage discrimination is not practiced, an unlikely combination. A union wage hike might have the same effect. However, the markets where minimum-wage hikes raise existing wages are typically rather competitive. Thus, increased unemployment is the normal result when minimum wages are increased.

5. **Unions** have traditionally organized into craft or industrial unions. The *American Federation of Labor* (AFL) was the bulwark of craft unions; industrial unions composed the *Congress of Industrial Organizations* (CIO). Frequent jurisdictional disputes over which organization would represent particular workers caused the two to merge into the AFL-CIO in 1955.

6. To protect their prerogatives as sole bargaining agents for workers, unions and their leaders use several kinds of agreements with organized firms. **Closed shops** require workers to be union members as a precondition for employment. At the other end of the spectrum, **open shops** permit union and nonunion members to work side by side. This arrangement is quite unsatisfactory to unions because nonmembers receive the benefits of collective bargaining but need not pay union dues. **Union shops** are compromises between closed and open shops. The employer can hire union or nonunion workers, but an employee must join the union within some specified period (usually 30 days) to retain the job. The Taft-Hartley Act of 1947 outlawed the closed shop and permitted individual states to pass right-to-work laws forbidding union shops. In many of these states, **agency shops** have been created to protect unions from free riders. Workers may choose not to belong to the union but must pay dues.

7. Unionism developed in a hostile environment. The Great Depression shifted public policy in favor of collective bargaining. As trade unionism grew, many felt that unions became corrupt and too powerful, and tighter organizing and financial reporting constraints were imposed on labor organizations. The union movement was relatively stable from roughly 1950 until 1980, but since then, union membership has declined as a percentage of the total labor force. The labor force is increasingly employed in the service sector or consists of white-collar workers who are reluctant to join unions.

8. **Bilateral monopoly**, a very early model of collective bargaining, describes the limits to the wage bargaining process but provides little predictive power. Sir John Hicks's bargaining model predicts both final wage settlements and the duration of strikes.

9. Labor unions have typically employed three methods to increase the wages of their members: (*a*) reductions of the supply of workers to an industry, (*b*) establishing higher wages and then parceling out the available work to members, and (*c*) policies designed to increase demands for union labor.

10. **Wage differentials** between union and nonunion workers average roughly 10% to 15%. Some people blame inflation on excessive union wage demands. Large wage hikes in key industries may set the pattern for other industries. Higher wages may raise unemployment and induce public officials to pursue expansionary macroeconomic policies, further intensifying inflationary pressures. Since organized labor represents less than one worker out of seven, it is unlikely that unionism explains much inflation.

11. A small percentage of collective bargaining negotiations end in *strikes*, and most of these are short. Strikes often impose costs on individuals and firms that are not direct parties to labor negotiations. Strikes may cause shortages, shipping delays, or losses of perishable products.

12. Public employee unions frequently mix politics and collective bargaining to win their demands. Public officials negotiating contracts are seldom those who are responsible for developing government budgets; thus, they may have only weak incentives to resist union wage demands.

QUESTIONS FOR THOUGHT AND DISCUSSION

1. Many firms view salary information as confidential. Can you cite reasons for this practice other than wage discrimination? Do you believe these other reasons are valid?

2. Some economists argue that by permitting collective bargaining, we condone monopoly despite Sherman Antitrust Act prohibitions of monopolies. Is there anything inherently more palatable about labor monopolies than about product monopolies? By encouraging unions to expand through various laws protecting collective bargaining, are we creating what John Kenneth Galbraith has called "countervailing power," where big unions bargaining for workers offset the effects of concentrated industry? Is there any reason to suspect that the two forces, big labor and big business, will not combine like OPEC to gouge the little consumer? What forces, if any, keep this from happening?

3. In the 1980s, union membership declined steadily. What do you think accounts for the reduction in union membership during this period? Do you foresee labor unions recovering from this decline, or will it continue? Why do you think so?

4. The Taft-Hartley Act outlaws the closed shop, yet in some industries or occupations it is almost impossible to find a job unless you belong to a union. Are these unions doing something illegal? How do you explain this apparent contradiction between the law and reality? Why would employers agree to hire only union members if they did not have to?

5. Some economists argue that the most effective union to date is the American Medical Association. Does the AMA operate like a labor union? In what ways? Name other professional societies that perform the same functions as unions for their members. Should these associations be subjected to the same democratic standards and financial reporting standards that are applied to unions? How do you think medical doctors would feel if the AMA changed its name to United Medical Doctors of America, Amalgamated Brotherhood of Medical Doctors, or some similar moniker?

Chapter 30

Rent, Interest, Profits, and Capitalization

Entrepreneur   Monosony

Discrimination

Implicit contracts

Wage   VMP = MRP

Human capital

S_L

Great fortunes are usually based, not on wages, but rather on rents on land, interest on capital, or entrepreneurial profit. This chapter describes these nonwage sources of income. Most people rely primarily on wage income, which may explain why most people are not rich.

Market forces shape rates for rents, interest, and profit much as they determine workers wages. The derived demands for all resources are based on output prices and on each resource's marginal contribution in producing goods and services consumers want. This production entails transforming materials so that they become more valuable in form, space, time, or possession. Market prices direct these transformations.

Resources are also altered to enhance value. Human capital, for example, makes labor more valuable, which partially motivates your quest for a degree. Most workers try to learn skills that will increase wage incomes. Similarly, potential income gains motivate owners of nonlabor resources to carefully mold their assets. Investment in capital, for example, can take many forms; whether new capital will be hand tools, buildings, measuring instruments, or industrial robots de-pends on which form of capital is expected to be most profitable. Entrepreneurs try to develop special expertise in areas they forecast as prof-itable, and landowners plant their acreage or build shopping malls on it so that their land is most valuably used.

Markets for capital, land, and entrepre-neurial talent tend to be even more competitive than labor markets. Geography and habit often limit workers' mobility, but investors compete in international markets, rapidly shifting financial capital between investments when even slight differentials arise in rates of return; economic capital follows soon thereafter. Entrepreneurs respond quickly to the slightest whiff of a profit opportunity. Although land cannot move geo-graphically, flows of other resources when higher resource payments beckon make land mobile between uses if not spaces.

Our first task in this chapter is an overview of how different mixes of resources affect the out-puts of typical production processes. Second, we will examine the nature of economic rent and the role it plays in allocating resources. We then turn to explanations of how interest rates are determined and to the sources of economic profits. Finally, we investigate capitalization, which transforms predictable rents, interest, or profits into wealth. As you work through this chapter, keep in mind that markets for capital, entrepreneurship, and land are all relatively competitive and tend to conform to the principles of marginal productivity theory discussed earlier.

RESOURCE RATIOS AND PRODUCTIVITY

The amounts and types of other resources used in a production process are major determinants of labor productivity. For example, even unskilled workers in the United States work with much more capital and consequently produce far more than their counterparts in, say, India. Thus, American trash collectors each process more garbage than Indian trash collectors because Americans use more trucks, crushers, and other equipment. The relatively high amount of capital per worker in industrialized countries is a major reason that workers in advanced nations enjoy higher wages on average than do workers in less developed economies.

The flip side is that capital productivity rises as the number of workers per machine grows. Large amounts of capital per worker in the United States mean that labor per unit of capital is low relative to developing countries such as India. Thus, while output per worker is high in the United States relative to India, output per unit of capital is probably higher in India. In the United States, hand shovels often lay idle on construction projects; in India, a shovel typically is more productive and may be used three shifts every day. The upshot of this is that labor productivity and wages tend to be higher the greater the capital-to-labor ratio, while interest payments and the productivity of capital tend to be higher the lower the capital-to-labor ratio.

This broad notion holds for virtually all resource ratios: (*a*) capital is more productive and highly paid the greater the amounts of labor, entrepreneurial talent, or land working with capital; (*b*) entrepreneurs will be more productive and highly remunerated the fewer the entrepreneurs attempting to use other given resources; and (*c*) land will be more productive and draw higher rents the more capital and labor are used to work the land. For example, relative to vast desolate ranches on which a few cowhands try to keep track of a few scattered cattle, small flower farms covered with greenhouses and automatic watering equipment produce much more value per acre.

The general principles of marginal productivity govern the markets for labor, land, capital, and entrepreneurial talent, but each market has unique characteristics. The last two chapters outlined some specifics of labor markets, so we will now examine these other markets.

ECONOMIC RENTS

"Rent" usually conjures up payments to landlords or prices charged for temporary use of a videotape or a truck at the local Rent-All. As seems too often true, economists have taken a perfectly good word, "rent," and attached their own special meaning to it.

> **Economic rent** is realized whenever the owner of any resource is paid more than the minimum necessary to elicit the quantity supplied of that productive resource.

Thus, economic rent broadly applies to parts of many payments to resource owners.

Economic rents may have little to do with apartment leases or similar rental values. For example, many rock musicians spend years paying their dues, that is, working for peanuts in smoke-filled bars and generally hustling just to get by. If they hit it big and begin to pull down seven figures annually, there is an enormous difference between their superstar incomes and the small amounts for which they were once willing to play music. Economists view such differences as economic rents. Land is about the only resource, however, that generates "pure" economic rents.

Pure Land Rents

One unique characteristic of land is its absolutely fixed supply. The land available to society cannot grow even if payments to landowners rise to infinity; the supply is perfectly inelastic at Q_S in Figure 1. If demand is D_0 rent per acre will be τ_0 and total rent is area $0acf$. If new technology enhanced land's physical productivity, or if higher output prices boosted the derived demand for land to D_1, rent per acre would rise to τ_1, yielding total rent equal to the area $0bef$. What will rent for raw land be if demand is D_2? Zero, and some land will be idle (df). Owners of this vacant land are earning negative rents; they are having to shell out payments (taxes and maintenance) to keep the land. In summary, all payments received for the fixed supply of land are pure rents determined solely by the strength of demand.

The clearest examples of pure economic rents are payments for use of unimproved land. Note that when people construct dikes or drain swamps, they create capital, not new land. (Recall that any improvement increasing the productivity of natural resources is classified as capital.) Consequently, the supply of land is perfectly inelastic, so changes in demand yield proportional changes in land rents. Demands and rental rates for different parcels of land differ according to their locations and their physical characteristics.

• **Location Rents** Why is a vacant square block in Manhattan worth more than an acre of prime Kansas wheat land? Transportation costs are a major reason. Looked at from a different perspective, the customer populations differ, causing different values. One facet of *location rents* is that if a seller can locate so that customers bear lower transportation costs than are incurred in buying from a competitor, the advantageously located seller can charge more for the goods and services she produces.

Suppose that you owned an isolated Kansas farm and replicated a chunk of downtown Manhattan on the north forty, including a hamburger stand. If you cut the price charged at your hamburger stand by half and put on an advertising campaign worthy of Ronald McDonald, your sales would fall far short of those by your New York rival. The reason is that for the average hamburger buyer, the total cost of a hamburger (including transportation costs) would be far less at the New York stand than at yours. New Yorkers would become regular customers only if you charged such a low price for hamburgers that transportation costs were overcome. Fat chance!

Another facet of location rents is that a firm is able to pay lower prices for inputs if it locates so that its input suppliers (workers, for example) gain from lower transportation costs than would be incurred in selling to a competing firm. When being in business at a particular location gives a firm the ability to charge more to its customers or to pay less to its suppliers, the owner of the location will become aware of these advantages and charge rents sufficiently high that only normal profits are received by the firm.

For example, suppose you lease a building in a rundown area of Chicago to establish a fancy French restaurant. Then suppose that a huge luxury hotel unexpectedly locates in the next block; business would boom and you might profit immensely in the short run. When your lease is up,

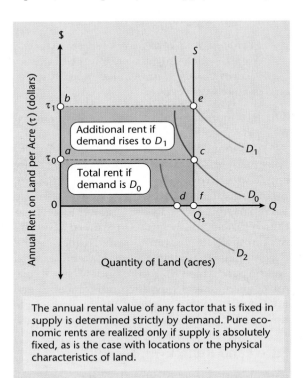

The annual rental value of any factor that is fixed in supply is determined strictly by demand. Pure economic rents are realized only if supply is absolutely fixed, as is the case with locations or the physical characteristics of land.

FIGURE 1   Economic Rent for Raw Land

however, your landlord will raise your rent to capture the increased profitability of the location. Economic rents of this type, known as **location** (or *site*) **rents**, are illustrated in Figure 2. Actual rents per month for a two-bedroom flat in selected cities are shown in the table in this figure.

• **Rents from Physical Characteristics**   Marginal productivities and the rental rates of parcels of land reflect differences in fertility or the values of minerals the land holds. Some land is not used at all. Windswept deserts and Arctic tundra are examples of land so barren and remote that its marginal productivity is effectively zero.

David Ricardo, who originated the theory of pure rent, observed that marginal (barely useful) land commands zero rent whenever equally productive parcels are vacant. For example, you could always live rent free at an oasis in the Sahara if at least one comparable oasis were vacant. If the owner tried to charge any positive rent, you would move to a vacant oasis. The production cost saved by using more productive land versus marginal land equals the rental value per period of the more productive land.

Competition for cost reductions from particular sites permits a landowner to charge rent reflecting the productivity differences between superior land and the marginal (zero rent) land. Ricardo viewed land rent as an *unearned surplus* because its fixed supply would be available even at a zero price. Henry George gained fame by arguing that this unearned surplus to landowners could be taxed without creating economic inefficiency.

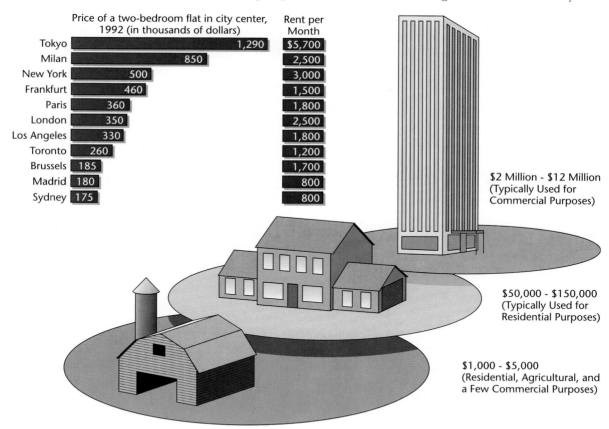

Price of a two-bedroom flat in city center, 1992 (in thousands of dollars)	Rent per Month
Tokyo — 1,290	$5,700
Milan — 850	2,500
New York — 500	3,000
Frankfurt — 460	1,500
Paris — 360	1,800
London — 350	2,500
Los Angeles — 330	1,800
Toronto — 260	1,200
Brussels — 185	1,700
Madrid — 180	800
Sydney — 175	800

$2 Million - $12 Million (Typically Used for Commercial Purposes)

$50,000 - $150,000 (Typically Used for Residential Purposes)

$1,000 - $5,000 (Residential, Agricultural, and a Few Commercial Purposes)

Market values and rental rates for land are influenced strongly by where a particular parcel is located. As we move further and further from hubs of business activity, economic rents for land tend to decline.

FIGURE 2   Value of Acre of Land, Depending upon Location

BIOGRAPHY

Henry George: The Single Tax Movement

High birth rates and the arrival of millions of immigrants caused rapid growth of the nineteenth-century American economy. Fertile frontier lands were homesteaded, and urban land values boomed. Henry George (1839–1897) and his followers believed landowners unjustly reaped major benefits from economic growth, which George perceived as rightfully belonging to society in general. In *Progress and Poverty* (1879), George proposed a **single tax** on land equal to the surplus that landowners were receiving and thought these revenues could finance all government spending. His reasoning is illustrated in Figure 3.

Equilibrium rent per acre before the land tax is τ_0 (point *a*). A tax equal to half of annual rent would cut the net rent per acre to landowners to τ_1. They cannot change the supply of land to drive up its rental rate. Attempts to raise rents would fail, because surpluses of vacant land would develop. Rent that can be charged land users is strictly demand determined, so landowners cannot avoid the full burden of a pure land tax.

How would a land tax affect allocation? If untaxed land were used optimally, the most profitable uses would remain so after imposing the tax. (If you are able to keep half of all rent, 50% of the *highest* possible economic rent is the best you can do.) Thus, land taxes seem allocatively neutral.

The central thrust of George's economics is that land rent can be taxed heavily without distorting production incentives. George felt that "nothing short of making land common property can permanently relieve poverty and check the tendency of wages to the starvation point." He proposed to do this not by directly nationalizing land, but by the roundabout method of taking away the unearned income that propri-

etors enjoyed from land rents.

Land nationalization schemes were common in George's day, but he generally opposed government intervention and proposed leaving land titles in individual ownership, merely taxing all land at 100% of its rental value. This levy should be, according to George, a single tax to replace all other taxes. *Progress and Poverty* became his era's bestselling work on economics and the bible of the single-tax movement.

A single tax on land sounds appealing, but it suffers from several flaws: (*a*) potential revenue would probably not cover today's total government spending; (*b*) administration would be complex, because distinguishing the values of land from its improvements—clearing, irrigation, buildings—is quite difficult; (*c*) rent does provide resource owners with incentives to find users who most highly value the resources; and (*d*) land is not the only resource that generates economic rents. A single tax on land rent would impose the full burden of paying for government on landowners. This seems unfair from the vantage point of current landowners.

George's single-tax movement reached its apex in his 1886 race for mayor of New York City. Running as the candidate of the United Labor Party, George finished second, but there was wide speculation that he might have won an honest ballot count. Henry George died during another run at the mayor's office in 1897, but he left his imprint on economic reform movements at home and abroad.

Landowners alone bear the full burdens of land taxes, because the total amount competitive renters will pay to use land is determined strictly by its productivity. If landlords try to shift a land tax forward in the form of higher rental rates, surplus land will be available, along with pressures for rent reductions. For example, if landlords tried to raise their rental rate to τ_0, there would be surplus land. Equilibrium rents on land are always all the market will bear.

FIGURE 3   Effect of a Tax on Land: Landowners Bear the Burden

Rents to Other Resources

The concept of economic rent originated with David Ricardo's analysis of corn and the land used to produce it. Economic rents are received, however, whenever a resource owner is paid more than the minimum necessary to induce a given amount of the resource. Thus, many owners of scarce resources earn economic rents. The economic rents received when resource supply curves are imperfectly elastic are illustrated in Figure 4, which portrays a positively sloped labor supply curve for professional wrestlers.

Equilibrium occurs at point *e* when 450 wrestlers work for annual incomes averaging $80,000, but only very reluctant wrestlers (those making up the labor supply near point *e*) are paid the bare minimums necessary for their services. Other wrestlers would work for less and so receive economic rents as surpluses above their minimum acceptance wages. For example,

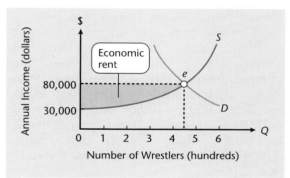

Economic rents are realized whenever a supplier of a resource receives more than the minimum necessary to make the factor available to the market. Thus, the area above the supply curve but below the price line is economic rent, which is sometimes called the supplier's surplus. In markets for output, such areas represent producer surplus, which is the flip side of consumer surplus. Recall that consumer surplus is the area below a demand curve but above the price line. It is the difference between what a buyer would willingly pay for a specific quantity of a good and the amount actually paid because goods can be bought at a uniform price.

FIGURE 4   Economic Rent and Professional Wrestlers

if Hulk Hogan were willing to work for $50,000 annually (his actual salary is $80,000), his economic rent is $30,000. Total rents to wrestlers equal the shaded area above the supply curve but below the wage rate.

Rents and Efficiency

Economic rent is any surplus to a resource owner when income exceeds the opportunity cost of providing the resource to society as a whole. Economic rents are fairly common because most productive resources are at least partially fixed: their supplies are not perfectly elastic for the entire economy. This fixity generates economic rents.

People who view the income distribution as unfair often target high incomes from interest, profit, or rent. Referring to multimillion-dollar-a-year sports figures or movie stars, they express sentiments such as "No one is worth that much." Do rents serve any purpose beyond enrichment of the owners of land or specialized talents? If not, these surpluses can be completely taxed by government with no net loss to society. But both the short- and long-run consequences of taxing economic rents might actually cause inefficient allocations of resources.

• **Short-Run Allocation**   Even in the short run, the drive to maximize economic rent creates incentives for resource owners to use their productive resources in the most valuable ways possible and to maintain them properly. Suppose that you own a city block that will potentially rent for $1 million annually. If rents were taxed 100%, would incentives exist to seek the highest bidder so that the land would be put to its most valuable use? Absolutely not.

Henry George argued that land would be used efficiently even if 50% taxes on rent were imposed because half is better than nothing. When we consider transaction costs, however, his analysis falters. If the tax were 99.99%, for example, the $100 received if you found the $1 million bidder for use of your land would be unlikely to overcome your transaction costs. You might simply let your land lie idle. But what if the site tax were only 80%? Or 32%? Any tax rate, however low, reduces the incentive that motivates landowners to incur the transaction costs required to put land to its most valuable use.

Some corporate CEOs, movie stars, musicians, novelists, and athletes realize incomes that seem outrageous. Much of such income is economic rent, so why not impose 100% taxes on annual incomes over $1,000,000? (The Deficit Reduction Act of 1993 eliminated the deductibility of executive salaries over $1,000,000. Business can pay salaries in excess of $1 million, but it cannot deduct this excess as a legitimate business expense against federal income tax liabilities.) This question is partially answered if you ponder how you would react were you in this position. High income tax rates explain why many English actors and rock stars have emigrated to Switzerland, the United States, and Ireland (where income tax rates are zero for royalties from books and records).

Another problem is that parts of even extraordinary incomes are not pure rents. If emigration seems unattractive, why bother to be worth more than $1,000,000 annually? Great actors might study their lines less diligently or do fewer films. Might opera singers begin to smoke or fail to avoid colds? Would successful authors write as much? Would sports superstars play as hard or often? Would they happily play in industrial towns, or might most gravitate to sunny resort areas? Some might still strive to excel out of personal pride, but after a certain point, we suspect that cold cash motivates most people whose specialized skills earn large economic rents.

In summary, rents are important even in the short run, because they are incentives to maintain rent-generating resources, and because they are important in ensuring that those who most highly value scarce resources are able to use them.

• **Long-Run Allocation** Many resources that draw economic rents because they are semifixed in the short run are far from fixed for the economy as a whole over the long haul. Prospects of high income motivate people to invest in assets that subsequently command economic rent. Today's opportunity costs become tomorrow's fixed costs, as resources jell into fixed assets. For example, medical students undergo years of expensive training in hopes of high economic rents once their M.D. degrees are in hand. Investors in buildings or capital equipment draw economic rents over the useful lives of these assets.

Would tomorrow's superstar athletes have as much incentive to polish their skills if the economic rents enjoyed by basketball's Shaquille O'Neal, tennis's Steffi Graf, or football's Emmitt Smith were taxed away? No. Would the lawyers of the next generation be as skilled as Alan Dershowitz or Lawrence Tribe if the incomes of top attorneys were limited because they are economic rents? Whence would come future Luciano Pavarottis, Danielle Steeles, or Bill Cosbys? The long-run effects of taxing all economic rent would be disastrous because there would be fewer incentives to invest in oneself or in capital equipment; the entire economy would stagnate.

It should come as no surprise that the annual rental value of any resource is tied closely to its selling price, which is the wealth associated with owning a resource or other asset. Before we discuss capitalization, which is the process of translating rents or other income flows into wealth, you need an understanding of interest and profits, which also may be capitalized through the process described near the end of this chapter.

INTEREST

You may have deposits in a bank account that draw interest. Why does your bank pay interest? The answer seems obvious: banks make loans at higher interest rates than they pay depositors. Most loans, however, are made to business investors who buy capital—machines or buildings. Thus, interest is ultimately a payment to providers of economic capital. Interest payments are somewhat roundabout in advanced economies, being spread among those who own capital directly and others whose saving and financial investment make it possible for society to accumulate economic capital.

Interest Rates

We will focus on interest payments to holders of financial capital to simplify our analysis. Similar reasoning applies to direct owners of economic capital.

> *Nominal interest rates* are the percentage of monetary premiums paid per time period for the use of money.

The ultimate lenders are those who save by spending less than their income. If you pay a dime annually for each dollar you owe on a car loan, the annual interest rate is 10%. (The people you truly owe are depositors in the lending institution.) Because of differences in borrowers and debt instruments—car loans, mortgages, government or corporate bonds, and so on—there are many nominal interest rates at any given time. These IOUs are a large component of our financial capital. Interest rates vary among these financial instruments because of the following:

1. *Risk.* Different borrowers have different probabilities of defaulting on their loans. Naturally, higher risk premiums in the interest rate are charged the greater the risk of default.
2. *Maturity.* Interest rates are generally higher the longer it will take to retire a loan, in part because lenders have sets of expectations that become increasingly uncertain as the time period considered becomes longer.
3. *Liquidity.* Better developed markets for specific debt instruments drive interest rates down, because the transaction costs incurred in buying or selling such IOUs will be lower. Competition among lenders to grant certain types of loans facilitates liquidity.

Interest rates commonly range from a government-subsidized 5% annually to a loan shark's 5% weekly. References to "the rate of interest" usually mean the nominal interest rate charged annually on long-term (20- to 30-year) riskless loans. Interest rates on negotiable long-term government bonds or those charged to "prime" borrowers are reasonable approximations of this concept.

Changes in the price level drive wedges between nominal and real interest rates.

> *The real interest rate* is the percentage of purchasing power annually paid by borrowers to lenders.

Real interest rates can be roughly computed by subtracting the percentage annual rate of inflation from nominal interest rates. For example, 8% nominal interest yields only about 5% real interest if annual inflation is 3%.

Markets for Financial Capital

Interest is a payment to providers of economic capital. Saving makes new capital supplies available; thus, the ultimate capital suppliers are savers. Just what factors determine the interest rate? After adjusting for inflation, the real interest rate depends on the following:

1. *Premiums savers require to delay gratification.* Most of us want goods now instead of later, unless we are rewarded for waiting. If 5% more goods are required to get typical savers to wait a year to consume their income, real interest rates gravitate toward 5%.
2. *Premiums required for sacrificing liquidity.* Less-liquid assets generate higher rates of return, or we would all hold cash.
3. *Productivity of new capital.* If new capital reproduces 6% of its value in new goods each year, interest rates tend toward 6%.

The first two items are reflected in the supplies of *loanable funds*; item 3 is reflected in the demand for loanable funds.

The total demand for loanable funds in the United States depends on the plans for borrowing by domestic consumers, government, and business and by foreigners. The supply depends on (*a*) plans for saving by individual households, (*b*) international flows of financial capital (by which foreign savers can make loans to U.S. borrowers, or vice versa), and (*c*) the monetary policy of the central bank.

Keep in mind that markets for loanable funds are affected by government deficits and debt, monetary policies, and international capital flows, but these are macroeconomic topics. The analysis of this section would not change in a meaningful way if we considered all the roles played by all the entities just listed. Therefore, for simplicity we will focus on household plans to save as sources of loanable funds and on business borrowing as a use of loanable funds.

• **Demands for Loanable Funds** Some business borrowing is to cover current operating expenses, but we will concentrate on the investment plans that absorb the bulk of business borrowing. Firms construct buildings, buy machinery, or purposely increase inventories only if they expect to profit by doing so. Firms can finance these investments with funds from (*a*) retained earnings, (*b*) direct sales of the company's stock, (*c*) sales of new bonds, or (*d*) loans from financial institutions. Naturally, the depositors (savers) are the real lenders. The third approach is called *debt capital*. To simplify our analysis even further, we will focus on debt capital. Our analysis would change little if we separately considered each form of financial capital. Keep in mind that financial capital is merely a tool used to secure purchasing power over a wide range of goods, including economic (physical) capital.

Business investors demand funds for a variety of investments, each of which is expected to yield profits to the borrower. Just as the demand for labor depends on labor's marginal productivity, the demand for capital depends on its marginal productivity. Capital's marginal productivity (its *MRP*) as a percentage of expenditures on capital is known as the **rate of return on investment** (*r*). Like the demands for other resources, the demand for capital is a derived demand.

The demand for capital goods generates demand for loanable funds to finance new investment. In Figure 5, this demand for loanable funds is expressed in terms of rates of return and interest rates. One explanation for the negative slope of demand curves for capital and loanable funds is that, for the economy as a

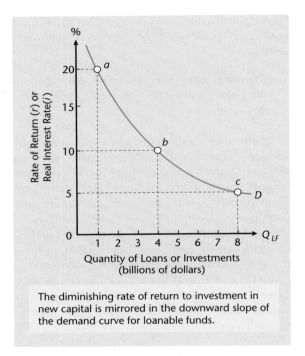

FIGURE 5 The Demand Curve for Debt Capital (Loanable Funds)

The diminishing rate of return to investment in new capital is mirrored in the downward slope of the demand curve for loanable funds.

whole, greater investment causes more and more capital to be used with fixed amounts of land and labor. The law of diminishing marginal returns then causes successive doses of capital to be decreasingly productive.

An alternative approach is to recognize that firms rank potential investment projects from the highest expected rate of return to the lowest. Assuming that funds from retained earnings or new stock offerings are insufficient, these projects underpin the demand for loanable funds shown in Figure 5. Only a few projects will yield a 20% rate of return or greater ($1 billion worth in Figure 5). As the rate of return requirement falls, firms find that more projects are advantageous. If interest costs fall to 10%, $4 billion worth of projects are profitable (point *b*); $8 billion in new investments generate rates of return of at least 5% (point *c*).

Construction costs and equipment costs are obviously important determinants of business investment. Because the supply curves for capital goods are positively sloped, their costs and prices tend to rise during prosperity as demand for investment goods increases, choking off short-term surges in investment. Conversely, declines in the costs of investment goods during economic downturns slow the fall of investment spending.

Investors do most of the borrowing in this country, but consumers and all levels of government also borrow substantially. Consumer purchases of homes and automobiles fall sharply when interest rates rise. Although the federal government's borrowing seems unaffected by interest rates, state and local governments borrow more to finance schools, parks, and roads when their interest costs are less. Thus, when consumer, investor, and government demands for loanable funds are combined, the market demand curve slopes downward. As with all other markets, however, demand is only half of the story.

- **Supplies of Loanable Funds** The supply of loanable funds is positively related to the price received (interest). The ultimate lenders (savers who supply loanable funds) receive interest for the use of their funds. The major alternative for saver—lenders is current consumption, but a few, who value liquidity highly or who expect a financial crash, may hoard their savings. High interest rates confront individuals with high opportunity costs of current consumption or hoarding. As a result, many save (providing funds to the capital market) and use their future wealth (amount saved plus interest) for consumption at a later time.

- **Equilibrium Interest Rates** Equilibrium in the financial capital market is shown in Figure 6. The initial demand for funds, D_0 reflects the rates of return expected by business (plus consumer or government borrowing). It is negatively sloped because investments become less profitable as interest rates rise. The initial supply curve S_0 is positively sloped because household saving grows as interest rates paid savers rise (the opportunity costs of current consumption rise).

FIGURE 6 The Market for Loanable Funds

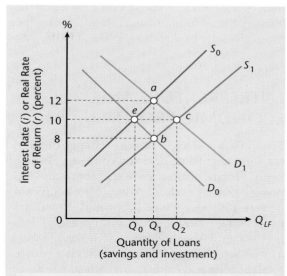

Increases in saving will increase the supply of loanable funds and decrease the interest rate (point *b*). Reduced anxiety about the future tends to expand both the demand and the supply of loanable funds (point *c*).

The rate of return on new investment equals the interest rate in equilibrium, which occurs at the intersection of the demand (D_0) and supply (S_0) curves in Figure 6 (point *e*). The initial equilibrium rate of return and interest rate will be 10%, and the quantity of investment loans will equal Q_0. Suppose that expected returns on new capital investments rise so that the demand for loanable funds increases to D_1. Equilibrium interest and investment loans would rise to 12% and Q_1, respectively (point *a*). When investors grow more optimistic, expected rates of return, interest rates, and financial investments all rise.

Similarly, suppose households decide to delay consumption and save more. When families increase the rate at which they postpone consumption, the loanable funds available for investment rise, supply shifts from S_0 to S_1 and interest rates fall (point *b*).

In summary, interest rewards households who save for deferring their consumption and for sacrificing liquidity. Interest is also a return to capital that depends on capital's marginal productivity. The interest rate charged on a particular financial instrument depends on its liquidity and length of time to maturity, and on lenders' perceptions of the probability of default.

ENTREPRENEURS AND ECONOMIC PROFIT

Economic profit and a desire to change the world are fundamental motives for entrepreneurs who establish firms to innovate new products and technologies in a capitalist economy. Most people misunderstand this role of profit and substantially overestimate average profit, both per sales dollar and as a return on invested capital. You know that a firm's accounting profit is the difference between total revenue and explicit costs, which pay for the use of resources not owned by the firm. Only after subtracting implicit costs (opportunity costs of resources owners provide to operate a firm) from accounting profit do we have pure economic profit, which is also a pure rent to the firm's owners.

> ***Economic profit*** *is revenue exceeding all opportunity costs for resources.*

In a purely competitive and unchanging economy in which transaction costs were zero, economic profit would always be zero; implicit payments to sustain owner-provided resources would absorb all accounting profits. In reality, transaction costs are significant, and the future is uncertain. Many changes are wrought by entrepreneurial quests for profits. Moreover, monopoly power is commonplace. This leads to the major sources of pure economic profits: (*a*) monopoly power, (*b*) innovation, and (*c*) uncertainty.

Monopoly Profit

Monopoly power enables some firms to generate total revenue far in excess of the opportunity costs of the resources used. But can a monopolist continually enjoy economic profit? Transaction costs, uncertainty, and entry barriers create short-run profit opportunities. *Monopoly profit* may persist into the long run if barriers prevent entry by competitors, but profits will stimulate resource flows that eliminate monopoly profit in markets where there is a threat of potential new entry (contestable markets). If so, profit will have served its function by signaling where society desired greater production. If barriers preclude entry in the long run, economy-wide efficiency will not occur, but the drive for monopoly profit does encourage least-cost production.

The capitalization processes described in a moment suggest that profit is realized primarily by the owners when a firm secures a monopoly position. Predictable profits are capitalized in the long run into a higher market value (and thus higher opportunity costs) for ownership of the monopoly; subsequent owners can expect only normal profits.

Rewards for Innovation

Innovation is another source of profit.

> ***Innovation*** *involves the development and implementation of a new product or production process or the opening of a new market.*

A firm is likely to profit if it is among the first to introduce a successful good or a more efficient technology. Profits fall when competitors mimic successful innovators. Thomas Edison, for example, became rich when he established General Electric as the outlet for his genius, but GE now faces hordes of competitors and realizes only normal profits.

Invention and innovation are not synonymous; each is a part of the process of change. Some highly successful inventions have been innovated by firms not directly associated with the inventor. You may never have heard of Gilbert Hyatt, but in 1990, the courts and the U.S. Patent Office recognized him as a primary inventor of modern computer chips. The microchip makers who launched a revolution in how we live by innovating his chips wound up paying him royalties only after extended bouts in court. Sam Walton pioneered discount stores in small communities, propelling his company, Wal-Mart, to the top and making himself a billionaire into the process. On a smaller scale, one Colorado sixth-grader developed and marketed biodegradable golf tees.

Joseph Schumpeter first expressed the innovation theory of profits to help explain the business cycle.[1] Entrepreneurs attempt to capitalize on new profit opportunities created by a significant innovation, and their collective investments fuel economic booms. Once the advantages from the innovation are fully absorbed, however, investment declines, pushing the economy into a downturn to await another major innovation.

Risk Bearing and Uncertainty

If the likelihood of some occurrence is fairly predictable, many people will adjust in similar ways, so only normal rates of return can be expected. Buying insurance is one adjustment against life's possible hazards, or you might *self-insure* and take your chances. Some aspects of the future, however, seem totally unpredictable. If fortune smiles, unexpected profit may be your reward for bearing the risk of just being in a line of business, or you may be clobbered if disaster unexpectedly strikes your industry.

The economist Frank Knight first distinguished *risk* from *uncertainty*.[2]

> **Risk** *exists when the probability of a given event can be estimated.*

For example, if a firm can reliably predict that, on average, a production process will yield 3 defective units out of 100, it can adjust for these risks by considering losses due to defects as a normal cost of doing business. Similarly, the probabilities of fire, some accidents, or the death of a key executive can be fairly reliably predicted, and insurance is available. Again, these risks will be reflected in production costs and output prices.

Uncertainty, on the other hand, forces entrepreneurs to weigh imperfect information and base their decisions on subjective judgments.

> **Uncertainty** *exists when a potential occurrence is so unpredictable that forecasts are unavoidably almost pure guesswork.*

According to Frank Knight, profits are rewards for bearing uncertainty. Entrepreneurs invest in an expectation of generating sufficient revenues to cover all costs, including allowances for all risks, but the unfolding of time may yield events beyond any entrepreneur's wildest hopes or fears. Uncertainty makes it impossible to predict economic profits or losses.

The Economic Role of Profits

Uncertainty, innovation, and monopoly power are major sources of economic profit, but what functions do profits perform? Economic profits signal that prices exceed average costs and indicate that social welfare can be improved by shifting resources from unprofitable to profitable endeavors. Conversely, industry-wide economic losses signal that too many resources are devoted to particular forms of production and could beneficially be shifted elsewhere.

Profits are also a stimulus for efficiency. Entrepreneurs' desires for profits cause costs to be cut wherever possible, freeing resources for other uses. Competition forces profits down to normal levels as imitators mimic successful firms, whether success is derived from being in a certain product line or from using a more efficient technology. Competition also punishes relatively inefficient high-cost firms with economic losses.

Profits also reward the entrepreneurs who innovate new products and technologies in an uncertain business environment. The drive for entrepreneurial profit propels society along a path of economic growth and progress. Predictable rents, interest, or profits are translated into

---

[1]Joseph A. Schumpeter, *Business Cycles: A Theoretical, Historical, and Statistical Analysis of the Capitalist Process* (New York: McGraw-Hill, 1939).

[2]Frank H. Knight, *Risk, Uncertainty, and Profit* (Boston: Houghton-Mifflin, 1921).

wealth through *capitalization* processes when resources that generate these income flows can be sold. In the next section, we examine the mechanics of how competition for income streams determines the market values of income-generating assets.

CAPITALIZING INCOME STREAMS

Suppose you manage a rock group called Mutant Larvae, currently being booked as a warm-up act for more popular bands. The group's third album suddenly goes platinum and phones begin to ring. Promoters want Larvae to headline upcoming concerts, but it is solidly booked for the next six months at $5,000 per appearance. Who will benefit from the group's popularity during the next six months? Promoters who contracted with your band prior to its hit album will profit by selling out their concerts even if they raise ticket prices. How long will these economic profits (which could also be considered rents) continue to be received by individual concert promoters?

Being a smart promoter yourself, you will quit booking Larvae as an opening act and will raise its fee when you negotiate future contracts so individual concert promoters will earn only normal profits. This *capitalizes* rents from the group's popularity. The group's fee now reflects the higher ticket prices and attendance for each performance. If you held exclusive rights to book the group, you could sell the contract for a fat profit.

> *Capitalization* is the transformation of future income streams into current value or wealth and quickly eliminates economic profits.

Similar capitalization processes occur in farming. If international grain prices soar, farmers temporarily enjoy economic profits. But the price of farmland rises when expected profits are capitalized into higher land values. Even farmers who own their land find the opportunity cost of holding their land rises, squeezing out the economic profit derived from farming. Their higher wealth naturally would keep them from mourning this fate.

Present Values and Rates of Return

Investors prefer more income to less, and they want it sooner rather than later. Thus, the capitalized value of an income stream will be larger (*a*) the greater the income stream and (*b*) the more quickly income is realized. Truly understanding these relationships requires knowing how to calculate present values and rates of return.

• **Present Values** Economic investment generates future output and yields an income stream to the investor. The income stream per period as a percentage of the dollar outlay for a capital good is the rate of return. Determining whether an investment will be profitable requires calculating its *present value*, which is the value today of all expected future income.

> The **present value** of an asset is the discounted value today of the expected income stream associated with the asset.

Suppose you were offered a guaranteed $100 payable one year from today and that your savings account earned 6% interest annually. What is the most you would willingly pay for this IOU? Certainly less than $100. You can calculate the amount at which you will do equally well by having your funds in either the savings account or this IOU by answering this question: How much money would I have to put in the bank at a 6% annual interest rate so that when the interest earned in one year is added to the original amount, the total equals $100? This problem boils down to $1.06(PV) = \$100$, where PV stands for present value. If you divide both sides of this equation by 1.06, $PV = \$100/1.06$, you have the answer. Similar questions can be answered for any interest rate, any time period, or any amount of money using the following formula:

Present Value

$$PV = \frac{Y_1}{\left(1+i\right)^1} + \frac{Y_2}{\left(1+i\right)^2} + \text{L} + \frac{Y_n}{\left(1+i\right)^n}$$

$$= \sum_{t=1}^{n} \frac{Y_t}{\left(1+i\right)^t}$$

Are Lottery Tickets Sucker Bets?

Maybe we need "truth-in-winning" laws. Truth-in-lending laws force financial institutions to disclose all interest and miscellaneous costs to borrowers. But similar standards apply only inconsistently to state lotteries, magazine subscription sweepstakes, and similar schemes aimed at people afflicted with get-rich-quick mentalities.

The sad reality is that winning $1,000,000 in a state lottery won't even come close to making you a millionaire. The biggest reason is that lottery commissions typically spread top prizes across 20 checks and 19 years of payments. (You get a first check when you win, and then one at the end of each of the next 19 years.) State governments effectively collect the interest on your winnings. Another consideration is taxes. State, federal, and local taxes usually absorb at least 40% of your prize. Thus, winning $1,000,000 usually generates annual checks of roughly $30,000 because taxes are withheld. Still a tidy sum, but what is

this income stream worth today?

Suppose 10% is the standard interest rate. Your winnings are worth $30,000 plus $30,000/1.10 plus $30,000/(1.10^2) plus . . . plus $30,000/(1.10^{19}), or a grand total of $282,732. When interest rates and taxes are considered properly, it would take a cool $3,569,184 as an announced prize to yield a present value of $1,000,000 and truly make the winner a millionaire.

What are the odds against getting rich by buying lottery tickets? Typical state lotteries brag that they pay out half of their revenues in prizes. Most gloss over taxes and the length of time for payout. In fact, lottery commissions usually buy annuities from financial institutions to handle payoffs to winners across time. They pay less than 30% of the face value of the announced winnings for these annuities. And then the states collect taxes on your winnings. Consequently, on average, "the house" collects roughly 75% to cover its expenses out of all rev-

enues from lottery tickets.

On the other hand, roughly 3% of each bet, on average, goes to cover the operations of a gambling casino in Las Vegas or Atlantic City. For example, the average payout to craps players is $35 paid out for every $36 that gamblers bet. Casinos support their operations by collecting $1 out of each $36 bet. Unlike states that collect state income taxes from winners, however, casinos don't collect a "casino tax."

This analysis suggests that, if you cannot control the impulse to gamble, you are likely to do much better by dealing with private organizations instead of a state government. Lottery tickets are a terrible gambling strategy, shunned by economists, statisticians, or almost anyone with any sense about what payoffs should be to warrant a financial investment. Most lottery tickets are, unfortunately, sold to misguided dreamers and poor people who don't know about better investments.

where: Y_t = payment expected at time t; i = annual interest rate or discount rate; t = time period; n = number of periods when payments are expected; and Σ = an arithmetic operator meaning "sum across."

If you use a 6% interest rate to discount the $PV = \$100/1.06$, which equals $94.34. This amount in a savings account paying 6% interest would yield $94.34 \times (0.06) = \$5.66$, at the end of the year your principal plus interest would total to $94.34 + $5.66, which is $100. If you had to wait two years for the $100, what is the most you would pay, assuming the interest rate is 6%? The answer is $89, because $100/[1 + .06]^2 = \$89$. Naturally, an IOU paying $100 next

year plus $100 two years hence would be worth $94.34 + $89.00 = $183.34.

State legislatures came under tremendous pressure during the 1980s to hold taxes in check. Many responded by enacting state lotteries. Federal truth-in-lending laws were enacted to help borrowers avoid misunderstanding about interest rates and present values. Focus 1 indicates how misleading state lotteries are because their advertising fails to reflect the importance of discounting future income streams.

• **Perpetuities** The present value formula may appear formidable, but there is a shortcut in calculating present values if the annual income expected from an asset is fixed into the indefinite future at a constant Y_t. Such assets, known as perpetuities, are computed with the following equation:

Present Value for Perpetuities

$$PV = \frac{Y_t}{i}$$

Thus, if a parcel of land is expected to generate annual rent of $10,000 forever and the interest rate is 10% (0.10), the parcel's present value is $100,000. If a government bond promises to pay $1,000 annually forever to its owner and the interest rate is 8% it is worth $12,500. Bonds of this type, called *consols*, are issued by the Bank of England.

• **Rates of Return**   While present value calculations are very important to financial analysts, investors are more often interested in rate of return analysis, which facilitates quick and dirty comparisons of alternative investments. If you are majoring in accounting or finance or are just interested in investment analysis, you should pay special attention to both present value and rate of return formulas—you will undoubtedly see them again.[3]

> The **rate of return** is the annual return to an asset expressed as a percentage of the asset's price.

Investors usually have some idea of the income stream they might expect from an investment. We can determine the rate of return (r) by solving the following formula:

Rate of Return Calculation

$$P = \sum_{t=0}^{n} \frac{Y_t}{\left(1 + r\right)^t}$$

where P equals the price of the investment good, r equals the annual rate of return, and all other variables are as defined earlier. Since we know price (P) and expected income in each time pe-

riod. (Y_t), the only unknown is r, the rate of return. For example, if an asset selling for $100 today will pay $110 a year from today, the rate of return is 10%. A $112 payment in a year yields a rate of return of 12%. Thus, the larger the expected income in each time period, the greater the rate of return for a given price.

• **Comparing Present Values and Rates of Return**   How are present values and rates of return related to each other and to the capitalization process? If the present value is at least as great as the price ($PV \geq P$), then the expected rate of return is at least as great as the interest rate ($r \geq i$); you will invest because the asset appears profitable. You will not invest if an asset's price exceeds your estimate of present value because the expected rate of return will be less than the market rate of interest.

Generally, we know the price (P), the going interest rate (i), and the income expected each year (Y_1) when we evaluate an investment.

Break-Even Investments

$$PV = \sum_{t=0}^{n} \frac{Y_t}{\left(1 + r\right)^t}$$

When this equation holds, an investment is a *break-even* proposition. For example, if an investor could expect $224 one year hence and the interest rate were 12%, a price of $200 makes an investment a break-even proposition. However, your assessment of the present value of an asset may be either higher or lower than the going price. Similarly, you may estimate the rate of return as either above or below the market interest rate.

Present value calculations solve for the current worth of an income stream by discounting expected future income with the market rate of interest, both of which we know. Rate of return analysis also assumes that we know how much income to expect in the future and when it will be received, but solves for an unknown *implicit* interest rate (r) while using the known current price to arrive at a solution.

---

[3]You may want to keep this book as a simple introduction to this very complex topic.

Parallels in calculations of present values and rates of return may make it seem that maximizing one is equivalent to maximizing the other. Unfortunately, this perception can be misleading and result in misplaced investment priorities. Consider two one-time financial investments. Suppose that you have exactly $1,000 available. Your first option is a coupon for $10 guaranteed to quadruple to $40 in one day, a 300% return that is almost immediate. Unfortunately, buying the $10 coupon will prevent you from exercising your second risk-free option: your $1,000 will double in a day, yielding only a 100% return. Despite the fact that you must forgo the investment with the higher rate of return, doubling the $1,000 investment is clearly preferable to quadrupling a $10 investment over the same period.

Which of the following is more valuable as an investment? (*a*) A $5,000 investment in a Christmas tree lot will double your funds by generating a rate of return of 100%, but only for one month. (*b*) A $1 billion investment in a vitamin pill plant will generate a 1% net return per month forever. Even though the annualized return from the tree lot exceeds 1,200% (because of compounding), the investment in the pill factory is much more valuable. The key to sound investment is, "When in doubt, maximize present values—not rates of return."

Capitalization and Competition

There is tremendous competition for profits. If you are astute, several other astute investors will probably assess any given investment much as you do. If present value appears to substantially exceed price, there may be bidding wars that rapidly drive the price toward present value. Even if you do manage to pick up what you view as a bargain, you certainly would not then sell it for less than its present value to you.

Thus, the equilibrium price of any asset is its present value. Moreover, competition causes the rate of return expected from any asset, after adjusting for risk, to equal the market rate of interest. The process that discounts expected future income by the interest rate to arrive at present value and price is *capitalization*.

How might you use your knowledge of the capitalization process? Assume you own 1,000 shares of a wildcat oil company earning $1 per share per year. If market conditions required a 10% rate of return, shares of stock would sell for $10. What if the firm hit a gusher expected to triple its annual earnings? Stock shares would quickly rise to roughly $30 after the gusher was announced. What rate of return would be expected by people who bought stock after this discovery? Roughly 10% just as before. Similar capitalization processes determine the prices of all sorts of economic resources and financial investments. We suggested earlier that any predictable income stream is quickly capitalized. Focus 2 describes how capitalization enriches people who establish successful enterprises.

One possible road to riches requires finding assets for which the current owners have underestimated future earning power. You can then purchase these assets relatively cheaply. When the true earning capacity of the assets becomes known, you can become rich by selling the assets for considerably more. One roadblock that makes this a difficult avenue to wealth, however, is vigorous competition from many other bright bargain hunters.

At times, attempts to discover bargains lead people who acquire *insider information* about financial securities to break the law. Ivan Boesky acquired notoriety and millions of dollars as an *inside trader*, trading (illegally) based on inside information he procured. Profit is likely for anyone who acts on information about events that will affect the values of assets in predictable ways—but only if they act before that information is widely publicized. The case discussed in Focus 3 shows the effort people will extend to obtain information ahead of other investors.

THE MARGINAL PRODUCTIVITY THEORY OF INCOME DISTRIBUTION

We know that least cost production requires profit-maximizing firms to use combinations of resources so that the marginal physical products

Capitalization and the NFL

Professional football's domination by the National Football League (a cartel) went largely unchallenged from the league's establishment in 1920 until the 1960s. The NFL had 14 teams spread across the country in major cities by 1960. Several other cities sought NFL franchises, but established owners resisted growing pressure for expansion. (Cartel members recognize that increased output reduces prices.)

The sport's growing popularity and the advent of televised games (primarily on CBS and NBC) boosted revenue, attracting a group of wealthy fans who decided to compete with the NFL by launching the American Football League. These entrepreneurs were pre-pared to suffer initial losses in hopes of ultimate success in competing with the NFL. Each prospective owner ventured $25,000 for a franchise to start a team, locating largely in population centers neglected by the NFL. The AFL negotiated TV contracts of its own (primarily with ABC) and quickly proved competitive, drawing sell-out crowds in Denver, Buffalo, San Diego, and other second-tier markets. A bidding war for players ensued, and by 1965, the NFL capitulated to a merger.

Each $25,000 investment by an original AFL owner is now worth roughly $160 to 220 million. Does this huge increase mean that investment in an NFL franchise today would be enormously profitable? Capitalization explains why the answer is no. The NFL and then the AFL were enormously profitable for their original owners. Huge profits are possible for the entrepreneurs who start sports franchises and watch them succeed. But people who subsequently buy pieces of paper called "franchises" for millions of dollars can expect only normal returns. Capitalization causes the prices of franchises to equal the present value of expected returns. Thus, a buyer of an established franchise can expect only normal returns on investment.

---

of particular resources are proportional to the prices of the resources. This concept translates into the *principle of equal marginal productivities per dollar*:

$$\frac{MPP_L}{w} = \frac{MPP_K}{r} = \ldots$$

This is one application of the law of equal marginal advantage to production. Multiplying all *MPPs* by the price (*P*) of output reveals that competitive firms must operate so that the values of the marginal products of all resources (*VMP* = *P* × MPP) are proportional to their prices:

$$\frac{VMP_L}{w} = \frac{VMP_K}{r} = \ldots$$

But resource prices are equal to marginal factor costs if resource markets are competitive, and the market compels competitive firms to pay resource owners incomes equal to the resources' *VMPs*, so

$$\frac{VMP_L}{MFC_L} = \frac{VMP_K}{MFC_K} = \ldots$$

This suggests that a competitive market system tends to divide income according to the productive contribution of each individual's resources. Of course, product or resource markets are seldom purely competitive, but this brief review does identify some central tendencies for the distribution of income in a capitalist economy.

This *marginal productivity theory of income distribution* also points to a key for personal wealth. People will be relatively prosperous if they control a lot of resources that make valuable productive contributions to output. Incentives embedded in the structures of wages, rents, interest incomes from capital, and profits are sig-

Capitalizing on Insider Information

The Securities and Exchange Commission (SEC) forbids trading securities on the basis of **insider information;** knowledge not available to the general public about events that affect securities prices (e.g., lawsuits, new product development, or plans for mergers or takeovers). Insiders presumably could get a jump, allowing them to profit by buying or selling before information concerning profits was available to the public. The judge's ruling in SEC v. Materia (1984) illustrates a typical case of insider trading.

Our era aptly has been styled the "age of information." Francis Bacon recognized nearly 400 years ago that "knowledge is power," but only in the last generation has it risen to the equivalent of the coin of the realm. Nowhere is this commodity more valuable or volatile than in the world of high finance, where facts worth fortunes while secret may be rendered worthless once revealed.

Anthony Materia was employed by a printer of financial documents, including many concerning proposed tender (merger) offers. Because even a hint of an upcoming tender offer may send the price of the target company's stock soaring, the identity of a target is zealously guarded. It is customary, therefore, for offerors (or their law firms) to omit information that might identify a merger target until the last possible moment. Code names are used, blanks are left unfilled until the eve of publication, and misinformation may even be included in early drafts. In sum, a quick reading of preliminary paperwork would not reveal this confidential information.

In his job as a copyholder, Materia read clients' drafts aloud to a proofreader, who ensured that page proofs conformed to the copy received from the client. Despite scrupulous efforts to keep confidential information secret, Materia divined the identities of at least four tender offer targets between December 1980 and September 1982. He purchased stock within hours of discovery, and within days—after the offer had been made public—he sold his holdings at substantial gains.

Determined to combat securities fraud, Congress enacted comprehensive yet open-ended statutes capable of adaptation and refinement. In recent years, developments in capital formation and novel means of effecting corporate combinations have spawned a new genre of confidential information. Courts are increasingly called upon to address a myriad of issues regarding the use of such data. We do not believe the drafters of the Securities Exchange Act of 1934—envisaging as they did an open and honest market—would have countenanced the activities engaged in by Anthony Materia.

nals about how to alter resources and allocate them so that they are used most valuably.

Marginal productivity theory encapsulates a lot of information about incentives in a market economy. For example, interest rate differentials may cause you to shift funds from a savings account into a money market fund. Higher interest rates may induce you to consume less and save more. If you enjoy art, economics, finance, and philosophy about equally well, pay differentials may channel you toward the more remunerative of these areas of study. Pay differentials are, for better or worse, signals about how society values (at the margin) having more people in particular occupations.[4] Consequently, musicians whose personal preferences run to classical music may perform rock, and serious artists may be forced to live off of income generated by painting houses. This theory cannot even hint, however, at the most equitable income distribution—a normative question that is addressed in the next chapter.

---

[4]Artists and philosophers might use the *paradox of value* to argue that, just as water is absolutely more valuable (has more total utility) than diamonds (which have higher marginal values and prices), philosophy and the arts are absolutely more valuable to society than finance or economics. Relative prices and wage structures, however, are based on marginal valuations.

CHAPTER REVIEW: KEY POINTS

1. **Economic rent** exists whenever resource owners receive more than the minimum required for them to supply given amounts of the resource.

2. Land has a unique economic characteristic: it is fixed in supply. Thus, its supply curve is perfectly inelastic, and all payments for the use of land are *pure rent*. Land rents vary by location and particular physical characteristics, such as fertility or stores of minerals.

3. Land is not unique in generating economic rents. Any resource paid more than the minimum required to elicit its availability also generates economic rents.

4. Single taxers, inspired by Henry George, proposed a 100% tax on land rent as a *single tax* to finance all government spending. They argue that taxing this unearned surplus would not distort the allocation of land and thus would not hinder economic efficiency. The single-tax proposal suffers from (*a*) inability to finance the entire public sector, (*b*) administrative problems in distinguishing land values arising out of improvements made by owners from rent as an unearned surplus, and (*c*) reduced incentives for landowners to put their land to the best possible uses if rent is taxed away.

5. Economic rent promotes economic efficiency by providing resource owners with incentives to put their assets to the most valuable uses.

6. **Nominal interest rates** are the percentage annual premiums paid to borrow funds. Interest rates on financial instruments vary according to (*a*) risk, (*b*) maturity, and (*c*) liquidity. The interest rate normally means the rate on a long-term riskless bond.

7. In the long run, **real interest rates** (which are measured by purchasing power) depend on (*a*) premiums required to induce savers to delay consumption, (*b*) desires for liquidity, and (*c*) the productivity of capital. These factors determine interest rates through markets for *loanable funds*.

8. Pure **economic profits** are the residual after adjusting accounting profits for the opportunity cost of resources provided by a firm's owners. Profit may arise from *monopoly power*, from bearing business *uncertainty*, or from *innovation*.

9. Profits are a driving force in a capitalist economy, channeling resources to their most productive uses and stimulating progress, as entrepreneurs innovate and endure business uncertainty. Profits induce efficiency; competitive firms that do not produce at the lowest possible cost will suffer economic losses.

10. **Present values** are the sums of the discounted values of future income that may be expected from owning an asset. The present value of an asset and its price will be identical in equilibrium. If the present value exceeds price, then the asset is a profitable investment because the expected *rate of return* exceeds the interest rate. **Capitalization** is the process whereby prices gravitate toward present values of assets.

QUESTIONS FOR THOUGHT AND DISCUSSION

1. Economic rents and economic profits are both surpluses in excess of opportunity costs from the vantage point of society as a whole. They are unnecessary to secure resources socially. Rent on the land used by any firm is a true opportunity cost to that firm, however, although economic profits are not. Can you reconcile the apparent contradiction that rents are often opportunity costs to the individual user but not to the entire society?

2. Land taxes may not cause gross misallocations of land, but property taxes are widely perceived as dissuading owners from improving land in an optimal fashion. High property taxes are also blamed for the deterioration of the urban cores of large cities. How elastic is the supply of improvements to land with respect to the supply elasticity of land per se? How might land values be distinguished from improvements if land taxes replaced property taxes?

3. Accounting profits generally exceed economic profits because accountants may fail to consider implicit costs. Can you think of activities that might generate implicit revenues so that economic profits would exceed accounting profits? Might this explain how firms in some competitive lines of business continually generate accounting losses but continue to operate?

4. Some people who start a successful enterprise encounter major difficulties in managing their companies once the firm is on its feet. For example, Steve Wozniak and Steven Jobs built Apple Computers from a tiny operation housed in a garage into a billion-dollar concern between 1976 and 1981, but professional managers and stockholders had banded together and ousted both from leadership of the company by 1985. What are the differences in the personalities required to be innovative entrepreneurs and to be professional managers? Is it likely that one person can embody both sets of attributes? Can you cite other cases in which people who were strong starters were weak finishers? Where a strong starter established a series of successful companies, but was never able to maintain control once success was enjoyed? Where strong starters proved quite capable of effective management once an enterprise was successful?

5. Assume the federal government issues a bond that pays $1,000 per year forever. If the general level of interest rates is 10%, what will be the price of the bond when issued? After the bond is issued, if interest rates rise to 20%, what will happen to the price of the bond? What will happen if interest rates fall to 5%?

Entrepreneur   Monosony

Discrimination

Implicit
contracts

Wage $VMP = MRP$

Chapter 31

Income Distribution and Poverty

Human capital

Most of us wake up knowing that we will have full bellies and roofs to sleep under that night. But haunting images of starving children and the homeless regularly appear on television. Many of the world's people suffer from malnutrition and live in squalor. It is not surprising that poor people tend to be less healthy and die younger than those who command more resources. In the United States, slum dwellers consume much less than prosperous suburbanites do, and the incomes of migrant farm workers fall far below the national average. Overseas, the opulence enjoyed by some wealthy people contrasts even more starkly with the lives of the impoverished.

Why is the relative prosperity that most Americans, Japanese, and Western Europeans enjoy so rare elsewhere? Why are some people poor, while others consume conspicuously and extravagantly? Do prosperous people have a duty to share with the less fortunate? If voluntary sharing seems inadequate, should government, on behalf of the people it represents, redistribute income and wealth? Do government redistributions of income provide disin-

centives to work to both those receiving aid and those who ultimately provide aid?

Whether money can buy happiness is the first issue addressed in this chapter. We then present some alternative ethical criteria that address redistributing income and wealth. Then we examine the distribution of income with a focus on how the distribution has changed both here and abroad over the last two decades. Finally, we turn to a discussion of poverty, describe current American welfare programs, and look at proposed reforms. A majority of people in more fortunate circumstances favor aid to the poor but are concerned that disincentives to work are embedded in welfare programs. We will consider whether aid programs provide for the needy without creating incentives for a permanent underclass.

PROSPERITY AND HAPPINESS

Would most of us like more wealth than we have? Almost certainly. Jeremy Bentham, the utilitarian philosopher, offered two important propositions about wealth and utility. The first is widely accepted: All else being equal, more income or wealth makes most people happier. Bentham's second proposition is much more controversial: On average, additional income means more to the poor than to the rich. That is, income itself may be subject to the law of diminishing marginal utility. We will deal with these issues in turn.

Does Money Buy Happiness?

Are the rich happier than the poor? Soap operas, pulp magazines, and bad novels often suggest that the price of being rich is a life of pain and suffering. Wouldn't most of us gladly risk such misery?

Numerous studies indicate that, on average, health and longevity are positively related to income and wealth. Prosperous people also tend to rate themselves as happier than people who are not, as the study reported in Figure 1 shows. People were asked how happy they were. The responses shown in Panel A were assigned weights of +2 for "very happy," +1 for "pretty happy," and zero for "not too happy," leading to the *utility score* in Panel B.[1] Utility scores climb as income rises, supporting Bentham's idea that higher income yields greater happiness, although there is a possibility of reverse causation: cheerful people may get better jobs and do better financially.

A 1993 study of thousands of Asians reported by the Associated Press suggests that money isn't everything. Culture, for example, can be very important. The study found that 94% of people in impoverished Indonesia described themselves as "happy," while only 64% of people in affluent Japan described themselves as happy; fully one-third of the Japanese surveyed described their lives as miserable.

---

[1] Note that the scores reported in Figure 1 are what economists refer to as *ordinal* measures—they merely set a rank order of first group, second group, and third group. Thus, these measures are not as precise as *cardinal* measures, whereby we can, for example, measure something's weight as 1.42 kilograms. (An ordinal ranking of weight might be lightest, medium, heaviest.)

FIGURE 1   Income and Happiness

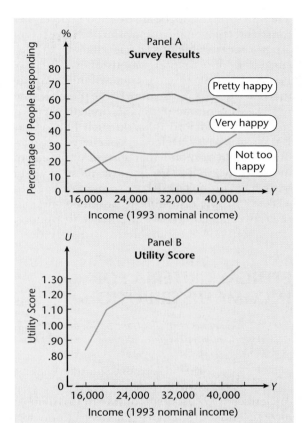

In Panel A, the percentage of people who rate themselves "pretty happy" seems unaffected by income. The response "very happy," however, is far more common for people with higher incomes, and relatively few high income people say they are "not too happy." Many low-income people consider themselves "not-too-happy," while few are "very-happy." This suggests that general satisfaction with life is positively related to income, as shown in Panel B. Panel B's utility scores are the averages for each income category if "very happy" is assigned a value of +2, "pretty happy" a value of +1, and "not too happy" a value of 0.

Source: Drawn from a survey of Illinois residents, reported in N.M Bradburn and D. Caplovitz, *Report on Happiness* (Chicago: Aldine, 1965). Updated to1993 dollars by authors.

Do Extra Dollars Mean More to the Poor Than to the Rich?

This question cannot be answered objectively because interpersonal comparisons of satisfaction are not measurable in any scientific way (as discussed in our chapter, "Consumer Choice"). People favoring greater equality might argue that extra dollars mean more to the poor because necessities generate more *utils* (imaginary measures of satisfaction) than do such luxuries as BMWs or jewelry. Defenders of current distributions could respond that income must mean more to the well-to-do because most of them work hard for it. The debate spins in circles, but a "best" income distribution cannot be scientifically ascertained. Wide differences in opinion exist about how income should be distributed.

ETHICAL CRITERIA FOR INCOME DISTRIBUTION

When wealth is centralized, the people are dispersed. When wealth is distributed, the people are brought together.

The Analects of Confucius, Book 14

Ancient controversies surround fair divisions of income and output. Uneven distribution has been thought unfair by most have-nots—and by many conscience-stricken haves as well. At least three schools of thought offer competing answers. One normative view is that income should be based on contribution (or marginal productivity); a second, that income should be distributed according to need; and a third, that income should be distributed equally.

The Contribution Standard

He that will not work shall not eat.

John Smith,
The General Historie of Virginia (1624)

In a competitive environment, income is allocated in proportion to the values of the marginal products and amounts of resources people sup-

ply. Marginal productivity theory (discussed in the preceding chapter) underpins the *contribution standard*, whose advocates believe that rewarding contribution is both equitable and efficient. A contribution standard recognizes that income incentives encourage work effort, investment, and attempts to profit by serving other people's demands.

> The **contribution (marginal productivity) standard** is the idea that income should be distributed according to the productivity of one's resources.

This standard assumes that markets accurately gauge productivity. Thus, who gets how much is determined by impersonal market forces, without the favoritism inherent in centralized decision-making. Income differences generated by a contribution standard are not a disadvantage, according to its champions, in part because people with high incomes save proportionally more, facilitating investment and economic growth. The rich and the poor alike gain according to the cliché, "A rising tide lifts all boats." Moreover, inequality is equitable if it results from smarter or harder work, longer hours, or higher rates of saving and investing.

A contribution standard uses carrots (income) to reward productivity, instead of the sticks (punishment for sloth) common under other systems. Should a cabdriver who works 60-hour weeks subsidize one who works only 30 hours? Should a factory worker who draws interest from savings squeezed from a slim paycheck share the interest with others who spend everything they make? Advocates of the contribution standard answer no to such questions, asserting that the standard is compatible with capitalism, sets efficient incentives for production and economic growth, and maximizes individual freedom.

Opponents of the contribution standard, however, wonder how well markets measure productivity. They question high pay for pro athletes and corporate CEOs relative to teachers and others doing society's work, and they argue that the very young, the very old, and the handicapped among us must share in our income if our society is to be fair and humane.

The Needs Standard

From each according to ability, to each according to needs.

Louis Blanc

Some people lack physical or mental attributes or skills to be very productive, while wealthy heirs, by resource ownership alone, claim to be productive. Citing such perceived inequities, many opponents of a contribution standard favor ensuring that everyone's needs are met.

*The **needs standard** asserts that income should be distributed "to each according to needs."[2]*

Blanc's slogan inspired Marxist revolutionaries for over a century, ultimately governing the nominal policies of countries containing one-third of humanity. Marxism's ongoing collapse in Eastern Europe and China is testimony to obstacles in implementing a needs standard.[3] Assessing needs is unavoidably imprecise and requires an immense bureaucracy likely to favor political entrepreneurs. Production incentives are also a problem. How many people would work diligently if distribution were strictly by need? Is it proper to replace economic incentives with government coercion?

Trade-offs between efficiency and equity can be heart wrenching (see Focus 1). Most people agree that at least the basic needs of those who cannot provide for themselves must be accommodated, because we should not allow or-phans, the aged, the severely handicapped, or society's misfits to starve. Whether capable but lazy people should be guaranteed the necessities of life is a separate issue.

The Equality Standard

Dividing income equally avoids the great disparities in income that come about under the contribution standard and dispenses with the huge bureaucracy required for a needs standard.

*The **equality standard** asserts that income should be distributed equally across the population.*

All an equality standard requires is accurate national income accounting and a census of population: divide national income by population, then mail each family a check for its share. Moreover, there is an economic rationale that under certain conditions an equal distribution of income generates the maximum economic welfare possible in a society.

Suppose you were the utilitarian ruler of a country with a fixed national income and were intent on maximizing social happiness. You suspect that some citizens would be reasonably happy with very little, while others would gain great happiness from higher monetary incomes. Unfortunately, you cannot measure any person's gain in happiness from a higher money income, nor can you objectively compare happiness between individuals. If you try to find out who would gain the most from more than an equal share, most people will exaggerate their needs, and some may lie to you. If you are convinced that each person gains from higher income but that, on average, the poor gain more than the rich, then expected happiness of the community is maximized if you simply divide all income equally.

Like distribution according to need, however, equal sharing of income erodes personal incentives for productivity. One ideal of socialism is to replace the selfish individuals assumed in conventional economic theory with people filled with desire to work for the betterment of all humanity. Attempts to educate masses of people into altruistic modes of behavior have uniformly

---

[2]An interesting historical note is that Marx viewed distribution according to need as an objective to be implemented only after a "dictatorship of the proletariat" gave way to "pure communism." According to Marx, the most glaring inequity of capitalism is that workers are paid less than the value of their *average* products because exploitative capitalists steal any production in excess of subsistence wages. Thus, Marx was an advocate of a productivity standard, were productivity was defined by average rather than marginal products. After Marx's death, John Bates Clark developed marginal productivity theory and the argument that payments to owners of their resources' marginal products would absorb all production. It would be interesting, were it possible, to know what Marx's own reaction would have been to Clark's rebuttal of the exploitation doctrine.

[3]Other aspects of an equality standard of distribution were introduced in Chapter 2.

Focus 1

Pie Makers vs. Pie Splitters

Orthodox Marxists believe that a proper blend of equality and need is the only fair criterion for distributing income. They view capitalist-style freedom as a facade; rich capitalists have freedom to exploit workers and hog most consumer goods, while the *proletariat* (working class) only has freedom to suffer in silence. Capitalism's alleged efficiency has been vilified as an empty shell that masks extreme inequalities of income, manipulative advertising, and a general exploitation of consumers and workers.

This overall characterization of capitalism was an article of faith among the leaders who led Marxist revolutions and installed communism. Official hostility to exploitation put a strange supply-side spin on economic activity. Restaurant employees' rights to stable jobs and income, for exam-

ple, preceded the rights of customers. Consequently, service was almost uniformly poor, because servers received the same incomes regardless of whether customers were satisfied and regardless of the restaurant's revenues. Under capitalism, consumer sovereignty yields a demand-side orientation. This means that restaurant employees who fail to render prompt and courteous service with good food experience low incomes and job instability.

Most of these same countries (e.g., Eastern Europe, China, and Vietnam) have now decided that the fundamental orientation of workers toward their jobs must change, and the leaders have sought greater efficiency and growth through increased reliance on market forces. For example, in China, experiments with markets are being broadened after great

success in the limited sectors originally targeted in the 1980s. But many ideologues and bureaucrats who feel attacked by market experiments have counterattacked, focusing on the high incomes earned by ambitious entrepreneurs.

After decades of being conditioned that income differentials reflect exploitation, many citizens cannot stand the idea that anyone deserves more income than anyone else. Hard-liners in some countries have proposed narrow limits on income differentials in response to growing inequalities in income. Progressive leaders are treading political high wires, trying to balance new incentives for productivity against the entrenched interests of bureaucrats whose jobs are threatened because they are inefficient.

failed, with the result that enforced production quotas have often replaced income incentives for production.

Inequality and Inequity

Life is unfair.

John F. Kennedy (1960)

People differ in natural ability and opportunity, in the times when and places where they were born, in age, race, sex, and religion. Most of all, they differ in luck. Some face discrimination; some are maimed or die in car wrecks or wars; and some are homely, demented, or physicaly or mentally impaired. Others are attractive, healthy, bright, buy winning lottery tickets, or are born with silver spoons in their mouths. Whether inequality is inherently inequitable or unfair is a

normative issue that varies according to individual judgments and from case to case.

Many sources of inequality may seem inequitable to some people but simply cannot be eliminated. A genius cannot transfer IQ points to someone less intellectually gifted, for example, nor can a world-class sprinter give speed to us slowpokes. Other apparent inequities may be partially remedied through government policies or social reforms. The inequity of slavery ended with the Civil War, and discrimination by religion, race, or sex is now illegal in education, housing, and employment.

No society ever achieves a consensus that everyone is treated fairly because equity is unavoidably normative and subjective. Suppose everyone agreed with the idea of *horizontal equity*: equals should be treated equally. Even this might do little to resolve equity because every person is somewhat unique. Advocates of the contribution standard argue that inequality of income or wealth is frequently justified by differences in individuals' productivity. Yet difficulties in specifying equity when people and circumstances differ have caused critics of a contribution standard to focus on any inequality as evidence of inequity.

INCOME DISTRIBUTION IN THE UNITED STATES

Just how unequal is the U.S. income distribution? Table 1 shows *pretax* and *pretransfer* distri-butions of income since 1967. Changes appear to proceed only at a snail's pace. Because taxes are mildly progressive while transfers tend to be regressive, Table 1 understates the share of net income received by people at the bottom and overstates the share of people at the top.

Measures of Income Distribution

Before we explore how much tax and transfer policies reduce inequality, we need to examine the three major measures used to compare distributions of income or wealth.

TABLE 1 The Distribution of Pretax and Pretransfer Household Income

| Year | Number (thous.) | Percent distribution of aggregate income Quintiles | | | | | Median (1990) | Gini ratio |
		Lowest	Second	Third	Fourth	Fifth		
1992		3.8	9.4	15.9	24.1	46.8	$30,786	.430
1991		3.8	9.5	16.0	24.2	46.5	31,034	.425
1990	94,312	3.9	9.6	15.9	24.0	46.6	29,943	.428
1989	93,347	3.8	9.5	15.8	24.0	46.8	30,468	.431
1988	92,830	3.8	9.6	16.0	24.3	46.3	30,079	.427
1987	91,124	3.8	9.6	16.1	24.3	46.2	29,984	.426
1986	89,479	3.8	9.7	16.2	24.3	46.1	29,690	.425
1985	88,458	3.9	9.8	16.2	24.4	45.6	28,688	.419
1984	86,789	4.0	9.9	16.3	24.6	45.2	28,197	.415
1983	85,290	4.0	9.9	16.4	24.6	45.1	27,581	.414
1982	83,918	4.0	10.0	16.5	24.5	45.0	27,577	.412
1981	83,527	4.1	10.1	16.7	24.8	44.4	27,669	.406
1980	82,368	4.2	10.2	16.8	24.8	44.1	28,125	.403
1979	80,776	4.1	10.2	16.8	24.7	44.2	29,074	.404
1978	77,330	4.2	10.2	16.9	24.7	44.1	29,168	.402
1977	76,030	4.2	10.2	16.9	24.7	44.0	28,067	.402
1976	74,142	4.3	10.3	17.0	24.7	43.7	27,913	.398
1975	72,867	4.3	10.4	17.0	24.7	43.6	27,442	.397
1974	71,163	4.3	10.6	17.0	24.6	43.5	28,197	.395
1973	69,859	4.2	10.5	17.1	24.6	43.6	29,108	.397
1972	68,251	4.1	10.5	17.1	24.5	43.9	28,545	.401
1971	66,676	4.1	10.6	17.3	24.5	43.5	27,377	.396
1970	64,778	4.1	10.8	17.4	24.5	43.3	27,640	.394
1969	63,401	4.1	10.9	17.5	24.5	43.0	27,828	.391
1968	62,214	4.2	11.1	17.5	24.4	42.8	26,844	.388
1967	60,813	4.0	10.8	17.3	24.2	43.8	25,719	.399

Source: U.S. Bureau of the Census, Current Population Reports, Series P60-184. *Money Income of Households, Families, and Persons in the United States: 1992*, U.S. Government Printing Office, Washington, D.C., 1993.

NOTE: Median household income has been deflated by the CPI-U-X1.

• **Lorenz Curves** The changes in the income distribution and the extent of inequality reported in Table 1 are hard to trace. Lorenz curves, developed by a German statistician, allow visual comparisons between distributions across time and between countries.

*A **Lorenz curve** shows the cumulative percentage distribution of income or wealth in a society.*

Cumulative percentages of families and family incomes before taxes and transfers are on the axes of the Lorenz curve in Figure 2. Quintile data (like that in Table 1) are sequentially summed to form the cumulative distribution. For example, if the bottom 20% and the second lowest 20% of the population receive 5% and 11% of all income, respectively, then the lowest 40% of the population receives 16% of total income. And if the middle 20% gets 17% of total income, then the lowest 60% of the population receives 33% (5 + 11 + 17 = 33). And so on.

If the Lorenz curve were a diagonal like the straight line 0*e*, then income would be distributed evenly: each fifth of the population would receive one-fifth of income. If one family had all income while the rest of us had nothing, the Lorenz curve would be identical to the bottom and right-hand axes—line 0*fe*. The Lorenz curve for the United States is the curved line 0*abcde*. Area *A* reflects inequality; the larger this area, the more unequal the income distribution.

• **The Gini Coefficient** A related measure of income concentration is the *Gini index* or *coefficient*, a statistical measure derived from the Lorenz curve.

*The **Gini index** or **coefficient** is the ratio of the area between the line of perfect equality (diagonal) and the Lorenz curve to the total area under the diagonal.*

In Figure 2, the Gini index would be the ratio of area *A* to area *A* plus area *B* or,

$$\text{Gini index} = \frac{A}{A + B}$$

The Gini index ranges from 0 (perfect equality) to 1 (perfect inequality).

FIGURE 2 Lorenz Curve (Income Before Taxes and Transfers)

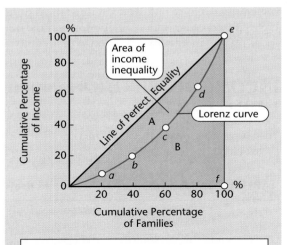

Approximate Income Distribution		Cumulative Income Distribution		
Group	% of Total Income	Group	% of Total Income	Point In Figure Above
Lowest 20%	5	First 20%	5	*a*
Second 20%	11	First 40%	16	*b*
Middle 20%	17	First 60%	33	*c*
Fourth 20%	24	First 80%	57	*d*
Highest 20%	43	Total	100	*e*

Lorenz curves illustrate unequal distribution. In this figure, the cumulative shares of pretax income are shown (on the vertical axis) for ever larger proportions of the population, beginning at the bottom of the income ladder. The area between the Lorenz curve and the 45° reference line indicates the extent of inequality.

Perfect equality can never be attained, if only because lifetime earnings patterns prevent continuously equal income distributions. Younger families typically earn less than more established families, primarily because of differences in work experience and past saving. Thus, even if every family had identical lifetime incomes, inequality would exist at every point in time because of typical age—earnings differences.

- **Relative Income** The Bureau of the Census recently began reporting a new measure called *relative income* to describe the distribution of income.

> *Relative income* measures the extent to which a person's income diverges from median income for the country.

For example, a person with a relative income of 0.25 has only one-fourth of median (middle) income while someone with a relative income of 3.0 has three times the middle income. Relative income is reported for three categories:

1. *Low Relative Income*: income less than one-half of median income.
2. *High Relative Income*: income at least twice that of median income.
3. *Middle Relative Income*: income between low and high relative income.

The relative income measure is particularly good at showing changes in the income distribution over time. Figure 3 uses relative income to highlight the major changes that have occurred in income patterns over the past three decades. Both tails (high and low relative income groups) have grown, resulting in a shrinking middle.

This brief look at the three income distribution measures suggests that, over the last few decades, pretax income has become more unequally distributed and the middle class is becoming smaller as more families become either rich or poor. In the next section we examine demographic, economic, and social trends to explain some reasons for these changes in our income distribution.

The Changing Distribution of Income

The state of economic development powerfully influences relative distributions of income, with more advanced countries tending to have greater income equality. For example, Figure 4 indicates that distribution is more equal in such countries as the United States, Japan, and West Germany than in such countries as Mexico, Turkey, Brazil, and Bangladesh. The average Gini coefficient for the developed nations shown is .337, while for the developing countries illustrated, it is .462 or nearly 40% more severe.

The gradual shift toward greater inequality in the United States in the last two decades is shown by the *pretax* Gini coefficients shown in Table 1 and the changes in relative income

Source: U.S. Bureau of the Census, Current Population Reports, Series P-60, No. 177, *Trends in Relative Income: 1964 to 1989,* (Washington D.C.: U.S. Government Printing Office), 1991. Estimates for 1994 by the authors.

Relative income measures the extent to which people's incomes differ from median income. In the last two decades, both low and high relative income groups have grown. The middle class has shrunk from 70 percent of the population to roughly 60 percent.

FIGURE 3   Relative Income (1964–1993)

FIGURE 4 Gini Index Numbers for Selected Countries

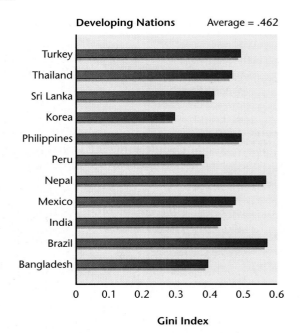

The Gini coefficients in this figure indicate that developing nations usually have problems because of both low income and severe inequality. Developed nations have more equally distributed incomes than do undeveloped nations. Data is for 1980–83.

shown in Figure 3. These shifts are in sharp contrast to earlier decades, when incomes rose at faster rates and were increasingly spread evenly across the income distribution.

Several factors account for the bulk of this rising income inequality.[4] First, baby boomers became adults and entered the labor force during the 1970s and 1980s. Over 75 million boomers entered the labor force, shifting the labor supply curve to the right, depressing average wage incomes, and increasing poverty rates and income inequality.

Second, Americas' industrial structure has shifted away from goods producing (manufacturing) to services (see Panel A of Figure 5). During this same period, union membership fell, the pay gap between well educated and poorly educated adults widened, and the composition of our imports and exports changed. Service industries typically pay less than manufacturing, employers are

---

[4]U.S. Bureau of the Census, "*Studies in the Distribution of Income*," Current Population Reports, series P60–183 (Washington, D.C.: U.S. Government Printing Office, 1992).

increasingly willing to pay wage premiums for highly skilled and highly educated workers, and our imports embody more unskilled labor than our exports. These changes all combined to raise incomes of the highest earners while lowering incomes of the bottom earning quintile.

Third, as Panel B of Figure 5 shows, married-couple households as a percentage of total households have fallen over this period. Rising divorce rates and births out of wedlock have reduced married couples as a percentage of total families from 70% in 1970 to 60% in 1990. Further, the percentage of married-couple households in which the wife was working increased by roughly 50% over the last two decades. These two trends mean that fewer households include married couples, and, in these fewer households, both partners are working, so earnings are rising relatively faster for this population cohort. Families in which both adult members are working tend to be in the higher income quintiles, and single parent families are more often poor.

In summary, the middle class is shrinking because of (*a*) a large labor supply increase from baby

FIGURE 5 Reasons for the Growing Inequality in the Distribution of Income

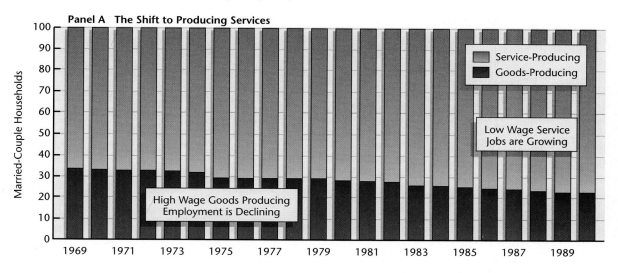

Panel A   The Shift to Producing Services

Service-Producing
Goods-Producing

Low Wage Service Jobs are Growing

High Wage Goods Producing Employment is Declining

Panel B   The Decline of Married-Couple Households and the Rise of Two-Earner Households

Married-Couple Households as Percentage of Total

Percentage of Married-Couple Households in Which Wife is Employed

JUST MARRIED!

The shrinking middle class is partly due to baby boomers entering labor markets and depressing wages, the continuing shift of our economy from a high-wage manufacturing emphasis to the low-wage service sector, the increase in low income single parent families and the rise in high income two earner families.

boomers that has depressed wages and income (for younger groups), (*b*) a growing service sector, (*c*) rising single-parent families, and (*d*) an expanding number of two-earner families.

Adjusting Income for Taxes and Transfers

U.S. Census Department surveys traditionally focused on pretax incomes and failed to con-

sider tax payments, unrealized capital gains, and benefits from government transfer programs. A recent study by the Department of Commerce shows that taxes, government transfers, and other government programs substantially affect the level and distribution of income.[5]

[5]U.S. Bureau of the Census, "Measuring the Effect of Benefits and Taxes on Income and Poverty: 1992," *Current Population Reports*, series P-60, no. 186-RD (Washington, D.C.: U.S. Government Printing Office, 1993).

FIGURE 6 Adjusting Lorenz Curves for Taxes and Transfers

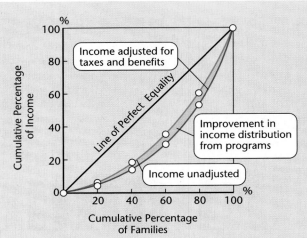

Quintiles	Money Income Current Measure	Money Income Adjusted for Taxes and Benefits
Top	48.80	43.30
Second	24.10	23.90
Third	15.90	16.70
Fourth	9.40	11.00
Lowest	3.80	5.10
Gini coefficient	0.43	0.38
Number below poverty (thousands)	36,880	26,533

When income is adjusted for tax payments and transfers, the distribution of income becomes more equal and the number of people below poverty line drops by roughly 30%.
Source: U.S. Bureau of the Census, *Current Population Reports*, series P-60, no. 186-RD, "*Measuring the Effect of Benefits and Taxes on Income and Poverty: 1992*," (Washington, D.C.: U.S. Government Printing Office, 1993).

As Figure 6 shows, after taxes, transfers, and capital gains are considered, the Gini index for 1992 drops by over 10% and the number of people living below the poverty line falls nearly 30%.

Transfer payments and the U.S. tax structure (which, overall, is progressive) have resulted in a somewhat more equal distribution of income. Some people, however, feel that redistribution schemes should focus on wealth instead of income, because income and prosperity are only roughly correlated.

The Distribution of Wealth

Wealth is the sum of financial assets and economic capital minus liabilities. Median household wealth in 1988 was nearly $36,000.[6] These assets include motor vehicles, real estate, stocks, mutual fund shares, and so on.

Do poor people occasionally have high incomes? Do wealthy people sometimes experience low incomes? The surprising answer to both questions is yes. Wealth is cumulative unspent income and is a stock variable, while income is a flow variable.[7] Wealth tends to generate income, but some high-income people don't save and never achieve wealth; you may have read about high-rolling financiers or big lottery winners declaring bankruptcy. On the other hand, some wealthy people occasionally have low-income years. (Donald Trump had negative income of roughly $1 billion during 1989 and 1990.) This is common for retirees, among others. Most welfare programs are intended for people plagued by both little wealth and low income.

Measures of wealth are unavoidably crude, but a 1991 Bureau of the Census study indicates that the lowest fifth of households owned under

---

[6]U.S. Bureau of the Census, *Household Wealth and Asset Ownership: 1988* (Washington, D.C.: U.S. Government Printing Office, 1990).

[7]*Stock variables* are timeless, while *flow variables* lack meaning without a time period. A millionaire's assets exceed debts by at least $1 million, and time is irrelevant. It matters greatly, however, whether you make $100 hourly or annually.

0.5% of all assets in 1988, while the top 20% held 38% of wealth, excluding pension plans, jewelry, and household furnishings.[8] White families average ten times as much wealth as African-American, and eight times as much as Hispanic-Americans. Only 2% of minority families were classified as wealthy, while 14% of whites were in the richest bracket. The wealthy tend to be professional or self-employed and in two-parent families. The poor tend to be uneducated and in broken homes. The major determinant of wealth, however, seems to be age. Many of those classified as poor are children. Typical heads of wealthy families are older than 55, while families headed by young parents are often poor. Time allows you to acquire wealth—another good reason to prefer growing older to its alternative.

Determinants of Income Distribution

Now that we have looked at snapshots of how income and wealth are distributed, we need to explore why some people are rich and some are poor. Many rich people inherit fortunes. (The most valuable talent anyone could have might be aptitude at parent selection.) Their productive assets can generate income with no labor efforts by the owners, so heirs to fortunes generally land in high-income brackets. Rent, interest, and corporate profit account for only about one-fifth of all income, but the bulk flows to the top 2% of the populace.

Income differentials also arise because, contrary to slogans and wishful thinking, we are not all created equal. Some of us are born with talents that especially suit us for remunerative careers. This is most obvious in entertainment or professional sports. Frustration will be your only reward if you cannot carry a tune but try to sing professionally, or stand less than 6 feet 8 inches tall and pursue a career as a center in the National Basketball Association. Levels of energy, motivation, amiability, and insight also separate individuals. Some people make choices

that seem to doom them to poverty. For example, perpetual students in esoteric disciplines, most artists, actors, and musicians, and some ministers select occupations for psychic income, not financial remuneration. Discrimination based on race, sex, age, ethnic background, height, or general appearance also causes differences in the options available to otherwise equally gifted individuals.

Occupational restrictions may also keep qualified people out of some jobs. For example, doctors are the highest paid professionals, on average, but medical practice requires specialized education, and the slots available in medical schools are limited. Some people step into management of a family business, while others bounce from job to job for years before settling into one that suits them. Finally, luck may play a major role in who gets a high-paying job and who doesn't—although some people seem to manufacture their own luck.

POVERTY IN AMERICA

Some people view poverty as evidence of the inequity of capitalism. In their minds, any economy generating almost $7 trillion in output should not allow the squalor and deprivation seen in our urban ghettos and many rural communities. Too often, children raised in poverty have few role models to show the way out of a life in which opportunities seem limited for education and, ultimately, good jobs.

Critics of this position note that the poor in the United States are not nearly as destitute as the down-and-out in India, North Africa, or other less developed regions. Defenders of our current distribution also point out that most of the "poor" in this country have televisions, refrigerators, and other items considered luxuries in most other countries. Focus 2 points out that poverty is far from an absolute concept; our views of poverty in part depend on average standards of living in a society.

What Does Poor Mean?

Identifying the poor requires a definition of poverty. The 20% of our population with the

---

[8]All studies of wealth, including this one, ignore human capital. In equilibrium, wealth and income are proportional if human capital is included in wealth.

Poverty: A Relative Concept

Friend: How's your spouse?

Economist: Relative to what?

An Unknown Pundit

This quip reflects a tendency among economists to measure almost everything relative to some alternative. *Poverty*, which is a lack of wealth or material comfort, is no exception. Everyone might agree that anyone without the physical means to sustain normal life is absolutely impoverished, but beyond that definition, poverty seems a relative concept determined by time and place. For example, many Americans below our official poverty line have amenities enjoyed only by the wealthy in less developed countries and seem prosperous relative to beggars and slum dwellers in some countries.

Consider how standards of living have changed over the centuries. The average lifespan of Europeans who survived childhood 1,000 years ago was less than 45 years. People in developed economies now typically live into their 70s because of advances in nutrition and medicine. Polio, cholera, smallpox, diphtheria, and leprosy are now extinct or quite rare in developed economies. Canning and refrigeration make it possible to store food for long periods, and the growth of commerce has enriched diets throughout the world. Even the nobility of medieval times did not have access to things that many Americans who are classified as poverty-stricken take for granted: aspirin, fast-food restaurants, telephones, running water, automobiles, electric lighting, indoor plumbing, garbage collection, paved roads, public education and transportation, antibiotics, grocery stores, "painless" dentistry, television, and central heating for their homes; this list could be extended for several pages.

Some Americans at society's bottom rungs—the homeless—do lead miserable lives, but for those in a position to receive food stamps and transfer payments, life on the dole is at least physically tolerable in most advanced economies. Suppose that you had to choose between (*a*) the physical comforts of a typical U.S. family relying on welfare for all its income in 1995 and (*b*) the standard of living enjoyed by noble members of King Arthur's court. If you ignore the trappings of power enjoyed by feudal nobility, we suspect that you would be reluctant to trade the range of choices available to most poor Americans for life in a damp and drafty castle.

This does not mean that poor Americans have a soft life. There is no doubt that the most destitute people in our society are often homeless, cold, and hungry. Our point, instead, is that poverty is in part determined by cultural norms, of which material comforts are only one dimension. Wealth and income ultimately provide their holders with freedom, power, and deference from others. Poor people have relatively less power and fewer choices over their lives.

lowest income is sometimes viewed as impoverished, but such an approach makes poverty incurable. Other definitions rely on estimates of the costs for families of various sizes and compositions of a minimal diet needed for life: soybeans, liver, lard, and other basic products. Such bland menus contain adequate nutrients but would quickly bore anyone. You may have heard of the *poverty line*.

The **poverty line** *is an index estimating the costs to secure minimal requirements for food, shelter, fuel, clothing, and transportation.*

This index is adjusted for family size, sex and age of the family head, number of minor children, and whether residence is rural or urban. Poverty thresholds in 1992 for various families are presented in Table 2. The poverty threshold for an average family of four now is nearly $15,000 in annual income.

Historically, one family in eight has been impoverished on average, but there is tremendous turnover among the poor. During a typical decade, more than 90% of the poor population changes; some people fall into poverty, replacing others who move above the

TABLE 2 Poverty Threshold Levels by Size of Family and Sex of Head of Household, 1992

Size of Family Unit	Threshold
One person (unrelated individual)	$ 7,134
15 to 64 years	7,299
65 years and over	6,729
Two persons	9,137
Householder 15 to 64 years	9,443
Householder 65 years and over	8,487
Three persons	11,187
Four persons	14,335
Five persons	16,592
Six persons	19,137
Seven persons	21,594
Eight persons	24,053
Nine persons or more	28,745

Source: Social Security Administration, 1993.

poverty line. Despite policies intended to reduce inequality, roughly 1% to 2% of all people remain destitute year after year.

Profiles of Poverty

F. Scott Fitzgerald once asserted, "The rich are different from you and me." Ernest Hemingway replied, "Yes, they are different. They have more money." This exchange can be turned upside down. Are the poor inherently different from the rich, or do they simply have much lower incomes?

Numerous studies indicate that certain personal characteristics are closely related to poverty. Some characteristics are not matters of choice: African-Americans, Hispanics, Native Americans, and new immigrants tend to be impoverished more often than are members of other population groups. This area of study is a normative mine field, and it is important to remember that correlation may not imply causation. The poor have relatively less education and labor participation, greater rates of illness and physical or mental disability, relatively more children, and heads of household who are more

often female, very young, or very old, as reflected in Figure 7.

The most important determinant of income seems to be the relationship of the family (or individual) to the labor market. Some of the poor are too young or too old to work, and some are too physically or mentally impaired to hold a job. But income opportunities are crucial if people who are mature and healthy are to be able to cure their own poverty. If jobs are the key, then government policies to maintain full employment might reduce poverty by providing job opportunities for many of the less fortunate. However, high employment alone will not solve the problem of poverty. Unless discrimination is a barrier, job openings are generally won by those who are most willing and qualified to work. Many poor people who are healthy and willing lack the experience, training, and education required to find a good job.

Moreover, there are regional pockets of unemployment and poverty caused by the decline of some industries; Appalachian coal mining from the 1920s into the 1970s is an example. Centers for such smokestack industries as steel and automobiles experienced similar problems in the 1980s, although these industries are now slowly recovering. Finally, as Figure 7 illustrates, poverty is not confined to the urban core. Poverty is uniformly higher in rural areas.

Government as a Provider for the Poor

Private charity alleviates some poverty, but many people see government aid as the only real remedy for poor people's misery. Reducing poverty has aspects of a public good (discussed in detail in the next chapter). You and I may both be distressed because people are hungry and homeless. If your private donations help ease this problem, I may feel a little better because I will encounter fewer panhandlers who ask for my spare change and see fewer stories about the poor on the news. Thus, I am less likely to contribute to charitable causes if I know that you do. These public good aspects of *private* giving mean that it is probably inadequate relative to society's desires to cure poverty—private

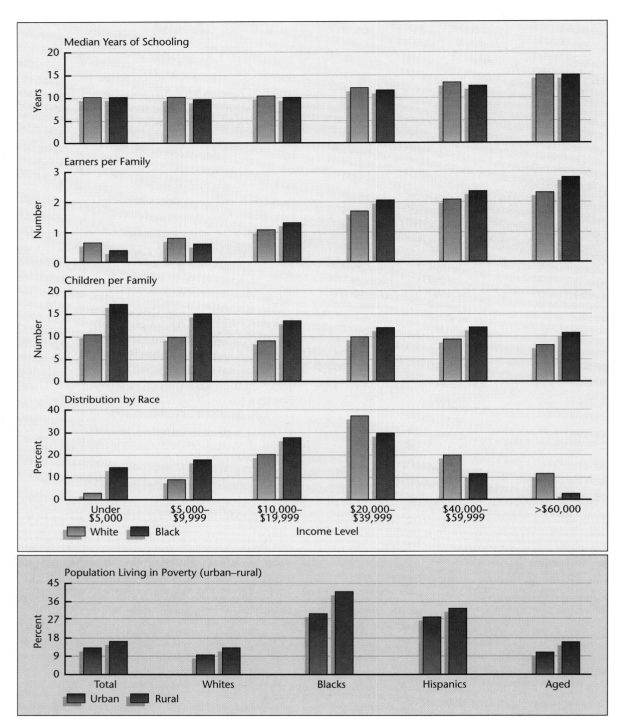

Source: U.S. Department of Commerce, Bureau of the Census, *Current Population Reports,* P-60, No. 185, *Poverty in the United States: 1992* (Washington D.C.: U.S. Government Printing Office), 1993 and *Business Week,* December 6, 1993, p. 28.

Caucasian families with few children and more than one highly-educated worker tend to have the highest incomes. African-American families with numerous children, few workers, and low levels of education are commonly caught in poverty. Poverty is not exclusively an urban phenomenon. In fact, poverty rates for all groups are higher in rural areas.

FIGURE 7 Poverty and Family Characteristics and Location

charity to reduce poverty will be insufficient. Government action may be required to provide a more efficient solution.

The government attack on poverty has been two-pronged, stressing job opportunities where practical and instituting income maintenance programs for those who cannot or will not work. Rapid economic growth may provide the biggest boost to standards of living for those at the bottom of the economic ladder. Figure 8 indicates that the percentage of families below the poverty line dropped after President Johnson launched a war on poverty in 1964. Federal funding for most welfare programs has grown continuously ever since, but over 30 million people remain below the poverty line. Poverty rates among African-American families have consistently been almost three times greater than those for Caucasian families.

A sharp jump in unemployment combined with reductions in the growth of social spending during the early 1980s worsened the plight of many people at the bottom of the income scale. This precipitated pressures for more federal funding from many who were concerned about poverty, but these pressures were offset somewhat by opponents of welfare spending. Opposition still continues from a growing chorus of critics who are skeptical that poverty can be cured by throwing money at it. Their view is that welfare programs have yielded limited gains to some poor people and have fostered among many recipients an unhealthy dependence on government, while reducing work incentives among both taxpayers and welfare recipients.

Types of Poverty

Some analysts divide the poor into *involuntary* and *voluntary* groupings. Involuntary poverty occurs if people cannot provide for themselves; those who voluntarily choose poverty could earn adequate income but rely on welfare programs instead. One study suggests that welfare programs are so generous that by the mid-1980s, each additional $4,000 in government transfer payments caused one additional family to vol-

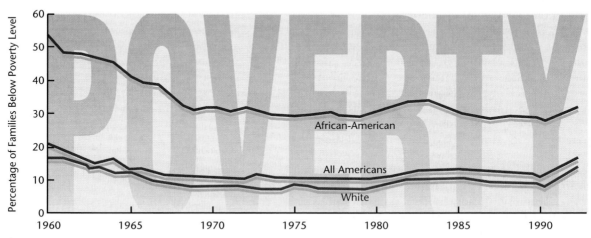

Source: U.S. Bureau of the Census, *Current Population Reports,* P-60, No. 185, *Poverty in the United States: 1992* (Washington D.C.: U.S. Government Printing Office). 1993.

Today roughly 13 percent of all families in the United States have incomes below the poverty level. Social programs developed in the 1960s probably account for much of the gradual reduction in measured poverty line increases. The number of people living in poverty is about 30 percent less when you include in-kind government transfers as income. Finally, these data indicate that African-American families on average are almost three times as likely to be poor as are their white counterparts.

FIGURE 8 Percentage of U.S. Families Who Are Poor, 1960—1989

untarily choose poverty.[9] How might higher welfare payments cause people to accept lower total income? Do you know workers who hate their jobs and would gladly quit working if society freely gave them half their current income? Similar choices may explain why some people are voluntarily poor.

Alternative Views of Poverty

Some critics of welfare programs cite evidence that the poor tend to commit more crimes and be less able, less motivated, less mobile, more reproductive, and less educated than the general population. To these critics, the high incidence of poverty among certain racial or ethnic groups reflects flaws in the cultural norms of these groups. There are, after all, prosperous members of every group. The success stories of many recent immigrants, especially from Southeast Asia, Jamaica, and Cuba, are cited as evidence that welfare is unnecessary. To these critics, the basic problem is failure to conform to a work ethic that has enabled other members of these same groups to succeed. In effect, these critics argue that many poor people are responsible for much of their own misery, and that most welfare payments waste taxpayers' money and reinforce the bad choices made by most of those who wind up poor.

A counterargument is that blaming the poor for their problems is misguided, that poor youngsters are obvious victims of poverty, and that immobility, nonparticipation in the labor force, and lack of education often reflect either outright discrimination or lack of opportunity (for education, employment, etc.). Moreover, many of the aged poor have been poor all their lives, many large families were poor before they became large, and so on. If members of certain groups are denied equal chances to participate in the economy, those who lack skills or suffer from discrimination will remain poor. Studies suggest that racial discrimination may have accounted for as much as 40% of poverty in the 1960s, but more recent studies yield substantially lower estimates, an indication that discrimination may be abating.[10]

Economic Discrimination

Most of us agree that it is wrong to discriminate on the bases of sex, race, or other characteristics irrelevant to economic contribution or personal worth.

> *Economic discrimination occurs when equivalent resources (labor) receive different payments (wages), even though their potential productive contributions are identical.*

There are many reasons for discrimination in labor markets. *Personal discrimination*, or *bigotry*, may play a major role, whether it is an employer's bigotry or the fear of bigotry from potential customers or other workers.[11] Bigotry may underpin economic discrimination to partially account for the lower average wages of women and members of some minority groups.

Economic discrimination in labor markets takes several forms. Members of certain groups may suffer because

1. *Wage discrimination* causes them to be paid less for equal work than members of other groups.
2. *Employment discrimination* excludes them from certain jobs.
3. *Occupational discrimination* bars them from certain occupations.
4. *Human capital discrimination* denies equal access to education or on-the-job training.

---

[9]L. Gallaway, R. Vedder, and T. Foster, "The New Structural Poverty: A Quantitative Analysis," in *War on Poverty—Victory or Defeat?* Hearings before the Joint Economic Committee, 20 June 1985 (Washington, D.C.: U.S. Government Printing Office, 1986).

[10]See J. Haworth, J. Gwartney, and C. Haworth, "Earnings, Productivity, and Changes in Employment Discrimination During the 1960s," *American Economic Review*, March 1975, pp. 158–168; and J. Long, "Earnings, Productivity, and Changes in Employment Discrimination During the 1960s: Additional Evidence," *American Economic Review*, March 1977, pp. 225–227. Thomas Sowell, in *Ethnic America*, (New York: Basic Books, 1981), provides estimates that discrimination accounted for only about 10% of black-white wage differentials by the late 1970s. For a look at employee benefits and discrimination see B. F. Kiker and Sherrie Rhine, "Fringe Benefits and the Earnings Equation," *Journal of Human Resources*, 1987, pp. 126–137.

[11]Discrimination may also occur because of customs or language. See Kevin Lang, "A Language Theory of Discrimination," *Quarterly Journal of Economics*, 1986, pp. 363–382.

5. Outright *bigotry* is manifested in discrimination that fosters inequitable housing conditions, higher prices, and reduced medical care, for example.

Although bigotry stimulates the other four types of discrimination, it is not necessarily their only cause. Different groups, for example, may have different cultural norms about the values of education or hard work. Another problem is that different types of discrimination tend to reinforce each other. For example, low prospective wages yield reduced incentives for investment in human capital, ultimately widening income differences.

The battle against discrimination predates the American Revolution. (Antislavery groups date back to colonial America.) From the time of President Lincoln's Emancipation Proclamation through the present, we have slowly marched toward an era in which government enforces a variety of civil rights legislation intended to ensure equal access to such things as education, housing, and employment opportunities. The existence of these laws, however, may not translate into color-blind or gender-neutral practices in many parts of our day-to-day world.

Legal controversy has marked almost all policies intended to achieve equal opportunity (e.g., busing children to integrate our schools and *affirmative action* plans imposed to overcome occupational, wage, and employment discrimination). Although the path to equal opportunity has been rocky, major progress has been made on the civil rights front in recent decades. Disagreements continue, however, about the extent to which discrimination accounts for income differentials between groups, what kinds of discrimination are involved, and what policies will best remedy its effects.[12] One approach emphasizes welfare pro-

_____

[12]Thomas Sowell, for one (in his *Ethnic America*), has argued that affirmative action has been more hindrance than help to members of minority groups. For example, he suggests that other people who encounter minorities in professional positions or high-level jobs commonly assume that these individuals gained their status, not from competency, but to fill some quota. A prospective employer may thus discount the previous experience of minority applicants who might otherwise be perfect for particular jobs and who would get these jobs were it not for the presumption that their previous experience was based solely on affirmative action requirements.

grams to compensate the victims of such historical social policies as segregation or slavery, although extensive welfare programs are also advocated on other grounds.

PUBLIC POLICIES TO ELIMINATE POVERTY

Just who is on welfare? Who should receive welfare? How much? Such questions are meaningless without a definition of welfare.

> ***Welfare*** *is received by anyone for whom the ratio of the personal benefits received (B) from government programs relative to the taxes paid (T) are greater than for average taxpayers.*

People are on welfare, for example, if they receive 2% of the total benefits from government programs but only pay 1% of the taxes used to support government. Our welfare system is an amalgam of many programs. In fact, people who are quite wealthy may be on welfare. For example, even after considering interest rates, some wealthy recipients contributed far less to Social Security when they were working than they receive after reaching retirement age. Most welfare recipients are, however, in low-income groups.

Aid to Families with Dependent Children

Aid to Families with Dependent Children (AFDC) is federally mandated, but administered by state and local governments. Explosive growth in AFDC rolls over the past two decades has been attributed to (*a*) relaxed requirements that increased the number of eligible families, (*b*) reductions in the social stigma from being on welfare, (*c*) work *disincentives* and pressures to dissolve families that are inherent in AFDC payment structures, and (*d*) payment differentials that cause the poor to flock into areas where welfare benefits are the most generous. The rapid growth in enrollment has created widespread concern that the AFDC system is out of control.

Panel A in Figure 9 illustrates the work disincentive effects of the original AFDC programs. Assume that, if a given family has no earnings, the annual AFDC grant is $5,000 (point *a* in Panel A). If the family earns up to an additional $5,000, the basic grant remains the same (point *b*). When the family's earnings exceed $5,000, however, AFDC grants are reduced dollar for dollar, so this poor family gains nothing by earning between $5,000 and $10,000 yearly (points *d* to *e*). Even worse, extra income is taxed and there may be losses of *in-kind subsidies* (Medicaid, food stamps, or public housing subsidies). This opens up the possibility that if family members work, a welfare family's spendable income could fall faster than its earnings grew.

Poor families were often penalized for working, so many followed the path of least re-sistance. AFDC benefits are especially skimpy if families include an able-bodied male, which pressures many males to abandon their wives and kids. Panel A shows that a 100% payment reduction on earned income over $5,000 is equivalent to a 100% marginal tax rate on earned income. Families do not gain from higher earnings if the entire increase goes to the government. These disincentives in AFDC and similar programs have contributed to the "welfare mess," as it has been labeled.

In the late 1970s, modest reforms of AFDC rules were aimed at cutting the implicit tax rate of over 100% faced by many poor families, but further changes during 1981 to 1983 reversed some of these reforms. Average marginal tax rates on AFDC benefits are now estimated at around 50%. Today's regulations are less dis-

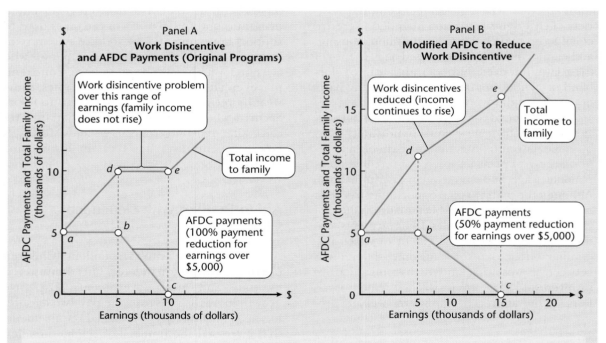

Can your take-home income fall if you earn more? When welfare programs are disjointedly tied to family income, the answer is yes. This incentive not to work is gradually being remedied, but Panel A reflects that this was a severe problem in the early 1970s. Under current regulations, the poor may face a marginal tax rate of 50% or more on additional income from employment, as shown in Panel B. While this still acts as a disincentive to work, it is much less severe than in the early 1970s when the adjusted marginal tax rate was often more than 100% for the working poor.

FIGURE 9   Work Disincentives and Welfare Programs

tortive than earlier programs in this respect. Panel B of Figure 9 shows how lower implicit tax rates allow greater work incentives. As earnings exceed $5,000, benefits fall at a rate of only $0.50 per $1, not dollar for dollar. Labor earnings now raise welfare families' spendable income; this was a rarity under the early system.

AFDC, unemployment compensation, and Social Security are among the many welfare programs that dispense cash grants. Other systems attempt to aid the poor through in-kind subsidies, including public housing, food stamps, Medicare and Medicaid, and various education, training, and rehabilitation programs. In-kind subsidies generally entail relatively high administrative costs and implicitly assume that recipients are incompetent to manage money were it given directly to them.

Most economists are skeptical of this reasoning and view in-kind payments as inefficient. For example, it costs taxpayers roughly $1.12 to give a poor family a food stamp with a face value of $1. The $1 food coupon is worth less than $1 to most recipients because it cannot be used for purchases other than food. Cash grant programs will typically provide benefits to poor people that are closer to their costs to taxpayers. Thus, in-kind transfers are relatively inefficient forms of welfare.

Another problem area is that many government transfer programs are based on criteria other than poverty. If farmers, the elderly, families headed by single women, members of certain minority groups, or the disabled tend to be poor, it does not follow that separate programs are required for each group. Programs to aid the blind, the infirm, the aged, or members of minority groups do not exclude the wealthy handicapped, the wealthy aged, or wealthy minorities. Similarly, there are affluent farmers, bankers, and TV station owners who are welfare recipients by our definition of welfare. They benefit from special subsidies or regulations bearing no relation to the taxes they pay.

In the 1930s, many of the aged were poor. Social Security has largely ameliorated this problem. Today, poverty is far more frequently a problem for the young, especially in families headed by single females.

Welfare Reform

Transfer payments of various types (including those for health care) have been the fastest growing component of government outlays in the United States since World War II. A number of reforms have been proposed. Some are intended to cut the growth of transfer payments; other reforms would redistribute more income to the poor.

• **Workfare** The hardship of the Great Depression resulted in a national system of *unemployment compensation* administered by state agencies. Unfortunately, the side effects may be as undesirable as the broken families and idleness generated by AFDC. Erratic employment patterns are encouraged, some income goes unreported, and some people who are not truly interested in work during some periods claim to be looking for jobs, biasing unemployment statistics upwards and, perhaps, misdirecting macroeconomic policy.

Some who believe that the welfare system as a whole encourages idleness advocate **workfare** to replace welfare. Workfare programs require able-bodied people who seek unemployment compensation or other public assistance to do jobs for the local government units that dole out such benefits. Wisconsin, for example, is one of several states that have adopted workfare requirements. To critics, one major drawback of such programs is that workfare may require parents to leave small children unattended. Thus, there is pressure for daycare programs to accommodate those impoverished parents.

• **Consolidation** The current welfare system is mired in excessive regulations, and income maintenance programs are fragmented among AFDC, unemployment compensation, Medicaid, food stamps, public housing, Social Security, and private charity. Ridding welfare programs of the work disincentives embedded in current policies is one major task of welfare reform; another is to reduce duplication and contain costs, perhaps by placing the welfare system under a single administrative umbrella. Some major programs are not based on income and thus benefit people who are not poor. There may be substantial gains from consolidation—both for taxpayers and for impoverished recipients. For these reasons, many economists favor a negative income tax approach (discussed below) to replace existing programs. Overall, we want the truly poor to get more aid, but where possible, we wish to preserve incentives for them to earn income on their own.

● **Family Allowance Plans** Many European nations and most British Commonwealth countries now have *family allowance plans* (FAPs).

*Transfer payments from **family allowance plans** are based on the number of minor children in a family and are usually adequate to feed and clothe each child.*

Family allowance plans provide basic income floors, but the incomes from these plans are then taxed as normal income and the progressivity of income taxes shrinks the FAP subsidy as a family's income rises.

Poverty seems especially harmful to children, so family allowance plans were proposed by the Nixon, Ford, and Carter administrations. A family allowance plan would be less of an administrative nightmare than the current welfare system. It would provide greater incentives for work than the many welfare programs that now confront the poor with very high implicit marginal tax rates; poor people's net incomes would always rise if they worked. Finally, it would eliminate situations where some poor people are technically ineligible for welfare but pay taxes to provide welfare to people who are better-off. (For example, an impoverished family headed by a low-wage working male may pay taxes to provide AFDC for a family without a working head of household. Average AFDC payments often exceed the family income of the working male.) Insufficient income for a given family unit, including children, would be the sole criterion for net (after-tax) receipts of welfare.

● **Negative Income Taxes** Negative income taxes (NITs) are variants of family allowance plans.

Negative income tax plans begin with an income floor. The level of assistance is reduced as additional income is earned by the family, but less than dollar for dollar.

A typical NIT plan is shown in Figure 10. The basic NIT floor on family income in this example is $6,000, and as the family earns an additional dollar, NIT benefits fall by $0.40. This negative income tax rate is 40%. When the family earns $15,000 on its own, NIT benefits are zero [$6,000 – ($15,000 × 0.40) = $0]. Beyond $15,000, the family pays positive taxes. Most economists envision these plans replacing all other income assistance plans. They would be administered through the Internal Revenue Service.

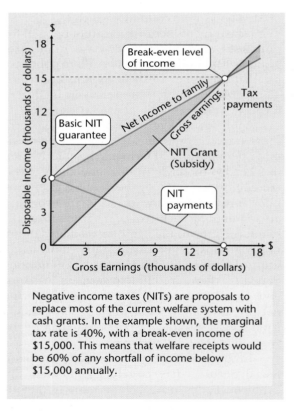

Negative income taxes (NITs) are proposals to replace most of the current welfare system with cash grants. In the example shown, the marginal tax rate is 40%, with a break-even income of $15,000. This means that welfare receipts would be 60% of any shortfall of income below $15,000 annually.

FIGURE 10   Negative Income Taxes

Negative income taxes would be simple to administer and would eliminate the need to dovetail numerous programs, but like any form of income assistance, NITs must balance equity and efficiency. This entails setting support levels that preserve work incentives, provide equitable income floors, and minimize administrative costs. Equity considerations might dictate high support flows, while efficient work incentives require low negative marginal tax rates. The cost of a program escalates when these attributes are combined. Reduced disincentives for work may, however, cut costs by making many of the poor less reliant on the public dole. Moreover, if an NIT plan replaced the current hodgepodge of welfare programs, administrative costs should fall, allowing higher income floors or reductions in taxes, or both.

Negative income tax plans have not been adopted in the United States, but the incorporation of earned income credits into the U.S. income tax codes reflects the general incentive philosophy of negative income taxes. The earned income tax credit program provides tax credits or a tax refund to poor working Americans, even if they owe no taxes. In effect, this is a negative income tax (subsidy) program to the working poor with children. Families earning up to $30,000 a year are covered by the program, but the amount of credit declines as income rises.

Public Policies, Progress, and Poverty

Annual spending on social programs rose from $29.5 billion to more than $600 billion between 1960 and 1990, but the number of people living below the poverty line actually grew over this period. Architects of the antipoverty programs enacted in 1964 often assigned responsibility to society for poor people's woes and saw welfare programs as compensation for social injustice. Many people maintain similar attitudes today and advocate further expansion of these programs to remedy poverty. However, some critics of our welfare system paradoxically blame much of current poverty on attitudes and programs instituted during the 1960s. Prominent among these critics are Thomas Sowell, an economist, and Charles Murray, a political scientist.

In his 1984 book, *Losing Ground*, Murray cites evidence of deterioration in the quality of life among many groups that seem stuck at the bottom. Between 1960 and 1965, African-American students' academic aptitude test scores rose from 68% to 79% of the average scores of whites; 1965 was the peak year for both groups. The average scores of African-American students on these tests had fallen to less than half of white norms by 1980. Annual rates of violent crime rose from 161 to 666 per 100,000 people between 1960 and 1988 (violent crime falls disproportionately on the poor). One African-American child in five was born to an unmarried mother in the 1950s; over half of all African-American infants today are illegitimate, and rates of white illegitimacy have risen from less than 1 in 50 to over 1 in 5. Four out of five white families include a married couple; the rate for African-American families has fallen sharply, to only one out of two.

The basic problem, according to many critics (Charles Murray, Thomas Sowell, and others), is that the rhetoric supporting many welfare programs implies that the poor bear no responsibility for alleviating their own poverty and that no stigma should be attached to being on welfare. This point of view means that the poor should not be expected to do anything for themselves; it is society's responsibility to lift people out of poverty.

These critics contend that such attitudes cause many poor people to feel like victims who cannot deal with their own problems and who psychically cannot claim credit for their accomplishments. They become trapped in a culture of poverty. Few avenues of escape are open through which to gain any sense of personal pride. The result is that some welfare families may remain on welfare for generations, suspended in a childish state of dependence on a system that is encouraged by social workers. Bureaucrats may be more interested in increasing the number of people in their programs than in reducing reliance on welfare. The goals of equity and efficiency may both suffer as a consequence.

What solutions are available? Few critics of the current welfare system favor abandonment of all welfare programs. Cutting all public assistance to zero would flood the nation's streets with many more millions of destitute and desperate people. Instead, most of these reformers propose that programs be restructured to provide more incentives for poor people to work, keep their families together, and diligently pursue education and on-the-job training. Most of all, welfare programs should seek to instill in poor people a sense that they control their own destinies. In the words of Murray, "The lesson is not that we can do no good at all, but that we must pick our shots."

Some of the welfare reforms proposed by President Clinton in 1994 were intended to more generously address the needs of those who cannot help themselves (the involuntarily impoverished). Parts of this proposal would be financed by a new federal tax on gambling. At the same time, some proposed reforms were aimed at reducing incentives for welfare dependency (the problem of voluntary poverty). Nevertheless, President Clinton's proposals would increase total spending to combat poverty and the social problems with which it is associated; a broad sense of despair and hopelessness; high rates of illiteracy, crime, and teen pregnancy; too many single-parent families; a wide lack of marketable skills; and prolonged joblessness for too many poor Americans. The next chapter focuses on how public programs are developed and financed.

CHAPTER REVIEW: KEY POINTS

1. **Lorenz curves** are one way to portray inequality. Lorenz curves for income are graphical representations of the cumulative percentages of income received by cumulative percentages of families. If the Lorenz curve is a straight-line diagonal, the income distribution is perfectly equal. Deviations from this diagonal reflect inequality in distribution.

2. A related statistical measure of income inequality is the **Gini index** or **coefficient**. The Gini index is defined as the ratio of the area between the line of perfect equality and the Lorenz curve to the total area under the line of perfect equality. The Gini index varies from 0 (perfect equality) to 1 (perfect inequality).

3. The **relative income** concept measures the extent to which income is above or below median income. A growing percentage of Americans are making more than twice the median income, but more and more are making less than half of median income. The result has been a shrinking middle class.

4. Since 1970, income distribution in the United States has become more unequal as shown by pretax and pretransfer Gini coefficients. Developed nations, in general, tend to have more equal distributions of income than do developing nations.

5. The Social Security Administration has developed income indices that define **poverty lines** for various family sizes, ages, and locations.

6. The causes of *poverty* are many and varied. Relative to more prosperous families, the poor tend to have less education, fewer earners, and more children. These characteristics of the poor are not necessarily the causes of poverty. **Discrimination** may be an important factor. Persistent discrimination reduces incentives to invest in education and other marketable skills. Discrimination is often cited as the primary reason that a relatively large proportion of African American families are in the lower income categories.

7. The major government program to fight poverty is **Aid to Families with Dependent Children** (AFDC). A floor on family income is established, but as the family earns additional income, reductions of AFDC benefits often pose extreme *disincentives* for work. Given the large number of different programs designed to help the poor, $1 increases in earned income sometimes result in more than $1 of lost benefits.

8. **Negative income tax plans** (NITs) have been suggested as solutions to the "welfare mess." Negative income tax proposals provide a floor on income; as additional income is earned, benefits are reduced, but by less than the additional income earned. In general, NIT plans consolidate numerous programs under one administra- tive roof and might allow either reduced costs or increased benefits. NIT plans have not been widely adopted, but NIT incentives have been adapted to many programs and provide the basic rationale for earned income tax credits aimed at keeping low-income, working Americans above the poverty line.

QUESTIONS FOR THOUGHT AND DISCUSSION

1. Suppose that you were in charge of an overcrowded lifeboat filled with the survivors of a shipwreck. Unless some passengers leave the boat, all will perish. Would it be fair for you to allocate the spaces available to the highest bidders? Would this be efficient? If not, would it be fairer or more efficient were a few affluent passengers able to persuade a sufficient number of poorer people to relinquish their space by offering contracts guaranteeing prosperity for the volunteers' families? If not, what other allocative mechanism would be fairer or more efficient? Why?

2. What would you expect to happen to the Lorenz curve for a country (*a*) if a more progressive tax system was instituted? (*b*) If education levels for all citizens became roughly equal? (*c*) If economic discrimination was significantly reduced?

3. Society devotes increasing amounts of resources to medical care for critical and sometimes incurable diseases or injuries. It is not unusual, for example, for the medical expenses of a very premature infant to exceed $1 million, and yet, even if it survives, the long-term consequences for the child are often tragic. Many parents cannot afford such outlays, and hospitals often simply treat these costs as overhead costs to be borne by other patients. Is this use of society's resources appropriate? What are some possible opportunity costs? Is this equitable? Why or why not?

4. In John Rawls' *A Theory of Justice* (Cambridge, Harvard, MA: University Press, 1971), he proposes the following mental exercise as an approach for deciding how society might be made fairer. Suppose you were given a computer with a data bank containing every economic mechanism ever tried and every theory ever proposed to answer the questions of What? How? and For whom? You also have the advice of any social philosopher, living or dead. Your task is to design a just society, and you must address many issues, including distributing wealth and income. Your final overall plan will be instituted worldwide. The hook is that your position in the world will then be decided randomly, providing a powerful incentive for you to consider the final positions of all people. What are some changes you would make to current social institutions?

5. In *Anarchy, State, and Utopia* (New York: Basic Books, 1974), Rawls' colleague, Robert Nozick, argues that over time individuals acquire inalienable rights. His *entitlement theory of justice* is an ethical argument for the adage that "possession is nine-tenths of the law." In Nozick's view, you are entitled to your property unless it can be proven that you, or the people who transferred it to you, unethically acquired it. He concludes that government redistributions of wealth or income are ethically wrong, because they violate people's basic rights to choose how their property will be used. In his words, "There is no justified sacrifice of some of us for others." Do you think that historical events ethically justify the degree of inequality that now exists? Why or why not?

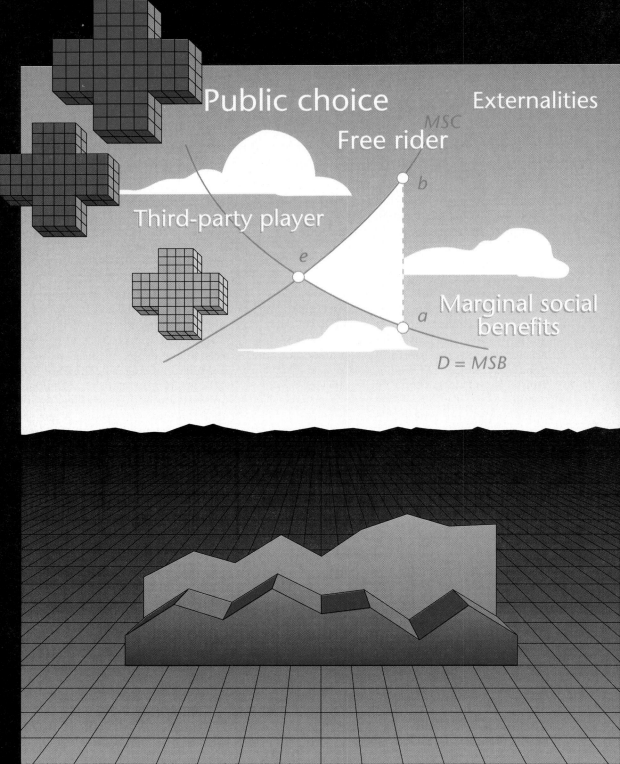

Part 9

Modern Microeconomic Issues

We have examined how markets tend to operate efficiently when (*a*) numerous potential buyers and sellers with freedom of entry and exit compete vigorously, (*b*) information is symmetric and widespread, (*c*) economies of scale are insignificant, and (*d*) external effects from transactions are negligible. Our primary concerns in this part of the book are assessments of market failures and the government policies intended to overcome them. *Market failures* arise from excessive market power, asymmetric information that promotes strategic behavior, or external (spillover) effects on parties not involved in particular transactions. (Some analysts also classify inequitable income distributions as market failures—an issue treated in the preceding chapter.)

The notion that government policies will efficiently cure market failures is often unrealistic. Political mechanisms may yield allocative results that are superior to those of the marketplace in some cases, but not in others. The magnitude of specific market failures should be weighed against the intensity of *government failure*, which occurs because public policies are often plagued by such problems as inadequate information, political pressures from special-interest groups, or inefficient incentive structures for government bureaucrats.

We begin this part by developing a framework to evaluate policy. In the first chapter, we consider rationales for governmental action by investigating areas in which the market may fail to allocate resources acceptably. Then, we survey the U.S. tax system, measuring both current taxes and recent tax reforms against principles of efficiency and equity. In the second chapter, we focus on *public choice*, an approach offering insights into government failure by analyzing political behavior from an economic perspective. In the third chapter, we examine the issues of resources management and environmental quality. Problems of health care are our major concerns in the last chapter.

Applying microeconomic tools to the areas covered in this part of the book should familiarize you with applied economic analysis, but we barely scratch the surface of the kinds of problems into which microeconomics can offer valuable insights. In previous parts of this book, you have seen that microeconomic tools can also be fruitfully deployed to develop insights into issues ranging from national defense to agriculture to energy to crime and punishment. But looking at all possible problem areas in depth would require a book twice as long as this one and a course twice as long as the one in which your are enrolled, exhausting your pocketbooks and the patience of your professors and our publishers. You will have opportunities to study many of these topics if you take further courses in economics.

Chapter 32

Market Failure and Public Finance

Business transactions would be much less certain if firms had the freedom to specify the meaning of "a pound," or to define all terms in any contracts signed. Thus, a pure laissez-faire system would be economically inefficient without some basic regulations. Government simplifies our lives by setting standards for money and weights and measures and by enforcing contracts. Efficiency is facilitated by certainty about the rules of business and clearly specified property rights.

The rationale for government action becomes even more powerful when the marketplace is perceived to fail despite a stable legal environment. Consumers may be exploited if firms exercise excessive market power (e.g., if public utilities rates were unregulated). Firms with monopsony power may exploit workers (e.g., a textile mill operated by abusive managers who dominate employment in a small town). Another problem is that private markets cannot efficiently coordinate private decisions about the production and delivery of some broad types of goods, including such things as national defense, the administration of justice, or a cleaner environment.

In this chapter, we categorize types of *market failure* and identify appropriate government corrections for certain types of failures. Once a need for government is recognized, we address who should pay for it and how. We will survey several types of taxes to assess how well our current system conforms to normative principles of taxation. In the next chapter, we explore political decision-making and *government failure*. There, you will find some answers to why public policy so often deviates from the ideals described in this chapter.

ECONOMIC ROLES FOR GOVERNMENT

Government policy has become a standard prescription to correct for unstable, inequitable, or inefficient market outcomes. In addition to maintaining a stable legal environment for economic activity, widely accepted goals for government now include

1. Ensuring full employment, a stable price level, and a secure and growing standard of living. (*Instability* is the first category of market failure.)
2. Facilitating equity through redistributions of income. (Potential *inequity* is a second broad type of market failure.)
3. Promoting market competition and allocating resources to meet public wants efficiently. (The third major type of market failure is potential *allocative inefficiency* because of excessive market power or because certain goods will not be optimally provided in purely private markets.)

Stability, the first goal, is primarily a macroeconomic topic. Policies intended to achieve *equity*, the second goal, were addressed in the preceding chapter. Antitrust policies (again, covered in an earlier chapter) promote *efficiency* through competition. Our focus in this chapter is how government allocates resources to provide for public wants.

Government in the United States now directly allocates roughly one-fifth of our national output in attempts to meet these goals. Another 15% is redistributed through *transfer payments*, which include such outlays as welfare payments and loans to farmers or students. Figure 1 provides estimates of the size and recent growth of total government activity. These estimates ignore certain costs of government, such as those incurred by firms in complying with government regulations, and the opportunity costs of some resources held by government (e.g., national parks).

MARKET FAILURE: ALLOCATION

Competitive markets usually perform well when all parties to a transaction pay for the benefits they receive and are compensated for their costs. For example, if you buy a warm coat for protection from cold winter days, the people who produce your coat are paid for this use of their

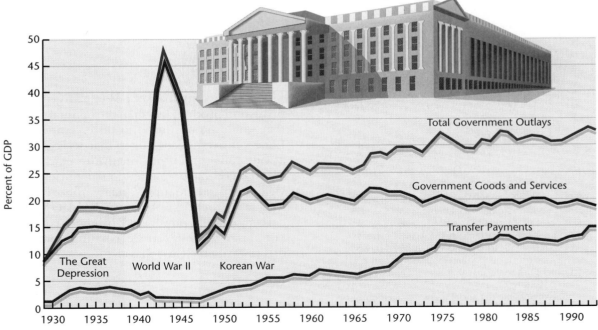

Source: Economic Reports of the President 1984–1994.

Government outlays relative to GDP have grown erratically from a base of less than 10 percent in 1929. After reaching almost half of GDP during World War II, outlays fell substantially, but not for long. Since 1960, government ouutlays have risen from about 25 percent of GDP to almost one-third today. Recent growth of government has been dominated by increases in transfer payments. These figures ignore the indirect cost of government regulation and the opportunity cost of government assets.

FIGURE 1 The Growth of Government Spending

resources. Unfortunately, securing payments for some types of goods is difficult, and identifying those who incur costs can also be a problem. No private firm, for example, could sell you cleaner air by using less-polluting production processes without simultaneously providing cleaner air for your neighbors. Nor could a neighbor privately buy national defense without protecting you.

Competitive markets allocate most standard goods so that marginal social benefits equal marginal social costs, as at point *a* in Figure 2. Allocative failure occurs when equilibrium marginal social benefits and costs diverge. Any market equilibrium except that at point *a* represents an allocative failure. Improper pricing and output occurs when private markets are afflicted with any of three basic types of problems.

Our monopoly chapter showed how *market power* may create inefficiency, with suboptimal output and excessive prices. But even competitive markets may yield failures that seem to justify government action. *Externalities* (pollution is an example) can warp price signals so that production costs or our demands are inaccurately reflected. Another difficulty, the *public goods* problem, results when shared consumption is possible but people cannot be denied access to the benefits from a good. National defense is an example.

Government may correct market failures by (*a*) promoting competition; (*b*) modifying the composition of private outputs through taxes, subsidies, or regulations; or (*c*) directly providing certain goods. (Some cynics argue that ideal adjustments are highly unlikely because government is hopelessly inefficient, but only philosophical anarchists argue that government provision of certain goods never improves efficiency.)

Economic efficiency requires that marginal social cost equal marginal social benefits (*MSC* = *MSB* at point *a*). Market failure occurs when *MSC* and *MSB* diverge. For example, the *MSC* of increasing output from Q_0 to Q_2 units equals point b, while the *MSB* from the Q_2 unit equals only point c, entailing a net social loss that is avoidable by restricting output to Q_0 units. A symmetric failure to exploit all possible net social gains occurs if output is below Q_0 units.

FIGURE 2   Socially Optimal Price and Quantity and Market Failure

Monopoly Power

Private firms with market power charge higher prices and produce less than the optimal output that would be produced in pure competition. Long-run average cost curves that decline across a wide range of output relative to market demand may make competition inefficient and yield a natural monopoly (many utility companies are examples). Antitrust legislation may curb monopoly power and promote competition, or regulation can steer natural monopolists toward efficient behavior.

Externalities

Some benefits or costs of certain activities *spill over* to parties not directly involved in the activity. These spillover benefits and costs are *externalities*.

Externalities *are the benefits conferred or costs imposed on a third party not directly participating in a transaction.*

This type of market inefficiency is common when market prices and outputs fail to reflect these third parties' preferences. For example, oil refineries emit hydrocarbons and foul the water. Some of these pollutants are absorbed by microorganisms and work their way up the ecological chain, damaging everyone's health so that people who do not buy oil bear some of the costs of refining it. And the air can become almost impossible to breathe. Most human activities generate externalities, some trivial and some of major concern. Noxious fumes and the noise from takeoffs and landings near airports annoy neighbors and reduce property values, loud rock concerts disrupt nearby residents, and so on. All forms of pollution—chemical, air, noise, and litter—are *negative externalities*.

Pollution and obnoxious billboards would be even more prevalent if markets were unregulated. Commuting would be more dangerous if drivers continually negotiated for the right-of-way, and big city traffic might suffer terminal gridlock. Deadly epidemics might decimate our populace if all immunizations were voluntary. You may have heard of Typhoid Mary, a restaurant worker who infected thousands of people in her day.

Negative externalities tend to be ignored when producers decide how much to produce, so the prices charged reflect only the producers' private costs. Thus, pollution-generating goods tend to be overproduced and underpriced. No government could absolutely prohibit all pollution because such policies would be inconsistent with life—all human activities generate at least some pollution. [Physicists refer to this concept as *entropy*. The second law of thermodynamics states that every process entails shifts from more organized forms of energy and matter (e.g., coal) into less organized forms (e.g., heat and smoke)]. Trade-offs exist between the cleaner environment most of us would like and the higher levels of consumption most of us desire.

Positive externalities that spill over from an activity may also create inefficiency. For example, Neighborhood Watch programs help suppress burglaries. You are less likely to suffer from a burglary if you are alert, and your neighbors are also less likely to be burglarized. But you may ignore our benefits when you decide how much attention to pay to suspicious characters casing the neighborhood. Thus, positive externalities tend to be ignored in private market decisions, resulting in underproduction and overpricing of the goods that generate positive externalities; the value to society exceeds the costs individuals willingly pay when they are uncompensated for external benefits.

Let's consider negative externalities in more detail. Garbage accumulating around the Slob family's property is shown in Figure 3. Suppose this family ignores informal social pressure to maintain their home. When they decide how often to have trash hauled away, the Slobs ignore noxious odors, declines in the values of adjacent property, and their neighbors' exposure to diseases. Unless they are compelled to consider these external costs, the Slobs will choose point a, leaving Q_0 garbage around their home, on average, at a private cost of P_0 per unit. Society might just legally require them to have all their trash hauled off instantly, but this would ignore benefits to the Slobs (or even ourselves) of being able to let the garbage pile up temporarily instead of having it removed at all times. After all, the Slobs are members of society. What we would like is to ensure that they consider the effects on their neighbors from stockpiling trash.

Demand curve D reflects the Slobs' gains from littering their home, tidying up only occasionally instead of being fastidious at all times. The *MSC* curve reflects losses from litter suffered by both the Slobs and their neighbors, with the *MC* curve reflecting only the Slobs' marginal private cost. Suppose the Slobs could legally store trash, and the vertical distance bc between the cost curves represents the external costs that the Slobs are inflicting on their neighbors. Their neighbors would willingly pay this amount to them to reduce trash accumulation to socially optimal level Q_1. If neighbors could legally limit the Slobs' debris, this vertical distance is the price the neighbors would charge the Slobs for

FIGURE 3 The Costs and Benefits of the Slob Family's Garbage

Living next to a slob is never pleasant. In economic jargon, slobs impose external costs on their neighbors and would be less slovenly if they took their neighbors' discomfort into account. Note that the Slob family in our example has a positive demand for garbage lying around. If they didn't want to store garbage, they would pay more and have it hauled away.

accumulating garbage. Note that the optimal amount of trash is not zero. After all, we all keep a little garbage on hand, even on days when garbage is collected.

How to deal with externalities is addressed in detail in our chapter on environmental quality. It is time to examine the market failure that seems to require the most of government—the public goods problem.

Public Goods

A desire for more shoes can be cured by a trip to a shoe store. But suppose you want more public parks or a stronger national defense. If you voluntarily send a check to the National Park Service or the Department of Defense, even if they spend your money wisely you will not have appreciably better access to parks or be noticeably better defended. The problem is that these are examples of public goods. **Public goods** are both *nonrival*, because people can consume the same units of such goods simultaneously, and

nonexclusive, because denying people access to such goods is prohibitively expensive.

> A **public good** can be enjoyed by numerous individuals at the same time (**nonrivalry**); once a public good is available, denying access to a consumer is prohibitively expensive (**nonexclusion**).

Prisons are examples of public goods because keeping violent criminals behind bars makes the world safer for the rest of us. We need not compete with each other to use public goods once they are produced because public goods do not involve rivalry. Most goods are **private goods** that are *rival* and *exclusive*.

• **Rivalry and Nonrivalry** Consumption exhausts a *rival good* so that no one else can consume the same unit. No one else can consume a particular apple if you eat it first. You cannot use my ski pants if I am wearing them. Food and clothing are rival goods. We can, however, enjoy the same TV program without rivalry. When your TV receives signals, it does not affect the signals to mine. A police patrol can simultaneously protect both you and your neighbor from burglars. Police protection and TV broadcasts are examples of *nonrival goods.*

Because consuming a rival good such as an apple uses up scarce resources, it is efficient that consumers pay for each unit consumed. On the other hand, for such nonrival goods as TV broadcast signals, hours spent in front of the TV do not diminish those signals. Compelling people to pay for TV signals based on their level of consumption would discourage consumption without any offsetting benefit, thus introducing inefficiency. (Although some critics of the tube would disagree.)

• **Exclusion and Nonexclusion** Restaurants can refuse to serve you unless you wear a shirt and shoes. A theater can require you to buy a ticket before seeing a film. Movies and meals are *exclusive goods.* But if the Air Force protects you from attacks by foreign enemies, your neighbor is protected automatically. The Air Force cannot guard you against attack and not protect your neighbor. National defense is a *nonexclusive good.* Nonexclusion occurs whenever it is prohibitively expensive to prevent people from enjoying a good once it is provided.

Government provides most public goods. For example, our legal system enables all of us to resolve most disputes without constantly resorting to violence. Other public goods include traffic lights, weather reports, AIDS research, democratic government, and national defense. Once the military is maintained and ready, every person in the United States consumes defense services simultaneously, and we all receive this protection whether we pay taxes or not, and whether we want it or not! An important note: public provision does not require public production. For example, government increasingly relies on private contractors to maintain streets, collect trash, and staff our prisons and public hospitals. Table 1 summarizes the four basic categories of goods and services.

TABLE 1 Categories of Goods: Rivalry and Exclusion

	Rival	Nonrival
Exclusive	**Pure Private Goods** Will be efficiently provided by the market: • cola • candy bars • automobiles • CDs	**Excess Capacity** Market will provide, but government regulation may be used to attain efficiency if economies of scale are significant: • theaters • airline flights • rapid transit trips • natural monopolies?
Nonexclusive	**Environmental Problems** Regulation normally used to solve, but assignment of property rights is sometimes used: • congestion • air, water and noise pollution • overfishing • overuse of commons	**Pure Public Goods** Less than efficient amounts are provided unless government intervenes: • national defense • flood control projects • weather forecasts • infectious disease control

Providing for Public Goods

Nonexclusive and nonrival goods differ markedly from private goods, so constructing demand curves for public goods requires a different approach than does construction of market demand curves for private goods.

• **Private vs. Public Demands** Recall that market demands for most goods are *horizontal* summations of individual demand curves: the quantities demanded at each price are summed. This is how the individual demands of Alan and Beth for lobsters, a private good, are summed in Panel A of Figure 4. The total demand for a public good, however, is a *vertical* summation of individual demand curves, as shown in Panel B. We all gain by having extra police patrols cruising our neighborhood at night, so our demand for this extra surveillance reflects the dollar amount we would collectively pay for it. A total demand curve for a public good is constructed by adding the funds we each would willingly pay for each possible amount of the good.

• **Optimal Public Goods** How do we ascertain how much of a public good to provide? Alan's (*A*) and Beth's (*B*) individual demands for police patrols are shown together with their total demand curve in Panel B of Figure 4. We assume that neither is trying to be a free rider, so both reveal their demands for police patrols. The total demand is the vertical summation of Alan's and Beth's demands. Suppose that costs are $6 per patrol. If three patrols are provided each night, Alan values each patrol at $4, while Beth values each at $2. The $6 cost per patrol could be covered if each paid in proportion to their gains [($4 × 3) + ($2 × 3) = $18].

Contrast this with optimal provision of private goods in Panel A; each individual pays the same price per unit, but each consumes different amounts. Alan consumes 35 pounds of lobster annually at $2 per pound, while Beth buys only 25 pounds at that price.

The preceding solution to public goods assumes that individuals willingly reveal their

FIGURE 4 Market Demands for Private and Public Goods

We all face the same prices for private goods but buy different amounts, so the market demand is the horizontal sum of individual demands (Panel A). We all consume the same public goods but value them differently, so the total demand for public goods requires vertically summing individual demands (Panel B). Revenue adequate for optimal amounts of a public good are generated if each person pays his or her marginal benefit from the good (in dollars) times the amount of the good provided. In this case, three patrols nightly at $6 per patrol could be secured if Beth paid $6 and Alan paid $12.

preferences. Further, it suggests that we could pay for these public goods by taxing individuals in proportion to the benefits received. This benefit approach is not, however, easily translated into the real world of taxes, nor is it the primary basis of taxation.

TAXATION

Taxes are the price we pay for civilization.

Oliver Wendell Holmes, Jr.

Taxes finance most of government spending. Many Americans complain about high taxes, but Figure 5 indicates that residents in most developed economies pay relatively more.

Who should pay how much of which taxes? Equity is a slippery concept, but precise terminology helps in analyzing fairness in taxation. Two somewhat contradictory principles broadly address equity in distributing tax burdens. The *benefit principle* favors taxes in accord with people's benefits from government spending; the

ability-to-pay principle advocates taxes in accord with one's wealth or income.

The Benefit Principle

The *benefit principle* is an ancient doctrine that taxes should be in proportion to the benefits individuals receive from government.

> The **benefit principle of taxation** taxes people in proportion to the marginal benefits they receive from a governmentally provided good.

This principle conforms to a universal gut feeling that you should pay for what you get. Revenues just adequate for optimal provision in our police patrol example can be secured by levying taxes so that people share costs in proportion to their marginal benefits.

Taxation according to marginal benefits is, unfortunately, impractical for most pure public goods. The public sector provides an incredible array of goods; collecting all the information re-

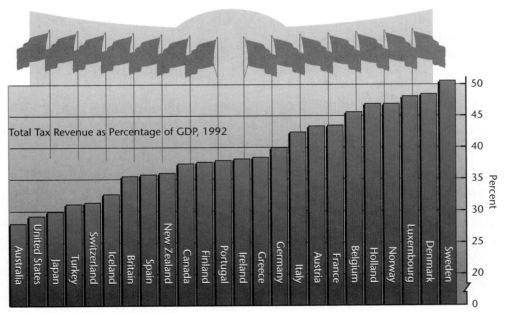

Total Tax Revenue as Percentage of GDP, 1992

Sources: OECD and *The Economist,* September 4, 1993.

Australia, Japan and the United States have the lowest tax burdens of the developed nations. The Scandinavian countries (Sweden, Denmark and Norway) have the highest burdens, but they also have huge public sectors.

FIGURE: 5   Tax Rates as Percentages of GDP—International

quired for appropriately different taxes is prohibitively costly. People cannot be excluded from enjoying the benefits whether they paid taxes or not. These characteristics of public goods lead to the free rider problem.

• **Free Rider Problems** Suppose taxes were based strictly on your reported benefits from a public good. Some people might assert that they want little or none of it. Crafty types might even try to get tax credits by asserting that the good harms them. Once other people agree to buy a public good, free riders can enjoy it without cost.

*The **free rider** problem arises when people evade paying for goods that are nonexclusive; they can use such goods without payment.*

A few people might voluntarily contribute funds for a nonrival good from which exclusion was impossible. The erratic success of public TV is one example. More commonly, however, voluntary contributions would be insufficient for private firms to accommodate our collective demands for a nonexclusive good. There is little incentive to reveal your demands for safer highways, cleaner air, better schools, or cancer research if you will be taxed accordingly. Why not be a free rider? Widespread free riding may preclude some public goods. Private firms could not adequately market them, so government provides most public goods and forces us to pay for them through taxes.

• **User Charges** General tax revenues are used to pay for most goods government provides, but the benefit approach to funding public goods is a basis for user charges that relate taxes to expected benefits. When a governmentally provided good has the exclusive characteristics of a private good, benefits can be approximated, with users being charged the costs of service. Examples include bus fares and entry fees for public museums, zoos, parks, or toll roads. Gasoline taxes are also roughly proportional to benefits; owners of heavy trucks or

drivers of huge gas hogs pay more gas taxes than do drivers of fuel-efficient compact cars, but they also put more wear and tear on the highways that gasoline taxes support.

Although the benefit principle of taxation is often inapplicable because individuals' preferences for public goods are concealed, general tax revenues are often used to fund activities where user charges could easily be applied. For example, should vegetarians pay for meat inspections? User charges imposed on meat-packers would be shifted forward to meat buyers. Similarly, federal tests of new medicines could be billed to the pharmaceutical companies that want to market them. If airports, air traffic controllers, and airplane safety inspectors were paid for exclusively by carriers, these tax burdens would not be borne by people who benefit little from air transport.

Political and practical difficulties, however, are not the only drawbacks of benefit taxes. Benefit taxation may conflict with other types of concerns about equity.

The Ability-to-Pay Principle

An alternative to the benefit principle of taxation is the idea that taxes should be proportional to one's *ability to pay*.

*The **ability-to-pay principle** suggests that the fairest tax is one based on your financial ability to support government activities.*

Taxes can be related to income in three basic ways:

1. A tax is **progressive** if higher incomes are taxed more proportionally than lower incomes.
2. **Proportional** taxes are a fixed percentage of income.
3. A tax is **regressive** if the percentage of income paid as taxes falls as income rises.

The benefit and ability-to-pay principles, though seemingly inconsistent, may lead to similar policies. Rich people may benefit more than the poor from such public goods as national defense or police and fire protection because rich people stand to lose more from disasters. They drive more miles on public roads and ring up more frequent flyer bonuses when flying out of publicly supported airports. Thus, both the benefit and the ability-to-pay principles may support the rich paying more taxes than the poor.

• **Vertical Equity** Vertical equity is the idea that a rich person should pay more taxes than a poor one for each to bear the same burden in supporting government.

> *Vertical equity* asserts that people better able to pay higher taxes should do so.

Implementing vertical equity in any tax system involves deciding who should pay higher rates and then writing tax laws that actually collect this amount from the correct people. Wealth and income are normally viewed as good measures of one's ability to pay taxes. Progressive taxation is, however, unnecessary for vertical equity; even regressive tax systems might satisfy this equity principle as long as the rich paid more in absolute terms.

• **Horizontal Equity** The Fourteenth Amendment to our Constitution (the Equal Protection clause) states, "nor shall any State deprive any person of life, liberty, or property, without due process of law; nor deny to any person within its jurisdiction the *equal* protection of the laws." This concept that equals must be treated equally is now known as *horizontal equity.*

> *Horizontal equity* requires that individuals who are equal in all important respects be treated equally.

Implementing a horizontally equitable tax system first requires identifying what constitutes equal circumstances—income, wealth, age, or marital status? Then we must specify what equal treatment means. Does equal treatment mean equal tax rates or equal tax payments over a lifetime?

Equity in our tax system requires both horizontal and vertical equity. Horizontal equity dictates that equals should pay equal taxes; vertical equity means that unequals should be treated unequally. Vertical equity is at the heart of the ability-to-pay principle.

TAX BURDENS AND EFFICIENCY

Apparent inequity in the tax system is a major concern, but economists focus their studies on inefficiency, an area permitting greater precision. In his *Wealth of Nations*, Adam Smith suggested that efficiency in taxation requires taxes to be certain (unavoidable) and convenient and that collection costs be minimized relative to the tax yield.

Government's net tax revenues ideally would exactly equal costs incurred by taxpayers. Taxpayers' costs unavoidably exceed net government revenues, however, because of (*a*) government's *administrative costs* (e.g., operating expenses for the Internal Revenue Service) and (*b*) taxpayers' *compliance costs* (e.g., time absorbed in keeping records for taxes and filling out tax reports, or payments to tax lawyers and accountants).

Total costs of a tax, however, include other, more subtle costs and ultimately equal the losses of disposable (after-tax) income and purchasing power to taxpayers. Consider an untaxed individual who enjoys a certain standard of living, including current levels of government services. Now impose a tax on that person.

> The **total burden** of a tax equals the amount that would have to be paid the individual on whom the burden falls to make that person just as well off with the tax as without it.

Differences between total tax burdens and net government revenues reflect inefficiency.

Excess Burdens

If high state taxes on beer cause New Yorkers to drive to New Jersey to buy their brew, then the total tax burden includes not only the revenues actually collected by New York, but also the time and transportation costs to the New Yorkers who avoid the tax. If some of these commuters wind up dying in traffic accidents, or if they drunkenly kill other people, then this loss of life is also a part of the total burden of the tax. Excess burdens arise whenever people are made worse off than the losses imposed by the tax funds actually collected from them.

> The **excess burden** of a tax is the difference between the total burden and the tax revenue collected by government.

In addition to administrative and compliance costs, taxes impose excess burdens if they distort the prices faced by consumers, workers, savers, investors, or business decision-makers.

Kyoto, Japan, imposed taxes on visitors to Buddhist temples in 1985. Most temple priests strongly opposed the tax as a violation of their religious principles and initially let visitors in free rather than pay the tax. But the priests eventually closed the temple doors to visitors, the city collected no revenue, and tourism declined (an excess burden). Finally, the city abolished the tax.

Supply and demand analysis can allow us to scrutinize excess burdens. In Figure 6, S_0 and D_0 reflect the nontaxed supply and demand for quarts of milk. For simplicity, we assume constant production costs at P_0 per quart. Suppose a tax of t per quart were imposed on milk. This tax shifts the supply curve to S_1 from the buyer's perspective. As buyers and sellers adjust to this tax, consumers watch the price of a quart of milk rise from P_0 to P_1 while the amount sold falls from Q_0 to Q_1. At Q_1 quarts monthly, the difference between the price paid by the buyer (P_1) and the price received by the seller (P_0) exactly equals tax t. Prior to the tax, consumers paid $0aef$ for Q_0 quarts of milk, but would have willingly paid $0def$. Thus, they enjoyed a consumer surplus of ade. The rise in the consumers' price

FIGURE 6   The Excess Burden of a Tax

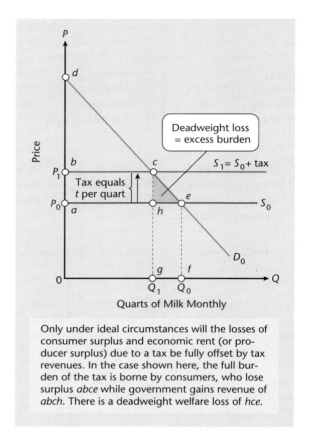

Only under ideal circumstances will the losses of consumer surplus and economic rent (or producer surplus) due to a tax be fully offset by tax revenues. In the case shown here, the full burden of the tax is borne by consumers, who lose surplus *abce* while government gains revenue of *abch*. There is a deadweight welfare loss of *hce*.

to P_1 shrinks consumer surplus by the area below the consumer demand curve but above the original price (P_0) and below the new price (P_1). The consumer surplus lost equals the trapezoid *abce*.

Government, however, gains monthly revenues of t per bottle for Q_1 quarts of milk, a total of area *abch*, which it can use to meet taxpayers' wants. The total loss of consumer surplus minus the gains to government equals area *hce* (*abce* − *abch*). The triangle *hce* is a *deadweight loss* to society from this tax; it is an excess burden. These losses, however, may be more than offset by consumer surpluses from government services provided with the tax revenues. Of course, if government spending is inefficient, this graph of excess burden may understate consumers' losses. Government ideally minimizes the excess burdens incurred in securing any given total of tax revenues.

Neutrality

The neutrality principle combines and extends Adam Smith's certainty, convenience, and economy principles. Ideally, the costs of transferring purchasing power from private hands into the public purse are minimized.

> A **neutral tax** distorts neither consumer buying patterns nor the production methods used by firms. Its total burden just equals the tax revenue collected, there are no excess burdens.

Tax neutrality requires that the tax directly cause only income effects, not substitution effects.[1] That is, a neutral tax does not induce behavior to avoid the tax; behavior changes only because of lost purchasing power. This requires that taxes be unavoidable.

No action by taxpayers (perhaps at the behest of their accountants or lawyers) should enable them to avoid payment, and the only impact on taxpayers should be declines in their purchasing power. For example, tax structures should not encourage fringe benefits in work contracts instead of direct wage payments or financial investment in tax-free municipal bonds rather than capital equipment. Nor should it encourage consumption of housing instead of groceries or clothes. (Our tax system has done all these things.) Taxes that directly alter the relative benefits and costs facing consumers or business decision-makers are nonneutral and inefficient. A neutral tax will be more certain, convenient, and economical than a nonneutral tax.

All taxes, unfortunately, induce substitution effects by directly altering relative prices, thereby changing the behavior of consumers and firms. As a result, taxes are often evaluated by their relative neutrality. Because all taxes are somewhat flawed, economists normally try to

---

[1]You may want to review the discussion of income and substitution effects from the chapter on consumer choice.

specify which are the most nearly neutral (those with the smallest excess burdens) and least inequitable in generating governmental revenues.

THE CURRENT TAX SYSTEM

Old taxes are the best taxes.

A Legislator's Proverb

Current sources of tax revenues at the federal and state levels are indicated in Figure 7. Just how efficient and equitable are the important taxes now used by our federal, state, and local governments?

Personal Income Taxes

One flaw of progressive personal income taxes is that rising marginal tax rates create disincentives that discourage investment and work effort. Another is that our complex Internal Revenue Code creates loopholes that allow individuals and corporations to legally avoid taxes. Tax *avoidance* is legal, but high marginal rates also provide huge incentives for tax *evasion*: the illegal nonpayment of taxes. Disincentives, tax evasion, and legal loopholes erode the tax base and cause legislators to raise tax rates. For example, if erosion of the base causes a tax rate of 50% to be applied to only half of potential untaxed income, then the rate could be dropped to 25% if all income were taxed.

Our five-step progressive income tax system is an example of an ability-to-pay tax, but loopholes erode its progressivity. Several studies indicate, however, that even after allowing for the heavier exploitation of loopholes by high-income families than by low-income families, the incidence of our income tax is, on average, mildly progressive. Not all loopholes, however, are designed only for the rich. For example, mortgage interest is deducted by more than 90% of all families who itemize deductions. Moreover, as Focus 1 indicates, the idea that loopholes offer huge advantages for those who use them is grossly exaggerated, primarily be-

FIGURE 7 Revenue Sources for Federal, State, and Local Governments

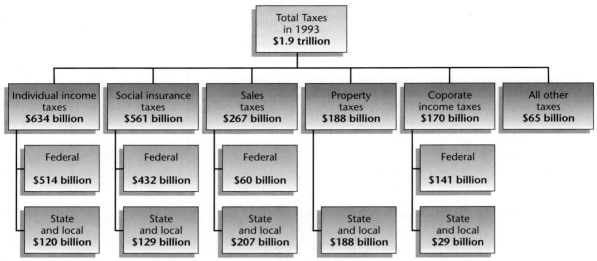

Source: "Our Tax Bill" from Associated Press, March 28, 1994. Reprinted by permission of AP/Wide World Photos.

The federal government relies almost exclusively on income and payroll taxes for revenues. State and local governments, on the other hand, get the bulk of their revenues from property and sales taxes, from user fees, and from the federal government through grants-in-aid.

cause artificially stimulated competition causes overinvestment in tax-sheltered areas.

You know how complicated computing your federal tax liability can be if you have ever filed a Form 1040 (the long form). Some state income tax computations are even more complex. Most economists favor eliminating almost all exemptions, credits, and deductions except for necessary business expenses. Then tax rates could be lowered substantially and still yield the same tax revenues. This would eliminate much of the vertical and horizontal inequity in income taxes and would substantially reduce the inefficiencies caused by preferential tax treatments for some sources of income.

For all the flaws of our income tax system, there seems to be widespread support for income taxation with some degree of progressivity. Few Americans favor abolishing the Sixteenth Amendment, which authorized income taxes. The major bone of contention is how to simplify income taxes and make them fairer.

The 1986 Tax Reform Act represented the most complete revamping of our tax system in decades. Income taxes were eliminated for most low-income families, and the bill replaced the 15 tax brackets under the old system (ranging from

11% to 50%) with two basic brackets (15% and 28%), and a temporary surcharge (an extra 5%) that applied primarily to upper-middle-income taxpayers. Revisions in 1990 intended to help limit the soaring federal budget deficit converted this surcharge into a permanent third bracket of 31% that applied to higher incomes. The Omnibus Budget Reconciliation Act of 1993 added two new brackets; taxable income above $115,000 for individuals and $140,000 for couples will be taxed at 36% and all income above $250,000 will be taxed at 39.6%. Table 2 details the current tax rates for various filing categories.

The 1986 tax reform was not intended to lower most people's taxes. Its major advantages are consistency and (alleged) simplicity. Major loopholes were closed, allowing sharp cuts in individual and corporate tax rates. *Consistency* (loophole closure) was expected to rebuild public confidence that people in similar circumstances pay similar taxes (horizontal equity), and that high-income families pay their fair share (vertical equity). *Simplicity* reduces the need to keep detailed accounting records. (Some studies report that such accounting absorbs resources equal to 1% to 2% of personal income.)

Tax Loopholes: Private Benefits and Public Costs

Most people perceive tax loopholes as mechanisms that allow rich people to escape their fair share of the tax burden. But do the rich really gain much from loopholes? Contrary to the implications of tidbits that frequently appear in the media (e.g., reports that "Daddy Warbucks only paid $314.83 in taxes last year on his billion-dollar income"), few people gain very much by using tax loopholes. Here is an example to show why.

Assume that most investors were in a 50% tax bracket and that all investment markets were initially in equilibrium and could be expected to yield after-tax rates of return equal to 10%. Now suppose that the Turkey Farmers Association persuaded Congress to declare that frozen turkeys were vital to the national defense and that income from turkey farming should be exempted from all federal taxes.

This raises the after-tax rate of return from turkeys to 20% and many investors could be expected to try to take advantage of this loophole. As money flowed into turkey farms, however, the resulting sharp drop in turkey prices would be paralleled by a decline in the rate of return from turkey farming. Simultaneously, invest-

ment in other areas would decline because of outflows of resources into turkey farming. In these nonfavored areas, the prices of goods would rise, and this would be paralleled by increases in rates of return for these goods. The law of equal marginal advantage implies that the final equilibrium would entail equal after-tax rates of return from all investments, including turkey farming.

Those who used this loophole would gain very little from it. Such loopholes ultimately only shift resources into tax-sheltered areas, which means that fewer resources are available to less-favored industries than market forces alone indicate are optimal. Overall tax loopholes reduce government revenues, but loophole users' gains are trivial. And the distorted structure of national output reflects loopholes instead of consumer preferences.

If loopholes ultimately provide so little gain to those who use them, then why do proposals to plug loopholes arouse such outrage? The answer is that closing a loophole can impose huge losses on people who currently use them. For example, many people have bought expensive houses because interest on mortgages is

deductible from taxable income. This deductibility has artificially raised the demand for houses and pushed up real estate prices. Were this deduction eliminated, current homeowners would lose, not only because of higher taxes, but because housing prices might plummet as well.

Who gains from loopholes? In large measure, the gainers are those who acquire specialized resources before favorable tax laws are enacted. They can become wealthy when the values of tax-sheltered areas are capitalized. Another group that gains are the tax attorneys, CPAs, and financial planners who advise people who want to avoid taxes. But even this group gains very little because most are competent people who would have been successful in other areas had tax loopholes never existed.

Tax reform historically has meant providing relief to groups that seem overburdened because of loopholes enjoyed by too many other groups. This has caused incredible complexity in the tax codes as loopholes have piled on top of loopholes over time, a situation only partially remedied by the Tax Reform Act of 1986.

Most income is now taxed more uniformly, regardless of source. Loophole closure refocused investments toward real values instead of a frantic search for loopholes. The new law, however, largely retained deductibility for real estate interest and property taxes, the two major middle-class loopholes. Pressure from state and local governments also caused interest income from state and municipal bonds to remain tax exempt. Nevertheless, most public finance experts perceived the 1986 tax reform as a major

step in the direction of efficiency and equity. Unfortunately, taxes remain about as difficult as ever to calculate (although slick computer programs have simplified filling out forms by taxpayers who are computer literate).

Social Security Taxes

You may be surprised to learn that the *Social Security* tax is expected to be the single largest

TABLE 2 Personal Income Tax Rates on Taxable Income

Rates	Taxable Income			
	Married filing jointly	**Head of household**	**Single**	**Married filing separately**
15%	0–$36,900	0–$29,600	0–$22,100	0-$18,450
28	$36,900–$89,150	$29,600–$76,400	$22,100–$53,500	$18,450–$44,575
31	$89,150–$140,000	$76,400–$127,500	$53,500–115,000	$44,575–$70,000
36	$140,000–$250,000	$127,500–$250,000	$115,000–$250,000	$70,000–$125,000
39.6	over $250,000	over $250,000	over $250,000	over $125,000

Source: Internal Revenue Service and Warren Esanu et al., *Guide to Income Tax, 1994 Edition* (Yonkers, N.Y.: Consumer Reports Books, 1993).

source of federal revenues by the year 2000. Social Security taxes, unemployment compensation, and workmen's disability taxes are *payroll taxes*; that is, they are based primarily on the payrolls that firms pay. Try this multiple-choice question: The Social Security tax is borne by (*a*) workers, (*b*) employers, (*c*) consumers, (*d*) a 50/50 split between workers and employers, (*e*) a 50/50 split between workers and consumers.

The idea that Social Security taxes are split 50/50 by employers and employees is a myth. This is the legal incidence of the tax, which requires employers and employees each to pay 7.65% of the first $57,600 in wage income for Social Security. In addition, both pay 1.45% of the first $135,000 in wage income for Medicare. Table 3 shows how this tax has changed over the years.[2] The simple fact is that the full tax is prob-

ably borne by workers. Here is an example to show why.[3]

Suppose that you work for ABC Corporation and your marginal revenue product is $800 weekly. If there are no other employment expenses to consider, competition forces ABC to pay you $800 weekly. Now suppose you insist that ABC send $50 to your Aunt Mary each week. The firm, however, will not retain your services unless you agree to allow them to deduct it from your check; if the law dictates that they send checks for $50 to the widowed aunts of all employees, they will cut wages correspondingly. It makes no sense to keep an employee worth only $800 if total employment costs exceed $800 weekly. Likewise,

[2]Of course, firms cannot pay taxes; only people can. To make this myth consistent, the firm's share is presumably forward-shifted to customers as higher prices.

[3]Most studies conclude that the after-tax wage elasticity of the aggregate supply of labor is approximately zero. You might review our discussion of tax incidence in our chapter on elasticity to construct a formal proof that payroll taxes will, consequently, be borne primarily by labor.

TABLE 3 Social Security Tax Hikes

Year	Maximum Covered Base ($)	Tax Rate* (percentage)	Maximum Amount of Tax*
1934	2,000	2.0	$40
1970	7,800	9.6	748
1975	14,100	11.7	1,650
1980	25,900	12.3	3,176
1985	39,600	14.1	5,584
1990	51,300	15.3	7,850
1994	57,600 (Social Security)	15.3	
	135,000 (Medicare)	2.9	12,728

Source: Social Security Administration, 1994.

*Half of these rates and amounts are legally levied on employers; the other half are legally borne by employees.

if money also must be sent to Uncle Sam because you are employed, you will bear this full burden: your gross salary will shrink by the amount of the tax.

Social Security has been pay-as-you-go for decades. Thus, current workers' taxes cover benefits to retirees. Even the entry of baby boomers into labor markets did not ease the growing tax burden, as the ranks of older Americans have swollen. Burdens on younger workers may become horrendous when boomers begin reaching age 65 in 2011.

Critics are dismayed that 65-year-old retirees who draw $100,000 in investment income can extract transfers from 18-year-old dishwashers working for minimum wages. Among many reform proposals are (a) raising the minimum age for retirement benefits, (b) eliminating benefits to the wealthy or subjecting Social Security payments to income taxes, (c) having all revenues come from general revenues, and (d) replacing Social Security with a negative income tax plan whereby people receive payments if they earn below a certain level of income. Pressure will mount to modify the system as the population of older people continues to grow, raising payroll tax burdens.

Sales and Excise Taxes

Sales taxes are percentage taxes broadly levied on dollar sales volumes, primarily by state and local governments. If sales taxes cover all goods, they are reasonably neutral and efficient. Sales taxes are not neutral, however, to the extent that they exempt items such as food, housing, or labor services. They distort relative prices and economic behavior.

Excise taxes are selectively applied to items like telephone calls, utility bills, and gasoline. Some excise taxes, called *sin taxes* (e.g., on cigarettes and liquor), are especially popular ways to raise revenues. Again, price distortions create economic inefficiency. A 10% tax on luxury cars and yachts was enacted in 1991. The tax on yachts was rescinded in 1994 after yacht sales plummeted, leaving thousands of workers unemployed (many of them relatively unskilled).

Sales and excise taxes are widely attacked as regressive because the proportion of income spent on taxed goods is higher for the poor than for the rich. Consequently, such basic necessities as food are often tax-exempt. Those who attack tax regressivity often advocate soaking rich corporations. Unfortunately, this strategy may backfire.

Corporate Income Taxes

Corporate accounting profits are taxed at the rates shown in Table 4 and, when initially levied, are borne by stockholders. However, consumers bear much of this tax burden in the long run, because *corporate income taxes* apply to accounting profits, which are largely normal profits, not economic profits. This tax raises costs and ultimately prices because normal profits are a long-run production cost. Moreover, even a tax on pure profit may ultimately be borne in part by consumers because aggregate investment is squelched; a reduced capital stock drives up prices in the long run.

The tax distorts prices to the extent that it is forward shifted; that is, the prices of goods manufactured primarily by corporations are raised relative to the prices of goods most often produced by unincorporated firms. A sad irony is that if, relative to rich people, poor people devote larger shares of income to the mass-produced goods supplied by corporations, the tax burden is regressive. People who think that corporate income taxes soak the rich are probably wrong.

People will buy corporate stock reluctantly if the tax is backward shifted. (Firms cannot truly

TABLE 4   Corporate Tax Rates

Taxable Income	Rate (percentage)
$0–50,000	15
50,001–75,000	25
75,001–100,000	34
100,001–335,000	39
335,000–10,000,000	34
Over 10,000,000	35

Source: Internal Revenue Service, 1994.

pay taxes; only people—in this case, stockholders—can.) The corporate sector will shrink relative to noncorporate firms until after-tax rates of return are equalized.

The inefficiency of the corporate income tax makes it extremely unpopular among most economists. One proposed reform is to eliminate corporate income taxes and allocate corporate profits to stockholders, who would then pay normal personal income taxes on their shares of corporate profits. Economists from across the political spectrum differ little in their dislike of the corporate income tax, but politicians almost universally favor it because their constituents often see the tax as a way for the little guy to get even with big business.

Property Taxes

The supply of land is perfectly inelastic. Thus, *land taxes* are relatively neutral; a tax on pure land rent has almost no effect on rental rates for land relative to other resources or goods. People often mistakenly apply this reasoning to property taxes, which are, however, among the least popular levies of all.

A *property tax* is based on the value of landholdings *plus* capital improvements. The supply of land may be perfectly inelastic, but improvements are very elastically supplied in the long run. Suppose you own prime land in an area with high property taxes. If you put a new building on it, you will pay higher taxes. Thus, the property tax is a disincentive to development. Similarly, if you are a slum landlord with tenants whose poverty limits the rents you can charge, will you repair or modernize your buildings if your tax bill jumps substantially as a consequence? Unlikely! Many students of the urban scene attribute part of the decay of central cities to high property taxes.

Inheritance and Gift Taxes

The Federal unified inheritance and gift tax rates are presented in Table 5. These taxes are progressive, but the first $600,000 on an estate

TABLE 5 Unified Transfer Tax for Lifetime Gifts and Estates

Taxable Estate (above $600,000) or Gift	Marginal Tax Rate (percent)
$0–10,000	18
10,000–20,000	20
20,000–40,000	22
40,000–60,000	24
60,000–80,000	26
80,000–100,000	28
100,000–150,000	30
150,000–250,000	32
250,000–500,000	34
500,000–750,000	37
750,000–1,000,000	39
1,000,000–1,250,000	41
1,250,000–1,500,000	43
1,500,000–2,000,000	45
2,000,000–2,500,000	49
2,500,000–3,000,000	50
Over 3,000,000	55

Source: Internal Revenue Service, 1994.

and the first $10,000 of any gift annually are tax-exempt. You might think that inheritance taxes could be avoided by giving your heirs the money, but *gift taxes* plug that loophole.

Extremely wealthy individuals avoid some of the inheritance tax in other ways. For one thing, they can establish irrevocable trusts that delay disbursements of estates until long after a person's death—to, say, their great grandchildren. This is one of several loopholes that make the inheritance tax an "optional tax" in the words of some critics. One proposed reform of the income and inheritance tax systems is to merge them. That is, any inheritances or gifts would simply be treated as taxable income.

TAX REFORM PROPOSALS

Rankings of the fairness of various taxes yield similar responses from both the public and tax experts. Virtually no taxes are thought fair. Our overview suggests that flawed taxes have historically outweighed equitable and efficient taxes.

The Microeconomics of Bloated Government

Polls indicate that an overwhelming majority of Americans want a smaller, but more efficient, government. Paradoxically, we simultaneously want better schools, roads and bridges, police and fire protection, and on and on. A majority of Americans now favor a more active role for government in providing affordable health care for all. But will a government medical-care program reduce the one-seventh of our GDP now devoted to health care? Unlikely. Can we afford the amount of government services that most of us would like? There is mounting evidence that the answer may be no.

Every national election is filled with political promises that, "if elected, I will get the federal deficit under control." Nevertheless, the deficit exceeded $200 billion in 1993, and federal debt exceeded $4 trillion—a burden of roughly $16,000 for every U.S. citizen. Yet being in favor of tax cuts has usually paved the way to election year victory [e.g., President Reagan (1980 and 1984) and President Bush (1988)], while hints that tax hikes may be necessary has spelled defeat (Walter Mondale

in 1984, Michael Dukakis in 1988). The election of President Clinton in 1992 may signal a growing concern about the deficit and a willingness to consider higher tax rates. However, President Bush's 1990 reversal of his 1988 pledge, "Read my lips—no new taxes," may have been significant.

How do victorious candidates propose to eliminate federal deficits without raising taxes? Apparently, most voters believe that promises to cut wasteful spending can be fulfilled. But we also tend to believe that wasteful government spending is that which benefits other people, not ourselves. For example, farmers may view $10 billion to support agriculture as warranted, while favoring cuts in programs that benefit the urban poor. People whose income depends on big defense contracts tend to favor continued big defense budgets, despite the demise of the USSR as much of a threat to world peace. Naturally, most teachers and the parents of school-aged children want more money to flow into education. Many of us apparently fail to recognize that all of these

demands for more government sum to the big government that we have, not smaller government that we perceive as the proper size to serve our individual needs.

Another problem that may, in part, account for our growing discontent with government is that we dislike the specific taxes government relies on and the hassle associated with filling out all the forms government imposes to monitor collection processes. We'd like the burden imposed on other groups; tax the rich is a popular theme. But who are the rich folks we'd like to pay more taxes? Surveys addressing this question typically find that the answer depends on who is asked the question, with most people defining those who should pay more taxes by the receipt of roughly 20% more income than the respondent receives. In the next chapter, we use economic analysis to address political aspects of government. By the time you've finished it, you should have a better feel for why government so often lacks the tax revenues to pay for its outlays.

Widespread discontent (addressed in Focus 2) has led to some proposed reforms to harmonize our tax system more closely with widely accepted tax principles: equity, neutrality, and simplicity.

Value-Added Taxes

Our tax system warps incentives, stifles economic performance, and, at times, has been so loaded with loopholes that large parts of it should probably be abandoned. Social Security and corporate income taxes are among possible targets for abolition. But what might replace

revenues generated by these taxes? A favorite contender is the value-added tax.

Value-added taxes (VATs) resemble sales taxes but apply only to differences between a firm's sales and its purchases from other firms.

Thus, a VAT is a fixed percentage of a firm's payments for resources and is not applied to intermediate products the firm purchases from other firms.

A major virtue of the VAT is that it is reasonably neutral. Another is that tax evasion is extremely difficult, which partially accounts for its use in much of Europe. A drawback is that VATs are largely hidden; final customers may be unaware of the VAT embodied in the price of a product. A normative objection is that, like sales taxes, VATs may be somewhat regressive. Finally, VATs require more cumbersome accounting than sales taxes because VATs must be paid at several levels of output. Nonetheless, value-added taxes are probably more efficient and less inequitable than corporate income taxes, Social Security taxes, or a number of other levies in the government's toolbox.

Flat Rate Taxes

Many critics claim that attempts to make income taxes highly progressive are self-defeating. They argue first that high marginal tax rates discourage investment and so, in the long run, actually hold down the incomes of most "working stiffs," or those whose productivity would be enhanced were they working with more capital. The obsolescence of British manufacturing and the comparatively slow growth of British wages from World War II through the 1970s are cited as examples of this problem. (The British economy began its recovery after tax rates were sharply reduced in the early 1980s.)

A second difficulty is that high marginal tax rates increase the payoff from lobbying for new loopholes, which can reduce the true progressivity of the tax system to a mere shadow of the nominal rates. Few high-income individuals fail to exploit loopholes. Progressivity has been combined with complex loopholes so that even tax experts have often been uncertain as to how much they owed. A third problem is that high marginal tax rates are incentives for (illegal) tax evasion.

One proposed answer for all these problems is the *flat rate tax*. Some analysts have suggested that a flat income tax of roughly 20% with no exemptions or deductions would (a) generate more revenue than the current tax system, (b) eliminate most tax evasion, (c) cut the amount of paperwork required from firms and house-

FIGURE 8   A Progressive Approach to the Flat Tax

This 20% flat tax is progressive because, with a standard deduction of $10,000, the percentage of income paid as taxes rises continuously as income rises. Note that the vertical intercept is at -$2,000; this approach is compatible with the negative income tax described in the preceding chapter as a possible partial cure for the welfare mess.

holds, and (d) cure the ulcers and headaches common around April 15 of each year. Critics of this proposal fear that a flat income tax system would be an inequitable retreat from society's fight against poverty.

However, one variant of the flat tax proposal that could retain substantial progressivity would entail merely enacting substantial standard deductions that would be similar to those in current income taxes. Figure 8 illustrates how a flat tax rate of 20% would be progressive after a $10,000 deduction. Zero taxes are paid at the $10,000 income level (point *a*), but $2,000 in taxes are collected at the $20,000 income level (10% of income at point *b*). At a $40,000 income, the tax would be $6,000 (15% of income at point *c*). For people with a $100,000 income, the tax would be $18,000 (18% at point *d*). As you can see, this approach combines the simplicity of a flat tax with progressivity, which most Americans seem to favor.

Consumption Taxes

Other critics argue that the major flaw in our current tax system is that, in a shortsighted quest for greater equality, progressive income taxes kill the goose that lays the golden eggs. These critics view disparities in consumption levels, not income, as the root of social inequity. They argue that resource use (*consumption*) is more appropriate as a measure of ability to pay than are potential claims to resources (*income*). Major drawbacks to taxing income are the severe disincentives to save and invest. The critics' solution is to allow all saving as a deduction from taxes, effectively replacing income taxes with a tax on consumption alone. Consequently, people with incomes of $1,000,000 per year would be taxed on the full amount if they spent it on Rolls-Royces, furs, jewelry, and other extravagances. Investing almost all of a $1,000,000 income, on the other hand, would result in negligible taxes.

A *consumption tax* could be as progressive as any income tax system, so problems of regressivity are not necessarily raised. Moreover, according to the advocates of this approach, the resulting increase in saving and investment would greatly enhance labor productivity, and technological breakthroughs would allow substantial economic growth.

We have looked at the types of government activities that can be rationalized as proper cures for market failures and have examined various tax structures. Questions about why government spending and taxes so frequently depart from the ideal have been addressed only peripherally, however. Many of these questions are answered when we look at the political dimensions of policymaking. The next chapter examines political behavior from an economic perspective.

CHAPTER REVIEW: KEY POINTS

1. The economic goals of government are to
   a. Provide a stable legal environment, promote competition, and provide efficiently for public wants.
   b. Stabilize income, employment, and prices.
   c. Redistribute income and wealth equitably.
2. When marginal social benefits and marginal social costs diverge, **market failure** occurs. In such cases, government may be used to provide the socially optimal quantities of some goods and to limit economic bads.
3. **Externalities** occur when private calculations of benefits or costs differ from the benefits or costs to society because third parties gain or lose from a transaction.
4. **Nonrivalry** means that a good is not used up when any individual enjoys it; a beautiful sunset is an example. **Nonexclusion** means that it is prohibitively expensive to deny access to a good. Note, however, that public provision does not require public production. Private firms often produce goods that government then distributes.
5. A good that is both nonrival and nonexclusive is a **pure public good**. Public goods will be less than optimally provided by the market system, if they are provided at all, because of attempts to *free ride*. A rival but nonexclusive good embodies *externalities* that often hinder the efficiency of market solutions.
6. The demand for a pure public good is the **vertical summation** of individual demand curves because all can enjoy the good simultaneously, while demands for private goods are summed horizontally. Adequate revenue for optimal quantities of public goods is generated if people pay taxes equal to their marginal benefits from

public goods multiplied by the amounts of these goods provided.

7. The **benefit principle of taxation** suggests that people should pay taxes in proportion to the marginal benefits they receive from a governmentally provided good.

8. The **ability-to-pay principle of taxation** requires taxes in proportion to people's income, their wealth, or, possibly, their consumption. This principle is closely related to the idea that government policies should move the income distribution closer to equality than is the market distribution of income.

9. The principle of **horizontal equity** suggests that equals should pay equal taxes; **vertical equity** requires higher taxes on the wealthy than on the poor.

10. If the loss to a taxpayer exceeds the government revenue gained, there is an **excess burden** of taxation. **Neutral taxes** impose only income, not substitution, effects and impose no excess burdens.

11. Our five-step **personal income tax** system is nominally progressive, but various loopholes make it somewhat inefficient and inequitable.

12. **Social Security taxes** are the second largest and fastest growing sources of federal revenues. They and other **payroll taxes** may be borne primarily by workers. Moreover, they are regressive, typically declining proportionately as personal income rises.

13. **Sales taxes** are reasonably efficient but, like income taxes, are marred by numerous exemptions. Many **excise taxes** apply to sins or luxuries. Unless they are based on a benefit principle of taxation (for example, public zoo ticket fees or gasoline taxes), they tend to cause inefficiency and be regressive. (Poor people smoke and drink as much, by volume, as rich people.)

14. The **corporate income tax** discriminates against the corporate form of business and against the goods produced primarily by corporations. In the long run, most of this tax is probably forward shifted to consumers. Thus, in the minds of most experts, this tax tends to be both inefficient and inequitable.

15. **Property taxes** provide disincentives for improvement and are blamed by some for the deterioration of central cities.

16. **Inheritance** and **gift taxes** have high and progressive rates, but they can be avoided because these tax laws are riddled with loopholes.

17. A **value-added tax (VAT)** is similar to a sales tax in that it is forward shifted. VATs only apply to the value added by each firm. VATs, **flat rate taxes**, and progressive **consumption taxes** (not income taxes) have been proposed as replacements for corporate income and/or Social Security taxes.

QUESTIONS FOR THOUGHT AND DISCUSSION

1. Indicate which of the following goods seem to be pure private goods, which are pure public goods, which generate positive externalities, which generate negative externalities, and which are likely to be produced by natural monopolies. Some goods may be hard to classify; they may fall into more than one category because production creates one type of effect, while consumption creates a different type of effect.
   a. deodorant soap
   b. electricity generated by atomic power
   c. lawn fertilizer
   d. radishes
   e. surf boards
   f. garlic
   g. cancer research

h. speeding tickets
i. kindergarten
j. heavy metal concerts

2. Why do fewer apartment dwellers voluntarily install smoke alarms than would be socially optimal? Does this justify regulations requiring smoke alarms? Will the number of smoke alarms in private homes be optimal without government regulation? How might pressure from neighbors and insurance companies eliminate the need for such regulations?

3. Can you think of ways to induce people to reveal their preferences for certain public goods so that they will not be free riders? Try this for such things as schools, highways, and national defense.

4. Many people support the sentiments of tax resisters who refuse to pay income taxes. If resistance became more widespread, what would happen to the tax burdens of those who conscientiously pay all of their legal tax liabilities? What are the effects (psychological and otherwise) on someone who pays taxes honestly when someone else defends cheating because "everybody does it"? Do honest people subsidize tax cheats?

5. One popular proposal is to entirely replace the current tax system with a single, flat rate income tax. What are the virtues of this proposal? The drawbacks? The advocates of this approach managed to tilt tax legislation in their favor during the 1980s. By how much did changes in income tax rates in 1993 restore the nominal progressivity of our tax structure? Does elimination of tax loopholes increase or decrease the actual progressivity of income taxes? Why?

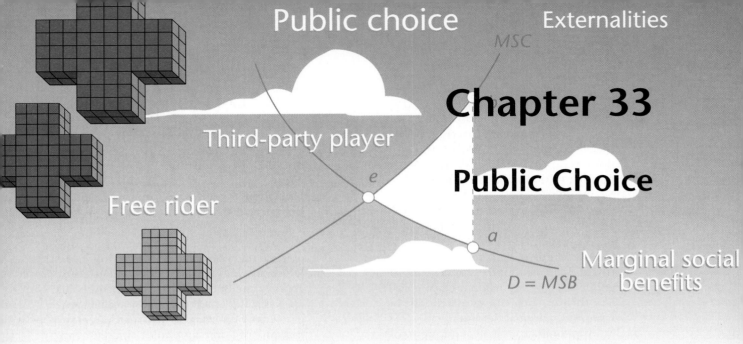

Public choice

Externalities

MSC

Third-party player

e

Chapter 33

Free rider

Public Choice

a

$D = MSB$

Marginal social benefits

Eternal optimists may think that government can infallibly cure the market failures described in the preceding chapter, but government policies are also often marred by inefficiency and inequity. No allocative mechanism works perfectly. Selecting the best mechanism for the task at hand usually involves trade-offs. Choosing government to remedy market failures, for example, may mean that the flexibility of markets is lost and that *government failure* creates a new set of problems.

Economists increasingly apply their insights to the processes of government.

> **Public choice** *analysis examines political behavior from an economic perspective.*

Specialists in public choice believe that the motives behind people's behavior in the political arena differ little from those behind their performance in the private sector, equal proportions of saints and greedy sinners are found among workers, voters, union leaders, bureaucrats, professors, business tycoons, and politicians.

Asymmetric information poses at least as much of a problem for efficient allocation through political processes as it does for efficient allocations through markets. The principal–agent problem rears its head in the issue of how well or poorly elected officials (agents) serve the interests of their constituents (principals). Government policymaking cannot be divorced from such realities as lobbying by special-interest groups, the desires of incumbents to be reelected, or bureaucratic inertia.

Our first topic in this chapter is private political behavior. Why do so few people vote, and why do so many seem oblivious to political issues? Then we investigate alternative voting systems. Is majority rule superior to unanimity or point voting in reflecting voters' preferences? Our next broad area is political competition: government as a mechanism through which special-interest groups compete for scarce resources. Finally, we look at government bureaucracy, focusing on ways in which individuals may serve their private interests when they lack profit motives for efficiency.

PRIVATE CITIZENS AND POLITICS

Consumers vote with dollars for the things they want in private transactions, but each consumer has different numbers of dollar votes. In modern democracies, adult citizens (except convicted felons) have equal rights to vote, so their opinions theoretically carry equal weight. Then why do so many people seem indifferent about politics?

Rational Voter Apathy

An election-year cliché is that "every vote counts." If people were always rational and if the outcome of every election hung on every vote and were crucial for everyone, then all eligible citizens would vote. We would not hear TV commentators lamenting voter apathy after every election.

Fewer than 10% of adult U.S. citizens bother to go to the polls in most local elections. Even in hotly contested national elections, a 60% turnout is rare. Many Americans evidently conclude that the personal costs of voting outweigh the personal benefits. The following is one explanation for why many people judge that voting is not worth the effort.

Suppose opinion polls indicate that 70 million people plan to vote in the next presidential election and that voters are split 50/50 between the Republican and Democratic candidates. This split maximizes the probability that your vote would matter if presidents were elected by popular vote. What is the probability that a single vote would swing this election? The probability of an exact 50/50 split of the vote is identical with the probability of flipping a coin 70 million times and obtaining exactly 35 million heads and 35 million tails: infinitesimal. Even if only 1,000 people voted, the probability that you might be the tie breaker if you were the 1,001st voter is less than 1%. The probability that any single voter will be the tie breaker is, of course, much lower the larger the number of votes.

The transaction costs of voting are not trivial when you consider the time and resources used to register, walk or drive to the polls, wait in line, learn about candidates and issues, and so on. This raises the question of why so many people do vote. Although the costs of voting are low, the probability of one vote swinging any important election is nearly zero. Some people argue that if you don't vote, you have no right to complain, but there is no law or religious commandment to that effect.

One possible explanation for widespread apathy is that most people living in democracies are reasonably content and are skeptical that the outcome of any election is likely to change their lives very much. People living in dictatorships often correctly believe, however, that democratic voting will allow people more control over their lives. People who defy thugs and bullets to vote are asserting their belief in the outcomes of voting as a group process. Few of them believe that each individual vote is highly likely to change the outcome of every election.

• **Why Many People Do Vote**   The preceding analysis makes it seem almost irrational to vote. Major elections, however, usually draw a majority of eligible voters. Some people may vote because political campaigns resemble spectator sports; the stakes are generally higher, but voting is a bit like cheering for your favorite football team or buying a ticket to a game. Others view voting as a democratic duty. Most voters like to think of themselves as good citizens or feel guilty if they don't vote. Just as no soldier alone is likely to win or lose a war, no single vote is likely to swing a major election. Nevertheless, most soldiers and voters derive some pleasure from participating in group processes that shape history.

Apathetic nonvoters who contend that individual votes don't matter are statistically correct. It may even be fortunate that many people don't vote. Voting is most likely among people with intense political preferences and least likely among people who are indifferent about politics and who know relatively little about the issues.

Rational Political Ignorance and Asymmetric Information

Better the devil you know than the devil you don't.

Unknown

Can you name even five people who were on the ballot in the last election? How much did you know about the candidates' positions on budget deficits? Immigration? Gun control? If you are typical, your answer to these and similar questions is not much.

> ***Rational ignorance*** *occurs when people decide that the marginal costs of more information exceed its marginal benefits.*

Information is costly. The future is uncertain. Therefore, consumers and producers operate with only imperfect information about markets. They are, to some degree, *rationally ignorant*. Similarly, voters rely on information that is far from perfect. The personal payoff from in-depth knowledge about all the candidates and issues decided in any important election is trivial and generally far less significant than the benefits of information about market choices. For example, textile import quotas now cost consumers billions of dollars annually. If your share is only $5 to $10 and the probability of influencing an election with your vote is negligible, then the time and effort required to learn about candidates' positions on import quotas so that you can vote wisely probably exceed the personal benefits from a more informed vote. There are, however, significant personal benefits in knowing about the quality and price of clothing you buy.

Rational ignorance on the parts of most voters compounds the principal–agent problem that can arise from asymmetric information. Election results share many attributes of public goods: your president is my president, we share the same sets of laws, and so on. Managers of firms have substantially greater incentives to monitor employees to prevent shirking than voters have to monitor the positions and activities of political candidates and elected officials.

Reports in the daily media can help voters monitor politicians, but most citizens do not keep close track of campaign events or the voting records of their elected officials. (Although special-interest groups certainly pay close attention if they think they will be affected.) The public goods aspects of elections create incentives for free riders who either don't vote or rely on other voters to acquire knowledge about the candidates and issues. Thus, we should not be surprised that many voters select candidates based on charisma–a flashing smile and a shock of wavy hair or an impression that a certain candidate is dependable, experienced, or reflective. Small wonder that every major political campaign abounds with public relations flacks.

We have examined why so many people fail to vote, and why so many who do vote are relatively ignorant about political issues. Let's survey some of the different methods by which candidates and proposals can be chosen.

SYSTEMS OF VOTING

Although single votes have little direct influence on elections, those of us fortunate enough to live in democracies can vote to collectively determine who will govern. But how accurately are voters' preferences reflected by election results? Does the system of voting matter?

Majority Rule

Any group of a dozen or more people will find it difficult to agree on almost anything. Group decisions tend to be middle-of-the-road compromises that are often inconsistent with any individual's preferences.

> ***Majority rule*** *voting systems require votes from 50% plus one of the voters.*

Whenever we vote and use a simple majority rule, we can be almost certain members on the minority side of the vote will perceive that their interests were harmed by the outcome of the election. (Otherwise, they would have voted with the majority; votes reflect expectations of gain or fears of loss.) Majority voting may even result in economic inefficiency, since the minority's losses may outweigh all gains to the side able to swing a majority of votes.

• Potential Inefficiencies

Although majority voting can be efficient, the example in Table 1 points out the possibility of inefficient results. Proposal X is defeated even though its benefits outweigh the costs by $300, but Proposal Y passes despite costs ($2,000) exceeding benefits ($1,700) by $300.

Notice that if supporters of Proposal X shared their gains with the potential losers, all could gain from its passage; if opponents of Proposal Y compensated the potential gainers, all could gain from its defeat. Thus, passage of Proposal X and defeat of Y would both be efficient moves. Majority rule voting yields inefficiency on both proposals, however, because it is illegal to pay money for votes. This is one reason for secret ballots. Markets for votes might shrink the inefficiency inherent in many voting situations, but a market approach to voting is widely viewed as unethical or inequitable.

The basic problem is that *intensities of preference* are easily registered in markets, but not by a majority rule. You can buy more or fewer pizzas based on the intensity of your preferences, but even if you passionately care who is elected dogcatcher, your vote counts no more than that of someone who randomly casts a vote that offsets yours.

• Potential Inconsistencies

Majority rule voting can yield inconsistent results, especially if choices are narrowed by sequential elections (e.g., party primaries). It is, for example, common for analysts to claim that Republican Smith could beat any Democrat in a presidential election, but that she has no chance because hardcore Republicans will nominate Mr. Jones, who cannot beat any Democrat. Table 2 illustrates this point by considering a three-party system. Assume that the voters are roughly divided into thirds between the Tory, Whig, and Populist parties, and that the ultimate winner must receive over 50% of the vote. If no one receives a clear majority, then a runoff election is held between the top two candidates.

Suppose that Tory voters despise Populists and will vote for Whigs if there are no Tories in a runoff election. Whig voters, however, vote for Populist Party candidates over Tory candidates in runoff elections. To complete this circle, Populist voters will support Tory over Whig candidates. Table 2 shows the potential results if no candidate receives a clear majority in an initial election. Tory candidates win against Whigs in runoff elections, who would win against Populists, who, in turn, would beat the Tories.

Some analysts believe that the possible inconsistencies apparent in these results of ma-

TABLE 1 Inefficient Outcomes under a Simple Majority Rule

A Beneficial Proposal (X) Is Defeated					An Excessively Costly Proposal (Y) Is Adopted				
			Votes					**Votes**	
Individual	**Benefits**	**Tax Cost**	**Aye**	**Nay**	**Individual**	**Benefits**	**Tax Cost**	**Aye**	**Nay**
A	$700	$400	X		A	$425	$400	X	
B	600	400	X		B	575	400	X	
C	350	400		X	C	450	400	X	
D	375	400		X	D	150	400		X
E	275	400		X	E	100	400		X
Total	$2,300	$2,000	2	3	Total	$1,700	$2,000	3	2

TABLE 2 Potential Inconsistencies in Voting

	Parties in Runoff		
	Tory vs. Whig	Whig vs. Populist	Populist vs. Tory
Tory voter preferences	Tory	Whig	Tory
Whig voter preferences	Whig	Whig	Populist
Populist voter preferences	Tory	Populist	Populist
Winner	Tory	Whig	Populist

jority rule voting may also foment instability, with parties taking turns being in power. This is known as the *voting cycle* phenomenon. An alternative explanation for voting cycles is that voters do not want any party to have a monopoly on political power. This may partially explain for example, why voters have elected Republican presidents in five of the seven national elections since 1968, while Democrats have held fairly consistent majorities in both the U.S. Senate and the House of Representatives, as well as a majority of governorships. Nevertheless, voting cycles and the resulting flip-flops in policies often create chaos for long-range planning by consumers, workers, and business investors and managers. Unstable policies would be less of a problem if changes required unanimous votes.

Unanimity

Some decisions are deemed so important that society requires more than a simple majority vote; minority opinions are weighed more heavily in determining critical social policies. A constitutional amendment requires either a constitutional convention called by three-fourths of all state legislatures, or their ratification of an amendment approved by two-thirds of the members of both the U.S. Senate and the House of Representatives. Similar congressional votes are required to override a presidential veto. In most states, a jury trying a criminal case must reach a unanimous verdict, or the case must be either retried or abandoned by the prosecutor. In such situations, requiring *unanimity* or near unanimity limits exploitation of a minority. Moreover, any legal changes under pure unanimity rules presumably would benefit every-

one or they would never be adopted. Thus, any changes would clearly improve economic efficiency.

One difficulty with requiring unanimity is that individuals who, on balance, are relatively unaffected by some proposal could withhold their votes to exert leverage over potential gainers from the proposed change. In a sense, requiring unanimity gives everyone the power to say, "It's my ball, so we play by my rules or we don't play." Although some people might negotiate disproportionate gains for themselves simply because of their political leverage, no voter would ever expect to lose from any unanimous vote.

A far more serious problem is that a unanimity rule is biased in favor of the existing situation. Unanimity might operate well if an overwhelming majority view the current situation as equitable, but it totally blocks political remedies for inequity, leaving only informal negotiation, violence, or the market as avenues open for people to pursue what they perceive as justice. For example, a unanimity requirement precludes any redistribution of income or wealth other than one that is strictly voluntary. (Under a unanimity rule, slavery would still exist. Persuading every slave owner to agree to its abolition would be extremely difficult without a resort to violence.) A final flaw is that even though a unanimity rule protects the existing rights of minorities, it also provides only crude indications of the intensity of people's preferences.

Point Voting

One proposal to reflect the intensities of preferences better than any "one person, one vote" rule is the use of *point voting*.

Point voting assigns equal numbers of points to all voters, which they can allocate among various issues as they see fit.

Voters ideally would allocate their points in proportion to their intensities of preference, that is, in proportion to their net expected gains or losses from given proposals. Thus, if individuals A, B, C, D, and E each have 100 points to allocate between the proposals in Table 1, they would ideally vote as in Table 3. Proposal X passes and Proposal Y fails; these results reverse the inefficient results under simple majority rule voting. Since Proposal X yields net benefits while Proposal Y's costs exceed its benefits, these ideal point voting results are preferable to the results of a simple majority rule.

A major flaw in point voting is that people might skew their voting points toward issues that they expected to be close, figuring that others would ensure the passage or failure of issues not expected to be close. For example, suppose you favored more spending on both national defense and medical research. If you expected a landslide vote on a national defense proposal but a close vote on medical research, you would probably place all your votes for medical research. Point voting systems are flawed when, instead of voting their true preferences, people try to forecast the outcomes of elections and then vote strategically. Election results would con-

form neither to the majority's will nor to reasonable benefit-cost decision-making.

No matter which voting system is used, most people view government as failing if election results do not reflect voters' preferences. All voting systems are somewhat flawed in this regard, but the overwhelming use of majority rule voting has evolved out of two centuries of experimentation with other voting systems. We have examined voting from the perspectives of citizens. The other side of this equation is how electoral processes shape political campaigns and policies of the candidates and private interests who want to influence government policy.

POLITICIANS AND PARTIES

Politics is the art of compromise.

Unknown

Some candidates seek office to mold policy to their ideals, hoping to make this a better world. Their constituents' interests are primary concerns. Political opportunists, on the other hand, may care far more about simply acquiring power and prestige. The first step towards election for either type of candidate is to project an image voters will support. One obstacle is that no one can be all things to all people. Any position on almost any issue will offend some voters. All serious candidates, whether idealists or oppor-

TABLE 3   The Results from Table 1 if Determined by Point Voting*

	Proposal X		Votes			Proposal Y		Votes	
Individual	Benefits	Tax Cost	Aye	Nay	Individual	Benefits	Tax Cost	Aye	Nay
A	$700	$400	92		A	$425	$400	8	
B	600	400	53		B	575	400	47	
C	350	400		50	C	450	400	50	
D	330	400		9	D	150	400		91
E	320	400		20	E	100	400		80
Total	$2,300	$2,000	145	79	Total	$1,700	$2,000	105	171

*Ideal point voting would mean that all voters would apportion their votes based on net benefits (benefits – costs). For example, Individual A's net benefits from Proposal X are $300 ($700 – $400); net benefits for Proposal Y are $25 ($425 – $400). Thus,

Individual A's voting pattern would be 92 votes $\left(\dfrac{\$300}{\$325} \times 100 \right)$ for Proposal X and 8 Votes $\left(\dfrac{\$25}{\$325} \times 100 \right)$ for Proposal Y.

tunists, are pressured to compromise in predictable ways on a wide range of issues.

Lumpiness in Voting

I voted for the lesser of two evils.

Unknown

Consumers operating in the marketplace can fine-tune their purchases to closely match their tastes and preferences. Even with such "lumpy" purchases as automobiles, you can buy a slightly bigger or smaller car, with more or fewer options, and keep it longer than your neighbor does or trade it in sooner. Such fine gradations are not available in the political arena.

You might prefer Madison's stands on education and welfare reform, for example, while favoring Monroe's views on international relations. Voting is a *lumpy decision,* somewhat akin to tie-in sales contracts that require buying some things you do not want to get the things you desire. Casting a vote involves trade-offs because you cannot vote for a set of positions other than those taken by one of the candidates.

This is one reason that most public figures either state their positions on controversial issues in inoffensive terms or they waffle, avoiding direct answers to barbed questions aimed at them by reporters or their political opponents. This is an important example of the distortive effects of asymmetric information in the political arena. Rational ignorance among voters and the complexity of most issues are two other reasons that politicians frequently sidestep taking a stand. A fourth reason is that most serious political candidates strive for a moderate image.

The Median Voter Model

Differences among candidates are often more form than substance. It seems that all favor a strong national defense, adequate welfare for the truly needy, a balanced budget, and low taxes. Positions soon become as predictable as calls to support motherhood, apple pie, and the flag.

Why do party platforms and political speeches so often seem like photocopies of one another?

> *The **median voter model** suggests that the median voter must be captured to achieve a majority vote, and it helps explain why political parties and candidates so often seem interchangeable.*

The median voter model partially explains similarities among political parties and candidates. In Figure 1, we assume that the preferences and voting patterns of individuals can be ranked very simply and are normally distributed along a continuum from the extreme left (revolutionary communism, perhaps) to the extreme right (fascism?). Point *M* is in the precise

The bell-shaped curve is based on the assumption that voters are normally distributed from left-wing to right-wing political positions. A right-wing candidate at point *R* gains more by moving toward the political center at point *M*, but is likely to lose substantial support from a move from *R* to the more extreme *R*₁. These losses of votes will be maximized if this candidate's opponent moves to a position just to the left of the candidate's position. The respective potential losses and gains pressure right-wing candidates and parties to move toward middle-of-the-road positions. Naturally, similar pressures would cause a serious left-wing candidate to shift toward the political center at point *M*.

FIGURE 1   How Candidates and Parties Are Pushed to the Middle of the Road

center of this spectrum and identifies the median voter—exactly half of all voters lie to the left, with the other half being to the right of this position.

Consider two candidates running for an office. The median voter can provide the margin of victory if the winner must receive 50% plus 1 votes. Thus, the candidate who adopts positions on the issues closest to point M captures the median vote and wins the election. Regardless of their initial positions (say, L and R, respectively), both candidates find that shifting their positions slightly toward point M boosts their standings in public opinion polls. Figure 1 also uses a slightly right-wing candidate to illustrate how movements toward the extremes lose votes, while shifts to the center gain votes. The same would be true of a left-wing candidate. As the candidates each try to maximize their expected votes, each creeps toward point M. Ultimately, their positions may be almost indistinguishable.

You might think that a new third candidate could win this race by entering at, say, point L, leaving the original candidates to split the votes from halfway between points L and M all the way to the extreme right. But this third candidate would also find that moving toward point M increases support by voters. This suggests that, ultimately, virtually all serious candidates for election gravitate toward point M. Similar forces are at work in elections ranging from that for president of a local PTA to the U.S. presidency, pressuring not only political candidates, but political parties as well, to gradually adopt middle-of-the-road policies.

The median voter model grossly oversimplifies the dynamic world of politics; otherwise, there would be no differences between candidates or party platforms. Among other reasons, differences exist because

1. The opinions of voters on various issues never fall along a simple array from left to right, and their opinions are only loosely correlated. For example, there may be no predictable connections between people's opinions on welfare, the environment, international trade, and law-and-order issues.

2. Voter distributions change, so it is impossible for politicians to know exactly where the median voter is on any controversial issue at any point in time.
3. Some politicians do have strong personal beliefs about some issues.

The median voter model also tends to break down because of low voter turnout and rational political ignorance. If a majority of eligible voters apathetically stay away from the polls, then the deciding votes in an election may be cast by well-informed political activists who belong to narrow special-interest groups. In spite of these qualifications, the median voter model helps explain the middle-of-the-road clustering of politicians and parties, which ignores the preferences of vast numbers of less moderate voters. It also hints at reasons for the dominance of the two-party system.

Two-Party Systems

That voters' preferences shift over time also helps explain *voting cycles*, that is, why political control tends to swing between two parties in most democratic countries. Normally, one party locates slightly to the left of center, with the other being slightly right of center. Each then advertises itself as the party of the future and hopes that circumstances will move more voters in its direction.

The two parties, being reasonably comfortable with each other, then compete through expensive campaigns. A typical congressional campaign now requires a war chest of over $1 million. One recent U.S. Senate candidate in New York spent $14 million campaigning for a job paying less than $200,000 annually—*and lost*. Campaign spending on television spots alone now exceeds $100 million in presidential election years. Such barriers frustrate third-party challenges to either dominant party. Another technique to bar entry is to make it difficult for a third party to get on the ballot. For example, the dominant parties may enact laws requiring that petitions be signed by huge numbers of voters before the third party can be on the ballot if it received less than 5% of the votes in a prior election.

Third parties tend to be launched from the extremes of the political spectrum and to be based on single issues. If a third party begins to attract more voters than either dominant party expected, the closest major party normally adopts a moderate version of the third party's position. If leaders of a third party seriously want political power, it tends to become more moderate and is eventually absorbed by the closest major party. Thus, mature democracies usually operate under the control of two major parties. Third parties rarely displace major parties, and then only when a major party fails to respond to changes in voter preferences.

Two-party systems also tend to foster political stability. Italy has numerous parties, and there have been more governments than years since the end of World War II. As we have seen, politicians and political parties tend toward the middle of the road in an effort to capture votes. Once politicians are in office, can we expect them to shed their self-interest and work primarily for the common good of their constituents?

POLITICAL ALLOCATION

Two things you never want to see made are sausages and laws.

Otto von Bismarck

Asymmetric information, rational political ignorance, low voter turnouts, lumpiness in voting for a candidate, and the tendency for parties and politicians to cluster around middle-of-the-road positions are among the reasons government policies only weakly mirror voter preferences. Lobbying and protracted negotiations among elected representatives are among the mechanisms that result in budgets and laws intended to balance the desires of *special-interest groups*, including those of voters. These mechanisms sometimes provide pressures for policies to more closely conform to voter preferences, but at other times they exacerbate problems inherent in political allocations of resources and incomes.

Logrolling

Economists generally favor most forms of voluntary exchange because both sides expect to gain or no trade occurs.

*Legislators commonly trade votes to obtain passage of proposals they favor, a process known as **logrolling**.*

For example, one legislator might want more funding to clean up the environment, while another seeks higher agricultural price supports. Trading votes may enable both to get what they want. Logrolling may also be beneficial by allowing legislators to register their *intensities of preference*. Votes about matters upon which a legislator is reasonably indifferent are traded for votes on proposed legislation about which the lawmaker feels strongly. This process can aid in the attainment of efficiency by allowing strongly held minority views to overcome weak opposition by the majority.

Economists recognize, however, that some exchanges may not be socially beneficial. An extreme case would be an agreement wherein you trade part of your loot from a bank robbery for my services as a lookout and getaway driver. Society's problem is that we are not the only people affected by this transaction: our victims' losses must be considered. Less dramatic but similarly damaging trades can take place through logrolling that results in pork barrel legislation.

__Pork barrel legislation__ uses tax revenues from taxpayers everywhere to fund projects that primarily benefit people in a narrower geographic area.

Many federal projects generate benefits that are largely local. For example, Arizonans make up about 1% of our population and pay about 1% of federal taxes. Even if a canal system to convey water into dry parts of Arizona would cost $2 billion but generate benefits of only $1 billion, constituents would pressure Arizona's senators and representatives to support federal funds to build it. Arizonans would pay only 1% of the costs while receiving most of the benefits—a good deal for Arizonans, but a crummy deal for other voters.

Most pork barrel legislation is packaged with other pieces of pork and then tied to laws that are national in scope. Presidents cannot selectively veto parts of a law and so must either accept or veto the entire package. This is why some states have passed line-item veto legislation and why there is pressure to do this at the national level.

> A **line-item veto** allows the executive branch (e.g., governors or, if enacted nationally, the president) to delete specific items in an appropriations bill before signing it.

Logrolling by lawmakers sympathetic to the goals of special interests is only one mechanism that interest groups use to secure policies they favor.

Special Interests

Majority rule voting tends to slight minority interests, but determined political minorities are often able to impose policies weakly opposed by a majority of voters. For example, opinion polls consistently indicate that most Americans favor some restrictions on private firearms. Yet, for decades, the National Rifle Association successfully blocked national gun control legislation. Why? Typical voters cared relatively little about gun control and were rationally ignorant of most candidates' positions on this issue. Thus, gun fanciers whose votes and contributions may be based on this issue alone made most politicians leery of pushing gun control. Finally, the alarm among voters about increased crime and violence swayed Congress to enact the Brady Handgun Control Act of 1993. Similarly, people who feel strongly about abortion, prayer in schools, or protecting our steel industry from foreign competition may have disproportionally strong voices in determining certain social policies.

Voting is not the only way for special interests to accomplish their political goals. Money

talks, and big money talks loudly. Campaign funds from a well-heeled minority may sway who gets elected, shading some politicians' positions on certain issues. Alternatively, campaign volunteers can beat the bushes to get other voters to support specific candidates. Money and bodies also may be used to propagandize for important minority issues. And then logrolling comes into play when politicians try to pass legislation favored by the interest groups that back them, including pork barrel projects for the folks in their home districts.

As we indicated earlier, one way a democracy can reflect intense preferences is for a minority to exert vigorous pressure and attain policies it favors. Much legislation enacted to benefit interest groups, however, may bear inefficiently high social costs.

Rent Seeking

People are self-interested and try to manipulate allocative mechanisms to enrich themselves. In competitive markets, this normally entails trying to produce better goods at lower costs. This boosts society's production and potential consumption. Government can be similarly beneficial by setting rules to correct market failures, but economic legislation and regulation often seem tailored for special-interest groups. One problem with this is that the gains to special-interest groups are often less than the costs to the general public. Indeed, inefficiency in collective decision-making arises primarily because the benefits accrue to small cohesive groups, while the costs are spread across a relatively anonymous, heterogeneous, and poorly informed public.

> **Rent seeking** is the term applied to attempts by interest groups to manipulate public policy for their own gain.

The interest group's benefits are usually overshadowed by losses to the larger public. Recall that economic rent is any income received in excess of the minimum required to secure the resources that people make available. Figure 2

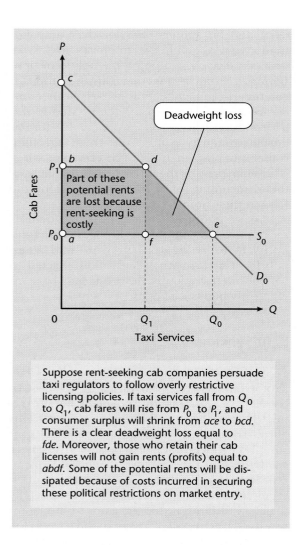

Suppose rent-seeking cab companies persuade taxi regulators to follow overly restrictive licensing policies. If taxi services fall from Q_0 to Q_1, cab fares will rise from P_0 to P_1, and consumer surplus will shrink from ace to bcd. There is a clear deadweight loss equal to fde. Moreover, those who retain their cab licenses will not gain rents (profits) equal to $abdf$. Some of the potential rents will be dissipated because of costs incurred in securing these political restrictions on market entry.

FIGURE 2   Why Rent Seekers' Gains Are Less than the Resulting Social Losses

uses overly restrictive licensing of taxicabs to show why rent-seeking behavior is often economically inefficient and reduces social well-being.

Suppose the taxi market is initially in a competitive equilibrium, with supply S_0 being perfectly elastic at price P_0, and that demand is D_0. Consumer surplus equals triangle ace, and cab companies cover all their costs, including a normal return on their investment. If major taxi operators thought that regulators could be

persuaded to restrict competition, they could follow a rent-seeking strategy. They might cite horror stories to prove that some unwary tourists were gouged by unethical drivers as evidence of the evils of cutthroat competition. Suppose that taxi licenses were restricted to Q_1, and were granted only to solid, reputable companies. Cab fares would rise to P_1, shrinking consumer surplus to bcd. The loss of consumer surplus equals the trapezoid $abde$.

At first glance, society's deadweight loss appears to equal triangle fde, with taxi companies reaping economic rent equal to $abdf$. Rent seeking, however, also absorbs resources directly, shrinking the gains of taxi firms and increasing the deadweight loss to society. Interest groups incur costs when seeking favorable policies and devote resources to mold laws and regulations as long as the expected marginal gains exceed the expected marginal costs. Consultants, lawyers, and professional lobbyists are hired by the parties on all sides of many issues; time and money is absorbed by hearings in front of regulatory boards or legislative committees. In some cases, crooked lawmakers or regulators who recognize the potential gains may solicit bribes for favorable policies. None of these costs are incurred productively. The net result of rent-seeking behavior is a continuing social loss for as long as inefficient policies are in place, plus losses equal to the costs incurred by interest groups to secure favorable laws or regulations or to oppose unfavorable ones.

We have now discussed voting procedures, political campaigning, and the legislative process from a public choice perspective. Once laws are made, they must be administered. This brings us to the topic of government bureaucracy.

BUREAUCRACY

A government could print a good edition of Shakespeare's works, but it could not get them written.

Alfred Marshall

Whether private or public, large organizations develop extensive formal operating rules or managerial coordination becomes impossible. The resulting mountains of red tape cause many people to view bureaucracy as almost synonymous with mindless inefficiency.

*Any large task-oriented organization is a **bureaucracy**.*

The federal government is by far our largest employer. State and local governments also hire their share of workers, as shown in Table 4. Federal, state, and local governments employ over one out of six American workers. Most government employees work in the agencies, or *bureaus*, that implement the laws passed by legislatures. Note that most of the growth of government employment in recent years has come at the state or local level—primarily, more teachers, social workers, police officers, firefighters, and so on.

Many government bureaucrats work hard because they believe deeply in the mission of their agency. Economic theory suggests, however, that the best starting point for analysis of behavior is the assumption of self-interest. Anyone who has worked in a large organization knows that opportunities for raises and promotions are closely tied to the organization's fortunes; prosperity and growth yield larger personnel budgets in both public and private bureaucracies. Thus, we can expect career employees of any large organization to push for growth and to fight budget cuts.

Many government agencies have worse reputations than business bureaucracies. Incentive structures may be the reason. Divisions of private firms are usually profit centers, with growth depending on serving more customers better and at lower cost. Ascertaining efficiency is much harder in government bureaus that use tax revenues to cover costs. Legislators tend to consider whether a public service is provided adequately. If not, a standard solution is to boost funding. Thus, paradoxically, inefficiency may swell a bureau's budget. Competition drives the opposite trend in the private sector.

After reviewing 50 international studies of cost differences between publicly and privately provided services, Dennis Mueller, a public choice specialist, concluded, "The evidence that public provision of a service reduces the efficiency of its provision seems overwhelming."[1] In 40 out of 50 cases, public sector enterprises were significantly less efficient than their private counterparts, and in only two cases were public agencies relatively more efficient. Figure 3 presents a sample of the results of these studies.

Have you noticed that it is often easier to buy auto insurance than to get a license for a new car? That the time absorbed in buying 10 bags of groceries is often less than the time spent waiting in a line at the Post Office to buy a roll of stamps? Rewards for efficiency are few in government bureaucracies and may cause relative inefficiency because (*a*) services may be supplied to the public at the convenience of government employees rather than vice versa and (*b*) government tends to pay relatively high prices. The basic problem probably originates with the warped incentives common in many government bureaus. You may have read about outrageous cost overruns in Department of Defense contracts. Focus 1 details some reasons for such apparent waste.

TABLE 4   Government Employment

	Millions of Government Employees		
	1970	1981	1993
Federal	5.0	4.5	4.5
Military	2.1	1.7	1.6
Civilian	2.9	2.8	2.9
State	2.8	3.6	4.5
Local	7.4	9.6	11.5
Total	15.2	17.7	20.5

Sources: U. S. Department of Commerce, Bureau of Economic Analysis, *Business Statistics, 1963–1991* (Washington DC: U.S. Government Printing Office, June 1992); and U.S. Department of Commerce, *Survey of Current Business*, February 1994.

---

[1]Dennis C. Mueller, *Public Choice II* (New York: Cambridge University Press, 1989).

FIGURE 3 Public Versus Private Provision of Comparable Services

INDUSTRY (COUNTRY)

Percentage by which Public Sector Costs
Exceed Private Sector Costs

Source: Dennis C. Mueller, *Public Choice II* (New York: Cambridge University Press), *1989, pp. 262–265.*

Many studies of public versus private provision of goods and services support the notion that efficiency declines when goods or services are provided publicly. The bars above represent ranges of costs. A value of 0 indicates that the service is provided at the same cost whether provided by a public or a private entity.

Empire Building

> It is a commonplace observation that work expands so as to fill the time available for its completion. Politicians and taxpayers have assumed with occasional phases of doubt that a rising total in the number of civil servants must reflect a growing volume of work to be done. Cynics, in questioning this belief, have imagined that the multiplication of officials must have left some of them idle or all of them able to work for shorter hours. But this is a matter in which faith and doubt seem equally misplaced. The fact is that the number of the officials and the quantity of the work to be done are not related to each other at all.

C. Northcote Parkinson[2]

Salary and status in a bureaucracy tend to be positively related to the numbers and levels of employees a manager supervises and the budget for which the manager is responsible. Thus, managers at all levels have incentives to acquire as many employees as possible, a practice termed *empire building*. In business, this usually

---

[2]C. Northcote Parkinson, "Parkinson's Law," *The Economist*, November 1955.

requires showing that your division has extraordinary profit potential. In government bureaus, however, it normally requires persuading legislators of the enormity of the problem your agency is supposed to cure. Thus, law enforcement officials predictably talk about organized crime and anarchy in the streets; educators decry teacher shortages and growing demands on our schools; admirals and generals stress world unrest; agriculture officials lament the plight of the family farmer—the ways bureaucrats try to build demands for their services seem endless.

The Growth of Government

Few experts in any field ever conclude that their area will be of less concern in the foreseeable future. Thus, there are few credible witnesses to dispute claims that society needs to devote more resources in any number of directions. This is another instance of asymmetric information and principal—agent problems in governmental processes. The result is that legislators,

Government Contracts

Military contracts for new weapons systems are almost uniformly plagued by mammoth cost over-runs. The Department of Defense (DOD) has paid $400 for $17 hammers, $56 for 8 cent Allen wrenches, and $27 for screws that hardware stores sell for less than a dime. Prices for custom-built items in aircraft are even more startling: $600 armrests and toilet covers, $400 ashtrays, and $17,000 coffeepots. The U.S. Army abandoned its unserviceable Sergeant York battle tank after sinking almost $8 billion into the project.

Critics cite examples of this sort to indict defense contractors for price gouging and to cite all of the bureaucrats who administered these contracts for incompetence. If the basic problems were this simple, the solution would be incredibly straightforward: prosecute dishonest contractors and deny them future contracts, and hire competent administrators.

Some contracts require delivery of weapons systems years into the future, and inflation may drive up costs. For high-tech weapons, it takes 8 to 16 years to go from concept exploration to full-scale production and deployment. Many weapon systems are obsolete by the time they are battle ready. Contract specifications are often vague because designs are still on the drawing board. Bids on such projects cannot be ironclad.

The nature of government contracting, however, may make problems of this type unavoidable. Defense procurement, for example, is characterized by (a) all or nothing competition (if an aircraft company loses or does not bid on a new stealth bomber, it may not have another opportunity for 20 years), (b) high technological demands and product precision uncertainty (many projects are vaguely specified initially, but have

demanding requirements in the end), (c) unpredictable funding because of changing world events and the political nature of long-term contracts, and (d) heavy capital requirements.

A recent study summarized the precarious world of defense contracting:
The buyer can pressure the seller to reduce prices or threaten to stop purchasing altogether, leaving the seller with heavy capital outlays that reap no returns. Suppliers are clearly reluctant to make such investments for fear of exploitation. Inducements to do so include charging higher prices (to compensate for the risk) and writing long-term contracts with stiff penalty clauses for buyer withdrawal. . . . [D]efense transactions have an implicit third party. Not only are a producer and a military buyer involved, but the U.S. Congress as well, with the latter intermittenly withholding funding [to force] . . . changes in the procurement. Not surprisingly, with Congress reluctant to permit multiyear contracts, recourse to higher selling prices is a main inducement for firms to remain as defense contractors.

Some problems with government contracting lurk in bureaucratic behavior. C. Northcote Parkinson, an English writer, developed "laws" of bureaucracy, one of which is "work expands to absorb the time available." As a project unfolds, specifications tend to grow excessively complex, which can be extremely costly. This occurs because many bureaucrats try to stay (or look) busy. One easy way to stay busy is to constantly write directives that detail the work of people you supervise. One DOD recipe for fruitcake is an unintentionally comic example—it took 18 pages. The recipe for a modern aircraft carrier runs to hundreds of thousands of pages. If

the ratio of overspecification for fruitcake holds for U.S. Navy ships, the excess costs from this problem alone sum to billions of dollars. Doing business with the Pentagon is not easy. Reporting and oversight by DOD is thick and burdensome. So much so, that from 1982 to 1987 (the height of the Reagan defense buildup), the number of defense suppliers fell by two-thirds.**

Another problem is that contractors and contract administrators may share interests that violate the public interest. For example, many retired generals and admirals ultimately go to work for defense contractors. If you were about to retire as a high-ranking military officer, might you be understanding about exorbitant costs incurred by a contractor in accommodating your design changes, especially if that firm was a major employer of someone with your expertise?

Such problems are not unique to the military. Government office buildings, flood control projects, highways, and nuclear power plants also often entail sloppy work and cost overruns. Between 1989 and 1994, the cost of constructing the new Denver International Airport rose from $1.8 billion to almost $4 billion dollars, and it was a year behind schedule.

We can only touch on some problems of government procurement; a detailed discussion would take volumes. The ultimate problem is inadequate incentives for efficiency. The costs of the resulting inefficiencies are borne by taxpayers.

*Donald L. Losman and Shu-jan Liang, *The Promise of American Industry*, (Westport, CT: Quorum Books), 1990, pp. 126--127.
**James Blackwell et al., *Deterrence in Decay*, (Washington, D.C.: Center for Strategic and International Studies, May 1989), p. 31.

many of whom might want to slash taxes, are inundated with well-documented requests for more funding in support of almost all programs.

Pressing social problems seem to beget new programs that acquire lives of their own, even if the original problem fades away. Trying to identify areas to cut is often an exercise in frustration. Interest groups (including bureaucrats) become accustomed to programs that benefit them and always want more rather than less. Attempts to cut any spending category provoke intense lobbying. One common strategy used by bureau chiefs to combat proposed budget cuts is to assert that any cuts threaten a bureau's most popular services. This usually arouses loud support from the bureau's clients. This was one tactic used by some opponents of attempts to cut military spending in the early 1990s. When military bases were scheduled to be closed, local merchants made sure that their elected officials worked long and hard to keep open facilities that were the hub of local commerce. The predictable result of the political processes described in this chapter? Government grows and grows, with no end in sight.

Public choice analysis identifies a number of problems inherent in political processes. Voting only crudely signals citizens' preferences and is flawed by apathy and rational ignorance; candidates base campaigns on image instead of substance; legislation is diverted from efficiently satisfying public wants by logrolling, pork barrel projects, and rent seeking; and bureaucratization yields incentives for sloth and artificial growth.

MARKET FAILURE VS. GOVERNMENT FAILURE

We have discussed how markets operate and how they may fail. This part of the book focuses on the tasks of government and why it may fail to accomplish these tasks appropriately. Most economic issues can be placed on a continuum that stretches from problems efficiently resolved in markets on one end, to issues that seem to re-

TABLE 5 Market Failures vs. Political Failures

Market Failure	Political Failure
1. Uncertainty about the future.	1. Uncertainty about the future.
2. Rational ignorance about consuming and investing.	2. Rational political ignorance.
3. Free riders for public goods.	3. Rational apathy and nonvoting.
4. Asymmetric information and principal–agent problems (e.g., between firms and employees).	4. Asymmetric information and principal–agent problems (e.g., between constituents and their elected representatives).
5. Externalities and pollution.	5. Tie-in-sales aspects of voting. All voting systems fail to fine-tune spending patterns to reflect the intensities of voters' preferences.
6. Monopoly power.	6. Disproportionate political power for special interests.
7. Inequity in the distributions of income and wealth.	7. Majorities may inefficiently or inequitably vote against interests of minorities.
8. Fosters greediness and unhealthy competitiveness.	8. Fosters bureaucracy and empire building.

quire collective action at the other extreme. Whether a particular issue is best resolved in markets or through government is sometimes murky in the broad middle of this continuum. The answer may depend largely on the relative speed and precision with which these allocative mechanisms correct errors or adjust to changing circumstances.

Self-Corrections

On average, markets tend to respond quickly and efficiently to changes in consumer wants and to mistakes made by business decision-makers. For example, if markets fail to synchronize the plans of the buyers and sellers of a pure private good (thermal underwear or guacamole dip, for example), price adjustments tend to cure the resulting shortages or surpluses rather quickly. On the other hand, markets may never adequately provide such public goods as national defense, so these goods are provided through government.

Political adjustments are inherently slow in a democracy, however. When an elected official becomes extremely unpopular, voters must normally wait for the next election to throw the rascal out: coups or assassinations are undemocratic. If a legislature enacts a disastrous policy, it may take years to repair the damage by changing the law. Once on the books, laws, regulations, and spending programs are hard to remove. Even though political solutions may be slow and inexact, government policy may be superior to private decision-making when markets fail because of concentrated economic power, nonrivalry, nonexclusion, or inequity. Table 5 summarizes some failings of both the marketplace and government as allocative mechanisms.

We will examine some of the public policies that the government pursues to deal with some possible market failures in the next two chapters. As you read this material, keep in mind the simple lesson of the current chapter: markets sometimes perform poorly, but so does government.

CHAPTER REVIEW: KEY POINTS

1. No allocative mechanism works perfectly. Just as markets fail in some cases, forces within all political systems can prevent government from reflecting the preferences of the people governed. **Public choice analysis** entails economic analysis of political behavior.

2. The probability that one vote will swing a major election is close to infinitesimal. Because the personal payoffs from voting are small, many people do not vote, nor do most find it personally worthwhile to inform themselves on a broad range of social issues. This is known as **rational political ignorance** and tends to be even more prevalent than the lack of information confronted when people make market decisions. *Asymmetric information* and principal–agent problems also pervade political processes.

3. All voting systems are flawed in that economic efficiency may be lost through political decision-making. **Majority rule** voting tends to impose losses on those taking minority positions; this is inefficient if their losses exceed the majority's gains. Majority rule may also lead to inconsistent or unstable political choices.

4. A **unanimity** rule ensures that all changes in laws are efficient, because everyone must expect to gain before acquiescing to a change. People who are reasonably indifferent about a policy change, however, might require excessive compensation for agreeing to the change from those who stand to gain much from the change. This would make changing policies a very cumbersome and time-consuming process. Moreover, a unanimity rule assumes that the initial situation is equitable, which may be untrue.

5. **Point voting** would allow voters to indicate their preferences by allocating votes in proportion to how strongly they felt about some issues relative to others. This system is flawed, however, by the potential for strategic behavior; people might not vote their preferences per se, tending instead to weigh their votes according to how they expected others to vote.

6. Voting is a *lumpy* process; we cannot pick and choose among the political stances taken by the candidates for an office. The market permits us to fine-tune our decisions, but we generally can choose only a single candidate or platform when we vote.

7. Attempts to maximize their chances for election cause candidates and political parties to try to attract the **median voter**, whose vote tends to determine the outcomes of elections. Rational ignorance among voters causes many candidates to avoid taking stands on issues while attempting to project a moderate image. Political competition for the support of the median voter causes candidates and parties to cluster around *middle-of-the-road* positions and creates pressures for a *two-party system*.

8. **Logrolling** occurs when lawmakers trade votes. This allows legislators to register the intensities of their preferences, because they trade votes about which they care little for votes on things about which they feel strongly. Logrolling can, however, re-sult in inefficient amounts of **pork barrel legislation**, which occurs when projects that have primarily local benefits are paid for by a broader taxpaying public.

9. One proposed check on pork barrel legislation is to grant the president the right of a **line-item veto**, whereby the chief executive can delete items from a spending bill before signing it.

10. **Special-interest groups** may be overrepresented because of low voter turnouts, widespread rational political ignorance, and intense lobbying. However, intensities of preference may be better reflected in political decisions because of this overrepresentation.

11. **Rent-seeking** involves attempts by special-interest groups to manipulate government policies for private gain, even though the social costs of special laws or regulations would exceed the expected benefits to the interest group that seeks economic rents.

12. The efficiency of most government **bureaucracies** is hard to measure, and the absence of a profit motive reduces incentives for efficiency in the public sector. Managerial salaries and perks are often tied to the numbers of employees supervised and the size of the agency budget, which leads to **empire building** and further growth of government.

QUESTIONS FOR THOUGHT AND DISCUSSION

1. Why will radical candidates tend to moderate their positions if they want to increase their prospects for election?

2. It is illegal to buy votes in the United States. Can you explain why this ban on the sale of votes is economically inefficient? Would it be desirable to make it legal for people to sell their votes? Why or why not?

3. Several positions are sometimes filled through a single election. For example, the top three (or five or seven) vote getters might be elected to a school board or as a county commissioners. Why do some voters cast their ballots for fewer than the number of candidates who will gain office, even if they have preferences among those for whom they don't vote?

4. Medical doctors are sometimes accused of building the demands for their services by exaggerating minor health problems and heightening the concerns of their patients. How might high-level government bureaucrats enhance the sizes and powers of their agencies through similar processes? What political institutions would they need to manipulate? Can you cite any cases where this type of thing seems to have occurred?

5. The market system and government are both allocative mechanisms. What are some advantages and disadvantages of each? In what areas now dominated by market forces should government assume a greater role, if any? In what areas should government allow market forces greater latitude? Why?

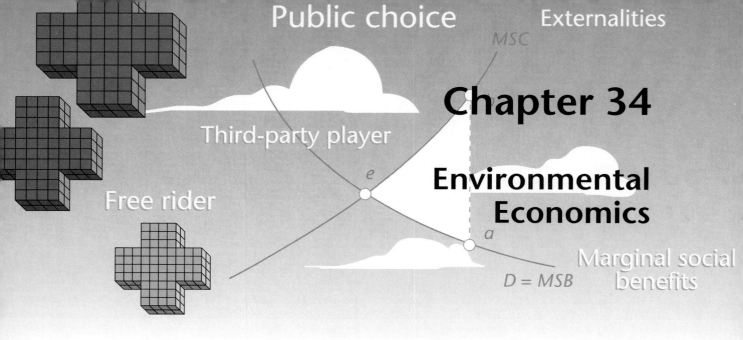

Public choice   Externalities

MSC

Third-party player

Free rider

e

Chapter 34

Environmental Economics

a

$D = MSB$

Marginal social benefits

Three Billion Years Plus a Few Minutes

ooze
cohesion, opulence
twinges, space, undulations
slithering, boring, hatching, germination
increase, complexity, blooming, coordination, cooperation
predation, parasitism, migration, competition, adaptation, selection
crowding, starvation, disease, populations, diversity, camouflage, mimicry
specialization, reduction, exclusion, conversion, blight, drought
pressure, defeat, decline, smoke, decimation
explosion, abuse, ignorance, teeming
contamination, residual, choking
silence, stillness
ooze

William T. Barry, from *Reflection*

William Barry's poem hints that the earth may turn into a dead planet over the long haul. Is this inevitable? Campaigns to improve environmental quality are in a race against population growth and production processes that convert raw resources into waste. At current population growth rates of 1.7% annually, world population will exceed 6 billion by the year 2000. Some resources needed to sustain life as we know it are already strained at the seams. As we try to stretch the earth's carrying capacity through extensive resource use, environmental decay and resource depletion rear their ugly heads. Mountains of garbage and problems like acid rain, nuclear waste, and oil spills become increasingly obvious, and environmentalists warn us about emerging dangers from ozone depletion, the greenhouse effect, and global warming.

Developed economies in Europe, North America, and Japan contain only one-third of the world's population but use almost four-fifths of all resources and generate about two-thirds of all pollutants. Despite ambitious development plans in emerging economies to boost per capita output to the levels enjoyed in developed economies, they produce less, so they use relatively fewer resources. However, their technologies tend to be dirtier, so they produce relatively more pollution per unit of GDP.

Raw materials entering production and consumption systems are ultimately converted into goods, noxious gases, dirty water, solid wastes, heat, or radiation. Some resources seem about to vanish, so attaining a uniformly high

Solid Waste Recycling

The problem with waste is that everyone wants you to pick it up and no one wants you to put it down.
        William Ruckelshaus
        (former EPA Director)

Recycling and waste management are growth industries. Americans will discard over 150 million tons of solid waste this year—enough to fill 80 lanes of garbage trucks extending from coast to coast. Nearly half of all states will fill their existing landfills by the year 2000. Stiff environmental regulations make average costs for new landfills nearly $60 million, but a NIMBY (not in my backyard) syndrome largely prevents their development. Figure 1 indicates the composition of this 150 million tons of garbage.

Moral suasion has swayed the American psyche favorably toward recycling as a remedy for environmental waste. Paper, plastics, metals, and glass are popular candidates for recycling. Aluminum cans represent a huge success cited by proponents of recycling. Virgin aluminum from bauxite is ten times more expensive than ingots from recycled cans. The relatively high prices paid for scrap aluminum have resulted in more than half of all aluminum beverage cans being recycled.

Too many recycling efforts, unfortunately, merely alter the form and place of environmental decay. Filtering airborne and waterborne pollutants, for example, results in dirty filters and mounds of solid waste. Burning solid waste, in turn, increases air pollution. Most cities have abandoned experiments with incinerators, which reflected attempts to increase the longevity of existing landfill space and produce energy as a by-product. Los Angeles, for example, dropped its incinerator project after one study indicated that burning trash might cause one additional Californian to develop cancer each year.

Consider paper and cardboard, which represent nearly 40% of all solid waste. Too few recycling paper mills are available to accomplish the recycling many municipalities now mandate; only eight mills are operating, and most are too remote from urban centers for cost-effective collection and transport. Buyer reluctance to use recycled newsprint—because it tears easily, disrupting tight deadlines by jamming high-speed presses— is another problem.

Paper bundles presented for recycling vary in quality. Recycling is impeded by dirty bundles: mixtures of newsprint, shopping bags,

junk mail, cardboard, catalogs, phone books, magazines, and so on. Equipment cannot satisfactorily sort dirty bundles, necessitating human labor. Clean bundles fetch $12 per ton, but municipalities are charged $20 per ton for the processing of dirty bundles. Teaching consumers who conscientiously try to recycle about the importance of keeping bundles clean is a key to making it economically viable. More than a million tons of dirty bundles of newsprint awaited recycling in 1994.

Restructuring local government trash collection policies might enhance the success of recycling efforts. Most cities charge flat fees or pay for garbage collection through property taxes. To homeowners or tenants, adding additional cans for trash pickups entails only the cost of a new can and the effort required to move it to the curb. Some cities now use a per-can charge to encourage citizens to recycle and to be selective in the products they purchase. Residents who pay by their volume of trash tend to avoid relatively small products enclosed in large bulky packages. Trash collection has declined by an average of 25% in cities where per-can fees have been instituted. One rising problem that was predictable, however, is an increasing tendency for people to secretly dump their trash by the roadside or in business dumpsters in attempts to avoid these fees.

Per-trash-can fees, taxes on nonrecyclables, deposits on cans and bottles, and rewards for trash separation are only a few steps toward meeting the EPA goal of recycling 25% of our trash by 1995. Ensuring that recycling does not simply trade one form of pollution for a worse form of pollution is vital, as are the appropriate incentives for consumers, firms, and government agencies.

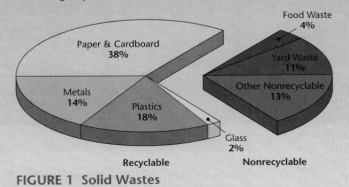

FIGURE 1 Solid Wastes

quality of life may require either massive recycling or technological advances based on resources that are now unusable. The issue of recycling is addressed in Focus 1. Enhanced environmental quality entails sacrifice; by raising the explicit costs and prices of many goods, controlling pollution disrupts traditional ways of doing things and often foments a political backlash.

Categorizing externalities relative to other economic activities is our first task in this chapter. How property rights evolve and how ambiguous property rights cause environmental problems are our next topics. Our attention then turns to types of externalities, and we describe how to determine optimal amounts of pollution. This chapter ends by examining alternative approaches to pollution and current U.S. environmental policies.

MARKET FAILURE AND THE ENVIRONMENT

Environmental problems usually reflect market failures that originate from the technical characteristics of certain goods or in the nature of their production. We will look at some of these characteristics before considering environmental issues in detail.

Characteristics of Goods

The rival-nonrival and exclusive-nonexclusive relationships (discussed earlier, in the chapter, "Market Failure and Public Finance") are combined in goods in various ways.

• **Private, Public, and Excess Capacity Goods** Goods that are both rival and exclusive are pure private goods and tend to be efficiently provided by the marketplace. Most goods, from apples to zithers, are pure private goods. Pure public goods are both nonexclusive and nonrival. Weather forecasts on TV, for example, are nonrival, simultaneously benefiting all who want to make plans for picnics. Forecasts are also nonexclusive: preventing this information from spreading is virtually impossible. Private meteorologists can do little to prevent people from passing weather forecasts along. Hence, the U.S. Weather Service is the major source of basic weather information. Nonexclusivity makes it hard for private forecasters to survive.

A combination of nonrivalry and exclusiveness generally entails excess capacity. Theaters with empty seats or airline flights with unsold tickets offer examples of nonrival goods, but you can be excluded from flying or enjoying movies. Unless economies of scale are so significant that market power is concentrated (e.g., the monopoly problem), competitive markets normally provide these goods efficiently. However, crowding may diminish the enjoyment of some goods (e.g., theaters or public parks) when more and more people try to use them. Congestion and environmental decay often emerge when this occurs.

• **Environmental Problems** Congestion and nonexclusion from the use of some scarce goods are keys to environmental breakdown. All allocative systems, including markets, almost uniformly fail when the costs of excluding a person who does not pay to use a good are prohibitive relative to the value of that good. A nonexclusive but rival good is typically overused, if it is provided at all.[1] If I enjoy scenery but also value the roadside as a garbage site, I may toss soda pop cans out my window as I drive down the highway. The resultant eyesore and the costs of cleaning up my litter are borne by taxpayers at large; my personal costs are trivial. (Most antilitter laws are only weakly enforced.) In some jurisdictions, people required to do community service (instead of jail time) spend their hours picking up roadside litter.

Public parks on holidays and traffic congestion are examples of rival but nonexclusive activities. It sometimes seems that everyone wants to drive during rush hour or on holidays.

---

[1] Firms cannot profit from and, consequently, will not produce goods if people can enjoy the goods regardless of whether they pay.

Limiting access to roads is seldom feasible, so many commuters sit idle, with their engines running and emitting air pollutants.

Abuse of the environment becomes rampant when both nonexclusion and rivalry for resource usage are present. In England, everyone once had access to certain fields for grazing that were held in common, but these *commons* were often treated as though no one owned them. The **tragedy of the commons** occurred because individuals lacked the personal ownership incentives to maintain the property, so pasture land that was common property was typically overused and rundown. Modern examples of the tragedy of the commons include the extinction of various species because of overfishing and overwhaling in international waters.

Despite the nonexclusivity of environmental quality, Focus 1 suggests that many Americans are increasingly so concerned about this issue that they incur personal costs to recycle the solid waste that threatens to bury us under mountains of garbage.

Pollution as a Public Bad, Abatement as a Public Good

A public good, once produced, benefits many people, none of whom can be excluded from enjoying its use. *Pollution abatement* (reduction) generally fits this definition. Everyone in Los Angeles could enjoy a clearer view of the horizon and breath more easily if smog were eliminated. Thus, environmental quality is a public good. The public good and externality aspects of pollution and its control suggest that government policies may be needed to steer production and consumption toward optimal levels.

We dealt with public goods and excess capacity (e.g., natural monopoly) problems in previous chapters. Many economists view pollution as a problem that might be resolved if all natural resources were private property so that owners had incentives to manage these environmental resources properly.

THE EVOLUTION OF PROPERTY RIGHTS

The evolution of environmental policy in the United States is a textbook case of development of *property rights* to scarce resources and of government involvement in this activity.

> ***Private property rights*** *assign individuals or organizations the rights to control access to certain resources or assets, including rights to charge for their use.*

Property rights usually develop in stages: (*a*) common access and nonscarcity, (*b*) common access and scarcity, (*c*) agency restrictions, and (*d*) fee-simple property rights.

Common access resources are available on a first-come, first-served basis. Vast buffalo herds that once roamed North America, for example, were treated by most Native American tribes as held in common. Scarcity is not a problem until growth of population and output create overuse. These resources are then quickly depleted or become congested or polluted. Buffalo were massacred as railroads and cities penetrated the American West. Other examples of the abuse of the commons include the dumping of waste in the ocean, or such activities as littering the highways and loud noises in residential neighborhoods.

Most modern economies are now beyond the common access and scarcity stage, because the greater productivity possible from restricted resource use causes abandonment of common-use policies. The enclosure movement in England and range wars between cattle ranchers and sheepherders in the old American West offer examples of conflicts during transitions from common use to limited use. We usually then move on to fee-simple property rights.

Fee-simple property rights allow the owner to use property in any fashion, including sale or destruction, as long as others' physical property (but not necessarily the financial value) is unaffected. (The term "fee-simple" means that monetary payments usually accompany transfers of ownership.) Evolution from common access and nonscarcity to scarcity (and overuse) of a resource usually leads to a system of property rights. Fee-simple property rights are basic for the attainment of economic efficiency in a competitive market economy. Market failure is common whenever fee-simple property rights seem impractical.

Property rights are efficient social remedies to externalities. Two major reasons why property rights sometimes fail to develop are that certain types of property rights might be (a) very costly to define and enforce and (b) traded in ways that hinder the value of property owned by others. When definition and enforcement of rights to property are excessively costly, public control or legal conventions tend to govern allocation. Stoplights, nontransferable hunting licenses, pro rata shares of common-pool oil leases, and technological restrictions on ocean fishing are all cases where a system of fee-simple property rights appears so costly that reasonably efficient alternatives to markets have developed.

Political intervention is also common when one person's actions reduce the value—but not the physical characteristics—of another's property. Such cases involve *pecuniary* (monetary) externalities. If your job pays $10 an hour and I offer to do it for $5 an hour, your labor becomes less valuable. Thus, labor market access is legally restricted; immigration policies and child labor laws are examples. If you sell milk for $2 a gallon and I offer to sell it for $1 a gallon, the market value of your milk (and your dairy) declines.

Transactions in many markets are controlled after high-price producers secure laws limiting competition from low-price producers. Protecting pecuniary interests and not merely the physical rights of others tends to be inefficient; production costs are generally excessive. If an external effect is strictly pecuniary rather than physical, all parties pay the same prices, which efficiently tend to equal marginal social costs. For example, if growing competition from burger chains for the potato crop raises potato prices in grocery stores, the price hikes merely reflect greater social demands for potatoes.

Property Rights and Environmental Quality

Abuse of shared resources—clean air and water, scenic beauty, or peace and quiet—creates decay. Smog, foul water, litter, and airport noise are evidence that overuse of common property may fail to lead to efficient social institutions such as fully specified property rights. The debate continues about how much purity to seek and what techniques to use.

At one pole, some critics view "greedy capitalism" as the root cause of environmental decay and economic analysis as irrelevant. Fervent environmentalists were among the leading opponents of the 1993 North American Free Trade Agreement (NAFTA), on the grounds that increased production in Mexico, with its less stringent environmental standards, would be counterproductive. The basic position of these environmentalists tends to be "forbid all pollution." The view that capitalistic markets are the basic problem, however, is contradicted by recent revelations about environmental disasters in countries that once followed avowedly socialist policies. For example, the nuclear meltdown at Chernobyl in the Ukraine reflected lack of environmental safeguards. Parts of Romania and Poland (Silesia) are among the most polluted regions on earth, being covered with soot emitted because factories strove to meet output quotas set without regard for the environmental consequences.

At the opposite pole are those who believe that fully specified property rights harmonize economic activity. These people believe that if individuals are assigned full rights to control specific resources, a market economy will arrive at an equilibrium with a healthy and efficient ecology. We will examine both extreme views and some intermediate positions as well; but first, let us readdress externalities, the origin of many environmental problems.

EXTERNALITIES

Competition tends to maximize both individual welfare and the public interest if only the parties *directly* involved in transactions are affected; marginal social benefits tend to equal marginal social costs.[2] But if external parties are physically (and not merely monetarily) affected, market prices and quantities usually fail to account for their preferences and social welfare may not be efficiently served.

> *Externalities* occur when private calculations of costs or benefits differ from the costs or benefits to society. Externalities are present whenever third parties gain without paying for their marginal benefits or lose without being compensated for the harm they endure.

Of course, payments by external beneficiaries or compensation for external costs transforms a third party into a participant in a transaction, effectively internalizing the externality. For example, if my neighbors agreed to accept my offer of $1,000 to let me put a neon sign on my house, irritation about the neon sign would be internalized. And if such payments were necessary, the neighbors' preferences would be recognized, and I would be less likely to put up the sign. Only *uncompensated* externalities create inefficiency. Such externalities may emerge from either consumption or production.

External Benefits

Some *external benefits* originate in production. For example, a pharmaceutical firm might develop knowledge to cure some deadly disease. Legal monopolies on knowledge are prohibited, however, so the firm could not prevent competitors from using the knowledge. Only techniques uniquely embedded in some commodity or piece of equipment are patentable.

External benefits occur not only in production, but in consumption as well. If you landscape your yard, your neighbors may benefit without sharing in your expenses. Their property values rise, and they gain more attractive

---

[2]Perhaps naively, this statement assumes that the distribution of income is not a problem. We treated issues of income distribution in an earlier chapter.

scenery, sweet-smelling flowers, and the like. If your family is inoculated against a contagious disease, your neighbors gain because their chances of contracting the disease decline. If you study economics in your spare time, you may enjoy a happier and more productive life. But if, at the same time, you become a more informed voter and better citizen, these gains are shared with people throughout this country. These are just a few examples of possible external benefits from consumption.

Without compensation to those who generate external benefits, activities that embody positive externalities may be less than optimal. For example, applied research may be profitable for a private firm because specific applications are patentable, but basic research is seldom pursued privately because the broad benefits of new knowledge cannot be marketed by the researchers. Similarly, children gain from education, but others also gain if education improves citizenship. If education were strictly private, it might be overpriced, and far fewer people would extend their schooling. People would quit buying education as soon as another unit of learning cost more than they expected it to be worth to them. They would not consider gains to their neighbors when deciding how much education to obtain.

From the consumption side, suppose that planting flowering trees in your yard boosts both your personal satisfaction and the value of your property. Your private demand for flowering trees is shown in Figure 2 as demand curve D_p. You can purchase all the trees that you desire for P_0 and plant Q_0 trees. Your neighbors may enjoy the trees nearly as much as you do, and the value of their property may be enhanced by your trees.

Demand curve D_S incorporates your private demand plus the social benefits to your neighbors from your flowering trees. The marginal social benefits of your actions are the sum of any private benefits to you plus any external benefits enjoyed by other people. Getting these other people to pay for their benefits is, unfortunately, very difficult.

Maximum social welfare occurs when marginal social benefits and costs are equal, so optimal planting of trees would be Q_S. But you may not plant Q_S trees unless you are compensated for your investment beyond Q_0. This could be accomplished if the government subsidizes tree planting by bc dollars per tree. Without compensation covering the external benefits to your neighbors, you all will miss an opportunity to gain with no one losing. The reason is that in your private decision-making, you tend to weigh your private costs and benefits much more heavily than any external benefits, which are usually ignored.

One cure for potential underproduction is communal arrangements, which may be either implicit or explicit. Implicit agreements occur when neighbors encourage each other to improve their properties through such things as informal and friendly competition: who has the nicest house, the prettiest lawn, and so on.

Implicit agreements tend to work best when only a few people are involved. Explicit agreements (community covenants or zoning) are more common when larger numbers must cooperate; all residents of some subdivisions may be required to have so many square feet of living space, or they may be prohibited from painting their homes other than approved colors, or each may agree to spend a certain amount on landscaping, and so on. In general, as the number of people affected by an externality grows, restrictions on behavior tend to become more formal and less flexible.

External Costs

Pollution can arise from either consumption or production. Water pollution flows primarily from production processes; air and noise pollution result about equally from both. For example, both industrial wastes and the residues from washing dishes flow into sewer systems and then into our water supplies. Automobiles, smokestack industries, and coal-fired electricity generation all contribute to the smog that engulfs many major cities and results in corrosive acid rain that falls on even some remote regions of our world. Many forms of production generate external costs. Examples include noise pollution near airports, unsightly billboards and junkyards, and factories that belch noxious smoke.

Suppose farmers use pesticides on artichoke crops and then irrigate their fields, washing pesticide onto adjacent properties and into nearby streams because enforceable property rights to water are absent. If pesticide works its way up the ecological chain—harming your fishing and health—then you, who may never eat artichokes, partially bear the cost of artichoke production. Assume all farmers exude external costs of $2 per pound of artichokes when using chemical sprays. In Figure 3, the supply curve S_0 is based only on farmers' costs, but the marginal social cost (MSC) is $2 higher.

Suppose artichoke farmers are now taxed $2 per pound to cover all social costs of production if harmful pesticides are used. The price initially rises from $5 per pound to $6, and out-

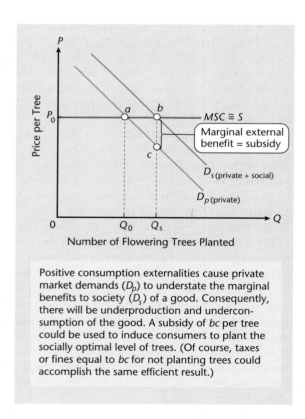

Positive consumption externalities cause private market demands (D_p) to understate the marginal benefits to society (D_s) of a good. Consequently, there will be underproduction and underconsumption of the good. A subsidy of bc per tree could be used to induce consumers to plant the socially optimal level of trees. (Of course, taxes or fines equal to bc for not planting trees could accomplish the same efficient result.)

FIGURE 2 **Positive Consumption Externalities**

put falls to 60,000 tons. Why prices rise and output falls is straightforward. There is a $2 vertical shift of supply from S_0 to MSC when farmers' private costs rise $2 per pound. Farmers formerly grew 100,000 tons annually at private costs of $5 per pound, which are now $2 per pound more for each output level when harmful sprays are used.

Unfortunately for artichoke growers, consumers would not continue to buy 100,000 tons if the price climbed to $7 per pound. The higher production costs will cause marginal farmers to fail, as consumers reduce artichoke consumption to 60,000 tons annually and the price rises to $6 per pound. Equilibrium moves from point a to point b in the short run, but farmers will look for ways to avoid this $2 pollution charge. Suppose that in the long run they discover nonpolluting organic sprays costing $1 more than inorganic sprays. When they use the organic sprays to avoid the $2 tax, the supply of artichokes will rise from MSC to S_1.

The ultimate optimal output in Figure 3 is 80,000 tons of artichokes at a price of $5.50 per pound (point c). At this price, consumers buy and farmers sell what they want, and society's resources are used efficiently. Competitive markets fail to achieve such results if large numbers of people are harmed or large numbers of people pollute.

What can we conclude from this analysis? First, external costs cause the private market to oversupply the good because full costs are not borne by customers (point a). That is, the social costs of production (total private costs plus any external costs) are not charged to consumers. Second, if consumers pay full costs, less is produced and consumed (point b). Third, when a pollution charge is imposed, producers will seek ways to reduce their level of pollution if this reduces their total costs, which now include any external costs (point c).

Could any lone individual reduce pesticide pollution? You might pay farmers to stop or sue for damages. But lawsuits often involve transaction costs (attorney fees, etc.) that exceed the damage done. For example, individually suing all air polluters in Los Angeles would be very costly relative to the potential personal recom-

FIGURE 3   Pollution Costs: Market Equilibrium with External Costs

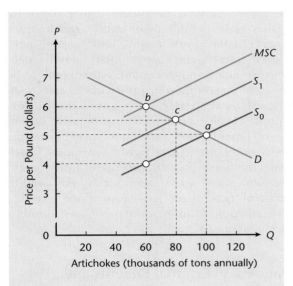

In economic parlance, most pollution is a problem of external costs of production. Suppose the market is initially at point a, where S_0 reflects only private costs. If the producers and consumers of polluting goods are forced to bear any external costs, their adjustments (*internalization*) may be to adopt nonpolluting (but more privately expensive) modes of production, as reflected in supply curve S_1 and the movement from a to c. If such changes in production processes are not feasible, production will fall more and price will rise more, as shown in the movement from a to b, when taxes are used to equate private and social costs. The full cost of cleanup is reflected in the marginal social cost (MSC) curve.

pense for the harm done. People may seek legal remedies, however, when damages are extreme. The key is to force each firm to *internalize* (fully consider) the costs of pollution to innocent third parties.

Internalization *is the process of adjusting prices and output to reflect all external costs or benefits.*

If each buyer of a good pays full production costs, including environmental damages, then externalities are internalized, yielding optimal amounts of production and consumption.

Consider such problems as drunk and reckless drivers, loud neighbors who party until dawn, violent criminals, or litterbugs. These are market failures in the sense that consumption-based external costs are imposed on other people. Similar annoyances and dangers might be even more common in a pure laissez-faire society. Many analysts, however, view these as examples of government failure because one of government's basic tasks in a market economy is to protect broad legal rights to property, which may include rights to peaceful and tidy neighborhoods and safe streets. Society has tried to control tendencies to overproduce external bads through zoning, social regulation, or other legal sanctions.

Summary: External Benefits and Costs

Purely private markets produce too much (or too little) of a good when external costs (or benefits) are present. Externalities cause market failures, because people tend to weigh their private costs and benefits far more heavily than the costs borne or benefits received by outsiders. People maximize their personal welfare by equating the marginal private benefit from an action with its marginal private costs. This is quite rational, because trying to identify and negotiate with any potential third parties may be prohibitively costly and because nonexclusivity for environmental quality would make such negotiations futile. Thus, market demands mirror marginal private benefits, while market supplies reflect marginal private costs.

Society tries to compel decision-makers to internalize externalities by assigning certain legal rights, through taxes or subsidies, or via mandates or prohibition. Pollutants are the most conspicuous examples of negative externalities. Firms ideally internalize any pollution costs, so consumers ultimately pay full production costs: private plus external costs. The growth and diverse characteristics of pollution have stimulated numerous public policies.

ALTERNATIVE SOLUTIONS TO POLLUTION

Nearly everyone recognizes that environmental decay must be controlled. That is where agreement ends. Extreme conservationists argue for a pristine environment and view the social benefits from abatement as overwhelming. To them, only technological limits should be allowed to constrain abatement; economic analysis is irrelevant. Others argue for looser environmental standards and oppose many current regulations as overly stringent and costly.

Is Zero Pollution Optimal?

Optimal outputs require marginal social benefits and costs to be equated. This occurs when all pollution costs are internalized; if they are borne by the consumers and producers of goods whose production or use generates pollution, users and makers will weigh these costs and their decisions will be both personally and socially efficient.

Zero pollution sounds great, but your first question should be, "What would it cost?" If perfect purity were costless, we would all demand an immediate end to pollution; but the costs of 100% purity are prohibitive. Trade-offs exist between environmental quality on the one hand and goods required for even modest standards of living on the other. What is optimal pollution? Figure 4 provides an answer using cost-benefit analysis, which compares the costs and benefits of an activity—in this case, pollution abatement.

Panel A of Figure 4 depicts the total benefits and costs from pollution abatement. The total social benefit curve reflects the fact that an increasingly clean environment yields decreasingly valuable additional benefits as we approach 100% purity. This is reflected in a downward sloping marginal social benefit (*MSB*) curve in Panel B. Enormous gains may be realized from eliminating deadly pollutants, but as the environment grows increasingly clean, we become increasingly tolerant of minor residual pollutants. Virtually no one, for example, would be willing to swim in a sewer, but few refuse to swim in a reasonably clean public pool loaded with tiny children. Society's marginal benefit is the sum of all benefits to individuals from each reduction in pollution. Our "output"

from pollution abatement translates into a given percentage reduction in pollution. Hence, as we move out along the horizontal axis, more abatement is achieved, and the environment becomes cleaner.

The total costs of abatement in Panel A rise as we expand efforts to reduce pollution. In Panel B, the positively sloped marginal social cost (*MSC*) of reducing pollution reflects diminishing marginal returns and increasing marginal costs. More ambitious attempts to reduce pollution entail ever greater sacrifices of resources. For example, the ash spewing from a chimney might be reduced by 20% by installing a crude chimney filter. (Big chunks are easy to screen.) Achieving a 40% reduction, however, requires a second filter with finer mesh to remove smaller particles, and this filter would require more frequent replacement. Each subsequent filter to reduce pollution even further would have to be even finer and would require even more frequent replacement. Achieving zero pollution is virtually impossible. Maximizing social welfare requires that *MSB* = *MSC* at point *e* in our example. To extend abatement beyond the optimal level (0*f*) would waste resources because further reductions in pollution cost more than they are worth.

This analysis contradicts the notion that society should completely eliminate pollution regardless of costs. To push pollution control until the total benefits equaled the total costs (point *b* in Panel A) would mean that the last bit of cleanup effort would cost society *ac* (in Panel B), while yielding additional benefits of only *ad*. Society, by cleaning up beyond the optimal level of 0*f* percent to 0*a* percent receives additional benefits of *feda* (Panel B) but uses resources worth *feca* to complete the job, which wastes resources equal in value to shaded area *dec*.

Another implication is that optimal pollution levels will vary for different regions of the country depending on their respective benefits and costs. Regions particularly vulnerable to smog may want to impose especially stringent emissions standards. Densely populated areas (like Los Angeles) faced with severe auto pollution may choose to limit travel (no-drive days, commuter lanes) or to subsidize mass transit that would not be optimal in Wyoming. Focus 2 in-

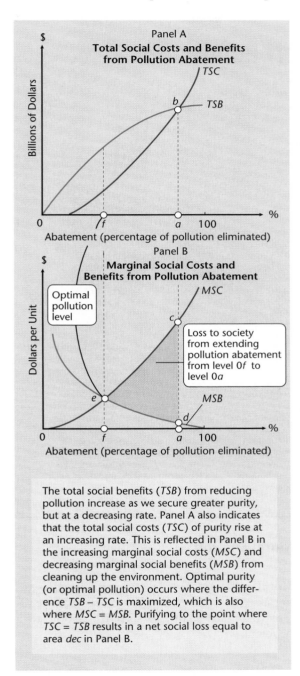

The total social benefits (*TSB*) from reducing pollution increase as we secure greater purity, but at a decreasing rate. Panel A also indicates that the total social costs (*TSC*) of purity rise at an increasing rate. This is reflected in Panel B in the increasing marginal social costs (*MSC*) and decreasing marginal social benefits (*MSB*) from cleaning up the environment. Optimal purity (or optimal pollution) occurs where the difference *TSB* – *TSC* is maximized, which is also where *MSC* = *MSB*. Purifying to the point where *TSC* = *TSB* results in a net social loss equal to area *dec* in Panel B.

FIGURE 4   Determining the Optimal Level of Pollution

Should We Export Pollution?

The aroma of Charles Dickens' London was a pungent mix of barnyard, smoke, coal dust, fish market, and refinery. Almost 3 million Londoners relied on over 200,000 horses for basic transportation; wood and coal fires heated homes and provided energy for industry; raw sewage and kitchen slop flowed down open gutters into the Thames River. The drapes of Paliament were regularly drenched with water to prevent members from being overwhelmed by the stench.

London's atmosphere is now much more agreeable, primarily because environmental quality is a luxury good. Thus, London, Rome, and New York are cleaner than Bombay, Mexico City, or Hong Kong. High per capita income yields rules that banish dirtier forms of production. People living in less prosperous regions are less picky; they welcome even unpleasant industries that will provide jobs and income. For example, destitute local communities in the United States may lobby legislators to locate prisons nearby; some poor areas have been competing to be sites for radioactive waste dumps.

Political leaders whose major priorities are growth and development for their countries frequently tolerate lax safety and environmental standards to simulate production or to attract industry. It is not surprising that the two most catastrophic industrial accidents ever recorded occurred in (a) Bhopal, India, when over 2000 died and thousands became invalids after a toxic industrial gas was released, and (b) the Soviet Union, during the 1986 meltdown of a nuclear power plant at Chernobyl.

Environmental and safety standards tend to be lower in less developed countries. This suggests that environmental quality in the United States and other advanced economies would improve if we imported more goods that entail substantial pollution from poorer countries that seem more willing to tolerate wastes. Laws to forbid importing goods that were not produced under environmental regulations as stringent as those in the United States have, however, been proposed by several groups on a variety of grounds.

1. Environmentalists who are concerned that our entire planet is being polluted see exporting pollution as a shortsighted solution that will only delay and worsen an ultimate reckoning with the problem of environmental decay. (But not all pollution is ultimately global. Some is primarily local.)

2. Exporting dirty and dangerous industries is perceived as an immoral way to exploit the poverty of the less developed nations. (But are our morals preserved if our policies keep people in less developed countries impoverished?)

3. Domestic industries (and their workers), which must meet strict U.S. environmental standards, contend that allowing foreign competition that does not face similar standards is unfair. (A parallel of this view would be arguing that garbage dumps should be spread uniformly across land in country clubs and remote land that is barren.)

The ultimate question is whether developed countries that, because of their prosperity, demand high levels of environmental quality have any right to prohibit less prosperous countries from producing goods that entail substantial pollution. It may be that the comparative advantages of less advanced countries are strongly shaped by greater tolerance for environmental degradation.

dicates that trade-offs between production and environmental quality may also affect the locations of certain industries.

The methods available to reduce pollution can be categorized according to their degree of intervention in the market process. The least interventionist is moral suasion, followed by various market techniques, then tax and subsidy incentives, and finally, outright government regulation and prohibition. We will examine each of these approaches.

Moral Suasion

Moral suasion lacks legal authority; its goals are to persuade offenders to voluntarily reduce offensive practices and to sensitize people to a problem.

> *Moral suasion* is social pressure to persuade people or institutions to act in some particular manner.

For example, "Don't Be a Litterbug" and "Don't Mess with Texas" campaigns have succeeded in reducing trash along public highways. Public hostility now restricts smoking to limited areas. Adverse publicity or threatened boycotts were the primary methods available early in the environmental movement and may persuade some polluters to desist. Moral suasion has limited power, however, because many goods are marketed nationally, public information campaigns are expensive, and voluntary boycotts ask people to act against their own interests.

Attempts to exert moral suasion have spawned several books rating the environmental record of business firms. Some companies have attempted to turn environmental activism to their advantage by advertising the firms' accomplishments or by introducing environmentally friendly products or services. Few books, however, have addressed the government's record on the environment, which, at times, has been dismal.

For example, the U.S. government built plutonium triggers for nuclear warheads from the 1950s through the 1980s at the Rocky Flats plant a few miles North of Denver, Colorado. As the plant was being phased down and converted to other uses in the early 1990s, inspectors revealed that hundreds of pounds of lethal plutonium dust were clogging the plant's system of air ducts, and an area exceeding 30 square miles was so contaminated by radiation that it was unfit for human habitation. In 1994, the Department of Energy officials in charge of Rocky Flats were still wrestling with a plan to clean up this mess.

Effluent Charges and Subsidies

Many economists favor tax penalties or *effluent charges* to curb environmental decay. This modified use of the market relies on price incentives to optimally allocate resources when externalities are present. Government sets the fee (charge) on pollution or the reward for reducing pollution, and polluters are allowed to adjust without overt coercion.

- **Effluent Charges** The effluent charge approach is illustrated in Figure 5. Suppose that a group of polluting manufacturers is located on a public lake that could also be used for recreation and fishing. Water pollution reduces the enjoyment derived from boating, skiing, fishing, and picnics.

Assume that community leaders estimate external costs per unit of effluent at $1 when only optimal pollution occurs. To attain optimal rates of discharge into the lake, the community charges the firms $1 per unit of discharge. The MC curve shows the firms' costs of reducing pollution. Given the $1-per-unit effluent charge, firms will reduce their effluents by E_0 units. The firms will not remove more than E_0 effluents because the removal cost (MC) exceeds the $1 effluent charge at quantities exceeding E_0.

- **Subsidizing Abatement** The government might use subsidies (the opposite of taxes) to encourage pollution abatement. Federal grants to pay for pollution control equipment have been used extensively to subsidize cleanups of sewage facilities run by state or local government. These sewer systems are now required to charge for

MC is the marginal cost of effluent control for this firm. Imposing an effluent charge of $1 per unit of effluent discharged on this firm will result in it incurring total control costs of $0ab$ to reduce E_0 amount of effluents.

FIGURE 5   Effluent Charges

their services based on measured use as a condition for receiving these federal funds.

Subsidies to private firms that reduce pollution ultimately subsidize the firms' customers, but are unlikely to be effective unless the subsidies make abatement profitable. Subsidies to encourage private pollution abatement could take such forms as grants to pay for equipment, tax credits, or rapid depreciation allowances. Substantial political opposition to subsidizing private pollution abatement has, however, sharply limited such subsidies.

Market Solutions

Many economists argue appropriately specified property rights would efficiently resolve all environmental problems. Much private property is owned only in a limited way. For example, you may own a car, but there are numerous restrictions on its use. Similar limits apply to ownership of land and buildings, guns, or ham radio equipment.

• **Lawsuits for Damages** One role of government in a market economy is enforcement of property rights. You could sue harmful polluters if property rights were assigned to protect you from being damaged by pollution. Lawsuits may work fairly well when pollution can be traced directly to a given polluter and the damage can be shown to be caused by that party's effluent. But suppose that a firm had the right to pollute. Your only remedy might be to pay the firm to reduce pollution–if it were worth it to you.

Who has rights to use the environment? This was a crucial issue in the 1879 case of *Sturges* v. *Bridgman*.[3] Sturges, a doctor whose office abutted those already occupied by Bridgman, a confectioner, added an examination room next to the confectioner's kitchen. Noisy equipment kept the doctor from examining patients with a stethoscope in the new room, so he sued to prevent the confectioner from operating the equipment. An injunction was granted on the grounds that the machinery imposed external costs on the doctor. (Consider the possibility, however, that this injunction imposed external costs on the candy maker, who previously had the right to operate noisy equipment.)

Both private and public lawsuits to protect the environment have some advantages. First, victims of pollutants may be compensated for their losses–and they may not have other enforcement methods. Firms have incentives to clean up if the compensation paid exceeds the costs of cleaning up. Second, successful lawsuits alert other polluters to new liability limits, encouraging these firms to adopt cost-justified precautions to avoid future damage claims.

Using the courts to enforce rights to pollute or to be protected from pollution has several disadvantages. First, legal procedures are slow and costly. Cases tried today have been initiated, on average, two to four years earlier. Furthermore, such solutions are impractical if the damaged party lacks the resources to bring a suit. These solutions alone may leave society saddled with excessive waste. A slightly different problem is that if there are numerous polluters and pollutees, it may be difficult to determine who harmed whom and to what degree. Lawsuits would face almost insurmountable difficulties in solving problems of fouled air in crowded industrial areas.

On a more positive note, legal precedents can alter the behavior of other firms, which may reduce their emissions to avoid costly litigation. Legal remedies work best where the number of polluters is small and their victims are few and easily identified. But residents of Love Canal, New York, and Times Beach, Missouri, personally experienced the chaos of areas polluted by toxic chemicals. Fearful for their own health and that of their children, and faced by plummeting property values and a maze of red tape when they sought restitution, these victims learned how hard it can be to correct the harm done by even easily identified polluters if the pollution happened long ago.

---

[3]U.S. Supreme Court Case 11 Ch. D. 852 (1879). For a detailed analysis of this case, see Ronald Coase, "The Problem of Social Costs," *The Journal of Law and Economics*, vol. 3, October 1960.

• **Assigning Pollution Rights** A second approach based on market forces is for the public sector to sell licenses to discharge wastes.

> **Pollution rights** are licenses to discharge given amounts of waste products.

Ronald Coase, was awarded the Nobel Prize for, among other things, showing that an equilibrium pollution level is optimal, and this equilibrium is unaffected by whether pollution rights are assigned to the polluter or the harmed party as long as those affected (*a*) are easily identified, (*b*) have roughly the same bargaining power, and (*c*) can bargain without cost.[4] In this view, the environment is just another productive resource.

This bargaining process is reflected in Figure 6. The demand for *pollution rights*, D_0 slopes downward. Pollution is Q_0 if the environment can be used freely as a garbage dump. Quotas might be auctioned if the community decided to allow only Q_e pollution. Business demands to pollute reflect how the production of pollution contributes to a firm's revenues and profits. A firm willing to pay only P_a for each right to pollute (point *a*) undoubtedly can curtail pollution for P_a or less per unit of effluent. Businesses would be willing to pay P_e each for Q_e pollution rights. If purity lovers would be hurt more than P_e by each unit of pollution, they could buy and retain the pollution rights. In this way, the initial sale of these rights would generate revenue for the community. If an auction were held and Q_e rights were sold, then excessive pollution ($Q_0 - Q_e$) would be eliminated.

What if other firms wanted to set up locally after the Q_e pollution rights had already been sold? They could buy rights from the owners of existing pollution rights. This might require buying an acutely dirty plant, shutting it down, and transferring its pollution rights to a new plant. Alternatively, a new firm could pay existing firms to install more antipollution equipment. Both techniques shift the demand for the right to contaminate from D_0 to D_1 in Figure 6.

[4]R. H. Coase, "The Problem of Social Cost," *The Journal of Law and Economics*, vol. 3, 1960.

The value of pollution rights rises, but not the level of waste. Consumers of goods entailing pollution pay full production costs as higher costs of polluting are shifted forward.

This approach has several advantages. First, polluters have incentives to clean up. Little administration other than monitoring is required. And if the government decides later to reduce pollution, it can repurchase existing rights–or if it becomes more accepting of pollution, it may sell even more rights as a revenue source. This approach can confer significant cost advantages to firms that implement relatively clean technologies. It may be a cheap and attractive alternative to direct regulation, and it works reasonably well in a relatively enclosed environment, like a lake under the control of local authorities. But administration is more difficult when spillovers are more extensive. Another flaw is that some voters and politicians equate pollution with sin and are outraged at the idea of allowing economic reasoning to dominate what is for them a moral issue. Even these moralists, however, would probably

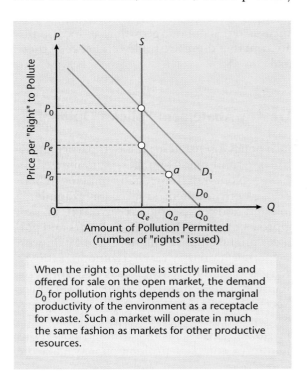

When the right to pollute is strictly limited and offered for sale on the open market, the demand D_0 for pollution rights depends on the marginal productivity of the environment as a receptacle for waste. Such a market will operate in much the same fashion as markets for other productive resources.

FIGURE 6 A Market for Pollution Rights

agree that selling pollution rights is better than giving them away for free.

Regulations and Prohibition

Direct regulation is a politically popular remedy for environmental damage. Complete prohibition may be desirable in the case of extremely dangerous materials (e.g., plutonium or other powerful carcinogens). When total bans on certain pollutants are too costly relative to the benefits, the government limits noxious wastes through regulations and standards.

Regulation is costly to administer and provides firms no incentives to reduce pollution once a standard is met. Every stringent rule incites imaginative attempts to discover loopholes around it. This typically results in an incredibly complex patchwork of directives to prevent cheating or avoidance. In some instances, there may be no acceptable alternatives to direct regulation. We need to recognize, however, that the quality of life depends at least as much on production and economic growth as it does on purity, and that there are trade-offs between these goals.

Are Any Abatement Policies Optimal?

Each policy discussed so far has its particular advantages and disadvantages, summarized in Table 1. None is the best for all situations. Where a closed environment (a lake, for example) is polluted and few people are involved, market approaches tend to be viable. Polluters and pollutees might simply be allowed to bargain with each other until they reach a solution. Effluent charges or subsidy schemes may also work efficiently. But these approaches break down where aspects of public goods arise. Standards and regulations may be appropriate if a problem is widespread and diverse. With extremely hazardous substances, complete prohibition may make the most sense.

Securing adequate energy supplies and bolstering economic growth are increasingly balanced against environmental protection and the quality of life as we move toward the twenty-first century. The history of environmental protection in the United States suggests that the Environmental Protection Agency increasingly relies on market solutions to prevent environmental deterioration. Although regulation remains the major weapon, most studies suggest that market incentives instead of regulations provide cost savings of as much as 50% per unit of pollution abated.

U.S. ENVIRONMENTAL POLICIES

We have examined various techniques to reduce pollution. As we noted earlier, political lags and other difficulties mean that sound economic policies are embraced only slowly, if at all, and transitions are often turbulent. Environmental protection in accord with modern economic analysis generally faces substantial obstacles, both technical and political.

Pollution Control in the United States

By the late 1960s, it was obvious that the United States had moved into the second phase of property rights: the tragedy of the commons. Environmental degradation had spread beyond isolated cities like Gary, Indiana, and Pittsburgh (which, incidentally, have made great strides toward improved air quality). Congress more formally delineated rights to use the environment by enacting environmental legislation for both water and air.

Arguments about environmental regulation can be rancorous. Environmentalists are often accused of shunning cost-benefit calculations in favor of rigid regulations requiring greater purity. Many environmentalists complain that bureaucrats fail to aggressively combat pollution. For example, turmoil at the EPA in the 1980s reflected outrage that regulators were selling out to polluting industries. This rhetoric has been counterbalanced: firms faced with high costs of cleaning up oppose EPA regulations by loudly criticizing the ineptitude of

TABLE 1 Summary and Evaluation of Some Environmental Policies

Policy Option	Advantages	Disadvantages
Moral suasion	Least disruptive to market processes. Educates and sensitizes people to the nature of environmental problems. Permits individual choice.	Ineffective in reducing pollution levels.
Market solutions		
1. Lawsuits	Private lawsuits enable victims to recover.	It may be difficult to prove in a lawsuit who damaged whom. Lawsuits can be expensive.
2. Pollution rights	Requires little government intervention. Reduces pollution to a given level depending upon the policy established. Relatively easy to administer.	Sometimes hard to develop good estimates of external costs for particular pollutants and polluters. License to pollute is politically unpopular. Typically requires a closed environment to administer effectively.
Taxes or Subsidies		
1. Effluent changes	Largest polluters have greatest incentives to reduce pollution. Generates revenue to further clean up environment.	Sometimes difficult to estimate appropriate charge. Monitoring compliance can be expensive, especially when large numbers of polluters are involved.
2. Subsidies	Relatively easy to administer.	Politically unpopular.
Direct regulation	Can be used to keep extremely harmful pollution below dangerous levels. Standards can preserve horizontal equity of the program. Politically most popular.	Once standard is met, polluter has no incentive to reduce pollution below standard (important if standard is above the socially optimal level). Administrative regulation often quite complex and cumbersome. Most interventionist in scope. Large bureaucracy is created to administer program. Does not generate its own revenue. Can become captive agency of particular special-interest groups. Generates incentives to creatively sidestep the regulation.

environmental managers. In spite of this furor, environmental policy appears to follow a smooth and predictable path.

The first step in moving past common, unrestricted use of the environment entails identifying causes of such problems as air pollution. Smog was first noticed in the 1940s as a haze against foothills east of Los Angeles. Smog was first thought a passing thing, but pressure slowly mounted to clean the persistent brown cloud. One problem was that no one could identify the nature of smog, that is, where it came from or what its effects might be. By 1951, however, a Cal Tech study fingered auto emissions as the major culprit.

When the EPA was first charged with responsibility for environmental quality, it viewed mandatory cleanup by all polluters as the only practical approach. Abatement was initially treated on a case-by-case basis, but uniform rules seemed necessary on two grounds. First, the EPA expected its mandates to be easily monitored. Second, uniform standards legally treat the affected parties equally and are nondiscriminatory constitutionally, even if they dictate unequal burdens of pollution control.

During this period of uniform pollution control, society learned more about pollution and how to measure it, paving the way for marketable pollution rights to emerge. At the same time, political obstacles shaped mandatory rules and standards. Special-interest groups lobbied for rules to benefit them. Surprisingly, special-interest groups frequently pressed for increased environmental purity; it is a mistake to think that regulations harm all firms. Some are harmed and some are not. For example, control over pollution in steel making entails substantial economies of scale. Thus, big firms tend to advocate tough rules that drive their smaller competitors out of business. The demise of small firms promotes environmental quality. Firms in polluted regions want pollution control requirements to be as burdensome on firms in cleaner areas. This also enhances environmental protection, but at significant cost. In most cases, special-interest pressures have caused inefficient regulation.

Despite special-interest groups, there has been a steady movement toward more convenient and transferable environmental property rights. The EPA allowed the *bubble concept* to be implemented in many situations in the 1970s. "Bubble" refers to a performance standard imposed for the area surrounding a plant or a group of adjacent plants, as opposed to the standards that were originally imposed on each specific source within a plant.

> The **bubble concept** *allows firms to transfer pollution rights between sources within a plant as long as a prescribed standard of environmental quality is met.*

There is a continuing evolution from the bubble concept to pollution rights that are marketable between plants. The gains from exchange that exist within a plant are also available between plants. Some permits to pollute are also now marketable.

> An **offset policy** *allows a new firm to enter an overpolluted area by inducing other firms to reduce emissions. Air quality must show a net improvement, and the new firm must meet all individual standards imposed on existing firms.*

What this means is that a new entrant can bargain with existing firms, paying them either to shut down or to employ better pollution controls. For example, a California firm was permitted to build a 40,000-barrel-per-day oil terminal after paying $250,000 for an offset created when a local chemical plant closed.[5] Such offsets are now advertised for sale in the *Wall Street Journal*. The 1990 Clean Air Act specifically permits coal-burning utilities to overcomply with sulfur dioxide standards and then sell their extra pollution rights. Recently, Northeast Utilities of Connecticut donated to the American Lung Association the company's pollution rights—rights to release 10,000 tons of acid-rain creating chemicals. A recent extension of offsets is described in Focus 3.

Although market solutions have crept into the regulatory postures of agencies like the EPA, there are still many inefficiencies that exist only to enhance the wealth of special interests. For instance, the bubble concept applies only to old plants, not new ones. New-versus-old disparities in environmental controls are a recurrent theme. Another example of special-interest effects is that the net improvement in the environment necessary to qualify an offset as legal is a political football often kicked from one end of the field to the other. Firms with offsets for sale commonly try to influence regulators to require great improvements in environmental quality before allowing a new firm to enter a blighted area; this drives up the value of existing rights to pollute.

---

[5]Tom Tietenberg, *Environmental and Natural Resource Economics*, 3rd ed. (New York: HarperCollins, 1992), p. 351.

Pollution Abatement and High Prices for Clunkers

Serious joggers and people with lung problems sometimes find the air in urban areas almost unbreathable. Automotive emissions are universally identified as the primary culprit, accounting for as much as 90% of carbon monoxide and other air pollutants. Regular tune-ups to pass mandatory emissions inspections have become an annual ritual for many car owners in smoggy metropolitan areas.

Many firms, however, emit more pollutants than any individual car. Controlling firms' emissions took a slightly different tack. For decades, state environmental agencies and the EPA traced pollutants to major sources, setting rigid standards to force offending firms to reduce their emissions. In highly competitive industries based on relatively dirty technologies, staggering compliance costs often forced firms to close their doors. Some environmentalists might respond with, "Good riddance," but owners were often bankrupted, thousands of workers lost their jobs, and the buyers of the goods these firms produced were forced to switch to higher-priced substitutes.

Is there a more efficient solution to excessive air pollution than forcing firms to reduce their pollutants? An innovative approach to pollution offsets may be a key in answering this question. Instead of requiring a firm to reduce its own emissions, the EPA can require major polluters to reduce pollution in a congested area but leaves each firm discretion about how to control emissions.

In some cases, this flexibility permits the EPA to require a bit more abatement than would be reasonable if all reductions had to

be accomplished within the firm itself. If the firm finds a way to reduce pollution externally for less than it would cost internally, (a) the firm can be more profitable, (b) its workers can have greater job security, (c) its customers can face lower prices, and (d) local residents can enjoy cleaner air.

Firms bought pollution offsets from other firms for several years before, in 1990, an obvious abatement technique was discovered that regulators ultimately allowed. Although more than three-fourths of all miles driven are in newer cars, 80% of all automotive emissions flow from the exhaust pipes of cars produced before 1983. Emissions standards were negligible for cars produced before 1975, and cars produced between 1975 and 1983 were subject to standards that were relatively lax when compared to the emissions standards imposed for 1983 and newer models.

Firms faced with meeting an abatement standard can now buy clunkers, take them off the road, and have the savings in pollution credited to their accounts. Since 1990, tens of thousands of older vehicles have met the crusher, primarily in California.

State and local government agencies are also getting into the act, primarily in areas that have failed to meet EPA regional standards for decades. In Denver, for example, bad days at least occasionally exceeded EPA mandatory ceilings in every year from 1974 to 1994. Although Denver's air quality improved steadily after 1980, the EPA grace period passed and officials throughout the Denver metropolitan area came under extreme pressure from the EPA (e.g., threats of losses of federal

highway funding). Among the possible remedies proposed for Denver were compulsory carpooling for employees at major employers, prohibitions on the driving of older vehicles on high pollution days, high taxes on downtown parking, and requirements that tuition at all local colleges be increased to include a mandatory bus pass. The local police were forbidden to auction off older vehicles they had confiscated from convicted criminals.

Denver merchants worried that these draconian measures would erode downtown retailing. With the encouragement of local officials, some firms bought old cars to get them off the road. Total Petroleum, for example, paid $750 each for more than 1,000 smoke belchers that the owners were able to drive to a collection point. Everyone gained, especially the owners of clunkers that were still drivable but well down the road to the junkyard.

Is it possible for you to gain from this approach to pollution offsets? If you think an aggressive offset program might be instituted in your town because of pressure from the EPA, you might try stockpiling a few clunkers if you can buy them cheaply. Then, when offsets reach a premium price, sell the clunkers for a healthy profit. Of course, you will be competing with junkyards that already have a comparative advantage in this type of speculation. The chapter entitled "Rent, Interest, Profits, and Capitalization" should have taught you that these sorts of windfalls are unlikely if markets are reasonably competitive, and we can assure you, profit seekers abound in our market economy.

The Future of Environmental Protection

We can reasonably expect continuing improvements to environmental quality. As the EPA and the other regulatory agencies become more adept at their jobs, pollution control will cost less per unit, and a substitution effect will cause society to demand more purity. Increases in national income will also drive demand for environmental quality, which is income elastic. This helps explain why such laws as the Clean Air Act of 1990 mandate improved environmental quality, but how far and how fast we are willing to go has limits. In 1990, the high costs expected with the sweeping "big green" initiative to set substantially higher environmental standards caused Californians to vote it down, and New Yorkers defeated a $2 billion environmental bond issue.

Markets for pollution permits are unlikely to ever be as unregulated as those for cars or land. Certain restrictions will probably remain, to sustain the wealth of special-interest groups. Even the market for land is regulated. Zoning ordinances and other laws protect the value of certain locations vis-à-vis others. It should be no surprise to find this same effect in air pollution rights. Finally, it seems likely that pollution taxes will never be a widespread method to allocate the environment for the disposal of waste. In contrast, both uniform standards and marketable pollution permits endow the regulated firms with this value. Political processes will probably never completely wrest this value from them.

To summarize the economics of environmental quality, we first must recognize that the environment is a scarce resource that has competing uses. Second, the political process weighs the cost of property rights definition and enforcement—and the profitability to special-interest groups from property rights restrictions—against the inherent efficiency of private property ownership. Our experience in the environmental arena chronicles the changing equilibrium of these forces. As property rights become more completely defined and easily enforced, society is increasingly likely to use private property assignments to allocate use of our environment.

CHAPTER REVIEW: KEY POINTS

1. Goods that are purely rival and exclusive are pure private goods. Such goods (e.g., ice cream or umbrellas) are usually efficiently provided in a private market system. Goods that are nonrival but exclusive entail excess capacity and are also efficiently provided by markets unless elements of natural monopoly are present. A good that is both nonrival and nonexclusive is a pure public good. Public goods will be less than optimally provided by the market system, if they are provided at all, because of attempts to *free ride*.

2. A rival but nonexclusive good embodies **externalities** that often hinder the efficiency of market solutions. Pollution may be the problem if externalities are negative (costly); underproduction may result if externalities are positive (beneficial).

3. The four stages in the development of **property rights** are (a) common access and non-scarcity, (b) common access and scarcity, (c)

agency restrictions, and (*d*) fee-simple property rights. *Fee-simple property rights* mean that you can do anything you want with your property so long as you do no physical damage to the property of others.

4. *Positive externalities* occur when an activity confers benefits on external third parties. Too few such activities are undertaken because private decision-makers tend to ignore the external benefits.

5. Pollution situations in which damaged third parties are uncompensated, and hence unconsidered, are examples of *negative externalities*. Negative externalities impose costs on third parties. Too many activities generating negative externalities are undertaken, because private decision-makers weigh the costs imposed on others too lightly, if at all.

6. Environmental quality is a public good, and controlling environmental pollution is costly. There are trade-offs between protecting the environment and producing goods that generate pollution, so the **optimal pollution** level is greater than zero.

7. *Pollution abatement* may occur through negotiation, **moral suasion** (jawboning and bad publicity), effluent charges, subsidies, lawsuits, the assignment of pollution rights, and government regulation. No single solution applies to all situations of negative externalities; they must generally be resolved on a case-by-case basis.

8. *Pollution rights* might be auctioned and then made transferable. The Environmental Protection Agency initially relied heavily on direct regulation through pollution ceilings but is increasingly using property rights solutions to control environmental deterioration.

9. The **bubble concept** sets a pollution performance standard for a plant. A firm can transfer rights to pollute within or between plants inside the bubble as long as the standard is met.

10. The **offset policy** allows new firms that wish to produce in a polluted area to operate if they can induce existing firms to reduce air pollutants to offset the newcomer's emissions.

QUESTIONS FOR THOUGHT AND DISCUSSION

1. Far more species of plants and animals (e.g., dinosaurs) have become extinct than exist in the world today. Is concern about the potential extinction of certain species sufficient reason to bar economic development? A few years ago, for example, a subspecies of the snail darter (a minnow-like fish) was discovered in a river scheduled to be dammed. Construction of the multimillion-dollar dam was halted to preserve this subspecies. If you believe in animal rights, do these rights extend to all species? For example, if you had the last samples on earth of the viruses that generate smallpox or AIDS, would you reason that these species should be preserved?

2. Why are chickens, pigs, and cows in no danger of extinction despite their system-atic slaughter to provide food for hungry people, while many edible wild animals are increasingly rare despite much lower kill rates (relative to total population) each year?

3. You are an ardent environmentalist who is shocked to learn that the government will soon begin selling rights to pollute. You and your friends express moral outrage that someone could be given the right to pollute at a time when environmental quality is threatened on many fronts. How might you, your friends, and others with similar views use the government's program to increase environmental quality?

4. Some analysts insist that external costs are so inherently bilateral that determining who is the polluter and who is the pollu-

tee is hard. If a polluter is the one who imposes costs on others, then the people who benefit when regulation secures greater purity are the polluters, because they impose cleanup costs on firms and their customers. In this view, whether a firm should pay for pollution abatement or whether those who desire purity should bribe the firm to install pollution abatement equipment is entirely arbitrary. Moreover, the government need not interfere, because, in this view, the parties will privately bargain to reach an optimal solution. What problems do you see with this approach to environmental quality?

5. Suppose a smelly feedlot for cattle was located in a remote area long before a builder placed a housing development next to it. Should the right to be smelly inure to the feedlot owner, or should the right to clean country air be conferred on new home buyers? How could the real estate developer or the new home buyers reduce or eliminate the aroma of cattle if the feedlot had the right to stink up the area? How might the feedlot preserve the right to operate if homeowners were awarded rights to clean air? Why might the final amount of barnyard odor be the same in equilibrium regardless of which party was granted these rights to air quality?

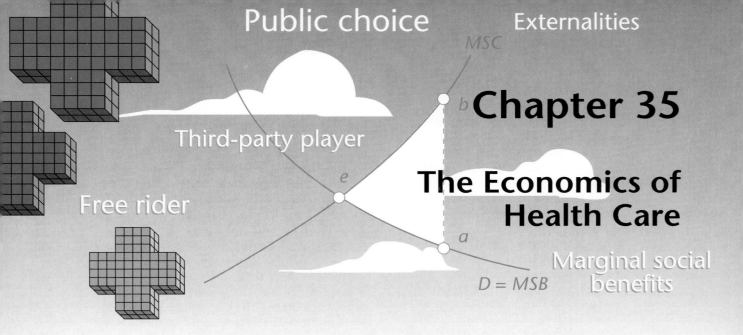

Public choice   Externalities

MSC

Third-party player

Free rider

b

Chapter 35

The Economics of Health Care

e

a

D = MSB   Marginal social benefits

The only way to keep your health is to eat what you don't want, drink what you don't like, and do what you'd rather not.

Mark Twain

The plague wiped out one-third of the populace of Europe and parts of Africa and Asia in the fourteenth century. No other cataclysm–including war–has ever swept away such a large percentage of the world's population in as short a period. But this earlier health-care crisis now seems like ancient history. Medical technologies now available are among the triumphs of modern science. Diseases that once ravaged the population have been eliminated or largely contained, among them, smallpox, polio, diphtheria, typhoid, and plague. Nevertheless, concern about health care is high and rising, especially among Americans. Why?

The emergence of AIDS and other new diseases is among the reasons health care is now viewed as a critical issue, as is a resurgence of some ancient diseases because certain strains of bacteria and viruses have become drug resistant (e.g., tuberculosis and malaria). Another source

of concern is that modern medicine now enables most of us to live longer. Many people fear bankruptcy if costly treatments that would prolong life are not covered by insurance. These sorts of concerns date back to antiquity, but certain interrelated factors come to the fore when experts itemize pressing issues for health-care reform: (*a*) soaring costs, (*b*) uneven quality, and (*c*) lack of universal access, or inadequate health insurance coverage for many Americans.

How we prioritize health-care problems depends on our positions. For most firms and many employees, rising health insurance costs despite decreasing coverage are a major concern. For many of the poor and for the uninsured, access is a central issue. Access to care is generally available, but too often, too little health care is accessible too late. For taxpayers, rising shares of tax dollars are absorbed by outlays for Medicare and Medicaid. For health-care providers (e.g., doctors and hospitals), major issues include (*a*) the growth of bureaucracy to oversee payments, leading to micromanagement of medical decisions; (*b*) the prospect of price controls in the guise of *cost containment*, and (*c*) malpractice suits that, regardless of fault, often arise from poor outcomes. (Some of us acknowledge the inevitable only reluctantly, but everyone ultimately recognizes that we all eventually die—a basic health problem beyond medical remedies.)

As is true of so many other economic issues, concerns about health care can be boiled down to trade-offs between *efficiency* (cost containment) and *equity* (improved access). Thus, health-care reform predictably has broad support in the abstract, but little consensus exists about concrete directions for specific reforms.

HEALTH CARE TODAY: SOME VITAL SIGNS

Annual spending on health care in the United States exceeds $1 trillion. It is not surprising that Americans have strong opinions about an industry that now absorbs more than 15 cents out of every dollar of our gross domestic product (GDP)—a share three times higher than it was

in the 1950s, as shown in Figure 1. Although specifying any cause-and-effect relationships entails some speculation, the high and rising costs of health care have been accompanied by certain benefits. We are, on average, healthier than we have ever been. Today, American men typically live to age 72, and women, to age 79, an increase in life expectancy of roughly five years since 1960. Roughly 85% of Americans are covered by some form of medical insurance, compared to less than one-third in 1960. Our medical technology is the most advanced anywhere in the world; foreigners afflicted by especially complex diseases often come to the United States for treatment. One issue, of course, is whether we live longer because we spend more on health care, or do we spend more because we are living longer?

When weighing the costs and benefits of our health-care system, one important point is that for every health-care *expenditure*, there is a health-care *income*. The health-care industry consists of more than just doctors and nurses

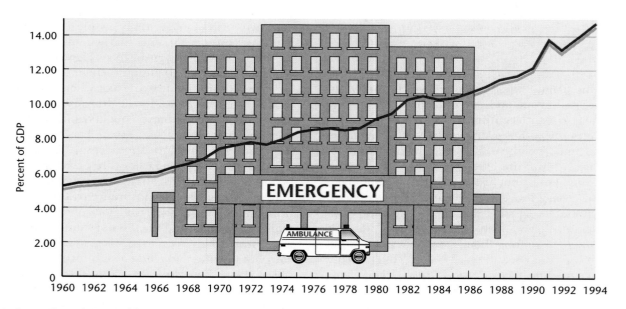

Source: *Economic Report of the President,* 1994 and Organization for Economic Co-operation and Development. *Health Care Systems in Transition: The Search for Efficiency,* 1990.

Health care spending as a percentage of U.S. Gross Domestic Product has roughly tripled, from about 5 percent in 1960 to over 15 percent today. Over the same period, the average life span of Americans has increased by five years. But whether rising health expenditures have increased longivity or whether an aging population has driven up health care costs cannot be discerned from these data.

FIGURE 1   Health Care Spending as a Percent of GDP

and hospitals; nursing homes, dentistry, pharmaceutical firms that make medicines, laboratories that do tests, and equipment makers whose specialties range from eyeglasses to X-ray machines and CAT scanners are all in health care. This industry employs roughly 9 million workers, dwarfing most other industries, and all the talk about health-care reform has put health professionals on the defensive.

The growth of health care is not the sole source of concern among Americans. For example, the entertainment industry (e.g., theme parks, blockbuster films, and professional sports) has grown as rapidly, and proposals to restructure entertainment are as scarce as hen's teeth. People buy medical care to improve or maintain their health. In this sense, health care resembles other purchases. Nicer homes, safer cars, and tastier food can improve our lives. But health care is qualitatively different because of (a) *uncertainty*—nobody can confidently forecast the likelihood of every potential life-threatening (and costly) illness; (b) *asymmetric information*—knowledge gaps between us and our physicians are vast when compared to most other products, and, finally, (c) *externalities*—in part because of potential contagion and higher health insurance rates, as individuals we are more concerned about whether the health needs of others are met than, say, with the quality of their furniture. The potential severity of uncertainty, asymmetric information, and externalities all combine to differentiate health care from most other purchases.

Our next task is a discussion of trends in health-care expenditures and access. We then examine characteristics that distinguish the health-care market from other markets. Next, we analyze the role of health insurance (both public and private). Then we focus on the respective strengths and weaknesses of how some other countries organize, provide, and finance health-care. Finally, we examine the various health-care reform proposals for the United States.

TRENDS IN SPENDING AND ACCESS

Rapidly rising health-care expenditures (the efficiency issue) and limited access (the equity issue) are worldwide problems. Almost 15% of Americans (35 million) lack health-care insurance. In most other developed nations, universal access is theoretically the norm, but rapidly rising expenditures are compelling these countries to ration or curtail services. The issues of high medical costs and limits to access are even more severe in less-developed parts of the world.

The Growth of Spending on Health

Our real *per capita* health-care spending has nearly quadrupled in the latter half of the twentieth century. In 1950, Americans typically spent about $840 (adjusted to 1990 dollars) on health care. Today, that number exceeds $2,600. In contrast to the 15% of U.S. GDP now spent on health care (refer to Figure 1), developed European nations typically spend only 7% to 9% of their GDPs, and Europeans are about as healthy (statistically) as Americans. However, the inflation of health-care costs is a global problem from which no nation emerges unscathed.

Two-thirds of current U.S. health-care expenditures are for hospital and physician services (shown in Figure 2). Bureaucratic and administrative costs are growing at an especially rapid clip. Estimates of the proportions of each category reported in Table 1 that are attributable to administrative costs are not available separately, but every expert in this area recognizes that administrative costs persistently outstrip growth rates for total health-care costs. On average, processing by insurance companies now absorbs 17% of all outlays on health care.[1] When the time hospital clerks take processing paperwork is added to the time health-care professionals devote to filling out forms instead of caring for patients, at least one-fourth of all health-care costs are probably administrative, and as much as one-third of the recent inflation of health-care costs may be attributable to increased paperwork.

---

[1] P. Barton et al., *Colorado Medicaid Reform Study*, (Denver: Office of the Governor, 1993), p. 542.

FIGURE 2 The Distribution of Health Care Spending

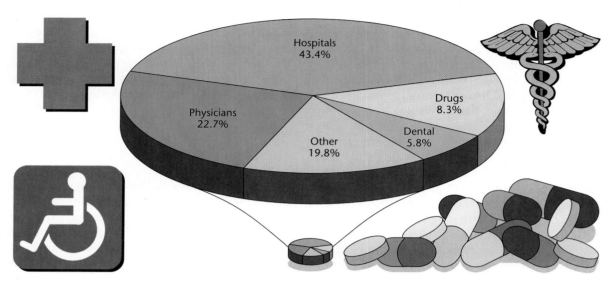

Over two-thirds of spending on health care is for hospital and physician services.

TABLE 1 Real Per Capita Health Care Expenditures (1990 Dollars)

Year	Total	Hospital		Physician		Drug		Dental		Other	
	$	$	%	$	%	$	%	$	%	$	%
1950	836.98	487.29	58.2	175.41	21.0	58.51	7.0	50.28	6.0	65.49	7.8
1955	950.04	529.76	55.8	199.06	21.0	65.63	6.9	61.52	6.5	94.07	9.9
1960	1,058.23	573.39	54.2	235.56	22.3	84.61	8.0	66.07	6.2	98.60	9.3
1965	1,419.23	725.96	51.2	299.68	21.1	126.77	8.9	82.06	5.8	184.76	13.0
1970	1,450.84	700.40	48.3	317.76	21.9	180.54	12.4	98.15	6.8	153.99	10.6
1975	1,709.73	833.61	48.8	362.92	21.2	236.70	13.8	109.83	6.4	166.67	9.7
1980	1,901.83	911.37	47.9	386.94	20.3	249.98	13.1	133.47	7.0	222.07	11.6
1985	1995.79	877.11	43.9	436.66	21.9	220.71	11.1	125.21	6.3	336.10	16.8
1990	2,329.54	1,010.72	43.4	528.57	22.7	193.26	8.3	135.24	5.8	461.75	19.8

Note: "Other" includes such professional services as optometry, prosthetics, and nursing home care. Sources: Charles Phelps, *Health Economics* (NY: HarperCollins Publishers, 1992) and Paul Feldstein, *Health Care Economics* (Albany: Delmar Publishers, 1993), and author updates.

Real per capita spending on all categories of health-care services has risen. The changing proportions in Table 1 reflect the fact that many procedures for which surgery and hospital stays were previously the norm now rely on new drug therapies. Notice the 700% growth in the "other" category of expenditures. All other categories have declined in importance when compared to "other," which covers such diverse professional services as eyeglasses, medical appliances, and nursing home care. Almost 80% of this expenditure growth is for nursing home care as our population has aged.

Recall that receipts or spending equal $P \times Q$, where P = prices and Q = quantities. Thus, rising per capita health-care expenditures reflect a combination of higher *prices* and higher *quantities* (for a given *quality*). Although separating spending changes into changes in prices and changes in service levels (quantity) is complex, if we ignore changes in quality for a moment, we can analyze the price-change side using the Consumer Price Index (CPI) and its medical component. Changes in health-care prices reflect both changes due to overall inflation and price changes specific to health care. Table 2 takes you step-by-step through calculations for the decades between 1960 and 1990. Per capita health-care spending rose about 10% annually across these three decades (shown on line 1). Part of this rise was due to general inflation (line 2), and part, to prices rising especially fast in the health-care sector (line 4). Subtracting these two rates of price change leaves the change in per capita consumption of health-care services (quantity). This rise in quantity consumed partially reflects both the rising health-care needs of an aging population, and partially, the increasing costs of new medical technologies.

• **Problems in Measuring Health-Care Costs**
Table 2 indicates that the quantity of services grew most rapidly during the 1960s and 1970s, but slowed to a 2.2% average annual growth during the 1980s. However, much of the rising cost of medical care may reflect quality improvements not accounted for in the government's statistics. For example, new drugs enter the CPI market basket each year, but there is no previous price for them. The Bureau of Labor Statistics (BLS), which computes the CPI, treats the previous price for a new drug as a weighted average of all other drugs in the sample. If new

drugs have therapeutic qualities absent in earlier drugs, then this method will typically overstate price increases for drugs–and for health care in general.

Another deficiency is that if a new drug priced above the average is a substitute for costly hospitalization, the CPI will still rise even though true costs to treat that ailment have fallen. For example, clozapine, an expensive drug, has proven effective for schizophrenia. Clozapine sharply reduces the need for psychiatric hospitalization and allows many patients to go home. And lithotripsy (ultrasound treatment to pulverize and dislodge kidney stones) has higher monetary costs than surgery, but it shortens hospital stays, allowing patients to return to their lives and their work. This reduces total costs because patients' opportunity costs must be considered. Thus, lithotripsy is usually a bargain. But some new drugs may be complements to existing medical procedures, increasing their use. For example, drugs to reduce rejection rates for transplants may encourage frequent and expensive transplant surgeries, raising the overall cost of medical care.[2]

Similarly, it is difficult to measure quality in hospital and physician services and the breadth of insurance coverage. Rising hospital costs may reflect lower ratios of nurses to patients or more sophisticated diagnostic testing. In recent decades, more diagnostic testing and surgeries

[2]D. Cleeton, V. Goepfrich, and B. Weisbrod, "What Does the Consumer Price Index for Prescription Drugs Really Measure?" *Health Care Financing Review*, Spring 1992, p. 45–51.

TABLE 2 Average Annual Percent Change in Health-Care Expenditures Per Capita, Prices and Quantities, 1960–1990

Line	Item	1961–1970	1971–1980	1981–1990
1	Health-care expenditures per capita	9.2	11.9	9.2
2	Minus: Economy-wide inflation	2.2	6.2	4.6
3	Equals: Expenditures per capita corrected for inflation	6.9	5.4	4.4
4	Minus: Health-care price increases in excess of inflation	1.7	1.6	2.3
5	Equals: Growth in quantity of health care per capita	5.1	3.8	2.2

Source: *Economic Report of the President*, 1993, p. 147.

Note: Columns do not sum both because of rounding and because price-quantity interaction terms have been omitted.

have shifted to outpatient sites. Thus, hospitalized patients are, on average, much sicker than those of 20 years ago. Rising physician fees may reflect higher quality because physicians are more specialized. Hikes in insurance rates may reflect higher medical service costs, rising administrative costs, broader policy coverage, or increased usage by policyholders.[3] Some of these trends obviously represent quality improvements ignored by BLS. The result is that the rise in health-care costs is probably overstated by the medical component of the CPI in line 4 of Table 2.

Another problem in measuring health-care costs is that some types of spending are hard to classify, especially when comparing total spending on health care between countries. For example, elderly Americans increasingly reside in nursing homes. All outlays for their care are included when total spending on health care is calculated. But should it be? Inclusion of spending for their food and shelter is questionable. Moreover, in earlier times, most elderly Americans stayed with family members. In many foreign countries (e.g., Japan), this is still the custom; nursing homes are a rarity. Thus, the shift of elderly Americans into nursing homes causes overstatement (*a*) in the overall growth of health-care spending in the United States and (*b*) relative to spending on health care in other countries. The point here is that all aggregate data on the prices of health care and on total health expenditures must be handled with care. As we shall see, the growth of health-care expenditures may partially stem from increasing amounts of overconsumption. However, Table 2 suggests that rapidly rising health-care prices and costs may induce self-correcting competitive forces.

• **Managed Care** Breaking down medical spending as we have suggests that the rapid growth in the amount of medical care consumed appears to be slowing. The recent decline in the growth of quantity consumed may arise in part

from efforts by insurers and firms to cut costs (*a*) through *utilization reviews* (which assess the efficiency of specific procedures in an attempt to limit those that yield zero or little benefit when applied to patients with certain ailments) and (*b*) by shifting employees into such managed care systems as *health maintenance organizations* (HMOs).

Health maintenance organizations (HMOs) typically contract with large firms to cover the health-care needs of employees and their families for a fixed fee per person covered by the contract.

Early reports on HMOs suggested that managed care did decrease utilization (quantity) and expenditures. However, more recent studies suggest that employees who selected HMOs had less utilization and lower expenditures than the average before they enrolled in managed care. Two possibilities are that (*a*) people with healthy lifestyles are more likely to enroll in HMOs or (*b*) HMOs try to select patient populations that are healthier than average. This is "cherry picking," or *favorable selection*, the reverse of the adverse selection described earlier in this book. Thus, studies that fail to adjust HMO utilization for pre-enrollment averages overestimate how effectively managed care reduces utilization.

• **The Role of the Federal Government** The federal government's role in health care was once largely limited to the funding of medical research, veterans hospitals, and attempts to control contagious diseases (by the Public Health Service). But this role for government has expanded with each passing decade. Much of the 5.1% annual growth in the *quantity* of medical care consumed in the 1960s followed enactment of Medicare and Medicaid as federally funded programs in 1965.

*Through **Medicare**, government subsidizes medical insurance for all Americans over 65 years of age and for many disabled workers as well. **Medicaid** mandates shared state and federal funding of health care for the poor.*

---

[3]P. Feldstein, *Health Care Economics*, 4th ed. (Albany, NY: Delmar Publishers, 1993), p. 61–64.

Older people tend to be heavy users of health-care services, so covering the aged automatically boosted the demand for health care. Many poor people are also unhealthy, so Medicaid also added to the growth of expenditures for health care.

• **The Spread of Health Insurance**   In 1950, less than one-third of all workers and their families had health insurance. Few families purchased private health insurance because health care was relatively much less costly than it is today, and because insurance rates were high relative to the expected costs of health care for relatively healthy families. Put simply, *adverse selection* was a problem. People who purchased health insurance tended to be those who were unhealthy, while healthy people largely chose to self-insure. Thus, health insurance was viewed as an uneconomical luxury by most Americans.

The surge in health-care costs that followed the adoption of Medicare heightened workers' anxiety about affordable medical care. Consequently, unions and the managers of large firms began to view health insurance as a major and very valuable tax-free fringe benefit. From 1970 to 1994, over 40 million people were added to payrolls; those employed have risen from 57% of all Americans in 1970 to 62% today. Most workers and their families are now covered by health insurance provided through employers. The combined forces of Medicare and the spread of insurance should make it no surprise that health-care spending rose.

• **The Issue of Quality**   The preceding analysis presumes a constant technology and quality of medical care across the last four decades, which is, of course, incorrect. For example, organ transplants and heart bypass surgery are comparatively recent innovations. Thus, part of the rising demand for medical care is due to new procedures and technologies. One way improvements in the quality of health care stimulates demand is that people who are inherently not very healthy live much longer and, throughout their longer lives, absorb more health-care resources each year.

Another way new technologies (embodying higher quality) stimulate the demand for health care is that procedures are available to alleviate ailments that the patient would simply have endured in an earlier time. For example, liposuction has made it possible for people to quickly lose unwanted (or inconveniently located) poundage. And hip or knee joint replacements have allowed millions of older Americans to walk away from their wheelchairs or to store their canes and walkers in a closet.

However, new technology and improved quality are not always synonymous, although they have been so perceived in the past. Unfocused use of technology or technology not linked to improved outcomes may represent an increase in quantity with no improvement in quality. For instance, widespread use of fetal ultrasonography for all pregnancies does not necessarily yield improved birth outcomes. The federal Office of Technology Assessment estimates that only one-fifth of all medical technologies have been reliably tested to be effective in improving patient outcomes. However, current research is now focusing on answering such important questions as whether physical therapy is better than home exercise, whether some heart surgery procedures are better than others, or whether bone marrow transplants extend the lives of cancer patients.

The growing share of income devoted to health care suggests that health care is income elastic. The income elasticity of demand for health care is roughly 1.3, so the share of spending on health care will probably continue to rise as per capita income grows in the future.[4] So what can we conclude? First, as a nation, we now consume more *real per capita* health-care services than ever before. Much of this growth has occurred during the relative prosperity that followed World War II, and much of it may be attributable to government's increased role in

---

[4]Organization for Economic Co-operation and Development, *Health Care Systems in Transition: The Search for Efficiency* (Paris: OECD, 1990). Also see Charles Carlstrom, "The Government Role in the Health Care Industry: Past, Present, and Future" *Economic Commentary* (Cleveland Ohio: Federal Reserve Bank of Cleveland), 1 June 1994.

health care (e.g., from Medicare coverage as most citizens live longer and grow older).

HEALTH-CARE ACCESS

Among the first questions a new patient is asked is, "Do you have insurance?" The vast majority is covered by health insurance, but one American in seven does not have insurance and many others are underinsured. Lack of insurance often means that, except for emergencies, people receive care only on a cash basis. Consequently, many of the nearly poor simply go without proper health care or delay care until they become insured. Many of the uninsured do rely on care from hospital emergency rooms (ERs). These facilities prioritize incoming patients according to severity, so treatment in an ER is often incredibly slow, especially for patients with minor ailments. ERs are also very costly to operate when dealing with minor cuts and sprains or symptoms of flu or colds. Thus, high utilization of ERs has contributed to the overall costs of health care.

• **The Uninsured** The distribution of insurance coverage shown in Figure 3 indicates that most American workers and their families are insured through their employers. Medicaid covers roughly half of all people living below the poverty line, but many others, including large numbers of children, go without coverage. Although the "certified" poor are covered by Medicaid, many families living below the poverty line are uninsured, as are many younger workers previously covered under parental health plans.

Another uninsured group consists of people with *preexisting conditions* (e.g., diabetes or a history of cancer) that virtually preclude private insurance. Preexisting conditions are excluded in a majority of insurance plans for individual families, and covering an employee with a family member debilitated by a costly disease may increase premiums for small firms. The irony for people with these problems is that it is for just

FIGURE 3 Health Insurance Coverage

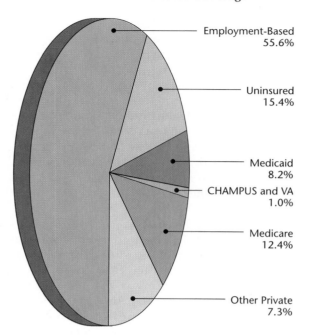

Employment-Based
55.6%

Uninsured
15.4%

Medicaid
8.2%

CHAMPUS and VA
1.0%

Medicare
12.4%

Other Private
7.3%

Note: Other includes, for example, privately purchased health insurance and the Department of Veterans Affairs.
Source: Economic Report of the President, 1994

Nearly two-thirds of health insurance coverage in the United States is provided by employers. The government (through Medicare and Medicaid) provides insurance to roughly half of those remaining. At any moment in time, over 15% (35 million people) are without medical insurance. Further, over any two-year period, nearly 1 in 4 will be without insurance. These people typically rely on hospital emergency rooms for treatment.

such conditions that insurance seems imperative. (More about this in a moment.) Further, preexisting conditions often tie people insured through their employers to particular jobs. Since new policies will not cover illnesses that were manifest before the policy went into effect, workers with family members who have chronic conditions may feel compelled to remain with their current employers, even when they have opportunities to work elsewhere for higher pay or in an otherwise preferable work environment.

• **The Problem of Cost Shifting** Hospitals seldom collect on their billings to uninsured patients, so insured patients or those who pay cash are charged higher prices for medical care.

> **Cost shifting** occurs when patients who pay less than the costs of their medical care are subsidized through higher charges to patients who do pay full costs.

Cost shifting results not only when indigent patients overuse access through hospital emergency rooms, but also because some government programs (e.g., Medicaid) pay only a fraction of total medical costs. This means that doctor fees and hospital bills are driven up for patients who do pay, and insurance rates are consequently increased as well.

• **The Changing Economy**   Some people have never had health insurance, so this fact alone cannot explain the relatively recent groundswell of support for universal access or coverage. One concern is the accelerating rate of structural change. Employment has become less secure because of corporate restructuring, the globalization of markets, and a rising tide of laws that have driven up the costs to firms of hiring employees (e.g., pension funding laws, higher Social Security taxes, and the Family Leave Act). Worries about health-care coverage have risen correspondingly. More and more employers have attempted to offset rising costs of covering full-time employees by employing more temporary and part-time employees, who are seldom covered by health insurance. Many people once covered by excellent health-care plans now work for smaller firms (or for themselves) that provide, at best, limited insurance coverage that does not cover preexisting conditions.

The result? Calls for reform ring out not only from the uninsured, but also from many who are now covered by broad insurance policies. The pressure is for *guaranteed access* to comprehensive coverage that is *portable* (stays with the individual worker) and *affordable*. To see how this might be accomplished, we must first look at the nature of health care itself and then examine our present health-care markets.

WHAT IS UNIQUE ABOUT HEALTH CARE?[5]

Competitive markets usually translate consumer demands into powerful price incentives for firms to efficiently provide products and to improve profit opportunities through innovation. But, as we saw in earlier chapters, some markets contain elements of market failure, including (a) uncertainty, (b) externalities, (c) imperfect information, or (d) monopoly and monopsony power. Examples of these are (a) some uncertainty always exists about whether a new movie is worth your time; (b) automobiles create pollution; (c) at least one trip to a restaurant is usually required to ascertain the quality of the food and the service; and (d) most public utilities are monopolies. But unlike most product markets, the health-care industry embodies all four of these elements of market failure.

Uncertainty in Health Care

Many health-care decisions arise from such apparently random events as unforeseen illnesses, car accidents, or broken limbs resulting from such seemingly normal (and safe) activities as walking down stairs. Random elements in health and illness stimulate desires in all of us to have our health needs met in some predictable fashion. And the process of aging always plays a role. This has led many to argue that access to adequate health care is an inherent human right.

Added to the uncertain incidence of many illnesses is general uncertainty about medical costs. For example, in recent years, many parents have been shocked when doctor and hospital charges have doubled–or more–with each new child born into a family. The costs of care can range from a few pennies for aspirin to treat a headache to a fortune that can be exhausted in attempts to solve a severe heart or kidney problem. This increases people's anxiety about health care. Hospital and physician

---

[5]This section closely follows analysis by Charles Phelps, *Health Economics* (New York: HarperCollins, 1992).

Sticker Shock in Medicine

What do heart bypass surgery and new cars have in common? Both have outrageously high sticker prices that most consumers ignore. Differences between sticker prices and actual prices are often sensationalized and are cited as potential sources of savings by reformers who favor infusing these markets with either more competition or price controls.

Consider a recent survey of the costs of heart bypass surgery in Pennsylvania.* One hospital charged $21,000 while another, located at a medical school, charged $84,000. Critics condemn this $63,000 difference as a symptom of waste and inefficiency. This difference, however, is like the exaggerated sticker price for new automobiles: the actual selling price is typically far lower. In the

real world of health-care purchases, Medicare and Medicaid (40% of the market) unilaterally set prices, and large insurance firms (another 35% of the market) are able to negotiate deep discounts from these "list" prices. Medicare, Medicaid, and large insurance carriers all possess some monopsony power and account for over three-quarters of all hospital revenues. Like fleet buyers of automobiles, they never pay the sticker price. After adjusting for these discounts, the average prices per procedure actually received by these two hospitals differed by only $5,700—they received $18,221 and $23,974 respectively.

Since virtually nobody pays full prices, why do hospitals inflate their bills? Hospitals attempt to collect these full charges from

smaller insurance companies and from those who can pay, but who lack insurance. This is clearly an example of price discrimination. More importantly, since many people have insurance that requires a copayment, hospitals can often collect a copayment equal to a percentage of the sticker price. For example, the 20% copayment charged the patient is based on the full-payment price, not what big insurance companies can negotiate. This practice of basing the copayment on the sticker price and not the actual price paid is now the subject of a large class-action lawsuit to force hospitals to return the copayment overcharges to patients.

* Reported in *The New Mexican,* 13 October 1993.

charges for the same service can vary enormously (see Focus 1). These variations may be due to the mix of treatments, the severity of any patient's illness, and the perceived status of the institution performing the services. But, in any event, a patient undergoing a procedure often has little idea about how much will be charged.

Almost everyone recognizes that medicine is not an exact science, but therapies for the same illness vary to a surprising degree. One study showed how strongly the probability of being hospitalized for certain procedures depends on location.[6] Over 85,000 cases at 16 major uni-

versity and large community hospitals were addressed. These are hospitals where medical knowledge could be assumed to be at state-of-the-art levels. Doctors, however, disagreed systematically about proper procedures. For thirty specific surgical procedures, the range in admission rates for the population in the market area between the lowest and highest admitting hospitals was 500%. This strongly suggests that your odds of being hospitalized for these specific illnesses varied by over five times, depending on where you live.

Risk and uncertainty can often be buffered by insurance. For example, auto insurance partially protects drivers from the financial consequences of a collision. While we would like to be guaranteed good health, such guarantees are impossible. Health insurance or guaranteed access to medical services, however, does reduce the financial burden associated with purchasing

[6]J. Wennberg, "Small Area Analysis and the Medical Care Outcome Problem," in *Research Methodology: Strengthening Causal Interpretation of Non-Experimental Data,* ed. L. Sechrest et al. (Rockville: Dept. of H. H. S., 1990), p. 177–213. This study is summarized in C. Phelps, "Diffusion of Information in Medical Care," *Journal of Economic Perspectives,* Summer 1992, p. 23–42.

medical care. Due to the uncertain nature of illness, health-care markets have evolved to include either substantial private insurance or government provision or financing.

Health-Care Externalities

How selfishly soever man may be supposed, there are evidently some principles in his nature which interest him in the fortune of others, and render their happiness necessary to him, though he derives nothing from it except for the pleasure of seeing it.

Adam Smith, *The Theory of Moral Sentiments* (1759)

Health-care externalities have been recognized for centuries. We all benefit when other people have flu shots or vaccination against polio. Public health agencies were established to eradicate or reduce the effects of communicable diseases. Perhaps the biggest bang for the health-care buck comes from public water and sewage treatment.[7]

There is a growing consensus that basic medical care should be available to all, regardless of ability to pay. Many see health care as a fundamental right. Most of us feel better if we know that the less fortunate will be cared for in times of catastrophic illness, instead of being left to die. Part of this new consensus has developed from this altruistic *caring externality*, and part has developed from recognition that catastrophic illnesses may be random, the selfish notion that if we are in such a situation, our health-care needs will be covered.

Asymmetric Information

Physicians often spend a decade or more after college acquiring knowledge and skills needed to practice their medical specialties. As a result,

most Americans rely heavily on the expertise of their doctors. This is a classic case of the *principal–agent* problem covered in earlier chapters. One problem posed by asymmetric information is that patients may have only a vague sense about how qualified a physician is.

Another problem is that providers may use their superior knowledge to influence demand in their self-interest. This possibility is at the heart of many policy controversies.

> ***Supplier-induced demand (SID)*** *occurs when an agent (a doctor) uses superior knowledge to induce a principal (a patient) to buy more of a good or service.*

Patients (principals) rely on doctors (agents) to guide medical care treatment. Most doctors are still paid on a *fee-for-service* basis.

> ***Fee for service*** *entails payment tailored to each treatment.* ***Capitation*** *is the practice of charging a fixed fee to provide medical services to a patient for a year at a time.*

In a sense, capitation is like the pricing for the buffet at an all-you-can-eat restaurant, while fee for service is like ordering a la carte.

Capitation embodies substantial incentives for care providers to minimize the resource costs of health care. However, in a fee-for-service arrangement, the doctor as an agent has financial incentives to extend services beyond the amount the patient would want if the patient had the same information as the doctor. For example, doctors with financial interests in medical laboratories may order redundant tests to bolster lab revenues. Supplier-induced demand has been shown to affect the rate of C-sections (delivery of a baby by operation), with insured women having far more than the uninsured, even in the same hospital. However, we should note that in addition to price (a C-section being more costly), the convenience for the insured patient of scheduling a birth may be a consideration.

Is resource allocation more efficiently achieved through prices and consumer choice on the demand side? Or are regulatory controls

---

[7]In many developing nations, average life spans are increased most efficiently (at least cost) through modest spending on water and sewage disposal systems. See P. Passell, "Health Care in the Rich and Poor Lands: Some Issues are the Same," *The New York Times*, 8 July 1993, p. D2.

needed on the supply side? Obviously, the more important supplier-induced demand is, the less efficient will be markets based on consumer sovereignty. However, the excessive demand that might foster overuse of health resources may be offset by restrictions on the supply of physicians.

Monopoly and Monopsony Power

Health-care markets are permeated by players with at least some degree of monopoly or monopsony power, or both. For example, the American Medical Association (AMA) has a certain amount of market control over the supply of physicians, some hospitals have monopsony power in nursing markets, major health insurers (e.g., Blue Cross and Blue Shield) may exercise monopsony power as purchasers of health services, and some pharmaceutical companies have market power as providers of powerful therapeutic drugs for which almost no close substitutes exist. Only individual consumers are largely bereft of market power. In this section, we will look at some possible consequences of the exercise of market power in health care.

• **Monopoly Power and Physician Supply** In the mid-1800s, the American Medical Association focused on getting states to license physicians. After accomplishing this goal by the early 1900s, the AMA turned its attention to control of medical schools. In 1910, the Flexner Report, sponsored by the Carnegie Foundation at the urging of the AMA, persuaded lawmakers that all physicians should be required to attend first-class medical schools before they could enter practice, with the AMA having power to determine what "first class" meant. The number of medical schools was cut in half by 1940.

Next, the AMA was able to raise more barriers to entry into the practice of medicine when it gained control over internship and residency processes and over board certifications. In addition, the AMA has lobbied successfully to limit competition from substitute providers, including optometrists, podiatrists, and chiropractors. For example, physicians were prohibited from referring patients to or accepting referrals from chiropractors, and chiropractors were denied the privilege of practicing in hospitals.[8] Historically, nearly half of those applying to medical school have been denied entry. This excess demand for a medical degree is evidence that the AMA, through its lobbying of state legislatures, substantially limited the supply of physicians.

The supplier-induced demand hypothesis described a moment ago suggests that physicians can exploit superior knowledge, vis-à-vis that of patients, to inefficiently boost demands for health care. This is shown as the shift of demand from D_0 in Figure 4 to demand curve D_1 where D_0 represents the demand that would exist if patients and physicians had identical knowledge. The AMA's ability to restrict the supply of physicians' services is shown by supply curve S_1 which is much less than the supply S_0 that would exist in the absence of the AMA's market power.

Whether the total amount of physicians' services purchased by patients is more or less than the amount that would be transacted if this market were purely competitive is ambiguous in Figure 4. However, the price of physicians' services is clearly artificially high, and so are physicians' incomes. According to critics, these forces contribute to the abnormally high returns to an investment in medical education: roughly double that from investments in other advanced degrees.

The extent of uncertainty, externalities, asymmetric information, and market power in medical care make it somewhat unique and have driven much of the government regulation in this market. Uncertainty has stimulated use of insurance (both public and private) to protect consumers' pocketbooks and peace of mind. Public health considerations from externalities have been another source of pressure for universal health-care coverage. All of these factors have contributed to rising medical care costs over the last few decades.

---

[8]S. Folland et al., *The Economics of Health and Health Care*, (New York: Macmillan 1993), p. 655.

FIGURE 4 Supplier-Induced Demand, the AMA Monopoly, and the Price of Physician Services

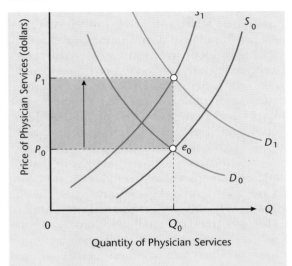

Asymmetry of information yields supplier-induced demand shown as the shift from D_0 to D_1. Limited slots in medical school limit the supply of doctors, shown as the shift from S_0 to S_1. Relative to the equilibrium e_0 that would exist if this market were competitive and if information were equal, the effects of these shifts on the amounts of physician services consumed is ambiguous, but prices for physician services and incomes for physicians are unambiguously higher.

THE HEALTH-CARE MARKET

Medical care is a growth industry. In this section we examine how improved health care is produced and try to specify why spending on medical care has grown. Spending on health has grown because (*a*) the growth of private and public medical insurance increasingly reduces the *per episode* cost of medical care, (*b*) the subsidies to employers (and individuals) from the tax-free treatment of health-care benefits paid by employers encourage use, (*c*) rapidly improving (and costly) technologies and new treatments stimulate demand, and (*d*) aging and other de-mographic changes occurring in our economy boost demand.

The Production of Health

Health care is only one input that influences our overall health. Other factors include our biological makeup (our genetic predisposition to specific illnesses) and our lifestyles (exercise, food intake, smoking, stress, etc.). An underlying desire for health creates our demand for health-care services. In the event of illness, health-care inputs are used to maintain and restore health.

The production function for health shown in Panel A of Figure 5 specifies the relationship between health status (*H*) and various medical inputs (*m*). We have lumped physician, hospital, drugs, and all medical care services into one single input, health care. This approach treats the production of health as parallel to the production of sand and gravel discussed in the chapter "Production and Costs."

With zero spending on health care ($m = 0$) health status is point *a*. Through preventive health care (e.g., vaccinations and regular checkups) and by treating various ailments, health status rises, but at a diminishing rate. Health is subject to the law of diminishing returns (Panel B). As more people are immunized, the spread of contagious diseases is slowed and the marginal benefits from immunizing an additional citizen are reduced. Similar declines in marginal benefits apply to individuals as we use more and more antibiotics to cure a specific set of illnesses. We may even develop resistance to additional antibiotics, so that marginal benefits eventually became negative. For example, as more people are treated in hospitals, eventually, the increased probabilities of provider errors or contracting diseases may yield only negative net benefits.

Further, once comprehensive medical care is provided to all, *moral hazard* problems potentially arise, reducing our personal efforts to remain healthy. Just as seat belts and air bags may give some drivers the confidence to speed or drive recklessly, guarantees that care will be

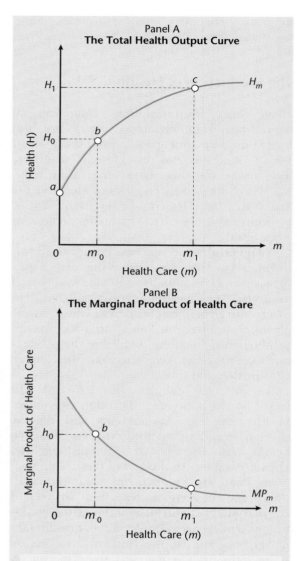

Panel A
The Total Health Output Curve

Health (H) — vertical axis

H_1 ...... c ...... H_m

H_0 ...... b

a

0 .... m_0 .... m_1 .... m

Health Care (m)

Panel B
The Marginal Product of Health Care

Marginal Product of Health Care — vertical axis

h_0 ...... b

h_1 ...... c ...... MP_m

0 .... m_0 .... m_1 .... m

Health Care (m)

The production function of health in Panel A shows the relationship between health status (H) and various medical care inputs lumped into one single input, health care (m). Health status increases with additional health-care inputs, but at a declining rate. Panel B shows that the production of health faces the law of diminishing returns; the marginal product of health care declines as health-care inputs are expanded.

FIGURE 5   The Production of Health

available reduce the costs of smoking, hang-gliding, and other activities that can endanger health. Thus, by the time we use m_1 units of health care, their marginal productivity in Panel B is only h_1, which is much below the marginal benefits from initial inputs of medical care.

Throughout this century, life expectancy has been strongly related to per capita income, as shown in Figure 6. However, the marginal benefits to life span from added income decline sharply as income rises. The lengthening life expectancy in this figure also reflects the impact of advancing medical technology.

Your health is determined by your genetic makeup, environmental influences, how you choose to live, and, to a lesser degree, by the amount of health services you consume. Most of us buy health care to combat serious illness, but this care is usually paid for by an insurance provider. Since 85% of Americans are covered by some form of insurance, how insurance interacts with health-care providers and patients is crucial for understanding health care in the United States.

The Role of Health Insurance

*If I bought groceries the way we pay for health care,
I'd eat better and so would my dog.*

Senator Phil Gramm (1993)

Uncertainty about individual illness caused private markets for health insurance to develop early in this century. However, before the federal government introduced Medicare in 1965, relatively few families were insured. The majority were *self-insured*; that is, they were not covered by a health insurance policy–they paid their own bills. This helped curb higher prices because the entire cost of medical services falls on self-insuring consumers. Quantity demanded falls when out-of-pocket costs (or prices) rise. In fact, as recently as 1960, 56% of all medical expenses were covered by out-of-pocket payments from individuals, in contrast to less than 20% today.

FIGURE 6 Income, Technological Progress and Life Expectancy

Source: Jee-Peng Tan and Kenneth Hill. "The Foundation for Better Health", *Finance & Development, September 1993,* pp. 14–16. Data from *World Developement Report 1993,* World Bank.

This figure shows that income and life expectancy are positively related, but only at a diminishing rate. Higher incomes have more of an impact in poor countries because added resources can be used to buy basic necessities (food, shelter and better sanitation). These expenditures yield big results. Technological change has the effect of improving the entire relationship for both rich and poor countries.

Note: International dollars are derived from national currencies, not by use of exchange rates but by assessment of purchasing power. The effect is to raise the incomes of poorer countries, often substantially. Data refer to all individual countries for which estimates could be made.

• **Insurance Companies** Many people might be willing to take an even bet of a small amount of money on the flip of a coin. However, only a few high rollers are willing to bet thousands of dollars with only even odds of winning. Most of us want the probable outcome of risky activities to favor us substantially or we just don't want to play. This widespread characteristic is called *risk aversion,* and it provides insurance companies with opportunities for profit.

> *The Insurance Principle: Most of us are willing to pay to avoid some financial consequences of taking risks, so insurance companies can sell*

us a guarantee against risks for a fee large enough to cover their claims and operating costs and still make a profit.

No one can predict with certainty who will be next to suffer a catastrophic illness. Thus, insurance policy buyers contribute toward a fund to compensate the person afflicted. Insurance companies can provide this service and expect to make profits as long as the fee (or premium) exceeds the amount they might have to pay multiplied by the probability of payment. No insurance company will knowingly sell policies at rates so low that, given the expected risk of a payout, it will probably lose money. This fact distresses people concerned about the screening strategies insurance companies use to exclude some people from standard health coverage because of potentially costly preexisting conditions such as diabetes. Few complain, however, when nonsmokers receive preferential rates. From an insurance perspective, both are simply risk-adjusted premiums.

• **Insurance and Price Elasticity of Demand**
Insurance coverage usually involves a mixture of *coinsurance* (the patient pays x percent of the total bill) and a *deductible* (the patient pays the first y dollars). The higher the deductible, the more powerfully market forces curb price hikes for minor medical care. If you must pay the first $250 of annual medical care, for each trip to the doctor you will balance benefits against the full price charged. After this initial $250 expense (the deductible) is incurred, health plans typically pay 80% of extra medical care for that year until some maximum is reached. Thus, families pay 20% of all bills until they have spent, say, $5,250 ($5,000 maximum plus the $250 deductible). Thereafter, insurance pays 100%. Beyond the initial $250 deductible (or if you are reasonably certain your family's health outlays will exceed $250), your implicit new price for medical care is far lower, and, at the margin, you will consume more services.

The effect of coinsurance is a little different. In Figure 7, an uninsured patient's demand for medical care is D_0. If the original price for the service is P_0, market quantity demanded will be Q_0 (point a). Now assume the patient is covered with insurance that pays two-thirds of the bill. The patient pays only one-third. For such consumers, the price is now $P_{1/3}$ and they will purchase quantity Q_1 (point b) of medical care. The result is that at a market price of P_0, consumers now purchase Q_1 units (point c). This gives us one point on the new demand curve for medical care with insurance, D_1. If insurance pays the entire bill (zero copayment), consumers will demand Q_2 levels of health care. Thus, the effect of health insurance is to rotate the demand curve clockwise at point d, resulting in a less elastic demand than the original curve. If medical care were free, would the demand be perfectly inelastic? Probably not, since transaction costs for patients are not zero.

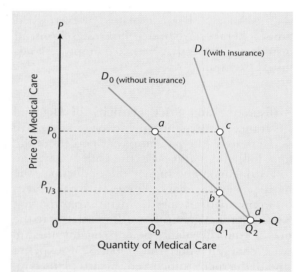

Insurance shifts the demand curve from D_0 (without insurance) to D_1 (with insurance). Without insurance, the patient would have to pay P_0 and would purchase Q_0 medical services (point a). Because insurance pays two-thirds of the bill, the effective price to the patient is $P_{1/3}$ and the quantity of medical care demanded rises to Q_1 at point b. Thus, the quantity of medical care demanded at a total price P_0 increases from point a to point c. Thus, insurance coverage reduces the price elasticity of demand for medical care.

FIGURE 7   Effect of Insurance on Demand for Medical Care

• **Moral Hazard and Insurance**   The problem of moral hazard also drives up health insurance costs. Moral hazard arises, first, because insurance reduces financial costs. Although good health is also motivated by many nonfinancial considerations, insurance coverage diminishes the incentive to adopt a healthier lifestyle, which increases the probability of illness or injury–and costly treatment. Second, artificially lower prices encourage more intensive use than would be efficient. A wedge is driven between the total cost of medical services and the value of (consumers' willingness to pay for) these same services. Consequently, inefficient (artificially low) price signals are transmitted to consumers.[9]

• **Medical Malpractice Awards**   Huge awards in malpractice cases have driven up the costs of medical malpractice insurance, most notably in obstetrics. This, according to critics, has led to the practice of *defensive medicine*, where doctors may order relatively unnecessary tests. The goal of defensive medicine is to definitively rule out any condition (however rare) that, if undetected, would lead to a costly malpractice suit. Insurance pays most of these costs, so few patients object. Defensive medicine, however, is difficult to detect; more extensive use of modern tests may signal defensive medicine, but it may simply reflect advances in medical technologies. Nevertheless, this is another form of moral hazard that adds to the rising cost of medical care. Many critics have called for reforms that make it more difficult to prove a malpractice claim and that put caps on malpractice awards by juries.

• **Low-Benefit High-Cost Care**   The spread of insurance (both public and private) has led to what some observers call *low-benefit high-cost care*. For many illnesses, a long menu of treatments is available, with declining marginal benefits from extending or expanding therapies. For ex-

---

[9]C. Donaldson and K. Gerard, *Economics of Health Care Financing: The Visible Hand* (New York: St. Martin's Press, 1993), p. 31–35.

ample, a headache is not relieved more quickly if you take full doses of aspirin and ibuprofen. In fact, this approach is likely to make you quite ill. This is reflected in the negative slope of the marginal benefits curve shown in Figure 8.

Paralleling other forms of production, health care faces rising marginal costs. Thus, in Figure 8, society faces a rising marginal cost curve. Optimally, society would choose Q_0 care at a price of P_0 (point e). At this point the marginal benefits from care just equal marginal costs. However, since insurance reduces the cost per episode, the effective price to consumers is P_1 (point a), and consumers (following their agent-doctor's advice) consume Q_1 units at a marginal cost of P_2 (point b). Because insurance payments reduce prices to consumers, they demand too much care, resulting in low additional benefits at a higher resource cost. Thus, high-cost low-benefit care results in a welfare loss to society equal to area eba.

To enter practice, physicians take the Hippocratic oath, which directs doctors to pursue all possible benefits for their patients *irrespective* of costs. And, with insurance paying a large portion of the cost, this often means prolonging treatment until marginal benefits approach zero.

> The **third-party payer problem**: Insurance or other subsidies for consuming health care (or any other good) boost effective demand by reducing the price paid by the consumer while raising the price received by the provider.

When the third-party payer problem is combined with physicians' financial incentives under a fee-for-service arrangement (the supplier-induced demand problem), medical care clearly is quite likely to be significantly overused. (This analysis suggests the quantity of physician services purchased as depicted back in Figure 4 will be unambiguously higher, and the prices of these services—and physician incomes—will be enhanced even more than is indicated in that figure.)

• **Adverse Selection and Insurance** Adverse selection arises in the insurance market because

FIGURE 8   Marginal Benefits and Marginal Costs of Various Levels of Health Care and the Optimal Level of Care

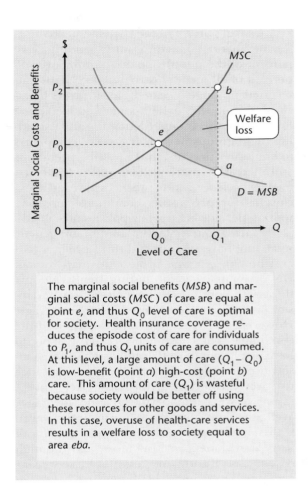

The marginal social benefits (*MSB*) and marginal social costs (*MSC*) of care are equal at point *e*, and thus Q_0 level of care is optimal for society. Health insurance coverage reduces the episode cost of care for individuals to P_1, and thus Q_1 units of care are consumed. At this level, a large amount of care ($Q_1 - Q_0$) is low-benefit (point *a*) high-cost (point *b*) care. This amount of care (Q_1) is wasteful because society would be better off using these resources for other goods and services. In this case, overuse of health-care services results in a welfare loss to society equal to area *eba*.

buyers of insurance may have a better idea about their general health than insurers do. Healthy young people do not wish to pay average insurance rates when they perceive low probability of using the coverage. On the other hand, people with ill health will jump at any chance to buy insurance at these rates. Thus, many young people with lower incomes who are without employer-provided insurance choose to self-insure. Insurance companies cannot perfectly isolate high-risk individuals who have preexisting conditions. In addition, insurers for small companies and individuals use age and sex profiles to establish *risk bands* that predict typical payouts and then adjust insurance rates accordingly.

Another problem for insurers is that each year a small portion of the population accounts for the bulk of all medical care spending. Two percent of the population account for over 40 percent of all medical care outlays.[10] This pattern sets up huge incentives for insurers to exclude people who exhibit a marked likelihood for being in this group. Identifying and excluding these groups permits insurance companies to limit their payouts, thus lowering premiums and increasing market share and profitability. Such experience-rating practices have led to exclusions for preexisting conditions and long waiting periods before new policies take effect.

Fears about potential misuse of genetic screening have surrounded the $2 billion federal human genome project (to map human DNA). Simple genetic testing might identify those with a predisposition for an illness, and insurers might use such tests to limit coverage. However, such screening and exclusion of the conditions that consumers are most likely to have would significantly reduce the value of insurance to most individuals. We buy insurance to cover the future; if the most likely future events are excluded, why buy the coverage? Well, we might continue to buy insurance (even with some limitations on coverage) because of fears about unexpected illnesses and the high cost of care. But the net result of these screens would be a growing pool of uninsured. This, in all likelihood, will lead to government restrictions on exclusionary practices, or it may lead to government coverage of those excluded by private insurance.

• Administrative Costs and the Size of the Pool

Insurance companies collect premiums and pay benefits with the goal of generating surpluses after covering administration costs along the way. The surplus compensates the company for bearing risk (in some years, benefits exceed costs); the administrative fee covers the actual administrative costs of marketing policies, collecting premiums, and paying benefits.

Group health policies average administrative fees of roughly 15% to 20%. For very large groups (e.g., Medicaid or United Auto Workers), administrative fees may fall to as low as 5%. Nongroup or private individual policies (where adverse selection is a serious problem) often involve administrative fees that match expected benefit payments. This means that half of all premiums are absorbed in administrative costs. Figure 9 provides estimates of average administrative fees for group plans based on the number of employees in the insured firm.

For hospitals and doctors, the existence of thousands of insurers with their separate paperwork and payment rules is a bureaucratic nightmare. A recent study concluded that about one-quarter of current medical care costs in the United States arise from marketing, underwriting, and other insurance administrative expenses and the myriad of insurance forms (both private and public) that doctors and hospitals must complete to get paid.[11] Advocates of a *single payer system* [similar to the one in Canada, where each province (state) acts as a single insurance company for its entire population] argue that much of this would be eliminated if the United States abandoned its reliance on widely diverse policies from a multitude of private insurance companies.

In 1994, President Clinton proposed *healthcare alliances* that would cover huge pools of workers to reduce the average administrative costs of health care. All alliances would use a single standard insurance form. He argued that we can free the resources to permit universal access by wringing out inefficiencies in the present system. However, how to tackle rising administrative costs remains extremely controversial.

---

[10]See H. Aaron, *Serious and Unstable Condition: Financing America's Health Care* (Washington, D.C.: The Brookings Institution, 1991), p. 51; and M. Berk and A. Monheit, "The Concentration of Health Expenditures: An Update," *Health Affairs*, Winter 1992, pp. 145–149.

[11]S. Woolhandler, *et al.*, "Administrative Costs in U.S. Hospitals", *New England Journal of Medicine*; 5 August 1993, pp. 400–403.

FIGURE 9 Insurer Administrative Fees and Size of Firm

Source: Hay & Higgins—estimates for *Congressional Research Service,* 1993

As the number of employees in the firm grows, the administrative cost associated with the health insurance declines as a percent of the total premiums.

• **Medicare and Medicaid** In 1965, Congress passed the Medicare bill creating universal health insurance for persons over 65 and included Medicaid, a program that created federal-state joint ventures to cover some categories of the poor. Medicare has since been expanded to include persons permanently disabled for at least two years and those with potentially fatal kidney ailments. Today the costs of Medicare and Medicaid have become a dominant health cost issue. Table 3 illustrates why.

Total real per capita health-care spending in the United States (as we saw in Table 1) roughly doubled between 1965 and 1994. In contrast, as Table 3 shows, real per capita Medicare spending more than quadrupled. In 1993 alone, taxpayers spent over $6,000 per Medicare enrollee. Interestingly, the real per capita spending on Medicaid patients has been roughly constant since the program's introduction. But more and more people are covered by Medicaid.

That Medicare coverage is costly should not be surprising: average medical expenses rise with age. Figure 10 shows health-care expenditures by age. A survey by the Health Care Finance Administration concluded that nearly 29% of all Medicare funds are spent on older Americans in the *last* year of their lives. Rising Medicare costs have been targets of recent deficit reduction legislation. Both the 1990 and 1993

TABLE 3 Real per Enrollee Medicare and Medicaid Spending, 1965–1990

| Year | Real Spending Per Enrollee (1990 Dollars) | |
	Medicare	Medicaid
1965	$ 1,297	NA
1970	3,557	$ 2,597
1975	4,881	2,358
1980	5,526	2,445
1985	5,806	2,499
1990	5,631	2,752

FIGURE 10 Per Capita Health Care Spending by Age, 1987

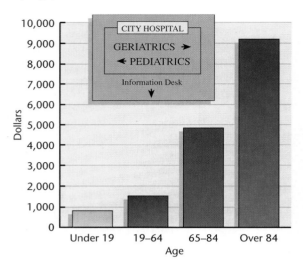

Health care spending per capita is significantly higher for older Americans.

Deficit Reduction Acts had provisions designed to reduce the cost of Medicare (e.g., new regulations focused on setting ceilings on physician and hospital payments), but both raised payroll taxes to support Medicare spending.[12]

Income Taxes and Health-Care Spending

Employer-provided fringe benefits have always been exempt from federal income taxes. As a consequence, employees can avoid taxes by shifting some of their wages into employer-paid health insurance and health services. For example, if your federal marginal tax rate is 28% while your state marginal income tax rate is 5% and if Social Security taxes are 7% then your combined marginal tax rate is 40% (28% + 5% + 7%). As a result, when $1 is shifted from tax-able wages into fringe benefits, you sacrifice only 60 cents in after-tax take-home pay. This 40 cent difference is implicitly a tax subsidy.

Employees will naturally be willing to purchase more health insurance and health services for 60 cents on the dollar, and employers have been happy to accommodate. And much of the spending by individuals on health care is tax deductible. One result of these subsidies is overconsumption of health insurance and health services, contributing to rising health-care costs. These subsidies currently cost the federal government roughly $65 billion a year in lost revenue and are the third largest government health-care subsidy, behind Medicare and Medicaid.[13] Because federal and most state income tax rates are progressive, this subsidy is most valuable to individuals in higher income brackets. As Figure 11 shows, higher income individuals receive better health-care benefits and, thus, receive a larger tax subsidy.[14]

The government encourages overconsumption by its tax subsidy of employer-provided health insurance, driving up the prices for private individuals who purchase health coverage. And finally, as we will see next, excessive health insurance provides incentives that favor expensive medical technologies instead of lower-cost medical care solutions.

Technology and the Cost of Health Care

The human body has become increasingly like an automobile, with replacements available for an ever growing number of parts—an arm or a leg, at about $2,000, an elbow at $1,200, an ear at $10,000, and a heart at $50,000–$80,000. They are even available in small, medium, large and extra large sizes. "Installation," of course, is extra, and as with auto parts, is typically many times greater than the price of the part.

Burton Weisbrod

---

[12]The 1990 law extended a 2.9% Medicare payroll tax to wages up to $125,000. The 1993 law eliminated the cap on wages. The 1990 law raised Medicare premiums and deductibles and cut payments to doctors and hospitals.

[13]L. Burman and J. Rodgers, "Tax Preferences and Employment-Based Health Insurance," *National Tax Journal*, September 1992, pp. 331–56.

[14]B. Fox, L. Taylor, and M. Yucel, "America's Health Care Problem: An Economic Perspective," *Federal Reserve Bank of Dallas: Economic Review*, Third Quarter, 1993, pp. 21–31.

FIGURE 11   Employer Provided Health Benefits and the Estimated Tax Subsidy (1991)

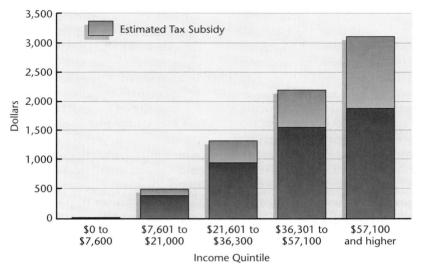

Source: U.S. Department of Commerce, Bureau of the Census and Beverly Fox, Lori Taylor and Mine Yucel, "America's Health Care Problem: An Economic Perspective." *Federal Reserve Bank of Dallas: Economic Review,* Third Quarter,1993, p.26.

Because marginal tax rates rise with rising income, the subsidy from federal tax exclusion of medical benefits rises as income increases.

Medical technology has advanced beyond the wildest dreams of our great grandparents. Less than a half a century ago, doctors' roles were primarily diagnostic: they identified an illness, predicted a likely outcome, and acted as tour guides as the illness ran its natural course. Drugs and therapies were in their infancy. Today, doctors can transplant organs, and many new drugs reduce the need for invasive surgery. Just a decade ago, heart and liver transplants were available only in a few medical centers. Now, many thousands of transplants are done annually all over the country. There is a growing consensus among economists that the rapid growth and proliferation of medical techniques is the principal cause of rapidly rising health-care costs.[15] New medical technology affects spending in several ways.

[15]Aaron, op. cit. and B. Weisbrod "The Health Care Quadrilemma: An Essay on Technological Change, Insurance, Quality of Care, and Cost Containment," *Journal of Economic Literature,* June 1991, pp. 523–552

• Technology's Impact on Treatment Costs
First, new technology opens up alternative choices for treatment. Treatments such as angioplasty (used to open clogged arteries), microsurgery, and arthroscopy exemplify procedures recently added to the menu. In some cases, these advances are clearly beneficial, quickly allowing patients to resume enjoyable and productive lives. Other new techniques, however, may represent high-cost, low-benefit treatment. Advances in technology frequently push back medical frontiers, permitting doctors to treat conditions that would have been fatal more quickly in an earlier era. To the extent that technology prolongs the lives of patients who are inherently quite ill, it often adds to the total costs. Older, less certain methods might yield the same outcome, but at lower cost and with less agony to all concerned.

Second, many technological breakthroughs cut the costs of treating common ailments in ways that may ultimately increase total medical spending. For example, antibiotics save many of us from certain death for various illnesses.

Result? We later succumb to more costly ailments. In addition, antibiotics are complementary inputs to many cancer treatments. Chemotherapy and radiation destroys the body's natural defenses. Without antibiotics, such treatments could be as lethal as the cancers themselves.[16]

Third, new diagnostic technologies like magnetic resonance imaging (MRI) permit doctors to acquire diagnostic information that previously entailed rare and dangerous surgery. For example, computerized axial tomography (CAT scans) and MRI equipment involve extremely high fixed costs and low variable costs. Consequently, there are tremendous incentives to use the equipment to spread overhead across increased volume. In addition, these expensive scanning techniques are essentially without risk. The result is that savings in surgical costs may be more than offset by the costs of newer, high-volume diagnostic scanning.

• **Insurance, Medical Technology, and Rising Medical Costs** Typical cities now have fewer five-star restaurants than five-star hospitals equipped to provide organ transplants, CAT scans, and other high-tech treatments. Why so few outstanding restaurants? The answer can be found by imagining what would happen if employers issued every worker in America a meal ticket permitting employees and their families to eat in *any* restaurant at any time, as often as they wished. All employees would do is leave the tip. Five-star restaurants would pop up like convenience stores. Five-star home food delivery services would supplant Domino's Pizza (unless Domino's upgraded its menus). Home cooked meals would become endangered species. Why cook? For the cost of a tip, you can enjoy a piping hot gourmet meal delivered to your door.

As public and private insurance has expanded to cover nearly all treatments (no matter what the cost), technology has advanced. The question of causation is in doubt, but we can speculate that the demand for medical insurance depends on technology and the treatments available. Costly high-tech treatments increase the demand for insurance, and vice versa. At the same time, spending on medical research and development (R&D) will depend on the availability of insurance to finance health care in the future. When a new high-tech treatment is developed, pressure grows for insurance policies to cover the treatment. Competition compels insurance companies to cover such treatments to maintain their market shares. Pharmaceutical and medical equipment companies know this and finance immense R&D projects with confidence that, once a successful treatment is developed, insurance payments will be made available *no matter what the cost*. Thus, firms expect solid rates of return on their R&D dollars.

The insurance and R&D relationship has an unfortunate bias in favor of high-tech, high-cost treatments. There is some evidence that by merely eliminating care that provides little or no benefit, health-care expenditures could be reduced by nearly 30%.[17] For example, while tests for prostate specific antigens (PSA) can help monitor recurrence in cancer patients, they are not cost-effective in screening patients without histories of prostate cancer. When trials were still underway (the R&D component), insurance companies were prematurely pressured to pay for PSA testing on healthy males. Most of this pressure came from the insured population, who, individually, did not pick up the tab. Many other countries understandably have tried to contain rising health-care costs by limiting the use of high-tech treatments.

• **Summary** What can we conclude from our review of this market? First, our demand for health care derives from desires for health and is subject to declining marginal benefits. Second, uncertainty about the need for health care, its high costs, and its significant subsidy from fed-

---

[16]Aaron, op. cit.

[17]See R. Brook and M. Vaiana, *Appropriateness of Care: A Chart Book*, report prepared for the National Health Policy Forum (Washington D.C: June 1989); J. Wennberg, "Outcomes Research, Cost Containment, and the Fear of Health Care Rationing," *New England Journal of Medicine*, 25 October 1990, pp. 1202–04; and H. Aaron, op. cit.

eral income tax treatment have led to widespread employer-provided insurance. Health insurance coverage reduces the elasticity of demands for health care, so low-benefit high-cost care is commonplace.

Third, the widespread existence of large numbers of insurance companies fosters substantial administrative fees and a maze of reimbursement rules and paperwork. Further, since small numbers of people account for the bulk of medical spending, insurance companies have tried to exclude these groups of individuals to reduce insurance payouts. This permits the company to reduce average premiums, increasing its market share and profitability.

Finally, the widespread existence of insurance has stimulated high-tech treatments. The knowledge that insurers will be forced to cover a new treatment regardless of cost has led to a "field of dreams" scenario: develop a high-tech solution to some problem and insured patients will demand its use.

All these factors have contributed to a general overuse of health services, high-tech treatments, and rapidly rising costs. This has resulted in a clamor for guaranteed access to high-quality health care at affordable prices. Before we examine the reform proposals being considered by Congress, we need to survey how these issues are dealt with in other developed nations to see what we can learn.

INTERNATIONAL COMPARISONS

The United States appears to spend more on health care than other major nations, both in terms of absolute dollars and relative to Gross Domestic Product. Although health-care spending has risen rapidly in other countries since 1960, the gap between the United States and most other countries appears to be growing. However, as Figure 12 shows, health-care spending has grown not only in the United States, but in other countries as well.

Proponents of health-care reform argue that we get less for our money than in other countries. The issue of whether we are getting our money's worth is difficult. Comparisons of

FIGURE 12   Growth in Real Per Capita Health Care Spending in Selected Countries—1960 to 1990

Source: *Organization for Economic Cooperation and Development* and *Economic Report of the President,* 1993.

All five countries have faced rising health care expenses in the last three decades. The United States and Canada, however, are the only countries that have not reduced their growth rates for health care outlays in the past decade.

health-care spending and outcomes between countries are complicated because (*a*) much of the spending data is not truly comparable; (*b*) measuring health-care outcomes is difficult and uncertain; (*c*) differences in social, medical, cultural, demographic, and economic conditions cloud the analysis; and (*d*) as we have seen, the United States spends more on high-tech care

Health-Care Spending and Outcomes

Table 4 presents health-care spending and outcome data for the United States, Canada, Great Britain, Germany, and Japan. These five countries run the gamut from reliance on a relatively free market provision of health care (U.S.) to almost completely socialized medicine (G.B.).

The data in Table 4 show that the United States spends two to three times more per capita than these other countries and, in some cases, nearly twice the percentage of GDP. Some observers have suggested that this is simply a case where the United States is richer and our income elasticity of demand for health care may exceed those in other countries. However, the small differences in income elasticities reported suggest that greater income alone cannot explain the differences in spending (the range of income elasticities is only from 1.1 to 1.3).

These data also suggest that our health-care outcomes are worse than in the other countries. While the United States is at the bottom of the pack in the outcome measures shown (infant and perinatal mortality rates and life expectancies at birth), in part this is because we choose to pay for poor outcomes rather than preventive care. Another reason is that, in the United States, more high-risk pregnancies are brought to term, which in other countries would have resulted in spontaneous abortions. We are in the middle of the countries listed when it comes to life expectancy for the 60- to 80-year-old population (not shown in the table). Thus, when you reach 60 or 80, your life expectancy improves in the U.S. relative to other countries. This is because the United States spends more on high-tech care for the elderly than any other country.

These data do not present a very pretty picture of health care in America. But critics of these data note that our population is much larger than that of most countries, much more culturally diverse, and it contains a relatively large proportion of elderly. Further, the United States spends more on medical research and development per capita than any other country. In large measure, these other countries may be getting a free ride on American research efforts.

What can we learn from how health care is organized and financed in these other coun-

TABLE 4 Health-Care Spending and Outcomes for Five Selected Countries, 1987

Country	Per Capita Health-Care Spending (U.S. adjusted dollars)*	Percentage of GDP	Income Elasticity of Demand	Infant Mortality Rate†	Perinatal Mortality Rate‡	Life Expectancy at Birth	
						Male	Female
United States	$2,051	11.2	1.3	1.00	1.00	71.5	78.3
Canada	1,483	8.6	1.2	0.79	0.84	73.0	79.8
Great Britain	758	6.1	1.1	0.91	0.88	71.9	77.6
Germany	1,093	8.2	1.1	0.83	0.73	71.8	78.4
Japan	915	6.9	1.3	0.50	0.66	75.6	81.4

Source: Organization for Economic Co-Operation and Development, *Health Care Systems in Transition: The Search for Efficiency* (Paris: OECD), 1990.

*Health-care spending is adjusted (converted) to dollars using prevailing exchange rates. This crudely permits comparisons of spending across countries.

†Death rate of infants under one year of age per 100 live and still births.

‡Late fetal and neonatal deaths per 100 live and still births.

tries? Since health-care provision and financing in these four countries is different and covers the spectrum, let's examine each country in more detail.

Great Britain

Since World War II, the British National Health Service has been the prototype for socialized medicine. Health care is financed from general tax revenues; nearly all health care is free, although low copayments are required for some services. Health care is organized around hospitals and office-based doctors. Government-owned hospitals employ their own doctors and operate from global government budgets. The British government sets a limit on total spending, and all health care must be financed within this *global budget*. (This does not include out-of-pocket health expenditures by those who choose the private health market.) Global budgets force doctors to make hard decisions. For example, critics have recently focused on the death of a smoker who was refused bypass surgery in Great Britain because, according to the doctors involved, "Smokers don't benefit from heart bypass surgery *as much as* non-smokers."

Office-based physicians are paid annual fees (*capitations*) per patient that are adjusted by age. All specialists are salaried and see only patients referred to them from office-based general practitioners. Visits with doctors are short, waiting lists for nonemergency procedures are long, and Britain offers relatively few high-tech services. A very small but growing private market exists, but few hospitals will service the privately insured.

Canada

Canada, like Britain, provides health care to all citizens, which is funded by general tax revenues. Unlike Britain, Canadian national health insurance (called Medicare) is administered by the provinces (states). Canada historically used private markets and, until 1971, relied primarily on employer-provided health insurance. It is now essentially illegal for hospitals and doctors

to accept private payments from patients. Hospitals must survive within a global budget and are subject to extensive regulations on their charges. Hospitals must get provincial approval (the equivalent of state government approval in the United States) to purchase new equipment. The result has been that Canadian hospitals have adopted new high-technology equipment at a much slower pace than American hospitals.

Bureaucratic inefficiencies are common. According to one observer, ". . . dogs at the York Central Hospital in metropolitan Toronto were able to get CAT scans immediately while humans were put on a waiting list. The reason? Canadian patients are not allowed to pay for CAT scans . . . [but] dog owners were. . . ."[18] But, overall, the Canadian system has very low per capita administrative costs—only one-fifth of those in the United States.

Doctors are paid fees based on a negotiated schedule; provincial associations of Canadian MDs collectively bargain with provincial government agencies. Micromanagement, however, is far less than in the United States, resulting in lower administrative costs. Doctors' fees have risen less rapidly than in the United States. Since physicians' incomes equal $P \times Q$, critics charge that one result of low fees (P) is that doctors increase the quantity of services (Q) provided at these lower fees. This is cited as evidence of supplier-induced demand in the Canadian system. Like Britain, waiting lines for nonessential procedures are relatively long, and patients needing high-tech treatments or elective surgeries are often referred (or self-refer) to the United States.[19]

Germany

All workers in Germany must carry health-care insurance. They can select from over 1,000 re-

---

[18]J. Arnett, "Canada's Single-Payer Health Scheme a Singular Failure," *The Wall Street Journal*, 6 August, 1993, p. A7.

[19]According to a recent survey reported in the *New England Journal of Medicine*, one-third of Canada's doctors have sent patients outside the country for treatment during the past five years. See J. Arnett, ibid.

gional or occupation-based not-for-profit "sickness funds." Each is financed by payroll taxes that vary substantially. High-income individuals can purchase private insurance instead, and roughly one-third of all Germans now do. The nonworking poor have insurance through these same sickness funds, paid for by general revenues. Federal unemployment insurance pays the sickness fund fees for the unemployed, and retired people pay sickness fund fees via their pensions and are charged the average sickness fund rate.

Doctors belong to regional associations that negotiate lump-sum global budgets with the individual funds. Doctors are either hospital or office based. Those working for hospitals are paid salaries and may practice only in the hospital, while those doctors who are office based are paid a fee for service from the regional association. If, during the year, doctors' payments exceed the global budget, fees go down to adjust to the negotiated annual budget. Doctor visits are brief and more frequent than in many other countries.

Hospitals are paid operating costs negotiated from the various sickness funds. Capital equipment is purchased by funds provided by the state governments. As a result, Germany lacks significant new high-technology equipment. Since nearly one-third of Germans have private insurance, many hospitals provide special facilities to care for these patients.

Japan

The Japanese system parallels that of Germany in that employees and retirees have health-care insurance provided by their current or former employers, with protection for the remainder of the population provided by a national health insurance plan. Japanese plans have copayments of 20% for hospital care and 30% for office visits, and all have monthly catastrophic illness caps of roughly $400. Japanese patients are required to pay their copayments up to a maximum of $400 per month. Beyond that, insurance covers all costs.

Hospitals are primarily private and nonprofit, hire their own physicians, and run their own clinics. Outside physicians are not allowed to practice in hospitals; many of them fear that they will lose their patients to hospital clinics if they refer patients to a hospital. Further, MDs in Japan both *prescribe* and *sell* drugs. As a result, Japan has the *lowest* hospitalization rate of any industrialized nation and the *highest* level of prescription drug use. Private MDs are on a fee-for-service basis and, because of price controls, typically require patients to come back more often, resulting in a high office-visit rate. Few doctors in Japan book appointments; patients just show up and wait (about one hour on average).

Japan has a low-cost medical system with better-than-average outcomes. As Table 4 indicates, its infant and perinatal mortality rates are the lowest and life expectancies are the highest for the five countries listed. (The superior health of the Japanese may be partially attributable to a relatively low-fat diet.)

Evaluating the Various Health-Care Systems

There is a growing consensus that everyone should enjoy some minimum level of access to health care and that basic care should be provided according to need, not ability to pay. This has been the general philosophy in most European countries for decades. In addition, there is a growing feeling that all Americans should be protected from financial catastrophes that modern medical care can inflict on those without coverage.

Most Americans continue to desire the freedom to choose their physicians, hospitals, and treatments. This is viewed as desirable for both the privately and publicly insured. Health-care providers, on the other hand, seek the maximum autonomy possible, while purchasers of medical care services and insurance are demanding that costs be contained.

These goals are in conflict. They represent the classic equity versus efficiency trade-off discussed earlier in this chapter. Universal coverage without regard to ability to pay is an equity goal. (Note, however, that if society subsidizes treatments for certain illnesses, say diabetes, then all taxpayers will subsidize both rich diabetics and poor ones, and some of the funds to cover the treatment of a rich diabetic will come from poor people who are healthy. Does this seem fair? Many people would answer no.) Once universal access has been achieved (as it has in most European countries), the agenda turns to efficiency and reasonable rationing policies.

For most countries, rationing follows cost control like night follows day. In America, high rates for private insurance ration individuals and small firms out of the market. Business resistance to high premiums brings reduced coverage. For example, copayments are rising, there are low limits on insurance payments for some procedures (e.g., orthodontia), the use of generic (or cheaper) drugs is mandated, and some procedures may be excluded from insurance (e.g., psychiatric care or experimental therapies). Increasingly, insurers insist on selecting physicians or HMOs that agree to very low fees or fixed prices per patient covered per year (capitation).

As technology advances, increasing both the choice of treatments and costs, rationing will become even more direct and explicit. Health-care bureaucrats, for example, will set more restrictive criteria for heart bypass surgery (smokers versus nonsmokers–the British debate), withhold treatment for liver disease for alcoholics, and so on. As one doctor put it, "we may well be on the slippery slope to withholding treatment for the unmotivated and unfit."

Cost control may ultimately require limits on the number of doctors allowed to practice. If we apply standard supply and demand analysis to health care, we would assume that increasing the supply of practicing doctors would lower the fees for service. However, recent studies in both the United States and Canada suggest that, even with stringent cost controls, total physician compensation (cost) rises with the number of doctors practicing within a given area. Analysts suggest that doctors try to maintain their incomes by ordering more services and providing easier access to care. For most patients, personal inconvenience is a major cost. Doctors and hospitals recognize this and have introduced shorter and less invasive solutions, and they increasingly emphasize outpatient care and home visits by nurses. This has also resulted in part from Medicare's strict price controls on inpatient care. Thus, average hospital stays for most procedures have been cut dramatically over recent decades. Cost control pressures from insurers have been partly responsible for these changes in hospitalization rates and lengths of stay.

• Centralized Systems

A brief evaluation of the strengths and weaknesses of both market-oriented, decentralized systems and centralized, government-mandated or provided services will help us to anticipate the effects of health-care reform in America. When government intervenes, presumably to solve some of the market failures inherent in a private market for medical care, there are unintended and unwanted side effects. This is another example of the law of unintended consequences.

Governments initially attempted to correct market failure with regulation. Early on, self-regulation was encouraged. For example, professional codes of conduct (and the accompanying monopoly of supply) for highly skilled health-care workers were permitted. Professional associations (e.g., the American Medical Association) set standards, limited entrance into professional schools, administered licensure, and often controlled professional lives by setting prices and restricting such practices as advertising. Self-regulation, in general, has not adequately negated market failure in medical care markets, and access continues to be a problem.

Where universal access has been accomplished through compulsory health insurance financed by premiums based on income or wages (with a subsidy for the poor), the result has often been rapid growth of public spending. The U.S. government's experience with Medicare is an example. To counter rising costs, governments have often enacted command-and-control regulations designed to limit medical care cost increases, but bureaucratic controls can seriously distort health-care markets. When price ceilings are introduced, health-care providers do respond by increasing the quantity (or reducing the quality or both) of service (e.g., increased hours per week and the use of such midlevel "physician extenders" as physician's assistants and nurse practitioners).

The ultimate centralized systems are those in which the government has completely taken over health care, putting doctors on salary and providing medical care through public clinics and hospitals. At its best, this approach can provide high quality health care at a reasonable cost. At its worst, queues are long; elective procedures are pruned; and service is impersonal, slow, and provided by a weakly motivated staff in ill-equipped facilities. These systems are slow to adopt costly new technologies and always confront the possibility of being corrupted by private (under-the-table) payments for preferential treatment.

• **Decentralized Systems** Competitive markets can efficiently allocate resources and goods in most markets. In private competitive markets, consumers balance the marginal benefits from any good or service with its marginal cost. Producers are forced to adopt efficient means of producing the product. Some observers argue that, with appropriate redistributions of income, competitive markets could efficiently provide health care, since medical care is just another personal service.

As we have seen, however, the unpredictable nature of an individual's health-care needs, the spread of insurance with its accompanying moral hazard and adverse selection problems, and asymmetry of information have all contributed to inefficient overprovision of health care. When the government entered the health-care market with Medicare and Medicaid in 1965, the likelihood that America would return to relatively free markets in this industry evaporated. Health-care reform will undoubtedly make government a bigger player in this industry. Markets and competitive pressures provide checks on inefficiency and encourage innovation. Reform policies and programs should be designed that, while improving access, promote efficiency. This clearly poses a difficult challenge for policymakers.

LESSONS FOR HEALTH-CARE REFORM

When faced with difficult approval decisions, FDA reviewers often ask for costly, elaborate new studies. If anyone is hurt by a new drug, after all, it will be front-page news. But if 10,000 people die because approval is delayed, the public will never know.

Murray Weidenbaum

Many Americans seem eager for some sort of reform. With 85% of us already insured, any reform will probably be incremental. Few people are willing to lose their current comprehensive insurance. What can we conclude that Americans want from their health-care system? Low cost, no paperwork, no waiting, the best technology, and continued freedom to choose their own doctors and hospitals. Any politically viable reform must improve on the current system.

What have we learned from examining the U.S. health-care industry and how health care is financed and delivered abroad? First, we know that insurance entails moral hazards where people overuse medical care, disregarding how low the benefits are from some treatments. They can also downplay the effect of lifestyles on their overall health. Because most health-care dollars are spent on a small percentage of the population, insurance companies try to develop screening devices to exclude high-risk groups and individuals. Because of these problems, achieving universal access through private insurance is difficult. Any reform that sets coverage for all as a priority must either provide or mandate insurance coverage.

Second, administrative functions in insurance companies and government appear to absorb nearly a quarter of our health-care resources. Individual or small group coverage entails significantly higher administrative costs and returns (as much at 50% of the premium).

Thus, any reform will probably endeavor to standardize insurance policies, coverage, claims, and other forms, and to expand the size of the pools covered.

Third, when any third party (e.g., insurers) pays the bills, people will fail to efficiently balance their private marginal benefits against society's marginal costs. Inevitably, any reform will attack these incentives through limits to coverage, possibly providing only catastrophic coverage and no coverage for chronic ailments that involve high-cost, low-benefit treatment. Global budgets would force health-care providers to deal with these issues. The result is quite likely to be some form of rationing, either using prices as in the current system, or by setting standards to withhold services in some cases. Any reform must correct for incentives that reward high-cost low-benefit care, but few Americans are willing to surrender their shot at living if they could be beneficiaries of some "miracle" of modern medicine.

Current Health-Care Reform Initiatives

Most health-care reform proposals provide for nearly universal coverage within some specified period. Since most health insurance is currently provided by employers, most reform plans rely heavily on firms to continue providing protection to employees, with some form of government subsidy to cover the poor or the nearly-poor who work.

Most proposals set some standard for a benefits package for all Americans. These packages cover most health needs, including minimal mental health services. Most of these packages provide less than Medicaid and may not address care for the disabled (mentally, physically, or developmentally) or long-term care. Most of the plans attack the small-group administrative-cost problem by moving toward health alliances: state-wide insurance buying groups. Some proposals add global budgeting caps to limit the growth in annual health-care expenditures.

Since an additional 35 million people are likely to eventually have comprehensive health coverage, unless current inefficiencies in the system can be reduced, a larger share of GDP will ultimately be devoted to this sector. The best estimates available suggest that any reform proposal which brings all citizens under the health-care umbrella will likely cost roughly 15% to 20% more, assuming that benefits are not reduced. That would mean that $150 billion to $200 billion more per year in real resources would be devoted to health care in this country.

CHAPTER REVIEW: KEY POINTS

1. The major issues driving the call for health-care reform are high and rapidly rising costs for care (*efficiency*) and the nearly 35 million people uninsured (*equity*).

2. The **uncertainty** of individuals' needs for medical treatment has resulted in heavy reliance on comprehensive health insurance. Added to this is the massive restructuring taking place in corporate America. Jobs are less secure, and more part-time workers have replaced full-time employees, making the problem of access to health care more acute.

3. Public health-care **externalities** are widespread. Because people are often concerned with their neighbor's access to care, there is a growing consensus in America that all individuals have a *right* to quality medical care regardless of their ability to pay.

4. Significant **asymmetries of information** between patients and medical personnel

make it virtually impossible for patients to evaluate the efficacy of certain types of medical care. This problem is exacerbated by the incentives faced by doctors under the current **fee-for-service** system, because doctors have an economic incentive to expand the level of services provided each patient. This problem is known as **supplier-induced demand**, or **SID. Capitation** systems of payment (fixed annual fees per patient) embody incentives to hold down the costs of health care.

5. The health-care industry is rife with market power on the parts of almost all players except individual patients. Market power (e.g., licensing) enhances the incomes of MDs.

6. Health care is only one input into the production of health. Health-care services, like other inputs, are subject to the law of diminishing returns: the benefits from additional health-care spending eventually decline.

7. Widespread reliance on medical insurance reduces the elasticity of demand for medical treatment and increases the quantity of medical services consumed. Factors other than medical care enhance a person's overall state of health, but insurance reduces our incentives (creates a moral hazard) to maintain a healthier lifestyle.

8. Because insurance significantly reduces the cost of treatment to the patient, and the medical profession's *Hippocratic oath* mandates provision of *all* beneficial care, many analysts contend that this industry provides too much **high-cost low-benefit** care.

9. Private (non-group) insurance is prohibitively expensive for most individuals because the costs of administering individual health plans are huge, and adverse selec-

tion problems abound. *Adverse selection* arises because individuals have better information than insurance companies about their general health. People in poor health gladly purchase insurance at average prices, while those in good health are more likely to self-insure (or, if they won't accept insurance, join managed care). This raises the average risk of the pool, causing prices to rise, further causing more healthy people to self-insure, and so on.

10. The demand for medical care began a sharp climb when government entered the market, with **Medicare** and **Medicaid** insuring two very high-risk groups, the elderly and the destitute. Today, nearly half of all medical care spending is accounted for by these federal programs. In addition, income tax rules heavily subsidize employer-provided health insurance. Many critics charge that this has led to excessive insurance coverage and overuse of the health-care system.

11. Widespread comprehensive health-care coverage has encouraged the rapid development of high-technology treatments. This has contributed to rising health-care costs.

12. Relative to other industrialized nations, the United States spends two to three times more on health care, both in absolute dollars and as a percentage of GDP. Unfortunately, our health-care outcomes (life expectancies and infant mortality rates) are worse than in many other countries. This may be due to the data not being comparable, and to differences in social, cultural, economic, and demographic conditions. These data also ignore the fact that the United States is a world leader in medical research and development.

QUESTIONS FOR THOUGHT AND DISCUSSION

1. Health-care spending as a percentage of GDP has tripled over the last few decades. Many supporters of health-care reform forecast that over 20% of GDP will be spend on health care by the year 2000 if we fail to enact reforms. Is this sort of forecasting meaningful? What forces might mitigate the growth of health-care spending in the future?

2. Price ceilings have been proposed as one way to curb the growth of spending on medical care. What might be some side effects of ceilings on physician and hospital charges?

3. Suppose an amazing machine were developed that could perfectly forecast every disease or injury an individual will ever experience. How would this affect the insurance industry?

4. Dan Callahan[20] argues, "The elderly have already lived out a full life. They have not been denied (at least because of their age) the opportunities of living a life; and death deprives them of less than a child or young person who has had no such opportunity. Not only does it seem justifiable to work harder, and to take more chances, to save and rehabilitate the life of a sick child, but also to allocate more resources to those conditions that bring premature death than to those that bring death after a long life." Such problems must be addressed because health-care spending is limited. Is this issue more about ethics or economics? Discuss the role of decision-making at the margin in Callahan's argument.

5. John Braun[21] asserts, "Blaming hospitals and physicians for the increasing costs of health care makes about as much sense as blaming the police for the cost of crime. Hospitals and physicians treat disease; they do not cause it!" Is John Braun correct? Why or why not? What economic arguments can be made against such a comparison?

---

[20]D. Callahan, *Setting Limits* (New York: Simon & Schuster, 1987).

[21]J. Braun, *American Medical News*, 11 March 1988.

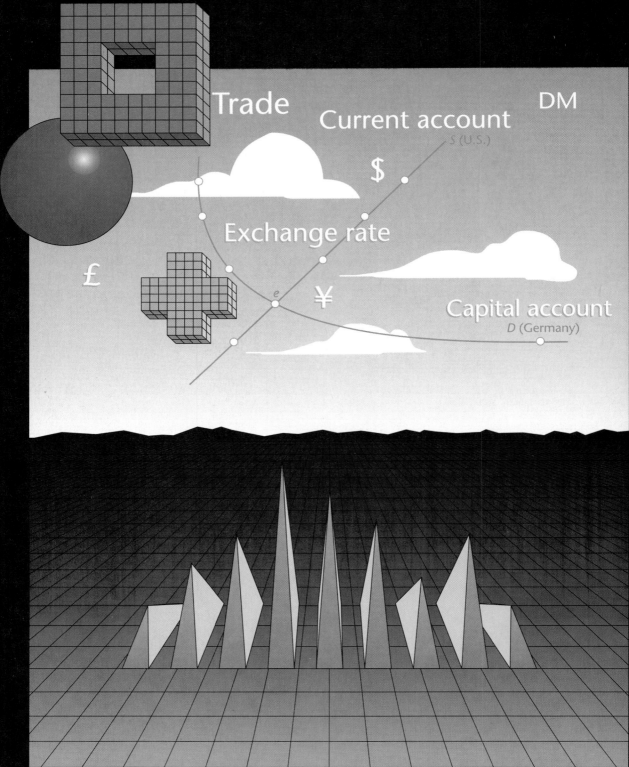

The International Economy

International trade is growing faster than domestic production and income almost everywhere in the world. Virtually every aspect of daily life is affected—from the composition of our diets to the purchasing power of our income to the jobs we choose to issues of war and peace. We cannot be oblivious to economic developments outside our national borders if we are to enjoy at least the standards of living of past generations of Americans, and, if history is a guide, we should be able to live even more prosperously. This is one reason this book is permeated with international issues and examples. Our purpose in the last part of this book is to provide an integrated perspective on how international trade and finance affect people's well-being around the world.

Gains from specialized production and exchange according to comparative advantage were introduced in Chapter 2. But other types of gains from trade may be even more important. These gains help explain why most national economies are increasingly interdependent and prosperous, and why economic systems seem to be converging. Nevertheless, many people everywhere continue to sing the protectionist's song, "Restrict imports of 'cheap' foreign goods." How almost everyone ultimately gains from international trade and why restricting trade is usually foolish are among the major topics we address in the next chapter.

You can now buy stocks and bonds in American, Japanese, or Italian corporations through stock exchanges in Sydney, London, or Hong Kong (and soon, perhaps, in Moscow or Beijing). International financial developments crucially affect job opportunities and patterns of economic growth, among other things. The ongoing internationalization of capital markets has made currency exchange rates and the value of the dollar an issue not only for those fortunate enough to travel abroad, but for all of us. Capital flows and the different mechanisms that can be used to pay for imports are at the heart of our discussion in the last chapter.

The quality of your life will be affected by sweeping changes in international trade and finance far more than your parents' lives have been, but undoubtedly far less than will be the lives of your own children. The world economy is growing fiercely competitive, but the rush of global events opens up opportunities as well. Knowing something about international trends can provide you with both absolute and comparative advantages over the majority of people, many of whom seem only vaguely aware of these developments.

Trade

Current account

DM

S (U.S.)

Chapter 36

Exchange rate

International Trade

D (Germany)

£

$

¥

e

Capital account

Specialized production and exchange yield enormous benefits. The gain to both Hawaiians and Texans from trading sugar for oil is an obvious example. Similar advantages arise from transactions whether the people with whom we deal are Americans or foreigners. The exchange of goods and services across national boundaries is called **international trade**. Trade is generally a positive-sum game; both sides expect to gain or they do not trade. International transactions are somewhat more complex than domestic trade, however, because of differences in currencies and national policies.

In this chapter, we discuss some advantages and possible disadvantages of commerce between traders separated by international borders. We also evaluate some arguments against free trade and consider the effects of policies that restrict trade.

THE SIZE AND SCOPE OF TRADE

International trade grows in importance year after year, ranging, among industrialized nations, from 10% to 12% of U.S. national income to roughly 30% in Great Britain. Few Americans, however, pay much attention to how international trade affects our daily lives. We drink Colombian coffee, cocoa from Ghana, or tea from Sri Lanka; wear Swiss watches and clothes made in China; watch TVs made in Japan; and burn gasoline refined from Arab oil in Hyundais, Fiats, or Toyotas. Most of our shoes, the graphite in our pencils, and even the elastic in our underwear come from abroad.

Foreign countries are markets for our production, so U.S. exports are one source of Aggregate Demand. Imports add to our Aggregate Supply; they are sources of consumption goods (e.g., Sony Walkman headsets) and investment goods (e.g., Korean steel I-beams). At the same time, they detract from Aggregate Demand, making marketing more difficult for domestic producers who compete with imports. Consequently, macroeconomic policy must consider the impact of international trade on domestic unemployment, inflation, economic growth, and our Gross Domestic Product (GDP).

The importance of international trade in several major trading nations is shown in Figure

1. The sheer size of the United States makes it the world's single most important international trader; our exports and imports each exceeded $700 billion in 1994. Generally, however, trade is even more crucial to small countries than to large ones.

WHY DO NATIONS TRADE?

The United States has a highly skilled work force, an unmatched stock of capital equipment, and vast amounts of fertile land and raw materials. Even though our national income is more than twice that of our nearest competitor, U.S. exports and imports have each averaged over 10% of national income in recent years. Figure 2 reveals which countries are our major trading partners.

Why do Americans even bother to trade with the rest of the world? All trade is motivated by expectations of gain: either increased income or reduced costs. The global value of income and output is maximized if the opportunity costs of producing everything everywhere are minimized. International trade is a mechanism for consumers to get goods at lower cost without having to travel to where the goods are produced, and for resource owners (e.g., labor) to receive higher income without having to relocate to wherever their outputs are most advantageously consumed. Efficient patterns of trade permit higher standards of living for people everywhere.

Curiously, we both import (to reduce costs) and export (to boost incomes) many goods that are close substitutes for each other. For example, while we are the world's biggest car importer, we are also its third largest car exporter. The composition of U.S. foreign trade (indicated in Figure 3) is evidence that trade can be advantageous even when self-sufficiency is possible.

	United States	United Kingdom	Germany	France	Italy	Canada	Japan	Russia	China	OPEC	Eastern Europe
Imports	11.6	20.9	23.0	18.3	15.6	23.1	6.3	10.1	18.8	19.6	28.3
Exports	10.4	18.0	24.2	18.0	14.7	24.3	9.2	10.3	19.8	18.6	24.7

Percentages of GDP

Source: *Economic Report of the President,* 1994; *Direction of Trade Statistics Yearbook* (Washington: International Monetary Fund) 1993.

The United States is both the world's largest exporter and it's largest importer, but trade is less important to us as a percentage of GDP than it is to most other developed nations. Surprisingly, Japan is not especially dependent on foreign trade. Trade is especialy vital, however, for such highly specialized countries as OPEC member nations. China and former "Eastern bloc" countries have historically been insignificant as traders, but this is changing dramatically as the twenty-first century approaches.

FIGURE 1   Imports and Exports of Selected Countries as Percentages of GDP, 1992—1993

FIGURE 2　Major U.S. Trading Partners, 1993

Source: *Economic Report of the President,* 1994; *Direction of Trade Statistics Yearbook* (Washington: International Monetary Fund) 1993
(*Note:* All figures presented here are in billions of U.S. dollars.)

The Concept of Absolute Advantage

The notion of *absolute advantage* emerges from differences in the abilities of individuals and nations to produce goods from given resources. For example, one Arabian worker can get more oil out of 10 acres of Arab land than can one Georgian working 10 acres in Georgia. However, the Georgian might be able to raise more peanuts per acre than the Arab can. In this case, the Arab has an absolute advantage in oil production, while the Georgian has an absolute advantage in peanut growing. Obviously, each could gain from specialized production and trade. Parallel reasoning led Adam Smith and other early economists to attempt to state a broad principle.

> The *"principle" of absolute advantage* asserts that nations gain by producing goods that require fewer domestic resources and exchanging their surpluses for goods produced abroad with fewer resources.

This approach is incomplete, however, because it ignores the gains that may be available through trade even though one party has an absolute advantage in producing almost all goods (or, in a simple model, each of two goods).

Specialization and Comparative Advantage

Suppose U.S. workers can produce either four silk blouses or eight electric drills daily, while Chinese workers average only two silk blouses or one drill. An absolute advantage approach offers no way for Americans to gain from trade. The *law of comparative advantage* developed by David Ricardo shows how trade can enrich people in both countries even if American workers have absolute advantages in both goods.

> The *law of comparative advantage:* Mutually beneficial trade is always possible between nations whose pretrade relative costs and prices differ.

FIGURE 3   The Percentage Composition of U.S. Exports and Imports, 1993

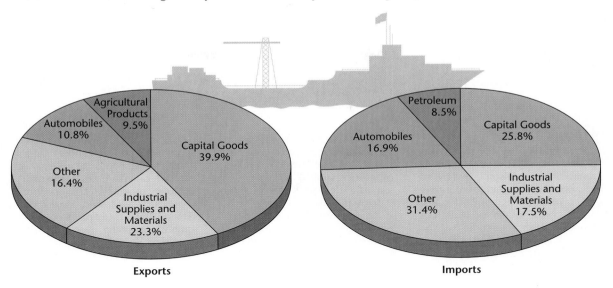

Exports   Imports

Source: *Economic Report of the President,* 1994.

The composition of our trade appears roughly balanced, except for net imports of fuels and minerals and net exports of capital goods and agricultural products. Each of these very broad categories, however, disguises a rich diversity of imports and exports.

Table 1 helps illustrate this key concept in international trade. Without trade, two drills are sacrificed to produce each silk blouse in the United States, while in China, each blouse costs only half of a drill. Imagine that you could costlessly move between these countries and that you initially had one blouse. You could begin by trading it for two U.S. drills and then trade the drills for four Chinese blouses, for which you would receive eight U.S. drills, and so on. China increasingly would specialize in blouse making and the United States, in drill production. As long as the costs of blouses relative to drills did not change (price ratios of 2:1 in the United States and 1:2 in China), no one in either country would lose and you would gain. You might

even become rich. Thus, this example shows how trade enhances efficiency.

• **The Terms of Trade**   Arbitrageurs (introduced in Chapter 4) can risklessly profit by buying low and selling high if relative price differentials between markets exceed the transaction costs incurred with intermarket transfers of goods. We need to insert a bit more realism into our example, because vigorous competition would eventually eliminate any pure economic profit from your attempts to arbitrage. Most of the potential gains would actually have been shared by Americans and Chinese. Moreover, the prices of drills relative to blouses were artificially assumed constant in both the United States and China.

TABLE 1   Outputs per Worker and Their Costs

Country	Pretrade Costs				Free Trade Costs
	Electric Drills per Worker	**Blouses per Worker**	**Drills per Blouse**	**Blouses per Drill**	
United States	8	4	2/1	1/2	1:1
China	1	2	1/2	2/1	1:1

David Ricardo: Foundations for International Trade

David Ricardo's (1772–1823) genius was illustrated in both the practical world of affairs and in the realm of ideas. Disinherited by his wealthy Jewish father for marrying a Quaker at the age of 21, Ricardo and his bride joined the Unitarian church, which at the time was viewed as a radical sect.

Ricardo successfully pursued a career as a stockjobber and then as a loan contractor, and when he was forty-two, his accumulated wealth permitted him to retire from business. Bored with the idle life, he turned his attention to politics and intellectual pursuits. After a hesitant beginning as a writer on economic subjects, Ricardo etched his name on the pages of history by publishing a treatise, *On the Principles of Political Economy and Taxation*. He was not an ac-

complished writer, having a heavy-handed, obscure, and abstract style. Nevertheless, the force of his logic almost immediately attracted a close-knit band of gifted if dogmatic disciples.

Ricardo's appeal was based on his ability to cast a wide assortment of serious problems into simple analytical models that considered only a few strategic variables but yielded sweeping conclusions of a very practical nature. One example of Ricardo's penetrating insight concerns the doctrine of comparative costs. Earlier economists had taught that it pays a country to concentrate on the production of those goods it can produce using fewer resources than any other country and to import those goods that can be produced abroad using fewer resources. Ricardo developed the

following not-so-obvious implication of this doctrine: under free trade, not all goods are necessarily produced in countries where their absolute production cost (in terms of resources) is lowest. He demonstrated that it could pay a country to import something, even though it could produce the same product with fewer resources at home. Ricardo's demonstration rests on the idea of relative efficiency, or comparative costs.

Ricardo's principle is developed in greater detail in the present chapter, but it is important to note that the core of all free trade arguments harks back to this Ricardian concept. Ricardo's discussion of land rent and his analysis of taxation were also trailbreaking works that place modern economists forever in his debt.

Arbitrage tends to equalize relative prices in all markets by boosting demand in the market with the lower price, driving that price up, and boosting supply in the market with the higher price, sending it down. In international trade, low-cost producers export, while high-cost producers face increased competition from imports. The phrase *terms of trade* refers to the prices of exported goods relative to imported goods:

$$terms\ of\ trade\ =\ \frac{prices\ of\ exports}{prices\ of\ imports}$$

In our example, drills initially cost only half a blouse in the United States but two blouses in China, while blouses cost two drills in the United States but only half a drill in China. Intuitively,

terms of trade should end up between the two countries' relative pretrade production costs at, say, a 1:1 price ratio in both countries. American consumers gain by buying "cheap" imported Chinese blouses, while China's consumers gain by buying "cheap" imported U.S. drills. At the same time, U.S. drill makers export at what they perceive is a premium price and Chinese blouse makers also perceive themselves as being paid premium prices for their exports. These types of cost savings and income growth are the foundations for the gains from trade.

GAINS FROM TRADE

Most gains from trade are distributed between producers of goods that are exported and consumers of goods that are imported. People everywhere, however, gain from trade in several ways. Gains from trade are realized internationally because of (*a*) specialization according to comparative advantage, (*b*) the uniqueness of certain resources, (*c*) gains from scale achievable through expanded markets, (*d*) the spread of technology, (*e*) accelerated capital formation, (*f*) accelerated innovation, and (*g*) improved international political stability.

Specialization Gains

People gain even if they could produce imported goods, because through specialization, their incomes and purchasing power rise. Access to export markets makes what people produce more valuable. Even those who do not work directly on exported goods ultimately have higher incomes because of increased demands in resource markets. Moreover, they are able to buy goods at lower opportunity costs than if they relied solely on domestic production.

> *Specialization gains from trade arise from producing and selling goods in which you have a comparative advantage and buying other goods from other parties who can produce them at lower cost.*

In our example, U.S. drill makers and blouse consumers would gain as the price of drills relative to blouses rose. (The U.S. price of blouses falls.) Similarly, Chinese blouse makers and drill buyers gain when the relative prices of blouses rise. Chinese blouse buyers and U.S. blouse producers might seem to lose, and so might Chinese makers and U.S. buyers of drills. In a moment we will show that these short-run gains from trade alone generally outweigh losses that arise because some people who compete with imports suffer disruptions to their lives and temporary losses of income.

Uniqueness Gains

Nature fails to provide local sources of some resources in certain regions. For example, diamonds, chromium, tin, petroleum, bauxite, and other minerals are not distributed smoothly across the earth's surface. Technology may also differ substantially between countries. International trade makes goods available that simply could not be produced domestically.

> *The **uniqueness gains** from trade arise from trading for goods that are not available from local sources.*

Uniqueness gains underpin trade for certain minerals and many foods, fibers, and animal products, such as bananas, coffee, silk, and frozen fish.

Gains from Scale

Adam Smith was the first economist to note that specialization is limited by the size of the market. Moving beyond domestic markets into international markets facilitates specialization that, in turn, allows expanded production. This occurs, in part, because least cost production for some goods requires output levels that exceed market demands within a single country.

> *Gains from scale occur when access to export markets stimulates production of larger amounts of goods at lower average costs.*

For example, Haiti would not, by itself, support an aluminum mill with sufficient capacity to produce at efficiently low costs. Nor is there sufficient demand for clocks in Switzerland alone to allow efficient production. Gains from scale include product diversity, which allows demands to be served that are skimpy in even the largest countries. Not even the U.S. market is large enough alone to justify research, development, and production of medicines to treat extremely exotic diseases; the U.S. market demand would be strictly below the average cost curve for production.

Long-Run Dynamic Gains

The purchasing power of national income grows immediately when imports expand, but long-run changes wrought by trade may be even more important than this short-run effect.

Long-run dynamic gains occur when trade accelerates economic growth and development.

Long-run improvements occur when (*a*) trade spreads technology, or (*b*) higher income from trade accelerates capital formation, or (*c*) entrepreneurs are stimulated to innovate by both competition from imports and the increased profit opportunities potentially available from export markets. These dynamic gains from trade are especially apparent in the rapid economic development of Japan and other Pacific Rim countries.

• **The Spread of Technology** Trade spreads technology that would be known only locally if each country operated in isolation. Technological advances tend to be infectious: one researcher's discovery is improved upon by another, who stimulates a third, ad infinitum. Imagine how primitive life would be if every national group had to rediscover the wheel, electricity, and the advantages of indoor plumbing.

• **Capital Formation** Dynamic gains also arise because trade boosts the value of national output, making it easier for people to save and invest. In less developed nations, higher real income from trade can enable people to move beyond bare subsistence; increased saving allows new capital formation that can provide a way to break out of the vicious circle of poverty in which many countries are mired.

• **Innovation** Fierce competition stimulates entrepreneurial efforts to lower costs, improve existing output, and create entirely new products. Firms facing competition from low-cost imports have powerful incentives to innovate. International trade also whets competitive instincts, in part by providing new markets that broaden profit opportunities. Experimentation with new forms of production and the innovation that results provide workers with a learning-by-doing environment, which sparks more rapid rates of economic growth and development.

International Political Stability

International trade also enhances international relations. To the extent that trade improves our standard of living, it also makes us more dependent upon people in other nations and them on us.

Political gains from trade arise when economic interdependency facilitates international political stability.

Cessation of trade between warring countries eliminates mutual benefits and is one cost of hostilities. Thus, interdependencies created by trade reduce the likelihood of war because higher costs reduce the amounts demanded for any activity. Just as mountain climbers attached by ropes may argue, but try to avoid potentially suicidal violence, mutually beneficial trade is a powerful incentive for peaceful negotiation. International trade in military hardware (e.g., munitions sales to Iraq before 1990) may be an exception to the principle that trade fosters peace.

NET GAINS FROM SPECIALIZATION

Some types of gains from trade seem obvious. We turn now to demonstrating those that may seem less clear. Specialization gains generally confer *net* gains to the participants—even in the short run, total gains exceed all losses. Comparative advantage is the key to identifying these net gains. Returning to our example where Chinese blouses were traded for U.S. drills, we will use a simple short-run model suggesting who shares in the net gains from trade. We consider only two countries, but the logic holds if we consider any country vis-à-vis the rest of the world or a host of goods instead of only two. In fact, the net gains available from trade rise as the number of traded goods rises and as the number of traders (people in different trading countries) grows.

We will begin with the following assumptions:

1. Production possibilities curves for both China and the United States have constant opportunity costs but reflect different technologies.
2. Only two goods (drills and blouses) are produced and traded.
3. Goods, but not resources, can move freely between countries, while resources can move freely only between domestic industries.
4. All prices are perfectly flexible.

These simplifying assumptions may seem unrealistic, but they are used only to illustrate a point; most can be relaxed without changing the basic analysis.

Let us begin with aggregate production relationships for the United States and China similar to those outlined in Table 1. We will assume that workers in the United States can produce 400 million blouses or 800 million drills annually, or any combination in between, maintaining constant opportunity costs of two blouses per drill. Similarly, Chinese workers are able to produce 400 million drills or 800 million blouses annually, because we assume China's labor force is four times as large as ours.

Constant production costs yield linear production possibilities frontiers (*PPFs*) like those shown as solid lines in Figure 4. These frontiers can also be thought of as *consumption possibilities frontiers* (*CPFs*) because, without trade, neither country could sustain consumption beyond these boundaries. Suppose that both countries are originally producing and consuming at points *a* in

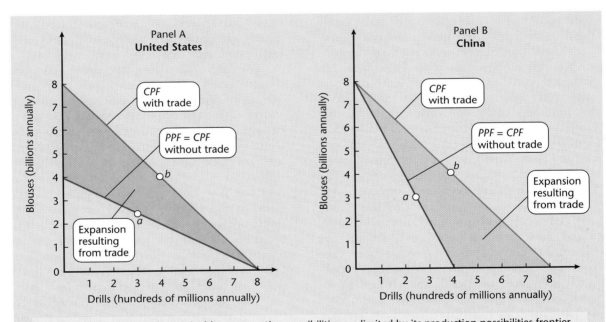

Prior to trade, a country's sustainable consumption possibilities are limited by its production possibilities frontier. When trade commences, both trading partners experience net gains from trade because, by specializing in those goods they produce at lowest relative cost and by importing those things that they find costly to make themselves, they can each consume more of all goods. Thus, their consumption possibilities expand beyond their production possibilities, just as we gain individually by trading with others instead of relying strictly on what we personally produce.

FIGURE 4   How Trade Expands Consumption Possibilities

TABLE 2 Specialization Gains from Trade

Country Commodity	(1) Production After Trade (millions)	+	(2) Exports (−) or Imports (+) (millions)	=	(3) Consumption After Trade (millions) (2) + (3)	−	(4) Output and Consumption before trade (millions)	=	(5) Gains from Trade (millions) (4) − (1)
United States									
drills	800		400		400		300		100
blouses	0		400		400		250		150
China									
drills	0		400		400		250		150
blouses	800		400		100		300		100

Column 1 indicates the respective outputs of the U.S. and China with trade. Once trade commences, Americans export 400 million drills and import 400 million blouses (column 2). (Terms of trade are one to one.) Thus, U.S. consumptions equals production minus exports plus imports, or 400 million each of drills and blouses (column 3). Subtracting pretrade American consumption of 300 million drills and 250 million blouses (column 4) leaves yields U.S. gains from trade—free trade permits Americans to consume 150 million extra blouses and 100 million more drills (column 5). Chinese enjoy similar net gains from trade.

both panels of Figure 4, which graphically reflects column 4 of Table 2. Finally, assume that the final trading ratio is one drill for one blouse.

The United States will specialize in the good with lowest domestic costs: drills, with annual production at 800 million units. Each drill now may be traded for a blouse, so a total of up to 800 million drills plus blouses might be consumed. The U.S. *CPF* expands as shown in Panel A of Figure 4. Symmetrically, China will specialize in blouse production (800 million annually) and, by trading blouses for drills, can expand its consumption to any combination of blouses and drills along the red *CPF* in Panel B.

A simplifying assumption reflected in Figure 4 and Table 2 is that people everywhere have identical tastes, so after trade commences, each country consumes at points *b* in both panels. Table 2 outlines the specific gains from trade to each country. Americans consume an additional 100 million drills and 150 million more blouses. Similar gains are realized in China.

Note that people in both nations can consume more of *both* goods. This possibility exists with any specialization and exchange, whether within a country or internationally. An example at the level of an individual family is the homebuilder whose family has a nicer house than if it had to produce not only its own home, but also

its own food, clothing, and all the other amenities of life. Diversion into these other activities and away from its area of expertise could easily cause the family to live in a hovel.

Moving toward free trade resembles economic growth driven by technological advances. We can consume more even though no more resources are available than previously; even in the short run, both countries' gains from free trade typically outweigh any losses. The final terms of trade are 1:1 in our example, although they need not fall precisely at the midpoint of no-trade prices. All prices are shaped by both demand and supply. The production possibilities frontiers used address only the supply side, but explicitly considering differences in demand would not change our conclusion that trade confers net gains on all trading parties. People will not trade unless they expect to benefit.

The magnitudes of gains from trade between nations are positively related to the differences in comparative advantages among the trading groups.

Short-Run Gainers and Potential Losers

You may lose if the price of your output falls relative to the prices of the things you buy. Thus, economists talk about an "adverse change in the terms of trade" whenever export prices fall relative to import prices. For example, an adverse change in the U.S. terms of trade occurred when the price of imported oil skyrocketed after Iraq invaded Kuwait in 1990, while vigorous international competition precluded similar hikes in our export prices.

When trade expands, changes in the relative prices of imports and exports benefit some people and harm others, even though, on balance, the gains exceed any losses. Some individuals may suffer adverse changes in their individual terms of trade if trade exposes their output to competition from foreigners whose production costs are lower. A simple demand and supply model of the international blouse market will illuminate why some people dislike certain aspects of trade. We will abandon the confines of our constant-cost model and, for simplicity, assume that the dollar is the world currency.

Figure 5 depicts market demands and supplies for blouses in the United States (Panel A) and in China (Panel C). Without trade, U.S. blouse prices would be $80, or 2 drills. At every price below $80, there is an excess demand (*XD*) for blouses in the United States. Domestic producers are willing to supply fewer blouses than American buyers would purchase. This excess demand (the horizontal distance between the supply and demand curves) is graphed as XD_a in the center panel of Figure 5 and indicates how many blouses would be imported at various prices.

In China blouses would cost only $40 each, or half a drill, with no sales to the U.S. market. At prices exceeding $40, Chinese blouse makers are willing to sell more blouses than Chinese consumers are willing and able to buy. This surplus, or excess supply (the horizontal distance between the supply and demand curves), is graphed as XS_c in the center panel of Figure 5

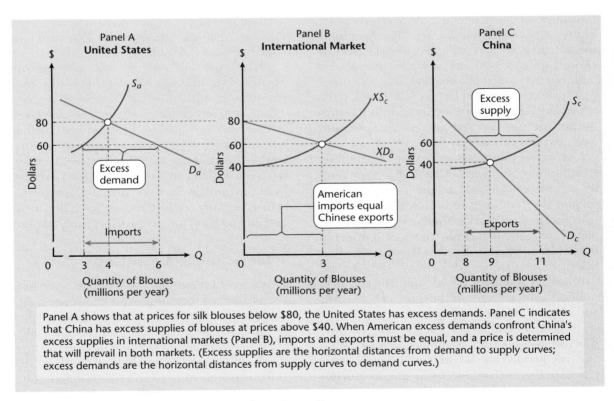

Panel A shows that at prices for silk blouses below $80, the United States has excess demands. Panel C indicates that China has excess supplies of blouses at prices above $40. When American excess demands confront China's excess supplies in international markets (Panel B), imports and exports must be equal, and a price is determined that will prevail in both markets. (Excess supplies are the horizontal distances from demand to supply curves; excess demands are the horizontal distances from supply curves to demand curves.)

FIGURE 5   International Excess Demands and Supplies

and indicates how many Chinese blouses are available for export at prices greater than $40.

Equilibrium between our willingness to import and China's willingness to export occurs when our excess demand equals their excess supply. Blouses will sell for $60 in both the United States and China with free trade; annual Chinese output will rise to 11 million blouses, while U.S. output drops by 1 million blouses. Moreover, Chinese purchases of blouses decline by 1 million, while American blouse buying rises by 2 million annually.

Individual Gainers and Losers

Who gains from trade? Chinese blouse makers sell more blouses at higher prices. American blouse buyers also gain; the price of a blouse in the United States has dropped from $80 down to $60, and purchases have risen. Now, for possible short-run losers: American blouse makers may lose when the price falls to $60 (from $80), and Chinese blouse buyers may lose as the price rises to $60. Blouse ownership in China could decline because of the higher price, but higher Chinese income would tend to boost purchases of blouses. The net effect is uncertain. American blouse output falls, but note that world blouse production has risen by 1 million units. Even former U.S. blouse makers tend to gain when they move into the production of drills, where the United States possesses a comparative advantage.

Because Americans are buying $180 million worth of blouses from China ($60 × 3 million), we will have balanced trade if we export $180 million worth of drills to China. If we drew figures for the drill market similar to Figure 5, we would conclude that trade causes drill prices to fall in China, while drill prices rise in the United States; employment and output of the Chinese drill industry declines, but less than the U.S. drill industry grows. There will be more of both drills and blouses after trade commences.

Table 3 summarizes gainers and possible short-term losers from trading drills for blouses, and vice versa. You should keep in mind, however, that this analysis only looks at short-run *specialization* gains and losses and that it only balances one import against one export. In a world of

TABLE 3 Gainers from Specialization and Potential Short-Run Losers from Trade

Country	Gainers	Possible Losers
United States	drill sellers blouse buyers	drill buyers blouse sellers
China	drill buyers blouses sellers	drill sellers blouse buyers

People who purchase low-price imports gain from trade, while people who rely on production of the good for income may lose in the short run.

millions of imports and exports, even those whose income falls because of lower-priced import competition for the good they produce also gain when they buy imports—including goods they personally produce—at lower prices. For example, competition from imported clothing may shrink textile workers' income, but they gain when they buy low-priced imports of oil, cars, VCRs, . . ., *and* clothes. When uniqueness, scale, dynamic, and political gains from trade are considered as well, it is hard to imagine anyone who ultimately loses from international trade.

Can we be fairly sure that gains to the four groups of winners more than offset the losses to the four groups of potential losers? We can. Trade expands global production of each good. Because both countries' consumption possibilities frontiers grow, gainers in each country could (but seldom do) compensate the losers from trade so that every man, woman, and child in both countries gained. If I gain $50 from a transaction that causes you to lose $20, we are both ahead if I share my gain by giving you $25.

Trade Adjustment Assistance

Most successful movements to restrict trade have been launched by groups who lose because they operate at comparative disadvantages when forced to compete with foreign producers. They are effective politically because they are strongly opposed to importing certain goods. Suppose that 100,000 people would lose $10,000 apiece annually if restrictions on textiles imports were eliminated (a total of $1 billion), while 200 million other

Americans will shell out an average of an extra $10 a year for clothing (a total of $2 billion) if textile imports continue to be restricted. You have 100,000 people who will vote for or against politicians based largely on their platforms on textile quotas, and 200 million people who are, for the most part, oblivious to their personal losses and politicians' positions on trade.

Let us see why trade restrictions are inefficient and what might be done to ensure that everyone gains from free trade. In our example, if the 200 million consumers each contributed $6 annually to a relief fund for the 100,000 textile workers, each textile worker could receive $12,000 annually. If we set up the relief fund only with the precondition that textiles be freely imported, textile workers would gain ($2,000 each) and so would textile consumers ($4 each annually). Clearly, this would be a move in the direction of economic efficiency: everyone gains, and no one loses.

Examples like this have driven *trade adjustment assistance* legislation, which is intended to provide retraining and financial assistance for workers displaced because of liberalized international trade. Unfortunately, it is quite difficult to identify who loses from lower trade barriers. Congress has seldom funded these programs adequately, and they have been among the first items on the chopping block when politicians have tried to balance the budget. However, in 1993, the Clinton administration negotiated numerous pieces of aid to various regions and industries when passage of the North American Free Trade Agreement (NAFTA) appeared to be in trouble with the Congress. Nevertheless, sentiment for trade restrictions remains a strongly held minority position in the United States. Support for higher trade barriers is voiced by many unions and managers of industries facing foreign competition.

ARGUMENTS AGAINST FREE TRADE

Goods tend to be produced at minimum opportunity cost and then traded by their producers for other goods that are subjectively more valuable to them. Recent high growth rates in many emerging countries (e.g., China, Malaysia, and Indonesia) that have begun focusing on international trade are evidence that free trade tends to maximize the value of the world's production. Then why is free trade the exception instead of the general practice? The answer lies in arguments *against* free trade and *for* import barriers against foreign goods. Some arguments are partially valid, but others verge on the irrational. All too commonly, irrational arguments prove persuasive, or semivalid charges against free trade are applied incorrectly. It is also unfortunate that most trade barriers protect domestic industries in incredibly inefficient ways. We will begin by examining relatively weak arguments for trade barriers and then work up the ladder to more telling thrusts against free trade.

Nationalism

"Buy American" campaigns (or pleas to shop at hometown merchants) entail asking or requiring people to act against their own interests. For example, advertising from the International Ladies' Garment Workers' Union (ILGWU) exhort us to save American jobs by buying domestic instead of imported apparel. Policymakers who yield to such nationalistic arguments cut us off from gains from exchange to, for example, subsidize domestic producers or depress foreigners' incomes. At times, such policies may generate psychic income (e.g., by defending cultural identity or national heritage), but higher costs or lower quality diminish our economic power. Thus, most trade restrictions are contrary to our real national interests.

The Exploitation Doctrine

Some people perceive trade as a zero-sum game. They reason that if one trader gains, the other must lose. Thus, if we gain, we must be exploiting our trading partner. Such reasoning may hold for poker or roulette, but the gains from trade we just described indicate that people on both sides of an exchange gain. Transactions do not occur without expectations of gain. The belief that people in less developed countries lose absolutely and so are exploited when they trade with people in developed countries is clearly wrong.

A more sophisticated argument is that trade results in relative oppression because the stronger party's gains far outweigh benefits to a weaker trader. This argument is normally wrong because gains from trade are generally greatest in small countries; the less your trade affects the terms of trade offered by your trading partners, the greater your ability to exploit differences in the relative opportunity costs of production. For example, Monaco, a tiny country, relies heavily on trade and might be impoverished but for the world market. The United States and Germany, on the other hand, have wide internal markets and rich resource mixes. These giants rely less on trade than countries like Monaco or Switzerland. Imagine how destitute the United Arab Emirates might be without trade. Their natural resources consist largely of sand, oil, and more sand. Through trade, their per capita income has, at times, exceeded that enjoyed by typical Americans.

Retaliation

Many countries restrict imports from the United States, so why shouldn't we retaliate with barriers against their exports? This argument is often directed at Japan, which severely restricts imports of U.S. machinery and agricultural goods. One problem is that this notion ignores the harm done to U.S. consumers by retaliatory policies. When we restrict imports, we reduce the amounts of goods available to Americans and domestic prices rise.

Nevertheless, in some situations, our threat to retaliate against foreign governments' trade barriers can tip international negotiations so that their markets are opened to American exports. Just as workers' rights to strike must be exercised occasionally for the threat of a strike to have weight in union negotiations with management, the threat of retaliation against foreign

trade barriers may be viable only if we occasionally do retaliate.

But retaliation is an effective negotiating tool only if other countries adopt freer trade policies, just as a strike harms union workers if it fails to yield a better work contract. And just as a permanent strike would harm workers, we normally compound the damage done by foreign trade restrictions if we retaliate with policies that are maintained in the long run. We may harm foreign producers, but we harm ourselves as well. In fact, some analysts argue that the worldwide depression of the 1930s was substantially worsened because of escalating retaliation by many major trading nations; they fear that a major trade war could cause another global depression.

Antidumping

The accusation that foreign producers compete unfairly by "dumping" is raised almost every time an American producer is undersold.

> ***Dumping*** *occurs when a country exports at lower prices than those charged within the exporting country.*

Dumping might arise from price discrimination, which entails charging desperate (domestic) buyers more than less desperate (foreign) buyers. In such a case, consumers in the country "dumped on" benefit from the discriminatory policy. Alternatively, a foreign government may try to create jobs by subsidizing exports. (Japan is often accused of such policies.) Finally, *predatory dumping* means that a seller tries to establish a worldwide monopoly by driving competitors out of the market. Presumably, prices could then be raised to yield monopoly profits.

There is scant evidence of dumping, however, and if it does occur, the customers who buy at lower prices are major beneficiaries. Congress has enacted laws against foreign producers dumping in U.S. markets. Should our government protect us from low prices? Dumping is legally inferred whenever imports are sold below cost. In one case, Mexican tomato growers were barred from U.S. markets because they were selling below cost. The sad fact was that a bumper crop had depressed the price so much that tomatoes sold below cost in Mexico. Mexican tomato growers had to sell the tomatoes before they spoiled. Banning U.S. imports simply compounded losses to Mexican farmers.

Infant Industries

Although loud clamoring for protection is now heard from "senile" industries, a slightly more valid but still misleading argument for trade restrictions is protection of *infant industries*. Shortly after the American Revolution, Alexander Hamilton argued that British industrial superiority only reflected a head start over American economic development, and that protection of infant industries from low-cost British competition was necessary for this country's industrialization.

Figure 6 shows what happens if production costs decline as industrialization proceeds. If the world price is P_w for some commodity and average production costs follow path AC_0 over time, eventually declining to P_w, then in the long run a protected infant industry will mature, be competitive in the world market, and not require protection. Notice, however, that if consumers buy constant quantities of the protected good in each period, across time they cumulatively lose an amount equal to the red area below AC_0 and above P_w. This loss is inefficient because these burdens are not offset by lower costs after the industry is established.

A path like AC_1 is necessary for the efficient establishment of a new industry. The discounted value of the long-run lower costs (shaded blue) must exceed the initial losses (red). Of course, if entrepreneurs perceive that in the long run they will achieve average production costs that are sufficiently below world prices, they will build the new industry without protection. Even if the infant industry argument is occasionally semi-valid, it would be better to subsidize the industry than to protect it with trade barriers.

The infant industry argument contains only the barest kernel of logic and is largely invalid,

FIGURE 6 The Error in Infant Industry Arguments

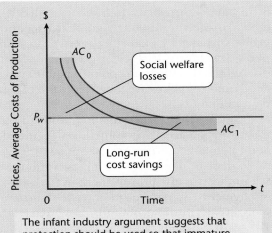

The infant industry argument suggests that protection should be used so that immature industries can become competitive in the world market. However, tariffs or quotas designed to buffer infant industries from foreign competition will cause losses of social welfare (the red area) unless they are offset by extraordinarily low costs (the blue area) in the long run. Of course, if such cost savings are possible, there is no need for protection, because profit-seekers will invest in this industry anyway.

but it has been used by many less developed countries to justify protectionist policies. The almost uniform result is inefficient production and little or no growth in per capita income. For example, protection of a government-subsidized Indian automobile plant was rationalized by an infant industry argument in the 1970s. The factory ultimately produced only a few vehicles that resembled cheap Fiats, but average production cost exceeded that for a Mercedes-Benz. This high price tag illustrates how ignoring comparative advantages can lead to financial disaster. Indians would have been far better off if their government had focused on the production of goods that used labor (its abundant factor) more intensively and capital (its scarce resource) less—a course of action the Indian government adopted in 1991, along with substantial deregulation. India's growth rate accelerated after its liberalization of international trade.

Trade and Payments Deficits

Anxiety about imbalances of trade or payments is, in part, a throwback to a theory called *mercantilism*. Mercantilists argued that a country grows stronger by exporting more than it imports, drawing the balances in gold. Adam Smith discredited this theory by pointing out that real goods and resources are the true wealth of a nation, not money.

Nevertheless, concerns about trade or payments imbalances are sometimes legitimate. Some people advocate tariffs or quotas to reduce these deficits. The resulting misallocations are seldom worth any improvement in the balance of payments. When we run a trade deficit and there are net outflows of funds that "weaken the dollar," it is usually better to allow natural market adjustments to rectify the imbalance.

Moreover, there is the threat that other countries will retaliate if we impose trade barriers. Finally, shouldn't we be happy that foreigners are willing to sell us more than we sell them—if they are willing to take dirty green paper for the difference? Just as decapitation will cure the common cold, trade barriers may cure deficits in the balances of trade or payments, but better remedies are available.

Job Destruction

Ross Perot got a lot of mileage during the 1992 presidential campaign by predicting "giant sucking noises as industries and jobs move south" to Mexico if NAFTA were enacted. (NAFTA passed anyway.) The view that imports slice into domestic employment is based on simplistic logic: we will produce goods ourselves if we don't import them. One obvious fallacy is if imports reduce employment, exports expand it. In fact, one major study suggests that even more jobs are created in export industries than are lost because of imports.

Another problem is that import barriers invite retaliation that destroys jobs in export industries. In fact, trade barriers frequently trade good jobs for bad jobs. When imports threaten an industry's survival, the marketplace is sig-

naling that the industry is relatively inefficient and may be senile. Trade barriers sustain comparatively inefficient industries and retard more efficient growth. Resource owners will ultimately be better paid if their resources are moved into areas in which they have comparative advantages.

Even if maintaining employment in certain industries is a national priority for some reason, trade barriers are incredibly inefficient ways to promote employment. The prices of the goods protected by import barriers rise far more than the incomes of protected workers. Several studies indicate that "voluntary" limits on auto exports from Japan boosted U.S. carmakers' share of domestic sales by 6% to 8% but raised American car prices by an average of $400 to $600, while Japanese import prices rose by between $2,000 and $3,800 apiece.[1] The result? Each American autoworker's job saved by trade restrictions cost U.S. car buyers almost $200,000. Table 4 presents a set of estimates of the costs of saving jobs through trade barriers.

These numbers may seem astounding, but trade barriers cause American consumers to lose in many ways, most of which are hidden.

1. Consumers subsidize U.S. industries and resource suppliers (e.g., workers) that lack comparative advantages in areas protected by trade barriers.
2. The market power of some domestic producers is protected, enabling them to restrict output and raise prices.
3. Nontariff trade barriers subsidize efficient foreign suppliers, substantially worsening our balance of payments.
4. Trade barriers help foreign producers exercise monopoly power that enriches them to the tune of billions of dollars each year. (An irony is that U.S. restrictions on imports generate monopoly profits for foreign firms, while our antitrust laws are only one aspect of official policies to promote domestic competition.)

---

[1] Robert W. Crandall, "Import Quotas and the Automobile Industry: The Costs of Protectionism," *The Brookings Review*, Summer 1984, pp. 62–74.

TABLE 4   The Costs of Jobs Saved by Protectionism

Industry	Estimated Total Costs ($ millions)	Number of Jobs Saved	Annual Cost per Job Saved ($)
Apparel and textiles	24,500	169,000	145,000
Automobiles	5,800	39,700	173,000
Book manufacturing	500	5,000	100,000
Ceramic tile	130	347	400,000
Corn brooms	10	105	100,000
Dairy products	500	25,000	220,000
Fishing (tuna)	—	—	240,000
Glassware	20	100	200,000
Luggage	211	226	934,000
Maritime	3,000	11,100	270,000
Shoes	—	—	38,000
Steel	6,800	15,800	430,000
Sugar	900	15,000	60,000

Sources: S. Nosar, "The High Costs of Protectionism," *N.Y. Times,* 2 November 93 C2; G. Hufbauer et al. *Trade Protection in the United States:31 Case Studies* (Washington D.C.: Institute for International Economics 1986); FTC studies cited by P. Gramm, "New Protection = Old Sophistry," *Wall Street Journal,* 4 October 1985 p. 21, plus author calculations.

To illustrate how inefficient trade barriers are as a way to protect jobs, consider policies that might provide jobs for 1,000 American diamond miners. The United States has a few sparse diamond fields. Barriers causing mediocre diamonds to cost $20,000 per carat could spur domestic diamond mining in some regions. South Africa and Russia, however, would realize huge profits by selling in U.S. markets. The high costs of trade barriers suggest that other policies to protect workers' incomes are more efficient. For example, Table 4 suggests that, for most protected industries, one-time trade adjustment assistance of $50,000 per worker displaced by freer trade would be a bargain.

Harmful Income Redistribution

The United States is commonly perceived as having relatively less labor but more capital than the rest of the world. The *Hechscher-Ohlin model* of trade suggests that goods requiring heavy doses of a country's abundant resources will be exported and goods intensive in a country's scarcest resources will be imported. A corollary of this theory is that owners of resources that are more plentiful nationally than worldwide garner all short-run specialization gains from trade, while owners of resources that are relatively abundant internationally but scarce domestically suffer short-run losses from the specialization caused by freer trade.

This approach has been interpreted as suggesting that U.S. workers face stiffer competition from low-wage foreign labor because of trade, while American capital owners gain potential foreign customers. Thus, American wages are driven down by trade while returns to capital rise; only capital owners enjoy the net specialization gains from trade.

Capital owners could more than compensate workers for income shrinkage caused by trade, but our institutions are not geared for such transfers (e.g., failure to fund trade adjustment assistance). Hence, working-class people suffer while the rich get richer. This theory may help explain some American labor unions' support for trade barriers. If we are truly concerned about income inequality, however, we should not ignore the gains to poor foreign workers when their products are exported, nor should we forget the uniqueness, scale, dynamic, and political benefits of trade.

The Hechscher-Ohlin model has often been misapplied by ignoring some major sources of U.S. comparative advantage. A partial rebuttal to the idea that capitalists gain from trade while American labor loses is that, more than other types of resources, the United States has relative abundances of rich farm land and labor that is adept with sophisticated technology. These resources are relatively scarce in the rest of the world, so American agricultural incomes and the incomes of highly skilled workers are enhanced by international trade. The post–World War II burst of industrialization of Western Europe and Japan has shifted this country's gains from trade away from capitalists toward highly skilled workers and farmers. Less developed countries have also benefited enormously from increased competition among modern industrial powers for raw materials.

The Hechscher-Ohlin approach suggests that resource differentials largely determine the composition of imports and exports. Four decades of studies aimed at predicting the composition of trade from this model have, however, yielded mixed results. This prompted Michael Porter and his associates at the Harvard Business School to analyze trade patterns at a very detailed level. His conclusions are addressed in Focus 1.

Exploiting Monopoly and Monopsony Power

A country that is a major importer or exporter of a good can flex its muscle through trade restrictions to drive prices up or down. For example, a country having monopoly power might be able to impose an export tariff (tax) that would be borne in part by "foreign devils." If so, it is conceivable that the citizens of the exporting country would gain.

The monopolistic or monopsonistic unit may gain tremendously by manipulating its output or purchases (and, consequently, prices), but only by imposing even greater losses on its customers or suppliers. For example, OPEC jacked up oil prices by over 1,000% during the 1970s by agreeing to raise prices and restrict the outputs of member countries. They prospered for a period, but at the cost of worldwide economic recession that was especially hard on less developed countries. Brazil and Colombia, somewhat less successfully, combined to raise coffee prices, but only at considerable cost to coffee drinkers.

It would be naive to expect altruism to deter countries from exercising their economic clout. A country's leaders should nevertheless be leery of muscling its trading partners, because abuse of monopoly or monopsony power invites retaliation and raises the specter of disastrous trade wars.

Diversity

Volatile demands or supplies can be devastating if a country specializes in only a few major outputs. Colombia's reliance on coffee is one example. Droughts, floods, or coffee blight can easily wipe out a year's income, or large harvests in Brazil might severely depress world prices. Diversification is one way of spreading the risk, just as farmers rotate their crops to rest the soil and spread their risks.

Protection of developing industries may encourage diversity, but at some cost in efficiency. These efficiency losses might be thought of as insurance premiums, but diversification could be encouraged at far less cost by production subsidies. On rare occasions diversification may be a valid goal for narrowly specialized countries, but not in the United States and other richly varied economies. Even small countries' diversification policies have often been so misdirected that opportunities for development were lost.

National Defense

Domestic access to certain products is crucial for our national defense, so we might want to protect such industries as aircraft or weapons from foreign competition. This argument is often

Sources of Comparative and Competitive Advantages

Traditional models to explain why nations import certain goods and export others focus on different mixes of resources between countries. Australia, for example, has vast tracts of arable land but a relatively sparse population, while China is densely populated and much of its land is unsuited for agriculture. Thus, Australia predictably exports wool and grain to China, while importing such labor-intensive goods as Chinese textiles.

The conventional model also implies that countries with relatively abundant natural resources should be prosperous, while those with fewer natural resources should be relatively poor—a prediction refuted by lower per capita incomes in such resource-rich countries as Mexico or Brazil when compared with the prosperity of such barren and overpopulated locales as Japan or Taiwan. Japan, for example, is a leading steel exporter despite its relative scarcity of fossil fuels and iron ore.

Such paradoxes raise questions about sources of comparative advantage. In the words of Michael Porter,* "How can we explain why Germany is the home base for so many of the world's leading makers of printing presses, luxury cars, and chemicals? Why is tiny Switzerland the home base for international leaders in pharmaceuticals, chocolate, and trading? Why are leaders in heavy trucks and mining equipment based in Sweden? Why has America produced the preeminent international competitors in personal computers, software, credit cards, and movies? Why are Italian firms so strong in ceramic tiles, ski boots, packaging machinery, and factory automation equipment? What makes Japanese firms so dominant in consumer electronics, cameras, robotics, and facsimile machines?"

Porter headed a research team that examined over a hundred industries spread across ten major countries. He concluded that basic resources (e.g., raw land and minerals) are much less important in explaining the international competitiveness of an industry than are advanced resources (sophisticated technology and a work force that is highly motivated and specialized, but adaptable). Comparative advantages arise primarily from how efficiently and effectively these advanced resources are deployed.

Other important determinants of comparative advantage Porter identified include (a) robust domestic demand that allows an industry to get started, (b) internationally competitive suppliers and related industries, and (c) vigorous domestic competition that forces firms to achieve high quality for both products and customer service.

Porter found that government subsidies or protection from foreign competitors usually create only anemic industries that require continuous government support. He argues that international success for an industry is facilitated if government policies merely (a) encourage domestic rivalry, (b) invest heavily in human resource skills that enhance productivity, and (c) emphasize quality as a national priority. With this minimal sort of government intervention, areas of comparative advantage are then best decided in the international marketplace.

*Michael E. Porter, *The Competitive Advantage of Nations* (New York: The Free Press, 1990).

misused and results in perverse policies. For example, the idea that we should not depend on foreign oil has been used for the past century to justify "Drain America First" policies that actually increased our long-run dependence on foreign oil suppliers.

We have only discussed import barriers to this point. National defense may provide more legitimate reasons for bans on exports of critical products and materials. Sales of scrap metal to Japan prior to World War II were clearly shortsighted. It would be equally foolish to allow terrorists or the Mafia to buy atomic weapons on a free market basis.

One final note: one major gain from trade is that mutual interdependence improves the prospects for peace. The costs of conflict increase, providing incentives to avoid war. Freer trade promotes international harmony and reduces the need for defense spending.

TRADE BARRIERS

A number of mechanisms are used as barriers to free trade, but the most important are *tariffs* and *quotas*. Each can be imposed on either imports or exports, but restrictions on imports are far more common than export barriers.

Tariffs

In the United States, tariffs on exports are forbidden by the Constitution.

> A **tariff** is a special tax that applies only to goods traded internationally.

Import tariffs raise the domestic prices of goods and stimulate domestic production. The United States is a major trader in most goods, so U.S. import tariffs also tend to drive down the incomes of foreign producers.

Suppose that we have a tariff on imported steel of $25 per ton, that the international price is $100 a ton, and that U.S. demands and supplies of steel are as depicted in Figure 7. Without the tariff, the United States domestic production would be 100 million tons annually, with imports equaling 60 million tons of steel (160 million – 100 million). The $25-per-ton tariff allows American steel makers to boost production to 120 million tons, but cuts domestic steel usage by 20 million tons (to 140 million) while imports fall 40 million tons. As a result of the tariff, U.S. steel consumers now pay more for less steel. Government collects revenues from the tariff equal to the shaded area *abfe*, or $500 million ($25 × 20 million).

Nontariff Barriers

International negotiations to reduce trade barriers (e.g., GATT, the General Agreement on Tariffs and Trade) historically focused on tariffs. The result has been growth of nontariff barriers against imports. For example, rigid U.S. regulatory standards have been used to limit automobile imports and drive up their prices. You might think this is appropriate, but a hint that

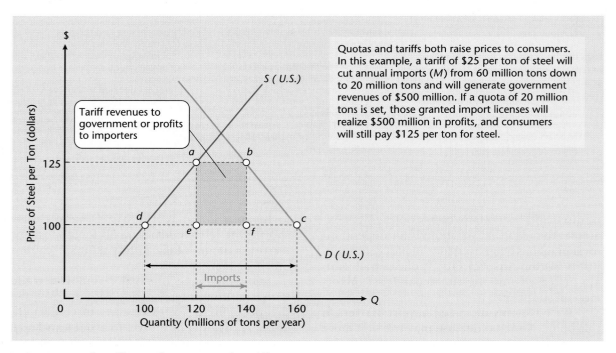

Quotas and tariffs both raise prices to consumers. In this example, a tariff of $25 per ton of steel will cut annual imports (*M*) from 60 million tons down to 20 million tons and will generate government revenues of $500 million. If a quota of 20 million tons is set, those granted import licenses will realize $500 million in profits, and consumers will still pay $125 per ton for steel.

FIGURE 7   The Effects of Quotas and Tariffs

safety or environmental standards may not be the real issue arises from the fact that Japanese standards drive up the prices of U.S. car exports to Japan even more. Both U.S. and Japanese carmakers have lobbied for regulations disadvantageous to foreign producers.

The latest round of GATT negotiations–the Uruguay round–involved almost all trading nations, accounting for over 90% of all international trade. This round of GATT took aim at reducing both tariff and nontariff barriers to trade and was completed in 1994. Among other issues were international standards for the protection of intellectual property rights; the pirating of music, software, and written works has been a major problem over the past two decades. Although the latest GATT treaty helped make patterns of trade significantly freer, negotiations prompted by various interest groups from different countries left significant barriers in place. For example, France insisted on limits to U.S. exports of films, music, and other forms of entertainment. And the United States retained the right to restrict imports based on antidumping laws. Thus, the United States still maintains nontariff barriers against such varied goods as apparel, electronics, and automobiles.

• **Quotas** Quotas are the most common nontariff barriers to trade.

> *Quotas* limit the amounts of goods that may be imported or exported.

Both quotas and tariffs inefficiently raise the prices of imported goods so that potential gains from trade are not fully realized, but the side effects of quotas make them especially harmful. Let us investigate why this is so.

Suppose the $25 tariff in Figure 7 were replaced by an import quota of 20 million tons annually. The domestic price remains at $125 per ton, but government would collect no revenues. Importers who secured import licenses would collectively pick off profits of $500 million: 20 million tons of steel costing $100 per ton could be sold for $125 a ton. These potential profits make import licenses very valuable and provide substantial inducements for bribery and corruption.

• **Voluntary Export Restrictions** The United States has traditionally been a cheerleader for freer international trade. Our actual policies, however, have been a bit schizophrenic. Fear of a trade war coupled with international treaties (instigated by the United States) to reduce tariffs have made it difficult for U.S. policymakers to bow to political pressures for protectionism by raising tariffs. This has diverted most industries (along with their unions) that want protection from imports into lobbying for *voluntary export restrictions* (VERs). Our government threatens foreign industries with import barriers unless they restrict exports. VERs are voluntary only in the sense that you voluntarily give up your money when a mugger points a gun at you and says "Your money or your life."

Japan imposed quotas on textile exports to the United States in the 1970s and on its auto exports in the 1980s. We indicated earlier that restrictions on auto imports from Japan saved American autoworkers' jobs at a cost of from $150,000 to $241,000 each. Curiously, the Japanese auto industry gained. The preceding analysis of quotas shows how. Limits on auto exports raised the prices Japanese firms received for exported vehicles and boosted their profits by billions of dollars. These profits would have been converted into U.S. tax revenues if tariffs had been used instead of quotas.

The Japanese reaction to this VER illustrates how regulation provokes unanticipated adjustments that may defeat its stated purpose. The goal of the VER was to protect American jobs and reduce the U.S. trade deficit, but it only limited the number of Japanese exports–not their value. Consequently, Japanese carmakers focused on exporting more luxurious lines: Toyota Land Cruisers and the new Acura, Lexus, and Infiniti vehicles. Thus, some of the import pressure on economy cars was shifted to another market segment. But Korean Hyundais, for example, were not subject to quotas, so they partially replaced low-end Japanese exports in American garages. Even voluntary quotas have unpredictable results.

Regional Economic Integration

Just as TV broadcasts and fast-food restaurant chains are slowly reducing differences in regional dialects and in how towns look from Maine to Texas to Hawaii, the gains from trade and advances in telecommunications are blurring international borders and differences of language and culture. Groups of countries increasingly adopt common economic policies. OPEC, for example, sets oil prices for its 17 member countries (with erratic success). An even more significant trend is *regional economic integration*, whereby agreements tear down trade barriers between neighboring countries. This may be a baby step toward free trade throughout the world.

The European Community
Germany, France, Italy, Belgium, the Netherlands, and Luxembourg launched the European Community (EC) in 1967. They have since been joined by the United

Kingdom, Ireland, Denmark, Greece, Spain, and Portugal on a slow (and sometimes erratic) path toward full economic integration. (See Figure 8.) Barriers restricting trade and capital flows have virtually disappeared. Leaders in a number of former Eastern bloc countries have recently indicated desires to join the EC, where an official but still weak European Community government is at work on laws to govern commercial activity in all EC countries.

The European Currency Unit (ECU) was established in 1979 to stabilize financial dealings among EC countries and would represent a giant step toward a common monetary system. In 1993, however, a majority of European countries indicated that they wanted to maintain more national sovereignty and rejected a quicker pace toward full monetary integration.

The North American Community
Trade between the United States and Canada flourished after most trade barriers and restrictions on resource flows were removed in 1989. Mexico joined this economic union in 1993, although northward movements of more Mexican labor remains limited under NAFTA. Ongoing policies to privatize enterprises historically mismanaged by government bureaucracies have recently reawakened interest in Mexican stocks and bonds after a decade of pessimism caused by its enormous international indebtedness.

Prospects
Japan and South Korea have similar free trade agreements, and they are negotiating with China and other Pacific Rim countries. Tariff barriers that restricted trade with Russia and other former Eastern bloc countries have been largely dismantled, and negotiations are underway to reach accommodation with the EC and North American economic unions. Leaders in a number of countries in Central and South America have expressed interest in expanding NAFTA to a Pan-American economic union that would extend from Tierra del Fuego (the southern tip of Chile) to the Arctic circle.

From a global perspective, regional economic integration has the disadvantage of erecting uniform trade barriers against outsiders. Nevertheless, the potential gains from even freer trade are so powerful that the next logical step is negotiated reductions of trade barriers between the emerging blocs of traders. The GATT treaty concluded in 1994 represents a major step in this direction. There is reason to be optimistic that the full gains available from free trade throughout most of the world may ultimately be realized.

1. Austria, 1973
2. Belgium, 1967
3. Denmark, 1973
4. Ireland, 1973
5. France, 1967
6. Germany, 1967
7. Greece, 1981
8. The Netherlands,1967
9. Italy, 1967
10. Luxemburg, 1967
11. Portugal, 1986
12. Spain, 1986
13. United Kingdom, 1973

FIGURE 8 The European Community

Another problem is that rigid quotas fail to accommodate changes in demand. Growth in demand can be met by imports with a tariff system, but not under import quotas. Finally, relative to tariffs, quotas retard the incentives of foreign producers to cut costs and produce better products by doing research and innovation. Conclusion: from the perspective of the citizen or taxpayer, tariffs are preferable to quotas. However, either mechanism causes substantial economic inefficiency.

A FINAL ARGUMENT FOR FREER TRADE

Perfect government policies might, in an ideal world, achieve any feasible set of goals we choose. Optimal trade barriers could efficiently exploit our own monopoly or monopsony power and counter that exercised by foreigners. Ideal barriers might also be constructed to protect American jobs, incomes, and infant industries, bolster our national defense, rectify trade and payments imbalances, and offset unfair practices by foreign governments.

In the real world, however, most trade barriers are enacted because of pressures from special interests. These barriers depress our national income, stimulate foreign retaliation and hostility against the United States, endanger jobs in U.S. export industries, and reduce competition for domestic firms that exercise monopoly power. Nor has the growth of nontariff barriers to trade prevented enormous and growing trade and payments deficits.

A major reason U.S. trade policies are so far from ideal is that specific trade barriers strongly affect the incomes of members of special-interest groups who are willing to work hard in the political arena for their passage. But members of the general public are politically apathetic about such things as import quotas on shoes, because their individual well-being is affected relatively little. The result is mounting pressure for protectionism that will inefficiently benefit the few at much higher cost to the broad public. Focus 2 points out, however, that recent international agreements may pave the way for freer international trade.

International trade is a major source of economic growth and development. At the same time, consumer demands grow and broaden as consumers' incomes increase, so trade tends to expand as the world economy grows. Trade also increases interdependence and improves international relations. In this chapter we have explored the gains from trade and exposed fallacies behind most arguments against free trade. We hope you will remember these discussions when people debate trade policies.

CHAPTER REVIEW: KEY POINTS

1. **International trade** is important to people throughout the world. The smaller and less diversified an economy is, the greater is the importance of its international trade.

2. The **law of comparative advantage** suggests that there will be net gains to all trading parties whenever their pretrade relative opportunity costs and price structures differ between goods.

3. A country's **consumption possibilities frontier (CPF)** expands beyond its production possibilities frontier (*PPF*) with the onset of trade or with the removal of trade restrictions.

4. The **terms of trade** are the prices of exports relative to the costs of imports. An adverse change in the terms of trade lowers a country's CPF, while a favorable change in the terms of trade expands it.

5. Gains from trade arise because international transactions (*a*) provide **unique** goods that would not otherwise be available, (*b*) allow highly specialized industries to exploit **economies of scale**, (*c*) speed the spread of **technology** and facilitate **capital accumulation** and **entrepreneurial innovation**, (*d*) encourage more **peaceful international relations**, and (*e*) facilitate

specialization according to comparative advantage.

6. Domestic producers of imported goods may suffer short-term losses from trade, as do domestic consumers of exported goods. However, their losses are overshadowed by the specialization gains to the consumers of imports and the producers of exports. The gainers could always use parts of their gains to compensate the losers so that, on balance, no one loses. Moreover, **uniqueness, scale, dynamic**, and **political gains** from trade make it unlikely that anyone loses from trade in the long run.

7. Even the most valid of the arguments against free trade are substantially overworked. The arguments that are semivalid include the ideas that (*a*) the income redistributions from trade are undesirable; (*b*) desirable diversity within a narrow economy is hampered by free trade; (*c*) national defense requires restrictions to avoid dependence on foreign sources and (more validly) export restrictions to keep certain technologies out of the hands of potential enemies; and (*d*) major exporters of a commodity can exercise monopolistic power by restricting exports, while important consuming nations can exercise monopsonistic power through import restrictions.

8. Any exercise of international monopoly or monopsony power invites **retaliation** and causes worldwide economic inefficiency. Those who lose because of trade restrictions will lose far more than is gained by the "winners."

9. If trade is to be restricted, **tariffs** are preferable to **quotas** or other **nontariff barriers** because of the higher tax revenues and the smaller incentives for bribery and corruption.

10. **Trade adjustment assistance** is one way that the gainers from trade might compensate the losers so that all would gain. However, the difficulty of identifying the losers and past failures to fund these programs adequately have resulted in continuing pressures for trade restrictions.

QUESTIONS FOR THOUGHT AND DISCUSSION

1. What would happen to standards of living in the United States if all foreign trade were prohibited? How significant do you think this would be? In what areas would the impact be the strongest?

2. How is smuggling related to import tariffs and quotas? (Positively, negatively, or not at all?) Does smuggling increase social welfare or decrease it? If your answer is that it depends on the types of goods smuggled, for which types of goods would smuggling increase welfare? What types of goods justify barriers against importation?

3. How do a nation's endowments of labor, natural resources, and capital shape the outputs in which it has comparative advantages? What influence might weather have? Can you think of other determinants of a country's areas of comparative advantage?

4. The Hechscher-Ohlin model of international trade has been extended to "prove" that international transactions tend to equalize factor payments (e.g., the purchasing power of wages and rates of return to capital). Since World War II, the rapid growth in labor incomes in Japan and Western Europe relative to that in the United States seems to support this theory. What mechanisms tend to equalize resource payments?

5. Most models of international trade assume that goods move across international borders but people and capital do not. Can you use the principles you have learned in this chapter to explain immigration patterns and international capital flows?

Trade Current account DM

Chapter 37

International Finance

S (U.S.)

Exchange rate

£

$ ¥

e

D (Germany)

Capital account

Would you enjoy a European vacation? Some lucky students can afford it and will go next summer. Others will go only after they retire, if ever. A major influence on the cost of touring Paris or Rome is the dollar's *exchange rate*; its value relative to French francs or Italian lire. A high-valued dollar reduces our costs for a European tour and more of us fly overseas, but a lower exchange rate raises the cost of foreign travel so more of us stay home. Of course, a low-valued dollar makes travel in America a bargain for foreign tourists, and the Grand Canyon, Disneyland, and similar spots will be more crowded than usual.

Most of us are more familiar with exchange rates than with other aspects of *international finance*, which covers such issues as (*a*) the consequences of flows of funds for purposes of speculation or to finance international trade in goods or resources and (*b*) how these transactions are funded when one set of traders is based in a country that uses, say, dinars or pesos, while their trading partners customarily deal in yen or dollars. The first topic in this chapter is the relationship between international trade and in-

ternational finance. Then we turn to the nature of balance of payments accounts.

How prices are set when traders use different currencies is our next concern. A key to this puzzle involves looking at different ways that exchange rates between currencies can be determined. Exchange rates translate *all* wages and prices in one country's currency into their values in other countries' currencies. Our final task in this chapter is an overview of influences on the international value of the dollar during the past few years. This will complete the framework you need to interpret recent imbalances in our international payments.

BALANCES OF PAYMENTS AND TRADE

Many Americans cannot identify how they personally have been affected by persistent deficits in the international trade or payments of the United States. Trade deficits or surpluses provide starting points for understanding international finance.

If the dollar value of merchandise imports exceeds that for exports of U.S. merchandise, then the United States experiences a **balance of trade deficit**. But if the dollar value of our merchandise exports exceeds the monetary value of imports, there is a **balance of trade surplus**.

There is no special reason for inflows of dollars from sales of U.S. exports to precisely match outflows of dollars for purchases of imports. Because one country's imports are another's exports, the total of all trade deficits in some countries must exactly balance surpluses in other countries. Thus, when the United States runs a trade deficit, some other countries must run surpluses.

Accounting for international transactions in merchandise and services is the first step in building our balance of payments accounts.

Our **balance of payments accounts** summarize flows of payments between the United States and foreigners with whom it deals.

Transactions that cause U.S. citizens to send funds abroad drive this account toward a deficit; transactions generating inflows of funds move the balance of payments toward a surplus.

A **deficit** occurs in our balance of payments if monetary outflows from the United States exceed money inflows; a **surplus** occurs if the inflows exceed the outflows.

Table 1 outlines the U.S. balance of payments account, which covers two major categories: the current account and the capital account. The *current account* deals with transfers

TABLE 1   The U.S. Balance of Payments Accounts, 1993

	Receipts(+)	Payments(–)	Balance
Current Account			
(1) Merchandise Exports	+440		
(2) Merchandise Imports		–536	
Trade Balance (1 – 2)			–96
(3) Net Investment Income	+6		
(4) Net Services	+56		
(5) Net Unilateral Transfers		–33	
Current Account Transfers (1 + 2 + 3 + 4 + 5)			–66
Capital Account			
(6) Capital Outflows		+53	
(7) Capital Inflows	+89		
(8) Statistical Discrepancy			+12
Capital Account Balances (6 + 7 +8)			+24
Official Reserves Transactions Balance (1 + 2 + 3 + 4 + 5 + 6 + 7 + 8)			–42
Method of Financing			
(9) Increase U.S. Official Reserve Assets (–)		+2	
(10) Increase in Foreign Official Assets (+)	+41		
Total Financing of Surplus			+42
Sum of (1) through (10)			0

Source: *Survey of Current Business,* April 1994
Note: Totals may not sum precisely because of rounding

and trade in goods and services. The *capital account* records transactions in such items as stocks and bonds, or investments in physical capital. These accounts are balanced by changes in U.S. holdings of foreign currencies or net outflows of U.S. money, items 9 and 10 in this table.

The Current Account

Only merchandise shipments are considered when computing the balance of trade, but dollar for dollar, sales of services or international transfers have roughly equivalent macroeconomic effects. Many people intuitively believe that international trade occurs only in merchandise, not services. Nevertheless, a French tourist who exchanges francs for dollars and then gets a haircut in a Chicago barbershop before returning to Paris is effectively importing that haircut, and the barber is, perhaps unknowingly, an exporter. Foreign students who pay tuition after exchanging their national currencies for dollars are importing education to their countries.

Net investment income (item 3 in Table 1) refers to net flows of income from foreign investments, that is, any differences between funds Americans who have invested abroad are paid and the funds paid to foreigners as returns on their investments in the United States. Transfer payments (item 5) include cash gifts between individuals that cross international borders and other unilateral transfers, such as foreign aid or pension payments to workers who have retired abroad. Just as you receive interest (an *inflow*) only long after your funds have been deposited in a bank (an *outflow*), the inflows of investment income in the current account reflect earlier investments abroad by Americans (outflows).

The Capital Account

The capital account summarizes patterns of inflows and outflows of investment funds. Foreign investments historically account for most net outflows of U.S. financial capital. For example, deposits to a Swiss bank account or purchases of stock on the Hong Kong exchange by Americans

cause outflows of funds. Symmetrically, if a Japanese firm builds an auto assembly plant in the United States or buys U.S. Treasury bonds, funds flow into the United States.

Statistical discrepancies (item 8 in Table 1) are large because many transactions are not recorded–such transactions as smuggling (dollars for cocaine) are a mystery, and learning what foreign tourists buy after trading their money for dollars is close to impossible. Purchases of U.S. securities by foreigners are also largely unmonitored, in part because data collection has not kept pace with international flows of funds. Flows of foreign investment leave many governments in the dark. The British government, for example, was dismayed to learn that its claim to being among the world's three biggest creditor nations was no longer true by 1991 because its statistical discrepancy account was dominated by net capital inflows for much of the 1980s.

Note that the bulk of any deficit in the current account (imports – exports) translates into forces that tend to yield a surplus in the capital account, which means that foreigners acquire ownership of American stocks, bonds, real estate, and production facilities (economic capital). After we sum all transactions that draw money into the United States and subtract those that send funds abroad, we have the payments surplus or deficit, which summarizes net international transactions. As the last line in Table 1 shows, a country's overall balance must be zero.

Imbalances of Payments

The immense federal budget deficits of recent years have contributed to persistent balance of payments deficits. In Chapter 15, we showed that if net private domestic saving $(S - I)$ failed to cover a budget deficit $(G - T)$, then that deficit must be financed by foreigners:

$$S + T - I - G = X - M$$

(Recall that M = imports, X = exports, S = domestic saving, I = investment, G = government outlays, and T = tax revenues.)

Our domestic saving and taxes have not covered domestic investment and government outlays in recent years ($S + T < I + G$), so the United States has run large deficits in its current account ($X - M < 0$). Many of this country's trading partners have used surpluses in their balances of trade (their current accounts) to buy U.S. financial assets (Treasury bonds, corporate stocks and bonds, or real estate). Foreign financial investment in the United States has helped Americans live beyond their current incomes in recent years.

The preceding government budget constraint can be rearranged to isolate the current account of the U.S. balance of payments:

$$M - X = (I - S) + (G - T)$$

Thus, reversing deficits in our current account (i.e., moving $M - X$ toward zero) requires higher taxes, more domestic saving (greater S = less consumption), declines in government outlays (G), or less private investment (I). International economists call these harsh choices the *absorption* problem. The implication of the absorption problem is that, if higher taxes or cuts in government outlays are not politically feasible and if Americans refuse to reduce our consumption, then we must rely on inflows of foreign financial capital to sustain healthy domestic investment, but ownership of U.S. economic and financial resources is "exported" in the process.

One way to attract foreign capital is through high interest rates that make investments in U.S. financial assets more attractive. International flows of funds are controlled by forces operating in international financial markets. International borrowing and lending (which can be thought of as trade across time) and international risk sharing in investments have grown in importance at incredible rates in recent years. The relative strengths of supplies and demands for a country's money are reflected in the relative prices of national currencies, that is, their exchange rates.

EXCHANGE RATES

Diversity in all its forms–social, linguistic, and economic–has been a force for human progress because different cultural perspectives widen the range of insights into how the world works and offer different options (e.g., Nigerian music, Chinese art, and Mexican cuisine) that enrich people everywhere. Nevertheless, diversity raises transaction costs. For example, different languages or currencies increase information costs between potential transactors. Most American students who have enrolled in a foreign language class only because it was required have, on occasion, mused that the world would be much simpler "if everyone just spoke English." In economic parlance, information might be more efficiently produced. (Of course, students elsewhere think that their's should be the chosen language.)

Similarly, transaction costs for trade would be lower if people everywhere used the same currency. But should pesos, yen, or dollars be used for the world's financial system? Controversy about which government would control the supply of money preclude a standard world currency as surely as geographic and cultural differences preclude a worldwide language. Thus, most international transactions require exchanging the currency of the buyer for the currency of the seller. For example, Americans usually want dollars, so foreign customers who buy from us must acquire U.S. dollars. They express their demands for dollars by supplying their own currencies. Similarly, we demand foreign goods, make loans to foreigners, or invest abroad by supplying dollars, which translates into demands for foreign currencies. The relative demands and supplies of various currencies determine their relative prices, or exchange rates.

Suppose you buy Brazilian coffee. Your grocer accepts dollars to pay the wholesaler, who probably pays U.S. dollars to the importer. But most Brazilian coffee growers do not want dollars from the importer; they want *reals* (which replaced Brazilian cruzeiros in July 1994) to pay their workers and suppliers. Dollars must be traded for reals. Thus, your purchase is ultimately translated into a demand for reals in international money markets and, simultaneously, into a supply of dollars.

> *The price of one currency (reals) in terms of another (dollars) is called the **nominal exchange rate**.*

If $1 trades for 200 reals, then the real is priced at half a cent ($0.005) and the nominal Brazilian exchange rate is 200. It takes 200 reals for a Brazilian to buy U.S. goods worth $1. Exchange rates are reciprocals: if $1 = 200 reals, then 1 real = 1/200th of a dollar.

Nominal Exchange Rates vs. Real Exchange Rates

Problems inherent in using nominal exchange rates to adjust incomes in different countries so that standards of living can be compared were described in Chapter 8. In the short run, the domestic purchasing power of different currencies may not be in accord with nominal exchange rates. Adjusting exchange rates for relative purchasing power yields the *real exchange rate*.

Let's reconsider payments between Americans and Brazilians. For simplicity, we assume that trade is competitive and unmarred by barriers to trade and that transaction costs are zero. If so, after adjusting for exchange rates, real costs for all goods must be identical in both the United States and Brazil. Assume further that dollar prices of all goods produced in the United States move proportionally with the U.S. price level P_A, and that real prices for all goods produced in Brazil move proportionally with the Brazilian price level P_B, so the ratio P_A/P_B reflects the cost of living in the U.S. relative to the cost of living in Brazil. In long-run equilibrium, nominal exchange rates would be proportional to the cost of living. Thus, if the long-run equilibrium exchange rate were $1 = 200 reals, then the price level in Brazil stated in reals would be 200 times higher than if it were based on dollars; $P_A = 1/200 \, P_B$ and $P_B = 200 P_A$, so $P_A/P_B = 1/200$.

If the exchange rate is $1 = 200 reals and a pound of prime coffee costs 600 reals in Brazil, then it must cost $3 in the United States. Now consider a Brazilian baker who wants to buy American wheat. She will pay reals for the wheat, but American wheat farmers must be paid in dollars. If American wheat is $8 per bushel, how much is this in reals? You should be able to compute the Brazilian price of wheat as 1600 reals per bushel.

> *The relative price of foreign goods (e.g., coffee) in terms of domestic goods (wheat) is the **real exchange rate**, which equals*

$$\left[\frac{\text{Price level}_{\text{domestic}}}{\text{Price level}_{\text{foreign}}} \right] \times \left[\begin{array}{c} \text{nominal} \\ \text{exchange} \\ \text{rate} \end{array} \right]$$

Each pound of coffee Brazilians export will "buy" 3/8 of a bushel of wheat, or alternatively, Brazilians must export 8/3 of a pound of coffee for each bushel of wheat they import from the United States. Because it is never true that all goods are exactly proportionally priced between countries, the real exchange rate is different for most pairs of goods. Consequently, real exchange rates are usually calculated as indices of the prices of exports relative to the prices of imports.

Nominal exchange rates translate all prices in one currency into their values in another currency. Suppose that, relative to real exchange rates, the nominal exchange rate of the dollar for the yen is low. For example, if typical production facilities that cost $10 million in the United States cost 1,200 million yen (¥) to set up in Japan, then any nominal exchange rate that had fewer than 120¥ per dollar would be low relative to the real exchange rate. A low nominal exchange rate for the dollar would make investment in the United States attractive to Japanese investors, so Japanese financial capital would flow into the United States.

Huge federal budget deficits in the 1980s increased U.S. reliance on foreign capital. These massive deficits partially explain why real interest rates in the early 1980s were high in the United States, making U.S. financial investments so attractive to foreign investors that a flood of capital inflows from abroad bolstered the dollar's exchange rate. However, our large budget deficits have created a persistent need to attract more foreign capital, which ultimately resulted in a certain amount of saturation, and the dollar's exchange rate fell during 1985 to 1988.

The dollar's recovery by 1991 allowed Americans to buy more yen per dollar–and more Minoltas and Toyotas. The Japanese who had invested in the United States and who "cashed out" received more yen when selling their dollar assets; their investments were more profitable than expected. But Japanese investors who held on to their U.S. assets were out of luck when the dollar again fell on international markets during 1993. What looks like a good foreign investment if exchange rates are stable may be spectacular if the foreign currency's exchange rate rises, or a miserable dog if it falls. An exchange rate can rise through a currency's *appreciation* or *revaluation*, or it can fall through a currency's *depreciation* or *devaluation*.

Currency Appreciation and Depreciation

Exchange rates respond to changes in supplies and demands much as other prices do. Table 2 shows cross exchange rates in September 1994 for nine major currencies.

*There is **appreciation** of a nation's currency if market forces cause foreign currencies to become cheaper.*

For example, if the real's price fell from $0.004 to $0.002, a dollar would buy twice as many reals and, thus, has appreciated, and the real has depreciated.

***Depreciation** of the domestic currency (e.g., dollars in the United States) means that foreign currencies have grown in value.*

A depreciated dollar buys fewer reals (and less coffee) than previously.

Revaluation and Devaluation

Until 1971, exchange rates between major currencies were governed by the Treaty of Bretton Woods (1946), but such agreements cannot survive gross inconsistencies with market forces

*When fixed exchange rates are adjusted, the currency that appreciates is **revalued**, and the depreciating currency is **devalued**.*

In an earlier era, many currencies were based on a *gold standard*, by which a government guaranteed to exchange a fixed amount of currency for a fixed amount of gold. Gold standards automatically yield fixed international exchange rates.

TABLE 2   Cross Exchange Rates for Some Major Currencies

Key Currency Cross Rates   Late New York Trading Sept. 19, 1994

	Dollar	Pound	SFranc	Guilder	Peso	Yen	Lira	D-Mark	FFranc	CdnDlr
Canada	1.3508	2.1201	1.05088	.77780	.39689	.01371	.00086	.87222	.25523	....
France	5.2925	8.307	4.1174	3.0474	1.55502	.05373	.00338	3.4174	....	3.9180
Germany	1.5487	2.4307	1.2048	.89175	.45503	.01572	.00099	....	.29262	1.1465
Italy	1564.0	2454.7	1216.74	900.56	459.53	15.877	....	1009.88	295.51	1157.8
Japan	98.51	154.61	76.638	56.723	28.944	....	.06299	63.608	18.613	72.93
Mexico	3.4035	5.3418	2.6478	1.9598	....	.03455	.00218	2.1976	.6431	2.5196
Netherlands	1.7367	2.7258	1.3511	....	.51027	.01763	.00111	1.1214	.32814	1.2857
Switzerland	1.2854	2.0174	....	.74014	.37767	.01305	.00082	.82999	.24287	.9516
U.K.	.63715	....	.49568	.36687	.18720	.00647	.00041	.41141	.12039	.47168
U.S.	....	1.5695	.77797	.57580	.29382	.01015	.00064	.64570	.18895	.74030

Source: Dow Jones Telerate Inc.

[The gold in an English pound traded for its equivalent amount of gold in an American double eagle ($20 gold coin) when both countries backed their currency with gold through the 1920s.]

Even today, some exchange rates are fixed and occasionally must be adjusted. For example, in recent years, exchange rates among European Community (EC) currencies have been pegged within narrow bands and tend to float in unison with respect to other currencies. This was intended as a first step toward a common currency (the European Currency Unit, or ECU) for use throughout the EC, replacing the pound, the franc, the DM, and the rest. When German reunification in 1991 boosted both public and private needs for funds to invest, German interest rates rose, attracting foreign investors. This raised the demand for DMs relative to other currencies. Under a flexible exchange rate system, the DM would quickly have appreciated. However, in the European Monetary System's (EMS) "pegged" exchange rate system, relative to such currencies as the pound (£), the DM approached the upper edge of the acceptable fluctuation band.

Despite efforts of several central banks to defend the pound (by buying £s), the British were left with a dilemma: either devalue the pound to remain in the EMS, or abandon the EMS in favor of a market-determined flexible exchange rate. In 1992, Britain quit the EMS. Other EMS countries faced similar pressures and responded by devaluing their currencies or widening the bands within which exchange rates could fluctuate. The end result? Europe monetary integration lost momentum that, if all had gone according to plan, would have resulted in a common currency within a decade or so. As you can see, realizing how market forces affect exchange rates is fundamental to understanding how the international economy operates.

DEMANDS AND SUPPLIES OF CURRENCIES

Demands for foreign money (collectively known as *foreign exchange*) resemble domestic demands for money. Most demands for foreign exchange are based on international transactions in goods, resources, or financial investments, but some key currencies (primarily the dollar) are also demanded by foreigners for precautionary reasons or because they are viewed as stable assets. (Transaction, precautionary, and asset demands for money were discussed in Chapter 14.)

For simplicity, assume the only two currencies are U.S. dollars ($) and German deutsche marks (DM). Our demand for deutsche marks is mirrored in our willingness to supply dollars. To see this, consider point *a* in both panels of Figure 1, which shows that if the exchange rate is one for one, we are willing to supply $1 billion for DM1 billion. When we can get DM2 for $1 (point *b* in Panel A), we are willing to supply $2 billion to get DM4 billion (each DM costs $0.50 at point *b* in Panel B). And so on. Comparing the matched points between Panels A and B will confirm that information in one is duplicated in the other.

It is hard to overemphasize the critical point that the demand for dollars is the supply of DM, and that the demand for DM is the supply of dollars. Changes in exchange rates cause movements along international supply and demand curves for a currency, paralleling how price changes cause changes in quantities demanded or supplied along supply and demand curves for goods. And, just as we treat certain influences as constant when constructing standard demand curves, isolating the effects of exchange rates on the quantity of dollars demanded to build the German demand curve for dollars requires holding constant (*a*) the prices of substitutes (foreign goods are the relevant substitutes), (*b*) foreign incomes, (*c*) foreign tastes and preferences, (*d*) expectations about exchange rate changes and relative inflation rates in both countries, (*e*) the dollar prices of U.S. goods, and (*f*) interest rates in both countries.

Symmetrically, we hold U.S. incomes, prices, preferences, expectations, and foreign prices in DM constant to draw the U.S. supply curve of dollars. Changes in these variables shift the demand or supply of dollars. Although we fix the dollar prices of U.S. goods in the United States and the DM prices of German goods in Germany, dollar prices for imports from Germany and DM prices for our exports change

FIGURE 1 The U.S. Supply of Dollars and Its Mirror Image: The Demand for Foreign Exchange

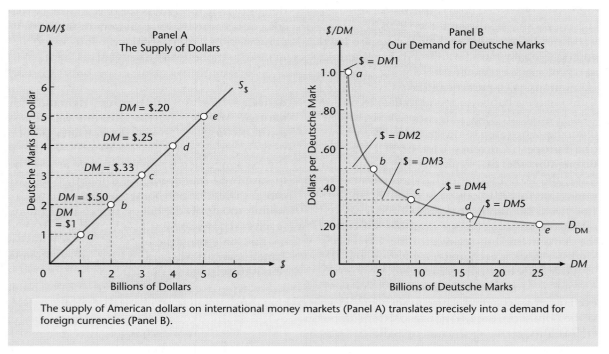

The supply of American dollars on international money markets (Panel A) translates precisely into a demand for foreign currencies (Panel B).

proportionally if exchange rates fluctuate. This is the key to why demand and supply curves of dollars (or DM) slope down and up, respectively.[1] Table 3 summarizes how these variables affect the international demands and supplies of dollars.

The Supply of Currencies

The supply of dollars in Panel A of Figure 1 is based on Americans' offers to buy foreign currencies, which we then use to buy foreign goods and services or to invest abroad. This supply curve slopes upward because increases in the price of dollars in terms of deutsche marks (DM/$ rises) imply that the dollar will buy more German goods, raising the demand for these goods and, thus, the demand for DM. This increases the supply of dollars offered for sale on

---
[1] Technically, this requires that international demands and supplies of goods be elastic, conditions that we assume are met throughout our exposition in this chapter.

the foreign exchange market. Conversely, a decline in the price of the dollar is equivalent to a rise in the price of the deutsche mark (DM/$ falls), which raises the U.S. cost of imports from Germany. Many previous American buyers of imports may drop out of the market or shift to substitutes (movements such as $e \rightarrow d \rightarrow c \rightarrow b \rightarrow a$).

The Demand for Currencies

Our transaction demand for deutsche marks in Panel B of Figure 1 is really a demand by U.S. citizens to buy German goods and to invest overseas. We measure the price of the DM in terms of dollars, and this demand curve slopes downward. If DM become more costly in terms of dollars, prices for German goods and investments rise in dollars and U.S. citizens will buy fewer German goods and invest less abroad. When U.S. citizens buy more U.S. goods and invest more domestically, they demand fewer DM. When DM are cheaper, U.S. citizens will buy

TABLE 3 Shifts in International Demands and Supplies of a Currency

Foreign demands for dollars rise, increasing the dollar's exchange rate, if
1. The domestic prices of goods in other countries rise.
2. The incomes of foreigners rise.
3. Foreigners' tastes for American products increase.
4. Foreigners expect the exchange rate of the dollar to rise.
5. Relatively rapid U.S. inflation is expected (Foreigners know the "buy low, sell high" rule.)
6. The dollar prices of U.S. goods fall (e.g. deflation in the U.S.)
7. Investment in the U.S. appears more profitable (e.g. U.S. interest rates rise).

The supply of U.S. dollars on international markets grows, lowering the dollar's exchange rate, if
1. The domestic prices of American outputs increase (e.g. inflation).
2. National Income in the United States increases.
3. Americans increasingly prefer imported goods.
4. Americans expect exchange rate of the dollar to fall.
5. Inflation expected abroad (e.g., we might expect prices for BMWs to rise).
6. Prices for imported goods fall (e.g., deflation abroad).
7. Foreign investments appear more profitable.

Naturally, reversals of the movements listed here would reverse the effects on exchange rates as described.

more of them because imports from Germany will be cheaper, as will dollar investments in Germany.

Equilibrium Exchange Rates

The supply curve of dollars is actually a flipped over demand curve for foreign currencies as shown in Panel B of Figure 1. (Remember that exchange rates are the reciprocals of each other.) We offer (supply) dollars to buy foreign exchange and, ultimately, foreign goods. The demand curve for dollars is similarly an inverted supply curve of the foreign currency. This means we can look at the same market with either set of curves. That is, our demand for foreign currency (Panel B of Figure 1) mirrors our supply of dollars (Panel A of Figure 1).

Interactions between supply and demand determine equilibrium exchange rates and quantities of dollars and foreign currencies. The foreign demands for dollars (in Panel A of Figure 2) are the supplies of foreign currencies (Panel B), and equilibrium for the German DM occurs at $0.50. This is the same as saying that

the equilibrium price of the dollar is DM2. Even if the exchange rates of the dollar and deutsche mark are in equilibrium, international transactions in the current and capital accounts may still yield net flows of foreign exchange between countries.

We have shown that you need to look at only one market to know precisely what is happening in the other. In the rest of this section, we will look only at the dollar market; no additional information is gained by looking at the market for DM (used here to represent all foreign currencies).

Foreign Demands for Dollars

Among reasons why the United States has been able to run persistent balance of payments deficits are our size, our importance in world trade, and our political and economic stability. This has created transactions, precautionary, and asset demands for the dollar as a key international money used for many international transactions, even if no U.S. citizens are involved. Thus, if all motives for foreigners to want

FIGURE 2 The Relationships Between Our Supply of Dollars and Demands for Foreign Exchange and Supplies of Foreign Exchange

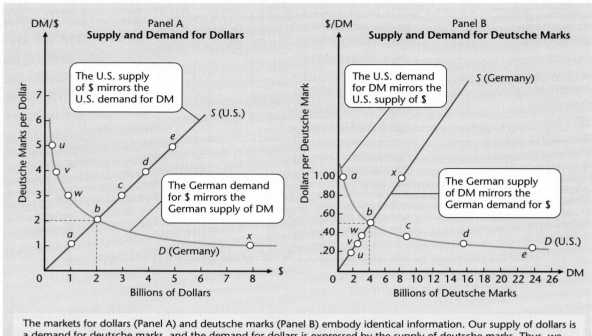

The markets for dollars (Panel A) and deutsche marks (Panel B) embody identical information. Our supply of dollars is a demand for deutsche marks, and the demand for dollars is expressed by the supply of deutsche marks. Thus, we only need to look at the market for one currency in order to know precisely the state of the market for the other currency.

dollars are considered, net outflows of funds can occur at equilibrium exchange rates where the quantity of dollars demanded equals the quantity supplied.

• **Transactions Demands** The dollar has historically been so convertible that foreigners often require dollars when they sell to other foreigners. Suppose Brazilians want Saudi oil but lack sufficient Saudi riyals, but Saudis are unwilling to accept Brazilian reals. Dollars solve this dilemma: OPEC, for example, states oil prices in dollars, so the Saudis will take dollars for their oil. Arrangements of this sort create international transaction demands for dollars; few other currencies are accepted as international mediums of exchange, and none as widely as the dollar. The international acceptability of U.S.

dollars drives foreigners to seek dollars even if they have no plans to buy U.S. exports.

• **Precautionary and Asset Demands** Rich foreigners who fear revolutions or chaos in their own countries may acquire dollars (or, frequently, gold) for precautionary reasons. Deposed dictators commonly flee their countries carrying suitcases filled with dollars (e.g., General Cedras's departure from Haiti in 1994). Foreign economic instability may also be a source of asset demands for dollars. For example, Israelis or Brazilians may use dollar-denominated securities to hedge against rapid inflation in their own countries.

The point is that persistent deficits in the U.S. balance of payments may not signal a disequilibrium. Foreigners may want dollars more than they want the U.S. goods the dollars would buy. We are a major world banker and supply dollars the way other countries supply cars or cameras. In a sense, dollars may be the major U.S. export, and Americans gain substantially by the payments deficit. Production costs for dollars are trivial, and our economy gains enormous *seigniorage* (profit from printing money) by supplying international money. However, increasing sophistication in international capital markets is slowly eroding our ability to make these profits.

Curing Exchange Rate Disequilibria

There are occasions, however, when imbalances of payments signal disequilibrium. We need to examine how foreign exchange markets can bring international supplies and demands of a currency into balance. Suppose that the exchange rate of the dollar for the DM is artificially held below equilibrium at, say, $0.25 per DM (DM4 per dollar) as shown in Figure 3. Relative to equilibrium, German DM are too cheap and dollars are too expensive. Situations like this

offer one explanation for imbalances of international payments. In this example, there is a *surplus* of dollars on international markets, and the United States will experience a *deficit* of payments. Germany runs a compensating balance of payments *surplus*; if we constructed a graph depicting the DM market, it would show a *shortage* of DM internationally. Be sure that you understand how surpluses of a currency imply that the issuing country experiences a balance of payments deficit, while a currency shortage implies a surplus in a country's balance of payments. This terminology can be confusing unless you are very focused.

Regardless of what causes deficits or surpluses in a country's balance of payments, there are four basic ways of dealing with these imbalances. We can (*a*) allow changes in exchange rates, (*b*) adopt controls to ration foreign exchange, (*c*) follow macroeconomic policies to shift the supply or demand curves for foreign exchange, or (*d*) allow flows of money from deficit to surplus countries. Each mechanism has been used in some regions during some periods.

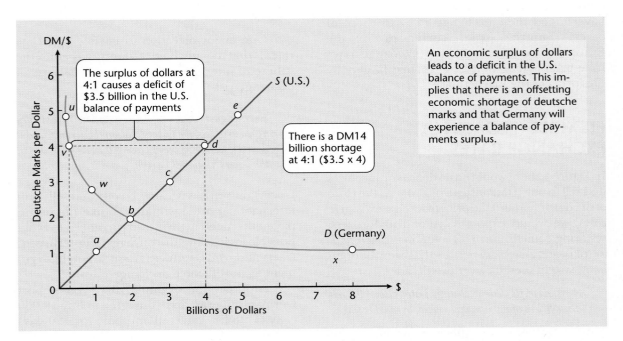

An economic surplus of dollars leads to a deficit in the U.S. balance of payments. This implies that there is an offsetting economic shortage of deutsche marks and that Germany will experience a balance of payments surplus.

FIGURE 3 U.S. Balance of Payments Deficit Caused by Exchange Rates that Do Not Yield Equilibrium

FIXED EXCHANGE RATES

Most payments, whether domestic or international, were made in currencies denominated in gold until World War I.

Fixed amounts of each currency can be exchanged for given amounts of gold under an ideal **gold standard** *so that all exchange rates are also fixed.*

A gold standard makes exchanging one currency for any other easy because their values in gold are all fixed. An ounce of gold exchanges for an ounce of gold. But the supply of gold did not keep pace with the volume of transactions in rapidly growing economies, so countries everywhere abandoned the gold standard early in this century and turned to *fiat* (paper) *money*.

Worldwide abandonment of gold-backed money in favor of fiat currencies raises this issue: what are the appropriate exchange rates between currencies? One answer to this question is given if governments intervene through *fixed exchange rate* agreements (price controls) or other regulations intended to stabilize exchange rates. Alternatively, it can be left to supply and demand. Since 1973, although some countries have linked their exchange rates to those of other countries (e.g., currencies in the European Community), most exchange rates have been *flexible*–that is, governed largely by the forces of the marketplace.

FLEXIBLE (FLOATING) EXCHANGE RATES

In Figure 4, there would be no deficits or surpluses if $1 fell to only DM2 instead of DM4. As the price of the dollar fell (and the price of foreign exchange rose), we would export more and import less, restoring equilibrium. This solution is called *flexible* (or floating) *exchange rates* and has been the dominant system used for over two decades.

A system of **flexible exchange rates** *allows the relative prices of currencies to be set by market forces.*

Thus, international supplies and demands for various currencies now largely determine exchange rates.

FIGURE 4   Flexible Exchange Rates: A Market Solution to Balance of Payments Deficits

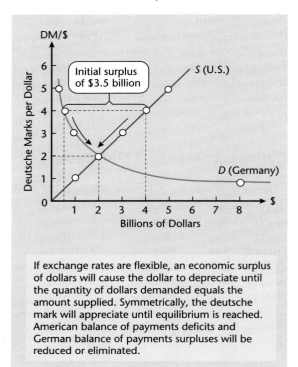

If exchange rates are flexible, an economic surplus of dollars will cause the dollar to depreciate until the quantity of dollars demanded equals the amount supplied. Symmetrically, the deutsche mark will appreciate until equilibrium is reached. American balance of payments deficits and German balance of payments surpluses will be reduced or eliminated.

One major objection to flexible exchange rates is that too much uncertainty may enter the sphere of international transactions because of exchange risk.

Exchange risk *arises because sellers lose if they agree to accept the buyers' national currency and it depreciates, while buyers lose if they agree to pay in the sellers' national currency and it appreciates.*

Uncertainty arises because buyers and sellers in international trade would each like the future payments stated in their own currencies to avoid possible losses. This discourages long-term contracts and, thus, reduces trade–a potent argument against flexible exchange rates.

Suppose, for example, that you import German cameras, and you agree to buy 10,000 cameras to be delivered and paid for 120 days from today. If the contract specified payment in DM and the DM appreciated in the next four months, you would wind up paying more dollars for the DM marks due than you expected. On the other hand, if dollar payments were specified and the DM appreciated, the exporter would receive fewer DM than expected.

Defenders of flexibility counter this objection by pointing out that importers and exporters can insure against exchange risk by dealing in forward markets that match future inflows against future outflows of dollars.

*In a **forward market** for currencies, sellers can contract to receive the currency desired in exchange for the currency received from buyers, or a buyer can contract to secure the currency desired by the seller.*

This insurance against exchange risk, however, involves transaction costs absent were exchange rates absolutely fixed. An even more critical failing is that forward markets exist for only a few currencies, and even these are available for only limited future periods, as Table 4 illustrates.

Critics also charge that flexible rates encourage destabilizing speculation, but it is unlikely that speculation is destabilizing in the long run. Destabilizing speculation implies that, on average, speculators forecast in a systematically incorrect way. Destabilizing speculation would (a) raise prices by adding to demand when prices would otherwise have reached their peaks and (b) reduce prices by adding to supply when prices would otherwise have been at their lowest. Thus, destabilizing speculation is equivalent to buying high and selling low, and these speculators will go broke in the long run. Stabilizing speculation, on the other hand, tends to reward correct forecasts.[2] Exchange rates are set in international markets in which trades in foreign exchange are overwhelmingly dominated by currency arbitrageurs and speculators.

The Lively Market for Foreign Exchange

Overall, the United States, with its $7 trillion annual GDP, is the world's #1 importer and exporter. It is also the world's #1 in net international payments; as you learned in

---

[2]If this seems unclear, please review our discussion of speculation in Chapter 4.

Chapter 15, the United States was the world's #1 creditor nation before 1981, but persistent federal deficits helped make it the world's #1 debtor nation by 1990. Despite its pivotal role internationally, U.S. balance of payments accounts display numbers that seem puny when weighed against total transactions in foreign exchange. Almost $1 trillion flows across international borders on an average business <u>day</u>. However, only about 4% of flows through the markets for foreign exchange are attributable to trade or movements of economic (physical) capital. What else accounts for these tidal waves of funds? The answer is (a) *arbitrage* to make exchange rates consistent and (b) *speculation* based on forecasts of where exchange rates might move.

• **Exchange Rate Arbitrage** Suppose you were a currency trader in New York and that, at current exchange rates, a dollar buys either 100 yen or 5 French francs (a ratio of $1 : 100¥ : 5F). Further suppose that these are equilibrium exchange rates, but the exchange rate between the yen and the franc is 25 to 1, not the 20 to 1 (or 100¥ : 5F) consistent with equilibrium exchange rates. This discrepancy opens the door for arbitrage—the prospect of a riskless return!

You would immediately convert any francs you had into yen, receiving 100 yen for every 4 francs you spent. Then convert the yen to dollars at the 100 to 1 ratio. Each $1 would have cost only 4 francs, not the 5 it would have cost if you traded the francs directly for dollars. Then you would buy 5 francs for each dollar, for a net return of 1 extra franc for every 4 francs you had initially. If you could, you would infinitely repeat this *triangular arbitrage* process to eventually become infinitely rich, exchanging 4F for 100¥ for $1 dollar for 5F, and so on. Unfortunately, however, as thousands of other currency traders also traded francs for yen for dollars, the supply of francs would grow, along with demands for yen and dollars. The franc would fall toward the 20 to 1 ratio for yen consistent with the $1 : 100¥ : 5F equilibrium set of exchange rates.

Operators in international capital markets are constantly alert for discrepancies between exchange rates. Disparities of less than 1% can quickly set billions of dollars worth of foreign

TABLE 4   The Wall Street Journal Tuesday, September 19, 1994

CURRENCY TRADING

EXCHANGE RATES

Monday, September 19, 1994

The New York foreign exchange selling rates below apply to trading among banks in amounts of $1 million and more, as quoted at 3 p.m. Eastern time by Bankers Trust Co., Dow Jones Telerate Inc. and other sources. Retail transactions provide fewer units of foreign currency per dollar.

Country	U.S. $ equiv. Mon.	U.S. $ equiv. Fri.	Currency per U.S. $ Mon.	Currency per U.S. $ Fri.
Argentina (Peso)	1.01	1.01	.99	.99
Australia (Dollar)	.7421	.7445	1.3475	1.3432
Austria (Schilling)	.09175	.09206	10.90	10.86
Bahrain (Dinar)	2.6518	2.6518	.3771	.3771
Belgium (Franc)	.03137	.03149	31.88	31.75
Brazil (Real)	1.1750881	1.0989011	.85	.91
Britain (Pound)	1.5700	1.5810	.6369	.6325
30-Day Forward	1.5693	1.5800	.6372	.6329
90-Day Forward	1.5672	1.5781	.6381	.6337
180-Day Forward	1.5634	1.5751	.6396	.6349
Canada (Dollar)	.7406	.7407	1.3503	1.3500
30-Day Forward	.7404	.7405	1.3507	1.3505
90-Day Forward	.7400	.7395	1.3514	1.3522
180-Day Forward	.7389	.7378	1.3533	1.3554
Czech. Rep. (Koruna)				
Commercial rate	.0358153	.0359028	27.9210	27.8530
Chile (Peso)	.002475	.002461	404.10	406.36
China (Renminbi)	.115221	.115221	8.6790	8.6790
Colombia (Peso)	.001191	.001216	839.50	822.50
Denmark (Krone)	.1640	.1643	6.0984	6.0879
Ecuador (Sucre)				
Floating rate	.000447	.000448	2236.04	2233.04
Finland (Markka)	.20307	.20221	4.9244	4.9453
France (Franc)	.18902	.18941	5.2905	5.2795
30-Day Forward	.18893	.18932	5.2930	5.2822
90-Day Forward	.18875	.18913	5.2979	5.2875
180-Day Forward	.18860	.18891	5.3023	5.2935
Germany (Mark)	.6457	.6481	1.5488	1.5430
30-Day Forward	.6456	.6480	1.5490	1.5431
90-Day Forward	.6456	.6480	1.5490	1.5431
180-Day Forward	.6462	.6483	1.5475	1.5425
Greece (Drachma)	.004241	.004255	235.80	235.00
Hong Kong (Dollar)	.12942	.12941	7.7270	7.7275
Hungary (Forint)	.0092618	.0092370	107.9700	108.2600
India (Rupee)	.03212	.03212	31.13	31.13
Indonesia (Rupiah)	.0004598	.0004596	2175.00	2176.04
Ireland (Punt)	1.5518	1.5548	.6444	.6432
Israel (Shekel)	.3298	.3298	3.0320	3.0320
Italy (Lira)	.0006393	.0006415	1564.31	1558.82

Country	U.S. $ equiv. Mon.	U.S. $ equiv. Fri.	Currency per U.S. $ Mon.	Currency per U.S. $ Fri.
Japan (Yen)	.010147	.010111	98.55	98.90
30-Day Forward	.010167	.010131	98.36	98.71
90-Day Forward	.010217	.010178	97.88	98.25
180-Day Forward	.010300	.010259	97.09	97.48
Jordan (Dinar)	1.4682	1.4682	.6811	.6811
Kuwait (Dinar)	3.3617	3.3619	.2975	.2975
Lebanon (Pound)	.000600	.000599	1668.00	1669.00
Malaysia (Ringgit)	.3912	.3913	2.5560	2.5555
Malta (Lira)	2.7397	2.7360	.3650	.3655
Mexico (Peso)				
Floating rate	.2938152	.2935564	3.4035	3.4065
Netherland (Guilder)	.5758	.5780	1.7366	1.7301
New Zealand (Dollar)	.6037	.6040	1.6565	1.6556
Norway (Krone)	.1472	.1477	6.7923	6.7715
Pakistan (Rupee)	.0327	.0327	30.58	30.58
Peru (New Sol)	.4545	.4515	2.20	2.21
Philippines (Peso)	.03953	.03857	25.30	25.93
Poland (Zloty)	.00004328	.00004335	23108.00	23066.00
Portugal (Escudo)	.006346	.006360	157.59	157.23
Saudi Arabia (Riyal)	.26664	.26665	3.7504	3.7503
Singapore (Dollar)	.6756	.6743	1.4801	1.4830
Slovak Rep. (Koruna)	.0319183	.0319183	31.3300	31.3300
South Africa (Rand)				
Commercial rate	.2821	.2816	3.5452	3.5515
Financial rate	.2275	.2264	4.3950	4.4170
South Korea (Won)	.0012505	.0012513	799.70	799.20
Spain (Peseta)	.007784	.007796	128.47	128.27
Sweden (Krona)	.1343	.1346	7.4443	7.4295
Switzerland (Franc)	.7779	.7813	1.2855	1.2800
30-Day Forward	.7786	.7819	1.2844	1.2789
90-Day Forward	.7798	.7831	1.2823	1.2770
180-Day Forward	.7821	.7852	1.2786	1.2735
Taiwan (Dollar)	.038121	.038153	26.23	26.21
Thailand (Baht)	.04006	.03854	24.96	25.95
Turkey (Lira)	.0000296	.0000296	33804.17	33804.17
United Arab (Dirham)	.2723	.2723	3.6725	3.6725
Uruguay (New Peso)				
Financial	.194363	.194363	5.15	5.15
Venezuela (Bolivar)	.00590	.00590	169.57	169.57
— — —				
SDR	1.46732	1.46335	.68151	.68336
ECU	1.23130	1.23490	....	....

Special Drawing Rights (SDR) are based on exchange rates for the U.S., German, British, French and Japanese currencies. Source: International Monetary Fund.

European Currency Unit (ECU) is based on a basket of community currencies.

FUTURES PRICES

	Open	High	Low	Settle	Change	Lifetime High	Lifetime Low	Open Interest

CURRENCY

JAPAN YEN (CME)—12.5 million yen; $ per yen (.00)

	Open	High	Low	Settle	Change	Lifetime High	Lifetime Low	Open Interest
Sept	1.0120	1.0160	1.0120	1.0133	+ .0022	1.0408	.8942	28,091
Dec	1.0180	1.0230	1.0179	1.0218	+ .0039	1.0490	.9525	41,381
Mr95	1.0295	1.0303	1.0260	1.0294	+ .0039	1.0560	.9680	2,274
June	1.0360	1.0380	1.0360	1.0385	+ .0039	1.0670	.9915	449

Est vol 22,265; vol Fri 32,787; open int 72,278, +1,084.

DEUTSCHEMARK (CME)—125,000 marks; $ per mark

	Open	High	Low	Settle	Change	Lifetime High	Lifetime Low	Open Interest
Sept	.6473	.6478	.6442	.6445	− .0037	.6595	.5364	56,318
Dec	.6481	.6487	.6428	.6455	− .0026	.6606	.5351	74,915
Mr95	.6450	.6471	.6447	.6461	− .0026	.6595	.5798	3,838
June				.6467	− .0027	.6595	.5980	477

Est vol 47,947; vol Fri 64,252; open int 135,558, +2,730.

CANADIAN DOLLAR (CME)—100,000 dlrs.; $ per Can $

	Open	High	Low	Settle	Change	Lifetime High	Lifetime Low	Open Interest
Sept	.7393	.7403	.7393	.7401	− .0006	.7740	.7068	7,666
Dec	.7392	.7400	.7386	.7398	− .0003	.7670	.7038	42,624
Mr95	.7387	.7387	.7385	.7389	− .0003	.7618	.7020	1,031
June	....	....	....	.7376	− .0003	.7600	.6990	444
Sept	....	....	....	.7358	− .0003	.7250	.6965	303

Est vol 2,938; vol Fri 7,159; open int 52,090, −181.

BRITISH POUND (CME)—62,500 pds.; $ per pound

	Open	High	Low	Settle	Change	Lifetime High	Lifetime Low	Open Interest
Sept	1.5740	1.5756	1.5696	1.5696	− .0116	1.5880	1.4440	20,469
Dec	1.5770	1.5796	1.5608	1.5672	− .0116	1.5848	1.4400	31,306
Mr95	1.5700	1.5700	1.5580	1.5636	− .0118	1.5790	1.4530	259

Est vol 11,708; vol Fri 20,730; open int 52,041, +2,754.

SWISS FRANC (CME)—125,000 francs; $ per franc

	Open	High	Low	Settle	Change	Lifetime High	Lifetime Low	Open Interest
Sept	.7790	.7802	.7760	.7760	− .0057	.7894	.6590	17,670
Dec	.7830	.7845	.7753	.7794	− .0043	.7905	.6885	37,882
Mr95	.7845	.7845	.7790	.7817	− .0043	.7920	.7287	537

Est vol 23,116; vol Fri 40,131; open int 56,119, +1,829.

AUSTRALIAN DOLLAR (CME)—100,000 dlrs.; $ per A.$

	Open	High	Low	Settle	Change	Lifetime High	Lifetime Low	Open Interest
Sept	.7433	.7435	.7433	.7435	− .0016	.7476	.6645	4,499
Dec	.7420	.7429	.7409	.7411	− .0025	.7455	.6965	6,115

Est vol 425; vol Fri 946; open int 10,643, −70.

U.S. DOLLAR INDEX (FINEX)—1,000 times USDX

	Open	High	Low	Settle	Change	Lifetime High	Lifetime Low	Open Interest
Sept	87.62	88.02	87.65	87.85	+ .28	98.55	86.85	947
Dec	87.85	88.43	87.81	88.14	+ .31	99.00	87.08	3,872
Mr95	....	....	....	88.34	+ .31	96.65	88.00	3,008

Est vol 2,000; vol Fri 9,420; open int 7,860, −3,555.

The index: High 88.11; Low 87.54; Close 87.84 +.27

exchange in motion. Thus, discrepancies between exchange rates tend to be both miniscule and quickly eliminated by triangular arbitrage.

• **Speculation and Exchange Rates** You learned in Chapter 4 that speculation always entails risk. Suppose you view the dollar as overrated and expect it to depreciate relative to the English pound (currently, say, $1:1£). This is identical to expecting the pound to appreciate. You may gain by trading your dollars for pounds and then holding on until the pound rises. If you are right and the ratio moves to $1.20 : 1£ before you reconvert to dollars, your return is 20%. But if you are wrong and the exchange rate moves to, say, $1 : 0.80£, you lose. Each original $1 will have withered to about 80¢. The more faith you have in your ability to predict exchange rate movements, the more prone you will be to speculate in the forward market for foreign exchange, which holds prospects for even greater profit—but only if you prove right more often than you get clobbered for being wrong.

Arbitrage and speculation in foreign exchange have been estimated to account for roughly 96% of international flows of funds, but these transactions merely involve swaps of financial capital (pieces of paper or their electronic counterparts) and, dollar-for-dollar, have far less real impact than the flows of money spent on goods traded internationally, or on transnational investments in physical capital. Arbitrage and speculation tend to be focused on short-run considerations. Moreover, gross flows of funds do not enter balance of payments ledgers; only net flows are recorded in the capital account—not arbitrage or speculation per se. Thus, when exchange rates are flexible, long-run trends are determined primarily by dynamic changes in patterns of international trade and shifts in real international investment.

MACROECONOMIC CORRECTIONS

We have been focusing on how adjustments occur when exchange rates are flexible, but other possibilities must be considered. A balance of payments deficit will evaporate if the supply and demand curves shown in Figure 5 shift to intersect at an equilibrium exchange of DM4 instead of DM2. This cure for deficits or surpluses relies on macroeconomic adjustments.

Imbalances of payments caused by disequilibrium may be cured through **macroadjustments** *to Aggregate Demand that change nominal GDP (which equals PQ) or, in the longer run, by adjustments to Aggregate Supply.*

One option is for the deficit country to follow contractionary macroeconomic policies; domestic Aggregate Demand, including the demand for imported goods, will shrink. The resulting recessionary fall in output or deflation of domestic prices, or both, will cause the deficit country to import less. These are adjustments that operate through changes in the balance of trade, or the current account. An alternative is for adjustment through the capital account. For example, contractionary monetary policies might increase U.S. interest rates, increasing the inflow of financial capital. Either contractionary monetary or fiscal policies reduce the international supply of dollars, shown in Figure 5, or the disequilibrium could be cured through expansionary policies in Germany.

Contractionary macro policies also induce lower prices for U.S. exports and encourage foreigners to buy more from us. The supply of foreign currency (DM) grows along with foreigners' demands for dollars. (Remember that the supply curve of DM mirrors the demand for dollars.) The original deficit in payments (distance *ab*) is eliminated as the economy moves from disequilibrium in the balance of payments (point *d*) to equilibrium (point *c*).

Some experts argue that deficits pose few problems; after all, deficit countries actually export money, which has a very low production cost, and receive goods and services embodying much higher production costs. These analysts recommend that the balance of payments surpluses in some countries be cured with expansionary macroeconomic policies, causing domestic prices to rise in surplus countries and the prices of their imports to fall; their surpluses of receipts from international trade would therefore be eliminated.

FIGURE 5   Using Macroeconomic Adjustment to Eliminate Deficits

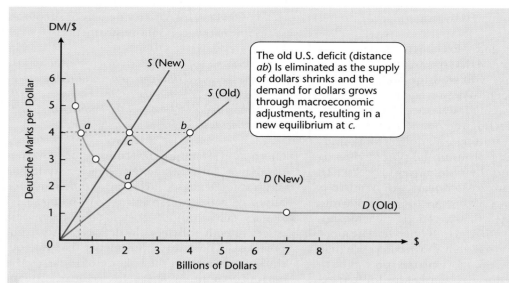

The old U.S. deficit (distance *ab*) Is eliminated as the supply of dollars shrinks and the demand for dollars grows through macroeconomic adjustments, resulting in a new equilibrium at *c*.

Flows of funds from imbalances of payments tend to expand Aggregate Demands in surplus countries. If all countries are close to full employment, the prices of domestic goods in surplus countries will rise, making imports better buys. The resulting growth in imports will be reflected in rising demands for the currencies of deficit countries. At the same time, monetary outflows tend to reduce Aggregate Demand in deficit countries. There will be decreases in the prices of domestic goods relative to imports, and the international supplies of deficit countries' currencies will decline as imports fall. Thus, the exchange rate remains stable, with all adjustments coming in the form of higher prices in countries that initially experienced surpluses and lower prices in deficit countries. This solution poses no special problem if prices are perfectly flexible. If prices are sticky downward, however, macroeconomic adjustments may impose severe hardships.

These sorts of *macroadjustments* are automatic under a gold standard, which was the policy of most developed countries in the half-century preceding World War I. Payments deficits reduced a country's supply of gold money; surpluses increased it. But because macropolicy–based corrections require deflation and stimulate unemployment in countries experiencing a deficit, they tend to be unpopular with the people who live in those countries. Nor do most leaders of countries having excessive surpluses in their balances of payments welcome the suggestion that expansionary or inflationary macroeconomic policies are in order.

For example, from 1960 to 1982, foreign finance ministers often urged the U.S. government to adopt contractionary policies to cure our chronic payments deficits. We offered counterproposals that their governments should use expansionary policies to cure their chronic surpluses, and they predictably ignored us. An intriguing about-face followed when contractionary U.S. monetary policies slowed U.S. inflation and boosted the exchange rate of the dollar in the early 1980s: foreign governments urged us to follow more expansionary policies to fight a worldwide recession that was, in part, attributable to U.S. counterinflationary policies. A foreign diplomat compared dealing with the United States to "sharing a bed with an elephant; you must be careful when you nudge the beast to get it to roll over."

EXCHANGE CONTROLS

We might ration foreign exchange to cure deficits. At $0.25 per DM, only DM2 billion (at point *a* in Figure 6, worth $500 million) are available to Americans, but they would like to buy DM16 billion ($4 billion at point *b*) worth of German goods.

FIGURE 6 Using Exchange Controls to Prevent Currency Flows When Deficits Occur

Only $0.5 billion in DM are available (DM2 billion) to be allocated if exchange controls are used

If currency flows are used $3.5 billion flows abroad in dollars or in previously accumulated or borrowed DM or gold

Exchange controls can be used to artificially maintain the price of a currency above the equilibrium exchange rate, but this requires government rationing of the limited foreign exchange that is available. Alternatively, persistent balance of payments deficits may permit an exchange rate to be above equilibrium if the deficit country can borrow from surplus countries or draw down its stocks of gold or previously acquired foreign currencies.

The U.S. government could allocate the available DM2 billion among would-be importers through licenses, or it could curb some imports by using quotas or tariffs. Many Americans wanting to tour Germany or buy German cameras or VWs would have to do without.

Such techniques are called *exchange controls* and today, are most commonly used only in underdeveloped countries.[3]

> ***Exchange controls*** *allow access to foreign exchange only to favored industries or individuals and make it illegal to exchange foreign for domestic currencies except through the government's banks at official exchange rates.*

Exchange controls are extremely inefficient and share many of the failings of quotas (described in the preceding chapter). Controls must be exercised through some government agency, and they

create powerful incentives for smuggling, bribery, graft, black-marketeering, and corruption.

Fixed Exchange Rates Revisited

Our earlier discussions of price controls indicated that if prices are fixed above their equilibrium values, there will be surpluses, while if the price of a good is held below its equilibrium value, there will be a shortage of that good. The same results hold for international currency markets.

If we have accumulated reserves of foreign exchange, or if we can beg, borrow, or steal reserves of foreign currencies from our friends and allies (i.e., if we can persuade them to accept and hold our currency), then we can rely on international flows of currencies or debt as the fourth and final solution to a balance of payments deficit.

> ***Currency*** *or* ***debt flows*** *can accommodate imbalances of international payments.*

---

[3]The world can crudely be divided into developed nations, developing nations, less developed nations, and underdeveloped countries. Exchange controls are most frequently enforced in the least developed of these categories.

In Figure 6, $0.5 billion dollars (DM2 billion) of our annual foreign exchange needs are met by regular inflows of foreign currency. How can we accommodate our remaining $3.5 billion (DM14 billion) outflow of funds? One system requires an international agreement to fix exchange rates.

The Bretton Woods Agreement established the International Monetary Fund in 1946, along with a system of fixed exchange rates. (The International Monetary Fund lingers on, but the fixed exchange rate died of natural causes during 1971–1973.) Under the Breton Woods Agreement, most nations pegged the value of their currency to the dollar, which the United States agreed to redeem for gold at $35 per ounce. Because the values of all major currencies were pegged to the dollar (and, thus, to gold), these currencies were fixed relative to each other as well.

The U.S. Treasury used some of the gold it had acquired over the previous century to pay parts of chronic deficits experienced from 1951 into the 1970s. Most of these deficits, however, were absorbed by foreign central banks when our trading partners bought the surplus dollars. Our theoretical willingness to redeem at least some dollars for gold and the willingness of our trading partners to absorb surplus dollars were key to the fixed exchange rate system of this period.

*A system of **fixed exchange rates** requires governments to establish and maintain constant relative values for their currencies.*

Figure 7 shows how foreign governments (e.g., Germany) can ensure that our currency will never fall below certain values if they buy the dollars sent out as our balance of payments deficits. Similarly, we can set floors for the values of their currencies if we buy their money when they run deficits. In our example, the German government can supply DM or other currencies "on loan" to the United States and

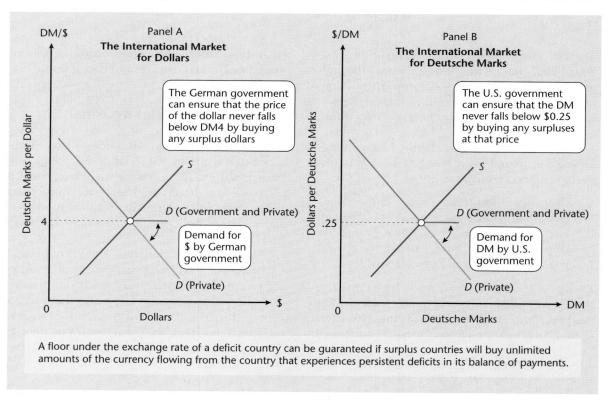

A floor under the exchange rate of a deficit country can be guaranteed if surplus countries will buy unlimited amounts of the currency flowing from the country that experiences persistent deficits in its balance of payments.

FIGURE 7   Fixing Exchange Rates Through International Agreement

take the excess dollars off the market. (Germany accumulates $ reserves.) This enables the two countries to maintain *fixed exchange rates.*

Persistent U.S. deficits will cause growing piles of American dollars to accumulate in German banks. The widespread acceptability of the dollar may enable Germans to use U.S. currency to pay for their imports, but then these dollars wind up consuming space in other foreign central banks. There is a limit to the amount of dollars foreign governments will absorb. This imposes downward pressure on the dollar. After a saturation point is reached, surplus dollars will return via the capital account of the U.S. balance of payments when foreigners begin buying Treasury bonds, corporate securities, U.S. firms, or U.S. real estate, or foreigners may simply invest and establish production facilities in the United States.

Fixed exchange rates pose no special problems as long as they reflect relative supplies and demands for currencies—that is, if their values are the same as flexible exchange rates would be. Even if fixed exchange rates are initially in equilibrium, however, different macropolicies or growth rates between countries, or changes in technologies or tastes, will change relative supplies and demands of currencies. Shortages and surpluses emerge amid persistent disequilibria in balances of payments when fixed exchange rates fail to reflect true demands and supplies.

Macroeconomic problems such as inflation or recessionary pressure tend to be extremely contagious when exchange rates are fixed. A country running payments deficits in its current account "exports" money, so it may tend to have less inflation than if its international payments were balanced. (In a sense, the export of money enables deficit countries to "export" inflationary pressure.) But countries with persistent current account deficits also experience drains on Aggregate Demand that can exacerbate pressures for excessive unemployment.

This contagiousness of macroeconomic woes is substantially less under a system of flexible exchange rates. When exchange rates are flexible, flows of capital may only be a symptom that investors in the country that runs a current account surplus want to invest in the countries that run deficits, perhaps because of perceptions that returns to investment are higher abroad—and not because of fundamental macroeconomic problems in the deficit country.

In summary, there are four basic ways to deal with surpluses or deficits in balances of payments: change the price (float), ration (control), shift the curves (macroadjustment), or allow currency flows. Similar solutions apply equally to surpluses or shortages of wheat, gasoline, teachers, or skateboards. You can add a lot of frills, but this simple supply and demand analysis is what the complex world of international finance is really all about.

The Dirty Float: 1973 to ?

Most exchange rates have been flexible for over two decades, but with some government intervention. In reasonably competitive markets for goods and services, surpluses or shortages are cured by price changes. Floating systems allow exchange rates to vary, so it would seem that U.S. balance of payments deficits (surpluses of dollars) should be cured automatically if they are signs of disequilibrium. But why have U.S. payments deficits persisted if imbalances of payments should vanish automatically?

We indicated earlier that a partial answer is that foreigners have often wanted U.S. dollars even more than they wanted American goods; deficits in our international payments may be signs of economic and political health. But parts of U.S. deficits may reflect international imbalances, because governments constantly intervene in markets for foreign exchange.

EXPLAINING PERSISTENT U.S. PAYMENTS DEFICITS

If a country runs large and persistent deficits, foreign banks will accumulate substantial amounts of that country's currency when foreign suppliers exchange the payments they receive for their own money. Why have foreign private and central banks permitted the United

States to run persistent balance of payments deficits?

The answer to this question is multifaceted. First, between 1946 and 1971, the dollar was the only major currency redeemable for gold, at least for purposes of international payments. Foreign central banks could present $35 to the U.S. Treasury and demand one ounce of gold. It was illegal for Americans who were not jewelers, coin collectors, or dentists to own gold bullion, bars, or coins between 1933 and 1973. Any American gold not used industrially or in teeth or jewelry was used to back the dollar for international transactions.

The United States was the only major country with its manufacturing capacity intact at the end of World War II. We supplied much of the world's needs and generally demanded payment in gold because most other currencies were either unstable or worthless. Hence, as we entered the 1950s, the United States had substantial gold on hand. The dollar was a nearly perfect substitute for gold for purposes of international payments because it was redeemable for gold.

This meant that our money was often viewed as at least as valuable as the American goods that might be bought with it by, say, the Italians; people in other countries would cheerfully accept dollars when they would not accept lire in payment for Italian purchases. In a sense, the convertibility of U.S. dollars into gold (under a partial reserve system much like that used by commercial banks) enabled the United States to create international money.

After World War II, international trade grew far more rapidly than the quantity of gold available for international payments. The acceptability of the U.S. dollar as an international *key currency* made it possible for the U.S. Treasury and the Fed to accommodate increasing world demands for an international medium of exchange by simply printing money. Americans gained through *seigniorage* (differences between money's face value and its production cost) from this ability to print international money because we were able to export less than the total value of the goods we imported. In a sense, we consumed more than we

produced. The difference was made up by the dollars we printed that circulated among foreign countries, seldom being redeemed for American output or resources. The international acceptability of the dollar was a major reason that the United States was able to run persistent and large deficits between 1951 and the present.

The relative prices of most currencies in international exchange markets presumably have been set by supply and demand since 1973. We may still run deficits under a floating exchange rate system, however, if foreigners commonly demand our dollars instead of American goods and services. Even so, foreign demand for dollars as insurance or as an internationally accepted means of payment does not even come close to explaining the magnitudes of our persistent balance of payments deficits.

The central banks and treasuries of a number of countries have often accumulated dollars to limit declines in the exchange rate of the dollar; the float has been a dirty float. Why would foreign governments (e.g., Japan) wish to maintain high prices for imports from the United States and concomitant low prices for Japanese products exported to Americans? Part of the answer is that employment and growth in the Japanese and some other economies are heavily dependent on their export industries. In addition, the Japanese farmers and manufacturers who compete with imports from the United States are very powerful politically.

When the Japanese central bank buys and holds the dollars we have paid for Japanese exports, the effect is the same as a tariff on their imports and a subsidy on their exports. This Japanese policy of acquiring growing amounts of dollars has resulted in subsidies to American consumers by Japanese consumers. Until Japanese taxpayers and voters catch on, we may continue to gain at their expense.[4] Curiously, our government pressured the Japanese gov-

---

[4]This support for the dollar can be viewed as a hidden subsidy that for years, Japan and Germany used to induce the United States to provide defense services. Tens of thousands of American soldiers have been stationed in Germany since World War II, but the demise of the USSR has resulted in major reductions in these forces.

FIGURE 8 The Dance of the U.S. Dollar

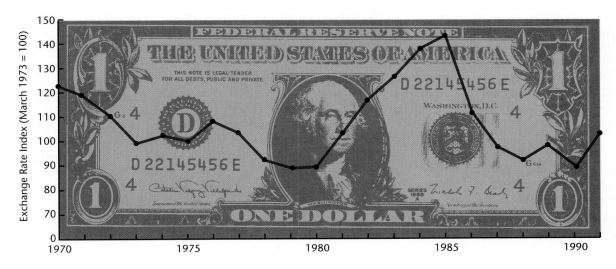

Source: *Economic Report of the President,* 1991.

The overall depreciation of the dollar relative to the average of other major curencies during the 1970s reflected the maturation of other currencies, the declining prestige of the United States, problems with inflation, the deterioration of our terms of trade as the prices of imports grew faster than the prices of our exports (e.g., oil imports versus machinery exports), rising concerns about the future of the dollar and of the American economy, and a host of other problems. The dollar's strong recovery during the early 1980s signaled a reversal of this downward spiral.

ernment to adopt policies to eliminate the U.S. trade deficit with Japan.

In sum, the United States has been able to run balance of payments deficits fairly consistently for over three decades because

1. Until the 1970s, fixed exchange rates under the Bretton Woods Agreement were adjusted only to cure fundamental disequilibria. Most major trading countries found it advantageous to maintain the dollar's primacy until inflation in the 1960s and the vitality of some other currencies doomed the fixed exchange rate system that had been based on a sound dollar.
2. The dollar has been used extensively as an international medium of exchange.
3. Dollar holdings have been viewed as insurance in unstable countries.
4. Such countries as Japan and Germany supported the dollar at artificially high exchange rates to boost U.S. demand for their

exports. These policies increased employment and economic growth in these countries.[5]

The Dance of the Dollar

The dollar was the world's key currency from World War II into the 1960s. The exchange rate of the dollar fell relative to most major currencies during the 1970s, hitting its low in 1978, but it recovered steadily until 1985, as Figure 8 demonstrates. Why did the dollar fall during the 1970s? Why did it recover, then weaken again after 1985 and, finally, bounce back a bit again in the 1990s? Several explanations are all at least partially correct.

---

[5] During the 1970s, our government urged foreign governments to run budget deficits, increase their money supplies, and reduce trade barriers against American products, among other measures.

We know that the price of anything will fall if supply grows relative to demand, and vice versa. Some explanations for the initial fall of the dollar focus on reduced desires by foreigners to hold dollars; others focus on increased supplies of dollars in international markets. Although growing supplies and falling demands for the dollar (or vice versa) are interrelated, we will deal first with factors that alter international demands for dollars.

Inflation and Exchange Rates

The 1970s were an inflationary era, not only in the United States, but around the world. When our inflation abated in the early 1980s, the dollar's exchange rate rose—at least, for a while. (Of course, U.S. inflation has been less of an issue from 1983 to the present.)

• **Relative Inflation** When prices increase faster in the United States than elsewhere, we buy more imports and supply more dollars internationally, but demands for our exports and dollars fall. This line of reasoning leads to a classical explanation for falling exchange rates; relatively rapid inflation in the United States during the 1970s reduced foreign demands for dollars. Coupled with an increased supply of dollars, the dollar's exchange rate predictably declined. Then, as U.S. inflation abated in the early 1980s, the dollar began to recover. Thus, relative inflation causes depreciation of a currency, while less than the average of international inflation causes exchange rate appreciation, a factor that bodes well for the dollar through the rest of the 1990s.

• **Expectations** An international perception in the 1970s was that, more than any other major country, the United States was committed to expansionary and, consequently, inflationary policies. Increased income, whether real or inflated, boosts dollar demands for imports (by U.S. residents). If other countries are not expected to follow similarly expansionary policies, pressures grow for the dollar to depreciate.[6] U.S. inflation

throughout the 1970s generated international expectations of continued inflationary policies and relative inflation in this country. Such expectations led foreigners to treat dollars as hot potatoes; their dollar holdings fell dramatically at times during 1974 through 1980.

There has been downward pressure on the dollar when international money managers have expected the United States to experience both continued relative inflation and substantial balance of trade deficits. When U.S. monetary growth began to slow in 1979, the dollar began its recovery. An American recession during 1981 to 1983 spread to the rest of the world as it choked off our demands for imports and constricted the international supply of dollars. High U.S. interest rates also attracted short-term financial investments by foreigners, further strengthening the dollar. It seems ironic that recessions bolster the dollar, but they do.

By 1985, the exchange rate of the dollar was so high that foreign finance ministers and American policymakers were alarmed. They adopted policies to depreciate the dollar. Accordingly, foreign central banks sold dollars on international markets, increasing the supply to private financiers. Fear that the United States might resume more expansionary macropolicies caused many private financial institutions to be leery of holding many dollars. Coupled with record deficits in the U.S. balances of payments and trade that caused the international supply of dollars to swell, the dollar drifted down from 1985 to 1988. Nevertheless, the dollar had largely recovered by 1991, although U.S. prosperity combined with a severe recession in Japan caused the dollar to continue to depreciate relative to the yen through 1994.

Budget Deficits and Anemic Saving

We previously discussed how federal budget deficits and inadequate private domestic saving create pressure for borrowing from foreigners, which may take the form of foreign investments in the United States. (If $S + T < I + G$, then $X < M$.) But foreigners will buy assets in the United States only if this appears more profitable than invest-

---

[6]This action reduces the exchange rate of the dollar and, by increasing the prices of our imports and decreasing the prices of U.S. exports, eliminates the deficits.

ment elsewhere. Thus, high interest rates in the United States attract foreign sources of financial capital. If the exchange rate of the dollar appreciates, these foreign investors gain, but if it depreciates, they lose. One way for foreigners to feel that investment in the U.S. is secure is for the exchange rate of the dollar to be so low that they think it likely that it will only rise. For example, a high value for the yen and a low value for the dollar stimulated massive Japanese purchases of U.S. real estate, banks, and communication companies during the late 1980s.

From World War I until 1980, the United States experienced far more trade surpluses than deficits, so American investors poured waves of investment funds into foreign assets. The United States became the world's greatest creditor nation because current account surpluses (net exports) engender capital account deficits (U.S. investments abroad). However, persistent federal budget deficits (our last surplus was experienced in 1969) create pressures for capital inflows to the United States (capital account surpluses, and rising foreign ownership) to offset current account deficits. But capital tends to flow into countries where the expected rate of return is the highest, after adjustment for normal business risks, relative inflation, and exchange rate risk. High interest rates are one way to attract foreign capital. Another is through lower exchange rates. Federal deficits pushed down the dollar in the late 1970s and again during 1985 through 1988.

Portfolio Adjustments

For some time after World War II, the U.S. dollar and gold were viewed as the only stable international mediums of exchange. The world's supply of gold grew more slowly than the volume of international transactions. Consequently, institutions like central banks and international corporations were happy to use the dollars made available by our balance of payments deficits to meet their transaction demands for money and desires for liquid assets.

Economic instability in the United States beginning during the Vietnam conflict diminished confidence in the dollar. During the same period, numerous industrialized economies throughout the world matured or reached full recovery from World War II; their currencies became attractive parts of the portfolios of many countries' central banks, competing with the dollar as a reserve asset. The growing availability of good substitutes for dollars led financial institutions around the world to diversify, holding smaller proportions of their assets in dollars.

When the dollar began to depreciate a little during the mid-1970s, it fell off the pedestal that had caused so many countries to hold dollars. The huge proportion of international reserves held by foreign central banks in the form of U.S. currency caused the dollar overhang to collapse. For example, in 1977 alone, almost 60% of the dollars held by OPEC countries were exchanged for other currencies, intensifying pressure for the dollar to fall.

Several countries attempted in the late 1970s to price their exports (e.g., OPEC oil) on an index of such strong foreign currencies as the Swiss franc and German deutsche mark. These experiments temporarily weakened the dollar because it was less demanded for international transactions, but they ultimately failed, forcing renewed reliance on the dollar as the world's key currency and further bolstering the dollar's recovery in the early 1980s.

Oil and the Balance of Trade

Our cumulative payments deficits during the 1970s added almost 30% to the total amount of dollars held abroad. Substantial parts of payments deficits over this period were attributable to oil imports. The international price of oil grew sharply when OPEC exercised its muscles between 1973 and 1981. Because American production technology is extremely energy intensive, higher oil prices only slowly reduced our oil imports. The dollar value of oil imports grew dramatically, worsening our balance of payments deficit. This—and our own increasing preferences for Japanese electronics, cameras, and cars—pushed down the exchange rate of the dollar. But by the early 1980s, our imports of crude oil were declining and the dollar began showing considerable strength in international financial markets.

Critics of those who view OPEC as a major player on the international financial scene point out, however, that the strength of the dollar in the early 1980s was primarily attributable to high interest rates. Most of the demand for the dollar was manifested through the capital account, not the current account, as would be the case if merchandise trade were the driving force. Clearly, the effect of oil on exchange rates has waned considerably in the 1980s and 1990s.

The Monetarist Explanation

All the preceding factors provide parts of a solution to the temporary decline of the dollar. Predictably, some monetarists attribute the slide of the dollar to too rapid growth in the U.S. money supply (and declining rates of monetary growth were credited with its recovery). We will use the deutsche mark (DM) to explain the monetarist mechanism. The reasoning goes that if the supply of dollars grows relative to the demand for dollars faster than the supply of DM grows relative to the demand for them, then the dollar will depreciate relative to the DM.

The problem with this approach is that, while it is unquestionably true, it has little explanatory value. In fact, during 1985 to 1988 the U.S. money supply grew less rapidly than the money supplies of virtually any other major country, yet the dollar danced downward relative to almost every major currency. Monetarists were unable to explain the declining demand for the dollar, other than by vague references to

inflation. Then, the dollar's recovery since 1990 was attributed to diminishing inflation.

In summary, among possible explanations for the decline of the dollar during the 1970s were:

1. Relative inflation of the dollar
2. Expectations that inflation in the United States would remain higher than elsewhere
3. Expected continuation of trade deficits
4. Persistent and growing federal budget deficits
5. Adjustments of international portfolios against the dollar
6. Modest depreciation causing the dollar to lose its "halo"
7. Larger trade deficits caused by high oil prices
8. Too rapid monetary growth in the United States

The dollar's recovery in the 1980s apparently occurred because of reversals of a number of these factors. Different phases of the swings of the dollar in recent years can be partially explained by different parts of items 1 through 8. Each explanation seems logically plausible, yet none alone is a satisfactory explanation for the swings in the exchange rate of the dollar, and some are even contrary to the evidence.

The ebb and flow of international financial markets are almost impossible to follow if you focus too much on any single explanation. However, if you remind yourself that the key to understanding almost any part of economics is in interpreting how supplies and demands are influenced by specific events, you are half-way home. And that is the thought we wish to leave with you as you conclude this final chapter.

CHAPTER REVIEW: KEY POINTS

1. Since we have no world currency, we must establish the value of each national currency in terms of all others. The **exchange rate** is the value of one currency in terms of another.

2. **Balance of payments** accounts record the flows of money into and out of a country and provide information about trade relationships among countries.

3. Flows of merchandise and services are summarized in the **current account** of the balance of payments. The **capital account** summarizes international investments and swaps of ownership (for, e.g., financial se-

curities, real estate, and production facilities) between domestic and foreign entities.

4. **Flexible**, or floating, systems of **exchange rates** permit the values of currencies to be set by market forces. If a country experiences a balance of payments surplus under such a system, it is an indication that the country's citizens or government desire foreign currencies.

5. When its current exchange rate is too high relative to equilibrium, a country tends to experience a deficit in its balance of payments. Outflows of funds create surpluses of the currency in world financial markets. The exchange rate for the currency will decline if a flexible rate is in operation. This mechanism is reversed to cure balance of payments surpluses if the exchange rate for a currency is below equilibrium.

6. A fixed exchange rate system imposes price ceilings and floors on currencies, often resulting in persistent disequilibria in balances of payments. **Macroadjustments** are the cure.

7. Explanations for the decline of the dollar in the 1970s range from relative inflation to expectations of continued inflation and payments deficits to federal budget deficits to the emergence of other strong international currencies to the formation of oil cartels to too rapid monetary growth. Opposite trends then strengthened the dollar. Each of these explanations bears the germ of truth, but none alone is adequate to explain the dance of the dollar over the past 30 years.

QUESTIONS FOR THOUGHT AND DISCUSSION

1. Recent growth of foreign investment in the United States alarms many Americans. There are calls to sharply limit foreign holdings of U.S. assets, but in periods when U.S. investment abroad has been vigorous, there are complaints that we are exporting jobs to low-wage countries. Can you offer arguments that justify both special limits on U.S. investment by foreigners and on foreign investments by Americans? Or should investors be allowed to place their capital wherever they think it will yield the largest profit?

2. Calculate all possible exchange rates if a U.S. dollar ($) will buy 2 deutsche marks (DM), or a British pound (£), or 6 French francs (F), or 120 Japanese yen (¥).

3. One popular myth is that surpluses in the balances of trade and payments are good omens, while deficits are symptoms that a country may be suffering from economic anemia. Yet persistent U.S. current account deficits during the past two decades may have been unavoidable simply because of the relative vigor of the American economy. How is this so? How have Americans gained from the trade deficit? From the payments deficit? How have they lost from these deficits? On balance, have the gains outweighed the losses?

4. Conventional theories of international finance suggest that imbalances of payments are signs of disequilibrium. Conventional monetarists favored flexible exchange rates as a cure. A recent theory called "global monetarism," however, hypothesizes that surpluses can be expected when people in some countries want more money more than they want more goods, while people in other countries have "too much" money and willingly trade some of their money for imports. How might persistent surpluses or deficits occur in equilibrium?

5. Global monetarists also favor fixed exchange rates, arguing that flexible rates make no more sense than reducing the price of the quarter relative to the penny if there are surpluses of quarters and shortages of pennies. What are the major differences, if any, between these situations? Do these economists have a point? What mechanisms are available to accommodate deficits or surpluses under fixed exchange rates? What are the implications of fixed exchange rates for the independence of macroeconomic policies?

Epilogue

Where do you go from here? A few of you may regret having taken economics; others may feel that the time it took to prepare for this course was well spent, but you have no intention of extending your formal training in economics. Still others may choose to take three or four more courses in this field. We can promise those of you who fit into any of these categories that you will encounter economic concepts repeatedly, regardless of the path your life takes.

But this epilogue is really addressed to those few students who find the analytical methods we use and the problems we tackle so intriguing that you are considering a career as an economist. We are grateful that there are so few of you; otherwise, the supply of economists might be so great that those of us who love economic reasoning would not be able to live comfortably while doing the work we like best. John Maynard Keynes once issued a challenge to aspiring economists that we would like to echo:

The study of economics does not seem to require any specialized gifts of an unusual order. Is it not, intellectually regarded, a very easy subject compared with the higher branches of philosophy and pure science? Yet good, or even competent, economists are the rarest of birds. An easy subject, at which few excel! The paradox finds its explanation, perhaps, in that the master economist must possess a rare combination of gifts. He must be a mathematician, historian, statesman, philosopher—in some degree. He must understand symbols and speak in words. He must contemplate the particular in terms of the general, and touch abstract and concrete in the same flight of thought. He must study the present in the light of the past for the purposes of the future. No part of man's nature or institutions must lie entirely outside his regard. He must be purposeful and disinterested in a simultaneous mood; as aloof and incorruptible as an artist, yet sometimes as near the earth as a politician.

J. M. Keynes (1924)

Everyone who wishes to be an economist would do well to pursue the lofty goals implicit in Keynes's essay.

Glossary

Ability to Pay Principle The idea that the rich should pay more taxes than the poor. (See also Benefit Principle of Taxation.)

Absolute Advantage The idea that nations should produce goods that absorb fewer resources than in other countries and exchange their surpluses for goods produced with fewer resources elsewhere; replaced by the Law of Comparative Advantage.

Absolute Price The monetary price of a good. (See also Relative Price.)

Absorption Problem Government spending must be funded by taxes, private saving, or imports, or by reduced investment or exports: $G = S + T + M - I - X$.

Activism The Keynesian notion that Aggregate Demand should be adjusted by goverment macroeconomic policy to offset shocks to Aggregate Demand or Aggregate Supply. "Fine-tuning" is an extreme version of this approach.

Administration Lag The period that passes before discretionary policy changes can be implemented. Monetary policy can be implemented quickly through the Fed's Federal Open Market Committee; fiscal policies entail long administration lags because discretionary changes in taxes or government expenditures require changing the law.

Administrative Costs of Regulation Include the salaries of government workers, inspectors, office supplies, etc. (See also Compliance Costs of Government Regulation.)

Adverse Selection Occurs when a party to a contract has been deceived about the qualities it expects to receive from a transaction.

Aggregate Demand Curve The negative relationship that exists between the general price level (P) and the quantity demanded (Q) of total national output.

Aggregate Expenditures The sum of consumption, investment, government purchases, and net exports [$C + I + G + (X - M)$].

Aggregate Expenditures Curve The relationship between Aggregate Expenditures and income; positively sloped because income induces spending. Sometimes known as a Keynesian cross diagram.

Aggregate Supply Curve A positive relationship between real national production (Q) and the absolute price level (P).

Aid to Families with Dependent Children (AFDC) A major program designed to alleviate poverty; originally this program was characterized by a payment structure which provided overwhelming incentives for recipients not to work.

Allocative Mechanisms Alternative modes for a society to use in deciding how inputs will be allocated among competing ends and how incomes and production will be distributed.

Anarchism The idea that government should be eliminated, leaving people largely free to do as they pleased. Anarchists believe that social harmony would evolve naturally through cooperative efforts. Most philosophical anarchists recognize the importance of private property rights and, hence, completely disavow social ownership.

Appreciation of a Currency When the exchange rate (price) of a currency increases as measured by its exchange rates with other currencies.

Arbitrage The risklessly profitable process of buying a good at a lower price in one market and selling the same good at a higher price in another market; forces relative prices of the same good toward equality in all markets.

Artificial Barriers to Entry Significant barriers to entry that are not caused by natural market forces. Government or existing firms erect these barriers to exclude competition.

Asset Demand for Money Exists because people (*a*) perceive money as riskless relative to alternative assets, (*b*) confront transaction costs in acquiring other assets that exceed their expected rate of return, and (*c*) expect the prices of alternative assets to fall in the near future.

Asymmetric Information When people have different levels of knowledge about a bargaining situation.

Automatic (Built-in) Stabilizers Government tax and spending mechanisms that automatically drive the federal budget into deficit when the economy slumps or into a surplus when inflationary pressures build; tend to stabilize economic activity.

Automation Technological advances that replace human labor by machinery.

Autonomous Expenditure Spending unrelated to income; occurs at zero income. Investment, government purchases, net exports, and part of consumer spending are all treated as autonomous in very simple Keynesian models.

Autonomous Spending Multiplier The number which, when multiplied by the sum of all autonomous spending, yields equilibrium income; in simple Keynesian models, this multiplier equals the reciprocal of the marginal propensity to save.

Average Fixed Cost (AFC) Total fixed cost (TFC) per unit of output (Q); TFC/Q graphs as a rectangular hyperbola.

Average Physical Product of Labor (APP_L) Production per worker; equals total output (Q) divided by labor (L); Q/L.

Average Propensity to Consume (APC) The proportion of disposable income consumed; $APC = C/Y_d$.

Average Propensity to Save (APS) The proportion of disposable income saved; $APS = S/Y_d$.

Average Revenue Revenue per unit of output; synonym for price in the absence of price discrimination; equals total revenue (TR) divided by output: TR/Q.

Average Revenue Product Revenue per unit of an input; computed by dividing a given total revenue (TR) by the amounts of given resources [e.g., workers (L)] generating this revenue (e.g., TR/L).

Average Total Cost (ATC) Total cost incurred per unit of output; often termed *average cost* or *unit cost*; $ATC = AVC + AFC$, or TC/Q.

Average Variable Costs (AVC) Variable cost per unit of output; equals TVC/Q. (See also Variable Costs.)

Bad Anything the consumption of which decreases human happiness.

Balance of Payments A record of the payments between a country and the countries with which it trades. Balance of payments deficits occur when a country's payments of money to foreigners exceed its receipts from foreigners. A balance of payments surplus occurs when a country's receipts from foreigners exceed its payments to foreigners.

Balance of Trade (deficit, surplus) The relationship between a country's annual exports and imports. A deficit in the balance of trade exists when the dollar value of a country's imports exceeds the value of its exports. A surplus in the balance of trade exists when the dollar value of a country's exports exceeds the dollar value of its imports. Differs from balance of payments because foreign investment flows and loans, among other things, affect payments.

Barrier to Entry A significant obstacle of some sort that either discourages or prevents the entry of firms into an industry.

Barter Trading goods for other goods rather than money.

Basic Economic Problem Scarcity, which means that fewer goods are freely available than people want to consume.

Basic Economic Questions *What* economic goods will be produced, *when* and *how* resources will be used for which types of production, and *who* will get to use the goods.

Benefit Principle of Taxation The idea that individuals should be taxed in proportion to the marginal benefits that they receive from governmentally provided commodities and services. (See also Ability to Pay.)

Bilateral Monopoly Occurs when a monopoly supplier confronts a monopsonistic buyer.

Black Market Transactions that violate legal price ceilings.

Blacklisting Circulation by employers of lists to bar hiring of union organizers or other "troublemakers." Now illegal.

Block Pricing Price discrimination for utility rates.

Board of Governors The governing body of the Federal Reserve System. Six regular board members are appointed to staggered 14-year terms of office; the Chair is appointed to a 4-year term.

Bonds Promises by government or corporations to pay certain amounts of money by specific future dates.

Break-even Point The rate of output at which total revenue equals total cost.

Breton Woods Agreement (1944) Established both the International Monetary Fund and a fixed exchange rate system with the dollar as the world's key currency. Other nations agreed to peg their currencies to the dollar.

Budget Deficits or Surpluses Occur, respectively, when government outlays exceed or fall below government revenues.

Budget Line A line showing various combinations of goods that cost the same amount as the consumer's income.

Bureaucracy A large organization with many employees, called bureaucrats; tends to be governed by many rules and regulations, called red tape.

Business Cycles Alternating periods of expansion and contraction in economic activity.

Business Firms Centers of production; they sell goods in output markets and buy services in resource markets.

Buyers' Market Occurs when the prevailing market price lies above the equilibrium price, resulting in a surplus.

Capital All physical improvements made to natural resources that facilitate production, including buildings and all machinery and equipment.

Capital Deepening When the percentage growth of the capital stock exceeds the growth rate of the labor force; real per capita output normally rises.

Capital Widening When the labor force and the capital stock experience identical percentage rates of growth.

Capitalism An economic system based on private property rights and emphasizing private, as opposed to governmental or collective, decision-making. (See also Laissez-Faire, Socialism.)

Capitalization The process whereby income streams are transformed into wealth, resulting in the elimination of economic profits.

Cartel An organization of firms that jointly make decisions about prices and production for the entire group; usually attempts to charge monopoly prices and limit production to monopoly rates of output. OPEC is an example.

Caveat Emptor An ancient legal doctrine that suggests that buyers are the best judges of whether or not they receive full value from the goods they purchase and should bear the consequences of their own decisions; it means "let the buyer beware."

Caveat Venditor A legal doctrine reflected in prohibitions against fraud and in sellers' legal liability for damages if unknown dangers lurk in a product; a Latin phrase meaning "let the seller beware."

Celler-Kefauver Antimerger Act (1950) This act made it illegal for major firms to acquire the stock or assets of their competitors.

Central Bank An institution whose function it is to make a nation's financial system operate as smoothly as possible; serves as the government's banker.

Central Planning or Centralized Decision-making Major economic decisions are made by some central authority, as in the former Soviet Union.

Certificates of Deposit (CDs) Very long-term, high-value savings accounts issued by financial institutions.

Christian Socialism Emphasizes the virtues and dignity of work and advocates labor unionization; rejects the violent means to overthrow capitalism advocated by radical socialists and communists.

Circular Flow Model Shows interactions between households and firms. Households are centers for wealth holding and consumption and buy goods from the firms that produce them; firms buy resources from households in order to produce goods and services.

Classical Theory A systematic study of the functioning of a market economy which concluded that, in the long run, the economy would always attain full employment at equilibrium GDP, assuming the validity of Say's Law and flexible wages, prices, and interest rates.

Clayton Act (1914) Specified offenses more precisely than did the Sherman Act (1890); the Clayton Act forbade price discrimination and interlocking directorates, exempted collective bargaining from antitrust actions, and exempted agricultural associations so that nonprofit corporations could be formed without violating antitrust laws.

Closed Shop A firm that has agreed to hire only union members; these agreements are illegal under the Taft-Hartley Act.

Coinsurance Medical insurance where the patient pays x percent of the cost of medical treatment. This is often coupled with a deductible where the patient pays the first y dollars of any medical treatment of the first y dollars of any medical treatment or the first y

dollars of medical treatment within a given period of time (usually a calendar year.

Collective Bargaining   The process by which workers who are members of a labor union negotiate with an employer to set wages, hours, and working conditions.

Command Economy   These economic systems resolve the basic economic questions through central planning; allocations of inputs and distributions of goods are coordinated by a bureaucracy.

Commodity   Any tangible produced good that may be owned.

Commodity Money   Has substantial value independently of what it will buy. Gold and silver coins are examples.

Common Stock   Ownership shares in a corporation.

Communism   An idealized classless society in which all people would live and work under the condition "from each according to ability, to each according to needs"; under communism, all nonhuman property would be owned collectively.

Comparable Worth   The idea that jobs typically filled by women should generate wages equal to those paid to men with comparable skills.

Comparative Advantage, Law of   Mutually beneficial trade can always take place between two countries (or individuals) whose pretrade cost and price structures differ.

Competition   A process driving price close to opportunity cost. Pure competition requires (*a*) numerous potential buyers and sellers; (*b*) homogenous outputs or inputs, precluding nonprice competition; (*c*) each buyer and seller to be small relative to the market so that no single decision will influence the price of the item or service; and (*d*) an absence of long-run barriers to entry or to exit. (See also Contestable Markets Theory.)

Complementary Goods   Goods that are consumed together, such as tennis racquets and balls; a negative cross price elasticity of demand exists between complementary goods.

Compliance Costs of Government Regulation   Costs incurred mainly by the private sector (and also by state and local governments) in the process of complying with regulations. (See also Administrative Costs of Regulation.)

Concentration Ratio   The percentage of some aspect of market power (e.g., sales) wielded by the leading four or eight firms in an industry.

Conglomerate   A firm that operates in several different industries.

Constant Cost Industry   The long-run industry supply curve is horizontal; constant per unit production costs are incurred for every output level because the supplies of all the resources used are perfectly price elastic.

Consumer Equilibrium (the Cardinal Utility approach)   A consumer maximizes total utility when the last cents spent on each good yield the same number of utils of satisfaction; no reallocation of spending will increase total utility.

Consumer Equilibrium (the Indifference Curve approach)   Consumer maximizes satisfaction upon reaching tangency between their budget constraint lines and the highest attainable indifference curves.

Consumer Price Index (*CPI*)   A statistical comparison, over time, in the prices of goods bought by typical urban consumers; the base year equals 100, with subsequent changes in the price level reflecting inflation (over 100) or deflation (under 100).

Consumer Surplus   A gain to consumers arising from differences between the amounts of money they would willingly pay to consume goods and the amounts that they must pay in order to consume the good; the area below their demand curves but above the price line.

Consumption   Spending by households for goods used to gratify human wants; the major component of Aggregate Demand.

Contestable Markets Theory   Suggests that all advantages of pure competition as a market structure are realized if freedom of entry and exit exists, and that the number of firms currently in a market is less important for efficiency than the threat of potential new entrants. (See also Competition.)

Contingent Labor Force   Contingent workers include part-time employees, the self-employed and temporary workers.

Contraction (Recession)   A decline in economic activity; unemployment and inventories rise unexpectedly.

Contribution Standard   The idea that income should be distributed according to the productivity of one's resources.

Corporation   An organization formed under state law that is considered a legal person distinct and separate from its owners.

Cost-Push Inflation Upward price level movements that originate on the supply side of the economy; cost-push cycles of inflation generate clockwise adjustment paths of inflation versus real output.

Costs of Unemployment, Economic Include the opportunity costs of the output unemployed workers could have produced were they employed.

Credit A promise to pay at some future date is exchanged for money.

Cross Price Elasticity of Demand A measure of the responsiveness of the quantity demanded of one good to changes in the price of another; computed by dividing the percentage change in quantity demanded of a good by the percentage change in price of another good: $\%\Delta Q_x \div \%\Delta P_y$; positive for substitute goods, but negative for complementary goods.

Crowding-Out Hypothesis The idea that increases in governmental spending inevitably cause reductions in private consumption or investment. (See also Absorption Problem.)

Crude Quantity Theory of Money A monetary theory that the price level is exactly proportional to the nominal money supply (M).

Currency Coins and paper money.

Cyclical Deficit The difference between government revenues and outlays that emerges when the macroeconomy operates below its potential. (See also Structural Deficit.)

Cyclical Unemployment Unemployment that results from a recession.

Decentralized Decision-making When most decisions about what to produce, when and how to produce, and who gets to use output are determined in private markets.

Decentralized Socialism Economic systems characterized by social ownership of resources, but which rely on markets to resolve the economic problem by setting equilibrium prices and quantities.

Decrease in Demand An entire demand curve shifting downward and to the left; occurs only if one or more of the nonprice determinants of demand change. Less will be purchased at each possible price.

Decrease in Supply The entire supply curve shifts to the left; occurs only if one of the non-price determinants of supply changes so that less will be available at each possible price.

Decreasing Cost Industry An industry for which the long-run supply curve is negatively sloped, reflecting declines in per unit costs as production in the industry increases.

Deflating Using a price index to adjust monetary values for changes that occur to the price level over time; dividing the nominal values of a time series for a variable by (1% of) the price level during the period in which the nominal variable occurs.

Deflationary Gap See Recessionary Gap.

Demand Purchases of a good that people are actually willing and able to make, given the prices and choices available to them.

Demand Curve A graph of the maximum quantities of a good that people are willing to purchase at various market prices.

Demand Deposits Funds kept in a financial institution that by law must be available upon the depositor's demand; checking accounts.

Demand, Law of The quantity demanded of an economic good varies inversely with its price.

Demand Price The highest price that buyers are willing and able to pay for a specific amount of a good or resource. Also known as subjective price. (See also Supply Price.)

Demand Schedule A table reflecting the maximum quantities of a given good or resource that will be purchased at various market prices.

Demand-Side or Demand-Pull Inflation Hikes in the price level that originate from growth of Aggregate Demand; caused by excessively rapid increases in the growth rate of the nominal money supply or upward shifts in autonomous real expenditures; demand-pull inflation generates a counterclockwise adjustment path of inflation versus real output.

Depreciation The amount of capital used up during a period. In GDP accounting, known as the capital consumption allowance.

Depreciation of a Currency A decrease in the value of one currency measured in terms of its exchange rates with other currencies.

Depression A sharp and sustained decline in business activity.

Derived Demand The demand for a resource that exists because of its productivity; resource demands are derived from demands for output.

Devaluation of a Currency Occurs when exchange rates are either "pegged" or fixed under a gold standard and some government decides to decrease the gold content of its currency; not synonymous with depreciation of currency.

Development, Economic Qualitative changes in an economic system; economic development occurs when there are improvements in either the quality of life or the quality of goods, or both.

Dialectical Materialism Karl Marx's explanation of historical change; all massive social and cultural changes are determined by contradictions that exist in the ways that societies produce, exchange, distribute, and consume goods; for the most part, these contradictions are embedded in conflicts that exist between the different classes in society.

Diminishing Marginal Returns, Law of When additional equal units of a variable input are applied to fixed inputs, a point is inevitably reached where total output increases at a diminishing rate as additional units of the variable input are applied to the fixed inputs; diminishing marginal returns are pervasive even in the long run because it is virtually impossible to vary all influences on production both proportionally and simultaneously.

Diminishing Marginal Utility, Principle of Consumption of successive units of a good eventually causes an additional unit of the good to yield less satisfaction than that of the preceding unit.

Diminishing Returns, Law of The further any activity is extended, the more difficult (and costly) it is to extend it further.

Dirty Float Occurs when governments intervene in a "floating" foreign exchange market in order to stabilize exchange rates.

Discount Rate (*d*) The interest rate the Fed charges member banks to borrow money from Fed "discount windows."

Discretionary Fiscal Policy Deliberate changes in government spending and tax policies for economic stabilization purposes.

Discrimination, Economic Occurs when equivalent units of a resource receive different rates of remuneration even though their potential marginal contributions to total output are the same.

Diseconomies of Scale A firm's average costs rise as output rises.

Disequilibrium When the forces for change in a system are not in balance.

Disincentives Penalties that discourage an activity; often applied to government policies that discourage productive activities.

Disinflation A significant decrease in the rate of inflation; this normally creates pressures for recessions.

Disposable Personal Income (*DPI*) The after-tax income households receive in a given year; equals consumption plus saving ($C + S$).

Dissaving Negative saving; occurs when desired consumption exceeds income; families go in debt or draw down past savings to afford their purchases.

Distortion Costs of Inflation Losses from distorted decisions caused when inflation warps relative prices and reduces certainty.

Divestiture When court orders require large corporations to break down into smaller independent companies.

Division of Labor Specialization of labor by task; for example, when one person designs a computer program, another writes the computer code, a third debugs the program, a fourth writes the user manual, a fifth copies the program to diskettes, a sixth packages and ships the programs, and so on.

Dominant Strategy In game theory, a player's best response, no matter what strategy other players might pick.

Double Coincidence of Wants A requirement of barter that you must locate someone who has what you want and who wants what you have to transact.

Dumping When a country sells an export for less than the price charged domestically for that good; may result from international price discrimination, which entails charging desperate domestic buyers more than indifferent foreign buyers; predatory dumping occurs when a country tries to drive competitors out of a market to establish a monopoly.

Durable Goods Consumer goods that are useful for more than one year.

Economic Growth A positive quantitative change in an economic system; occurs when a society acquires greater productive capacity that can be used for consumption or investment.

Economic Incidence of a Tax The final burden of a tax; that is, who actually pays the tax through lower purchasing power.

Economic (Capital) Investment Purchases of new output that can be used for further production. The four basic types of new capital are (*a*) new business structures, (*b*) new residential structures, (*c*) new machinery and equipment, and (*d*) inventory accumulation.

Economic Profit The excess of revenues over the opportunity costs of the resources employed; these profits reward an entrepreneur if they exceed the minimum necessary to continue the firm's existence, and are a premium for bearing risk and innovating.

Economic Rent Surpluses reaped by owners of a resource if it is paid more than the minimum necessary to elicit the supply of the resource.

Economics The study of how individuals and societies allocate their limited resources in attempts to satisfy their unlimited wants.

Economies of Scale When long-run average costs fall as output rises.

Economies of Scope Cost savings realized because certain types of production are complementary.

Efficiency, Economic Occurs when the opportunity cost of some specific amount of a good is at its lowest possible value and when maximum production from given resources and costs is achieved; implies that gains to anyone entail losses to someone else.

Efficient Markets Theory The idea that all possible gains that are foreseeable will be exploited by private individuals.

Efficiency Wages Wages that exceed market-clearing wages which are intended to raise the costs of dismissal and reduce shirking by employees.

Egalitarianism The idea that everyone should have the same income.

Elasticity The sensitivity of one variable relative to some other variable. [See also Income Elasticity of Demand, Price Elasticity of Demand (or Supply).]

Eminent Domain Government's legal right to acquire property without the previous owner agreeing to the price government pays.

Empire Building Exaggerating the difficulty of the mission of a bureaucracy so that the budget of the agency will be expanded.

Employment Act of 1946 Established the Council of Economic Advisors and set priorities of full employment with price level stability, but provided few directives about how to achieve such goals.

Employment Discrimination Occurs when particular groups suffer a higher incidence of unemployment than other groups.

Entrepreneurship The organizing function which combines the services provided by other resources so that goods are produced.

Entry and Exit into an Industry If there are no barriers to entry and exit, entry into an industry by outside competitors or exit of existing firms continue until economic profits are zero; positive profits attract new entrants, while economic losses cause exit from an industry. Potential entry by competitors is the key to "contestable" markets theory.

Equal Distribution of Income Standard One ethical criterion for distributing income and wealth; assumes that an extra dollar means more to the poor than to the rich, and ignores the disincentives for production that occur when incomes are independent of productivity.

Equal Marginal Advantage, Law of Efficiency requires similar resources to be used to equally advantage. In consumption, the last cent spent on any good must yield the same satisfaction as the last cent spent on any other good. In production, the last cent spent on any resource must yield the same output as the last cent spent on any other resource.

Equal Marginal Productivities per Dollar, Principle of The last few cents spent on any resource must yield the same additional output as the last few cents spent on any other resource. This is a requirement for least cost production and maximum profit.

Equal Marginal Utilities per Dollar, Principle of The last few cents spent on any good yield identical amounts of satisfaction or utility; algebraically, this requires $MU_1/P_1 = MU_2/P_2 = \ldots = MU_m/P_m$, where the subscripts 1 through $m - 1$ denote commodities and m denotes money.

Equation of Exchange $MV = PQ$, where M denotes the nominal money supply, V denotes the income velocity of money, P denotes an index for the general price level, and Q denotes real output; a tautology, since it is true by definition.

Equilibrium Exists when the pressures that bring about change in the market system are in balance. *Macroeconomic equilibrium* is when desired demand expenditure equals actual income or output. *Microeconomic equilibrium* is when the quantities of a good or resource demanded and supplied are equal.

Equilibrium (Market-Clearing) Price The market price that clears the market.

Equilibrium Quantity The quantity of a good marketed at the equilibrium price.

Equity Fairness, a normative concept; value judgments are inherent in specifying what is fair.

Escalator Clauses Contractual obligations specifying that future payments of money will be adjusted for price-level changes.

Excess Burdens of a Tax The amounts by which the total burden of a tax exceeds government revenue yielded by the tax.

Excess Demand The amount by which the quantity demanded exceeds the quantity supplied when the prevailing market price lies below the market-clearing price; normally associated with shortages.

Excess Reserves (*XR*) The amounts by which banks' legal (total) reserves exceed their required reserves.

Excess Supply The amount by which the quantity supplied exceeds the quantity demanded when the prevailing market price lies above the market-clearing price; normally associated with surpluses.

Exchange Controls Legal limits on the ability to buy or sell foreign currencies; frequently stimulate black markets for foreign money.

Exchange Rate The value of one currency expressed in terms of another currency, or some combination of other currencies.

Excise Tax A per unit tax levied on a specific good.

Exclusive Good A good is exclusive if people can be denied access at a relatively low cost; if these people do not pay, they may be excluded from consuming the good.

Expansion (Recovery) The phase of the business cycle when economic activity begins to increase; employment rises, inventories fall unexpectedly.

Expected Rate of Inflation The percentage annual rate at which economic transactors expect the general price level to rise.

Expenditure Approach to Estimating GDP GDP equals the sum of personal consumption, investment, government purchases of commodities and services, and net exports: $GDP = C + I + G + (X - M)$.

Explicit Costs Outlays of funds to individuals or firms external to the producer; some examples are wages paid employees, rent payments, utility bills, and purchases of intermediate goods.

Exploitation Payment of wages less than the value of the marginal product of labor. May result from a firm's monopsony power as a hirer of labor, or because a firm has monopoly power.

Exports Goods manufactured in this country and purchased by foreigners.

External Supply Shocks These shocks, which originate outside the economy, shift the Aggregate Supply curve to the left; rising production costs create pressures for supply-side (cost-push) inflation and increasing unemployment.

Externalities Market failures that occur whenever some activity affects economic transactors who are not directly involved in the activity. Pollution is an example of a negative externality; education generates positive externalities to the extent that all of society gains from being a part of a more educated populace. External costs and benefits are largely ignored by individual decision-makers.

Fabian Socialism This socialist theory advocates nationalizing only heavy industry; all other property would be privately owned, although extensive welfare programs would ensure that people's needs were met.

Family Allowance Plan (FAP) Many European nations countries now have family allowance plans based on the number of minor children in a family; these payments are usually adequate to feed and to clothe each child in the family and are made regardless of the family's income.

Featherbedding The employment of workers who are not in productive jobs; normally a result of union pressure or inefficient government regulation.

Federal Funds Market A privately operated network that enables banks to borrow or lend large amounts of money for very short periods.

Federal Open Market Committee (FOMC) The policymaking body within the Federal Reserve System.

Federal Reserve System (Fed) Central bank of the United States; created by Congress in 1913 to buffer financial crises by acting as a bankers' bank and lender of last resort; the Fed's primary role is conducting monetary policy.

Federal Trade Commission (FTC) Act (1914) Created the FTC and empowered it to challenge any "unfair methods of competition . . . , and unfair or deceptive acts or practices in or affecting commerce."

Fee-for-service This entails medical payments (usually to doctors) that are tailored to the specific treatment. (See Health Maintenance Organizations).

Fiat Money Money that is worthless as a commodity and which has value only because of its use as a medium of exchange.

Final Goods Goods bought by the consumers or investors who ultimately use them.

Financial Capital Securities; paper claims to goods or resources.

Financial Intermediation The process by which household saving is made available through financial institutions to those desiring to spend in excess of their income (especially investors).

Financial Investment Paper documents representing financial claims on assets, created when purchases of stocks, bonds, and real estate are made.

Fine-tuning Government attempts to make the economy function as smoothly as possible by frequently changing both monetary and fiscal policies to offset even minor fluctuations in economic activity.

Firm An entity that operates one or more plants and which buys productive resources from households.

Fiscal drag A tendency to generate budget surpluses in a growing economy, assuming that government spending and tax rates remain unchanged; arising because of our progressive income tax, fiscal drag retards growth of Aggregate Demand.

Fiscal Policy Policies for government spending or setting tax rates or revenues to either stimulate or contract economic activity; intended to offset cyclical fluctuations in economic activity.

Fisher Effect Adjustments of nominal interest rates as borrowers and lenders compensate for expected inflation in order to secure some equilibrium "real" rate of interest.

Fixed Costs The total of all costs not related to the level of production; fixed costs are also known as historical, sunk, or overhead costs and are irrelevant for rational decision-making.

Fixed Exchange Rates A system in which international agreements set the values of all currencies in terms of one another; the exchange rates of currencies are not allowed to respond to changes in the relative supplies and demands for the currencies; balance of payments surpluses and deficits occur in a fixed exchange rate system when equilibrium exchange rates differ from the fixed (pegged) exchange rates and can be eliminated only through adjustments of Aggregate Demands or Aggregate Supplies.

Flexible (Floating) Exchange Rates The major alternative to a system of fixed exchange rates; under this exchange rate system, markets for individual currencies determine their equilibrium and actual exchange rates.

Flexible Wages, Prices, and Interest Rates According to classical theory, full employment is guaranteed by the existence of perfectly flexible wages, prices, and interest rates. (See also Say's Law.)

Flow Variable An economic variable that is only meaningful if measured over a period of time; income and production are examples.

Foreign Exchange A stock of foreign currencies held as an asset.

Foreign Sector Substitution Effect Tendency to import more and export less in response to an increase in the price level, and to invest more abroad and less domestically because a higher price level normally entails higher domestic production costs. Partially accounts for the negative slope of the Aggregate Demand curve. (See also Wealth Effect and Interest Rate Effect.)

Forward (Futures) Markets Markets in which contracts to deliver currencies or products at some future date are bought and sold.

Fractional Reserve Banking System A banking system in which banks are legally required to hold only a fraction of their demand deposit liabilities in the form of reserves.

Free Enterprise System Agreements to trade are made by private buyers and sellers; ownership of resources is private, not social.

Free Good A good for which the quantity demanded fails to exceed the quantity available at a price of zero.

Free-Rider Problem   Encountered in the consumption of public goods; refers to the lack of incentives for people to reveal their true preferences for public goods once these goods are provided; nonexclusive goods can be consumed at a zero price by those who contribute nothing to cover their production costs.

Frictional Unemployment   Unemployment that exists because no one possesses perfect knowledge concerning job opportunities or free mobility between places of employment; lends a certain flexibility to the economy.

Functional Distribution of Income   A breakdown of total income into the proportions paid to owners of various types of resources.

Functional Finance   The view that balance in the economy is important and that imbalance in the federal budget is not important.

Future Goods   Investments (postponed consumption) that boost productive capacity.

Gains from Scale   Cost savings realized because international trade enables firms to become larger because they serve larger markets.

Gains from Specialization of Labor   The extra output yielded when workers combine different types of expertise to perform a particular task.

Gains from Trade   Improvements in human welfare because trading parties gain by acquiring (*a*) unique goods that they could not produce; (*b*) goods at lower costs than could be yielded by own-production; (*c*) transfers of technology; (*d*) greater income that, through higher saving, stimulates investment; (*e*) gains from economies of scale made possible by larger markets; and (*f*) calmer relations with other people because of mutual interdependence.

Galloping Inflation   Increases in the price level at double-digit rates annually.

Game Theory   A technique that requires assessing the potential gains and losses from all possible strategies by all participants in some activity so that the most likely combinations of choices and outcomes can be ascertained.

General Equilibrium Analysis   A method of analysis that not only looks at the direct effects of some variables on others, but also at indirect effects and feedbacks among the economic variables.

General Training   Training that increases the productivity of a worker equally for numerous possible places of employment.

GDP (Implicit Price) Deflator   A price index composed largely of components from the *CPI* and *PPI*; used to adjust nominal GDP for changes in the price level.

GDP Gap   The amount by which current GDP is below full-employment GDP.

Gold Standard   Money may be exchanged at a fixed rate for gold; for example, until 1933, one ounce of gold could be bought from the U.S. Treasury for $35 or sold to it for $35.

Good   Anything which satisfies a human want and, in so doing, increases human happiness.

Gresham's Law   Bad money drives out good.

Grim Strategy   In game theory, entails refusal to commit to a position until other players commit to a position.

Gross Domestic Product (GDP)   The value of all production that takes place in a country annually, regardless of whether the resources used are owned domestically or by foreigners. GDP replaced Gross National Product in 1991 as the primary measure used to report U.S. production.

Gross National Product (GNP)   The value of all output produced by resources owned by the citizens of a country. The standard measure for U.S. production until 1991. (See also Gross Domestic Product.)

Health Maintenance Organizations (HMOs)   These health organizations typically cover the health needs of their members for a fixed fee per person.

Herfindahl-Hirschman Index (HHI)   The sum of the squares of the market shares of the firms in an industry; HHIs are now used as a guideline for antitrust actions.

Hoarding   Holding money in idle cash balances; money that is hoarded is not spent on consumption or investment; causes velocity to fall.

Horizontal Combination   A firm which has numerous plants producing identical or similar products.

Household Income   Used for consumption, saving, or taxes.

Households Individuals or family units that provide input services and that are the ultimate storehouses of wealth; they purchase goods in the output markets, and they sell resources in input markets.

Human Capital Improvements made in the labor embodied in human beings; people invest in human capital so that their labor services become both more productive and more highly paid.

Human Capital Discrimination Reduces access by certain groups to schooling, on-the-job training, or to human capital investments.

Humphrey-Hawkins (Full Employment and Balanced Growth) Act (1978) Augments the Employment Act of 1946 by (*a*) identifying specific economic priorities; (*b*) directing the president to establish goals based on those priorities; and (*c*) creating procedures to improve the coordination and development of economic policy between the president, the Congress, and the Federal Reserve System.

Hyperinflation Increases in the price level at rates exceeding 50% per month.

Idle Cash Balances Money that is hoarded.

Impact Lag The period that passes before newly implemented changes in policy have an impact on economic activity; the impact lag of tax policy is short relative to that of monetary policy.

Implicit Labor Contract Unspoken agreements between firms and workers that the firm will continue to provide jobs when economic conditions are poor if the employee does not demand huge wage increases during periods of prosperity.

Implicit Costs The opportunity costs of all resources that a firm's owner makes available for production without direct outlays of money; examples are the values of the entrepreneur's funds, labor, and land tied up in the firm.

Imports Goods produced in foreign countries and consumed or invested domestically.

Income Approach to Estimating GDP GDP is the sum of personal consumption, total saving, and total taxes; $GDP = C + S + T$.

Income Effect Changes in consumption patterns arising because price changes also change the purchasing power of money incomes; may be positive, negative, or zero.

Income Elasticity of Demand A measure of the responsiveness of the quantity demanded of a good to changes in real income; computed by dividing the percentage change in the quantity demanded of a good by the percentage change in real income: $\%\Delta Q_{xod}/\%\Delta Y$.

Income Velocity (*V*) of Money $V = PQ/M$; the number of times annually that the average unit of money changes hands during the process of purchasing GDP (*PQ*).

Incomes Policies Measures intended to curb inflation without reducing Aggregate Demand expenditures; these policies include moral suasion, wage and price guidelines, and wage and price controls.

Increase in Demand When the entire demand curve shifts upward and to the right; more will be purchased at every price; occurs only if one of the nonprice determinants of demand changes.

Increase in Supply When the entire supply curve shifts rightwards; buyers will be offered more at every price; occurs only if a nonprice determinant of supply changes.

Increasing Cost Industry An industry whose long-run supply curve is an upwardly sloping line; higher costs per unit are incurred as production in the industry increases.

Index Numbers Numbers used to make relative comparisons of a specific variable between time periods.

Indicative Planning France, whose economy is primarily capitalistic, has used indicative planning, which entails trying to coordinate economic activity by setting production targets for major industries.

Indifference Curve A line connecting the various combinations of two goods that yield the same total utility; the consumer is indifferent among the various bundles of goods along an indifference curve.

Indirect Business Taxes Various taxes that are viewed by business firms as costs of production; are not part of National Income since they are not resource payments. Examples are sales and excise taxes.

Induced Expenditures Expenditures that depend on income.

Industrial Policy Government uses subsidies, tax breaks, and protection from foreign competition to support "target industries" that have high productivity, strong "linkages," or future importance.

Industry   All firms that compete in some product market.

Industry Interest Theory of Regulation   Regulation of industry serves not the public interest, but instead serves the particular interests of the regulated industries.

Infant Industry Argument for Tariffs   The notion that emerging industries need to be protected from more efficient, established, foreign competitors.

Inferior Good   A good for which the income elasticity of demand is negative; the demand for this type of economic good varies inversely with real income; technically, a good for which the income effect of a price change is negative.

Inflation   Upward movements of the absolute price level.

Inflationary Gap   The amount by which autonomous expenditures exceed those necessary for full employment income or output.

Informative Advertising   Accurate information provided to consumers so that good economic choices can be made at lowered transaction costs; not a waste of resources.

In-Kind Transfers   Welfare paid, not as cash, but rather as, for example, food stamps, educational grants, or housing allowances.

Innovation   In the 1930s, Joseph Schumpeter argued that progress in capitalist systems is driven by major innovations, including (*a*) introduction of a new good, or new quality in a familiar product; (*b*) introduction of new technology; (*c*) opening of a new market; (*d*) discovery of a major source of raw materials; and (*e*) reorganization of a major industry.

Inputs   Resources used in the production process, such as labor and raw or semifinished materials.

Insurance Principle   Since most people are willing to pay to avoid some financial risk, insurance companies sell guarantees against such risks, charging a fee high enough to cover administrative costs and earn a profit.

Interest   Payments per time period for the use of capital services.

Interest Rate Effect   The Aggregate Demand curve slopes down in part because higher price levels increase the interest rate, which reduces purchases; dollar amounts to finance a given investment grow, while the nominal supply of loanable funds available does not.

Intermediaries   Firms that convey goods from the ultimate producer to the ultimate user. Intermediaries are profitable only if they reduce transaction costs.

Intermediate Goods   Semiprocessed goods used in the production of other economic goods.

International Trade   Exchanges of goods across national boundaries; facilitates efficient uses of the world's scarce resources.

Investment   Additions to the economy's real capital stock, that is, all final purchases of capital equipment (machinery, tools, etc.), all residential or commercial construction, and changes in inventories.

Invisible Hand   Adam Smith's term for automatic market adjustments toward equilibrium.

Involuntary Saving   Occurs when government policies decrease consumption in order to stimulate capital accumulation; governments can force individuals to save a portion of their income through taxation, inflationary financing of government expenditures, or by setting low wages and high prices.

Jawboning   Oratory used by policymakers to persuade people or institutions to act against their individual interests; especially common as an exhortation to hold prices below equilibrium levels.

Joint Profit Maximization   A cartel of oligopolistic firms tries to share the profits that a monopoly would make if it controlled the industry.

Key Currency   An international medium of exchange; use of the U.S. dollar as an international medium of exchange has been a major reason the U.S. was able to run persistently large balance of payments deficits after 1951.

Keynes Effect   The initial decreases (or increases) in both the nominal interest rate and the real interest rate brought about by an increase (or decrease) in the rate of growth of the nominal money supply.

Keynesian Fiscal Policy   Policies designed to combat the problems associated with inadequate Aggregate Demand.

Keynesian Government Growth Ratchet The tendency for government to grow because policymakers cut taxes and expand spending during economic downturns but do not raise taxes or cut spending during inflationary episodes.

Keynesian Investment Schedule The idea that investment demand is insensitive to movements of the interest rate, but very sensitive to changes in expectations.

Keynesian Liquidity Preference The idea that the demand for money is extremely sensitive to interest rate movements and may even become horizontal at very low interest rates.

Keynesian Model A framework used to describe how output responds to changes in Aggregate Demand; generally ignores price level changes.

Keynesian Monetary Transmission Mechanism The idea that changes in the nominal money supply affect consumer spending only indirectly; money → interest rate → investment → income represents the chain of events emanating from a change in the money supply's rate of growth.

Keynesian Theory Specifies that macroeconomic adjustments involve changes in quantities below full employment and that price level changes only become the major adjustment mechanism when Aggregate Demand grows at full employment.

Keynes' Fundamental Psychological Law of Consumption Consumption expenditures increase as income rises, but by a smaller amount.

Kinked Demand Curve Model An oligopolistic pricing model that explains noncollusive oligopolistic behavior and predicts stickiness or rigidity of prices in oligopolistic industries.

Labor Labor services are typically measured in terms of the total amount of time worked during a given interval.

Labor Force Participation Rate (LFPR) The proportion of a population in the labor force; computed by dividing the labor force by the total population.

Labor Theory of Value The idea that the value of anything is exactly proportional to the labor time socially necessary for its production; this approach was the standard economic explanation of price until late in the 1800s and is still an article of faith among Marxists.

Labor Unions A worker organization that negotiates labor contracts with firms' managers to set wages and the conditions of work.

Laffer Curve A figure showing that very high tax rates may so discourage productive efforts that fewer tax revenues are collected than if tax rates were substantially lower.

Laissez-Faire This philosophy embraces the notion that a market system operates most efficiently when government minimizes its activity in the economy; according to this philosophy, governments should provide national defense and police protection, specify property rights, and enforce contracts drawn up between economic agents—and little or nothing else. (See also Capitalism, Socialism.)

Land Includes all natural resources, such as unimproved land, minerals, water, air, timber, wildlife, and fertility of the soil.

Legal Barriers to Entry Governmentally erected barriers to entry into an industry; these barriers maintain monopoly power by legally prohibiting or limiting competition from other firms; barriers include patents, copyrights, and licensing or bonding restrictions.

Legal Incidence of a Tax Falls on the party who legally must pay the tax to government, but the economic burdens may be shifted to others. (See Economic Incidence.)

Legal Reserves Total bank reserves; the sum of bankers' required reserves and excess reserves.

Lemons Market The notion that adverse selection will cause the market for used cars to be dominated by bad used cars (lemons) because asymmetric information causes good used cars ("cream puffs") and lemons to sell for the same prices. Sometimes generalized to other markets, for example, labor markets.

Lerner Index of Monopoly Power (LMP) An estimate of monopoly power using the percent by which price of output exceeds marginal cost; monopoly power is then measured as: $(P - MC)/P$.

Libertarianism A philosophy based on the notion that individual freedom is the most important social goal; libertarianism emphasizes the inherently coercive nature of government and urges reliance on the free market system to resolve nearly every human problem.

Limit Pricing   Occurs when firms that possess monopoly power set a profitable price that is low enough to discourage potential entrants.

Liquidity   How easy (costless) it is to turn an asset into cash; the transaction costs entailed in the purchase or sale of an asset is directly related to its illiquidity.

Liquidity Preference   The total demand for money in a Keynesian model; derived by summing the transactions, precautionary, and asset (speculative) demands for money.

Liquidity Trap   The horizontal portion of the Keynesian liquidity preference curve; occurs only when economic transactors choose to hold all increases in the nominal money supply in idle cash balances; it is doubtful if perfect liquidity traps have ever existed.

Logrolling   When legislators trade votes.

Long Run (LR)   A period of sufficient duration for all feasible adjustments to any event to be completed.

Long-Run Average Cost Curve (*LRAC*)   A curve showing the minimum average costs of producing each level of output after adjusting all resource inputs, including the size of the plant.

Long Wave Theory of Business Cycles   A theory of long (50 to 60 year) waves in economic activity was developed in the 1920s by a Russian economist named Kondratieff.

Lorenz Curve   A Lorenz curve shows the degree of inequality that exists in distributions of income or wealth in a particular society.

M1   = currency + demand deposits in commercial banks + all interest paying checkable accounts.

M2   = M1 + time deposits.

M3   = M2 + long-term deposits (Certificates of Deposit, or CDs).

Macroeconomic Equilibrium   Occurs at the price level where Aggregate Supply and Aggregate Demand are equal; when this occurs, the economy is stationary.

Macroeconomics   The branch of economics concerned with aggregate variables such as the levels of total economic activity, unemployment, inflation, the balance of payments, economic growth and development, the money supply, and the federal budget.

Majority Rule   When the winning side of a vote must capture 50% plus one vote.

Malthusian Prognosis   Reverend Thomas Malthus, an early nineteenth century English economist, promulgated the dismal notion that all workers were doomed to live a subsistence existence; in formulating his forecast, Malthus neglected to consider the favorable impact of technological advances on the world's ability to produce food.

Margin Requirements   A Fed tool that sets the legal minimum percentage down payments required for purchases of stock.

Marginal Cost = Marginal Revenue   ($MC = MR$) A condition required for maximum profits. Typically, $MR > MC$ for units prior to the $MR = MC$ level of output, so extra output boosts profits or cuts losses. Higher output levels than the $MR = MC$ level entail $MR < MC$ and would not be produced.

Marginal Cost (*MC*)   The change in total cost associated with producing an additional unit of output; computed by dividing the change in total cost (ΔTC) by the change in output (ΔQ): $MC = \Delta TC/\Delta Q = \Delta TVC/\Delta Q$.

Marginal Physical Product of Labor (*MPP_L*)   The additional output produced by an additional unit of labor; computed by dividing the change in total output (ΔQ) by the change in labor (ΔL): $\Delta Q/\Delta L$.

Marginal Propensity to Consume (*MPC*)   The change in saving brought about by a small change in disposable income ($MPC = \Delta C/\Delta Y_d$).

Marginal Propensity to Save (*MPS*)   The change in saving brought about by a small change in disposable income ($MPS = \Delta S/\Delta Y_d$).

Marginal Resource (or Marginal Factor) Cost (*MRC*)   The additional cost incurred in purchasing the services of an additional unit of a productive input; computed by dividing the change in total cost of production (ΔTC) by the change in input (ΔN), that is, $\Delta TC/\Delta N$; also computed by dividing the change in total variable costs of production (ΔTVC) by the change in input (ΔN), that is, $\Delta TVC/\Delta N$.

Marginal Revenue (*MR*)   The additional revenue associated with selling an additional unit of output; computed by dividing the change in total revenue by the change in output: $MR = \Delta TR/\Delta Q$.

Marginal Revenue Product (*MRP*)   The additional total revenue generated by an added unit of a variable input; computed by dividing the change in total revenue (ΔTR) by the change in input (ΔN), that is $\Delta TR/\Delta N$; or by multiplying marginal revenue by the marginal physical product of a resource, that is, $MR \times MPP_N$.

Marginal Social Benefits (MSB) Computed by summing the marginal private benefits and the marginal external benefits, if any, from consuming additional units of commodities or services.

Marginal Social Costs The sum of marginal private costs and any marginal external costs incurred in producing additional units of a good.

Marginal Utility (MU) The added utility or satisfaction derived by a consumer from the consumption of an additional unit of a good.

Marginalism The idea that decisions are based on the effects of small changes from a current situation.

Market Mechanisms that enable buyers and sellers to strike bargains and to transact.

Market Demand Curve A graphic representation totaling all individual demand curves; it is derived for most goods by horizontally summing all individual demand curves.

Market Economies Systems that rely on market interaction of supplies and demands to resolve the economic problem; the price system is used to coordinate the diverse plans of consumers and producers.

Market Equilibrium When neither shortages nor surpluses exist because, at the prevailing price, the quantities demanded and supplied are equal.

Market Failure When the market resolution of an economic problem is inefficient, inequitable, or unstable.

Market Period An interval too short to allow changes in decisions about amounts of output, so that only prices may be varied.

Market Power See Monopoly Power, Monopsony Power.

Market Price The price that is confronted in the market whether we buy or not.

Market Supply Curve A figure derived by horizontally summing all individual supply curves.

Market System See Capitalism, Free Enterprise System.

Maximizing Behavior *Homo sapiens* are perceived as human calculators who strive to maximize pleasure and to minimize pain.

Measure of (Net) Economic Welfare (MEW) A welfare measure obtained after deducting from GDP items that do not contribute to economic welfare and adding items that do, but which are not counted in GDP.

Measure of Value and Unit of Account The function performed by money as a common denominator through which the relative prices of goods are stated; reduces the information costs associated with exchange.

Median Voter Model Suggests that the median voter must be captured to achieve a majority of the vote, and attempts to explain why political parties and candidates tend to be so similar and why two parties tend to dominate electoral processes.

Medicaid A federal program that mandates shared state and federal funding for health care for the poor.

Medicare A federal government plan that subsidizes medical insurance for Americans over 65 years of age, and for the disabled.

Medium of Exchange The most important service that money provides; refers to standard items used to execute transactions.

Menu (Repricing) Costs of Inflation The costs in time and effort incurred in redesigning rate schedules and repricing goods.

Mercantilism A discredited economic doctrine that fostered imperialism and advocated surpluses in a country's balance of trade.

Merger The joining of two or more firms into a single firm.

Microeconomics The branch of economics that focuses on individual decision-making; the allocation of resources; and how prices, production, and the distribution of income are determined.

Mid-Point Bases Used in elasticity calculations to avoid ambiguity in measuring percentage changes to variables. An average of the beginning and ending period is used as the base from which relative changes are measured.

Minimum Efficient Scale (MES) The quantity of output at which a firm first minimizes average total cost (ATC).

Mixed Economies Societies in which some allocations rely on the market system while others rely on government or some other allocative mechanism.

Model The structure of a theory.

Monetarism The idea that erratic growth in the money supply is the major cause of macroeconomic instability.

Monetarist Monetary Transmission Mechanism The idea that changes in the growth rate of the nominal money supply affect private spending directly; an increase in the money supply yields a proportional rise in nominal GDP; $MS \rightarrow (C + I) \rightarrow Y$ is the causal chain emanating from a change in the monetary growth rate.

Monetary Base or High-Powered Money (MB) The total of bank reserves plus currency held by the nonbanking public.

Monetary Growth Rule The idea that the economy will be relatively stable if the money supply is set to grow at a low fixed percentage rate regardless of short-run economic conditions.

Money Illusion Decision-makers suffer from money illusion if their decisions are based on movements of the monetary values of economic variables rather than on the real values of the variables.

Money Multiplier (m_p, m_a) Potentially equals the reciprocal of the reserve requirement ratio ($m_p = 1/rr$); the number which, when multiplied by a change in total reserves, yields the potential change in the money supply. Actually, $m_a = MS/MB$ because of currency holdings of the public, excess reserves, and other leakages.

Monopolistic Competition An industry in which many firms sell slightly differentiated goods and there is freedom of entry or exit; monopolistic competition resembles pure competition, but goods are heterogeneous and each firm possesses a bit of monopoly power.

Monopoly The lone seller of a good that has no close substitutes.

Monopoly Power Possessed whenever a seller can force prices up by restricting output.

Monopsonist The sole buyer of a particular good or resource.

Monopsony Power Possessed whenever a buyer can force price down by restricting purchases.

Moral hazard When a contract creates an incentive for opportunistic behavior that raises the costs or lowers the benefits to the other party.

Moral Suasion See Jawboning.

Multiplier Effect The total change in spending that results when new autonomous spending boosts income, which, in turn, is spent, creating more income, and so on. (See also Autonomous Expenditures Multiplier.)

Nash Equilibrium A strategy combination in game theory where no player has a net incentive to change unless other players change.

National Banks Banks chartered by the Comptroller of the Currency that must be members of the Federal Reserve System.

National Debt The value of government bonds in the hands of the public or foreigners.

National Income (NI) A measure of economic activity computed by summing all resource incomes; equals the sum of wages and salaries, rents, interest, and corporate and noncorporate incomes.

Natural Barriers to Entry Significant barriers to entry that result from the nature of the economic good or from the cost structure inherent in its production.

Natural Monopoly A market in which only one seller can most efficiently produce an economic good; the production process is characterized by tremendously large fixed costs and relatively small variable costs; emerges where the market demand is small relative to the economies of scale.

Natural Rate Theory The notion that the economy is inherently stable and that unemployment and real interest will coincide with their natural rates in the long run. According to this theory, traditional Keynesian policy goals are unattainable because attempts to drive down unemployment or real interest rates more than can be reconciled with people's preferences are self-defeating in the long run.

Negative Externality When a market transaction imposes costs on third parties not directly involved in any aspect of the exchange.

Negative Income Taxes (NIT) Negative income tax plans represent attempts to reconcile equity and efficiency considerations in resolving the problems posed by income inequality and poverty; the negative income tax plan maintains incentives for recipients to work to earn additional income.

Net Domestic Product (NDP) The net value of commodities and services produced in the economy after adjusting for the fact that we have used up productive capacity; equals GDP minus depreciation; also equals National Income (NI) plus indirect business taxes. (See also Net National Product.)

Net Investment Gross investment minus depreciation; represents net additions to an economy's capital stock or productive capacity.

Net National Product (NNP) The net value of commodities and services produced by resources owned by the citizens of a country after adjusting for the fact that we have used up productive capacity; equals Gross National Product minus depreciation; also roughly equals National Income (NI) plus indirect business taxes.

Neutral Tax Imposition of a neutral tax distorts neither consumer buying patterns nor the methods used by firms in the conduct of their business; in other words, the imposition of a neutral tax does not distort relative prices by inducing substitution effects.

New Classical Macroeconomics Modern theories that extend classical theories of competitive markets; normally supports laissez-faire macroeconomic policies.

New Industrial Organization (new I-O) In contrast to the more traditional Structure-Conduct-Performance (SCP) approach, new I-O deemphasizes the numbers of competitors in an industry and stresses (*a*) how economic interactions can be better modeled with *game theory*, (*b*) how *asymmetric information* among transactors shapes business decisions and market structures, and (*c*) how *strategies* develop in response to the specifics of different competitive environments.

New Keynesian Economics Macroeconomic theories that blend traditional Keynesian insights with more elements of classical macroeconomic theory. New Keynesians continue to emphasize quantity rather than price adjustments to macroeconomic disturbances and to focus on efficiency wages and other impediments to perfect wage-price flexibility. However, far more than traditional Keynesians, new Keynesians accept the notion that changes in the money supply are important in explaining both inflation and recession, and they are less "activist" in their approaches to macroeconomic policymaking.

Nominal Rate of Interest The average annual percentage monetary premium paid for the use of money.

Nominal Values The current dollar values of economic variables.

Nondiscretionary Fiscal Policy See Automatic Stabilizers.

Nondurable Goods Goods that are used up in less than one year.

Noneconomic Costs of Unemployment Include the psychological trauma of being unemployed and the social unrest unemployment engenders.

Nonexclusive Good A good is nonexclusive if a person can enjoy it without paying for the right to consume; the result when it is relatively expensive to prevent individuals from consuming a good.

Nonrival Good A good is nonrival if consumption of the good by an individual does not prevent consumption of the same unit of that good by other people.

Normal Good Any good with a positive income elasticity of demand.

Normal Profits A normal cost of production; income that entrepreneurs must receive to make production worthwhile to them.

Normative Economics Deals with values and addresses what should be rather than what is.

Occam's Razor The "principle of parsimony," which suggests that the simplest workable theories are also the best and most useful.

Occupational Crowding This occurs when women and members of other disadvantaged groups are forced into low-wage occupations.

Occupational Discrimination Exclusion of certain groups from particular occupations.

Oligopoly A market in which several large firms control most of an industry's output. The few firms that constitute the industry must each consider other firms' reactions before setting its policies; mutually interdependent behavior is the unique characteristic of oligopoly; the importance of predictability leads to cooperation between firms. Pure oligopolies produce homogeneous outputs, while impure oligopolies produce slightly differentiated outputs.

Open Market Operations When the Fed's Open Market Committee buys and sells U.S. bonds; these operations determine the size of the money supply by altering the amounts of reserves in the banking system.

Open Shop A firm that employs workers without considering union membership.

Opportunity Cost The value of the next best opportunity to a good or to some activity.

Opportunity Cost of Money Keynesians view the true price of money as the interest rate, since the closest alternatives to money as an asset are stocks, bonds, and other assets that pay interest. Monetarists argue, instead, that the true price of money is the reciprocal of the absolute price level—the purchasing power of money—since money is a substitute for all other goods and assets.

Outputs Transformed materials; the results of production.

Paradox of Thrift The possibility suggested by Keynes that an increase in saving at all income levels (depicted by an upward shift of the saving function) may cause equilibrium income or output to decrease and could result in less saving rather than more.

Parity The idea that government subsidies should be used to ensure that agricultural goods' prices are stable relative to other prices.

Partial Equilibrium Analysis A method of economic analysis that looks at the direct effects of some chosen variables on others, assuming other influences are constant.

Partnership An unincorporated firm formed by two or more persons.

Passive Policy Setting permanent policies (e.g., a monetary growth rule) and allowing the market system to adjust to any temporary shocks to the economy.

Patents Legal barriers to entry that extend to their holders a renewable right to produce an economic good for 17 years and that prohibit the production of the good by other firms; intended to promote research and development of new goods and technologies.

Payoff Matrix In game theory, a table that matches sets of gains or losses when players choose from the options available to them. The payoff to any player from selecting a particular option depends on the option(s) selected by other players.

Peak (Boom) The phase of the business cycle when a preponderance of measures of economic activity are at their high points.

Per Capita Income A crude measure of economic well-being computed by dividing National Income by the population.

Perfectly Price Elastic Demand or Supply Curves Horizontal lines at the current market price; perfectly price elastic demand or supply curves have a price elasticity of infinity at every point.

Permanent Income (Wealth) The average income expected over one's lifetime. According to Milton Friedman, permanent income explains a person's patterns of consumption and money holdings.

Perpetuity A bond that will pay a fixed amount of money each year until it is purchased by the government that issued it.

Personal Discrimination Bigotry; generates inequitable housing conditions, higher prices for comparable goods, reduced medical care, and other problems.

Persuasive Advertising Designed to persuade or to mislead consumers rather than to inform them; entails a waste of resources.

Phillips Curve An inverse statistical relationship between the rate of change of the general price level and the rate of unemployment. In 1959, A. W. Phillips, an English economist, reported an empirical foundation for the idea that policymakers faced a permanent trade-off between unemployment and inflation. During the 1970s, the Phillips curve proved highly unstable.

Planned Injections Equal to Planned Withdrawals A condition necessary for macroeconomic equilibrium. Injections include all forms of autonomous spending; withdrawals represent such dilutions from spending streams as saving or taxation.

Planned or Intended Investment The amount of investment that business firms desire to make at each income level, assuming that business expectations remain unchanged.

Planned or Intended Saving The amounts of saving desired at each income level, assuming that savers' expectations remain constant.

Plant A production facility with a specific location; it may be involved in processing, fabrication, assembly, wholesale, or retail.

Plurality When the outcome of an election is determined by which side gets the most votes; a majority is unnecessary.

Point Voting When each voter is assigned a certain number of votes and can cast them among various electoral issues depending on the intensity of preferences.

Political Business Cycles Swings in economic activity that occur when macroeconomic policies are manipulated to improve incumbents' chances of reelection. The economy booms before elections and stagnates after them.

Pollution In economic parlance, a negative externality.

Pollution Abatement Programs Techniques used to reduce pollution.

Pork Barrel Legislation that yields benefits that are primarily local, but where funding is by the national government.

Positive Economics Value-free descriptions of and predictions about relationships among economic variables.

Positive Externality Occurs when a market activity bestows benefits on economic transactors who are not direct parties to the activity.

Potential GDP What an economy could produce at high rates of utilization of all resources; full-employment GDP approximates potential GDP.

Precautionary Demand for Money The amount of money that economic transactors desire to hold to cover unexpected expenses; is positively related to income or wealth.

Predatory Behavior Behavior by firms that attempt to drive rivals from an industry or to deter entry. Predatory tactics include low prices, expanded output, aggressive advertising, cloning rival products, and overly rapid technologoical innovation.

Present Value The present value of any asset is the value now of the income stream expected from the asset, discounted by the interest rate; the demand price of the asset.

Pretrade Costs The rate of exchange that exists domestically between two goods prior to international trade; also referred to as the domestic terms of trade; given by the slope at each point along the production possibility frontier.

Price Ceiling A maximum legal price set at the behest of buyers.

Price Discrimination Occurs when essentially the same good is sold at different prices, and price differentials do not reflect different production costs; perfect price discrimination absorbs all potential consumer surplus derived from consuming a good.

Price Elasticity of Demand (or Supply) Measures of the responsiveness of the quantity of a good demanded (or supplied) to changes in the price of the good; roughly computed by dividing percentage changes in quantities of a good demanded (or supplied) by the percentage changes in its price: $\%\Delta Q_d \div \%\Delta P$ (or $\%\Delta Q_s \div \%\Delta P$. To see how these percentage changes are calculated, however, see Mid-Point Bases. (See also Elasticity, Income Elasticity of Demand.)

Price Floor A minimum legal price set at the behest of sellers.

Price Taker or Quantity Adjuster A competitive buyer or seller whose actions do not affect prices; they can choose only among quantities.

Principal–Agent Problem When an agent (e.g., an employee) pursues personal goals that conflict with the principal's (e.g., the employer's) contractual rights.

Prisoners' Dilemma A noncooperative "game" in which every player's dominant strategy imposes losses on all other players. The result is that all players lose relative to the payoffs available if all players followed cooperative strategies.

Private Debt Debts owed by consumers or business firms.

Private Ownership System Resources are privately owned.

Privatization The conversion of a government activity into a private business.

Product Differentiation When consumers perceive differences in competing goods. Real differences in similar products may be related to durability, styling, or other physical characteristics; imaginary differences result from advertising or the imaginations of consumers. Firms use product differentiation to try to shift the demands for their products to the right and to decrease the price elasticity of the demands for their goods.

Production Occurs when materials are transformed in ways that make them more valuable.

Production Function The technical relationship that exists between inputs and outputs; allows all inputs to vary as different rates of production are achieved; not synonymous with total product curve.

Production Possibility Frontier (*PPF*) A curve showing the various combinations of goods that an economy could produce, assuming a fixed technology, full employment, and efficient resource utilization.

Profit The excess of a firm's total revenues over total cost; accounting profits consider only the explicit costs incurred by a firm; economists view total costs in terms of opportunity costs, which include both explicit and implicit costs; is a return to entrepreneurs for bearing uncertainty and innovating.

Progressive Taxes Tax rates which vary directly with income, so that the proportion of income devoted to taxes rises as income rises.

Promotional Profits The increases in the values of stock controlled by individuals who engineer a merger.

Property Rights Legal rights that people possess over property; the broadest of property rights are *fee-simple* property rights that allow individuals (*a*) to use goods in any manner so long as other people's property rights are not violated, (*b*) to exchange these property rights for others, and (*c*) to deny the use of their goods to others.

Property Tax A tax based on the value of capital improvements and land.

Proportional Taxes Tax rates that do not vary with income; the same percentage of income is collected in taxes regardless of the income level.

Proprietors Individuals in business for themselves.

Psychic Income Value of nonmonetary satisfaction gained from an activity.

Psychological Theories of the Business Cycle Focus on the herd instincts of human beings coupled with prolonged periods of optimism or pessimism.

Public Choice Economic interpretations of political behavior.

Public Debt Created when government spends more than it collects in tax revenue; the public debt grows when government sells bonds to the public in order to finance a deficit.

Public Good A public good is a good that can be consumed by more than one individual at a time (nonrivalry) and whose consumption cannot be denied a consumer who desires it (nonexclusion) once the good is provided.

Public Interest Theory of Regulation This theory suggests that government should control unethical business practices and regulate businesses plagued by such market failures as (*a*) externalities or (*b*) monopoly power derived from economies of scale.

Quantity Demanded The amount of a good purchased at a given price.

Quantity Supplied The amount of a good supplied at a given price.

Quantity Theory of Money The idea that the dominant determinant of the price level is the money supply. An extreme version attributes all inflation to excessive monetary growth.

Queuing Allocating goods or resources on a first-come, first-served basis. This tends to result in queues (lining up for access).

Quota A quantitative restriction on trade; the imposition of quotas raises the prices of imported goods and causes failure to fully realize potential gains from international trade.

Rate Base The value of a regulated firm's capital stock to which an acceptable, or fair, rate of return applies.

Rate of Return The annualized average size of the income stream per time period as a percentage of the dollar outlay for an investment.

Rational Expectations The notion that markets operate so efficiently that policy goals will not be achieved, even in the short run, unless the timing and the effects of demand-management policies come as surprises to the public.

Rational Ignorance Decision-makers will search for information only as long as the expected benefit exceeds the expected cost and, thus, may choose to be rationally ignorant of much information.

Real Business Cycles Some new classical macroeconomists contend that external shocks to Aggregate Supply are permanent and do not merely represent temporary departures from a long-run trend of economic growth. Concludes that activist policies are unwarranted.

Real Rate of Interest The annual percentage premium of purchasing power paid by a borrower to a lender for the use of money; the amount of extra goods, expressed in percentage terms, that can be enjoyed if consumption is delayed; computed by adjusting the nominal interest rate for the rate of general price change.

Real Values The current dollar value of economic variables after adjustment for price level changes. (See also Deflating.)

Recession Modern name for a depression.

Recessionary Gap A deficiency in autonomous expenditure that, if filled, would be multiplied so that full-employment output was achieved.

Recognition Lag Arises because policymakers' perceptions about current economic conditions are clouded, and time and effort are required to gather, compile, process, and interpret data to gain some feeling for any widespread changes in economic activity; applies equally to both monetary and fiscal policies.

Regressive Taxes Tax rates which vary inversely with income, so that tax payments decline relative to income as income rises.

Reindustrialization See Industrial Policy.

Relative Income A measure of the extent to which a person's income diverges from median income for the country.

Relative Price Price of a good in terms of another good. (See also Absolute Price.)

Rent Payments per time period for the services of land. (See also Economic Rent.)

Rent Seeking Attempts by special interest groups to shape public policies to their advantage, even though such policies may impose excessive costs on the general public.

Required Reserves (*RR*) The reserves that banks are legally required to hold against their deposits.

Reserve Requirement Ratio (*rr*) The fraction of its deposit liabilities that a bank must hold in reserves.

Reserves The amounts of money held in a bank's vault or on deposit at the Fed to meet withdrawals of deposits.

Resources Land, labor, capital, and entrepreneurship.

Ricardian Equivalence The idea that people will adjust so that whether government spending is financed by taxes or bonds is irrelevant.

Risk The likelihood of an event for which a probability can reasonably be estimated. (See Uncertainty.)

Rival Good A good is rival if consumption of a unit of the good by one individual exhausts that particular unit so that another individual cannot consume it.

Robinson-Patman Act (1936) Strengthened the Clayton Act's limits on price discrimination; however, it permitted discounts if they could be justified by differences in costs of production or if they were introduced as "good faith" efforts to meet competition.

Rule of Reason The rule of reason approach to the Sherman Act permitted certain restrictive practices of a firm despite their anticompetitive effects if the firm could prove that its conduct was based on sound business practice and was secondary to its primary business practices.

Rule of 72 The time required for some variable to double is calculated by dividing its percentage annual growth rate into 72. This approach adjusts for compounding (e.g., interest on interest).

Sales Tax A percentage tax that is typically levied on the sales value of most commodities and services.

Saving The change in one's total wealth over some period of time.

Say's Law "Supply creates its own demand"; that is, the very act of producing a product creates an equivalent amount of demand, since people do not work for the sake of work alone; named after the classical economist, Jean Baptiste Say.

Scarce Good A good for which the quantity demanded exceeds the amount available at a zero monetary price.

Scarcity A state that results because resources are limited and cannot accommodate all of our unlimited wants.

Screening When a principal examines the qualifications of a potential agent before offering the agent a contract.

Seasonal Unemployment Unemployment that varies with the season.

Seigniorage The profits made by goverments when they coin or print money.

Sellers' Market When the prevailing market price lies below the equilibrium price, resulting in a shortage.

Services Intangible economic goods.

Sherman Antitrust Act (1890) Our first antitrust law; specifies that "every contract, combination in the form of trust or otherwise, or conspiracy, in restraint of trade or commerce among the several States, or with foreign nations, is hereby declared illegal"; and, according to the second section, "every person who shall monopolize, or attempt to monopolize . . . shall be deemed guilty of a felony."

Shifted Backward A tax is shifted backward when its economic incidence falls on owners of resources supplied to the firm.

Shifted Forward A tax is said to be shifted forward when the economic incidence of the tax falls on the consumer.

Shirking A principal–agent problem that occurs when an agent (e.g., an employee) fails to perform because the principal (e.g., an employer) cannot adequately monitor the agent's performance.

Shocks An external shock (e.g., war or bad weather) causes macroeconomic disequilibrium by disrupting Aggregate Supply.

Shortage Occurs if some people cannot buy all of an economic good for which they are willing to pay the going price.

Short Run (SR) An analytic period of time in which at least one resource is fixed so that firms can neither enter nor leave the marketplace; a firm can shut its plant down, but it cannot leave the industry.

Shutdown Point The price-output combination at which total revenue equals total variable costs; in the short run, the firm must at least cover the variable costs of production; if it cannot, then it will shut down and minimize its losses by incurring only fixed costs.

Signaling Behavior by agents to communicate special qualifications that will elicit the offer of a contract from a principal.

Socialism A system characterized by collective ownership of property and government allocation of resources. (See also Capitalism, Laissez-Faire.)

Socially Necessary Labor The Marxist concept that includes not only direct labor time, but also the labor time used to construct factories and to produce capital equipment; Marxists view all commodities and capital as congealed labor.

Special Interest Groups Groups that can gain from public policies that may not be in accord with the interests of other groups or society as a whole.

Specialization When different resources (e.g., people's labor) are used to produce different goods. This is most advantageous when resources are allocated so that every good is produced at the lowest possible opportunity cost.

Specific Training Training that a firm provides a worker that only increases the productivity of the worker for that firm.

Speculative Demand for Money Inversely related to the interest rate; refers to the amount of money that economic transactors desire to hold at alternative interest rates for the purpose of speculating against movements in the prices of stocks or bonds.

Speculators Intermediaries who buy a good in the hope of selling it at a higher price at a later point in time. Profitable speculation tends to reduce price volatility and the risks to others of doing business.

Spillovers (Externalities) When benefits or costs are bestowed upon third parties who are not part of a transaction; produce false price signals and lead to nonoptimal decisions.

Stabilization Attempts to use macroeconomic policy to achieve full employment, price stability, and economic growth.

Stagflation The simultaneous occurrence of high rates of inflation and high rates of unemployment; stagflation, or inflationary recession, occurs during both demand-induced and supply-induced cycles of inflation when Aggregate Supply declines relative to Aggregate Demand.

Standard Industry Classification (SIC) Codes Categories developed by the Bureau of Census in order to classify industries.

Standard of Deferred Payment Money performs this function by being acceptable in the payment of contractual obligations involving future payments.

State Banks Banks that are chartered by state governments; they have the option of becoming members of the Federal Reserve System.

Statutory (Legal) Incidence of a Tax Falls on the party responsible for paying the tax, but a tax's economic incidence may be shifted.

Sticky Wages Partially account for the positive slope of short-run Aggregate Supply curves. "Stickiness" occurs when nominal wages fail to adjust to changes in market conditions as rapidly as prices do. Wage stickiness can result from (*a*) reluctance of individual workers to accept wage cuts when the value of their productivity has fallen, (*b*) the prevalence of implicit or explicit long-term contracts between workers and firms, or (*c*) efficiency wages—employers may try to secure the loyalty of career employees by paying wages rates that exceed those that would prevail in purely competitive labor markets.

Stock See Common Stock.

Stock Variable An economic variable that can be measured holding time constant.

Store of Value Money is a store of value in that, except for inflation, it is a relatively riskless way of holding wealth.

Strategic Behavior Ascertaining how other people ("players" in game theory) are likely to behave, and then following tactics to maximize your gain or minimize any harm to you.

Structural Deficit The budget shortfall that would result because of the design of current government tax and outlay programs, were the economy operating at its capacity. (See also Cyclical Deficit.)

Structural Unemployment Unemployment that arises because workers do not possess the skills required for existing job opportunities.

Structure-Conduct-Performance Paradigm The theory that *market structure* almost rigidly determines each firm's *conduct* (output decisions and pricing behavior), which yields an industry's overall *performance* (e.g., its efficiency and profitability).

Subsistence Theory of Wages The theory that classical economists used to explain how wage rates were determined; this theory suggests that wages would be sufficient to meet the biological needs of workers, with only minor adjustments to meet the social and customary needs of workers.

Substitute Goods Goods that are substituted one for another in consumption; positive cross price elasticities of demand exist between substitute goods.

Substitution Effect The change in the pattern of consumption brought about by a change in the relative price structure; the substitution effect of a price change is always negative, for consumers will always substitute cheaper goods for more expensive goods; the substitution effect is generally so powerful that it serves as the theoretical underpinning for the law of demand.

Superior (Luxury) Good A good for which the income elasticity of demand is greater than one; that is, the demand for this kind of economic good is very sensitive to real income changes.

Supplier Induced Demand (*SID*) This is a particular application of the principal–agent problem in the medical care market. It occurs when an agent (a doctor) uses superior knowledge to induce a principal (a patient) to buy more medical care than is necessary.

Supply The amounts of goods or resources that producers or owners are willing to sell in the market under various conditions.

Supply Curve A graphic representation of the maximum quantities of a good or resources that producers or owners are willing to supply at various market prices.

Supply, Law of The quantity of an economic good supplied varies directly with the price of the economic good.

Supply Price The lowest price at which sellers are willing to make a specific quantity of a good available. (See also Demand Price.)

Supply-Side Economics A reemphasis on the importance of the effects of government policies on Aggregate Supply; rebuts Keynesian emphasis on Aggregate Expenditures.

Surplus, or Excess Supply The excess of the quantity supplied over the quantity demanded at a given price.

Surplus Value The difference between the total value of what workers produce and what workers are paid for their labor services; surplus value is expropriated by the capitalists, according to Marxists; surplus value is the sum of rent, interest, and profits.

Survival Principle The idea that the most efficient firms in an industry are those that remain viable over time; the optimal size of firms is indicated by the size of the firm that survives in an industry over time.

Syndicalism A revolutionary sociopolitical theory that advocates the overthrow of government and the reorganization of society into syndicates, which are effectively industrywide trade unions.

Taft-Hartley Act (1947) This legislation amended the Wagner Act and made certain labor union practices unfair, outlawed the closed shop, and permitted individual states to pass "right-to-work" laws that ban union shops.

Tariff A tax on internationally traded goods; the imposition of tariffs raises the prices of imported goods and prevents full realization of potential gains from international trade.

Team Production Most complex forms of production cannot be accomplished efficiently (or at all) by lone individuals or families. Firms coordinate team production to (*a*) reduce transaction costs and (*b*) exploit economies of scale.

Technological Change Occurs when a given stock of productive inputs produces a greater quantity of output, or when a given amount of output can be produced with fewer productive inputs; refers to greater efficiency in market processes, improved knowledge concerning the use of productive inputs in production, the advent of completely new production processes, improvements in the quality of human and nonhuman resources, and new inventions and innovations. The idea of progress is tightly bound up in the process of technological change.

Terms of Trade The prices of exported goods relative to imported goods after international trade has commenced.

Theory A testable hypothesis concerning the way in which observable facts are related.

Third-Party Payer Problem Medical insurance pays the bulk of health-care expenses, boosting effective demand by reducing the price paid by consumers while raising the price received by providers.

Tie-In Sales Attempts by firms to exploit their market power by using tie-in sales agreements that require customers to buy another product as a condition for buying the monopolized good.

Tit-for-Tat In game theory, a strategy that begins cooperatively. Thereafter, in any period, tit-for-tat entails echoing what the opponent did in the previous period.

Total Burdens of a Tax The amounts of money that individuals would have to be paid to make them just as well off with the tax as without.

Total Cost All costs to the firm of producing a particular rate of output; computed by multiplying the quantity of a good produced by the per unit cost of producing the good.

Total Product Curve The technical relationship that exists between production and various levels of one input, assuming that other resources are held constant.

Total Revenue The dollar value of a firm's sales; computed by multiplying the quantity of a good sold by its per unit price.

Total Revenue Minus Total Cost ($TR - TC$) Approach The profit-maximizing firm will produce the rate of output at which total revenue most greatly exceeds total cost.

Trade Adjustment Assistance Provides retraining and financial assistance for workers disemployed because of liberalized international trade.

Transaction Costs The costs associated with gathering information about products and transporting goods and people geographically or between markets.

Transactions Demand for Money The amount of money that economic transactors desire to hold in order to execute expected transactions; is positively related to income and wealth.

Transfer Payments Transfers of income from one set of households to another set through such programs as welfare payments, social security, and food stamps.

Trap of Underdevelopment Less developed countries typically remain underdeveloped for the following reasons: (*a*) high rates of population growth that result in low per capita incomes, (*b*) negligible capital accumulation because of low saving rates fostered by low per capita incomes, (*c*) rather primitive products are purchased by consumers, and (*d*) low labor productivity.

Trough (Depression) Phase of the business cycle when most measures of economic activity are at their low point.

Unanimity A requirement that all voters agree before new policies are implemented.

Uncertainty When a reasonable estimate cannot be made of the probability that some event will occur. (See also Risk.)

Unemployment When an individual wants work but is without a job.

Unintended Inventory Changes A balancing item for the economy, these changes in inventories resolve any differences between the planned saving and planned investment functions and assure that actual saving and actual investment are equal at all times.

Union Shop A firm that will hire nonunion workers, but joining the union is a requirement for continued employment.

Uniqueness Gains Arise because exchange allows traders to secure goods not available from local sources in reasonable quantities at reasonable prices.

Usury Law A legal ceiling on the interest rates that lenders may charge borrowers.

Util An imaginary unit of measurement of satisfaction.

Utilitarianism A philosophy developed in England during the 1800s by Jeremy Bentham, an eccentric English philosopher and social reformer; this school of thought embraced the notion that satisfactions or utilities of individuals could be measured, and it sought "the greatest happiness for the greatest number."

Utopian Socialism All property would be collectively owned and all decisions would be democratic.

Value Added The excess of a firm's revenues over the amount it pays to other firms for intermediate goods; used to calculate GDP and, in much of Europe, as a major base for taxes.

Value-Added Approach to Estimating GDP GDP equals the sum of the values added to economic goods at each level of production.

Value of Money The purchasing power of money, which is determined by the interaction of the supply of and demand for money.

Value of the Marginal Product (*VMP*) The value to society of the output produced by an additional unit of a variable input; computed by multiplying the price of output (P_x) by the marginal physical product of a unit of input (MPP_N): that is, $VMP = (P_x) \times (MPP_N)$.

Variable Costs Costs that vary with the level of production; variable costs are also known as direct costs or prime costs and are the only costs that rational decision-makers consider.

Vertical Combination A firm having different plants producing products at different production levels within an industry.

Voluntary Saving The voluntary decisions of individuals to defer consumption until some future date.

Voluntary Unemployment The frictional unemployment that exists when everyone who wants to work at the prevailing wage rate has a job or can find one rapidly.

Wage Differentials Differences in wages that may reflect differences in training, human capital, personalities, occupations, and economic discrimination.

Wage Discrimination Occurs when members of a particular group are paid less than are members of other groups for doing equal work.

Wage Stickiness See Sticky Wages, Efficiency Wages.

Wage-Price Controls Legal restrictions most often used to keep prices from coinciding with their equilibrium levels.

Wages Payments per time period for labor services.

Wagner Act(1935) Guaranteed labor the right to organize independent unions and made a company's refusal to negotiate with an elected union an unfair labor practice.

Wealth The discounted present values of income streams that are paid to the owner of an asset.

Wealth Effect The Aggregate Demand curve slopes down, in part, because higher price levels reduce the purchasing power of such financial assets as money or bonds, and vice versa.

Webb-Pomerene Act (1918) Exempts export trade associations from antitrust litigation.

Winner's Curse A theory that vigorously competitive situations are likely to impose losses on the winning bidder because the winning bidder is probably ignorant of information possessed by other bidders.

X-Efficiency Excessive costs created by managerial sloppiness when a firm has some market power.

Yellow-Dog Contracts Contracts that were widely used by business firms during the antiunion years to prevent the formation of labor unions by their employees; as a condition of employment, workers were forced to sign a yellow-dog contract, which was an agreement not to join a labor organization.

Zero Economic Profit The long-run equilibrium state of pure competition. All opportunity costs are covered by revenues, but there will be no net resource movements because no better opportunities exist elsewhere.

Name Index*

*Some names recur so frequently in this book (e.g., Adam Smith, John Maynard Keynes, and Milton Friedman) that not all references to them in the text are cited here.

Subject Index

Pollution (continued)
  as a public bad, 773
  effluent charges, 781
  is optimal zero? 778-780
  lawsuits for damages, 782
  market solutions to, 782-784
  offset policy, 786
  regulation, 329, 625, 784-788
  "rights", 783-784
  subsidizing abatement, 781-782, 787
  and trade, 788
Population
  and business cycles, 109-110
  and diminishing returns, 426
  and Malthus, 427-428
  S curves and growth, 109-110, 426
  and the work force, 134, 426-428
  in underdeveloped countries, 428, 440-442
Population growth, 66, 427
Pork barrel legislation, 760-761
Portfolio adjustments (international trade), 869
Positive economics, 18-19
Positive externality, 625
Positive relationship, 228
Positive-sum-games, 594, 824
Potential GDP, 226-227
Potential money multiplier, 271-272
Poverty in America, 715
  and discrimination, 720-721
  involuntary, 719
  line, 716-717
  profiles of, 717
  programs, 717-719
  public policy to eliminate, 717, 721-726
  as relative concept, 717
  types of, 719-720
  voluntary, 719-720
  War on, 719
Precautionary demand for money, 299, 856
Predatory pricing behavior, 599-601
Prehistory, 436
Present value, 696-697
  and lotteries, 329
Price
  absolute, 12, 20
  change and income effects, 60, 474, 549
  demand, 59
  equilibrium, 589
  as incentives/disincentives, 14, 460
  as information, 13-14
  of life
  marginal revenue, 564
  and marginal utility, 468-470, 472-473
  market, 59
  as rationing devices, 14
  relative, 12-14, 20, 50
  short run, 545, 585
  stickiness, 140, 218, 324, 384
  and substitition effects, 60, 473-474
  versus quantity adjustments, 218
Price ceiling, 89, 626
Price/cost dynamics, 87, 119-120, 549-550
Price consumption curve, 488
Price controls, 78, 81, 624, 858
Price discrimination, 573, 667
  arbitrage, 573-574

and efficiency, 624
  profits from, 574-575
  requirements for, 573-574
Price elasticity of demand, 62, 449-450, 584, 564, 640
Price elasticity of supply, 458-459
Price floor, 90-92, 626
Price index numbers, 154-159
Price level, 19, 20, 194-195, 229, 354
  (See also Inflation)
  adjustments, 218
  and Classical theory, 194
  crude monetary theory of, 304-306
Price maker, 563
Price and quality, 479-480, 624
Price rigidity (stickiness), 140, 218, 324, 384, 589
Price system, 589, 590
Price taker, 535, 554
Primitive culture, 436-437
Principal, 502-503, 653
Principal/agent problem, 502-503, 523, 752
  shirking, 364, 503, 653, 655
Principle of absolute advantage, 827
Prisoners' dilemma, 594-595
Private budget constraints, 328
  corporations, 328
Private good, 772
Private property rights, 50-52, 773-774
Private sector, 33
Privatization, 53, 54, 491
Producer cooperatives, 497
Producer Price Index (PPI), 158
Product differentiation, 479, 582-584
Production, 6, 121, 492, Chapter 23
  economic costs of, 35, 501-502, 513, 623, 776, 777-778
  least cost, 521-522
  team, 400, 505
Production efficiency, 39, 495, 650
Production function, 509-510
Production possiblities and trade, 37-41, 831
Production possibilities frontier, 21, 32, 37, 361
  and crowding out, 333-335
  and diminishing returns, 39-41
  and economic growth, 37-39, 41-47, 426
  and international trade, 46-47, 831
  and opportunity costs, 37, 40-41
  resources, 333
  scarcity, 41
  technology, 41, 361-363
Productive inefficiency (market power), 39, 586
Productive resources, 6
Productivity and inflation, 372-375, 380
Profit maximization for competitive firm, 537-538, 540-542, 648
Profit maximization for a monopolist, 564-566, 567-568, 585
Profits, 8, Chapter 30
  and costs, 500-502
  economic, 500-502, 548-579, 694
  and innovation, 694-695
  as market signals, 548-549
  maximization, 95, 500, 537-542, 648
  and monopoly, 585, 694
  in national income, 176
  normal, 501-502

payment to entrepreneurship, 8
  and price discrimination, 549, 585
  and risk, 695
  role of, 695-696
  and uncertainty, 695
Progressive tax, 100, 738
Property rights, 50, 773-774
Property rights and environment, 773-774
Property rights, fee-simple, 50, 773-774
Property tax, 746
Proportional tax, 101
Proprietor's income, 175-176
Proprietorship, 496
Protectionism, and inefficiency, 838
Psychological theories of the business cycle, 112-113
Public choice, 628, 752, Chapter 33
Public choice theory of regulation, 628
Public debt, 326, 337-344, Chapter 15
  benefits of, 342
  burdens on future generations, 341
  foreign holding, 338-339
  interest on, 339-341
  must it be repaid? 341-342
  recent growth, 327-328
  remeasuring, 342-344
Public finance, Chapters 15, 32
Public goods, 99, 732, 734-736, 772
Public interest theory of regulation, 623-626
Public sector, 33, 387
Public utilities, See Natural monopoly
Pure competition, 534, 555, 564, 582, 586, 594, 607, Chapters 24, 26
  (See also Competition)
  evaluation of, 535, 554-555
  long run, 550-552
  supply curve, 552-554
Pure monopoly, 561, 563, Chapter 25
  (See also Monopoly)

Quadrants (mathematical), 24
Quality and Prices, 479-480
Quantity adjusters, 218, 554 (See also Price takers)
Quantity vs. price adjustment (macro), 218
Queuing, 47-48, 90
Quotas
  as barriers to trade, 588, 842-843

Racial discrimination, See Discrimination
Raiders, corporate, 611
Random selection, 48
Rate of interest, See Interest rate
Rate of return, 117, 205, 314-315, 692, 698-699
Rate structure of utilities, 624
Rational choice and information, 477
Rational expectations, 396-400
  limitations, 398-400
Rational ignorance, 101-102, 472, 477-479, 753
Real business cycles, 400-401
Real money, 283-285, 313
Real rate of interest, 392, 691
Real values, 155-156
Real wages, 359

National Income and Related Statistics for Selected Years, 1929-1993

Basic National Income Accounts **	1970	1971	1972	1973	1974	1975	1976	1977	1978	1979
Personal Consumption Expenditures*	646.5	700.3	767.8	848.1	927.7	1024.9	1143.1	1271.5	1421.2	1583.7
Gross Private Domestic Investment*	150.3	175.5	205.6	243.1	245.8	226.0	286.4	358.3	434.0	480.2
Government Purchases*	212.7	224.3	241.5	257.7	288.3	321.4	341.3	368.0	403.6	448.5
Net Exports*	1.2	-3.0	-8.0	0.6	-3.1	13.6	-2.3	-23.7	-26.1	-23.8
SUM to: **Gross Domestic Product** **	1010.7	1097.2	1207.0	1349.6	1458.6	1585.9	1768.4	1974.1	2232.7	2488.6
MINUS: Depreciation Allowance*	49.7	54.6	61.0	66.2	77.5	93.3	103.8	116.2	132.3	153.0
EQUALS: **Net Domestic Product**	961.0	1042.6	1146.0	1283.4	1381.1	1492.6	1664.6	1857.9	2100.4	2335.6
MINUS: Indirect Business Taxes*	58.8	64.5	69.2	76.3	81.4	87.4	95.1	104.1	114.6	123.3
EQUALS: **National Income**	902.2	978.1	1076.8	1207.1	1299.7	1405.2	1569.5	1753.8	1985.8	2212.3
MINUS: Social Security Contributions	62.2	68.9	79.0	97.6	110.5	118.5	134.5	149.8	171.8	197.8
MINUS: Corporate Income Taxes*	27.2	29.9	33.8	40.2	42.2	41.5	53.0	59.9	67.1	69.6
MINUS: Undistributed Corp. Profits*	12.5	18.7	24.7	37.3	45.2	43.6	56.6	66.8	79.1	86.7
PLUS: Transfer Payments*	84.6	100.0	111.8	127.9	151.4	190.2	208.3	223.4	241.6	270.7
EQUALS: **Personal Income**	884.9	960.6	1051.1	1159.9	1253.2	1391.8	1533.7	1700.7	1909.4	2128.9
MINUS: Personal Taxes*	109.0	108.7	132.0	140.6	159.1	156.4	182.3	210.0	240.1	280.2
EQUALS: **Disposable Income**	775.9	851.9	919.1	1019.3	1094.1	1235.4	1351.4	1490.7	1669.3	1848.7
REAL GDP (in $1987 Billions)	2873.9	2955.9	3107.1	3268.6	3248.1	3221.7	3380.8	3533.3	3703.5	3796.8
Real Per Capita Disposable Income	$9,073	$9,331	$9,671	$10,183	$9,924	$9,904	$10,190	$10,426	$10,802	$10,727
Annual Percent Change in Per Capita DI	1.7	2.8	3.6	5.3	-2.5	-0.2	2.9	2.3	3.6	-0.7
Money and the Price Level										
Consumer Price Index (1982-4 = 100)	38.8	40.5	41.8	44.4	49.3	53.8	56.9	60.6	65.2	72.6
Percentage Inflation Rate	5.7	4.4	3.2	6.2	11.0	9.1	5.8	6.5	7.6	11.3
Supply of Money, M1*	214.4	228.3	249.2	262.8	274.3	287.5	306.3	331.1	358.2	382.5
Population / Labor Force										
Population (Millions)	205.1	207.7	209.9	211.9	213.9	216.0	218.0	220.2	222.6	225.1
Civilian Labor Force (Millions)	82.8	84.4	87.0	89.4	91.9	93.8	96.2	99.0	102.3	105.0
Unemployment (Millions)	4.1	5.0	4.9	4.4	5.2	7.9	4.4	7.0	6.2	6.1
Percent Unemployment / Total Labor	4.9	5.9	5.6	4.9	5.6	8.5	7.7	7.1	6.1	5.8
International Trade										
Exports*	57.0	59.3	66.2	91.8	124.3	136.3	148.9	158.8	186.1	228.9
Imports*	55.8	62.3	74.2	91.2	127.5	122.7	151.1	182.4	212.3	252.7
The Federal Budget										
Federal Government Receipts*	192.8	187.1	207.3	230.8	263.2	279.1	298.1	355.6	399.6	463.3
Federal Outlays*	195.6	210.2	230.7	245.7	269.4	332.3	371.8	409.2	458.7	503.5
Federal Surplus (+) or Deficit (-)*	-2.8	-23.0	-23.4	-14.9	-6.1	-53.2	-73.7	-53.7	-59.2	-40.2

*Billions of Dollars